A GUIDE TO INTERNATIONAL ESTATE PLANNING

Drafting, Compliance, and Administration Strategies

Second Edition

Leigh-Alexandra Basha, Editor

SECTION OF REAL PROPERTY | TRUST & ESTATE LAW

AMERICAN BAR ASSOCIATION
Defending Liberty
Pursuing Justice

Cover by Jill Tedhams/ABA Publishing.

Printed in the United States of America

17 16 15 14 13 5 4 3 2 1

Library of Congress Cataloging-in-Publication Data

A guide to international estate planning / Edited by Leigh-Alexandra Basha.—2nd ed.

p. cm.

ISBN 978-1-62722-267-9

1. Estate planning—United States. 2. Inheritance and transfer tax—Law and legislation—United States. 3. Investments, Foreign—Taxation—Law and legislation—United States. 4. Double taxation—United States. 5. Conflict of laws—Estate planning—United States. 6. Conflict of laws—Inheritance and succession—United States. I. Basha, Leigh-Alexandra, editor. II. Schoenblum, Jeffrey A. Guide to international estate planning

KF750.A21575 2013

346.7305—dc23

2013037325

Discounts are available for books ordered in bulk. Special consideration is given to state bars, CLE programs, and other bar-related organizations. Inquire at ABA Publishing, American Bar Association, 321 North Clark Street, Chicago, Illinois 60654-7598.

www.ShopABA.org

Contents

CHAPTER 7
U.S. Taxation of Foreign Trusts, Trusts with Non-U.S. Grantors and Their U.S. Beneficiaries 127

Ellen K. Harrison, Elyse G. Kirschner, and Carlyn S. McCaffrey

CHAPTER 19
Ethics in International Estate Planning 647
Christopher M. Reimer

CHAPTER 20
Asset Protection Trusts 687
Gideon Rothschild

Media/Books Products Committee

Real Property, Trust and Estate Law
Media/Books Products Committee
Candace M. Cunningham, *Editor-in-Chief*
Phyllis M. Rubinstein, *Editor-in-Chief Emeritus*
Aen Walker Webster, *Editor-in-Chief Emeritus*

Real Property
Richard M. Frome, *Managing Editor*
Amy E. McShane, *Acquisitions Editor*
April Condon, *Acquisitions Editor*
Cynthia Boyer Blakeslee, *Books Editor*
Marcia Charney, *Acquisitions Editor*
Thomas D. Kearns, *Books Editor*
Troy Rule, *Acquisitions Editor*
Carla Moynihan, *Books Editor*

Trust and Estate
Carolyn P. Vinson, *Managing Editor*
Michael A. Kirtland, *Acquisitions Editor*
Harold W. Pskowski, *Acquisitions Editor*
Nancy E. Shurtz, *Senior Books Editor*
Marianne R. Kayan, *Books Editor*
Amy Morris Hess, *Acquisitions Editor*
Elizabeth Lindsay-Ochoa, *Acquisitions Editor*
Aen Walker Webster, *Acquisitions Editor*

Introduction

This book was first published in 2000. In the last decade, we have seen extraordinary changes in the international arena. The world has become far more global as our clients work, live, and marry without borders. We have experienced the European Union and its new regulations, more tax treaties have been negotiated, and we now have more transparency than ever. This book is intended to serve as a resource for practitioners having a specific inquiry or for those looking for general guidance on a topic in international planning, tax, succession, compliance, and other issues affecting private clients. Since the book was first published, we have added chapters on FATF and anti-money laundering and offshore compliance and chapters from several foreign jurisdictions to provide comparative insights on different topics.

A Guide to International Estate Planning: Drafting, Compliance, and Administration Strategies is comprised of twenty-two chapters organized into eight overarching parts. Part I affords an overview. Robert C. Lawrence, III of Walker, Jones, Lawrence, Duggan & Savage, P.C. and Elisa Shevlin Rizzo of Fiduciary Trust Company International address the conflict of laws issues that are central in determining which country's laws will govern the disposition of a donor or decedent's wealth. In Chapter 2, Henry Christensen, III of McDermott Will & Emery and Toni Ann Kruse explore the basic transfer tax rules for nonresident aliens as well as for citizens and resident aliens.

Building upon this foundation, Part II consists of chapters that address two critical topics regarding testamentary disposition of wealth. First, in Chapter 3, Barbara R. Hauser discusses the perennial, much-debated question of whether multiple wills, typically a domicile and situs wills, should be utilized in international estate planning. While some have argued in favor of this approach, others have argued for a single will, and then only when a nontestamentary substitute, such as a trust, is not appropriate as the ultimate receptacle and management tool for the client's global wealth. Following Barbara Hauser's analysis of the multiple wills issue, G. Warren Whitaker and Dina Kapur Sanna both of Day Pitney explore the nontax and tax complexities associated with probate and/or administration of a multinational estate.

Part III of the book focuses on the central concerns of marital and familial rights and protections. Chapter 5, which is the second chapter contributed by Robert C. Lawrence, III and Elisa Shevlin Rizzo, dovetails with their earlier discussion of conflicts of law in Chapter 1. Lawrence and Rizzo explain the civil law protections afforded the spouse in terms of community property rights and also the protections afforded other family members, such as children, in terms of forced heirship. In addition to explaining the principles and operation of these protections, Lawrence and Rizzo also analyze the jurisprudence that has developed in the United States as a result of courts being petitioned to enforce these foreign spousal and family protections with respect to U.S. assets. In Chapter 6, Joshua A. Rubenstein of Katten Muchin Rosenman updates Professor Jeffrey A. Schoenblum's chapter and explores in depth the topic. This chapter considers what rights spouses have under different legal systems on a comparative basis and which regime governs when the spouses have had marital domiciles in more than one country or own property situated in more than one jurisdiction. Since marital property regimes seriously curtail the amount of property susceptible to free disposition, the topic cannot be ignored by attorneys representing a married client, a deceased spouse's estate, or the surviving spouse or other family members.

Part IV focuses on important tax issues in detail. First, in Chapter 7, Carlyn S. McCaffrey and Elyse G. Kirschner both of McDermott Will & Emery and Ellen K. Harrison of Pillsbury Winthrop Shaw Pittman deal with the extraordinarily intricate rules of the Internal Revenue Code with respect to foreign trusts, trusts with non-U.S. grantors, and U.S. beneficiaries of such trusts. In Chapter 8, Douglas L. Siegler of Sutherland, Asbill & Brennan analyzes with the same acumen the tax problems associated with the disposition of wealth by a U.S. citizen to a noncitizen spouse. This chapter is nothing short of encyclopedic in the treatment of its subject matter. In Chapter 9, Donald D. Kozusko and Richard A. Fava both of Kozusko Harris Vetter Wareh Duncan LLP proceed to consider the estate planning measures an individual should consider pursuing prior to immigrating to the United States. As the authors demonstrate with their subtle insights, taking the appropriate steps beforehand can yield dramatic benefits down the road. In Chapter 10, Michael G. Pfeifer of Caplin & Drysdale Chartered, offers a thorough analysis of the tax, as well as certain other nontax concerns, confronted when the U.S. citizen or resident emigrates or expatriates.

Part V focuses on U.S. tax treaties. In Chapter 11, Barbara Hauser analyzes the often-neglected, but quite important, estate and gift tax bilateral treaties entered into by the United States. In Chapter 12, William B. Sherman and Summer A. LePree both of Holland & Knight consider the more numerous income tax conventions. They emphasize those provisions of the income tax treaties impacting most prominently on the individual with multinational investments or family members abroad.

In Part VI, attention turns to trusts and alternative vehicles for the international and offshore client. In Chapter 13, Alec R. Anderson of Conyers Dill and Pearman paints a vivid and incisive portrait of the offshore world and the vehicles and jurisdictions that can be utilized to benefit clients. Following this, in Chapter 14, Anne J. O'Brien and Cara M. Koss both of Arnold and Porter update David Hayton's chapter and deal with the role letters of wishes play in facilitating the carrying out of a settlor's goals, while technically keeping the typically offshore trustee independent of the settlor for various tax and nontax reasons. The authors also explore the evolving legal precedents onshore and offshore with respect to the issues raised by the use of letters of wishes. An increasingly vital aspect of international trusts is developed in Chapter 15. Specifically, Frans Sonneveldt and Mike Vrijomed both of Mazars (the Netherlands), Stefano Guiso Gallisay of Studio Legale Ughi e Nunziante (Italy), Line-Alexa Glotin of UGGC & Associes (France), Sonia Velasco Menal and Carlos Ara Triadu both of Cuatrecasas Abogados SRL (Spain), and Gerd Kostrzewa of Heuking Kuehn Luer Wojtek (Germany) elucidate the current trends in European taxation of trusts. They share the laws of their respective jurisdictions to point out the different approaches being taken as European jurisdictions struggle to define the tax ramifications to settlor, trustee, and beneficiary of trusts with links to civil law countries in which the common law trust historically has not been recognized by the domestic law.

Part VII takes a look at the unique problems associated with estate planning when any one of three countries with many cross-border ties with the United States is involved. In Chapter 16, Mary Ann Bueschkens and Lucindia E. Main both of Heenan Blaikie and Jason P. Trenton of McDermott Will & Emery update the chapter originally written by Wolfe D. Goodman and consider the unique planning problems and different tax systems involved when dealing with a person who has U.S. and Canadian affiliations and/or property. Chapter 17 by Michelle B. Graham and Laura M. Nava both of McKenna Long & Aldridge affords the same consideration to estate planning involving the United States and Mexico. Finally, in Chapter 18, Richard Cassell and Penelope Williams both of Withers, focus on U.S.–United Kingdom estate planning considerations.

Part VIII examines the ever-changing world of transparency and disclosure and their impact on practitioners and clients. Chapter 19 by Christopher M. Reamer of Long Reimer Winegar examines the ethical challenges practitioners face in the international field. In Chapter 20, Gideon Rothschild of Moses & Singer looks at offshore planning opportunities for protecting clients' assets. In Chapter 21, Kevin L. Shepherd of Venable examines the changing world of transparency, due diligence, and heightened scrutiny by lawyers as gatekeepers. Given the vastly changing world of tax transparency, in Chapter 22, Justin Ransome, Marianne Kayan, Ben S. Wright, Ashley Weyenberg, and Caryn Gross all of Ernst & Young look at the compliance burdens client face when they have anything foreign and how to deal with clients seeking to make a voluntary disclosure to the Internal Revenue Service.

Undoubtedly, as we go to press, tax, regulatory, and other laws will have changed. As practitioners, such changes are our major challenge. Given that our clients and their issues are far more international and multinational, we at least have a place to start in analyzing their complex planning and other issues. I wish to thank all the authors and editors who assisted in this process including Ted Ahlgren, Andrew Stone, and Marianne Kargan to bring the international estate planning world to these pages.

Leigh-Alexandra Basha
September 24, 2013

PART I
Overview

Basic Conflict of Laws Principles

1

Robert C. Lawrence, III
Elisa Shevlin Rizzo

I. Introduction

This chapter provides an overview of some of the conflict of laws issues and attendant considerations that may arise in working with multinational clients.[1] It addresses opportunities available to the international investor under the laws of certain states of the United States. Specifically, it sets forth the extent to which courts of the United States enforce legal rights, obligations, or claims affecting a nonresident alien's assets located within the United States when such rights, obligations, or claims arise under the laws of foreign jurisdictions, which often are civil law jurisdictions.

Generally, the principles of conflict of laws provide guidelines to determine whether a court of the forum jurisdiction will apply its law or the laws of another interested jurisdiction to a dispute. This inquiry often requires a court to make a choice that may be affected by public policy considerations of the forum jurisdiction. Conflict of laws principles, moreover, may extend to many aspects of a case, such as judicial jurisdiction,

1. This chapter is adapted from ROBERT C. LAWRENCE, III, INTERNATIONAL TAX AND ESTATE PLANNING ch. 1 (3d ed. 1999), which contains a detailed discussion of conflict of laws issues in the context of international estate planning.

characterization of property, choice of law, and the recognition and enforcement of foreign judgments.

II. Conflict of Laws Issues

A. Determining Affiliation

1. Introduction

The traditional ordering process for determining choice of law issues in common law jurisdictions is that the law of the jurisdiction of domicile governs the disposition of personal property (often referred to as movables), and the law of the situs governs the disposition of real property (often referred to as immovables).[2] Civil law jurisdictions, however, often refer to nationality for determining choice of law issues. These three principles are described below.

2. Domicile

The determination of a client's domicile is the threshold question in determining many of the rights and obligations of the parties, the characterization of property, the validity and construction of a will, the place of probate, and other planning issues. Domicile is a legal construct that describes the relationship between an individual and a particular locality or country. While there is no uniform definition of domicile, under the laws of most common law jurisdictions, domicile consists of two elements that must exist concurrently: (1) physical presence in the jurisdiction and (2) the intent to remain indefinitely.[3] This common law definition has been codified in one form or another in both federal and state laws. For example, under New York law, "domicile" is defined as "a fixed, permanent and principal home to which a person wherever temporarily located always intends to return."[4]

There are certain legal presumptions that are helpful to determine a person's domicile. Domicile may be examined in terms of the following categories: domicile of origin, domicile by operation of law, and domicile of choice. Some common law jurisdictions recognize the concept of "domicile of origin." Domicile of origin is the domicile the law assigns to each person at birth—generally, the domicile of the father in the case of a legitimate child and of the mother in the case of an illegitimate child.[5] Domicile may also be assigned by operation of law. For example, at common law, a married woman was presumed to have the same domicile as her husband.[6] However, this rule has evolved, and today, in most common law jurisdictions, a husband and wife may have different domiciles even if they are not

2. Hereafter, the term "movable" is used in this chapter interchangeably with the term "personal property," and the term "immovable" is used interchangeably with "real property."

3. 25 Am. Jur. 2d *Domicil* § 1 (2012); 28 C.J.S. *Domicile* § 1 (2004).

4. N.Y. Surr. Ct. Proc. Act § 103[15] (Lexis Nexis 2012).

5. Restatement (Second) Conflict of Laws § 14 (1971).

6. Lawrence, International Tax and Estate Planning, *supra* note 1, § 1:3.1[B]

living apart from one another. A third type of domicile is "domicile of choice." One who is legally capable of changing his or her domicile may acquire a domicile of choice by being physically present in a new jurisdiction and possessing the intent to remain there indefinitely.[7]

With domicile of choice, both elements must exist concurrently—neither physical presence in the jurisdiction nor intention to remain alone is sufficient to effectuate a change in domicile.[8] In determining whether the individual has the requisite intent, courts generally focus on factors such as the individual's social and business contacts, type of home, church membership, voting registration, place of driver's license and car registration, and other similar elements that demonstrate that the individual has a close and settled relationship with a particular locality. Declarations of domicile—whether formal declarations, such as in a will or trust instrument, or informal statements—are also admissible as evidence but are given less weight because of the self-serving nature of such statements.[9]

Determining one's domicile may be difficult, in part because the concept of domicile resembles and is often confused with the concept of "residence." Residence does not, however, generally involve the requisite attitude of mind and requires only physical presence in a particular locality or an actual place of abode there.[10] Therefore, it is commonly said that a person can have several residences but only one domicile.[11] Further confusing matters, the terms "residence" and "domicile" are often used interchangeably but with differing meanings in various types of statutes.[12] In particular, tax statutes often cause confusion by using the principles of residence and domicile for imposing taxes. A good example is the U.S. federal estate and gift tax scheme. The Internal Revenue Code adopts residence as the basis of taxation, but the Treasury Regulations indicate that the term residence is to be interpreted to mean domicile.[13]

---

7. 25 Am. Jur. 2d *Domicil* § 6; Restatement (Second) Conflict of Laws § 15.

8. 25 Am. Jur. 2d *Domicil* § 14.

9. Restatement (Second) Conflict of Laws ch. 2, Special Note on Evidence for Establishment of a Domicil of Choice; *see also* Kjarstad v. State, 703 P.2d 1167 (Alaska 1985); *In re* Esser's Will, 239 N.Y.S.2d 585 (Sur. Ct. 1963); Meltzer v. Commonwealth Unemployment Compensation Bd. of Review, 471 A.2d 157 (Pa. Commw. Ct. 1984).

10. *See* Stacher v. United States, 258 F.2d 112 (9th Cir.), *cert. denied*, 358 U.S. 907 (1958); Weible v. United States, 244 F.2d 158 (9th Cir. 1957). *See also* Restatement (Second) Conflict of Laws § 30—factors include amount of time spent in the locality, the nature of the abode (fixed or temporary), attitude of mind, and activities in the locality.

11. 25 Am Jur. 2d *Domicil* § 1 (2012). Farmers Mut. Ins. Co. v. Tucker, 576 S.E.2d 261 (W. Va. 2002).

12. Restatement (Second) Conflict of Laws § 11, cmt. k notes that, as used in various U.S. statutes, the term "residence" may be interpreted (1) as the equivalent of domicile, (2) as a domicil where one actually dwells, or (3) as the place where one dwells without regard to domicile.

13. I.R.C. § 2001. Treas. Reg. § 20.0-1(b)(1) defines a "resident" decedent as "a decedent who, at the time of his death, had his domicile in the United States. . . . A person acquires a domicile in a place by living there, for even a brief period of time, with no definite present intention of later removing therefrom. Residence without the requisite intention to remain indefinitely will not suffice to constitute domicile, nor will intention to change domicile effect such a change unless

3. Nationality

While domicile is the criterion used in common law jurisdictions to determine certain conflict of laws issues, the estate planner should be aware that other jurisdictions employ the concept of nationality.[14] In such jurisdictions, the determination of one's nationality may be conditioned on one's political allegiance, parentage, place of birth, or naturalization.[15] Thus, a person may be domiciled in one country, yet may be a national of another country. As with domicile, different jurisdictions may apply different standards in determining an individual's nationality. Thus, two or more countries may claim an individual as its national. Furthermore, some jurisdictions, such as Switzerland, employ a mixed system of domicile and nationality, whereby the domiciliary rule is applied to both foreigners living within the jurisdiction and its nationals living abroad.[16] Although generally nationality does not play a significant role in conflict of laws analyses by U.S. courts, it is an area of law with which a multinational estate planner should be familiar.

4. Situs

Conflict of laws questions relating to immovables are generally decided in accordance with the law of the jurisdiction in which such property is situated.[17] The situs rule is based upon the rationale that the situs jurisdiction has the greatest interest in controlling the administration of property located within its borders.

B. Bases of Jurisdiction of a U.S. Court

An important initial consideration is the selection of the court and thereby the jurisdiction in which to probate or establish a decedent's will. The general rule of probate or establishment is that a will should be probated or established in the first instance at the testator's domicile.[18] However, because each jurisdiction has the power to administer and dispose of property located there, a will may frequently be probated in a jurisdiction where the testator left property.[19] A

---

accompanied by actual removal." Conversely, a "nonresident" decedent is defined as "a decedent who, at the time of his death, had his domicile outside the United States." Treas. Reg. § 20.0-1(b)(2). *See also* LAWRENCE, INTERNATIONAL TAX AND ESTATE PLANNING, *supra* note 1, § 1:3.1.

14. Jurisdictions that employ a nationality standard include many Western European counties, most of Eastern Europe, the Middle East, and Latin America, as well as Japan. For a general discussion of nationality issues in multinational estate planning, see CHARLES STEVENSON ET AL., INTERNATIONAL ESTATE PLANNING ch. 2 (1992).

15. *See id.* § 2.05; 1 JEFFREY A. SCHOENBLUM, MULTISTATE AND MULTINATIONAL ESTATE PLANNING § 12.02[c] (2D ED. 1999).

16. STEVENSON ET AL., *supra* note 14, § 2.05[2].

17. RESTATEMENT (SECOND) CONFLICT OF LAWS § 239 (1971).

18. D.E. Evins, *Annotation, Probate, in State Where Assets Are Found, of Will of Nonresident Which Has Not Been Admitted to Probate in State of Domicile*, 20 A.L.R.3d 1033 (1968). N.Y. SURR. CT. PROC. ACT § 205(a) provides in pertinent part: "The surrogate's court of any county has jurisdiction over the estate of a decedent who was a domiciliary of the state at the time of his death, disappearance or internment."

19. *See* N.Y. SURR. CT. PROC. ACT § 1605(1); Pullman's Palace Car v. Pennsylvania, 141 U.S. 18 (1891); *In re* Estrem's Estate, 107 P.2d 36 (Cal. 1940).

number of states have statutes that authorize the court to exercise original jurisdiction over the will of a nonresident decedent,[20] and it is not unusual for a non-U.S. domiciliary to direct probate of his or her will under the laws of a particular state. Thus, in *Montgomery v. National Savings & Trust*, the Court of Appeals for the District of Columbia Circuit affirmed the decision of the United States District Court for the District of Columbia, which admitted to probate an "American will" of a decedent domiciled in Italy that disposed of stocks, bonds, and cash located in the District.[21] Similarly, a New York surrogate's court exercised jurisdiction over the will of a testator, domiciled in Peru, who directed New York as a place of probate, left assets in New York, and named a New York beneficiary and executor.[22] Likewise, jurisdiction over the will of a Swiss domiciliary in New York was deemed proper where the decedent left 90 percent of his assets in New York and the will requested that New York law apply to its probate.[23] Many courts, however, have said that they are not required to grant original probate, even though authorized by statute. Thus, a court will grant original probate in the exercise of sound discretion, depending on the facts and circumstances of each case and considerations of comity. A court, for example, may wish to await the action of a court in the decedent's domicile and may deny original probate if most of the major contacts are in another jurisdiction.[24]

Original probate of a will of a nonresident may be denied if the will has already been admitted to probate at the testator's domicile.[25] In such case, the

20. Several states have express statutes authorizing the exercise of original probate over the will of a nondomiciliary who has left property in the state. *See, e.g.*, N.Y. Surr. Ct. Proc. Act § 1605(1); R.I. Gen. Laws § 33-7-25; Tex Prob. Code § 103; Wis. Stat. § 868.01.

21. Montgomery v. Nat'l Sav. & Trust, 356 F.2d 806 (D.C. Cir. 1966); *see also In re* Cates, N.Y.L.J., June 25, 1980, at 11, col. 2, *aff'd*, 80 A.D.2d 1003 (Sur. Ct. 1981) (New York County Surrogate exercised jurisdiction to probate will executed in Haiti by decedent who had an apartment and other property in New York, but who was assumed by court to have been domiciled in Haiti for purposes of decision); *In re* Goldstein's Will, 310 N.Y.S.2d 602 (App. Div. 1970) (abuse of discretion to refuse jurisdiction to probate will drafted by New York lawyer, which had New York attesting witnesses, where all assets were located in New York, most of witnesses preferred New York probate, and fiduciaries named under will were disqualified under law of descendant's Florida domicile); *In re* Estate of Nelson, 475 N.Y.S.2d 194 (Sur. Ct. 1984) (court exercised jurisdiction over estate even though assets were brought into jurisdiction after testator's death).

22. *In re* Estate of Chopitea, 228 N.Y.S.2d 104 (Sur. Ct. 1962).

23. *In re* Estate of Vischer, 280 N.Y.S.2d 49 (Sur. Ct. 1967). Jurisdiction was upheld even though the Swiss-U.S. Treaty had been interpreted to provide that all controversies between successors to property be decided by the laws of decedent's domicile in *In re* Estate of Rougeron, 217 N.E.2d 639 (N.Y.), *cert. denied*, 385 U.S. 899 (1966).

24. For example, in *In re* Estate of Brunner, 339 N.Y.S.2d 506 (Sur. Ct. 1973), a New York surrogate's court declined jurisdiction over a will executed in New York despite a clause requesting that New York law apply. The testator died a domiciliary of France. The decedent's only New York asset was a single small bank account. Most of the decedent's other assets were located in France, and the decedent did not own a New York residence. The court held that the bank account was an insufficient basis for jurisdiction and emphasized both the need to rely on French law to administer the will and the fact that any witnesses necessary to testify as to the capacity of the testator would also be in France.

25. *In re* Estate of Wachman, 238 N.Y.S.2d 112 (Sur. Ct. 1963); N.Y. Surr. Ct. Proc. Act § 1605.

nondomiciliary jurisdiction is generally limited to the exercise of ancillary jurisdiction. However, this rule is subject to certain exceptions. For example, under New York law,[26] a court may exercise original probate jurisdiction over the will of a nondomiciliary if (1) ancillary probate would be unduly inconvenient, expensive, or impossible under the circumstances,[27] (2) the laws of the decedent's domicile discriminate against New York domiciliaries,[28] or (3) the will expressly directs probate in New York.[29] As a planning matter, if a nondomiciliary testator wishes for probate and administration in a particular state, the planner would be well advised to have his or her client establish as much of a nexus with that state as possible. At the least, the client should maintain substantial assets within the jurisdiction, appoint an executor who is present therein, and direct that probate be therein.

---

26. N.Y. Surr. Ct. Proc. Act § 1605(2).

27. *In re* Estate of Turton, 15 N.Y.S.2d 131 (Sur. Ct. 1961), a New York surrogate's court refused to dismiss a petition for original probate of the will of a testator, allegedly domiciled in British Honduras, even though proceedings for probate were still pending in British Honduras. The court based its decision on three factors: (1) the amount of time that had elapsed since the will was offered for original probate in British Honduras, (2) the question of domicile remained unresolved and (3) substantial expense had already been incurred in handling the estate in New York.

28. In *In re* Estate of Siegel, 373 N.Y.S.2d 812 (Sur. Ct. 1975), the court concluded that because Florida law discriminated against the appointment of the nominated trustee, the Marine Midland Bank, a New York domiciliary, it would admit the will of a Florida domiciliary to original probate even though the will had been admitted to probate in Florida. *See also In re* Estate of Brown, 436 N.YS.2d 132 (Sur. Ct. 1981) (upholding exercise of jurisdiction by New York court where Florida, the decedent's domicile, discriminated against the petitioner by prohibiting him from being appointed executor in Florida because he was a nonresident).

29. In *In re* Estate of Renard (*Renard I*), 417 N.Y.S.2d 155 (Sur. Ct.), *aff'd*, 418 N.Y.S.2d 553 (1979), involving a domiciliary of France whose New York will requested probate in New York (there was a later French will dealing with French property), the court retained jurisdiction. The court stated that the fact that the New York will had already been admitted to probate in France was entitled to careful consideration, but noted that (1) substantial assets were located in New York, (2) nominated executors were New York residents, (3) opposing the forced heirship claim of the decedent's son in France would prove burdensome for the interested legatees, and (4) the proceedings were brought in good faith and without the intent to thwart French law.

Some of these factors were originally applied in *In re* Will of Heller-Baghero, 258 N.E.2d 717 (N.Y. 1970), although that case did not involve the same statutory provision because a 1962 will, rather than the 1964 will offered for probate in New York, had been established (the equivalent of admission to probate) at the testator's domicile, Austria. Thus, unlike *Renard I*, no statute governed the question. Upon appeal, the New York Court of Appeals held that the surrogate properly exercised jurisdiction to probate the 1964 will. The court reasoned that jurisdiction was proper because (1) the issue of the validity of the 1964 will had not been foreclosed in Austria, (2) 90 percent of the assets were located in New York, (3) the executor and two legatees were New York residents, and (4) the proceedings were brought in New York in good faith, with no suggestion of an attempt to thwart Austrian laws. Although the objectants relied on case law denying original probate of the will of a nonresident, the court maintained that it was a rule of ad hoc discretion, and that the facts of this case were strong enough to justify the assumption of jurisdiction. The case demonstrates the wide discretion given to the court to entertain probate. *See also In re* Will of Nelson, 475 N.Y.S.2d 194 (Sur. Ct. 1984). Factors the court considered in this case in accepting jurisdiction were the wishes of the testator, the convenience of fiduciaries and beneficiaries, and pending litigation in New York relating to the estate.

C. Choice of Law

1. Overview

Once a court accepts jurisdiction, it must determine what law to apply to a given issue, such as the construction, validity, or interpretation of a will (or trust instrument). Each planner has to analyze the facts and circumstances and plan the result of this determination. The analysis is a two-step process: characterizing the property interest and choosing the appropriate law to be applied.

2. Classification of Property

As an initial matter, the court determines under its local law whether the property involved is immovable or movable. The distinction between immovables and movables is basic to conflict of laws analysis and estate planning, yet the laws governing such classifications vary. For example, some jurisdictions may classify a partnership interest in a partnership that owns real estate as intangible personal property; others may classify it as an interest in real property.[30] Similar issues may also arise with respect to leasehold interests in real property. For example, under New York law, leaseholds are generally characterized as real property and thus are governed by the law of the situs.[31] It should be of some comfort, however, that often two interested jurisdictions will characterize a property interest in the same way.

3. Choice of Law Approaches

Once a determination has been made as to whether the property is immovable or movable, the second step in the choice of law analysis is to determine whether the court will apply the law of its own jurisdiction or the law of another jurisdiction to govern the distribution and administration of an estate or certain of its components. Many issues that arise in the administration of an estate are procedural rather than substantive and are uniformly decided by the local law of the forum, regardless of the nature of the dispute or identity of the parties.

The procedural-substantive distinction is purely one of convenience. Procedural matters are concerned with the management of litigation in the courts of a particular jurisdiction. Procedural matters include the form of action, timing for filing or responding to pleadings or motions, evidentiary questions, methods of service, means of enforcing a judgment, and similar rules concerned with administration that presumably do not affect the substantive outcome of the case, and, as to them, the forum is considered to have the most significant relationship.[32] In contrast, matters of substance pertain to the legal relations or rights of the

---

30. *See* Note, *Problematic Definitions of Property in Multistate Death Taxation*, 90 Harv. L. Rev. 1656 (1977). *See also* Southeast Bank, N.A. v. Lawrence, 489 N.E.2d 744 (N.Y. 1985). The court determined that the right of publicity is personal property, thus Florida, not New York law, would apply to a question of whether a theater owner could use the name of a famous deceased playwright.

31. *In re* Hadelman's Estate, 143 N.Y.S.2d 396 (Sur. Ct. 1955).

32. *See, e.g.*, Eugene Scoles & Peter Hay, Conflict of Laws 57–67 (2d ed. 1992); Restatement (Second) Conflict of Laws § 122 (1971).

parties. As such, they are determinative of the outcome of the dispute and are generally decided in accordance with the law of the jurisdiction having the most significant relationship to the dispute or particular issue.[33]

As pointed out, it is sometimes difficult to determine which law a court will apply to the facts of a particular case. In some areas of the law, courts have changed from the traditional approach of applying the law of the situs to immovables and the law of the domicile to movables to a modern approach based on the purposes and policies of the particular jurisdiction. The goal of the modern approach is to determine, from the facts of each case, which jurisdiction has the most significant relationship to the given situation.[34] The *Restatement (Second) of Conflict of Laws* has listed the important factors to be considered as:

- the needs of the interstate and international system;
- relevant policies of the forum;
- relevant policies of the interested states or countries and the relative interests of those places in the particular issue;
- protection of justified expectations;
- basic policies underlying the particular field of law;
- predictability and uniformity of result; and
- ease in the application and determination of the law.[35]

As noted, however, choice of law analysis in property succession is, to a large extent, governed by the traditional rules, which are applied with great consistency. Moreover, many jurisdictions, such as New York, have adopted comprehensive statutes to direct the courts' choice of law.[36] This does not, however, conflict with the current trend in many areas of the law to identify the jurisdiction with the most significant relationship to the issue. On the contrary, the durability of the doctrinal rules in the area of property succession is explicable by applying the above-listed factors to a given situation. In most cases, such an application will lead to the same predictable result as an application of the traditional rules, although some recent decisions reflect a deviation by some courts from these rules when the balancing of the relevant policies of the different jurisdictions indicates a certain decision should be reached.[37]

4. *Renvoi*

The approach of a jurisdiction to choice of law issues, particularly to *renvoi*, is crucial in determining the law applicable to each part of an estate plan. The doctrine of *renvoi* provides that a forum apply not only the substantive law of the

33. Scoles & Hay *supra* note 32, at 57–67.

34. *See, e.g.*, Babcock v. Jackson, 191 N.E.2d 279 (N.Y. 1963); Willis L.M. Reese, *Choice of Law: Rules or Approach*, 57 Cornell L. Rev. 315 (1972).

35. Restatement (Second) Conflict of Laws § 6 (1971).

36. N.Y. Est. Powers & Trusts Law § 3-5.1.

37. *See, e.g.*, *In re* Estate of Clark, 281 N.Y.S.2d 180 (1967), *aff'd*, 236 N.E.2d 152 (N.Y. 1968). *Cf.* Rudow v. Fogel, 426 N.E.2d 155 (Mass. App. Ct. 1981).

state of reference but also its conflicts rules: in other words, its whole law. Simply stated, if *renvoi* is applied, the forum essentially sits as a foreign court in order to reach a result consistent with the "whole" law—choice of law and local law—of the other jurisdiction.[38] Of course, the choice of law rule of the foreign jurisdiction may then direct the application of its own local law, that of the original forum, or even the law of a third jurisdiction.

Renvoi is often applied to the validity and effect of transfers of both immovable and movable property. It is especially important in planning for the succession of immovable property because the local laws of the various jurisdictions may differ significantly.[39]

There are essentially three approaches to *renvoi*. First, some countries reject it outright and, when directed by their own choice of law rule to apply the law of another jurisdiction, apply only the substantive (local) law of that jurisdiction. The second and more common approach is "single-reference" *renvoi* whereby a forum looks to the choice of law rule of the foreign jurisdiction to which it is directed by its own conflicts rule as well as the foreign jurisdiction's substantive (local) law.[40] Under the third approach, some jurisdictions may, in certain cases, apply "double-reference" *renvoi*. Like "single-reference" *renvoi*, the forum first looks to the conflicts rule of the foreign jurisdiction, Country X, to which it is directed by its own choice of law. However, the forum will determine whether Country X would also apply *renvoi* to the issue had it been initially brought in a court there.

---

38. *See generally* RESTATEMENT (SECOND) CONFLICT OF LAWS § 8 (1971); Erwin Griswold, *Renvoi Revisited*, 51 HARV. L. REV. 1165 (1938). The comments to the Restatement go on to explain that "[w]hen a court is directed by its choice-of-law rules to determine a particular issue in accordance with its own law, the word 'law' means the local law of the forum. If, in this context, 'law' were to be interpreted as meaning the entire law of the forum, the court would be referred back to its own choice-of-law rules and would be back at the place where it began." RESTATEMENT (SECOND) CONFLICT OF LAWS § 8, cmt. c.

39. For example, many civil law jurisdictions apply a single or unitary law to all assets (whether immovable or movable) of a decedent. Depending upon the jurisdiction, this unitary law is the law of the decedent's nationality or last domicile. In contrast, common law countries differentiate the law to be applied according to whether the assets are characterized as immovables or movables. If a court in County A, a unitary law jurisdiction that accepts *renvoi*, assumes jurisdiction over the administration of a will of an English national, it would look to the law of England, including its choice of laws rules. This follows because Country A's own choice of law rule is to apply the "law" of the nationality; because Country A accepts *renvoi*, "law" refers to choice of law as well as local law. Because English choice of law would apply the law of the last domicile to movables and the law of the situs to immovables, the court in County A will do the same. In contrast, a court in County B, a unitary law jurisdiction that does not accept *renvoi*, administering the will of the same English national, would simply apply the substantive law of England. For further discussion, see LAWRENCE, *supra* note 1, § 1:5.5; Eugene Scoles & Max Rheinstein, *Conflict Avoidance in Succession Planning*, 21 L. & CONTEMP. PROBS. 499, 499–501 (1956).

40. For example, in *In re* Schneider's Estate (*Schneider*), 96 N.Y.S.2d 652 (Sur. Ct. 1950), *aff'd on reh'g*, 100 N.Y.S.2d 371 (Sur. Ct. 1950), a New York court was required to determine the validity of a testamentary disposition of real property in Switzerland by a New York domiciliary. The forum looked to Swiss choice of law and concluded that under the Swiss unity-of-succession principle, the Swiss courts would apply the law of the testator's domicile to all of his real and personal property. Accordingly, the court employed "single-reference" *renvoi* and applied New York local law to uphold the disposition of the real property.

If it would, the forum will then apply the choice of law, rather than the local law, of the jurisdiction it is then directed to by the conflicts rule of Country X.[41] The "perpetual loop" or "Ping-Pong" effect frequently mentioned in connection with "double-reference" *renvoi* creates more of a problem in theory than in practice.[42]

5. Special Considerations with Respect to Wills

Many choice of law issues arise with regard to wills. Before discussing these issues, it should be noted that at least under the common law system, the intent of the testator has paramount importance, and if the testator specifically designates the applicable law, a court will generally honor it. For the sake of simplicity, the following discussion assumes that the forum is a common law jurisdiction.

The two main choice of law principles in a testamentary context are (1) that the law of the situs of real property governs the validity and effect of its disposition[43] and (2) that the law of the testator's last domicile governs the validity and effect of the disposition of personal property, tangible and intangible, wherever situated.[44] The rationale is simple. As to real property, it is assumed that the situs jurisdiction has the greatest interest in who holds title to the property and that only a court of that jurisdiction can issue an enforceable decree affecting title. Therefore, it is likely that a foreign judgment that does not respect the laws of the situs will be denied enforcement by the situs jurisdiction.[45] As to personal property, the courts are more interested in the intent of the testator in disposing of his or her property. It is presumed that the testator is most familiar with the laws of his or her domicile, that the will has been prepared accordingly, and that the jurisdiction of domicile has the greatest relationship to the testator and the estate with regard to such personal property.

---

41. Thus, if the New York court in *Schneider* had employed "double-reference" *renvoi*, and assuming it determined that Switzerland would also apply *renvoi* to the issue, the court would ultimately have applied the local law of Switzerland to the realty, in conformance with New York choice of law. *See, e.g.*, *In re* Annesley, [1926] 1 Ch. 692 (Eng.). The essential difference in the two approaches is that the single-reference *renvoi* assumes that the country to which the forum is directed by the forum's choice of law does not accept *renvoi*. The double-reference approach, by contrast, takes into account the foreign country's actual approach to *renvoi*. This approach is also known as "sitting and judging."

42. In theory, a perpetual loop can only occur if the forum and the jurisdiction to which the forum looks both practice the double-reference approach, and their respective conflicts rules point to each other for the applicable law. In reality, such an occurrence is extremely rare and would ultimately be resolved by resorting to the local policy of the forum toward the substantive issue.

43. Restatement (Second) Conflict of Laws § 239 (1971); *see, e.g.*, *In re* Barrie's Estate, 35 N.W.2d 658 (Iowa), *cert. denied sub nom.* Hodge v. First Presbyterian Church, 338 U.S. 815, *reh'g denied*, 338 U.S. 881 (1949). *But see In re* Estate of Janney, 446 A.2d 1265 (Pa. 1982). In *Janney*, the Pennsylvania court would not give effect to New Jersey law, which had subsequently been superseded, notwithstanding the fact that the controversy centered upon proceeds from the sale of real property in New Jersey when the law was in effect. *See also* Restatement (Second) Conflict of Laws § 239 cmt. c (1971).

44. Restatement (Second) Conflict of Laws § 263 (1971); Scoles & Hay, *supra* note 32, at 812.

45. *See, e.g.*, *Schneider*, 96 N.Y.S.2d 652, *supra* note 40.

In applying the law of the situs or domicile to the disposition of property, an estate planner must always consider the possibility of *renvoi.*[46] Unless another jurisdiction is considered to have a more dominant interest in the particular issue, however, the general presumption is that a court in the jurisdiction of situs will apply its local law to the disposition of real property and a court in the jurisdiction of domicile will apply its local law to the disposition of personal property.[47]

(a) Formal Validity, Revocation, and Testamentary Capacity. Questions concerning statutory formalities, revocation, and capacity are decided by the normal application of the laws of the situs or domicile.[48] The situs jurisdiction, for example, is under no obligation to give effect to a disposition of real property if the will does not comply with its local requirements, even if the will has been executed in accordance with all formalities of the testator's domicile. Similarly, a forum may test the formal validity of a will disposing of personal property by the law of the testator's domicile.[49]

To mitigate the harsh results that might follow from the strict application of these rules, many jurisdictions have expanded the test of formal validity. Thus, many courts will uphold a will or testamentary instrument if it complies with the requirements of any jurisdiction that is significantly related to the will. This includes the testator's domicile at the time of execution, the situs of the assets, or the forum.[50] Statutes in more than thirty states provide for alternative places of reference with respect to questions of proper execution of a testamentary instrument.[51]

The courts in the jurisdictions of situs (as to real property) and domicile (as to personal property) normally apply their own local laws to the issue of the validity of the revocation of a testamentary instrument, either by physical act or by operation of law.[52] Some states have extended the effect of their statutes to uphold revocations that are valid in the jurisdiction where the act occurs.[53] In civil law

46. *See supra* text accompanying notes 40–42; *Schneider*, 96 N.Y.S.2d 652.

47. Restatement (Second) Conflict of Laws §§ 239(2), 263(2) (1971). Of course, the result is different if these courts do not subscribe to situs/domicile principles of succession. In that case, the reference may be back to the forum or a third jurisdiction.

48. *See generally* George Stumberg, Conflict of Laws 375–78 (3d ed. 1968); *In re* Estate of Georg, 298 F. Supp. 741 (D.V.I. 1969).

49. *See, e.g.*, Moultrie v. Hunt, 23 N.Y. 394 (1861).

50. *See* John B. Rees, Jr., *American Will Statutes: II*, 46 Va. L. Rev. 856, 905–06 (1960).

51. *Id.*; *see, e.g.*, N.Y. Est. Powers & Trusts Law § 3-5.1; Ill. Comp. Stat. Ann. ch. 755, § 5/7-1. *See generally* Alice M. Bright, *Permitting a Non-Resident to Choose a Place of Probate*, 85 Tr. & Est. 865 (1956). England has also adopted a very liberal provision for providing alternative places of reference. *See* England Wills Act 1967, H & 12 Eliz. 2, ch. 044.

52. *See* Martin Wolff, Private International Law 206–09 (2d ed. 1950); Sternberg v. St. Louis Union Trust Co., 163 F.2d 714 (8th Cir.), *cert. denied*, 332 U.S. 843 (1947).

53. *See* Restatement (Second) Conflict of Laws §§ 239–43 (1971); *In re* Barrie's Estate, 73 N.E.2d 654 (Ill. 1947).

countries, an intentional act of revocation is generally effective if it complies with the formalities of the place where it occurs.[54]

In response to the need for uniform international regulation, the Hague Conference on Private International Law met in 1960 to draft certain conflicts rules relating to the form of testamentary dispositions.[55] Nineteen countries participated and a multireference rule for recognizing the validity of the execution of wills was adopted.[56] Under article 1 of the Convention on the Conflicts of Laws Relating to the Form of Testamentary Dispositions, a testamentary disposition is formally valid if it complies with the internal law of (1) the place of execution, (2) the nationality of the testator either at the time of execution or of death,[57] (3) the place where the testator had a habitual residence either at the time of the disposition (execution) or of death, and (4) the situs if the assets are real property. These same places of reference are also applied to the formal validity of a revocation.

On questions of capacity, of either the testator or the beneficiary, the courts in the jurisdictions of situs (as to real property) or domicile (as to personal property) generally apply their local law unless it is clear that another jurisdiction has the stronger interest. The situs jurisdiction may impose various restrictions, for example, as to the capacity of aliens or foreign corporations to hold title to real property.[58] Because of the obvious interest of the situs jurisdiction as to who holds title to real property within its jurisdiction, courts can be expected to apply their own local law regardless of the law of other interested jurisdictions.

Statutes providing alternative places of reference on issues of formal validity should also be considered with respect to capacity. If a will is admitted to probate

---

54. *See* Scoles & Rheinstein, *supra* note 39, at 499, 505.

55. *See generally* Kurt Nadelmann, *The Hague Conference on Private International Law, Ninth Session*, 9 AM. J. COMP. LAW 583 (1960).

56. The Ninth Session of the Hague Conference was comprised of representatives of the governments of eighteen member states—Austria, Belgium, Denmark, Finland, France, West Germany, Greece, Italy, Japan, Luxembourg, the Netherlands, Norway, Portugal, Spain, Sweden, Switzerland, the United Kingdom, and Yugoslavia. The United States sent an observer delegation. To date, the Convention on the Conflicts of Laws Relating to the Form of Testamentary Dispositions has been entered into force by forty-one contracting states including the following member states: Australia, Austria, Belgium, China, Croatia, Denmark, Estonia, Finland, the former Yugoslav Republic of Macedonia, France, Germany, Greece, Ireland, Israel, Japan, Luxembourg, the Netherlands, Norway, Poland, Slovenia, Spain, Sweden, Switzerland, Turkey, and the United Kingdom. The Convention has also been entered into force by a number of nonmember states, including Antigua and Barbuda, Botswana, Fiji, Grenada and Mauritius. For a full status report, see Hague Conference on Private International Law, Full Status Report Convention #11, http://www.hcch.net/index_en.php?act=conventions.status&cid=40 (last visited Oct. 12, 2012).

57. Whether the testator had his or her domicile in a particular place under article I is to be determined by the law of that place. Article 9, however, allows contracting states to reserve the right to determine where the testator was domiciled according to foreign law.

58. *See, e.g.*, Carpenter v. Bell, 34 S.W. 209 (Tenn. 1896). This issue is discussed in detail in LAWRENCE, *supra* note 1, Chapter 3.

because it was properly executed in another jurisdiction, the forum may also refer questions of capacity to the local law of that jurisdiction.[59]

(b) Interpretation and Construction. Interpretation and construction are distinct processes to help the courts determine the meaning and effect of words contained in a testamentary instrument.

Interpretation, the more common practice, is the attempt to discover the actual meaning and intent of the testator. It is therefore a question of fact and does not give rise to choice of law problems. Instead, a court looks at such factors as who drafted the instrument, the context in which the words were used, and the circumstances under which the instrument was drafted. In considering these factors a court is bound only by the evidentiary rules of the forum.[60]

If the intent of the testator or the draftsperson cannot be ascertained from the document or the evidence considered in its interpretation, the court will assign a legal meaning to the language in accordance with the rules of construction of the applicable legal system. These rules vary significantly among jurisdictions and important choice of law issues may arise. Typical examples are the legal significance of terms, such as "heirs" and "issue," or whether a certain phrase effected an equitable conversion of property.[61]

In practice, with respect to real property, the courts of the jurisdictions of situs are divided on whether to apply their own local law or the law of the domicile at execution.[62] The latter law is clearly more relevant if the goal of construction is to carry out the presumed intention of the testator. Interestingly, the English rule presumes that the law of the domicile at execution will govern construction of the entire instrument in the absence of contrary evidence as to the testator's intent.[63]

Similar confusion exists with respect to the disposition of personal property. Usually the courts apply the law in the jurisdiction of the testator's last domicile.[64] Sometimes, however, the courts in the jurisdiction of domicile may apply the law of the testator's domicile at the time of execution of the will.[65]

---

59. *See, e.g.*, Wilcoxen v. United States, 310 F. Supp. 1006 (W.D. Kan. 1969); *In re* Estate of Taylor, 391 A.2d 991 (Pa. 1978). However, not all states follow this general rule. New York provides that the formal validity of a will of a decedent not domiciled in New York at his or her death may be tested under the laws of New York, the jurisdiction in which the will was executed (at the time of execution), and the jurisdiction in which the decedent was domiciled (either at death or at execution). N.Y. Est. Powers & Trusts Law § 3-5.1(c). However, questions as to such decedent's general capacity will be examined under New York law. *Id.* § 3-5.1(h).

60. *See* Willis L.M. Reese & Maurice Rosenberg, Cases and Materials on Conflict of Laws 798 (8th ed. 1984).

61. *Id.* at 800; *see* Clarke v. Clarke, 178 U.S. 186 (1900).

62. *See* Reese & Rosenberg, *supra* note 61, at 789.

63. *See* P.M. North & J.J. Fawcett, Private International Law 851–53 (11th ed. 1987).

64. *See* Restatement (Second) Conflict of Laws § 264 (1971); Scoles & Hay, *supra* note 32, at 818.

65. *See, e.g.*, Hamilton Nat'l Bank v. Hutcheson, 357 F. Supp. 114 (E.D. Tenn. 1973), *aff'd*, 492 F.2d 1243 (6th Cir. 1974); Scoles & Hay, *supra* note 32, at 819.

Fortunately for the estate planner, the goal of construction is primarily to carry out the presumed intent of the testator, and the courts are disposed to give effect to an explicit direction that the will be construed according to the laws of a particular jurisdiction.[66] Generally, the courts construe such a direction to refer to the local law, rather than the choice of law, of the designated jurisdiction. The planner should, therefore, consider the inclusion of such a provision in a will disposing of multinational assets.

(c) Substantive Validity. The intrinsic or substantive validity of a testamentary plan or specific disposition presents the most fertile ground for choice of law problems and potentially the most severe pitfalls for the planner. Again, the general conflict of laws rule concerning the effect and validity of a testamentary disposition is also that the law of the situs governs as to real property[67] and that the law of the decedent's last domicile governs as to all personal property, tangible and intangible.[68] Although courts in the jurisdictions of situs (as to real property) and domicile (as to personal property) will usually apply their own local law, the possible application of the doctrine of *renvoi* must not be overlooked.

For example, in *Schneider*, where a New York domiciliary died leaving real property in Switzerland, the New York court looked to Swiss conflicts law with regard to the disposition of the real property and held that under Swiss unity of succession principles the Swiss courts would apply the law of the testator's last domicile to all assets of the deceased, even real property.[69] Accordingly, the court applied New York local law to uphold a disposition of real property that was invalid under the law of the situs.[70]

Despite the deference of courts to the traditional choice of law principles on dispositions of real and personal property, the U.S. Supreme Court recognized early on that the intent of the testator should govern. If the testator clearly intends the law of a jurisdiction other than that which would normally apply to control the disposition of the testator's assets, that intent should be controlling.[71] Several states, including New York, Illinois, Florida, New Jersey, and Connecticut, have statutes that permit a nondomiciliary testator to elect to have the laws of that jurisdiction govern the effect of testamentary dispositions of personal

---

66. *See* Restatement (Second) Conflict of Laws §§ 224, 240, 264 (1971); Second Bank-State St. Trust Co. v. Weston, 174 N.E.2d 763 (Mass. 1961).

67. Restatement (Second) Conflict of Laws § 239 (1971).

68. *Id.* § 263; *In re* Weiss' Will, 64 N.Y.S.2d 331 (Sur. Ct. 1946).

69. *See Schneider*, *supra* note 40 and accompanying text.

70. Significantly, the realty had been liquidated prior to probate, and the funds representing the realty had been remitted to New York for disposition. It should be clear at this point that if the issue had been the disposition of the realty itself and the New York court had incorrectly construed Swiss law, the Swiss courts would probably have denied enforcement of the New York decree.

71. Harrison v. Nixon, 34 U.S. 483 (1835).

property having a situs therein;[72] other jurisdictions have reached the same result by judicial decision.[73]

(d) 1989 Hague Convention on Succession. In 1989, the Hague Convention on the Law Applicable to Succession to the Estate of Deceased Persons (1989 Convention) approved a draft of conflict rules to regulate matters concerning the devolution of property.[74] To date the proposal has not been ratified by the United States, and only Argentina, Luxembourg, the Netherlands, and Switzerland have signed the Convention.[75]

Very generally, the 1989 Convention provides conflict rules for countries that are parties, absent a specific designation of applicable law by the testator. It abandons the traditional distinctions between immovable and movable property and abolishes concepts of domicile and situs, substituting the concepts of "habitual residence" and "nationality" and applying these concepts to both immovable and movable property.

The 1989 Convention sets forth the testator's right to designate the law that will govern succession to the "whole of [the] estate." The testator may choose either the law of habitual residence or nationality at the time the testator makes his or her will, or the law of habitual residence or nationality at the time of his or her death. Moreover, the testator may incorporate by reference into the will the substantive law of any legal system to govern particular assets within his or her estate. However, a testator may not designate a law applicable to particular assets that would contravene the succession principles of the law governing the whole estate.[76]

6. Special Considerations with Respect to Trusts

Many civil law jurisdictions do not recognize the concept of a trust. In 1984, the Hague Conference on Private International Law adopted a Convention on the Law Applicable to Trusts and Their Recognition (the 1984 Convention).[77] One

---

72. N.Y. Est. Powers & Trusts Law § 3-5.1(h); 755 Ill. Comp. Stat. Ann. 5/7-6; Fla. Stat. Ann. § 731.106; N.J. Stat. Ann. § 3B:3-33; Conn. Gen. Stat. § 45a-287(c).

73. *See* Lanius v. Fletcher, 101 S.W. 1076 (Tex. 1907); *In re* Chappell's Estate, 213 P. 684 (Wash. 1923).

74. *See* Convention on the Law Applicable to Succession to the Estates of Deceased Persons, Aug. 1, 1989, 28 I.L.M. 150 (1989), *reprinted in* 2 Proceedings of the Sixteenth Session of the Hague Conference on Private International Law 515 (1990). As of October 12, 2012, the 1989 Convention on Succession was not in force. *See* http://www.hcch.net/index_en.php?act=conventions.status&cid=62 (last visited Oct. 12, 2012).

75. Henry Christensen, International Estate Planning § 5.06[4] (2d. ed. 1999). A full status report of the 1989 Convention is available at http://www.hcch.net/index_en.php?act=conventions.status&cid=62 (last visited May 31, 2012).

76. For further discussion of the 1989 Convention, see Lawrence, *supra* note 1, § 1.5.11.

77. Hague Convention on the Law Applicable to Trusts and their Recognition, Hague Conference on Private International Law, 15th Sess., Final Act (concluded July 1, 1985), *reprinted in* 23 I.L.M. 1388 (1984) (full text also available at http://www.hcch.net/index_en.php?act=conventions.text&cid=59 (last visited Oct. 12, 2012). On May 8, 1987, the U.S. Secretary of State's Advisory Committee on

of the main purposes of the 1984 Convention was to assist civil law countries in interpreting trust instruments.[78] Pursuant to the choice of law provisions of the 1984 Convention, a trust should be governed by the law chosen by the settlor as evidenced by the written trust instrument. If no applicable law is designated, then the trust should be governed by the law of the jurisdiction with which the trust is most closely connected.[79] However, the 1984 Convention also recognizes that certain severable aspects of the trust might be governed by different laws.[80]

The settlor's right to choose the governing law of a trust is subject, however, to certain limitations. Very generally, the 1984 Convention provides that its provisions will not prevent the application of certain mandatory laws, such as the rights of minors, marital rights, succession rights, transfer of title, creditors' rights, the protection of third parties acting in good faith, and economic regulations, such as exchange or export controls.[81] Moreover, the 1984 Convention does not require civil law jurisdictions to adopt the concept of the trust; therefore, to the extent that the most significant elements of the trust are closely connected with a country that does not have such an institution, the country will not be required to recognize the trust.[82]

III. Summary

This chapter is designed to provide the multinational estate planner with an overview of how choice of law principles are utilized in determining which law will apply, as well as how the courts in the United States and certain common law jurisdictions determine rights, obligations, or claims to a nonresident alien's property arising under foreign law.[83] As an initial matter, an estate planner should be familiar with the conflict of laws issues that may arise if a non-U.S. resident has investments or other property situated in the United States and develop a plan that provides as much predictability as possible. This may involve not only choice of law issues but also selection of a favorable jurisdiction.

Private International Law unanimously approved the Trusts Convention. However, the United States has not yet ratified the Trusts Convention. To date, the Trusts Convention is in force in Australia, Canada, Hong Kong, Luxembourg, Malta, Monaco, Switzerland, the United Kingdom, Italy, and the Netherlands. See http://www.hcch.net/index_en.php?act=conventions.status&cid=59 for a full status report on the Trusts Convention. For a general discussion of the Trusts Convention, see David J. Hayton, *Developing The Hague Trusts Convention within Mainland Europe*, 3 CHASE J., NO. 1 (1999).

78. 23 I.L.M at 1388–89 (introductory note).

79. *Id.* at 1389–90.

80. *Id.* at 1390.

81. *Id.* at 1390–91.

82. *Id.* at 1390.

83. When dealing with multinational situations, local counsel should always be consulted when developing an estate plan for any non-U.S. resident with investments in the United States.

2 Current Rules for the United States Income and Transfer Taxation of Nonresident Alien Individuals

Henry Christensen, III
Toni Ann Kruse

I. Introduction

This chapter provides an introduction to and overview of the current United States federal tax rules for the estate, gift, and generation-skipping transfer taxation (hereafter, transfer taxation except in the context of a specific tax) of nonresident alien individuals.The chapter also provides an introduction to the rules of federal income taxation and compares the incidence of income tax to the incidence of transfer tax for a nonresident alien individual.

This book does not focus upon state taxation, but foreign readers should remember that the United States consists of fifty sovereign states and that each state has its own system of taxation. A nonresident alien individual obligated to pay income or transfer tax to the United States federal government may also be obligated to pay tax to a state of the United States and, in the case of income tax in a few cases, to a city of the United States. Such a tax is unlikely to be owed if the incidence of federal tax is based on passive ownership of an intangible (a dividend or a share of stock) sourced or sited in the United States, but a state tax may be owed, particularly if real estate is located in the state or a business is directly or indirectly conducted (as through a partnership) in the state.

The United States is unique among major countries in subjecting to transfer taxation all of a citizen's worldwide assets, wherever the citizen is resident. All of our major trading partners subject transfers of assets located in the jurisdiction to estate tax (and, in some cases, gift tax), but they only tax an individual's worldwide transfers if he or she is resident in the jurisdiction. For this reason, double taxation may arise if a United States citizen dies domiciled in a foreign jurisdiction that imposes an estate tax. However, with the exception of its worldwide transfer taxation of citizens, no matter where resident, the United States' transfer tax rules are not dissimilar to those of other major countries in that the transfer tax applies on a worldwide basis to the property of residents and on a situs basis to the property of nonresident aliens. Similarly, for income tax purposes, the United States taxes its citizens and residents on their worldwide income but taxes nonresident aliens solely on their U.S.-source income. Residence for gift and estate tax purposes and residence for income tax purposes are not the same, as described below.

II. Bases for Taxation

A. Citizenship

Except in connection with special rules applicable to expatriates[1] and to citizens of the United States who are citizens solely by reason of their being citizens of possessions of the United States,[2] the question of who is a "citizen" of the United States is usually easy to answer. All persons born or naturalized in the United States and subject to its jurisdiction are citizens of the United States. (Thus, a child born in the United States to parents who are diplomats of a foreign country, and therefore not subject to the jurisdiction of the United States, is not a United States citizen.) In addition, the following are U.S. citizens at birth:

1. persons born outside of the United States of parents, both of whom are citizens of the United States and one of whom has had a residence in the United States or one of its outlying possessions prior to the birth of such persons;

1. See brief discussion *infra* text accompanying notes 89–92 and extended discussion *infra* Chapter 10.

2. See discussion *infra* text accompanying notes 23–26.

2. persons born outside of the United States and its outlying possessions of parents, one of whom is a citizen of the United States who has been physically present in the United States or one of its outlying possessions for a continuous period of one year prior to the birth of such persons, and the other of whom is a national but not a citizen of the United States; and
3. persons born outside of the United States and its outlying possessions of parents, one of whom is an alien, and the other a citizen of the United States who, prior to the birth of such persons, was physically present in the United States or its outlying possessions for a period or periods totaling not less than five years, at least two of which were after attaining the age of fourteen years. There are other provisions of narrower application.

In addition, of course, one can become a naturalized citizen of the United States.[3] Generally one must have been a lawful permanent resident for at least five years in order to be naturalized as a citizen.

While the United States formerly imposed strict limitations on dual nationality, it is now relatively common for a person to hold dual citizenship in the United States and another country, and for U.S. tax purposes, the person is considered a U.S. citizen, fully subject to the U.S. income and transfer tax. The only limitation upon dual nationality now in the United States is that a United States citizen will lose his or her citizenship if he or she takes an oath of allegiance to another country or takes actions regarding citizenship of another country (such as serving in the armed forces), which by their nature preclude dual nationality.[4]

B. Residence in the United States for Income Tax Purposes

Since January 1, 1985, the rules for determining residence in the United States for income tax purposes have been set by statute and are relatively easy to apply. Under the provisions of the Internal Revenue Code (I.R.C.) § 7701(b), an alien individual is treated as a resident alien of the United States for income tax purposes if he or she satisfies either one of two tests: (1) the lawful permanent resident test or (2) the substantial presence test. A lawful permanent resident alien can also elect resident status for the first year of residence from the first day he or she is actually present in the United States, under most circumstances, if he or she wishes to do so. A lawful permanent resident is an individual holding a "green card" or visa entitling him or her to permanent residence, and the ability to work, in the United States. An alien who is a lawful permanent resident of the United States is subject to United States income tax upon his or her worldwide income, just as a citizen, for as long as he or she holds the green card, whether or not the alien is actually resident in the United States in any one or more years during the period that he

3. 8 U.S.C. § 1427.
4. 8 U.S.C. § 1481.

or she holds the green card.[5] Special rules apply during the first and last years of residency in the United States.[6]

As discussed further below, abandoning permanent resident status requires more than simply relinquishing the holder's "green card," and depending on the number of years in which this has been held, such surrender may have tax consequences. The substantial presence test simply looks to the number of days an alien has spent in the United States during the calendar year and two preceding calendar years. A new determination of residence for U.S. income tax purposes is made annually. Assuming the individual is not lawfully admitted for permanent residence (i.e., a green card holder), the alien is a nonresident if the *weighted* number of days spent in the United States in the current and two preceding years combined is less than 183 days or the individual spent less than 31 days in the United States during the current year. The weighted number is determined by adding to the total number of days the alien is present in the current year, one-third of the number of days he or she was present in the preceding year, and one-sixth of the number of days he or she was present in the second preceding year.[7] This test is often referred to as the "120-day test," because if an alien never spends more than 120 days per year in the United States, he or she will never meet the prerequisites of the substantial presence test and will not be deemed to be a United States resident. This is because every day spent in the current year, counted as a full day, starts the computation with 120 days; every day in the prior year, counted as one-third of a day, adds 40 days to the computation; and every day in the second preceding year, counted as one-sixth of a day, adds 20 days to the computation, giving a total of 180 days, or less than 183 days.

If an individual meets both the weighted 183-day test and the 31 days in the current year test, the individual is deemed to be a resident of the United States in the current year (unless he or she meets one of the exceptions discussed in the following paragraph) and will be taxed upon his or her worldwide income in the current year. Even if the weighted aggregate of three years exceeds 183 days, the individual is a nonresident if he or she is in the United States for less than 31 days in the current year. Thus, if the individual was present in the United States for 330 days in

5. I.R.C. § 7701(b)(1)(A)(i).

6. *Id.* § 7701(b)(2). Residency status for the green card test generally begins on the first day of the year that the alien is physically present in the United States with a lawful permanent resident visa, and ends on the last day on which the alien holds a lawful permanent resident visa (subject to certain exceptions for dual-residents under the treaty "tie-breaker" rules, and certain "long-term" residents under the expatriation rules). In the case of the substantial presence test, by its terms, the test refers to the first day of physical presence for the initial year. If an alien either satisfies the substantial presence rest in a given year, or makes a "first-year" election under I.R.C. § 7701(b)(4) to be treated as a U.S. resident starting from their date of entry into the U.S. in a year in which they would not generally be considered a resident under the substantial presence test, their date of entry into the U.S. will be their residency starting date. Thereafter, the alien will be deemed a U.S. resident for the entire year that he or she meets the substantial presence test, and a nonresident alien for the entire year that he or she does not meet the test (subject to exceptions under the "closer connection" rule discussed *infra* text accompanying notes 13 and 14).

7. *Id.* § 7701(b)(3)(A); Treas. Reg. § 301.7701(b)-1(c).

each of the two preceding years, but only 30 days in the current year, the *weighted* number of days for the three-year period is 195 days (55 days plus 110 days plus 30 days), but because the number of days in the current year is less than 31, the alien is a nonresident for the current year.[8] Again, determinations under the substantial presence test are made annually so that an alien individual may be found to be a resident of the United States in one year and a nonresident in the succeeding year, based upon days spent in the United States in each year. This can have important consequences in the timing of realization of income and permit an alien who has been resident in the United States for some years to avoid tax upon income in the current year, if he or she wishes, by staying below the 31-day threshold.

There are a number of important exceptions to the substantial presence test in determining whether an alien individual is resident in the United States for income tax purposes. Most apply to how one counts days "present" in the United States, but one exception allows the alien to spend more days here.

First, foreign government-related individuals, teachers, teacher trainees, students, and professional athletes in the U.S. temporarily to compete in a charitable sports event, so long as they are legally within the United States and always acting within the scope of their visa, are not deemed "present" here at all and thus do not trigger the 120-day calendar. An individual claiming such status who otherwise would have met the substantial presence test must timely file a Form 8843 claiming the exemption. (This requirement that Form 8843 be filed does not apply to diplomats or students.)[9]

Second, commuters from Canada or Mexico are not "present" in the United States on days they commute here.[10]

Third, a day spent in transit through the United States (e.g., from Europe to Mexico through a New York City airport) does not count if it is only transit and the alien does not have meetings (even in the airport) or visit friends here on the transit day.[11] The alien cannot be present in the United States for more than twenty-four hours in order for a transit day not to count.

Finally, an alien who is forced to prolong a stay here because of an unforeseen medical condition that arose while in the United States and prevents departure is not "present" here for the days after the medical condition arose so long as the alien did intend to leave.[12] The alien must timely file a Form 8843 setting forth the facts and attach a doctor's certificate.

While each of the foregoing exceptions goes to establishing "exempt" days that do not count toward the substantial presence test, the "closer connection" test grants the alien the ability to spend more days here every year. The substantial presence test is based on a weighted, three-year total of more than 182 days. Under the closer connection test, an individual can spend a total of up to 182 days in the

8. Treas. Reg. § 301.7701(b)-1(c)(4).
9. I.R.C. § 7701(b)(5). Treas. Reg. § 301.7701(b)-8(a).
10. I.R.C. § 7701(b)(7)(B).
11. *Id.* § 7701(b)(7)(C); Treas. Reg. § 301.7701(b)-3(d).
12. I.R.C. § 7701(b)(3)(D); Treas. Reg. § 301.7701(b)-3(c).

United States every year if he or she demonstrates to the Internal Revenue Service (the Service) that he or she has a tax home (as that concept is understood in I.R.C. § 162(a)(2)) in another country and, based upon all of the facts and circumstances, maintains a closer connection to that country than to the United States.[13] In order to claim this exception, an individual must timely file a Form 8840 each year, setting forth all of the facts upon which the claim is based and disclosing the number of days spent in the United States and in the "home" country. It is not necessary that the taxpayer have spent more days in the "home" country than in the United States, but the total connections must be closer. A Form 8840 must be filed currently to be valid. It cannot be filed later if the IRS is subsequently auditing the taxpayer.[14]

C. Residence in the United States for Transfer Tax Purposes

For estate tax purposes, I.R.C. § 2001(a) provides: "A tax is hereby imposed on the transfer of the taxable estate of every decedent who is a citizen or resident of the United States." "Residence" in the United States is not defined by the Internal Revenue Code (the Code) for transfer tax purposes. Instead, for estate tax purposes, the regulations provide that

> [a] "resident" decedent is a decedent who, at the time of his death, had his domicile in the United States. The term United States, as used in the Estate Tax Regulations, includes only the States and the District of Columbia [and not the territories or possessions of the United States]. A person acquires a domicile in a place by living there, for even a brief period of time, with no definite present intention of later removing therefrom. Residence without the requisite intention to remain indefinitely will not suffice to constitute domicile, nor will intention to change domicile effect such a change unless accompanied by actual removal.[15]

The test, then, is a subjective one based on the alien's intent. While statements of intent as to domicile are relevant, the determination of domicile is to be made based upon all the facts.

For example, in one often-cited case, *Estate of Nienhuys v. Commissioner*,[16] the Tax Court held that a Dutch citizen who had come to the United States on a business trip in 1940 and was unable to return home because of the German invasion of Holland did not die domiciled in the United States, even though he stayed here until 1946. The facts showed that although the decedent could have returned to Holland after the war, his health was poor, there were food shortages in Holland, and he did not want to return in the winter. Based upon all of these facts, it was determined that he had never established the requisite intention to remain

13. I.R.C. § 7701(b)(3)(B); Treas. Reg. § 301.7701(b)-2.

14. Treas. Reg. § 301.7701(b)-8(d)(1).

15. Treas. Reg. § 20.0-1(b)(1). Similar domicile rules apply to the imposition of gift tax. Treas. Reg. § 25.2501-1(b).

16. Estate of Nienhuys v. Comm'r, 17 T.C. 1149 (1952).

permanently in the United States. Though the decedent had remained legally in the United States for six years and had no present plan to leave, he had an intention to return to Holland as soon as he could.

The courts have also recognized that an alien can spend part of every year in the United States without becoming domiciled here. In *Estate of Paquette v. Commissioner*,[17] the decedent, a Canadian citizen domiciled in Montreal, began coming to Florida with his wife every winter. He established a pattern of spending six months a year in Montreal and six months in Florida and continued it for many years. Upon his death (in Florida) in 1975, the Tax Court determined that he had never intended to change his domicile to Florida.

In contrast, in Revenue Ruling 80-209,[18] the Internal Revenue Service was presented with an illegal alien who died resident in the United States, although he had never legally been admitted to residence here. While at all times subject to deportation, the decedent had lived in the United States for nineteen years, had owned a home in the United States for fourteen years, and was active in community affairs. The Internal Revenue Service ruled that he had established the requisite intent to remain in the United States (even if illegally) and never leave and that he was therefore domiciled in the United States and subject to the payment of U.S. estate tax on his worldwide assets.

If a decedent is a resident of the United States under this definition, the Code subjects to estate tax his or her entire worldwide estate. I.R.C. § 2031(a) provides: "The value of the gross estate of the decedent shall be determined by including to the extent provided for in this part, the value at the time of his death of all property, real or personal, tangible or intangible, wherever situated."

For gift tax purposes, the Code works differently. Gift tax is imposed upon all transfers of property by gift by all individuals, resident or nonresident.[19] I.R.C. § 2501(a)(1) provides: "A tax, computed as provided in Section 2502, is hereby imposed for each calendar year on the transfer of property by gift during such calendar year by any individual, resident or nonresident."

Nevertheless, I.R.C. § 2501(a)(2) promptly excludes from taxation in the United States all transfers of intangible property by nonresident aliens. The definition of "residence" for gift tax purposes is the same as it is for estate tax purposes.[20] Thus, while at first blush the gift tax is more inclusive than the estate tax, in practical effect, it is far less inclusive, and it is clearly in the interest of nonresident aliens of the United States owning stocks, bonds, or other intangible

17. Estate of Paquette v. Comm'r, T.C.M. (P-H) 1983-571 (1983).

18. Rev. Rul. 80-209, 1980-2 C.B. 248.

19. For those unfamiliar with the United States gift tax, it is important to remember that the Treasury Regulations provide: "Donative intent on the part of the transferor is not an essential element in the application of the gift tax to the transfer." Treas. Reg. § 25.2511-1(g)(1). The issue thus becomes one of whether the transfer was for less than full and fair consideration and, if so, whether, based on the relationships of the parties and all of the facts and circumstances, the transfer was a gift and not just a bad bargain.

20. Treas. Reg. § 25.2501-1(b).

assets in the United States to give those assets away during their lifetime rather than hold them until their death, if, as a personal matter, they can afford and wish to give the assets away during their lifetime and do not want to sell the U.S. assets (reinvesting the proceeds in non-U.S. situs assets) or hold the assets in offshore corporations (see discussion below).

It is important to remember that for U.S. transfer tax purposes, the citizenship or residency of the estate beneficiary or donee is of no consequence. Tax is imposed upon the decedent or donor, not the recipient, and is based upon the citizenship or residence of the decedent or donor or, if he or she is a nonresident alien, the situs of the assets.

Finally, for generation-skipping tax purposes, I.R.C. § 2601 imposes the tax "on every generation skipping transfer." Again, the statute does not distinguish between U.S. persons and nonresident aliens. However, I.R.C. § 2663(2) requires the Secretary of the Treasury to adopt "regulations (consistent with the principles of chapters 11 and 12) providing for the application of this chapter [the tax on generation-skipping transfers] in the case of transferors who are nonresidents not citizens of the United States." By regulations adopted on December 26, 1995, the Treasury has provided that the generation-skipping transfer tax applies to transfers by a nonresident alien during his or her lifetime or upon death to the extent the gift or estate tax would apply to the transfer.[21] Thus, for example, if a nonresident alien of the United States gave stock in a German corporation to his U.S. citizen grandchild during his lifetime or upon his death, there would be no generation-skipping transfer tax. The same result (no tax) would apply if the subject of the lifetime gift was stock in an American corporation, because gifts by a nonresident alien of intangible personal property are not subject to gift tax. But, if a nonresident alien of the United States makes a testamentary gift to his nonresident alien grandchild of stock in an American corporation, the bequest is subject to both estate tax and generation-skipping transfer tax.[22]

D. Special Rule for Citizens of Possessions of the United States

Special rules under I.R.C. §§ 2208 and 2209 apply to the estate taxation of citizens of the United States who are citizens and residents of possessions of the United States. A decedent who was a citizen of the United States and a resident of a U.S. possession is considered a "citizen" of the United States at his or her death *unless* he or she acquired United States citizenship solely by reason of being a citizen of such U.S. possession or birth or residence within the possession,[23] and is deemed a nonresident alien of the United States if he or she acquired United

21. Treas. Reg. § 26.2663-2.

22. Treas. Reg. § 26.2263-2(d), Example 2. Gifts of real estate will be subject to the generation-skipping transfer tax whether made inter vivos or upon death. *Id.* Example 1.

23. I.R.C. § 2208. Possessions of the United States for this purpose are Puerto Rico, the Virgin Islands, Guam, American Samoa, the Northern Marianas, Okinawa, and the Marshall Islands.

States citizenship solely by reason of being a citizen of the possession or birth or residence there.[24]

There are regulations and rulings applying these provisions and somewhat expanding their scope. Most important, the Service has ruled that a U.S. citizen who died resident in a U.S. possession was not a citizen for estate tax purposes at death, even though the U.S. possession in which he or she died resident was not the same U.S. possession as that in which he was born and thereby acquired U.S. citizenship.[25] The Treasury has provided by regulations that a U.S. citizen who became a citizen by becoming naturalized after moving to a possession also is not a U.S. citizen for estate tax purposes.[26]

III. U.S. Income Taxation of Nonresident Aliens

As a general matter, a nonresident alien of the United States (or a foreign corporation) pays United States income taxes only upon income paid from sources within the United States. The rules are set out in subchapter N of chapter 1 of the Internal Revenue Code (§§ 861 through 884). Special rules exist under § 897 (as discussed *infra* Section V) for certain direct or indirect dispositions of interests held by a nonresident alien in United States real property.

Generally, a nonresident alien's income from the conduct of a trade or business within the United States (so-called "effectively connected income") or from the performance of personal services within the United States is taxed at ordinary graduated rates of tax.[27] Income from fixed or determinable sources within the United States (dividends, interest, royalties, and the like) is taxed at flat 30 percent rates (or reduced treaty rates) by withholding at the source upon the periodic income payment.[28] Income from the sale or exchange of capital assets located in the United States other than real estate is subjected to tax at the same 30 percent rate, but only if the recipient was present in the United States for more than 182 days both in the year the taxable gain was effected and in the year the income was collected, if it is collected in a future year.[29] These provisions are affected by treaties. As discussed further below, additional withholding tax provisions may apply under the HIRE Act of 2010.

A. Income Connected with the Conduct of a Trade or Business

Income from a U.S. trade or business, which is taxed at ordinary graduated rates, is generally of one of three kinds.

24. I.R.C. § 2209.
25. Rev. Rul. 74-25, 1974-1 C.B. 284.
26. Treas. Reg. § 20.2209-1, Example 5.
27. I.R.C. § 871(b).
28. I.R.C. §§ 871(a), 1441.
29. Treas. Reg. § 1.871-7(d)(2).

1. Personal Services

A nonresident alien individual's income from the conduct of a U.S. trade or business includes income from the performance of personal services within the United States at any time during the tax year. However, a nonresident alien individual performing personal services in the United States is not engaged in a U.S. trade or business if the services are performed for a foreign employer, the aggregate compensation does not exceed $3,000, and the nonresident alien employee is present in the United States for no more than 90 days during the tax year.[30] Most full bilateral treatises allow an individual to spend up to 182 days a year in the United States and to earn an unlimited amount without U.S. income tax if the taxpayer's employer is based in his or her country of residence.[31]

2. Trading in Securities or Commodities

Under the rules of I.R.C. § 864(b)(2), a foreign person who trades in stocks, securities, or commodities in the United States is not treated as conducting a U.S. trade or business (and is therefore not subject to U.S. income tax on his or her "effectively connected income" from the securities or commodities trading) if the foreign person does not have an office in the United States through which, or under the direction of which, the securities transactions are effected. Under the safe harbor rules of I.R.C. §§ 864(b)(2)(A)(ii) and 864(b)(2)(B)(ii), however, a foreign individual, corporation, or trust is not treated as conducting a U.S. trade or business even if he or she or it has an office in the United States through which, or by direction of which, the transactions in stocks, securities, or commodities are effected, *provided* the transactions are for the taxpayer's own account.

3. Facts and Circumstances Test

In determining whether a taxpayer is engaged in a trade or business in the United States, activities of the taxpayer, other than performing personal services (Section 1 above) and trading in securities and commodities (Section 2 above) are examined in the light of the facts and circumstances of each case. The Internal Revenue Service does not issue advance rulings or determination letters on a taxpayer's status in the conduct of a U.S. trade or business. The facts and circumstances test examines the nature and extent of the taxpayer's economic activities and contacts within the United States. A U.S. trade or business does not include isolated and nonrecurring transactions by a nonresident alien in the United States absent a profit motive. The taxpayer must have been, during some substantial portion of the tax year, regularly and continuously transacting business in the United States.

---

30. I.R.C. § 864(b)(1). Under many treaties, such as that with the United Kingdom, these results are altered and the employee may be present in the United States for up to 182 days, and earn more money, before he is subject to tax in the United States.

31. *See, e.g.*, Convention Between the Government of the United States of America and the Government of the United Kingdom of Great Britain and Northern Ireland for the Avoidance of Double Taxation and the Prevention of Fiscal Evasion with Respect to Taxes on Income and on Capital Gains, art. 14.

B. Income Not Connected with a U.S. Trade or Business

If the taxpayer is a nonresident alien of the United States, the alien pays U.S. withholding tax at flat rates on U.S. source income not connected with the conduct of a trade or business.[32] U.S. source income means income paid by United States payors. The Code makes important exceptions to the taxation of U.S. source income, encouraging certain types of investments. Taxable passive U.S. source income includes interest, dividends, rent, royalties, original issue discount, one-half of U.S. social security benefits received, and most other more specialized categories of income.

While dividends, interest, and rents are self-explanatory, certain of these categories of income require further explanation.

1. Original Issue Discount

Original issue discount, the difference between the issue price and the stated redemption price at maturity of a bond or other evidence of indebtedness purchased by an investor, is subject to U.S. income tax in the hands of a nonresident alien investor unless it is paid on a short-term obligation payable within 183 days of its original issue or paid on a tax-exempt obligation.[33]

2. Portfolio Debt

More important, all interest paid to a nonresident alien, whether "coupon" or other interest payments actually made or deemed paid as original issue discount, is exempt from tax if it is portfolio interest income: that is, interest paid on fixed income securities purchased by a nonresident alien to be held in his or her investment portfolio. Portfolio interest paid to a nonresident alien is not subject to withholding.Portfolio interest is defined as any interest, including original issue discount, that would be subject to tax under I.R.C. § 871(a) but for I.R.C. § 871(h) and is either:

1. Interest on nonregistered obligations of the type described in I.R.C. § 163(f)(2)(B), which are obligations for which there are arrangements designed to ensure that such obligations will be sold or resold only to nonresident aliens and, if the obligation is in bearer form, interest on such obligations is only payable outside the United States; or
2. Interest on a registered obligation (with respect to which the U.S. person obligor would normally have to deduct and withhold tax) with respect to

32. Although prior law was otherwise, under current law, a nonresident alien pays U.S. income tax on U.S. source income not connected with the conduct of a U.S. trade or business at a flat 30 percent rate whether or not the alien is conducting a U.S. trade or business. If the alien is conducting a U.S. trade or business, he or she must keep records of which classes of U.S. source income are connected with a U.S. trade or business and which are not, and each is taxed at its own rates, with its own deductions. Treas. Reg. § 1.871-8(a).

33. I.R.C. § 871(g)(1)(B).

which the withholding agent has received a statement that the beneficial owner is not a U.S. person.

Note that bearer bonds issued after March 18, 2012, are not considered portfolio debt, and the interest on such bonds thus is not exempt from tax.[34]

Most long-term U.S. Treasury and corporate obligations are issued in registered form and qualify as an instrument bearing "portfolio interest," and thus are exempt from withholding tax once the withholding agent receives a certification that the owner is a nonresident alien. Interest paid by United States individuals on borrowings from nonresident aliens can also be made exempt from tax if the note is drafted in conformity with the portfolio debt rules.

3. Interest on Bank Deposits

Generally, interest paid to nonresident aliens on deposits with banks, savings and loan associations, and insurance companies in the United States is exempted from income taxation by specific statutory exception in I.R.C. § 871(i).

4. Gain on Sale of a Capital Asset

As noted above, a nonresident alien's U.S. source gain from the sale or exchange of personal property that is a capital asset is subject to tax at 30 percent (or lower treaty rate) of the net gain if the gain is not otherwise taken into account as income effectively connected with a U.S. trade or business, but only if the alien recipient is physically present in the United States for 183 days or more during the tax year in which the property is sold or exchanged *and* the tax year in which the gain is received.[35]

IV. U.S. Transfer Taxation of Nonresident Aliens

The rules for transfer taxation of nonresident aliens are similar to those for the income taxation of nonresident aliens, except that the property must have a situs in the United States rather than the income having a source in the United States. The principles are obviously similar. This discussion first focuses upon estate tax, then gift tax, and finally generation-skipping transfer tax.

A. Estate Tax

The estate taxation of nonresident aliens is covered by subchapter B of chapter 11 of I.R.C. (§§ 2101–2108). The rules are as follows:

1. Situs of Various Classes of Assets

(a) Tangible Property. All tangible property, both real and personal that is located in the United States at the time of a nonresident alien decedent's death

34. H.R. 2847, the Hiring Incentives to Restore Employment (HIRE) Act, § 502.
35. Treas. Reg. § 1.871-7(d)(2).

and that would be included in the estate of a citizen or resident alien, is also included in the gross estate of a nonresident alien.[36] Works of art are not included in the estate of a nonresident alien if they are imported into the United States solely for exhibition at a public gallery or museum and are either on exhibition or en route to or from the exhibition at the time of the decedent's death.[37]

Personal property accompanying a nonresident alien who dies while temporarily visiting the United States is not included in such nonresident alien's estate.[38]

Real property is deemed to have its situs in the place where it is located. Issues do arise in determining what constitutes real property. For purposes of the estate tax, the determination of what constitutes real property is made under United States law rather than the law of the place where the interest is located.[39] Real property includes land, buildings, improvements, and fixtures. It also includes crops, timber cutting rights, and mineral rights (but not certain extracted commodities and minerals). Generally, a condominium apartment is deemed to be real estate located within the United States. A cooperative apartment is generally treated as intangible personal property and so is not subject to tax within the United States (including gift tax upon inter vivos transfer), although the stock in the cooperative apartment corporation (see below) is subject to estate tax, as stock of a U.S. corporation, if owned directly by a resident of a non-treaty country.

(b) Corporate Stock. Whether intangible personal property is situated within the United States and thus subject to estate tax in the estate of a nonresident alien depends less on the location of the paper evidencing title to the property than on the nature of the property interest owned by the decedent. Shares of stock issued by a domestic corporation are property within the United States; shares of stock issued by a foreign corporation are not.[40] If a foreign corporation is formed by a nonresident alien in order to hold U.S. situs property, care must be taken to assure that the foreign corporation, not the nonresident alien shareholder, is the true owner of that property and that corporate formalities are followed. The Treasury Department has recently announced that it is studying many aspects of the situs rules as they relate to nonresident alien decedents, but in particular the rules applicable to interests in partnerships and in wholly owned foreign corporations.

(c) Proceeds of Life Insurance. Proceeds of insurance on the nonresident alien decedent's life are not property within the United States regardless of whether the company issuing the life insurance policy is a domestic or foreign company.[41]

36. Treas. Reg. § 20.2104-1(a).
37. I.R.C. § 2105(c).
38. *See, e.g.*, Delaney v. Murchie, 177 F.2d 444 (1st Cir. 1944).
39. Estate of de Perigny v. Comm'r, 9 T.C. 782 (1947) (holding 99-year lease to real estate to be "real property" for federal estate tax purposes).
40. I.R.C. § 2104(a).
41. I.R.C. § 2105(a).

Note, however, that the insurance must be on the life of the decedent. If a nonresident alien decedent dies owning an interest in a life insurance policy on the life of another issued by a United States company, it is U.S. situs property included in the gross estate at whatever its value may be.[42] Recent guidance in the form of Revenue Rulings 2009-13 and 2009-14 has provided significant additional clarity as to the taxation of various transactions involving life insurance.

(d) Debt Obligations. Generally, debt obligations of U.S. persons or of the United States or any state or political subdivision of the United States are property within the United States subject to estate tax. However, there is a major exception to this rule. Debt obligations are not "located in the United States" if, without regard to the general requirement that the obligor not be a U.S. person, the interest thereon would have been treated as portfolio interest exempt from United States income tax if the decedent had received that interest before he died.[43] Similarly, bank deposits, the interest on which is not subject to income tax, are not subject to estate tax by the United States.[44] The estate tax rules here generally follow the income tax rules—if the interest was not subject to income tax in the hands of a nonresident alien, the principal is not subject to estate tax.

(e) Copyrights, Patents, and Trademarks. Treasury regulations indicate only that intangibles have a non-U.S. situs if they are not issued by or enforceable against a resident of the United States or a domestic corporation or governmental unit. Pursuant to law and international conventions, copyrights, patents, and trademarks are enforceable in most parts of the world, including the United States, and often have an international, multinational registry. Thus, the treasury regulations do not provide a good basis for analysis.

A general rule of thumb is, therefore, that such interests may be subject to estate tax in the United States if the primary patent, copyright, or license was issued in the United States, but the results are very fact-specific. Estate tax treaties generally resolve ambiguities in this area, but most countries have no estate tax treaty with the United States.

(f) Partnership Interests. When dealing with a possible partnership interest, an initial question is how to classify the particular entity. The "check the box" rules on entity classification are of great utility in determining whether a particular entity is a corporation or a partnership.[45] These rules apply to classify an entity for United States transfer tax purposes as well as income tax purposes. If it is a partnership, the position of the United States government has long been that a

42. Treas. Reg. § 20.2104-1(a)(7).
43. I.R.C. § 2105(b)(3).
44. I.R.C. § 2105(b)(1).
45. Treas. Reg. §§ 301.7701-1 to 301.7701-3 (effective Jan. 1, 1997).

partnership is deemed "sited" in the United States or outside of the United States based upon where the partnership primarily does business; however, there are other theories under which the situs of a partnership may be determined, and the situs of such an interest can be difficult to determine with certainty.[46] Generally, the United States Treasury has examined partnerships on an entity basis, rather than an assets basis, in determining their situs for estate tax purposes and has not looked through the entity. The issue is under study by the Treasury for possible revision, particularly in this age of international partnerships.

(g) Trust and Estate Interests. Unlike partnerships, interests in trusts are examined according to the situs of the assets rather than the situs of the trust. That is, Treasury does look through a trust. If a nonresident alien has a beneficial interest in a trust that itself has interests deemed to be situated in the United States, the nonresident alien's interest in the U.S. assets is included in his gross estate, even if the trust itself is a foreign trust. The foreign assets of the trust are not generally subject to U.S. tax, except in certain cases where § 2104(b) requires this result.[47]

If a U.S. trust's investments are in a U.S.-based common trust fund, the shares or units of the common trust fund owned by the trust are situated in the United States regardless of where the assets owned by the common trust fund are located *if* the common trust fund is located in the United States.[48] Interests in mutual funds are deemed located in the United States if they are organized in corporate form and the corporation is a U.S. corporation. On the other hand, interests in mutual funds organized as partnerships or as trusts are looked through, and only those assets located in the United States or from U.S. issuers are deemed located in the United States for estate tax purposes.[49]

(h) Other Intangible Personal Property. All intangible personal property, the written evidence of which is not treated as the property itself, is property located within the United States if it is issued by, or enforceable against, a resident of the United States or a domestic corporation or government unit.

2. Rates of Tax

Until November 10, 1988, nonresident aliens of the United States had their U.S. estates subjected to U.S. estate tax on their own rate schedule, up to a maximum rate of 30 percent.[50] Since November 10, 1988, nonresident aliens have been subject to U.S. estate tax at the same graduated rates applicable to citizens or residents of

46. Rev. Rul. 55-701, 1955-2 C.B. 836.
47. *See* Comm'r v. Nevius, 76 F.2d 109 (2d Cir. 1935).
48. Rev. Rul. 55-163, 1995-1 C.B. 674.
49. I.R.S. Priv. Ltr. Rul. 9748004 (Aug. 19, 1997).
50. Prior I.R.C. § 2101(d), repealed effective for estates of decedents dying after November 10, 1988, by Pub. L. No. 100-647, 102 Stat. 3342, § 5032(c) (1988).

the United States (thus, up to a maximum rate in 2013 of 40 percent), although the tax applies only to assets located in the United States.

3. Deductions

Nonresident aliens are entitled to only limited deductions for estate tax purposes. General expenses of administration, debts, taxes, funeral expenses, and losses of the worldwide estate are deductible from the U.S. estate in the proportion the U.S. estate bears to the worldwide estate. It is immaterial whether the deduction was incurred in the United States. Thus, if a nonresident alien has a worldwide gross estate valued at $1 million, of which his U.S. gross estate is valued at $100,000, 10 percent of his debts, taxes, and funeral and administration expenses are deductible, regardless of whether they are directly attributable to the administration of the U.S. estate, so long as there is full disclosure on the estate tax return of the worldwide estate and the worldwide expenses.[51] (Many executors of nonresident aliens' estates choose not to claim this deduction because they do not wish to disclose the worldwide assets.) Nonrecourse mortgages, which encumber U.S. situs assets, are fully deductible for U.S. estate tax purposes, without disclosure of the worldwide estate.

(a) Charitable Deductions. A nonresident alien decedent is entitled to a charitable deduction without limit as to the portion of the estate located in the United States, *provided*:

1. In the case of a charitable contribution to a corporation, the deduction is available only for gifts or bequests to U.S. corporations; and
2. In the case of a charitable contribution to a trust or foundation, the deduction is available only to the extent that the gift or bequest requires the charity to spend the money within the United States. Bequests to charitable corporations that are U.S. corporations may be spent anywhere.

No charitable contribution deduction is allowed for gifts of foreign situs property to a U.S. charity. The gift must be of property that was included in the gross estate.[52] As with the deduction for debts, expenses, and taxes, the charitable deduction is allowed only if the executor discloses the entire worldwide estate, but there is no percentage limitation for the charitable deduction.

(b) Marital Deduction. The estate of a nonresident alien may claim a marital deduction, without limit, under the same rules that apply to citizens and residents of the United States, but only for bequests of property that was subject to tax in the United States. A bequest to a U.S. citizen spouse is eligible for the marital deduction if paid directly or in a fashion otherwise deductible under I.R.C. § 2056. A bequest to a noncitizen spouse is eligible for deduction only if paid to a qualified

---

51. I.R.C. § 2106(a)(1); Treas. Reg. § 20.2106-2.
52. I.R.C. § 2106(a)(2); Treas. Reg. § 20.2106-1(a)(2); I.R.S. TAM 9040003 (June 27, 1990).

domestic trust (QDOT) under rules similar to those applicable to United States citizens making bequests to noncitizen spouses under I.R.C. § 2056A.[53] Some estate tax treaties, such as the United States-France treaty, expand the marital deduction.

(c) State Death Tax Deduction. Nonresident alien decedents' estates can also claim a deduction for state death taxes paid, but such deduction is subject to a special limitation. The allowable deduction is limited to the amount that bears the same ratio to the state death taxes as the value of the taxable estate for state tax purposes bears to the value of the total gross estate.[54]

4. Estate Tax Credits

Nonresident alien estates are entitled to a unified credit equal to the amount of tax due on a $60,000 estate, or $13,000 in 2013.[55] This contrasts to the $2,045,800 unified credit allowed the estate of a U.S. citizen or resident in 2013.

B. Gift Tax

As noted above, chapter 12 of the Internal Revenue Code (Gift Tax) differs from chapter 11 (Estate Tax) in that it generally applies both to persons and nonresidents. By its terms, chapter 12 applies to nonresident aliens with respect to all gifts of property (whatever the situs of such property), but in fact it applies only with respect to gifts of property that has a U.S. situs. The application of the gift tax is further limited by I.R.C. § 2501(a)(2), which provides that the gift tax shall not apply to gifts of intangible property by nonresident alien donors, except those who have expatriated from the United States. In practical effect, I.R.C. § 2501(a)(2) is providing that all intangible property is deemed to have a foreign situs for gift tax purposes for gifts made by nonresident alien donors.

While the Code does not speak of situs of property for gift tax purposes, the Treasury Regulations state expressly that for a nonresident alien donor, the gift tax applies only to gifts of real estate and tangible personal property located in the United States.[56]

The citizenship or residence of the donee is of no consequence for estate or gift tax purposes. Thus, a nonresident alien making gifts of property to his U.S. resident or citizen children need not declare or pay tax upon the gifts. Under changes made to the Internal Revenue Code in 1996,[57] the U.S. resident or citizen children must declare their receipt of the gifts[58] so that the Internal Revenue Service has a record of the gifts having been made. However, the gifts are not subject to the payment of gift tax by the donees or the donors. The gifts may be subject to

53. I.R.C. § 2106(a)(3); Treas. Reg. § 20.2106-1(a)(3).

54. I.R.C. § 2016(a)(4).

55. I.R.C. § 2102(b)(1).

56. Treas. Reg. §§ 25.2511-1(b), 25.2511-3.

57. I.R.C. § 6039F, enacted effective for gifts received after August 20, 1996, by Pub. L. No. 104-188, § 1905(a) (1996).

58. *See* discussion *infra* text accompanying note 80 and Chapter 7.

income tax in the hands of the donees if it is found that the source of the money used to make gifts was in fact nongrantor foreign trusts rather than the individual donor making the gift.[59]

1. Annual Exclusion

The annual exclusion for the first $10,000 (adjusted for inflation, the amount is $14,000 in 2013) of gifts of present interests in property to each donee is available to every donor, whether or not a U.S. citizen or resident.[60] The exclusion applies to gifts of otherwise taxable property so that a nonresident alien donor could give each donee each year $14,000 (in 2013) of property otherwise subject to U.S. gift tax, and an unlimited amount of intangible property not subject to U.S. gift tax.

2. Rate of Tax

The rate of tax imposed upon nonresident alien donors has, since 1988, been the same for nonresident alien donors as for citizens and residents.

3. Unified Credit against Gift Tax

There is no unified credit against gift tax for gifts by nonresident aliens. A nonresident alien donor must begin paying gift tax as soon as his or her gifts of U.S. situs property exceed the $14,000 (in 2013) annual exclusion.

4. Charitable Deduction

I.R.C. § 2522 distinguishes between the charitable deduction for gift tax purposes for gifts by citizens or residents and for gifts by nonresident aliens. Nonresident aliens may obtain a charitable deduction for U.S. gift tax purposes only if the gift is of U.S. situs property and (1) if the donee is corporation, it must be a U.S. corporation; or (2) if the donee is a trust or foundation, wherever organized, the donee must spend the gift within the United States. Thus, the gift tax charitable contribution deduction rules are the same as the estate tax charitable contribution rules.

5. Marital Deduction

Under I.R.C. § 2523(i), the unlimited gift tax marital deduction is limited to gifts made to United States citizens. If the donee spouse is not a United States citizen, the 2013 annual exclusion amount is $143,000, not $14,000. This is available to both U.S. persons and nonresident alien donors, but again, a nonresident alien donor would not be subject to the payment of the U.S. gift tax in any event unless the gift were of U.S. situs property.

6. Gift Splitting by Spouses for Gifts to Third Parties

While the availability of the marital deductions for gifts to a spouse depends upon the citizenship of the donee spouse, gift splitting for gifts by a husband and wife to third parties depends upon citizenship or *residence* of both spouses. The

---

59. *See* I.R.C. § 643(h).
60. I.R.C. § 2503(b); Treas. Reg. § 25.2503-2(a).

regulations make clear that the issue is residence or citizenship of both spouses at the date of the gift.[61] A nonresident alien is not entitled to split gifts.

C. Generation-Skipping Transfers

The generation-skipping transfer tax is an extra, prohibitive tax at a flat rate of 40 percent (the maximum estate tax rate in 2013) imposed upon donative transfers to grandchildren or further descendants or, in the case of transfers to nonfamily members, to donees whose "generation assignment" is to a generation twice removed from the donor's, generations by statute being set at 25 years.[62]

There was initially considerable debate as to whether the generation-skipping transfer tax, when enacted in 1986, would apply and, if it would, the extent to which it would apply to gifts by nonresident aliens. On December 26, 1995, the Treasury Department enacted final regulations, as required by I.R.C. § 2663, which imposed a generation-skipping transfer tax upon transfers by nonresident alien donors based solely on the situs of the property transferred under the applicable estate and gift tax rules.[63] Thus, a transfer by gift to a grandchild of stock in a U.S. corporation is not subject to the generation-skipping transfer tax because it is not subject to gift tax. On the other hand, a transfer upon death by a nonresident alien donor to his nonresident alien grandchild of stock in a U.S. corporation is subject to both the estate tax and the generation-skipping tax.[64] Obviously, such transfers are to be avoided.

Transfers otherwise subject to the generation-skipping transfer tax are exempt from the tax, up to a cumulative total of otherwise taxable transfers of $5.25 million per donor in 2013, at the election of the donor.[65] This exemption is available to nonresident alien donors, against their otherwise taxable gifts.[66]

V. U.S. Income Taxation of Dispositions by Nonresident Aliens of U.S.-Situs Real Property

The Foreign Investment in Real Property Tax Act (FIRPTA)[67] was enacted by Congress in 1980.[68] Prior to this time, gains upon the sale of U.S. situs real property by nonresident aliens had been taxed like gains upon the sale of any other U.S. situs capital asset—they were subject to U.S. income tax only if the nonresident alien

61. I.R.C. § 2513(a)(1); Treas. Reg. § 25.2513-1(b)(2).
62. I.R.C. § 2651(d).
63. Treas. Reg. § 26.2663-2.
64. I.R.C. § 26.2663-2(d), Example 2.
65. I.R.C. § 2631.
66. Treas. Reg. § 26.2663-2(a).
67. *See* I.R.C. § 897.
68. Pub. L. No. 96-499, 94 Stat. 2682, § 1122(a) (1980).

owner was present in the United States for more than 182 days in the year of sale (and, if different, the year of collection of the sale proceeds).[69]

FIRPTA was enacted because of increasing purchases of U.S. real estate, particularly farmland, by nonresident alien investors in the 1970s, and a perception by Congress that this class of investment by nonresident aliens was not in the interest of U.S. taxpayers because it was increasing the cost of purchase of a limited resource, land. The statute was enacted to subject this class of investment to income tax upon disposition, regardless of whether the nonresident alien was present in the United States in the year of disposition of the real property.

Under FIRPTA, the gain or loss upon disposition of "a United States real property interest" is subjected to income tax, as if the gain or loss were effectively connected with the conduct of a trade or business in the United States, and taxed under I.R.C. § 871(b)(1).[70]

"United States real property interests" include both directly held interests in land, buildings, mines, farms, and other "real estate" and interests in certain corporations, other than publicly traded securities in such corporations, 50 percent or more of whose assets consist of United States real property interests.

Minimum tax rules of I.R.C. § 55 apply to calculation of the FIRPTA tax, and U.S. purchasers of FIRPTA interests are generally required to withhold 10 percent of the gross purchase price of the asset from a foreign purchaser and remit the amount to the Internal Revenue Service with a FIRPTA information return,[71] unless the seller delivers a withholding certificate that reduces or eliminates the withholding requirement.[72] A nonresident alien seller of a United States real property interest is required to file a United States federal income tax return Form 1040NR, even if the withholding of 10 percent of the gross sales proceeds equals or exceeds the tax due.[73]

Congress in 1980 gave the Treasury Department statutory authority to require annual information returns by all nonresident alien owners of United States real property interests,[74] but Treasury to date has adopted no regulations requiring such reporting.

69. *See* discussion *supra* text accompanying note 35.

70. I.R.C. § 897.

71. I.R.C. § 1445. The transferee files Form 8288, disclosing the transaction, with the 10 percent withheld tax and two copies of Form 8288-A, one of which is stamped for use by the seller as a receipt for use with his tax return. Treas. Reg. § 1.445-1(f)(2).

72. Treas. Reg. § 1.1445-3.

73. I.R.C. § 1.6012-1(b)(2).

74. I.R.C. § 6039C, enacted effective June 19, 1980, by Pub. L. No. 96-499, 94 Stat. 2687, § 1123(a) (1980).

VI. Returns Required to Be Filed by Nonresident Aliens or Persons Related to Nonresident Aliens

A. Income Tax Returns

Every nonresident alien individual who engages in a trade or business in the United States during the tax year[75] (whether or not he or she has any taxable income), or who has any income subject to U.S. income tax, must file a return (Form 1040NR). The return must be filed with the Internal Revenue Service Center by the fifteenth day of the fourth month following the end of the taxpayer's fiscal year (thus by April 15 for calendar year taxpayers) if the taxpayer had income from wages, and by the fifteenth day of the sixth month in all other cases.[76] Any taxes due must be paid with the return to the extent not previously withheld by the paying agent.

An important exception to the requirement that a nonresident alien file an income tax return allows the taxpayer to avoid filing a return if all of his or her income was passive income subject to withholding at the source and if the applicable tax was in fact fully withheld.[77] This exception does not apply to a taxpayer with income effectively connected with the conduct of a U.S. trade or business or with FIRPTA income, in both of which cases a return must be filed.

B. Estate Tax Returns

The executor of the estate of a nonresident alien decedent having U.S. situs assets in excess of $60,000 must file Form 706-NA.[78] The return must be filed within nine months of the date of death of the decedent. Any taxes due must be paid with the return. Extensions are available for delayed payment of tax and filing of a return, upon proper request for an extension filed before the due date.

A Form 706-NA must disclose all of the assets of the decedent situated in the United States and, if deductions are sought for the payment of debts, expenses, and taxes, must disclose all of the worldwide assets and deductions.

A Form 706-NA must be filed by the "executor," which is defined by I.R.C. § 2203 as the executor or administrator of the decedent's estate, duly appointed, qualified and acting in the United States or, if none, then any person in actual or constructive possession in the United States of assets of the decedent. In certain cases, this can mean that persons who would not ordinarily consider themselves to be a U.S. executor may nevertheless effectively be deemed to be acting as such.

75. Treas. Reg. § 1.6012-1(b).
76. I.R.C. § 6072(c); Treas. Reg. § 1.6072-1(c).
77. Treas. Reg. § 1.6012-1(b)(2).
78. I.R.C. § 6018(a)(2); Treas. Reg. § 20.6018-3(b).

C. Gift Tax Returns

A nonresident alien donor making a gift subject to the U.S. gift tax must file a Form 709, U.S. Gift Tax Return, by April 15 of the year following the year of the gift.

D. Generation-Skipping Transfer Tax Returns

There is no separate return for generation-skipping transfer tax. A transfer subject to the tax is disclosed on the estate or gift tax return that is otherwise due.

E. Income Tax Returns by Foreign Estates and Trusts

Foreign estates are generally taxed in the same way as nonresident alien individuals and therefore must file a Form 1040NR, in the same circumstances as an individual would have to file.

Foreign trusts are now subject to detailed reporting provisions under I.R.C. § 6048.[79] The rules are different for trusts created by U.S. persons and for trusts created by non-U.S. persons. In the case of trusts created by non-U.S. persons, the rules focus upon determining whether a U.S. beneficiary has received a distribution (whether deemed or actual) constituting taxable income and, in particular, an accumulation distribution of a prior year's income from a foreign trust.

F. Returns of U.S. Beneficiaries of Gifts and Trusts

Individuals who are U.S. persons and receive gifts exceeding $100,000 in any year from a nonresident alien individual, or exceeding $10,000 (adjusted for inflation, $15,102 in 2013) in any year from a foreign person other than an individual,[80] or who receive direct or indirect distributions in any amount from a foreign trust,[81] must file a Form 3520 by April 15 of the year following receipt of the payment, disclosing the gift.

G. Liens for Payment of Estate and Gift Taxes

A special lien for the payment of United States federal estate and gift taxes attaches automatically, without the filing of a notice of lien, to property that is the subject of a taxable transfer upon death or by gift, and remains upon the property for a period of ten years following the death of the decedent or date of the gift.[82] The lien is automatically discharged from property purchased by a third party for full and fair consideration from a holder other than the executor of the estate or a beneficiary who has received property from the executor. In all other cases, the owner of the property (the executor of the decedent's estate or a donee or beneficiary) must apply to the Internal Revenue Service for a discharge of the special ten-year lien for payment of estate and gift taxes. The Treasury Regulations specifically forbid a domestic corporation or its transfer agent to transfer shares

79. For a more detailed discussion, see *infra* Chapter 7.

80. I.R.C. § 6039F.

81. I.R.C. § 6048.

82. I.R.C. § 6324.

registered in the name of a nonresident decedent (regardless of citizenship) to one other than a domestic executor or administrator without the submission of a transfer certificate, releasing the lien, issued by the Internal Revenue Service.[83]

VII. Treaty Impact

The United States has bilateral income tax treaties with its major trading partners and an increasing number of third world nations. The purpose of such treaties is to reduce double taxation, to allocate primary taxing authority to the nation having a closer connection to the taxpayer or the category of income, and to facilitate cooperative tax administration by the two nations.[84] Most treaties reduce from 30 percent to 15 percent or less the flat withholding rate of tax on classes of passive income, and many allow a nonresident alien to spend more time in the United States before being taxed as a resident.

The United States has estate (and sometimes gift) tax treaties with only sixteen countries, and many of these, such as the dual estate tax treaty with Japan, are outmoded. As in the case of bilateral income tax treaties, the purpose of dual estate tax treaties is to reduce double taxation, to allocate primary taxing authority between the two nations, and to facilitate cooperative tax administration.[85]

VIII. Expatriation to Avoid Tax

The estate, gift, and income tax regimes have long contained provisions that impact the taxation of nonresident aliens who are deemed to have expatriated to avoid tax. Under current law, as changed by the Heroes Earning Assistance and Relief Tax Act of 2008 (the Heart Act), a "mark-to-market" exit tax is imposed on a "covered expatriate," whereby such expatriate must recognize and pay tax on unrealized gain in excess of $600,000 (adjusted for inflation, $663,000 in 2013).[86] All worldwide property of a covered expatriate is deemed to be sold for its fair market value on the day before expatriation. A "covered expatriate" is a person who, after June 17, 2008, renounces U.S. citizenship or who, as a long-term lawful permanent resident, gives up his or her green card entitling him or her to permanent resident status[87] in the United States; who meets certain minimum income

83. Treas. Reg. § 20.6325-1.

84. For a further consideration of the income tax treaties, see *infra* Chapter 12.

85. For a further consideration of the estate and gift tax treaties, see *infra* Chapter 11.

86. *See* I.R.C. § 877A.

87. "Long-term" residents are those who have had permanent resident status for at least eight of the last fifteen years. I.R.C. § 877A(g)(5).

and assets thresholds;[88] or who fails to certify compliance with U.S. tax obligations for the prior five years.

The Heart Act also imposes a tax on "covered gifts and bequests" (in excess of the $14,000 annual exclusion, adjusted for inflation) by covered expatriates to U.S. citizens or residents, with certain exceptions.[89] Tax will be imposed on the recipient[90] of the covered gift or bequest at the highest gift or estate tax then in effect[91] (40 percent in 2013). This tax will be reduced by the amount of any gift or estate tax paid to a foreign country with respect to the gift or bequest.[92] A transfer that normally would attract a generation-skipping transfer (GST) tax in addition to a gift or estate tax (i.e., a transfer from grandparent to grandchild) will be subject only to gift tax or estate tax.

88. The individual must have had an average annual net income tax of at least $ 155,000 (in 2013) for the five years preceding expatriation and a net worth of at least $ 2,000,000. I.R.C. § 877(a)(g)(1).

89. I.R.C. § 2801.

90. *Id.* § 2801(b).

91. *Id.* § 2801(a)(1).

92. *Id.* § 2801(d).

PART

II

Wills, Probate, and Administration

The Use of Multiple ("Situs") Wills

3

Barbara Hauser*

I. Introduction

The use of multiple wills is a difficult subject. For United States lawyers,[1] though, it is an even more difficult subject. The U.S. estate planner has been trained that a client has only one will in effect at a time. When other countries are involved, this may not always be the best approach.

This chapter deals with when and how the client may be better served by having more than one will in effect at a time. If there is going to be more than one will, however, extreme caution must be exercised in the coordination of the wills. It is, in the author's opinion, imperative that knowledgeable local counsel be consulted in each such case.[2]

Finally, several examples of laws in other countries will be mentioned. These are intended to provide illustrations of the

* With appreciation to Robert C. Lawrence, III, for his review of the original chapter.

1. The author will refer to United States lawyers in place of the more common "American" lawyers out of deference to the other countries in North, South, and Central America.

2. In fact, particular practitioners will be acknowledged in footnotes to this chapter since they, and others not named, have been invaluable. The author expresses special gratitude to the memory of Wolfe D. Goodman, who consistently provided generous guidance.

many differences that exist in this field. In any particular case, local counsel should be consulted. Not only do the laws change, but they also may not operate in practice the way they read in legal treatises.

II. Prevalent Mistakes

A. Accidental Revocation

Before discussing the considerations in favor of having more than one will in effect at a time, it is appropriate to alert the practitioner to what is perhaps the most common mistake in this area—accidental revocation. In all of the standard will forms in the United States, there is likely to be a version of one or more of the following: "I make this my Last Will and Testament," "I hereby revoke and replace all other Wills and Codicils made heretofore by me," "This, my last Will . . . ," or "Last Will and Testament of . . . ."

The inclusion of any of these phrases would revoke other wills, even when that was not intended. These phrases are so standard in wills in the United States that they are used without particular concern or attention, and in fact are unlikely to be mentioned to clients. It is also rare for the U.S. adviser to ask whether there is a will (or more than one) in existence in another country. Clients from other countries, moreover, may be so accustomed to having a local will wherever they own assets that they see no reason to mention it to the new lawyer. The author has even found that a long-standing U.S. client prepared a handwritten will for some property in Italy that seemed not worth mentioning to the author. Thus, U.S. lawyers routinely cause the unintended revocation of all prior plans.

The only exception to this accidental revocation might be when the other will includes a specific phrase providing that it can be revoked only by a later will that refers specifically to the other will, which is sometimes recommended by those who practice in this field.[3] From a client's perspective, however, there would be a substantial risk that the prior will and its restriction on revocation could be forgotten over time. One might also argue that a client cannot effectively restrict his or her own freedom to make new wills. The client may in fact intend a new will to replace completely the prior will, and may even forget to mention the prior will. Unfortunately, in that case, it is possible that the prior will continue to be in effect, and it is nearly certain that the two wills will be inconsistent with each other.

B. "Pour Over" Wills (and Their Revocable Trusts)

The second most common mistake made by U.S. lawyers in this field is the use of a revocable trust (and its brief accompanying will, "pouring" any assets not transferred during life to the revocable trust) in the attempt to avoid probate in other

3. In discussions with the author, Robert Muckelstone has cautioned, however, that Japanese law may prohibit a testator from restricting the testator's power of revocation.

countries. In many European countries, the trust is not a recognized legal relationship, and a will that refers to a trust for its dispositive provisions could cause significant problems in civil law jurisdictions.[4] In addition, those other countries may not have a probate system, so the goal of avoiding probate might be illusory.

III. "Situs" Wills: Reasons to Consider the Use of Multiple Wills

The word "situs" refers to "location." A "situs" will deals with, and only with, those assets that are considered to be located within that country. The category considered most often for situs wills is "immovable" property, consisting generally of land, buildings, long-term leaseholds, and fixtures.[5] Depending on the jurisdiction in which the property is located, however, "immovables" could include mortgages on real property even when a portfolio of mortgages is held as an investment. For example,the right of a mortgage holder is treated as immovable in England and Ontario, but as movable in New Zealand and Australia.[6]

It is particularly important to use clear and effective legal terms in the case of immovables because the succession to land is highly regulated by the jurisdiction in which the land is located. As stated in a leading English treatise on private international law:[7] "At the end of the day, only the law of the situs can control the way in which land, which constitutes part of the situs itself, is transferred."[8]

A. Elimination of Some Administration Expenses

It may be true that a local will will simplify the administration and its attendant expenses. In jurisdictions that impose an administration charge based on a percentage of assets under administration, reducing the amount of assets under administration will directly reduce those fees.

B. Clearer Application of Relevant Law

When a will is prepared in a particular jurisdiction, the drafter of the will is familiar with the local legal rules. If the will contains legal terms that are familiar in that jurisdiction, it is presumed that the subsequent administration will be clearly understood in that jurisdiction.

4. In fact, most European countries do not have "probate" anyway; therefore, the initial reason for using a revocable trust to avoid probate of the foreign assets should be examined in each case.

5. *See also supra* Chapter 1 pertaining to choice of law for assistance in deciding which country's definition would be used for "immovable."

6. P.M. North & J.J. Fawcett, Cheshire and North's Private International Law 923 (13th ed. 1999).

7. This term is used in England; in the United States, the more common term is conflict of laws.

8. North & Fawcett, *supra* note 6, at 929.

C. Translations

Translation is actually a prime concern, and one that is not often mentioned. If a United States will is used to transfer assets in another country, that country will likely require an official translation of the will. As noted below, it can be nearly impossible to translate some of the terms in a will. It may also happen that the client will have a "situs" will in a jurisdiction such as France where "notarial" wills must be understood by the witnesses. If that will is written in English (for the benefit of the client), it may not be valid on the grounds that the witnesses in France did not understand it.[9]

In the field of inheritance and succession, there are many different systems around the world. Each system uses its own technical terms, which are almost impossible to translate outside of that particular system. In addition, the author is continually surprised by how the same English word can have an entirely different meaning in the British legal system.

D. Selection of Law

It is sometimes suggested that a benefit of using a "situs" will is that the client may be able to select the law that is to govern with respect to the assets covered by that will. This becomes especially important if the local law would otherwise apply its forced heirship rules.[10] For example, a home in Switzerland would normally be subject to Swiss forced heirship laws, but Swiss law offers someone who is a national of a different country the option of choosing the law of their nationality to apply.

E. Requirements for Validity

When a will is executed in a particular country, it might be assumed that the requirements relating to its formal validity will have been met. Even this is not a simple issue though, because the applicable law relating to the formalities of execution may be the law of the domicile or the law of the situs of the property.[11] See discussion *infra* relating to execution requirements.

F. Need of an Original Will by the Probate Court

It may happen that a local jurisdiction will require the production of the original will, which could become difficult. For example, one situation where there was only one will involved an English will that had been "lodged for probate" in England. There were substantial bank accounts in the United States, but the probate

9. *See* 1 Jeffrey A. Schoenblum, Multistate and Multinational Estate Planning § 15.02[B], at 861 (2d ed. 1999).

10. See *supra* Chapter 1 and *infra* Chapter 5, respectively, dealing with conflict of laws and forced heirship rules for a more extensive discussion of these issues.

11. See *supra* Chapter 1 for a more extensive discussion of the conflict of laws.

court in New York would not appoint the U.S. executor without examining the original will, which the English court would not release.[12]

G. Confidentiality—If Administration Is Confined to Certain Assets

Many clients who interact with other legal systems have a strong preference for not disclosing all of their assets to any one jurisdiction (and often to any one adviser either). In terms of any client to whom the United States estate tax would apply on a worldwide basis, this is not a relevant goal because there will be U.S. federal estate taxation on worldwide assets. In fact, if the client is a nonresident alien owning real estate in the United States and wishing to have a situs will in the United States to dispose only of that property, the planner should also advise the client that any indebtedness on the property (other than nonrecourse indebtedness) will be subtracted from the value only as a proportionate amount of the client's worldwide assets, which must then be disclosed on the U.S. estate tax return.[13] Most wills refer to the residuary assets in general terms[14] and usually do not specify what those assets are or where they are located. If a situs will specifies, however, that it applies only to assets located within a certain jurisdiction, the administration in that jurisdiction would be confined to those assets.

H. Simpler Administration in Each Jurisdiction

This is not a simple area either. Although it makes sense to assume that a local will will be simpler to administer in that jurisdiction, that may not be the case. For example, a Swiss court will not accept for probate a Swiss will, covering Swiss bank accounts, if the testator was not domiciled in Switzerland. The only exception is when the foreign court "does not deal with (such assets)."[15] On the other hand, a personal representative appointed in accordance with a U.S. will by a U.S. court will not be allowed to deal with any property located in England unless the representative obtains a special grant from an English court: "It is an absolute rule that the status of an administrator appointed by a foreign court is not recognized in England."[16]

12. This particular matter was resolved by entrusting the original to an English solicitor acting as an officer of the court who personally delivered it to the New York court for inspection and copying.

13. I.R.C. § 2106(a)(1).

14. For example, "I leave all the 'rest, residue, and remainder' of property 'owned by me or in which I have any interest whatsoever' and 'wherever located'" is a common disposition.

15. Art. 88 al. 1 LDIP (with thanks to C. Alain Burnand).

16. North & Fawcett, *supra* note 6, at 981.

IV. Choice of Law Issues

There are several particular issues in the area of choice of law.[17] A few illustrations from other legal systems will be given in the discussion that follows.[18] Knowledgeable local counsel should always be consulted.

A. Capacity

The general issue of capacity is whether or not the person who made a will had the capacity to make a valid will.[19] Issues of capacity include whether the person was of sufficient age, whether the person had sufficient mental capacity, and whether the person was under any duress or undue influence.

England uses the law of the domicile of the deceased at the time the will was made to determine the capacity to make a will.[20]

Sharia law provides that every adult Muslim with reasoning ability has capacity to make a will. The determination of becoming an adult depends, however, on particular systems of Sharia law, as follows:

1. A Hanafi, Nabali, or Shafi'i Muslim is adult upon attaining puberty;
2. A Sunni Muslim is presumed to attain puberty no later than age fifteen; and
3. The Maliki system uses the "age of discernment," which is age ten.[21]

Under the Uniform Probate Code, a person who is eighteen may make a will.[22] In France, the age is sixteen.[23]

B. Bequest to Witness

There are many cases dealing with the validity of bequests to witnesses. This does not affect the validity of a will but does affect the validity of a particular bequest. In some jurisdictions, bequests to witnesses are void. In others, they are permitted.

C. Revocation Effected by Marriage

Under the Uniform Probate Code (the UPC),[24] a marriage subsequent to the making of a will does not effect a revocation of that will. In Scotland, a will is not revoked by a subsequent marriage.[25] In France, a will is not revoked by a subse-

17. *See also supra* Chapter 1.

18. For a more extensive discussion, see *supra* Chapter 1.

19. A separate issue of capacity is whether or not the legatee has the capacity to receive the property.

20. John G. Collier, Conflict of Laws 270 (2d ed. 1996).

21. David Pearl & Werner Menski, Muslim Family Law 450–51 (3d ed. 1998).

22. Unif. Probate Code § 2-501.

23. Brice Dickson, Introduction to French Law 234 (1994).

24. However, an omitted spouse is entitled to his or her intestate share, as if the testator died without a will. *See* Unif. Probate Code § 2-301.

25. Collier, *supra* note 20, at 273.

quent marriage, although being sentenced to life imprisonment will revoke a will.[26] In England, a will is revoked by marriage unless the will states that it is made in contemplation of marriage.[27] Incidentally, if these rules are considered to be rules of testamentary law, they will generally be determined by the law of the testator's domicile at the date of death. If they are rules relating to the matrimony, though (as seems more likely), they will generally be determined by the law of the domicile at the time of marriage.[28]

D. Revocation Effected by Divorce

In most jurisdictions, a divorce decree will effect a revocation of the bequests to the former spouse. Some divorce decrees will also cancel the appointment to serve as executor. The definition of divorce may vary, and such revocation or cancellation may include the time when a petition is filed.

E. Bequests to Charities or Others

In France, many charities cannot accept a bequest unless they first obtain governmental approval.[29] In Austria and several other countries, bequests to charities are subject to tax.[30] In France, doctors who have taken care of a testator cannot inherit under a will made during treatment.[31]

V. Property That Can Be Disposed of by Will

A question that is seldom encountered by United States lawyers is whether the testator has the right to dispose of his or her property. This should also be addressed. For example, under Sharia law, a Muslim cannot dispose by will of more than one-third of the surplus of his or her estate after payment of funeral expenses and debts. Any bequests in excess of that amount require the consent of the heirs after the testator's death.[32]

A. Marital Rights and Regimes

In the United States, most states provide by statute, such as the UPC,[33] that a surviving spouse has the right to "elect against" the will if he or she has not been left a certain minimum amount. In the states with community property laws, a spouse

26. Dickson, *supra* note 23, at 234.

27. North & Fawcett, *supra* note 6, at 998.

28. *Id.*

29. Dickson, *supra* note 23, at 235.

30. *See, e.g.*, Friedrich Schwank, *Non-Profit Organizations in Austria: A Fiscal Study* (1997), *in* Austria 4.1, 4.7, Collection of Conference Papers of the International Academy of Estate and Trust Law.

31. Dickson, *supra* note 23, at 235.

32. With thanks to Ravinder Singhania.

33. Unif. Probate Code § 2-202.

is allowed to dispose of only his or her own separate property and his or her share of the community property (i.e., one-half).

In other countries, there are different marital "regimes" that restrict the amount of property the testator can dispose of. For example, in France, it is not simple to determine the rights each spouse has to dispose of property. They are assumed to have chosen as the one law that will govern their property rights throughout their marriage, regardless of later moves or changes in nationality, the law of the place where they settle their first matrimonial domicile. They may, however, have entered into a contract (which they can also change during the marriage) to elect to continue with separate property or to have community property.[34]

B. Forced Heirship

There is a separate chapter in this book addressing forced heirship (*see* Chapter 5). It is relevant here, though, to emphasize that in many countries, there is little freedom to dispose of a large portion of one's assets. Testamentary freedom of disposition seems to be a principle firmly rooted in the common law system and generally repudiated in the civil law system. In France, for example, the portion that must be left to children is referred to as the "reserve," and the testator may only dispose of the rest, aptly called the "*quotite disponible.*" This can also affect the validity of lifetime gifts, which can be "clawed back" if the amount left at death is not sufficient under the forced heirship rules.[35]

C. Other Restrictions

There are a number of other restrictions on the transfer of property. In some cases, the local country may have seized or frozen the assets. In some cases, the owner who returns to claim assets may not be permitted to leave again. In China, there are three categories of property ownership: the state, the community, and the individual, who owns only his or her "personal" property. In some countries, it still appears that women are not treated as owners of property of which they can dispose. On the death of a Muslim, non-Muslim heirs are excluded from any share of the estate, unless there is a bequest under a will.[36]

VI. Drafting Concerns

A. Nonrevocation Provision

As mentioned at the beginning of this chapter, the most common error in drafting a will is the accidental revocation of other wills. The initial language in most forms states: "I hereby revoke and replace . . . ." That clause will have to be omitted if

34. With thanks to Daniel Angenieux, a French *notaire*.
35. *See infra* Chapter 5.
36. PEARL & MENSKI, *supra* note 21, at 468–69.

another will is intended to remain in effect. The practitioner should also consider whether or not to refer specifically to that other will, including its date. An alternative approach would be to restrict a will to assets located in the situs jurisdiction and to state that it is not to apply to any assets outside that jurisdiction.

B. Statement of Residency

Wills in the United States almost always begin with "I [name of testator], a resident of [name of county], [state] . . . ." This is a statement that needs some thought if more than one country is involved. On the one hand, some recommend that no domicile or residence should be named in a will on the grounds that there will be more flexibility to claim a particular residency or domicile in the future.[37] On the other hand, the author has sometimes used that section of the will to state for the record that a client, for example, is "a citizen of X country, temporarily residing in the United States while on a work assignment." Some have used the phrase "temporarily sojourning" in the local jurisdiction.

C. Coordination of Beneficiaries

Often when separate wills are used, the assets located in one country are given to one set of beneficiaries, and the assets in another country, dealt with by a will in that country, are left to a different set of beneficiaries. What then often happens is that some of the assets are sold, the proceeds are relocated, and the originally intended beneficiaries are left with no assets to inherit. This is simply a more complex version of what happens when domestic clients name different children on different bank accounts, sometimes in place of having a will. It is important to review multiple wills and asset ownership every few years.

D. Allocation of Tax Liability

An obvious trap is the allocation of estate or inheritance tax liability. If there are separate wills disposing of different assets, there will no longer be a unified residue to use for the payment of taxes. A fair amount of work may be involved in estimating what the taxes will be and from which country, and then to tailor a specific allocation clause. If there are references to other wills, some of the desired confidentiality may be lost. In addition, the client may move or change ownership, and the allocation that was written may turn out to be inappropriate.

E. Responsibility for Tax Payment

An issue of great concern to those who are named as executors or administrators in a multiple will scenario is which of them will be treated as responsible, by which country, for the payment of the estate taxes.[38] In the worst case, there could

---

37. This is the view stated by Robert Lawrence and Jeffrey Schoenblum. *See, e.g.*, Robert C. Lawrence III, International Tax and Estate Planning § 8.04[a] (3d ed. 1996); 1 Schoenblum, *supra* note 9, § 8.05 at 354–55.

38. There may also be issues relating to final income taxes of the decedent.

be an executor who is responsible for the payment of the majority of the taxes but who has authority over very few of the assets.[39] Robert Lawrence suggests that the executor in the "primary" jurisdiction should be authorized in the will to pay the debts and expenses in the other jurisdictions, provided that the other jurisdictions certify as to those expenses.[40]

F. Authority to Administer

When assets are spread among two or more countries, the will should also indicate which executor has the authority to administer assets in which country. There may also be provisions authorizing ancillary administrations and procedures for appointing and replacing those executors or administrators.

G. Critical Definitions

If there are any special circumstances relating to any beneficiary, particularly to the category of children, the adviser should consider including specific definitions in the will (such as those that are commonly included in trusts in the United States). The construction of the meaning of a term, such as "my children," will generally be decided by the law of the domicile of the testator at the time the will was made.[41] If the primary concern is to arrive at the intent of the testator, there may be cases in which the words were intended to have the meaning they have under another jurisdiction, such as the situs jurisdiction for a disposition of land.

Gifts or bequests to "my children," in some jurisdictions, will refer only to "legitimate" children (who can be defined a number of ways);[42] in others, the term may include all illegitimate children. In one South African case, it was held that the children of a polygamous union, born when the father was domiciled in India, were legitimate under the law of Natal, the domicile of the father at this death.[43] Adopted children may or may not be included. The legal effect of adoptions can also vary. In France, for example, there are two forms of adoption: under one form, the adoptee continues to have inheritance rights from the natural parents in addition to having them from the adoptive parents; under the other form, the first inheritance rights are replaced by the second.[44] Under Sharia law, adoption is not recognized. The author suggests that the particular term "my children" be defined with great specificity in the will.

With respect to the term "husband," "wife," or "spouse," it is also wise to name the particular person and perhaps even to add a phrase that the person "shall be

39. With thanks to Joseph Field.

40. Lawrence, *supra* note 37, at § 8-14.

41. North & Fawcett, *supra* note 6, at 1002.

42. Even the simple definition of being a child who is born during a legitimate marriage can involve a determination of whether or not the marriage was legitimate and under which law. Often a child who is born "illegitimate" because the parents were not married can later become "legitimate" upon the subsequent marriage of those parents.

43. Seedat's Executors v. The Master 1917 AD 302, *cited in* North & Fawcett, *supra* note 6, at 891.

44. Dickson, *supra* note 23, at 225–26.

considered to be my spouse for all purposes in this will." Otherwise, there could be a risk that the applicable law would produce a result that the person thought to be a spouse was not a spouse. This scenario can arise, for example, if a divorce in one jurisdiction is not recognized in another jurisdiction, resulting in an invalid subsequent marriage. Jurisdictions are also changing in their recognition of same-gender marriages.

VII. Formalities of Execution

The practitioner is not expected to know the requirements of proper execution of a will from another jurisdiction. When there are multiple wills, however, and the foreign wills need to be considered, an initial determination will have to be made as to whether a particular foreign will is valid.

A. Recognized Classifications of Wills

The initial question is whether the document is in a form that is recognized as a will by the relevant jurisdiction.

Under the UPC, a testator must be at least eighteen years of age and "of sound mind." The will must be in writing and signed by two witnesses.

The form of a will can vary by country. For example, in France, there are three prescribed written forms, as follows:

1. Holographic. This is a will entirely in the handwriting of the testator, who must sign it and date it. It is the most commonly used form of will in France.
2. Notarial (or "authentic"). This is a will drafted by a notary in the presence of two witnesses or another *notaire* (who will then know the contents of the will) and signed by the testator, two witnesses, and the drafting *notaire*.
3. Mystic (or "secret"). The will, written by or for the testator, is put in a sealed envelope and then presented to *a notaire* and two witnesses, and all four sign the envelope.

In Switzerland, it is also still possible to have an "oral" will if the testator is in danger of death, but the validity of the will ceases fourteen days after the danger has passed.

B. Validity of Formalities of Execution

The initial question, as with so many other issues in this field, is which law governs.[45]

1. Local Law

To refer to "local" law is not always sufficient. There may well be, as there is in the United States, a further subdivision of jurisdictions that govern formalities of

45. See *supra* Chapter 1 for a more complete discussion.

execution issues.[46] Switzerland, for example, is a federation of twenty-six separate "cantons," which have shared jurisdiction with the federal government on issues of taxation, but only the federal government has jurisdiction over family and property law. In Canada, there are provinces. In addition to those geographic jurisdictions, there may also be religious or community (or even tribal) laws that apply. It is important to consult with a knowledgeable local practitioner. Even the rules about who can be a witness vary by jurisdiction. For example, in France, a beneficiary may not be a witness, and neither may the relatives of beneficiaries or the clerks of the *notaire*.[47]

2. Uniform Probate Code

In 1969, the UPC was approved by the National Conference of Commissioners on Uniform State Laws in the United States and the American Bar Association House of Delegates. It has since been adopted by about one-third of the states in the United States, often with amendments. With respect to "international" wills, a state that has adopted the UPC gives three alternatives under which to establish the validity of a will with respect to the formalities of execution:

1. It satisfies the regular UPC requirements;
2. It was executed in compliance with the law of any of the following:
   (a) the place of execution;
   (b) the testator's domicile at the time of execution;
   (c) the testator's place of abode at the time of execution;
   (d) the place of the testator's nationality at the time of execution;
   (e) the testator's domicile at the time of death;
   (f) the testator's place of abode at the time of death;
   (g) the testator's nationality at the time of death; or
3. It complies with the Uniform International Wills Act, which is contained within the UPC but is designed to be adopted as a separate act by states that may not have adopted the UPC. The Act applies, however, only among those states that have adopted it. Although some fourteen states and the District of Columbia (in the United States), and the U.S. Virgin Islands have adopted this as a separate act, the author is not aware of any foreign jurisdiction that has adopted it. Thus, the practitioner should not be misled by the title of the Act.

3. The Washington Convention

In 1973, the International Institute for the Unification of Private Law convened a Conference on Wills in Washington, D.C., with members from forty-two countries. The resulting Convention, the "Convention providing a Uniform Law on the Form

46. Robert Lawrence notes that he often sees references to "the U.S." when it should be a reference to a particular state within the United States.

47. Dickson, *supra* note 23, at 234.

of an International Will," was signed by eleven of those countries[48] subject to ratification." After being ratified or acceded to by five countries, the Convention enters into force with respect to those countries." At the present time, it has been ratified by only three countries: Belgium, Ecuador, and France. It has been acceded to by nine countries (including Canada,[49] and Italy), and thus is in effect with respect to those twelve countries.[50] The Washington Convention was finally ratified by the United States Senate in 1991, with a proposal to enact enabling legislation, but it is not in effect in any state in the United States.[51]

4. The Hague Convention on Form of Testamentary Dispositions

The Hague Conference on Private International Law has adopted four conventions in the estate planning field. They become effective after three member countries have ratified them. Once they are in effect, they apply to, and only to, the countries that at some time have ratified them or acceded to them.

(a) Application of the Convention. The Hague Convention on the Conflicts of Laws relating to the Form of Testamentary Dispositions was adopted in 1961 but has never been ratified by the United States, although it is in effect in forty other countries. Those include Australia, Belgium, Denmark, France, Germany, Italy, Japan, the Netherlands, Norway, Spain, Sweden, Switzerland, and the United Kingdom.

(b) Provisions of the Convention. The purpose of the Convention is to recognize as valid, in terms of the formalities of execution, a will that complies with the domestic law of any one of the following:

1. The place where the testator made the will;
2. The nationality of the testator, either at the time of making the will or at the time of death;
3. The domicile of the testator, either at the time of making the will or at the time of death;
4. The place of "habitual residence," either at the time of making the will or at the time of death; or
5. With respect to immovable assets, the place where they are situated.

---

48. Belgium,Czechoslovakia, Ecuador, France, Holy See, Iran, Laos, Sierra Leone, Taiwan, the United Kingdom, the United States, and the United Soviet Socialist Republic.

49. Originally only for Manitoba and Newfoundland, then extended to Ontario, Alberta, Saskatchewan, Prince Edward Island, New Brunswick, and, most recently, Nova Scotia.

50. *See* 2 SCHOENBLUM, *supra* note 9, at app. L, at 1194–96 (reprinting record of U.S. Dep't of State). The United States is the official depositary of accessions and ratifications to the Convention.

51. However, a similar set of provisions is incorporated in the Uniform Probate Code and has been enacted by a number of states. *See* UNIF. PROBATE CODE art. II, pt. 10.

5. The European Union

The European Union has been struggling for several years with the inefficiencies and confusion caused by the potential application of the different laws of so many member countries. In particular, the conflicts between English common law and continental versions of civil law seem difficult to harmonize.

VIII. Conclusion

Many fine practitioners will conclude that the risks and pitfalls in the use of multiple wills greatly outnumber the possible benefits. This is not an area to enter without a great amount of thought and special attention to complex coordination. The author's best advice is practical: ask a local "international" practitioner in the other jurisdiction if the will you are proposing to use would cause any concerns in that other country.

Estate Administration and Postmortem Planning Considerations for the International Client

4

G. Warren Whitaker
Dina Kapur Sanna*

I. Introduction

Probate and administration in connection with cross-border estates raise a wide range of legal issues that by definition necessarily touch two or more different jurisdictions. In addressing these issues, certain basic distinctions may be drawn between the approaches of common and civil law jurisdictions. Typically, within the various jurisdictions involved, there are even further distinctions regardless of common or civil law classification.

The extent to which the law of a particular jurisdiction controls probate and administration is based on jurisdictional limitations. These limitations set the level of liability, both for claims of ordinary creditors and for outstanding taxes.

Moreover, interrelated with estate administration is the matter of postmortem estate planning, which in turn gives rise to

* The original chapter was authored in 1999 by William Newton and was updated and revised in 2013 by G. Warren Whitaker and Dina Kapur Sanna with the assistance of their colleague, Immeke M. Schmidt.

issues touching on estate situs, distributions to estate beneficiaries, foreign and domestic trusts, and foreign corporate liquidation and dissolution.

II. Common and Civil Law Jurisdictions Contrasted

A. Common Law Jurisdictions

In common law jurisdictions, probate is the judicial proceeding for proving and establishing the validity of a purported will. Its principal function is to establish that the instrument is indeed the last will and to affirm the validity of legal rights flowing from its terms.[1]

Once the will has been admitted to probate, the formal estate administration may begin. Estate administration in common law jurisdictions is the process of collecting assets of the decedent and paying the decedent's debts, including any outstanding taxes, until all debts are paid or all assets are exhausted. Payment of any remaining balance to the beneficiaries is termed distribution.[2]

The estate is administered by an estate fiduciary referred to as an executor or an administrator. An executor is nominated by the decedent in the will. The nomination must be ratified by the probate court to qualify the executor to serve. An administrator is appointed if the decedent dies intestate or no competent executor is designated in the decedent's will. In certain jurisdictions, executors and administrators are known as personal representatives.[3] Estate fiduciaries occupy a position of trust and stand in a fiduciary relationship relative to those interested in the estate—the creditors and beneficiaries.

In general, a duly appointed executor or administrator has no authority (apart from comity) to enter a foreign jurisdiction and exercise official functions over property located there. Correlatively, the executor or administrator should not be charged with loss of assets located in a foreign jurisdiction over which he or she has no control and which never come into the executor's or administrator's hands.[4] Even so, in the case of a closely held foreign corporation, the personal representative must exercise due care in connection with voting the corporate stock, especially if the corporation is engaged in business activities in a foreign jurisdiction.[5] Personal property located in a foreign jurisdiction but brought into

---

1. *See generally* William Newton, International Income Tax and Estate Planning § 11.02 (2d ed. 2012).

2. *See, e.g.*, Ross v. Beacham, 33 F. Supp. 3, 6 (W.D. S.C. 1940); *In re* Estate of Jones, 588 P.2d 960, 962 (Kan. Ct. App. 1979).

3. For U.S. estate tax purposes, if there is no estate fiduciary that has been duly qualified within the United States, then a person in actual or constructive possession of any property of a decedent having a U.S. situs is considered an executor for estate tax purposes and is liable for any estate taxes until receipt of an IRS-issued transfer certificate (Form 5173). 26 C.F.R. §§ 20.2203-1, 20-6018-2.

4. *See, e.g.*, *In re* Estate of Withington, 140 P.2d 482 (Cal. Ct. App. 1943) (court refused to charge executor of estate of California domiciliary with loss of money on deposit with Mexican bank).

5. *See, e.g.*, *In re* Estate of Massaglia, 113 Cal. Rptr. 751 (1974).

the local jurisdiction is subject to the local court's equity power to protect and preserve assets for the ultimate beneficiaries.[6]

B. Civil Law Jurisdictions

Civil law probate and administration differ significantly from their common law counterparts. First, because surviving family members by statute are commonly and inflexibly assigned a sizable share of the estate under forced heirship principles, the role of a will is diminished and minimized. Second, due to the civil law concept of universal succession, which treats the decedent's property as descending directly to the beneficiaries, there typically is no probate of a will.[7] Although there is variation among civil law jurisdictions, in general, a certificate of heirship or inheritance is issued to the beneficiaries identifying them and stating what portion of the estate is to be distributed to each, and the beneficiaries are often charged with responsibility for administration of the estate rather than an appointed executor or administrator.

Only if there is a controversy and a beneficiary petitions for a determination of an extant will's validity does probate occur. In such a case, the probate court makes a complete inquiry into the issue of validity. That inquiry may include identification of the beneficiaries and their relationship to the decedent.

The certificate of heirship or inheritance is prima facie proof of the estate distribution. A third party relying on the certificate in good faith is protected. This includes debtors of the decedent who, in reliance on the certificate, make payment directly to the estate. Where the estate consists of real property, a certificate may be required in order to replace the decedent's name in the real property records with that of the beneficiaries.

Civil law administration is minimized significantly as compared to that at common law. This is due to the principle of universal succession, which, on death of the decedent, vests title to both real and personal property directly and immediately in the decedent's beneficiaries.[8] In addition to receiving title, the beneficiaries ordinarily become personally liable for the decedent's debts. Where the decedent's liabilities exceed assets, the beneficiaries may petition for appointment of an executor if one was designated in the will, or an administrator if no executor was designated. By appointing an executor or administrator, the beneficiaries limit liability to their allocable portion of the decedent's estate. Otherwise, the beneficiaries will be personally liable for the excess.

The decedent's creditors may also conclude that appointment of an administrator is necessary. This is the case especially where the beneficiaries themselves are in a weak financial position. Otherwise, the decedent's assets may

6. *See, e.g.*, Kaltsas v. Kaltsas, 497 N.E.2d 26 (Mass. 1986) (property subject to domiciliary administration in Greece but brought into Massachusetts subject to local court's equity jurisdiction).

7. *See generally* Newton, *supra* note 1, §§ 11.05, 11.06.

8. *See, e.g.*, Estate of de Eissengarthen v. Comm'r, 10 T.C. 1277, 1278–79 (1948) (under Swiss law, property of decedent becomes by force of law that of beneficiaries designated in will).

be dissipated by an irresponsible beneficiary or attached by the creditors of a beneficiary. The appointment of an administrator may preclude these unfortunate results.

If the estate has United States beneficiaries, creating the potential for shifting the income tax burden between those beneficiaries and an ostensible foreign estate through income accumulation, it may be prudent to formally undertake steps to open a foreign estate proceeding to enhance the likelihood of having a foreign rather than domestic estate situs for United States income taxation. Otherwise, the principle of universal succession may preclude existence of an estate such that income is taxed to the beneficiaries from the outset. Even so, beneficiaries of property in civil law jurisdictions arguably, in effect, assume the position of administrator of the estate for payment of debts, so the estate rather than the beneficiaries should be considered the requisite taxpayer.

C. Convention Concerning International Administration of Estates of Deceased Persons

The Convention Concerning International Administration of Estates of Deceased Persons (the "Hague Convention") resulted from the 1972 Hague Conference on Private International Law. Its purpose is to facilitate collection of assets located abroad and is intended to bridge the gap between common and civil law administration.[9]

The Hague Convention applies only to personal or movable property. It designates a foreign fiduciary to act as personal representative of the estate. The fiduciary's authority for administration is evidenced by an international certificate, which should specify detailed information about the decedent, the fiduciary, the powers of the fiduciary, and the identity of the issuing jurisdiction.

The certificate is issued by the jurisdiction of the decedent's habitual residence. A jurisdiction in which the decedent's assets are situated may refuse recognition of the certificate only under certain circumstances.[10]

Where administration is governed by territorial units of a jurisdiction, the Hague Convention may apply to any one or more of those units. An example would be the federal system of the United States, where the territorial units are the fifty states. The Hague Convention has not been widely adopted, and indeed the United States is not a party to this convention.

9. *See generally* NEWTON, *supra* note 1, § 11.11.

10. Circumstances in which a jurisdiction may refuse recognition are the following: the certificate is not authentic or is in improper form; the certificate was not prepared by an authority with jurisdiction; the jurisdiction refusing recognition also claims the decedent as a habitual resident; the decedent was a national of the jurisdiction refusing recognition; the certificate is incompatible with a decision on the merits, rendered or recognized in the requested jurisdiction; incompatible certificates are issued; or recognition of the certificate would be manifestly incompatible with the public policy of the refusing jurisdiction.

III. Jurisdictional Authority

A. General Considerations

A decedent may have owned property situated in a number of different jurisdictions. These may include both common and civil law jurisdictions and may include both the jurisdiction of the decedent's domicile and situs jurisdictions where the decedent's assets are located.

In either event, any jurisdiction in which the decedent's assets are located at death—whether domiciliary or situs—has full and plenary power over those assets for purposes of probate and administration. However, a jurisdiction may voluntarily refrain from exercising the full authority over assets that it is otherwise entitled to exercise. This voluntary reduction of the level of authority is based on the principle of comity.

In common law jurisdictions, rights, powers, and responsibilities of an executor or administrator appointed in one jurisdiction to administer property located in another vary substantially and are subject to different theoretical approaches, but the starting point is to focus on the jurisdiction of domicile, which is termed "domiciliary administration."[11] If assets owned by the decedent are located outside the jurisdiction of his domicile, separate administration may be required, which is termed "ancillary administration." Whether ancillary administration is required depends in part on the nature of situs assets as real or personal and if personal, tangible, or intangible. In general, common law jurisdictions tend to exercise situs jurisdiction to the fullest practicable extent.[12]

In civil law jurisdictions, the authority of the domiciliary fiduciary of the estate, if one has been appointed, to administer foreign situs property situated in civil law jurisdictions ordinarily is independent of whether the property is personal or real. In civil law jurisdictions, estate administration treats all of the decedent's property as situated in the jurisdiction of the decedent's country of either nationality or domicile. Nationality is the jurisdictional nexus most often adopted.[13]

B. Validity of Wills and Choice of Law

If a decedent owns property in a number of jurisdictions, he may have a single will disposing of his worldwide property, or multiple wills to cover each of the jurisdictions in which he owns property. The issue for a decedent owning property in multiple jurisdictions who has only executed one will (for example, in the jurisdiction of his domicile) is whether that will is valid in the other jurisdiction or jurisdictions in which his property is located. The answer raises two issues: the form of the will and its substantive provisions.

---

11. *See generally* Newton, *supra* note 1, § 11.04.

12. *Id.*

13. *See generally* Newton, *supra* note 1, § 11.07; *see, e.g.*, Neill H. Alford Jr., *Collecting a Decedent's Assets Without Ancillary Administration*, 18 Sw. L.J. 329, 369 (1964).

1. Validity of Wills

Regarding the formal validity of a will, the question is whether one jurisdiction will accept a will of another jurisdiction as a valid will.

(a) Washington Convention (International Will Statute). Depending on the jurisdiction, the Washington Convention on Laws and Wills (the "Washington Convention," also known as the "International Will Statute")[14] may provide the answer. Under the Washington Convention, each adopting jurisdiction will accept wills executed in conformity with the convention's requirements.[15] The purpose of the convention is to provide testators with a way of making wills that will be valid as to form in all countries joining the Washington Convention. The U.S. is a signatory to the Washington Convention, but it must be adopted by each state under the Uniform International Wills Act. Fewer than half of the U.S. states have adopted the Uniform International Wills Act.[16] The Washington Convention has no effect on the substantive validity of the will.

(b) The Hague Convention on Form. The Hague Convention Relating to the Form of Testamentary Disposition of 1961 (the "Hague Convention on Form") may also provide an answer. This convention was the precursor to the Washington Convention and had similar aims. In countries that have adopted the Hague Convention on Form (which includes most of Europe but not the United States), a will is deemed valid if it satisfies the formalities for validity in any of the following jurisdictions: (i) the place where the will was executed; (ii) the country of which the testator was a national when he executed the will or at his death; (iii) the place in which the testator was domiciled when he executed the will or at his death; (iv) the habitual residence of the testator when he executed the will or at his death; or (v) in the case of immovables, the situs of the property.[17]

In countries that have not adopted the Washington Convention or the Hague Convention on Form, it is uncertain which law applies to determine whether the will is formally valid. Generally speaking, common law countries that have not adopted the Hague Convention on Form take an approach similar to English law regarding the formal validity of wills. Civil law countries, on the other hand, follow a nationality principle in choice of law matters.[18]

2. Choice of Law

The substantive validity of a will turns on choice of law rules in both jurisdictions. Matters of substance pertain to the legal relations or rights of the parties,

14. Uniform International Wills Act, 8 U.L.A. 281 (Supp. 1998 & 2005).

15. *See generally* Leigh Alexandra Basha, When a Marriage Goes Global: International Estate Planning Aspects of Marital Planning and Dissolution pt. XIII (2012).

16. New York, for example, has not adopted the Uniform International Wills Act.

17. The Hague Convention, Oct. 5, 1961, art. 1, 510 U.N.T.S. 1977.

18. *See* Basha, *supra* note 15.

which include forced heirship rules, a spouse's right of election, and community property.

Under traditional choice of law principles in the United States, the law that the forum court will apply to most succession issues depends on whether the property is characterized as real or personal. Generally, the law of the situs governs the succession of real property, and the law of the decedent's domicile at death governs the disposition of personal property. In contrast, many civil law countries base their choice of laws, rules, and succession law on a person's citizenship.[19]

In recent years, several courts in the United States have moved away from the traditional choice of law rules to an approach that weighs the interests of the jurisdictions involved and applies the laws of the jurisdiction with the predominant interest.[20] However, in the area of succession of property, the traditional choice of law rules have been applied consistently in U.S. courts.[21] The traditional choice of law rules have also been codified in several states, including New York, as described below.

(a) *Renvoi*. When there is a conflict of choice of law rules, the doctrine of *renvoi* may come into play. *Renvoi* arises when the conflict of law rules in one jurisdiction refer a matter to the law of another jurisdiction. If only the substantive (local) law of the other jurisdiction is applied, there is no *renvoi*. However, if the entire law of the other jurisdiction is applied (including the substantive law and the choice of law rules), *renvoi* comes into play. *Renvoi* is used in many civil law countries, but traditionally is not applied by courts in the United States.[22] The potential application of *renvoi* is a complicated factor that must be considered in the conflicts analysis.[23]

(b) The Hague Convention on Succession. In the 1989 Hague Convention on the Law Applicable to Succession to the Estates of Deceased Persons (the "Hague Convention on Succession"),[24] choice of law issues relating to substantive succession law matters are addressed by development of uniform choice of law rules for substantive succession law matters. The Hague Convention on Succession is not in force in the United States. To date, only Argentina, Luxembourg, the Netherlands, and Switzerland have signed the Hague Convention on Succession, and only the Netherlands has ratified it.

---

19. *Id.*

20. *See generally* Henry Christensen III, International Estate Planning ch. 5 (2d ed. 1999); *see* Restatement (Second) of Conflict of Laws § 6(2); *see generally* discussion *supra* chapter 1.

21. *Id.*

22. *Id.*

23. *Id.*

24. *See* Convention on the Law Applicable to Succession to the Estates of Deceased Persons, Aug. 1, 1989, 28 I.L.M. 150, *reprinted in* 2 Proceedings of the Sixteenth Session of the Hague Conference on Private International Law 515 (1990).

(c) European Succession Regulation (Brussels IV).[25] Brussels IV came into force on August 17, 2012, and will apply to the estates of individuals dying on or after August 17, 2015. Brussels IV applies to succession of the estates of deceased persons resident in the European Union only, except for the United Kingdom, Ireland, and Denmark, which have each opted out of the legislation. The purpose of the regulation is to simplify the procedures in cross-border succession in the European Union and to provide certainty with respect to the law that will govern succession.

Generally, under Brussels IV, the law of the last habitual residence of a decedent would apply to the succession, unless the decedent chooses the law of his or her nationality to apply. In addition, *renvoi* should no longer be relevant under Brussels IV. Another benefit of Brussels IV is that it establishes a European Certificate of Succession that will provide proof of heirship without the need for further documentation.

C. Original Probate in Situs Jurisdiction

A situs jurisdiction may authorize original probate of a decedent's will, although there has been separate probate in the jurisdiction of domicile. Arguments advanced for full application of situs authority include protection of local assets and creditors.

1. Prerequisite for Probate—Execution in Accordance with Situs Formalities

The classic conflict of laws rule is that a will in respect of realty must be executed in accordance with formalities of the situs[26] of the realty, and a will in respect of personal property must be executed in accordance with formalities of the decedent's domicile.[27]

In *In re Panousseris' Will*,[28] the will was executed by the decedent only in the presence of his attorney. It was placed in an envelope and sealed with five seals bearing the decedent's personal imprint. Two days later, the will was taken to a notary. The decedent stated in the presence of the notary and three witnesses that the envelope contained his will.[29] Delaware law required that every will be attested and subscribed in the testator's presence by two or more credible witnesses. The issue was whether the signatures on the envelope were an integral part of the will. The court held that they were not, but rather that they were part of the handing-over ceremony required by Greek law. The result was that the

25. Regulation (EU) No 650/2012 of the European Parliament and of the Council of 4 July 2012 on jurisdiction, applicable law, recognition and enforcement of decisions and acceptance and enforcement of authentic instruments in matters of succession and on the creation of a European Certificate of Succession (OJ n. L 201, p 107 ff.).

26. *In re* Panousseris' Will, 151 A.2d 518 (Del. 1959).

27. *Id.*

28. *Id.*

29. *Id.* at 520.

decedent's Greek will did not control the disposition of the decedent's real property located in Delaware.

In Florida, any will—other than a holographic or nuncupative will, executed by a nondomiciliary of Florida—is valid and effective for purposes of Florida law only if executed in conformity with Florida law or the law of the place of execution.[30] The statute creates a gap because it invalidates wills otherwise valid under the law of the testator's domicile, abode, or nationality, either at the time of execution or death.

By contrast, the Uniform Probate Code provides that a will is valid if executed in accordance with local law, the law of the place of execution, or *the law of domicile, abode, or nationality, either at time of execution or death* without otherwise qualifying its application.[31]

New York law is similar to the Uniform Probate Code. Under New York law, a will disposing of personal property, wherever situated, or real property situated in New York, made within or without New York by a domiciliary or non-domiciliary, is formally valid and admissible to probate if it is in writing and signed by the testator and is executed and attested in accordance with the local law of New York, the jurisdiction in which the will was executed, or the jurisdiction in which the testator was domiciled, either at the time of execution or of death.[32]

The fact that a will or trust is executed in a foreign language with which the testator had little familiarity may be important in showing that a will was never intended at all, thus raising the potential for contest.[33]

2. Situs Jurisdictions Emphasize a Number of Important Factors in Allowing Original and Situs Probate

The general rule of probate is that a will should be probated in the first instance at the testator's domicile.[34] However, where situs assets exist and the will at issue designates local substantive law as controlling, the potential for original or situs probate is enhanced. This is especially the case where a local statute provides for designation of controlling substantive law, such as in New York.[35] Many courts,

---

30. Fla. Stat. Ann. § 732.502(2).

31. *See* Unif. Probate Code § 2-506 (emphasis added). *See also* Ariz. Rev. Stat. Ann. § 14-2506; Cal. Probate Code § 6113 (adopting Uniform Probate Code in this respect). The Uniform Probate Code has been adopted, at least in part, by eighteen states. Numerous other states have adopted the Uniform Probate Code in an incomplete form.

32. *See* N.Y. Est. Powers & Trusts Law § 3-5.1(c).

33. *See, e.g.*, Miltenberger v. Miltenberger, 78 Mo. 27 (1883) (English will executed by testatrix who understood German and French held invalid); Kittleson's Estate v. Kittleson, 173 N.W. 161 (S.D. 1919) (English will executed by testator who understood Norwegian held invalid). Furthermore, local statutes may exist that expressly require the testator to understand the language in which the will is written. *See, e.g.*, Gonzales v. Gonzales, 13 La. 104 (1839) (English will invalid under Louisiana statute). *See generally* Wade R. Habeeb, *Wills: Testator's Illiteracy or Lack of Knowledge of Language in Which Will Is Written as Affecting Its Validity*, 37 A.L.R. 3d 889, § 12[a] (1971).

34. *See generally* Robert C. Lawrence, International Tax & Estate Planning: A Practical Guide for Multinational Investors § 7:6 (3d ed. 2012).

35. N.Y. Est. Powers & Trusts Law § 3-5.1(h).

however, have said that they are not required to grant original probate, even though a statute authorizes it, simply because some assets are located within its jurisdiction. A court will grant original probate in its discretion depending on the facts and circumstances and considerations of comity.[36] For example, a court may wish to await the action of a court in the decedent's domicile and may deny original probate if most of the major contacts are with another jurisdiction.[37]

In *In re Heller-Baghero*,[38] the court authorized situs probate in New York of the 1964 will of an Austrian domiciliary though Austrian courts had already assumed jurisdiction of an earlier 1962 will. In so doing, the court emphasized several key factors: some 90 percent of the assets were in New York, the executor named in the will and one of the two legatees were residents of New York, and evidence that probate of the 1964 will in Austria would entail extensive litigation. The court further emphasized that the proponent of the 1964 will did not participate in the Austrian court proceedings.

An analogous result was reached in *In re Estate of Vischer*,[39] where again approximately 90 percent of the decedent nondomiciliary's assets were in New York with the balance in Switzerland and Vermont. Because of the substantial property within its jurisdiction, New York exercised situs authority and allowed probate of the decedent's will.

In contrast, in *In re Estate of Brunner*,[40] the court disallowed situs probate in New York despite a clause in the will requesting that New York law apply. The decedent was a United States citizen domiciled in France. The total estate was estimated to have a value of between $1 million and $2 million, but the New York situs assets were worth less than $1,000. The court held that the bank account was an insufficient basis for jurisdiction and emphasized the need to rely on French law to administer the will and the fact that any witnesses necessary to testify as to the capacity of the testator would also be in France.

Protection of local creditors is an additional key factor in authorizing situs probate. *Emmerich v. May*[41] disregarded administrative provisions of Netherlands law to ensure collection of New York situs taxes. The decedent was domiciled in the Netherlands at death and left securities situated in New York. The sole beneficiary contended that under Netherlands civil law he was entitled to immediate possession without the need for situs administration in New York. The New York administrator argued that title to the securities vested in him on the decedent's death rather than in the beneficiary. The administrator further emphasized that local administration was needed because situs taxes remained unpaid.

---

36. *See generally* Lawrence, *supra* note 34.
37. *Id.*
38. *In re* Heller-Baghero, 310 N.Y.S.2d 313 (1970).
39. *In re* Estate of Vischer, 280 N.Y.S.2d 49 (Sur. Ct. 1967).
40. *In re* Estate of Brunner, 339 N.Y.S.2d 506 (Sur. Ct. 1973).
41. Emmerich v. May, 130 F. Supp. 426 (S.D.N.Y. 1955) (involving ancillary administration and not original probate).

The court in *Emmerich* distinguished between administration and distribution. It emphasized that in many common law jurisdictions, such as New York, administration of personalty is tied to situs and distribution relates to domicile. Only when administration is completed and the decedent's taxes are paid may remaining assets be distributed to the beneficiaries. The distinction, the court emphasized, was analogous to the one between substance and procedure: "The forum's procedural rules determine the point in time when the substantive rules of another state are to be permitted to operate."[42] Because the situs of the securities was in New York, administration under New York procedural rules was necessary before distribution could take place under the law of the Netherlands—the law of domicile.

This is not to say that property must always be transferred to the jurisdiction of domicile before distribution to intended beneficiaries. In *In re Estate of Censor*,[43] the decedent left property in Israel and the United States. The property in Israel was to be distributed in one manner and that in the United States in another. The issue was whether the New York court would follow the general rule of transmitting the assets to the domiciliary fiduciary in Israel for distribution. On examining the most important factor, the testatrix's intent, it was determined there was no intent to transmit funds to Israel, only to have a redistribution to beneficiaries in the United States. The court resolved the matter of debts and administrative expenses in Israel by allocating all debts and expenses pro rata against the combined assets in Israel and the United States and, after deducting the charges, directing distribution of the United States assets to the designated United States beneficiaries.

3. New York Original Probate Statute

(a) Original Probate When Will Not Previously Admitted to Probate in Testator's Domicile. Under § 1605 of the New York Surrogate's Court Procedure Act (SCPA), the court has discretion to admit a nondomiciliary's will to original probate if the decedent had property in New York and the will disposes of such property. If, however, the nondomiciliary's will has already been admitted to probate or refused probate in the decedent's domicile, then the court's ability to admit the will to original probate is restricted.[44]

Under SCPA § 1605(1), a nondomiciliary's will may be admitted to original probate in New York at the discretion of the court if the will:

1. operates upon New York property belonging to the decedent at his death;
2. was validly executed for probate in New York;
3. has not already been admitted to probate in the decedent's domicile; and
4. was not denied probate in the decedent's domicile.

42. *Id.* at 430.
43. *In re* Estate of Censor, N.Y.L.J., Vol. 203, May 1, 1990, at 22 (Sur. Ct. Nassau County).
44. *See generally* Warren's Heaton on Surrogate's Court Practice § 47.08.

If the above criteria are met, the court will consider whether to grant original probate based on the factors applied in the *Heller-Baghero* case,[45] such as: the nominated executor's and the beneficiaries' residence; the location of the decedent's assets; the residence of the attesting witnesses; any consent; and the decedent's intent. Even if all of the factors weigh in favor of original probate in New York, the court will generally deny original probate if there is already a contested probate proceeding pending in the state of decedent's domicile.[46]

In *In re Terry*,[47] the court granted original probate to the will of a Florida domiciliary where the assets consisted solely of property located in New York, the distributees were the same under New York and Florida law, and it was alleged that the will had not been and would not be offered for probate in Florida.

Related to *Heller-Baghero* is the scenario in which the decedent has intentionally created two wills. For example, the testator may have one will that covers the property in his foreign domicile and a separate will regarding his New York property. In such a case, the surrogate has the jurisdiction to grant original probate to the New York will, resulting in separate probate proceedings for the New York and foreign estates.

Under SCPA § 1605(3), a will that by judgment or decree has been denied probate or establishment in the decedent's domicile will not be admitted to original probate in New York except if the denial is solely for a cause that is not a ground for rejection of probate in New York.

(b) Original Probate When Will Previously Admitted to Probate in Testator's Domicile. If a will has already been probated or established in the decedent's domicile, a court will only admit it to original probate in New York if (i) ancillary probate would be inconvenient or impossible, (ii) the testator directed in his will that it should be offered for probate in New York, or (iii) the laws of the decedent's domicile discriminate against domiciliaries of New York either as beneficiaries or fiduciaries. In addition, the criteria of SCPA § 1605(1) must be met. If the foregoing factors are not met, the principle of comity favors deference to the domicile once its jurisdiction has been invoked.

In re Estate of Renard[48] provides illustration. There, the testatrix was domiciled in France at her death and left substantial personal property situated in New York. This property was specifically subject to her New York situs will, which, pursuant to New York statute, expressly spelled out that New York substantive law controlled. The effect of allowing original situs probate was to cut off French forced share rights and thereby reduce the amount otherwise passing to the decedent's son. Original probate in New York was challenged by the decedent's son on the

45. *Hellerl-Baghero*, 310 N.Y.S.2d 313.

46. *See* WARREN'S HEATON, *supra* note 44; *In re* Nevai, 788 N.Y.S.2d 843 (Sur. Ct. 2005), *aff'd*, 28 A.D.3d 561 (N.Y. App. Div. 2006).

47. *In re* Terry, N.Y.L.J., Vol. 231, Feb. 2, 2004 at 17 (Sur. Ct. Suffolk Country).

48. *In re* Estate of Renard, 417 N.Y.S.2d 155 (Sur. Ct.), *aff'd*, 418 N.Y.S.2d 553 (1979).

grounds that the decedent's domicile of France had assumed jurisdiction over the will. The court held that New York probate was authorized as the will directed that it be admitted to probate in New York and construed under the laws of New York. Additionally, 80 percent of the decedent's assets were located in New York, and the nominated executors were New York residents. Also, the proof of the New York will would have entailed extensive litigation in the decedent's domicile, and thus it was "only natural" for the executors to pursue probate in New York.

In *In re Estate of Brown*,[49] the court allowed original probate of a Florida domiciliary's will because Florida law disallowed any nonresident from qualifying as an estate fiduciary unless the nominated fiduciary was of a specified relationship to the decedent. Because the nominated fiduciary in the decedent's will was a New York resident and was not related to the decedent, he could not serve as the fiduciary following the probate in Florida. In addition, the decedent had approximately 50 percent of her assets in New York, and the will was drafted and executed in New York while she was a New York domiciliary.

D. Effect of Res Judicata

A situs jurisdiction may voluntarily exercise less power over property in its territory than that to which it is otherwise entitled. An example is res judicata. This principle, when applied between sovereign jurisdictions, is not mandatory but is based on comity. In contrast with international law, the Full Faith and Credit Clause of the United States Constitution *requires* each state of the United States to give effect to judgments rendered by sister states provided *in personam* jurisdiction existed.

Res judicata rests on the theory that identical parties should not be allowed to relitigate a matter previously adjudicated. *In re Hahnel*[50] relied on this principle. There, two wills were at issue—a holographic will validated by the German courts and an earlier executed New York will that had not yet been presented for probate. All parties in interest had participated in the German proceeding. When the unsuccessful party sought to present the earlier will for probate in New York, the prevailing party in Germany objected. The New York court, relying on res judicata, concluded the parties had had their day in court.

Res judicata was also applied in *Watts v. Swiss Bank Corp.*[51] Rather than a will, the issue was whether French-forced heirship rights applied to a bank account in New York held in joint names of the decedent and his wife with right of survivorship. A declaratory judgment action was initiated in France in which all parties were treated as participating. The French court concluded that French law controlled, and the New York court held that it was bound by the French judgment.

49. Estate of Brown, 436 N.Y.S.2d 132 (Sur. Ct. 1986).
50. *In re* Hahnel, 389 N.Y.S.2d 970 (Sur. Ct. 1976), *aff'd*, 395 N.Y.S.2d 395 (App. Div. 1977).
51. Watts v. Swiss Bank Corp., 265 N.E.2d 739 (N.Y 1970).

In contrast, where all parties do not participate in the earlier proceeding, res judicata is inapplicable. This is illustrated by *In re Gifford's Will*,[52] where the testatrix died in France leaving a holographic will. The will left her personal effects to Mr. Constantino Gavazzi. Pursuant to the will, a French court entered an order vesting the testatrix's property in Mr. Gavazzi. The order was entered ex parte, without notice to or participation by the decedent's husband, who resided in New York. Mr. Gavazzi applied to the New York court for ancillary letters with respect to New York situs property. He contended that he was entitled to possession of all the decedent's property. The New York court denied the application, pointing out that "[n]o *ex parte* determination . . . can conclusively bind the courts of this State."[53]

IV. Postmortem Estate Planning Considerations Involving Estate Situs and Distributions to Beneficiaries

During the period of administration, an estate is subject to income taxation. The extent of income taxation by the United States depends on whether the estate is classified for income tax purposes as domestic or foreign. A domestic estate is taxed on its worldwide income. By contrast, foreign estates are taxed as non-United States persons, typically only on U.S.-source fixed and determinable annual or periodical income and income effectively connected with a United States trade or business.

A. Criteria for Distinguishing between Domestic and Foreign Estates

For federal income tax purposes, a "foreign estate" is defined in the U.S. Code at Title 27, Section 7701(a)(31) as an entity that is not subject to U.S. taxation on income that is neither from U.S. sources nor effectively connected with a U.S. trade or business. Although 1996 legislation set forth objective criteria for determining the tax situs of a trust, it did not change the definition of tax situs of an estate. Accordingly, the vagueness of the above definition remains, and the tax situs of an estate is highly fact specific, turning on the totality of facts and circumstances of each case.

In Revenue Ruling 62-154, the IRS indicated that a nonresident alien's estate that is subject to domiciliary administration in a foreign country is not automatically a foreign estate. Rather, consideration is given to all facts and circumstances, including the citizenship and residency of the ancillary administrator and the extent and duration of his activities in the United States.[54] This analysis has been applied in several private letter rulings that follow.

52. *In re* Gifford's Will, 18 N.E.2d 663 (N.Y. 1939).

53. *Id.* at 666.

54. *See, e.g.*, Rev. Rul. 62-154, 1962-2 C.B.148.

Private Letter Ruling 7917087 concluded that the estate of a nonresident alien decedent was foreign, although substantial property passed under both the foreign and the United States wills, and the ancillary administrator was a United States institution. In reaching this conclusion, the ruling emphasized that the executor's activities did not constitute a U.S. trade or business and were of short duration, limited to paying debts and administrative expenses and immediately thereafter distributing estate proceeds under the United States will to the designated foreign beneficiary. Similarly, the estate of a nonresident alien in Private Letter Ruling 7918118 was foreign, although, due to universal succession, there was no domiciliary administration in the foreign jurisdiction and there was ancillary administration by a United States person in the United States.

By contrast, the fact that decedent was a United States citizen at death—subject to worldwide income taxation—does not alone cause the estate to be domestic rather than foreign.[55]

From a review of these rulings, the following factors appear most relevant:

1. The domicile of the decedent at the time of death and the situs of domiciliary administration;
2. The primary location of the major assets held in the decedent's estate;
3. The nationality and residence of the fiduciaries who are responsible for the administration and management of the estate of the decedent; and
4. The extent and duration of their activities in the United States.

It is clear that a decedent has only one estate even if he has multiple wills and multiple administrations to direct property transfers in several countries.[56] In Revenue Ruling 64-307, the estate at issue was held to be domestic, although 80 percent of the decedent's property was located abroad. The ruling further concluded that a decedent had only one estate for income taxation, even though two wills existed—one disposing of property in the United States and the other disposing of property in a foreign country.

B. Income Taxation of Estate Versus Distributions to Beneficiaries

1. United States Citizen or Resident Beneficiaries

An estate is treated as a separate taxable entity. In the case of a domestic estate, both the estate and the United States citizen or resident beneficiaries are subject to worldwide income taxation. However, the throwback rules that apply to foreign and other qualified trusts are inapplicable to estates. Thus, there is potential for shifting the income tax burden between the estate and its beneficiaries depending

55. *See, e.g.*, Rev. Rul. 81-112, 1981-1 C.B. 598 (foreign estate arose where United States citizen had been resident of foreign jurisdiction for substantial period of time and decedent's contacts were all focused in that jurisdiction) and I.R.S. Priv. Ltr. Rul. 8524010 (Feb. 19, 1985) (analogous result where United States citizen-decedent resided continuously in foreign jurisdiction for eight years prior to death).

56. Rev. Rul. 64-307, 1964-2 C.B. 163.

on which is in the higher tax bracket. The extent to which this can be done is limited by the duration of the estate administration. The benefit of shifting the income tax burden to the estate is problematic at this time because, in the case of an estate, the various income tax brackets are activated at much lower taxable income thresholds than for individuals.[57]

By contrast, because a foreign estate is taxed in the same manner as a nonresident alien individual, it can generate income that is not subject to United States income taxation, including capital gains.[58] Such income does not constitute part of the estate's distributable net income[59] and can be passed through to the United States beneficiaries in the same year free of tax. Moreover, U.S.-source income that qualifies for an exemption from tax under law (such as portfolio interest and bank deposit income) or an applicable tax treaty can be accumulated in the foreign estate and distributed in a subsequent year to United States beneficiaries free of tax due to the absence of the throwback rules.

Revenue Ruling 68-621 illustrates the taxation of a foreign estate that computes its income under the usual rules for nonresident alien individuals. The estate in that ruling sold some securities in the United States and distributed the gains, along with certain dividend income, to nonresident alien beneficiaries. The I.R.S. concluded that the estate was taxable at a flat 30 percent rate on its U.S.-source dividends and, because it had a U.S. ancillary administrator present in this country for 183 days or more of the taxable year, on its capital gains from sales and exchanges within the United States.[60] The estate was entitled to a distribution deduction, and the beneficiaries had corresponding income inclusion, measured by the estate's distributable net income, but the nonresident alien beneficiaries did not have to include the capital gains in their income if they did not meet the 183-day presence rule of § 871(a)(2). Since the ruling, the Taxpayer Relief Act of 1997 has amended § 641(b) to provide that a foreign trust or estate is treated as a nonresident who is not present in the United States at any time for purposes of § 871(a)(2), despite the presence of a U.S. ancillary administrator.[61]

Once an estate has come into existence, it may continue as long as required for the administrator or executor to perform the ordinary duties of administration, such as collection of assets and payment of debts, taxes, legacies, and bequests, whether that period is longer or shorter than the period specified under the applicable local law for settlement of estates.[62] The IRS may terminate an estate if administration has been unreasonably prolonged.

---

57. *Compare* I.R.C. § 1(e) *with* § 1(a)–(d).

58. Capital gains (other than gains on the disposition of U.S. real property or effectively connected income) are not taxable to a nonresident alien who is not present for 183 days in the United States. I.R.C. § 871(a)(2).

59. I.R.C. § 643(a) defines "distributable net income" as the taxable income of an estate or trust computed with certain modifications specified therein.

60. Rev. Rul. 68-621, 1968-2 C.B. 286.

61. Pub. L. 105-34, § 1601(i)(3)(B) (effective for tax years beginning after 1996).

62. *See* Treas. Reg. § 1.641(b)-3.

2. Nonresident Alien Beneficiaries

For a domestic estate that generates income, the portion of its distributable net income that does not consist of U.S.-source fixed and determinable annual or periodical income or income effectively connected with a United States trade or business should not be accumulated but should be distributed currently to the estate's nonresident alien beneficiaries. In this event, the income will be attributable but not taxed to the nonresident alien beneficiaries.[63] If instead that income is accumulated and not distributed currently, taxation to the estate results with no relief to the nonresident alien beneficiaries on distribution.[64]

In the case of foreign estates with nonresident alien beneficiaries, the matter of accumulation versus current distribution is basically immaterial, though conceivably there may be some theoretical potential for shifting U.S.-source income between the *two*, depending on whether progressive rates are applicable.

C. Transfers of Appreciated Property by United States Person to Foreign Estate or Trust

The Taxpayer Relief Act of 1997 repealed the prior 35 percent excise tax and replaced it with § 684. This provision requires a United States person to recognize gain on the transfer of appreciated property to a foreign estate or trust. A United States person for this purpose means a United States citizen or resident, a domestic partnership, a domestic corporation, a domestic estate, or a domestic trust.[65] There are exceptions for fair market value transfers, transfers to foreign grantor trusts, transfers to foreign charitable trusts, and transfers at death where the assets received a basis step-up. Because of the broad reach of § 679, which treats a foreign trust as a grantor trust with respect to a U.S. transferor if the trust has or could have a U.S. beneficiary, § 684 rarely applies to lifetime transfers. However, on the U.S. grantor's death when the foreign trust becomes a nongrantor trust, § 684 can apply to cause recognition of gain if the assets did not receive a date of death basis step-up.[66]

---

63. Martin-Montis Trust v. Comm'r, 75 T.C. 381 (1980) (current distribution of U.S. bank interest retains character in hands of nonresident beneficiaries under conduit rules of trust taxation and qualifies under § 861(a)(1)(A) for exclusion from tax as foreign-source income); Rev. Rul. 81-244, 1981-2 C.B. 151 (interest income on U.S. bank deposits distributed by simple trust currently to nonresident alien income beneficiary retains its tax-free character in the nonresident beneficiary's hands under conduit rules).

64. Rev. Rul. 86-76, 1986-1 C.B. 284 (domestic estate taxable as a complex trust on U.S. bank interest received that was not distributed or required to be distributed in tax year of receipt to nonresident alien beneficiaries; domestic trust entitled to deduction under § 662(a) for the interest currently distributed, which retained its character in hands of nonresident beneficiaries as foreign-source income). *See* I.R.S. Priv. Ltr. Rul. 8324015 (Mar. 8, 1983) (same).

65. I.R.C. § 7701(a)(30).

66. CCA 200445025 (Nov. 5, 2004) (deemed transfer on termination of foreign grantor trust status).

V. Postmortem Estate Planning Considerations Involving Trusts and Foreign Corporations

While a foreign trust qualifies as a grantor trust with respect to a nonresident alien, for U.S. federal income tax purposes, he will be treated as owning the assets of the trust, including the stock of the foreign corporation. On the grantor's death, however, the trust becomes a nongrantor trust, and indirect ownership rules under the Controlled Foreign Corporation (CFC) and Passive Foreign Investment Company (PFIC) regimes will treat the U.S. beneficiaries as owners of the foreign corporation. These rules are commonly referred to as the "anti-deferral rules," because they penalize U.S. shareholders from deferring tax through accumulating income in foreign corporations. The anti-deferral rules can impose punitive tax consequences on U.S. shareholders of foreign corporations that accumulate income generated from passive investments. Prior to 2004, there was a third set of rules known as the Foreign Personal Holding Company Rules (FPHC) that applied, but they were repealed by the American Jobs Creation Act of 2004, Pub. L. 357, effective for taxable years of foreign corporations beginning after December 31, 2004.

A. Impact of Controlled Foreign Corporation (CFC) and Passive Foreign Investment Company (PFIC) Provisions

One set of anti-deferral rules are the CFC rules. A foreign corporation is a CFC if more than 50 percent of the vote or value of its stock is held by U.S. shareholders, each owning (or deemed under the attribution rules to own) at least 10 percent of the voting stock.[67] If a foreign corporation is a CFC for an uninterrupted period of thirty days in a taxable year, U.S. shareholders are required to include their pro rata share of the foreign corporation's "Subpart F income" in their gross income each year, as a deemed dividend.[68] In addition, on deemed or actual liquidation (or certain other actual or deemed stock dispositions) of a CFC, the U.S. shareholder may be taxed at ordinary income rates on his pro rata share of the unrealized appreciation in the corporation.[69] Subpart F income consists of many categories of income, the most relevant of which is "foreign personal holding company income," which includes investment income, such as dividends, interest, and capital gains.

Another set of anti-deferral rules is the PFIC rules. A foreign corporation is a PFIC if 75 percent or more of its gross income is passive income or 50 percent or more of its assets are passive assets.[70] Passive income includes foreign personal holding company income. Unless a U.S. shareholder make an election to be taxed currently on his share of PFIC income or gain, he is taxed on a disposition of, or excess distribution with respect to, his PFIC stock. An excess distribution is the

67. I.R.C. § 957(a).
68. *Id.* § 951(a).
69. *Id.* § 1248.
70. *Id.* § 1297(a).

amount by which the distribution exceeds 125 percent of the average of the prior three years of distributions. In general terms, the gain on disposition or excess distribution is thrown back over the U.S. shareholder's holding period in the PFIC, taxed as ordinary income, and the tax draws an interest charge. In the event there is an overlap and a corporation is both a CFC and PFIC, the CFC rules take precedent with respect to a 10 percent or greater U.S. shareholder.[71]

Both sets of rules have indirect ownership principles, providing that a U.S. beneficiary of a foreign nongrantor trust is treated as owning the stock of the foreign corporation in proportion to his interest in the trust.[72] Proportionality is determined by facts and circumstances with an emphasis on who is entitled or eligible to receive income distributions.[73] It is difficult to determine proportionality in the context of a wholly discretionary trust. Guidance under the now repealed FPHC rules suggests that relevant facts and circumstances include "pattern of past distributions, appropriate mortality assumptions, the trustee's fiduciary duties and the relationships among the trustees and beneficiaries."[74] This analysis was adopted by the I.R.S. in a 2007 private letter ruling applying the PFIC indirect ownership rules to a discretionary foreign nongrantor trust. In that ruling, the I.R.S. looked at the pattern of equal distributions and the settlor's letter of wishes evidencing an intent to divide up the relevant assets equally, followed by subsequent actions taken by the trustee to effect this division equally between U.S. and foreign beneficiaries.[75] Therefore, distribution history and subsequent actions following the disposition of the PFIC can be important factors in determining which beneficiary was the indirect owner of the PFIC.

As noted, Subpart F income is taxable only if the foreign corporation is a CFC for more than thirty consecutive days during the corporation's taxable year. Thus, one planning strategy involves liquidating the foreign corporation within twenty-nine days of the nonresident, nondomiciliary settlor's death and the conversion of the trust to a nongrantor trust. The enactment of the check-the-box regime permits certain eligible foreign entities to elect their status for U.S. tax purposes.[76] If a foreign corporation elects to be disregarded, this has the effect of a deemed liquidation for U.S. tax purposes. The election can be made retroactive 75 days, thereby permitting a 104-day period after the nonresident, nondomiciliary's death in which to act. Assuming there was an outside basis step-up at death, the deemed liquidation will not give rise to capital gains in the hands of the trust. Outside

71. *Id.* § 1297(d) (effective for the portion of the U.S. shareholder's holding period after December 31, 1997).

72. *Id.* §§ 958(a)(2), 1298(a)(3).

73. I.R.S. Field Service Advice Mem. 199952014 (Sept. 23, 1999) and I.R.S. Priv. Let. Rul. 8748043 (Sept. 1, 1987). *See also* Treas. Reg. §1.958-1(c)(2) (where the purpose of the determination is to attribute income of a CFC to a U.S. shareholder, his interest in the income of the corporation is most relevant).

74. I.R.S. Priv. Ltr. Rul. 9024076 (Mar. 21, 1990).

75. I.R.S. Tech. Adv. Mem. 200733024 (Aug. 17, 2007).

76. Treas. Reg. § 301.7701-3.

basis is a reference to the basis of the stock in the hands of the shareholder trust. Generally speaking, property—even foreign situs property of a nonresident, non-domiciliary alien—that either was acquired or passed from a decedent receives a step-up in basis equal to fair market value at the valuation date. For property in trust to obtain a basis step-up, however, the nonresident, nondomiciliary settlor must retain certain powers over the trust.[77]

The PFIC rules will not preclude an outside basis step-up if the decedent was a nonresident alien at all times during the holding period of the stock.[78] Inside basis refers to the basis of internal corporate assets in the hands of the corporation. If the liquidation occurs within twenty-nine days of death and the corporation holds no foreign investment funds that could themselves be considered PFICs, the gain realized to the corporation on the deemed liquidation will not be taxable to the U.S. beneficiaries. If the corporation holds foreign investment funds that are considered PFICs, the liquidation could give rise to an indirect disposition of those PFICs. Therefore, a further strategy is for the trust to hold U.S. situs assets such as shares of U.S. corporations in a foreign holding company, and to hold assets that have a foreign situs for United States estate taxation, such as investment fund PFICs, which are classified as foreign corporations for U.S. tax purposes, outside the foreign holding company. In this way, the PFICs themselves receive the basis step-up and can be disposed of after death for little or no gain.

Where appropriate inter vivos steps have been taken to avoid holding investment fund PFICs in the foreign corporation, and assuming the settlor retains powers providing for an outside basis step-up, little or no gain should result on liquidation. Moreover, any gain that is realized by the trust may be washed away if the trustee makes an election under § 645 for the trust to be treated as part of the nonresident, nondomiciliary's estate for income tax purposes. This election is available only to qualified revocable trusts that were treated as owned by the decedent under § 676 (without regard to spousal attribution). If made, this election permits the trust to be taxed as an estate for income tax purposes so that foreign-source income and capital gains are not part of its distributable net income, and the throwback rules do not apply for the period during which the estate is open and the election is in effect.

Parenthetically, if all of the beneficiaries under this scenario were nonresident aliens rather than United States citizens or residents, these provisions would be irrelevant in any event. If certain of the beneficiaries were nonresident aliens and others were United States citizens or residents, criteria of both the CFC and PFIC rules may be present, depending on actual and constructive shareholder ownership. Though complex, consideration under this scenario could be given to redeeming the interests of the U.S. citizen and resident beneficiaries.

77. *See* Rev. Rul. 84-139, 1984-2 C.B. 168.
78. *Id.* § 1291(e)(2).

B. Domestication Versus Nondomestication of Foreign Trust

The presence of United States beneficiaries raises the issue of whether on the death of the settlor, when a foreign grantor trust becomes a nongrantor trust, its tax residency should be changed from foreign to domestic. Where the beneficiaries are foreign, the shifting of situs to the United States usually does not make sense.

If the beneficiaries include United States persons, a number of important United States income tax considerations arise as part of the process of determining whether domestication is appropriate. This is particularly so where income is to be accumulated and not distributed currently. In this case, both the throwback rules and the § 668 interest charge apply. Moreover, where the accumulated income includes capital gain, the gains lose capital gain character and become taxed in the U.S. beneficiary's hands as ordinary income on subsequent distributions in a later year. Under this scenario, a shift in residency from foreign to domestic, though not mandatory, is worthy of careful consideration.

If all distributions to U.S. beneficiaries will be made from current rather than accumulated income, these considerations may be irrelevant. This could occur where the requirements of the U.S. beneficiaries are relatively modest, perhaps due to other assets personally owned or where the beneficiary will be paid all trust income each year. Further, consideration should be given to whether the U.S. beneficiaries intend to remain in the United States permanently or only on an interim basis and to the status of subsequent generations of beneficiaries as United States or foreign persons.

Residency of the trust can be changed in two ways: the trust can "migrate" to the United States by changing trust situs, governing law, and trustees from foreign to domestic persons, or it can "decant" into an existing domestic trust. A migration is not treated as an immediate taxable event, whereas a decantation is treated as a distribution from a foreign trust to a U.S. trust that carries out income, and therefore can, if there is UNI, trigger imposition of the throwback tax at the time the trust is decanted. Still, a decantation may be preferable in some cases to a migration, as the throwback rules continue to apply to the undistributed net income carried over through migration to domestic trusts that were once foreign.[79]

C. Distributions from Domestic Nongrantor Trusts to Foreign Beneficiaries

A United States individual settlor may create a domestic inter vivos grantor trust that has nonresident alien beneficiaries. When the settlor dies and the trust becomes nongrantor, the issue becomes how best to minimize the overall level of United States income taxation.

79. I.R.C. § 665(c); Rev. Rul. 91-6, 1991-1 C.B. 89.

In addressing this issue, it is emphasized that a domestic nongrantor trust is taxed as a United States resident on its worldwide income that is accumulated in the trust and not distributed currently. While the nonresident alien trust beneficiary receives, on ultimate distribution, a reduction in tax by that previously paid by the trust, to the extent the tax imposed on the trust exceeds that of the beneficiary, no refund is available.[80] This is illustrated in *Maximov v. United States*.[81] There, the grantor and all beneficiaries were citizens and residents of the United Kingdom. The trust was domestic. Capital gain was realized, which was accumulated and taxed directly to the trust. Article XIV of the former United States-United Kingdom income tax treaty exempted capital gain from United States taxation; however, because the trust was domestic, it was not a resident of the United Kingdom and thus was unable to claim the exemption.

Private Letter Ruling 7933075 extends further than *Maximov*. There, a domestic trust with Canadian beneficiaries accumulated capital gain. Because the trust was domestic, the capital gain exemption under article VIII of the former Canadian treaty was unavailable. The ruling held that not only was the exemption unavailable, but also that due to I.R.C. § 666(e), any refund was precluded.

By contrast, if capital gain realized (for example, by a domestic trust from the sale or exchange of publicly traded stock or other categories of income that are not taxed to a foreign person) is distributed currently to a nonresident alien beneficiary rather than being accumulated, the distribution as measured by distributable net income retains its character in the beneficiary's hands.[82] As noted above, a nonresident alien is typically not taxed on most U.S. source capital gain, including gain derived from sale or disposition of publicly traded stock of a U.S. corporation, or on foreign-source income. Note, for this purpose, the criteria of § 871(a)(2) should not be satisfied because, in the case of a current distribution of capital gain, the status of the beneficiary should control.

Given that such a current distribution of capital gain is typically not taxed by the United States in a nonresident alien beneficiary's hands, the focus next shifts to the mechanics of effecting the distribution pursuant to the terms of the domestic trust at issue. In this regard, the Treasury Regulations provide that capital gains are included in distributable net income (DNI) in a domestic trust in three circumstances: (i) when allocated to fiduciary accounting income; (ii) when allocated to principal but treated consistently by the fiduciary on the trust's books, records, and tax returns as part of the distribution to the beneficiary, or (iii) when allocated to principal but actually distributed to a beneficiary or used by the fiduciary in determining the amount that is distributed or required to be distributed to a beneficiary. If such allocation occurs (i) by a mandatory direction under local law and the governing instrument or (ii) pursuant to the reasonable and impartial exercise of discretion by the fiduciary under a power granted under local law or

80. *Id.* § 666(e).

81. Maximov v. United States, 373 U.S. 49 (1963).

82. *See* Rev. Rul. 81-244, 1981-2 C.B. 151; Rev. Rul. 72-12, 1972-1 C.B. 440.

the governing instrument (if not prohibited by local law), then the capital gains so allocated will be attributable to the nonresident alien beneficiary rather than to the domestic trust. Caution is urged in making such allocations in that the Treasury Regulations and examples provided therein take a strong bias in favor of generally excluding capital gain from DNI of a domestic trust.[83]

Even so, if the trust contains provisions authorizing distributions pursuant to an ascertainable standard, a "5 and 5 power," or discretionary power, it may be feasible to make *non-Kenan*[84] distributions of appreciated capital gain assets in kind. That is, rather than having the trust sell the appreciated asset, the asset is distributed directly to the nonresident alien beneficiary pursuant to trust distribution provisions. While the beneficiary takes a carryover basis,[85] this usually is immaterial since nonresident aliens are not typically taxed by the United States on capital gain other than gain on the sale of U.S. real property. Accordingly, the beneficiary may individually sell the capital asset and personally realize the gain under this scenario without United States income taxation. Immediate sale may be particularly advisable if the distributed asset is otherwise United States situs property for purposes of the United States estate tax. This is so because in contrast with United States citizens or domiciliary aliens, the credit equivalent exemption of a nondomiciliary alien is only $60,000.[86]

D. Postmortem Estate Planning as Related to Qualified Domestic Trusts (QDOTs)

Even though a decedent does not leave property to a surviving noncitizen spouse in a QDOT, the marital deduction nevertheless remains available if the surviving spouse either actually transfers or irrevocably assigns the property to a trust subsequently created by the surviving spouse or the executor, which otherwise meets the basic QDOT requirements.[87] The transfer or assignment must be completed prior to the filing of the estate tax return or before the last day for which the QDOT election may be made.[88]

Moreover, the QDOT tax on distributions to or upon death of the surviving spouse is itself inapplicable if the noncitizen surviving spouse subsequently becomes a United States citizen, provided:

1. the spouse was domiciled in the United States at all times after the death of the decedent and before becoming a United States citizen, or no taxable distributions were made from the QDOT before the spouse became a citizen, and

83. *See* Treas. Reg. § 1.643(a)-3(a) and (b).
84. Kenan v. Comm'r, 114 F.2d 217 (2d Cir. 1940).
85. I.R.C. § 643(e)(1).
86. *Id.* § 2102(c)(1).
87. Treas. Reg. § 20.2056A-2(b)(2).
88. *Id.*

2. the United States trustee of the QDOT notifies the Internal Revenue Service and certifies in writing that the spouse has become a citizen.[89]

Additionally, a special election precludes imposition of the QDOT estate tax even if the surviving spouse was not at all times domiciled in the United States and a taxable distribution was made. For this treatment to be available, the surviving spouse, on or before April 15 of the year following that in which citizenship was acquired, must elect (1) to treat taxable distributions occurring prior to the election as taxable gifts for estate and gift taxation, and (2) to reduce the spouse's unified credit by the amount of the decedent's unified credit applied to reduce the QDOT estate tax imposed on distributions prior to the taxable year of acquisition of citizenship.[90]

89. *Id.* § 20.2056A-10(a).
90. *Id.* § 20.2056A-10(b).

PART III

Marital and Family Rights

5 Enforcement of Spousal and Forced Heirship Rights in U.S. Courts

Robert C. Lawrence, III
Elisa Shevlin Rizzo

I. Introduction

This chapter will discuss specifically the principles that apply when a surviving spouse or protected heir seeks to enforce in the United States the right to a share of the estate granted by another country. A testator's estate plan may contravene such rights, and, therefore, if the testator's plan is to succeed, the planner will need to select an appropriate strategy to ensure the plan's administration in a favorable jurisdiction.

II. General Considerations

An initial but frequently overlooked issue in developing a testator's estate plan is determining whether the testator has an interest in property that will be subject to spousal and forced heirship claims. The estate planner should be aware of not only the testator's current domicile but also whether the testator previously resided in any other states or foreign jurisdictions. If the testator is married, the estate planner should inquire about where the marriage took place. In all instances, the estate planner should determine the identity and character of any property owned by the testator, how the property was acquired, and, if purchased, the source of funds used to acquire the property and how the property is titled.

In particular, the estate planner should be aware of the distinction between community and separate property under U.S. law. The question concerning the community or separate character of property carries far-reaching implications, because, generally, U.S. community property states recognize spousal rights only in property characterized as community property. Moreover, the characterization of property as community or separate property may have an impact upon determining the rights of surviving spouses and forced heirs. These matters are discussed more fully below.

The estate planner should also be aware that under the laws of the states of the United States, the recognition of forced heirship rights remains limited to the property system of the state of Louisiana, which, unlike the other forty-nine states, traces its legal principles to the French Civil Code. Thus, the question presented by a claim to enforce forced heirship rights against a nonresident alien's property located within other U.S. community property states or common law states requires the courts of such states to evaluate rights that are alien to their succession laws.

Before discussing the disposition of forced heirship claims in such state courts, however, it is essential to distinguish forced heirship rights from the analogous concept of spousal inheritance rights. As a rule, a surviving spouse generally has certain rights to a portion of the decedent's estate. In contrast, nonspouse beneficiaries are provided little, if any protection. Constraints on the ability of a testator to disinherit his or her spouse have been recognized and enforced in the United States for centuries, originating with common law dower and curtesy rights. Today, state legislatures generally (although not entirely) have replaced dower and curtesy with statutory spousal inheritance provisions, such as elective share statutes and community property regimes.[1]

III. Spousal Inheritance

A. Overview

At common law, a surviving spouse was protected by the systems of dower and curtesy, which gave the surviving spouse the right to occupy and use a portion of real property owned by the decedent spouse during the marriage. These common law principles have largely been replaced with statutory provisions guaranteeing a surviving spouse's right to share in at least a portion of the decedent's estate. Where a decedent dies intestate (without a will), the disposition of the decedent's

1. *See* 1 Jeffrey A. Schoenblum, Multistate and Multinational Estate Planning § 10.01 (2d ed. 1999).

property is usually governed by statute. Such provisions generally provide for the receipt of a portion of the decedent's estate by the surviving spouse. Moreover, where a decedent dies testate (with a will), similar statutory protections frequently enable a surviving spouse to "elect" against the will and take a share determined by law. The extent of the surviving spouse's intestate or elective share often depends upon whether the decedent was survived by children or issue.

B. Characterization of Property

The characterization of property is an issue to be resolved by courts when determining spousal rights to property owned by a nonresident alien and located within a U.S. jurisdiction. The threshold characterization problem carries significant implications because classifying property as movable, as opposed to immovable, often triggers divergent choice of law analyses. As might be expected, leaseholds, mortgages, and equitable conversions of immovables present difficult characterization questions.[2] In an attempt to simplify characterization, some courts may apply the local law of the situs in a manner comparable to the application of the local law of the forum to procedural issues, while others may apply the "whole law" of the situs, including its conflicts rules.[3]

In accordance with traditional conflicts of law rules, U.S. court decisions regarding spousal (and forced heirship) rights in property of nonresident alien decedents depend on the type of property involved. For immovables, as indicated above, the law of the situs generally governs as to whether the surviving spouse is entitled to a share, as well as the amount of such share.[4] Moreover, the court of the jurisdiction in which the nonresident alien's will is probated (most likely the decedent's domicile at death) ordinarily defers to the situs jurisdiction in matters concerning immovables.[5] The law of the decedent's last domicile generally governs the disposition of movables, both tangible and intangible property, wherever situated. However, this traditional rule of applying the law of the decedent's domicile is subject to three major exceptions: (1) where a statute of the situs jurisdiction provides for original jurisdiction over the will of a nonresident, including the authority to admit the will to original probate and to govern both movables and immovables located within the state;[6] (2) where a court in the situs jurisdiction

---

2. *Id.*

3. *Id.*; *see also supra* Chapter 1.

4. The Restatement adopts the situs rule. RESTATEMENT (SECOND) OF CONFLICT OF LAWS § 242 (1971). *See also In re* Estate of Swanson, 397 So. 2d. 465, 466 (Fla. Dist. Ct. App. 1981) (situs rule under the Uniform Probate Code); ROBERT C. LAWRENCE III, INTERNATIONAL TAX AND ESTATE PLANNING § 1:5[f] (3d ed. 1999).

5. *See* SCHOENBLUM, *supra* note 1, § 10.04.

6. In such a case, the state would apply its own dower, elective share, or community property rules. *See, e.g.*, N.Y. SURR. CT. PROC. ACT § 1605; *In re* Estate of Gould, 1 Ohio Op. 2d 366 (Hamilton County Prob. Ct. 1956), *aff'd*, 140 N.E.2d 801 (Ohio Ct. App. 1956); Bolton v. Barnett, 95 So. 721 (Miss. 1923) (discussed in SCHOENBLUM, *supra* note 1, § 10.05).

applies the "whole law" of the situs jurisdiction, including its conflicts rules;[7] and (3) the Restatement approach under which the court applies the "whole law" of the domicile jurisdiction, including its conflicts rules.[8]

C. Special Considerations with Respect to Community Property

Most civil law jurisdictions and a number of U.S. states recognize the system of community property.[9] The estate planner should be familiar with the general rules regarding community property as the estates of non-U.S. residents frequently contain significant amounts of community property, and any person who lived or owned real property in a community property jurisdiction is likely to discover that a portion of the assets held in his or her name is subject to a one-half, undivided interest in his or her spouse.[10]

The system of community property is founded on the theory that marriage is a conjugal partnership whereby a husband and wife should share equally in the fruits of their common labor upon the termination of the marriage either by death or divorce. Under the laws of most community property jurisdictions, any property brought by a spouse into the marriage is referred to as "separate" property, and any property acquired during the marriage is "community" property.

Consistent with choice of law rules applicable in noncommunity property jurisdictions, a surviving spouse's rights in a nonresident alien's property having a connection with one of the ten U.S. community property states (or civil law jurisdictions recognizing community property) depend on the characterization of the property as an immovable or movable. To determine the initial effect of marriage upon the property rights of spouses in questions involving immovables, courts ordinarily apply the law of the situs.[11] However, application of the situs law of a community property jurisdiction may not yield the result that immovables acquired after marriage are community in character.[12]

---

7. This alternative, however, often results in the application of the domicile principle because the conflicts rules of the situs jurisdiction typically direct the court to apply the law of the decedent's domicile to the disposition of such movables. *See, e.g.*, Robert A. Leflar et al., American Conflicts Law § 232 (4th ed. 1986).

8. *See* Restatement (Second) of Conflict of Laws § 265(1) (1971).

9. The nine U.S. states traditionally classified as community property states are: Arizona, California, Idaho, Louisiana, Nevada, New Mexico, Texas, Washington, and Wisconsin. Additionally, Alaska has adopted an elective form of the community property system. Alaska Stat. § 34.77.030 (1999). For a thorough discussion of the history and evolution of community property law in the United States, see Lawrence, *supra* note 4, ch. 4; William Q. DeFuniak & Michael J. Vaughn, Principles of Community Property (2d ed. 1971).

10. *See generally* Scott Greene, *Comparison of the Property Aspects of Community Property and Common Law Marital Property Systems and Their Relative Compatibility with the Current View of the Marriage Relationship and the Rights of Women*, 13 Creighton L. Rev. 118 (1979).

11. Restatement (Second) of Conflict of Laws § 233 (1971).

12. *See* Rau v. Rau, 432 P.2d 910 (Ariz. 1967) (real property in Arizona acquired with funds earned in a noncommunity property state not community property). *But see* Steczo v. Steczo, 659 P.2d 1344 (Ariz. 1983) (*Rau* rule negated by Ariz. Rev. Stat. § 25-318, which provides that property acquired by

With regard to the effect of marriage on spousal property rights in movables, courts (including the court exercising jurisdiction over such property) commonly refer to the law of the marital domicile.[13] Of course, defining the marital domicile may prove problematic given the antiquated nature of the traditional rule, which deems the husband's domicile to be the marital domicile.[14] The characterization rules concerning spousal rights in movables acquired after marriage often point to the domicile of the spouses at the time of the property's acquisition.[15] However, some jurisdictions may apply the law of the first domicile after the marriage because such domicile may be deemed to continue.

Any income from property is also subject to classification as community or separate property. In general, income from separate property remains separate property. In some jurisdictions, such as Texas, Louisiana, Wisconsin, and Idaho, however, income from most separate property is classified as community property.

Complications may arise when a couple moves from a community property jurisdiction to a common law jurisdiction. Upon the termination of the marriage, it becomes necessary to determine whether and to what extent the community interest in property that was subject to community property rights survived the change of the marital domicile. As discussed above, with respect to immovables, courts generally apply the law of the situs of the property, regardless of the marital domicile. Thus, if a couple resides in a common law state but owns real property in a community property state, such property will be deemed to be community property. With respect to movables, most courts follow the rule that property retains its character as community or separate property following a change of domicile.[16]

However, further complications may arise in determining property interests if, after a change in the marital domicile from a community property state to a common law state, community property is exchanged for new property. As a general rule, if the common law jurisdiction recognized the community property rights in the original property, it will trace the character of the source of funds used to purchase or acquire the new property.[17] Thus, if land in a common law state was purchased with funds acquired by the spouses while domiciled in a community property state, a court of the situs generally will hold that the spouses have the same marital interest in the land as they had in the funds.[18]

---

either spouse outside Arizona is deemed to be community property if the property would have been community property if it had been acquired in Arizona).

13. RESTATEMENT (SECOND) OF CONFLICT OF LAWS § 257 (1971).

14. *See* LEFLAR ET AL., *supra* note 7, § 232; DEFUNIAK & VAUGHN, *supra* note 9, § 91.

15. *See, e.g.*, *In re* Succession of Dunham, 408 So. 2d 888 (La. 1981).

16. The RESTATEMENT has also apparently adopted this position. RESTATEMENT (SECOND) OF CONFLICT OF LAWS § 259 (1971). *See generally* LAWRENCE, *supra* note 4, § 4:4.2[b].

17. *See, e.g.*, *Rau*, 432 P.2d 910; Barber v. Barber, 331 P.2d 628, 631 (Cal. 1958) (local law applied in absence of a foreign source of funds). For further discussion, see LAWRENCE, *supra* note 4, § 4:4.2[c].

18. RESTATEMENT (SECOND) OF CONFLICT OF LAWS § 234, cmt. a (1971).

As a general matter, in a United States community property jurisdiction, upon termination of a marriage by the death of a spouse, each spouse is entitled to his or her separate property and one-half of the community property.[19] It is important to note, however, that different jurisdictions and community property systems may produce divergent results. For example, in certain foreign jurisdictions, all property, regardless of how acquired after marriage, is treated as community property.[20] As a consequence of these different rules, the multinational estate planner must carefully examine the spousal inheritance and conflicts provisions of any U.S. state in which a client seeks to own property in order to avoid results contrary to the client's intent.

D. Enforcement of Spousal Inheritance Rights

As noted above, the courts in the United States have long recognized restrictions on a testator's ability to disinherit his or her spouse and generally seek to protect a spouse's right of election. In *In re Estate of Clark*, the New York Court of Appeals held that a testator may not unilaterally impair or reduce a spouse's right under the law of his or her last domicile to take an elective share of the estate.[21] The testator, a Virginia domiciliary, created a testamentary trust for his wife that satisfied his wife's right of election under New York law[22] but not under Virginia law. The testator had most of his assets in New York, and the will directed New York law to govern. The court upheld the spouse's right of election under Virginia law, which entitled her to more of the estate than provided for in the testamentary trust. The rationale was that a spouse's right of election was not a "testamentary disposition" to be governed by New York law, the testator's choice of law, as contemplated in § 47 of New York's Decedent Estate Law (the predecessor to § 3-5.1(h) of the New York Estates, Powers and Trusts Law). Instead, it was a restriction on the right of the decedent to make such a disposition in contravention of the spouse's right. Rather than refer to the traditional rule, the court weighed the points of contact and concluded that Virginia had the predominant, if not the sole, interest in having its law apply. As noted previously, this approach to the law of conflicts is becoming increasingly popular among courts.

Although in theory there should be no distinction between the rights of spouses and those of descendants and ascendants, some courts have reached different results for spouses and descendants and ascendants. The *Clark* decision appears to be consistent with the decisions of sister states on the spouse's right of election.[23] However, there is no conflict in public policy here. Most common

19. Lawrence, *supra* note 4, § 4:3.1.

20. For example, in Belgium and South Africa, all property acquired after marriage is treated as community property. *See* Schoenblum, *supra* note 1, § 10.14.2 & n.9. *See also infra* Chapter 6.

21. *In re* Clark, 281 N.Y.S.2d 180 (App. Div. 1967), *aff'd*, 236 N.E.2d 152 (N.Y. 1968).

22. Now, N.Y. Est. Powers & Trusts Law § 5-1.1, 5-1.1A.

23. *See* Restatement (Second) of Conflict of Laws § 265 (1971).

law jurisdictions, at least in the United States, afford statutory protection to the spouse against the intention of the testator to leave little or nothing to the spouse.

Courts have not only responded to an invocation of foreign domiciliary law by a disinherited spouse, but have also at times applied the law of the situs in order to protect the spouse. For example, in *In re Estate of Gould*, a testator domiciled in Bermuda left personal property in Ohio, the jurisdiction of original probate of his will.[24] The court honored his spouse's right of election under Ohio law, even though the law of Bermuda gave her no such right. Similarly, in *In re Smith's Estate*, the decedent, a U.S. citizen domiciled in Spain, bequeathed personal property situated in New York to his children and did not leave anything to his wife.[25] The will provided that New York law should apply. Although under Spanish law, the wife was only entitled to a life estate in a portion of the decedent's property, under New York law, she was entitled to outright ownership in one-third of the decedent's property. Thus, the court applied New York law, and thereby, the decedent's wife was entitled to a greater proportion of the decedent's estate than she would have been had the decedent specified that Spanish law apply, even though it was apparent that the decedent's testamentary plan was to diminish his wife's rights to share in his estate.[26]

It is exceedingly difficult to disinherit a spouse merely by designating a foreign law to apply. Although, apparently, other states with statutes similar to New York's have yet to rule on this point, they are likely to exercise similar restraint.[27] Interestingly, the last sentences of the applicable Illinois and Florida statutes allow their courts either to order distribution of the assets or to remit them to the domiciliary states for distribution.[28]

However, the courts will not always apply the law that is more favorable to the surviving spouse. For example, in *In re Estate of Crichton*, decided six months before *Clark*, the New York Court of Appeals resorted to a "points of contact" analysis to determine the applicable law.[29] This case involved a New York domiciliary who made no provision in his will for his wife. Most of his estate consisted of personal property located in Louisiana. The widow invoked Louisiana community property laws under which she was entitled to a share of the assets.[30] In deciding whether the law of the marital domicile, New York, or the law of the

24. *Gould*, 1 Ohio Op. 2d 366.

25. *In re* Smith's Estate, 48 N.Y.S.2d 631 (Sur. Ct. 1944).

26. Schoenblum reconciles the *Clark* and *Smith* decisions by asserting that, taken together, the two cases can be read as sanctioning choice of law clauses when the result will be beneficial to the surviving spouse, but not when they will operate to the surviving spouse's detriment. SCHOENBLUM, *supra* note 1, § 10.07.

27. *But see In re* Chappell's Estate, 213 P. 684 (Wash. 1923).

28. ILL. COMP. STAT. ANN., ch. 755, § 5/7-6; FLA. STAT. ANN. § 731.106.

29. *In re* Estate of Crichton, 267 N.Y.S.2d 706 (Sur. Ct.), *aff'd*, 272 N.Y.S.2d 987 (App. Div. 1966), *aff'd*, 288 N.E.2d 799 (N.Y. 1967).

30. LA. CIV. CODE ANN. art. 2334 (former art. 2400).

situs, Louisiana, should apply, the court determined that since all the significant contacts were with New York, it had the paramount interest and its law should apply.[31]

Two additional points may be worth mentioning. First, *Clark* involved two sister states, the difference being not an inconsistent statutory policy but the amount of property subject to the right of election. Second, in addition to the policy of protecting the spouse, common to most jurisdictions, some argument can be made for not creating a system in which sister states compete with each other to attract assets. When the competition is between two countries, there may be different policy considerations.

IV. Forced Heirship Rights

A. Overview

Unlike the respect U.S. courts generally accord spousal inheritance rights, they generally resist enforcing forced heirship rights in property located in the United States. This judicial antipathy is rooted in the public policy of all U.S. states, other than Louisiana, that disfavor the concept of forced heirship. As mentioned above, Louisiana law is based on principles of civil law that recognize the concept of forced heirship.[32]

It is a basic principle in many civil law jurisdictions that the majority of an individual's property (the "reserved portion") must pass upon his or her death to the individual's descendants, immediately and unconditionally, in equal shares per stirpes regardless of the individual's wishes.[33] Thus, in such jurisdictions, an individual's power of testamentary disposition is generally limited to the portion of his estate (the disposable portion) that does not pass to the forced heirs. The size of the disposable portion depends upon whether the individual is survived by descendants or ascendants and, if so, by how many.[34] Only when the individual is not survived by descendants or ascendants is all of the individual's estate freely disposable.

During an individual's lifetime, in principle, gifts may be made only from the disposable portion of his or her estate. However, the disposable and reserved portions of the decedent's estate cannot be calculated until after death. Thus,

31. The law of New York provides that the law of the matrimonial domicile governs as to the ownership of personal property by husband and wife. However, the matrimonial domicile in New York is defined as the domicile of the husband. *See Estate of Crichton*, 267 N.Y.S.2d at 709.

32. The interest of the decedent's children is frequently referred to as the "legitime." For a thorough discussion of forced heirship, see Antony Duckworth, *An Offshore View of Forced Heirship: Global Conflict and Its Planning Implications* (on file with the author).

33. *Id.*

34. *See generally* Walter Ryser, *Forced Heirship in Civil Law and Family Relief Legislation in Common Law: Traps to Be Avoided When Emigrating to a Civil Law Country (Table and Questionnaire), in* SWITZERLAND 15.3, COLLECTION OF CONFERENCE PAPERS OF THE INTERNATIONAL ACADEMY OF ESTATE AND TRUST LAW.

property that was the subject of a lifetime gift may have to be reduced or returned.[35] This is the principle known as "clawback."

Under the clawback rule, if the decedent's actual estate at the time of death is sufficient to provide for the forced shares due to the decedent's forced heirs, lifetime gifts are safe from clawback. However, if the amounts due to the forced heirs exceed the decedent's actual estate, lifetime gifts are subject to reduction (or clawback) in order to make up the deficit.[36] In such a situation, the recipients of the most recent gifts and, thereafter, the recipients of earlier gifts, are obligated to compensate the forced heirs. Although the clawback rules do not generally invalidate a gift, a gift may be challenged if the purpose of the gift was to avoid forced heirship rights.

Clawback poses some serious threats to a well-considered estate plan. First, in many jurisdictions, there is no time limitation upon the forced heirs' right to clawback inter vivos gifts.[37] Thus, depending upon the laws of the civil law jurisdiction, forced heirs may recover property disposed of by the decedent, twenty, thirty, or more years before his death. Second, clawback requires the donee to compensate the forced heirs regardless of whether the donee still owns the property and whether others have acted in reliance on the disposition. Thus, clawback has the effect of making all gratuitous transactions and the property rights arising from such transactions uncertain until the decedent's death. Title to the property remains conditional, even in the hands of subsequent purchasers, until the decedent's death and the expiration of the applicable statute of limitations for forced heirship claims. Third, in calculating the forced share, an heir need not include the value of any gifts made by the decedent in trust for the heir's benefit. Moreover, the forced heirs' rights to clawback cannot be waived. Thus, if an individual dies subject to a forced heirship jurisdiction, the forced heirs may interfere with the disposition of foreign property and with rights governed by other jurisdictions.[38]

B. Characterization of Property

As is the case with spousal inheritance rights, a preliminary consideration in determining the rights of forced heirs is whether the property is immovable or movable. As noted previously and as a general rule, the law of the situs applies to the disposition of immovables, while the law of the decedent's domicile governs the disposition of movables.[39] Consequently, movable property situated in a

35. The French Civil Code sets forth a complex statutory plan by which inter vivos and certain testamentary dispositions may be reduced. *See* Schoenblum, *supra* note 1, § 12.02[A].

36. *See* Duckworth, *supra* note 32.

37. However, under Austrian law, an inter vivos gift made more than two years before the succession is opened will not be included in computing the reserved portion of the decedent's estate. Likewise, the time limit under Swiss law is generally five years. *See* Ryser, *supra* note 34.

38. See Duckworth, *supra* note 32, for further explanation of these issues.

39. For example, the French forced heirship rules apply to (1) movables (wherever situated) owned by a French domiciliary and (2) immovables situated in France, regardless of the decedent's domicile. *See, e.g.*, *In re* Russell's Estate, 159 N.Y.S.2d 651 (Sur. Ct. 1956); Schoenblum, *supra* note 1, § 12.02[A]; Duckworth, *supra* note 32.

common law jurisdiction may be subject to forced heirship claims if the decedent was a domiciliary of a civil law jurisdiction. Thus, in determining forced heirship rights, the law of the decedent's domicile may become extremely important when the decedent is a domiciliary of a civil law jurisdiction.

C. Enforcement of Forced Heirship Rights

As noted above, the courts in the United States are generally reluctant to enforce forced heirship rights asserted by the heirs of a decedent. The case *In re Estate of Renard* exemplifies the general trend of U.S. courts not to recognize forced heirship rights.[40] For the purpose of the present discussion, the relevant issue in *Renard* concerned the assertion of forced heirship rights in bank and brokerage accounts located in New York and disposed of by a will executed in France under which the testator (a U.S. citizen and a French domiciliary) designated the application of New York law. The forced heirship claim was made by the testator's son who resided in California but held joint U.S./French citizenship. In rejecting the son's contention that French law entitled him to a forced share of the accounts, the New York courts relied upon a New York statute that permits testators to choose New York law to determine the validity and effect of the disposition of assets deemed located in New York. The court concluded that § 3-5.1(h) of the New York Estates, Powers and Trusts Law was intended to permit a decedent to avoid forced heirship rights of a foreign jurisdiction in movables by directing the application of New York law.[41] Hence, *Renard* established that New York will not recognize forced heirship claims in assets located in New York when the testator has designated New York law to govern the disposition of these assets.

In a similar context, a Florida district court of appeal overturned a lower court holding that had permitted the enforcement of forced heirship rights arising under Venezuelan law in Totten trust accounts,[42] jointly owned by the decedent and two sons, which were located in a Florida bank.[43] The reviewing court noted that Florida statutory law directed the disposition of joint bank accounts in accordance with the law of the situs, regardless of the domicile of any joint owner.

40. *In re* Estate of Renard, 437 N.Y.S.2d 860 (Sur. Ct. 1981), *aff'd*, 447 N.Y.S.2d 573 (App. Div. 1981), *aff'd*, 439 N.E.2d 341 (N.Y. 1982).

41. The court also noted that, in view of the decedent's long residence in New York and the son's nonresidence in France, the New York policy allowing freedom of disposition of property should prevail. However, Judge Cooke's dissent indicates that this was not the basis on which the majority of the court of appeals reached its decision to sustain the surrogate's court decision.

42. Totten trusts, also referred to as savings account trusts, are bank savings accounts that the depositor, O, opens in the name of "O, as trustee for A." During O's lifetime, O retains the right to withdraw the funds, and A is entitled to the amount on deposit at O's death. *In re* Totten, 71 N.E. 748 (N.Y. 1904).

43. Sanchez v. Sanchez De Davila, 547 So. 2d 943, 945 (Fla. Dist. Ct. App. 1989). *But see* Nahar v. Nahar, 656 So. 2d 225 (Fla. Dist. Ct. App. 1995) (upholding decision of The Hague with respect to forced heirship claim brought under the laws of Aruba by the adult children of a decedent [determined by The Hague to be domiciled in Aruba despite his residence in Florida] who owned bank accounts situated in Florida).

Because the accounts were situated in Florida, the court applied Florida law, which defeated the forced heirship claims of the heirs who were not parties to the account by vesting ownership of the accounts solely in the surviving joint tenants.

The inconsistent treatment of forced heirship and spousal rights in property may create tension in those jurisdictions that have failed to recognize forced heirship claims. For example, at least one commentator suggests that the *Renard* decision overturns, de facto, *Clark*, in which the court applied the law of the decedent's domicile to determine spousal inheritance rights in New York property even though the testator specified that New York law apply to the disposition of such property.[44] However, even assuming *Clark* was overturned by *Renard* (which the authors do not believe is the case), the application of the New York elective share statute to a nonresident decedent's New York property would afford future surviving spouses instituting claims similar to that of *Clark* protection against disinheritance. Additionally, it should be noted that *Renard* failed to expressly overturn *Clark* and, to date, has not been applied to defeat non-New York spousal inheritance laws.

V. Testamentary Substitutes

The enforcement of spousal or forced heirship rights may also arise in connection with testamentary substitutes, such as inter vivos trusts. It may be possible for a non-U.S. domiciliary to avoid spousal and forced heirship claims arising under the laws of his or her domicile by using testamentary substitutes such as inter vivos trusts, Totten trusts, and joint and survivor bank accounts. With respect to spousal elective rights statutes currently in effect in almost all *common* law states, revocable inter vivos trusts and gifts *causa mortis* may be included in the deceased spouse's estate against which the survivor may elect. Such statutes, however, generally do not extend to inter vivos transfers occurring well in advance of death.[45]

Consistent with the rules applicable to testamentary transfers, New York courts have applied New York law to disputes involving assets located in New York where the parties have designated New York law to apply. Thus, in the case of *Wyatt v. Fulrath*, the New York court determined that New York law applied to a joint bank account that was located in New York, that was governed by an agreement under which full title would pass to the survivor, and that was governed by

44. *See* Robert A. Hendrickson, *Choice of Law Directions for Disposing of Assets Situated Elsewhere Than the Domicile of Their Owner—The Refractions of* Renard, 18 Real Prop. Prob. & Tr. J. 407 (1983). *See also* Schoenblum, *supra* note 1, § 10.07 (*Clark* implicitly overruled by *Renard* on ground that statutory language, which previously allowed New York choice of law clause with regard to "testamentary dispositions," had been revised to allow choice of law clause with respect to disposition of decedent's property).

45. *See generally* J.R. Kemper, Annotation, *Validity of Inter Vivos Trust Established by One Spouse Which Impairs the Other Spouse's Distributive Share of Other Statutory Rights in Property*, 39 A.L.R.3d. 14, 22 (1971).

New York law.[46] This result obtained even though application of New York law contradicted Spanish community property law, the law of the couple's domicile, under which the surviving spouse's interest in the account would have been limited to one-half. Similarly, in *Hutchinson v. Ross*, a New York court determined that New York law governed the validity of an inter vivos trust that was situated in New York and had been established by a domiciliary of Quebec, even though the trust's dispositive provisions violated the law of Quebec.[47]

The courts do appear to be drawing a distinction between testamentary and inter vivos transfers. For example, the *Clark* decision was distinguished from *Wyatt* and *Hutchison*, both of which involved spouses, on the ground that the latter cases were inter vivos transfers and were governed by the law of the situs.[48]

In the case of inter vivos trusts, the courts seem to look to the law of the situs of the trust, especially when it is designated as the governing law, to determine the rights of spouses.[49] For example, in *Rose v. St. Louis Union Trust Co.*, the Illinois court found that Missouri law applied to determine the validity of an inter vivos trust established in Missouri and to which the decedent, an Illinois domiciliary, had bequeathed 40 percent of his testamentary estate.[50] Similarly, in *Johnson v. La Grange State Bank*, the Supreme Court of Illinois applied Illinois law to determine the rights of the surviving husband (who was an Illinois domiciliary) in an inter vivos trust previously established by his wife in Illinois before she died as a Florida domiciliary.[51] The lower court had determined that Illinois, not Florida, had the greater interest in having its law applied to the issue. However, some commentators and the Restatement (Second) of Conflict of Laws assert that the law of the last domicile might control these issues under certain circumstances.[52]

---

46. Wyatt v. Fulrath, 211 N.E.2d 637 (N.Y. 1965).

47. Hutchinson v. Ross, 187 N.E. 65 (N.Y. 1933).

48. *Clark*, 281 N.Y.S.2d 180.

49. For example, in *De Werthein v. Gotlieb*, 594 N.Y.S.2d 230 (App. Div. 1993), the court applied New York law to defeat a spouse's rights with regard to a Totten trust. *See also Nahar*, 656 So. 2d at 230 (error for lower court to find Totten trust to be under jurisdiction of Dutch court; trust account held to be true trust account that vested upon decedent's death and passed according to terms of trust).

50. Rose v. St. Louis Union Trust Co., 253 N.E.2d 417 (Ill. 1969).

51. Johnson v. La Grange State Bank, 383 N.E.2d 185 (Ill. 1978). In *La Grange*, the deceased wife had named herself as trustee for life and had named an Illinois bank as successor trustee. Her entire (though insubstantial) probate estate poured over into the inter vivos trust. *Id.* at 189. *See also* Nat'l Shawmut Bank v. Cumming, 91 N.E.2d 337 (Mass. 1950) (validity of husband's transfer to fully revocable inter vivos trust effectuated three years before his death held to be controlled by law of Massachusetts, situs of trust, and not by law of Vermont, decedent's domicile at death); Kemper, *supra* note 45. For further discussion of this topic, see LAWRENCE, *supra* note 4, ch. 7.

52. *Clark*, 281 N.Y.S.2d 180; *see* RESTATEMENT (SECOND) OF CONFLICT OF LAWS § 244 (1971). With respect to revocable inter vivos trusts, some commentators and the Restatement suggest that when the trust is established for the purpose of avoiding the elective share rights of the jurisdiction of the decedent's last domicile, courts might choose to apply the law of the domicile as to the right of the issue of the surviving spouse to a share of the trust assets. *See* David Cavers, *Trusts Inter Vivos and the Conflict of Laws*, 44 HARV. L. REV. 161, 198 (1930). *See also* 5A SCOTT, LAW OF TRUSTS § 601, at 319–20 (4th ed. 1987) (suggesting that it might be proper to apply different law to different issues and that the law of the

Whether or not these distinctions will be upheld remains to be determined. It is arguable that distinguishing between inter vivos and testamentary dispositions, or for that matter between descendants and spouses, is counterproductive if the result is to defeat the policy of the jurisdiction having the primary interest. If the trend toward adopting a "points of contact" or "primary interest" test for choice of law purposes continues, these distinctions may be abandoned.

It is essential to recognize that *Wyatt* and *Hutchinson* exemplify the policy of New York that favors the recognition of designations of New York law in circumstances in which the dispute has a connection to New York state. In fact, New York's General Obligation Law statutorily extends this policy to allow parties to a contract relating to a transaction of at least $250,000 to designate the application of New York law to that contract even though the contract bears no relation to the state of New York.[53] Further, the statute provides that where the contract amount equals or exceeds $1 million, the parties may agree to litigate any dispute involving the contract in New York.[54]

There is at least one exception to the application of the designated law of New York. That exception concerns the recognition of valid final judgments of foreign countries or sister states. For example, in *Watts v. Swiss Bank Corp.*, the New York Court of Appeals recognized a previous decision of a French court regarding the disposition of property in a New York joint bank account which the parties agreed would be governed by New York law.[55] In barring the parties from relitigating the issue in New York, the court applied the principles of res judicata and comity.

Further, the Uniform Foreign Monetary Judgments Recognition Act[56] operates in New York and provides for the recognition and enforcement of foreign monetary judgments in the same manner that judgments of sister states warrant "full faith and credit." It should be noted that this Act requires foreign judgments to meet certain jurisdictional conditions and to comply with basic principles of due process of law. New York courts, nevertheless, may disregard judgments (1) when the foreign court lacked subject matter jurisdiction, (2) when the defendant did not receive notice in time to defend, (3) when obtained by fraud, (4) in the case of jurisdiction based on personal service, when the foreign forum was a seriously inconvenient forum for the trial of the action, (5) when the judgment conflicts with another final judgment or violates the public policy of New York, or (6) when

domicile might control forced zheirship issues); RESTATEMENT (SECOND) OF CONFLICT OF LAWS § 270 cmt. 3 (1971). However, the decisions cited by these commentators do not seem to support directly the view that the law of the last domicile should be controlling. In most cases where courts have confronted the problem, they appear to have denied the disinherited spouse's claim that the law of the domicile should be applied as opposed to the law of the situs of the trust, at least where the settlor has designated the situs law as the governing law.

53. N.Y. GEN OBLIG. LAW § 5-1401.

54. *Id.* § 5-1402.

55. Watts v. Swiss Bank Corp., 265 N.E.2d 270 (N.Y. 1970).

56. N.Y. C.P.L.R. §§ 5301–5309.

the parties agreed to settle the dispute in question in a manner other than by an action in the forum court.[57]

VI. Conclusion

As this chapter makes clear, spouses are generally accorded a preferred status by courts in the United States, and, thus, it may be difficult for a non-U.S. resident to defeat spousal claims to assets situated in the United States. On the other hand, because of public policy considerations that allow an individual to dispose freely of his or her assets, descendants and ascendants generally do not enjoy the same privileged status as do spouses.

As a general matter, inter vivos transfers in some jurisdictions, such as New York, are more likely to withstand claims brought by a surviving spouse or descendants. A multinational estate planner might recommend that a non-U.S. resident client with investments in the United States establish a trust in a jurisdiction such as New York. In such a case, the trust instrument should designate the law of New York as the governing law, and the client should establish as close a nexus as possible with New York. Thus, the trust assets should be situated in New York, and, ideally, the trustee should be a New York resident.

Of course, as indicated above, although a non-U.S. resident may attempt to and even succeed at circumventing spousal and forced heirship rights by designating that the law of a particular jurisdiction apply to assets situated therein, substantial uncertainty persists regarding which jurisdiction's law will control in disputes involving a non-U.S. resident's property.

57. *Id.* § 5304.

Theories of Marital Property on the International Stage*

6

Jeffrey A. Schoenblum
Joshua A. Rubenstein

I. Introduction

Most commonly, issues concerning the division of property between spouses arise because of divorce. This is not the focus of this chapter because, in the context of divorce, courts are often empowered to reallocate assets of the spouses regardless of ownership.[1] Keeping with the subject matter of this book, the focus is on rights of spouses at the death of either one. When one spouse dies, the survivor may claim ownership so that the property or a portion of it does not pass to other persons, such

* This discussion includes portions (as revised) of § 10.24, *Theories of Marital Property on the International Stage*, as excerpted from JEFFREY A. SCHOENBLUM, MULTISTATE AND MULTINATIONAL ESTATE PLANNING (2d ed. 1999), with permission of the publisher (Aspen Publishers, Inc.).

1. In the states of the United States, there has been widespread adoption of principles of equitable distribution. *See* Jana B. Singer, *Divorce Obligations and Bankruptcy Discharge: Rethinking the Support/Property Distinction*, 30 HARV. J. ON LEGIS. 43, 73 (1993); Michaela M. White, *Divorce After the Bankruptcy Reform Act of 1994: Can You Stay Warm After You Split the Blanket?*, 29 CREIGHTON L. REV. 617, 623 (1996). For an argument that this power to allocate misconceives the issue, see Joan Williams, *Is Coverture Dead? Beyond a New Theory of Alimony*, 82 GEO. L.J. 2227 (1994).

as children from a prior marriage. On the other hand, children may dispute a characterization of the surviving spouse as a partial owner of property based on community property ownership. Creditors as well as claimants under various family protection provisions may seek to reach all of the debtor's estate, asserting that it also includes property to which the surviving spouse asserts ownership.

As spouses move from one country to another or acquire property in different countries, the question that inevitably arises is how each spouse's rights in the property will be determined. Ordinarily, the country in which assets are located or can be controlled will ultimately be asked to decide the issue, although the possibility exists that it will honor an order issued by a court of another jurisdiction that it deems to have a law-determinative affiliation or link with the spouses.

In determining the rights of the parties, the courts of any jurisdiction will typically turn to its established legal doctrine, whether in the form of codes or cases. Commonly, development of the law in this area has been limited so that there are few precedents, and the codal rules are far from complete. Nevertheless, the approaches followed by different countries can be understood by exploring how they address a number of crucial foundational issues, which are discussed below.[2]

II. Mutability Versus Immutability

One of the great debates influencing the development of diverse positions involving marital property rights concerns the mutability of those rights. "Mutability" means the possibility that the property rights of the parties will be altered by a change in their law-determining affiliation. The matter need not be perceived as a pure mutability/immutability dichotomy. That is, a jurisdiction may adopt a rule of partial mutability/immutability. Under this regime, a change, for example, in domicile will mean a change in the governing law as it concerns only future acquisitions of property. On the other hand, the marital property rights prior to the change in domicile remain immutable.[3]

A theory of complete mutability would allow the spouses at any time, both before and after marriage, to exercise personal autonomy in deciding which law should govern their rights in property. They could enter into an agreement

2. For a particularly insightful article, see Friedrich K. Juenger, *Marital Property and the Conflict of Laws: A Tale of Two Countries*, 81 Colum. L. Rev. 1061 (1981). *See also* J. Thomas Oldham, *Conflict of Laws and Marital Property Rights*, 39 Baylor L. Rev. 1255 (1987); Michael S. Finch, *Choice-of-Law and Property*, 26 Stetson L. Rev. 257, 279–85 (1996). The Hague Conference on Private International Law has assembled excellent, although somewhat dated, materials, in connection with the Convention on the Law Applicable to Matrimonial Property Regimes. In particular, *see* Georges A.L. Droz, *Matrimonial Property Matters in Private International Law—Lessons and Conclusions Drawn from the Comparative Study*, *in* 2 Actes & Documents De La Treizieme Session: Matrimonial Property Regimes 111 (1978).

3. This is the regime followed throughout the United States. *See* 1 Jeffrey A. Schoenblum, Multistate and Multinational Estate Planning § 10.21[C] (2d e d. 1999).

specifying which law would govern and would not be subject to local public policy concerns. Total mutability of this sort does not exist in any developed country.[4]

To the extent that the spouses cannot specify their choice of law in a written agreement,[5] total mutability would require that as the spouses changed the law determining affiliation[6], the law governing their marital property rights would also change. Generally, this would create an intolerable situation in terms of the reliance interests of spouses worldwide and might actually discourage international mobility. There would be no certainty as to what law governs marital rights unless the spouses could be certain that they would never leave the original marital state. Nevertheless, in Switzerland, an aspect of this principle of total mutability is enforced. Article 55 of the Swiss Statute on Private International Law of 1987[7] makes the law of the new domicile retroactive to the time of the marriage. However, this effect is tempered by the right of the spouses at any time to enter into a written agreement excluding this retroactivity.[8] Retroactivity is also defeated by an earlier agreement to maintain existing governing law or by a marriage contract specifying the respective rights of the spouses.[9]

A pure immutability principle would also be unacceptable for many immigrant nations.[10] Although spouses may have left behind for good a former jurisdiction, its law would still govern their rights in assets acquired in the new jurisdiction.[11] Not only would this put immense pressure on the immigrant nation's courts in seeking to grasp and apply correctly the former jurisdiction's law, with potentially many such foreign laws to master, but it also would have the perverse effect of applying the very property regime that many of these immigrants had fled.[12]

---

4. For a discussion of the restrictions imposed by states in the United States on the designation of a governing law, see *id.* § 10.21[D].

5. The spouses might not succeed in the designation of a controlling law for a number of reasons: the governing law might bar them completely from doing so, a particular jurisdiction in which property was located might refuse to recognize a designation, or the particular choice of law might not be recognized because of the lack of a sufficient relationship to the spouses.

6. This affiliation most commonly would be domicile, nationality, or habitual residence. *See* Schoenblum, *supra* note 3, § 10.24[B].

7. Switzerland: Statute on Private International Law, 29 I.L.M. 1244, 1263 (1990).

8. *Id.* art. 55:1.

9. *Id.* art. 55:2. Still, article 55 has been described by one leading authority as a "radically different and revolutionary solution." *See* Georges A.L. Droz, *Regards sur le droit international prive compare*, 229 Recueil Des Cours D'Academie De Droit International 212 (1991).

10. Juenger, *supra* note 2, at 1071.

11. France is an immigrant nation but only allows change to the point of the marriage. *See infra* text accompanying note 13. In effect, then, it condemns its immigrants to their prior matrimonial property law, at least if they are not refugees. A case demonstrating the French approach is Cour d'appel Paris, 1re ch., Nov. 3, 1993, 1994 J.D.I. 148, note Mariel Revillard (involving Swiss husband and French wife governed by Cuban law despite his later adoption of French nationality). For the case of the treatment of refugees in conflict of laws generally, see Schoenblum, *supra* note 3, § 9.08.

12. One of two French exceptions to immutability involves refugees. *See* Droz, *supra* note 9, at 210 n.422. However, this exception is recognized only in very narrow circumstances. Thus, in one case, an effort by a Romanian couple, who had become French nationals, to have their matrimonial property regime altered, was rejected. The spouses had married in Romania in 1937 and had lived

While most countries have, therefore, gone the partial mutability/immutability route, the compromises struck differ from one jurisdiction to another. The classical French model, for example, endorses mutability, but only up to the point of marriage.[13] In other words, the persons are free to designate any governing law prior to the marriage. However, once married, they are not free to alter the law designated.[14] If no law is designated, then the law "tacitly" agreed to by the parties controls.[15] Significantly, under the classical French system, even after a move to a new domicile[16] and the acquisition of "new" assets there, these "new" assets will be governed by the "old" law. Exceptions exist in two cases: where the governing

---

there until 1964. *See* Cour d'appel Paris, 1re ch., July 5, 1990, 1992 J.D.I. 373, 378, 380, note Laurence Idot. Although Germany generally follows a nationality rule (*see* Introductory Act to the Civil Code arts. 14 & 15 in the GERMAN CIVIL CODE (Simon L. Goren trans., rev. ed. 1994), even it preserves special treatment for displaced persons and refugees. *See* Act of Aug. 4, 1969, Concerning the Matrimonial Property Regime of Displaced Persons and Refugees. See SCHOENBLUM, *supra* note 3, § 9.08, for other choice of law problems involving the law governing refugees.

13. The origin of this rule is the *Consilium* 53 of 1525, *in* C. MOLINAEUS, CONSILIA ET RESPONSA 251 (2d ed. 1568) (discussed in Juenger, *supra* note 2, at 1062). The jurist DeMoulin wrote: "It is not inappropriate that the law of Paris should thereby, indirectly, have a ubiquitous effect, even with respect to goods and property that have a situs outside the territory of the coutume and of the parties' domicile." Presently, France is party to the Hague Convention on the Law Applicable to Matrimonial Property Regimes, Mar. 14, 1978. The Convention, which entered into force on January 9, 1992, is considerably more complex. *See* SCHOENBLUM, *supra* note 3, § 10.24[K]. Article 6 of the Convention alters the French classical rule of postmarital immutability.

14. This rule is breached in some jurisdictions otherwise committed to immutability. For example, Belgian courts have been willing to apply Belgian law where the spouses have settled permanently in Belgium. *See, e.g.*, Trib. civ. Gaud, Sept. 10, 1987, 1986 J.D.I. 177–78, note L.B. They have also shown a willingness to avoid the application of a foreign law by classifying the matter as one of procedure governed by the law of the forum. *See, e.g.*, Trib. civ. Anvers, Mar. 31, 1988, 1996 J.D.I. 177, note L.B.

15. This law may not, however, be the law of the country where the spouses first settle. *See, e.g.*, Cass. civ. 1re, Oct. 9, 1991, Rev. crit. D.P. I 479 (Fr.), and note Georges Khairallah (rejecting first matrimonial domicile, including place of marriage celebration, if spouses are there simply for convenience or do not have serious localization of interests there; thus, Pakistan was not law-determining country, even though French woman and German man married and lived there for several months while German husband was on business assignment).

16. Considerable controversy surrounds the determination of domicile. Many French courts have invoked the standard of *la loi du premier domicile matrimonial* (the law of the first matrimonial domicile). However, this tends to freeze in place the first home of the parties after marriage. This was the case involving two French nationals who were married in the United States (Texas), where the husband was studying. After fifteen months in the United States, they moved to France, where they lived as a couple for a number of years. Nevertheless, the court found their domicile to be in Texas since at the time of the marriage, they manifested an intent to localize their "pecuniary interests" in the United States. *See* Cour d'appel Versailles, le ch., Apr. 11, 1991, 1992 J.D.I. 378, note, Laurence Idot.

Suppose the couple marry in country X but agree to establish a domicile in country Y "as soon as possible." Under these circumstances, English courts have been prepared to consider this agreement and not consider the place of marriage as the first marital domicile of the parties. *See In re* Egerton's Will Trusts, [1956] 2 All E.R. 817 (Eng.) (English husband retired from army and moved to France where wife was domiciled). *But see supra* note 14.

law itself allows for change and where there are exceptional circumstances, such as in the case of refugees.[17]

This principle of postmarital immutability, however, must be distinguished from the reference to facts occurring after marriage that may help establish what the intent of the couple was at the time of marriage. It should also be recognized that premarital acts that may seem to represent a choice of law may not be regarded as such. These points are developed in a decision of the Cour de Cassation (the highest appellate court) of France involving a Moroccan man who married a French woman. They attached to the *Acte de mariage* (marriage document) at the time of their marriage, a *certificat de coutume*, which is an affidavit or memorandum of foreign law that need not be in any particular form. Prepared by the Moroccan consul, it stated that in the Arab world, "marriage is based on the regime of separate property." Subsequently, the parties settled in France. The following year, the husband registered with the Registry of Commerce for Rennes and indicated that his marriage was governed by the French community property regime. Several years later, the spouses acquired a house, at which time the notary confirmed that they were married under *la communaute d'acquets* (community of acquisitions) set forth in the Civil Code beginning with article 1400. Many years later, the husband was involved in a creditor action, and the liquidator sought to sell the house. The husband claimed the house belonged to his wife under the separate property regime indicated at the time of marriage. Challenging the assertion that the couple had a community property regime as indicated in the Commercial Registry, he pointed out that the parties were not able to alter the governing law after marriage.

The court rejected the husband's position. It described the *certificat de coutume* as a simple administrative requirement at the time of marriage,[18] which, in the absence of an express manifestation of intent, was not an adoption of Moroccan law. Rather, the subsequent acts, including the statement in the Commercial Registry and the notarization restatement at the time of the acquisition of the house, established and clarified the intent of the spouses at the time of their marriage. Thus, the case is important primarily for two reasons. It emphasizes the

17. *See, e.g.*, Cour d'appel Paris, 1re ch., July 5, 1990, note Laurence Idot. Even when the governing law allows for change, there has been considerable litigation over whether that law or the newly chosen law determines the modalities by which the change is properly effected. *See, e.g.*, Cour d'appel Chambery, ch. civ., June 20, 1995, 1996 J.D.I. 663 (Fr.). *See also* Cour d'appel Colmar, ch. civ., Jan. 19, 1993, 1993 Rev. crit. D.P. I 281, note Paul Lagarde (Fr.). In this particular case, the court held that the governing German law allowed a change of the governing law to French law. In accomplishing this change, German law did not require submission to homologation (confirmatory court determination), but French law did. The court concluded that the change in governing law had not been properly effected due to the failure to submit it to homologation. The note by Paul Lagarde suggests that even more difficult problems of this sort are posed under the Hague Convention on the Law Applicable to Matrimonial Regimes, which is considered in SCHOENBLUM, *supra* note 3, § 10.24[B].

18. The Registry office requires information to be given to French officials officiating over marriages as to the provisions of the marriage law of a foreigner's country. *See* Cass. civ., 1re ch., Dec. 13, 1994, 1995 Rev. crit. D.P. I 319, 322–23, note Mariel Revillard (Fr.).

significance of executing at the time of the marriage a document satisfactory to establish a choice of law regarding marital property.[19] Second, it demonstrates how a subsequent expression of governing law may actually be viewed as proof of initial intent. This may be helpful where the parties failed to make a choice of law at the time of marriage and do not want to be bound by the law that is applied in the absence of an express choice.[20] Under French law, that choice of law will typically be the first matrimonial domicile where the spouses have fixed their pecuniary interests.[21]

A variation on the French system has been endorsed in England and, therefore, is followed in much of the Commonwealth. The source of the English rule is *De Nichols v. Curlier.*[22] The House of Lords held that a wife who had married in France was entitled to assert French community property rights upon the death of her husband. The Lords so held even though the spouses had left France and had become domiciled in England, where the husband became a United Kingdom citizen. As a result of this decision, the husband was defeated in effectuating his estate plan, which was to leave his considerable wealth in a trust pursuant to which his wife would receive only a life interest.

In reaching its decision, the House of Lords reversed the Court of Appeal, which had pronounced a theory of total mutability.[23] As in France, the House of Lords found a tacit agreement of the spouses, by marrying in France, to have France's property laws apply. The English approach appears to incorporate the *whole* law of the governing jurisdiction. Thus, if French law would allow a choice of another law in the case under discussion, then so would the English courts.[24]

Even though the United States and the United Kingdom are both common law jurisdictions, the American approach differs markedly from the English approach. The crucial U.S. precedent is *Saul v. His Creditors*,[25] which relied on earlier Spanish

19. As to what is a satisfactory document and which law determines this, see *supra* note 17.

20. Cass. civ., 1re ch., Dec. 13, 1994, 1995 Rev. crit. D.P. I 319 (Fr.). *See also* Cass. civ., 1e ch., Oct. 9, 1991, 1992 Rev. crit. D.P. I 479, note Georges Khairallah (Fr.) (court recognizes that *circumstances posterieures* (subsequent circumstances) can be taken into account in determining relevant law; included in such circumstances is declaration before a notary after marriage, choosing in this case Alabama law to govern spouses' marital property rights).

21. Cass. civ. 1re ch., Dec. 13, 1994, 1995 Rev. crit. D.P. I 319, 324, note Mariel Revillard (Fr.).

22. De Nichols v. Curlier, [1900] A.C. 21.

23. *In re* De Nichols, [1898] 2 Ch. 60, 62–63. The Court of Appeal had itself reversed the Chancery Division.

24. This is the English "foreign court" theory of *renvoi.* It is also known as "double *renvoi*" or "total *renvoi.*" *See generally* P.M. North & J.J. Fawcett, Cheshire and North's Private International Law (12th ed. 1992). Note that France does not follow this approach. Indeed, French law expressly repudiates *renvoi* in cases involving matrimonial property. *See, e.g.*, Cass. civ., 1re ch., Jan. 27, 1969, 1969 Rev. crit. D.P. I 710, note Deruppe (Fr.); Judgment of Feb. 1, 1972, Cass. civ., 1re, 1972 Rev. crit. D.P. I 644, note Wiederkehr (Fr.). *See also* Yvon Loussouarn & Pierre Bourel, Droit International Prive 339 (3d ed. 1988). *See also infra* text accompanying note 42; *supra* Chapter 1.

25. Saul v. His Creditors, 5 Mart. (n.s.) 569 (La. 1827). *See also* Murphy's Heirs v. Murphy, 5 Mart. (o.s.) 83 (La. 1817); Gale v. Davis' Heirs, 4 Mart. (o.s.) 645, 649 (La. 1817).

authority.[26] This case endorsed the principle of postmarital mutability as well as premarital mutability. Following a change of marital domicile, new acquisitions would be governed by the marital property law of the new marital domicile. On the other hand, the principle of mutability did not extend to assets acquired prior to the change of domicile. These assets remained governed by the marital property law of the domicile at the time of acquisition.[27]

Thus, under the American approach uniformly followed throughout the United States at the present time,[28] the result in *De Nichols v. Curlier*[29] would be different. The widow would not be entitled to French community property rights, except as to property acquired while the marital domicile was in France. English marital property law would control with respect to assets acquired after the spouses established their English marital domicile.[30]

One major criticism of the American approach is that it requires accurate record keeping of the dates of acquisition of items and domicile at that time. In the case of intangible assets, complex tracing problems must be confronted to the extent capital has been added, profit earned, or debts incurred in a subsequent domicile.[31]

The German approach is akin to the American approach. Under article 1408(1) of the German Civil Code, the spouses "may cancel or alter the matrimonial regime after concluding the marriage."[32] By way of contrast, Japan follows the classical French model. Pursuant to articles 755, 756, and 758 of the Civil Code, if no contract has been entered into and registered before the notification of marriage, the "[p]roperty relations between husband and wife cannot be changed after the notification of marriage."[33]

Both the classical French and English approaches are premised on the express designation of a governing law by the spouses or their "tacit" agreement

---

26. *See* Gregorio Lopez de Tovar, Las Siete Partidas Glosadas, Partida IV, tit. 11, ley 24 (1551). However, prior authority had enunciated a different view. *See* Alfonso el Sabio, Las Siete Partidas, Partida IV, tit. 11, ley 24 (1265), *reprinted in* LAS SIETE PARTIDAS 941–52 (S. Scott trans. 1931) ("We decree that the contract which they made with one another shall be valid in the way which they agree upon, before or at the time when they married, and shall not be interfered with, by any contrary custom existing in the country where they went to reside").

27. As has been pointed out by Professor Juenger, the theoretical basis for this approach is the statutist theory that marital property rights laws are "real statutes" that have no extraterritorial effect. *See* Juenger, *supra* note 2, at 1068.

28. *See* SCHOENBLUM, *supra* note 3, § 10.02.

29. *See supra* text accompanying notes 22–24.

30. This would have reduced the widow's rights since English law was less generous than French law. Most assets in value were acquired after the move to England.

31. *See* Droz, *supra* note 9, at 215. For a further discussion *see* SCHOENBLUM, *supra* note 3, § 10.13.

32. *See* Introductory Act to the Civil Code art. 1408(1), in the GERMAN CIV. CODE (Simon L. Goren trans., rev. ed. 1994).

33. *See* Civil Code art. 758:1, in BASIC JAPANESE LAWS (Hiroshi Oda ed. 1997).

on the day of marriage.[34] Other countries tending to immutability simply assign as governing law the nationality of one or both of the spouses on the day of the marriage. To the extent nationality is relied upon, there is far less opportunity to choose, short of an antenuptial agreement.[35] For example, the German private international law requires application of the nationality law "at the time of the marriage."[36] The same is true in Spain.[37] On the other hand, if the spouses alter their nationality, their property rights may change under some systems of law. This appears to be the case under articles 29 and 30 of the Italian statute regarding private international law.[38]

III. Party Autonomy

As previously discussed, both the classical French-English approach as well as the approach of the states of the United States, recognize party autonomy. It just ends earlier under the French-English model. By the time the estate planner sees the couple, it may well be too late to draft an agreement or choose a governing law. Thus, unmarried clients should be alerted to the overriding significance of an antenuptial agreement for persons marrying and establishing their initial marital domicile in these jurisdictions. A review of any other jurisdiction's laws pertinent to clients must also be pursued, since the other jurisdiction may follow the French-English model.[39]

Although the Netherlands is, like France, a party to the Hague Convention on the Law Applicable to Matrimonial Property Regimes, if that Convention does not apply, no changes in governing law can be made by the spouses after their marriage.[40]

---

34. As noted, this intent has been established in some, but by no means most, cases by subsequent circumstances. *See supra* text accompanying notes 14–16. *See also* the Israeli Spouses (Property Relations) Law, 1973 § 15 ("property relations between spouses shall be governed by the law of the domicile at the time of the solemnization of the marriage").

35. *See, e.g.*, Introductory Act to the Civil Code arts. 14 & 15, *in* the GERMAN CIV. CODE (Simon L. Goren trans., rev. ed. 1994).

36. *Id.* art. 15(1).

37. *See* JULIO ROMANACH JR., CIVIL CODE OF SPAIN, Preliminary Title, art. 9.2 (1994). *See also* Peruvian Civil Code of 1984, art. 2078, *translated in* 24 I.L.M. 997, 1008 (1985) ("The change of domicile does not alter the law competent to govern the relationships of the spouses with regard to property acquired before or after the change").

38. *See* Law No. 218 of May 31, 1995, *translated in* 2 THE ITALIAN CIV. CODE, App. F, Booklet 14 (Mario Beltramo ed., rev. ed. 1996).

39. *See* Droz, *supra* note 9, at 215. For a further discussion, see *supra* notes 13–24.

40. This rule is based on the famous case of Chelouche/Van Leer, Dec. 10, 1976, 1977 NJ 275, 27 NETH. INT'L L. REV. 244 (1980). *See also* RENE VAN ROOIJ & MAURICE V. POLAK, PRIVATE INTERNATIONAL LAWI THE NETHERLANDS 197 (1987). In *Chelouche*, an American entrepreneur of Dutch origin married a French woman. Although quite peripatetic, they spent most of their time in the Netherlands. The Hoge Raad (Supreme Court) stated the general principle of immutability. However, it made an "exception" in this case and refused to apply its own law because the Dutch community of estates regime was unknown

Note should also be taken of the fact that France and many other civil law jurisdictions do not recognize dépeçage with regard to the designation of governing law.[41] Thus, not only must a choice of law be made prior to the marriage, but there also must be a single choice of law with respect to all property. This would not be the case in England, thus indicating another major difference between the generally consistent approaches of French and English courts.[42] The French approach also differs in this regard with the approach in a number of states of the United States. In these states, the spouses can have local assets, such as bank accounts or real property, governed by local law, even though other assets are governed by the law of the marital domicile.[43]

The freedom to choose governing law in the United States, as well as under the classical French-English model, has already been reviewed.[44] In other countries, the freedom to choose is also often permitted, although with particular restrictions. Again turning to the example of Germany, the spouses may choose the law of a state of which one of them is a national[45] or habitually resident,[46] or the law of the forum where the property is located in the case of immovable property.[47] Italy's law largely parallels the German approach.[48] Spanish law is more restrictive; prior to marriage, the parties may select either one's national law or law of his or her habitual residence.[49]

IV. Scission between Real Property and Personal Property

The ordinary scission between personal and real property recognized in succession matters applies as well in the marital property context in the United States[50]

to the legal systems with which the spouses were connected prior to marriage. The circumstances in which "special circumstances" will be found are unclear. *See* TH. M. DE BOER & R. KOTTING, *Private International Law, in* INTRODUCTION TO DUTCH LAW FOR FOREIGN LAWYERS 219, 231 (Jeroen Chorus et al. eds., 2d rev. ed. 1993). The principles set forth in *Chelouche* were re-endorsed in HR, Judgment of Mar. 22, 1981, 1981 NJ 335.

41. *See generally* SCHOENBLUM, *supra* note 3, § 15.07. For a more complete discussion of depecage, see *id.*, ch. 15, n.588.

42. See *supra* note 24 for the differences relating to *renvoi.*

43. *See, e.g.*, N.Y. EST. POWERS & TRUSTS LAW § 3-5.1. *See also* Wyatt v. Fulrath, 211 N.E.2d 637 (N.Y. 1965); Hutchison v. Ross, 187 N.E. 65, 71 (N.Y. 1933). See the discussion of these cases in SCHOENBLUM, *supra* note 3, § 10.13.

44. *See supra* text accompanying note 39.

45. Introductory Act to the Civil Code art. 15(1), in the GERMAN CIV. CODE (Simon L. Goren trans., rev. ed. 1994).

46. *Id.* art. 15(2).

47. *Id.* art. 15(3).

48. Law No. 218 of May 31, 1995, *translated in* 2 THE ITALIAN CIV. CODE, App. F, Booklet 14 (Mario Beltramo ed., rev. ed. 1996).

49. JULIO ROMANACH JR., CIVIL CODE OF SPAIN, Preliminary Title, art. 9.2 (1994).

50. *See* SCHOENBLUM, *supra* note 3, § 10.05.

and England.[51] Thus, in these jurisdictions, real property is governed by the law of the situs, regardless of the marital domicile. In this respect, notions of mutability are overridden by sovereignty principles.

By way of contrast, and despite observance of scission in succession matters, France opts for the principle of unity of the marital property regime. With one exception,[52] French courts have routinely and consistently taken this position.[53]

Despite the foregoing, a "source" rule has developed. Pursuant to this rule, some jurisdictions will trace back to the origin of the funds used to acquire the real property. If those funding assets were, for example, community property, the same will be true of the real property, even if acquired in the name of a single spouse.[54]

Many countries, in addition to France, do not distinguish between the law governing real and personal property. Unlike France, their preference for unity parallels their approach in succession matters. For example, Greece applies a unified approach to succession pursuant to article 28 of the Civil Code.[55] With respect to the matrimonial property regime, the high court of Greece decided in one case[56] that a French husband had a community interest in an immovable in Greece acquired by his Greek wife during their marriage. The Greek court applied the Greek conflict of laws rule in force then, which looked to the nationality of the husband at the time of the marriage. Thus, the French marital property regime controlled.

Importantly, however, the court was not prepared to recognize the authority of a French court's judgment finding that the French community law applied. While the practical outcome was the same, the Greek courts alone were held to have authority over rights in Greek real property.[57] Thus, the fact that a court is prepared to pursue a unified approach in this realm should not be taken as a willingness to surrender complete authority to decide the rights in property under its control.

---

51. The principle was established in English law by the House of Lords in *Welch v. Tennent*, [1891] A.C. 639 (involving spouses' separation in which Scottish domiciliary claimed Scottish law rather than law of situs, England, applied; argument was rejected).

52. Trib. civ., Orleans, Judgment of Feb. 27, 1951, 1954 Rev. crit. D.P. I 358, note Batiffol (Fr.).

53. *See, e.g.*, Cour d'appel Paris, Oct. 31, 1991, 1992 J.D.I. 373, note Laurence Idot (English marital property law applied to French real property, the spouses having been domiciled in England from their marriage in 1972 until the acquisition of the property in 1982); Cour d'appel Versailles, 1re ch., Apr. 11, 1991, 1992 J.D.I. 378, note Laurence Idot (French couple married in the United States and lived there for fifteen months; concluding that "at the moment of marriage, the spouses manifested an intent to localize their pecuniary interests in the U.S.," the court treated the French real property as governed by New York law; this approach was taken despite notarial practice of recognizing matrimonial domicile only after a stay of two years).

54. *See* Juenger, *supra* note 2, at 1073–74.

55. See Phaedon John Kozyris, *Conflict of Laws, Nationality, International Jurisdiction and Recognition and Enforcement of Judgments and Awards*, *in* Introduction to Greek Law 301, 307 (Konstantinos D. Kerameus & Phaedon J. Kozyris eds., 2d rev. ed. 1993).

56. Areios Pagos (Supreme Court), Judgment No. 12/1986, 1992 J.D.I. 206, note Ph.D.

57. *Id.* at 206.

A country consisting of several law-determining political subdivisions may have internally conflicting rules on the scission issue. An excellent example is Canada. Ontario does not distinguish between real and personal marital property. The last common habitual residence governs both.[58] On the other hand, several other provinces, such as British Columbia, do draw this distinction.[59]

V. *Renvoi*

Notwithstanding the absence of scission in most civil law systems, it can result from application of *renvoi*. For example, Italy generally does not distinguish between personal and real property. However, article 13, 1.(a) of the Italian private international law provides for *renvoi*. Thus, if the law of another country is applied and it treats real and personal property differently, the effect is to bring scission into Italian law.[60]

This position, however, should be contrasted with that of France. The French courts have almost uniformly held that there is to be no *renvoi*, even when French real property is involved.[61] This determination has been made in cases of mixed English-French or U.S.-French couples with English or a U.S. state marital property regime.[62] This result is based on a belief in the unity of the marital property regime and a desire for simplicity.[63] *Renvoi* would undermine these objectives.

There can be no certainty as to which law will ultimately determine marital property rights without knowledge of the situs state's position on *renvoi*. For example, article 32 of the Greek Civil Code rejects *renvoi*.[64] Thus, when reference to a governing law is made, it is the domestic marital property law of that particular state. On the other hand, Spain permits a single *renvoi*. That is, if the country of the governing law would look to another governing law rather than its own internal law, then Spain will do the same.[65] However, it will not allow for a second

58. R.S.O. 1990, C.F.3, 5.15. *See also* Pershadsingh v. Pershadsingh, [1987] 40 D.L.R. (4th) 681. For a further consideration of "last common habitual residence," see Maharaj v. Maharaj, 1996 Ont. C.J. Lexis 2676 (Ont. Ct. S. July 7, 1996).

59. *See, e.g.*, Tezcan v. Tezcan, [1990] 44 B.C.L.R. 2d 343 (involving Turkish nationals who had married in Turkey years before).

60. *See generally* Tito Ballarino, *Personnes, famille, regimes matrimoniaux et successions dans la loi de reforme du droit international prive italien*, 1996 Rev. crit. D.P. I 21, 36 (discussing matter in context of succession to assets of French citizen, domiciled in Italy, with real property in England).

61. *See supra* text accompanying note 52.

62. *See id.*

63. *Id.*

64. *See also* Phaedon John Kozyris, *Conflict of Laws, Nationality, International Jurisdiction and Recognition and Enforcement of Judgments and Awards*, *in* INTRODUCTION TO GREEK LAW 301, 307 (Konstantinos D. Kerameus & Phaedon J. Kozyris eds., 2d rev. ed. 1993). A similar result follows in the Japanese law. *See* The Civil Code art. 32, *in* BASIC JAPANESE LAWS (Hiroshi Oda ed. 1997) (providing special rule to this effect with regard to matrimonial property).

65. JULIO ROMANACH JR., CIVIL CODE OF SPAIN, Preliminary Title, art. 12.2 (1994).

renvoi; if the second country would look to a third country, Spain will not go that far. It will apply the internal law of the second country.

A crucial distinction exists between *renvoi* and the determination of mutability based on the governing law. For example, France does not endorse *renvoi*. If the marital regime of country X is deemed to apply, only its internal law applies, and any reference country X's law would make to country Y's law is ignored. On the other hand, if, under the internal law of country X, the parties' matrimonial regime can be changed by the spouses after marriage, then French courts will recognize a postmarital change, even though internal French law follows a rule of immutability.[66]

VI. The Law-Determining Affiliation

To the extent that the parties do not or are not permitted to choose a governing law, a determination may have to be made as to what law governs the property rights of the spouses. A forum exercising effective control over property will not necessarily apply its own internal law.[67] As in other multijurisdictional matters, the forum may well refer to the law of another jurisdiction with what are deemed to be crucial ties. However, different jurisdictions have settled on quite different law-determining affiliations. The states of the United States, France, and England all look to domicile[68] with respect to personal property, and the states of the United States and England look to the situs with regard to real property. France maintains the unity of choice of law with respect to the matrimonial regime, looking to the initial matrimonial domicile.[69]

Other jurisdictions look to nationality, or even habitual residence,[70] as the law-determinative affiliation. However, unlike choice of law involving succession matters, there are two individuals with affiliations in marital property situations. If the spouses have different law-determinative affiliations, which one's should govern? In this regard, the traditional rule has been that the husband's nationality controls. With the equalization of status between husband and wife, new

66. *See, e.g.*, Cour d'appel Paris, fre ch., July 5, 1990, 1992 J.D.I. 378, 382, note Laurence Idot (citing numerous authorities for this well-established exception to the immutability principle, the only other one recognized in French law being the special case of refugees).

67. On the other hand, it may well do so, at least when the parties to the dispute do not raise the choice of law issue. *See, e.g.*, Cour d'appel Abidjan, Feb. 22, 1974, 1991 J.D.I. 1017–18 (Ivory Coast). The forum may also apply its own law in the exercise of the jurisdiction's police power, as when a third-party creditor is seeking to enforce a claim against a spouse and the other spouse asserts a community property interest under a different system of law. *See id.* (involving two French nationals married in France but living in Abidjan, where one was involved in hotel business and had outstanding obligations).

68. The French concept of domicile differs from both the American and English concepts, which also differ from each other. *See* SCHOENBLUM, *supra* note 3, § 9.02[A] & § 9.02 n.12.

69. *See supra* text accompanying notes 13, 52–53.

70. *See infra* note 71.

tie-breaking rules[71] have been incorporated into many, but by no means all, private international laws.

A typical example is the German law. Article 15 of the Act on the Revision of the Private International Law,[72] relating to the choice of the marital property regime, incorporates the rules of article 14 pertaining to the general legal effects of marriage. Under article 14, if the spouses were last nationals of the same country during marriage, then that country's law governs so long as one spouse is still a national of that country.[73] If neither spouse is still a national at the relevant time, then consideration is given to the law of the jurisdiction in which both spouses have their habitual residence.[74] If they last had their habitual residence in the state during marriage and one still "resides" there, its law governs. If there is no relevant habitual residence, the law of the state "with which the spouses mutually are most closely connected in some other manner" controls.[75] Obviously, the exact meaning of this last concept is far from clear, introducing considerable uncertainty into the process.[76]

In contrast to German law, the Italian solution is more straightforward, although not necessarily more certain in outcome. Pursuant to article 30, proprietary relations between the spouses are governed by the law applicable to the personal relations of spouses. Article 29 addresses this matter. The law of the country of common citizenship governs.[77] If the parties have different nationalities or multiple common nationalities, marital property is governed "by the law of the State in which the matrimonial life is mainly located."[78]

---

71. In Belgium, the law was changed by the courts from the nationality of the husband to the residence of the spouses. This precipitated a further dispute as to the retroactivity of the new choice of law rule. It was held not retroactive all the way back to the date of the marriage in a case involving an Italian husband and a Belgian wife. *See* Cour de cassation de Belgique, Judgment of Sept. 9, 1993, 1996 J.D.I. 178, note N.W (Bel.).

72. 27 I.L.M. 1, 12 (1988).

73. *Id.* art. 14(1)(1). Similar issues are confronted by jurisdictions that employ domicile or habitual residence as the law-determinative standard. However, problems arise more commonly under the nationality standard since spouses more commonly have different nationalities than different domiciles or habitual residences. *See, e.g.*, Switzerland: Statute on Private International Law, art. 54:2–3, 29 I.L.M. 1244, 1263 (1990). Under Swiss law, the initial reference is made to the spouses' common domicile. If there is no common domicile, the spouses' common national law applies. If there is no commonality there either, the Swiss regime of separate assets applies.

74. For a discussion of the meaning of habitual residence, see SCHOENBLUM, *supra* note 3, §§ 9.06 and 15.07[D].

75. 27 I.L.M. 1, 12, art. 14(1)3. *See also* the Japanese Horei for a similar approach, in The Civil Code arts. 14 & 15, in BASIC JAPANESE LAWS (Hiroshi Oda ed. 1997).

76. These provisions allowing for a change in governing law must be contrasted with article 1409 of the Civil Code, which provides, in connection with a marriage contract, that the "matrimonial regime may not be determined by reference to a law no longer in force or to a foreign one." This creates the curious problem of how a law can be changed if the regime does not allow a change in the governing law. *See* Cour d'appel Colmar, ch. civ., Jan. 19, 1993, 1995 Rev. Crit. D.P. I 281, note Paul Lagarde (Fr.).

77. Law No. 218 of May 31, 1995, *translated in* 2 THE ITALIAN CIVIL CODE, App. F, Booklet 14, art. 29(1) (Mario Beltramo ed., rev. ed. 1996).

78. *Id.* art. 29:2.

Both the German and Italian approaches contemplate the evolution of affiliations during the married life that may ultimately affect the determination of spousal rights. Thus, references to the "last" marital nationality or habitual residence during marriage means that the first such nationality or habitual residence need not be the last for purposes of determining matters such as what property each owns at death. These principles are consistent with the German and Italian civil codes, which allow for contractual change of the matrimonial regime after marriage.[79]

The Spanish Civil Code takes a very different approach. Under article 9.2, the common personal law of the spouses controls. Pursuant to article 9.1, the common personal law is defined as their nationality. If they have different nationalities, "the common habitual residence immediately subsequent to the [marriage] celebration" applies, "and, in the absence of that residence, [the marital property is governed] by the law of the place of celebration of the marriage."[80] Thus, the Spanish rules place considerable emphasis on the immutability principle. In the interest of certainty, a fallback of the law of the place where the marriage was celebrated is designated, even though that jurisdiction could very well have little to do with where the spouses live their lives together. This is the case with many Latin American countries as well.

In the case of a country in which marital property law is determined at the provincial or state level, there may be conflicting approaches taken by the political subdivisions, just as on related matters such as the scission question.[81] In Canada, for example, certain provinces employ the domicile standard. British Columbia is one such province.[82] Others prescribe the last habitual residence, as set forth, for example, in the Saskatchewan Matrimonial Property Act.[83] As for the distinction between domicile and habitual residence in this context, one court has described the latter standard as domicile without the *animus manendi* (intention to remain) in the future.[84]

VII. Formalities and Capacity to Contract

As to the formalities required to be observed for a valid marital agreement, each civil law state takes a somewhat different approach. The German law sim-

79. *See supra* note 17 for a discussion of the German law. The Italian law is provided for in art. 210 of the Civil Code. Law No. 218 of May 31, 1995, *reprinted in* 1 THE ITALIAN CIVIL CODE art. 210 (Mario Beltramo ed., rev. ed. 1996).

80. JULIO ROMANACH JR., CIVIL CODE OF SPAIN, Preliminary Title, art. 9.2 (1994).

81. *See* SCHOENBLUM, *supra* note 3, § 15.07[C].

82. *See, e.g.*, Tezcan v. Tezcan, [1990] 44 B.C.L.R. (2d) 343.

83. S.S. 1980, c. 9, § 22(1).

84. Adderson v. Adderson, [1987] 36 D.L.R. (4th) 631 (Ct. App. Alberta). For a further discussion of the habitual residence standard, see SCHOENBLUM, *supra* note 3, §§ 19.06 and 15.07[D].

ply requires that the choice of law be notarized.[85] However, notarization is not required if the marital agreement is not undertaken in Germany. Rather, the formalities will be valid in Germany as well if they comply with the requirements for marriage contracts under the law chosen or the "forum in which the choice of law was made."[86]

Under article 30 of the Italian law,[87] the fact that the agreement is valid under Italian law is apparently not relevant. Rather, it must be valid under either the law chosen or the state where the agreement was reached.

Capacity to enter into marital property contracts is generally determined under the personal law of the party. In the case of countries that look to nationality, this same law of nationality would determine whether an individual had the capacity to enter into the agreement.[88] In the case of common law countries, the usual contractual choice of law rules should apply.[89]

The crucial point is that capacity is generally not determined on the basis of a number of choice of law options, any one of which validates the agreement. The rule as to capacity is much less flexible.[90] Different choice of law rules apply in the case of determining governing law with regard to the agreement itself than apply to capacity to enter into the agreement.

VIII. Publicity and Enforcement by and against Third Persons

Although there is no such requirement in the states of the United States, most civil law jurisdictions have a publication requirement with respect to any marital property agreement. Absent the required publication, the agreement is not binding with regard to third persons.[91] Some of these systems are national in nature and do not provide a mechanism for the disclosure of information on an international level. Moreover, certain countries do not give effect to any foreign laws insofar as

85. Introductory Act to the Civil Code art. 14(4), *in* GERMAN CIV. CODE (Simon L. Goren trans., rev. ed. 1994).

86. *Id.*

87. Law No. 218 of May 31, 1995, *translated in* 2 THE ITALIAN CIVIL CODE, App. F, Booklet 14, art. 30(2) (Mario Beltramo ed., rev. ed. 1996).

88. *See, e.g.*, Federal Republic of Germany: Act on the Revision of the Private International Law, art. 7(1), 27 I.L.M. 1, 11 (1988); Law No. 218 of May 31, 1995, *translated in* 2 THE ITALIAN CIVIL CODE, App. F, Booklet 14, art. 20 (Mario Beltramo ed., rev. ed. 1996).

89. *See, e.g.*, *In re* Estate of Brown, 955 S.W.2d 940, 945 (Mo. 1997).

90. *Id.* (citing RESTATEMENT (SECOND) CONFLICT OF LAWS § 187 cmt.(d). (1971), stating that: "[A] person cannot vest himself with contractual capacity by stating in the contract that he has such capacity"). In the event that the parties to the agreement are governed by different laws and each has capacity under his or her own, each can probably specify that capacity shall be governed by that particular law. *See* RESTATEMENT (SECOND) CONFLICT OF LAWS § 187 cmt. i (1971).

91. *See* Droz, *supra* note 2, at 115.

they affect domestic third persons. In other words, international aspects of the contract are entirely *inter partes*.

An example of the latter approach is Japan's. Under Japanese conflicts law, a "matrimonial property system governed by the law of a foreign country cannot make a juristic act done in Japan or in respect of property situated in Japan valid as against a third party acting in good faith."[92] The third person must be acting in good faith. Furthermore, the rule only applies to property situated in Japan[93] or to acts performed there. Thus, with regard to some property, third persons will be bound as to publicity. With respect to other property, only the parties will be bound. Crucially, if the matrimonial property contract is registered in Japan, it is completely binding on third persons.[94] The Italian law takes a more protective stance vis-à-vis third persons. The agreement can be enforced against third persons "only if the latter were informed about the foreign law, or if they ignored it by their own fault."[95] There is no exception for registration. Accordingly, a burden would appear to be on spouses not only to inform persons with whom they are dealing about the agreement, but also to bring to their attention the relevant provisions of the governing foreign law. In the case of real property, nevertheless, the "disclosure modalities" of the state in which the property is situated are to be used. If these are observed, all rights are enforceable with respect to third persons.

Yet a third approach is exemplified by Switzerland.[96] Generally, the consequences of the "matrimonial regime" on the legal relationship of one of the spouses and a third party will be based on the law of the state in which the relevant spouse was domiciled "at the time the relationship began."[97] Nevertheless, "if the third party already knew or should have known about this law at the time the legal relationship began," the law applicable to the matrimonial regime will be controlling with respect to a third person.[98] There is no provision here for publication. No distinction is made between personal and real property nor between Swiss-situs and non-Swiss-situs property. Rather than a good faith test, a test based on what the third person should have known is imposed. There is no obligation to inform the third person about foreign law.

The particular provisions regarding third persons must not be overlooked. Improper notice may enable the third person to avoid the consequences of the foreign matrimonial property regime that might otherwise apply. Moreover, even

92. The Civil Code art. 15:2, *in* BASIC JAPANESE LAWS (Hiroshi Oda ed. 1997).

93. Presumably, this is to be determined under Japanese law.

94. The Civil Code art. 15:3, *in* BASIC JAPANESE LAWS (Hiroshi Oda ed. 1997).

95. Law No. 218 of May 31, 1995, *translated in* 2 THE ITALIAN CIVIL CODE, App. F, Booklet 14, art. 30(3) (Mario Beltramo ed., rev. ed. 1996).

96. Switzerland: Statute on Private International Law, art. 57, 29 I.L.M. 1244, 1263 (1990).

97. *Id.* art. 57:1.

98. *Id.* art. 57:2.

public notification may not suffice when the court considers important public policy concerns, including protection of certain creditors, to be involved.[99]

IX. The Border Territory between Matrimonial Property and Succession to Property at Death

The choice of law rules regarding the matrimonial property regime may differ substantially from the choice of law rules affecting succession at the death of a spouse. This may result in a characterization problem at death. Depending on whether distribution via matrimonial property or succession is involved, very different rights of survivors in the property may result.[100]

The conflict over characterization is exemplified by the handling of the rights of the surviving spouse with regard to usufruct[101] or an elective share. These are typically regarded as controlled by succession law.[102] Nevertheless, certain jurisdictions regard them as part of the marital property regime. In some cases, the country may even determine the spouse's rights in the estate based on the law of the situs of the property.[103] This might occur where, as in the Nordic countries, the community continues between the surviving spouse and heirs.[104]

In addition to the question of characterization of certain rights, principles subsumed under each regime may clash. Generally, this conflict can be readily resolved in an entirely domestic context. However, the problem becomes far more complex when one jurisdiction's law is deemed to govern the marital property regime and another, or several others, the succession to the worldwide estate. One situation in which this might arise is where the spouse is entitled to a forced heirship right of a limited percentage of the decedent's assets based on the choice of law rules governing succession at the death of the decedent. On the other hand, the governing marital property law may recognize a marital agreement awarding all or most property to one spouse at the death of the other.[105] Failure to recognize the potential for this clash of conflicting choices of law may lead to some faulty conclusions as to the ultimate disposition of the estate.

99. *See, e.g.*, Cour d'appel, Abidjan,, Judgment of Feb. 22, 1974, 1991 J.D.I. 1017 (Ivory Coast) (even though husband published notices that he was not responsible for wife's debts and they were both French nationals, court concluded husband's obligation for wife's debt was not governed by French marital property regime since public policy concerns meant that husband could not be protected under internal Ivory Coast law).

100. This problem is also discussed in SCHOENBLUM, *supra* note 3, § 15.02[E], in connection with the Hague Convention on Succession to Decedents' Estates.

101. For a discussion of this concept, see *id.* § 18.03.

102. Droz, *supra* note 2, at 111.

103. *Id.* at 116.

104. *Id.* at 88.

105. *Id.* Of course, the contract may actually limit the surviving spouse's rights so that the surviving spouse will wish to assert a statutory right.

The existence of these varied succession and matrimonial property laws will also have a tremendously complicating effect on estate administration. Most notably, which rules should be implemented first: the succession rules of country X or the marital property rules of country Y? There is really no persuasive guidance on these matters at the present time.

X. Intertemporal Conflicts

A particularly pressing problem in connection with marital property rights may be generated when a law governing certain property is altered. For example, suppose the forum determines that spouses are governed by the law of country X, where they had their first spousal domicile but from which they have since departed. Then, subsequently, the law of country X is changed as to spousal property rights. Under these circumstances, the question that arises is whether the spouse's marital property rights should be fixed based on the law in effect when they married and were domiciled in X or as currently modified.

The issue is extremely complex and has elicited many different responses. It has attracted a great deal of attention with regard to countries that have experienced great political upheaval. For example, after World War II, many of the eastern European countries shifted from separate property regimes to socialist-inspired community property regimes. A similar shift occurred in Italy in 1975. In an effort to equalize the rights of men and women, Switzerland altered its marital property laws in 1988.

The position in the common law countries appears to be one of giving effect to changes introduced in the governing law.[106] The French position, likewise, is that the law, as modified, applies.[107] This is also true for a number of other civil law jurisdictions.[108] The one exception is for refugees. Thus, a Russian who was under a pre-Soviet marital regime but had fled the country would be allowed to retain the pre-Soviet matrimonial regime.[109] By way of contrast, Germany has provided that if the refugee is "domiciled" in Germany, its matrimonial property regime applies.[110] In contrast, in *Proschek v. Proschazka*,[111] the Quebec court of appeals reversed prior precedent and held that the new Polish law applied rather than the one in effect at the time of the marriage in 1922.

Changes may occur as well in the forum's choice of law rules. These, too, raise an intertemporal conflict. Should the forum apply its former rule in force when the

106. *See, e.g.*, *id.* at 213 n.432.

107. *See, e.g.*, Cour d'appel Paris, July 2, 1954, 1954 Rev. crit. D.P. I 810, note Batiffol.

108. *See, e.g.*, Cass., Judgment of Sept. 9, 1993, 1996 J.D.I. 178, note N.W. (Belgium). The Belgian high court concluded that Italian law, as modified, applied; Sup. Ct., Judgment of Mar. 19, 1968 (Sweden), as reported in Droz, *supra* note 9, at 213.

109. *See, e.g.*, Cass. civ., 1re ch., Dec. 1, 1969, 1970 J.D.I. 306, note Ponsard (1970) (Fr.).

110. *See* Droz, *supra* note 9, at 214.

111. Proschek v. Proschazka, [1973] C.A. 410.

spouses married, especially if the country follows the immutability principle? If a change has been made for essential public policy reasons, such as the equality of the sexes, how should this be taken into account? For example, if the forum's law now refuses to prefer the husband's nationality, does this change the law governing the spouse's property under the control of the forum? This was the question confronted by the high court of Belgium in 1995. The court opted for simplicity and certainty in concluding that the old choice of law rule still applied.[112]

The same principle has been followed with respect to stateless persons who suffered from Nazi persecution. For example, the Hoge Raad, the Netherlands' Supreme Court, has held that despite that country's strong commitment to immutability of the governing matrimonial law, it would not apply German law based on the postwar restoration of German citizenship to a man who had married when he had previously been deprived of that citizenship and had been left stateless.[113]

XI. Immediate and Secondary Questions

A recent development has been the growing challenge to choice of foreign law through the invocation of the police power (public policy) exception. Through this route, the forum avoids the application of foreign law. This development often seems motivated by a desire to afford protection to a spouse or creditors who would not fare as well under the law designated by a contract as a result of the right application of the forum's choice of law rules with regard to matrimonial property regimes.

The issue arises because each country typically regulates the interaction of spouses within their borders. Certain matters, such as support, the preservation of the family home, the joint obligation for debts incurred by either one for a child's education, and the like,[114] are commonly described as laws of immediate application. They are also known as "primary rules" because the duties they impose cannot be avoided, whether or not there is a marital property agreement choosing a different law or simply not incorporating these rules. They also apply uniformly to all spouses, covering foreign nationals as well.[115] Indeed, article 226 of the French Civil Code provides that these rules apply "whatever be the matrimonial regime of the spouses."[116]

112. Cass., Sept. 19, 1995, 1996 J.D.I. 178, note N.W. (Bel.).

113. HR April 20, 1979, 1980 N.J. 527. *See* also VAN ROOIJ & POLAK, *supra* note 40, at 197–98.

114. Droz, *supra* note 9, at 220–21 (discussing matter in context of FRENCH CIVIL CODE, especially ch. VI dealing with the duties and rights of spouses).

115. *See generally* YVON LOUSSOUARN & PIERRE BOUREL, DROIT INTERNATIONAL PRIVE 486–89 (3d ed. 1988).

116. *See* THE FRENCH CIVIL CODE, art. 226 (John H. Crabb trans., rev. ed. 1995). *See generally* Cass., 1re ch., Oct. 20, 1987, 1988 J.D.I. 444, note A. Huet (Fr.) ("article 212 *et seq.* of the civil code are subject to territorial application"). For cases in other countries reaching a similar conclusion, see, e.g., Cass., Judgment of May 25, 1992, 1996 J.D.I. 175, note L.B. (Bel.); Cour d'appel, Abidjan, Judgment of Feb. 22, 1974, 1991 J.D.I. 1017 (Ivory Coast).

A number of jurisdictions have actually gone further by demarcating the subject property of matrimonial property laws and indicating that the regime set forth applies, regardless of the spouses' otherwise governing matrimonial regime. For example, article 462.10 of the Quebec Civil Code takes this approach.[117]

XII. International Treaties and Conventions

One approach to resolving the variety of questions raised in connection with marital property is to address these matters in bilateral and multilateral conventions. Indeed, before concluding that a particular country's conflicts rules apply, a determination must be made as to whether a bilateral treaty alters these rules in the particular case. France, especially, has entered into a number of such treaties.[118] The Nordic Convention of February 6, 1931, is a multilateral agreement that regulates rights between the Scandinavian countries. It is premised on the applicability of the law of the domicile. No differentiation is made between real and personal property. Upon a change of domicile, the governing law changes, although prior vested marital property rights remain unchanged.

The Hague Convention of July 17,1905, on the Law Applicable to the Personal and Patrimonial Consequences of Marriage[119] sought to address the problem as well on a multilateral basis. The husband's national law was favored, as was the permanence of the governing law. Nevertheless, a change of nationality was allowed to effect a change in law with regard to subsequently acquired assets.

There were serious problems with this convention. Notably, it only applied to parties at the convention. This created a confusing situation. For example, in the case of the Netherlands, spouses to whom the Convention applied, based on the husband's nationality, had a different set of conflicts rules applied than did spouses where the husband was from a country not subject to the Convention. These aspects of the Convention—its limited applicability, its reference to the *husband's* domicile, and the adherence to the immutability principle—were all abandoned with the denunciation of the Convention on August 25, 1977,[120] and the entry into force of a new Hague Convention fifteen years later.

117. Interesting and unresolved questions arise if property is not classified as matrimonial property. If regarded as obligations or debts, such as involving support, the judgment of the forum may have to be enforced under European Community Law. Thus, the outcomes may be quite different depending on the characterization of the item involved. *See* Droz, *supra* note 2, at 71–72, 194–95.

118. See, for example, Franco-Yugoslav Convention of May 18, 1971, which looks to the law of the spouses' common nationality and, if none, to their common domicile. On the other hand, the Franco-Polish Convention of April 5, 1967, provides for application of the spouses' common domicile. If they had none, then the law of common nationality applies, and, if none, then the law of the last common domicile applies. These outcomes can be overridden by a choice of law in a contract of the place where the contract was entered into. *See* Droz, *supra* note 2, at 118–19.

119. This Convention is discussed in Alfred E. Von Overbeck, Report of the Special Commission, Droz, *supra* note 9, at 139.

120. de Boer & Kotting, *supra* note 40, at 230–31.

On September 1, 1992, the Hague Convention on the Law Applicable to Matrimonial Property Regimes[121] entered into force. This Convention has been ratified by very few countries.[122] Nevertheless, it is important because of the adherence of two countries, France and Netherlands, the laws of which have thereby changed dramatically. This does not mean that the traditional rules of these jurisdictions no longer apply at all. They still do apply generally for spouses married prior to the conventions entering into force.[123] On the other hand, the Convention applies even when the nationality or habitual residence of the spouses, or the law otherwise to be applied, is of a noncontracting state.[124]

There are several themes embodied in the Convention. First, the spouses have the freedom to designate the internal law to govern them prior to their marriage. They are free to choose the law of one of their nationalities or habitual residence. Alternatively, they can choose the law of the first state where at least one of the spouses establishes an habitual residence after the marriage.[125]

As a general matter, dépeçage is prohibited.[126] The one exception pertains to immovables. The spouses may specify that the law of the situs is to govern. They may also declare that subsequently acquired immovable property will also be governed by its situs.[127]

In the event that the spouses fail to make a choice of law before marriage, their matrimonial property regime will be the internal law of the first common habitual residence after their marriage.[128] Notwithstanding the foregoing, the internal law of the common state of nationality will govern under certain circumstances, including where the spouses have a common nationality and:

---

121. Article 29 specifies that the Convention enters into force "on the first day of the third calendar month after the deposit of the third instrument of ratification, acceptance, approval or accession referred to in Articles 22 and 23." This occurred in 1992. *See* Final Act, 1 Actes & Documents De La Treizieme Session: Matrimonial Property Regimes 319, 325 (1978).

122. The three countries are France, the Netherlands, and Luxembourg. *See* 44 Neth. Int'l. L. Rev. 283 (1997). Apparently, with respect to the Netherlands, the Convention has only been accepted "for the Kingdom in Europe." *Id.*

123. Article 21. *See* Cour d'appel Paris, fre ch., Judgment of Nov. 3, 1993, 1994 J.D.I. 148, 153–56, note Mariel Revillard. *See generally* Cass. civ., fre ch., Dec. 13, 1994, 1995 Rev. crit. D.P. I 321, note Mariel Revillard (in France, Convention applies to persons married on September 1, 1992, or thereafter). While countries have the power, pursuant to article 21, to impose the Convention on persons married earlier, none of the countries to which the Convention applies have done so. Cour d'appel Paris, lre ch., Nov. 3, 1993, 1994 J.D.I. 149, 154, note Mariel Revillard. This actually further complicates the choice of law picture.

124. Article 2. This represents a dramatic change from the earlier Hague Convention of 1905 on the Law Applicable to the Personal and Patrimonial Consequences of Marriage. *See supra* text accompanying note 121.

125. Article 3.

126. *See generally* Schoenblum, *supra* note 3, § 15.07.

127. Article 3 (flush paragraph after "3").

128. Article 4.

1. that country has made a declaration that its law should apply to its common national spouses;[129]
2. that country, although not a party to the convention, applies its internal law; the spouses had their first habitual residence after marriage in a country making the declaration referred to above; or, though not party to the convention, the country follows the nationality principle;[130] or
3. the spouses do not establish their first habitual residence after marriage in the same state.[131]

The spouses are also given the opportunity to agree after marriage to a governing law. However, their choices are limited to the internal law of the state of which either is a national[132] or is an habitual resident at the time of designation.[133] With respect to immovables, the same approach as in article 3 is followed. The spouses may designate the law of the situs. They are not required to make this choice as to all immovables. Finally, they can also indicate that immovables acquired in the future will be subject to situs law.[134]

The convention leaves unanswered which law determines whether the spouses can change the governing law. In one case, a couple who had married and lived in Cuba for many years settled in France, and both became French nationals.[135] The question raised was whether the governing law could be changed from Cuban to French law. Cuban law bars any postmarital change in the law governing the matrimonial property regime. Ordinarily, under the classical French approach, this would have barred a change of controlling law.[136] As a result of its ratification of the Convention, that limitation was held no longer to apply in France. The court assumed that French law allowed a change in the law of the matrimonial regime.[137] Still largely unsettled is the question of which law determines whether

---

129. Articles 4:1 and 5. For example, the Netherlands has made such a declaration. *See infra* text accompanying notes 150–152. There is an exception to the application of this national law if the spouses have been habitual residents of another state for five years prior to their marriage and that state has not made the same declaration or does not apply the nationality principle under its own private international rules.

130. Article 4:2.

131. Article 4:3.

132. Article 6:1.

133. Article 6:2.

134. Article 6 (flush paragraph after "2"). This provision refers to the "law" of the place where the immovables are situated. Since it does not expressly refer to that state's internal law, it may include the conflicts law of the situs jurisdiction. This is left unclear by the Convention. It is not addressed in the accompanying report either. *See* Droz, *supra* note 2, at 357, 359–60.

135. *See* Cour d'appel Paris, fre ch., Nov. 3, 1993, 1994 J.D.I. 148, note Mariel Revillard.

136. *See supra* note 13.

137. As urged by Mariel Revillard (*see supra* note 135), any other result could severely limit the significance of French ratification of the Convention since many countries follow the immutability principle. Indeed, another commentator has described a reference to the original governing law as "not applicable, by definition . . . ." *See* Cour d'appel Chambery, June 20, 1995, 1996 J.D.I. 663, 669, note Eric Kerckhove (Fr.). Yet how can the Convention allow for a change in choice of law but not provide for a change in the matrimonial property regime? Kerckhove argues that it must be implied.

the Convention will apply. If Cuban law controlled, no change could be made. If an automatic change in law is brought about by article 7 of the Convention, so that French law applied, then what about France's requirement under article 1397 of the French Civil Code that a change in regime can only be accomplished after two years? Does the Convention require reference to these internal law requirements? Even if so, should the two-year period be counted from the time of the automatic change under the Convention or retroactively from the date of the marriage? These issues raise difficulties that have not yet been conclusively decided. In the case under consideration, however, the court seemed to bypass them, simply allowing for a change in the law.[138]

Suppose the parties move to another state, never having designated a governing law. With respect to assets subsequently acquired,[139] the new habitual residence will govern if:

1. the parties are or become nationals of the new habitual residence;
2. this has been their habitual residence for ten years;
3. at the time of the marriage, their common nationality applied because they did not have a common habitual residence at the time.[140]

Relations with third persons are generally determined by the applicable law under the Convention. Nevertheless, a contracting state can protect a third person or a spouse, if habitually resident there, by imposing publication requirements or other safeguards.[141] The same type of rule is applied with regard to the state in which an immovable is situated.[142]

As to form, the designation of a choice of law must be explicitly stated in writing or be implied necessarily from the other provisions of a marriage contract.[143] The form of the express stipulation must conform with the internal law of the stipulated governing law. Alternatively, it may satisfy the requirements of the internal law of the place where the contract was entered. However, in all events, the designation of a choice of law must be in writing and be dated and signed by

Id. at 668. Droz argues for a two-stage process. First, the Convention, beginning with article 10, tells how the change of law is accomplished. Second, the conditions of the new law must be observed for a change in the matrimonial regime. *See id. See also* Georges A. Droz, *Les Nouvelles regles de conflit francaises en matiere de regimes matrimoniaux*, 1992 Rev. Crit. D.P. I 631 no. 41.

138. *See supra* note 135. Indeed, the parties were not technically covered by the Convention, thus suggesting the possibility of its application by willing courts to spouses married prior to September 1, 1992, permitting those who have a domicile in France and French nationality to change the governing law.

139. Article 8.

140. Article 7.

141. *See, e.g., infra* note 152 (relating to special Dutch legislation). For publication generally, *see* SCHOENBLUM, *supra* note 3, § 10.24[G].

142. Article 9.

143. An example of an implied choice would be when the contract refers to a specific provision in the governing civil code allowing such a choice. *See* Droz, *supra* note 2, at 371. *See generally* art. 11.

both spouses.[144] The marriage contract itself must be valid formally under the internal law of the state governing the matrimonial property regime. Alternatively, however, it may be valid under the place where the contract was entered into. In either event, the bare minimum is that it, too, must be "in writing, dated and signed by both spouses."[145]

While the parties generally have the freedom to specify their choice consistent with the provisions of the convention, no designation need be given effect in a contracting state if "it is manifestly incompatible with public policy ('ordre public')." The precise parameters of this concept are unclear, although it roughly approximates the public policy exception in the United States.[146]

If a change of law is effected automatically under article 7 of the Convention, the question arises whether the internal rules of the new law control as to the procedure for accomplishing a change in matrimonial property regime. For example, will a notarized document or court procedure be required? Alternatively, does it occur automatically under the terms of the Convention? This question remains unanswered. However, some French jurisprudence suggests a bypassing of internal law formalities.[147]

A series of Convention provisions relate to the problems raised by a country with autonomous systems of law, such as the United States. If the country has its own rules for determining which territorial unit's law should apply, those rules control. If there are no such rules, then the last common habitual residence of each spouse controls.[148] This common habitual residence need not have existed at the same time. For example, if a man from New York marries a woman from Texas, and the man attended the University of California at Los Angeles from 1960 to 1963 and the woman attended the University of California at Berkeley from 1968 to 1970, then California law will control, even though they have both long since left the state and were actually there at different times.[149] Of course, the spouses would be free to designate a controlling law under the terms of the convention.

The ratification of the Convention has created a particularly confusing situation in the Netherlands regarding the choice of law question. In large part, this has been fostered by the fact that the Netherlands had previously ratified the 1905 Convention.[150] The Hoge Raad (Supreme Court) held in 1981 that the former Convention will continue to apply to persons married prior to August 23, 1977, when

144. Article 13.

145. Article 12.

146. For a discussion of this concept in the context of other Hague Conventions, see SCHOENBLUM, *supra* note 3, § 15.07[K]. For the increasing propensity in certain countries to override the otherwise valid choice of law by asserting the police power exception, see *supra* text accompanying note 67.

147. *See* Cour d'appel Paris, 1re ch., Nov. 3, 1993, 1994 J.D.I. 148, note Mariel Revillard; Cour d'appel Chambery, ch. civ., June 20, 1995, 1996 J.D.I. 668–69, note Eric Kerckhove (Fr.), for a discussion of the question, though not directly pertinent to the case itself.

148. Article 16.

149. Droz, *supra* note 2, at 375.

150. *See supra* notes 119–120.

the Netherlands repudiated the earlier convention. Since the new Convention was not signed until October 10, 1988, and did not enter into force until September 1, 1992, there was a gap of several years. This period, as well as the prior period, to the extent that the 1905 Convention does not apply, is governed by the principles set forth in the *Chelouche* case.[151] The Hoge Raad (Supreme Court) held that these principles apply retroactively, except where the 1905 Convention still applies. As for the 1992 Convention, the Netherlands enacted the *Wet Conflictenrecht Huwelijksvermogens* regime, which implements the Convention's choice of law rules, retains the nationality principle in certain cases pursuant to article 5 of the convention, and introduces certain additional rules relating to third parties.[152]

---

151. *See supra* note 40.
152. *See* DE BOER & KOTTING, *supra* note 40, at 219, 231 & n.37.

PART IV

Special Tax Considerations

7

U.S. Taxation of Foreign Trusts, Trusts with Non-U.S. Grantors and Their U.S. Beneficiaries*

Ellen K. Harrison
Elyse G. Kirschner
Carlyn S. McCaffrey

The Small Business Job Protection Act of 1996 (the 1996 Act)[1] made significant changes to the rules applicable to foreign trusts and trusts established by non-U.S. persons. These rules were intended to prevent tax avoidance through the use of foreign trusts and the exploitation of the grantor trust rules. The 1996 Act imposes an array of reporting requirements and harsh penalties on those who fail to comply with these requirements; increases the interest charge imposed on taxes paid on distributions of accumulated income from foreign trusts; treats loans of cash from foreign trusts as distributions; expands the kinds of gifts that can be treated as indirect transfers from foreign trusts; limits the circumstances in which a non-U.S. person will be treated as the owner of a trust under the grantor trust rules; and allows certain gifts to be recharacterized as taxable distributions from corporations, partnerships, or trusts. Curiously, the 1996 Act encourages the creation of foreign trusts by its adoption of a

---

1. The Small Business Job Protection Act of 1996 was enacted on August 20, 1996. Pub. L. No. 104-188, 110 Stat. 1755 (1996).

set of criteria for foreignness that is both more objective than the criteria formerly used and biased in favor of foreign status.

The penalties applicable to U.S. persons who fail to timely report their gratuitous transfers to foreign trusts and the reporting requirements applicable to such persons and to the U.S. beneficiaries of foreign trusts have been significantly enhanced by the Hiring Incentives to Restore Employment Act of 2010 (the 2010 HIRE Act).[2] The 2010 HIRE Act also treats the uncompensated use of assets owned by a trust as a deemed distribution.

This chapter discusses how to create foreign trusts; examines their exposure and the exposure of their U.S. grantors and beneficiaries to U.S. income tax; describes the reporting requirements imposed on their creators, their beneficiaries, and the trusts themselves; explains the grantor trust rules applicable to non-U.S. persons and immigrants; and covers anti-avoidance provisions that require reporting of foreign gifts, redefine who is the grantor, and recharacterize purported gifts from "intermediaries" and from partnerships, foreign corporations, and certain trusts. In addition to explaining these rules, it also considers the extent to which foreign trusts continue to be useful planning tools for U.S. persons.

I. How to Create a Foreign Trust

A. How to Determine Whether a Trust Is a Foreign Trust

1. Before the 1996 Act

Before the 1996 Act, there was no clear standard for determining a trust's nationality. The former statutory definition consisted only of a statement that a foreign trust is a trust

> the income of which, from sources without the United States which is not effectively connected with the conduct of a trade or business within the United States, is not includible in gross income under subtitle A.[3]

This statement is merely descriptive of the consequences of foreign trust status and gives no guidance as to how to determine its existence.[4]

Judicial and administrative authority partially filled the definitional void by establishing a test that required weighing of a trust's foreign contacts against its

---

2. The Hiring Incentives to Restore Employment Act was enacted on March 18, 2010, Pub. L. No. 111-147.

3. Code § 7701(a)(31) before amendment by the 1996 Act. References in this chapter to "Code §" are to sections of the Internal Revenue Code of 1986, *as amended* (the Code). References to "Treas. Reg. §" are to sections of the Treasury regulations promulgated thereunder.

4. Curiously, the domestic or foreign status of an estate continues to be governed by the same provision. Code § 7701(a)(31)(A).

U.S. contacts.[5] The guidance these authorities provided was of little help in determining the foreign or domestic status of trusts with both foreign and domestic contacts.

2. After the 1996 Act

Code § 7701(a)(30)(E) and (31)(B) attempts to provide clarity, but in a way that creates a strong statutory bias in favor of foreignness.

Under Code § 7701(a)(30)(E) and (31)(B), a trust is a foreign trust unless both of the following conditions are satisfied: (1) a court or courts within the United States must be able to exercise primary supervision over administration of the trust; and (2) one or more U.S. persons have the authority to control all substantial decisions of the trust.[6]

Under this test, a trust may be a foreign trust even if it was created by a U.S. person, all of its assets are located in the United States, and all of its beneficiaries are U.S. persons. It only takes one foreign person who has control over one "substantial" type of trust decision. Consider the following example.

> ***Example 1:*** Jenny, a U.S. citizen and resident of New York, created a trust for the benefit of her children, all of whom are U.S. citizens and residents. She named the Gotham Trust Company, a New York corporation, and her brother Pat, a citizen and resident of Ireland, as co-trustees. The trust instrument gave Pat the right to determine the ages at which each of the children would receive his or her share of the trust fund. It directed that the trust funds be maintained in the United States in the custody of Gotham and that the laws of the State of New York were to govern the trust's administration.

Despite its significant U.S. contacts, the law will treat Jenny's trust as a foreign trust since an obviously substantial decision is controlled by a foreign fiduciary.[7] This definition fulfills the goal of the U.S. Department of Treasury (Treasury Department or Treasury), which was to

5. *See, e.g.*, B. W. Jones Trust v. Comm'r, 132 F.2d 914 (4th Cir. 1943); First Nat'l City Bank v. IRS, 271 F.2d 616 (2d Cir. 1959), *cert. denied*, 361 U.S. 948 (1960); Rev. Rul. 60-181, 1960-1 C.B. 257.

6. The Administration's explanation of this rule issued in connection with its original proposal offered some protection from this harsh rule by expressing an intention that the Internal Revenue Service would allow a trust "a reasonable period of time to adjust for inadvertent changes in fiduciaries (e.g., a U.S. trustee dies or abruptly resigns when a trust has two U.S. fiduciaries and one foreign fiduciary)." U.S. Dep't of Treasury, *General Explanations of the Administration's Revenue Proposals* 25 (Feb. 7, 1995). The Joint Committee Explanation offers similar comfort. Joint Comm. on Taxation, *General Explanation of Tax Legislation Enacted in the 104th Congress* (JCS-12-6), Dec. 18, 1996, at 274. The Administration's intention is reflected in Treas. Reg. § 301.7701-7(d)(2). The 1996 Act's version of the definition referred to "fiduciaries" rather than persons. Section 1601(i)(3)(A) of the Taxpayer Relief Act of 1997 changed the word "fiduciaries" to "persons."

7. A trust that is treated as a foreign trust for federal tax purposes under the new rule may continue to be a local trust for state income tax purposes. For example, although Jenny's trust may pay no federal income tax, it will continue to be subject to New York State income tax because it was created by a resident of New York and has a New York trustee. N.Y. Tax Law § 605(b)(3).

increase the flexibility of settlors and trust administrators to decide where to locate and in what assets to invest. For example, if the location of the administration of the trust were no longer a relevant criterion, settlors of foreign trusts would be able to choose whether to administer the trusts in the United States or abroad based on non-tax considerations.[8]

It is understood that one of the principal objectives Treasury sought to achieve by implementing this new definition was to level the competitive playing field for trust business between U.S. and foreign institutions. Under the former definition, a foreign person who might have preferred to use a U.S. financial institution as trustee was generally reluctant to do so because of the likelihood that the trust would have been taxed as a U.S. domestic trust. A foreign person can now easily use a U.S. financial institution without creating a domestic trust.[9]

Although Code § 7701(a)(30)(E) and (31)(B) establish a more objective method for determining whether a trust is domestic or foreign, they fall short of establishing the bright-line test that was intended.

(a) The Treasury Regulations. Some clarity is provided by Treas. Reg. § 301.7701-7, which is applicable to trusts for taxable years ending after February 2, 1999.[10] The regulations provide that a trust is a U.S. person on any day that the trust meets both the "court test" and the "control test."

(b) The Court Test. The court test is the regulatory interpretation of the statutory requirement that "a court or courts within the United States is able to exercise primary supervision over administration of the trust." The final Treasury Regulations (the "7701 Regulations") provide a safe harbor for the court test, under which a trust satisfies the court test if the following three requirements are met:

1. The trust instrument does not direct that the trust be administered outside the United States;
2. The trust in fact is administered exclusively in the United States; and
3. The trust is not subject to an automatic migration provision described in Treas. Reg. § 301.7701-7(c)(4)(ii).

According to the preamble to the 7701 Regulations, the Internal Revenue Service (the IRS) included the court test safe harbor in the 7701 Regulations because it recognized the difficulty in determining whether the courts of a particular state

8. Treasury Dep't, *General Explanation of the Administration's Fiscal Year 1996 Revenue Proposals* 25 (Feb. 7, 1995).

9. This understanding is based on conversations with David K. Sutherland, former Associate International Tax Counsel and a principal draftsperson of the new statutory definition.

10. Treas. Reg. § 301.7701-7 may be relied on by trusts for taxable years beginning after December 31, 1996, and by trusts whose trustees have elected under § 1907(a)(3)(B) of the 1996 Act to apply Code § 7701(a)(30) and (31) to the trusts for taxable years ending after August 20, 1996. *See also* Notice 96-65.

would assert primary supervision over the administration of a trust if that trust had never appeared before any court in that state.

Treas. Reg. § 301.7701-7(c)(3) provides the following definitions critical to the application of the court test:

1. "Court" includes federal as well as state and local courts.
2. "United States" means the fifty states and the District of Columbia.
3. "Is able to exercise" means "that a court has or would have the authority under applicable law to render orders or judgments resolving issues concerning administration of the trust."
4. "Primary supervision" means the judicial "authority to determine substantially all issues regarding the administration of the entire trust . . . notwithstanding the fact that another court has jurisdiction over a trustee, a beneficiary, or trust property."
5. "Administration" means "the carrying out of the duties imposed by the terms of the trust instrument and applicable law, including maintaining the books and records of the trust, filing tax returns, managing and investing the assets of the trust, defending the trust from suits by creditors, and determining the amount and timing of distributions."

Treas. Reg. § 301.7701-7(c)(4) describes four types of trusts that satisfy the court test and one that does not. The four types of trusts that satisfy the court test are:

1. Trusts that are registered in a court within the United States by an authorized fiduciary under a state statute substantially similar to the Uniform Probate Code, art. VII, Trust Administration, now superseded by the Uniform Trust Code, and withdrawn from the UPC in 2010.[11]
2. Testamentary trusts, if all fiduciaries of the trust have been qualified as trustees by a court within the United States.
3. Inter vivos trusts, if the fiduciaries and/or beneficiaries take steps with a court in the United States to cause the administration of the trust to be subject to the primary supervision of such court.
4. Trusts that are subject to primary supervision with respect to their administration by both a U.S. court and a foreign court.

This list of trusts that satisfy the court test is not intended to be an exclusive list. Thus, other types of trust may also satisfy the test.

The Regulations specify that a trust whose trust instrument contains a provision that would cause the trust to migrate from the United States if a U.S. court

11. Section 7-201 of the Uniform Probate Code gave exclusive jurisdiction over the internal affairs of a trust to the courts of a state in which a trust is registered. Sixteen states have adopted the Uniform Probate Code in its entirety (in some cases with significant modifications). They are Alaska, Arizona, Colorado, Florida, Hawaii, Idaho, Maine, Michigan, Minnesota, Montana, Nebraska, New Mexico, North Dakota, South Carolina, South Dakota, and Utah. 8 U.L.A. 1 (West Supp. 1998).

attempted to assert jurisdiction over it or otherwise attempted to supervise its administration, either directly or indirectly does not satisfy the court test. However, a trust will not fail the court test solely because "the trust instrument provides that the trust will migrate from the United States only in the case of foreign invasion of the United States or widespread confiscation or nationalization of property in the United States."[12]

(c) The Control Test. The control test is the regulatory explanation of the statutory requirement that "one or more United States persons have the authority to control all substantial decisions of the trust." Treas. Reg. § 301.7701-7(d)(1)(ii) provides the following critical definitions:

1. "United States person" means a U.S. person within the meaning of Code § 7701(a)(30).
2. "Substantial decisions" means all decisions other than ministerial decisions that any person, whether acting in a fiduciary capacity or not, is authorized or required to make under the terms of the trust instrument or applicable law. Such decisions include, but are not limited to:
   a. the timing and amount of distributions;
   b. the selection of beneficiaries;
   c. the power to determine whether receipts are allocable to income or principal;
   d. the power to terminate the trust;
   e. the power to compromise, arbitrate, or abandon claims of the trust and to decide whether to sue on behalf of or defend suits against the trust;
   f. the power to remove, add, or replace a trustee;
   g. the power to appoint a successor trustee (even if such power is not accompanied by an unrestricted power to remove a trustee) unless the appointment power is limited in such a way that it cannot be exercised in a manner that would alter the trust's residency; and
   h. the power to make investment decisions.[13]
3. Ministerial decisions "include decisions regarding details such as the bookkeeping, the collection of rents, and the execution of investment decisions" made by the fiduciaries.
4. "Control" means "the power, by vote or otherwise, to make all of the substantial decisions of the trust, with no other person having the power to veto any of the substantial decisions."

12. Treas. Reg. § 301.7701-7(c)(4)(ii).

13. If a U.S. person hires an investment adviser on behalf of the trust and can terminate at will such adviser's power to make investment decisions, the U.S. person will be treated as retaining control over the investment decisions made by the investment adviser. Treas. Reg. § 301.7701-7(d)(1)(ii)(J).

Certain employee benefit and investment trusts will be deemed to satisfy the control test so long as U.S. *fiduciaries* control all of the substantial decisions to be made by trust fiduciaries.[14]

(d) Reversing an Unintended Loss of U.S. Status. If a trustee whose status caused a trust to be treated as a U.S. (or foreign) trust inadvertently ceases to be a trustee or ceases to be a U.S. (or foreign) person (e.g., through death, incapacity, resignation, change in residence, or change in trust powers), the regulations provide the trust twelve months from the date of such cessation to make whatever changes are necessary to give control over all substantial decisions of the trust to persons such that the trust's U.S. or foreign status will be maintained.[15] If the change is made within this period of time, the trust will be treated as having maintained its status even during the time when one or more substantial decisions were not controlled by U.S. (or foreign) persons. If the change is not made within this time period, the trust will be treated as having lost its status on the date the trustee lost her status or ceased to serve as trustee. The appropriate district director has the power to extend this time period for reasonable cause.

B. Creation of and Transfer of Property to a Foreign Trust by a U.S. Person

1. Tax Consequences of Creation and Transfer

No tax consequences are imposed on a U.S. person on account of her creation of a foreign trust, but, under some circumstances, income tax may be imposed on her transfer of property to a foreign trust, whether that trust was created by her or by another. Code § 684[16] treats a transfer of property by a U.S. person to a foreign trust as a sale or exchange for an amount equal to the fair market value of the property transferred and requires that the transferor recognize gain (but not loss) on the excess of such fair market value over her basis in the transferred property. This rule does not apply to the extent that any person (including the transferor) is treated as the owner of such trust under Code § 671.

2. Tax Treatment during the Life of a U.S. Creator or Transferor

(a) Grantor Trust Treatment under § 679. If a foreign trust to which a U.S. person has made any direct or indirect gratuitous transfers has one or more U.S.

---

14. Such employee benefit trusts include qualified trusts described in Code § 401(a); trusts described in Code § 457(g); trusts that are individual retirement accounts described in Code § 408(a); trusts that are individual retirement accounts described in § 408(k) or (p); trusts that are Roth IRAs described in Code § 408A; trusts that are educational retirement accounts described in Code § 530; trusts that are voluntary employees' beneficiary associations described in Code § 501(c)(9); group trusts described in Rev. Rul. 81-100; investment trusts classified as a trust under Treas. Reg. § 301.7701-4 provided certain conditions are met; and such additional categories of trusts designated by the IRS.

15. Treas. Reg. § 301.7701-7(d)(2).

16. Code § 684 was added to the Code by the 1997 Act.

beneficiaries, Code § 679 treats the trust as a so-called "grantor trust" owned by the U.S. person within the meaning of Code § 671 to the extent of her transfer.[17]

A transfer is not a gratuitous transfer if it was made for full fair market value. For purposes of determining whether full fair market value has been received, if the transferor (or, in certain cases, the guarantor) is the grantor or a beneficiary of the trust (or a person related within the meaning of Code § 643(i)(2)(B) to any grantor or beneficiary of the trust), any obligation issued by the trust (or by certain related persons) is disregarded, except as provided in the regulations.[18] Treasury Regulations provide that certain "qualified obligations" will be recognized as consideration.[19] An obligation is a qualified obligation only if:

> (i) The obligation is reduced to writing by an express written agreement; (ii) The term of the obligation does not exceed five years (for purposes of determining the term of an obligation, the obligation's maturity date is the last possible date that the obligation can be outstanding under the terms of the obligation); (iii) All payments on the obligation are denominated in U.S. dollars; (iv) The yield to maturity is not less than 100 percent of the applicable Federal rate and not greater than 130 percent of the applicable Federal rate (the applicable Federal rate for an obligation is the applicable Federal rate in effect under section 1274(d) for the day on which the obligation is issued, as published in the Internal Revenue Bulletin); (v) The U.S. transferor extends the period for assessment of any income tax or transfer tax attributable to the transfer and any consequential income tax changes for each year that the obligation is outstanding, to a date not earlier than three years after the maturity date of the obligation (this extension is not necessary if the maturity date of the obligation does not extend beyond the end of the U.S. person's taxable year and is paid within such period); when properly executed and filed, such an agreement is deemed to be consented to by the Service Center Director or the Assistant Commissioner (International) for purposes of § 301.6501(c)-1(d) of this chapter; and (vi) The U.S. transferor reports the status of the loan, including principal and interest payments, on Form 3520 for each year that the loan is outstanding.[20]

---

17. Code § 679(a)(1). This section does not apply to trusts that are described in Code § 6048(a)(3)(B)(ii). Trusts that are described in Code § 6048(a)(3)(B)(ii) are either trusts that are described in Code §§ 402(b), 404(a)(4), or 404A (relating to deferred compensation trusts) or trusts determined by the Treasury to be described in § 501(a)(3) (relating to charitable trusts). The regulations under Code § 679 have expanded the protection for transfers to charitable trusts to apply to any foreign trust described in § 501(c)(3) determined without regard to whether the Treasury has determined it is so described and determined without regard to Code § 508(a). Treas. Reg. § 1.679-4(a)(3).

18. Code § 679(a)(3)(A)(i).

19. Treas. Reg. § 1.679-4(d).

20. *Id.*; *see also* Notice 97-34 (discussed further below).

Section 679 applies to both direct and indirect transfers to foreign trusts. If a U.S. person transfers property to another person and that person transfers property to a foreign trust, the second transfer will be treated as an indirect transfer by the U.S. person to the foreign trust if the transfers were part of a plan, the principal purposes of which is to avoid U.S. income tax. The regulations deem the principal purpose of tax avoidance to exist if the U.S. person is related to a beneficiary of the foreign trust (or has another relationship with a beneficiary that establishes a reasonable basis for the transferor making a gratuitous transfer to the foreign trust) and the U.S. person cannot demonstrate that (1) the other person (the intermediary) has a relationship with a beneficiary that establishes a reasonable basis for the intermediary making a gratuitous transfer to the trust; (2) the intermediary acted independently of the U.S. person; (3) the intermediary is not an agent of the U.S. person; and (4) the intermediary timely complied with the reporting requirements of § 6048 of the Code.[21] According to the regulations, if a bank loans money to a foreign trust and the loan would not have been made unless the U.S. person had deposited funds with the bank, the bank is an intermediary.[22]

Section 679 applies if a U.S. person makes a constructive transfer to a foreign trust.[23] A constructive transfer includes an assumption or satisfaction of a foreign trust's obligation to a third party. A U.S. person who is related to a beneficiary of a foreign trust and who guarantees a loan to the trust is treated as making a transfer to the foreign trust equal to the portion of the obligation guaranteed.[24] A guarantee includes any arrangement under which a person, directly or indirectly, assures on a conditional or unconditional basis the payment of another person's obligation. A commitment to contribute capital to the debtor or otherwise maintain its financial viability is a guarantee even if the arrangement is not a legally binding obligation or is subject to a contingency that has not yet occurred.[25]

Transfers by U.S. persons to entities owned by a foreign trust are treated as transfers to the foreign trust followed by a transfer by the trust to the entity unless the U.S. person is not related to a trust beneficiary or the U.S. person demonstrates that the transfer is attributable to the U.S. person's ownership interest in the entity.[26] For example, if a foreign trust and a U.S. person jointly fund a corporation, each taking back stock proportionate to their transfers, Code § 679 is not applicable.

A trust is treated as having a U.S. beneficiary in any year in which income or corpus may be paid to or for the benefit of, or accumulated for future distribution to or for the benefit of, a U.S. person, or in any year in which, if the trust terminated, any part of the income or corpus could be paid to or for the benefit of a U.S.

21. Treas. Reg. § 1.679-3(c)(2)(i).
22. *Id.* § 1.679-3(c)(5), Example 3.
23. *Id.* § 1.679-3(d).
24. *Id.* § 1.679-3(e)(4).
25. *Id.*
26. Treas. Reg. § 1.679-3(f).

person.[27] According to the regulations, Code § 679 applies even if no distribution may be made to a U.S. person until after the grantor's death or to a person who is a U.S. person until he or she ceases to be a U.S. person.[28] If the terms of the trust permit the trust to be amended to make a U.S. person a beneficiary, the trust will be treated as having a U.S. beneficiary.[29] For this purpose, the term "U.S. person" includes a controlled foreign corporation as defined in Code § 957(a), a foreign partnership with one or more U.S. partners, and a trust or estate, one or more beneficiaries of which are U.S. persons.[30]

A beneficiary who first became a U.S. person more than five years after a gratuitous transfer to a trust will not be treated as a U.S. person for purposes of that transfer.[31] The exception is not applicable if the person at any previous time was a U.S. person.[32]

The test for determining whether a foreign trust has a U.S. beneficiary is done on a year-by-year basis. If a foreign trust has no U.S. beneficiaries in one year and acquires one in a subsequent year, the U.S. gratuitous transferor will be required to include in her gross income in such year an amount equal to all the undistributed net income of the trust at the end of the prior year that is attributed to her transfer or transfers to the trust.[33] Code § 679 will cease to apply on January 1 of the year following the year when it no longer has U.S. beneficiaries. The grantor will be treated as transferring assets to the foreign trust on January 1, and Code § 684 will require the transferor to realize income and gain as if the assets had been sold.[34]

(b) Hiring Incentives to Restore Employment Act of 2010. The 2010 HIRE Act contains the following amendments to § 679, most of which seem to do nothing more than codify certain regulatory provisions designed to increase the likelihood that a trust created by a U.S. person will be treated as having a U.S. beneficiary in any particular taxable year.

1. Section 531(a) of the 2010 HIRE Act amends § 679(c)(1) to provide that income will be treated as accumulated for the benefit of a U.S. person in a particular year even if the U.S. person's interest in the trust is contingent on a future event. The section replicates the provision in Treas. Reg. § 1.679-2(a)(2)(i), which provides that the determination of whether income or corpus may be paid or accumulated to or for the benefit of a U.S. person is made "without regard to whether a U.S. person's interest in the trust

27. Code § 679(c)(1).
28. Treas. Reg. § 1.679-2(a)(2), Examples 4 and 13.
29. Treas. Reg. § 1.679-2(a)(4)(ii)(A).
30. Code § 679(c)(2).
31. *Id.* § 679(c)(3).
32. Treas. Reg. § 1.679-2(a)(3), Example 2.
33. Code § 679(b).
34. Treas. Reg. § 1.679-2(c)(2).

income or corpus is contingent on a future event." The prior regulations under Section 679 also contain an exception for contingent interests that are so remote as to be negligible.[35] It is unclear whether this exception will apply to the new Code provision.

2. Section 531(b) amends § 679(c) to provide that if any person has the discretion to make a distribution from the trust to or for the benefit of any person, the trust will be treated as having a U.S. beneficiary unless the class in whose favor the power can be exercised is specifically identified and no member of the class is a U.S. person in such year. This provision states the rule that is illustrated by an example in the regulations. The example concludes that a trust will be treated as having a U.S. beneficiary when the trustee has the discretion to distribute income to any person who is studying ancient Greek because it is possible that a U.S. person will receive trust income.[36]
3. Section 531(c) amends § 679(c) to provide that a trust will be treated as having a U.S. beneficiary if any U.S. transferor to the trust is involved in any agreement, written, oral or otherwise, that may result in trust income or corpus being paid or accumulated to or for the benefit of a U.S. person. Because this provision requires the involvement of the transferor in the agreement, it appears to be a narrower application of the rule of Treas. Reg. § 1.679-2(a)(4), which states that all written and oral agreements and understandings relating to the trust are to be taken into account in determining whether a trust has a U.S. beneficiary. The technical explanation of the HIRE Act issued by the Joint Committee on Taxation, however, broadens the provision by stating that it is assumed "that a transferor of property to the trust is generally directly or indirectly involved with agreements regarding the accumulation or disposition of the income and corpus of the trust."[37]
4. Section 532 of the 2010 HIRE Act amends § 679 to permit the IRS to treat a foreign trust to which a U.S. person has made a transfer as having a U.S. beneficiary unless the transferor submits to the IRS such information as it requires and demonstrates to Treasury's satisfaction that the trust has no U.S. beneficiary.[38]
5. Section 533 of the 2010 HIRE Act amends § 679 to provide that a loan of cash or marketable securities or the use of any other property from a foreign trust to a U.S. person "shall be treated as paid or accumulated for the

35. *Id.* § 1.679-2(a)(2)(ii).

36. *Id.* § 1.679-2(a)(2)(iii), Example 10.

37. Joint Committee on Taxation, *Technical Explanation of the Revenue Provisions Contained in Senate Amendment 3310, the "Hiring Incentives to Restore Employment Act," Under Consideration by the Senate,* (JCX-4-10), Feb. 23, 2010, at 72 [hereinafter the Joint Committee's HIRE Act Explanation].

38. This new provision appears to supersede the normal rule of § 7491 that puts the burden of proof as to factual issues on the Internal Revenue Service when a taxpayer introduces credible evidence with respect to a factual issue and satisfies certain record-keeping requirements.

benefit of a United States person, whether or not the person to whom the loan is made is a trust beneficiary unless the U.S. borrower pays market value interest or rent." Presumably, this means that the trust would be treated as having a U.S. beneficiary. If such a loan is made to a person who is not a beneficiary, the loan would contravene the trust terms. This new rule is similar to Treas. Reg. § 1.679-2(a)(4)(ii)(C), which provides that, "[if] the parties to the trust ignore the terms of the trust instrument, or if it is reasonably expected that they will do so, all benefits that have been, or are reasonably expected to be, provided to a U.S. person must be taken into account."

3. Tax Treatment at the Death of U.S. "Owner" of a Foreign Trust

The death of a U.S. person who was treated as the owner of a foreign trust during her lifetime may be a gain recognition event under Code § 684. Until the U.S. person's death, she was the owner of the property for U.S. income tax purposes under Code § 671. Her death terminates the trust's grantor trust status. Treas. Reg. § 1.1001-2(c), Example 5, treats the termination of grantor trust status as a transfer of the trust property by the grantor.[39] If this regulation is applied to Code § 684, and if it applies to terminations caused by death, the deceased U.S. person will be treated as having made a transfer to a foreign trust at the moment of her death. Treasury Regulations under Code § 684 confirm this tax treatment for the U.S. owner, except that the regulations provide that the transfer to the foreign trust will be treated as having occurred *immediately before* the U.S. owner's death.[40] Treasury Regulation § 1.684-3(c) provides an exception to this gain recognition rule in instances where the trust property is included in the U.S. owner's gross estate for U.S. estate tax purposes and the basis of the property in the hands of the foreign trust is determined under Code § 1014(a).

It may be possible to avoid the risk that gain will be recognized upon the death of a foreign trust's U.S. owner by giving a U.S. person, perhaps a U.S. trust, the right to withdraw the foreign trust's property immediately before the death of the U.S. person.[41] The withdrawal power would give the deceased U.S. person the protection of Code § 684(b).[42] Code § 684(b) excepts transfers to trusts to the extent such trusts are owned by any person (other than a foreign nongrantor trust) under Code § 671.

A transfer by the will of a U.S. decedent of property to a foreign nongrantor trust generally will not be subject to Code § 684 if Code §1014 applies in the year of the decedent's death. This is so because the estate will receive the property from the decedent with a basis adjustment under Code § 1014. If the estate transfers

39. *See also* Madorin v. Comm'r, 84 T.C. 667 (1985), and Rev. Rul. 77-402, 1977-2 C.B. 222.

40. Treas. Reg. § 1.684-2(e), Example 2.

41. A trust will be treated as an owner of another trust to the extent it has the power to withdraw that trust's assets. Treas. Reg. § 1.671-2(e)(6), Example 8.

42. See Treas. Reg. § 1.684.2(e), Example 2, which implies that the death of a U.S. grantor will not trigger Code § 684 if, as of the date of death, another person is treated as the owner of the trust.

the property before any post-death appreciation occurs, there will be no gain to which Code § 684 can apply. Even if there were gain, to the extent the distribution carries out the gain to a foreign beneficiary, the gain should avoid U.S. tax.

4. Tax Treatment after Death of U.S. Person

After the death of the U.S. person who has made transfers to a foreign trust, the trust will no longer be subject to Code § 679 and will be treated as a foreign non-grantor trust.

5. Reporting Requirements

A U.S. person who creates a foreign trust or who transfers property to a foreign trust, other than a transfer in exchange for consideration equal to the full value of the transferred property, is required to report the creation or transfer on Form 3520.[43] For purposes of determining whether full consideration has been received, notes issued by the trust or related persons (or in certain cases guaranteed by the same) are to be disregarded to the same extent they are disregarded for purposes of Code § 679 (a)(3), as discussed above. Qualified obligations, as defined in Treas. Reg. § 1.679-4(d), will be treated as consideration, but an obligation will be treated as qualified only if reported.[44]

Form 3520 is due at the same time the U.S. person's income tax return is due for the year in which such creation or transfer took place. Failure to file may subject a transferor to a penalty equal to 35 percent of the amount transferred.[45] For reports required to be filed after December 31, 2009, the 2010 HIRE Act requires a minimum penalty of $10,000, not to exceed the gross reportable amount.[46]

A U.S. person who is treated as the owner, within the meaning of Code § 671, of a foreign trust is required to ensure that the trust files an annual return that sets forth a full accounting of all trust activities and operations for each year that she is treated as owner.[47] The 2010 HIRE Act added, for years beginning after March 18, 2010, a separate requirement that the U.S. owner of the foreign trust supply such information as the Treasury prescribes with respect to such trust.[48] The U.S. "owner" is required to disclose on Form 3520 the existence of the trust, its taxpayer identification number, the names of other persons who are considered "owners" of the trust, the Code section that causes the trust to be treated as owned by the U.S. person and others who are treated as owners, the country in which the trust was created, and the date of creation. Form 3520 is due at the same time the U.S. person's income tax return is due. The information required to be furnished by the trust must be disclosed on Form 3520-A, which is due on each March 15 following the year for which reporting is required. If Form 3520-A is not

43. Code § 6048(a); Notice 97-34, 1997-2 C.B. 422.
44. Treas. Reg. § 1.679-4(d)(1)(vi).
45. Code § 6677(a).
46. *Id.* § 6048(a).
47. *Id.* § 6048(b).
48. *Id.*

filed, the U.S. person who is treated as the owner may be liable for a penalty equal to 5 percent of the value of the trust assets that are treated as owned by her.[49]

The executor of the estate of a U.S. person who transfers property to a foreign trust at her death—who was treated as the owner of a foreign trust during her lifetime or whose estate includes, for estate tax purposes, any portion of a foreign trust—must report the death and the transfers on Form 3520.[50] Form 3520 is due at the same time the executor's income tax return is due for the year in which the decedent's death occurred. Failure to file may subject the executor to a penalty equal to 35 percent of the amount transferred.[51]

6. Treatment of Trusts That Become Foreign Trusts

(a) In General. If a U.S. trust with U.S. beneficiaries becomes a foreign trust during the life of a U.S. person who has made a gratuitous transfer to it, the trust and the U.S. person will be treated in the same manner they would have been treated under Code § 679 if the trust had been a foreign trust when the transfers were made.[52]

If a U.S. trust becomes a foreign trust (1) at a time when there is no living U.S. person who ever made a gratuitous transfers to it or if it has no U.S. beneficiaries and (2) if it is not treated as owned by another person within the meaning of Code § 671, the trust will be treated as having transferred all of its assets to a foreign trust immediately before becoming a foreign trust.[53] As a result, Code § 684(a) will treat it as having sold all of its assets for an amount equal to their fair market value. Gain is recognized on an asset by asset basis, but losses are not deductible.[54]

(b) Reporting Requirements. A U.S. trust that becomes a foreign trust is required to report its change of status on Form 3520.[55] Form 3520 is due at the same time as the trust's income tax return is due for the year in which the transfer took place. Failure to file may subject a trust to a penalty equal to 35 percent of the amount transferred.[56]

(c) Treatment of Distributions by U.S. Trusts to Foreign Trusts. When a U.S. trust transfers property to a foreign trust, unless the foreign trust is treated as owned by another person within the meaning of Code § 671, the transfer will be treated in the same manner as a transfer by an individual to a foreign trust. This means that the transfer will be treated as a sale or exchange and that the trust will be treated

49. *Id.* § 6677(b).
50. *Id.* § 6048(a).
51. *Id.* § 6677(a).
52. *Id.* § 679(a)(5).
53. *Id.* § 684(c).
54. Treas. Reg. § 1.684-1(a)(2).
55. Code § 6048(a).
56. *Id.* § 6677(a).

as having recognized gain equal to the excess of the fair market value of the property transferred over the trust's adjusted basis in the transferred property.

If, however, the transferee foreign trust is a beneficiary of the U.S. trust and the transfer is treated as a distribution to a beneficiary within the meaning of Code § 661(a), the application of Code § 684 will result in no income tax liability if the U.S. trust's capital gains are included in its distributable net income in the year of the distribution. This would be so because the U.S. trust would receive a distribution deduction equal to the amount of income recognized on the distribution.[57] Treas. Reg. § 1.643(a)(3) describes the rules for determining when a trust's capital gains are included in its distributable net income. Inclusion in distributable net income of all the capital gains recognized by a trust in the year of its termination will always be required because all of the trust's remaining assets (including its capital gains) will be distributed in that year.[58]

C. Creation of a Foreign Trust by a Non-U.S. Person

Neither Code § 684(a) nor Code § 679 applies to a transfer to a foreign trust by a non-U.S. person (except in certain instances under § 679(a)(4), as discussed *infra*). As a result, no U.S. income tax will be imposed on such transfer. The trust's

57. It is possible that the IRS would take the position that a U.S. trust that makes a distribution to a foreign trust that has one or more U.S. beneficiaries and that is not terminated by the distribution becomes the deemed owner of the foreign trust under Code § 679. A literal application of Code § 679 appears to compel this result. The following consequences would flow from a successful assertion of this position: (1) no distribution deduction would be available because the trust would be treated as having made a distribution to itself; (2) Code § 684 would not apply because the foreign trust would be treated as owned by another person (the distributing U.S. trust); and (3) the foreign trust's income attributable to that distribution would be treated for U.S. income tax purposes as the income of the U.S. trust. Although the foreign trust is treated as being owned by the U.S. trust, its income distributed to U.S. beneficiaries would not be taxed to them unless the distribution is treated as being made by the domestic trust to the beneficiaries via the foreign trust. (Compare, e.g., (1) the treatment of a distribution to a beneficiary that is made from a grantor trust as a transfer by the grantor to the beneficiary, which, in the case of the grantor who is an individual is treated for income tax purposes as a gift and (2) a distribution to a beneficiary that is made from a trust to which an entity has made a gratuitous contribution, which may be treated and taxed as a distribution from the entity directly to the beneficiary under Treas. Reg. § 1.672(f)-4(c)). If the distribution from the foreign trust is treated as being made from the domestic trust, then income of the domestic trust should carry out to the beneficiaries under the normal rules of Code §§ 661 and 662. However, if the domestic trust was never a foreign trust, the throwback tax should not be applicable to a distribution attributed to the domestic trust, because a distribution from such a trust is not subject to the throwback rules and interest charges. On the other hand, if the distribution is treated as being made from the foreign trust (and not indirectly made from the domestic trust), to the extent that the income of the foreign trust is "owned by" the domestic trust as a result of the application of Code § 679, the throwback tax will not apply, because the foreign trust will not have any undistributed net income. As a practical matter, treating the domestic trust as the owner of a foreign trust under § 679 does not seem to be a good position for the IRS to take because, if the U.S. trust lacked sufficient assets to pay the income tax on the foreign trust's income, the IRS seems to have no available way under the Code of collecting the tax. If Code § 679 does not apply, then Code § 684 will apply, which may produce a better result.

58. Treas. Reg. § 1.643(a)(3)(e), Example 7.

income will be treated for U.S. income tax purposes as if earned by a foreign non-grantor trust unless Code § 672(f) applies to the trust. Prior to the 1996 Act, trusts created by non-U.S. persons were subject to the so-called "grantor trust" rules set forth in Code §§ 671–679 to the same extent as trusts created by U.S. persons. The application of the grantor trust rules shifted the trust's income, for virtually all U.S. income tax purposes, from the trust to its grantor.

As discussed more fully below, Code § 672(f), which was added by the 1996 Act, denies grantor trust status to trusts with non-U.S. grantors unless (1) the grantor retains the right—exercisable either unilaterally or with the consent of another person who is a related or subordinate party who is subservient to the grantor—to revoke the trust; or (2) the only amounts permitted to be distributed from the trust during the grantor's life are amounts distributable to the grantor or her spouse.[59]

II. Tax Treatment of Foreign Nongrantor Trusts

A. In General

Nongrantor trusts calculate their taxable incomes in the same manner as individuals with certain modifications set forth in Code §§ 642, 643, 651, and 661. For this purpose, foreign nongrantor trusts are treated as nonresident individuals who are not present in the United States at any time.[60]

B. Gross Income

The gross income of a foreign nongrantor trust consists only of (1) gross income derived from sources within the United States that is not effectively connected

59. Code § 672(f). Trusts with foreign grantors that were in existence on September 19, 1995, and that were treated as grantor trusts under Code § 676 (relating to trusts, the property of which may be returned to the grantor) or Code § 677 (relating to trusts, the income from which may be paid to the grantor or her spouse) other than Code § 677(c) (relating to trusts, the income from which may be used to pay life insurance premiums on the life of the grantor or her spouse) will continue to be treated as grantor trusts except to the extent transfers were made to such trusts after September 19, 1995. Pub. L. No. 104-188, § 1904(d)(2), 110 Stat. 1755.

60. Code § 641(b). Code § 871(a)(2) provides that a nonresident alien individual who is present in the United States for a period of 183 days or more in a taxable year is subject to a 30 percent tax on her net capital gains allocable to sources within the United States. Under Code § 865(a)(1), income from the sale of personal property is generally sourced according to the residence of the seller. But, under Code § 865(e)(2)(A), a nonresident alien who maintains an office in the United States has U.S.-source income to the extent she sells personal property attributable to that office. Prior to the 1997 Act, it was unclear whether a trust that was a foreign trust within the meaning of new Code § 7701(a)(31) but that had a U.S. trustee with an office in the United States would be treated as having U.S.-source income to the extent that trustee directed the sale of personal property. *See* Eileen Caufield Schwab & Dyke M. Davies, *Tax Risks When U.S. Fiduciary Acts as Trustee of Foreign Trust*, N.Y. L.J. (Jan. 7, 1997). Section 641(b) was amended by the 1997 Act to provide that, in determining the income of a foreign trust, the trust shall be treated as a nonresident alien individual who is not present in the United States at any time.

with the conduct of a trade or business within the United States and (2) gross income that is effectively connected with the conduct of a trade or business within the United States.[61]

Gross income from sources within the United States includes:

- interest from the United States (or any of its agencies), the District of Columbia, noncorporate residents of the United States, and domestic corporations;[62]
- dividends from domestic corporations;[63]
- rentals and royalties from property located in the United States, including rentals or royalties for the use in the United States of patents, copyrights, secret processes and formulas, good will, trademarks, trade brands, franchises, and the like; and[64]
- gains from the disposition of U.S. real estate.[65]

C. Imposition of U.S. Income Tax

Foreign nongrantor trusts are subject to U.S. income tax on the types of income described below:

1. Income Effectively Connected with U.S. Trade or Business

Foreign nongrantor trusts are taxable on taxable income that is effectively connected with the conduct of a trade or business within the United States.[66]

Although it is unlikely that a foreign nongrantor trust would be engaged directly in a trade or business, some foreign trusts may have this type of income as a result of investments in partnerships that engage in U.S. trades or businesses. A foreign nongrantor trust that is a general or limited partner in a partnership engaged in a U.S. trade or business is deemed to be engaged in that trade or business.[67]

2. Election with Respect to Income from Real Property

In addition, a foreign nongrantor trust that receives income from real property located in the United States may make an election to treat all such income as income effectively connected with a U.S. trade or business if the property is held for the production of income.[68] In the absence of such an election, this income would be taxed on the basis of gross receipts unreduced by any deductions.

---

61. Code § 872(a).
62. *Id.* § 861(a)(1).
63. *Id.* § 861(a)(2).
64. *Id.* § 861(a)(4).
65. *Id.* § 861(a)(5).
66. *Id.* § 871(b).
67. *Id.* § 875(1); Rev. Rul. 91-32, 1991-1 C.B. 107; Rev. Rul. 85-60, 1985-1 C.B. 187. Treas. Reg. § 1.864-2(c)(2)(ii) excepts partnerships that trade in securities for their own accounts unless they are dealers.
68. Code § 871(d)(1).

3. Disposition of U.S. Real Property Interests

Gains of a foreign nongrantor trust from the disposition of "United States real property interests" are treated as income that is effectively connected with a U.S. trade or business.[69] For this purpose, a "United States real property interest" is "any interest, other than an interest solely as a creditor, in either:

i) real property located in the United States or the Virgin Islands, or
ii) a domestic corporation unless it is established that the corporation was not a U.S. real property holding corporation within the period described in § 897(c)(1)(A)(ii)."[70]

The term "interests in real property" includes fee ownership and co-ownership of leaseholds of land and improvements thereon, personal property associated with the use of real estate, and options to acquire such land, improvements, leaseholds, and personal property.[71]

A U.S. real property holding corporation is any corporation unless the value of its U.S. real property interests is less than 50 percent of the sum of the value of all of its real property interests plus the value of all of its assets that are used or held for use in its trade or business.[72]

A foreign nongrantor trust's receipt of consideration for the disposition of a partnership interest in a partnership that holds any U.S. real property interests is treated as consideration received for the disposition of a U.S. real property interest to the extent attributable to U.S. real property interests.[73]

4. Fixed or Determinable Annual or Periodic Income

Foreign nongrantor trusts are taxed on their U.S.-source fixed or determinable annual or periodic income such as interest, dividends, rents, annuities, and the like.[74] They are also taxed on their U.S.-source gains from certain timber, coal, and iron ore transactions;[75] on their U.S.-source gains from the sale or exchange of patents, copyrights, secret processes and formulas, good will, trademarks, trade brands, franchises, and similar property to the extent the gains are from payments that are contingent on the use of the transferred interest;[76] and, subject to the important exceptions described below, on their original issue discount from U.S. sources.[77] These forms of income are all subject to the same type of taxation,

---

69. Code § 897(a).
70. Treas. Reg. § 1.897-1(c)(1); *see* Code § 897(c)(1).
71. Code § 897(c)(6).
72. *Id.* § 897(c)(2). Shares of any class of securities that are regularly traded on an established securities market will not be treated as a United States real property interest except as to a person who holds more than 5 percent of the stock. Code § 897(c)(3).
73. Code § 897(g); Notice 88-72, 1988-2 C.B. 383.
74. Code § 871(a)(1)(A).
75. *Id.* § 871(a)(1)(B).
76. *Id.* § 871(a)(1)(D).
77. *Id.* § 871(a)(1)(C).

except to the extent that they are effectively connected with a U.S. trade or business. For convenience, they are referred to in this chapter as "fixed or determinable annual or periodic income."

5. Other Gains

Nonresident aliens who are present within the United States for 183 days or more in a particular taxable year are normally subject to tax on gains derived from sources within the United States from the sale of capital assets.[78] As discussed above, Code § 641(b) prevents this rule from applying to foreign nongrantor trusts. It provides that, for purposes of calculating the taxable income of a foreign trust, the trust shall be treated as a nonresident alien individual who is not present in the United States at any time. Thus, even though the trustees of a foreign nongrantor trust reside permanently in the United States, the trust will be treated for U.S. income tax purposes as if the trustees had never been present in the United States.

6. Exceptions

No U.S. income tax will be imposed on a foreign nongrantor trust's receipt of so-called "portfolio interest" unless such income is effectively connected with the conduct of a U.S. trade or business.[79] For this purpose, portfolio interest is interest (including original issue discount) that is paid on certain obligations of U.S. persons issued after July 18, 1984.[80] If issued in proper form, interest paid by a

78. *Id.* § 871(a)(2). Income from the sale of personal property (other than inventory property) attributable to an office or other fixed place of business in the United States that is maintained by a nonresident in the United States is U.S. source income. See Code § 865(e)(2).

79. Code § 871(h).

80. With certain exceptions, interest payable on two types of obligations is eligible for the portfolio debt exception, bearer debt, but only if it is described in Code § 163(f)(2)(B) and the regulations under that section, and debt issued in registered form if the payee has provided the obligor with a statement that the owner of the obligation is not a U.S. person for U.S. income tax purposes. These requirements are intended to decrease the possibility that U.S. persons will acquire and fail to pay tax on such obligations. The portfolio debt exception is not available for interest on obligations issued by a corporation if the nonresident alien and certain related parties own 10 percent or more of the voting stock or for interest on obligations issued by a partnership if the nonresident alien and certain related parties own 10 percent or more of the capital or profits interest. The portfolio debt exception is also not available for contingent interest, i.e., interest that is determined with reference to receipts, cash flow, income profits, and the like of the obligor.

Foreign targeted bearer debt is eligible for the portfolio debt exception. Foreign targeted bearer debt is debt that meets the following requirements:

(1) There are arrangements reasonably designed to ensure that the obligation will be sold (or resold in connection with the original issue) only to a person who is not a U.S. person;
(2) Interest on the obligation is payable only outside the United States and its possessions; and
(3) The face of the obligation bears the legend that "[a]ny United States person who holds this obligation will be subject to limitations under the United States income tax laws, including the limitations provided in section 165(j) and 1287(a) of the Internal Revenue Code." Treas. Reg. § 1.163-5(c).

U.S. person in a debt instrument issued to reflect that person's borrowings from a foreign trust should qualify for the exception.

- No U.S. income tax will be imposed on a foreign nongrantor trust's receipt of interest from a U.S. bank, savings and loan association, insurance company, or similar institution unless such income is effectively connected with the conduct of a U.S. trade or business.[81]
- No U.S. income tax will be imposed on a foreign nongrantor trust's receipt of original issue discount income on obligations that mature in 183 days or less from the date of original issue unless such income is effectively connected with the conduct of a U.S. trade or business.[82]
- No U.S. income tax will be imposed on a foreign nongrantor trust's receipt of any interest-related dividend or short-term capital gain dividend from a regulated investment company.[83]

D. Deductions

1. Income Effectively Connected with U.S. Trade or Business

In computing a foreign nongrantor trust's taxable income that is effectively connected with the conduct of a trade or business within the U.S., the trust is entitled to reduce its gross income so connected (or treated as so connected) by the deductions that are "connected" with such income.[84] The proper apportionment and allocation of deductions for this purpose is determined in accordance with Treas. Reg. § 1.873-1. In addition, the trust is also entitled to deduct against its effectively connected income the following:

- the deduction for losses allowed by Code § 165(c)(3) if the loss occurred with respect to property located in the United States;
- the deduction for charitable contributions allowed by Code § 170; and
- the deduction for personal exemptions allowed by Code § 151.[85]

Section 502 of the 2010 HIRE Act repeals the foreign targeted bearer debt exception for debt issued after March 18, 2012.

Debt is considered to be issued in registered form if:

(1) The obligation is registered as to principal and interest with the issuer or its agent, and transfer of the obligation may be accomplished only by surrender of the old instrument and reissuance to the new holder;
(2) The right to principal and interest may be transferred only through a book entry system maintained by the issuer or its agent that identifies the owner of an interest in the obligation; or
(3) It is registered as to principal and interest with the issuer or its agent and may be transferred by either of the methods described in (1) or (2). Treas. Reg. § 5f.103-1(c).

81. Code § 871(i).

82. *Id.* §§ 871(a)(1)(C), 871(g)(1).

83. *Id.* § 871(k). The exception for short-term capital gain dividends is not applicable to dividends with respect to a taxable year of a regulated investment company that begins after December 31, 2009.

84. *Id.* § 873(a).

85. *Id.* § 873(b).

Nothing in the Code or the regulations indicates whether the distributions made to beneficiaries by a foreign nongrantor trust with income effectively connected to the conduct of a trade or business within the United States are connected with such income and are therefore deductible under Code §§ 651 and 661.

It is appropriate to permit a foreign nongrantor trust to deduct that portion of its distributions to beneficiaries that consist of effectively connected income. In determining the portion of a distribution that consists of effectively connected income, the distribution should be treated as consisting of the same portion of effectively connected income as the total of the trust's effectively connected income bears to the trust's total income. The IRS seems to take this approach.[86]

2. Other Income

No deductions are permitted against U.S.-source fixed or determinable annual or periodic income, except to the extent that such income is effectively connected to a U.S. trade or business.

3. Foreign Tax Credit

A foreign nongrantor trust engaged in a trade or business within the United States (either directly or through investments in partnerships that are so engaged) that pays foreign income, war profits, or excess profits taxes on income that is effectively connected with such trade or business may, subject to certain limitations, credit the foreign tax against its U.S. income tax liability.[87] Alternatively, it may deduct such taxes.[88]

The total amount of the credit:

- is limited to the proportion of the U.S. tax against which such credit is taken as the trust's taxable income from foreign sources bears to its entire taxable income effectively connected with its U.S. trade or business;[89]
- may not be used against any income tax imposed on income not effectively connected with such business;[90] and
- is not allowed to the extent it is properly allocable under Code § 901(b)(5) to the trust's beneficiaries.[91]

In some cases, foreign income, war profits, or excess profits taxes will be imposed on the foreign grantor of a foreign nongrantor trust rather than on the trust itself. This would occur, for example, if the trust were treated as "owned" by its grantor under foreign tax rules similar to the so-called grantor trust rules set forth in Code §§ 671–679. There is no mechanism in the Code that permits the foreign nongrantor trust to credit the taxes paid by the grantor against the trust's U.S. income tax.[92]

86. *See, e.g.*, Rev. Rul. 85-60, 1985-1 C.B. 187.
87. Code §§ 901(b)(4), 906(a).
88. *Id.* § 164(a)(3). If the trust claims the credit, the deduction is not permitted. *Id.* § 275(a)(4).
89. *Id.* §§ 904(a) and 906(b)(2).
90. *Id.* § 906(b)(3).
91. *Id.* § 642(a).
92. *Id.* § 901(b)(5). *See* p. 32.

Until the 1996 Act's imposition of significant limitations on the availability of grantor trust status for trusts created by non-U.S. persons, the absence of a credit mechanism was unlikely to be a problem. This was so because the U.S. grantor trust system is so broad that any trust treated as owned by its grantor under foreign tax law was also likely to be treated as owned by its grantor under U.S. tax law. Under current U.S. law, the absence of a credit mechanism can result in serious foreign tax credit misallocations.[93]

E. Tax Rates

1. Income Effectively Connected to a U.S. Trade or Business

This type of income is subject to the normal tax rates applicable to trusts under Code § 1 or Code § 55.[94] As of 2013, Code § 1(e) imposes a maximum tax rate of 39.6 percent; Code § 1(h) imposes maximum tax rates between 20 percent and 28 percent on long-term capital gains and 20 percent on qualified dividend income.

2. Other Income

U.S.-source fixed or determinable annual or periodic income, except to the extent such income is effectively connected to a U.S. trade or business, is subject to tax at a flat rate of 30 percent.[95] The currently applicable reduction in the maximum tax rates applicable to dividend income to 20 percent[96] does not apply to income received by a foreign trust or any other nonresident alien.

F. Withholding

1. Income Effectively Connected with U.S. Trade or Business

Withholding is generally not required for income (including fixed or determinable annual or periodic income) to the extent it is effectively connected with a U.S. trade or business. Withholding obligations are, however, imposed on partnerships that have taxable income that is effectively connected (or treated as effectively connected) with the conduct of a U.S. trade or business if such income is allocable under Code § 704 to a foreign partner.[97] The withholding rate applicable to foreign nongrantor trusts that are partners in such partnerships is the highest rate of tax specified in Code § 1.[98]

---

93. See discussion at Section III.B.2.d of credit that may be allowed to a foreign trust by regulation for foreign taxes imposed on its foreign grantor in certain circumstances.

94. Code § 871(b)(1).

95. *Id.* § 871(a).

96. Section 302 of the Jobs and Growth Tax Relief Reconciliation Act of 2003 (Pub. L. No. 108-27) added paragraph (11) to § 1(h) of the Code. This paragraph provides that the term "net capital gain" means "net capital gain . . . increased by qualified dividend income."

97. Code § 1446(a). Such a partnership is required to file Form 8804 and to send Form 8805 to each such foreign partner.

98. *Id.* § 1446(b).

2. U.S. Real Property Interests

The transferee of a disposition by a foreign person of a U.S. real property interest is required to withhold. The withholding rate is 10 percent of the gross amount realized.[99]

3. Fixed or Determinable Annual or Periodic Income

Code § 1441(a) requires any person paying any of the items of income listed in Code § 1441(b) to withhold a 30 percent tax (or lower treaty rate) to the extent such income constitutes gross income from U.S. sources of any nonresident alien individual or of any foreign partnership[100] unless such income is effectively connected with the conduct of a U.S. trade or business.[101] The income items listed in Code § 1441(b) are the various kinds of fixed or determinable annual or periodic income. Code § 1442 imposes a similar requirement with respect to the income of foreign corporations. Curiously, neither section refers to withholding with respect to the income of trusts. Nevertheless, the regulations state that income paid to a foreign trust is subject to the withholding requirements of Code § 1441. In general, withholding will be required unless the person paying any of the items listed in Code § 1441(b) has received appropriate documentation indicating that withholding is not required (or that a lower rate of withholding applies) and the person does not have any reason to believe that the documentation is inaccurate.[102]

G. Effect of Tax Treaties

The principles described above may apply differently to foreign nongrantor trusts that are residents of countries with which the United States has an income tax treaty. For example, most income tax treaties to which the U.S. is a party reduce the tax imposed on dividends not effectively connected to a U.S. trade or business from 30 percent to 15 percent.

H. Taxable Year; Reporting

1. Taxable Year and Estimated Tax Payments

Foreign nongrantor trusts must adopt a calendar taxable year and are required to make estimated income tax payments in the same manner as U.S. trusts.[103]

2. U.S. Nonresident Alien Income Tax Return—Form 1040NR

The trustee of a foreign nongrantor trust is required to file Form 1040NR for a particular year if:

---

99. *Id.* § 1445(a). The transferee is required to file Form 8288 and to furnish Form 8288-A to the transferee.

100. The person withholding is required to file Form 1042 and to furnish Form 1042-S to the person from whom tax is withheld.

101. Code § 1441(c)(1).

102. Treas. Reg. § 1.1441-5(e).

103. Code §§ 6654(a) and 6654(l); Notice 87-32, 1987-1 C.B. 477.

- the trust was engaged in trade or business in the United States during such year even if no income was derived from such trade or business; or
- the trust had income in such year that is subject to tax in the United States unless the trust's liability for such tax is fully satisfied by withholding.[104]

If a foreign nongrantor trust is required to file Form 1040NR for a particular year, the return must be filed by the fifteenth day of the sixth month following the close of the year if the trust does not have an office or place of business in the United States. If the trust does have an office or place of business in the United States, it must file its Form 1040NR by the fifteenth day of the fourth month following the close of the year.[105]

3. Report of Foreign Bank and Financial Accounts—Form TD F 90-22.1

A U.S. trustee of a foreign nongrantor trust must file Form TD F 90-22.1 if she has a financial interest in or signature authority or other authority over any financial accounts, including bank, securities, or other types of financial accounts in a foreign country if the value of such accounts exceeds, in the aggregate, $10,000. A person has a financial interest in any such account if she has legal title to it. Trustees generally have legal title to accounts in which trust funds are invested. In addition, if legal title to an account is held by a corporation or partnership and the trustee owns more than 50 percent of the corporation or partnership, the trustee will be treated as having a financial interest in such account. A person has signature authority over an account if she can control the disposition of account property by the delivery of a document signed by her and one or more other persons. A person has other authority over an account if she can control such disposition by direct communication to the person with whom the account is maintained.

Form TD F 90-22.1 must be filed by June 30 of the year following the year in which the U.S. person had such financial interest or signature or other authority.

4. Taxpayer Identification Numbers

Code § 6109 requires persons to obtain a U.S. identifying number to the extent required by regulations. Treas. Reg. § 301.6109-1(b) requires a foreign nongrantor trust (or any other nonresident alien) to obtain a U.S. taxpayer identification number if:

- it has income effectively connected with a U.S. trade or business or has a U.S. office or place of business;
- it files a U.S. income tax return or refund claim; or,
- after December 31, 1998, it furnishes a withholding certificate claiming a reduced tax rate under a treaty (other than for dividends and interest from stocks and debt that are actively traded and certain other securities), or

104. Treas. Reg. § 1.6012-1(b).
105. *Id.* § 1.6072-1; T.D. 7426.

an exemption from withholding from income that is effectively connected with a U.S. trade or business.

III. Tax Treatment of U.S. Beneficiaries of Foreign Nongrantor Trusts

A. In General

U.S. taxpayers who are beneficiaries of foreign nongrantor trusts may be subject to U.S. income taxes on distributions of cash or other property received from such trusts. In some cases, loans made to them or to persons related to them from such trusts will be treated as distributions.

The determination of the U.S. tax liability of a U.S. beneficiary with respect to distributions and loans depends on a number of factors, including (1) whether the distribution was made during a year in which the foreign nongrantor trust earned income and the relationship between the size of that income and the value of the distributions made in that year to the U.S. beneficiary and to other trust beneficiaries; (2) whether, if the amount of the trust's distributions exceeded the amount of its income for the year of distribution, the trust had undistributed income accumulated from prior years; and (3) whether the trust previously paid U.S. income tax or foreign income tax.

U.S. beneficiaries of foreign trusts may also be subject to tax on income earned by certain corporations whose shares are owned by the trust. The types of corporations that are the source of such potential liability are controlled foreign corporations and passive foreign investment companies. This subject is discussed more fully below.

B. Distributions of Income in the Year Earned

1. General Rules

(a) Distributable Net Income. A U.S. beneficiary of a foreign nongrantor trust is required to include in her gross income for any particular year:

(1) the amount of any trust income in such year required to be distributed to her from a so-called "simple trust" (whether or not actually distributed to her) to the extent of her share of the trust's distributable net income (DNI) for the year;[106]

(2) the amount of any trust income required to be distributed to her in such year from any other foreign nongrantor trust, a "complex trust" (whether

106. Code § 652(a). The term "simple trust" refers to a nongrantor trust that is required to distribute income, is not permitted to make payments to charity, and, in the year for which the characterization is made, makes no principal distributions.

or not actually distributed to her), to the extent of her share of the trust's DNI for the year;[107] and

(3) any other amount required to be distributed to her (whether or not actually distributed to her) or properly and actually distributed to her from a foreign complex trust in a such year to the extent of her share of the trust's DNI for such year.[108]

(b) Determining a Beneficiary's Share of DNI. In the case of a simple trust, if the amount of income distributions required to be made exceeds the trust's DNI, each beneficiary shares in the trust's DNI in the proportion that the amount of income required to be distributed to her bears to the amount of income required to be distributed to all beneficiaries.[109] The same rule applies to income distributions from complex trusts.[110]

If a complex trust's DNI exceeds the amount of income required to be distributed to its beneficiaries, and if there are other amounts either required to be distributed or properly distributed to a beneficiary, that beneficiary will share in the trust's remaining DNI in the proportion that the amount of the trust's distribution (or required distribution) to her bears to the amount of all such distributions (or required distributions) to all beneficiaries.[111]

Consider the following example.

> ***Example 2:*** Kate is a U.S. beneficiary of a foreign nongrantor trust (FNT). Under the terms of the trust, all income is (and always has been) required to be distributed currently to Kate's mother, M, a nonresident alien. The trustees are permitted to make principal distributions to Kate. In 2010, the trust's income (and its DNI) consisted of $100,000 of dividends from foreign corporations, all of which were distributed to M. The FNT has never had any income from capital gains. The trustees made a principal distribution of $100,000 to Kate. Kate is not required to include any portion of the $100,000 distribution in her gross income.

(c) Meaning of "Income." For purposes of these rules, the term "income" (unless part of the phrase "taxable income," "distributable net income," "undistributed net income," or "gross income") means the amount of income for the taxable year of the trust determined under the terms of the governing instrument and applicable local law.[112] To avoid confusion, this chapter refers to "income" as "trust accounting income." The term "income" or "trust accounting income" is generally used to describe, for local law purposes, the amount required or permitted to be

107. *Id.* § 662(a)(1). The term "complex trust" refers to a nongrantor trust other than a simple trust.

108. *Id.* § 662(a)(2).

109. *Id.* § 652(a).

110. *Id.* § 662(a)(1).

111. *Id.* § 662(a)(2).

112. *Id.* § 643(b).

distributed to current trust beneficiaries when the terms of the trust instrument require or permit trust income, but not trust principal, to be distributed to such beneficiaries. The items that are included in the term "income" or "trust accounting income" vary from jurisdiction to jurisdiction. There is no standard federal definition. The term generally includes items such as dividends and similar distributions made with respect to investments in business or investment entities, interest, and rent. It generally excludes gains from the disposition of property. Trust provisions that define income in a manner that departs fundamentally from local law are not recognized for purposes of this definition.[113]

(d) Sixty-five Day Election. At the trustee's election, an amount that is properly paid to a beneficiary within sixty-five days after the end of a taxable year will be treated as having been paid to her within such taxable year.[114] The amount to which the election applies may not exceed the amount of income of the trust for the prior taxable year or the DNI for such year, if greater, reduced by amounts paid, credited, or required to be distributed in such year calculated without regard to the election.[115]

(e) Specific Gifts. An amount that the trust instrument requires to be paid to a beneficiary as a gift of a specific sum of money or of specific property and that is actually paid to her all at once or in no more than three installments is not treated as a distribution and, therefore, is not included in the gross income of the U.S. beneficiary. This exception does not apply to amounts that can be paid only from trust income.[116]

Consider the following example.

> ***Example 3:*** Pat is a U.S. beneficiary of a foreign nongrantor trust. The terms of the trust document require the trustees of the FNT to pay Pat $1 million on his thirtieth birthday. Pat reached age thirty during 2010, a year in which the FNT's income and DNI exceeded $1 million. The FNT's principal in that year was worth $10 million. Pat is not required to include the $1 million paid to him by the FNT in his gross income.

(f) Distributions of Property Other Than Cash. The amount of any distribution to a beneficiary of property other than cash (other than a required distribution of trust accounting income or other fixed amount[117]) is the lesser of the trust's basis in the property or its value at the time of distribution unless the trustee

113. Treas. Reg. § 1.643(b)-1.

114. Code § 663(b).

115. Treas. Reg. § 1.663(b)-1(a)(2).

116. Code § 663(a)(1).

117. The distribution of appreciated property by a trustee to a beneficiary in satisfaction of the beneficiary's right to receive trust accounting income or other fixed amount is a recognition event. Kenan v. Comm'r, 114 F.2d 217 (2d Cir. 1940); Suisman v. Eaton, 15 F. Supp. 113 (D. Conn. 1935), *aff'd per curiam*, 83 F.2d 1019 (2d Cir.), *cert. denied*, 299 U.S. 573 (1936). *Cf.* Treas. Reg.§ 1.664-1(d)(5).

makes an election to recognize gain on the distribution. If the trustee makes such an election, the amount of the distribution will be the value of the property. The trust will recognize gain equal to the excess of the value of the property over its basis. If the trustee does not make the election, the beneficiary's basis will be the same as the trust's basis.[118]

Consider the following example:

> ***Example 4:*** Jenny is a U.S. beneficiary of FNT, a foreign nongrantor trust. During 2010, the trustees of FNT distributed 100 shares of X corporation stock to her. The shares were worth $1,000,000 at the time of distribution. The trust's basis in the shares was $1,000. FNT's income and DNI in 2010 exceeded $1,000,000. The trustees did not make the election described above to recognize gain on the distribution. Jenny will not be required to include any amount in excess of $1,000 in her gross income on account of the distribution. Her basis in the X shares will be $1,000.

These general rules are no different than the rules that apply to U.S. beneficiaries of U.S. nongrantor trusts.

However, a trust must recognize gain on the distribution of appreciated property to a "covered expatriate" who is subject to tax under § 877A in an amount equal to the excess of the property's then fair market value over basis.[119]

2. Special Rules Applicable to Nongrantor Trusts That Are Foreign

(a) Different Definition of Distributable Net Income. Generally, the DNI of a U.S. nongrantor trust for a particular year is equal to its taxable income for that year adjusted (1) by adding to taxable income the amount deducted as a personal exemption, the amount of its tax exempt income, and the amount of the trust's deduction for distributions to beneficiaries and (2) by subtracting from taxable income the trust's capital gains except to the extent such capital gains are "paid, credited or required to be distributed to any beneficiary during the taxable year."[120]

The DNI of a foreign nongrantor trust includes its capital gains.[121] In addition, a foreign nongrantor trust's DNI includes the amount of its income from non-U.S. sources reduced by amounts that would be deductible in connection with such income in the absence of Code § 265[122] and the amount that was excluded from its gross income by treaty under Code § 894.[123]

---

118. Code § 643(e).

119. *Id.* § 877A(f)(1)(B). The trustee is required to withhold 30 percent of the taxable portion of the distribution. In the case of a U.S. trust, the "taxable portion" would not ordinarily include the amount of gain triggered by the distribution. Code § 877A applies to certain persons who expatriate on or after June 17, 2008.

120. Code § 643(a)(3).

121. *Id.* § 643(a)(6)(C).

122. *Id.* § 643(a)(6)(A).

123. *Id.* § 643(a)(6)(B).

Consider the following example

> ***Example 5:*** John is a U.S. beneficiary of a foreign nongrantor trust. During 2010, the trust had foreign-source dividend income of $10,000 and long-term capital gain from the sale of securities of $10,000. Its U.S. gross income and taxable income is zero. The trust distributed $15,000 to John. It neither made nor was required to make distributions to any other beneficiary. The trust's DNI was $20,000. John's gross income from the trust, therefore, is $15,000. If the FNT had been a U.S. trust, its DNI would have been only $10,000, and John's gross income on account of his distribution from the trust would have been $10,000.

(b) Tax Character of Distributions. The tax character of distributions received by a beneficiary in a particular year reflects the character of the trust's income for that year proportionately.[124]

> ***Example 6:*** John, the U.S. taxpayer in the above example who received a $15,000 distribution from an FNT, which had dividend income of $5,000, interest income of $5,000, and long-term capital gains of $10,000, will be treated as having received dividend income of $3,750, interest income of $3,750, and long-term capital gains of $7,500. The dividend income may be eligible for the 20 percent maximum rate of tax on qualified dividend income.

If the trust document or local law requires that particular types of trust income be allocated to particular beneficiaries, and if such requirement has economic significance independent of the tax consequences, the character of the amounts received by the beneficiaries will reflect such required allocation.[125]

> ***Example 7:*** The terms the foreign nongrantor trust described in the example above required that all of the FNT's dividend and interest income be distributed annually to F, John's nonresident alien father. F will be treated as having received all of the ordinary income included in the trust's DNI. John's $15,000 distribution, therefore, will consist of $10,000 of long-term capital gains. The balance of $5,000 will not be included in his gross income.

(c) Credit for U.S. Withholding Tax. As discussed above, if the foreign nongrantor trust had fixed or determinable annual or periodic income or income from the disposition of U.S. real property interests, it is likely that the trust paid U.S. income tax on such income through withholding under Code § 1441 or Code § 1445. The IRS takes the position that a U.S. beneficiary who receives a distribution from a foreign nongrantor trust that includes U.S.-source income from which U.S. tax has been withheld must include in her gross income not only the amount she actually

124. *Id.* §§ 652(b) and 662(b).

125. *Id.*; Treas. Reg. §§ 1.652(b)-2(a) and 662(b)-1.

receives but also the amount of the withheld tax. She may then credit the withheld tax against her personal income tax liability.[126]

> ***Example 8:*** FNT, the foreign nongrantor trust described in the above Example 7, had, in addition to its $10,000 of foreign-source dividend income and $10,000 of long-term capital gains, $10,000 of dividends on U.S. securities from which $3,000 of tax was withheld. The FNT distributed $13,500 to John. John will be treated as having received a distribution of $15,000 consisting of foreign-source dividend income of $5,000, long-term capital gains of $5,000, and U.S. dividend income of $5,000. The U.S. dividend income has been "grossed-up" by his $1,500 share of the taxes withheld from it. The $1,500 will be credited against his U.S. income tax.

(d) Credit for Foreign Income Taxes Paid by Trust. A U.S. person who pays income, war profits, or excess profits tax to a foreign country may credit the amount of such taxes against her U.S. income tax liability or may claim such taxes as an itemized deduction.[127] The total amount of the credit allowed to be taken is limited by the proportion her aggregate taxable income from foreign sources bears to her entire taxable income.[128]

If a foreign nongrantor trust pays such foreign taxes, its U.S. beneficiaries who receive distributions of income on which such taxes have been paid may elect to take a credit for the share of foreign taxes attributable to their share of the income or a deduction.[129] The credit is subject to the limits described above.

Neither the Code nor the regulations explain whether the beneficiary must include in her gross income the amount of foreign taxes paid with respect to the income distributed to her if she elects to take the credit. The IRS's internal position seems to require such inclusion. The current edition of the IRS's foreign trust training manual provides the following guidance for its agents:

> While many foreign trusts are established in countries having no income taxes, such as Bermuda or the Bahamas, some are established in countries with income taxes. Some also pay taxes to other countries where they have investments.
>
> In either case, a U.S. citizen or resident taxed on the income of such a trust may claim credit for his/her allocable share of foreign income taxes paid by the trust. If the credit is claimed, the amount of income reported should be grossed up to include the foreign taxes paid.

---

126. Treas. Reg. §§ 1.1441-3(f) and 1.1462-1(b); Rev. Rul. 56-30, 1956-1 C.B. 646; Rev. Rul. 55-414, 1955-1 C.B. 385.

127. Code §§ 901(a) and 164(a)(3). An election to take the credit precludes the deduction. *Id.* § 275(a)(4).

128. *Id.* § 904(a).

129. *Id.* § 901(b)(5).

The taxpayer may deduct the taxes instead if he/she chooses. Failure to gross up trust income should be regarded as an election to take a deduction.[130]

If foreign income, war profits, or excess profits taxes are imposed on a foreign nongrantor trust's non-U.S. grantor or on another non-U.S. person rather than on the trust itself, and if the trust would have been treated as owned by the grantor or such other person under subpart E of the Code but for Code § 672(f), Code § 901(b)(5) may permit these taxes to be treated for foreign tax credit purposes as if they had been imposed on the trust. Unfortunately, the implementation of this portion of Code § 901(b)(5) appears to require regulatory action, which has not yet occurred.

C. Distribution of Income Accumulated in a Prior Year—the "Throwback Rules"

1. In General

If a foreign nongrantor trust makes distributions in excess of its DNI for a particular year, the U.S. beneficiaries who receive such distributions are likely to be required to include those distributions in their gross incomes, may be required to calculate their U.S. income tax on such distributions under a complex rule generally referred to as the "throwback rule," and may be subject to interest on these taxes.

2. Accumulation Distributions

(a) In General. The throwback rule and its accompanying interest charge apply only if the foreign nongrantor trust has made an "accumulation distribution." An accumulation distribution is a distribution under Code § 661(a)(2) (dealing with amounts properly paid or credited or required to be distributed other than trust accounting income required to be distributed currently) to the extent such distribution exceeds the trust's DNI for the year reduced (but not below zero) by trust accounting income required to be distributed currently.[131]

The following two important exceptions to this definition may be applicable to distributions from foreign nongrantor trusts.

130. "Foreign Trusts and the IRS," 1997 Training 3325-002 (05-97), 98 TNI 149-44. The manual cites no authority for this conclusion. Its discussion on the topic is similar to Howard Zaritsky's speculation as to how the issue should be resolved in Zaritsky, U.S. Taxation of Foreign Estates, Trusts and Beneficiaries, 854 T.M. A-32.

131. Code § 665(b).

(b) Exceptions

(i) Specific Gifts. A distribution in satisfaction of a gift of a specific sum of money or of specific property described in Code § 663(a)(1) (described above) is not an accumulation distribution.[132]

Example 9: The foreign nongrantor trust described above of which Pat is a beneficiary had no DNI in the year in which Pat reached age thirty. The trustees distributed the sum of $1 million to Pat as they were required to do under the terms of the trust instrument. The distribution to Pat is not an accumulation distribution.

(ii) Distributions Not in Excess of Trust Accounting Income. Distributions that do not exceed trust accounting income in the year in which they are made are not accumulation distributions. The Code establishes this exception with the following text:

If the amounts properly paid, credited, or required to be distributed by the trust for the taxable year do not exceed the income of the trust for such year, there shall be no accumulation distribution for such year.[133]

This principle is illustrated by the following example:

> ***Example 10:*** Isaac is a U.S. beneficiary of a foreign nongrantor trust. The terms of the trust permit the trustees to distribute income and principal to any one or more beneficiaries at such times and in such amounts that they believe appropriate. In 2010, the FNT received $100,000 in dividends from foreign corporations. It paid trustee commissions of $60,000, $40,000 of which was allocable to principal and $20,000 of which was allocable to income. Its trust accounting income for the year was $80,000, $100,000 reduced by the $20,000 of expenses chargeable to income. Its DNI was $40,000, $100,000 reduced by the total amount of the trustee commissions. The trustee distributed $80,000 to Isaac. The distribution is not an accumulation distribution because it is not in excess of trust accounting income.

(c) Default Method of Calculating an Accumulation Distribution. In some cases, the U.S. beneficiary of a foreign nongrantor trust will not have received sufficient information about her distribution and the trust to enable her to determine whether she has received an accumulation distribution. Notice 97-34,[134] and the current version of IRS Form 3520 (2012) gives her a so-called "default" method of making this determination. A beneficiary is required to use this method if the trust

132. Treas. Reg. § 1.665(b)-1A(c)(1).
133. Code § 665(b). The word "income" in this quotation refers to "trust accounting income."
134. 1997-1 C.B. 422.

did not provide her with a Foreign Nongrantor Trust Beneficiary Statement.[135] If the trust did provide her with such a statement, she may elect to use the default method.

The required steps of the default method are as follows.

Step 1—Calculate the total amount of distributions the beneficiary has received from the foreign nongrantor trust during the three prior years.
Step 2—Multiply the total by 1.25.
Step 3—Divide the product determined in Step 2 by the lesser of 3 or the number of years the trust has been in existence (other than those years in which it was treated as a grantor trust).

The amount treated as a distribution of current income will be the smaller of the actual distribution or the amount determined in Step 3. The balance of the distribution will be treated as an accumulation distribution. If the default method is used, the number of years used for purposes of calculating the interest charge under Code § 688, as discussed below, will be one-half of the number of years the trust has been in existence.[136]

Consider the following example.

Example 11: Joshua is the beneficiary of a foreign nongrantor trust that has been in existence since 1998. At the end of 2006, the FNT had assets worth $20 million. In each of the years 1998 through 2006, the FNT earned $1 million. Assume the FNT has no income in 2007, 2008, 2009, and 2010 and that the FNT distributes $2 million to Joshua in each such year. The amount of Joshua's accumulation distribution in each year would be $2 million under Code § 665(b). His situation would be improved considerably by using the default method.

In 2007, the accumulation distribution under the default method would be the full $2 million because there were no distributions in any of the prior three years.

In 2008, the amount of the accumulation distribution is reduced to $1,166,667 ($2,000,000 - ($2,000,000 x 1.25/3)).
In 2009, the amount of the accumulation distribution is reduced to $333,333 ($2,000,000 - ($4,000,000 x 1.25/3)).

---

135. IRS Form 3520, Line 30 (2012). Presumably, the IRS's authority for enforcing this requirement is found in Code § 6048(c)(2)(A), which provides:

If adequate records are not provided to the Secretary to determine the proper treatment of any distribution from a foreign trust, such distribution shall be treated as an accumulation distribution includible in the gross income of the distributee under chapter 1.

The information that must be furnished in a Foreign Grantor Trust Beneficiary Statement is described below.

136. Code § 6048(c)(2)(B).

In 2010, the amount of the accumulation distribution is reduced to 0 ($2,000,000 - (6,000,000 x 1.25/3).

Because the default method of calculating the amount of an accumulation distribution can have the effect of significantly reducing that amount, the use of this method can significantly reduce the interest imposed on the taxes paid on accumulation distributions.

(d) Undistributed Net Income

(i) In General. Undistributed net income (UNI) limits the amount of an accumulation distribution that will be subject to tax. If a foreign nongrantor trust has no UNI, no tax will be imposed on its accumulation distributions. A trust's UNI for any particular year is equal to the amount by which its DNI for such year exceeds the sum of:

- the amount of trust accounting income required to be distributed in such year;
- the amount of any other amount properly paid or credited or required to be distributed for such year; and
- the amount of any taxes imposed on the trust that are attributable to its DNI for the year.[137]

(ii) Addition of Taxes. The taxes taken into account in the UNI calculation include U.S. income taxes and foreign income, war profits, and excess profits taxes that are imposed on the trust and that are allocable to the undistributed portion of the trust's DNI.[138] In addition, if any such taxes are imposed on a foreign nongrantor trust's non-U.S. grantor or any other non-U.S. person, and if that person would have been treated as the owner of the trust under the normal grantor trust rules but is prevented from being treated as the owner by Code § 672(f), these taxes may also reduce the trust's UNI.[139] Unfortunately, the effectiveness of the portion of the Code that permits such reduction appears to require regulatory action, which has not yet occurred.

(iii) Reduction of UNI. The original UNI for a particular year of a trust will be reduced by accumulation distributions made in later years to the extent that such distributions are deemed to have been made in such year under Code § 666(a).[140] A distribution paid or used for charitable purposes within the meaning of Code § 642(c) is not treated as an accumulation distribution.[141] As a result, such distributions do not reduce UNI.

If distributions are made under the default method that in fact exceed DNI, do those distributions reduce UNI for purposes of determining whether there is an

137. *Id.* § 665(a).
138. *Id.* § 665(d).
139. *Id.* § 665(d)(2).
140. Treas. Reg. § 1.665(a)-1A(c).
141. *Id* § 1.665(b)-1A(c)(2).

accumulation distribution in the final year of the trust if the trust then switches to the actual method. Consider the following example.

> ***Example 12:*** A trust worth $2,000X has $60x of UNI at the beginning of 2010. In 2010, the trust has gain of $100x, which is distributed to beneficiaries. The trust has no DNI in any subsequent year but distributes $41.67x in 2011 and $18.33x in 2012 using the default method so that there is no accumulation distribution. The trust terminates in 2013 and distributes the balance of the assets. If the distributions made under the default method carry out UNI (which the distributions would have done had the default method not been used), then there is no accumulation distribution in 2013. This seems to be the correct result and the logical consequence of allowing trusts to revert to the actual method in the final year of the trust.

(iv) Default Method of Calculating UNI. If the U.S. beneficiary of a foreign nongrantor trust uses the default method of calculating her accumulation distribution, the instructions for Internal Revenue Service Form 3520, in effect, require her to assume that the trust's UNI is at least equal to the amount of the accumulation distribution.

(e) Calculation of Throwback Tax on an Accumulation Distribution

(i) In General. If a beneficiary has received an accumulation distribution from a foreign nongrantor trust, her tax, the "throwback tax" on the distribution, can be calculated by following the complex series of steps outlined below. The steps are intended to produce a rough approximation of the tax the beneficiary would have been required to pay if the foreign nongrantor trust had paid income to her in the year earned instead of accumulating it and paying it to her in a later year.

(ii) The Steps. Step 1—Allocate the accumulation distribution among the preceding years of the trust for which there is any remaining UNI, starting with the earliest such year.[142] If the amount of the accumulation distribution exceeds the UNI for the earliest year, the excess is allocated to the next year for which there is any remaining UNI. The process continues in the same manner until all of the accumulation distribution has been allocated to a preceding year. Each portion of an accumulation distribution allocated to a particular preceding year is deemed to have been distributed on the last day of such year.

> ***Example 13:*** Michael is a U.S. beneficiary of a foreign nongrantor trust. The FNT was created in 1997 by Michael's non-U.S. mother. The FNT distributed $100,000 to Michael in 2004, a year in which the FNT's DNI and trust accounting income was $20,000. Therefore, $80,000 of the distribution is

142. Code § 666(a). If the trust's records are not sufficient to establish which years have UNI, the accumulation distribution will be allocated to the earliest year that the trust was in existence. *Id.* § 666(d).

treated as an accumulation distribution. The FNT's DNI, none of which was distributed, in each of its preceding years was as follows:

1997—$4,000
1998—$20,000
1999—$30,000
2000–$40,000

Michael's $80,000 accumulation distribution is deemed to have been made $4,000 on the last day of 1997, $20,000 on the last day of 1998, $30,000 on the last day of 1999, and $26,000 on the last day of 2000.

Step 2—Add to the amount deemed under Step 1 to have been distributed on the last day of a preceding year the taxes that were imposed on such amounts in such year.[143] Such taxes include U.S. income taxes and foreign income, war profits, and excess profits taxes.[144]

Example 14: Assume that the FNT described in the preceding example paid taxes in each of its preceding taxable years equal to 40 percent of its DNI. The total amount deemed to have been distributed to Michael on the last day of each 1997, 1998, 1999, and 2000 will be $5,600, $28,000, $42,000, and $36,400, respectively. The total amount deemed distributed or "thrown back" will be $112,000.

Step 3—Determine the number of preceding taxable years in which a distribution is deemed to have been made.[145] For purposes of this calculation, if any year's deemed distribution is less than 25 percent of the total amount of the accumulation distribution divided by the number of preceding taxable years to which the accumulation distribution is allocated, that year will not be included.[146]

Example 15: In the above example, the number of preceding taxable years in which a distribution is deemed to have been made will be three. The year 1997 is disregarded because the amount of the accumulation distribution allocated to that year ($4,000) is less than 25 percent of the total accumulation distribution ($80,000) divided by the number of years to which the distribution is deemed allocated (four).

---

143. *Id.* § 666(b), (c).

144. *Id.* § 665(d). If the beneficiary has received distributions from more than two trusts that are deemed to have been distributed to her on the last day of the same preceding taxable year, the taxes that were imposed on the third trust and any additional trusts because of such amounts are not deemed to have been distributed to the beneficiary. *Id.* § 667(c). This is detrimental to the beneficiary rather than beneficial because the consequence of the failure to treat taxes as having been distributed is the loss of the ability to use the taxes as a credit against the tax on the accumulation distribution. *Id.* §§ 667(b) and 667(d). For purposes of this rule, a distribution from a trust deemed to have been distributed on the last day of a particular preceding year will be disregarded unless, when added to any previous distributions for such year, it equals or exceeds $1,000. *Id.* § 667(c)(2).

145. *Id.* § 667(b)(1)(A).

146. *Id.* § 667(b)(3).

Step 4—Identify the beneficiary's computation years. The computation years are those three of the beneficiary's five immediately preceding taxable years left after eliminating the year in which his income was the highest and the year in which his income was the lowest.[147]

> ***Example 16:*** Assume in the above example that Michael's taxable income in 1999 was $50,000, in 2000 was $100,000, in 2001 was $200,000, in 2002 was $150,000, and in 2003 was $175,000. The year of the highest taxable income, 2001, and the year of the lowest taxable income, 1999, are eliminated. Michael's three computation years are the remaining years, 2000, 2002, and 2003.

Step 5—Determine the average annual distribution amount by dividing the amount deemed distributed (the amount of the accumulation distribution plus the amount of taxes deemed distributed) by the number of preceding years in which the distribution is deemed to have been made as determined under Step 3.[148]

> ***Example 17:*** In the above example, the amount deemed distributed is $112,000, and the number of preceding years in which the distribution is deemed to have been made is three. The average annual distribution amount is $37,333.

Step 6—Determine the amount by which the beneficiary's income tax would have increased in each of the three computation years if the annual distribution amount had been added to his taxable income in each of such years.[149] In making this calculation, no differentiation is made among the various types of income that were included in the foreign nongrantor trust's UNI (other than tax-exempt income). Thus, for example, if a portion of the trust's UNI was long-term capital gain, the beneficiary will not receive the advantage of the lower rate that generally applies to such gains. If any foreign income, war profits, or excess profits taxes were added in Step 2 to the amount deemed to have been distributed, the amount of such taxes may be allowed as a credit against the increase in tax calculated in this step.[150]

---

147. *Id.* § 667(b)(1)(B).

148. *Id.* § 667(b)(1)(C).

149. *Id.* § 667(b)(1)(D). Code § 1411, which was added to the Code by the 2010 Health Care Act (the Patient Protection and Affordable Care Act), as amended by the 2010 Health Care Reconciliation Act (the Health Care and Education Reconciliation Act of 2010), imposes an extra tax equal to 3.8 percent of an individual's net investment income to the extent her modified adjusted gross income exceeds a threshold amount of $250,000 in the case of married individuals filing joint returns and $200,000 in the case of unmarried individuals filing as single. This new tax is effective for taxable years beginning after 2012. Because Code § 667(b) calculates the throwback tax with reference to an individual's "taxable income," it appears that the 3.8 percent tax will not apply to accumulation distributions.

150. Code § 667(d).

> ***Example 18:*** Assume that Michael's income tax would have been increased by \$15,200, \$16,500, and \$16,600 in each of the three computation years.

Step 7—Determine the average tax increase by dividing the sum of the three increases by three.[151]

> ***Example 19:*** Michael's average tax increase is \$16,100 (\$48,300 divided by three).

Step 8—Multiply the average tax increase by the number of preceding taxable years in which the distribution is deemed to have been made as determined under Step 3.[152]

> ***Example 20:*** Michael's average tax increase, \$16,100, is multiplied by three. The product is \$48,300.

Step 9—Subtract from the product obtained in Step 8 the amount of any U.S. income taxes that were added in Step 2 to the amount deemed distributed to the beneficiary.[153] The result is the amount of the beneficiary's throwback tax.

> ***Example 21:*** Assume that \$25,000 of the total taxes added to Michael's deemed distribution were U.S. income taxes. The \$25,000 is subtracted from \$48,300, leaving a throwback tax of \$23,300.

(iii) Use of the Steps with the Default Method. If the U.S. beneficiary of a foreign nongrantor trust uses the default method of calculating her accumulation distribution, it is unclear how she would calculate her throwback tax using these nine steps. The difficulty is that the default method contains no instructions for determining the number of years to which the distribution is to be thrown back. In the absence of detailed information, the appropriate approach might be to treat the distribution as having been thrown back in equal shares to one-half the total number of years the trust has been in existence. This approach would be consistent with the method used to calculate the interest charge when the default method is used.

3. Calculation of the Interest Charge

(a) In General. If a foreign nongrantor trust makes a distribution to a U.S. beneficiary that is subject to a throwback tax, the tax is increased by an interest charge determined under Code § 668.[154]

(b) Before the 1996 Act. Before the 1996 Act, the throwback tax imposed on distributions from foreign trusts was subject to a 6 percent simple interest charge.[155] For purposes of the interest calculation, an accumulation distribution

151. *Id.*
152. *Id.* § 667(b)(1).
153. *Id.* § 667(b).
154. *Id.* § 667(a)(3).
155. Prior Code § 668.

was deemed to have been made from the earliest period or periods with respect to which the trust had UNI. For example, if a foreign nongrantor trust made an accumulation distribution in 1994 of $25,000, and if its UNI for 1990 (after adjustment for any prior accumulation distributions) was $50,000, for purposes of the interest calculation, the distribution would be deemed to have been made entirely from the income accumulated in 1990, and four years' worth of interest would be charged. If the tax on the distribution was $10,000, the interest charge would have been $2,400. Code § 668(b) limited the total interest charge to the excess of the amount of the taxed distribution over the tax charged on such distribution. Thus, in this example, the interest charge could not exceed $15,000 ($25,000, the amount of the distribution), reduced by $10,000, the amount of the tax on the distribution.

(c) After the 1996 Act. Code § 668, as amended by the 1996 Act, modified the interest rate charged on the tax imposed on distributions of accumulated income by foreign trusts and completely changed the calculation method. The interest rate will be the floating rates applied under Code § 6621 to underpayments of tax. In addition, interest will be compounded daily and will be calculated over a specially calculated number of years rather than with reference to the length of time between the year of the earliest undistributed accumulations and the year of distribution.[156] The number of years over which interest is calculated is determined by the following rather complicated process designed to produce a "dollar-weighted" number of years.

Step 1—the UNI for each year must be multiplied by the number of years between such year and the year of the distribution (counting the year of the accumulation but not the year of distribution).

Step 2—all products calculated in the first step must be added together.

Step 3—the sum of such products calculated in the second step must be divided by the aggregate amount of the trust's undistributed income. The quotient is to be rounded to the nearest half-year.[157]

For purposes of this calculation, an accumulation distribution is treated as having come proportionately from each year with respect to which there is UNI (other than a year during which the beneficiary was not a U.S. person) rather than from the earliest accumulation years. This change has the effect of reducing the interest charge on earlier distributions but will prevent the trustees from arranging for distributions from earlier years to be made to beneficiaries who are likely to pay less tax and, therefore, less interest.

The process may be illustrated by the following example.

> ***Example 22:*** The FNT, a foreign trust created in 1996, made no distributions before 2002. It had income of $0 in 2001, $60 in 2000, $124 in 1999, $87 in 1998, $54 in 1997, and $25 in 1996. Its total UNI in 2002 was the sum

156. Code § 668(a).
157. Line 50, IRS Form 3520 (2005).

of these amounts or $350. It had no income in 2002 and distributed $286 in that year to its U.S. beneficiary, Tyler. The FNT's weighted UNI is $1,260, as shown in the chart below:

[1]	[2]	[3]	[4]
Year	# of Years Since That Year	UNI From Each Year	Weighted UNI
			[2] x [3]
2001	1	$ -	$ -
2000	2	$ 60.00	$ 120.00
1999	3	$ 124.00	$ 372.00
1998	4	$ 87.00	$ 348.00
1997	5	$ 54.00	$ 270.00
1996	6	$ 25.00	$ 150.00
Totals		$ 350.00	$1,260.00

To determine the weighted number of years, the weighted UNI figure is divided by the total UNI figure, producing, in this example, a weighted number of years of 3.6, which is to be rounded to the nearest half year, or 3.5.[158]

Tyler's income tax on his accumulation distribution was $100. He will calculate his interest over a 3.5 year period ending on the applicable date. The applicable date, according to the instructions in Form 3520, is June 30 of the year in which the distribution was made.[159] Total interest is calculated in the manner illustrated by the chart below:

From	To	Rate	# of Days	Interest	Interest
					+
					Principal
					$ 100.00
1-Jan-99	31-Mar-99	7.0%	90.00	$1.74	$101.74
1-Apr-99	31-Mar-00	8.0%	366.00	$8.50	$110.24

158. The figures in this example are derived from the instructions to Form 3520 (2002).

159. Alternatively, if the taxpayer received only one accumulation distribution during the year, she may use the date of the distribution as the applicable date.

1-Apr-00	31-Mar-01	9.0%	365.00	$10.38	$120.62
1-Apr-01	30-Jun-01	8.0%	91.00	$2.43	$123.05
1-Jul-01	31-Dec-01	7.0%	184.00	$4.42	$127.47
1-Jan-02	30-Jun-02	6.0%	181.00	$3.85	$131.32
Total			1,277.00	$31.32	

Alternatively, Tyler may use the chart contained in the instructions to Form 3520 to calculate his interest. The chart produces total interest of only 29.998 percent rather than 31.12 percent.

The chart below shows the various Code § 6621 rates in effect from January 1, 1996, through March 31, 2013.[160]

From	Through	Rate
January 1, 1996	March 31, 1996	9%
April 1, 1996	June 30, 1996	8%
July 1, 1996	March 31, 1998	9%
April 1, 1998	December 31, 1998	8%
January 1, 1999	March 31, 1999	7%
April 1, 1999	March 31, 2000	8%
April 1, 2000	March 31, 2001	9%
April 1, 2001	June 30, 2001	8%
July 1, 2001	December 31, 2001	7%
January 1, 2002	December 31, 2002	6%
January 1, 2003	September 30, 2003	5%
October 1, 2003	March 31, 2004	4%
April 1, 2004	June 31, 2004	5%
July 1, 2004	September 30, 2004	4%
October 1, 2004	March 31, 2005	5%
April 1, 2005	September 30, 2005	6%
October 1, 2005	June 30, 2006	7%
July 1, 2006	September 30, 2006	8%
January 1, 2008	March 31, 2008	7%
April 1, 2008	June 30, 2008	6%
July 1, 2008	September 30, 2008	5%
October 1, 2008	December 31, 2008	6%
January 1, 2009	March 31, 2009	5%

160. Rev. Rul. 2012-8.

From	Through	Rate
April 1, 2009	January 1, 2011	4%
January 1, 2011	March 31, 2011	3%
April 1, 2011	September 30, 2011	4%
October 1, 2011	September 30, 2013	3%

Code § 668(b) remains unchanged. Thus, total interest charges can never exceed the amount of the accumulation distribution reduced by the tax imposed on it.

If the interest calculation period includes any years before 1996, a possibility that will become increasingly unlikely given the peculiar method of determining the calculation period, the interest rate applicable to that period will be 6 percent. The interest will not be compounded except as to that portion of the interest calculation period after 1995.[161]

(d) The Default Method. If the U.S. beneficiary uses the default method of calculating her accumulation distribution, the period over which interest is calculated is one-half the number of years the trust has been in existence as a foreign nongrantor trust.[162]

The application of the new default interest rule can be draconian. If, for example, the interest rate on underpayments is 5 percent, and if the U.S. beneficiary's tax rate is 35 percent, the entire amount of the distribution from a trust that has been in existence for forty-six or more years will be consumed by taxes and interest.[163] Interest charges, however, can be reduced by spreading distributions over a number of years and using the default method rather than the exact method of calculating the amount of the accumulation distributions. As illustrated by Example 11, use of the default method will, with a pattern of equal annual distributions, eliminate accumulation distributions after a period of three years.

(e) Observation. For families who view their trusts as semi-perpetual arrangements, the interest charge is not likely to be significant. Their trustees are likely to be able to arrange investment and distribution patterns in order to avoid accumulation distributions. No matter how many years a foreign nongrantor trust is permitted to accumulate income free of U.S. income tax, its U.S. beneficiaries will never be subject to an interest charge unless they receive an accumulation

161. Code § 668(a)(6).

162. IRS Form 3520, Line 38 (2005). A similar rule exists under Code § 666(d) and provides that if adequate records are not available to determine the years within which income was accumulated, a distribution of accumulated income shall be deemed to have come from income accumulated in the first year of the trust's existence. Presumably, the rule in Code § 6048(c)(2)(B) supersedes Code § 666(d) for foreign trusts.

163. A twenty-year trust requires that interest be calculated over a ten-year period. Interest calculated at a rate of 9 percent compounded daily on a tax of $40 (the assumed tax on a hypothetical distribution of $100) over a ten-year period will be approximately $60.

distribution. Distributions that do not exceed the greater of the trust's trust accounting income or DNI in the year of distribution will not be treated as accumulation distributions, and, therefore, the income tax they attract will not be subject to an interest charge.

4. Distributions of Income Accumulated before Beneficiary Became a U.S. Resident

If a U.S. person receives an accumulation distribution that is attributable to periods before she became a U.S. resident, the interest charge on the accumulation distribution is computed by excluding the years in which she was a foreign person. Code § 668(a)(4). For example, if a trust accumulated $25,000 of income each year from 2000 to 2005, and a foreign person moved to the United States in 2004 and in 2006 received an accumulation distribution of $125,000, the interest charge would apply only for 2004 and 2005.

However, a question arises as to whether the person who moved to the United States in 2004 should be taxed at all on the income accumulated prior to 2004, assuming it is not U.S.-source income.[164] Code § 667(a) establishes the general rule that an accumulation distribution allocated to a particular preceding taxable year is to be taxed, when distributed, to the extent that such amounts "would have been included in the income of such beneficiary under § 662(a)(2) (and, with respect to any tax exempt interest to which § 103 applies, under § 662(b)) if such total had been paid to such beneficiary on the last day of such preceding taxable year." This rule abandons the usual rule in Code § 662(b) that the character (and presumably the source) of income taxable to a beneficiary is determined by the source and character of the income of the trust, with the limited exception for tax-exempt interest. If the character of the non-U.S. source income were preserved for purposes of computing the tax on an accumulation distribution made to a U.S. person, then the person who received an accumulation distribution attributable to non-U.S. source income accumulated in a year in which such person was not a U.S. person would not be subject to tax. Unfortunately, Code § 667 does not expressly so provide, although it should as a matter of tax policy. Note that Code § 667(d) and (e) preserve the character rule for other purposes, namely, calculation of the allowable foreign tax credit and distributions from a foreign trust to a nonresident alien. Code § 667(e) appears to apply only if the person is a nonresident alien at the time of the distribution. Unless Code § 667(e) can be broadly interpreted to preserve the character rule for distributions to a U.S. person that are attributable to income accumulated in the foreign trust in years in which the U.S. taxpayer was a nonresident alien, then the U.S. immigrant is unfairly penalized for tax avoidance

---

164. *See* Jose L. Nunez & Andrea L. Mirabito, *Just Off the Boat, Trust Fund in Hand,* TRUSTS & ESTATES (Dec. 2005); *See also* NORMAN H. LANE & HOWARD M. ZARITSKY, FEDERAL INCOME TAXATION OF TRUSTS AND ESTATES § 6.06(6)(b) (1993) (regarding the application of the throwback rules with respect to a beneficiary who was not taxable in some of the base period years).

that did not occur.[165] The provisions of Code § 668(a)(2) (waiving the interest charge for distributions allocable to a year in which the beneficiary was not a U.S. person) would not be necessary if the accumulated income in the year were not subject to U.S. tax.

D. Loans Treated as Distributions

1. In General

Code § 643(i), which was added to the Code by the 1996 Act, treats, except as provided in regulations, a foreign trust's loans of cash (including foreign currencies and cash equivalents) or marketable securities to any U.S. grantor or beneficiary of the trust or to any other U.S. person who is related to such a grantor or beneficiary as a distribution.[166] For this purpose, a person is related to another person if the relationship between them would result in loss disallowance under Code § 267 or Code § 707(b).

If the loan is made to a person who is not the grantor or a beneficiary, it is not treated as a distribution to the borrower but instead is treated as a distribution to the grantor or beneficiary to whom the borrower is related.[167] The logic of this provision is difficult to see. It has the effect of separating the tax consequences from the economic enjoyment of the deemed distribution.

Congress apparently intended that Treasury would create regulatory exceptions to this rule to protect loans that are commercially reasonable.[168] Although

165. The unfair application of the accumulation distribution rules is not limited to this situation. For example, suppose a typical Canadian marital trust pays all income to a Canadian widow and accumulates capital gain. Upon the widow's death, the trust terminates and distributes to U.S. children. The children will be taxed under the accumulation distribution rules on gains that were accumulated in the trust. Gains were not accumulated in the trust to avoid U.S. tax. Gains were accumulated to preserve principal and because distributions to anyone other than the spouse is prohibited in order to qualify under Canadian law to defer capital gains at death. Had the assets passed outright to the widow rather than to the marital trust, the children would not be taxed on the gains (realized or unrealized) that accrued as of the date of their mother's death.

166. Code § 643(i). This provision did not apply to the loan of tangible property such as vacation homes, automobiles, and boats until the enactment of the 2010 HIRE Act on March 18, 2010. An earlier version of the foreign trust legislation that was passed in 1996 would have treated the loan of such property as a distribution of its use value. H.R. 981, 104th Cong. § 207(d) (1995). Prior to the HIRE Act of 2010, there was no existing authority holding that a beneficiary's rent-free use of a residence or other asset owned by a trust is a constructive distribution to the beneficiary. *See, e.g.*, Comm'r v. Plant, 76 F.2d 8 (2d Cir. 1935) (trust income expended for maintenance of property in which beneficiary resided held not income taxable to beneficiary); Alfred I. duPont Testamentary Trust v. Comm'r, 66 T.C. 761 (1976), *aff'd per curiam*, 574 F.2d 1332 (5th Cir. 1978) (same); Sparrow v. Comm'r, 18 B.T.A. 1 (1929) (on similar facts, allowing income tax deductions by trustees for cost of repairs to property on grounds that widow's right to occupy did not amount to a legal life estate). *See also* IRS Notice 97-34 (discussing constructive distributions from foreign trusts to U.S. beneficiaries, but silent regarding the rent-free use of trust-owned assets).

167. A person is related to a grantor or beneficiary if, under Code § 267, their relationship would result in a disallowance of losses for transactions between them. For this purpose, Code § 267(c)(4) is to be applied as if the family of an individual includes the spouses of her family members. Code § 643(i)(2)(B).

168. H.R. Rep. No. 737, at 334 (1996).

such regulations have yet to be issued, the IRS signaled its thinking on this subject in Notice 97-34.[169] The Notice states that the regulations will provide that a loan to a U.S. beneficiary (or a U.S. person related to a beneficiary) will be treated as a distribution unless it is a "qualified obligation." As discussed above, an obligation is a qualified obligation only if:

> (i) The obligation is reduced to writing by an express written agreement; (ii) The term of the obligation does not exceed five years (for purposes of determining the term of an obligation, the obligation's maturity date is the last possible date that the obligation can be outstanding under the terms of the obligation); (iii) All payments on the obligation are denominated in U.S. dollars; (iv) The yield to maturity of the obligation is not less than 100 percent of the applicable Federal rate and not greater than 130 percent of the applicable Federal rate (the applicable Federal rate for an obligation is the applicable Federal rate in effect under section 1274(d) for the day on which the obligation is issued, as published in the Internal Revenue Bulletin); (v) The U.S. person extends the period for assessment of any income tax attributable to the loan and any consequential income tax changes for each year that the obligation is outstanding, to a date not earlier than three years after the maturity date of the obligation issued in consideration for the loan (this extension is not necessary if the maturity date of the obligation does not extend beyond the end of the U.S. person's taxable year and is paid within such period); when properly executed and filed, such an agreement will be deemed to be consented to by the Service Center Director or the Assistant Commissioner (International) for purposes of § 301.6501(c)-1(d); and (vi) The U.S. person reports the status of the obligation, including principal and interest payments, on Form 3520 for each year that the obligation is outstanding.

Section 533 of the 2010 HIRE Act, effective March 19, 2010, extended the reach of Code § 643(i).[170] The section now treats loans of any property by a foreign trust to the grantor, beneficiary or a U.S. person related to the grantor or a beneficiary as a distribution. In the case of loans of property other than cash or marketable securities, the provision does not apply "to the extent that the trust is paid the fair market value of such use within a reasonable period of time of such use."[171]

169. 1997-1 C.B. 422.

170. The tax-free use of tangible personal property or real estate owned by a foreign trust was identified as an abuse. "Loans that are treated as trust distributions under U.S. tax law should be expanded to include, not just cash and securities as under present law, but also loans of real estate and personal property of any kind, including artwork, furnishings and jewelry." *Tax Haven Abuses: The Enablers, the Tools and Secrecy*, Minority & Majority Staff Report of the Permanent Subcommittee on Investigations, Aug. 1, 2006, at 10.

171. Code § 643(i)(2)(E).

2. Repayment of Loans

When a loan that has been treated as a distribution under Code § 643(i) is repaid, Code § 643(i)(3) disregards the repayment for all purposes of "this title." More precisely,

> any subsequent transaction between the trust and the original borrower regarding the principal of the loan (by way of complete or partial repayment, satisfaction, cancellation, discharge, or otherwise) shall be disregarded for purposes of this title.[172]

This is a curious provision. The "title" referred to includes not only the income tax provisions but the estate, gift, and generation-skipping transfer tax provisions as well. A literal application of Code § 643(i)(3) would permit a foreign trust created by a U.S. person to make a loan to a grandchild beneficiary of the trust's creator and to subsequently cancel that loan without any generation-skipping transfer tax consequences. The loan itself would not be treated as a taxable distribution for generation-skipping transfer tax purposes, because it is offset by a corresponding obligation running from the grandchild to the trust. The trust's subsequent cancellation would not be treated as a taxable distribution, because Code § 643(i)(3) requires that it be ignored. This provision should be amended to change its reference to "title" to "subtitle."

3. Amount of the Distribution

In gauging the impact of the loan provision as it applies to loans of marketable securities, it is important to keep in mind how Code § 643(e) treats the distribution of property in kind. Under Code § 643(e), unless the trustee elects otherwise, the amount of a distribution other than cash is the lesser of the trust's basis in the distributed property or its fair market value. The new rule does not seem to change this result. Thus, if a foreign trust lends marketable securities with a basis of 10 and a fair market value of 100 to a U.S. beneficiary, the amount treated as a distribution under Code § 643(i) would be 10, not 100, unless the trustee elects to recognize gain on the distribution.

E. Indirect Transfers from Foreign Trusts

1. Distributions through "Intermediaries"

Code § 643(h), which was added by the 1996 Act, treats a U.S. person who receives property from a person as having received the property directly from a foreign trust if the property she received was derived directly or indirectly from a foreign trust. This provision does not apply if the person from whom she received the property was the grantor of the trust. The intent of this provision is to prevent U.S. persons from avoiding income tax on their share of trust distributions by arranging for the distributions to be routed to them through another person.

---

172. *Id.* § 643(i)(3).

Since 1962, the Code has contained a rule intended to prevent the use of intermediaries as a means of circumventing the general rules that tax U.S. persons on distributions from foreign trusts created by U.S. persons. Former Code § 665(c) provided that:

> For purposes of this subpart, any amount paid to a United States person which is from a payor who is not a United States person and which is derived directly or indirectly from a foreign trust created by a United States person shall be deemed in the year of payment to have been directly paid by the foreign trust.

The language of former Code § 665(c) was broader than needed to accomplish the statutory objective. The Treasury, however, perhaps in recognition of the unnecessary breadth of the provisions, brought it within reasonable boundaries by regulation. Treasury Regulation § 1.665(c)-1A(b) provided that the section would not apply

> if the distribution is received by such beneficiary under circumstances indicating lack of intent on the part of the parties to circumvent the purposes for which section 7 of the Revenue Act of 1962 . . . was enacted.

New Code § 643(h) extends the scope of the old rule (1) to amounts derived from trusts created by non-U.S. persons (other than amounts received from the grantor of certain foreign trusts) and (2) to payments received from U.S. persons. It provides as follows:

> For purposes of this part, any amount paid to a United States person which is derived directly or indirectly from a foreign trust of which the payor is not the grantor shall be deemed in the year of payment to have been directly paid by the foreign trust to such United States person.

The expansion of the rule to trusts created by non-U.S. persons was presumably necessary to prevent what would otherwise have been a means of circumventing other provisions of the 1996 Act, which enhance the tax penalties imposed on the receipt of distributions of accumulated income from foreign trusts that are not taxed as grantor trusts under Code § 679 or otherwise.[173]

The reason for extending the rule to payments received from U.S. persons is less urgent. Foreign trust payments channeled through U.S. persons would, in the absence of new Code § 643(h), already have been exposed to U.S. taxation and, in the case of accumulation distributions, to the 1996 Act's additional costs imposed on the receipt of such distributions.

The Treasury has issued regulations under Code § 643(h).[174] The regulations treat distributions from trusts as being made through intermediaries only if the

173. *See id.* § 668.

174. Treas. Reg. § 1.643(h)-1.

transaction has a principal purpose of avoiding U.S. tax. The regulations create a presumption of tax avoidance if *all* of the following factors are present:

1. The U.S. person who received property from the intermediary is related to the grantor of the foreign trust or has another relationship with the grantor of the foreign trust that establishes a reasonable basis for concluding that the grantor would make a gratuitous transfer to the U.S. person. For example, if the U.S. person is a child of the grantor of the foreign trust, this factor would be satisfied.
2. An intermediary received a distribution from a foreign trust and, within a four-year period beginning two years before the distribution, transferred to a U.S. person the same property, proceeds from the disposition of such property, or property "in substitution for" such property.
   a. Example 5 of Treas. Reg. § 1.643(h)-1(g) illustrates a transfer of property to a U.S. person in substitution for property distributed to an intermediary. The substitute property was shares of stock of equivalent value to shares distributed from the trust, but in different companies.
   b. Example 6 of Treas. Reg. § 1.643(h)-1(g) demonstrates that a bank is viewed as an intermediary if it lends money to a U.S. person and the loan is secured by the trust's deposit of funds in the bank if it can be shown that the bank would not have loaned funds to the U.S. person without the security interest in the trust's deposit. Note that the bank has not received a "distribution" from a foreign trust, but rather a deposit. However, the loan is deemed to have been made from the trust.
3. The U.S. person cannot demonstrate to the satisfaction of the IRS that:
   a. the intermediary has a relationship with the U.S. person that establishes a reasonable basis for concluding that the intermediary would also make a gratuitous transfer to the U.S. person;
   b. the intermediary acted independently of the grantor and the trustee of the foreign trust;
   c. the intermediary was not the agent of the U.S. person; and
   d. the U.S. person properly reported the gift under Code § 6049F (required if the gift was made by a foreign person and the recipient received aggregate foreign gifts in excess of the reportable threshold).

Examples in the regulations indicate that a U.S. person who receives property from a nonresident alien parent who received a distribution from a foreign trust funded by a grandparent will have to demonstrate more than a family relationship to the intermediary to avoid the nonresident alien parent being treated as an intermediary. If there is a pattern of giving, and if the intermediary has other sources of income from which the transfer may have derived, that, plus the family relationship, apparently will be sufficient to avoid the parent being treated as an intermediary.[175] Less evidence is required to show that a *resident* alien parent did not act as an intermediary.[176]

Example 2 of Treas. Reg. § 1.643(h)-1(g) demonstrates that a U.S. person who is treated as having received a distribution from a foreign trust through an intermediary need not be a beneficiary of the foreign trust. In that example, GM created a trust for her children. A distribution was made to the child, who was a nonresident alien. The beneficiary made a gift to her daughter who was a U.S. resident. The grantor's granddaughter was treated as having received a distribution from the foreign trust even though she was not a beneficiary.

2. The Grantor Is Not an "Intermediary"

Under the Code, a grantor is never an intermediary. Treas. Reg. § 1.643(h)-1(b)(2) limits the exception to instances in which "the intermediary is the grantor of the portion of the trust from which the property that is transferred is derived." The regulations do not discuss how the portion rules are to be applied in this context.

The portion rules apply to determine what portion of a trust a grantor is deemed to own for income tax purposes. The rules do not explain how one determines who is the grantor of a portion of a trust. Consider, for example, a trust created by gift of community property. If a distribution is made to just one of the spouses, will the distribution qualify in full for the exception to the intermediary rule? If the trustee separately accounts for trust shares, presumably the answer is yes.

If a person creates or nominally funds a trust on behalf of another person, both are considered "grantors," but the nominal grantor is not treated as the owner of any portion of the trust.[177] Although the intermediary regulations use the term "grantor" and not the term "owner," if nominal grantors were able to serve as intermediaries, the intermediary rule would be simple to circumvent.

It is not clear whether the grantor must actively participate in the transfer of funds for the exception to the intermediary rule to apply. For example, if the trust makes a distribution to an account in the joint names of the grantor and a beneficiary, and the beneficiary withdraws funds, it would be reasonable to treat the distribution as made through the grantor because the bank should not be treated as an intermediary in this situation.

3. Agency Principles Control Issue of Timing and Amount of Income

Under the regulations, if a distribution is treated as being made through an intermediary, the intermediary is considered to be the agent of the trust unless the facts show that the intermediary was the agent of the U.S. person. Where the intermediary is considered to be the agent of the trust, the U.S. person includes the

175. *See id.* § 1.643(h)-1(g), Example 3.
176. *See id.* § 1.643(h)-1(g), Example 7.
177. *Id.* § 1.671-2(e)(5).

cash or property he or she receives from the intermediary in income in the year in which the U.S. person receives the cash or property, even if the distribution was made to an intermediary in an earlier taxable year. If the property distributed from the foreign trust is worth more by the time the U.S. person receives it, the increased amount is included in income. If the property has declined in value, the U.S. person reports the lower value. If the intermediary has paid foreign taxes with respect to the cash or property distributed from the foreign trust, the U.S. person treats such taxes as if imposed on the trust for purposes of Code § 665(d)(2).[178]

If the intermediary is the agent of the U.S. person, the U.S. person includes the cash or property distributed to the intermediary in the U.S. person's income when her agent receives the distribution. Any income accruing on such cash or property between the time the intermediary receives it and the time the U.S. person receives it is also taxable to the U.S. person. If any foreign taxes were owed by the intermediary with respect to such cash or property, the taxes are creditable by the U.S. person as if the taxes were imposed on the U.S. person. Usual agency principles are applied to determine whether the intermediary is the agent of the U.S. person.[179]

If a person who receives a distribution from a foreign trust is deemed to be an intermediary, the intermediary may exclude the distribution from gross income.[180] The regulations fail to exclude from the intermediary's gross income any income accruing on the property distributed from the foreign trust before it is transferred to the U.S. person, although presumably this was intended.

A *de minimis* exception applies where the aggregate amount of distributions to a U.S. person in one taxable year that are made from foreign trusts, either directly or through one or more intermediaries, does not exceed $10,000.[181]

F. Treatment of Income of Controlled Foreign Corporations and Passive Foreign Investment Companies

1. In General

The U.S. beneficiaries of a foreign nongrantor trust may be subject to tax on income earned by controlled foreign corporations (CFCs) and passive foreign investment companies (PFICs) whose shares are held by the trust.[182] The CFC and PFIC rules, also called the "anti-deferral regimes," eliminate the deferral of U.S. income tax that generally exists for U.S. shareholders of domestic corporations (i.e., shareholders are not subject to income tax on corporate income until

178. *Id.* § 1.643(h)-1(c)(1).

179. *Id.* § 1.643(h)-1(c)(2).

180. *Id.* § 1.643(h)-1(c)(3).

181. *Id.* § 1.643(h)-1(d).

182. The American Jobs Creation Act of 2004, which was enacted on October 22, 2004 (Pub. L. No. 108-357, 118 Stat. 1418) (the 2004 Act), repealed the foreign personal holding company rules under Code §§ 551–558. The repeal is effective for taxable years of foreign corporations beginning after December 31, 2004.

dividends are paid to them). These anti-deferral regimes require that certain types of passive income of CFCs or PFICs be taxed to their U.S. shareholders currently, whether or not distributions are made to them.

2. The Anti-Deferral Regimes

(a) Controlled Foreign Corporations. A foreign corporation is a CFC if more than 50 percent (by vote or value) of its stock is owned by "United States shareholders."[183] For purposes of this definition, a "United States shareholder" is a United States person[184] who owns—either directly, through one or more foreign entities,[185]or through the application of certain constructive ownership rules[186]—at least 10 percent of the total combined voting power of all classes of stock entitled to vote.[187] For purposes of determining whether a United States shareholder meets the 10 percent test, the constructive ownership rules of Code § 318, as modified by Code § 958(b), apply. Under these rules, the shareholder will be deemed to own stock that is owned directly or indirectly by members of her family who are also U.S. persons, and will be deemed to own her proportionate share of any stock owned directly or indirectly by a partnership, estate, or trust in which she has an interest, or by a corporation if she owned, directly or indirectly, 50 percent or more of the value of its stock.[188] For purposes of Code § 318, the members of a shareholder's family include only her spouse, children, grandchildren, and parents.[189]

A U.S. person who owns directly or through a foreign entity shares of a foreign corporation that is a CFC for an uninterrupted period of more than thirty days during any taxable year and who owns shares in such corporation on the last day in such year on which the corporation is a CFC must include in gross income for each year her pro rata share of the CFC's subpart F income.[190] A shareholder's pro rata share of a CFC's subpart F income is the amount that would have been distributed with respect to the stock that such shareholder directly or indirectly (but not constructively) owns if, on the last day of the taxable year, the CFC had distributed all of its subpart F income pro rata to its shareholders.[191] Subpart F income includes certain types of insurance income, foreign base company income, international boycott income, and foreign bribe-produced income.[192] This includes foreign personal holding company income (FPHCI), which, subject to some important exceptions,

---

183. Code § 957(a).

184. The term "United States person" generally has the same meaning assigned to it by Code § 7701(a)(30). It includes individuals who are citizens or residents of the United States, domestic partnerships, domestic corporations, and estates or trusts other than foreign estates and trusts.

185. Code § 958(a).

186. *Id.* § 958(b).

187. *Id.* § 951(b).

188. *Id.* § 318(a).

189. *Id.* § 318(a)(1).

190. *Id.* § 951(a).

191. *Id.* § 951(a)(2).

192. *Id.* § 952(a).

generally includes, among other things, dividends, interest, royalties, rents, annuities, gains from the sale or exchange of certain types of property, gains from commodities, foreign currency gains, profits from the purchases and sales of certain types of personal property, and income from the performance of certain services for or on behalf of a related person outside the CFC's country of incorporation.[193]

For taxable years of foreign corporations beginning before January 1, 2005, an alternate, anti-deferral regime known as the foreign personal holding company (FPHC) regime could apply to tax a shareholder who owned shares of a foreign corporation that was not reached by the CFC rules.[194] The FPHC rules potentially applied to a smaller group of foreign corporations because they applied to a corporation only if at least 50 percent of its gross income was FPHCI. But, corporations that satisfied the gross income test were more likely to satisfy the U.S. ownership test of the FPHC regime than the U.S. ownership test of the CFC regime because of the FPHC's more expansive version of the constructive ownership rules. Under the FPHC rules, a U.S. person was deemed to own all shares of a foreign corporation owned by her spouse, ancestors, descendants, and siblings, whether or not such family members were U.S. persons, as well as all shares owned by any partner of hers, no matter how large the partnership nor how small her interest in it. Additionally, the FPHC rules applied to tax a U.S. person with shares in an FPHC on her share of the corporation's income for a particular year no matter how many days in the taxable year the corporation was an FPHC. In contrast, the CFC rules operate to tax a U.S. person in a particular year only if the corporation is a CFC for at least thirty continuous days in such year.

(b) Passive Foreign Investment Companies. A U.S. shareholder who is not subject to current tax under the CFC regime may still be subject to the PFIC regime. A foreign corporation is a PFIC if (1) 75 percent or more of its gross income for the taxable year is passive income or (2) the average percentage of assets (by value) held by the corporation for the production of passive income is at least 50 percent.[195] Passive income generally means income that would be FPHCI under subpart F.[196] Generally, a U.S. person who owns any interest in a PFIC will be subject to ordinary income tax on gain from disposing of PFIC stock and will be subject to an interest charge on the income tax imposed on such gain and on distributions from the PFIC.[197] For purposes of this provision, a disposition of shares in a PFIC by a foreign nongrantor trust may be treated as a disposition of PFIC stock by

193. *Id.* § 954(a) and (c) A *de minimis* rule provides that if, in any particular year, a CFC's foreign base company income and its gross insurance income are less than the lesser of (1) 5 percent of its gross income or (2) $1 million, no part of its income will be treated as foreign base company income or insurance income. *Id.* § 954(b)(3). Special rules are provided for CFCs that have more than one class of stock with different dividend rights.

194. *Id.* §§ 551–558 (repealed by the 2004 Act).

195. Code § 1297(a).

196. *Id.* § 1297(b).

197. *Id.* § 1291.

the trust's U.S. beneficiaries. Similarly, a distribution of property from a PFIC to the foreign nongrantor trust may be treated as a distribution to its U.S. beneficiaries.[198] The specific tax consequences to a U.S. shareholder depend on whether or not she makes a "qualified electing fund" election or a mark-to-market election (with respect to regularly traded securities).[199]

Under the Offshore Voluntary Disclosure Program in effect at the time of publication of this chapter, through which taxpayers may declare unreported offshore income and assets and pay tax, interest, and penalties (including a fixed "offshore" penalty based on the highest value of the offshore assets within the covered period) to resolve prior non-compliance with respect to such offshore income and assets, a taxpayer may calculate tax on a basis that is consistent with a mark-to-market election allowed in Code § 1296 but without the need to reconstruct historical data.[200] Instead, the PFIC tax is computed as of the end of 2003 (or the first year covered by the disclosure, if later) or the end of the first year PFIC shares were owned, if later, assuming a basis as negotiated between the taxpayer and the IRS, if records are not available. Gains are taxed at 20 percent instead of the rate called for under Code § 1291, and interest on the deferred tax is calculated at 7 percent for the first year instead of the rate under Code § 1291(c).

3. The Attribution, Indirect, and Constructive Ownership Rules

The CFC regime contains indirect and constructive ownership rules that are used to determine both whether a corporation is a CFC and the extent to which U.S. persons will be taxed on its income.[201] Similarly, the PFIC regime contains attribution rules that are used to determine the extent to which U.S. persons will be taxed on distributions and dispositions.[202] In both cases, these rules provide that stock in a foreign corporation owned by a foreign nongrantor trust will be considered as owned proportionately by its beneficiaries.[203] When the beneficiaries of a foreign nongrantor trust have fixed interests in the trust, applying the constructive ownership rules is simple.

> ***Example 23:*** A foreign nongrantor trust established in 2004 has three beneficiaries, Michael, Isaac, and Tyler. Each beneficiary is entitled to one-third of the FNT's income each year. At the end of the FNT's ten-year term, the trust fund will be distributed equally among the three benefi-

---

198. *Id.* § 1298(b)(5)(A).

199. *Id.* §§ 1293–1295.

200. FAQ 10 on IRS web page on voluntary disclosure. http://www.irs.gov/Individuals/International-Taxpayers/Offshore-Voluntary-Disclosure-Program-Frequently-Asked-Questions-and-Answers (last visited July 24, 2013). In certain instances, this Program also allows a taxpayer to disregard the existence of a foreign trust or foreign corporations, including CFCs. See FAQ 29.

201. Code § 958(a), (b); Code § 554(a).

202. *Id.* § 1298(a).

203. *Id.* § 958(a)(2) (CFC attribution rules); *Id.* § 554(a)(1) (foreign personal holding company attribution rules). The PFIC regime contains constructive ownership rules that apply to determine the extent to which U.S. persons will be treated as owning its stock. *Id.* § 1298(a)(3).

ciaries. Michael and Tyler are U.S. persons; Isaac is not. The FNT holds 100 percent of the stock of a foreign corporation (FC). In 2005, eighty (80 percent) percent of FC's gross income is FPHCI. Under the attribution rules discussed above, Michael, Isaac, and Tyler will each be considered as owning 33-1/3 percent of the shares of FC. As a result, in 2005, FC will be classified as a CFC. FC will also be a PFIC because of its percentage of passive income. Michael and Tyler, however, will be taxed only under the CFC regime, which takes precedence over the PFIC regime.[204]

Matters are more complicated when beneficial interests are divided temporally. Suppose, for example, that in Example 23, on the death of the first of Michael, Isaac, and Tyler to die, the FNT was to terminate and all of its property was to be distributed to Cathlyn, a non-U.S. person. Suppose further that the actuarial value of the income interests in the trust were equal to 30 percent of the value of the trust and the actuarial value of the remainder interest, 70 percent. Do Michael and Isaac, the two U.S. persons, each now indirectly own only 10 percent of FC?

The regulations under the former FPHC rules deal only with trusts the beneficiaries of which own both present and future interests in equal shares.[205] The IRS has ruled, however, that a beneficiary's proportionate ownership is to be determined with reference to her proportionate actuarial interest in the trust.[206] There are no final regulations interpreting the PFIC attribution rules. Proposed regulations suggest that the determination of a person's indirect ownership should be made on the basis of all the facts and circumstances.[207] The CFC regulations establish two different approaches. The first construes Code § 958(a), the subsection that determines both whether the beneficiary will be subject to tax on a CFC's income and whether the corporation whose shares are owned by the trust is a CFC. It states that the determination of a person's proportionate interest in a foreign trust will be made on the basis of all of the facts and circumstances.[208] The second construes Code § 958(b), the subsection that applies for purposes of determining whether a corporation is a CFC. It states that stock owned directly or indirectly by a trust will be considered as owned by its beneficiaries in proportion to the actuarial interests of such beneficiaries in the trust.[209]

The IRS provided some guidance on this issue in Field Service Advice 199952014.[210] Without stating whether the actuarial allocation rule might simultaneously apply for purposes of Code § 958(b), the IRS determined that, for purposes of Code § 958(a), the trust beneficiaries who were entitled to receive all

204. *See* Treas. Reg. § 1.958-1(d), Example 3.
205. Treas. Reg. § 1.554-1; Treas. Reg. § 1.552-3; Treas. Reg. § 1.544-2.
206. Rev. Rul. 62-155, 1962-2 C.B. 132.
207. Prop. Reg. § 1.1291-1(b)(8)(i).
208. Treas. Reg. § 1.958-1(c)(2).
209. *Id.* § 1.958-2(c)(1)(ii)(a).
210. FSA 199952014 (Sept. 23, 1999).

current income should be treated as owning all of the stock owned by the trust. The remainder beneficiaries were treated as owning no stock.

In the personal holding company context, the IRS has also provided some guidance as to discretionary trusts. Applying the attribution rules in the context of a foreign nongrantor trust becomes more difficult when the trust is a discretionary trust. The trustees of such a trust have complete discretion to distribute income and/or principal among the beneficiaries. The beneficiaries do not have fixed interests in the trusts that can be easily calculated.

In Private Letter Ruling 9024076,[211] the IRS described several relevant facts and circumstances to be considered in determining the actuarial interest of a beneficiary in a discretionary trust for purposes of Code § 544 (concerning personal holding companies). These facts include (1) the pattern of past distributions, (2) appropriate mortality assumptions, (3) the trustee's fiduciary duties, and (4) the relationships among the trustees and beneficiaries. According to the IRS, if it is possible to discern a pattern of past distributions, each beneficiary receiving distributions under such pattern will be deemed to own an income interest in the trust in the same proportion that the amount of distributions she receives bears to the total amount of the distribution. Each beneficiary's income interest can then be determined on an actuarial basis with reference to the mortality tables as if the trustees were required to distribute the income to such beneficiary over the remainder of her life.

In Technical Advice Memorandum 200733024, the IRS applied the facts-and-circumstances test to treat beneficiaries of a foreign trust as indirectly owning shares of a PFIC owned by the trust in the same proportion as the historic patterns of distributions. When the trust liquidated its interest in the PFIC, the beneficiaries were treated and taxed as if they had disposed of the PFIC shares of which they were the indirect beneficial owners.

If the beneficiaries are treated as the indirect owners of shares held in a trust, the beneficiaries may be obligated to file information returns required of CFC shareholders (Form 5471) and PFIC shareholders (Form 8621).[212]

4. Planning Techniques

If U.S. beneficiaries receive shares of CFCs on the death of a nonresident alien, their retention of the shares will subject them to current income tax at ordinary income tax rates on their pro rata share of certain corporate income whether or

211. I.R.S. Priv. Ltr. Rul. 9024076 (Mar. 21, 1990).

212. Although reporting was previously required based on the occurrence of a triggering event, such as the sale or disposition of the PFIC, the 2010 HIRE Act enacted Code § 1298(f) to expand the filing obligations of PFIC shareholders. Therefore, a U.S. beneficiary attributed an interest in a PFIC held by a trust will now generally be subject to annual reporting requirements on IRS Form 8621 ("*Information Return by a Shareholder of a Passive Foreign Investment Company or Qualified Electing Fund*"), regardless of whether the trust sells or disposes of the PFIC. The IRS promptly suspended this filing requirement pending the release of an updated form and regulations. Notice 2010-34, 2010-7 IRB 612; Notice 2011-55, 2011-29 IRB 53; *see also* instructions to Form 8621(December, 2012).

not the income is distributed to them. If, in order to avoid this result, they liquidate the corporation, they will be taxed on their share of the unrealized appreciation in the corporation's assets on liquidation, and, if their share of the value of the assets received on liquidation exceeds their basis in the stock of the corporation, on that gain as well.[213]

The tax on the unrealized appreciation in the corporation's assets can be avoided by liquidating the corporation within thirty days of the death of the non-U.S. person. The liquidation will be timely if it prevents the corporation from having been a CFC for thirty days or more during the year of death of the non-U.S. person. For purposes of counting the thirty days, the date of death of the non-U.S. person is excluded and the date of the liquidation is included. For example, if a nonresident alien dies on September 1, bequeathing her 100 percent ownership in a foreign corporation to her U.S. daughter, a liquidation of the corporation on or before September 30 would be timely, but liquidation on or after October 1 would not.[214]

The thirty-day time limit can effectively be extended by using a corporation that would be classified as a partnership or a disregarded entity for U.S. income tax purposes if an appropriate election is made.[215] Within seventy-five days after the death of the nonresident alien, the foreign corporation would file an election to be classified as a partnership for U.S. income tax purposes effective two days after the death of the nonresident alien. The effect of the election will be to treat the corporation as having distributed all of its assets and liabilities to its U.S. shareholder in complete liquidation of the corporation on the day before the effective date of the election.[216] The corporation will be treated as recognizing gain to the extent the fair market value of its assets exceeds its basis in those

213. If the liquidation takes place shortly after the death of the nonresident alien, the basis adjustment normally applicable under Code § 1014 will often eliminate the tax on the unrealized gain with respect to the shares of stock. *See* discussion *infra* Section IV.E.

214. Treas. Reg. § 1.951-1(a), (f).

215. Treas. Reg. § 301.7701-2 classifies, for U.S. income tax purposes, a foreign business entity, other than an entity that is automatically classified as a "*per se*" corporation under Treas. Reg. § 301.7701-2(b), as a partnership if it has more than one member, at least one of which does not have limited liability, or as an association taxable as a corporation if all of its members have limited liability. If the entity has only one member and that member does not have limited liability, the entity is disregarded as an entity separate from its owner. A business entity is, generally, any entity other than an entity properly classified as a trust. Foreign entities that are automatically classified as corporations include the Société Anonyme in Belgium, France, and Switzerland; the Aktiengellschaft in Austria, Germany, and Switzerland; the Sociedad Anónima in Mexico and Spain; and the Public Limited Company in the United Kingdom. If a foreign entity is not automatically classified as a corporation, but is classified as an association taxable as a corporation because all of its members have limited liability, it may elect to be classified either as a partnership or a disregarded entity, depending on the number of members, by filing Form 8832 with the appropriate IRS service center. The election made on Form 8832 will be effective on the date specified on the form, provided the effective date may not be more than seventy-five days prior to or more than twelve months after the form is filed.

216. Treas. Reg. § 301.7701-3(g)(1)(iii).

assets,[217] but will not pay U.S. income tax on this gain because it is not subject to U.S. income tax. The basis of the corporation's assets in the hands of its U.S. shareholder will be the fair market value of the assets on the day before the effective day of the election.[218] The deemed receipt by the shareholder of the corporation's assets will be treated as amounts received in exchange for her stock.[219] Any gain recognized, however, should be minimal if the basis of the stock of the corporation was adjusted under Code § 1014 to the value as of the date of death of the nonresident alien.[220]

IV. Tax Treatment of U.S. Beneficiaries of Grantor Trusts with Foreign Grantors

A. Background

The 1996 Act limited the circumstances in which a person who is not a U.S. citizen or resident (foreign person) will be treated as the owner of a trust under the grantor trust rules.

Under prior law, a foreign person was treated as the owner of a trust under Code §§ 673–678 to the same extent as a U.S. person, whether the trust was foreign or domestic. Only Code § 679 was limited to U.S. grantors. If a foreign person was treated as the owner of the income, then (1) the foreign grantor-owner was taxed on such income only under the limited rules for taxing nonresident alien individuals and foreign corporations, and (2) distributions from the trust to U.S. beneficiaries were treated as gifts from the foreign grantor-owner. Such gifts generally were not taxable to the U.S. beneficiary as income.[221] A gift tax would not be imposed so long as the subject matter of the gift was either intangible property or situated outside the United States.

B. Limitation on Grantor Trusts

Code § 672(f) prevents avoidance of U.S. income tax by limiting the circumstances in which foreign persons will be treated as the owner of trust assets under the grantor trust rules. Generally, the grantor trust rules will apply only if the rules result in an amount (if the trust as any income) being currently taken into account in computing the income of a U.S. person, except as provided in § 672(f)(2), as discussed further below.

---

217. Code § 311(b). U.S. income tax could be imposed, however, if the lower-tier corporation owns U.S. real estate.

218. Code § 334(a).

219. *Id.* § 331(a).

220. *Id.* § 1014. In the case of decedents dying before January 1, 2005, the Code § 1014 basis adjustment was not available for shares of FPHCs.

221. Rev. Rul. 69-70, 1969-1 C.B. 182.

C. Definition of Grantor

Treasury regulations define the term "grantor" as a person (which may include both an individual and a nonnatural person) who either creates a trust or directly or indirectly makes a "gratuitous transfer" of property to a trust.[222] Prior to the issuance of regulations on July 5, 2000, there was no clear definition of "grantor," which led to abuses.[223]

1. Accommodation Grantor

If a person creates or funds a trust on behalf of another person, both persons are treated as grantors, but only the person making gratuitous transfers may be treated as the owner of the trust. A person who is reimbursed for a gratuitous transfer is not treated as an owner of any portion of the trust. For example, if an attorney settles a trust for the benefit of a client's children, funds the trust with $5,000, and later receives reimbursement for such contribution, the attorney is a grantor who may have an obligation to report the creation of the foreign trust and the transfer of funds to the trust for purposes of Code § 6048, but the attorney is not treated as the owner of any portion of the trust.[224] If an accommodation grantor, such as the attorney in the above example, were treated as the grantor for purposes of the exception to the intermediary rule, the intermediary rule would be easily circumvented.[225] Distributions could be made from foreign trusts through accommodation grantors, and such transfers would be tax-free gifts to the U.S. donees. Applicable regulations seek to prevent this by limiting the exception to distributions from the "portion of the trust" of which the intermediary is the grantor.[226]

2. Gratuitous Transfer

A gratuitous transfer means a transfer other than a transfer made for fair market value or a distribution made by an entity, such as a corporation or partnership, in respect of an interest in such entity owned by a trust. For example, dividends received from a corporation in which a trust owns stock are not gratuitous transfers. A transfer for fair market value means a transfer in consideration for and equal to the value of (1) property received from the trust (other than an interest in the trust); (2) services rendered by the trust; or (3) the right to use property owned by the trust. A transfer may be gratuitous without regard to whether it is a gift for gift tax purposes and whether gain is recognized on the transfer.

3. "Grantor" Includes Purchasers

A grantor includes a person who acquires a beneficial interest in a trust from the grantor if the trust is one of the following: a fixed investment trust described

222. Treas. Reg. § 1.671-2(e).
223. T.D. 8890 (July 5, 2000).
224. Treas. Reg. §§ 1.671-2(e)(1) and 1.679-3(c); Treas. Reg. § 1.671-2(e)(6), Example 3.
225. Code § 643(h) excludes a grantor from the class of persons who are treated as intermediaries.
226. Treas. Reg. § 1.643(h)-1(b)(2).

in Treas. Reg. § 301.7701-4(c), a liquidating trust described in Treas. Reg. § 301.7701-4(d), or an environmental remediation trust described in Treas. Reg. § 301.7701-4(e).

4. Grantors Who Are Corporations or Partnerships

A corporation or partnership will be treated as the grantor of a trust established for a business purpose, such as to secure a legal obligation to an unrelated third party. However, if a corporation or partnership establishes a trust for a purpose other than a business purpose, the shareholder or partner on whose behalf the trust was deemed to have been established will be treated as constructively receiving the property and contributing it to the trust.[227]

5. Trusts Established by Other Trusts

If a trust makes a gratuitous transfer to another trust, the grantor of the transferor trust is treated as the grantor of the transferee trust *unless* a person with a general power of appointment over the transferor trust exercises the power in favor of another trust. When this occurs, the power holder is treated as the grantor of the transferee trust.[228] This rule applies even if the grantor of the transferor trust is treated as the owner of the transferor trust. This rule creates significant planning opportunities.

A power of appointment exercisable with the consent of a person who is not the grantor or an adverse party may be a general power. For example, suppose that A creates a foreign trust that is treated as being owned by A. Further suppose that B, who is a nonresident alien individual, has a general power of appointment over the trust exercisable with the consent of a protector who is related to A but who has no beneficial interest in the trust. If B exercises the power to appoint the trust assets to a new trust, B is treated as the grantor of the trust to which the assets have been appointed. Although B will not qualify as the owner of the trust unless the requirements of Code § 672(f)(2) are met, distributions through B may satisfy the exception to the intermediary rule in Code § 643(h) even if B is not treated as the owner of the trust.

Code § 672(f)(5) does not apply to make A the owner of the trust (even assuming that A was a beneficiary of the transferee trust) unless B would otherwise be treated as the owner of the trust.

Code § 679 treats A as the owner of the foreign transferee trust if A has transferred property to the trust, directly or indirectly, and the trust has a U.S. beneficiary, unless the transfer was for value. Has A indirectly transferred property to the trust established by B's exercise of B's power of appointment? Does Treas. Reg. § 1.671-2(e)(5) affect the analysis? That regulation makes B, and not A, the grantor of the transferee trust. Does this regulation preclude A from being treated as the transferor of the transferee trust for purposes of Code § 679?

227. *Id.* § 1.671-2(e)(4).
228. *Id.* § 1.671-2(e)(5).

If B's power was a limited power of appointment, A would continue to be treated as the grantor of the trust to which the assets were appointed.

6. Code § 678 Powers

The regulations clarify that a person who has the right to withdraw assets from the trust is not a "grantor." Although such a person would be treated as the owner of the trust under Code § 678 if he or she were a U.S. person, a foreign person who has an *unexercised* Code § 678 power will not be treated as the owner of a trust.[229]

However, if the person who has the Code § 678 power exercises the power to create a new trust, then he or she will qualify as the grantor. Even if he or she will not qualify as the owner of the trust, distributions may be made through the new grantor. The grantor is never treated as the intermediary.

Reg. § 1.671-2(e)(5) provides that a person who funds a trust by exercising a general power of appointment is the grantor. The general power of appointment, but not the Code § 678 power, can be subject to limitations on exercise. Therefore, a power of appointment may be more useful for changing the grantor.

However, there is a risk that a nominal grantor will not be treated as the grantor for purposes of the intermediary rule. In some cases, the more conservative course may be to give the grantor control over assets before they are resettled in a new trust so that there is less argument for challenging her status as a real grantor.

7. Trust as Owner of Another Trust

A trust can be treated as the owner of another trust under the grantor trust rules. For example, if Trust 1 funds Trust 2 pursuant to the exercise of the trustee's discretion, but the trustee of Trust 1 retains a power to revoke Trust 2 and revest the assets in Trust 1, Trust 1 will be treated as the owner of Trust 2 under Code § 678.[230]

D. Foreign Persons Not Treated as Owners

1. General Rule

Code § 672(f)(1) provides:

> Notwithstanding any other provision of this subpart, this subpart shall apply only to the extent such application results in an amount (if any) being currently taken into account (directly or through 1 or more entities) under this chapter in computing the income of a citizen or resident of the United States or a domestic corporation.

229. *Id.* § 1.671-2(e)(6), Example 4.
230. *Id.* § 1.671-2(e)(6), Example 8.

2. Exceptions to General Rule

Code § 672(f)(2) provides three exceptions to the general rule of Code § 672(f): (1) certain revocable trusts, (2) trusts that benefit only the grantor and the grantor's spouse, and (3) compensatory trusts. In addition, certain trusts in existence on September 19, 1995, are grandfathered from the new rules.

(a) Revocable Trust. A trust is exempt from Code § 672(f)(1) if it is revocable by the grantor alone or with the consent of a "related or subordinate party," as defined in Code § 672(c), who is subservient to the grantor.[231] In the event of the grantor's incapacity, the trust will continue to qualify as revocable if a guardian or other person has the power to revoke the trust on behalf of the grantor without the consent of any other person.

A related or subordinate party is a "nonadverse party" who is the grantor's parent, issue, sibling, or employee, or a corporation or employee of a corporation in which the stock holdings of the grantor and the trust are significant from the viewpoint of voting control, or a subordinate employee of a corporation in which the grantor is an executive. A nonadverse party is a person who does not have a sufficient beneficial interest in the trust to be adverse to the exercise of the power of revocation. Therefore, the exception in Code § 672(f)(1) may not apply where the grantor needs a beneficiary's consent to revoke the trust, even if, without regard to the "nonadverse party" requirement, the beneficiary is a related or subordinate party. However, if the beneficiary whose consent is required is the grantor's spouse, the spouse's adverse interest should be disregarded because any power or interest held by the grantor's spouse is treated as if held by the grantor.[232] It is not clear whether Code § 672(f) overrides Code § 672(e).

Persons within the category of related or subordinate are presumed to be subservient to the grantor unless shown by a preponderance of the evidence to be not subservient.[233]

De facto control over the person who holds the consent power is not sufficient. Example 3 of Treas. Reg. § 1.672(f)-3(a)(4) provides that where an independent trustee has the power to revest assets in the grantor and the grantor has the power to replace an independent bank with a related or subordinate trustee, the nonresident alien grantor will not be treated as the owner of the trust. Example 1 reaches the opposite conclusion where the bank serving as trustee is owned and controlled by the grantor's brother. The regulations are not consistent with the IRS rulings concerning when trustee powers are imputed to the grantor.[234] If the grantor has the power to remove the independent bank and appoint himself

231. The trust need not expressly state that it is "revocable" so long as the grantor has the power to "revest absolutely in the grantor title to the trust property . . . ." Code § 672(f)(2)(A)(i).

232. *Id.* § 672(e).

233. Treas. Reg. § 1.672(f)-3.

234. *See, e.g.*, Rev. Rul. 79-353, 1979-2 C.B. 325, *as modified by* Rev. Rul. 95-58, 1995-2 C.B. 191.

as trustee, the powers of the trustee should be imputed to the grantor, but the regulations suggest that the IRS would not agree.

Treas. Reg. § 1.672(f)-3(a)(2) requires that the revocation power must be exercisable for a period aggregating 183 days or more during the taxable year of the trust. If the year is less than 183 days, the 183-day requirement is met if the trust is revocable for each day of the short year.

Treas. Reg. § 1.672(f)-3(a)(1) provides that if a trust does not qualify for the limited exception for certain revocable trusts for a particular year, the trust will not qualify for the exception in any subsequent year, even if the trust is later revocable by the grantor. To avoid this result, the grantor could exercise the power and resettle the trust.

A beneficiary who has a withdrawal right is not treated as the *de facto* grantor. For example, a beneficiary who can withdraw all of the assets of a trust at any time is not defined as the grantor and thus cannot be treated as the owner of the trust under Code § 672(f)(2)(A)(i). If the beneficiary actually withdrew trust assets and funded a new trust, the beneficiary would be treated as the grantor-owner if she retained the same right to withdraw the assets from the new trust.

(b) Trust for the Benefit of Grantor or Spouse. A trust that benefits *only* the grantor or the grantor's spouse during the lifetime of the grantor is exempt from Code § 672(f)(1). If any amount is distributable to another person, even temporarily, the trust will not be a grantor trust under this exception. For example, if a trust benefits only the grantor except that distributions may be made to the grantor's child during the period the child attends graduate school, the trust will not be a grantor trust even after the child graduates.[235]

The regulations treat certain amounts that are distributable to discharge a legal obligation of the grantor or the grantor's spouse as distributable to the grantor or the grantor's spouse for purposes of determining the applicability of this exception.[236] If the obligation is owed to a person not related to the grantor or the grantor's spouse, the exception is applicable so long as it is enforceable under the local law of the jurisdiction where the grantor or the grantor's spouse resides. If, however, the obligee is a related person (other than a spouse who is legally separated from the grantor under a decree of divorce or separate maintenance), the exception will not apply unless "it was contracted, bona fide and for adequate and full consideration in money or money's worth"[237] or unless the related person is an individual who would be treated as a dependent of the grantor or the grantor's spouse under Code § 152(a)(1)–(9) if the grantor or the grantor's spouse provided more than half of her support and that individual is either permanently disabled or younger than nineteen years of age.

235. Treas. Reg. § 1.672(f)-3(b)(4), Example 3.
236. *Id.* § 1.672(f)-(3)(b)(2)(i).
237. *Id.* § 1.672(f)-(3)(b)(2)(ii).

For this purpose, a person is related to the grantor or the grantor's spouse if the relationship between them would result in a disallowance of losses under Code § 267 or § 707(b) with the following expansions of the relationships described in those provisions:

- For purposes of applying the family relationship rules of Code § 267, the family of an individual includes the individual's spouse; and
- For purposes of applying Code § 267 (other than Code § 267(f)) and Code § 707(b)(1), a 10 percent rather than a 50 percent interest is required.

The regulations do not address the consequences of divorce except to say that distributions pursuant to a decree of divorce or separate maintenance are deemed to satisfy the legal obligations of the grantor. Therefore, it is uncertain whether a trust that fails to terminate the beneficial interest of the grantor's spouse upon divorce will qualify for this exception to Code § 672(f)(1).

The exception in Code § 672(f)(2)(A)(ii) also applies to certain business trusts established by a corporation or other business entity. For example, a trust established by a corporation to secure a loan to finance an airplane will be a grantor trust under this exception if distributions may only be made to satisfy the legal obligations of the corporate grantor arising out of its loan, and upon satisfaction of the loan, the balance reverts to the corporate grantor.[238]

(c) Certain Compensatory Trusts. Compensatory trusts are exempt from Code § 672(f)(1). The final regulations clarify that compensatory trusts include those for self-employed persons (independent contractors) as well as employees.[239]

(d) Limited Grandfathering for Trusts Funded as of September 19, 1995. Code § 672(f)(1) does not apply to trusts that are grandfathered. Grandfathered trusts are trusts funded as of September 19, 1995, that were either:

- Treated as owned by the grantor because distributions could be made to the grantor or the grantor's spouse without the consent of an adverse party; or
- Treated as owned by the grantor because the trusts were revocable by the grantor without the consent of an adverse party. Unlike the exception in Code § 672(f)(2), the person whose consent is required to revoke can be independent and need not be related or subordinate.

According to a literal reading of the statute, grantor trust status continues as long as the trust otherwise would continue to be so treated under any of the basic grantor trust rules except as to any portion of the trust that is attributable to transfers to the trust that are made after September 19, 1995. However, applicable regulations add additional requirements.

---

238. *Id.* § 1.672(f)-3(b)(4), Example 6.
239. *Id.* § 1.672(f)-3(c).

According to Treas. Reg. § 1.672(f)-3(d), if any additions are made to a grandfathered trust and the additions are not separately accounted for, the *entire* trust ceases to be grandfathered. There is no basis for this in the statute. However, the regulations clarify that physical separation is not required to satisfy the separate accounting requirement. In addition, the regulations provide an extension of time to satisfy the separate accounting requirement. Separate accounting is satisfied if completed by the due date (including extensions) for the tax return of the trust for the first taxable year of the trust beginning after August 10, 1999. If the trust is not required to file a return, this regulation could be construed to suspend the separate accounting requirement until a return is required.

The statute says that Code § 672(f) does not apply to grandfathered trusts, with no requirement that the grandfathered trusts continue to satisfy the requirements for which grandfathered status was allowed. However, Treas. Reg. § 1.672(f)-3(a)(3) provides that a trust that was treated as being owned by the grantor under Code § 676 on September 19, 1995, will no longer be grandfathered if it thereafter ceases to satisfy Code § 676. For example, suppose that A, a nonresident alien, was the grantor of a revocable trust in existence on September 19, 1995. No subsequent additions were made to the trust after September 19, 1995, but A released her power to revoke the trust on January 1, 2000.[240] A retained a power of substitution described in Code § 675(4), which would cause the trust to be a grantor trust if Code § 672(f) did not apply. According to the regulations, the trust would cease to be grandfathered as of January 1, 2000.

Similarly, Treas. Reg. § 1.672(f)-3(b)(3) provides that a trust that was treated as owned by the grantor under § 677(a)(1) or (2) on September 19, 1995, will no longer be grandfathered if it thereafter ceases to satisfy § 677(a)(1) or (2). For example, if A, a nonresident alien, was a beneficiary of a foreign trust that was in existence on September 19, 1995, and A released A's beneficial interest on January 1, 2000, but retained a testamentary power of appointment, according to the regulations, the trust would cease to be grandfathered as of January 1, 2000.

3. Trusts Created by Certain Foreign Corporations

Code § 672(f)(3) provides that the rules of Code § 672(f)(1) do not apply to a CFC or a PFIC. This prevents such corporations from using foreign trusts to avoid U.S. tax.[241]

CFCs and PFICs are treated as domestic corporations for purposes of the grantor trust rules, but are treated as foreign corporations for purposes of Code § 672(f)(4). Code § 672(f)(4) gives the IRS the authority to recharacterize purported gifts to U.S. persons that are made directly or indirectly from foreign

240. To avoid the release of a power of revocation from being treated as a transfer to the trust, it would be prudent to continue to have a power of revocation exercisable with the consent of another person who need not be a related or subordinate party and who is subservient to the grantor.

241. Treas. Reg. § 1.672(f)-2(a) extends these rules to FPHCs. Because the rules relating to FPHCs were repealed by the 2004 Act, presumably this regulatory provision is no longer effective.

corporations. The regulations treat gifts to U.S. persons that are made from a trust funded by a foreign corporation as if made indirectly by such corporation if that incurs more U.S. tax.

The regulations further provide that the rules of Code § 672(f)(4) also will apply if the CFC or PFIC is not the grantor of a foreign trust but is treated as the owner of such trust under Code § 678. Purported gifts to U.S. persons from the foreign trust over which a CFC or PFIC has a Code § 678 power will be treated as indirectly made by such CFC or PFIC.[242]

For purposes of determining whether the character of income and assets of a corporation qualifies it to be classified as a PFIC, the rules of Code § 672(f) are ignored. That is, the assets held in the trust are treated as being held directly by the PFIC.[243]

E. Qualifying for a Basis Adjustment at the Grantor's Death

Under some circumstances, assets transferred by a nonresident alien to a trust will qualify for an adjustment to basis under Code § 1014, even though the assets are not subject to U.S. estate tax at the grantor's death.[244] Sections 1014(b)(2) and (3) provide a basis adjustment:

> Property transferred by the decedent during his lifetime in trust to pay the income for life to or on the order or direction of the decedent, with the right reserved to the decedent at all times before his death to revoke the trust; [and]
>
> . . .
>
> [P]roperty transferred by the decedent during his lifetime in trust to pay the income for life to or on the order or direction of the decedent with the right reserved to the decedent at all times before his death to make any change in the enjoyment thereof through the exercise of a power to alter, amend, or terminate the trust.[245]

The requirements of Code § 1014(b)(2) and (3) are different from the requirements to qualify a trust as a grantor trust under Code § 672(f). First, it is not clear that an irrevocable trust payable to or on the order or direction of the grantor will qualify for the exception for a trust that is payable only to the grantor or the grantor's spouse. As a matter of tax policy, this should not be a problem. Second, the grantor's retained power to alter, amend, or terminate a trust should not be exercisable to allow payment to anyone other than the grantor or the grantor's spouse during the grantor's lifetime. Code § 1014(b)(3) should be satisfied even

242. Treas. Reg. § 1.672(f)-2(b)(2).
243. *Id.* § 1.672(f)-2(c).
244. Rev. Rul. 84-139, 1984-2 C.B. 168; I.R.S. Priv. Ltr. Rul. 8904046 (November 1, 1988); Priv. Ltr. Rul. 201245006 (November 9, 2012).
245. Code § 1014(b)(2) and (3).

where the grantor's power to alter, amend, or terminate the trust applies to distributions made after the grantor's death.[246]

If a basis adjustment is not possible under Code § 1014(b)(2) or (3), another way to adjust the basis of assets is to invest trust assets through a foreign entity that is eligible to make a check-the-box election under Treas. Reg. § 301.7701-3. If the election is treated as a deemed liquidation, the assets will acquire a new basis equal to the fair market value of such assets on the deemed liquidation date.[247] An election may be made following the grantor's death to be effective before death, provided the election is filed within seventy-five days of the effective date.[248] However, the results of this would be disastrous for U.S. beneficiaries of the trust if they were taxable as constructive owners of the shares held by the foreign trust on the date of the deemed liquidation. U.S. beneficiaries should not be treated as constructive owners during the period that the trust was a grantor trust.[249]

F. Consequences of Expatriation

Unless the foreign trust is a grantor trust under the rules of § 672(f), a U.S. person who expatriates at a time when she is treated as the owner of a foreign trust will cease to be treated as the owner of the trust under the grantor trust rules when she expatriates. If the grantor ceases to be treated as the owner of the foreign trust, Code § 684 will treat the grantor as having sold all of the assets of the trust immediately before the trust ceases to be a grantor trust and will be required to recognize gain but not loss.[250]

> ***Example 24:*** Joshua moved to the United States in 2000 for temporary employment. He had established a foreign trust before becoming a U.S. resident. On the date of Joshua's immigration to the United States, the trust owned securities worth $1 million that had a basis of $700,000 and that had had a value of $900,000 when he first became a U. S. resident. The trust is an irrevocable discretionary trust for the benefit of Joshua and his family and thus is not a grantor trust under § 672(f) while Joshua is not

246. Priv. Ltr. Rul. 8904946, *supra* note 245.

247. Treas. Reg. § 301.7701-3(g). However, if the U.S. classification of the foreign entity as a corporation or disregarded entity was never relevant for U.S. tax purposes, the filing of the election could be treated as establishing the *initial* classification of the entity rather than as a liquidation so that a basis adjustment would not be allowed. *Id.* § 301.7701-3(d)(2).

248. An election may be filed with an effective date up to seventy-five days prior to the date of filing. Treas. Reg. § 301.7701-3(c)(1)(iii). Thus, an election can be made after the grantor's death that is effective prior to the grantor's death. If the election is treated as a deemed liquidation, the election would cause assets to acquire a new basis as of the effective date of liquidation. The election is made on Form 8832, and a taxpayer identification number is required in order to make the election.

249. A grantor is treated as actually owning the assets held by the grantor trust. Rev. Rul. 85-13, 1985-1 C.B. 184. Treas. Reg. § 1.958-1(b) attributes to the grantor ownership of shares in a CFC that are held by a grantor trust. Stock in a CFC owned or treated as being owned by a nonresident alien individual is not treated as constructively owned by a U.S. individual. Treas. Reg. § 1.958-2(b)(3). The attribution rules for a PFIC are similar but not as explicit.

250. Treas. Reg. § 1.684-2(e).

a U.S. person. However, while he is a U.S. person, the trust is a grantor trust. After two years, Joshua returns to his home in the United Kingdom. The trust assets have appreciated to $1.2 million. Joshua will recognize at least $500,000 of gain immediately before he is no longer treated as the owner of the trust, that is, immediately before he ceases to be treated as a U.S. person. Depending upon the circumstances, this may occur when he departs or on January 1 of the year following his departure. Joshua's gain includes appreciation that accrued before Joshua moved to the United States. Because the gain accrues immediately before Joshua ceases to be a U.S. person, he cannot avoid tax on non-U.S. source gains.

Joshua could avoid gain if the trust continued to qualify as a grantor trust after his residency terminated. Joshua could also avoid gain if the trust terminated immediately before he expatriated or if the trust became a U.S. trust prior to his expatriation. As discussed above at Section I.B.6.c of this chapter, the tax imposed by Code § 684 may be reduced or eliminated by a timely distribution by the trust to a nonresident alien beneficiary, which is deductible by the trust under Code § 661.

A person who expatriates may also be subject to tax under Code § 877A. That section applies only to a person who is a "covered expatriate." A "covered expatriate," with certain exceptions, including some exceptions based on income and net worth, is a U.S. citizen who gives up her citizenship or a long-term permanent resident of the United States who gives up her residency. A long-term permanent resident is a person who has been a permanent resident of the United States for all or a portion of eight years in the fifteen-year period prior to relinquishing residency. Code § 877A applies to expatriations that occur after June 17, 2008.

When a covered expatriate expatriates, Code § 877A treats her as having sold all of her property, including certain property held in a trust treated as owned by her under the grantor trust rules, for its fair market value. The following are some differences between the recognition rules imposed by Code § 877A and those imposed by Code § 684.

1. Code § 684 is applicable only to transfers to foreign trusts; Code § 684 is not applicable to transfers to domestic trusts. If both Code §§ 684 and 877A apply, then Code § 684 applies first.[251] This is unfortunate for the expatriate since the Code § 684 rules are harsher.
2. The property owned by the trust that is treated as owned by the expatriate for purposes of the mark-to-market tax is limited to property that would have been includable in her gross estate had she died at the time of expatriation and property that she is treated as beneficially owning under a facts-and-circumstances test (so that the expatriate would not be treated

251. Code § 877A(h)(3).

as owning any portion of the grantor trust in which she had no beneficial interest).[252]

3. The sale is deemed to have taken place on the day before the expatriation rather than immediately before the expatriation.
4. Code § 877A permits the covered expatriate to offset her gains with her deductible losses; Code § 684 does not.
5. Codes § 877A reduces the amount subject to tax by $668,000;[253] Code § 684 does not.
6. Code § 877A allows the payment of the expatriation tax to be deferred, with interest, if adequate security is provided, but no deferral is permitted by Code § 684.
7. Code § 877A permits the covered expatriate to use the fair market value of an asset on the date she became a U.S. resident as the basis for purposes of calculating gain if such fair market value is higher than the expatriate's basis.

If the trust is and remains a U.S. trust, Code § 684 will not apply.

G. Consequences of Immigration

1. Pre-immigration Trusts under Code § 679(a)(4)

Code § 679(a)(4) provides that if a foreign person becomes a U.S. resident within five years of directly or indirectly transferring property to a foreign trust, for purposes of Code §§ 679 and 6048, the grantor will be treated as if he or she funded the trust on the date her residency commenced. Code § 679(a) provides that a U.S. person who transfers property to a foreign trust shall be treated as the owner for a particular taxable year of the portion of the trust attributable to such property for such year if there is a U.S. beneficiary of any portion of such trust in such year. Grantor trust status under Code § 679 may be avoided, of course, by the trust migrating to the United States since the statute only applies to foreign trusts. However, as discussed below, Code § 679 is not the only basis upon which the new immigrant may be treated as the owner of the trust.

(a) Determination of Whether a Trust Has a U.S. Beneficiary. As discussed in Section I.B.2 of this chapter, the Code and regulations take an expansive view of when a trust has a U.S. beneficiary.

However, a beneficiary who *first* became a U.S. person more than five years after a transfer to a foreign trust will not be treated as a U.S. person for purposes of that transfer.[254]

---

252. *See* Notice 2009-85, 2009-45 I.R.B. 598 § 3.A, and Instructions to Form 8854 (2008).

253. The reduction amount is adjusted yearly for inflation. The $668,000 figure is the amount applicable to expatriations that took place in 2013. Rev. Proc. 2012-41.

254. Code § 679(c)(3); Treas. Reg. § 1.679-2(a)(3).

For purposes of Code § 679, the term "U.S. person" includes a controlled foreign corporation, as defined in Code § 957(a); a foreign partnership with one or more U.S. partners; and a trust or estate, one or more beneficiaries of which are U.S. persons.[255]

(b) Annual Test for Determining Whether a Foreign Trust Has a U.S. Beneficiary. If a foreign trust that has no U.S. beneficiary in one year acquires a U.S. beneficiary in a subsequent year, the U.S. grantor will be treated as receiving additional income in the year the trust acquires a U.S. beneficiary. The amount of additional income is equal to the UNI of the trust at the end of the preceding year. Such additional income is subject to the throwback tax, discussed above.[256]

If a foreign trust that has a U.S. beneficiary in one year ceases to have a U.S. beneficiary in a subsequent year, Code § 679 will cease to apply on January 1 of the subsequent year. The grantor will be treated as transferring all of the assets then in the foreign trust to the foreign trust on January 1, and Code § 684(a) will require the grantor to realize income and gain as if the trust assets had been sold.[257]

(c) Indirect and Constructive Transfers. As discussed in Section I.B.2 of this chapter, Code § 679 applies to indirect and constructive transfers to a foreign trust. The regulations under Code § 679 take an expansive view of indirect and constructive transfers.[258]

Transfers by a U.S. person to an entity owned by a foreign trust are treated as transfers to the foreign trust followed by a transfer by the foreign trust to the entity. This rule is not applicable, however, if the U.S. person is not related to a trust beneficiary or if the U.S. person demonstrates that the transfer is attributable to the U.S. person's ownership interest in the entity.[259] For example, if a foreign trust and a U.S. person jointly fund a corporation, each taking back stock proportionate to their transfers, Code § 679 is not applicable.

Transfers to a trust that are made by a corporation or partnership are treated as made by its shareholders or partners unless the trust serves a business purpose. For example, a corporation that funds a trust to secure a debt obligation serves a business purpose.[260]

If a person is treated as the owner of a trust (a transferor trust) that makes a transfer to a foreign trust (a transferee trust), the person who is treated as the owner of the transferor trust is treated under § 679 as making the transfer to the foreign transferee trust.[261] This result is slightly different from the portion of the § 671 regulations that defines the term "grantor." The § 671 regulations

255. Code § 679(c)(2).
256. *Id.* § 679(b); Treas. Reg. § 1.679-2(c)(1).
257. Treas. Reg. § 1.679-2(c)(2).
258. *Id.* § 1.679-3.
259. *Id.* § 1.679-3(f).
260. *Id.* § 1.671-2(e)(4).
261. *Id.* § 1.679-3(b).

provide that the grantor of a trust that makes a gratuitous transfer to another trust is the grantor of such trust to the extent of such transfer unless the transferee trust is funded by the exercise of a general power of appointment held by another person.[262] In the latter case, the power holder, rather than the grantor of the transferor trust, is treated as the grantor of the transferee trust.

The § 671 regulations, however, do not treat a person as the grantor of a transferee trust if the only reason that person was treated as the owner of the transferor trust was his, her, or its possession of a Code § 678 power. The power holder becomes the grantor of a transferee trust only if the transferee trust is funded as a result of the power holder's exercise of her general power of appointment. This portion of the § 671 regulations is inconsistent with the § 679 regulations. Regulations under Code § 679 treat the beneficiary as the owner of the foreign transferee trust whether or not the beneficiary exercised her general power of appointment to fund the transferee trust. Of course, if the beneficiary exercises her general power of appointment, the same result occurs under both sets of regulations—the beneficiary is treated as the owner.

(d) Deemed Transfer Date for Pre-Immigration Trusts. If a nonresident alien grantor transfers property to a foreign grantor trust more than five years before becoming a U.S. person and within five years of becoming a U.S. person, the trust is amended so that the trust ceases to be a grantor trust, the transfer to the trust is deemed to have been made within five years of immigrating to the United States, and Code § 679(a)(4) applies.[263] For example, if the trust was a revocable trust and the grantor released the power to revoke, the trust is deemed funded on the date the power of revocation is released.[264]

Because Code § 672(f) limits the circumstances in which a nonresident alien will be treated as the owner of a trust under the grantor trust rules, it also limits the circumstances in which an amendment to a trust will cause the trust to be subject to Code § 679(a)(4). For example, assume that a nonresident alien grantor and her husband and children are beneficiaries of a foreign nongrantor trust created more than five years prior to the family immigrating to the United States. If the grantor and her husband remain beneficiaries after the family immigrates, the trust will become a grantor trust under Code § 677. This is because Code § 672(f) will cease to apply to the grantor who has become a U.S. taxpayer. However, if, prior to becoming U.S. taxpayers, the grantor and her spouse renounce their beneficial interests in the trust so that Code § 677 will not apply, the trust may continue as a nongrantor trust after the family immigrates to the United States so long as the trust instrument contains no other provisions that would cause the grantor to be treated as owner. Code § 679 will not apply, because the trust was created more than five years prior to immigration.

---

262. *Id.* § 1.671-2(e).
263. *Id.* § 1.679-5(b)(1).
264. *See id.* § 1.679-5(c) Example 2.

(e) Treatment of Undistributed Income. If Code § 679(a)(4) applies, for purposes of Code §§ 679 and 6048, all UNI for periods prior to immigration to the United States is deemed contributed to the trust on the residency start date.[265] The statute provides that UNI that accrued before immigration is taken into account in determining the portion of the trust that is attributable to property transferred by such individual but "shall not otherwise be taken into account." The scope of the phrase "shall not otherwise be taken into account" is not entirely evident, nor is it explained by regulations.

It seems clear that the grantor will not be taxed on the undistributed income or the deemed transfer of the assets to the foreign trust on the date U.S. residency commences. It remains unclear, however, whether the UNI of the trust prior to immigration remains subject to the throwback tax upon later distribution to a U.S. beneficiary. Consider the following examples.

> ***Example 25:*** Sally, who is not a citizen or resident of the United States, contributes $100x to a foreign trust in 2008. Sally and her spouse and children are discretionary beneficiaries of the trust. On January 1, 2010, Sally and her husband become U.S. residents. At that time, the value of the trust is $125x of which $25x is UNI for 2008 and 2009. Suppose that a distribution of $15x is made to Sally on June 30, 2010, and that the 2010 income of the trust is $5x.
>
> Sally is treated as contributing $125x on January 1, 2010. She is treated as the owner of the trust and is taxable on 2010 income. However, Sally is not taxable on the $25x of UNI she is deemed to have conveyed to the trust on January 1, 2010. The distribution made to Sally in June 2010 should not be subject to the throwback tax because, under Code § 671, subpart D of subchapter J, the subpart that contains the throwback tax applies to a trust only to the extent the grantor trust rules of subpart E do not apply. Although § 679 does not explicitly address this question, it would be inconsistent to tax Sally on the receipt of property from the trust that she is deemed to own for income tax purposes under Revenue Ruling 85-13.

> ***Example 26:*** Assume the same facts described in Example 25, except assume that Sally is no longer living on June 30, 2010, when a distribution of $15x is made to Sally's daughter, Betty. Code § 679 is not applicable to the trust after Sally's death. In this case, it is unclear whether the throwback tax will apply to Betty's distribution. The distribution exceeds current income, but all prior UNI was deemed contributed by Sally on January 2010. The provision in Code § 679(a)(4)(B) that pre-immigration income shall not be taken into account for any purpose other than determining which portion of the trust the grantor will be treated as owning

265. Code § 679(a)(4)(B).

post-immigration lends some support to an argument that the throwback tax should not apply.

2. Treatment of Trusts That Become Grantor Trusts When the Grantor or Beneficiary Immigrates

(a) Grantor Trust Rules Applicable to U.S. Persons Will Commence to Apply. Even if Code § 679(a)(4) is not applicable, all of the other grantor trust rules would become applicable to trusts of which the immigrant is the grantor or a beneficiary after the immigrant becomes a U.S. person. Code § 672(f) will cease to apply to limit application of the grantor trust rules. Thus, the broad reach of Code §§ 673–678 will apply to potentially make the immigrant the owner of the trust. For example, the immigrant will be treated as the owner of the trust after becoming a U.S. person if she was the grantor of the trust and the immigrant or her spouse is a beneficiary, or if the immigrant has a withdrawal right described in Code § 678, even if the trust was funded more than five years before immigration occurred.

(b) Treatment of Pre-Immigration UNI When the Trust Becomes a Grantor Trust. It is not clear whether the UNI of a foreign trust that becomes a grantor trust under Code §§ 673–678 as a result of the immigration of a grantor or beneficiary is deemed added to the trust in a tax-free transaction as may occur in the case of trusts subject to Code § 679(a)(4). There are two other possibilities. One is that the UNI remains in the trust and may be subject to throwback tax when distributed to a U.S. beneficiary. This result would be inconsistent with the principle of Revenue Ruling 85-13—that the grantor is treated as actually owning the assets in a grantor trust. If so, it would be strange to tax a grantor-owner on the receipt of property she is deemed to own, or to treat another beneficiary as taxable on the receipt of assets deemed owned by the grantor rather than by the trust. In addition, it would be inconsistent with Code § 671, which provides that subpart D of subchapter J applies only to the extent that subpart E does not apply.

Another possibility is that there is a deemed distribution from the nongrantor trust to the grantor when the grantor becomes a U.S. person and therefore is treated as acquiring tax ownership of the trust assets under the grantor trust rules. A grantor is treated as actually owning the assets held in a grantor trust.[266] Therefore, one could take the position that when a nongrantor trust becomes a grantor trust, a deemed distribution occurs. It is well settled that a deemed transfer occurs when a grantor trust becomes a nongrantor trust.[267] To be consistent, arguably, the reverse should also be true, but there seems no authority for this proposition. If there were a deemed distribution, would the grantor have taxable income? Code § 679(a)(4) seems to preclude this possibility in the case

266. Rev. Rul. 85-13; 1985-1 C.B. 189.

267. *E.g.*, Madorin v. Comm'r, 84 T.C. 667 (1985); Treas. Reg. § 1.1001-2(c), Example 5.

of pre-immigration trusts because the deemed transfer to the trust is solely for purposes of §§ 679 and 6048. Why should older trusts be treated more harshly?

Notwithstanding the fact that a transfer is deemed to occur when a grantor trust becomes a nongrantor trust, which transfer can be a taxable event, apart from Code § 679(b), there is no authority for the reverse—that a deemed transfer to the grantor occurs when a nongrantor trust becomes a grantor trust or, even if it does, that this deemed transfer constitutes a taxable event. In Chief Counsel Advice 200923024 (Dec. 31, 2008), the taxpayer sold a partnership interest to a nongrantor trust in exchange for an annuity. Gain on the sale would be recognized as annuity payments were made. The trust received a cost basis in the partnership interest it purchased in exchange for the annuity even though recognition of gain to the seller was deferred and reported as the annuity payments were made. The partnership elected under Code § 754 to adjust the basis of partnership assets. The partnership owned appreciated securities which it then sold. The stepped-up basis on partnership assets avoided tax on the sale. In order to avoid the taxpayer having to recognize gain as annuity payments were made, the taxpayer arranged for the trusts to become grantor trusts. The IRS argued that in order to ensure that taxable income is recognized from the sale of the appreciated stock owned by the partnership, the conversion of the trust from nongrantor to grantor trust should be treated as a taxable transaction. The grantor should be treated as realizing income on the receipt of assets from the nongrantor trust. Even though the Chief Counsel viewed the transaction as abusive, the government's argument was rejected.

> Assuming the transaction in the present case is abusive, asserting that the conversion of a nongrantor trust to a grantor trust results in taxable income to the grantor would have an impact on non-abusive situations. A nongrantor trust may become a grantor trust in several situations: examples include the appointment of a related or subordinate trustee to replace an independent trustee as in the present case (§ 674); a borrowing of the trust corpus under § 675(3) . . . ; or the payment of the grantor's legal support obligations under § 677(b). No prior guidance dealing with these events has indicated that they result in taxable income to the deemed transferee (the owner of the grantor trust). Rev. Rul. 85-13 concluded that the grantor became the owner of the trust corpus which he had indirectly borrowed, and thus was taxable on the trust's income and, as the deemed owner of the trust assets, could not engage in a transaction with the trust that would be respected for income tax purposes. It did not conclude that the grantor realized the amount of the indirect borrowing or any portion of that amount as income under § 61 or any other section. Therefore, while we agree that this appears to be an abusive transaction, the Service should not take the position that the mere conversion of a nongrantor trust to a grantor trust results in taxable income to the grantor.

Because a conversion of a trust from nongrantor to grantor trust status can occur for a variety of common reasons, if the conversion were a taxable event, it is reasonable to expect that there would have been some authority supporting it. The absence of authority supports the proposition that such conversion has no immediate tax consequences.

In addition, Code § 679(b) supports the proposition that conversions to grantor trust status for any reason other than as provided for in § 679(b) are not taxable distributions to the grantor. Code § 679(b) specifically provides that when a foreign trust that is not a grantor trust under § 679 because it has no U.S. beneficiary subsequently acquires a U.S. beneficiary, the trust becomes a grantor trust, and the grantor is taxable on all of the undistributed net income of the trust.[268] If all conversions of nongrantor trusts to grantor trusts were deemed to be taxable distributions to the grantor, Code § 679(b) would be superfluous.

3. Pre-immigration Amendments to Obtain Grantor Trust Status

Post-immigration grantor trust status may be advantageous to U.S. beneficiaries. Suppose that a grantor created a trust more than five years before immigrating to the United States. The trust had substantial UNI when the grantor became a U.S. resident. If the trust remains a nongrantor trust, a distribution to a U.S. beneficiary that is deemed to carry out that UNI would be subject to throwback tax, as discussed below. However, if the trust becomes a grantor trust when the grantor becomes a U.S. resident, and if the conversion is not treated as a taxable distribution to the grantor, a subsequent distribution from the grantor trust to a U.S. beneficiary should not be taxable. If the grantor is treated as owning trust assets, then the beneficiary is treated as if she received a gift from the grantor rather than a distribution from a trust.[269] Thus, the change from nongrantor trust classification to grantor trust classification may avoid throwback tax on UNI that accrued before U.S. residency started. This result arguably is inconsistent with the purposes of Code § 672(f), which was intended to limit the use of the grantor trust rules to shield U.S. beneficiaries from income tax on trust distributions.

4. Pre-immigration Amendments to Prevent Grantor Trust Status

Suppose a grantor fully funded a trust more than five years before becoming a U.S. resident and is not treated as the owner of the trust due to the limitations in Code § 672(f), but would start to be treated as the owner after the grantor becomes a U.S. person and Code § 672(f) no longer applies. If, before becoming a U.S. person, all of the interests or powers that would make the trust a grantor trust after U.S. residency commences are released, then the trust will continue as a foreign nongrantor trust.

For example, suppose that *prior* to becoming a U.S. resident, the trust is modified to require the consent of an adverse party prior to making distributions to

268. *See also* Treas. Reg. § 1.679-2(c).
269. Rev. Rul. 69-70, 1969-1 C.B. 182.

the grantor and the grantor's spouse (and the trust was not otherwise a grantor trust). In that case, the trust would remain a foreign nongrantor trust even after the grantor became a U.S. resident. Form 3520 would not have to be filed except when distributions were made to U.S. persons. In effect, the income of the trust would be taxed in the United States only on a remittance basis.

Suppose instead that the modification to require the consent of an adverse party occurs *after* the grantor becomes a U.S. resident. Code § 679 would apply when the trust is modified because the cessation of the U.S. grantor's treatment as the owner of the foreign trust should be treated as a deemed transfer to a foreign trust by the U.S. grantor.[270]

5. Treatment of Pre-immigration UNI if a Trust Remains a Nongrantor Trust

As discussed above in Section III.C., the UNI of a foreign nongrantor trust is subject to throwback tax if and when distributed to U.S beneficiaries, including UNI attributable to periods prior to the grantor's immigration to the United States. This is true because the character of the income distributed to a U.S. beneficiary is disregarded (except for tax-exempt income). However, the interest charge on the throwback tax would not apply to tax on income attributed to a year in which the recipient was not a U.S. resident.[271] Thus, the use of a nongrantor trust for U.S. beneficiaries works best when the trust will not be distributing its UNI.

H. Shifting the Identity of the Grantor—Code § 672(f)(5)

Code § 672(f)(5) provides that if a foreign person funds a trust that would be a grantor trust, and a U.S. person who is a beneficiary made gratuitous transfers to such foreign person, the U.S. beneficiary will be treated as the grantor-owner of the trust.[272] The rule applies whether or not the beneficiary was a U.S. person at the time of the transfer to the foreign person, but only if the U.S. person making the gratuitous transfer to the foreign person is a beneficiary. For example, if A transfers assets to her brother B, who is a nonresident alien, before becoming a U.S. person, and B establishes a revocable trust for A and A's family, A will be treated as the grantor after she becomes a U.S. person.

Code § 672(f)(5) would not apply if A were not a beneficiary. For this purpose, however, the IRS views a person who may be added as a beneficiary as a "beneficiary."[273]

Code § 672(f)(5) does not by its terms contain any time constraints on applying this rule. However, if the U.S. beneficiary can demonstrate that the transfer

270. *Cf.* Treas. Reg. § 1.679-3(b); Madorin v. Comm'r, 84 T.C. 667 (1978).

271. Code § 668(a)(2).

272. The U.S. person will be considered the grantor under this section only to the extent that her transfers to the foreign person exceeded transfers from the foreign person to the U.S. person.

273. Treas. Reg. § 1.672(f)-5(a) refers to Code § 679 for the definition of "beneficiary." Code § 679 defines "beneficiary" very broadly to include, for example, persons who may be added as beneficiaries through the exercise of a power of appointment or power of amendment. *See* Treas. Reg. § 1.679-2(a)(2), Example 11; Treas. Reg. § 1.679-2(a)(4)(ii)(A).

to the foreign person was wholly unrelated to the funding of the trust, Code § 672(f)(5) will not apply.[274]

Transfers not in excess of the amount not treated as taxable gifts under Code § 2503(b) are disregarded.[275]

I. Comparison of Code §§ 672(f)(5) and 679(a)(4)

Code § 679(a)(4) applies whether or not the purported nonresident alien grantor for any other reason would be treated as the owner of the trust and whether or not the U.S. person is a beneficiary of the trust. For example, if A transfers assets to her brother, B, who is a nonresident alien, B funds a trust for the benefit of A's descendants, and A becomes a U.S. person within five years of making the transfer to B, then Code § 679(a)(4) will apply because A will be treated as indirectly funding the trust. Code § 672(f)(5) would not apply if B is not otherwise treated as the owner of the trust. (If the trust is irrevocable and benefits B's sister's descendants, the trust would not qualify as a grantor trust while B remained a nonresident alien.) Code § 672(f)(5) also would not apply if A were not a beneficiary of the trust. If A transferred the funds to B, and B funded the trust more than five years before A became a U.S. person, Code § 679(a)(4) would not apply—§ 679(a)(4) does not apply if the trust is funded more than five years before immigration to the United States.[276] It is not clear whether Code § 679(a)(4) applies if the U.S. person made a transfer to a nonresident alien person more than five years before immigration to the U.S. but the trust was funded within the five-year period before U.S. residency commenced.

Code § 672(f)(5) has an exception for transfers within the annual gift tax exclusion, but there is no dollar limitation for purposes of Code § 679(a)(4).

Code § 672(f)(5) has no time limit. Thus, if A transferred funds to B six years before moving to the United States and B created a revocable trust for A, Code § 672(f)(5) may apply to treat A as the owner of the trust.

V. Recharacterization of Purported Gifts

A. Purported Gift

A "purported gift or bequest" is any transfer, other than a transfer for fair market value, made from a corporation or a partnership to a person who is not a shareholder or a partner. If the purported donee is a shareholder or partner, a purported gift includes a distribution not consistent with the donee's interest in the partnership or corporation.[277]

274. Treas. Reg. § 1.672(f)-5(a).
275. *Id.*
276. Even if Code § 679(a)(4) is not applicable, the usual "intermediary" rules of Code § 679 are applicable. *See* Treas. Reg. § 1.679-3(c).
277. Treas. Reg. § 1.672(f)-4(d).

B. Purported Gifts from Partnerships

When a U.S. person receives a purported gift from a partnership (directly or indirectly), the entire amount must be included in the U.S. donee's gross income as ordinary income without regard to the amount of partnership income.[278]

C. Purported Gifts from Corporations

When a U.S. person receives a purported gift from a foreign corporation (directly or indirectly), the amount must be included in the U.S. donee's income as if it were a distribution from the foreign corporation. The distribution will be taxed as a dividend to the extent of earnings and profits and as a sale or exchange to the extent the amount exceeds earnings and profits. If the corporation is a PFIC, an interest charge may apply. If the distribution is taxed as a sale or exchange, the donee's basis will be deemed to be zero. The donee's holding period for determining whether any gain is short term or long term is equal to the weighted average of the holding periods of the actual shareholders (excluding the holding period of shareholders who treat the purported gift attributable to their interest as if received by and taxable to them). If the purported donee is a corporation, no "deemed paid" foreign tax credit will be allowed under Code § 902 to offset U.S. tax.

D. Exceptions

The following are exceptions to the above rules:

1. Donee Has No Relationship to Partners or Shareholders

The purported gift rules do not apply if the U.S. person receiving the purported gift has no family or other relationship to a partner or shareholder that establishes a reasonable basis for concluding that the partnership or foreign corporation would make a gratuitous transfer to the U.S. donee.[279]

2. Domestic Partnership Wholly Owned by U.S. Citizens or Residents or Domestic Corporations

If all beneficial owners of a domestic partnership are U.S. citizens or residents or domestic corporations, the purported gift rules do not apply.[280] This exception does not apply to foreign partnerships. For this purpose, a "domestic partnership" is a partnership created or organized under the laws of the United States or any state of the United States[281]

3. A U.S. Citizen or Resident Individual Owning the Shares or Interests Reports the Distribution and Gift

If a U.S. citizen or resident individual who directly or indirectly holds an interest in the partnership or foreign corporation treated the gift as a distribution to the

278. *Id.* § 1.672(f)-4.
279. *Id.* § 1.672(f)-4(d)(2)(ii).
280. *Id.* § 1.672(f)-4(b)(2).
281. *Id.* § 301.7701-5.

U.S. partner or shareholder and as a subsequent gift by such partner or shareholder to the U.S. donee, then the gift will not be taxable to the donee. There is no similar exception where the owner of the interest is a nonnatural person, such as a trust.[282]

4. Foreign Individual Owning the Shares or Interests Reports the Distribution and Gift and U.S. Donee Reports the Gift

If a nonresident alien individual partner or shareholder reported the distribution from the entity and the gift for purposes of the tax laws of such individual's country of residence, and the U.S. donee timely reported the gift in accordance with Code § 6039F, then the gift will not be taxable to the donee.[283] Example 1 of Treas. Reg. § 1.672(f)-4(g) suggests that if reporting in the foreign country is "not applicable" under the laws of such country, the exception may still be available.

5. Capital Contributions

The purported gift rules do not apply to contributions to the capital of a U.S. corporation described in Code § 118.[284]

6. Charities

The rule does not apply to payments made for an exempt purpose by donors who are charities and who have received determination letters of tax exempt status or to donees that are charities described in Code § 170(c).[285]

E. Gifts through Trusts Funded by Gratuitous Transfers from Partnerships or Foreign Corporations

If a partnership or foreign corporation creates and funds a trust, whether or not it is the entity or the partners or shareholders who are treated as the grantors of the trust (see Treas. Reg. § 1.671-2(e)(4) treating entities as the grantor of trusts established for business purposes and partners and shareholders as the grantor of trusts established for nonbusiness purposes), and then the trust makes a distribution to a U.S. person—

(a) The distribution is deemed made by the partnership or foreign corporation unless the rule in (b) applies.

(b) The distribution will be taxed as if it were made by the trust if the tax as so computed would be greater than the tax that would be imposed if it were treated as a distribution directly from the partnership or foreign corporation.[286]

(c) A distribution to a U.S. person from a trust funded by a foreign corporation or partnership will not be taxed as a purported gift by the entity or

282. *Id.* § 1.672(f)-4(b)(1)(i).
283. *Id.* § 1.672(f)-4(b)(1)(ii).
284. *Id.* § 1.672(f)-4(b)(3).
285. *Id.* § 1.672(f)-4(b)(4).
286. *Id.* § 1.672(f)-4(c)(2).

as a trust distribution if a U.S. donee demonstrates that the transfer has been taken into account for U.S. tax purposes by a U.S. citizen or resident or domestic corporation. No similar exception applies where a nonresident alien has reported the income. In Example 3 of Treas. Reg. § 1.672(f)-4(g), a purported gift to a U.S. person from a foreign trust funded by a foreign corporation is treated as subject to the accumulation distribution rules. The example does not mention whether a foreign shareholder reported the distribution and the gift. An inference can be drawn that the IRS considered this fact immaterial, since this information was mentioned in Example 1, where the distribution was made directly from the foreign corporation.

F. Affirmative Use

Treas. Reg. § 1.672(f)-4(e) provides that a taxpayer may not use the rules under Code § 672(f)(4) affirmatively to reduce the taxpayer's tax liability. The regulation purports to give the IRS authority to "depart from the rules of this section and recharacterize (for all purposes of the Internal Revenue Code) the transfer in accordance with its form or its economic substance."

G. De Minimis Rule

The purported gift rules do not apply if, during the taxable year of a U.S. donee, the aggregate amount of gifts and bequests received directly or indirectly (such as from trusts) from all partnerships or foreign corporations that are related does not exceed $10,000.[287] The amount must include gifts or bequests from persons that the U.S. donee knows or has reason to know are related to the partnership or foreign corporation within the definition of "related" in Code § 643(i).

H. Anti-avoidance Rule—Check the Box

The purported gift rules cannot be avoided by electing pass-through treatment for a single member entity. A single member entity that elects to be taxed as a sole proprietorship under the check the box regulations will be treated as a corporation for purposes of Treas. Reg. § 1.672(f)-4.[288] This rule gives the IRS latitude to recharacterize purported gifts made by such entities.

287. *Id.* § 1.672(f)-4(f). Although this regulation does not index the *de minimis* amount, Form 3520 does index the reporting threshold for purported gifts from partnerships and foreign corporations. The indexed amount for 2013 is $15,102. Rev. Proc. 2012-41.

288. Treas. Reg. § 1.672(f)-5(b).

VI. Reporting of Distributions from Foreign Trusts and Gifts from Foreign Persons

A. Reporting by U.S. Beneficiaries of Foreign Trusts Who Receive Distributions

A U.S. person (including a grantor) who receives, directly or indirectly, or is treated as receiving any distribution from a foreign trust must report to the IRS information regarding the name of the trust, the amount of distributions received from the trust, and such other information as the IRS may require.[289] Form 3520 is used to report distributions from foreign trusts.

In Notice 97-34,[290] the IRS describes the additional required information. Such information is to be set forth in either a Foreign Grantor Trust Beneficiary Statement or a Foreign Nongrantor Trust Beneficiary Statement.

1. Nontaxable Distributions Are Reportable

Reporting is required even if the foreign trust is a grantor trust and whether or not Code § 663(a) applies to the distribution.

2. Only Gratuitous Transfers Are Reportable

All gratuitous transfers are reportable. Trustee fees, for example, are not reportable. However, if the trustee fees paid to a beneficiary/trustee are excessive, the distribution is reportable. The reporting obligation is waived if the payee reports the amount as taxable compensation for services rendered.

3. Constructive Distributions

Indirect and constructive distributions are reportable. For example, if a beneficiary uses a credit card and the trust guarantees or pays the invoice, the amount charged on the card is treated as a distribution. A beneficiary who draws a check on a trust account is in receipt of a distribution. A beneficiary who receives a payment for services or property in excess of the value of such services or property is deemed to have received a distribution.

4. Knowledge that Trust Is Foreign

Reporting is required only if the U.S. beneficiary knows or has reason to know that the trust is a foreign trust.

5. Information Required

(a) IRS Discretion to Determine Tax. Code § 6048(c) provides that if adequate records are not provided (by the beneficiary or some other person) to enable the IRS to determine the proper tax treatment of any distribution received from a foreign trust, the distribution will be treated as a taxable accumulation distribution from a foreign nongrantor trust, subject to the throwback tax. For purposes of

289. Code § 6048(c).
290. 1997-1 C.B. 422.

determining the interest charge on the throwback tax, the deemed accumulation period will be one-half of the years the trust has been in existence.

(b) Appointment of Agent. To the extent provided in regulations, this rule will not apply if the foreign trust has appointed a U.S. agent for the purpose of responding to IRS inquiries. Any U.S. person may serve as the agent of the trust, including a grantor or a beneficiary. Although the appointment of a U.S. agent is not required, if an agent is not appointed, the IRS will have broad discretion to determine the amount of taxable income derived by the U.S. beneficiary from the trust. According to the "Blue Book" prepared by the staff of the Joint Committee on Taxation, Congress intended that the IRS's exercise of this authority will be subject to judicial review under an "arbitrary and capricious" standard, which provides a high degree of deference to the IRS.[291] A foreign trust that appoints such an agent will not be considered to have an office or permanent establishment in the United States, or to be engaged in a U.S. trade or business, solely because of the activities of the agent under Code § 6048. Notice 97-34 provides a form for the appointment of an agent.

(c) Beneficiary Statements. A U.S. beneficiary may avoid the presumption that a distribution is taxable as an accumulation distribution from a foreign nongrantor trust and therefore subject to the throwback tax if, with respect to the distribution, the beneficiary obtains from the foreign trust either (1) a Foreign Grantor Trust Beneficiary Statement to be attached to Form 3520, which would allow the beneficiary to treat the distribution as a nontaxable gift, (2) a Foreign Nongrantor Trust Beneficiary Statement to be attached to Form 3520, or (3) information regarding actual distributions from the trust for the prior three years ("default treatment"). Under the default treatment, a U.S. beneficiary will be allowed to treat a portion of the distribution as current income based on the average of distributions from the prior three years, with only the excess amount of the distribution treated as an accumulation distribution subject to the throwback tax. This rule is an adaptation of the rule for determining the interest charge on distributions from a passive foreign investment company.[292]

(d) Exceptions. Beneficiaries need not report (1) distributions from trusts taxable as compensation for services rendered that are reported as such on the recipient's federal income tax return or (2) distributions from foreign trusts received by a U.S. charitable organization, provided that such organization has a determination letter from the IRS (that has not been revoked) recognizing its tax-exempt status.

---

291. *See* Joint Comm. on Taxation, General Explanation of Tax Legislation Enacted in the 104th Congress (JCS-12-6), at 276 (Dec. 18, 1996).

292. *See* Code § 1291(b).

It is not clear whether loans from grantor trusts are reportable. Notice 97-34 provides:

> If a trust makes a loan to a grantor that causes the grantor to be treated as the owner of a portion of the trust under section 675(3), the loan will not be treated as a distribution under section 643(i) and will not be reportable under section 6048(c).

Code 643(i) treats loans and the uncompensated use of trust assets as distributions for purposes of subparts B, C, and D. These subparts do not apply to grantor trusts. Consequently, loans to a beneficiary from a grantor trust may not be reportable. Similarly, the uncompensated use by any beneficiary of trust assets owned by a grantor trust may not be reportable. However, Form 3520 does not "prompt" this result, and it is not clear why, as a matter of policy, an exception to the reporting requirements would be made for these transactions with grantor trusts when other distributions from grantor trusts are reportable.

(e) Penalties for Nonreporting. A U.S. beneficiary who fails to report distributions from a foreign trust under Code § 6048(c) will be subject to a penalty equal to the greater of $10,000 or 35 percent of the amount distributed.[293] Additional penalties can be imposed for continuing noncompliance. Although the total penalties may not exceed the reportable amount, the IRS may assess the penalties before the reportable amount is determined; and when the reportable amount is determined, the excess must be refunded. The IRS is authorized to assess and collect these penalties without prior judicial review.

The IRS is permitted to waive any penalty if the failure to file was due to reasonable cause and not willful neglect. The fact that a foreign jurisdiction would impose a civil or criminal penalty on any person for disclosing the required information will not be considered a reasonable cause for failure to file. Notice 97-34 clarifies that "reasonable cause" does not include refusal on the part of a foreign trustee to provide information. This is true whatever the reason, including difficulty in producing the required information or provisions in the trust instrument that prevent the disclosure of information.

These penalties generally apply to distributions received after August 20, 1996. The minimum penalty applies to returns required to be filed after March 18, 2010. Under the second voluntary disclosure initiative announced February 8, 2011, no penalty will be imposed for failure to file information returns, including Form 3520, if all income was reported and the Form is filed by August 31, 2011.[294] A third

293. *Id.* § 6677, *as amended by* § 535 of the 2010 HIRE Act.

294. FAQs 17 and 18 on IRS web page, http://www.irs.gov/Businesses/International-Businesses/2011-Offshore-Voluntary-Disclosure-Initiative-Frequently-Asked-Questions-and-Answers (last visited July 24, 2013).

voluntary disclosure program was announced on January 9, 2012, which is similar to the 2011 initiative, but it has no time limit.[295]

(f) Statute of Limitations. The statute of limitations does not begin to run until a return required by Code § 6048 is filed for an event or a period related to information required to be reported.[296] Section 512 of the 2010 HIRE Act increases the negligence penalty imposed by Code § 6662 from 20 percent to 40 percent for deficiencies attributable to an unreported foreign financial asset, which is defined as "any asset with respect to which information was required to be provided under section 6038, 6038B, 6038D, 6046A, or 6048 for such taxable year but was not provided by the taxpayer as required under the provisions of those sections." Section 512 is applicable to taxable years beginning after March 18, 2010.

This can result in divergent treatment, because for years closed prior to the date of enactment of the HIRE Act of 2012, only certain information returns may remain open, while for years still open as of that date, the entire return for that year may remain open as a result of failure to file these information returns.

If penalties for nonreporting could apply under both Code §§ 6677 and 6039F, the Code § 6677 penalty will be assessed and will reduce any penalty otherwise imposed under Code § 6039F.[297]

B. Reporting Gifts from Foreign Persons

Code § 6039F imposes information reporting requirements on any U.S. person (other than certain tax-exempt organizations) who, after August 20, 1996, receives, in the aggregate, gifts from foreign persons in excess of $10,000 in any taxable year.[298] A "gift" includes a bequest.[299] A foreign gift does not include an amount that is a "qualified transfer" under Code § 2503(e)(2) (a payment of tuition or medical expenses to a service provider) or any distribution from a foreign trust properly reported under Code § 6048. The $10,000 threshold is indexed for inflation after 1996. The threshold for 2013 is $15,102; however, as noted below, Notice 97-34 generally increases this reporting threshold to $100,000.[300]

1. Form 3520

Part IV of Form 3520 requires only a brief description of the property received, the fair market value of the property, and the date of the gift where the donor is an individual or an estate. Form 3520 does not ask for the name and address of the donor except where the foreign donor is a corporation or a partnership. The identity of a foreign donor who is a corporation or a partnership must be disclosed.

295. IR-2012-5. The announcement cautions, however, that the IRS may terminate the initiative at any time.

296. Code § 6501(c)(8).

297. Notice 97-34.

298. Code § 6039F.

299. *Id.* § 6039F(b).

300. Rev. Proc. 2012-41.

The form also asks whether the filer has any reason to believe that the foreign donor is acting as a nominee or intermediary for another person. Form 3520 does not indicate that a gift from a grantor should not be treated as gifts by an intermediary. Even though the identity of donors is not required in the case of donors who are individuals, it is important to note that upon request, the U.S. person may be required to provide additional information, including the identity of the donor.

2. Exceptions

Qualified tuition and medical payments are not taxable gifts under Code § 2503(e) and need not be reported. Distributions made from a foreign trust to a U.S. beneficiary that are reported by the U.S. beneficiary under Code § 6048(c) do not have to be reported again by the U.S. beneficiary under Code § 6039F.

3. Interaction of Code §§ 6039F and 6048

U.S. beneficiaries who receive distributions from foreign trusts should report the amounts under the trust reporting rules at Code § 6048(c) rather than the gift-reporting rules of Code § 6039F. This is true even if the trust is grantor trust and the distribution is treated as a gift under principles of substantive law.

4. Gifts to Trusts

U.S. beneficiaries are not required to report contributions by foreign persons to trusts in which the U.S. beneficiaries have an interest, unless the U.S. beneficiaries are treated as receiving the contribution in the year of transfer (i.e., a U.S. beneficiary has a Code § 678 power). A domestic trust that receives a contribution from a foreign person must report the gift unless the trust is treated as owned by a foreign person (e.g., a foreign person creates a U.S. revocable trust). According to Notice 97-34 and the instructions to Form 3520, a U.S. beneficiary who receives a distribution from a domestic grantor trust owned by a foreign grantor must report it under Code § 6039F as a gift from a foreign person (i.e., the deemed foreign owner of the domestic trust).

5. Reporting Thresholds

(a) Individuals and Estates. Notice 97-34 increases the statutory threshold for reporting gifts received from foreign individuals and foreign estates. The annual reporting threshold for the aggregate amount of gifts from a foreign individual or foreign estate is $100,000 with respect to that individual or estate. Once the $100,000 threshold is met, Form 3520 requires the U.S. donee to separately identify each gift in excess of $5,000; however, the U.S. donee is not required to identify the donor unless the IRS requests this information.

(b) Corporations and Partnerships. A U.S. person is required to report the receipt of purported gifts from foreign corporations and foreign partnerships if the aggregate amount of gifts from all such entities exceeds $10,000 (as adjusted for the cost of living under Code § 6039F(d)) in the taxable year. Once the $10,000 threshold is met, Form 3520 requires the U.S. donee to separately report all purported gifts from such entities, including the identity of the donor entity. Such purported gifts are subject to recharacterization under Code § 672(f)(4).

(c) Aggregation Rules. In calculating the threshold amounts with respect to a particular foreign person, a U.S. donee must aggregate gifts from foreign persons that he or she knows, or should know, are related (under Code § 643(i)(2)(B)). If the relevant reporting threshold is exceeded, the donee must (1) separately report each aggregated gift in excess of $5,000 from a foreign individual or foreign estate without identifying the donor, and (2) separately report each aggregated purported gift from a foreign corporation or foreign partnership, including the identity of the donor.

(d) Examples. Notice 97-34 provides two examples:

Example 14. A U.S. person, A, receives $90,000 from his or her nonresident alien spouse, B, and the following amounts from the spouse's siblings:

Sibling C	$40,000
Sibling D	two gifts, $4,000 and $3,000
Sibling E	$4,000

The total of gifts from related foreign individuals is $141,000. Reporting is required because the total exceeds $100,000. A must separately identify the gifts from B and C. A must identify the receipt of $7,000 from D but is not required to separately list information about each transaction. A is not required to separately identify information about E's gift. None of the donors need be identified.

Example 15. If U.S. citizen, A, receives a gift of $6,500 from his or her nonresident alien spouse, B, and a purported gift of $9,000 from a foreign corporation wholly owned by B, A must report the gifts because A has reason to know that the donors are related, and the aggregate amount, $15,500, exceeds the $10,000 (indexed to $15,102 in 2013) threshold for gifts from foreign corporations. A must separately identify each gift.

6. Penalties for Nonreporting

A U.S. person who fails to report such foreign gifts will be subject to penalties equal to 5 percent of each gift for each month of noncompliance (not to exceed 25 percent of the aggregate foreign gifts). The IRS is also authorized to determine the tax consequences of any unreported gift based on the information available to it. The Conference Report to the 1996 Act states that the IRS's exercise of this authority will be subject to review under an "arbitrary and capricious" standard. These sanctions will not apply if the failure to file was due to reasonable cause and not willful neglect.

C. Unified Reporting Forms

Form 3520 (Annual Return to Report Transactions with Foreign Trusts and Receipt of Certain Foreign Gifts) allows U.S. persons generally to use a single form to comply with all of the foreign trust and foreign gift reporting requirements. Form 3520-A is to be filed by or on behalf of U.S. grantor-owners of foreign trusts to report trust income.[301]

Generally, to avoid the penalties for nonreporting under Code §§ 6039F or 6677, taxpayers must file Form 3520 with the IRS Service Center in Ogden, Utah, by the due date of their income tax returns (including extensions). There is no separate extension available to file Form 3520; the extension of time to file Form 1040 controls the due date for Form 3520. Spouses may file jointly.

Form 3520-A must be filed in the IRS Service Center in Ogden, Utah by the fifteenth day of the third month following the end of the taxpayer's taxable year (i.e., by March 15, in the case of a calendar year taxpayer) or later if an extension is granted. An extension of time to file Form 3520-A is made on Form 7004; an extension of time to file Form 1040 does not extend the time to file Form 3520-A. A separate form is required for each trust, but spouses may file jointly.[302] Reporting must be done on a calendar year basis even if the foreign trust uses a different fiscal year.

D. Gifts from Covered Expatriates

A U.S. person (including a domestic trust) who directly or indirectly receives a gift or bequest from a covered expatriate (as defined in Code § 877A(g)(1)) whose expatriation date is on or after June 17, 2008, is subject to tax under Code § 2801. The tax is imposed at the highest rate under Code § 2001(c). The tax does not apply to gifts not in excess of the dollar amount of the annual exclusion allowed under Code § 2503(b) in the year of the gift, gifts, or bequests that would qualify for the marital or charitable deduction if the donor or decedent was a U.S. taxpayer, and to gifts or bequests that are otherwise subject to U.S. gift or estate tax provided that such gifts or bequests are reported on timely filed returns. The tax does not apply to gifts or bequests to foreign trusts (unless the trust elects to be treated as a domestic trust and pay the tax), but applies to distributions from foreign trusts to U.S. beneficiaries that are attributable to gifts or bequests from a covered expatriate. A credit is allowed for foreign gift or estate tax paid with respect to the same gift or bequest. A deduction is allowed under Code § 164 for income tax paid by the recipient of a distribution from a foreign trust that is includable in income.

301. Section 534 of the 2010 HIRE Act amends Code § 6048(b) to provide that a U.S. person who is treated as the owner of a foreign trust shall submit such information concerning the trust as the Secretary may require. This requirement is in addition to such person's obligation under Code § 6048(b) to ensure that the trust makes a return for the relevant year that fully accounts for all trust activities.

302. Treas. Reg. § 404.6048-1(a)(2).

Form 3520 asks whether the filer has received a gift or bequest from a covered expatriate. If the answer is "yes," Form 3520 directs the filer to also file Form 708, "U.S. Return of Tax for Gifts and Bequests Received from Expatriates," when the form becomes available. As of the date of this writing, no such form has been issued. The IRS announced that no tax payment would be due until further guidance was issued.[303]

VII. Reporting Foreign Financial Assets and Foreign Accounts

A. Bank Secrecy Act Reporting Requirements for Trust Beneficiaries

Section 5314 of Title 31 (the Bank Secrecy Act) of the United States Code requires a U.S. person to file Form TD F 90-22.1—Report of Foreign Bank Account (FBAR) to report all foreign bank accounts and foreign financial accounts in which he or she has a financial interest or signature authority if the aggregate value of the accounts exceeded $10,000 at any time during the year.[304] A financial account includes a bank account, a securities account, a mutual fund, or other pooled investment fund.

The instructions to the FBAR state that a U.S. person has an indirect financial interest in an account owned by the trust and is therefore required to file an FBAR report for foreign accounts held by the trust if he or she is the grantor and is treated as the owner of the trust under Code §§ 671–679 or if he or she has a present beneficial interest in more than 50 percent of the assets of the trust or receives more than 50 percent of the income of the trust.[305] Regulations issued by the Financial Crimes Enforcement Network (FinCEN), a bureau of the Treasury,[306] lighten trust beneficiaries' reporting obligations by providing that trust beneficiaries (other than those treated as owners under the grantor trust rules) do not have to file an FBAR report for financial assets held by trusts of which he or she is a beneficiary if the trust, trustee of the trust, or agent of the trust is a U.S. person and files an FBAR report disclosing the trust's foreign financial accounts.[307]

303. Notice 2009-85, 2009-45 IRB 598 (issued Oct. 15, 2009) and Announcement 2009-57, 2009-29 I.R.B. 158.

304. 31 U.S.C. § 5314.

305. The preamble to the final FBAR regulations at 76 Fed. Reg. 10234 (Feb. 16, 2011) makes it clear that a discretionary beneficiary and a remainder beneficiary are not required to file FBARs.

306. Treasury has delegated its authority to administer the Bank Secrecy Act to the director of FinCEN. By a Memorandum of Agreement between FinCEN and the Commissioner of the IRS, the authority to enforce the FBAR reporting requirements of the Bank Secrecy Act was re-delegated to the IRS.

307. Section 103.24(g)(5) of 31 C.F.R. pt. 103, 76 Fed. Reg. 10234 (Feb. 16, 2011).

The form must be received by June 30 of the year following the year in which the person possessed the interest obligating him or her to file an FBAR (timely mailing is not timely filing). No extensions of time to file are available.

The penalty for failure to file is $10,000. If the failure is willful, the penalty is the greater of $100,000 or 50 percent of the value of the account. Criminal penalties are up to $250,000 and five years in prison, and if the failure to file is part of a pattern of illegal activity, the penalty increases to up to $500,000 and up to ten years in prison. To avoid the penalty where the filer lacks adequate information, the IRS website suggests filing an incomplete return and an amended return filed later when the missing information becomes available. Answers to questions about FBAR issues can be obtained from an IRS website. Or, send questions to the e-mail address, FBARquestions@irs.gov.

On March 23, 2009, the IRS announced a voluntary disclosure initiative, which remained in effect until October 15, 2009.[308] A second voluntary disclosure program was announced on February 8, 2011.[309] Persons who participated in this new initiative were to pay a penalty capped at 25 percent of the highest account balance in unreported foreign accounts in the prior six years in lieu of all other penalties for failure to file information returns. This was 5 percent more than the maximum penalty under the first initiative. However, lower penalties apply in certain circumstances. As with the first initiative, income tax on unreported income, interest, and an accuracy penalty for the six-year period also would be owed. Participation in the voluntary disclosure program originally required that all forms be filed and taxes paid by August 31, 2011. However, on June 2, 2011, in an update to the initiative's Frequently Asked Questions web page, the IRS announced in FAQ 25.1 that taxpayers could request a ninety-day extension of time to file if they properly extended the statute of limitations, had made a good faith attempt to comply with the August 31, 2011, deadline, and filed a request for such an extension by August 31, 2011. A further extension of time—to September 9, 2011—was made as a result of Hurricane Irene. FAQs 17 and 18 explain that if late returns were filed by September 9, 2011, and no tax was due (all income was reported), no penalty will be imposed. FAQ 52 provided relief for U.S. citizens living abroad who have complied with the tax laws of the country of residence and have U.S. source income of $10,000 or less per year; the penalty for failure to file information returns would be only 5 percent of the highest financial account balance.

On January 9, 2012, the IRS announced a third offshore voluntary disclosure program (OVDP).[310] The third program is the same as the second initiative, except that the penalty rate was increased from 25 percent to 27.5 percent. The penalty applies to the highest account balance in the prior eight years. The lower penalty rates available to some taxpayers under the second initiative were not changed. A

308. The voluntary disclosure program initially closed on September 23, 2009, but was extended until October 15, 2009.

309. IR-2011-14 (Feb. 8, 2011).

310. IR-2012-5 (Jan. 9, 2012).

right to opt out of the program applies if the taxpayer believes that the penalties without the application of the OVDP would be lower.

B. Internal Revenue Code Reporting Requirements for Foreign Financial Assets

Section 511 of the 2010 HIRE Act added new § 6038D to the Code, effective for taxable years beginning after December 31, 2010.[311] Section 6038D(a) requires any individual who holds any interest in a specified foreign financial asset during any taxable year to attach to his or her income tax return for that year the information described in § 6038D(c) if the aggregate value of all such assets exceeds $50,000 on the last day of the taxable year, or $75,000 on any day during the taxable year, or $200,000 and $300,000 for an individual residing abroad. These thresholds increase to $100,000 and $150,000 for married individuals filing jointly who reside in the United States and $400,000 and $600,000 for those residing abroad.[312]

The definition of an interest in a specified foreign financial asset includes not only financial accounts maintained in foreign financial institutions but also, unless held in an account maintained by a domestic financial institution, any stock or security issued by a non-U.S. person, any financial instrument or contract held for investment that has an issuer or counterparty other than a U.S. person, and any interest in a foreign entity. The term "foreign entity" includes foreign trusts. According to instructions to draft Form 8938 and the temporary regulations, a taxpayer's interest in a nongrantor trust equals the sum of the amounts actually received in the taxable year plus the present value of a mandatory right to receive a distribution. If the taxpayer cannot determine the value of his or her interest in a foreign estate, the value is the amount actually received. If a Form 3520, 3520-A, 5471, 8621, or 8865 is filed, Form 8938 need only disclose the identity of the taxpayer and indicate that the information is on the other form. However, an FBAR and Form 8938 both must be filed in full; there is no relief from duplicative filing of these forms, which are filed with different agencies. In addition, the instructions create filing thresholds higher than provided for in the statute for married taxpayers and persons living abroad. The statute creates a presumption that the filing threshold is exceeded.

The penalty for failure to file is $10,000. Additional penalties apply if the failure to file continues after notice is given to the taxpayer. If the failure to file continues ninety days after notice is given to the taxpayer, the additional penalty is $10,000 per thirty-day period beginning after expiration of the ninety-day period. However, the penalty cannot exceed $50,000. The penalty may be waived if the failure was due to reasonable cause and not willful neglect.

311. Notice 2011-55 postponed the filing due date until a final form is issued. A draft Form 8938, "Statement of Specified Foreign Financial Assets," was released September 28, 2011. According to the instructions, a taxpayer was to attach the forms for both 2011 and 2012 to his or her tax return for 2012.

312. Treas. Reg. 1.6038D-2T.

The statute applies only to interests held directly by U.S. individuals or by individuals indirectly through disregarded entities. However, the statute gives the IRS authority to issue rules applying the statute to U.S. entities that are formed or availed of to avoid the foreign financial assets. For example, the IRS could issue rules making the statute applicable to U.S. trusts that own foreign financial assets. Temporary regulations have been issued that require reporting by certain such "specified domestic entities."[313]

Effective for taxable years beginning after March 18, 2010, the negligence penalty imposed by Code § 6662 increased from 20 percent to 40 percent if the deficiency is attributable to an unreported foreign financial asset.[314]

In addition, the statute of limitations will not commence to run until the return required by new Code § 6038D is filed for events and periods related to the information required on the return.[315] This statute is effective for all open years as of March 18, 2010. Section 513 of the 2010 HIRE Act also amended Code § 6501(e) to provide that the statute of limitations on assessment of a return is extended from three to six years if the taxpayer omitted more than $5,000 from gross income and the omission is attributable to assets with respect to which a return was required by Code § 6038D, whether or not the filing threshold for Code § 6038D is met.

313. *Id.* 1.6038D-6

314. Section 512 of the 2010 HIRE Act.

315. Code § 6501(c)(8), *as amended by* § 513 of the 2010 HIRE Act.

Planning for Transfers to Noncitizen Spouses

8

Douglas L. Siegler

I. Introduction

A. Prior Law

Prior to the enactment of the Technical and Miscellaneous Revenue Act of 1988 (TAMRA),[1] a donor who was a U.S. citizen or resident was allowed an unlimited federal *gift tax* marital deduction for the value of all gifts to his or her spouse, regardless of the donee spouse's citizenship.[2] The estate of a U.S. citizen or resident was allowed an unlimited federal *estate tax* marital deduction for the value of all property passing to the surviving spouse, regardless of the surviving spouse's citizenship.[3] No deduction was allowed in computing the taxable gifts of a nonresident alien donor or the taxable estate of a nonresident alien decedent for

---

1. Pub. L. No. 100-647, 102 Stat. 3342 (1988).

2. Prior § 2523(a) of the Internal Revenue Code of 1986. All section (§) references are to the Internal Revenue Code of 1986 (as amended), unless otherwise noted. Following *United States v. Windsor*, 570 U.S. ___ , 133 S. Ct. 2675 (2013) and Rev. Rul. 2013-17, __ I.R.B. __ (August 29, 2013), individuals of the same sex will be considered to be lawfully married under the Code as long as they were married in a state whose laws authorize the marriage of two individuals of the same sex, even if they are domiciled in a state that does not recognize the validity of same-sex marriages. For purposes of applying Rev. Rul. 2013-17, the term "state" means any domestic or foreign jurisdiction having the legal authority to sanction marriages.

3. § 2056(a).

the value of gifts or bequests to a spouse, even if the recipient spouse was a U.S. citizen.

The assumption underlying the allowance of the federal gift and estate tax marital deductions is that the property with respect to which the deduction is allowed would be includable in the estate of the recipient spouse to the extent not consumed or given away (perhaps as a taxable gift) prior to the spouse's death. Congress determined that although this assumption is generally valid where the surviving spouse is a U.S. citizen, who would therefore be subject to federal estate taxation on his worldwide assets, the situation was different where the surviving spouse was not a U.S. citizen because he could leave the United States, return to his country of origin, and thereby give up his U.S. residence. By doing so, he would be subject to federal estate taxation only on his U.S.-situs assets, rather than on worldwide property.[4] As a result, there was a greater likelihood that the property (which already had escaped federal estate tax at the death of the first spouse due to the availability of the unlimited marital deduction) could also escape the imposition of the federal estate tax at the death of the surviving spouse.[5]

Congress remedied this perceived loophole by:

- Denying the federal *estate tax* marital deduction for bequests to surviving spouses who were not U.S. citizens (noncitizen spouses) unless such property passes to or is placed into a "qualified domestic trust" (QDOT).[6]
- Denying the unlimited federal *gift tax* marital deduction for transfers to a noncitizen spouse and introducing an increased annual exclusion from the federal gift tax.[7]
- Making § 2040(b)—under which only half the value of property jointly held by spouses is includable in the gross estate of the first spouse to die, regardless of which spouse provided the consideration for the property—inapplicable to the estate of a decedent spouse where the surviving spouse is not a U.S. citizen.[8]
- Reenacting §§ 2515 (without the election provisions of §§ 2515(c)) and 2515A of the Internal Revenue Code of 1954 (the 1954 Code) to determine whether a gift results from the creation and termination (other than by death of a joint tenant) of a joint tenancy between spouses where the donee spouse is not a U.S. citizen.[9]

---

4. *See* § 2103.

5. *See* H.R. Rep. No. 795, 100th Cong. (1988) (1988 House Report). Note that following the enactment of the Health Insurance Portability and Accountability Act of 1996, Pub. L. No. 104-191, if the surviving spouse was a permanent U.S. resident (i.e., a "green card" holder), his departure could subject him to the amended expatriation provisions of §§ 877, 2107, and 2501. *See* Notice 97-19, 1997-1 C.B. 394.

6. § 2056(d).

7. § 2523(i)(1) and (i)(2).

8. § 2056(d)(1)(B).

9. *See* § 2523(i)(3).

TAMRA (as amended by the Omnibus Budget Reconciliation Act of 1989 (OBRA 1989)),[10] the Omnibus Budget Reconciliation Act of 1990 (OBRA 1990),[11] and the Taxpayer Relief Act of 1997 (TRA 1997),[12] and as interpreted and implemented by the final regulations—is a broad response to these perceived problems. It places substantial burdens and restrictions on recipient noncitizen spouses, creates technical inconsistencies with existing laws, and discriminates against noncitizen spouses rather than equalizing the tax treatment afforded citizen and noncitizen spouses.

B. Background

1. Statutory Provisions

Section 5033 of TAMRA restricts the availability of the federal estate and gift tax marital deduction where the recipient spouse or the donee spouse is not a U.S. citizen. These provisions were amended by OBRA 1989, OBRA 1990, and TRA 1997.

2. Proposed Regulations

On January 5, 1993, proposed regulations implementing these provisions were issued.[13] The proposed regulations provided practical guidance and answered many questions encountered by practitioners attempting to comply with the marital deduction limitations. However, in an effort to ensure collection of the deferred estate tax imposed on QDOTs, the proposed regulations imposed burdensome information and record-keeping requirements on QDOT trustees. In addition, the proposed regulations imposed numerous "governing instrument" requirements, under which the failure to include certain provisions prevented a trust from qualifying as a QDOT, even if the trust actually complied with the regulatory requirements.

3. Temporary and Final Regulations

On August 22, 1995, final and temporary regulations were issued.[14] The portion of the regulations issued in final form covered all the provisions introduced by the TAMRA legislation except those concerning security arrangements for the collection of the QDOT tax under § 2056A(a)(2) (the Security Requirements). The final regulations were comprehensive and generally responsive to many of the concerns raised in comments to the Treasury.

In recognition of the substantial changes that were made from the proposed regulations, the provisions governing the Security Requirements were issued in temporary and proposed form.[15] Final regulations governing the Security Requirements were issued on November 29, 1996.[16] Finally, on December 9, 1996, the IRS

10. Revenue Reconciliation Act of 1989, Pub. L. No. 101-239.
11. Revenue Reconciliation Act of 1990, Pub. L. No. 101-508.
12. Pub. L. No. 105-34.
13. 58 Fed. Reg. 305 (Jan. 5, 1993).
14. T.D. 8612, 60 Fed. Reg. 43,531 (Aug. 22, 1995).
15. 60 Fed. Reg. 43,554, 43,575 (Aug. 22, 1995).
16. T.D. 8686, 61 Fed. Reg. 60,551 (Nov. 29, 1996).

issued Revenue Procedure 96-54,[17] which included sample language that satisfies the Security Requirements.

II. Disallowance of Federal Estate Tax Marital Deduction

A. General Rule

In calculating the federal estate tax, the value of the gross estate is reduced, subject to application of the terminable interest rules of § 2056(b), by the value of all property passing to a surviving spouse.[18] However, if the surviving spouse is not a U.S. citizen at the date of death of the decedent spouse, no marital deduction is allowed to the decedent spouse's estate unless such property passes to the surviving spouse in a QDOT.[19]

In order for property passing to or for the benefit of a surviving spouse who is not a U.S. citizen at the date of the decedent spouse's death to qualify for the federal estate tax marital deduction, the regulations[20] impose two requirements:

1. The property must pass from the decedent to (or pursuant to)—
   a. a QDOT described in § 2056A and Treas. Reg. § 20.2056A-2;
   b. a trust that, although not meeting all of the requirements for a QDOT, is reformed after the decedent's death to meet the requirements of a QDOT;[21]
   c. the surviving spouse not in trust (e.g., by outright bequest or devise, by operation of law, or pursuant to the terms of a plan or arrangement) and, prior to the date that the estate tax return is filed and during the time that the QDOT election may be made (that is, no more than one year after the time prescribed by law, including extensions, for filing the return), the surviving spouse either actually transfers the property to a QDOT or irrevocably assigns the property to a QDOT;[22] or
   d. a plan or other arrangement that would have qualified for the marital deduction had the surviving spouse been a U.S. citizen and whose payments are not assignable or transferable to a QDOT, if the requirements of Treas. Reg. § 20.2056A-4(c) are met;[23] and
2. The executor of the decedent spouse's estate must make a timely QDOT election under Treas. Reg. § 20.2056A-3.[24]

17. 1996-2 C.B. 386.
18. § 2056(a); Treas. Reg. § 20.2056(a)-1(a).
19. §§ 2056(d)(1)(A) and 2056(d)(2)(A). *See* Fung v. Comm'r, 117 T.C. 247, 253 (2001), *aff'd*, 58 F. App'x 328 (9th Cir. 2003).
20. Treas. Reg. § 20.2056A-1(a).
21. *See id.* § 20.2056A-4(a) and discussion *infra* Section IV.
22. *See* Treas. Reg. § 20.2056A-4(b) and discussion *infra* Section V.
23. *See* discussion *infra* Section VI.
24. *See infra* Section III.C.3.

B. Treatment of Jointly Held Property (with Right of Survivorship) at Death

1. Rules Prior to TAMRA

Generally, the value of property titled jointly with right of survivorship or as tenants by the entireties is included in the gross estate of the first joint tenant to die except to the extent that the executor of the decedent's estate can demonstrate that the surviving joint tenant supplied the consideration for the property. Only one-half of the value of the property is included in the decedent's estate where the property was acquired by the joint tenants by gift, devise, bequest, or inheritance.[25]

In order to exclude such property from the estate, the decedent's executor must "submit[] facts sufficient to show that property was not acquired entirely with consideration furnished by the decedent, or was acquired by the decedent and the other joint owner or owners by gift, bequest, devise, or inheritance."[26]

Section 2040(b) provides that only one-half of the value of property owned by the decedent and his spouse as joint tenants or as tenants by the entireties is included in the decedent's estate, regardless of the amount of the consideration furnished by the decedent.[27] With respect to spousal joint tenancies created prior to the enactment of § 2040(b) in 1976, the provisions of § 2040(a) may be applicable.[28]

2. Legislative and Regulatory Amendments

TAMRA made § 2040(b) inapplicable to the estate of a decedent whose surviving spouse is not a U.S. citizen.[29] The effect of this provision, except as described below, is to require the decedent's executor to trace the consideration provided by each spouse in order to determine how much of the property must be included in the decedent's gross estate.

(a) Limited Grandfathering Relief. OBRA 1989 provided some relief from these burdensome tracing requirements. With respect to joint tenancies to which the "half-half" rule of § 2040(b) is inapplicable solely by reason of the TAMRA changes, consideration furnished for such interests by the decedent prior to July 14, 1988, to the extent treated at the time as a gift (for purposes of the federal gift tax) to the noncitizen surviving spouse, is treated as consideration furnished by the noncitizen spouse in applying § 2040(a).[30] Specifically § 7815(d)(16) of OBRA

---

25. § 2040(a); Treas. Reg. § 20.2040-1(a)(1), (2).

26. Treas. Reg. § 20.2040-1(a) (last sentence).

27. § 2040(b) (added by § 2002(c)(1) and (d)(3) of the Tax Reform Act of 1976).

28. *See, e.g.*, Gallenstein v. United States, 975 F.2d 286 (6th Cir. 1992) (holding that where the husband purchased real property with his own funds in 1955 and took title to the property in joint name with right of survivorship with his wife, the entire value of the property was included in his gross estate on his death in 1988). *See also* Patten v. United States, 116 F.3d 1029 (4th Cir. 1997).

29. § 2056(d)(1)(B); Treas. Reg. § 20.2056A-8(a)(1).

30. See discussion *infra* Section IX.B on the gift tax effects of creation of spousal joint tenancies.

1989 provides that consideration "shall be treated as consideration originally belonging to such [noncitizen] spouse and never acquired by such spouse from the decedent."[31]

OBRA 1990 further amended this grandfathering provision to provide that a transfer creating a spousal joint tenancy that would have constituted a gift to the noncitizen spouse had the donor been a U.S. citizen will be treated as consideration belonging to the donee spouse. For example, a nonresident alien provided all the consideration for the purchase of non-U.S. situs real property after December 31, 1981, and prior to July 14, 1988, and the property was titled in the name of the donor spouse and his noncitizen donee spouse. Under these facts, the noncitizen donee spouse will be treated, for purposes of § 2040(a), as having provided one-half of the consideration for the purchase of the property, even though there was no gift for federal gift tax purposes, because the transfer involved a "gift" of non-U.S. situs property by a non-U.S. citizen or resident.[32] In determining whether the consideration was a gift by the decedent under § 2511 for purposes of applying the grandfathering provision, the regulations presume that the decedent was a U.S. citizen at the time the consideration was furnished to the spouse.[33] Of course, if the donor spouse dies first, and if he or she is still a nonresident alien, presumably such property will not be includable in his or her gross estate.[34]

> ***Example 1:*** In 1987, D, a U.S. citizen, purchases real property and takes title in the names of D and S, D's spouse (a noncitizen, but a U.S. resident), as joint tenants with right of survivorship. In accordance with Treas. Reg. § 25.2511-1(h)(5), one-half the value of the property is a gift to S. D dies in 2012. Because S is not a U.S. citizen, the provisions of § 2040(a) determine the extent to which the real property is includable in D's gross estate. Because the joint tenancy was established before July 14, 1988, and under the applicable Code provisions and regulations the transfer was treated as a gift of one-half the property to S, one-half of the value of the property is deemed attributable to consideration furnished by S for purposes of § 2040(a). Accordingly, only one-half of the value of the property is includable in D's gross estate under § 2040(a).[35]

(b) Donee Spouse Dies First. The legislative history is silent on whether the same tracing rules must be applied where the decedent spouse is a noncitizen who provided none of the actual consideration for the purchase of jointly held property. Section 7815(d)(16) of OBRA 1989 addressed only the situation in which

---

31. *See also* Treas. Reg. § 20.2056A-8(a)(2) and -8(c), Example 1.
32. *See* §§ 2511(a) and 2501(a)(1), (2).
33. Treas. Reg. § 20.2056A-8(a)(2).
34. *See* § 2103.
35. *See* Treas. Reg. § 20.2056A-8(c), Example 1. *See also* I.R.S. Priv. Ltr. Rul. 9151044 (Sept. 26, 1991) (entire value of jointly titled residence purchased by decedent and his noncitizen spouse in 1977 with funds "all or substantially all" provided by decedent is included in decedent's gross estate).

the noncitizen spouse is the survivor and the decedent spouse provided the consideration. Under the literal language of § 7815(d)(16), the rule would not apply in the reverse situation. The regulations provide that the deemed consideration rule applies only when the donor spouse dies first. Where the donee spouse dies first, any portion of the consideration treated as a gift to the donee spouse/decedent at the creation of the tenancy (or subsequently), regardless of the date the tenancy was created, will not be treated as a consideration furnished by the donee spouse/decedent for purposes of applying § 2040(a).[36]

> ***Example 2:*** Assume the same facts as in the previous example, except it is S who dies in 2012, survived by D, who is not a U.S. citizen. For purposes of applying § 2040(a), D's gift to S at the creation of the tenancy will not be treated as consideration furnished by S toward the acquisition of the property. Accordingly, because S made no other contributions with respect to the property, no portion of the property is includable in S's gross estate.[37]

(c) Amount Required to Be Transferred to QDOT. If only a portion of the value of a jointly held property interest is includable in a decedent's gross estate, only that portion that is so includable may be transferred to a QDOT to obtain the estate tax marital deduction for the property.[38] If the surviving spouse becomes a U.S. citizen prior to the date on which the decedent spouse's federal estate tax return is filed, in accordance with the requirements of § 2056(d)(4) and Treas. Reg. § 20.2056A-1(b), then the "half-half" rule of § 2040(b) applies to determine the portion of spousal joint tenancy property that is to be included in the gross estate of the decedent spouse.[39]

(d) Proof of Consideration Furnished. The decedent's estate bears the burden of proof regarding the consideration furnished by the decedent and the surviving joint tenant.[40] The lapse of time and the failure to keep contemporaneous records may result in a lack of solid direct proof of which spouse provided the consideration. However, the regulations indicate that proof of the consideration furnished by the decedent and the surviving spouse toward the purchase price and improvements to jointly held property can be shown indirectly. For example, the regulations provide that when a down payment and subsequent mortgage payments and improvements are paid from a joint bank account held by the husband and wife, and the only funds deposited in the joint bank account are the earnings of the two spouses, proof of the approximate ratio of the earnings contributed to the bank account will be sufficient to establish the relative contributions of each

36. Treas. Reg. § 20.2056A-8(a)(2) (last sentence).

37. *Id.* § 20.2056A-8(c), Example 2.

38. *Id.* § 20.2056A-8(a)(3). *See, e.g.*, I.R.S. Priv. Ltr. Rul. 9551014 (Sept. 21, 1995) (limiting portion of jointly held property assignable to QDOT to portion determined to be included under Treas. Reg. § 20.2056A-8(a)(2)).

39. *See* Treas. Reg. § 20.2056A-8(b).

40. *Id.* § 20.2040-1(a)(2).

spouse to the consideration for the purchase of the property.[41] Furthermore, when the contribution of the surviving spouse to the purchase price of a parcel of real estate is limited to mortgage payments on which the spouses are jointly liable, the IRS has indicated that it will calculate the surviving spouse's contribution by multiplying the date-of-death value of the property by a fraction, the numerator of which is one-half of the date-of-death balance of the mortgage, and the denominator of which is the purchase price of the property.

> ***Example 3:*** D dies, survived by his noncitizen spouse, S. D and S purchased Blackacre in 1979 for $300,000, with D paying the entire $20,000 down payment. D and S are jointly liable on the mortgage. At D's death, the mortgage balance is $200,000, and the property is worth $500,000. The entire value of the property is included in D's estate except to the extent that D's estate can show that S provided the consideration. S's contribution to the purchase price, and thus the amount excluded for D's gross estate, will be $166,667, and the value included in D's gross estate will be $333,333, determined as follows:
>
> 500,000 - (500,000 x ½(200,000)).[42]
> 300,000

C. Allowance of Marital Deduction When Surviving Spouse Becomes a U.S. Citizen

The disallowance of the estate tax marital deduction under § 2056(d) will not apply, and the regular marital deduction rules of § 2056(a) will apply to the estate of the decedent spouse if two conditions are met:

- The surviving spouse becomes a U.S. citizen prior to the day on which the decedent's federal estate tax return is made; *and*
- The surviving spouse is a U.S. resident at all times after the date of death of the decedent spouse and before becoming a U.S. citizen.[43]

For purposes of qualifying for this exception, the surviving spouse is a "resident" only if he is a U.S. resident for purposes of the federal estate tax.[44] The status of the spouse as an income tax resident under § 7701(b) is not relevant to this determination except to the extent that the income tax residency of the spouse is pertinent in applying Treas. Reg. § 20.0-1(b)(1).[45] In this connection, the surviving spouse will not fail to qualify for the relief provided under § 2056(d)(4) merely

41. *See id.* § 20.2056-8(c), Example 3.
42. *See* I.R.S. Priv. Ltr. Rul. 9551014 (Sept. 21, 1995) (citing Rev. Rul. 79-302, 1979-2 C.B. 328).
43. § 2056(d)(4)(A) and (B) (added by OBRA 1989).
44. *See* Treas. Reg. § 20.0-1(b)(1). A resident decedent is a decedent who, at the time of his death, has his domicile in the United States. A person acquires domicile, for U.S. estate tax purposes, by living in a place, even for a brief period of time, with no definite present intention of moving therefrom. *See* Estate of Khan v. Comm'r, T.C.M. 1998-22.
45. Treas. Reg. § 20.2056A-1(b).

because he was temporarily out of the United States after the date of the decedent spouse's death and before the date on which U.S. citizenship was obtained.

The provisions of § 2056(d)(4) may provide only a limited escape from the application of the QDOT rules. The IRS has indicated that it will strictly interpret the requirement that the surviving spouse actually become a U.S. citizen prior to the date on which the federal estate tax return is filed. In Private Letter Ruling 9021037 (Feb. 23, 1990), the surviving spouse, who was a Canadian citizen, had applied for U.S. citizenship prior to the death of his wife and had represented that this application would likely be processed prior to the due date of the federal estate tax return. In addition, the surviving spouse claimed that his "history and continuing ties with the United States" should be considered to satisfy the concerns that prompted Congress to pass § 2056(d). The IRS ruled that the surviving spouse would nevertheless have to utilize a QDOT because the disallowance of the marital deduction under § 2056(d)(1) applies without exception to estates of decedents who die after November 10, 1988, if the surviving spouse is not a U.S. citizen. The fact that the surviving spouse has demonstrated loyalty by applying for citizenship or by other means is not sufficient to override the statute.

In addition, the preamble to the final regulations[46] rejected the suggestion of certain commentators that if the surviving spouse has filed an application for naturalization within a reasonable time after the decedent's death, then any late filing of the return pending the outcome of the citizenship process should be treated as due to reasonable cause for purposes of applying § 6651 (imposing penalties for failure to file return and the failure to pay tax). The IRS refused to adopt this suggestion, stating that the existence of reasonable cause for late filing and late payment should be determined on a case-by-case basis, applying standards as prescribed in current law.

As a practical matter, if the naturalization process was not initiated prior to the date of death of the decedent spouse, it may be difficult to complete the process within the nine months (or even fifteen months, with the automatic extension of time to file the federal estate tax return) following the decedent's death. Of course, if the surviving spouse becomes a U.S. citizen, and the provisions of § 20.2056A(b)(10) are satisfied, the QDOT can be terminated at that time.[47]

Notice, however, that for purposes of qualifying for the § 2056(d)(4) exception to the marital deduction limitations, the regulations state that a federal estate tax return filed prior to the due date (including extensions) is considered to be filed on the last date that the return is required to be filed, including extensions, and a late return is considered to be filed on the date it is actually filed.[48]

Comment: If an extension of time within which to file the federal estate tax return can be obtained, such an extension will extend the time during

46. T.D. 8612, 60 Fed. Reg. 43,531 (Apr. 22, 1995).
47. *See infra* Section VII.F.
48. Treas. Reg. § 20.2056A-1(b). *See also* I.R.S. Priv. Ltr. Rul. 9808022.

which the surviving spouse can obtain U.S. citizenship and avoid the marital deduction limitations of § 2056(d)(1). Further, under the regulations, a late-filed return has the effect of extending the time during which citizenship can be obtained. Of course, a late-filed return may give rise to penalties[49] and may prevent timely elections and allocations to be made.

III. Qualification as a QDOT

A. In General

The statute and the regulations set out numerous requirements for ensuring that a trust meets the requirement of a QDOT. Broadly speaking, these requirements fall into three categories: the Marital Deduction Requirements, the Statutory Requirements, and the Security Requirements to ensure collection of the QDOT tax.

B. Marital Deduction Requirements

There are three different methods by which the Marital Deduction Requirements can be satisfied, depending on the type of property involved and how it passes to the surviving spouse.

1. Property Passing Directly to a QDOT

If property passes from the decedent spouse to a QDOT, the trust must also qualify for the federal estate tax marital deduction under:

a. § 2056(b)(5) (as a life estate with power of appointment);
b. § 2056(b)(7) (as qualified terminable interest property, including joint and survivor annuities under § 2056(b)(7)(C));
c. § 2056(b)(8) (surviving spouse is the only noncharitable beneficiary of a charitable remainder trust); or
d. Treas. Reg. § 20.2056(c)-2(b)(1)(i)–(iii) (meeting the requirements of an estate trust).[50]

2. Property Passing Outright to Surviving Noncitizen Spouse

Property that passes outright to the surviving spouse in a manner that, but for the marital deduction limitations of § 2056(d)(1), would qualify for the marital

49. *See* § 6651(a)(1) and (a)(2). However, if, as a result of the delay, bequests to the surviving spouse qualify for the estate tax marital deduction and no estate tax is due, then no penalties will be imposed.

50. Treas. Reg. § 20.2056A-2(b)(1). An estate trust is a form of marital trust sanctioned by the regulations under § 2056. Unlike the requirements for a general power of appointment marital trust or a Qualified Terminable Interest Property (QTIP) trust, an estate trust does not mandate satisfaction of the "qualifying income interest for life." *See* Treas. Reg. §§ 20.2056(b)-5(f), 20.2056(b)-7(d). Instead, the estate trust allows for the accumulation of some portion or all of the trust income, provided that any such accumulated income be paid over to the surviving spouse's estate on his or her death.

deduction (e.g., proceeds of insurance payable to the spouse or property passing to the spouse by operation of law) qualifies for the estate tax marital deduction only if the surviving spouse actually transfers the property to, or irrevocably assigns the property to, a trust that meets the Statutory Requirements (discussed *infra* Section III.C) and the Security Requirements (discussed *infra* Section III.D).[51]

The transfer or irrevocable assignment of property to a QDOT must take place prior to the filing of the federal estate tax return and before the due date of the QDOT election.[52] Note that the trust to which the property is to be transferred need *not* meet the requirements for the federal estate tax marital deduction under §§ 2056(b)(5), 2056(b)(7), 2056(b)(8) or the requirements of an estate trust. In fact, the surviving spouse need not even be a beneficiary of such a QDOT. However, because the surviving spouse will be deemed to be the transferor of the property for purposes of the estate tax,[53] the retention by the spouse of rights to income or principal, or the holding of even a limited power of appointment over the trust property, will cause the QDOT property to be included in the spouse's gross estate.

3. Property Passing to the Noncitizen Surviving Spouse under a Nontransferable Plan or Arrangement

The regulations provide special rules for property passing from the decedent under a plan or other arrangement that will qualify for the marital deduction but for the limitations imposed by § 2056(d)(4) and payments from which are not assignable or transferable. Under these provisions, such nonassignable annuities or arrangements will be treated as satisfying the Marital Deduction Requirements, the Statutory Requirements, and the Security Requirements if the provisions of Treas. Reg. § 20.2056A-4(a) are satisfied.[54]

C. Statutory Requirements

1. Trustee

In order to qualify as a QDOT, the trust instrument must require that at least one trustee be an individual who is a U.S. citizen or a domestic corporation.[55] This constitutes a significant relaxation of the rule originally enacted in TAMRA, which required *all* trustees of a QDOT to be either U.S. citizens or domestic corporations.

OBRA 1989 amended § 2056A(a)(1) to provide that the trust instrument must require that no distribution from a QDOT be made without the approval of the

51. Treas. Reg. § 20.2056A-2(b)(2). *See* § 2056(d)(1)(B).

52. Treas. Reg. § 20.2056A-2(b)(2), § 2056(d)(1)(B). The provisions regarding transfers and assignments of property to a QDOT are discussed in detail in *infra* Section V.

53. *See* § 2056(d)(2)(B); Treas. Reg. § 20.2056A-4(b)(5).

54. *See* Treas. Reg. § 20.2056A-2(b)(3) and *infra* Section VI.

55. § 2056A(a)(1).

U.S. trustee. This requirement, read literally, created a potential conflict with the requirements of the marital deduction under § 2056(b)(5) and (b)(7).[56]

OBRA 1990 again amended the trustee requirement by bifurcating the provisions of § 2056A(a)(1). Following OBRA 1990, a QDOT must still require that at least one trustee be an individual who is a U.S. citizen or domestic corporation.[57] In addition, however, the trust instrument must provide that no distribution (other than income) may be made from the trust unless a U.S. trustee "has the right to withhold from such distribution" the QDOT tax imposed on the distribution.[58] OBRA 1990 also eliminated any potential conflict with the requirements of the marital deduction by making explicit that any provision of the QDOT that permits the trustee to withhold from any distribution an amount to pay the QDOT tax on such distribution will not cause the QDOT to fail to meet the requirements of §§ 2056(b)(5) and 2056(b)(7).[59]

These amendments were effective retroactively as if included in TAMRA. As a result, QDOTs drafted to comply with the prior requirements of § 2056A(a)(1)—as, for example, instruments that required the approval of the U.S. Trustee for all distributions—most probably will not satisfy the withholding requirements enacted by OBRA 1990. For a QDOT that is presently irrevocable, the trustee may have to reform the trust (either pursuant to a judicial reformation or pursuant to the terms of the trust instrument) in order to ensure that it meets the requirements of § 2056A(a)(1)(B).[60]

TRA 1997 enacted additional relief by providing that any trust executed prior to the November 5, 1990, date of enactment of OBRA 1990 will be treated

---

56. The prior law requirement that the U.S. trustee approve QDOT distributions would appear to run afoul of the mandatory income interest requirements of a general power of appointment marital deduction trust set out in § 20.2056(b)-5(f)(7) and the "qualifying income interest for life" requirement of a QTIP trust as set out in § 2056(b)(7)(B)(ii) and Treas. Reg. § 20.2056(b)-7(d). Moreover, the "approval" requirement may also be inconsistent with the general power of appointment marital trust insofar as § 2056(b)(5) requires that the surviving spouse's power to appoint the trust assets must be exercisable alone and in all events. *See* Treas. Reg. §§ 20.2056(b)-5(a)(3), (4) and 20.2056(b)-5(g). If the power of appointment could only be exercised with the consent of the U.S. trustee, this requirement would not be satisfied. It seems unlikely that Congress intended this result, especially given the explicit recognition in the legislative history that qualification of terminable interests for the marital deduction may, under § 2056(b)(5) and (b)(7), require the surviving spouse to have an income interest in the trust. H.R. REP. NO. 101-247, at 1431 n.97 (1989) (1989 House Report). More likely, what Congress intended by the approval requirement was to ensure that the U.S. trustee (1) be aware of any distribution from the QDOT and (2) be in a position to withhold the amount of any QDOT tax imposed.

57. § 2056A(a)(1)(A).

58. § 2056A(a)(1)(B).

59. *See* § 2056A(b)(14). *See, e.g.*, I.R.S. Priv. Ltr. Rul. 9620015 (Feb. 14, 1996) (marital trust qualified under § 2056(b)(8) notwithstanding withholding requirement).

60. Some transitional relief was provided to allow a reformation proceeding under § 2056(d)(5)(A)(ii) to be commenced at any time before May 5, 1991, the date six months after enactment of OBRA 1990, even if the federal estate tax return had previously been filed. *See* § 11701(1)(2) of OBRA 1990. *See also* H. REP. NO. 894, at 29, 101st Cong. (1990) (1990 House Technical Corrections Report). The reformation provisions are discussed *infra* Section IV.

as meeting the requirements of § 2056A(a)(1) if the instrument required that all trustees of the trust be individual U.S. citizens or domestic corporations. This provision is effective as if included in OBRA 1990. Again, however, trusts drawn to comply with the U.S. trustee "approval" requirement enacted in OBRA 1989 will likely not meet the requirements of § 2056A(a)(1) without a timely and effective reformation.

(a) Corporate Trustee. For purposes of the trustee requirements, a domestic corporation is a corporation that is created or organized under the laws of the United States or under the laws of any state or the District of Columbia.[61]

(b) Individual Trustee. If the U.S. Trustee is an individual U.S. citizen, the individual must have a tax home (as defined in § 911(d)(3)) in the United States.[62] The term "tax home" is defined as an individual's home for purposes of § 162(a)(2) (relating to travel expenses while away from home). An individual's tax home is considered to be located at his regular or principal (if more than one regular) place of business or, if the individual has no regular place of business, then at his regular place of abode in a real or substantial sense.[63]

Section 911(d)(3) provides that an individual shall not be treated as having a tax home in a foreign country for any period for which his abode is within the United States. However, the temporary presence of an individual in the United States, or maintenance of a dwelling in the United States by the individual (whether or not used by the individual's spouse or dependents) is not conclusive proof that the individual's abode is in the United States.[64]

2. Withholding Requirement

The trust instrument must provide that no distribution other than income may be made from the trust unless the U.S. Trustee has the right to withhold the amount of any QDOT tax imposed on such distribution.[65] There is apparently no requirement that the U.S. Trustee actually withhold the amount of such tax; rather, the trustee must simply be authorized to do so. As a practical matter, it will make sense for the trustee to actually withhold the amount of the QDOT tax to ensure that when the Form 706-QDT is filed, the trustee has sufficient funds with which to pay the QDOT tax. On the other hand, the trustee should be able to apply other trust assets in payment of the QDOT tax. However, where the trust assets are illiquid, it may be prudent to withhold the amount of the tax from the distribution.

61. Treas. Reg. § 20.2056A-2(c).
62. *Id.* § 20.2056A-2(d)(2).
63. *See id.* § 1.911-2(b).
64. *Id.* § 1.911-2(b).
65. § 2056A(a)(1)(B).

3. Election by Executor

The decedent spouse's executor must make an election to treat the trust as a QDOT. The election must be made on the federal estate tax return, in the form and manner set forth on the return, including applicable instructions.[66] Once made, the election is irrevocable.[67]

Under the current version of Schedule M of Form 706, the requirement that the executor signify the QDOT election by checking a box has been replaced with a provision that states that if the surviving spouse is not a U.S. citizen, the QDOT election is presumed to have been made with respect to any property passing to the noncitizen surviving spouse for which the marital deduction had been claimed, and the executor must affirmatively *elect out* of QDOT treatment. This provision of Form 706 is similar to the provisions governing the QTIP election and should decrease the incidence of the inadvertent failure to properly signify the QDOT election.

(a) Time Limitations. The election to treat a trust as a QDOT must be made on the last federal estate tax return filed before the due date (including extensions of time to file actually granted) or, if a timely return is not filed, on the first federal estate tax return filed after the due date.[68] However, in no case may the election be made on any return filed more than one year after the time prescribed by law (including extensions) for filing the return.[69]

(b) Partial QDOT Election. An election to treat a trust as a QDOT may not be made with respect to a specific portion of an entire trust that would otherwise qualify for the marital deduction but for the application of the marital deduction limitations of § 2056(d).[70] The preamble to the proposed regulations stated that such partial elections were not authorized by the statute and "would present computational difficulties in determining the deferred estate tax in the event of a distribution of corpus from the trust."[71] However, if the trust is actually severed in accordance with the applicable requirements of § 2056(b)(7), a QDOT election may be made for any one or more of the severed trusts.[72]

Under the QTIP regulations, a marital trust may be divided into separate trusts to reflect a partial QTIP election that has been made or is to be made if the

66. §§ 2056A(a)(3) and 2056A(d); Treas. Reg. § 20.2056A-3(a), -3(d); H.R. Rep. No. 1104 (1988) (Conf. Report) (1988 Conference Report).

67. Treas. Reg. § 20.2056A-3(a).

68. *Id.*

69. § 2056A(d). *See* I.R.S. Priv. Ltr. Rul. 9843030 (July 24, 1998).

70. Treas. Reg. § 20.2056A-3(b).

71. 58 Fed. Reg. 305 (Jan. 5, 1993).

72. Treas. Reg. § 20.2056A-3(b). *See* I.R.S. Priv. Ltr. Rul. 9505007 (Nov. 3, 1994) (allowing an extension of time within which to divide a QTIP trust and make QTIP and QDOT elections with respect to only one of the trusts). *See also* Gilpatric v. Cabour, 879 N.E.2d 1236 (Mass. 2008) (allowing a division of a marital trust under Massachusetts law to allow for a smaller QDOT election).

division is authorized under the governing instrument or is otherwise permissible under local law.[73] The regulations provide that the division of the trust must be done on a fractional or percentage basis to reflect the partial election (although the separate trusts need not be funded with a pro rata portion of each asset held by the undivided trust) and that a trust may be divided only if the fiduciary is required, either by applicable local law or by the express or implied provisions of the governing instrument, to fund the trust on the basis of the fair market value of the assets of the trust at the time of the division.[74]

(c) Protective QDOT Elections. A protective election to treat property as a QDOT may be made only if at the time the Form 706 is filed, the executor of the decedent spouse's estate reasonably believes there is a *bona fide* issue that concerns (1) the residency or citizenship of the decedent, (2) the citizenship of the surviving spouse, (3) whether an asset is includable in the decedent's estate, or (4) the amount or nature of the property the surviving spouse is entitled to receive.[75] Under the regulations, a "bona fide issue" arises if the estate is involved in a will contest, if there are questions concerning the inclusion in the gross estate of an asset which, if includable, would be eligible for the QDOT election, if there is uncertainty regarding the status of the decedent as a resident alien or a nonresident alien for estate tax purposes, or a similar controversy regarding the citizenship status of the surviving spouse.[76]

The protective election must be made within the time prescribed for making the QDOT election under § 2056A(d), i.e., on the last federal estate tax return filed before the due date (including extensions of time to file actually granted) or, if a timely return is not filed, on the first federal estate tax return filed after the due date (including extensions).[77]

There are numerous requirements for a valid protective QDOT election. The protective election must be made in a written statement signed by the executor under penalties of perjury. The written statement must be attached to the federal estate tax return and must identify the specific assets to which the protective election refers and the specific basis for making the protective election. Subject to these requirements, the protective election may be defined by means of a formula, such as the minimum amount necessary to reduce the estate tax to zero.[78] Once made, however, the protective election is irrevocable. By way of example, the regulations note that if a protective election is made because a *bona fide* question exists as to the includability of an asset in the decedent's gross estate, and if it is

73. Treas. Reg. § 20.2056(b)-7(b)(2)(ii).

74. *Id.*

75. *Id.* § 20.2056A-3(c).

76. *Id.*

77. Under the regulations, a protective election is in addition to, and is not in lieu of, the requirements in connection with the reformation provisions set forth in Treas. Reg. § 20.2056A-4.

78. Treas. Reg. § 20.2056A-3(c).

finally determined that the asset is so includable, the protective election becomes effective with respect to the asset and cannot be revoked.

> ***Comment:*** Notwithstanding the liberalization of the protective election provisions in the final regulations, the "*bona fide* issue" requirement is still a strict standard. It was hoped that final regulations would have allowed a protective QDOT election to be made whenever the executor has a legitimate question regarding any aspect of the marital deduction, including questions that could arise after the federal estate tax return is filed, such as during audit of the return. This position was not adopted by the regulations.

4. Situs and Administration Requirements

In order to qualify as a QDOT, the trust must be maintained under the laws of a U.S. state or the District of Columbia. A trust is treated as being maintained under the laws of a U.S. state or the District of Columbia if the records of the trust (or copies of such records) are kept in that state (or the District of Columbia). The administration of the trust must be governed by the particular laws of a U.S. state or the District of Columbia. Further, the trust may be established pursuant to an instrument executed under either the laws of a U.S. state or the District of Columbia or pursuant to an instrument executed under the laws of a foreign jurisdiction, such as a foreign will or trust, provided such instrument designates the law of a U.S. state or the District of Columbia as governing the administration of the trust and the designation is effective under the law of the designated jurisdiction.[79]

5. Trust Requirement

The QDOT must constitute an "ordinary trust," as that term is defined in Treas. Reg. § 301.7701-4(a), and not any other type of entity. Because bequests to the noncitizen spouse must be held in a QDOT in order to qualify for the marital deduction, where an active trade or business constitutes a significant portion of the QDOT assets, there is a possibility that the QDOT could lose its status as a trust and instead be treated as an association taxable as a corporation.[80] However, the regulations provide that for purposes of determining whether the trust meets the statutory requirements, the trust will not fail to constitute an ordinary trust solely because of the nature of the assets transferred to the trust, regardless of the trust's classification under the rules of Treas. Reg. §§ 301.7701-2 through 301.7701-4.

---

79. *Id.* § 20.2056A-2(a).

80. *See* I.R.S. Priv. Ltr. Rul. 9032014 (May 11, 1990), in which the IRS ruled that a trust to be funded primarily with stock of a foreign corporation would qualify as a QDOT, but did not address the trust-versus-association issue.

D. Security Requirements for Collection of the QDOT Tax

1. Introduction

A QDOT must meet the requirements prescribed by the regulations in order to ensure the collection of QDOT tax imposed on the trust.[81] The legislative history states Congress's expectation that such QDOT tax "Security Requirements" would require a sufficient portion of trust assets to be subject to U.S. jurisdiction so as to ensure that any QDOT tax imposed on the trust can be collected.[82] As an example, the legislative history provides that the regulations might require a portion of the trust property be physically situated in the U.S., or that the trustee be an institution with substantial U.S. assets.[83] Congress gave no guidance, however, regarding the effect of fluctuations in the value of the U.S. assets or changes in the financial condition of a corporate QDOT trustee on qualification of the trust as a QDOT.

As noted above in Section I.B, the Security Requirements were issued as part of the proposed regulations implementing §§ 2056(d) and 2056A. Although the remainder of these regulations were subsequently issued in final form, the security requirements contained so many changes from the proposed provisions that they were reissued in temporary form. The final regulations were a substantial improvement over the original proposed regulations, easing many of the requirements originally included by the IRS. However, the Security Requirements still contain many onerous provisions that seem excessive in view of the security concerns of the Treasury.

2. General Comments on the Regulations

(a) Governing Instrument Requirements. The regulations require a trust to include substantial governing instrument requirements in order to satisfy the Bank Trustee Requirement of Treas. Reg. § 20.2056A-2(d)(1)(i)(A), the Bond Requirement of Treas. Reg. § 20.2056A-2(d)(1)(i)(B), the Letter of Credit Requirement of Treas. Reg. § 20.2056A-2(d)(1)(i)(C), and the Foreign Real Property Requirement of Treas. Reg. § 20.2056A-2(d)(1)(ii). A trust that is in actual compliance with the requirements, but that does not explicitly include the required language, will *not* qualify as a QDOT.[84] In order to eliminate this potential hazard, the IRS has issued Rev. Proc. 96-54,[85] setting out model language that may be included in the governing trust instrument to ensure compliance with the Security Requirements.

> ***Comment:*** The existence of such a substantial number of governing instrument requirements increases the difficulty in drafting a QDOT and may render the resulting trust a cumbersome document that will have to include many detailed provisions that will likely never be applicable. In

81. § 2056A(a)(2).
82. 1988 Conference Report, *supra* note 66, at 115.
83. *Id.* at 114–15.
84. There are certain limited effective date exceptions to the application of the Security Requirements. *See infra* Section XI.B.2 and Treas. Reg. § 20.2056A-2(d)(6).
85. 1996-2 C.B. 336.

light of this problem, it seems clear that every QDOT should explicitly provide the trustee with the authority to amend the trust in any manner necessary to ensure that the trust meets all of the requirements of § 2056A, the applicable Treasury Regulations, any administrative pronouncements issued by the IRS under § 2056A, or any judicial decisions interpreting these provisions.

(b) Valuation and Indebtedness. Proper valuation is a key element in the application of the Security Requirements. Specifically, as discussed in Section III.B.3 below, whether the QDOT has assets in excess of, equal to, or less than $2 million is the threshold determination. In addition, the value of the QDOT assets determines the value of the bond or letter of credit needed in order to satisfy the Bond Requirement or the Letter of Credit Requirement of Treas. Reg. § 20.2056A-2(d)(1)(i)(B) or (C).

Under the regulations, the determination of whether a QDOT is a Large QDOT or a Small QDOT is made by measuring the fair market value of the assets passing to, or treated or deemed to have passed to, the QDOT (or in the form of a QDOT), "determined without reduction for any indebtedness with respect to the assets . . . ."[86] Likewise, the value of the bond to be furnished or a letter of credit to be undertaken must equal 65 percent of the fair market value of the trust assets "determined without regard to any indebtedness with respect to the assets . . . ."[87] In determining the value of the property passing to or held in the QDOT, it would seem reasonable that the value of any indebtedness should be deducted since the debt represents a reduction in the value of the property that would be subject to the QDOT tax. Moreover, the failure to deduct indebtedness can result in a double counting since the assets of the decedent's estate likely include the value of the proceeds of the indebtedness.

(c) Final Determination. As discussed in more detail below, numerous provisions of the Security Requirements apply the concept of values "as finally determined." The regulations set out the requirements for a final determination, relying largely on the mitigation provisions of § 1311. Specifically, the fair market value of an asset will be "finally determined" for purposes of the Security Requirements on the first to occur of:

(A) The entry of a decision, judgment, decree, or other order by any court of competent jurisdiction that has become final;
(B) The execution of a closing agreement made under § 7121;
(C) Any final disposition by the Internal Revenue Service of a claim for refund;

86. Treas. Reg. § 20.2056A-2(d)(1)(i) and (1)(ii).
87. *Id.* § 2056A-2(d)(1)(i)(B) and (C).

(D) The issuance of an estate tax closing letter (Form L-154 or equivalent) if no claim for refund is filed; or

(E) The expiration of the period of assessment.[88]

3. Rules Governing Classification as Large QDOT or Small QDOT

(a) General Rule. Under the Security Requirements, QDOTs are divided into two classes: those having assets at the date of death of the decedent spouse of $2 million or less (Small QDOTs) and those having assets in excess of $2 million at the decedent spouse's date of death (Large QDOTs).

The determination of whether a QDOT is a Small QDOT or a Large QDOT is based on the value, as of the date of death or as of the alternate valuation date available under § 2032, if applicable, of the assets passing, treated, or deemed to have passed to the QDOT. As noted above, this determination is to be made without reduction for any indebtedness with respect to such assets.[89] For purposes of determining whether the $2 million threshold is met, if more than one QDOT is established for the benefit of the surviving spouse, the fair market value of all trusts is aggregated.[90]

(b) Audit Adjustments. The regulations provide a grace period for valuation adjustments on audit. Specifically, if the value of the property passing or deemed to have passed to the QDOT, as reported on the decedent spouse's Form 706, is equal to or less than $2 million (i.e., a Small QDOT), but the fair market value of such property is finally determined to be in excess of $2 million (i.e., a Large QDOT), the U.S. Trustee is granted a reasonable period of time, not exceeding sixty days, within which to comply with the Bank Trustee Requirement, the Bond Requirement, or the Letter of Credit Requirement.[91] Note also, as discussed below in Section III.D.6, that a substantial understatement of the value of QDOT assets may result in a disallowance of the marital deduction in its entirety.

(c) Personal Residence Exclusion. In response to numerous concerns regarding the effect of residential real estate held in a QDOT, the regulations provide a special election to exclude the value of the surviving spouse's personal residence as well as any related furnishings from (a) the value of the property passing to the QDOT for purposes of determining whether the QDOT is a Large QDOT or a Small QDOT and (b) the size of the bond or letter of credit necessary to comply with the Bond Requirement or the Letter of Credit Requirement. Specifically, under the "Personal Residence Exclusion," in determining whether the $2 million threshold is met, the executor of the decedent spouse's estate may elect to

---

88. *Id.* § 20.2056A-2(d)(1)(iii).
89. *Id.* § 20.2056A-2(d)(1)(i) and (1)(ii).
90. *Id.* § 20.2056A-2(d)(1)(ii)(A).
91. *Id.* § 20.2056A-2(d)(1)(ii).

exclude up to $600,000 in value attributable to real property, wherever situated, as well as related furnishings that are owned directly by the QDOT.[92] Similarly, in connection with valuing the QDOT to determine the proper amount of the bond or of the letter of credit, up to $600,000 of the value of the QDOT attributable to a personal residence of the surviving spouse, as well as related furnishings, may be excluded.[93] The Personal Residence Exclusion does not apply, however, for purposes of determining whether the 35 percent test of the Foreign Real Property Exclusion is satisfied.[94]

For purposes of this exclusion, the term "personal residence" refers to the surviving spouse's principal residence, as that term is defined in § 1034, and one other residence of the surviving spouse.[95] The personal residence may include appurtenant structures used by the surviving spouse for residential purposes and adjacent land not in excess of that which is reasonably appropriate for residential purposes, taking into account the size and location of the residence. The residence may be located in or out of the United States,[96] must be available to the surviving noncitizen spouse at all times, and may not be rented to a third party, even when not occupied by the spouse.[97]

The term "related furnishings" refers to furniture and commonly included items such as appliances, fixtures, decorative items, and china "that are not beyond the value associated with normal household and decorative use." The regulations make clear that rare artwork, valuable antiques, and automobiles of any kind or class are not within the meaning of the term "related furnishings."[98]

In order to qualify for the exclusion, the residence must be owned directly by the QDOT.[99] Therefore, an interest in a residence held through another entity, such as a family limited partnership or limited liability company, would not qualify for the exclusion.

The Personal Residence Exclusion is claimed by attaching a written statement to the decedent spouse's estate tax return on which the QDOT election is made and clearly identifying any property with respect to which the election is made.[100] If the Personal Residence Exclusion is not claimed at the time of filing the federal estate tax return, such as where the Bond or the Letter of Credit Requirements are

92. *Id.* § 20.2056A-2(d)(iv)(A)

93. *Id.* § 20.2056A-2(d)(iv)(B).

94. *Id.* § 20.2056A-2(d)(iv)(C).

95. *See id.* § 20.2056A-2(d)(1)(iv)(D). *Cf.* Treas. Reg. § 25.270-25(c)(2) (defining a personal residence for purposes of a qualified personal residence trust under § 2702). This provision represents a significant expansion of the residence exclusion provided under the temporary regulations, which applied only to a spouse's principal residence. *See* Treas. Reg. § 20.2056A-2(d)(1)(iii)(D). Note that although TRA 1997 repealed § 1034, the definition of "principal residence" contained in the statute and regulations should continue to apply.

96. Treas. Reg. § 20.2056A-2(d)(1)(iv)(A), (B).

97. *Id.* § 20.2056A-2(d)(1)(iv)(D).

98. *Id.* § 20.2056A-2(d)(1)(iv)(E).

99. *Id.* § 20.2056A-2(d)(l)(iv)(A).

100. *Id.*

selected, the election must be attached to the Form 706-QDT.[101] Also, in order to cancel a Personal Residence Exclusion election that is in place, a statement must be attached to the Form 706-QDT.[102]

The potential disadvantage of making the election is that the U.S. trustee may have to file information statements for any year in which the residence is sold or ceases to be used as a personal residence. That statement, described below in Section III.D.10, requires the inclusion of extensive information concerning the assets held in the QDOT and their value.[103]

Generally, if the residence ceases to be used by or held for the use of the surviving spouse as a personal residence, or if the residence is sold during the term of the QDOT, the Personal Residence Exclusion ceases to apply unless the adjusted sales price is reinvested in a new personal residence within twelve months. If less than all of the adjusted sales price is reinvested in a new personal residence within the twelve-month period, the exclusion may continue to be claimed in an amount equal to the amount reinvested in a new personal residence plus the amount previously allocated to any other residence held in the QDOT that continues to apply for the exclusion.

Upon the sale of a personal residence, or if the residence ceases to be used by or held for the use of the spouse, the exclusion may be reallocated to another qualifying residence held in the QDOT or another QDOT created for the benefit of the spouse. The amount of such reallocation may allow for the full utilization of the $600,000 Personal Residence Exclusion, even if less than the full amount was previously claimed.[104]

Finally, if, as a result of the disallowance or reduction in the dollar value of the Personal Residence Exclusion claimed, a QDOT is reclassified as a Large QDOT, the requirements for a Large QDOT must be satisfied within 120 days after the effective date of cessation.[105]

4. QDOTs with Assets in Excess of $2 Million

If the QDOT is determined to be a Large QDOT, the governing instrument must require that the trust meet the Bank Trustee Requirement, the Bond Requirement, or the Letter of Credit Requirement. The QDOT may alternate between any one of these arrangements, provided that, at any given time, at least one of the arrangements is in effect. On the other hand, the trust instrument may also limit the available options to one or two of these alternate arrangements.[106]

(a) Bank Trustee Requirement. Under the Bank Trustee Requirement, the trust instrument must require that during the entire term of the QDOT, at least one U.S.

---

101. *Id.* § 20.2056A-2(d)(1)(iv)(B)
102. *Id.* § 20.2056A-2(d)(3)(iii)(B).
103. *Id.* § 20.2056A-2(d)(1)(iv)(F) and -2(d)(3)(i).
104. *Id.* § 20.2056A-2(d)(1)(iv)(G).
105. *Id.*
106. *Id.* § 20.2056A-2(d)(1)(i).

Trustee be a bank as defined under § 581. Alternatively, the U.S. Trustee may be the U.S. branch of a foreign bank, provided that the trust instrument also requires that during the entire term of the QDOT, a U.S. Trustee acts as a trustee with such foreign bank trustee.[107]

(b) Bond Requirement. Under the Bond Requirement, the QDOT must require that the U.S. Trustee furnish a bond in favor of the IRS in an amount equal to 65 percent of the fair market value of the trust assets, determined without regard to any indebtedness on the assets. The value of the QDOT assets is the value as finally determined, as of the decedent spouse's date of death or on the alternate valuation date under § 2032, if applicable.[108]

If a change is made on audit to the fair market value of the QDOT assets, the U.S. Trustee has up to sixty days within which to adjust the amount of the bond accordingly, provided that the penalty for substantial valuation understatement, discussed below in Section III.D.6, does not apply.[109] As discussed above, if the executor of the estate elects the Personal Residence Exclusion, the amount of the bond required in order to satisfy the Bond Requirement is calculated by excluding up to $600,000 in value attributable to real estate, wherever situated (and related furnishings), owned directly by the QDOT and used by the surviving spouse as the spouse's personal residence.[110]

The bond must remain in effect until termination of the trust and the payment of any QDOT tax liability finally determined to be due.

> ***Comment:*** This may require the bond to remain in effect until the running of the statute of limitations on collection of the QDOT tax, thereby resulting in an undue delay in the final distribution of the trust property.

The bond itself must be placed with a satisfactory surety and is subject to IRS review. Further, the bond may not be canceled, it must be for a term of at least one year, and it must be automatically renewable at the end of the term on an annual basis unless the IRS is notified at least sixty days prior to the end of the term. Under the regulations, the IRS must be given notice of nonrenewal at least sixty days prior to the end of the bond term, and the IRS will not draw on the bond if, within thirty days of receipt of the notice of failure to renew, the U.S. Trustee notifies the IRS that alternate Security Requirements will take effect immediately upon expiration of the bond.[111]

---

107. *Id.* § 20.2056A-2(d)(1)(i)(A).
108. *Id.* § 20.2056A-2(d)(1)(i)(B).
109. *Id.*
110. *Id.* § 20.2056A-2(d)(1)(iv)(B).
111. *Id.* § 20.2056A-2(d)(1)(i)(B)(1).

The final regulations include a sample form for the bond and require that the bond be in that form, in a form that follows that form in all material respects, or in any form approved by the IRS in published guidance.[112]

Payment on the bond is required at any time the IRS, in its sole discretion, determines that a taxable event with respect to the trust has occurred, that the trust no longer qualifies as a QDOT, or that a distribution subject to the QDOT tax has been made. The QDOT must also provide that if the IRS draws on the bond, neither the U.S. Trustee nor any other person will seek a return of any part of the remittance until April 15 of the calendar year following the year the bond is drawn upon. After that date, the remittance will be treated as a deposit that can be returned without interest if the U.S. Trustee requests it, unless the IRS determines that the collection of the QDOT tax is in jeopardy. However, any jeopardy assessment will first be credited to the QDOT tax as reported on the 706-QDT, then to any unpaid balance of the QDOT tax (plus interest and penalties) for the prior taxable years, with the balance of the bond amount returned to the U.S. Trustee.[113]

The bond must be filed with the decedent spouse's Form 706 (or 706-NA, as the case may be) unless an extension for filing the bond is granted under Treas. Reg. § 301.9100. The U.S. Trustee must also include a written statement listing the assets used to fund the QDOT and the value of these assets.[114]

> ***Comment:*** As a practical matter, it seems unlikely that the executor of the decedent spouse's estate will be able to list the specific assets that will secure the bond undertaking as of the date the Form 706 is filed. It seems reasonable to conclude that listing those assets included on the Form 706 from which the QDOT will be funded should satisfy the requirement.

(c) Letter of Credit Requirement. The third Security Requirement alternative for a Large QDOT is for the U.S. Trustee to furnish an irrevocable letter of credit. In order to satisfy the Letter of Credit Requirement, the QDOT must require the U.S. Trustee to provide a letter of credit issued by (1) a bank described, as in § 581, (2) the U.S. branch of a foreign bank, or (3) a foreign bank and confirmed by a bank as described in § 581.[115]

The letter of credit must be in an amount equal to 65 percent of the fair market value of the trust assets, determined without regard to any indebtedness on the trust assets. As with the Bond Requirement discussed above, the value of the QDOT assets is the date-of-death value of the QDOT (or the alternate valuation date value, if applicable), as finally determined. Subject to the substantial undervaluation penalty, discussed below, the U.S. Trustee has sixty days from the conclusion of the final determination of the value of property held on the QDOT

112. *Id.* § 20.2056A-2(d)(1)(i)(B)(2). No alternate bond language has been published by the Service.

113. *Id.* § 20.2056A-2(d)(1)(i)(B)(3).

114. *Id.* § 20.2056A-2(d)(1)(i)(B)(3) and (4).

115. *Id.* § 20.2056A-2(d)(1)(i)(C).

within which to adjust the value of the letter of credit to the estate tax value of the QDOT assets. In determining the value of the QDOT assets for purposes of the Letter of Credit Requirement, the executor may elect the Personal Residence Exclusion to exclude the value up to $600,000 of the spouse's primary residence.

The letter of credit must be irrevocable and must provide for sight payment. In addition, it must last for a term of at least one year and must be automatically renewable at the end of the term, "at least on an annual basis," unless notice of the failure to renew is received by the IRS at least sixty days prior to the end of the term.[116]

If the letter of credit is issued by the U.S. branch of a foreign bank, and the U.S. branch is closing, the branch of the foreign bank must notify the IRS of the closure, and the notice of closure must be mailed at least sixty days prior to the date of the closure.

> ***Comment:*** Query whether such information would be public sixty days prior to the happening of the event.

Upon the closure or nonrenewal of the letter of credit, the IRS will not draw on the letter of credit if, within thirty days of receipt of the notice of failure to renew or of closure, the U.S. trustee notifies the IRS that an alternate arrangement has been put in place.

The regulations include sample forms for an irrevocable letter of credit and a confirmation (to be used if the letter of credit is issued by a foreign bank).[117]

Governing instrument requirements similar to those included with respect to the Bond Requirement are included in the regulations for the Letter of Credit Requirement.[118]

5. QDOTs Having Assets of $2 Million or Less

If the fair market value of the property passing to the QDOT is finally determined, as of the date of the decedent spouse's death (or the alternate valuation date, if applicable), to be $2 million or less, then the trust will be classified as a Small QDOT. In order for a Small QDOT to satisfy the Security Requirements, the governing trust instrument must require that the trust meet either the Bank Trustee Requirement, the Bond Requirement, the Letter of Credit Requirement, or the Foreign Real Property Requirement.

(a) Foreign Real Property Requirement. The Foreign Real Property Requirement is satisfied where the governing instrument requires that no more than 35 percent of the fair market value of the trust assets, determined annually on the last day of the QDOT's taxable year, consists of real property that is owned by the trust and

116. *See id.* § 20.2056A-2(d)(1)(i)(C)(1). It is unclear how the annual renewal requirement would apply to a multiyear letter of credit.

117. *See id.* § 20.2056A-2(d)(1)(i)(C)(2), (3).

118. *See id.* § 20.2056A-2(d)(1)(i)(C)(4).

located outside of the United States. Note that the Personal Residence Exclusion, discussed above, does *not* apply for purposes of determining whether the 35 percent foreign real property threshold is satisfied.[119]

> ***Comment:*** Under these provisions, the attorney drafting a Small QDOT that holds no foreign real estate—a common fact pattern—can satisfy the Security Requirements simply by including a provision barring the trust from owning, directly or indirectly, foreign real property. By including such a provision, the trust will satisfy the Foreign Real Property Requirement without having to file annual information reports (discussed below). Further, so long as the instrument includes an amendment provision, the trustee should be able to bring the trust into compliance with the Security Requirements should circumstances change.

If, based on an examination of the decedent spouse's estate tax return, the value of the property passing to a Small QDOT is finally determined to be in excess of $2 million, the U.S. Trustee has a sixty-day grace period within which to satisfy the Security Requirements applicable to Large QDOTs. However, the substantial understatement penalty of Treas. Reg. § 20.2056A-2(d)(i)(D), discussed below in Section III.D.6 may apply.[120]

If, in any year, a Small QDOT is relying on the Foreign Real Property Requirement and the value on the last day of the QDOT's tax year of the foreign real property held in the QDOT exceeds 35 percent of the fair market value of the trust assets by virtue of either (1) distributions of QDOT principal during the year, (2) fluctuations in the value of foreign currency where the real estate is located, or (3) fluctuations in the value of trust assets, the QDOT will not be treated as failing to meet the Foreign Real Property Requirement—and, therefore, will not cease to be a QDOT—if at the end of the taxable year of the QDOT that immediately follows the year in which the 35 percent limit was exceeded, the trust is brought into compliance with the percentage limitations of the Foreign Real Property Requirement. Alternatively, the QDOT may elect to meet the requirements of an alternate arrangement, such as the Bank Trustee, Bond, or Letter of Credit.[121]

(b) Look-Through Rules. The regulations adopt a limited look-through rule that is applied solely for purposes of determining compliance with the 35 percent limitation of the Foreign Real Property Requirement.[122] Therefore, no look-through rule is required for a QDOT, whether Large or Small, that utilizes the Bank Trustee Requirement, Bond Requirement, or Letter of Credit Requirement.[123]

---

119. *Id.* § 20.2056A-2(d)(1)(iii)(C).

120. *Id.*

121. *Id.* § 20.2056A-2(d)(1)(ii)(D).

122. The proposed Security Requirements applied a look-through rule in all cases where the QDOT owned certain interests in corporations or partnerships to determine whether the trust was a Small QDOT or a Large QDOT. *See* Prop. Treas. Reg. § 20.2056A-2(d)(1)(ii)(B).

123. Treas. Reg. § 20.2056A-2(d)(1)(ii)(B).

When applicable, the look-through rule treats the QDOT as holding a pro rata share of all the assets owned by (a) a corporation having fifteen or fewer shareholders, where the QDOT owns more than 20 percent of the voting stock or the value of the corporation, or (b) a partnership having fifteen or fewer partners, where the QDOT owns more than 20 percent of the capital interest. In the case of a partnership, the QDOT's pro rata share of partnership assets is based on the greater of the QDOT's capital interest or profits interest in this partnership.[124]

> ***Comment:*** It would appear that minority and lack of marketability discounts would be unavailable in valuing the pro rata interest of the QDOT in a corporation or partnership.

The regulations contain an attribution rule that applies solely for applying the threshold shareholder/partner and percentage ownership tests. Specifically, all stock in a corporation and all interests in a partnership, as the case may be, owned or held for the benefit of the surviving spouse or any members of the surviving spouse's family (within the meaning of § 267(c)(4)) are treated as being owned by the QDOT.[125] The attribution rules do not apply, however, in measuring the QDOT's interest in the underlying assets of the corporation or partnership.[126] Interests owned by the QDOT in other entities (such as an interest in a trust or a limited liability company) are to be accorded treatment consistent with these attribution rules.[127]

When the application of the look-through rule results in deemed ownership of foreign real estate by a QDOT using the Foreign Real Property Requirement, the QDOT will have annual reporting obligations under Treas. Reg. § 20.2056A-2(d)(3).[128]

6. Substantial Undervaluation Provisions

As noted above, if final adjustments are made to the value of property passing to a QDOT from that reported on the decedent spouse's Form 706, and as a result, either (a) a QDOT originally qualifying as a Small QDOT is recharacterized as a Large QDOT or (b) the amount of the bond or the letter of credit must be increased, the U.S. Trustee has up to sixty days within which to make any required changes.[129] However the grace period may be unavailable where the value of property passing to the QDOT is substantially greater than that reported on the estate tax return. Specifically, if the value of the QDOT property reported on the decedent spouse's Form 706 is 50 percent or less of the amount finally determined

---

124. *Id.*

125. *Id.* Under § 267(c)(4), an individual's family includes siblings, spouses, ancestors, and lineal descendants.

126. Treas. Reg. § 20.2056A-2(d)(1)(ii)(B).

127. *Id.* § 20.2056A-2(d)(1)(ii)(C).

128. *Id.* § 20.2056A-2(d)(1)(ii)(C). See *infra* Section III.D.10 for a discussing of the reporting requirements.

129. *See* Treas. Reg. §§ 20.2056A-2(d)(1)(i)(B), (C) and § 20.2056A-2(d)(1)(ii).

to be the correct value of the property for federal estate tax purposes, the estate tax marital deduction will be disallowed *in its entirety.*[130] This penalty will not apply if there was reasonable cause for the undervaluation and the fiduciary of the estate acted in good faith, as determined by reference to the rules of Treas. Reg. § 1.6664–4(b).[131]

> ***Comment:*** In order to avoid the possible imposition of the disqualification penalty in these circumstances, it may make sense to make a protective QDOT election and/or protective assignment of property to the QDOT. This might be an especially effective strategy where the estate holds difficult-to-value assets, such as a partnership interests.

7. Anti-abuse Rule

Regardless of whether the QDOT utilizes the Bank Trustee Requirement, the Bond Requirement, the Letter of Credit Requirement, or the Foreign Real Property Requirement, if the trust utilizes any device or arrangement that has, as a principal purpose, the avoidance of liability for the QDOT tax or a prevention of the collection of the tax, the trust will immediately cease to qualify as a QDOT.[132] An example of the abuses intended to be reached by this rule is the selection of a U.S. Trustee that is domestic corporation established with insubstantial capitalization by the surviving spouse or members of the spouse's family.

> ***Comment:*** Given the lack of examples in the regulations as to what constitutes an abuse reached by this rule, and given the harshness of the penalty (immediate disqualification of the QDOT and imposition of the QDOT tax on the entire value of the property then held in the QDOT), it seems that the QDOT Trustee should be afforded some period in which to correct the improper practice after discovery.

8. Request for Alternate Arrangement or Waiver

The regulations state that if the IRS provides guidance pursuant to which a testator, executor, or U.S. Trustee may adopt an alternate plan or arrangement for the collection of the QDOT tax, and if such alternate plan or arrangement is properly adopted, then the QDOT will be treated as meeting the Security Requirements. Any such alternate plan arrangement will, in all cases, be subject to the anti-abuse rule described *supra* in Section III.D.7. Prior to the publication of such guidance, taxpayers may submit a request for a private letter ruling for the approval of any alternate plan or arrangement to ensure the collection of the QDOT tax.[133]

---

130. Tres Reg. § 20.2056A-2(d)(1)(i)(D)(1).
131. *Id.* § 20.2056A-2(d)(1)(i)(D)(2).
132. *Id.* § 20.2056A-2(d)(1)(v).
133. *Id.* § 20.2056A-2(d)(4). No such rulings have been granted.

9. Adjustment of Dollar Threshold and Exclusion

The IRS may increase or decrease the $2 million threshold for Large and Small QDOTs and for the $600,000 Personal Residence Exclusion.[134]

10. Annual Reporting Requirements

The final regulations substantially reduced the burden of the annual reporting requirements imposed on the U.S. Trustee from those included on the proposed regulations.

(a) When Required. The U.S. Trustee must file an annual report in any year in which the QDOT satisfies either one of the following criteria:

1 A QDOT relying on the Foreign Real Property Requirement for satisfaction of the Security Requirements owns directly or, after application of the look-through rule of Treas. Reg. § 20.2056A-2(d)(1)(ii)(B), is deemed to own, any foreign real estate on the last day of the taxable year of the QDOT; or

2 The personal residence previously subject to the personal residence exclusion is sold, or ceases to be used or held for use as a personal residence, during the year.[135]

(b) Required Information. Where the information report is required to be filed, it must include the name, address, and taxpayer identification number (if any) of the U.S. Trustee and of the QDOT, and a list summarizing the assets held by the QDOT, together with the fair market value of each listed QDOT asset determined as of the last day of the QDOT's taxable year.[136]

If the look-through rule applies to a Small QDOT attempting to satisfy the Foreign Real Property Requirement, the information statement must also identify the partnership, corporation, trust, or other entity, and list the QDOT's pro rata share of the assets owned by that entity as if directly owned by the QDOT.[137]

> ***Comment:*** If the QDOT does not hold a controlling interest in such a corporation, partnership, or other entity, it may be extremely difficult, if not impossible, for the QDOT Trustee to obtain such asset and valuation information about the entity.

If the personal residence previously subject to the Personal Residence Exclusion is sold during the taxable year, the information statement must include the date of sale, the adjusted sale price, and the extent to which the adjusted sale price has been or will be used to purchase a new personal residence. In addition, if or to the extent that the proceeds are not to be timely reinvested, the statement must indicate what steps will be taken to ensure that the QDOT meets the Security

134. *Id.* § 20.2056A-2(d)(5).
135. *See id.* § 20.2056A-2(d)(3)(i).
136. *Id.* §§ 20.2056A-2(d)(3)(iii)(A) and (B).
137. *Id.* § 20.2056A-2(d)(3)(ii)(B).

Requirements.[138] Similarly, if the personal residence ceases to be used as such by the surviving spouse during the year, the information statement must describe the steps that will be or have been taken to ensure that the QDOT complies with the Security Requirements.[139]

(c) Time and Manner of Filing the Information Statement. The information statement must be filed for any taxable year of the QDOT in which any of the events or conditions specified above for filing the statement have occurred or are satisfied. The information statement must be attached to Form 706-QDT, and must be filed no later than April 15 of the calendar year following the calendar year in which or with which the taxable year of the QDOT ends.[140] Form 706-QDT, with the statement attached, must be filed regardless of whether the form would otherwise be required to be filed.[141] Failure to timely file the information statement may subject the QDOT to the provisions of the anti-abuse rule of Treas. Reg. § 20.2056A-2(d)(1)(v), discussed above, the violation of which could result in termination of QDOT status and imposition of the QDOT tax on the entire value of the QDOT property at that time.[142]

E. Miscellaneous QDOT Issues

1. Who May Create a QDOT?

Section 2056(d)(2)(B) allows the marital deduction for property passing from the decedent spouse to the surviving noncitizen spouse if such property is transferred or irrevocably assigned to the QDOT prior to the date on which the federal estate tax return is made. The statute does not explicitly state whether only the decedent can create a QDOT or whether the noncitizen surviving spouse and/or the personal representative of the decedent spouse may create such a QDOT. The 1989 House Report states in a footnote that there is no requirement that the QDOT be created by the decedent and that, therefore, "the QDOT may be created by the executor or the surviving spouse."[143] This position is adopted in the final QDOT regulations.[144]

138. *Id.* § 20.2056A-2(d)(3)(iii)(C).

139. *Id.* § 20.2056A-2(d)(3)(iii)(D).

140. The time for filing the information statement can be extended under the rules provided by Treas. Reg. § 20.2056A-11(a). *See infra* Section VII.E.5.

141. Treas. Reg. § 20.2056A-2(d)(3)(ii).

142. *Id.*

143. 1989 House Report, at 1431 n.96. See *infra* Section V.K discussing the tax effects of the transfer by the surviving spouse of property to a QDOT.

144. *See* Treas. Reg. §§ 20.2056A-2(b)(2) (in order to qualify for the marital deduction, property passing directly to the surviving spouse must be transferred or assigned "to a trust (whether created by the decedent, the decedent's executor or by the surviving spouse)"; 20.2056A-4(b)(1) (QDOT to which nontrust marital transfer is made to a noncitizen surviving spouse may qualify for marital deduction if transferred or assigned to a QDOT "created by the decedent (during life or by will), by the surviving spouse, or by the executor.").

2. Conflicts of Interest in Making the QDOT Election

As with any discretionary postmortem actions affecting the tax liability of the decedent's estate, decisions regarding the qualification for the marital deduction of bequests and other testamentary transfers to the surviving noncitizen spouse may give rise to conflicts between and among beneficiaries and fiduciaries. The potential for conflict is driven primarily by the terms of the estate plan and the allocation of tax liability. For instance, if the estate taxes due at the death of the decedent spouse are to be borne by his residuary estate, the failure of the executor—who may be the surviving spouse—to make the QDOT election or to make only a partial election—will adversely affect the amount of property to be received by the residuary beneficiaries.

Where the surviving spouse is also the residuary beneficiary or one of several beneficiaries of a residuary trust, the potential for conflict may be diminished. However, if the residuary beneficiaries are persons other than the noncitizen spouse—the decedent spouse's children by a prior marriage or a Credit Shelter Trust for their benefit, for example—the decision as to whether or not to make the QDOT election or to reform a trust to allow the QDOT election to be made can put the surviving spouse and the other beneficiaries in direct conflict. Moreover, if the residuary beneficiary is a trust designed to capture the decedent's unified credit exemption amount, it is arguable that the ability of the noncitizen spouse to control whether and to what extent the QDOT election is made—and, therefore, the amount of property passing to the trust—is tantamount to a general power of appointment over the trust. An independent executor may mitigate some of the conflict, at least in respect to bequests under the decedent spouse's estate plan directly to a QDOT. However, even if the surviving spouse is not the executor of the decedent's estate, the surviving spouse retains control over whether to transfer jointly titled property or other nonprobate property to a QDOT and whether to take the necessary steps to qualify nonassignable annuities or other payments for the marital deduction. In these situations, equitable adjustments may be available to minimize adverse tax effects. However, the better course would be to thoroughly discuss these issues with the testator in the planning process and, if necessary, draft tax clauses that equitably apportion liability.

3. QDOT as S Corporation Shareholder

Only certain kinds of trusts are permissible shareholders of an electing small business corporation under subchapter S of the Code (an S corporation).[145] If a trust meets the requirements of a qualified subchapter S trust (a QSST) and the trust beneficiary makes the QSST election, then the trust will be a permissible S corporation shareholder.[146] However, care should be used when stock of an

145. *See* § 1361(c)(2).
146. *See* § 1361(d)(1).

S corporation is transferred to a QDOT, because § 1361(c)(2)(A) limits the time that shares of such stock may be held by a trust prior to the making of the QSST election.

In order to qualify as a QSST, the terms of the trust must require that (1) there be only one current income beneficiary of the trust, (2) principal distributions be made only to that beneficiary during the beneficiary's life, (3) the income interest terminates upon the first to occur of the death of the income beneficiary and the termination of the trust, and (4) upon termination of the trust prior to the death of the income beneficiary, all trust property must be distributed to the income beneficiary.[147] Finally, all of the income of the trust must be distributed currently to the income beneficiary, and the income beneficiary must be a U.S. citizen or resident.[148] Therefore, unless the surviving spouse is a U.S. resident, the QDOT will not qualify as a QSST, and the trust will not be a permissible S corporation shareholder.

If the surviving spouse is a U.S. resident, then a QDOT that qualifies as a general power of appointment marital trust or a QTIP trust should meet the requirements of a QSST, provided that the surviving spouse makes the election required under § 1361(d)(2). Likewise, an estate trust will qualify as a QSST if all trust income is actually distributed to the surviving spouse who is a U.S. resident. Alternatively, the trustee may be able to make the Electing Small Business Trust (ESBT) election under § 1361(c)(3) to qualify the trust as an eligible S corporation shareholder.

4. Foreign Trust Status

A QDOT trust may also be subject to the rules governing foreign trusts. For U.S. tax purposes, a foreign trust is any trust that does not satisfy both of the following tests:

- A court within the United States is able to exercise primary supervision over the administration of the trust (the court test), and
- One or more United States persons have the authority to control all substantial decisions of the trust (the control test).[149]

(a) Court Test. If a trust is to qualify as a QDOT, "the trust must be maintained under the laws of a state of the United States or the District of Columbia, and the administration of the trust must be governed by the laws of a particular state of the United States or the District of Columbia."[150] A trust is maintained in a particular state if the records (or copies of the records) of the trust are kept in that state.[151] Thus, a QDOT is likely to meet the court test, which is satisfied if:

147. *See* § 1361(d)(3)(A).
148. § 1361(d)(3)(B).
149. *See* §§ 7701(a)(31)(B), 7701(a)(30)(i)–(ii); Treas. Reg. § 301.7701-7.
150. Treas. Reg. § 20.2056A-2(a).
151. *Id.* § 20.2056A-2(a).

- The trust instrument does not direct that the trust be administered outside of the United States;
- The trust in fact is administered exclusively in the United States; and
- The trust is not subject to an automatic migration provision . . .[152]

For this purpose, administration "means the carrying out of the duties imposed by the terms of the trust instrument and applicable law, including maintaining the books and records of the trust, filing tax returns, managing and investing the assets of the trust, defending the trust from suits by creditors, and determining the amount and timing of the distributions."[153]

(b) Control Test. However, a QDOT may not satisfy the control test, which requires that one or more U.S. persons have the authority to control all substantial decisions of the trust. "Substantial decisions" include whether and when to distribute income or corpus; the amount of any distribution; the selection of any beneficiary; whether a receipt is allocable to income or principal; whether to terminate the trust; whether to compromise, arbitrate, or abandon claims of the trust; whether to sue on behalf of the trust or to defend suits against the trust; whether to remove, add, or replace a trustee; whether to appoint a successor trustee; and investment decisions.[154]

Because a QDOT requires only that one trustee be a U.S. person, it is possible that a QDOT will not satisfy the control test. For instance, the control test will be satisfied if there are three trustees, two of whom are U.S. persons, and if all decisions of the trustees are made by majority vote.[155] If, in such a situation, the trustees may only act by unanimous vote, or if the non-U.S. trustee possesses a veto over the actions of the U.S. trustees, the control test will not satisfied, and the trust will be characterized as a foreign trust.[156]

If foreign trust status is not desired, the QDOT should be drafted so that non-U.S. persons are not given the authority to control all substantial decisions of the trust.

IV. When Is Qualification as a QDOT Determined?—Provisions for Reformation

A. General Rules

The determination of whether a trust qualifies as a QDOT will be made generally as of the date on which the federal estate tax return is made.[157] However, if an

152. *Id.* § 301.7701-7(c)(1).
153. *Id.* § 301.7701-7(c)(3)(v).
154. *Id.* § 301.7701-7(d)(1)(ii)(A)–(J).
155. *Id.* § 301.7701-7(d)(1)(v), Example 2.
156. Treas. Reg. § 301.7701-7(d)(1)(v), Example 1. *See, e.g.*, I.R.S. Priv. Ltr. Rul. 199918039 (Feb. 8, 1999).
157. § 2056(d)(5)(A)(i).

interest in property passes from the decedent spouse to a trust for the benefit of a noncitizen surviving spouse, and if the trust otherwise qualifies for a marital deduction but for the provisions of § 2056(d)(1)(A), the property interest is treated as passing to the surviving spouse in a QDOT if the trust is reformed, either in accordance with the terms of the decedent's will or trust agreement, or pursuant to a judicial proceeding to meet the requirements of a QDOT.[158] For these purposes, the requirements of the QDOT include all applicable Marital Deduction Requirements, Statutory Requirements, and Security Requirements.[159]

A reformation pursuant to the terms of the decedent's will or trust instrument must be completed by the time prescribed for the filing of the decedent's estate tax return (including extensions). For this purpose, a return filed prior to the due date (including extensions) is considered to be filed on the last day that the return is required to be filed (including extensions), and a late return filed at any time after the due date is considered filed on the date that it is actually filed.[160]

> ***Comment:*** The inclusion of provisions in the QDOT authorizing the trustee to reform or modify the QDOT to meet the statutory or regulatory requirements of the QDOT should be sufficient to authorize such reformations and should alleviate the necessity of obtaining a judicial reformation of the trust.

A reformation pursuant to a judicial proceeding must be commenced on or before the due date (determined with regard to extensions actually granted) for filing the federal estate tax return for the decedent spouse's estate, regardless of the date on which the return is actually filed.[161]

Prior to the time that a judicial reformation of a trust is completed, the trust must be treated as a QDOT. Therefore, the trustee must file Form 706-QDT, pay any QDOT tax that becomes due, and file any annual statement that is required under the Security Requirements. The failure to comply with these requirements may cause the trust to be subject to the anti-abuse rule provided under Treas. Reg. § 20.2056A-2(d)(1)(v), discussed above in Section III.D.7.

If the judicial proceeding is terminated prior to the time the reformation is completed, the decedent's estate will be required to pay the resulting increased

---

158. § 2056(d)(5)(A)(ii); Treas. Reg. § 20.2056A-4(a)(1). *See* I.R.S. Priv. Ltr. Rul. 9848007 (July 27, 1998).

159. Treas. Reg. § 20.2056A-4(a)(1). *See supra* Section III.

160. Treas. Reg. § 20.2056A-4(a)(1).

161. *Id.* § 20.2056A-4(a)(2). *See, e.g.*, I.R.S. Priv. Ltr. Ruls. 199904023 (Oct. 30, 1998), 9848007 (July 27, 1998), 9148021 (Aug. 26, 1991). *Cf.* I.R.S. Priv. Ltr. Rul. 9017015, discussed above at Section III.C.1, where the executor initiated a court proceeding to reform decedent's will to create a trust that qualified as a QDOT, rather than modify an existing trust to qualify as a QDOT. Although the IRS discussed the reformation provisions, it seems clear that the executor's reformation of the outright bequest would not qualify under the precise language of § 2056(d)(5). The ruling request was submitted prior to the enactment of OBRA 1989 and, therefore, prior to the enactment of the reformation provisions of § 2056(d)(5). At that time, it was not clear that the decedent's executor or the surviving spouse could create a QDOT.

estate tax imposed on the decedent's estate (plus interest and any applicable penalties) that is due at the time of such termination as a result of the failure of the trust to comply with the marital deduction requirements of § 2056(d).[162]

If a reformation proceeding is commenced, the statute of limitations on assessment of a federal estate tax deficiency attributable to the failure of the trust to qualify as a QDOT will not close prior to the date that falls one year after the IRS is notified that the trust reformation has been completed or that the judicial proceeding has been terminated.[163]

The reformation (whether pursuant to a judicial proceeding or otherwise) must result in a trust that is effective under local law. Further, under the regulations, a reformed trust may be revocable by the spouse, or otherwise be subject to the spouse's power of appointment, provided that no person, including the spouse, has the power to amend the trust during the continued existence of the trust in a manner that would disqualify it as a QDOT.[164]

B. Limitations and Uses of Reformation Provisions

The reformation provisions provide some relief from the burden created by the absence of liberal grandfathering provisions and transition rules in the statute. In addition, they allow QDOTs drafted before the issuance of regulatory guidance to be amended to comport with those requirements.[165]

If property passes to a trust for the benefit of the noncitizen surviving spouse, and the trust does not qualify as a QDOT, the surviving spouse or the decedent's executor may not create a trust that meets the requirements of a QDOT and transfer the property to such a trust. The IRS takes the position that § 2056(d)(2)(B)(ii), discussed in Section V below, is "intended to cover a situation where property passes directly from the decedent to the surviving spouse under a will or the spouse receives nonprobate property."[166] In such a case, property can be transferred to a QDOT created by the surviving spouse or the decedent spouse's executor. However, if the decedent spouse makes a bequest to the surviving spouse in trust, and such trust does not conform to the requirements of § 2056A, then reformation of the recipient trust is the appropriate manner to ensure that the bequest qualifies for the estate tax marital deduction.

Note that the reformation provisions may not be applied to amend a trust to meet requirements for the marital deduction that are independent of the QDOT requirements.[167] In addition, the reformation provisions, as originally enacted, appear to have only prospective application. Therefore, they are of no assistance to estates that filed their federal estate tax returns prior to the December 19, 1989,

162. Treas. Reg. § 20.2056A-4(a)(2).
163. § 2056(d)(5)(B).
164. Treas. Reg. § 20.2056A-4(a)(2).
165. *See* I.R.S. Priv. Ltr. Rul. 199904023 (Oct. 30, 1998).
166. I.R.S. Priv. Ltr. Rul. 9043070 (Aug. 3, 1990).
167. 1989 House Report, at 1431.

effective date of OBRA 1989, because under § 2056(d)(5), the reformation must be commenced before the date of the federal estate tax return. This is a harsh result, especially given the liberalizing intent of the reformation provisions.

OBRA 1990 provided some relief by allowing reformation proceedings to be commenced prior to May 5, 1991, the date six months after the date of enactment of OBRA 1990, notwithstanding the prior filing of an estate tax return.[168]

V. Transfers by the Surviving Spouse of Outright Bequests and Nonprobate Property to a QDOT

A. Statutory Provisions

The decedent spouse can, through his or her will or by a trust or through beneficiary designations, direct that property must pass into a QDOT. Such property will qualify for the federal estate tax marital deduction because it is property passing to a surviving spouse in a QDOT in accordance with § 2056(d)(2)(A). Further, property passing to a noncitizen surviving spouse will be treated as passing to the spouse in a QDOT if either (1) the property is transferred to the QDOT before the date on which the federal estate tax return is made[169] or (2) the property is irrevocably assigned to the QDOT under an irrevocable assignment which is enforceable under local law and which is made on or before the date on which the return is made.[170] In addition, property may be treated as passing directly from the decedent to the QDOT if it is distributed pursuant to a settlement agreement that is negotiated at arm's length and represents the *bona fide* settlement of a legally enforceable claim.[171]

B. Effective Dates

Section 7815(d)(4)(B) of OBRA 1989 provides that property passing from decedents dying prior to December 19, 1989 (the date of enactment of OBRA 1989), will be treated as qualifying for the marital deduction if such property is transferred or irrevocably assigned to a QDOT within one year following the date of enactment. Persons dying after November 10, 1988, but whose federal estate tax returns were filed prior to enactment of OBRA 1989, were also allowed to avail themselves of the broader rules regarding assignments and transfers of probate property to a QDOT, and perhaps then amend their federal estate tax returns. In addition, OBRA 1990 provided some additional relief by allowing a proceeding to reform a trust to qualify as a QDOT to be commenced at any time prior to May 5, 1991, the date

168. § 11701(l)(2) of OBRA 1990. *See* 136 Cong. Rec. H7147 (daily ed. Aug. 3, 1990) (statement of Rep. Rostenkowski upon introduction of H.R. 5454).

169. § 2056(d)(2)(B)(i).

170. § 2056(d)(2)(B)(ii).

171. *See* I.R.S. Priv. Ltr. Ruls. 9845015 (Aug. 7, 1998), 9845016 (Aug. 7, 1998).

six months after the date of enactment of OBRA 1990, even if the estate tax return had previously been filed.[172]

C. Regulatory Provisions Governing Transfers of Property to a QDOT

1. General Rule

The special provisions allowing for the transfer of nontrust marital property to a QDOT apply with respect to interests in property passing outright from the decedent to a noncitizen surviving spouse, whether by bequest or devise, by operation of law, or pursuant to an annuity or other similar plan or arrangement. However, any such property interest passing to the surviving spouse must, but for the marital deduction limitations under § 2056(d), otherwise qualify for the estate tax marital deduction.[173]

2. Application of Marital Deduction Requirements to Transferee Trust

If the only property to be held in the QDOT is property transferred by the surviving spouse, the QDOT need not qualify for the federal estate tax marital deduction under § 2056(a); that is, the trust need not be a § 2056(b)(5) or § 2056(b)(7) trust or an estate trust. Therefore, the trust need not require the distribution of all income to the surviving spouse and can have current beneficiaries other than the surviving spouse. This rule applies, however, only if *all* the trust property has been transferred or assigned to the trust by the surviving spouse; if any property is or has been transferred to the QDOT by the decedent spouse, then the trust must include provisions necessary to ensure that all of the trust property qualifies for the marital deduction under § 2056.[174] Thus, if the decedent is a U.S. citizen and bequeaths property to a U.S. trust that is not a general power of appointment marital trust, a QTIP trust, or an estate trust (e.g., a credit shelter trust), that trust cannot be used as a transferee QDOT because after the trust is fully funded, a portion of the value of the property attributable to property bequeathed to the trust of the decedent will not qualify as a marital deduction under § 2056.

Likewise, if a nonresident alien decedent bequeaths non-U.S. situs assets to a trust created under his will, the surviving spouse may not transfer U.S.-situs assets passing to the spouse outside of the will to such a trust.[175]

D. Who May Make the Transfer

The regulations provide that the transfer of property to a QDOT may be made by the surviving spouse, the surviving spouse's legal representative (if the surviving spouse is incompetent), or the personal representative of the surviving spouse's estate (if the surviving spouse has died).[176]

172. § 11701(l)(2) of OBRA 1990.
173. Treas. Reg. § 20.2056A-4(b)(1).
174. *Id.*
175. *Id.*
176. *Id.*

E. When Must the Transfer to the QDOT Be Made?

Property passing from the decedent spouse to the noncitizen surviving spouse must be placed in or irrevocably assigned (in a manner enforceable under local law) to a QDOT "before the date on which the return of the tax imposed by this chapter is *made* . . . ."[177] The regulations provide that a property interest must be actually transferred to a QDOT "before the estate tax return is filed and on or before the last date prescribed by law that the QDOT election may be made,"[178] and that property may be assigned to a QDOT under an enforceable and irrevocable assignment "made on or before the date on which the return is filed and on or before the last date prescribed by law that the QDOT election may be made."[179]

> ***Comment:*** Thus, an extension of time within which to file the federal estate tax return also extends the time during which outright bequests and nonprobate property can be transferred or irrevocably assigned to a QDOT.[180]

F. Irrevocable Assignment of Property to a QDOT

Since the enactment of OBRA 1989, both probate and nonprobate property may be irrevocably assigned to a QDOT under an irrevocable assignment that is enforceable under local law.[181] The legislative history indicates that Congress intended the Treasury to use the regulatory authority granted to it under § 2056A(e) to provide rules regarding the treatment of property that is assigned to a QDOT but not actually transferred within a fixed period of time.[182] The 1989 House Report notes that such regulations might treat the failure to actually make the transfer of the assigned property interest to the QDOT as a trust distribution subject to an estate tax or as giving rise to disallowance of the marital deduction.

Property irrevocably assigned but not actually transferred to the QDOT before the estate tax return is filed must actually be conveyed and transferred to the QDOT under applicable local law before the administration of the decedent's estate is completed. If there is no administration of the decedent's estate (because, for example, none of the decedent's assets are subject to probate under local law), the actual conveyance of the property assigned to the QDOT must be

177. § 2056(d)(2)(B)(i) (emphasis added).

178. Treas. Reg. § 20.2056A-4(b)(1). Section 2056A(d) provides that in no case shall the election be made more than one year after the time prescribed for filing the federal estate tax return, with extensions.

179. Treas. Reg. § 20.2056A-4(b)(1).

180. *See* I.R.S. Priv. Ltr. Rul. 9148021 (Aug. 26, 1991) (outright residuary bequests to a noncitizen surviving spouse and nonprobate property passing to the surviving spouse, all of which were transferred to a QDOT after an extension of time to file the federal estate tax return was granted but prior to the timely filing of the return, satisfied the requirements of § 2056(d)(2)(B) and qualified for the marital deduction).

181. *See, e.g.*, I.R.S. Priv. Ltr. Rul. 200352005 (Dec. 26, 2003).

182. 1989 House Report, at 1431 n.95.

made on or before the date that is one year after the due date (including extensions) for filing the decedent spouse's Form 706.[183]

If an actual transfer to the QDOT is not timely made, § 2056(d)(1)(A) applies, and the marital deduction is not allowed.[184] Presumably, the disallowance of the marital deduction is limited to the property assigned but not actually transferred to the trust. The executor of the decedent's estate may request a private letter ruling from the IRS extending the time for completing the conveyance or waiving the actual conveyance under specified circumstances under Treas. Reg. § 301.9100-1(a).[185]

G. Special Rules for Transferable Annuities

For purposes of these assignment provisions, an assignment of rights under an annuity or other similar arrangement that is assignable or transferable is treated as though the property were actually transferred to the QDOT (regardless of the method of payment actually elected under such annuity or plan), even if the plan assets are not, in fact, transferred to a QDOT.[186]

For these purposes, individual retirement *annuities* described in § 408(b) are nonassignable annuities by virtue of application of § 408(b)(1) and thus do not come within this rule.[187] On the other hand, unless the terms of the account agreement provide otherwise, individual retirement *accounts* provided under § 408(a) are assignable and are subject to this special rule. However, for purposes of applying the special rules for nonassignable annuities, the surviving spouse may elect to treat individual retirement accounts as being nonassignable and therefore eligible for the procedures for such nonassignable annuities.[188]

The provisions regarding the assignment of rights under annuities or similar arrangements that are transferable apply solely for purposes of qualifying the annuity or account for the marital deduction under § 2056(b). The regulations note that reference should be made to other sections of the Code, e.g., §§ 408(d) and 4980A, to examine the consequences of an assignment for purposes of other provisions of the Code.[189]

183. Treas. Reg. § 20.2056A-4(b)(6).

184. *Id. See, e.g.*, I.R.S. Priv. Ltr. Rul. 200352005 (Dec. 26, 2003).

185. Treas. Reg. § 20.2056A-4(b)(6).

186. *Id.* § 20.2056A-4(b)(7)(i). See, e.g., I.R.S. Priv. Ltr. Ruls. 9544038 (Aug. 9, 1995), 9322005 (Feb. 24, 1993), and 9321032 (Feb. 24, 1993) for rulings in which the IRS allowed the marital deduction for payments by IRAs through a QTIP trust that also qualified as a QDOT. See also *infra* Section VI discussing qualification for the marital deduction of annuities and other similar payments that are not transferable or treated as being not transferable.

187. Treas. Reg. § 20.2056A-4(b)(7)(ii).

188. *Id.* § 20.2056A-4(b)(7)(iii). *See infra* Section VI.

189. Treas. Reg. § 20.2056A-4(b)(7)(iv). For example, the payment of IRA distributions to a QDOT that qualifies as a QTIP trust may bar the surviving spouse from electing under Treas. Reg. § 1.408-8, A-4(b) to treat the IRA as her own for purposes of determining the required beginning date. *See, e.g.*, I.R.S. Priv. Ltr. Ruls. 9322005 (Feb. 24, 1993) and 9321032 (Feb, 24, 1993). Note also that § 4980A was repealed by TRA 1997.

H. Special Provisions Governing Assignments and Transfers

A transfer or assignment of property to a QDOT must be in writing and must otherwise be in accordance with all local law requirements for such assignments or transfers. Copies of the transfer or assignment documentation must be submitted with the decedent's estate tax return.[190] The transfer or assignment may be of a specific asset or a group of assets, or a fractional share of either, or may be of a pecuniary amount.[191] If a transfer or assignment is of a specific asset or group of assets, only assets passing from the decedent to the spouse and included in the decedent's gross estate (or the proceeds from the sale, exchange, or conversion of such assets) may be transferred or assigned to the QDOT.[192]

The noncitizen surviving spouse may not transfer or assign to the QDOT property owned by the surviving spouse at the time of the decedent's spouse's death in lieu of property included in the decedent's estate that passes to the spouse (or in lieu of the proceeds from the sale, exchange, or conversion of such includable assets). Further, if only a portion of an asset is includable in the decedent's gross estate, the spouse may only transfer the portion of the asset that is includable to the transferee trust.[193]

A transfer or assignment of less than an entire interest in an asset or a group of assets may be expressed as a formula (such as the minimum amount necessary to reduce the estate tax to zero).[194] If the transfer or assignment is expressed in the form of a pecuniary amount (such as a fixed dollar amount or a formula designed to reduce the decedent spouse's estate tax to zero), the transfer or assignment must satisfy certain funding valuation requirements. Specifically, pecuniary formula assignments must require either that:

- Assets actually transferred to the QDOT in satisfaction of the transfer or assignment have an aggregate fair market value on the date of actual transfer to the QDOT amounting to no less than the amount of the pecuniary transfer or assignment;[195] or
- The assets actually transferred to the QDOT be fairly representative of appreciation or depreciation in the value of all property available for transfer to the QDOT between the valuation date and the date of actual transfer to the QDOT, if the assignment is to be satisfied by accounting for the assets on the basis of their fair market value as of some date before the date of actual transfer to the QDOT.[196]

---

190. Treas. Reg. § 20.2056A-4(b)(2).
191. *Id.*
192. *Id.* § 20.2056A-4(b)(3).
193. *Id.*
194. *Id.* § 20.2056A-4(b)(2).
195. *Id.* § 20.2056A-4(b)(4)(i).
196. *Id.* § 20.2056A-4(b)(4)(ii).

Example 4: D, a U.S. citizen, dies survived by his spouse, S, who is not a U.S. citizen at the time of D's death. Under the terms of D's will, the entire probate estate passes outright to S. Prior to the date D's estate tax return is filed and before the date that the QDOT election must be made, S establishes a QDOT and irrevocably assigns to the QDOT that portion of the gross estate necessary to reduce the estate tax to zero, taking into account all available credits and deductions. The assignment meets the requirements of Treas. Reg. § 20.2056A-4(b), assuming that the QDOT is funded no later than the date that administration of D's estate is completed.[197]

I. Protective Assignments of Property to a QDOT

1. The Problem

Section 2056(d)(2)(B) does not provide for protective assignments of property to a QDOT. Such protective assignments are critical when, at the date the decedent spouse's federal estate tax return is filed, valuation of assets is not conclusively determined. For example, the repeal of § 2040(b) if the surviving spouse is not a U.S. citizen[198] requires tracing of the consideration furnished by the respective spouses. This may be an extremely difficult task, and the executor's inability to substantiate to the satisfaction of an examining agent the amount of consideration furnished by the noncitizen spouse may, in the case of a large jointly held asset such as a residence, require the inclusion of the property in the gross estate of the decedent spouse at a time when the transfer to a QDOT will no longer be timely.

Protective assignments are also important when the decedent spouse's status as a U.S. domiciliary or a nonresident alien is unclear, because such status determines what property is subject to U.S. estate tax and whether the exemption equivalent of the decedent spouse's unified credit is the amount provided under § 2001 or § 2101, respectively.

2. Protective Assignments under the Regulations

A protective assignment of property to a QDOT may be made only if, at the date the estate tax return is filed, the executor of the decedent's estate reasonably believes that there is a "*bona fide* issue" that concerns either the residency or citizenship of the decedent, the citizenship of the surviving spouse, the includability of an asset in the decedent's gross estate, or the amount and nature of the property that the decedent's spouse is entitled to receive.[199] By way of example, the regulations provide that a protective assignment may be made (1) if, at the time the decedent's federal estate tax return is filed, the estate is involved in a *bona fide* will contest; (2) if there is uncertainty regarding the inclusion in the gross estate of an asset, which, if includable, would be eligible for the QDOT election; (3) where there is uncertainty regarding the status of the decedent as a resident

197. *Id.* § 20.2056A-4(d), Example 2.

198. § 2056(d)(1)(B).

199. Treas. Reg. § 20.2056A-4(b)(8).

alien or a nonresident alien for federal estate tax purposes; or (4) there is similar uncertainty regarding the citizenship status of the surviving spouse,.

Many of the provisions governing protective assignments of property to a QDOT are similar to those governing protective QDOT elections, discussed above in Section III.C.3.c. The protective assignment must identify the specific assets to which the assignment refers and the specific reason for the protective assignment, but may otherwise be defined by means of a formula (such as the minimum amount necessary to reduce the estate tax to zero). A copy of the assignment must be submitted with the decedent's estate tax return.[200] Once made, the protective assignment cannot be revoked. The regulations provide, by way of example, that if a protective assignment is made because a question exists as to the includability of an asset in the decedent's gross estate and it is later determined that the asset is so includable, the protective assignment becomes effective with respect to the asset and cannot be revoked.[201]

Protective assignments are, in all events, subject to the rules of Treas. Reg. § 20.2056A-4(b)(6), requiring that property assigned to a QDOT must, in general, be actually transferred to the QDOT prior to the completion of administration of the estate.[202]

J. Nontransferable Property

Because many civil law countries do not recognize trusts, the requirement that property passing to a noncitizen surviving spouse be held in a QDOT in order to qualify for the marital deduction may put the surviving spouse in a no-win situation. The problem is especially acute with respect to real property located in these countries. Prior to enactment of TRA 1997, neither the statutory provisions nor the legislative history explicitly addressed this problem, and no procedures were provided where the transfer of assets to a trust is not permitted.

One possible solution would be to include provisions in the decedent's estate planning instruments to allow the decedent's executor to transfer such assets into a corporation, partnership, or other entity. If such transfers are permitted under local law, and if there are no adverse tax consequences (such as excessive transfer taxes), then the stock or partnership interest could be transferred to a QDOT.[203]

> ***Comment:*** Note that under the final regulations governing collection of the QDOT tax (the Security Requirements), a Small QDOT relying on the

200. *Id.*

201. *See, e.g.*, I.R.S. Priv. Ltr. Rul. 200910019 (Nov. 20, 2008).

202. *But see* I.R.S. Priv. Ltr. Rul. 200448027 (July 29, 2004) (waiving the requirement of actual conveyance to the QDOT where the surviving spouse became a citizen before the assigned property was actually transferred to the QDOT).

203. *See* I.R.S. Priv. Ltr. Rul. 199918039 (Feb. 8, 1999) (marital deduction allowed for stock conveyed by surviving spouse to a QDOT where surviving spouse transferred foreign real property to foreign corporation in exchange for stock of the corporation).

Foreign Real Property Requirement may be subject to the look-through rule of Treas. Reg. § 20.2056A-2(d)(1)(ii)(B), where the trust owns 20 percent or more of the voting stock or value of a corporation having fifteen or fewer shareholders or 20 percent of the capital interest in a partnership with fifteen or fewer partners. If the look-through rule is applied, the QDOT will be treated as owning a pro rata portion of each asset owned by the corporation, partnership, or other entity to which the property is transferred. As a result, the QDOT may be unable to meet the Foreign Real Property Requirement if the entity owns a substantial amount of foreign real estate.[204]

In any case, the decedent's will should provide the executor with broad powers to incorporate businesses, and to join and create partnerships and joint ventures.[205]

The legislative history does indicate that the Treasury's regulatory authority granted under § 2056A(a)(2) to ensure the collection of any QDOT tax might require that either a sufficient portion of the trust assets be subject to U.S. jurisdiction or that the trustee be an institution with substantial U.S. assets.[206] However, there is nothing to indicate that this would require a complete prohibition against ownership of non-U.S. situs real property or other non-U.S. situs assets. As dis-

204. *See supra* Section III.D.

205. *But see* I.R.S. Priv. Ltr. Rul. 9101034 (Oct. 11, 1990). In this ruling, real and personal property were to be transferred to a trust for the benefit of the surviving, noncitizen spouse in settlement of claims by the surviving spouse against the estate. After setting out the provisions of the trust, the ruling stated that a provision of the trust authorizing the trustees "to form, at any time and from time to time, a corporation or other entity under the laws of any jurisdiction and to convey all or any part of the trust assets to such corporation or entity in exchange for property (including securities) of such corporation or entity and to continue to hold such property" would be deleted prior to the date on which the decedent spouse's federal estate tax return was made. No explanation was provided for this deletion.

Under the position taken in certain early letter rulings, a QDOT could be initially funded with stock of a foreign corporation, provided that the stock certificates were held in the United States by a U.S. Trustee and that the U.S. Trustee retains sufficient assets to pay any QDOT tax imposed on the trust. These rulings could be read to require stock or other evidence of ownership constituting a significant portion of the property transferred to the QDOT to be held by the U.S. Trustee. Although a similar position was adopted in the proposed regulations (*see* Prop. Treas. Reg. § 20.2056A-2(d)(3)), it was rejected in the final regulations.

Priv. Ltr. Rul. 9043070 (Aug. 3, 1990), which predated the final QDOT regulations, considered the issue of whether a QDOT may be permitted to hold foreign real property. In this ruling, the IRS concluded that a marital trust would qualify as a QDOT if it were reformed to include certain specific provisions, including a prohibition on the trustee "from investing in realty that is not situated in the United States." Likewise, in Priv. Ltr. Ruls. 9003030 (Oct. 24, 1989), 9044072 (Aug. 8, 1990), 9109021 (Nov. 30, 1990), and 9151044 (Sept. 26, 1991), the IRS concluded that trusts created by the surviving spouse that prohibited the trustee from investing in *any* property located outside the United States would qualify as a QDOT. *But see* I.R.S. Priv. Ltr. Rul. 8952005 (Sept. 20, 1989) (provisions of a QDOT created by the surviving spouse that met the requirements of § 2056A did not include the requirement that all trust property have a U.S. situs; there appears to be no basis for such an absolute prohibition).

206. *See supra* Section III.D.

cussed above at Section III.D.5, a Small QDOT that attempts to comply with the Foreign Real Property Requirement may hold up to 35 percent of the value of its assets in foreign real property.[207]

Some relief may be available in future regulations. TRA 1997 enacted § 2056A(c)(3), which authorizes issuance of regulations to define the term "trust" to include other arrangements having substantially the same effect as a trust.[208] The legislative history indicates Congress's understanding that such regulations would allow the marital deduction for a nontrust arrangement only when the United States could retain jurisdiction and adequate security to impose any transfer taxes on transfers of the property by the surviving spouse. The legislative history contemplates the adoption of bilateral tax treaties or closing agreement procedures under which the surviving spouse waives tax benefits, allows the United States to retain taxing jurisdiction over the property, and satisfies security requirements for payment of the tax.[209]

K. Effect of Transfer of Assignment on Other Tax Provisions

1. Statutory Provision

When the noncitizen spouse transfers or irrevocably assigns property to a QDOT, the surviving spouse could be viewed as the transferor of the property for purposes of other tax provisions. The statute provides that property passing from the decedent to the surviving spouse "shall be treated as passing to such spouse" in a QDOT if the transfer or assignment is made prior to the date on which the decedent spouse's federal estate tax return is made.[210]

The legislative history is silent on whether a deemed gift would occur at the date of transfer or assignment of property to a QDOT. The apparent intent of § 2056(d)(2)(B) is to provide a mechanism by which the decedent spouse's estate may receive a marital deduction for bequests to the noncitizen surviving spouse or for property passing to the noncitizen surviving spouse by operation of law (such as joint tenancy property). In addition, because property so transferred is treated as passing to the spouse in a QDOT, the result, at least from a federal estate tax policy perspective, should not be any different from the result when property passes directly to the trustee in a marital trust.

2. Regulatory Provisions

Under the regulations, however, property assigned or transferred to a QDOT pursuant to § 2056(d)(2)(B) is treated as passing from the decedent in a QDOT *solely* for purposes of § 2056(d)(2)(A). For all other purposes (e.g., income, gift, estate,

---

207. *See* Treas. Reg. § 20.2056A-2(d)(1)(ii).

208. TRA 1997 § 1312(a). The amendment is effective for decedents dying after August 5, 1997. TRA 1997 § 1312(b).

209. H. Rep. No. 148, 105th Cong., at 626–27 (1997).

210. § 2056(d)(2)(B).

generation-skipping transfer taxes),[211] the surviving spouse is treated as the transferor of the property to the QDOT.[212] The preamble to the proposed regulations stated that this treatment "comports with § 2056(d)(2)(B), which provides that property transferred or assigned by the spouse to a QDOT is treated as passing from the decedent to the QDOT *solely* for purposes of § 2056(d)(2)(A), and not for purposes of the income and transfer tax provisions of the Code."[213]

The final regulations retained this rule. The preamble states the Treasury's belief that this treatment is consistent with congressional intent as evidenced by the enactment of § 2056A(b)(15). This section exempts from the QDOT tax a distribution to the surviving spouse to the extent that the distribution is used to reimburse the surviving spouse for income taxes on an item of income from the trust to which the surviving spouse is not entitled under the terms of the trust. As discussed below in Section V.K.3, § 2056A(b)(15) was enacted out of concern that the surviving spouse would be treated as the owner of the trust property under the grantor trust rules and would, therefore, be taxed on trust income, including capital gains, that he would not be entitled to receive.

In an effort to ameliorate the harshness of this rule, the final regulations provide two additional provisions.

(a) Transfers by Disclaimer. The final regulations take the position that the decedent spouse will be treated as the transferor of property to a QDOT if the property passes to the QDOT by a transfer that satisfies the requirements of § 2518(c)(3). Therefore, if the decedent spouse's testamentary instruments provide for an outright bequest to the surviving spouse, with the provision that if and to the extent that he disclaims property, it will pass into a QDOT created under the decedent's will or revocable trust, then the surviving spouse will not be treated as the transferor of the property into the QDOT.[214]

(b) Application of Chapter 14 Valuation Rules. The final regulations amended Treas. Reg. § 25.2702-1(c) by adding an exception to the application of the chapter 14 valuation rules for transfers or assignments described in § 2056(d)(2)(B) by a noncitizen surviving spouse of property to a QDOT, if the surviving spouse retains an interest in the transferred property that is not otherwise a "qualified interest"[215] (as defined in § 2702(b)).

> ***Example 5:*** D's will bequeaths $700,000 outright to S, who is not a U.S. citizen. The bequest qualifies for a marital deduction under § 2056(a)

211. The regulations also include a reference to the excise tax imposed under § 1441. The § 1441 excise tax, imposed on certain transfers to foreign trusts, was repealed by TRA 1997 and replaced by new § 684. Presumably, the provisions governing the effect of transfers by the surviving spouse to a QDOT would also apply to transfers falling under the provisions of § 684.

212. Treas. Reg. § 20.2056A-4(b)(5).

213. 58 Fed. Reg. 305 (Jan. 5, 1993) (emphasis added).

214. Treas. Reg. § 20.2056A-4(b)(5).

215. *Id. See also* Treas. Reg. § 25.2702-1(c)(8).

except that it does not pass in a QDOT. S creates an irrevocable trust that meets the requirements for a QDOT and transfers the $700,000 to the QDOT. The QDOT instrument provides that S is entitled to all the income from the QDOT payable at least annually and that, upon the death of S, the property remaining in the QDOT is to be distributed to the grandchildren of D and S in equal shares. The trust instrument contains all other provisions required to qualify as a QDOT. On D's estate tax return, D's executor makes a QDOT election under § 2056A(a)(3). Solely for purposes of the marital deduction, the property is deemed to pass from D to the QDOT trust, and, therefore, D's estate is entitled to a marital deduction for the $700,000 value of the property passing from D to S. However, S's transfer of property to the QDOT is treated as a gift of the remainder interest for gift tax purposes, because S's transfer creates a vested remainder interest in the grandchildren of D and S. Accordingly, as of the date that S transfers the property to the QDOT, a gift tax is imposed on the present value of the remainder interest. In addition, at S's death, S is treated as the transferor of the property into the trust for estate tax and generation-skipping transfer tax purposes.[216] The trust is not eligible for a reverse QTIP election by D's estate under § 2652(a)(3) because a QTIP election cannot be made for the QDOT. This is so because the marital deduction is allowed under § 2056(a) for the outright bequest to the spouse, and the spouse is then separately treated as the transferor of the property to the QDOT.[217]

Comment: The provisions of § 2056(d)(2)(B) state only that "for purposes of subparagraph (A), such property shall be treated as passing to such spouse in a qualified domestic trust . . . ." There is no use of the term "solely" in the statute. Further, the legislative history is silent on whether a deemed gift would occur at the date of transfer or assignment of property to a QDOT. The apparent intent of § 2056(d)(2)(B) is to provide a mechanism by which the decedent spouse's estate may receive a marital deduction for bequests to the noncitizen surviving spouse or for property passing to the noncitizen surviving spouse by operation of law (such as joint tenancy property). In addition, because property so transferred is treated as passing to the spouse in a QDOT, the result, at least from a federal estate tax policy perspective, should not be any different from the result when property passes directly to the trustee in a marital trust.

Comment: The easiest way to avoid the adverse gift tax effects of this provision is to ensure that the surviving spouse has a special power of

216. *See, e.g.*, §§ 2036 and 2652(a)(1).
217. Treas. Reg. § 20.2056A-4(d), Example 5.

appointment over the property in the trust to which the property is transferred or irrevocably assigned, thereby avoiding a completed gift.[218]

3. Grantor Trust Status of QDOT Created by the Surviving Spouse

Where the noncitizen spouse creates a QDOT and transfers property to it, and with respect to any property added to a QDOT created by the decedent or by the decedent spouse's executor, the surviving spouse may be treated as the owner of the trust for purposes of the grantor trust rules.[219] Depending on the terms of the trust, the noncitizen spouse may be treated as the owner of any capital gains incurred by the trust. In that case, he or she will be liable for any income tax thereby due.

Under the provisions of § 2056A, as in effect prior to OBRA 1990, if the trust paid the capital gains tax for the surviving spouse, or distributed to the surviving spouse property in an amount equal to the tax due, the amount paid or distributed would itself be a distribution subject to the QDOT tax, even when the capital gains were not distributed to the surviving spouse. However, § 2056A(b)(15), added by OBRA 1990, changed this by providing that no QDOT tax shall be imposed under § 2056A(b)(1) on any distribution to the surviving spouse to the extent such distribution is made to reimburse the surviving spouse for any tax imposed by subtitle A of the Code on any item of income of the QDOT to which such surviving spouse is not entitled under the terms of the trust.[220] The legislative history explains that under this provision, "the QDT tax is not imposed upon any distribution to reimburse the spouse for Federal income tax paid on an item of income of the QDT to which the spouse is not entitled under the terms of the trust, e.g., capital gains if such gains are taxable to the spouse."[221]

VI. Special Rules for Nonassignable Annuities and Other Arrangements

A. Background

Under § 2056A(e), the Secretary of the Treasury is provided with broad regulatory authority to carry out the purposes of § 2056A. The Treasury is directed to "prescribe such regulations under which there may be treated as a qualified domestic trust any annuity or other payment which is includable in the decedent's gross

218. *See* Treas. Reg. § 20.2056A-4(d), Example 1. *See also* Priv. Ltr. Ruls. 9808022 (Nov. 19, 1997) (special power of appointment retained by surviving spouse), 9551014 (Sept. 21, 1995) (retention of general power of appointment by surviving spouse prevents gift tax on funding of QDOT by surviving spouse).

219. *See* §§ 671 *et seq.* Note that application of § 672(f) may, in certain circumstances, prevent a QDOT classified as a foreign trust from being a grantor trust.

220. § 11702(g)(2)(B) of OBRA 1990.

221. 1990 House Technical Corrections Report, *supra* note 60.

estate and is by its terms payable for life or a term of years."[222] The legislative history of OBRA 1989 makes explicit that this treatment is available only when the annuity or other payment would otherwise qualify for the marital deduction.[223] The legislative history also suggests that the payor of a joint and survivor annuity may be required to withhold amounts equal to the QDOT tax imposed on such distributions and meet other conditions to ensure collection of the tax.[224]

In addition, the regulatory authority granted under § 2056A(e) is to "be applied to property interests that cannot be transferred to a QDOT under Federal law."[225] This transfer restriction most commonly arises under the anti-alienation provisions contained the Retirement Equity Act of 1984 on qualified plans.[226] The legislative history failed to take account of those annuities or other payments that are transferable under federal law, but that are subject to transfer restrictions imposed by the plan itself, by state law, or by foreign law. The legislative history suggests that if the annuity or other payment is part of a nonqualified plan or is otherwise free of federal law transfer restrictions, then it may not itself be treated as a QDOT and must, therefore, actually be transferred to a QDOT in order to qualify for the marital deduction. However, so long as the conditions imposed by the regulations to ensure collection of the QDOT tax on nontransferable annuities and other payments are also imposed on those annuities and other payments that are transferable, there would appear to be no reason not to treat transferable annuities or other payments as QDOTs without actually placing them into a QDOT.

Further, if, under the retirement plan, the surviving spouse receives a lump sum at the death of the decedent spouse that he or she then rolls over to a spousal Individual Retirement Account (IRA), it is not clear from the legislative history whether the spousal IRA could be treated as a QDOT. However, in Private Letter Ruling 9109021 (Nov. 30, 1990), the surviving spouse irrevocably transferred funds received by her from the decedent spouse's IRA and the portion of a death benefit received by her from the decedent spouse's § 403(b) retirement plan into a spousal rollover individual retirement trust that qualified as a QDOT. The IRS ruled that, provided the transfer was irrevocable and completed prior to the date the decedent's estate tax return was filed, the transfer of such funds would qualify for the marital deduction. Also, in Private Letter Ruling 9151043 (Sept. 26, 1991), the noncitizen surviving spouse, who was designated as the beneficiary of two IRAs, irrevocably designated a QDOT created after the death of the decedent spouse as the beneficiary of the IRAs. The ruling held that the IRAs would be treated as assets of the QDOT and would qualify for the marital deduction. However, this ruling contains some questionable language and should be read carefully.

222. § 2056A(e).
223. H.R. No. 386, 101st Cong. 670 (1989) (1989 Conference Report).
224. 1989 House Report, at 1433.
225. 1989 Conference Report, at 670.
226. *See* §§ 401(a)(11), 417, and § 401(a)(13).

The final regulations note that the IRS will prescribe by administrative guidance the extent, if any, to which the provisions governing qualification of otherwise nonassignable annuities or other arrangements for the marital deduction apply to a rollover from a qualified trust to an eligible retirement plan within the meaning of § 402(c) or a distribution from an individual retirement annuity that is paid through an individual retirement account or an individual retirement annuity within the meaning of § 408(d)(3).[227]

B. Final Regulations Governing "Nonassignable Annuities or Other Payments"

1. Overview

The final regulations provide extensive detail regarding qualification of nonassignable annuities for the marital deduction. Under the final regulations, any "nonassignable annuity or other arrangement" will be treated as meeting the Marital Deduction Requirements,[228] the Statutory Requirements,[229] and the Security Requirements[230] if either the requirements of Treas. Reg. §§ 20.2056A-4(c)(2) (the Current Tax Method) or 20.2056A-4(c)(3) (the Roll Over Method) are satisfied.[231]

A "nonassignable annuity or other payment" is a plan, annuity, or other arrangement, whether qualified or not qualified under part I of subchapter D of chapter 1 of subtitle A of the Code (§§ 401–419A) that qualifies for the marital deduction but for the limitations of § 2056(d)(1)(A), and whose payments are not assignable or transferable to the QDOT under either federal law, state law, foreign law, or the terms of the plan or arrangement itself. An assignment meeting the requirements of Treas. Reg. § 20.2056A-(4)(b) of rights under annuities or similar arrangements that *are* transferable is treated as having been actually transferred to a QDOT regardless of the method of payment actually elected under an annuity or plan.[232]

As noted above, the final regulations clarify the treatment of individual retirement accounts and annuities as nonassignable annuities or other payments. Specifically, under Treas. Reg. § 20.2056A-4(b)(7), individual retirement *annuities* are classified as nonassignable because of provisions of § 408(b)(1). On the other hand, individual retirement *accounts* were determined to be assignable and are therefore subject to the rule discussed at Section V.G, above. However, under the final regulations, the surviving spouse may elect to treat the individual retirement account as being nonassignable, and therefore eligible for the special rules governing nonassignable annuities or payments.

227. Treas. Reg. § 20.2056A-4(c)(1) (last sentence). Such guidance has not been issued.
228. *See supra* Section III.B.
229. *See supra* Section III.C.
230. *See supra* Section III.D.
231. *See* I.R.S. Priv. Ltr. Rul. 1999904023 (Oct. 30, 1998).
232. Treas. Reg. § 20.2056A-4(c)(1).

2. The Current Tax Method

The requirements of the Current Tax Method are set out at Treas. Reg. § 20.2056A-4(c)(2). The Current Tax Method is intended to approximate the result that would occur if the plan or annuity arrangement itself constituted a QDOT and distributed a portion of corpus to the spouse annually. The Current Tax Method requires:

a. the noncitizen surviving spouse to agree to pay the QDOT tax due on the "corpus portion," as defined in Treas. Reg. § 20.2056A-4(c)(4) (*see infra* Section VI.B.6), of each nonassignable annuity or other payment received under the plan or arrangement;[233]
b. the executor of the decedent's estate to file with the estate tax return the information statement described in Treas. Reg. § 20.2056A-4(c)(5);[234]
c. the executor to file with the federal estate tax return the "Agreement To Pay Section 2056A Estate Tax."[235] That statement must be signed by the surviving spouse (or by the surviving spouse's legal representative if the surviving spouse is legally incompetent to sign the agreement) and must be in the form set out in Treas. Reg. § 20.2056A-4(c)(6)(ii); and
d. The executor to make the QDOT election under Treas. Reg. § 20.2056A-3 with respect to the nonassignable annuity or other payment.[236]

3. The Roll Over Method

The Roll Over Method is intended to approximate the same result as if the present value of the survivor benefit were transferred to a QDOT in a lump sum and, thereafter, the noncitizen spouse received the income from the QDOT. The requirements of the Roll Over Method are set out at Treas. Reg. § 20.2056A-4(c)(3) and are satisfied if:

a. the noncitizen surviving spouse agrees to roll over and transfer the corpus portion of each annuity payment to a QDOT, whether the QDOT is created by the decedent's will, the executor of the decedent's estate, or the surviving spouse;[237]
b. a QDOT for the benefit of the surviving spouse is established prior to the date the federal estate tax return is filed and on or prior to the last date prescribed by law for making the QDOT election;[238]
c. the executor of the decedent's estate files with the federal estate tax return the information statement described in Treas. Reg. § 20.2056A-4(c)(5);[239]

233. *Id.* § 20.2056A-4(c)(2)(i).
234. *Id.* § 20.2056A-4(c)(2)(ii).
235. *Id.* § 20.2056A-4(c)(2)(iii).
236. *Id.* § 20.2056A-4(c)(2)(iv).
237. *Id.* § 20.2056A-4(c)(3)(i).
238. *Id.* § 20.2056A-4(c)(3)(ii).
239. *Id.* § 20.2056A-4(c)(3)(iii).

d. the executor files with the estate tax return the "Agreement to Roll over Annuity Payments" described in Treas. Reg. § 20.2056A-4(c)(7).[240] That statement must be signed by the surviving spouse or by the legal representative of the surviving spouse if the surviving spouse is legally incompetent to sign the agreement and must be in the form set out in Treas. Reg. § 20.2056A-4(c)(7)(ii); and
e. the executor makes the election under Treas. Reg. § 20.2056A-3 with respect to the nonassignable annuity or other payment.[241]

Comment: In connection with the Roll Over Method, the surviving spouse may incur an income tax liability on the receipt of amounts that must then be transferred to the QDOT. Treas. Reg. § 20.2056A-5(c)(3)(iv)(A) exempts from the QDOT tax amounts paid from the QDOT (by actual payment or by withholding) to reimburse the spouse with respect to the income tax imposed on the amounts transferred to the QDOT under the Roll Over Method.[242]

Comment: It appears likely that the Roll Over Method will be the preferred option for a surviving spouse beneficiary of a nontransferable plan, because it provides a greater opportunity for deferral of the QDOT tax. This would clearly be the case when the surviving spouse is contemplating obtaining U.S. citizenship.

Comment: When the surviving spouse anticipates electing Roll Over treatment with respect to annuity payments, an issue may arise as to what actions are to be taken with respect to annuity payments received by the surviving spouse after the death of the decedent but prior to the filing of the federal estate tax return and the creation of the QDOT that will receive the corpus portion of the annuity payments. In Private Letter Ruling 199904023 (Oct. 30, 1998), the QDOT tax was paid on the corpus portion of the annuity payments received after the decedent's death and prior to the filing of decedent's estate tax return, in accordance with the Current Tax Method. On the Form 706, the executor properly made the Roll Over Method election and transferred the corpus portion of the annuity payments received thereafter to the QDOT. The regulations do not appear to require adoption of the Current Tax Method with respect to annuity payments received in the interim period ending with the filing of the federal estate tax return. It would seem reasonable that holding the corpus portion in a separate account pending creation of the QDOT and filing of the Form 706, followed by a timely remittance when the QDOT is completed, should satisfy the requirements of the Roll Over Method.

240. *Id.* § 20.2056A-4(c)(3)(iv).
241. *Id.* § 20.2056A-4(c)(3)(v).
242. *See, e.g.*, I.R.S. Priv. Ltr. Ruls. 9746049 (Aug. 15, 1997) and 9729040 (Apr. 23, 1997).

4. Failure to Comply with Agreements

Under the proposed regulations, both the Current Tax Agreement and the Rollover Agreement to be executed by the surviving spouse provided for the imposition of the QDOT tax on the entire remaining present value of the annuity upon the failure to pay the QDOT tax due or to file the Form 706-QDT. This rule was unnecessarily severe, especially because the surviving spouse would not have had access to the entire value of the plan on which the QDOT tax would be imposed. Under the terms of these agreements as adopted in the final regulations, the failure either to timely file Form 706-QDT or to timely pay the tax imposed on the corpus portion of any annuity payment (under the Current Tax Method) or to transfer any required amount with respect to any annuity payment or timely file the Form 706-QDT reporting the transfers in a year (in the case of the Roll Over Method) *may* cause the surviving spouse to become immediately liable to pay the QDOT tax on the entire remaining present value of the annuity. The regulations provide that the surviving spouse may apply for relief under Treas. Reg. § 301.9100-1 from the consequences of failing to timely file the QDOT tax return and to pay the QDOT tax necessary or to timely transfer the corpus portion of any annuity to the QDOT.

5. Foreign Plans or Arrangements

Under the final regulations, in the case of a plan or arrangement established and administered by a person or entity located outside the United States for the benefit of a surviving spouse of a nonresident alien decedent or a surviving spouse of a U.S. citizen who died domiciled outside of the United States, the surviving spouse must agree when requested by the District Director to enter into a security arrangement to secure any undertakings of the surviving spouse.

6. Determination of Corpus Portion of Annuity Payment

The regulations set out in step-by-step detail the manner in which to determine the corpus portion for purposes of applying the Current Tax Method and the Roll Over Method. Note that these rules do not apply when the surviving spouse is receiving amounts under a nonassignable plan or other arrangement other than in the form of an annuity, even if the Current Tax Method or the Roll Over Method is elected. This could occur when the surviving spouse rolls over plan balances into a Roll Over IRA before the required beginning date. In such cases, the determination of corpus and income is made as if the IRA were itself a trust, in accordance with the rules of § 2056A(c)(2) and the regulations.[243]

a. Corpus Portion. The "corpus portion" of each nonassignable annuity or other payment is the "corpus amount" of the annual payment divided by the total annual payment.
b. Corpus Amount. The "corpus amount" of the annual payment is determined in accordance with the following formula:

243. *See, e.g.*, I.R.S. Priv. Ltr. Ruls. 9746049 (Aug. 15, 1997) and 9729040 (Apr. 23, 1997).

$$\text{corpus amount} = \frac{\text{Total present value of annuity or other payment}}{\text{Expected annuity term}}$$

c. The "total present value of the annuity or other payment" is the present value of the nonassignable annuity or other payment as of the date of the decedent's death, determined in accordance with the interest rates and mortality data prescribed by § 7520.

d. The "expected annuity term" is the number of years that would be required for the scheduled payments to exhaust a hypothetical fund equal to the present value of the scheduled payments.

   (1) This is determined by first dividing the total present value of the payments by the annual payment.

   (2) From this quotient, the expected annuity term is derived by identifying the term of years that corresponds to the annuity factor equal to the quotient. This is determined by using column 1 of Table B, for the applicable interest rate, contained in IRS Publication 1457, "Actuarial Valuations" (May 2009). If the quotient obtained falls between two terms, the longer term is used.[244]

Example 6: At the time of D's death in March 2013, D is a participant in an employees' § 401(a) pension plan. On D's death, D's spouse S, a U.S. resident, becomes entitled to receive a survivor's annuity of $100,000 per year, payable monthly, for life. At the time of D's death, S is age sixty-five. Assume that under § 7520, the appropriate discount rate to be used for valuing annuities at D's date of death is 1.4 percent. The annuity factor at 1.4 percent for a person age sixty-five is 15.2163. The adjustment factor at 1.4 percent for monthly payments is 1.0064. Accordingly, the right to receive $100,000 a year on a monthly basis is equal to the right to receive $100,064 ($100,000 x 1.0064) on an annual basis.

The corpus portion of each annuity payment received by S is determined as follows:

1. First, *determine the annuity factor* for the number of years that would be required to exhaust a hypothetical fund that has a present value and a payout corresponding to S's interest in the payments under the plan, determined as follows:
   (a) Present value of S's annuity:
   $100,640 x 15.2163 = $1,531,368
   (b) Annuity Factor for Expected Annuity Term:
   $1,531,368/$100,640 = 15.2163
2. Second, *determine the number of years* that would be required for S's annuity to exhaust a hypothetical fund of $1,531,368. The term certain annuity

244. Treas. Reg. § 20.2056A-4(c)(4)(i) and (ii).

factor of 15.2163 falls between the annuity factors for seventeen and eighteen years in a 1.4 percent term certain annuity table (Column 1 of Table B, Aleph Volume, Publication 1457). Accordingly, the expected annuity term is eighteen years.

3. Third, *determine the corpus amount* by dividing the expected term of eighteen years into the present value of the hypothetical fund as follows:
   Corpus amount of annual payment:
   $1,531,368/18 = $85,076
4. Fourth, determine the corpus portion of each annuity payment by dividing the corpus amount of each annual payment by the annual annuity payment as follows:
   Corpus portion of each annuity payment:
   $85,076/100,640 = 0.845

Accordingly, 84.5 percent of each payment to S is deemed to be a distribution of corpus.[245]

> ***Comment:*** Lower interest rates increase dramatically the corpus portion of each payment. At higher § 7520 rates, e.g., 9 percent, the corpus portion will be closer to 50 percent.

7. Hardship Exemption

The final regulations include a hardship provision under both the Current Tax Method and the Roll Over Method. Specifically, if the financial circumstances of the surviving spouse are such that an amount equal to all or a portion of the corpus portion of a nonassignable annuity payment received by the spouse would be subject to the hardship exemption provided under Treas. Reg. § 20.2056A-5(c) if paid from a QDOT, then all or a corresponding part of the corpus portion will be exempt from either the current tax payment required under the Current Payment Method or the rollover required under the Roll Over Method.[246]

8. Information Statement

In addition to the requirements set out above, in order for a nonassignable annuity or other payment to qualify under either the Current Tax Method or the Roll Over Method, Treas. Reg. § 20.2056A-4(c)(5)(i) requires an extensive information statement, containing the information set out below, to be filed with the decedent spouse's federal estate tax return.

- Annuity source information.
  (1) Employment-related annuity. If the nonassignable annuity or other payment is employment related, the following information must be provided:

245. *See id.* § 20.2056A-4(d), Example 4.
246. *See id.* § 20.2056A-4(c)(2)(i) and (3)(i).

(a) the name and address of the employer;
(b) the date of retirement or other separation from employment of the decedent;
(c) the name and address of the pension fund, insurance company, or other obligor that is paying the annuity (or similar payment); and
(d) the identification number that the obligor has assigned to the annuity or other payment.[247]

(2) Annuity not employment related. If the nonassignable annuity or other payment is not employment related, the following information must be provided:
(a) the name and address of the person or entity paying the nonassignable annuity or other payment;
(b) the date of acquisition of the nonassignable annuity contract by the decedent or by the decedent and the surviving spouse; and
(c) the identification number, if any, that the obligor has assigned to the nonassignable annuity or other payment.[248]

- The total annuity amount payable each year.
  (1) The total amount payable annually under the nonassignable annuity or other arrangement;
  (2) A description of whether the annuity is payable on a monthly, quarterly, or other interval;
  (3) A description of any scheduled changes in the annuity payout amount.[249]
- The duration of the annuity.

A description of the term of the nonassignable annuity or other payment in years, if it is determined by a term certain, and the name, address, and birth date of any measuring life if the nonassignable annuity or other payment is determined by one or more lives.[250]

- The applicable market interest rate under § 7520.[251]
- Calculations showing the determination of corpus portion of each payment.[252]
- For the Roll Over, Method, the name and address of the U.S. Trustee and the name and taxpayer identification number of the QDOT.[253]
- Certification statement. The information statement must be signed under penalties of perjury by both the executor of the decedent's estate and by the surviving spouse (or the legal representative of the surviving spouse if the surviving spouse is legally incompetent) to certify as follows:

247. *Id.* § 20.2056A-4(c)(5)(ii)(A).
248. *Id.* § 20.2056A-4(c)(5)(ii)(B).
249. *Id.* § 20.2056A-4(c)(5)(iii).
250. *Id.* § 20.2056A-4(c)(5)(iv).
251. *Id.* § 20.2056A-4(c)(5)(v).
252. *Id.* § 20.2056A-4(c)(5)(vi).
253. *Id.* § 20.2056A-4(c)(5)(vii).

Under penalties of perjury, I hereby certify that, to the best of my knowledge and belief, the information reported in this information statement is true, correct and complete.[254]

VII. Taxation of QDOTs

A. Taxable Events

1. General Rule

The QDOT tax is imposed on certain distributions from a QDOT during the life of the surviving spouse,[255] and upon the value of the property remaining in the QDOT at the date of death of the surviving spouse.[256] In addition, if, at any time, there is no trustee who is a U.S. citizen or a domestic corporation, or if the QDOT fails to meet any other requirement imposed by § 2056A(a)(1) or by the Security Requirements, the QDOT tax will be imposed as if the surviving spouse died on the date the trust ceased to qualify as a QDOT.[257] Finally, any trust property that is used to pay the QDOT tax imposed under § 2056A(b)(1) is itself a distribution subject to the QDOT tax in the year that the tax is paid.[258]

2. Are Distributions of Accumulated Income Taxable Events?

There are situations in which all of the income of a QDOT may not be required to be distributed in order for a trust to qualify as a QDOT.[259] For example, where the QDOT is in the form of an estate trust all of the income need not be distributed to the surviving spouse. In addition, where the surviving spouse transfers property to a QDOT, and no property passed from the decedent spouse to the same trust, then the QDOT need not satisfy the mandatory income provisions of § 2056(b)(5) or § 2056(b)(7) in order to meet the Marital Deduction Requirement.[260] In these situations, a portion of a distribution from a QDOT may constitute accumulated income. There is no indication as to whether such a distribution will be treated as a tax-free distribution of income or a distribution of principal subject to the QDOT tax. Logically, it should be treated as a distribution of income; however, such amounts should be segregated by the trustee to avoid the need for tracing. Of course, if the trust is a QTIP trust or a general power of appointment marital trust, there would be no accumulated income because under either trust, income must be distributed to the surviving spouse no less frequently than annually.

254. *Id.* § 20.2056A-4(c)(5)(viii).
255. § 2056A(b)(1)(A) and Treas. Reg. § 20.2056A-5(b)(1).
256. § 2056A(b)(1)(B) and Treas. Reg. § 20.2056A-5(b)(2).
257. § 2056A(b)(4); Treas. Reg. § 20.2056A-5(b)(3).
258. § 2056A(b)(11); Treas. Reg. § 20.2056A-5(b)(1).
259. § 7815(d)(7)(A) of OBRA 1989.
260. *See supra* Section III.B.2.

B. Amount Subject to Tax

1. Lifetime Distributions of Principal

If a taxable event occurs during the surviving spouse's lifetime, the QDOT tax is imposed on the amount of money and the fair market value of the property that is distributed, including property distributed from the trust pursuant to the exercise of a power of appointment, and including any amount withheld from the distribution by the U.S. Trustee to pay the tax. If the QDOT tax is not withheld by the U.S. Trustee but is paid by the U.S. Trustee out of other assets of the QDOT, an amount equal to the tax so paid is treated as an additional distribution to the spouse in the year that the tax is paid.[261]

2. Death of the Surviving Spouse

The amount subject to tax at the death of the surviving spouse is the fair market value of the trust assets at the date of the spouse's death or on the alternate valuation date, if applicable. With respect to nonassignable plans or arrangements, any corpus portion amounts remaining in a QDOT after a surviving spouse's death are subject to the QDOT tax as well as any residual payments from a nonassignable plan or arrangement that are payable to the spouse's estate or to successor beneficiaries.[262]

3. Trust Ceases to Qualify as QDOT

If a taxable event occurs as a result of the trust ceasing to qualify as a QDOT, the amount of property subject to the QDOT tax is the fair market value of the trust assets on the date of disqualification.[263]

C. Amount of Tax

1. Rate of Tax

The amount of the QDOT tax imposed equals the federal estate tax that would have been imposed under § 2001 *on the estate of the decedent spouse* had such decedent's taxable estate been (a) increased by the sum of (i) the amount of property involved in the taxable event and (ii) the aggregate of the amounts involved in all previous taxable events with respect to all QDOTs of the decedent spouse, and (b) reduced by the federal estate tax that would have been imposed on the decedent spouse's estate had it been increased by the amount involved in all previous taxable events.[264] For purposes of applying this provision, the estate tax that would have been imposed on the decedent spouse's estate means the net tax after allowance of any available credits, including the unified credit (applicable credit amount) allowable under § 2010, the credit or deduction for state death taxes

261. Treas. Reg. § 20.2056A-5(b)(1).
262. *Id.* § 20.2056A-5(b)(2).
263. *Id.* § 20.2056A-5(b)(3).
264. § 2056A(b)(2)(A).

under § 2011 or § 2058, the credit for tax on prior transfers under § 2013, and the credit for foreign death taxes under § 2014.[265]

In the case of a nonresident alien decedent, the applicable credits are determined under § 2102.[266]

In making this calculation, for a decedent spouse dying before January 1, 2002, the 5 percent surtax that eliminates the benefits of the graduated estate tax rates and the unified credit under § 2001(c)(2) applies.[267]

The QDOT tax, net of any allowable credits, constitutes an estate tax for purposes of the income tax deduction provided under § 691(c)(2)(A).[268]

Example 7: D, a U.S. citizen, dies in 1997 with a gross estate of $1.2 million. Under D's will, a pecuniary bequest of $700,000 passes to a QDOT for the benefit of D's spouse, S, who is a resident but not a citizen of the United States. D's estate tax is computed as follows:

Gross estate	$1,200,000
Marital Deduction	(700,000)
Taxable Estate	$500,000
Gross Tax	$155,800
Less: Unified Credit	(155,800)
Net Tax	0

At S's subsequent death, the value of the corpus of the QDOT is $700,000. Assuming there were no taxable events during S's lifetime with respect to the QDOT, the QDOT tax imposed under § 2056A(b)(1)(B) is $235,000, computed as follows:

D's actual taxable estate	$ 500,000
QDOT property	700,000
Total	$1,200,000
Gross Tax	$ 427,800
Less: Unified Credit	(192,800)
Net Tax	$ 235,000
Less: Tax that would have been imposed on D's actual taxable estate of $500,000	0
Deferred Estate Tax	$ 235,000

265. Treas. Reg. § 20.2056A-6(a).

266. *Id.*

267. *Id.*

268. *Id.* This provision in the regulations is necessary since the § 691(c) deduction allows an income tax deduction for the estate tax imposed under §§ 2001 and 2101 on items of IRD, and the QDOT tax, although designated as an estate tax, is imposed under § 2056A(b).

2. Change in Rate of Tax

The QDOT tax is imposed at the highest marginal federal estate tax rate under § 2001 applicable to the estate of the decedent spouse, taking into account the amounts involved in all previous taxable events. It is not clear from the statute what happens if there is a change in the marginal federal estate tax rates or allowable unified credit between the death of the decedent spouse and the time of the taxable event. The statute refers only to "the tax which would have been imposed under § 2001 on the estate of the decedent."[269] However, the legislative history states that the amounts involved in taxable events are "subject to an estate tax based on the decedent's rates and unified credit."[270] Under the regulations, the tax is imposed in accordance with the rate schedule under § 2001 in effect at the date of the decedent spouse's death.[271] Therefore, changes in the unified credit and applicable credit amount, and changes in the top marginal estate tax rates, enacted by the TRA 1997,[272] the Economic Growth and Tax Relief Reconciliation Act of 2001 (EGTRRA),[273] the Tax Relief, Unemployment Insurance Reauthorization, and Job Creation Act of 2010 (TRUIRJCA),[274] and the American Taxpayer Relief Act of 2012 (ATRA)[275] will not affect the QDOT tax imposed on decedents dying during the full phase-in of the increased exclusion amount.

Similarly, the one-year repeal of the federal estate tax in 2010 did not prevent the imposition of QDOT tax on taxable events occurring in 2010 in respect of QDOTs created by decedents dying before 2010. Of course, a decedent whose death occurs in 2010, survived by a non-U.S. citizen spouse, would have no need to create a QDOT or make the QDOT election, thereby eliminating any QDOT tax exposure going forward.

3. Portability and the QDOT tax

a. TRUIRJCA[276] amended § 2010 to incorporate so-called "portability" of estate tax exemptions between spouses. Under portability, a citizen or resident's applicable credit amount is equal to his "basic exclusion amount" (the inflation-adjusted $5 million exclusion) plus, in the case of a surviving spouse, the deceased spousal unused exclusion, or DSUE"[277] Basically, then, provided the first spouse's estate properly elects portability,[278] the surviving spouse is entitled to her applicable credit amount plus any unused applica-

269. § 2056A(b)(2)(A)(i).
270. 1989 House Report, at 1431.
271. Treas. Reg. § 20.2056A-6(d).
272. TRA 1997, § 501.
273. EGTRRA, §§ 511, 521.
274. Pub. L. No. 111-312.
275. Pub. L. No. 112-240.
276. TRUIRJCA § 302(a)1).
277. § 2010(c)(2), (3).
278. *See* § 2010(c)(5)(A); Temp. Treas. Reg. § 20.2010-2T.

ble exclusion amount of the first spouse to die. Such amounts are applied against the surviving spouse's lifetime gifts and taxable estate.

b. Where the surviving spouse is a beneficiary of a QDOT created at the death of the first spouse to die, the fact that any QDOT tax is treated as a tax imposed on the first spouse's estate renders the computation of the first spouse's DSUE tentative, until the QDOT tax, if any, imposed on the QDOT is finally determined. This creates uncertainty as to how much of the DSUE is available to the surviving spouse and when such amount is available. The preamble to the proposed portability regulations[279] outlined certain alternative solutions:

> One proposal is to allow a decedent's DSUE amount to be computed and available to the surviving spouse as of the date of death of the decedent, without regard to the estate tax to be imposed by § 2056A. A second suggestion is to allow an executor of such an estate to elect portability with respect to only a portion of the DSUE amount so that an executor could reserve a portion of the decedent's DSUE amount for the estate tax to be imposed by § 2056A. A third proposal is to allow the decedent's applicable exclusion amount and the initially determined DSUE amount to be applied on a chronological, or first come, first served, basis; that is, by applying the decedent's applicable exclusion amount on the occurrence of a taxable event subject to the estate tax imposed by § 2056A and at the time of a transfer by the surviving spouse subject to the gift tax imposed by § 2501, in each case, to the extent applicable exclusion amount or DSUE amount, respectively, is available at such times.

c. However, the temporary regulations rejected these alternatives, concluding that "[e]ach of the proposals raises issues of fairness, complexity, and administrability. The applicable exclusion amount first and foremost belongs to the decedent. Portability of a DSUE amount allows a surviving spouse to use a decedent's exclusion amount only to the extent it is not used by that decedent. Accordingly, the temporary regulations allow the decedent's estate full availability of the decedent's applicable exclusion amount until such time as the final estate tax liability of the decedent is computed."

d. Under the temporary portability regulations, when property passes for the benefit of a surviving spouse in a QDOT, the DSUE amount of the decedent is computed on the decedent's estate tax return for the purpose of electing portability in the same manner as if the surviving spouse were a U.S. citizen. However, the DSUE amount of the decedent is tentative, and is redetermined upon the occurrence of a taxable event.[280]

279. T.D. 9593 (July 9, 2012).
280. Temp. Treas. Reg. § 20.2010-2T(c)(4).

e. Because the amount of the first spouse's DSUE is tentative, the temporary regulations provide that the surviving spouse may not use the DSUE until the occurrence of the final QDOT distribution or final other event (generally, the death of the surviving spouse or the earlier termination of all QDOTs for that surviving spouse) on which the QDOT tax is imposed.[281] However, the temporary regulations allow the decedent spouse's DSUE amount to be applied to the surviving spouse's taxable gifts made in the year of the surviving spouse's death, or if the terminating event occurs prior to the surviving spouse's death, then in the year of that terminating event and/or any subsequent year during the surviving spouse's life.[282]

Example 8: Husband (H), a U.S. citizen, dies in January 2011 having made no taxable gifts during his lifetime. H's gross estate is $3 million. H's wife (W) is a U.S. resident but not a citizen of the United States and, under H's will, a pecuniary bequest of $2 million passes to a QDOT for the benefit of W. H's executor timely files an estate tax return and makes the QDOT election for the property passing to the QDOT, and H's estate is allowed a marital deduction of $2 million under § 2056(d) for the value of that property. H's taxable estate is $1 million. On H's estate tax return, H's executor computes H's preliminary DSUE amount to be $4 million. No taxable events within the meaning of § 2056A occur during W's lifetime with respect to the QDOT. W makes a taxable gift of $1 million to X in December 2011 and a taxable gift of $1 million to Y in January 2012. W dies in September 2012, not having married again, when the value of the assets of the QDOT is $2.2 million.

H's DSUE amount is re-determined to be $1.8 million (the lesser of the $5 million basic exclusion amount in 2011, or the excess of H's $5 million applicable exclusion amount over $3.2 million (the sum of the $1 million taxable estate augmented by the $2.2 million of QDOT assets)). On W's gift tax return filed for 2011, W cannot apply any DSUE amount to the gift made to X. However, because W's gift to Y was made in the year that W died, W's executor will apply $1 million of H's re-determined DSUE amount to the gift on W's gift tax return filed for 2012. The remaining $800,000 of H's re-determined DSUE amount is included in W's applicable exclusion amount to be used in computing W's estate tax liability.[283]

Comment: Thus, the first spouse's DSUE will be fully available to the surviving spouse once she becomes a U.S. citizen and the QDOT is terminated.

281. *Id.* §§ 20.2010-3T(c)(2), 25.2505-2T(c)(2)(i).
282. *Id.* § 20.2505-2T(c)(2)(i).
283. *Id.* § 20.2505-2T(c)(2)(ii).

4. Tentative Tax Imposed When Decedent Spouse's Federal Estate Tax Not Determined

If, at the date the Form 706-QDT is filed, the federal estate tax imposed on the estate of the decedent spouse has not been finally determined, the QDOT tax imposed on the amount involved in the taxable event is determined based on the *highest* marginal estate tax rate in effect under § 2001 applicable to the decedent spouse's estate.[284] The tax on the decedent spouse's estate will not be finally determined for purposes of the tentative tax if, for example, the statute of limitations on the estate is still open, or if a judicial proceeding to determine the estate tax has not been completed.[285] The legislative history indicates that a tax may be finally determined by a closing agreement executed in accordance with § 7121.[286]

If, after the tax is finally determined on the decedent spouse's estate, a refund is due to the QDOT because the decedent spouse's marginal federal estate tax rate is determined to be lower than that applied to the calculation of the tentative QDOT tax, then the trustee may claim a refund or credit.[287] Such a refund or credit now bears interest; prior to the enactment of OBRA 1989, the statute made no provision for the payment of interest on a claim for refund of the tentative tax.[288] The claim for refund or credit must be filed within one year after the final determination of the federal estate tax on the decedent spouse's estate.[289]

5. Multiple QDOTs

(a) General Rules. OBRA 1989 enacted harsh rules when there is more than one QDOT created with respect to a decedent spouse, unless the decedent's executor designates either an individual who is a U.S. citizen or domestic corporation (the designated return filed) to be responsible for the filing of all returns of the QDOT tax imposed under § 2056A(b)(1) and the payment of any such tax.[290] If such "designated return filer" is appointed, or if such person fails to meet any applicable regulatory requirements, the QDOT tax imposed on the amount involved in any taxable event with respect to the QDOT will be determined by applying the highest marginal federal estate tax rate in effect at the date of the decedent spouse's death. However, there is no mechanism for the redetermination of the federal estate tax imposed as there is when a tentative QDOT tax is imposed under § 2056A(b)(2)(B). In addition, when no such appointment is made, or when the person appointed fails to meet the regulatory requirements, the exemption from the QDOT tax on distributions on account of hardship provided under § 2056A(b)(3)(B) will be unavailable.[291]

284. § 2056A(b)(2)(B)(i).
285. *See* 1988 Conference Report, at 115, n.1.
286. *Id.*
287. § 2056A(b)(2)(B)(ii).
288. *See* § 5033(a)(2) of TAMRA.
289. § 2056A(b)(2)(B)(ii).
290. § 2056A(b)(2)(C).
291. *See* § 2056A(b)(3)(B), discussed *infra* Section VII.D.3.

(b) Designation of Return Filer. The legislative history states Congress's intention that the regulations regarding designation of the person required to file the QDOT tax return and pay the QDOT tax shall ensure collection of the federal estate tax.[292] Under the regulations, the designated return filer must be a U.S. Trustee of the QDOT. If the U.S. Trustee is an individual, the individual must have a tax home (as defined in § 911(d)(3)) in the United States.[293] The designation of the designated return filer must be made on either the decedent spouse's federal estate tax return or on the first Form 706-QDT that is due and is filed by its prescribed date, including extensions.[294] At least sixty days before the due date for filing the Form 706-QDT, the U.S. Trustee(s) of each of the QDOTs must provide to the designated return filer all of the necessary information relating to distributions from their respective QDOTs.[295] The U.S. Trustee of each QDOT submits to the designated return filer a Schedule B to the Form 706-QDT setting out the required information.

Unless the decedent has provided for a successor designated filer, where the designated filer ceases to qualify as a U.S. Trustee or otherwise becomes unable to serve as a designated filer, the remaining trustees of each QDOT must select a qualifying designated successor (who is also a U.S. Trustee) prior to the due date for filing of Form 706-QDT, including extensions, and such selection must be indicated on the Form 706-QDT.[296]

(c) Allocation of QDOT Tax. The regulations provide that the QDOT tax due from each QDOT is to be allocated on a pro rata basis, based on the ratio of the amount that each distribution constituting a taxable event bears to the amount of all such distributions. However, this proration will not apply when a different allocation is required under the terms of the governing instrument or under local law.[297] It is unclear whether a non-pro rata allocation of the taxes is permissible when the governing instrument merely authorizes, but does not require, a different allocation of the tax. There appears to be no reason why the authorization of a non-pro rata allocation of any QDOT tax should not be respected.

D. Distributions Exempt from Tax

1. Distributions of Income

(a) Background and General Rules. Distributions of income from a QDOT to the noncitizen surviving spouse are not subject to the QDOT tax imposed under § 2056A(b)(1).[298] For purposes of the QDOT provisions, the term "income" has

292. 1989 House Report, at 1432–33.
293. *Id.* Treas. Reg. § 20.2056A-9. *See supra* Section III.C.1.
294. Treas. Reg. § 20.2056A-9.
295. *Id.*
296. *Id.*
297. *Id.*
298. § 2056A(b)(3)(A).

the same meaning as it has in § 643(b), subject to any regulatory modifications.[299] Section 643(b) states that for purposes of subchapter J of the Code, income is determined in accordance with the terms of the governing trust instrument and applicable local law. The Code allows the trustee, acting in good faith, to allocate certain types of income, including extraordinary dividends or taxable stock dividends, to trust corpus if, under local law or the trust instrument, such items would not be considered income.[300]

Prior to OBRA 1989, § 2056A(c)(2) did not explicitly provide the Secretary with authority to modify the definition of income for purposes of the QDOT provisions. The legislative history states:

> The Secretary of the Treasury is granted regulatory authority to modify the definition of income for purposes of determining the amount subject to the tax. The committee intends that such regulations define income so as to prevent avoidance of the estate tax. Thus, the characterization of income and corpus contained in the governing instrument would not control for purposes of the estate tax. For example, capital gain generally would not be treated as income for purposes of the estate tax on QDOTs, regardless of the characterization contained in the trust instrument.[301]

Under the prior regulations, "income" refers to income as defined in § 643(b), except that income does not include capital gains or other items that would be allocated to corpus under applicable local law governing the administration of trusts without regard to any specific trust provision to the contrary.[302] Where there is no statutory or case law regarding the allocation of items of income under the law governing the administration of the QDOT, the regulations take the position that the allocation must be governed by general principles of law (including but not limited to any uniform state acts such as the Uniform Principal and Income Act, or any restatement of applicable law).

(b) New § 643 Regulations. For tax years ending after January 2, 2004, the broad definition of income found in the revised § 643 regulations[303] applies and provides greater flexibility for QDOT beneficiaries. Specifically, the regulations provide that an allocation of amounts between income and principal pursuant to applicable local law will be respected if local law provides for a reasonable apportionment between income and remainder beneficiaries of the total return of the trust for the year, including ordinary income, tax-exempt income, capital gains, and appreciation. These provisions take one of two forms: a "unitrust provision," under which

---

299. *See* §§ 2056A(c)(2), 2056A(e).

300. § 643(b); Treas. Reg. § 1.643(b)-1.

301. 1989 House Report, at 1432.

302. Treas. Reg. § 20.2056A-5(c)(2). This would appear to include capital gains incurred on reinvested income.

303. T.D. 9102.

a state statute provides that income is a unitrust amount of no less than 3 percent and no more than 5 percent of the fair market value of the trust assets, and an "adjustment provision," under which a state statute permits the trustee to make adjustments between income and principal to fulfill the trustee's duty of impartiality between income and remainder beneficiaries.[304]

The final regulations also amended the provision of Treas. Reg. § 20.2056A-5 by adding the following provision:

> However, distributions made to the surviving spouse as the income beneficiary in conformance with applicable local law that defines the term income as a unitrust amount (or permits a right to income to be satisfied by such an amount), or that permits the trustee to adjust between principal and income to fulfill the trustee's duty of impartiality between income and principal beneficiaries, will be considered distributions of trust income if applicable local law provides for a reasonable apportionment between the income and remainder beneficiaries of the total return of the trust and meets the requirements of § 1.643(b)-1 of this chapter.[305]

The effect of the changes is that if a QDOT is administered in accordance with the law of a state that has adopted the Uniform Principal and Income Act[306] or under which the unitrust or adjustment provisions exist under state statute or by decisional law, the characterization of distributions in excess of the traditional measures of income will be respected for purposes of determining the portion of such distribution subject to the QDOT tax. For example, the adoption of a 5 percent unitrust payment will allow distributions to be classified as "income" for purposes of imposition of the QDOT tax, even though a portion of the distribution will include capital gains otherwise subject to the tax.

> ***Comment:*** The flexibility incorporated into the revised income regulations may allow significantly larger distributions to be made in the noncitizen spouse, when permitted under state law. Careful drafting and state forum shopping will be required to take advantage of the provisions.

2. Treatment of Income in Respect of a Decedent

Unless the IRS provides guidance to the contrary, income does not include items of income in respect of a decedent (IRD) as defined in § 691.[307] However, where the QDOT is designated by the decedent as a beneficiary of a pension or profit sharing plan or individual retirement account or annuity, the proceeds of which are payable to the QDOT in the form of an annuity, any payments received by the QDOT may be allocated between income and corpus, in accordance with the pro-

---

304. Treas. Reg. § 1.643(b)-1.
305. *Id.* § 20.02056A-5(c)(2).
306. 9 U.L.A. 45 (2002).
307. *Id.*

visions of Treas. Reg. § 20.2056A-4(c) regarding the determination of the corpus and income portions of each annuity payment.[308]

3. Principal Distributions on Account of Hardship

Distributions of trust corpus to the surviving spouse on account of "hardship" are also exempted from imposition of the QDOT tax.[309] Distributions made on account of hardship, although free from the QDOT tax, must be reported on Form 706-QDT even if it is the only distribution that occurred during the filing period.[310]

The exemption from the QDOT tax for distributions on account of hardship may be unavailable if there is more than one QDOT in existence with respect to a decedent spouse. Section 2056A(b)(2)(C) provides that where there is more than one QDOT in existence with respect to any decedent, the decedent spouse's executor must designate a person who is a U.S. citizen or a domestic corporation to be responsible for filing all returns and paying all QDOT Taxes due. In addition, the designated return filer must meet any requirements that may be prescribed in regulations. If no designated return filer is designated, or if the person fails to meet the regulatory requirements, the exemption from the QDOT tax for distributions on account of hardship will be unavailable.

There is no definition of "hardship" provided either in the statute or in the legislative history or in the instructions to Form 706-QDT. The regulations generally adopt a definition of "hardship" set out in Treas. Reg. § 1.401(k)-1(d)(2)(i) (involving permissible distributions from certain deferred compensation plans). Specifically, a distribution of principal is made on account of hardship if the distribution is made to the spouse from the QDOT in response to an immediate and substantial financial need relating to the spouse's health, maintenance, education, or support, or the health, maintenance, education, or support of any person to whom the surviving spouse is legally obligated to support. A distribution is not considered made on account of hardship if the amount distributed may be obtained from other sources that are reasonably available to the surviving spouse, e.g., the sale by the surviving spouse of personally owned, publicly traded stock or the cashing in of a certificate of deposit owned by the surviving spouse. For purposes of the application of the hardship exemption, assets such as a closely held business interest, real estate, or tangible personal property are not considered sources that are reasonably available to the surviving spouse.[311]

It is worth noting that legislation was introduced to expand the hardship exemption.[312] Under this proposal, annual distributions of trust principal of up to $100,000, reduced by the amount of income distributed to the surviving spouse

308. *Id.*

309. § 2056A(b)(3)(B).

310. *See* Treas. Reg. § 20.2056A-5(c)(1); Announcement 91-58, 1991-15 I.R.B. 39 (Apr. 15, 1991). *See infra* Section VII.E.3 for discussion of return filing requirements.

311. Treas. Reg. § 20.2056A-5(c)(1).

312. *See* H.R. 3299, 101st Cong. (1989).

during that year, could be made to a noncitizen spouse free of the QDOT tax.[313] This provision would have placed individuals who were not able to take advantage of the $100,000 annual exclusion for gifts permitted under § 2523(i) on a more equal basis with those who were able to make such gifts. In addition, as proposed under H.R. 3299, trust distributions made on behalf of the noncitizen spouse to any person for medical care of the spouse were not subject to the QDOT tax and were excluded in calculating the $100,000 limit on principal distributions.[314] The Senate Finance Committee stripped these two provisions and adopted the exclusion for hardship distributions only.[315] The failure to provide a certain level of tax-free principal distributions in the statute is clearly unfair to noncitizen surviving spouses of moderate wealth who are more likely to have to invade trust corpus for their support than wealthy noncitizen surviving spouses whose larger income stream will decrease or eliminate the need for corpus distributions.

4. Additional Distributions and Transactions Not Giving Rise to QDOT Tax

The regulations describe several additional distributions and transactions that do not require the imposition of the QDOT tax. This list is not intended to be exclusive.[316]

a. Payments for ordinary and necessary expenses of the QDOT, including bond premiums and letter of credit fees incurred if the Bond Requirement or Letter of Credit Requirement is utilized by the U.S. Trustee.
b. Payments to applicable governmental authorities for income tax or any other applicable tax imposed on the QDOT (other than a payment of the QDOT tax due on the occurrence of a taxable event). This provision allows for the QDOT tax-free payment of all income taxes—federal, state, local, and foreign—imposed on the QDOT.

Note that this provision applies when the QDOT tax imposed on the trust. When the QDOT is funded by an assignment of property by the surviving spouse, this provision will not apply if and to the extent that the QDOT is a grantor trust, because the tax liability falls on the spouse/grantor, and not the QDOT.[317]

On the other hand, the provision will likely apply if an item of IRD is made payable to the QDOT by the decedent spouse; in such a situation, all income taxes imposed on the QDOT should be payable with QDOT assets and not be subject to the QDOT tax.

c. Dispositions of trust assets by the trustees (such as sales, exchanges, or pledging as collateral) for full and adequate consideration in money or money's worth.

---

313. H.R. 3299, § 7815(d)(7)(B).
314. *Id.*
315. *See* S. 1750, 101st Cong., 1st Sess. § 6815(d)(7)(B) (1989).
316. Treas. Reg. § 20.2056A-5(c)(3).
317. *See* § 671.

d. In accordance with the provisions of § 2056A(b)(15), amounts paid from the QDOT to reimburse the surviving spouse for federal income taxes on any item of income of the QDOT to which the surviving spouse is not entitled under the terms of the trust. These distributions include, but under the regulations are not limited to:
   (1) amounts paid from the QDOT to reimburse the spouse for income taxes paid by the spouse (either by actual payment or through withholding) with respect to amounts received from a nonassignable annuity or other arrangement that are transferred by the spouse to a QDOT pursuant to Treas. Reg. § 20.2056A-4(c)(3); and
   (2) income taxes paid by the spouse (either by actual payment or withholding) with respect to amounts received in a lump sum distribution from a qualified plan if the lump sum distribution is then assigned by the surviving spouse to a QDOT.

The amount of the tax eligible for reimbursement under this provision is the difference between the actual income tax liability of the spouse and the spouse's income tax liability determined as if the item had not been included in the spouse's gross estate in the applicable tax year.[318] The IRS has ruled, however, that no § 2056A(b)(15) QDOT tax reimbursement will be allowed for amounts paid in connection with income earned on the assets transferred to the QDOT between the date of the decedent spouse's death and the transfer to the QDOT.[319]

E. Administrative Provisions

1. Liability for Tax

Each trustee of a QDOT is personally liable for the amount of any QDOT tax under rules similar to those in § 2204.[320] Under § 2204(b), a fiduciary other than an executor may be discharged from personal liability for taxes due for which he is personally liable by making a proper application to the Secretary of the Treasury and requesting a determination of the amount of any federal estate tax due for which a fiduciary is personally liable. After payment of any such tax and posting of a bond, if appropriate, the fiduciary is discharged from personal liability for any deficiency subsequently determined with respect to such tax.

2. Imposition of Withholding Requirement on Payors of Certain Annuities

The personal liability of the QDOT trustee creates a special problem with respect to an annuity or other payment treated as a QDOT and therefore not actually held in trust. Section 2056A(e) provides broad authority to issue regulations "necessary or appropriate to carry out the purposes of" § 2056A. With regard to joint and survivor annuities, the legislative history expands on this idea by noting that

318. Treas. Reg. § 20.2056A-5(c)(3)(iv) (last sentence).
319. *See* I.R.S. Priv. Ltr. Rul. 9235015 (May 23, 1997).
320. § 2056A(b)(6).

such annuities may be treated as a QDOT without actually being assigned to such a trust if the payor of the annuity withholds an amount equal to the distribution tax and meets other conditions designed to ensure collection of the tax.[321] The payor of the annuity is thus required to become a withholding agent with respect to the annuity. This may impose a significant administrative burden on private corporations and organizations providing such benefits.

3. QDOT Return Filing Requirements—Form 706-QDT

Form 706-QDT (U.S. Estate Tax Return for Qualified Domestic Trusts) is the form for making a return of taxable events and payment of the QDOT tax.

(a) Who Must File Form 706-QDT. The trustee is responsible for filing the Form 706-QDT and paying the QDOT tax if the surviving spouse is a beneficiary of only one QDOT, or the surviving spouse is the beneficiary of more than one QDOT but the decedent spouse's executor failed to appoint a designated return filer. If the surviving spouse is the beneficiary of more than one QDOT from a single decedent and that decedent has elected a designated return filer, the designated return filer is liable for filing the return and paying the QDOT tax, but the trustee must still complete Schedule B of the Form.

(b) Summary of Filing Instructions

1. The Form 706-QDT requests identifying information about the trustees, the designated return filer (if any), the surviving spouse, and the decedent spouse, as well as information about the federal estate tax return filed by the decedent spouse's estate.
2. Elections regarding alternate valuation, special use valuation, payment of estate tax in installments and the election to cease application of the QDOT tax when the surviving spouse becomes a citizen of the United States are all made on the Form 706-QDT.
3. The trustee of each QDOT in existence for the benefit of the surviving spouse must complete Schedule B. The trustee must state the amount of taxable distributions from that QDOT in prior years and describe in detail taxable distributions and distributions on account of hardship (even though not subject to the QDOT tax) during the current year.
4. If Form 706-QDT is being filed on account of the death of the surviving spouse or because the QDOT ceased to qualify as a QDOT during the year, the Form requires a detailed description of the property remaining in the QDOT and the property qualifying for the marital and charitable distributions.
5. If there is only one QDOT in existence for the surviving spouse, the information on Schedule B is used to determine the QDOT tax due for the year.

321. 1989 House Report, at 1433.

6. If there is more than one QDOT in existence for the surviving spouse, the trustees submit the information for all Schedule B's to the designated return filer, who summarizes all of the taxable events for all QDOTs during the year on Schedule A. This information is then used to determine the QDOT tax due for the year.

4. Due Date for Payment of Federal Estate Tax

The QDOT tax is due on the fifteenth day of the fourth month following the year in which the taxable event occurs.[322] The due date for any QDOT tax otherwise due on April 15, 1990, was extended indefinitely, due to the unavailability of Form 706-QDT.[323]

Form 706-QDT was originally issued with a date of March 1991. The IRS announced that the reporting date for taxable events occurring after November 10, 1988, and before January 1, 1991, would be September 16, 1991. For taxable events in years beginning after December 31, 1990, Form 706-QDT will be due by April 15 of the year following the year in which the taxable event occurred.[324]

Form 706-QDT is also used to report distributions of principal to a spouse on account of "hardship," even though the distributions are not subject to the QDOT tax and even though no other taxable event occurred during the tax year.[325] The QDOT tax on property held in the QDOT at the surviving spouse's death is due with the spouse's federal estate tax return, nine months from the date of death of the surviving spouse.[326]

QDOT tax due on any distributions that occur in the year of the surviving spouse's death are also due with the spouse's federal estate tax return.[327]

5. Extensions and Time to File Form 706-QDT and Pay the QDOT Tax

(a) Filing Extensions. An extension of not more than six months may be obtained for the filing of Form 706-QDT under § 6081(a) if the conditions specified in that section are satisfied.[328]

(b) Tax Payment Extensions. Pursuant to §§ 2056A(b)(10)(C) and 6161(a)(2), upon a showing of reasonable cause, the IRS may grant an extension of time for a reasonable period beyond the due date to pay any part of the QDOT tax that is imposed upon the surviving spouse's death and shown on the final Form 706-QDT, or any part of any installments of the tax under § 6166 (including any part of a deficiency prorated to any installment under that section). The extension may be granted for a reasonable period of time, not to exceed ten years from the date

322. § 2056A(b)(5)(A); Treas. Reg. § 20.2056A-11(a).
323. Announcement 90-39, 1990-12 I.R.B. 26 (Mar. 19, 1990).
324. Announcement 91-58, 1991-15 I.R.B. 39 (Apr. 15, 1991).
325. *Id.*; Treas. Reg. § 20.2056A-5(c).
326. § 2056A(b)(5)(B); Treas. Reg. § 20.2056A-11(b).
327. § 2056A(b)(5)(A).
328. Treas. Reg. §§ 20.2056A-11(a), (b).

prescribed for payment of the tax (or, in the case of an installment or part of a deficiency prorated to an installment, if later, not beyond the date that is twelve months after the due date for the last installment), by the District Director or the Director of the service center where the Form 706-QDT is filed.[329]

An extension of time beyond the due date to pay any part of the QDOT tax imposed on lifetime distributions under § 2056A(b)(1)(A), or imposed at the death of the surviving spouse under § 2056A(b)(1)(B), may be granted for a reasonable period of time, not to exceed six months (twelve months in the case of the QDOT tax imposed under § 2056A(b)(1)(B) at the surviving spouse's death), by the District Director or the Director of the service center where the Form 706-QDT is filed.[330]

6. Lien for QDOT Tax Due

Section 6324(a)(1) provides that unless paid in full sooner, or unless unenforceable by application of the statute of limitations, the federal estate tax imposed by chapter 11 of the Code shall be a lien upon the gross estate of the decedent for ten years from the date of death. No such lien shall apply to that part of the gross estate used to pay charges against the estate or expenses of administration of the estate that are allowed by any court having jurisdiction over the estate.

Any federal estate tax imposed on a QDOT under § 2056A(b)(1) is, for purposes of § 6324, treated as a federal estate tax imposed under chapter 11 with respect to a decedent dying on the date of the taxable event. In addition, the property subject to the taxable event shall be treated as the gross estate of such decedent.[331]

7. Liability for QDOT Tax

Under § 2056A(b)(6), each trustee (and not solely the U.S. Trustee(s)) of a QDOT is personally liable for the amount of the QDOT tax imposed in the case of any taxable event under § 2056A(b)(1). Each trustee is personally liable for the QDOT tax imposed on a taxable event with respect to that trustee's QDOT, but is not personally liable for any QDOT tax imposed on taxable events involving other QDOTs.[332] However, the assets of any QDOT are subject to collection for any QDOT tax resulting from a taxable event with respect to any other QDOT created by the same decedent. The trustee may also be personally liable as a withholding agent under § 1461 or other applicable provisions of the Code.[333]

8. Basis of Property Distributed from a QDOT

The provisions of § 1015, relating to the basis of property acquired by gift, are applied to determine the basis of property distributed in a taxable distribution

329. *Id.* § 20.2056A-11(c)(1).
330. *Id.* § 20.2056A-11(c)(2).
331. § 2056A(b)(8).
332. Treas. Reg. § 20.2056A-11(d).
333. *Id.*

from a QDOT. Section 1015(a) provides generally that the donee of a gift receives the lower of the donor's basis in the gifted property or the fair market value of the property. Section 1015(d) allows the basis of gifted property to be increased by that portion of the federal gift tax paid that is attributable to the appreciation in the gifted property immediately prior to the gift.

Under § 2056A(b)(13) and Treas. Reg. § 20.2056A-12, distributions from a QDOT during the life of the surviving spouse that give rise to a federal estate tax are treated as transfers by gifts, and the QDOT tax is treated as federal gift tax paid. Thus, the basis of the distributed property is increased (but not above fair market value) by the amount of the QDOT tax allocable to the appreciation in the value of the distributed property after the decedent's death.[334] Because the property held in a QDOT is treated as property passing from the decedent spouse, the property will have already received a basis equal to its value at the decedent's date of death.[335] Thus, there will be only a small benefit, in the first years after the decedent's death, from the step-up in basis for the QDOT tax paid.

In accordance with the provisions of § 2056A(b)(13), the regulations provide that in the case of any distribution from a QDOT on which the QDOT tax is imposed under § 2056A(b)(1)(A) on lifetime distributions to the surviving spouse, the distribution is treated as a transfer by gift for purposes of § 1015, and any QDOT tax paid is treated as a gift tax.[336] The regulations under § 1015 provide rules to implement this basis adjustment. Under these rules, any distribution from a QDOT during the noncitizen surviving spouse's lifetime on which the QDOT tax is imposed is treated as a transfer by gift, and any QDOT tax paid on the distribution is treated as a gift tax for purposes of applying the basis adjustment under § 1015(d)(6).[337]

Section 1015(d)(6) provides that the basis of gifted property in the hands of the donee is increased in an amount (not in excess of the amount of gift tax paid) that bears the same ratio to the amount of gift tax paid on the transfer as the net appreciation in value of the gift (that is, the amount by which the fair market value of the property exceeds the donor's adjusted basis immediately before the gift) bears to the amount of the gift.

> ***Example 9:*** In 1994, X, who has exhausted his unified credit, makes a gift to Y, an unrelated third party, of a parcel of real estate having a value for gift tax purposes of $100,000. X's adjusted basis in the real estate immediately before making the gift was $70,000. X also makes a gift the same year to Z, an unrelated third party, of a painting with a value for gift tax purposes of $70,000. X files a timely gift tax return with respect to which X paid gift tax in the amount of $55,500, computed as follows:

334. 1989 House Report, at 1433; Treas. Reg. § 1.1015-5(c)(1).
335. § 1014(a).
336. Treas. Reg. § 20.2056A-12.
337. *Id.* § 1.1015-5(c)(4).

Value of real estate given to Y	$ 100,000
Less: Annual exclusion	$_10,000
Included amount of gift (C)	$ 90,000
Value of painting given to Z	$ 70,000
Less: annual exclusion	$ 10,000
Included amount of gift	$ 60,000
Total included gifts (D)	$ 150,000
Total gift tax liability for gifts (B)	$ 55,500

In determining the gift tax paid with respect to the real estate given to Y, the amount of gift tax paid with respect to the gift of $100,000 is determined as follows:

__$90,000 (C)
$150,0000 (D) X $55,500 (B) = $33,300

The amount by which Y's basis in the real property is increased is determined as follows:

$30,000 (net appreciation) X $33,300 = $11,100
$90,000 (amount of gift)
Y's basis in the real property is $70,000 plus $11,100, or $81,100.[338]

Example 10: X dies, survived by his spouse, Y, who is not a U.S. citizen. In order to obtain the marital deduction for property passing to X's spouse, X established a QDOT in X's will. Subsequently, the trustee of the QDOT makes a distribution of principal from the QDOT in the form of shares of stock having a value of $70,000 and a basis of $50,000. The distribution is not made on account of hardship. No previous taxable distributions from the QDOT have been made. A QDOT tax is imposed and paid in the amount of $38,500 on the distribution. The amount by which Y's basis in the shares of stock is increased is determined as follows:

$20,000 (net appreciation)__ X $38,500 = $11,000
$70,000 (amount of distribution)
Y's basis in the stock is $50,000 plus $11,000, or $61,000.[339]

F. Cessation of Imposition of the QDOT Estate Tax: The Surviving Spouse Becomes a United States Citizen

1. Surviving Spouse Is a U.S. Resident

If the surviving spouse becomes a U.S. citizen after the decedent spouse's federal estate tax return is made, and the surviving spouse was a U.S. resident at the date of the decedent spouse's death and at all times thereafter, the QDOT tax is no

338. *Id.* § 1.1015-5(c)(5), Example 1.
339. *Id.* § 1.1015-5(c)(5), Example 2.

longer imposed on distributions to the spouse is no longer imposed, and there will be no federal estate tax imposed under § 2056A(b)(1)(B) at the death of the surviving spouse.[340] For purposes of qualifying for this provision, "residency" is defined by reference to Treas. Reg. § 20.0–1(b)(1).[341]

The U.S. Trustee(s) of the QDOT must notify the IRS and certify in writing that the surviving spouse has become a U.S. citizen.[342] Notice is to be made by filing a final Form 706-QDT on or before April 15 of the year following the year in which the surviving spouse becomes a U.S. citizen, unless an extension of time for filing is granted under § 6081.[343] An extension of time within which to file the required notice should be available under Treas. Reg. § 301.9100.[344]

2. Surviving Spouse Is Not a United States Resident

If the surviving spouse is not a U.S. resident[345] at all times following the death of the decedent spouse, different rules apply, depending on whether or not a QDOT tax was imposed on distributions from the QDOT that was made prior to the date on which the surviving spouse attained U.S. citizenship.

(a) QDOT Tax Had Not Been Imposed. If, prior to the surviving spouse's becoming a U.S. citizen, no QDOT tax had been imposed on any QDOT distribution, then, upon attaining citizenship, the QDOT tax will not be imposed on amounts involved in any taxable event, and no QDOT tax will be imposed upon the death of the surviving spouse.[346]

(b) QDOT Tax Had Been Imposed. If, however, a QDOT tax had been imposed on distributions from a QDOT, then to end application of the QDOT tax, the surviving spouse must elect to treat such distributions as taxable gifts for purposes of (1) the amount of prior taxable gifts in determining the estate tax imposed under § 2001 at the surviving spouse's death[347] and (2) calculating the amount of taxable gifts made by the surviving spouse in the year he attains U.S. citizenship and in

340. § 2056A(b)(12)(A); Treas. Reg. § 20.2056A-10(a)(1). The cessation of the imposition of the QDOT tax has no effect on the other marital trust provisions of §§ 2056(a) and (b). *See* I.R.S. Priv. Ltr. Ruls. 9848007 (July 27, 1998), 9826028 (Mar. 26, 1998), 9418014 (Feb. 2, 1994).

341. *See* Treas. Reg. § 20.2056A-1(b).

342. *Id.* § 20.2056A-10(a)(2).

343. *Id.* In Priv. Ltr. Rul. 9021037 (Feb. 23, 1990), the IRS arguably stated that the rule in § 2056A(b)(12)(A) applied only if the surviving spouse was a U.S. resident at all times after the decedent's death and that no QDOT tax had been imposed prior to the surviving spouse's having attained U.S. citizenship. This is an incorrect reading of the provisions of § 2056A (b)(12). In informal discussions with the IRS at the time the ruling was released, it was acknowledged that the requirements of §§ 2056A(b)(12)(A), (B), and (C) are alternate conditions and not conjunctive ones. Therefore, the statement referred to in Priv. Ltr. Rul. 9021037 is incorrect and should not appear in subsequent rulings.

344. *See infra* Section XII.B.7.d.

345. *See* Treas. Reg. § 20.2056A-1(b).

346. § 2056A(b)(12)(B); Treas. Reg. § 20.2056A-10(a)(1).

347. *See* § 2056A(b)(12)(C)(i)(I).

all future years.[348] In addition, the surviving spouse must elect to have his unified credit reduced for purposes of determining the surviving spouse's future federal gift and estate tax liability by the amount of the *decedent spouse's* unified credit allowed against such distributions.[349]

These elections are made on Line 4 of part II of Form 706-QDT filed on or before April 15 of the year following the year in which the surviving spouse becomes a citizen (unless an extension of time for filing is granted under § 6081) and attaching notification of the election to the return.[350] Section 9100 relief may be available to make the requisite elections and notification if they are not timely filed.

VIII. Death of the Noncitizen Surviving Spouse

A. Credit for Federal Estate Tax Paid

The death of the surviving spouse is a taxable event under § 2056A(b)(9), and the property remaining in the QDOT at that time is subject to federal estate tax as if it were included in the estate of the decedent spouse.[351] The property remaining in the QDOT at the death of the surviving spouse may also be included in his or her estate under § 2001 (if the surviving spouse was a U.S. resident at death) or § 2101 (if the surviving spouse was a nonresident alien). To avoid subjecting the property remaining in the QDOT to a double tax, Congress extended the protection of § 2013 to the estate of the surviving spouse.[352]

1. Calculating the § 2013 Credit

Section 2056(d)(3) provides that where (1) property passes to the surviving spouse from the decedent spouse, (2) such property would, but for the disallowance of § 2056(d), be eligible for the marital deduction from the decedent spouse's estate, and (3) the surviving spouse dies and his or her estate is subject to U.S. estate tax, then any federal estate tax paid, or treated as paid, under § 2056A(b)(7) by the decedent spouse with respect to such property shall be allowed as a credit under § 2013 to the estate of the surviving spouse. In calculating the credit, the percentage reductions in the available credit under § 2013(a) for elapsed time are disregarded.

Subject to certain adjustments, the credit allowed under § 2013(a) is the lesser of (1) the amount of federal estate tax attributable to the transferred property

348. § 2056A(b)(12)(C)(i)(II); Treas. Reg. § 20.2056A-10(b)(1). *See also* 1989 House Report, 1431–32.

349. § 2056A(b)(12)(C)(ii); Treas. Reg. § 20.2056A-10(b)(2).

350. Treas. Reg. § 20.2056A-10(b)(3).

351. *See* §§ 2056A(b)(1)(B) and 2056A(b)(2)(A).

352. *See also* I.R.S. Priv. Ltr. Rul. 9003030 (Oct. 24, 1989) ("The amount of estate tax imposed under § 2056A(b)(1)(A) is the tax that would have been imposed under § 2001 on the estate of [the decedent spouse] had the property been included in [the decedent spouse's] taxable estate").

in the decedent-transferor's estate (the First Limitation),[353] and (2) the amount of the federal estate tax attributable to the transferred property in the surviving spouse's estate (the Second Limitation).[354]

As originally enacted in TAMRA, in calculating the allowable credit, the net value of the property passing from the decedent spouse was reduced by the amount of the marital deduction allowed under § 2056, thereby reducing the amount of the credit available. Section 7815(d)(6)(B) of OBRA 1989 corrected the problem by providing in § 2056(d)(3) (flush language) that the credit is to be determined without deducting from the value of the property passing to the surviving spouse the value of the property that qualified for the marital deduction. The regulations take a position consistent with this change.[355]

In addition, a prerequisite to the credit under TAMRA was that the surviving spouse's estate be subject to the tax imposed under § 2001. Section 7815(d)(6)(A) of OBRA 1989 amended § 2056(d)(3) to require the estate of the surviving spouse to be subject to the tax imposed by "this Chapter," that is, chapter 11 of the Code, thereby making the credit available when the surviving spouse is a nonresident alien subject to estate tax under § 2101.

2. Application of § 2013 under the Regulations

(a) Property Subject to QDOT Election. Section 2056(d)(3) provides special rules for computing the § 2013 credit allowed with respect to property subject to a QDOT election. The amount of the credit is determined under § 2013 and the regulations thereunder, except that the First Limitation[356] is the amount of the QDOT tax imposed on distributions during the spouse's life and on the value of the trust corpus on the spouse's death.[357] In addition, in computing the Second Limitation[358] the value of the property transferred to the decedent[359] is deemed to be the value of the QDOT assets on the date of the surviving spouse's death, without reduction by the QDOT tax imposed at the time of the surviving spouse's death.[360]

The amount of the credit is determined without regard to the percentage limitations contained in § 2013(a).[361]

(b) Property Not Subject to QDOT Election. If (1) property includable in a decedent's gross estate passes to a noncitizen surviving spouse (the transferee), (2) no marital deduction is allowed to the decedent's estate for the property under § 2056(a) solely because the requirements of § 2056(d)(2) are not satisfied, and

353. § 2013(b); Treas. Reg. § 20.2013-2.
354. § 2013(c); Treas. Reg. § 20.2013-3.
355. *See* Treas. Reg. § 20.2056A-7(a).
356. § 2013(b) and Treas. Reg. §§ 20.2013-1(b), 20.2013-2.
357. Treas. Reg. § 20.2056A-7(a)(1).
358. *See* § 2013(c) and Treas. Reg. § 20.2013-3.
359. *See* § 2013(d) and Treas. Reg. § 20.2013-(4).
360. Treas. Reg. § 20.2056A-7(a)(2).
361. *Id.* § 20.2056A-7(a)(3).

(3) the surviving (transferee) spouse dies with an estate that is subject to tax under §§ 2001 or 2101, as the case may be, then any credit for tax on prior transfers allowable to the estate of the transferee spouse under § 2013 with respect to such property is determined in accordance with the rules of § 2013 and the regulations thereunder, except that the amount of the credit is determined without regard to the percentage limitations contained in § 2013(a).[362]

3. Efficiency of Credit

The application of the First Limitation and the Second Limitation on the allowance of the credit may cause the credit to fall short of its purpose of making the family unit whole.

With respect to the First Limitation, the allowance of the credit for state death taxes paid under § 2011 may reduce the size of the credit for previously taxed property available to the estate of the noncitizen surviving spouse under § 2056(d)(3). As noted above, the provisions of § 2056(d)(3) are intended to avoid the double taxation caused by the fact that property remaining in the QDOT at the death of the surviving spouse will not only be subject to federal estate tax as if it were included in the estate of the first spouse to die, but may also be subject to federal estate tax in the estate of the noncitizen surviving spouse under the normal marital deduction rules. However, the availability of the state death tax credit to the estate of the first spouse to die will effectively reduce the federal estate tax imposed on the estate of the first spouse to die. Therefore, because § 2013 credits the tax imposed under § 2001 on the transferee spouse's estate with all or a part of the federal estate tax paid by the transferor spouse's estate, the reduction in the federal estate treated as being paid by the first spouse to die because of the application of the state death tax credit will reduce the amount of the § 2013 credit available to the estate of the surviving spouse under § 2056(d)(3).

The effect of the Second Limitation on the credit is to decrease the maximum allowable § 2013 credit when the surviving spouse has fewer assets in his or her estate than the decedent-transferor spouse.

B. Allowance of Certain Tax Benefits

1. Disallowance Prior to OBRA 1989

As originally enacted in TAMRA, many federal estate tax benefits available in computing the federal estate tax liability of a decedent who is a U.S. citizen or resident were not allowed to a noncitizen surviving spouse. This was so because the QDOT tax imposed on QDOT assets at the death of the surviving spouse is treated as a tax on the estate of the decedent spouse.[363] In Private Letter Ruling 8942056 (July 25, 1989), for example, X created a QDOT under his will for the benefit of his spouse, Y. The QDOT qualified as a QTIP trust. Upon the death of Y, the property remaining in the QDOT was to be distributed to a § 501(c)(3) private foundation.

362. *Id.* § 20.2056A-7(b).
363. § 2056A(b)(7).

The taxpayer requested a ruling that Y's estate would be allowed a federal estate tax charitable deduction for the assets passing to the foundation. The IRS ruled that because the QDOT tax imposed on the assets remaining in the QDOT at the death of Y was treated as a tax imposed on X's estate, no federal estate tax charitable deduction would be allowed at Y's death.

2. Benefits Allowed

Section 7815(d)(9) of OBRA 1989 enacted § 2056A(b)(10) to allow certain benefits for purposes of the QDOT tax imposed at the death of the surviving spouse. The benefits are available if property with respect to which the benefits are claimed is includable in the estate of the surviving spouse (or would have been had the surviving spouse been a U.S. citizen or resident) and the requirements for those benefits were met, thereby ensuring that those benefits were allowable to the estate of the surviving spouse or would have been allowable if the surviving spouse were a U.S. citizen or resident at his death.[364]

3. Presumption of Residency

With regard to § 2056A(b)(10)(A), the regulations presume that the noncitizen spouse is a U.S. resident for purposes of determining whether the QDOT property is includable in the spouse's gross estate and for purposes of determining whether any of the credits, deductions, or deferral provisions are allowable with respect to the QDOT property to the estate of the spouse.[365]

The benefits allowable for purposes of determining the QDOT tax imposed at the death of the noncitizen spouse include those provided under §§ 2032 (alternate valuation date), 2032A (special use valuation), 2055 (federal estate tax charitable deduction), 2056 (federal estate tax marital deduction), and 6166 (payment of federal estate tax in installments), as well as § 2011 (credit for state death taxes) and 2014 (credit for foreign death taxes).[366] In addition, if the requirements of § 2056A(b)(10)(A) are met, and the estate of the surviving spouse meets the requirements of § 303, the QDOT will be entitled to redemption and capital gains treatment on the redemption of certain stock in payment of federal estate tax in accordance with § 303. In calculating the amount of redemptions for which the capital gains treatment afforded by that section is available, the QDOT tax is treated as federal estate tax payable with respect to the noncitizen spouse.[367]

4. Special Rule for Trusts Described in § 2056(b)(8)

In the case of a QDOT in which the spouse's interest qualifies for a marital deduction under § 2056(b)(8), the provisions of § 2056A(b)(10)(A) apply in determining

364. *See also* Treas. Reg. § 20.2056A-6(c)(1).

365. *Id.* § 20.2056A-6(c)(2).

366. § 2056A(b)(10)(A) (as amended by § 11702(g)(4) of OBRA 1990). Note that § 2056A(b)(10)(A) was not amended as part of TRA 1997. Therefore, it would appear that the benefits of §§ 2057 (qualified family owned business exclusion) and 2031(c) (qualified conservation easement) would be unavailable.

367. § 2056A(b)(10)(B).

the allowance of a charitable deduction in computing the deferred estate tax, notwithstanding that the QDOT is not includable in the spouse's gross estate.[368]

5. Credit for State and Foreign Death Taxes

In order for a credit to be finally allowed for either state death taxes under § 2011 or foreign death taxes under § 2014, the state or foreign jurisdiction must actually impose death taxes on the property subject to the QDOT tax and those taxes must actually be paid to the state or foreign jurisdiction. The credit allowable cannot exceed the state or foreign death taxes previously paid at the time of death of the first decedent, and any additional state or foreign taxes imposed on the surviving spouse's death on the QDOT property, other than taxes imposed on property includable in the spouse's gross estate.[369]

The regulations provide that if assets of the QDOT are included in the surviving spouse's gross estate (or would have been so includable if the spouse had been a U.S. resident) and state or foreign death taxes are paid by the spouse's estate with respect to the QDOT property, the taxes paid by the spouse's estate with respect to the QDOT are creditable to the extent allowable under §§ 2011 and 2014 in computing the QDOT tax. In addition, state or foreign death taxes previously paid by the first spouse's estate deemed allowable under §§ 2011 and 2014 are also creditable in computing the QDOT tax. The regulations provide substantial detail in the calculation of these credits.[370]

6. Alternate Valuation and Special Use Valuation

(a) In General. In order to claim the benefits of alternate valuation under § 2032, or special use valuation under § 2032A, for purposes of computing the QDOT tax, an election must be made on the Form 706-QDT that is filed with respect to the property remaining in the QDOT upon the death of the surviving spouse. In addition, the separate requirements for making the § 2032 and/or § 2032A elections under those sections and the regulations thereunder must be complied with except that, for this purpose, the surviving spouse is treated as a U.S. resident regardless of the surviving spouse's actual residency status.[371]

(b) Alternate Valuation. For purposes of the alternate valuation election under § 2032, the election may not be made unless the election decreases both the value of the property remaining in the QDOT upon the death of the surviving spouse and the net amount of QDOT tax due. Once made, the election is irrevocable.[372]

(c) Special Use Valuation. For purposes of § 2032A, the designated return filer (in the case of multiple QDOTs) or the U.S. Trustee may elect to value certain farm

368. Treas. Reg. § 20.2056A-6(c)(3).
369. *Id.* § 20.2056A-6(c)(4).
370. *See id.* § 20.2056A-6(b)(4) and -6(d), Example 2.
371. Treas. Reg. § 20.2056A-6(d)(5)(i).
372. *Id.* § 20.2056A-6(d)(5)(ii).

and closely held business real property at its farm or business use value, rather than its fair market value, if all of the requirements under § 2032A and the applicable regulations are met. For this purpose, the surviving spouse will be treated as a U.S. resident regardless of the spouse's actual residency status. The total value of property valued under § 2032A in the QDOT cannot be decreased from fair market value by more than $750,000.[373]

7. Extension of Time to Pay QDOT Tax

The provisions of § 6161(a)(2) (relating to extensions of time to pay the federal estate tax) are available with respect to the QDOT tax imposed upon the death of the surviving spouse.[374] The statute makes clear that the reference to the executor in § 6161(a)(2)(A) is to be treated as a reference to the QDOT trustee.

C. Double Taxation

When the QDOT is subject to a tax in a foreign country at the death of the surviving spouse, the fact that the QDOT tax is treated as tax on the estate of the first spouse to die would appear to subject the property held in the QDOT at the death of the surviving spouse to double taxation. At the death of the surviving spouse, a QDOT tax is paid on the property remaining in the QDOT at that time.[375] In addition, if the noncitizen spouse established domicile in a country that subjects the QDOT to its transfer tax, the estate of the noncitizen spouse will be subject to a second tax.

Although discussed in greater detail in Section X below, the United States. has a number of bilateral estate tax treaties in force. The primary purpose of these treaties is to prevent or reduce the incidence of double taxation, usually through the allowance of a credit. If the surviving spouse is domiciled at death in a country with which the United States has a treaty, and if that country subjects the QDOT to a death tax, the normal credit provisions will be of little assistance, since the only U.S. estate tax imposed on the estate of the noncitizen spouse will be that portion of the tax not eliminated by the credit provided by § 2013.[376] Further, § 2014 provides a credit against U.S. estate tax for the amount of any death taxes paid to a foreign country in respect of property that is included in the decedent's gross estate and has a situs, for federal estate tax purposes, in the foreign country. However, prior to the retroactive changes enacted in OBRA 1990, this credit could not have been used to reduce the double taxation on the QDOT because, as noted above, the QDOT tax is imposed on the estate of the first spouse to die, and not the noncitizen spouse's estate.

Some relief was provided by OBRA 1990. Section 2056A(b)(10)(A) (as amended by § 11702(g)(4) of OBRA 1990), now allows the benefit of the foreign

373. *Id.* § 20.2056A-6(d)(5)(iii).
374. § 2056A(b)(10)(C).
375. § 2056A(b)(1)(B).
376. *See supra* Section VIII.A.

death tax credit for purposes of the QDOT tax imposed at the death of the noncitizen spouse if such credit would otherwise be available with respect to the QDOT property to the noncitizen spouse's estate (or would have been allowable if the surviving spouse had been a U.S. citizen or resident).

D. Use of Spouse's Unified Credit and Federal Estate Tax Brackets

Because the federal estate tax imposed on a QDOT under § 2056A(b)(1) is treated as a tax imposed on the estate of the decedent spouse,[377] the surviving spouse (especially in a noncommunity property state) may be unable to fully use his or her unified credit and federal estate tax brackets. In a community property state, however, the surviving spouse should be able to use part or all of his unified credit and federal estate tax brackets because he will own one-half of the community property assets. The purpose of the QDOT provisions is to ensure that property passing to a noncitizen surviving spouse is subject to the federal estate tax at the death of the surviving spouse. However, treatment of the QDOT tax as a tax on the estate of the decedent spouse does not appear to be necessary to carry out the purpose of the statute and has the effect of discriminating against surviving spouses who opt to retain their foreign citizenship. In any case, as discussed in more detail below, these provisions suggest that property be transferred to the noncitizen spouse's ownership in order to facilitate use of his unified credit and estate tax brackets.

E. Generation-Skipping Transfer Tax

1. Who Is the Transferor?

Another result of the treatment of the estate tax imposed on a QDOT as a tax on the estate of the decedent spouse is to confuse the identity of the transferor for purposes of the generation-skipping transfer tax (GSTT).[378] For purposes of the GSTT, the "transferor" is the decedent, with respect to property subject to the Federal estate tax,[379] and the donor, with respect to any property subject to the Federal gift tax.[380] Thus, because the QDOT tax is treated as a tax on the estate of the decedent spouse, the noncitizen surviving spouse's $1 million exemption from the GSTT provided under § 2631(a) may be unavailable for property held in a QDOT.

On the other hand, because qualification as a QDOT requires the trust to meet the other marital deduction rules, it may also be a QTIP, a general testamentary power of appointment trust, or an estate trust. The property remaining in the QDOT at the death of the surviving spouse will, therefore, also be subject to federal estate tax in the estate of the surviving spouse. Because the property is "subject to the tax imposed by chapter 11" at the death of the surviving spouse (even

377. § 2056A(b)(7).
378. *See* §§ 2601 *et seq.*
379. § 2652(a)(1)(A).
380. § 2652(a)(1)(B).

though no federal estate tax may be paid by the estate of the surviving spouse), the surviving spouse should also be the transferor for purposes of the GSTT under § 2652(a)(1)(A).

2. Availability of the "Reverse" QTIP Election

In addition, § 2652(a)(3) allows a decedent's executor (or the donor spouse in the case of an inter vivos QTIP trust) to reverse the effect of the QTIP election so that the decedent (or the transferor spouse in the case of a gift) would be treated as the transferor for GSTT purposes, notwithstanding the subsequent inclusion of the QTIP in the donee spouse's estate. However, this election is available only when the property qualifies as a QTIP trust.[381] Therefore, if, under the decedent spouse's estate plan property is transferred to a QDOT, and valid QTIP election is made with respect to the trust, the reverse QTIP election should be available to ensure that the decedent's spouse remains the transferor for GSTT purposes.

However, if the QDOT is funded with property transferred or assigned by the surviving spouse, the regulations take the position that the surviving spouse is the transferor for all the purposes except for the provisions of § 2056(d)(2)(A) of the Code.[382] Thus, to the extent property is transferred to the QDOT by the surviving spouse, the regulations treat the surviving spouse as the transferor of the property for GST tax purposes.

Moreover, because property transferred to a QDOT by the surviving spouse is deemed to qualify for the marital deduction under § 2056(a) as an outright bequest to the spouse, the QTIP election is unavailable.[383] Therefore, the reverse QTIP election under § 2652(a)(3) is also unavailable.

IX. Federal Gift Tax on Transfers to Noncitizen Spouses

A. Limitation on the Marital Deduction for Gifts to Noncitizen Spouses

1. Extension of Gift Tax Marital Deduction to Nonresidents Alien Donors

Prior to the enactment of OBRA 1989, the federal gift tax marital deduction was available only for gifts made by U.S. citizens or residents.[384] A nonresident alien donor is now entitled to the same gift tax marital deduction available to a U.S.

381. §§ 2652(a)(3)(A) and (B).

382. *See* Treas. Reg. §§ 20.2056A-4(b)(5) and § 20.2056A-4(d), Example 5, and discussion *supra* at Section V.H.

383. *See* Treas. Reg. § 20.2056A-4(d), Example 5.

384. § 2523(a), prior to enactment of OBRA 1989.

citizen or resident.[385] This is consistent with the extension the federal estate tax marital deduction to the estates of nonresident alien decedents.[386]

2. Disallowance of Gift Tax Marital Deduction

For gifts made on or after July 14, 1988, TAMRA denied the unlimited federal gift tax marital deduction where the donee spouse is not a U.S. citizen.[387] The regulations make clear that the citizenship or domicile of the donor spouse at the time of the gift is irrelevant; therefore, so long as the donee spouse is a U.S. citizen at the time of the gift and the other provisions of § 2523 are met, the marital deduction will be allowed, regardless of whether the donor spouse is a U.S. citizen or U.S. resident.[388]

3. Annual Exclusion

In place of the marital deduction, the $10,000 annual exclusion provided under § 2503(b) is available for gifts to a noncitizen spouse and was increased to $100,000 annually.[389] For gifts made after June 29, 1989, the annual exclusion is available only for gifts that, but for the denial of the marital deduction under § 2523(i)(1), would qualify for the federal gift tax marital deduction.[390] Thus, gifts in trust to a noncitizen donee spouse must avoid the terminable interest rules of § 2523(b) and must be gifts of present interests in order to satisfy § 2503(b). The explanation to TCA 1990 states that "[i]t is intended that the entire $100,000 annual exclusion for gifts to a noncitizen spouse qualify as a present interest under § 2503(b), while only the additional $90,000 exclusion permitted noncitizen spouses must be transferred in a form that would qualify for the marital deduction if the donee spouse were a citizen."[391] The necessity of satisfying the present interest requirement is unclear.

The regulations under § 2503 now include provisions to take account of the increase in the annual exclusion afforded donors of gifts to noncitizen spouses. The first $100,000 of gifts made during the calendar year to a noncitizen donee spouse, other than gifts of future interests, are excludable in determining the total amount of gifts for the calendar year.[392] This rule applies to gifts made on or after July 14, 1988, and is subject to the provisions of any applicable gift tax treaty. As

385. *See* § 7815(d)(2) of OBRA 1989.

386. Section 2106(a)(3) (as amended by § 7815(d)(3) of OBRA 1989), allows the marital deduction in computing the federal estate tax liability of nonresident aliens in the amount that would be deductible with respect to U.S.-situs property under the principles of § 2056.

387. *See* § 2523(i)(1) (added by §§ 5033(b) and (d)(2) of TAMRA); Treas. Reg. § 25.2523(i)-1(a).

388. Treas. Reg. §§ 25.2523(i)-1(a), (c)(2).

389. § 2523(i)(2); Treas. Reg. §§ 25.2503-2(f)(1), 25.2523(i)-1(c).

390. § 7815(d)(1)(A) of OBRA 1989; Treas. Reg. § 25.2523(1)-1(c).

391. 136 Cong. Rec. H7147 (daily ed. Aug. 3, 1990) (statement of Rep. Rostenkowski introducing H.R. 5454).

392. Treas. Reg. § 25.2503-2(f)(1). Note that § 501(c) of TRA 1997 provides that the $10,000 annual exclusion amount will be indexed for inflation after 1998. The $100,000 annual exclusion for transfers to noncitizen spouses is also indexed for inflation. For 2013, the exemption was $143,000. *See* § 3.19(2) of Rev. Proc. 2012-41.

noted above, the donor's citizenship is not relevant; rather, it is the citizenship of the donee spouse at the time of the gift that is determinative of the application of these provisions.

> ***Example 11:*** D, a U.S. citizen, transfers a residence valued at $350,000 on December 20, 2013, to D's spouse, S, a resident alien. On January 31, 2014, S becomes a naturalized U.S. citizen. On D's federal gift tax return for 2013, D must include $207,000 as a gift ($350,000 transfer less $143,000 exclusion). Although S becomes a citizen in January, 2014, S is not a U.S. citizen at the time the transfer is made. Therefore, no gift tax marital deduction is allowable. However, the transfer does qualify for the $143,000 annual exclusion.[393]

Further, unless provided otherwise under an applicable estate and gift tax treaty, in the case of gifts made after June 29, 1989, the $100,000 exclusion provided in Treas. Reg. § 25.2503–2(f)(1) applies only if the gift in excess of the otherwise applicable ($10,000) annual exclusion is in a form that qualifies for the gift tax marital deduction under § 2523(a) but for the provisions of § 2523(i)(1) (disallowing the marital deduction if the donee spouse is not a U.S. citizen.)[394]

> ***Example 12:*** Assume the donee, S, is D's spouse and is not a U.S. citizen at the time of the gift. In 2013, D, a U.S. citizen, transfers to S, outright, 100 shares of X corporation stock valued for federal gift tax purposes at $200,000. The transfer is a gift of a present interest in property under § 2503(b). Additionally, the gift qualifies for the gift tax marital deduction but for the disallowance provision of § 2523(i)(1). Accordingly, $143,000 of the $200,000 gift is excluded from the total amount of gifts made during the calendar year by D for gift tax purposes.[395]

> ***Example 13:*** In 2013, D, a resident alien, transfers property valued at $500,000 in trust to S, who is also a resident alien. The trust instrument provides that the trust income is payable to S at least quarterly, and S has a testamentary general power to appoint the trust corpus. The transfer to S qualifies for the marital deduction under § 2523 but for the limitations of § 2523(i)(1). Because S has a life income interest in the trust, S has a present interest in a portion of the trust. Accordingly, D may exclude the present value of S's income interest (up to $143,000) from D's total 2013 calendar year gifts.[396]

> ***Example 14:*** The facts are the same as in the preceding example except that S does not have a testamentary general power to appoint the trust

---

393. Treas. Reg. § 25.2523(i)-1(d), Example 5.
394. *See also id.* § 25.2523(i)-1(c).
395. *Id.* § 25.2523(i)-1(d), Example 1.
396. *Id.* § 25.2523(i)-1(d), Example 3.

corpus. Instead, D's child, C, has a remainder interest in the trust. If S were a U.S. citizen, the transfer would qualify for the gift tax marital deduction if a QTIP election were made under § 2523(f)(4). However, because S is not a U.S. citizen, D may not make a QTIP election with respect to the property. Accordingly, the gift does not qualify for the gift tax marital deduction but for the disallowance provision of § 2523(i)(1). Therefore, the annual exclusion under § 2523(i)(2) is not available with respect to D's transfer in trust, and D may not exclude the present value of S's income interest in excess of $10,000 from D's total 2013 calendar year gifts.[397]

Comment: Interestingly, the conclusion reached by the IRS in the final regulations on these facts was the opposite of that reached in the proposed regulations. The IRS, applying a literal reading of the governing statute, reasoned that its original conclusion that the gift would qualify for the marital deduction was not consistent with the governing statute because the gift does not qualify for the marital deduction "but for" the application of § 2523(i)(1). Instead, the gift would only qualified for the marital deduction if the QTIP election were made. Because the election is unavailable if the donee spouse is not a U.S. citizen, the statutory requirement that only gifts that would have qualified for the marital deduction but for § 2523(i) are eligible for the increased annual exclusion was not satisfied. This requirement (which is intended to ensure that only gifts that would be includable in the spouse's gross estate at death qualified for the increased exclusion) was not satisfied in the example as proposed.[398]

4. Joint and Survivor Annuities

Prior to TAMRA, the irrevocable designation of a beneficiary of a joint and survivor annuity was a taxable gift. Where the beneficiary was a spouse, no federal gift tax marital deduction was available because the beneficiary's survivorship interest was a terminable interest. TAMRA changed the law so that a surviving spouse's interest in a joint and survivor annuity, under which only the surviving spouse has a right to receive payments under the annuity before the death of the surviving spouse, will qualify as QTIP property unless the decedent spouse's executor elects otherwise.[399] For federal gift tax purposes, the irrevocable designation of the surviving spouse as a beneficiary will be treated as a transfer of an interest that qualifies for the federal gift tax marital deduction, provided that only the donor spouse and the surviving spouse have the right to receive payments under the annuity prior to the death of the survivor.[400]

---

397. *Id.* § 25.2523(i)-1(d), Example 4.
398. T.D. 8612, Preamble, § 2, 60 Fed. Reg. 43,531 (Aug. 22, 1995).
399. § 2056(b)(7)(C).
400. § 2523(f)(6).

Because TAMRA repealed the federal gift tax marital deduction when the donee spouse is a noncitizen, § 2523(f)(6) only applies when the beneficiary spouse is a U.S. citizen.[401] Under this rule, the irrevocable designation of a noncitizen spouse as the beneficiary of a joint and survivor annuity would have resulted in a taxable gift, and since the gift is not a gift of a present interest, it would not qualify for the $100,000 annual exclusion.[402] However, OBRA 1990 cured this problem by excluding from the operation of § 2523(i) the "acquisition of rights under a joint and survivor annuity described in [§ 2523](f)(6)."[403]

> ***Example 15:*** Assume the donee, S, is D's spouse and is not a U.S. citizen at the time of the gift. In 2013, D, a U.S. citizen, retires from employment in the United States and elects to receive a reduced retirement annuity in order to provide S with a survivor annuity upon D's death. The transfer of rights to S in the joint and survivor annuity is a gift by D for gift tax purposes. However, under Treas. Reg. § 25.2523(i)-1(b), the gift qualifies for the gift tax marital deduction even though S is not a U.S. citizen.[404]

> ***Comment:*** The inapplicability of the gift tax marital deduction limitations to the creation of certain joint and survivor annuities may allow the proportioned spouse to transfer property through the designation of the noncitizen spouse as a survivor annuity beneficiary without the $100,000 annual gift tax limitation.

B. Federal Gift Tax Effects of Creation and Termination of Joint Tenancies[405]

1. Reenactment of Pre-ERTA Rules

TAMRA reenacted the rules of §§ 2515 and 2515A of the 1954 Code repealed by § 403(c)(3)(B) of ERTA (the Economic Recovery Tax Act of 1981), in determining whether and to what extent the creation and termination of a joint tenancy in real and personal property between a husband and wife constitute a taxable gift, when the donee spouse is not a U.S. citizen.[406] The rules for determining the federal gift and estate tax effects of the creation and termination of joint tenancies in different types of property under §§ 2515 and 2515A of the 1954 Code are discussed below.

Generally, § 2515(a) of the 1954 Code provided that the creation of a joint tenancy between spouses in *real property* would not be a taxable gift, regardless of

401. *See* § 2523(i)(1).

402. *See* § 2523(i)(2); § 7815(d)(1)(B) of OBRA.

403. § 11702(g)(1) of OBRA 1990; Treas. Reg. § 25.2523(i)-1(b).

404. Treas. Reg. § 25.2523(i)-1(d), Example 2.

405. The term "joint tenancy" refers to titled property owned as joint tenants with right of survivorship or as tenants by the entireties. Caution should be taken in relying on the conclusions stated in this section regarding the federal gift tax effects of creating and terminating spousal joint tenancies. The confusion in the legislative history, the lack of regulatory authority, and the absence of judicial and regulatory interpretation of the pertinent provisions make certainty in this area difficult.

406. § 5033(b) of TAMRA.

the amount of consideration furnished by each spouse. However, under prior law, provided the spouses with the right to elect to treat the creation of such tenancies in real property as a taxable gift to the extent the consideration furnished by one spouse exceeded that furnished by the other.[407] That election is not applicable under § 2523(i).[408]

Prior to its repeal, § 2515A of the 1954 Code provided that upon the creation of a joint tenancy between spouses in *personal property*, each spouse would be treated as the owner of one-half of the value of the property.[409]

The 1988 House Report stated:

> Under the bill, a gift between spouses does not occur by reason of the creation of a tenancy by the entirety or a joint tenancy with a right of survivorship. Upon the expiration of such a tenancy, however, there is a gift to the extent that the proportion of the total consideration furnished by a spouse multiplied by the proceeds of the termination exceeds the value of the proceeds received by that spouse.[410]

A footnote to the House bill added this statement: "Thus, the bill applies the law in effect prior to 1982 with respect to a tenancy in the entirety, except that there is no election to treat the creation of such a tenancy as a gift."[411]

This statement is correct only with respect to joint tenancies in real property; it is incorrect with respect to the creation of some tenancies in personal property. Given this inconsistency, therefore, it is unclear whether the creation of a joint tenancy in personal property gives rise to a gift at the time of creation and thereby reduces the amount of the $100,000 federal gift tax annual exclusion remaining.

There is even greater confusion when, at the death of the contributing spouse, the surviving spouse is not a U.S. citizen. As was discussed above in Section II.B, in applying § 2040(b) with respect to any consideration provided after December 31, 1976 (the effective date of § 2040(b)), and before July 14, 1988, the portion of joint tenancy property treated as a gift to the surviving spouse when the tenancy was created is treated as consideration furnished by the surviving spouse, and is therefore excluded from the decedent's estate. The 1989 House Report describes the law after enactment of TAMRA but prior to OBRA 1989 as follows:

> In determining estate tax, the value of gifts includable in the gross estate effectively is reduced by the value of the taxable gift when made. Thus for a joint tenancy created after [July 14, 1988], the amount included in the estate effectively is reduced by the amount transferred when the tenancy was created.[412]

---

407. § 2515(c) of the 1954 Code.
408. *See* Treas. Reg. § 25.2523(i)-2(a).
409. § 2515A(a) of the 1954 Code.
410. 1988 House Report, at 593.
411. *Id.* at n.193.
412. 1989 House Report, at 1428.

Given the confusion in the legislative history regarding the federal gift tax effects of the creation of joint tenancies in personal property (or additional contributions to such a joint tenancy) after July 13, 1988, the amount of such property excludable from the estate of the decedent's spouse is unclear.

2. Creation and Termination of Interests in Jointly Owned Property

(a) Real Property

(i) Creation of a Joint Tenancy. Generally, the creation of a joint tenancy in real property before January 1, 1982, and after July 13, 1988, between a husband and wife will not be treated as a taxable gift, regardless of the consideration furnished by either spouse.[413] With regard to such joint tenancies created before January 1, 1982, if the election available under § 2515(c) of the 1954 Code was made, then there would have been a gift upon the creation of the tenancy to the extent that the retained interest of either spouse was less than the portion of the consideration furnished by that spouse.[414]

The federal gift tax effects of the creation of a joint tenancy after December 31, 1981, and before July 14, 1988, depend on the rights accorded to the spouses under local law. If, under local law, the interests of the spouses may be unilaterally severed, then each spouse is treated as having a retained interest in one-half of the value of the property.[415] A spouse contributing more than one-half of the consideration for such property has therefore made a gift to the other spouse of the excess. If, however, such a unilateral severance is not allowable, as is often true of tenancies by the entirety, then the value of the retained interest of each spouse (and, therefore, the value of any gift) is made by determining the actuarial value of the respective spouse's interests, based on their ages and the IRS actuarial tables.[416] The actuarial factors to be used are those in effect at the date of creation of the tenancy.[417]

With respect to a joint interest where any amount was treated as being received from the decedent as a gift to a noncitizen spouse before July 14, 1988, it is treated as consideration furnished by the donee spouse for purposes of applying § 2040(a) (upon the death of the contributing spouse).[418]

(ii) Termination of Spousal Joint Tenancy in Real Property. Generally, upon the termination of a joint tenancy in real property, other than by reason of the death of one of the joint tenants, a spouse is treated as having made a taxable gift to the extent that the portion of the total consideration furnished by such spouse,

413. § 2515(a) of the 1954 Code; Treas. Reg. §§ 25.2515-1(b), 25.2523(i)-2(b)(1); Priv. Ltr. Rul. 9151044 (Sept. 26, 1991) (purchase of residence in 1977, no § 2515(c) election made).

414. Treas. Reg. § 25.2515-2(b).

415. *Id.* § 25.2515-2(b)(1).

416. *Id.* §§ 25.2515-2(b)(2) and (c).

417. *Id.*

418. *See supra* Section II.B.

multiplied by the proceeds from the termination, exceeds the value of the proceeds received by such spouse.[419]

With respect to joint tenancies in real property created prior to January 1, 1982, or after July 13, 1988, where the creation of the tenancy was not treated as a gift from the contributing spouse to the noncontributing spouse, there will be a gift to the extent that the noncontributing spouse receives an amount greater than the proceeds of the termination (that is, the value of the property at the date of termination) multiplied by the percentage of the consideration the noncontributing spouse provided in the purchase or improvement of the property.[420] Thus, if one spouse provided all the consideration for the purchase of the joint tenancy property, that spouse will be treated as having made a gift to the extent that the noncontributing spouse receives any proceeds upon termination.[421] Any amount received by a noncitizen spouse in excess of that spouse's portion of the proceeds will be a gift by the other spouse against which the $100,000 annual exclusion will be applied.[422]

If a joint tenancy was created after December 31, 1981, and before July 14, 1988, or if the election under § 2515(c) of the 1954 Code was made with respect to the creation of the joint tenancy prior to January 1, 1982, then the determination of the interest of the noncontributing spouse is dependent on local law.[423] Where, under local law, the interests of the joint tenants were unilaterally severable, each of the joint tenants is treated as having provided one-half of the consideration for the purchase of the joint tenancy property; therefore, the receipt by either of them of more than one-half of the proceeds on termination will be a taxable gift by the other joint tenant.[424] On the other hand, where the interests of the joint tenants are not unilaterally severable, the interests of the joint tenants in the property is determined using actuarial factors based on the respective ages of the joint tenants at the date of the severance.[425] Amounts received on termination of the joint tenancy in excess of their actuarial interest in the property (as determined at the time of termination of the tenancy) will be a gift by the other spouse.

(b) Personal Property—General Rule

(i) Gift at Creation of Joint Tenancy in Personal Property. Subject to the special rules described below in Section IX.B.3.a, the creation of a joint tenancy in personal property after December 31, 1953, is treated as a gift.

With respect to joint tenancies in personal property created prior to January 1, 1977, if the tenancy can be severed unilaterally by either tenant, there was a gift to the extent that the amount contributed by one of the spouses exceeds one-half

---

419. § 2515(b) of the 1954 Code; Treas. Reg. § 25.2523(i)-2(b)(2).
420. Treas. Reg. § 25.2515-3(a).
421. *Id.*
422. *See id.* § 25.2523(i)-2(b)(2)(i).
423. *See id.* §§ 25.2523(i)-2(b)(2)(ii), 25.2515-2.
424. *Id.* § 25.2515-3.
425. *Id.* § 25.2515-4(b).

the value of the property.[426] If no such unilateral severance is possible, the size of the gift was based on the excess of the consideration furnished over the actuarial value of the interest retained by the donor contributing spouse.

The value of the gift for joint tenancies created in personal property after December 31, 1976, and prior to January 1, 1982, is governed by § 2515A of the 1954 Code and is treated as a gift by the contributor spouse of one-half of the consideration furnished by that spouse.[427] Thus, if each spouse contributes one-half of the consideration, no gift will occur at the creation of the joint tenancy. This rule for post-1976 gifts applies regardless of whether the interest is unilaterally severable, because § 2515A(b) of the 1954 Code eliminated the need for actuarial computations except where values could not be reasonably ascertained without reference to the respective ages of the spouses. With respect to such tenancies created after December 31, 1981, the availability of the unlimited federal gift tax marital deduction eliminated any adverse gift tax effects.

Under the regulations, in the case of the creation (either by one spouse alone or by both spouses where at least one of the spouses is not a U.S. citizen) of a spousal joint tenancy in personal property, or additions to the value thereof in the form of improvements, reductions in the indebtedness thereof, or otherwise, the retained interest of each spouse, solely for purposes of determining whether there has been a gift by the donor to the spouse who is not a U.S. citizen at the time of the gift, is treated as one-half the value of the joint interest.[428]

The "half-half" rule does not apply with respect to any joint interest in property if the fair market value of the interest in property (determined as if each spouse had a right to sever) cannot reasonably be ascertained except by reference to the life expectancy of one or both spouses. In these cases, the determination of the gift tax consequences of the transaction may require use of actuarial principles.[429]

3. Effect of Termination of Joint Tenancy in Personal Property

Section 2515A of the 1954 Code contained no provisions for determining the federal gift tax effects of a termination of a joint tenancy in personal property. Some commentators have concluded that the regulations under § 2515 of the 1954 Code apply.[430] The IRS has taken this point of view on at least one occasion.[431] If the IRS applies the § 2515 regulations, then, when the interests of the tenants are severable under state law, there should be no gift upon the termination of the tenancy if the proceeds are divided evenly, regardless of the actual consideration furnished by the respective spouses. If, however, the interests of the spouses were not unilaterally severable under state law, there will be a gift to the extent that the pro-

426. *See id.* § 25.2511-1(h)(5).

427. § 2515A(a) of the 1954 Code.

428. *Id.* § 25.2523(i)-2(c).

429. *Id.* § 25.2523(i)-2(c)(2).

430. *See, e.g.*, Steven C. Gabrielson, *Estate and Gift Planning for Jointly Owned Property in the 1980's*, 38 N.Y.U. Inst. on Estate Planning § 41.02[3] (1980).

431. *See* I.R.S. Priv. Ltr. Rul. 7941046 (July 13, 1979).

ceeds received by one joint tenant are less than the actuarial value (determined at the time of termination) of his or her interest in the proceeds.

(a) Special Rules for Certain Types of Personal Property

(i) Joint Bank Accounts. The creation of joint bank accounts, where each spouse has the opportunity to withdraw funds without an obligation to repay such amounts, does not result in a taxable gift upon the creation of the joint tenancy.[432] The IRS has examined this issue several times, reaching different conclusions.[433] Under the rules relating to the federal gift tax effects of the creation and termination of joint tenancies in personal property, there will be a gift at the termination of the account or at the time of a withdrawal from the account to the extent that either spouse receives a greater portion of the account balance than he or she contributed, and there is no legal obligation to make a payment to the contributor spouse.

(ii) Joint Brokerage Accounts. This same rule applies with respect to certain joint brokerage accounts, where the account assets are held in the name of a nominee. Where, under the terms of the brokerage account agreement, each spouse can withdraw property held in the account unilaterally, and each spouse can direct the nominee to sell securities in the account and turn over the proceeds to either joint owner in his individual capacity, there is no gift upon the creation of the account.[434] There is a gift, however, where one spouse withdraws amounts in excess of that spouse's contributions to the account and the spouse has no legal obligation to make a repayment to the contributor spouse. There is also a gift upon termination of the account, after the death of one of the spouses, if one of the spouses receives a proportion of the proceeds in excess of that spouse's contribution to the account and there is no legal obligation on the spouse to make a repayment to the contributor spouse.[435] Where securities are held in nominee form and not in the special type of account described above, or if they are held in certificated form rather than in nominee name, the general rule with respect to personal property will apply.[436]

---

432. *See* Treas. Reg. § 25.2511-1(h)(4).

433. *Cf.* I.R.S. Gen. Couns. Mem. 36647 (Mar. 23, 1976) (concluding that under New York law, the creation of a joint bank account gives rise to a gift to the noncontributing spouse to the extent of one-half the value of the property contributed), I.R.S. Gen. Couns. Mem. 37310 (Nov. 2, 1977) (revoking Gen. Couns. Mem. 36647 and holding that under New York law, no gift occurs until the noncontributing spouse withdraws property from the account with no obligation to repay), and I.R.S. Gen. Couns. Mem. 37869 (Feb. 27, 1979) (proposing to revoke I.R.S. Gen. Couns. Mem. 37310 and reinstate I.R.S. Gen. Couns. Mem. 36647, but closing the project without opinion).

434. *See, e.g.*, I.R.S. Priv. Ltr. Rul. 9151044 (Sept. 26, 1991).

435. *See* Rev. Rul. 69-148, 1969-1 C.B. 226.

436. Treas. Reg. § 25.2511-1(h)(5).

X. Effect of Changes in the Federal Gift and Estate Tax Marital Deduction on Existing United States Tax Treaties

A. Existing U.S. Transfer Tax Treaties

The United States currently has bilateral transfer tax treaties in effect with sixteen countries: Australia, Austria, Denmark, Finland, France, Germany, Greece, Ireland, Italy, Japan, the Netherlands, Norway, Sweden, South Africa, Switzerland, and the United Kingdom. In addition, Protocols to the U.S.-Canada income tax treaty contain provisions governing the imposition of transborder death taxes. Generally, the purpose of these treaties is to prevent or minimize the double taxation of lifetime transfers and transfers at death by domiciliaries of the two contracting states. This is usually accomplished either by giving one country priority in taxing the property deemed by the treaty to be located in that country or by giving one country priority to tax the estate or the gifts of an individual, based on a determination of the decedent's or the donor's fiscal domicile. If application of the treaty gives rise to the imposition of a tax in both contracting states, a credit mechanism is usually adopted to minimize the burden of the double tax.

The imposition of taxes under more recent U.S. bilateral transfer tax treaties, such as the Danish and the Swedish estate and gift tax treaties, is also often limited by "nondiscrimination" provisions. These provisions typically require that the United States refrain from imposing different or more burdensome taxes on treaty-country citizens than those imposed on U.S. citizens. For instance, the estate and gift tax treaty with Denmark provides:

> Citizens of a Contracting State shall not be subjected in the other Contracting State to any taxation or any requirement connected therewith which is other or more burdensome than the taxation and connected requirements to which citizens of that other state in the same circumstances are or may be subjected.[437]

Some of the transfer tax treaties provide a marital deduction against the U.S. estate tax imposed on property passing from a decedent spouse who is not domiciled in the United States.

For example, the French estate and gift tax treaty provides that "[i]n the case of an individual who was domiciled in France there shall, for purposes of determining the United States tax, be allowed the same marital deduction in effect on" November 24, 1978 (the effective date of the treaty).[438] The available marital

437. Article 11(1) of the Denmark estate and gift tax treaty. *See also* art. 10(1)(a) of the United Kingdom estate and gift tax treaty.

438. Article 11(2) of the French estate and gift tax treaty. A Protocol the treaty, discussed below, was signed in December 2004.

deduction is thus limited to the greater of $250,000 or 50 percent of the decedent's adjusted gross estate, and the QTIP election is not available.[439]

The transfer tax treaty with Germany, prior to the negotiation of the 1999 Protocol, discussed below, provided that transfers of certain types of noncommunity property to a spouse by a citizen or domiciliary of one contracting state may be subject to tax by the other state only to the extent that the value of the property passing to the spouse exceeds 50 percent of the total value of the property subject to the tax in that other state.[440] Also, article 10(1) of the Netherlands estate and gift tax treaty provides the same marital deduction contained in the German treaty, but it is only available for property owned by a decedent who is a Dutch domiciliary or citizen under the treaty, which passes to the decedent's spouse and is subject to the U.S. estate tax.

Thus, under the treaty, if a decedent is domiciled in or a citizen of the Netherlands, the U.S. estate tax will be imposed on bequests of U.S.-situs property to the surviving spouse only to the extent that such bequests exceed 50 percent of the value of the property subject to U.S. estate tax. Similarly, article 8(8) of the Swedish estate and gift tax treaty provides that the U.S. estate tax imposed on noncommunity property transferred by a Swedish domiciliary to his or her surviving spouse shall be included in the U.S. estate tax base, but only to the extent the value of such property exceeds 50 percent of the value of the property subject to U.S. estate tax.

Under the United Kingdom treaty, property passing from a domiciliary or national of the United Kingdom that is subject to U.S. tax qualifies for the U.S. marital deduction to the extent a marital deduction would have been allowable if the decedent had been a U.S. domiciliary and the gross estate had been limited to the property subject to U.S. tax.[441] Likewise, if the donor or decedent is a U.S. domiciliary or national, transfers to a spouse that are subject to tax in the United Kingdom are entitled to an exemption equal to 50 percent of the value of the property transferred, provided that (1) the recipient spouse is not domiciled in the United Kingdom and (2) the transfer would have been eligible for the United Kingdom marital deduction had the spouse been domiciled there.[442]

Under the Danish estate and gift tax treaty, property that passes from a decedent who, under the treaty, is domiciled in Denmark qualifies for the U.S. marital deduction in computing the federal estate tax liability on the U.S.-situs property.[443] Likewise, if the surviving spouse elects, U.S. decedents are entitled to compute

---

439. *See* § 2056(c) of the 1954 Code, *repealed by* § 403(a)(1)(A) of ERTA.

440. Article 10(4) of the Germany estate and gift tax treaty. *See* I.R.S. Priv. Ltr. Rul. 9411023 (Dec. 16, 1993) (discussing the marital deduction provisions of the Germany-U.S. treaty).

441. Article 8(2) of the United Kingdom estate and gift tax treaty.

442. *Id.*, at art. 8(3).

443. Article 9(2)(a) of the Danish estate and gift tax treaty.

their Danish death taxes under the provisions of the Danish law regulating matrimonial rights that are applicable to the property.[444]

The legislative history of OBRA 1989 notes that when there is a conflict between a later statute and an earlier treaty provision, the statute prevails, even absent an explicit statement of congressional intent to override the treaty provision.[445] Therefore, except as provided by the three-year rule described in Section X.B.3 below, the changes to the marital deduction provisions enacted in TAMRA and OBRA 1989 will override conflicting provisions of earlier treaties.

B. OBRA 1989 Treaty Provisions

1. General Provisions

The legislative history of TAMRA states the conclusion of Congress that the TAMRA provisions do not violate any provision of an existing U.S. treaty, including any nondiscrimination provisions.[446] This is so because the nondiscrimination provisions are triggered only when the tax treatment imposed by one contracting state on a domiciliary of the other contracting state is more burdensome than the treatment imposed by that state on a domiciliary of that state. The changes to the marital deduction are based on the citizenship of the donor's or the decedent's spouse; therefore, because the tax is imposed without regard to the decedent's nationality, there is no discrimination.[447]Further, as the 1988 House Report points out, the nondiscrimination provisions would not apply even if the treaty focused on the citizenship of the transferee spouse, because beneficiaries who are U.S. citizens (and are thus subject to federal estate tax on their worldwide assets) are not similarly situated to noncitizen beneficiaries (who are subject to federal estate tax only on their United States situs assets).[448]

2. Effect of Marital Deduction Changes on Property Passing from Nonresident Aliens

Section 7815(d)(14) of OBRA 1989 provides that in the case of the estate of, or a gift by, a nonresident alien who was a resident of a country with which the U.S. has a tax treaty with respect to estate, gift, or inheritance taxes, the TAMRA amendments, as amended by OBRA 1989, shall not apply—and thus, the treaty provisions continue to apply—to the extent the legislative changes would be inconsistent with the provisions of any such treaty relating to the estate, gift, or inheritance marital deduction.

---

444. Article 9(2)(b) of the Danish estate tax treaty.

445. 1989 House Report, at 1435 (citing S. Rep. No. 100-445, 100th Cong. 316–28 (1988)).

446. 1988 House Report, at 593.

447. *Id.*

448. *Id.* Compare the nondiscrimination provision of the Swedish estate tax treaty, which states that "for purposes of United States taxation, United States citizens who are not residents of the United States are not in the same circumstances as citizens of Sweden who are not residents of the United States." Art. 10(1)(a) of the Swedish estate and gift tax treaty.

Citing the French and German treaties, the 1989 House Report states that those treaties were negotiated on the assumption that property passing to a surviving spouse from a nonresident alien donor or decedent did not, but for the treaty provisions, qualify for the marital deduction, and that with respect to bequests by nonresident aliens to noncitizen surviving spouses, TAMRA did not change that assumption. Therefore, there is no conflict between the treaty provisions and the amendments, and the treaty provisions should continue to apply. The legislative history concludes that with respect to property passing from nonresident aliens domiciled in a treaty country, the TAMRA amendments to the marital deduction should not apply to the extent inconsistent with the treaty provision.[449]

Query whether a determination that the provisions of TAMRA, as amended, do not apply by virtue of the treaty override provisions of § 7815(d)(14) of OBRA 1989 renders unavailable the provisions of TAMRA, as amended, that are beneficial to nonresident aliens with noncitizen spouses (e.g., the allowance of the gift tax marital deduction provided under § 2523(a) of the Code and the $100,000 annual exclusion for gifts to noncitizen spouses under § 2523(i)(2) of the Code)? Note that the final regulations take the position that when both a treaty marital deduction and the QDOT provisions are available to provide the estate with a marital deduction, the estate must choose either, but not both procedures.[450]

3. Effect of Marital Deduction Changes on Property Passing from United States Persons

The result of the above analysis is different with respect to U.S. donors and decedents. The denial of the marital deduction for property passing from a U.S. person to a noncitizen spouse is inconsistent with the assumptions on which the treaties were negotiated. Because conflicts between treaty provisions and subsequent statutes are to be resolved in favor of the statutes, the legislative history states Congress's conclusion that this change in U.S. internal laws should not "be frustrated by treaty provisions that when adopted provided a marital deduction no better than that available under U.S. internal law."[451] However, in order to provide the Treasury with time to renegotiate treaties where such conflicts exist, the 1988 repeal of the marital deduction with respect to property passing from a U.S. person to a noncitizen spouse does not apply to override a treaty provision until December 19, 1992, the date three years after the date of enactment of OBRA 1989.

4. Application of Treaties and QDOT Requirements

(a) Decedent Is a U.S. Citizen or Resident. Where, under a treaty, a decedent with a noncitizen surviving spouse is determined to be a U.S. citizen or resident, it seems clear, subject to the three-year rule discussed below, that property passing to the surviving spouse must be transferred to or irrevocably assigned to a QDOT.

449. 1989 House Report, at 1435.
450. Treas. Reg. § 20.2056A-1(c). *See also* I.R.S. Priv. Ltr. Rul. 9521031.
451. 1989 House Report, at 1435.

This is so because the changes to the U.S. marital deduction are inconsistent with the assumptions on which such tax treaties are based, and in case of such conflict, the provisions of the new legislation will be applied.[452] However, as noted above, the treaty provisions will continue to be applied until December 19, 1992, the date three years after enactment of OBRA 1989.

(b) Decedent Is a Foreign Domiciliary. If, however, the decedent is determined to be a nonresident alien with respect to the U.S. estate tax, but has property deemed to be U.S.-situs property under the treaty (as would normally be the case with U.S. business property or U.S. real property), the marital deduction provisions of the treaty would control. Therefore, if the decedent is domiciled in Denmark, the full value of property passing to the surviving spouse will qualify for the federal estate tax marital deduction on the same terms as it would if the decedent were a U.S. citizen. If under the applicable treaty the decedent is domiciled in Germany, Sweden, or the Netherlands, then only 50 percent of the U.S.-situs property would qualify for the federal estate tax marital deduction. Likewise, if the decedent is domiciled in France, the decedent's estate would be entitled to federal estate tax marital deduction of the greater of $250,000 or one-half of the value of the U.S.-situs property, and no QTIP election would be available. Under the United Kingdom treaty, U.S.-situs property qualifies for the U.S. marital deduction to the extent that a marital deduction would have been allowed had the decedent spouse been a U.S. citizen; therefore, if the surviving spouse is not a U.S. citizen, the decedent would have to transfer assets to a QDOT in order to qualify for the marital deduction.

(c) Recent Trends in Treaty-Based Marital Deductions. Negotiations have produced protocols to the U.S.-Canada income tax treaty, U.S.-German estate and gift tax treaty, and the U.S.-France estate and gift tax that provide limited relief against the hardship caused by the elimination of the federal estate tax marital deduction. Under article 19 of the Revised Protocol to the U.S.-Canadian income tax treaty,[453] relief from the marital deduction limitations is provided in two ways. First, the estate is given a unified credit against U.S. estate tax, in an amount bearing the same ratio to the maximum available unified credit as the total value of the gross estate issued in the United States bears to the total gross estate.[454] In addition, the treaty, as amended by the Revised Protocol, also allows a "marital credit," equal to the lesser of (1) the unified credit allowed to the decedent's estate and (2) the amount of the U.S. estate tax (exclusive of state death taxes) that would otherwise be imposed by the U.S. on the marital deduction property (based in the

---

452. *See* I.R.S. Priv. Ltr. Rul. 9411023 (Dec. 16, 1993).

453. Revised Protocol Amending the Convention between the United States and Canada with Respect to Taxes on Income and Capital (1995). Article 19 of the Protocol adds art. XXIX B to the Treaty.

454. Article XXIX B(2).

assumption that no QDOT election was made).[455] In order to claim the "marital" unified credit, the estate must irrevocably waive the right to make the QTIP and QDOT elections.[456]

The Protocol to the U.S.-German Estate and Gift Tax Treaty[457] adopts a similar approach. In addition to providing the estate of decedent domiciled in Germany with a pro rata portion of the unified credit, determined by reference to the portion of the estate located in the United States,[458] the 50 percent marital deduction provided under the prior treaty is revised. Specifically, the estate is allowed to elect a marital deduction equal to the lesser of (1) the value of property passing to the spouse that would have qualified for the federal estate tax marital deduction under U.S. domestic law if the surviving spouse were a U.S. citizen and all applicable elections (e.g., QTIP election) had been made and (2) the decedent's unified credit exclusion amount.[459] A Protocol to the United States-France Estate and Gift Tax Treaty incorporates similar changes.[460] In addition, the Protocol to the French treaty allows for the exclusion from the U.S. gross estate 50 percent of noncommunity property of the estate of a French domiciliary taxable by the United States solely on the basis of situs (e.g., U.S. real estate).[461]

XI. Effective Date Provisions

A. Effective Dates of Statutory Provisions

The general rule disallowing the marital deduction applies to the estates of decedents dying after November 10, 1988.[462] However, the marital deduction will be available if the surviving spouse becomes a U.S. citizen after the death of decedent spouse and prior to the date on which the decedent spouse's federal estate return is made, if the surviving spouse was a resident of the United States at the date of death of the decedent spouse and at all times thereafter until attaining U.S. citizenship.[463]

---

455. Article XXIX B(3) and (4).

456. This is similar to the rule of Treas. Reg. § 20.2056A-1(c), requiring the estate to elect either the treaty marital deduction or the QDOT provisions.

457. Protocol to the Convention between the United States and Germany for the Avoidance of Double Taxation with Respect to Taxes on Estates, Inheritances, and Gifts (1999).

458. Protocol, art. 3.

459. *Id.*

460. Protocol Amending the Convention between the United States and the French Republic for the Avoidance of Double Taxation and the Prevention of Fiscal Evasion with Respect to Taxes on Estates, Inheritances, and Gifts (2004).

461. *Id., amending* art. 11, para. 2 of the Treaty.

462. § 5033(d) of TAMRA.

463. *See* § 2056(d)(5); Treas. Reg. § 20.2056A-1(b).

1. Transitional Rules

TAMRA did not include any grandfathering provisions or transitional rules for application of §§ 2056(d) and 2056A. However, the legislative history to OBRA 1989 clarified that a surviving spouse or the decedent's executor could create a QDOT after the death of the decedent spouse. In addition, OBRA 1989 allows the decedent's executor to initiate reformation proceedings to amend a trust so as to qualify as a QDOT.[464] But the ability to reform a trust to ensure its qualification as a QDOT may be dependent on local law and the terms of the governing instrument, and relief may not be available. Further, the reformation provisions would not appear to provide relief if the marital bequest is in a form that (1) would not have met the requirements for the marital deduction, other than the QDOT provisions or (2) is an outright bequest to the noncitizen spouse, because the provision is stated in terms of changing "such trust."[465] However, if the noncitizen surviving spouse has received the property outright (whether as probate or nonprobate property), presumably he or she could create a QDOT to which a timely transfer of the property could be made.[466]

2. Irrevocable Trusts

Under OBRA, no relief is available for persons who created irrevocable trusts prior to the enactment of the marital deduction amendments. If these trusts are includable in the decedent's estate, the absence of any transitional relief may subject them to the QDOT requirements and potential federal estate tax many years after their execution.

B. Effective Date Provisions for Final Regulations

1. General Effective Date Provisions for QDOT Regulations

The final regulations are effective with respect to estates of decedents dying after August 22, 1995.[467] Presumably, with respect to estates of decedents dying on or before such date, taxpayers may rely on any reasonable interpretation of the statutory provisions.[468] In fact, the IRS has ruled that a QDOT created in 1992, prior to the issuance of any regulations or other guidance, the terms of which met

---

464. *See* § 2056(d)(4); Treas. Reg. §20.2056A-4(a).

465. § 2056(d)(5)(A)(ii).

466. In I.R.S. Priv. Ltr. Rul. 9017015 (Apr. 27, 1990), the decedent bequeathed one-half of his estate outright to his surviving spouse, who was not a U.S. citizen. Rather than having the executor create a trust that qualified as a QDOT, the executor petitioned the local probate court and obtained a reformation of the will itself. As reformed, the bequest to the noncitizen spouse was instead made to a testamentary trust created under the will that qualified for the marital deduction under § 2056A(a). As of the due date of the decedent spouse's estate tax return, the bequest to the surviving spouse met the requirements of §§ 2056(d)(2) and 2056A(a). Therefore, the marital deduction was allowed. It should be noted that this request was filed prior to enactment of OBRA 1989, although the IRS's analysis describes the provisions of §§ 2056 and 2056A as if the OBRA 1989 legislation were enacted at the time of the ruling request.

467. Treas. Reg. § 20.2056A-13(a).

468. Prop. Treas. Reg. § 20.2056A-13(a), PS-102-88, 58 Fed. Reg. 305 (Jan. 5, 1995).

the statutory requirements of § 2056A(a), "is not required . . . to meet the requirements of section 20.2056-1 through 13 of the estate tax regulations."[469]

2. Effective Date Provisions Regarding Payment of the QDOT Tax

Transition rules for reporting and paying the QDOT tax imposed under § 2056A(b)(1) are contained in Announcement 90-39,[470] and Announcement 91-58.[471] Announcement 90-39 provided that the due date for any QDOT tax otherwise due on April 15, 1990, was extended indefinitely due to the unavailability of Form 706-QDT. Following the release of the Form 706-QDT, the IRS released Announcement 91-58, which provided that the reporting date for taxable events occurring after November 10, 1988, and before January 1, 1991, would be September 16, 1991. For taxable events in years beginning after December 31, 1990, Form 706-QDT is due by April 15 of the year following the year in which the taxable event occurred.

3. Effective Dates of Final Regulations Governing Security Requirements for Collection of the QDOT Tax

(a) General Rule. There are special effective date rules governing application of the Security Requirements for collection of the QDOT tax. Generally, the regulations are effective for estates of decedents dying after February 19, 1996, the effective date of the temporary and proposed regulations.[472] The rules do provide some relief from the extensive governing instrument requirements included in the special provisions for the collection of the QDOT tax in the case of incompetency and irrevocability.

(b) Incompetency. A revocable trust or a testamentary trust is deemed to meet the governing instrument requirements of the Security Requirements notwithstanding that all provisions are not contained in the governing instrument, if the trust instrument (or will) was executed on or before November 20, 1995, and:

1. The testator or settler dies after February 19, 1996;
2. The testator or settlor is, on November 20, 1995, and at all times thereafter, under a legal disability to amend the will or trust instrument;
3. The will or trust instrument does not provide the executor or the U.S. Trustee with a power to amend the instrument in order to meet the requirements of § 2056A; and
4. The U.S. Trustee provides a written statement with the decedent spouse's federal estate tax return that the trust is being administered (or will be administered) so as to be in actual compliance with the requirements of Treas. Reg. § 20.2056A-2(d) and will continue to be administered so as to

469. I.R.S. Priv. Ltr. Rul. 9826028 (Mar. 6, 1998).

470. 1990-12 I.R.B. 26 (Mar. 19, 1990).

471. 1991-15 I.R.B. 39 (Apr. 15, 1991).

472. Treas. Reg. § 20.2056A-2(d)(6)(i). *See* 60 Fed. Reg. 43,554, 43,575 (Aug. 22, 1995). The effective date was 180 days after issuance of these regulations.

be in actual compliance for the duration of the trust. This statement must be binding on all successor trustees.[473]

(c) Irrevocable Trusts. An irrevocable trust is deemed to meet the governing instrument requirements of Treas. Reg. § 20.2056A-2(d) notwithstanding that all required provisions are not contained in the governing instrument if the trust was executed on or before November 20, 1995, and:

1. The settlor dies after February 19, 1996;
2. The trust instrument does not provide the U.S. Trustee with a power to amend the trust instrument in order to meet the requirements of § 2056A; and
3. The U.S. Trustee provides a written statement with the decedent spouse's federal estate tax return that the trust is being administered in actual compliance with the requirements of Treas. Reg. § 20.2056A-2(d) and will continue to be so administered, for the duration of the trust. This statement must be binding on all successor trustees.[474]

C. Effective Dates of Gift Tax Provisions

The regulations implementing the provisions of § 2523(i), disallowing the marital deduction for interspousal transfers when the donee spouse is not a U.S. citizen, and the gift tax effects of the creation and termination (other than by death) of spousal joint tenancies, are effective in the case of gifts made after August 22, 1995.[475] Presumably, any reasonable interpretation of the statutory provisions is allowed with respect to gifts made prior to the publication of final regulations.

XII. Planning for the Marital Deduction for Noncitizen Spouses

A. Lifetime Planning

1. Domicile Planning

It may be beneficial for persons who are not citizens but who have significant U.S.-situs property (and who do not have significant non-U.S. situs property) to take steps to establish U.S. domicile. Although by doing so they subject their worldwide estate to U.S. estate tax, they will be entitled to a full unified credit, rather than the $13,000 credit available to nonresident aliens.[476] Obviously, the desirability of establishing U.S. domicile must be determined on a case-by-case basis.

473. Treas. Reg. § 20.2056A-2(d)(6)(ii).
474. *Id.* § 20.2056-2(d)(6)(iii).
475. *Id.* § 25.2523(i)-3.
476. *Cf.* §§ 2010(a) and 2102(c).

Domicile is established, for federal estate tax purposes, by establishing physical presence in a place without the present intention of moving from that place.[477] The subjective aspect of domicile, that dealing with the intention to move, is based on an examination of all circumstances. The IRS will examine the duration of the individual's stay in the United States, the location of family and friends and important personal belongings, the center of the person's financial and business interests, and the size and location of the person's home.[478]

Although there are practical limits on the extent to which some of these features can be beneficially arranged, certain steps can be taken to increase the likelihood that the person will be treated as a U.S. domiciliary. For example, foreign bank accounts can be closed and the proceeds placed in a U.S. bank. If the person maintains homes both in the United States and in his home country, tangible property and other special personal items should be kept in the U.S. home. Revised U.S. wills, powers of attorney, advance medical directives, and other estate planning documents, each declaring that the individual is a U.S. domiciliary, should also be prepared and executed. In addition, the execution of an affidavit of U.S. residency, although arguably self-serving, could help demonstrate the intent of the individual to be treated as a U.S. domiciliary.

2. Unified Credit Planning

(a) General Planning Considerations. The limitation on the availability of the marital deduction for transfers to noncitizen spouses does not alter the need for each spouse to have sufficient property in his or her own name before a spouse dies in order to utilize both spouses' respective unified credits. (This is less of a problem in community property states if there are sufficient community assets.) This planning requirement remains critical when one or both of the spouses is a not a U.S. citizen. When both spouses are U.S. citizens, the process of rearranging the couple's assets, whether by outright gifts between spouses or by severance of jointly owned property, is relatively simple, because the unlimited marital deduction eliminates any adverse federal estate tax consequences. However, the elimination of the unlimited federal gift tax marital deduction for transfers to noncitizen spouses, its replacement with a $100,000 annual exclusion for such gift transfers, the reenactment of the rules of §§ 2515 and 2515A of the 1954 Code, and the uncertainty surrounding the law as to the amount of a gift when an old joint tenancy is severed, dictate careful planning in rearranging the couple's assets.

(b) Planning for Larger Estates. Where the spouses' combined assets are less than or equal to the spouses combined available exemption equivalents of their unified credits, the estates of the two spouses should, from a tax prospective, generally be equalized. However, when the combined assets exceed this amount,

477. Treas. Reg. § 20.0-1(b)(1).

478. *See, e.g.*, Rev. Rul. 80-209, 1980-2 C.B. 248.

it may be beneficial to rearrange the spouses' assets so that the noncitizen spouse has more than one-half of the property.

The more assets that the noncitizen spouse holds in his or her sole name, the less that will have to be placed in a QDOT at the death of the citizen spouse. Further, if the noncitizen spouse expects to leave the United States after the death of the first spouse to die, less property will be subject to the QDOT tax. Also, if the noncitizen spouse remains in the United States, his or her estate will be able to take advantage of the unified credit and graduated federal estate tax brackets. Finally, if the other spouse is a U.S. citizen, the noncitizen spouse can freely transfer assets to him or her through the unlimited marital deduction (without the use of a QDOT), if necessary, during life or at death without the imposition of the federal gift tax.[479]

(c) Generation-Skipping Transfer Tax Considerations. Where the spouses have combined assets in excess of $3 million, it is important, if generation-skipping transfers may be involved in the estate plan, that each spouse have sufficient assets in his or her sole name before the first spouse dies to utilize the $1.5 million exemption from the GSTT.[480] By doing so, the uncertainties created by the QDOT provisions regarding the identity of the transferor for purposes of allocating the generation-skipping transfer exemption[481] are minimized, and multigenerational transfers of property can be protected.

(d) Lifetime Gift Splitting. Often, the spouse holding the greater amount of assets is reluctant to make outright gifts of property to the noncitizen spouse. However, the noncitizen spouse's unified credit and GSTT exemption can still be utilized through inter vivos gift splitting by the spouses. If the spouse with the greater amount of assets is willing to make significant inter vivos gifts to third persons, such as the children and grandchildren of the marriage, the spouses can elect under § 2513 to have the gifts treated as being made one-half by each spouse, thereby utilizing the noncitizen spouse's unified credit and federal estate tax brackets. In addition, if the gift is made to children in trust or to grandchildren, the $1.5 million generation-skipping transfer exemption of the noncitizen spouse can also be allocated to one-half of these gifts. However, unless a gift tax treaty provides to the contrary, gift splitting is not available where one of the spouses is a nonresident alien for gift tax purposes.[482]

(e) Special Considerations. When First Spouse to Die Is U.S. Citizen or Resident. Notwithstanding the various asset strategies discussed above, when one of the

479. *See* I.R.S. Priv. Ltr. Rul. 9309023 (Dec. 3, 1992) discussing the tax effects of an inter vivos QTIP trust created by a noncitizen spouse for the benefit of her citizen spouse, the terms of which included a QDOT for the benefit of the donor spouse if the donor spouse survived the donee spouse.

480. *See* § 2631(a).

481. *See supra* Section VIII.E.

482. § 2513(a) (first sentence).

spouses is a U.S. citizen or resident who plans to remain in the United States and if the other noncitizen spouse plans to remain in the United States, it may be beneficial to have more, rather than less, assets held in the QDOT if the spouse who is a citizen or resident of the United States dies first. Because the QDOT tax is a tax imposed upon the estate of the first spouse to die, more property held in the QDOT will allow for a greater use of the first spouse's federal estate tax brackets.

When both spouses are U.S. citizens, the unified credit and federal estate tax brackets can only be utilized when there is a federal estate tax paid at the death of the first spouse to die. Therefore the QDOT tax presents an opportunity to use these brackets with the imposition of a tax upon a taxable event. However, in order for this strategy to be effective, the noncitizen surviving spouse must have sufficient assets in his sole name so as to utilize his unified credit and federal estate brackets. In community property states, this is less of a problem because the surviving spouse will own his share of the community property assets. Further, the surviving spouse must not intend to leave the United States after the death of the citizen spouse.

Calculations must be performed to determine whether holding a larger amount of assets in the QDOT is advantageous after taking into account the fact that the QDOT may also be taxed in both estates with an offsetting § 2013 credit, which may only be a partial offset due to the state death tax credit in the surviving spouse's estate. If the first spouse's unified credit was used against the QDOT rather than against a trust that will not be includable in the estate of the surviving spouse (such as a credit shelter trust), the first spouse's unified credit will probably be wasted. This is so because although the property will be taxed in the surviving spouse's estate, there will effectively be no offsetting § 2013 credit for tax on prior transfers with respect to that property because the first spouse paid no tax with respect to the property.

(f) Selecting Assets for Interspousal Transfers. In selecting assets to transfer to the noncitizen spouse, the estate planner must determine whether a QDOT would be particularly unsuited or impractical for certain assets. In particular, real estate and business interests that the noncitizen spouse may wish to retain control over rather than having to share control with a U.S. Trustee, should be transferred to the noncitizen spouse prior to the death of the other spouse. Further, it may be desirable to transfer to the noncitizen spouse during his life foreign-situs property that cannot, under the laws of the situs country, be transferred to a trust or that may not be held by a U.S. Trustee.[483] Similarly, the transfer of foreign real estate

483. Section 2056A(c)(3) authorizes the IRS to issue rules governing alternative arrangements for holding assets located in jurisdictions where trusts are not recognized. *See supra* Section V.J. However, no such relief has not yet been made available, and given the legislative history of the provision, it may be very narrow in scope.

to the noncitizen spouse may allow a Small QDOT to comply with the Foreign Real Property Requirement of the QDOT Security Requirements.[484]

3. Use of the Annual Exclusion

Only $100,000 of assets[485] can annually be transferred to the noncitizen spouse. For gifts after June 29, 1989, these transfers must be in a form that otherwise qualifies for the marital deduction.[486] The legislative history of the technical corrections provisions included in OBRA 1990 indicates that only $90,000 of the $100,000 annual exclusion gift needs to qualify for the marital deduction, but the entire $100,000 must be a present interest.[487] If the spouse with more property has significant sole name assets that can be easily divided and which can be accurately valued, such as traded securities or real estate, a program of annual $100,000 gifts to the noncitizen spouse is the easiest method by which sufficient sole name property may be placed in the name of the noncitizen spouse. If the spouse then contributes these sole name assets to a joint brokerage account, the respective contributions of the spouses should be easily determinable.[488] In order for transfers in trust to qualify, the trust must be in a form that (1) but for the TAMARA limitations qualifies for the federal gift tax marital deduction *and* (2) qualifies as a present interest under § 2503(b).

A general power of appointment marital trust would appear to satisfy this requirement. However, the regulations indicate that an inter vivos QTIP trust for the benefit of the noncitizen spouse would not qualify because this trust does not, but for the provisions in § 2523(i)(1), qualify for this gift tax marital deduction.[489]

4. Qualified Transfers

Transfers that constitute "qualified transfers" for purposes of § 2503(e) are not treated as transfers of property by gift. Such transfers include amounts paid on behalf of an individual that are either tuition payments made directly to the educational institution or payments made directly to the provider of medical care.[490] Because there does not appear to be any restriction on the identity or citizenship of the individual on whose behalf such payments are made, such payments could be made for the benefit of the noncitizen spouse over and above the annual exclusion limitation.

484. *See supra* Section III.D.

485. As noted above, the amount of this annual exclusion is indexed for inflation. For transfers made in 2010, the exclusion was $134,000.

486. *See* § 2523(i)(3); Treas. Reg. § 25.2523(i)-1(c)(1); § 7815(d)(1) of OBRA 1989.

487. *See* 136 CONG. REC. H7147 (daily ed. Aug. 3, 1990) (statement of Rep. Rostenkowski introducing H.R. 5445).

488. *See, e.g.*, I.R.S. Priv. Ltr. Rul. 9151044 (Sept. 26, 1991).

489. *See* Treas. Reg. § 25.2523(i)-1(d) (Example 4).

490. *See* § 2503(e)(2)(A) and (B). *See also* Treas. Reg. § 25.2503-6.

5. Jointly Owned Property

(a) General Considerations in Making Gifts of Jointly Owned Property. Often a married couple will own a large portion of their estate as joint tenants with right of survivorship or as tenants by the entireties. As discussed in Section IX.B above, the termination of such joint tenancies may have adverse federal gift tax consequences. In order to efficiently divide such assets, the estate planner must ascertain:

1. What types of property are available to be divided? Real property, bank and brokerage accounts are property commonly titled jointly with right of survivorship. However, significant items of tangible personal property, such as artwork and antiques, may also be available.
2. When was the property purchased?
3. Did the couple elect to treat the creation of the tenancy as a gift?
4. Who provided the consideration for the original purchase of the property, and if it was purchased with joint tenancy assets, who provided the consideration for that joint property?
5. How conclusive is the evidence of the consideration, and could the taxpayer meet the burden of proof if challenged by the IRS on the issue?
6. Who paid for improvements and the reduction of any indebtedness secured by the property, especially real estate?

In addition, the division of certain assets, especially the marital home, can have adverse consequences regarding probate, taxes, creditors' rights, homestead exemptions, and divorce and separation that must be explained to the clients when selecting assets for interspousal transfers. For instance, jointly owned property is not included in the probate estate and is therefore not subject to probate. However, the conversion of a joint tenancy to a tenancy in common will subject each spouse's portion of such property to probate, unless it is transferred to a revocable trust prior to death. Also, conversion of jointly owned property to tenancy in common property removes the protection provided to certain joint tenants under state law against the creditors of only one joint tenant. Further, such divisions necessarily allow each tenant to dispose of his or her share of the property, and may cause the property to be treated as sole name property in a subsequent marital dissolution.

To the extent a portion of the marital home is held in a QDOT after the death of the decedent spouse, if the noncitizen surviving spouse sells the home, the $250,000 exclusion provided under § 121(a) will be unavailable unless the surviving spouse is treated as the owner of the trust property under the grantor trust rules of §§ 671–678.[491] As a practical matter, however, the effect of this depends

491. Grantor trust status may arise where the surviving spouse transferred the residence to the QDOT in accordance with the provisions of § 2056(d)(2)(B) and therefore is treated as the transferor for all other tax purposes. *See* Treas. Reg. § 20.2056A-4(b)(1). *But see* § 672(f), which limits the application of the grantor trust rules in certain cases where the grantor is not a U.S. citizen or resident.

on the appreciation between the death of the first spouse to die and the time of the sale, because, under current law, the portion of the home held in the QDOT will have received a step-up (or -down) in basis at the death of the first spouse.

Finally, couples may be reluctant, for purely psychological reasons, to sever a joint tenancy in certain assets, such as the marital home or securities accounts intended for use during retirement.

(b) Severance of Joint Tenancies in Making Gifts to the Noncitizen Spouse

(i) Tracing Considerations. The need, in many cases, to trace the consideration used to purchase jointly owned property is perhaps the most onerous requirement of the marital deduction limitations. Because tracing has not been required in the past, records are often difficult to reconstruct. In addition, if the proceeds of one joint tenancy are rolled over into a new purchase also owned by the couple as joint tenants, one must examine the source of the consideration for the earlier purchase.[492] Therefore, especially in the case of the marital home, the rules may effectively require tracing of consideration back to the beginning of the marriage. And while this task may be easier when one spouse was the sole income earner during the entire marriage, this is not usually the case.

To the extent the spouses believe they can demonstrate a division of the source of the consideration for jointly held property, be it through transactions in bank and brokerage accounts, inheritances, or earnings histories of the couple, records supporting this conclusion should be collected, and affidavits should be prepared accurately reflecting how the consideration was provided. In addition, accurate appraisals of the property to be gifted, especially when real estate or artwork is involved, can be critical for withstanding a later challenge by the IRS.

(ii) Filing Federal Gift Tax Returns. Although it appears that the filing of a federal gift tax return will be unnecessary when the amount of annual gifts to a noncitizen spouse does not exceed $100,000,[493] there may be situations where the taxpayer wishes to disclose the gift and file a return. This is especially true when the property that is the subject of the spousal gift is a severed interest in jointly held property and there remains some doubt as to exactly how much of the consideration was furnished by each spouse. Prior to TRA 1997, the filing of a federal gift tax return started the running of the three-year statute of limitations.[494] If the federal gift tax return omitted items includable in the total gifts which exceeded 25 percent of the total amount of gifts stated in the return, the statute of limitations was six years.[495] However, disclosure of the particular gift on the gift tax return was not required to commence the statute of limitations.

---

492. *See* Treas. Reg. § 25.2515-1(d)(2)(ii).
493. *See* § 6019(a) and instructions to Form 709.
494. § 6501(a).
495. § 6501(e)(2).

Under § 2504(c), prior to TRA 1997 the running of the statute of limitations on a prior year's gift barred revaluation of that gift for purposes of determining the gift tax assessed or payable for any subsequent period, but only if a gift tax was assessed or paid in such prior year. Thus, if the donor spouse filed a gift tax return and the amount of gift tax due was less than his available unified credit, the gift tax was not treated as having been paid for purposes of § 2504(c). In this situation, while the IRS could not assess additional tax for the year of the gift after the statute of limitations had passed, it could increase the gift in determining the gift tax due on a transfer in a later year. When no federal gift tax return was filed for the year of the transfer, the statute of limitations did not begin to run and the federal gift tax could subsequently be imposed at any time.

Under TRA 1997[496], subject to the rule discussed in below, a post-August 5, 1997, gift for which the limitations period has passed cannot be revalued for purposes of determining the applicable gift and estate tax bracket and available unified credit even when the value of the gift as shown on the return does not result in any gift tax being assessed or owed (e.g., through use of the unified credit).[497] In order to revalue a gift that has been adequately disclosed on a gift tax return, the IRS must issue a final notice of redetermination of value (a final notice) within the statute of limitations applicable to the gift for gift tax purposes (generally, three years).[498]

However, this treatment is available only when the gift is adequately disclosed on the gift tax return. Thus, the statute of limitations will not run on an inadequately disclosed transfer made in calendar years ending after the date of enactment, regardless of whether a gift tax return was filed for other transfers in that same year. Regulations describe in detail the disclosure requirements.[499] However, the filing of a return may "red-flag" the transfer for the IRS.

6. Applying for United States Citizenship

One option that clearly avoids all of the issues raised by TAMRA is for the noncitizen spouse to apply for and obtain U.S. citizenship. The process takes some time, and it is unlikely that it could be completed prior to filing the federal estate tax return of the decedent spouse if not initiated prior to his death. However, the option of relinquishing citizenship of one's country of origin is not, in many cases, a viable alternative, especially when suggested solely for tax purposes.

---

496. § 506 of TRA 1997.

497. Technical correction legislation to TRA 1997 will likely clarify that this would be the case for gifts made after August 5, 1997, with respect to the value of prior gifts—even though the prior gifts preceded August 6, 1997.

498. §§ 2504(c) and 6501(c)(9).

499. See Treas. Reg. § 301.6501(c)-1(f), setting out the requirements for adequate disclosure of gifts.

7. Retirement Plan Assets

Qualified retirement plan benefits present some of the challenging issues when planning for a noncitizen surviving spouse. The potential application of both income taxes and the QDOT tax to payments from such plans, combined with the complexities surrounding qualification for the estate tax marital deduction of plan benefits payable to a trust, require careful analysis of the client's priorities and the tax consequences. Available alternatives include designating a marital trust that also qualifies as a QDOT as the beneficiary of the plan benefits; designating the noncitizen spouse as the plan beneficiary and relying on her to roll over the plan assets into a QDOT that qualifies as an IRA; having the surviving spouse assign an inherited IRA to a QDOT; or leaving the plan benefits in a form that does not qualify for the marital deduction and paying estate tax at the first spouse's death. In addition, where the benefits are not assignable (or, in the case of an IRA where the surviving spouse elects to treat the plan as nonassignable[500]), the surviving spouse can avail herself of the Roll Over and Current Tax Methods of § 20.2056A-4(c) in order to qualify the payment for the marital deduction.[501] As with many aspects of estate planning for the noncitizen spouse, practical issues may dominate the decision-making process, including the desirability of the spousal rollover, the level of control the decedent spouse wishes to retain over plan payments, the size of the plan, the ability to find a qualified trustee who will also serve as an IRA custodian, and the likelihood that the surviving spouse will become a U.S. citizen.

8. Miscellaneous Planning Issues

(a) Treaties. As outlined in Section X above, the planner must assess the effect of the provisions of any estate and gift tax treaty in existence with a client's country of citizenship. The treaty may be important in determining whether the client and his or her spouse will be treated as citizens or nonresident aliens of the U.S. for purposes of the federal estate tax. In addition, marital deduction provisions contained in those treaties may override the provisions of the federal marital deduction.[502] For example, the French estate tax treaty provides to a French domiciliary the marital deduction available on November 24, 1978. Therefore, a QTIP trust will not qualify as a marital deduction vehicle.

The final QDOT regulations also make clear that in the case of a decedent who is neither a U.S. resident nor citizen, where the QDOT provisions do not override the marital deduction provided under any such treaty, the estate may choose between the marital deduction provisions of the treaty and the marital deduction provisions of §§ 2056(d) and 2056A.[503] Furthermore, the specific provisions of the

500. *See id.* § 20.2056A-4(c)(1).

501. For an excellent analysis of these alternatives, see Natalie Choate, Life and Death Planning for Retirement Benefits (4th ed. 2002).

502. *See* OBRA § 7815(d)(14).

503. *See* Treas. Reg. § 20.2056A-1(c).

protocols to the U.S.-Canada income tax treaty and the U.S.-Germany estate and gift tax treaty, discussed above, may obviate the need for a QDOT in certain cases.

(b) Life Insurance. Except when the decedent-insured is a nonresident alien, proceeds of insurance policies on the life of the decedent over which the decedent retained incidents of ownership are included in his gross estate.[504] And even though such proceeds are nonprobate property, where the noncitizen surviving spouse is designated as the beneficiary, the proceeds will have to be transferred or assigned to a QDOT in order to qualify for the marital deduction. If, however, ownership of the insurance policy is transferred to the noncitizen spouse during the life of the insured spouse, and if the insured spouse lives for three years from the date of the transfer, the transfer of the proceeds to a QDOT will be unnecessary. On the other hand, if the insured transfers any incidents of ownership in a life insurance policy within three years of the insured's death, the proceeds of the policy are included in the estate of the decedent.[505]

A gift of an existing insurance policy to the noncitizen spouse may be an effective use of the annual federal gift tax exclusion, because the federal gift tax value of such a transfer is the cost of a comparable contract from the issuer, or, if that is not readily ascertainable (as when the policy has been in force for some time and premiums remain to be paid), the value of the policy for federal gift tax purposes is the interpolated terminal reserve value of the policy (which approximates the policy's cash value) plus a portion of the unearned premium.[506] Future premium payments by the donor spouse/insured will be gifts to the noncitizen spouse and will count against the annual exclusion. Of course, if the noncitizen spouse remains in the United States, and if he or she still has the proceeds at death, then they will be included in his or her gross estate. Nevertheless, such a transfer eliminates the need to hold the proceeds in a QDOT.

Further, the inclusion of the proceeds in the surviving spouse's estate can be avoided, regardless of whether he or she remains in the United States, if the policy is transferred to an irrevocable life insurance trust rather than outright to the noncitizen spouse, and the transferor spouse lives three years from the date the policy is transferred.[507] Such a trust should not, however, utilize the annual exclusion for gifts to the noncitizen spouse. That exclusion requires the spouse to have a nonterminable interest, thereby including the property in the donee spouse's estate. Alternatively, the noncitizen spouse can apply for and purchase a policy of insurance on the life of the citizen spouse. If the noncitizen spouse uses his own assets to pay policy premiums, and if he is not viewed as the agent of the

504. *See* §§ 2105(a) and 2042(a).
505. *See* § 2035(a)(2).
506. *See* Treas. Reg. § 25.2512-6.
507. *See* § 2035(a)(2).

insured, the application of the three-year rule should be avoidable.[508] If the noncitizen spouse predeceases the citizen spouse, he should bequeath the insurance policy to someone other than the insured, because the insured will have to again transfer the policy and live three years in order to avoid inclusion of the proceeds in his estate.[509] If the insured spouse predeceases the noncitizen spouse, and the noncitizen spouse remains in the United States, any portion of the policy proceeds not covered by the surviving spouse will be included in his estate.

If a noncitizen spouse does not want to have property held in a QDOT and is willing to pay the additional federal estate tax that will result at the death of the first spouse, the ownership of life insurance policy by the noncitizen spouse on the life the other spouse will provide the surviving spouse with a ready source of liquidity with which to pay the estate taxes arising at the death of the first spouse to die.

(c) Charitable Trust Planning. The regulations make clear that a marital trust that meets the requirements of § 2056(b)(8) can qualify as a QDOT.[510] Section 206(b)(8) provides an exception to the terminable interest rules of § 2056(b) when the surviving spouse is the only noncharitable beneficiary of a qualified charitable remainder trust described in § 664.[511]

Private Letter Ruling 9244013 (July 30, 1992) describes the interplay of the QDOT rules and the provisions of § 2056(b)(8) in connection with an inter vivos charitable remainder unitrust. In the ruling, the unitrust amount was payable to the grantor for his life, and, upon his death, to his spouse, if she survived him. The spouse was not a U.S. citizen. The surviving spouse's interest included provisions consistent with the QDOT requirements, including a provision that required the trustee to withhold the amount of any QDOT tax imposed on any distribution to the spouse. The ruling concluded:

- Any portion of a unitrust payment made from trust corpus will be subject to the QDOT tax.
- The requirement that the trustee withhold from the amount of any distribution to the spouse the amount of any QDOT tax imposed on the distribution will not conflict with the provisions of § 664, because the trustee is merely withholding a portion of the unitrust payment payable to the spouse; and

---

508. *See, e.g.*, Estate of Leder v. Comm'r, 89 T.C. 235 (1987), *aff'd*, 893 F.2d 237 (10th Cir. 1989); Estate of Headrick v. Comm'r, 93 T.C. 171 (1989), *aff'd*, 918 F.2d 1263 (6th Cir. 1990).

509. Of course, if the insured spouse is a nonresident alien, he can exclude the proceeds of the policy from his estate under § 2105(a).

510. *See* Treas. Reg. § 20.2056A-2(b)(1).

511. *See* I.R.S. Priv. Ltr. Ruls. 9845015 (Aug. 7, 1998), 9845016 (Aug. 7, 1998).

- The estate tax charitable deduction will be available in computing the QDOT tax imposed at the death of the surviving spouse.[512]

(d) Advance Private Letter Ruling. The National Office of the IRS will issue private letter rulings on proposed transactions involving QDOTs and on completed transactions before the return is filed.[513] However, no such prospective ruling will be issued on computations of tax, actuarial factors, and factual matters for prospective estates. Thus, the IRS is willing to issue a prospective ruling on whether the provisions of a trust will qualify as a QDOT.[514] Of course, if there is a change in the law subsequent to the issuance of the ruling, the ruling will no longer bind the IRS.[515]

B. Planning for a Noncitizen Surviving Spouse after the First Spouse's Death

Upon the decedent's death, if the surviving spouse is not a U.S. citizen, the executor and the surviving spouse must determine what action needs to be taken in order to qualify property passing to the surviving spouse for the marital deduction.

1. Spouse Becomes U.S. Citizen

The most basic option open to the surviving spouse is to become a U.S. citizen prior to the date on which the decedent's federal estate tax return is made. By doing so, no restrictions are imposed on property passing to the surviving spouse, provided the property is bequeathed and devised in a form that otherwise satisfies the requirements of the federal estate tax marital deduction. If the surviving spouse has not commenced naturalization procedures prior to the decedent's date of death, however, it may be very difficult to complete them prior to the due date of the decedent's federal estate tax return, even with extensions (assuming an extension would be granted for that purpose). Further, relinquishing citizenship may be an unpalatable solution for the surviving spouse. Of course, if the surviving spouse becomes a U.S. citizen after the date of the decedent spouse's federal estate tax return, the imposition of the QDOT tax can be eliminated in accordance with the conditions of § 2056A(b)(12).

2. No QDOT Created by Decedent

Where the decedent failed to create a marital trust, as when the marital bequest was an outright bequest to the surviving spouse, the decedent's executor or the surviving spouse must create a QDOT prior to the date on which the decedent's

512. See Treas. Reg. § 20.2056A-6(b)(3), making clear that where the surviving spouse's interest in a QDOT is in the form of a trust meeting the requirements of § 2056(b)(8), the provisions of § 2056A(b)(10)(A) apply in determining the allowance of a charitable deduction in computing the QDOT tax, even though the QDOT is not includable in the surviving spouse's estate.

513. *See, e.g.*, § 5.08 of Rev. Proc. 2010-1, 2010-1 I.R.B. 1, 12 (Jan. 4, 2010).

514. *See, e.g.*, I.R.S. Priv. Ltr. Rul. 9003030 (Oct. 24, 1989).

515. *See* § 11 of Rev. Proc. 2010-1.

federal estate tax return is made and must transfer or irrevocably assign the marital bequest property to the trust prior to such date.[516] The postmortem creation of a QDOT will also be necessary when the decedent spouse created a QDOT but the surviving spouse or the decedent's executor wish to place certain assets in a separate trust or a trust having different terms. In addition, when the decedent spouse's will provides for an outright bequest to a noncitizen surviving spouse, the executor may be able to initiate proceedings to reform the will and create a QDOT under that instrument.[517]

Under the regulations, if the property passing to the surviving spouse qualified for the estate tax marital deduction but for the marital deduction limitations of § 2056(d)(1)(A), then the QDOT created by the surviving spouse need not meet the marital deduction requirements of Treas. Reg. § 20.2056A-2(b). Thus, for example, the QDOT need not provide that the surviving spouse receive all—or, for that matter, any—of the QDOT income, as would be required if the QDOT needed to satisfy the requirements for a QTIP or a general power of appointment marital trust. However, because the regulations treat the surviving spouse as the transferor of the property transferred or assigned to a QDOT for all purposes other than § 2056(d), the surviving spouse must use care in drafting the QDOT to avoid or minimize adverse tax effects of the transfer or assignment.[518]

3. Decedent Created QDOT

If, under the decedent's will or other estate planning documents, property passing to the surviving spouse passes into a trust that meets the requirements of the marital deduction but fails to satisfy § 2056A(a) and the regulations, the executor of the decedent's estate or the trustee of the QDOT should reform the trust if the terms of the trust expressly allow for reformation or, if the terms of the trust do not allow for reformation, then initiate judicial proceedings to reform the trust. Such proceedings must be initiated prior to the due date of the decedent's federal estate tax return, determined with extensions of time to file.[519] Such reformations are limited to those necessary to qualify the trust as a QDOT and not to meet the other requirements of § 2056(a). If judicial proceedings are initiated, the statute of limitations cannot expire prior to the date one year after the executor notifies the Secretary of the Treasury that the trust has been changed or that the proceeding has been terminated.[520]

4. Assignments of Property to a QDOT

Probate and nonprobate property and property passing outright to the surviving spouse must be transferred or irrevocably assigned to a QDOT prior to the date

516. *See* § 2056(d)(2)(B); Treas. Reg. § 20.2056A-2(b)(2).
517. See I.R.S. Priv. Ltr. Rul. 9017015 (Apr. 27, 1990), discussed *supra* Section IV.A.
518. *See supra* Section V.H.
519. *See* § 2056(d)(5); Treas. Reg. § 20.2056A-4(a)(2).
520. *See* § 2056(d)(5)(B); Treas. Reg. § 20.2056A-4(a)(3).

on which the decedent's federal estate tax return is made.[521] Formula assignments and protective assignments, when permissible, should be considered. Further, should such assignments cannot be completed, a letter ruling seeking approval of an alternate arrangement should be considered.[522]

5. Appointment of Designated Return Filer

If more than one QDOT is created for the surviving spouse, the executor of the decedent spouse's estate must appoint a designated return filer. As noted in VII.C.4. above, the designated return filer must be a U.S. Trustee of the QDOT. The appointment of the designated return filer must be made on either the decedent spouse's federal estate tax return or on the first Form 706-QDT that is due and is filed by its prescribed date, including extensions.[523] Although the will or other estate planning documents may not contemplate more than one QDOT, multiple QDOTs may be arise where the surviving spouse creates a separate QDOT to hold nonprobate property or a separate trust is utilized to hold retirement plan or other annuity payments due to the surviving spouse. The failure to effectively appoint a qualified designated return filer will cause any QDOT tax to be imposed at the highest marginal federal estate tax rate in effect at the date of the decedent spouse's death[524] and prevent qualification of the hardship distribution allowance provided under § 2056A(b)(3)(B).[525]

6. Disclaimers

Planners should consider the use of qualified disclaimers under § 2518. If the noncitizen surviving spouse has sufficient assets prior to the death of the decedent spouse, a disclaimer of some portion or all of the property passing to the surviving spouse at the decedent's death may minimize or eliminate the need to transfer property to a QDOT. Also, disclaimers by beneficiaries of a trust created by the decedent spouse may enable a trust to meet the requirements of § 2056(b) and thereby allow the executor to make the QDOT election.[526]

Finally, the decedent spouse's will could provide that a disclaimer of property otherwise passing under the will outright to the surviving spouse passes into a QDOT for the surviving spouse's benefit. This use of the disclaimer allows the decedent spouse to be treated as the transferor of the property for all tax purposes, and the treatment of the surviving spouse as the transferor of the property for purposes other than the QDOT rules, should be avoided.[527]

---

521. § 2056(d)(2); Treas. Reg. § 20.2056A-4(b).
522. *See* Treas. Reg. § 20.2056A-4(b)(6). *See, e.g.*, I.R.S. Priv. Ltr. Rul. 200448027 (July 28, 2004).
523. *See* Treas. Reg. § 20.2056A-9.
524. § 2056A(b)(2)(C).
525. *See* § 2056A(b)(3)(B).
526. *See, e.g.*, I.R.S. Priv. Ltr. Rul. 9151044 (Sept. 26, 1991).
527. *See* Treas. Reg. § 20.2056A-4(b)(5).

7. Section 9100 Relief

(a) Standards for Relief. The IRS, in its discretion, may grant a reasonable extension of time within which to make a regulatory election, provided the taxpayer demonstrates that (1) the taxpayer acted reasonably and in good faith, and (2) granting relief will not prejudice the interests of the government.[528] For these purposes, a regulatory election refers to those elections and applications for relief from tax whose deadline is prescribed by regulations published in the Federal Register, or a revenue ruling, revenue procedure, notice, or announcement published in the Internal Revenue Bulletin. Under the regulations, an extension will be granted only if the taxpayer provides evidence, including affidavits, to establish that the taxpayer acted reasonably and in good faith, and that granting relief will not prejudice the interests of the government.[529]

(b) Late QDOT Elections. Section 2056A(d) provides that the election to treat a trust as a qualified domestic trust (QDOT) "shall be made by the executor on the return of tax imposed by section 2001. . . . No election may be made under this section on any return if such return is filed more than one year after the time prescribed by law (including extensions) for filing such return." The regulations governing the QDOT election, which are similar to those for the QTIP election, provide that the QDOT election is to made by the executor on the last federal estate tax return filed by the executor before the due date of the return, or, if a timely return is not filed, then on the first return filed after the due date.[530] Given the language of the regulations, then, it would seem likely that the QDOT election would not be viewed as an election the time for which is expressly provided for by statute. Therefore, when the provisions of §§ 2056(d) and 2056A of the Code are complied with, and the estate tax return claims a marital deduction for the value of the property transferred to a QDOT but the executor fails to elect to treat the trust as a QDOT, an extension of time to make the election under § 2056A(d) of the Code has been granted.[531]

Moreover, even when the estate tax return as originally filed failed to claim a marital deduction, an extension of time may be available within which to create a QDOT, assign property to the trust, and make the QDOT election. However, these actions will have to be completed within the one-year period for making the QDOT election.[532]

528. *Id.* § 301.9100-3(a).

529. *Id.* § 301.9100-1(b).

530. *Id.* § 20.2056A-3(a).

531. *See, e.g.*, I.R.S. Priv. Ltr. Ruls. 201103004 (Sept. 21, 2010), 200910019 (Nov. 20, 2008), 200821030 (Jan. 9, 2008), 200448027 (Nov. 26, 2004), 200211021 (Mar. 15, 2002), 200146015 (Nov. 16, 2001), 9718018 (Jan. 30, 1997), 9623044 (Mar. 11, 1996), 9547006 (Aug. 9, 1995).

532. *See, e.g.*, I.R.S. Priv. Ltr. Ruls. 201103004 (Sept. 21, 2010) (the IRS granted the taxpayer an additional 120 days within which to make the QDOT election when it found that when the taxpayer had relied on a qualified tax professional to prepare the Form 706 estate tax return, and that tax professional failed to elect QDOT treatment for a trust on the Form 706); 200712010 (Nov. 20, 2006); 9803020 (Oct. 20, 1997).

In the past, the IRS ruled that the QDOT election is a statutory election with respect to the one-year limit of § 2056A(d). As a result, § 9100 relief was not available to extend the time within which to make the QDOT election when the one-year period has passed.[533]

However, in the preamble to final regulations regarding the alternate valuation date election of § 2032,[534] which contain a similar one-year rule under § 2032(d)(2), the IRS announced that § 9100 relief would be available to extend the time within which to make a QDOT election, provided that the estate tax return itself was filed no later than one year after the due date, including extensions of time actually granted. Of course, statute of limitations must be checked carefully. In Private Letter Ruling 201052007, the IRS stated that § 301.9100-2(b) applies to requests for relief under §§ 2032(d) and 2056(A) if the taxpayer has timely filed Form 706 but failed to make an election and has taken the corrective actions as proscribed under § 301.9100-2(c).[535]

(c) Assignments of Property to a QDOT. In order to be treated as passing from the decedent into a QDOT (and therefore eligible for the QDOT election), property passing to the surviving spouse must be transferred to a QDOT "before the date on which the return of tax imposed by this chapter is made," or irrevocably assigned to the trust on or before such date.[536] In that connection, the IRS has granted requests for an extension of time within which to make an assignment of property.[537]

(d) Notification of U.S. Citizenship. Under § 2056A(b)(12), if the surviving spouse becomes a U.S. citizen and certain other conditions are met, the QDOT tax imposed under § 2056A(b)(1)(A) of the Code will not apply to taxable events occurring after that date. Regulations provide that the QDOT will no longer be subject to the imposition of the QDOT tax if the surviving spouse becomes a U.S. citizen and certain other conditions are satisfied. One of these conditions is that the U.S. trustee of the QDOT notifies the IRS and certifies in writing that the spouse has become a U.S. citizen. The trustee makes the notification by filing a final Form 706-QDT on or before April 15 of the calendar year following the year in

533. I.R.S. Priv. Ltr. Rul. 9843030 (July 24, 1998).

534. T.D. 9172, published January 4, 2005. *But see* I.R. S. Priv. Ltr. Rul. 201033023 (May 19, 2010) (denying § 9100 relief where the estate tax return was filed timely, but the § 2032 election was not filed within one year of the due date of the return.).

535. I.R.S. Priv. Ltr. Rul. 201052007 (Dec. 30, 2010).

536. *See* § 2056(d)(2)(B) of the Code; Treas. Reg. § 20.2056A-3(b)(1).

537. *See, e.g.*, I.R.S. Priv. Ltr. Ruls. 200910019 (Nov. 20, 2008), 200821030 (Jan. 9, 2008), 200712010 (Nov. 20, 2006), 200211021 (Mar. 15, 2002), 200146015 (Nov. 16, 2001), 9803020 (Oct. 20, 1997), 9718018 (Jan. 30, 1997), 9623044 (Mar. 11, 1996), 9547006 (Aug. 9, 1995), and TAM 9228001 (Feb. 20, 1992). *See also* I.R.S. Priv. Ltr. Ruls. 200448027 (Nov. 6, 2004) and 9834013 (May 21, 1998), ruling that when an extension of time within which to assign property to the QDOT is granted and the surviving spouse subsequently becomes a U.S. citizen, the IRS can waive the requirement for actual assignment of the property to the QDOT.

which the surviving spouse becomes a U.S. citizen, unless an extension of time for filing the return is granted under § 6081.[538] The IRS has determined that the filing of the notification is equivalent to an application for relief from tax; therefore, it has granted an extension of time within which to file the notification.[539]

(e) Bond and Letter of Credit Requirements. As discussed above, the Security Requirements imposed under § 2056A(a)(2) require the trust instrument governing a Large QDOT can provide that the U.S. Trustee furnish a bond in favor of the IRS in an amount equal to 65 percent of the fair market value of the trust assets, as finally determined, or furnish an irrevocable letter of credit issued by a bank in an amount equal to 65 percent of the fair market value of the trust assets, as finally determined.[540] The regulations provide that both the bond and the letter of credit must be filed with the decedent's Form 706 or 706-NA, unless an extension for filing the bond or the letter of credit "is granted under Section 301.9100 of this chapter."[541] Therefore, because the reference to § 9100 relief is expressly contained within the regulations, it seems clear that the IRS contemplates extensions of time within which to file the bond or the letter of credit requirement.[542]

(f) Nonassignable Plans and Annuities—Special Rules. Under the QDOT rules, in the case of a plan, annuity, or other arrangement that is not assignable or transferable (or is treated as such), the property passing under the plan from the decedent is treated as passing in the form of a QDOT if the requirements of Treas. Reg. § 20.2056–4(c)(2) are satisfied.[543] In order to satisfy these requirements, (1) the noncitizen surviving spouse must agree to pay on an annual basis the estate tax imposed under § 2056A(b)(1) due on the corpus portion, as defined in Treas. Reg. § 20.2056A-(c)(4), of each nonassignable annuity or other payment received under the plan or arrangement; (2) the executor must file with the estate tax return the information statement described in Treas. Reg. § 20.2056A-4(c)(5); (3) the executor must file with the estate tax return the Agreement to Pay Section 2056A Estate Tax described in Treas. Reg. § 20.2056A-4(c)(6); and (4) the executor must make the election under § 2056A(d) with respect to the nonassignable annuity or other payment.[544] The IRS has granted an extension of time within which to file the Agreement to Pay Section 2056A Estate Tax and the information statement required under these provisions.[545]

538. Treas. Reg. § 20.2056A-10(a).

539. *See* I.R.S. Priv. Ltr. Ruls. 201220017 (Jan. 26, 2012), 201140001 (June 28, 2011), 201032022 (Apr. 29, 2010), 200949009 (Aug. 13, 2009), 200719002 (Jan. 25, 2007), 200648022 (Aug. 10, 2006), 200451024 (Dec. 17, 2004), 200132013 (Aug. 10, 2001), 9624021 (Mar. 18, 1996).

540. *See* Treas. Reg. §§ 20.2056A-2(d)(1)(i)(B) and (C).

541. *Id.* §§ 20.2056A-2(d)(B)(4) and 2(d)(C)(5).

542. *See, e.g.*, I.R.S. Priv. Ltr. Rul. 9803017 (Oct. 17, 1997) (extension of time to file bond).

543. Treas. Reg. § 20.2056A-4(c)(1).

544. *See id.* § 20.2056A-4(c)(2)(i)–(iv).

545. *See* I.R.S. Priv. Ltr. Ruls. 200821030 (Jan. 9, 2008) and 200445010 (July 12, 2004).

Pre-Immigration Planning

9

Donald D. Kozusko
Richard A. Fava

Introduction

This chapter summarizes the U.S. tax rules and many of the associated planning considerations that would ordinarily apply to an individual who is not resident in the United States and is not a citizen of the United States (a so-called "non-resident alien" or NRA), but who is intending to immigrate to the United States. The discussion is divided into the following general categories and the associated planning considerations: (1) becoming subject to the U.S. transfer tax system as a U. S. resident upon leaving a low (or high) transfer tax jurisdiction and (2) becoming U.S. income tax resident upon leaving a low (or high) income tax jurisdiction. ("U.S. person" as used here means a U.S. citizen or a U.S. resident for income tax purposes and/or estate and gift tax purposes as the context requires).

I. Pre-Residency Planning for Transfer Taxes

A. U.S. Tax Burden Warrants Pre-Residency Planning

If the U.S. estate, gift, and generation-skipping transfer taxes apply to a gratuitous transfer by an NRA during life or at death, the cost to capital is high: the system imposes the same tax rates as for U.S. persons but with a greatly limited marital deduction and little or no unified credit for most gifts and bequests. However, the U.S. transfer tax system is usually avoidable by individuals who qualify as NRAs because it does not apply to non-U.S. property (including U.S. situs property held at death in offshore corporations), nor does it apply to gifts of intangible property (such as stocks). Moreover, modern treaties provide relief for residents of certain foreign countries with U.S. investments, principally by restricting the kinds of property subject to the U.S. estate tax. These special rules for NRAs serve legitimate tax policy goals, such as encouraging investments in U.S. markets.

As a result of these special rules, NRAs who have had no contact with the U.S. tax system other than as investors cannot easily appreciate the tax burden they will face if they become U.S. residents for tax purposes. Fortunately, these special rules also make it relatively easy for the NRA to rearrange assets free of U.S. tax before becoming a U.S. resident, in order to reduce future taxes. Pre-residency tax planning for NRAs often results in significant future tax savings.

B. Long-Term U.S. Residents Taxed as U.S. Citizens

An NRA expecting to reside in the United States for an extended period should realize that his or her future wealth transfers will generally be taxed much as those of a U.S. citizen are. Unlike the rules for transfers by NRAs, U.S. transfer taxes on gratuitous transfers by U.S. citizens and "residents" do not depend on the location or type of property. For this purpose, "residence" means "domicile," and a person acquires a U.S. "domicile" when physically present in the United States with the intention to permanently reside there (that is, with the intention to remain indefinitely rather than an intention to leave).[1]

Both physical presence and intention to remain must be proven, since a person's current domicile presumptively continues unless shown to change.[2] Ordinarily, this means that the immigrant must have also become a "lawful permanent resident" for visa purposes, but not necessarily.[3]

A particularly complex and burdensome set of rules applies when a person becomes a "long-term resident," as specially defined in the U.S. Internal Revenue Code (the Code), and then decides to end U.S. residency, either by physically moving or by electing the benefits of being treated as a resident of the person's "home" country under a treaty.[4] These individuals are treated like U.S. citizens who have given up their U.S. citizenship. Although these rules are written to apply to persons who change income tax residency, there also is a transfer tax element. For such an individual, future transfers of property to U.S. persons, whether by

1. Treas. Reg. § 20.0–1(b)(1).

2. *E.g.*, Estate of Kahn v. Comm'r, TC Memo 1998–22.

3. *See, e.g.*, Rev. Rul. 80-363 (G-4 visa); Rev. Rul. 80-209 (illegal alien); Toll v. Moreno, 397 A.2d 1009 (Md. 1979) (G-4); Castellon-Contreras v. INS, 45 F.3d 149 (7th Cir. 1994).

4. Code § 877A(g)(2).

way of gift or at death, are potentially subject to U.S. transfer tax in the hands of the recipient.[5]

Residents with longevity in the United States are also unlikely to obtain any relief from an estate and gift tax treaty between the United States and their "home" country. As a practical matter, the individuals are unlikely to qualify under a treaty as residents of their original "home" country, rather than as residents of the United States. In that case, they will not qualify for the more limited scope of U.S. taxation granted by the modern treaties (e.g., with the U.K., France, and Germany), which are more favorable than even the limited scope of U.S. taxation for NRAs who are not residents of treaty countries. In that respect, these longer-term residents of the United States are again like U.S. citizens. The United States has not agreed under its treaties to forgo the right to tax transfers by its citizens, wherever located, so U.S. citizens are taxed on worldwide transfers.

C. Gifts by NRA Usually Avoid Gift Tax

1. Scope of U.S. Gift Tax

Transfers by an NRA of tangible U.S. property are subject to gift tax, but transfers by an NRA of property considered situated outside the United States are not subject to the tax.[6] (This rule is the same for the estate tax, as discussed *infra* Section I.D). Transfers of intangibles by NRAs are not subject to U.S. *gift* tax, even if the intangibles are U.S. property (e.g., stock in a U.S. company).[7] As a result, only *real* property and *tangible* personal property *located* in the United States are subject to the U.S. gift tax.

The results can be severe if the gift tax applies, due to limitations on credits, exclusions, and deductions, as compared to gifts by a U.S. person. An NRA is not entitled to any gift tax unified credit at all. This tax benefit—which for tax year 2012 allowed up to $5 million in assets to pass free of tax under the Code—applies only to U.S. citizens and residents.[8] An NRA is entitled to the gift tax annual exclusion that allows tax-free gifts of $14,000 per year per donor per recipient (under current law[9]), but the NRA *cannot* double this amount by the common election to "split" gifts, even with a spouse who is a U.S. citizen.[10] Finally, the NRA's charitable gifts of U.S. property qualify for a gift tax deduction (i.e., tax free) only if made to a domestic U.S. charity.[11]

---

5. *See* Code §§ 877A and 2801 and *infra* Section IV.

6. Code § 2511(a). Property that has a U.S. "situs" is sometimes referred to as "U.S. property" or property "located" in the United States.

7. Code § 2501(a)(2).

8. *Id.* § 2505(a). The amount that can pass free of tax is inflation adjusted and more than $5 million ($5.25 million for 2013), but for purposes of simplicity, we will refer to it as $5 million.

9. The annual exclusion amount is indexed for inflation.

10. Code § 2513(a)(1).

11. *Id.* § 2522(b)(2).

The U.S. gift tax marital deduction is also likely to be limited for NRAs as a practical matter. NRAs are entitled to tax-free transfers under the U.S. gift tax marital deduction, just as a U.S. citizen, but no such deduction applies if the recipient spouse is not a U.S. citizen, regardless of the transferor's status.[12] A donor can make tax-free gifts to a noncitizen spouse of up to $143,000 *per year* under current law.[13] Gifts free of trust will usually qualify for this $143,000 exclusion. However, careful planning is needed for gifts in trust since the spouse's interest must be both a deductible interest under marital deduction concepts and a "present interest" under the annual exclusion.[14]

Thus, avoiding the gift tax by avoiding gifts of U.S. tangible property is critical. Even if a treaty applies to the NRA, it is unlikely to change this critical distinction. Most modern treaties generally allow the situs country to tax such transfers, for example, gifts of real estate located in the United States.

2. Property Conversions

Given this critical importance of the nature of the property at the time of the gift (tax-free except for tangible U.S. property), the inevitable question arises whether it is possible to rely on a "last minute" conversion of the property from such "taxable" property to "tax-free" property prior to making the gift. This question was addressed indirectly in *Davies v. Commissioner*,[15] where the NRA donor gifted cash to a family member who then purchased the donor's U.S. real estate pursuant to a prearranged plan. This was treated as a gift of U.S. real estate and taxed under the gift tax. (Under the law at the time, a sale of the real estate would have been tax-free under the income tax and would, of course, not be a gift at all.) Yet subsequent gifts of cash that were used by the family member to pay off a purchase money note to the donor were not treated as additional gifts of real estate because there was simply an expectation, not a requirement, that the cash be used for this purpose. The import of *Davies* is that the form of a transaction ought not to be disregarded simply because it was tax motivated if the steps had independent significance for other purposes. Absent unusual circumstances, a pre-gift conversion should be effective.[16]

12. *Id.* § 2523(a).

13. This amount is also indexed for inflation.

14. Code § 2523(i)(2); Treas. Reg. § 25.2523(b)-1 and (c)-1. *See* Treas. Reg. § 25.2523(i)-1, Examples 3 and 4.

15. 40 T.C. 525 (1963).

16. *Cf.* Pierre v. Comm'r, 133 T.C. No. 2 (Aug. 24, 2009) (cases collected in n.12 involving valuation discounts in a purely U.S. context, where the question was whether the gift is treated as a gift of illiquid interests in an entity or as gift of underlying liquid assets, in a case where assets were contributed to an entity shortly before taxpayer made the gift of interests in the entity); Pierre v. Comm'r, T.C.M. 2010-106 (RIA) (May 13, 2010) (simultaneous sales and gift combined for valuation purposes when nothing of "tax independent significance" separated the transactions). *See* D. Kozusko & S. Vetter, *Respect for "Form" as "Substance" in the U.S. Taxation of International Trusts*, 32 VAND. J. TRANSNAT'L L. 675, 686 (1999).

D. Clear Opportunities for Estate Tax Planning for NRAs

1. Benefits of Planning if NRA

The U.S. estate tax applies more broadly to an NRA than the U.S. gift tax, but can usually be avoided by proper planning. A significantly broader list of property is considered taxable in an NRA's estate, as compared to lifetime gifts. Code §§ 2103–2105. Generally, the property is subject to the estate tax if it has a U.S. situs (so-called "U.S. property" or property "located" in the United States). Generally speaking, U.S. real estate and tangible property physically located in the United States and securities or obligations issued by U.S. persons or entities are U.S. property and subject to tax unless specifically excluded by a special Code provision.

Most important, U.S. property includes stock in a U.S. company but not stock in a non-U.S. company. Thus, the NRA can avoid the estate tax by investing in U.S. property through an offshore holding company. U.S. estate tax rules do not "look through" these offshore holding companies except in special circumstances, and, as a result, it is commonly recommended that any investments in U.S. property by an NRA be made through an offshore company, usually owned in turn by an offshore trust.[17]

If the U.S. estate tax applies, the NRA's transfers are more severely taxed than those of a U.S. resident or citizen. The amount allowed for tax-free transfers is very low, and few estates qualify for the significant deductions applicable to U.S. residents. The NRA's estate tax credit under Code § 2102(b) is only $13,000 and exempts only the first $60,000 from estate tax, rather than the first $5.25 million allowed to U.S. citizens and residents as of tax year 2013. Thus, the net tax on a $500,000 U.S. estate of an NRA is almost $150,000. The deduction for debts and expenses of the estate is limited. Under Code § 2106(a)(1), the portion allowed is equal to the value of the U.S. property divided by the value of the decedent's entire worldwide estate. However, if the NRA owns U.S. property secured by nonrecourse debt (such as U.S. real estate secured by a nonrecourse mortgage), the entire amount of the debt can be deducted.

The estate tax charitable and marital deductions are also limited. Only transfers to a domestic U.S. charity qualify for the charitable estate tax deduction

17. The entity must have the characteristics of a corporation, and the form must be respected by the shareholder. *See* Estate of Swan v. Comm'r, 247 F.2d 144 (2d Cir. 1957) (Stiftungs formed and operated more like revocable trusts); Associate Chief Counsel Advice 2009-012 (Oct. 7, 2009) (Liechtenstein Stiftungs generally characterized as trusts). Also, the company should acquire the U.S. property, rather than having the shareholder (the NRA's trust) acquire the property and transfer it to the company. *See* Code § 2104(b). Otherwise, quite bizarre tax results might occur. In particular, an NRA decedent may have originally funded a trust with U.S. property and retained the right to amend the trust or receive trust income, causing the trust assets to be recaptured in the grantor's estate under Code §§ 2036 or 2038. The fact that the U.S. property is later converted to non-U.S. property *prior* to the grantor's actual death (by contribution to the non-U.S. corporation) does *not* change the result under the literal language of the Code. *See* TAM 9507044 (original transfer in 1923 while U.S. citizen; death in 1991, after grantor's expatriation).

under Code § 2106(a)(2). Transfers to or for a surviving spouse can qualify for the marital deduction under the same rules as for a U.S. citizen, but the property must pass to a special trust, the so-called QDOT, if the surviving spouse is not a U.S. citizen. As outlined below, this makes the marital deduction difficult to implement, of limited benefit, and much less flexible compared to the alternative of an offshore holding company.

2. QDOTs Are Effectively Useless

QDOTs are of limited use in most cases for serious tax planning by NRAs because of restrictive rules and limited benefit.[18] The requirements for qualifying as a QDOT under the Code and Treas. Reg. § 20.2056A-2 impose several restrictions that are unappealing in international planning. The two most troublesome limitations are imposed by the Code: (1) that the trust interest of the surviving spouse must qualify for the marital deduction (i.e., the surviving spouse must be the sole beneficiary during his or her life, and the trust must generally pay all income currently to the surviving spouse), and (2) under the special QDOT rule of Code § 2056A, a U.S. bank or U.S. citizen must be a trustee or co-trustee and must have the authority to withhold the deferred estate tax, pro rata, from almost all principal distributions.[19]

More fundamentally, using a QDOT *merely postpones the payment of tax until there is a later taxable event, which effectively ensures that the tax will be paid.* The entire trust is taxed if the trust ceases to qualify as a QDOT, and distributions of principal are subject to tax unless made on account of hardship or after the spouse has become a U.S. citizen. Upon a taxable event, the tax is computed using then current values and the same rate bracket as if the property were being taxed in the first decedent's estate (with a credit if the trust assets are also independently taxable in the surviving spouse's estate). The trustee's personal liability is the final element that ensures collection of the deferred tax. *All* of the trust property is subject to the special QDOT estate tax, wherever located, and the trustee is personally at risk if these assets are not available to pay all taxes when due, just as a U.S. executor in a domestic estate would be, but facing all of the complications of a multinational setting.

3. Treaty Protection

A modern treaty with the United States may provide substantial protection from the U.S. estate tax (although the number of countries having such treaties with the United States is limited). The scope of the estate tax as described above under the Code is reduced significantly for NRAs who qualify as residents of treaty countries that have a modern treaty with the United States (U.K., France, Germany, etc., as

18. *See* Michael Rosenberg, *Practical Tips for Dealing With Qualified Domestic Trusts*, 39 Est. Planning 28 (Nov. 20, 2012).

19. Treasury Regulations allow alternatives for assets initially passing to the spouse outright, but the trust approach and the alternatives are specifically and tightly restricted by Treas. Reg. § 20.2056A-1 *et. seq.*

compared to Japan, Switzerland, etc.). These treaties still allow the United States to tax its citizens wherever resident. Yet residents of treaty countries who are not citizens of the United States benefit from the treaty, because estate and gift taxation on their transfers is limited, generally, to transfers of U.S. real estate and to amounts associated with a "permanent establishment" located in the United States (a term of art akin to a fixed place of business of the decedent). Thus, these persons can transfer U.S. equities free of the U.S. estate tax. (Under Code § 2102(b)(2)(A), these residents may also be entitled to a pro rata share of the unified credit available to U.S. persons, but based on the ratio of U.S. property to all property, so the amount is usually not significant.) However, the treaty protection does not mean the NRA's estate passes free of tax. If a treaty applies, that usually means, as a practical matter, that the NRA is at risk for paying a high tax in the home country.

4. Change in Tax Burden If Not an NRA

The net result of the above-described rules is that the U.S. estate tax can be very expensive when it applies to assets of an NRA, and NRAs commonly need to use an offshore holding company to avoid U.S. estate tax on investments in U.S. property. This solution becomes useless, however, once the NRA becomes United States domiciled. At that point, the limitations of the QDOT will still apply, and the newly domiciled individual now faces the same estate tax regime as a U.S. citizen. This also means that, in most cases, the U.S.-domiciled individual will also be considered fully taxable in the United States even under U.S. treaties, so treaty protection will help only in avoiding non-U.S. tax on property "left behind" in other countries. For very wealthy U.S.-domiciled individuals, the result is only modestly better than the severe tax burden on an NRA who, for some reason, has not planned around the U.S. estate tax by using an offshore holding company. In short, the clear opportunity to avoid the U.S. estate tax has disappeared upon acquiring U.S. tax residence, and thus pre-residency planning is crucial.

E. Generation-Skipping Tax Planning Follows Gift and Estate Tax Planning

1. Scope of the GST

As required by Code § 2663, the scope of the generation-skipping tax (GST) follows the same pattern as the estate and gift tax on the underlying transfer.[20] Thus, a transfer by an NRA of non-U.S. situs property is not subject to the GST since it is not subject to estate or gift tax; but the GST applies when an NRA transfers U.S. situs property, except for intangibles transferred by gift. Treas. Reg. § 26.2663-2; § 26.2652-1(a)(2).

> ***Example 1:*** NRA grandparent transfers U.S. real property to grandchild. The gift or bequest is subject to U.S. gift or estate tax and thus also to the GST, unlike, for example, a gift of U.S. company stock.

20. Treas. Reg. § 26.2663-2(a) and (b).

> ***Example 2:*** NRA grandparent transfers U.S. real property in trust for child's benefit for life, remainder to grandchildren. Since the initial transfer to the trust, whether by gift or at death, was subject to the gift/estate tax, the trust is subject to the GST, to be imposed, for example, at the child's death.

Most important, the time for testing whether the tax applies is the same time as under the estate or gift tax, even though the "skip" transfer would often occur later. Specifically, the character of the property, and the nonresident alien status of the grantor, are tested only at the time of the transfer as determined for estate tax purposes (at death) or for gift tax purposes (when the gift is complete). Thus, the GST does not apply to transfers involving grantors who are NRAs and property situated outside the United States as of the time of the estate or gift transfer.

> ***Example 3:*** NRA gifts non-U.S. real estate or intangible property (e.g., U.S. company stock) to a trust for children and grandchildren. The GST does not apply—whether or not the beneficiaries are U.S. persons and whether or not the trust property or the grantor becomes U.S. situated or domiciled before a taxable distribution or termination occurs in favor of a grandchild. But if the transfer is not a completed gift, (see, e.g., Rev. Rul. 73-143) or is a gift with a retained interest for estate tax purposes, the time for testing whether the GST applies is delayed accordingly, applying traditional rules.

The ability to change the situs of property raises the question of whether a "step transaction" analysis could ever be applied to recharacterize what is transferred, e.g., to apply the GST to a gift of intangible or non-U.S. property that was promptly thereafter converted into U.S. tangible property.

> ***Example 4:*** NRA dies and leaves a valuable art collection located outside the United States to a U.S. resident grandchild. Does the grandchild have to delay bringing that property back to the United States where it would then become U.S. situs property?

> ***Example 5:*** NRA grandparent gives a U.S. resident grandchild non-U.S. securities pursuant to a prearranged plan to use those funds to purchase the grandparent's condominium in the United States worth $10 million with an equivalent tax basis, because it would be more costly for the NRA to pay the GST than the U.S. income tax on a sale of real estate.

The regulations originally proposed for the GST would have taxed the transfers in both of these examples under a so-called "anti-abuse" rule, but this proposal applied a rule based entirely on proximity in time and was deleted from the final regulations. Under the final regulations, it is clear that the same principles should apply to this question as under the estate and gift tax, but such precedent on "step transactions" is sparse. The fact of prearrangement might well be enough to apply the GST in the second example above, especially since the plan is to transfer U.S. property from the NRA donor as opposed to funding the purchase of U.S. property from a third party.[21] The application of this principle should be limited, however, because the principles of estate and gift taxation are necessarily very formalistic and rarely involve transactions with third parties where factors of economic significance and business purpose are more likely to exist. The same analysis should apply to a pre-transfer conversion from "taxable" property to "nontaxable" property. A statutory grant of authority to attack conversions was recently granted to the IRS by Congress, but that was limited to income taxation of tax-motivated expatriates.[22]

2. Exemption

There is some uncertainty as to the amount of the GST exemption that applies in the case of an NRA. The regulations provide that an NRA is entitled to a flat GST exemption of $1 million, with no cross-reference to any other section of the Code or regulations.[23] This was the amount in effect for transfers by U.S. persons when the regulations were adopted, and there is technically no reference to any of the inflation adjustments under prior law or that would pick up the ensuing changes to the applicable exclusion amount. Presumably, the intention of Code § 2663 was for the GST exemption available to an NRA to be equal to that available to a U.S. transferor, $5.25 million in 2013. The remainder of this discussion will assume that a GST exemption of $5 million is available to an NRA.

Apart from this question, GST planning for transfers by an NRA is similar to planning for transfers by a U.S. transferor, but some special rules apply. When the transfer by the NRA is fully subject to the GST, the same principles apply as for U.S. transferors, so the NRA will generally decide when the allocation is made.[24] When the transfer by the NRA is not subject to the GST, then the exemption is not, and cannot be, allocated. This makes the GST rules for NRAs very realistic. Because of the rules described above on the scope of the GST, NRAs need not be aware of the GST implications of their transfers unless the transfer otherwise requires the filing of U.S. gift or estate tax returns. For example, an NRA grandfather who has made a gift of non-U.S. property or intangibles worth $5 million to a U.S. grandchild need not file a U.S. gift tax return and need not allocate any GST exemption, because the GST simply does not apply. Similarly, a bequest of non-U.S. property avoids the estate tax, and therefore the GST, so the GST exemption is not needed. Finally, if the transfer is mixed, so that it is only partially subject to the GST, then a special rule for NRAs applies to calculate the inclusion ratio so that the tax can be imposed:

21. See the *Davies* case discussed *supra* Section I.C.
22. Code § 877(d)(2)(B). *See also* Code §§ 2701(b) and 877(d)(2)(E).
23. Treas. Reg. § 26.2663-2.
24. *See* Code § 2632.

Example 6: NRA grandparent establishes an irrevocable gift trust for the primary benefit of a U.S. child and funds it with $5 million in U.S. real estate and $5 million in bonds. The U.S. real estate is subject to gift tax and GST, but the bonds are not.

If the NRA allocates the full $5 million exemption to the trust, the inclusion ratio will be zero. The allocation is automatically matched by the regulations to the taxable U.S. portion of the trust.

If only $2.5 million is allocated, then 25 percent of each GST transfer will be taxed. The inclusion ratio is .25 because it is the number 1.00 less the applicable fraction, which is .75. The .75 applicable fraction is determined by adding together the value of the non-tax portion (the bonds) and the amount of the allocated exemption (a total of $7.5 million) and then dividing by the total trust value ($10 million).

The effect of this rule, as in the domestic context, is to encourage the creation of a separate trust in the amount of the allocated exemption as an administrative convenience and tax minimization device.

Example 7: Continuing on the same facts, if the GST exemption is allocated to assets of that value that are properly set aside in a separate trust, then the remaining portion subject to the GST can also be segregated in a separate trust and used to make distributions to the child that are not taxable under the GST (because there is no termination or distribution in favor of a grandchild).

F. Transfer Tax Planning Considerations

1. Domicile

An NRA may be domiciled in the United States for transfer tax purposes and yet not be U.S. tax resident in the United States for income tax purposes. This situation can occur when an individual has lived in the United States for many years using an A visa or G visa.[25] When the NRA severs ties with his or her home country and no longer intends to return there, domicile shifts to the United States. In addition, when someone has come to and worked in the United States for several years, they will ordinarily become a U.S. resident for income tax purposes unless they successfully claim residency in their home country under a treaty "tiebreaker" provision, usually on the grounds that they have closer connections to their permanent home and that has not changed.[26] In these kinds of cases, it is possible, or likely, that the "permanent home" has shifted and thus the individual also has become domiciled in the United States for transfer tax purposes. This uncertainty as to U.S. domicile should be considered by the NRA before making gifts.

25. *See supra* Section I.B.
26. *See infra* Section II.C.

For example, suppose an NRA comes to the United States to work in the technology industry and becomes resident for U.S. income tax purposes because there is no treaty available or the individual neglects to claim it, even though he or she may intend to return to his or her home country in a few years. Now suppose that the individual's employer grants stock to the individual, and the individual wants to gift some shares to family members. The gift will be subject to U.S. gift tax only if the individual has become domiciled in the United States (as noted above, the U.S. gift tax does not apply to gifts of intangible property by a non-U.S. citizen who is not domiciled in the United States). But given the uncertainty of the domicile question on the facts,[27] the individual should consider returning to his or her home country before making the gift in order to strengthen the argument that he or she was not U.S. domiciled when the gift was made.

2. QDOT Limitations

Pre-residency planning for noncitizen spouses should try to eliminate the need for a QDOT because the QDOT may, in the long run, produce unintended consequences or only modest benefits. The assets placed in a QDOT are not subject to U.S. estate tax upon the first death, but are subject to tax upon the death of the surviving spouse or other taxable event. This result may be acceptable if the surviving spouse remains domiciled in the United States. Yet the overall tax is likely to be higher, as a practical matter, than in the case of a marital trust for a U.S. citizen spouse, because any principal distributions from the QDOT during the surviving noncitizen spouse's life will usually be taxed, which is not the case for distributions during the lifetime of a U.S. citizen spouse. Moreover, the QDOT may result in an unexpected double tax. For example, if the surviving spouse later becomes subject to wealth transfer tax in another country, and the deferred QDOT tax is triggered by principal distributions to the surviving spouse, the other country's tax on the distributed assets will not be creditable against the QDOT tax under the foreign tax credit rules, even as the rules are augmented by § 2056A(b)(10). In addition, the foreign tax credit under § 2014 for residents of the United States does not grant a credit for non-U.S. tax on U.S. property, and it may be difficult to resolve issues between the two countries as to residency of the decedents and situs of property without considerable expense.

3. Pre-Residency Gifts

This is the primary field of opportunity in most cases of pre-immigration transfer tax planning. In typical domestic estate planning for wealthy individuals, the opportunities for using lifetime gifts to reduce later estate and generation-skipping taxes are circumscribed by the fixed nature of the unified credit amount sheltering the gift from transfer tax and burdened with an unavoidable measure of complexity and changing tax rules. The same difficulties will apply to an NRA once the individual acquires U.S. domicile, and, as a practical matter, the former

27. *E.g.*, Estate of Jack, 54 Fed. Cl. 590 (2002).

NRA is more likely to be handicapped by the rule that limits tax-free transfers to a spouse who is not a U.S. citizen. The pre-residency gift is the most powerful planning tool available to the NRA moving to the United States. The gift tax simply does not apply to a gift made prior to acquiring U.S. domicile, other than gifts of tangible property situated in the United States for tax purposes (which property also might be sold or restructured for gifting with no or minimal income tax consequences).

The use of pre-residency gifts allows a variety of transfers to be made to or for the benefit of the NRA's children—and noncitizen spouse—without a U.S. gift tax. The transfer must qualify as a completed gift for U.S. gift and estate tax purposes, passing the tests under Treas. Reg. § 25.2511–2 and escaping later estate tax under Code §§ 2036–2042. Under these rules, a transfer to a broadly discretionary trust would be a completed gift so long as the donor did not retain control over distributions. Under these standards, the donor could even retain the power to make investment decisions, other than voting closely held stock that is subject to Code § 2036(b). The retained power to make investment decisions, if held in a fiduciary capacity, will not cause the gift to be incomplete or subject to estate tax.[28] The donor might even be a discretionary beneficiary, in the same restricted manner now used in domestic planning for gifts to self-settled spendthrift trusts.

Given the virtually unlimited scale of the opportunity to make gifts from a pure tax viewpoint, details are critical. For example, it is important also to look to the nature of the property transferred, as well as the trust, to consider whether the gift will be complete prior to acquiring domicile.[29] Also, any existing trusts need to be scrutinized to determine whether, for example, a trust established by another family member provides the immigrating NRA with powers that would trigger income or estate tax if retained after becoming a U.S. person, such as certain rights to appoint or participate in distribution decisions that would shift distributions to the former NRA or reduce the value of the beneficial interest of the former NRA.

More fundamentally, serious judgments must be made about how to divide up the assets for planning in a practical manner that allows for opportune gifts but also for unexpected reversals in financial results over time, as well as for changes in the tax law, especially if the newly minted U.S. person would expect to live in the United States for a very long time, and possibly for a lifetime, or become a U.S. citizen. As a result, it is often useful to triage assets and associated planning into three categories, each with a different function: (1) one for long-term gifts, usually in trust, that are reliably planned to fall outside the scope of a later estate and generation-skipping tax; (2) one for continuing personal use with complete freedom to use the property or engage in later more typical U.S. domestic estate

28. *See* United States v. Byrum, 408 U.S. 125 (1972); Irizarry-Diaz, *Tax Considerations in Choice of Trustee*, 45 Tax Management Memorandum 283 (July 26, 2004); A. Acker, *Administrative Powers*, 820 TMP 3rd, § IX.

29. *See, e.g.*, Rev. Rul. 98-21, 1998-18 I.R.B. 7 (stock options).

planning; and (3) one for special gifts where the assurance of how the gift would be used or taxed later is less certain but where there is some greater measure of flexibility to adapt to changing circumstances in the future.

This third category blends flexibility with some opportunity for further tax savings. It could include, for example, gifts to a spouse or to a trust for a spouse with a limited power of appointment in the spouse and/or other trusted family members in succession. It could include a freeze gift as described immediately below. It could even include gifts to a self-settled asset protection trust. Such a trust might be appropriate in a situation where it would not be expected to ever make a distribution to the grantor, recognizing that the grantor would be subject to the retained interest rules of the estate tax if the grantor were to die while domiciled in the United States just as any other U.S. person, but also recognizing that the trust could provide a remote safety net for a time and that someone could be granted the power to remove the grantor as a beneficiary later in life.

This rough three-part division would then be planned and implemented after taking into account U.S. income tax planning, such as whether any of these gifts should be made to offshore trusts or whether existing offshore trusts established by the immigrating NRA or by others should be preserved for the benefit of immigrating or non-immigrating members of the family.

Even an incoming NRA moving from a high-tax country will usually find that these gifts will not trigger tax in the original home country, either because the gift tax there is nonexistent or limited in scope, or residency for gift tax purposes can be lost there before actually acquiring domicile in the United States. As noted earlier, to avoid U.S. tax, the gifted property must not be tangible U.S. property. Thus, the NRA would have to take steps first to transform any tangible U.S. property into non-U.S. property (for example, by using an offshore holding company) or into intangible property (such as through contribution to an LLC). The offshore holding company is usually less desirable because the donor and also persons benefited by the gift would usually later become U.S. residents for income tax purposes, and the offshore company structure would then likely cause difficulties if it held passive assets, due to the income tax and trust rules discussed below in Section III.D. The stock of the holding company would likely be considered held by the donor/grantor if in a trust or alternatively held by the U.S. donees whether or not transferred outright, and in any event, it would likely be treated as an equity interest in an investment company that is subject to special U.S. tax rules.

The special facts of each case can greatly influence the choice of a specific solution. For example, suppose, in a given case, it is useful to preserve for at least a short time an offshore private investment company that is taxed as a corporation for U.S. income tax purposes, but, nevertheless, that corporate structure is the ideal store of wealth to make gifts to family members already resident in the United States for income tax purposes. An example would be a family-owned corporation that must ultimately pass a share of its underlying net assets to U.S. persons or that represents the best source of underlying liquidity to finance personal needs in the United States. In such a case, it may be feasible for the offshore corporation to issue a debt security that is then gifted to the U.S. family members, or into a U.S. trust for their benefit. This is a tax-free gift of an intangible, but the debt does not carry the income tax complications inherent in an equity interest in a foreign corporation.

4. Pre-Residency Estate Freeze

One potentially valuable gift solution is the pre-residency estate freeze, which can be particularly useful for a large asset base or an NRA who might otherwise still be subject to gift tax on more direct gifts by the tax law of the original home country. An estate freeze provides an efficient vehicle to transfer future asset appreciation to family members, including those moving to the United States, while allowing the immigrating senior generation to retain an income stream. The advantage to the pre-resident NRA is that the freeze can be structured free of the comprehensive rules of chapter 14 of the Code, which treat all of the classic estate freeze structures as taxable gifts by valuing the retained frozen interest at zero, causing the gift of the subordinate growth interest to explode in value for gift tax purposes and which permit only certain restrictive structures to avoid this adverse gift tax result. Chapter 14, and Code §§ 2701 and 2702 in particular, do not present an obstacle to the incoming NRA so long as (1) those rules trigger the gift characterization before the NRA becomes U.S. domiciled, (2) the subject of the gift is not tangible property located in the U.S. for transfer tax purposes, and (3) there is no lingering retained interest or later disguised gift that would cause all or part of the value of the ownership interest of the next generation in the freeze structure to be recaptured as a later taxable transfer from the senior generation.[30] This favorable result is appropriate in view of the tax policy decision, made quite explicitly when chapter 14 was adopted, that estate freezes should be controlled by the gift tax rather than the estate tax.

As an example, the estate freeze structure could be a partnership in which, through the initial capitalization or a recapitalization, the pre-resident NRA retains a preferred interest that provides a current income stream to him or her for as long as the preferred interest is retained, while the common interest is owned by a trust for the NRA's family. After the immigrating NRA becomes U.S. domiciled, the preferred interest will be subject to U.S. estate tax, but the future growth will shift to the common interest. Through the trust, the benefit of this wealth shift could be set aside for children and multiple future generations as well as for the noncitizen spouse, and these beneficiaries could have continuing limited powers of appointment to adjust the benefit over time. Under ideal circumstances, the later estate tax on the preferred interest might also be avoided altogether. The preferred interest might be owned in a split interest between the senior generation and the younger generations, pursuant to a joint purchase that allows it to escape this

30. *See, e.g.*, Elizabeth Snyder v. Comm'r, 93 T.C. 529 (1989) (failure to convert stock resulted in gift, but not failure to exercise put).

later U.S. estate tax on the senior generation.[31] The structure also accommodates the ongoing cash needs of the NRA after becoming domiciled in the United States. In addition to the current income stream on the preferred interest, the NRA could initially retain and then later sell ownership interests to the entity or the other family members if and when the NRA needed additional cash, subject, of course, to income tax considerations. (For income tax reasons, this technique is more difficult to implement with a non-U.S. corporation that is a passive foreign investment company or controlled foreign corporation. *See infra* Section III.D.)

As another example, the Grantor-Retained Income Trust, the so-called "GRIT" in which the grantor retains an income interest in financial assets in trust for a period of years and the trust remainder constitutes a completed gift, is worth considering. In domestic estate planning, such a trust causes a gift of the entire trust assets under Code § 2702; the personal residence trust is the exception to this general rule. An NRA, on the other hand, could set up a pre-residency GRIT of the same kind that was more generally available prior to the enactment of chapter 14. The trust could hold high-growth and low-income financial investments that shifted growth to the next generation, rather than be limited to holding just a personal residence. Moreover, without being abusive, there is some opportunity for the trustee to modulate the income stream, preserving flexibility over time, just as any trustee should consider the needs of all the beneficiaries and their income tax considerations, including those of the grantor.

5. GST Planning

All NRAs with U.S. family members or U.S. situs assets should at least consider the following planning ideas, even if providing for non-U.S. beneficiaries, but these ideas are especially important for pre-residency gift transfers by an immigrating NRA. As described above, a property transfer by the NRA is never subject to the GST if it was not subject to the estate or gift tax. Pre-residency gifts of non-U.S. property or intangible property will be free of all transfer taxes and thus should be placed in generation-skipping trusts if tax planning for multiple generations is an important factor. As discussed above, property can be converted to non-U.S. or intangible property prior to making the gifts if it does not already qualify. Property that is more difficult to convert (e.g., appreciated U.S. real estate) should at least be segregated and not used to fund transfers to grandchildren if other property is available (to avoid incurring both the estate tax and the GST tax) or used only for trusts to which the GST exemption will be applied. If the NRA is transferring property that is subject to the estate or gift tax, the NRA should consider using a separate GST-exempt trust to take best advantage of the NRA's GST exemption.

The NRA should also consider whether any such property will be sheltered from the GST by the grandfather exception under Reg. § 26.2601-1(b) for trusts

31. *See, e.g.*, Wheeler v. United States, 116 F.3d 749 (5th Cir. 1997) (sale of remainder); J. Blattmachr & G. Slade, Partial Interests—GRATs, GRITs, QPRTs (Section 2702), 836 2nd TMP, sections I.A and VI.B (discussing joint purchases and GRITs prior to chapter 14 and *Wheeler*).

that were irrevocable as of September 25, 1985. Powers of appointment can be exercised in order to extend such existing grandfathered trusts, including the broad power often held by a trustee, in a fiduciary capacity in an offshore trust, to transfer assets to other trusts.

In designing or reviewing a long-term trust, remember also that a grant of a general power of appointment will create a new transferor in the power holder, even if the power is not exercised, so long as the power is validly exercisable.[32] Thus, for both estate and GST reasons, a long-term generation-skipping trust should avoid providing such powers for U.S. beneficiaries so that property of an unlimited amount can be held in trust, free of such taxes for multiple generations if originally funded by an NRA in an initial transfer that was not subject to U.S. estate or gift tax.

6. Philanthropy

The degree of regulation placed on family foundations by U.S. tax law would be surprising to most donors who have no prior experience with U.S. tax laws applicable to family philanthropy.[33] The NRA intending to immigrate to the U.S. may not have the motivation or opportunity to devote much effort or time to pre-residency planning for charitable purposes, but for those who do, the opportunity exists to leave assets in offshore structures by making completed pre-immigration gifts for U.S. purposes in order to later avoid the rules applicable to private foundations and supporting organizations and their substantial contributors. If the donor is willing to forgo the later U.S. income tax deduction in order to keep some part of the philanthropic funding outside of the reach of these U.S. regulatory rules, and if the donor also is willing to arrange decision making so that the gift is complete (i.e., the donor does not personally retain tainted distribution authority over the gifted funds), the funds can be transferred by pre-immigration gifts to and managed in an offshore corporation for future family giving; these offshore funds can be managed in a tax-free jurisdiction and co-invested with other family assets free of the self-dealing rules, political activity restrictions, and other constraints imposed on U.S. private foundations and supporting organizations. Note, however, that the offshore philanthropic entity must generally be in a corporate form (such as a corporation limited by guarantee and without shares) rather than in the form of a trust in order to avoid the grantor trust rules of Code § 679(a)(4) applicable to pre-immigration trusts that could benefit U.S. persons (whether or not family members).

32. Treas. Reg. § 26.2652-1(a)(5), Example 5.

33. *See* Jeffrey Haskell, *Private Equity in a Private Foundation: Tips for the Investor*, 39 Est. Planning 22 (Sept. 2012).

II. Pre-Residency Planning for U.S. Income Taxes

A. Change in Tax Burden

As with the U.S. transfer tax, the U.S. income tax is also comparatively benign for NRAs. The rates are relatively low, and the tax generally applies only to U.S.-source income, although sometimes on a gross rather than a net basis for NRAs. Most capital gains, (other than those from U.S. real estate) and so-called portfolio interest are exempt from U.S. income tax even if from U.S. sources. However, as in the transfer tax context, this favorable climate can darken dramatically if the NRA becomes a U.S. resident. Thus, pre-residency planning can be very useful. Moreover, much more so than in the transfer tax context, the NRA becomes resident in the United States for income tax purposes without any deliberate decision to acquire that status, causing serious tax consequences for the "accidental resident." Consequently, the rules for becoming a resident for U.S. income tax purposes are of special importance.

B. U.S. Citizens and Residents Taxed on Worldwide Income

The U.S. federal income tax system is applied to the worldwide income of a U.S. citizen or resident. The income subject to the U.S. income tax system is much more limited for NRAs than for U.S. persons. The income tax applies to an NRA primarily when the NRA receives income from U.S.-source investments, businesses, compensation for services, and so forth.

There are also numerous "carve-outs" from the taxable income of the NRA, which were usually enacted to promote investment in the United States, to facilitate enforcement, or to avoid enacting rules that cannot be enforced. The principal exemptions from taxation for an NRA are interest on U.S. bank accounts under Code § 871(i), interest on certain so-called "portfolio debt" instruments under Code § 871(h), and capital gains under Code §§ 865 and 871 (but not capital gains on real estate or stock in U.S. real estate holding companies under Code § 897 or capital gains of a person present in the United States for 183 days or more under Code § 871(a)(2)). These exceptions do not apply at all if the income is effectively connected with a U.S. trade or business.

Withholding tax at a 30 percent flat rate is collected at the source by the U.S. payor of dividends, interest, royalties, etc. (on a gross basis, without deductions, but generally reduced substantially by any applicable income tax treaty between the United States and the NRA's home country). Income effectively connected with a U.S. trade or business is subject generally to the same graduated rates applicable to all the income of U.S. citizens and residents. (Such "effectively connected" income is taxed on a net basis that allows related deductions, much like a U.S. citizen or resident, but real estate investments often require a special election to accomplish this because they may not be considered a trade or business for income tax purposes.)

C. Income Tax Residency Versus Estate and Gift Tax Domicile

It is possible to be domiciled in the United States, and thereby subject to U.S. estate and gift taxes, without being resident for income tax purposes. But the converse is more common—acquiring income tax residence without becoming domiciled in the United States. Under the "substantial presence" test of Code § 7701(b), income tax residency will be acquired by an individual who regularly conducts business, or otherwise maintains a physical presence, in the United States and does not engage in deliberate planning to avoid exceeding the limit on days spent in the United States, even if that person's permanent home is outside the United States. This is due to the "substantial presence" test.[34]

The "substantial presence" test really consists of two separate and alternative tests: the 183-day test and the three-year formula test. First, under the 183-day test, a person who is physically present in the U.S. for 183 days or more in a given calendar year and who does not qualify for any special treatment as a student, teacher, diplomat, etc., will be conclusively considered a U.S. income tax resident (unless a treaty "tiebreaker" is available).[35]

Second, the NRA must also be cognizant of the three-year formula test, under which it will still be difficult for the NRA to avoid residency, even with fewer days of presence, once the limit under a related three-year formula is exceeded. The formula limit is exceeded if the time spent in the United States is (1) at least thirty-one days in the current calendar year, *and* (2) the total days over the current year and the two prior calendar years exceeds 183 days (after multiplying days in the immediately prior year by one-third and days in the next prior year by one-sixth). If the formula limit is exceeded, the client will avoid U.S. income tax residency only if he or she can qualify for a treaty tiebreaker or qualify for the "closer connection/tax home" exception under Code § 7701(b)(3)(B)(ii), which applies if the taxpayer maintained closer ties to another country for the year in question and files the required statement substantiating that claim.[36]

Domicile for estate and gift tax purposes, unlike income tax residency, is based on "facts and circumstances" in all cases. Most important, domicile is presumed to continue in the foreign jurisdiction until it is established in the United

---

34. The alternative way that a person can become a U.S. income tax resident is the "green card" test: a lawful permanent resident of the U.S. for immigration purposes (a "green card" holder) is conclusively resident for income tax purposes. These persons will ordinarily also be considered domiciled in the United States.

35. Relief may be available to qualified residents of treaty countries. If a modern U.S. tax treaty applies, the income tax residency of an individual who is considered resident by the domestic law of both countries can be resolved under a treaty "tiebreaker" rule that generally looks first to where the individual has a permanent home, next to the center of vital interests, then to habitual abode, and then to citizenship. A person who is a U.S. income tax resident under the Code but not under the treaty tiebreaker rule can claim nonresident status for all purposes of computing his U.S. income tax liability, not just for treaty purposes. Treas. Reg. § 301.7701(b)(7)(a).

36. Treas. Reg. § 301.7701(b)-2.

States. This rule can decide a close case in the client's favor.[37] The location of business or employment activities does not necessarily determine domicile. Since domicile is less clearly related to current income-producing activities than the U.S. income tax concept of residency, it may be easier to maintain a foreign domicile in a country to which the client currently has no prohibitively expensive tax-producing affiliation.[38]

D. Effect of U.S. Income Tax Residency without U.S. Domicile

Acquiring U.S. income tax residency without a U.S. domicile usually means that transfers of non-U.S. situs property can still avoid the estate and gift tax, but will generate income tax liability. However, there are special rules for such cases that can lead to the following odd results. Bank accounts and portfolio debt will lose the special exemption not only from income taxes but also from estate taxes, due solely to the U.S. income tax residency.[39] Note also that interest on municipal bonds (issued by state and local governments) are exempt from the income tax under Code § 103, which applies to taxpayers in general, but the bonds are not protected from U.S. estate tax. Finally, gifts of intangibles and non-U.S. property by a nondomiciled U.S. resident for income tax purposes will still be exempt from gift taxes even if made while physically present in the United States. But it has been suggested from time to time that cash gifts do *not* qualify for this exception for intangibles. Moreover, because of income tax residency, transfers of property by a U.S. tax resident to non-U.S. corporations (Code § 367) and non-U.S. trusts (Code § 684) could trigger taxable gain as if the property were sold.

E. Temporary Loss of Residency

The U.S. tax laws contain a special anti-avoidance rule under Code § 7701(b)(10) that applies to certain non-U.S. citizens who temporarily abandon their status as a U.S. income tax resident alien. This provision applies to any alien individual who (1) is resident in the United States for a period of at least three consecutive years (the "initial residency period") and (2) thereafter ceases to be resident, but subsequently becomes a resident again before the close of the third calendar year after the end of the initial residency period. For example, if an alien individual resident in the United States from 2008 through 2010 abandoned U.S. residence on January 1, 2011, and subsequently reestablished residence on or before December 31, 2013, the individual would be covered by this provision.

---

37. *See* Estate of Paquette, T.C. Memo. 1983-571 (involving a Canadian who was much more than a "snowbird" in Florida, but held not to be domiciled there).

38. A treaty may also provide relief from the application of the U.S. transfer tax regime. Modern treaties (e.g., with the United Kingdom, France, and Germany) provide a tiebreaker rule much like the income tax treaties, but also provide a special protection (of varying degrees) for citizens of one country who had not been present in the other country for a substantial period of time before the gift or death.

39. Code § 2105(b).

This anti-avoidance rule can have a serious impact. An alien individual who falls within this provision generally will be subject to tax in the same manner as a resident alien on *all U.S. source* income or gains derived during the intervening period of nonresidence—including, for this purpose, all of the special source rules formerly applicable to expatriated citizens and long-term residents. Thus, U.S. income tax will apply to interest income on so-called portfolio debt and any gains from the sale or exchange of (1) property situated in the United States and (2) securities of U.S. issuers. In computing gain, the IRS has allowed the special step-up provision of § 877(e) to apply, so the original pre-residency appreciation can avoid tax.[40] Also, as is true for U.S. persons who surrender their U.S. citizenship, gains on U.S. property cannot be avoided by exchanging the property tax-free for non-U.S. property, and certain income in controlled foreign corporations will be attributed to the alien. *See* Section IV below.

The principal purpose of this anti-avoidance provision is to prevent resident aliens from avoiding tax on nonrecurring *U.S.-source* capital gains by temporarily abandoning resident status. Aside from this rule, U.S. domiciliaries or income tax residents who are not U.S. citizens and not long-term residents (*see* Section IV below) can immediately shift from worldwide taxation to the limited taxation applicable to NRAs under existing law. This rule is particularly important for persons who are not invested in immovable U.S. property (i.e., real estate).

F. Income Tax Planning Considerations

1. Becoming a U.S. Resident When Moving from a Low-Tax Jurisdiction

(a) Accelerating Income and Gains. An NRA from a low-tax jurisdiction who anticipates becoming a U.S. taxpayer should accelerate income prior to becoming a U.S. taxpayer and postpone deductions until after becoming a U.S. taxpayer. The accelerated income will be subject to tax, if at all, only in the NRA's home country, while the deductions can be used against the higher U.S. tax after U.S. residency is established.

There are several ways to accelerate income for U.S. income tax purposes. The owners of a private company can cause the company to declare a pre-residency dividend that clears out the company's earnings and profits account. Subsequent distributions from the company would constitute a return of capital to the shareholders and therefore are not subject to tax. After the dividend distribution, the shareholders could lend the funds back to the company if necessary.

Owners of companies that pay a regular dividend might consider accelerating that income stream by selling the dividend stream to a third party. In *Estate of Stranahan v. Commissioner*,[41] the taxpayer sold $122,000 worth of future dividends to his son for $115,000, which resulted in the father being taxed on the $115,000, while the subsequent dividends were taxable to the son when the dividends were

40. Notice 97-19, 1997-1 C.B. pt. XI.

41. 472 F.2d 867 (6th Cir. 1973), *rev'g and remanding* T.C. Memo. 1971-250.

paid. A variation on this transaction would be to pay for the dividend stream using an installment note.[42]

The NRA could also sell assets to a related or unrelated party in exchange for a note. If payments on the note extend beyond the taxable year of the sale, the installment sale rules of Code § 453 would apply. Those rules generally provide that gain is included in income when the payments are actually received. This rule was designed to postpone the tax burden associated with deferred payment sales until the taxpayer actually receives the corresponding payments. As applied to the pre-immigration sale of property by an NRA, the installment sale rules may have a detrimental impact by postponing the tax until the NRA is U.S. taxpayer resident. The Code provides that installment sale treatment is the default rule unless the taxpayer elects out of the installment method. The NRA, however, would have no reason to file a U.S. tax return to elect out of U.S. installment sale treatment, and the regulations do not provide a method for an NRA to elect out of the installment sale provisions. Under certain circumstances, if the NRA does not report the income after immigration into the United States, the IRS has in the past simply treated an NRA as having elected out of installment sale treatment.[43] Nonetheless, in order to ensure that the gain is in fact triggered prior to immigration into the United States, an NRA could dispose of the note, e.g., through a sale or exchange.[44]

The NRA holding appreciated securities traded on an established securities market may be able to accelerate that gain, and step-up the basis of the asset, by investing short against the box.[45] The Code provides that the appreciated securities will be treated as sold, and gain will be recognized, when the taxpayer enters into a short sale or an offsetting forward contract of the same or substantially the same property.[46] The taxpayer receives a stepped-up basis to account for the gain recognition.[47] Another possibility is a prepaid forward contract that is deliberately designed to be treated for U.S. purposes as a sale, yet gives the holder some room for sharing in future appreciation in value for a specified period.

(b) Restructuring Foreign Corporations. Owners of non-U.S. corporations should also be mindful of the controlled foreign corporation (CFC) and passive foreign investment company (PFIC) rules. *See* Section III.D below. The rules generally result in additional tax or, at a minimum, additional complexity for the U.S. taxpayer-shareholder of a foreign corporation. These rules can usually be avoided

42. *See* Boris I. Bittker & James S. Eustice, *Assignment of Dividend Income and Related Problems, in* Federal Income Taxation of Corporations and Shareholders ¶ 8.07[1][d] Sales (Thomson Reuters/WG&L, 7th ed. 2006 with updates through July 2013) (accessed on Checkpoint (www.checkpoint.riag.com) [August 12, 2013]).

43. *See* I.R.S. Priv. Ltr. Ruls. 8708002 (October 29, 1986) (taxpayer deemed to have elected out of installment method for pre-residency sale), 9412008 (December 20, 1993) (Canadian individual deemed to have elected out of installment method for pre-residency sale).

44. *See* Code § 453B.

45. *See id.* §§ 453(f)(2), 1259(a).

46. *See id.* § 1259(c)(1).

47. *See id.* § 1259(a)(2)(A).

through a pre-immigration restructuring of the offshore business entity into a disregarded entity or a partnership for U.S. tax purposes. This can often be accomplished merely by amending the entity's organizational documents to satisfy the default characterization under the "check-the-box" regulations, or by actually filing Form 8832 with the IRS to elect pass-through characterization. *See* Section III.F below. This restructuring typically will be treated as a liquidation for U.S. tax purposes, which means that the ownership interests in the reformed entity would have a fair market value basis. Thus, after immigration to the United States, the CFC and PFIC rules would not apply, and the ownership interests in the offshore entity could avoid the complications and adverse interest charges that flow from offshore passive investments in corporate form (although these interests may still be subject to information reporting under the rules applicable to non-U.S. partnerships and disregarded entities).

A related planning point would be to segregate passive offshore investments from any active business owned by the client. The CFC and PFIC rules generally do not apply to active businesses held in offshore corporations. Thus, if the pre-residency client wanted to maintain its active business ventures in the corporate form for U.S. tax purposes, it could do so.

(c) Postponing Deductions and Losses. There may be situations where an NRA from a low-tax jurisdiction needs to sell stocks or securities at a loss prior to immigration to the United States. In this circumstance, the NRA should use the wash sale rules of Code § 1091 to defer recognition of the loss. The wash sale rules effectively postpone the deduction by reducing the basis of the newly acquired stock or securities by the amount of the loss in the sold stock or securities. The loss is then triggered upon the subsequent sale of the newly acquired securities. As another example, an immigrating NRA who owns for U.S. tax purposes an offshore private investment company may have a higher cost basis in the stock of the corporation than is reflected in the inside basis of the company's assets; for example, prior dividends will not have reduced the basis of the stock but will have reduced what would have otherwise been the net liquidation value of the company's holdings. In such a case, it may be possible to liquidate the company shortly after the NRA becomes U.S. resident and trigger a loss (while avoiding adverse results under the rules applicable to CFCs and PFICS, as discussed below).

(d) Deferral of Current Income. If an NRA anticipates returning to the low-tax jurisdiction after a few years, the NRA could convert current income into a post-residency future income stream by purchasing financial products such as deferred annuities or life insurance.

(e) Stepping up the Basis of Illiquid Assets. Often, an NRA will own substantially appreciated illiquid assets, such as stock in a privately held company. It may be possible to trigger the gain in those assets prior to immigration, thereby stepping up the basis for U.S. tax purposes, without incurring U.S. income tax and without permanently disposing of the assets. The NRA may be able to accomplish this result under Code § 679 by selling the appreciated property to a non-U.S. trust.

Code § 679(a)(1) treats a U.S. person who transfers property to a non-U.S. trust as the owner of that property if the trust has U.S. beneficiaries. (Code § 679 is discussed below in Section III.A.) An NRA who makes a transfer to a non-U.S. trust within the five years prior to becoming a U.S. resident will be treated, under Code § 679(a)(1), as the owner of the assets transferred.[48] The property transferred to a non-U.S. trust, however, is not considered as being owned by the transferor if the transfer occurred in a fair market value exchange.[49] The NRA's transfer to the trust in exchange for an installment note should be respected as a sale if (1) the trust is not otherwise a grantor trust, (2) the sale is made at fair market value, and (3) the note constitutes a "qualified obligation" on the date that the NRA becomes a U.S. resident.[50] Upon receipt of the installment note from the trust, the NRA could elect out of installment sale treatment and recognize all gain in the year of the sale, thereby stepping up the basis of the asset transferred to the trust. After immigration to the United States, the foreign trust could even distribute the asset (or an appropriate portion) to the NRA in satisfaction of the note. The distribution would not trigger gain to the NRA, and the NRA would own the asset with a fair market value basis. There may, however, be gain to the trust if the trust is not otherwise a grantor trust under Code §§ 672 to 677, i.e., after the grantor has become a U.S. resident. In addition, the NRA would need to report on Form 3520 the outstanding note and payments made on the note.[51]

2. Becoming a U.S. Resident When Moving from a High-Tax Jurisdiction

An NRA coming to the United States from a high-tax jurisdiction should look for tax planning opportunities where transactions are characterized differently in the United States and the home country, so that under the home country tax law, the NRA is still deferring income but is at the same time accelerating income for U.S. tax purposes prior to becoming a U.S. taxpayer. Given the myriad of provisions in the Code that are designed to trigger income or that restrict the ability to engage in tax-free exchanges or other transactions, it is not uncommon to find that the tax law of the NRA's home country does not impose an income tax on events that do in fact trigger a tax under U.S. law. If such a mismatch cannot be found in the particular case, it may be necessary for the NRA from a high-tax jurisdiction to move to a third country with favorable tax laws prior to coming to the United States.

48. *Id.* § 679(a)(4); Prop. Treas. Reg. § 1.679-5(a).

49. Code § 679(a)(2)(B); Prop. Treas. Reg. § 1.679-4(a)(4).

50. Prop. Treas. Reg. § 1.679-4(d); *see also* I.R.S. Notice 97-34, 1997-1 C.B. 422; *General Explanation of Tax Legislation Enacted in 104th Congress: Joint Comm. on Taxation*, 104th Cong. 272 (Dec. 18, 1996).

51. Prop. Treas. Reg. § 1.679-4(d)(1)(vi).

III. Pre-Residency Planning for Foreign Trusts and Investment Companies

A. Trusts "Owned" by the Grantor (Grantor Trusts)

1. Benefits of Grantor Trusts

In the international context, U.S. grantor trust status may produce favorable results. If a trust funded by an NRA is treated as a grantor trust after applying the special rules of Code § 672(f), then it is likely that neither the trust nor the beneficiaries would pay U.S. income tax on its income during the lifetime of the NRA. Regardless of the situs of the trust, i.e., domestic or foreign, the grantor trust rules cause the NRA grantor to be treated as the owner of the trust, resulting in the trust's income and/or gains being attributed to the NRA for tax purposes.[52] As explained above in II.B., an NRA is subject to U.S. tax only on certain kinds of income.

U.S. beneficiaries of a foreign grantor trust created by a foreign grantor receive distributions free of U.S. income tax.[53] The same is true of a U.S.-based grantor trust.[54] The income and gains of a grantor trust are considered earned by the grantor, rather than the trust, and therefore do not become part of the accumulated income history of the trust. This prevents a U.S. trust beneficiary from being adversely taxed upon a later distribution of such accumulated income. The U.S. beneficiary treats the distribution for income tax purposes as if it came directly from the NRA grantor, and if it is a gift, the beneficiary does not include it in gross income.[55]

Similarly, the stock of a foreign corporation held by such a "grantor trust" is also considered to be owned by the NRA grantor and would not be attributed to the U.S. beneficiaries of the trust. As a result, such stock would generally not be considered stock of a controlled foreign corporation or passive foreign investment company, as explained below in section III.D, thereby avoiding adverse tax treatment.

2. Inbound Rules

In view of the above favorable results for U.S. beneficiaries of grantor trusts, certain inbound trust rules limit the extent to which a foreign person is treated as owner of the trust property under the grantor trust rules. (In this context, "inbound" is merely a convenient way to refer to payments from non-U.S. payors to U.S. recipients, as distinct from "outbound" payments moving in the other direction.) Due to the application of the special grantor trust rules of Code § 672(f)

52. Code § 671.

53. Rev. Rul. 69-70, 1969-1 C.B. 182.

54. *E.g.*, I.R.S. Priv. Ltr. Rul. 9152011 (Sept. 23, 1991) (U.S. grantor trust created by an NRA who invested in bank deposits at a domestic U.S. bank; no U.S. tax imposed on the trust income because NRA not taxable on bank account interest).

55. Code § 102.

and the grandfather protection for trusts in existence on September 19, 1995, a non-U.S. trust will be considered a grantor trust only if it falls into one of two categories.

The first category is where the trust is "revocable." If the trust is revocable, it must be revocable by the grantor or the grantor's spouse either (1) without anyone else's consent or (2) only with the consent of someone who is a "subservient" and "related" party (or simply a nonadverse party if the trust is grandfathered). Offshore trusts that are drafted as revocable trusts, however, often are written to require the consent of a protector who is unlikely to qualify as a "related" and "subservient" party.[56] The second category is a trust that permits distributions only to the grantor or the grantor's spouse during the grantor's life (unless the trust is grandfathered).[57]

Special rules also apply in identifying the grantor. An accommodation grantor, i.e., a person who creates or funds a trust on behalf of another, is treated as a grantor for purposes of Code § 671 but is not treated as the owner of the trust.[58] As grantor, the accommodating party will have a reporting obligation under Code § 6048.[59] Similarly, if a trust makes a gratuitous transfer to another trust, the grantor of the transferor trust is generally treated as the grantor of the transferee trust to the extent of the property transferred.[60]

Of particular relevance to pre-residency planning, certain persons may also be "deemed" to be a grantor under Code § 672 (f)(5). This special rule limits the tax effectiveness of certain grantor trusts established by non-U.S. persons for the benefit of U.S. beneficiaries, by treating the U.S. beneficiary as the grantor to the extent he or she has made direct or indirect gifts to the foreign grantor, whether or not prearranged or tax-motivated. The Treasury Department concluded that proof of prearrangement and tax avoidance was too difficult to obtain in this context, and Congress agreed. A simple example will illustrate the abuse (which might be colloquially referred to as the "Give and Go"): A and B are non-U.S. persons. A plans to immigrate to the United States, but A first makes a substantial gift to B, who then uses those funds to establish a trust under which A is a discretionary income beneficiary. The trust is revocable by B so that B would be treated as the owner of the trust under the grantor trust rules. A moves to the United States and then receives tax-free distributions from the trust. Code § 672(f)(5) puts an end to this by treating A (not B) as the grantor.

---

56. Treas. Reg.§ 1.672(f)-3(a).

57. *Id.* § 1.672(f)-3(b). The "grandfather" exception applies to trusts in existence on September 19, 1995, and that have not been funded since then or for which a separate account has been maintained for all such additions. *Id.* § 1.672(f)-3(a)(3).

58. *Id.* § 1.672-2T(e)(1).

59. *See* Code §§ 6048(a)(3) and 6048(a)(4).

60. Treas. Reg. § 1.672-2T(e)(5).

3. Outbound Rules

Special rules also apply to outbound grantor trusts. A U.S. person who transfers property to a foreign trust is treated as the owner of the transferred property if the trust has a U.S. beneficiary.[61] The trust is treated as having a U.S. beneficiary for the tax year unless (1) the trust terms provide that no part of the income or corpus of the trust may be paid to or accumulated for the benefit of a U.S. person, and (2) no part of the income or corpus of the trust may be paid to or for the benefit of a U.S. person if the trust terminates.[62]

These outbound rules may apply to an NRA who later immigrates to the United States. For transfers after February 6, 1995, a nonresident who becomes a U.S. resident within five years of directly or indirectly transferring property to a foreign trust is treated as a U.S. transferor for purposes of Code § 679(a)(1).[63] Such a person is treated as transferring the property to the foreign trust on the grantor's residency starting date (as determined under Code § 7701(b)(2)(A)). The amount deemed transferred is the portion of the trust (including undistributed earnings) attributable to the property previously transferred.[64] This does not mean that there is also a deemed transfer for other purposes of the Code. For example, there is nothing in the Code suggesting that the deemed transfer under § 679 should trigger gain under § 684 as if the person was in fact making a transfer as a U.S. resident.

The provisions of Code § 679 contain an exception for fair market value transfers. A transferor is not treated as the owner of a foreign trust with U.S. beneficiaries if the trust paid fair market value to the transferor for the property transferred.[65] Obligations issued by the trust, by any grantor, owner, or beneficiary of the trust, or by certain related persons, are generally not taken into account when applying this exception unless the obligation is a "qualified obligation."[66] Principal payments by the trust on any such obligations are taken into account on and after the date of the payment in determining the portion of the trust attributable to the property transferred.[67]

It is important to recognize that the § 679 five-year rule referenced above may undercut the qualified obligation exception to the extent that there is undistributed net income on the residency starting date attributable to the transferred property.[68] The undistributed net income is included in the amount deemed transferred on the residency starting date but ordinarily would not have been included in the amount of the qualified obligation executed years earlier. This mismatch

---

61. Code § 679(a)(1); Treas. Reg. § 1.679-1(a).
62. Code § 679(c)(1); Treas. Reg. § 1.679-2(a).
63. Code § 679(a)(4); Treas. Reg. § 1.679-5(a).
64. Code § 679(a)(4)(B); Treas. Reg. § 1.679-5(b)(2).
65. Code § 679(a)(2)(B); Treas. Reg. § 1.679-4(a)(4).
66. Treas. Reg. § 1.679-4(c); H.R. Conf. Rep. No. 737, 104th Congress 335 (1996); *see also* I.R.S. Notice 97-34, 1997-1 C.B. 422.
67. Code § 679(a)(3)(B); Treas. Reg. § 1.679-4(d)(6).
68. *See* Code § 679(a)(4)(B).

could cause the qualified obligation to be less than the "amount transferred," but that would be an anomalous result and runs counter to the statutory scheme. It is also important to recognize that the use of a qualified obligation does not necessarily prevent gain recognition under § 684. Under the regulations for § 684, a U.S. transferor must recognize gain upon the fair market value transfer of appreciated property to a *related* foreign trust, even if the trust pays for the property using a qualified obligation.[69] Under this regulation, the qualified obligation does not defer gain recognition, and the installment method is not available.

B. Current Income Distributions from Nongrantor Trusts

A nongrantor trust that is not resident in the United States for income tax purposes (a "foreign trust") is nevertheless governed by the same basic distributable net income (DNI) regime as domestic trusts when it makes a distribution. The foreign trust will be regarded for federal income tax purposes as a mere conduit to the extent it distributes (or is deemed to distribute) only amounts attributable to its DNI for the current tax year.[70] The tax treatment, therefore, will flow through to the beneficiaries, and the beneficiary will be taxed in roughly the same manner as if he or she had earned that distributed income directly.[71] This is the traditional rule for DNI, as defined in Code § 643, which is roughly equivalent to the trust's net ordinary income and other taxable income, as determined under U.S. income tax principles; however, the DNI of a foreign trust includes the excess of capital gains over capital losses.

C. Accumulation Distributions from Nongrantor Trusts

A number of special rules apply to distributions by a *foreign* nongrantor trust to a U.S. beneficiary if the trust has accumulated income. These rules basically levy an income tax at ordinary income tax rates, plus an interest charge on the tax that was previously deferred, to the extent there is an "accumulation distribution."

An accumulation distribution occurs when two conditions are satisfied: (1) distributions for the year exceed the current year's income (as measured for both income tax purposes and accounting purposes), and (2) there is undistributed net income (UNI) in the trust (*including undistributed capital gains*) from prior years during which the U.S. beneficiary now receiving the distribution was also then a U.S. person.[72] While the statutory analysis is complex, the consensus view of the commentators supports the conclusion that the tax on the accumulation should not apply in the distribution year if the beneficiary was not a U.S. person

---

69. *See* Treas. Reg. § 1.684-1(d), Example 5.

70. Code § 651(b) (limiting deduction to amount of DNI for the taxable year).

71. *Id.* § 652 (requiring that the amount of income for the taxable year that is required to be distributed by a trust under Code § 651 shall "be included in the gross income of the beneficiaries to whom the income is required to be distributed").

72. Code §§ 643(b), 652, 665(b), 666(a), and 667(last part of first sentence); Prop. Treas. Reg. § 1.652(b)-1 (character of amounts).

in the prior year of accumulation, a circumstance that seems likely in the context under consideration here.[73]

An accumulation distribution from a foreign trust can have serious adverse tax implications to a U.S. beneficiary. A distribution of more than the trust's current year income is almost certain to include an accumulation distribution because in calculating UNI, "income" includes foreign-source income even though such income is not taxable to the trust because it is not resident in the United States.[74] Capital gains also are taxed adversely when accumulated and later distributed from the foreign trusts. They are added to UNI in foreign trusts, and the substantially lower effective U.S. income tax rate on long-term capital gains under current law is lost because such accumulation distributions from a foreign trust are taxed as ordinary income at the higher rate. Code §§ 643(a)(6), 667(e). Finally, the trust may have expenses that are not deductible against income under U.S. tax law (e.g., expenses of maintaining a personal residence). Thus, income that is not taxable to the foreign trust, but that is taxable to the U.S. beneficiaries and not used for expenses that are *deductible* to the trust, will be considered UNI.

An accumulation distribution from a foreign trust also triggers an interest charge. Prior to 1996, an accumulation distribution was taxed at the U.S. beneficiaries' average marginal tax rate for the prior five years, plus interest computed at a fixed annual rate of 6 percent, with no compounding.[75] When an accumulation distribution involved amounts accumulated in more than one year, the deferral period for the 6 percent charge was the average number of years of deferral, but the average was not weighted to take into account the amount of the distribution from each year. In 1996, Congress provided for a nondeductible *compound* interest charge applied to the amount of tax that was effectively deferred during the time that the beneficiary receiving the distribution was a U.S. person (regardless of the beneficiary's age). The interest rate is 6 percent per year for distributions from accumulations attributed to the period prior to 1996, and that rate is applied on a compound basis as of January 1, 1996. For income earned and accumulated thereafter, the varying rate for tax underpayments applies.[76]

Although not technically limited to foreign trusts with accumulated income, a special rule for foreign trusts under Code § 643(i)(1) treats the use of a personal residence (or tangible property such as artwork) by a U.S. beneficiary (or grantor

73. J. Nuñez & A. Mirabito, *Just Off the Boat, Trust Fund in Hand*, Trusts & Estates (Dec. 2005); Zaritsky, Lane & Danforth, Federal Income Taxation of Estates and Trusts: Application of Throwback Rule When Beneficiary Was Not Taxable in Some Base Period Years ¶ 6.06[6][b] (3d ed. 2001, with updates through Nov. 2012) (online version accessed on Checkpoint (www.checkpoint.riag.com)). *But see* M. Spielman, U.S. International Estate Planning, Accumulation Trust Throwback Rules ¶ 5.08[2][a] (2012).

74. Code § 643(a)(6).

75. *Id.* §§ 666, 667(a) (referring to § 668 for the amount of interest); Code § 668(a) (prior to its amendment in the Small Business Job Protection Act of 1996, Pub. L. No. 104–88, § 1906(a), 110 Stat. 1755, 1914).

76. Code §§ 665(b) (defining "accumulation distribution"), 667(a)(3), 668, and 6621(a)(2) (explaining that the determination of interest rates is the rate applicable to underpayments of tax).

or related person) as a deemed distribution (unless fair market rent is paid). This result would be particularly troublesome for a trust with accumulated income because of the accumulation distribution rules, and the rule might be easily overlooked if an immigrating NRA has access to such property as a beneficiary of an offshore trust previously established by another family member.

D. U.S. Income Tax on U.S. Shareholders of Foreign Corporations

Several special U.S. tax provisions address ownership in non-U.S. corporations by U.S. persons, particularly investment companies or companies in a tax haven. Since the U.S. generally does not tax non-U.S. corporations on foreign-source income, these special U.S. tax rules are designed to prevent U.S. persons from using non-U.S. corporations to avoid tax by accumulating income offshore. These rules are principally, though not entirely, directed at the passive investment assets of non-U.S. corporations. The impact of these rules can be particularly disruptive if, for example, a non-U.S. trust in a tax haven jurisdiction owns one or more such passive investment corporations, and the trust has one or more U.S. beneficiaries governed by these rules, such as an NRA who has become U.S. resident without any related tax planning. Similarly, an NRA who holds such shares directly and plans to immigrate to the United States has a serious need for planning for these shares.

1. CFC

The controlled foreign corporation (CFC) rules require closely held U.S. ownership of the stock. In broad outline, a foreign corporation is a CFC if more than 50 percent of its stock, by value or vote, is owned directly, indirectly, or constructively by U.S. shareholders who, for CFC purposes, each hold or are deemed to hold 10 percent or more of the company's stock by vote.[77] Such a U.S. shareholder of a CFC must include in his own income the pro rata share of the CFC's income, including subpart F income (which in turn includes foreign personal holding company income with certain modifications, and sales and services income derived from transactions with related parties) and certain other items (such as any increase in the company's earnings invested in U.S. property).[78] Such U.S. shareholders are generally not simultaneously subject to the passive foreign investment company rules on the same stock.[79]

2. PFIC

As part of the Tax Reform Act of 1986, Congress passed the passive foreign investment company (PFIC) rules in order to reduce the opportunity to defer tax on passive income through widely held offshore corporate funds that avoided the CFC rules due to the lack of control by U.S. persons. Accordingly, a PFIC is

77. Code § 957 (delineating what constitutes a CFC).

78. *Id.* § 951.

79. *Id.* § 1296, *amended by* Code § 1121 of Taxpayer Relief Act of 1997, Pub. L. No. 105-34.

characterized by a passive income/assets test, but the stock ownership can be closely or widely held, and the percentage of U.S. ownership is irrelevant. A U.S. shareholder of a PFIC, such as a foreign mutual fund, must choose among a few unappealing alternatives: (1) current inclusion in income of the U.S. shareholder's pro rata share of current ordinary income and capital gains of the PFIC pursuant to a shareholder election (a so-called "qualified electing fund" or "QEF" election), under Code § 1295, (2) a "mark-to-market" election for marketable PFIC securities where gain is taxed annually at ordinary income rates under Code § 1296, or (3) upon a sale of the PFIC stock (or certain distributions to the shareholders), the imposition of ordinary income tax treatment and a compounding interest charge.[80] It is important to note that the interest charge is calculated on certain assumptions that are purportedly designed to estimate the deferral of U.S. tax on undistributed gains and income but seem instead to assume the greatest possible deferral and corresponding interest charge by treating the gain as earned equally over the deferral period.

E. Attribution of Investment Company Stock to U.S. Beneficiaries

In both of these offshore investment company provisions, Congress addressed ownership by foreign trusts. The CFC and PFIC rules each attribute stock owned by a trust to the beneficial owners of the trust.[81] In applying the CFC rules, it is important to distinguish between attribution for testing status and attribution for purposes of taxing corporate income to shareholders. The CFC rules have broad and detailed provisions attributing ownership among family members and to and from entities (trusts, corporations, partnerships) in order to test for CFC status. Attribution for income inclusion purposes is much more limited, but ownership by foreign entities generally cannot be used as a broad shield to allow the U.S. shareholder to avoid including CFC income in his or her personal income tax obligation. As indicated below, it is not clear how this last rule applies to include trust income in the income of beneficiaries. Attribution of ownership is generally not as important under the PFIC rules because U.S. control is irrelevant for PFIC testing purposes. However, the PFIC attribution rules of Code § 1298 do attribute ownership of PFIC stock held by an entity to the owner of the entity, proportionately, through multiple tiers, in order to impute ownership to a U.S. person for purposes of applying the alternative taxing regimes. In addition, when the PFIC rules measure the critical time period for computing the tax deferral and the related interest charge, Code §§ 1291(a)(3) and 1223(2) provide for "tacking" if the transferor passed on a carryover basis. Thus, a transfer by gift (or bequest, Code § 1291(e)) from one generation to the next will not purge the taint of the deferred tax and accumulating interest charge due on sale by an ultimate U.S. resident or citizen owner.

---

80. Code § 1291.

81. Code §§ 958(a)(2), 1298(b)(5); Treas. Reg. § 1.951-1 (as amended in 1983).

If applied literally, the PFIC attribution rules and related provisions in Code § 1298 could lead to severe results when applied to shares of stock held by a foreign nongrantor trust. The PFIC regime ordinarily does not cause phantom income in the absence of a cashless disposition of stock.[82] There is also no automatic deemed distribution to the shareholder, which is consistent with the concept that closely held ownership or U.S. control is irrelevant for defining a PFIC. However, if a U.S. beneficiary were attributed ownership of the PFIC stock owned by a foreign trust, does that mean that Code § 1298(b)(5) is applied literally, and the beneficiary could then be attributed phantom income when the PFIC pays a dividend *to the trust*? The beneficiary would be charged with income as if the beneficiary had actually received from the PFIC the portion of the dividend attributed to the beneficiary from the trust, even though the beneficiary may not actually be receiving any comparable distributions from the trust. The result would be quite different than the treatment of a U.S. beneficiary for whom trust income is being accumulated from other sources at the trust level (or in, say, investment partnerships) and also different from the treatment of an outright U.S. owner of PFIC shares. These persons are generally free of U.S. tax liability on the income until it is received, subject, of course, to an interest charge for deferral.

Any such formalistic attribution from the trust's share ownership to the beneficiaries can raise serious practical problems. For example, distributions from the trust may be needed by the U.S. beneficiary to pay the resulting taxes, and these tax payments to the U.S. government, and related reporting of information on the trust and the underlying corporation, can be disruptive to the confidentiality concerns of other branches of the family who may not have any similar obligation. Also, even if no distributions are required, a detailed information return may still be required by these foreign corporation rules.[83] Keep in mind that offshore nongrantor trusts are not funded by U.S. persons, and the U.S. beneficiary is unlikely to enjoy a clearly enforceable right to trust distributions, and, unlike a typical partner or stockholder, never voluntarily invested in the structure. There is usually no assurance that the taxable income at issue, even if paid in fact to the trust, will actually be paid out to the current U.S. beneficiaries then or at any future time, since beneficial interests in the customary offshore trust are largely indeterminate, and the trust language usually grants the trustee wide discretion over distributions.

The Code also contemplates that this issue will be addressed in regulations, but regulations have not been issued during the period of over twenty-five years since the PFIC provisions were enacted, nor has the core issue of income attribution been addressed in the regulations under the preexisting CFC regime. In both the CFC and PFIC regimes, the statute calls for the stock to be attributed "proportionately" to the beneficiaries, without any statutory reference to how the

82. Prop. Treas. Reg. 1.1291-3(b).

83. *See* Code § 1298(f); *but see* Notice 2011-55, 2011-29 I.R.B. 53 (suspending the filing requirement in certain circumstances pending release of new Form 8621).

proportion is measured. Sometimes the existing regulations refer again to attributing ownership to the beneficiaries "proportionately," without defining the term.[84]

This lack of guidance leads to uncertainty in determining income tax liability and raises the real concern that a U.S. beneficiary of a foreign nongrantor trust might be subject to current taxation on "phantom" income under the PFIC or CFC anti-deferral regimes. Arguably, there are at least three methods that could be used to attribute stock of a foreign corporation owned by a foreign trust to the trust beneficiaries: (1) actuarial, (2) pure current distributions, or (3) facts and circumstances, but it remains unclear which method could reasonably be applied to a particular set of facts.[85] It appears that with respect to the PFIC regime, the stance of the IRS is that a facts-and-circumstances test should apply.[86] This position was not pressed by the IRS in a court proceeding, however, and even if it fully succeeded in that case, which seems doubtful, it would not have provided much guidance, if at all, for application in other cases.

However, there is a fourth system available—the principles of subchapter J of the Code. If actual distributions were the key to attribution, and the delay was compensated for by an interest charge, then the PFIC rules, if not the CFC rules, would be harmonized with the rules for trust accumulations. The American College of Trust and Estate Counsel (ACTEC) has recommended this approach, which is discussed in Stephen K. Vetter, *ACTEC Proposals Integrate Subchapter J, PFIC Regime for Foreign Trusts*, TAX NOTES (Oct. 11, 2010). As ACTEC explains, the tax policy of both the CFC and PFIC rules and the legislative history of the PFIC regime favors a result that gives preeminence to the principles of distribution tracing of subchapter J and does not indicate that a free form application of "facts and circumstances" is appropriate in the absence of voting control held directly or indirectly by the beneficiaries in a manner that reflects CFC statutory policies.[87]

F. Pre-Residency Planning for Grantors and Beneficiaries

Due to the complexity and breadth of the above-described tax rules, several different paths can follow from the first steps taken by an NRA who has funded a foreign trust and intends to immigrate to the United States.

---

84. *See* Treas. Reg. §§ 1.958-1(c)(2) (as amended in 1983) and 1.958-2(c)(1)(ii)(a); *see also* Rev. Rul. 90-106, 1990-2 C.B. 162 (grantor trust); Prop. Treas. Reg. 1.1291-1(b)(8), pmbl. of Apr. 1, 1992 (suggestion to define "proportionate" for PFIC purposes by reference to the attribution rules in Treas. Reg. § 25.2701-6 concerning estate freezes); Treas. Reg. § 1.958-1(d), Example 3 (short-term trust holding of stock is to be attributed to vested beneficiary for CFC purposes, at least in testing U.S. control).

85. *See* Donald D. Kozusko & Stephen K. Vetter, *Respect for "Form" as "Substance" in U.S. Taxation of International Trusts*, 32 VAND. J. TRANSNAT'L L. 675, 700–03 (1999) (applying the various attribution methods).

86. *See* TAM 200733024. *See also* M. Read Moore, *Indirect Ownership of CFC and PFOC Shares by Beneficiaries of Foreign Trusts*, J. TAXATION (Feb. 2008).

87. ACTEC letter, 2010 TNT 183-21.

1. As discussed above in Section III.A, if the NRA funded the foreign trust within five years of immigration to the United States, the NRA will be deemed to have made a transfer to the foreign trust on the date the NRA becomes a U.S. income tax resident. To that extent, the NRA will be treated as the owner of the assets and fully subject to tax on the income from them regardless of where the assets are considered located, and the trust will be a foreign grantor trust, assuming that income could be distributed or used for future distribution to a U.S. person.[88]
2. If the NRA has not transferred assets to the foreign trust within the five years prior to immigration, there will be no deemed transfer to the trust upon the NRA's immigration to the United States. Assuming no transfers are made to the trust after the individual actually becomes income tax resident, Code § 679 does not apply. Code § 679 would also not apply if the trust could not benefit any U.S. persons.
3. Nevertheless, when the NRA becomes U.S. income tax resident, it is likely that the trust will become a grantor trust, even if Code § 679 does not apply. As a practical matter, Code § 672(f) will characterize most trusts as nongrantor trusts if the grantor is an NRA, but when the NRA becomes U.S. income tax resident, most of these trusts will become grantor trusts, usually under Code §§ 674, 677, or 678. If it is a grantor trust, the trust's holdings of corporate stock could cause application of the CFC or PFIC rules, leading to the risk of tax on phantom income to the now U.S. income tax resident grantor under the CFC rules or an adverse interest charge if the company is a PFIC and the stock is disposed of while the grantor is U.S. income tax resident. Also, departure from the United States might trigger a deemed disposition of the stock and consequent tax as a result of the PFIC rules under Code § 1298(b)(5). Even if these corporate shareholdings are restructured after the NRA becomes U.S. income tax resident, it may be too late to avoid adverse income tax consequences. The same result could occur, of course, if the NRA held such shares in outright ownership and moved to the United States.
4. Assuming the trust is not otherwise a grantor trust under Code § 671, or that the immigrating NRA is not in fact or law the grantor, the trust will be a foreign nongrantor trust. The foreign nongrantor trust could also be problematic if there are U.S. beneficiaries.
   (a) A foreign nongrantor trust with U.S. beneficiaries could run the risk of a tax on phantom income if the foreign trust owns investment company stock subject to the CFC or PFIC rules or an interest charge on distributions if the trust distributed accumulated income to a U.S. taxpayer.

88. *See* Code §§ 679(a)(4)(A), 679(a)(1).

   (b) If the foreign trust is expected to accumulate income, the trustee should weigh the benefits of remaining offshore versus bringing the trust into the United States.
5. Several factors should be considered when deciding whether to migrate a foreign nongrantor trust into the United States.
   (a) Leaving the trust offshore will allow the funds to accumulate tax-free. However, any distribution to a U.S. taxpayer of amounts accumulated offshore will be subject to an interest charge. As discussed in Section III.C above, the interest charge applies to the amount of tax that was effectively deferred during the time the U.S. beneficiary receiving the distribution was a U.S. person. Distributions of current income to a U.S. beneficiary are not subject to the interest charge. Similarly, distributions from accumulated capital gains (but not current year gains) will be taxed at ordinary income rates when received by a U.S. beneficiary.
   (b) Leaving the trust offshore for several years is one alternative that should be considered. It allows for tax-free accumulation. After several years, the trust could then start distributing current income (including capital gains). This strategy allows a larger asset base to build up offshore, which in turn generates more current income each year. Depending on the time horizon involved, the future income generated from the larger asset base may be advantageous, but it may take a high investment return or a long accumulation period offshore to in fact achieve this result.
   (c) Migrating the trust to the United States is an alternative to leaving the trust offshore. If the trust migrates to the United States, amounts accumulated offshore will retain their foreign character. Thus, after migration to the United States, a distribution to a U.S. beneficiary of amounts accumulated offshore will be subject to the adverse treatment of accumulation distributions from a foreign trust.[89] A pour over to other trusts (or non-U.S. beneficiaries) prior to the migration, or even after, may help to reduce the size of this problem. Trust income earned after the migration to the United States will be taxed to the trust if accumulated or to the beneficiary if distributed.
   (d) It will be difficult to maintain a trust as foreign if the U.S. beneficiaries are prone to use trust tangible property, such as a furnished residence, due to the deemed distribution rule if fair market rent is not paid for that use, or if the fair market rent is not easily determined or the property is in the United States.
6. Whether to migrate a foreign trust to the United States is a fact-specific decision that should account for whether the trust has or will acquire U.S. beneficiaries, how long the existing or potential U.S. beneficiaries will

89. *See* Rev. Rul. 91-6, 1991-1 CB 89.

remain U.S. income tax resident, and the trust's investment and distribution strategy both today and in the future. If the deferral period is very long and the trust generates a sufficient return on its assets, leaving the trust offshore for several years to build a large asset base and then distributing the larger future current income stream to U.S. beneficiaries may produce a better economic result than bringing the trust into the United States. The possibility of a change in U.S. tax law should also be considered.

7. In all cases, prior to immigrating, the NRA needs to know whether any investment companies owned by the trust will be subject to the PFIC or CFC tax regimes. If so, then the NRA should restructure the companies prior to immigrating in order to avoid application of the PFIC and CFC rules. For example, the investment entities can be reorganized as partnerships or limited liability companies. This conversion to partnership status could be accomplished through a check-the-box election or possibly through an amendment of the organizations' governing instrument.[90] If possible, a restructuring of the investment companies owned by the trust should be completed prior to the NRA's immigration into the United States, since the restructuring generally will be treated as a corporate liquidation for U.S. tax purposes. The liquidation will step up the basis of the investment assets, but could also trigger taxable income to U.S. beneficiaries of the trust that are deemed to own the company stock through the attribution rules (depending on the basis in the shares). The use of first-tier investment entities that are not corporations will not, however, eliminate all U.S. tax concerns. If the first-tier investment entities are invested in other investment funds organized as corporations, foreign hedge funds for example, these would generally be PFICs for U.S. tax purposes, and then the PFIC tax regime must again be considered.
8. Yet another possible outcome should be considered: the immigrant who has an attack of "resident's remorse." Application of the foreign grantor trust rules can result in odd and unfavorable results for the NRA who forms a foreign trust, immigrates to the United States and becomes a U.S. taxpayer, and then returns to his or her home country. We refer to this individual as the "round-trip NRA." Most individuals, in general, and wealthy immigrants to the United States, in particular, prefer to maintain flexibility. The following scenario suggests that setting up a pre-residency foreign trust will provide just the opposite result without careful planning.
   (a) Recall that the grantor trust rules generally apply to the extent that any portion of a trust, upon application of the grantor trust rules without regard to Code § 672(f), is treated as owned by a U.S. taxpayer.[91] The U.S. grantor trust rules generally do not apply to any portion of a trust

90. *See* Treas. Reg. § 301.7701-3(b)(2)(ii).
91. Code § 672(f)(1); Treas. Reg. §1.672(f)-1(a)(1).

that would otherwise be deemed as being owned by a foreign person. Application of these rules will generally result in foreign nongrantor trust treatment where, for example, an NRA grantor creates an irrevocable trust for the benefit of the grantor, the grantor's spouse, and the grantor's children.[92]

(b) Code § 679(a)(4) provides that a foreign grantor who becomes a U.S. resident within five years of directly or indirectly transferring property to a foreign trust is brought within the purview of the outbound foreign grantor trust rules. Under those rules, such a person is treated as transferring the property to a foreign trust on the grantor's residency starting date (as determined under Code § 7701(b)(2)(A)). The amount deemed transferred is the portion of the trust attributable to the property previously transferred.

(c) The combination of Code §§ 672(f) and 679 can result in a trap for the unwary round-trip NRA who creates a foreign trust just prior to becoming a U.S. resident. For example, assume that in 2010, an NRA grantor creates an irrevocable trust for the benefit of the grantor, the grantor's spouse, and the grantor's children. This trust would be a non-U.S. nongrantor trust (unless it is revocable without consent or with only limited consent, as discussed above in Section III.B). Now assume that the NRA becomes a U.S. income tax resident in 2014. Under Code § 679, the immigrant grantor is now treated as the U.S. grantor to a foreign grantor trust. Yet it is likely that grantor trust status exists solely due to the grantor's current status as a U.S. taxpayer, i.e., due to application of Code § 679. Now assume that the grantor abandons U.S. residency and returns to his or her home country. There is a real risk that abandoning U.S. residency status will be treated, under Code § 684, as a taxable transfer by a U.S. person to a foreign *nongrantor* trust because of the renewed application of § 672(f). The analysis is as follows: Code § 684 provides that any transfer of property by a U.S. person to a foreign trust is taxable, unless and to the extent the U.S. transferor (or other person) is considered to be the owner of the trust under the grantor trust rules.[93] When the round-trip NRA abandons U.S. taxpayer status, the foreign trust will no longer be a grantor trust due to Code § 672(f), and it appears that Code § 684 could require gain recognition upon departure from the United States. The IRS may simply argue that the NRA's departure should be deemed a taxable transfer by a U.S. taxpayer (i.e., the round-trip NRA prior to abandoning U.S. taxpayer status) to a

---

92. *See* Code § 672(f)(2)(A)(ii). This assumes that no U.S. beneficiaries have made gifts to the NRA grantor, and thus subsection (5) of Code § 672(f) does not apply.

93. *See* Code § 684(b); Treas. Reg. § 1.684-3(a).

> foreign nongrantor trust under Code § 684.[94] A transfer that is taxable under Code § 684 is treated as a sale or exchange of the property for its fair market value, and the U.S. transferor must recognize gain equal to the excess of the property's fair market value over its adjusted basis in the hands of the transferor.[95]

This result is inexplicably harsh and produces a result substantially worse than a pre-immigration plan that involved (1) a transfer to a foreign partnership[96] (2) a transfer to a PFIC,[97] or (3) simply leaving the assets in a non-U.S. brokerage or bank account. This round-trip NRA typically will be in a much worse position than the long-term U.S. resident subject to Code § 877A (application of Code § 877A is discussed in Section IV below). The long-term resident receives the benefit of the "inbound" step-up in basis under Code § 877(e)(3)(B) or perhaps a gain recognition agreement under Code § 877(d)(2)(c).[98] Neither of these is available to the round-trip NRA.

IV. Planning for Long-Term Residency

A. Expatriation Tax Regime on Surrender of Citizenship or Long-Term Residence

A special expatriation tax regime applies on the relinquishment of U.S. citizenship, or long-term U.S. residence, by individuals meeting certain tests.[99] These rules apply to a so-called "long-term" U.S. tax resident, which means someone who terminates U.S. income tax residency after holding a "green card" for at least eight of the last fifteen years ending with the year of expatriation. A long-term resident who terminates U.S. income tax residency will be subject to the expatriation tax regime (such a person is known as a "covered expatriate") if the individual (1) meets a net worth test, (2) meets a U.S. income tax liability test, or (3) fails to certify under penalty of perjury that all U.S. tax obligations were met for the five years prior to expatriation.

---

94. The regulations address a deemed transfer upon the death of the U.S. transferor, but those regulations do not address a deemed transfer upon the loss of U.S. taxpayer status. *See* Treas. Reg. § 1.684-3(c); *see also* Treas. Reg. § 1.684-2(e).

95. Code § 684(a); Treas. Reg. § 1.684-1(a)(1).

96. A pre-immigration transfer to a foreign partnership would have virtually no adverse tax consequences when the round-trip NRA departed from the United States.

97. A pre-immigration transfer to a foreign corporation could also result in a PFIC, but even PFIC treatment would not result in full gain recognition if the round-trip NRA departed from the United States even after becoming a long-term resident under Code § 877(e). *See also* Prop. Treas. Reg. § 1.1291-3(b)(2).

98. A gain recognition agreement typically allows a deferral of gain recognition until a disposition of the non-U.S. property. Code § 877(d)(2)(c).

99. Code § 877A.

B. Exit Tax

Under the expatriation tax regime of Code § 877A, an "exit tax" is imposed on a covered expatiate. The covered expatriate is deemed to have sold all of the assets that would be includible in the expatriate's estate as of the day before expatriation. Any gain in excess of an exemption amount ($668,000 in 2013, adjusted annually for inflation) is subject to U.S. income tax. For property held prior to becoming U.S. resident, the gain is limited to appreciation that occurred between the date the covered expatriate became a U.S. taxpayer and the date of expatriation.[100]

The assets that are subject to tax generally include all assets held in the individual's own name and certain trust interests. For example, if the covered expatriate is treated as the grantor of a trust, the assets of the trust are subject to the exit tax. There are certain items of income that are excluded from the exit tax and instead are subject to withholding tax when a distribution is made to the covered expatriate. These items generally include retirement accounts, deferred compensation, and beneficial interests in nongrantor trusts. However, the definition of nongrantor trust for these purposes is not the same as it is for other purposes under the Code.

C. Nongrantor Trusts

The expatriation tax rules define a nongrantor trust as any trust of which the covered expatriate is not the grantor for U.S. income tax purposes. So not only would this definition include a typical nongrantor trust, but it also includes a trust that is a grantor trust as to someone other than the expatriate.

With respect to any "nongrantor trust" of which the covered expatriate is a beneficiary on the day before expatriation, the expatriation tax rules impose a withholding obligation on the trustee. Prior to making a direct or indirect distribution to the covered expatriate, the trustee is required to withhold from the distribution 30 percent of the amount that would have been subject to U.S. tax if the covered expatriate was still a U.S. person. If the trustee makes a distribution of appreciated property, the trustee is deemed to have sold the property for fair market value and must recognize any gain.

It is important to note that these rules do not make a distinction between domestic and foreign nongrantor trusts. In addition, there is no time limit imposed on the withholding obligation. Thus, a covered expatriate who is a beneficiary of a nongrantor trust will continue to be subject to U.S. tax on distributions for an indefinite period of time.

D. Transfer Tax Rules

Not only is a covered expatriate potentially subject to an exit tax upon expatriation, but there are also U.S. transfer tax consequences that apply if the covered expatriate makes a gift or leaves a bequest to a U.S. citizen or resident. Under Code

100. *See* Notice 2009-85.

§ 2801, the U.S. recipient of a gift or bequest from a covered expatriate in excess of the annual exclusion amount ($14,000 for 2013, adjusted annually for inflation) is subject to U.S. transfer tax at the time of the gift or bequest at the highest gift or estate tax rate then in effect (40 percent for 2013). Certain exceptions to the transfer tax apply for gifts or bequests to U.S. charities or to a U.S. *citizen* spouse. For purposes of the transfer tax rules, a gift or bequest to a U.S. trust is subject to tax at the time it is made. In addition, gifts or bequests made to foreign trusts are also potentially subject to these transfer tax rules if a later distribution from the trust is made to a U.S. citizen or resident.

There is also no time limit imposed on the transfer tax provisions applicable to covered expatriates. As a result, gifts or bequests from a covered expatriate to U.S. recipients will be subject to U.S. transfer taxes indefinitely.

E. Treaty Application

The current expatriation tax regime was enacted in 2008. It is possible that this regime conflicts with U.S. treaty provisions regarding the taxation of former long-term residents. The expatriation rules themselves are silent as to their effect on treaties, and there is no relevant legislative history to the rules that provides any guidance. Historically, the IRS seemed to take the position that special rules for expatriates are not overridden by a treaty unless there is specific language to that effect. For example, U.S. tax treaties typically reserve the right to tax on the basis of citizenship. The IRS has taken the view that this reserved right applies also to taxing *former* citizens under the prior expatriation rules, even when the treaty language makes no reference to these rules.[101] The U.S. Tax Court has rejected this IRS position under the U.S.-Canadian Treaty in force as of 1978.[102] More recently, in the legislative history to the prior expatriation rules in 1996, Congress declared its "belief" that the rules as amended did not conflict with existing U.S. treaties and called upon the Treasury Department to identify and resolve any such conflicts by future treaty negotiations, and stated that any conflicts still remaining after ten years would be resolved in favor of the treaty.[103]

F. Planning Prior to Long-Term Residence

The expatriation tax regime of Code § 877A suggests two separate stages of planning. The first, discussed above, is pre-residency planning, i.e., planning that occurs before the NRA immigrates to the United States. The second important time period is after the NRA has moved to the United States, but during the first seven years that the individual has a green card and has not claimed income tax residency in his or her "home" country under a treaty. In these years, the now former NRA has become a U.S. income tax resident and likely has become domiciled in the United States. During these years, the former NRA who wants to preserve

101. Rev. Rul. 79-152.
102. Crow v. Comm'r, 85 T.C. 376 (1985).
103. Explanation of Conferees on H.R. 3448, at 244.

the flexibility to leave the United States without generating an exit tax should begin to take steps to avoid application of the expatriation tax regime of Code § 877A, which will apply if the former NRA becomes a long-term resident under Code § 877A(g)(5), which refers to § 877A(e)(2).

Even assuming this former NRA is domiciled in the United States, the individual can still leave before becoming a long-term resident and convert U.S. assets to non-U.S. assets after departure without triggering income tax or transfer tax. This individual can, for example, sell U.S. securities free of capital gains and avoid gift tax on any gift of intangibles, such as U.S. securities. The departure period may have to be several years, however, in order to avoid the three-year rule of § 7701(b)(10) that resources capital gains (*see* Section II.E above) and, if necessary, in order to reestablish a domicile outside the United States.[104]

Also, by not becoming a long-term resident, the individual will preserve the ability to make gifts, both outright and in trust, to or for the benefit of U.S. citizens and residents without incurring the transfer tax rules of Code § 2801.

However, if the individual cannot leave the United States (or surrender income tax residency) before becoming a long-term resident under Code § 877(e)(2), the individual will be subject to the exit tax under Code § 877A, assuming the individual exceeds the relevant thresholds. Additionally, the transfer tax rules under Code § 2801 will apply indefinitely to future gifts and bequests to U.S. recipients.

104. *See also* Code § 864(c)(6).

The Current State of Expatriation

10

Michael G. Pfeifer*

I. Introduction and Background

Section 301 of the Heroes Earnings Assistance and Relief Tax Act of 2008 (HEART or the Act)[1] dramatically alters the playing field for individuals who relinquish their U.S. citizenship or terminate their long-term U.S. residence (i.e., U.S. persons who "expatriate"). It does this by adding new §§ 877A and 2801 to the Code,[2] which, respectively, impose "mark-to-market" and "succession tax" regimes on such individuals.

Prior to HEART's enactment, expatriates generally were subject to a ten-year "alternative tax" regime on U.S.-source income, as defined, that was first introduced by the Foreign Investors Tax Act of 1966[3] (FITA). These rules were contained principally in §§ 877, 2107, and 2501 of the Code.

---

* The author wishes to acknowledge the assistance of Stephen C. Trow, Esq., of Trow & Rahal, P.C., in preparing the remarks regarding U.S. citizenship law appearing above. He also wishes to thank Dianne C. Mehany, Esq., and Stephen M. Pennartz, both of Caplin & Drysdale, for their assistance in the preparation of this chapter.

1. Pub. L. No. 110-245 (2008).

2. Except as otherwise indicated, all section references are to provisions of the U.S. Internal Revenue Code of 1986 (the Code), as amended, and to the Treasury Regulations issued thereunder.

3. Pub. L. No. 89-809 (1966).

In the intervening four-plus decades, the alternative tax regime was modified twice, first by the Health Insurance Portability and Accountability Act of 1996[4] (HIPAA) and then by the American Jobs Creation Act of 2004[5] (AJCA). Both of these Acts generally strengthened the income and transfer tax rules applicable to expatriates under the alternative tax regime.

However, despite these enhancements, the U.S. rules applicable to tax expatriation remained the subject of a continuing congressional debate that began in 1995, when the Clinton administration proposed a somewhat radical "exit tax" regime as part of its fiscal 1996 budget. The ensuing debate, which included claims calling the exit tax proposal a violation of international human rights comparable to the exit tax imposed on citizens of the former Soviet Union who sought to emigrate,[6] eventually focused on whether the tax opportunities and perceived abuses arising from expatriation can best be deterred or controlled through the alternative tax regime or whether an exit tax or mark-to-market regime would be more effective.[7] The enactment of the HEART Act's changes, which are generally effective from June 17, 2008, when President George W. Bush signed the legislation into law, appears to indicate that at least for the foreseeable future, the tax consequences of expatriation by U.S. persons will be governed by the mark-to-market and succession tax regimes.

II. Expatriation for Citizenship Law Purposes

Before diving into a brief history of the tax consequences of "expatriation" and a more in-depth explanation of the current rules, it is worth delving into the current meaning of the term for U.S. citizenship law purposes.

In common vernacular, an American living abroad is said to be an "expatriate." However, as a legal matter, an American citizen "expatriates" only when he or she

4. Pub. L. No. 104-191 (1996).

5. Pub. L. No. 108-357 (2004).

6. In fact, the two "exit taxes" had little in common. The tax proposed by the Clinton administration was intended to be levied on America's wealthiest taxpayers and did not seek to collect the tax as a condition of departure. The Soviet exit tax, in practice, was levied on many of that country's poorest taxpayers, who sought a better life in Israel or the West. Further, it was required to be paid before emigration would be approved. Finally, it is rumored that the Soviet government would not accept Russian rubles in payment but required payment to be made only in "hard" Western currencies.

7. The "mark-to-market" approach generally has been sponsored by the Senate. Prior to the HEART Act and its immediate 2007 antecedent, the Defenders of Freedom Tax Relief Act of 2007, H.R. 3997, 110th Cong., 1st Sess. (Senate Amendment, Dec. 12, 2007), the most recent mark-to-market proposal was contained in the Tax Relief Act of 2005, S. 2020, 109th Cong., 1st Sess. (2005). The provision went to conference in early 2006 but failed to be included in the Tax Increase Prevention and Reconciliation Act of 2005 (TIPRA), Pub. L. No. 109-222 (2006). The language of the Senate's 2005 bill was substantially identical to that of the Jumpstart Our Business Strength (JOBS) Act, S. 1637, 108th Cong., 2nd Sess. (2004), which vied in a prior conference with the House proposal contained in H.R. 4520, 108th Cong., 2nd Sess. (2004), that was incorporated into the AJCA virtually unchanged.

relinquishes, or otherwise loses, U.S. citizenship. Many Americans consider such an act to be unpatriotic, and in times of war or political turmoil,[8] that may, indeed, be part of the explanation. But there are many reasons American citizens expatriate. In recent decades, many have relinquished their U.S. citizenship because they were citizens and residents of foreign countries that do not recognize dual citizenship.[9] Still others are wealthy Americans who have chosen to expatriate to avoid what they perceive as unnecessarily high income or estate taxes or, perhaps, an excess of regulation and reporting.[10]

Though relatively few in number, it is these "economic" expatriates whose stories in the national press have at times inflamed Congress to tighten the tax laws pertaining to expatriation and overseas tax avoidance more generally. This phenomena has undoubtedly contributed to the recent spate of expatriations, especially in the case of what is often referred to as "accidental" Americans. These are individuals born and raised outside the United States who, through an accident of birth, are U.S. citizens but who do not identify with the United States and do not wish to be caught up in its offshore tax enforcement initiatives. Nor do they wish information regarding their financial affairs to be routinely exchanged with the U.S. tax authorities pursuant to the impending FATCA (Foreign Account Tax Compliance Act) reporting.

In order to fully understand the dynamic at work here, it is first necessary to determine who is and who is not a U.S. citizen. Citizenship generally can be obtained only in one of two ways: (1) by naturalization, which is an administrative process by which an individual affirmatively seeks to obtain U.S. nationality[11] and (2) by birth in the United States[12] or, in certain limited circumstances, by birth

8. *See, e.g.*, Tomas A. Tizon, *Vietnam-Era Activism Echoes Are Heard by U.S. Expatriates*, Ft. Lauderdale Sun-Sentinel, Mar. 26, 2005. As many as 50,000 Americans may have migrated to Canada during the Vietnam War. Approximately half are thought to have remained, even after President Carter granted amnesty to draft dodgers in 1977.

9. *See, e.g.*, *Dual Citizenship: Dutchmen Grounded*, Economist (Jan. 7, 2012). Many countries that formerly did not recognize dual citizenship, including, e.g., the Philippines and South Korea, now accept it, which seems to be a growing trend. However, many others, including a majority of African nations and Japan and Singapore in Asia, continue not to recognize dual citizenship. Still others try to find a middle ground: India requires emigrants to renounce their nationality of birth but provides them with an "overseas citizenship" that furnishes them with many rights enjoyed by full Indian citizens, but not the right to vote. Beginning in 2012, France required new citizens to sign an undertaking not to claim allegiance to another country while on French soil, but it does not bar dual citizenship.

10. *See., e.g.*, Karen de Witt, *Some of Rich Find a Passport Lost Is a Fortune Gained*, N.Y. Times, Apr. 12, 1995 (quoting former Treasury Department Assistant Secretary for Tax Policy Leslie B. Samuels as saying: "If you've gotten your riches from America, you should pay your fair share of taxes . . . . These expatriates are really like economic Benedict Arnolds.").

11. As this is a process undertaken voluntarily by an individual, it does not give rise to "accidental" nationality and will not be discussed herein.

12. Under 8 U.S.C. § 1401(a) (and the Fourteenth Amendment), all persons "born in the United States, and subject to the jurisdiction thereof" are American citizens at birth The sole exception to this rule is that an individual born in the United States to foreign parents having full diplomatic immunity will not be considered a U.S. citizen. Note, however, that a child born in the United States to foreign parents having only "official acts" immunity will be considered a U.S. citizen.

overseas to a parent who is a U.S. citizen. In the case of such births, wherever occurring, citizenship happens by operation of law, without application or necessary intent by the parents.

It is the circumstance of U.S. citizenship arising from a birth outside the United States that frequently catches people by surprise, resulting in the existence of many persons who simply did not know they were U.S. citizens until their status came to light in connection with an immigration, tax, or other similar administrative enquiry. Unlike the case of status arising from birth in the United States, the citizenship rules applicable to births overseas are not widely known. However, for more than seventy years, any person born abroad to two American citizen parents has been a U.S. citizen at birth, without the need of application or registration, so long as one parent had residence in the United States at *any* time prior to the child's birth.[13] Even if a person born overseas has only one American parent, he may be a U.S. citizen at birth in certain circumstances. The laws have evolved over the years, but since 1986, a person born abroad to one American citizen parent obtains U.S. citizenship at birth if that parent was physically present in the United States for a total of five years prior to the overseas birth. The parent need not have been a U.S. resident for the five years; mere physical presence is sufficient. Additionally, two of the five years spent in the United States must have been after the parent reached the age of fourteen years.[14] For foreign births occurring between 1941 and 1986, the American citizen parent was required to reside or be physically present in the United States for a total of ten years prior to the overseas birth of a child, with five of those years occurring after the parent reached the age of fourteen or sixteen years.[15] Lastly, from 1934 to 1941, a person born abroad to one American citizen parent received citizenship at birth if that parent was present in the United States at *any* time prior to the child's birth.[16] The point to emphasize is that, under current law, generations of unknowing "accidental" Americans may exist.

The U.S. Immigration and Nationality Act (INA) also establishes the methods by which a U.S. citizen might relinquish citizenship. The INA provides that a U.S. citizen will lose his citizenship by performing certain specified acts voluntarily and with the intention to thereby relinquish U.S. citizenship. Seven acts are considered "expatriating acts" by the INA. They are:

1. Naturalizing in a foreign state after reaching the age of eighteen;
2. Taking an oath, affirmation, or some other formal declaration of allegiance to a foreign country after reaching the age of eighteen;

13. 8 U.S.C. § 1401(b).

14. *Id.* § 1401(g).

15. In 1952, the requirements changed from residence to physical presence, and from sixteen years of age to fourteen.

16. Different rules apply to children born in a U.S. possession, or born to unmarried parents. Suffice it to say that the rules of citizenship are complex and not easily applied to persons born abroad to a U.S. parent in the last seventy-five years.

3. Serving in foreign armed forces if the person serves as a commissioned or noncommissioned officer, or that armed force is engaged in hostilities against the United States;
4. Accepting a foreign government position after reaching the age of eighteen if (1) the person has or acquires the nationality of that state, or (2) service in that position requires an oath of allegiance;
5. Formally renouncing U.S. nationality before a U.S. diplomatic or consular officer while abroad;
6. Submitting a formal written renunciation of U.S. nationality while in the United States during time of war; or
7. Conviction of treason, armed insurrection, or similar offense.

A person who commits any of the acts listed above is presumed to have done so voluntarily.[17] That person must also do so with the *specific and contemporaneous* intent to renounce his U.S. citizenship. Until 1990, a person who committed any of the above acts was also presumed to have done so with the intent to renounce his U.S. citizenship.[18] In fact, American consular offices routinely informed U.S. citizens abroad that committing any of these expatriating acts would result in loss of U.S. citizenship. Foreign government officials also frequently advised U.S. citizens who sought employment with a foreign government or to become a member of a professional organization licensed by a foreign government that swearing a required oath of foreign allegiance would relinquish any claims to U.S. citizenship. Many foreign governments also require that a person renounce his U.S. citizenship when swearing an oath of allegiance, as dual citizenship was not or is not permitted in certain instances.

In 1990, the Bureau of Consular Affairs adopted an alternate presumption for three of the expatriating acts detailed in the INA. It is now presumed that a U.S. citizen intends to retain his U.S. nationality even if he naturalizes in a foreign country, takes a routine oath of allegiance, or accepts anon-policy-level employment with a foreign government.[19] To turn these actions into an "expatriating act," a person must "affirmatively assert to a consular officer, after he or she has committed a potentially expatriating act, that it was his or her intent to relinquish U.S. citizenship."[20]

At first, the new presumption had a limited retroactive application. The Bureau of Consular Affairs initially gave persons who had presumptively lost their citizenship under the old rules the opportunity to have citizenship "reinstated." To do so, a person was required to submit a formal claim to the Department of State. Citizenship was reinstated so long as, at the time of the expatriating act, the person had not specified in writing that he intended to relinquish his U.S.

17. 8 U.S.C. § 1481(b).
18. *See* Bureau of Consular Affairs, Pub. Notice 2383, 61 Fed. Reg. 29,651 (June 12, 1996).
19. 22 C.F.R. § 50.30(a).
20. 22 C.F.R. § 50.40(a).

citizenship. Since few people did so, and because the presumption was automatic and did not require any formalization, citizenship could easily be retroactively reinstated.[21] The INA no longer requires a written request for retroactive reinstatement of U.S. citizenship. In fact, the INA now requires a person who committed an expatriating act after 1961 to establish, by a preponderance of the evidence, that he intended to relinquish his citizenship at that time. If the person traveled on a U.S. passport, voted, paid U.S. taxes, or otherwise registered a child as a U.S. citizen after the potential "expatriating act" occurred, that person could not claim he contemporaneously intended to relinquish his citizenship.

Whether done so informally prior to 1990 or in writing after 1990, scholars universally agree that prior to 1996, committing an "expatriating act" established the expatriation date for tax purposes as well.[22]

III. Expatriation for Tax Law Purposes: Prior Law

A. FITA: Original Provision

Section 877, as originally added to the Code by FITA, generally imposed tax, calculated at the higher of the rates applicable to nonresident aliens who were not former U.S. citizens, or at the rates applicable to U.S. citizens on the U.S.-source income of former U.S. citizens who expatriated for a principal purpose of tax avoidance for ten years following expatriation. Thus, it was necessary to make two calculations of tax to determine which led to a higher tax charge, and, hence, the method became known as the "alternative tax" regime. Congress's reason for introducing the provision was because FITA generally eliminated progressive taxation of the U.S. income of nonresident aliens not effectively connected to a trade or business, and Congress did not wish to encourage individuals to surrender their citizenship and move abroad.[23]

U.S.-source income, for this purpose, generally had its usual meaning under the Code but was defined to include gains from the sale or exchange of property (other than stock or debt obligations) located in the United States as well as gains from the sale or exchange of stock or debt obligations issued by domestic corporations or other U.S. persons. In addition, gains from the sale or exchange of property having a basis determined by reference to such property, in whole or part, was also treated as U.S.-source income for the ten-year period in order to catch gains from non-U.S. property acquired in nonrecognition transactions.

Under § 2107, also added by FITA, if an expatriate subject to the alternative tax regime of § 877 died within the ten years following expatriation, his U.S. estate

21. Bureau of Consular Affairs, Pub. Notice 2383, *supra* note 18.

22. *See generally* Joint Comm. on Taxation, Issues Presented by Proposals to Modify the Tax Treatment of Expatriation Pursuant to Pub. L. 104-7, JCS-17-95 No 6, 1995 WL 17828071 (I.R.S. June 1, 1995).

23. *See, e.g.*, S. Rep. No. 89-1707 (1966).

included—in addition to U.S. situs property generally subject to estate tax in the case of a nonresident alien decedent—shares held at the date of death comprising a 10 percent or greater direct or indirect interest[24] in a foreign corporation considered owned more than 50 percent by the decedent, directly, indirectly or constructively,[25] in proportion to the foreign corporation's underlying U.S. situated property. In addition, under § 2501(a)(3), as amended by FITA, the normal gift tax exclusion for intangible property of a nonresident alien did not apply in the case of transfers made within ten years of expatriation by an expatriate subject to § 877's alternative tax regime. Thus, such an individual was subject to gift tax on transfers of U.S. situs intangible property during the ten-year post-expatriation period.

For purposes of both the income and transfer tax provisions, if the IRS was able to show that it was reasonable to believe that a former U.S. citizen expatriated with a principal purpose of tax avoidance, the burden of proof on the issue was thrown back on the expatriate or, in the case of § 2107, his executor or personal representative.

Prior to the renewed interest in tax expatriation that commenced with the Clinton administration's exit tax proposal in February 1995, there were only two significant reported cases involving § 877 and its related expatriation provisions. In *Kronenberg v. Commissioner*,[26] the IRS prevailed in its claim that the taxpayer had a principal tax avoidance motive where he expatriated two days before receiving a large corporate liquidating distribution. However, in *Furstenberg v. Commissioner*,[27] the taxpayer was able to demonstrate to the satisfaction of the Tax Court that tax avoidance was not the taxpayer's principal motivation where she had "lifelong ties to Europe" and had married a foreign aristocrat, notwithstanding that she also sought tax advice prior to expatriation. The importance of the decision lies in the fact that the Tax Court held that to fall within the ambit of § 877 and its related provisions, a taxpayer's tax avoidance motive was required to be not just an important purpose of the expatriation but, indeed, "first in importance." It is likely that the IRS failed to bring many cases under § 877 because of the difficulties of proving a taxpayer's principal motivation within the meaning of the *Furstenberg* decision.

B. HIPAA: 1996 Modifications

The debate launched by the Clinton administration's 1995 exit tax proposal ultimately resulted in substantial changes to the tax expatriation rules, but not in the enactment of an exit tax. Shortly after legislation incorporating the administration's proposal appeared, House Ways and Means Committee Chairman Bill Archer proposed legislation that generally retained, but significantly strengthened, the

24. Within the meaning of § 958(a).
25. Within the meaning of § 958(a) and (b).
26. 64 T.C. 428 (1975).
27. 83 T.C. 755 (1984).

existing ten-year alternative tax regime. In part because Archer's proposal was "scored" by the staff of the Joint Committee on Taxation (JCT) to raise almost four times the revenue that the exit tax proposal was scored to raise, and also likely, in part, because the exit tax's proposal to tax income and gains not yet realized was considered to be a somewhat radical departure from existing U.S. tax policy, Archer's proposal carried the day and was enacted as part of HIPAA in 1996.[28]

HIPAA, which was generally applicable to expatriations occurring on or after February 6, 1995, made a number of significant changes to the alternative tax regime of § 877. First and foremost, the category of "covered expatriates" was enlarged to include "long-term resident aliens," defined as "lawful permanent residents" (i.e., green card holders) resident for tax purposes in eight of the prior fifteen taxable years.[29] Expatriation was considered to have occurred at the date prescribed for citizens under nationality law (i.e., as of the date of an expatriating act)[30] and for long-term residents under the tax residence rules.[31]

In order to avoid problems of proof raised by the *Furstenberg* decision, HIPAA also introduced the notion of "presumptive tax avoidance purpose" based on certain economic factors pertaining to a taxpayer. Thus, tax avoidance motive was presumed if an individual's net average U.S. income tax liability in the five years preceding expatriation was $100,000 or more ("income tax liability test") or if his net worth at expatriation exceeded $500,000 ("net worth test").[32] Exceptions were available for certain categories of individuals if they obtained a ruling from the IRS

28. In this regard, it is worth noting—and somewhat ironic—that § 2801, the HEART Act's succession tax provision (and likely the provision scored to raise most of the $411 million estimated to be raised under the new expatriation changes over the next ten years), was a direct result of the scoring of the original exit tax proposal. The succession tax provision—which is likely the most controversial part of the HEART Act changes—was added to the Clinton administration's exit tax proposal in 1996 by the Senate Finance Committee in order to compete with the Archer proposal that was ultimately enacted as part of HIPAA.

29. HIPAA § 501(f)(1) (adding new § 877(e)).

30. This was subject to an exception for citizens expatriating after February 5, 1994, who had not furnished a statement confirming their loss of citizenship to the Department of State (DOS) prior to February 6, 1995, the general effective date of the HIPAA expatriation changes. HIPAA § 511(g). Such individuals remained subject to § 877 for ten years following the furnishing of such statement.

31. Section 877(e) refers to § 7701(b)(6) for purposes of determining when an individual ceases to be a lawful permanent resident. That section provides that an individual granted lawful permanent resident status will remain a tax resident until such status has been revoked or administratively or judicially determined to have been abandoned. The regulations, at Treas. Reg. § 301.7701(b)-1(b), state that abandonment will be considered to occur as of the date an individual provides written notice of such action to the Immigration and Naturalization Service (INS) or a consular officer, or as of the date the INS (or a consular officer) issues an order of revocation or abandonment. (The role of the INS has now been taken over by the U.S. Citizen and Immigration Services (USCIS), an agency of the Department of Homeland Security (DHS)). Note that in the latter case, it is the *date of issuance* that marks cessation of residence and not the prior *effective date* of such an order.

32. HIPAA § 511(a), *amending* § 877(a)(2). Both figures were indexed for post-1996 years. For expatriations occurring in 2004, the year that the AJCA modified the expatriation rules, the figures were $124,000 and $622,000, respectively.

that tax avoidance was not a principal purpose of their expatriation.[33] In cases in which the IRS was unable to make a definitive determination, it was authorized to issue a limited ruling that lifted the statutory presumption, but left the taxpayer subject to subsequent examination, if the taxpayer's ruling request was considered to be complete and made in good faith.[34]

HIPAA also significantly enlarged the categories of income considered to be U.S.-source income. Thus, for example, income and gains derived from former controlled foreign corporations (CFCs) considered controlled by an expatriate within two years prior to expatriation were considered to be from U.S. sources if realized within the ten-year post-expatriation period.[35] Further, certain gains arising from otherwise nontaxable exchanges and "other similar occurrences" that resulted in a change of future income source from U.S. to non-U.S. were required to be recognized as U.S.-source income.[36] In addition, if, during the ten-year period following expatriation a taxpayer contributed property giving rise to U.S.-source income to a foreign corporation that, had the taxpayer remained a U.S. person, would have been a CFC, then the foreign corporation was disregarded and the expatriate was considered to receive the underlying U.S.-source income directly.[37]

HIPAA also introduced limited information reporting for individuals who expatriate in order to assist the IRS to administer the provisions. An expatriating U.S. citizen was required to provide an information statement, including a statement of net worth, to the DOS when disclosing an expatriating act; the DOS routinely forwarded these information returns to the IRS. A departing long-term resident was required to provide the same information statement directly to the IRS with his tax return for the year of expatriation.[38] Further, an expatriate was required to file a U.S. tax return, including a worldwide income statement, for any of the ten

---

33. HIPAA § 511(b)(1) (adding § 877(c)(2)). That provision set out the categories of expatriating *citizens* who could apply for a ruling. In Notice 97-19, 1997-1 C.B. 394 (the initial expatriation guidance that, *inter alia*, laid out the requirements of the ruling procedure), the IRS established substantially parallel classes of long-term residents who could apply for a ruling. These categories were modified somewhat in Notice 98-34, 1998-2 C.B. 29.

34. The IRS established the "complete good faith" ruling in Notice 98-34, *supra* note 33. The 2003 JCT Report, *infra* note 43, questioned whether this limited ruling position was supported by HIPAA's legislative history, and the IRS temporarily ceased issuing such rulings in 2003. When AJCA was enacted in October 2004, and it became clear that the expatriation ruling program would henceforth be eliminated, the IRS recommenced issuing "complete good faith" rulings in order to finish work on its backlog of suspended rulings.

35. HIPAA § 511(b)(1) (adding new § 877(d)(1)(C)). Such income was treated as U.S. source to the extent the former CFC's earnings and profits were attributable to an expatriate's stock accumulated while the expatriate met the control test.

36. HIPAA § 511(b)(1) (adding new § 877(d)(2)).

37. HIPAA § 511(b)(1) (adding new § 877(d)(4)).

38. HIPAA § 512(a) (adding new § 6039G). This statement was provided on Form 8854, "Expatriation Information Statement."

years following expatriation in which he had U.S.-source income subject to tax.[39] In addition, HIPAA required that the DOS furnish copies of the Certificate of Loss of Nationality (CLN) of expatriating citizens to the IRS and that names of such persons be published quarterly in the *Federal Register.* The immigration authorities were also required to furnish the names of all persons whose green cards were revoked or considered to have been administratively abandoned.[40]

Finally, the legislative history to the 1996 HIPAA expatriation changes indicates that the rules were intended to override inconsistent provisions of preexisting income and estate and gift tax treaties for ten years following enactment, or until August 21, 2006.[41] Since enactment of the 1996 changes, Treasury generally has added language excluding former U.S. citizens and long-term residents from treaty benefit to the "saving clause" of new or re-negotiated treaties and protocols.[42]

C. AJCA: 2004 Modifications

The 2004 AJCA generally adopted recommendations made by the staff of the JCT in a 2003 report[43] (2003 JCT Report) that was spawned by the expatriation debate.[44] After a thorough—and lengthy[45]—review of the effectiveness of the 1996 HIPAA changes, the JCT staff concluded that there had been little, if any, enforce-

39. This requirement was added by Notice 97-19, *supra* note 33. The Notice states that a failure to include a worldwide income statement will cause a return not to be considered a true and accurate return. The consequence of that, if a taxpayer's return is later examined, is a loss of entitlement to deductions and credits. *See generally* Treas. Reg. § 1.874-1.

40. HIPAA § 512(a) (adding new § 6039G(d)).

41. H. Rep. 145, 104th Cong. 30 (1995); H. Rep. 496, 104th Cong. 155 (1996). However, several treaties negotiated and signed before, but ratified after, HIPAA's date of enactment do not preserve the right of the United States to tax former long-term residents otherwise subject to § 877. *See, e.g.*, income tax treaties with Austria (1996), Ireland (1997), Luxembourg (1996), and Switzerland (1996). Thus, the intended treaty override has not been effective to bar the use of these treaties by former long-term residents emigrating to these countries.

42. *See, e.g.*, the post-August 21, 1996, treaties with Thailand and Venezuela, the new treaties with the United Kingdom, Japan, and Belgium, and the new protocols with Australia and Mexico, each of which reserves the right of the United States to tax former long-term residents subject to § 877. *See also* the December 2000 protocol to the estate and gift tax treaty with Germany, in which the "saving clause" was amended to preserve the right of the United States to tax the gifts and estates of former long-term residents for ten years following expatriation. Note that Germany, which also has a ten-year expatriation provision under domestic law, receives a reciprocal treaty benefit.

43. Joint Comm. on Taxation, *Review of the Present-Law Tax and Immigration Treatment of Relinquishment of Citizenship and Termination of Long-Term Residency*, JCS-2-03 (Feb. 2003).

44. The JCT Report was undertaken in response to a 1999 request by then Ways and Means Committee Chairman Bill Archer (R-TX) to evaluate the 1996 expatriation changes, which Archer had sponsored. Archer was responding to renewed calls by House Democrats (including, notably, the former Ways and Means Committee Chairman, Charles Rangel (D-NY)) to replace the HIPAA changes with a mark-to-market regime based largely on the original 1995 exit tax proposal of the Clinton administration.

45. The JCT Report was originally due in May 2000, and much work had been undertaken to meet the original due date, including a detailed report prepared by the Government Accounting Office (GAO) in May 2000. Why the JCT Report was not issued then is unclear. However, when the congressional Democrats again clamored for its release during 2002, considerable additional work had to be done to bring the information previously compiled up-to-date.

ment of the expatriation rules by the responsible agencies, principally the IRS. The staff also noted certain defects inherent in the 1996 HIPAA regime. However, rather than suggest a fundamental change to the expatriation rules (e.g., the mark-to-market regime), the JCT Report made a number of specific recommendations within the framework of the existing regime that were generally intended to make the rules easier to administer and enforce.

Thus, the AJCA generally left the ten-year alternative tax regime on U.S.-source income in place but made a number of important changes. In the first place, the AJCA removed the requirement that an individual have a principal tax avoidance purpose and eliminated the ruling procedure. The income tax liability test threshold was changed only slightly to "greater than" $124,000 (indexed annually beginning in 2005),[46] but the net worth test standard was increased substantially to $2,000,000 (not indexed).[47] In addition, the AJCA added a third test, providing that an expatriate certify that he has fully complied with all U.S. tax requirements for the five years preceding expatriation.[48] Exceptions to the provision were limited to certain dual nationals at birth having no "substantial contacts"[49] with the United States and minors expatriating before age 18 ½, who were born in the United States to noncitizen parents and who have not been in the United States more than thirty days in any of the ten years preceding expatriation.

The AJCA also amended the expatriation gift tax rules to add a provision that parallels the expatriation estate tax rule of § 2107 and imposes tax on gifts of shares of a foreign corporation considered to be controlled by the expatriate to the extent of such foreign corporation's underlying U.S. property during the ten-year post-expatriation period.[50]

---

46. The income tax liability test threshold for individuals expatriating in 2008, the year the HEART Act changes supplanted those made by the AJCA, was $139,000. Rev. Proc. 2007-66, 2007-45 I.R.B. 970, § 3.29 (Oct. 18, 2007). The current income tax liability test threshold for individuals expatriating in 2013 is $155,000. Rev. Proc. 2012-41, 2012-45 I.R.B. 539 (Oct. 18, 2012).

47. AJCA § 804(a)(1), *amending* § 877(a)(2).

48. AJCA § 804(a)(1) (adding new § 877(a)(2)(C)). The AJCA is silent as to when this certification must be made, but the requirement is now satisfied by completion and filing of Form 8854. The form's instructions indicate that an expatriating individual will be subject to tax under § 877 if he has not complied with his tax obligations, regardless of whether he meets the income tax liability or net worth thresholds. In Notice 2005-36, 2005 I.R.B. 1007 (Apr. 22, 2005), the IRS granted relief from the potentially prejudicial effect of the retroactive statutory change requiring certification of tax compliance for five years preceding expatriation by allowing individuals who expatriated after June 3, 2004, to treat the date they provided notice of expatriation to the DOS or DHS, respectively, as their expatriation date, provided that such persons filed a revised Form 8854 by June 15, 2005.

49. Under new § 877(c)(2)(B) (added by AJCA § 804(a)(1)), an individual is considered to have "substantial contacts" with the United States if he ever held a U.S. passport, was a U.S. tax resident within the meaning of § 7701(b), or spent more than thirty days in the United States in any of the ten years preceding expatriation. This exception is available only to individuals who were dual citizens at birth and remain a citizen of the other country.

50. AJCA § 804(d)(2) (adding new § 2501(a)(5)). As with § 2107 pertaining to the imposition of U.S. estate tax on shares of a closely held foreign corporation owning U.S. property, new § 2501(a)(3)(B) (added by AJCA § 804(d)(1)) affords a tax credit for foreign gift taxes imposed on a transfer.

In addition, the AJCA added a provision for determining when an individual is considered to have expatriated for *tax* purposes. New § 7701(n) provided that an individual will continue to be treated as a U.S. citizen or long-term resident until he both gives notice of his expatriation to the DOS or DHS, respectively, *and* furnishes an information statement required by amended § 6039G.[51] To give effect to this provision, the instructions to revised Form 8854 set out in some detail the specific acts by which U.S. citizenship and long-term residence may be terminated. The instructions then state very clearly that, notwithstanding the occurrence of these acts, the obligation to file U.S. tax returns and report worldwide income does not terminate until the later to occur of giving notice of these acts to the appropriate agency or filing Form 8854, which expressly has no filing due date for this purpose.[52]

Further, the AJCA strengthened the information reporting rules by requiring that an expatriate file an *annual* information statement for each of the ten post-expatriation years, regardless of whether the expatriate had any U.S.-source taxable income for such year.[53] The annual return requirement is also satisfied by filing revised Form 8854, which requires that a current balance sheet and worldwide income statement be prepared for each year.[54]

51. AJCA § 804(b) (adding new § 7701(n)). Section 6039G formerly required only that an expatriating citizen provide an initial information statement on the occurrence of the earliest of several events confirming the expatriating act. *See* former § 6039G(a), (c). The events were: (1) formal renunciation of nationality before a diplomatic or consular officer; (2) furnishing a statement of voluntary relinquishment confirming a prior event of expatriation; (3) issuance of a certificate of loss of nationality (CLN); or (4) a U.S. court's cancellation of a naturalized citizen's certificate of nationality. A former long-term resident was not required to submit the initial information statement until filing his tax return for the year of expatriation. *See* former § 6039G(f). The potential prejudice of this retroactive change to individuals expatriating after June 3, 2004, and before the issuance of guidance (especially to former long-term residents) was also relieved by the issuance of Notice 2005-36. *See supra* note 48. Note that the interplay between § 7701(n) and the requirement that an individual certify compliance with all tax obligations for the five years preceding expatriation, as set forth in Form 8854, raises a potentially interesting issue of tax compliance standards. What level of compliance is sufficient to permit an individual (possibly a long-term non-filer making a voluntary disclosure) conclusively to expatriate for tax purposes? Presumably, the normal compliance standards as set forth in, e.g., *Beard v. Commissioner*, 82 T.C. 766 (1984), *aff'd*, 793 F.2d 139 (6th Cir. 1986), will apply. A higher standard would make the statutory scheme unworkable.

52. Note that as originally enacted, § 7701(n) also unintentionally appeared to affect the residency termination of aliens who are not long-term residents within the ambit of § 877. This is because it required that *all* aliens terminating U.S. residence status provide notice of termination to the DHS. Although such notice is frequently provided by departing green card holders on DHS Form I-407, no comparable form is required to be filed by substantial presence aliens who terminate residence. This error was clarified by a technical correction contained in the Gulf Opportunity Zone Act of 2005 (GOZA), Pub. L. No. 109-135, § 403(v)(2).

53. AJCA § 804(e), *amending* § 6039G(a).

54. Annual information reporting is done on Form 8854, pt. III. If an expatriate has taxable U.S.-source income and is required to file Form 1040NR for the year, Form 8854 should be attached to it, and a second copy of the form filed with the IRS at Bensalem, PA. If an expatriate is not required to file a tax return for the year, Form 8854 must be filed only with the IRS at Bensalem, PA.

Finally, the AJCA added a new short-term residence rule to the expatriation tax provisions.[55] Under it, an individual otherwise subject to the tax expatriation rules will be subject to income and transfer taxes on his *worldwide* income and property as a U.S. citizen or resident during any of the ten post-expatriation years in which he is physically present in the United States for more than thirty days. This was the most controversial provision of the expatriation changes made by the AJCA and reflects a congressional view that if individuals wish to leave the U.S. taxing jurisdiction, they should "really leave" and should not be allowed to benefit from the generous provisions of § 7701(b) that generally permit an alien an average of 121 U.S. days per year without becoming a tax resident. A limited exception of up to thirty additional days of U.S. presence is permitted for certain expatriates performing services in the United States for an unrelated employer.[56]

IV. Omissions and Technical Issues under Prior Law

Although the HEART Act repeals the alternative tax regime prospectively[57] and thereby effectively renders moot many of the issues under prior law, because the prior rules continue to apply to individuals who expatriated under them and are still in their ten-year post-expatriation period, it remains necessary to understand prior law.

The issue most likely to come up under prior law concerns whether and when tax expatriation has occurred, especially in the case of long-term residents seeking to tiebreak their residence to a foreign country for tax purposes while holding on to their green cards for immigration purposes. This is due to the dual notice requirements established by former § 7701(n) in order to complete tax expatriation and the uncertain relationship between that section, § 877(e)(1), and the effective date of a residence tiebreaker claim under a tax treaty—is the claim effective when actually filed, or does it relate back to the end of the taxable year preceding the year for which the claim is made?

Another possible issue that could arise under prior law concerns whether and when the tax treaty override of the HIPAA changes ceased to apply. The legislative history to the AJCA makes no reference to the issue of treaty override. Presumably, since § 877, the fundamental taxing provision of the alternative tax regime, was neither materially amended nor reenacted by the AJCA, the 1996 treaty

55. AJCA § 804(c) (adding new § 877(g)).

56. The classes of individuals potentially entitled to this exception include only expatriates becoming a citizen or resident fully subject to tax of a country where they, their spouse, or either of their parents were born, or expatriates who have not spent more than thirty days in the United States in any of the ten years preceding expatriation. For this purpose, days of presence due to a medical condition arising while an individual is in the United States or while an individual is an "exempt individual" are disregarded. The exclusion of days as an "exempt individual" was another technical "clarification" of the AJCA rules by GOZA. *See* GOZA § 403(v)(1).

57. HEART Act § 301(d).

override provision remained intact only until August 21, 2006, the date that was ten years after the HIPAA changes were enacted.

V. HEART Act Changes

As previously indicated, the dramatic changes to the expatriation tax regime made by the HEART Act include both a mark-to-market tax regime to replace the former ten-year alternative tax regime on U.S.-source income[58] and a succession tax regime on gifts and bequests received by U.S. persons from a covered expatriate.[59] The latter provision, which is perhaps the most dramatic change made by the HEART Act, is scored to raise most of the revenue that the new legislation is expected to bring in but, as yet, has not been implemented due to the government's failure to issue any guidance.[60]

A. Section 877A: Mark-to-Market Tax

New § 877A replaces the former ten-year alternative tax regime on U.S.-source income of covered expatriates with a mark-to-market tax on gains in excess of $600,000 (indexed for years after 2008; for 2013, $668,000[61]) from a deemed sale of an individual's worldwide assets on the day prior to the individual's expatriation date. As under prior law, the term "covered expatriate" includes individuals who renounce or relinquish U.S. nationality or terminate their status as long-term lawful permanent residents (i.e., green card holders for at least eight of the fifteen taxable years preceding expatriation) and whose average net income tax liability for the five years preceding expatriation exceeds $124,000 indexed for inflation (for persons expatriating in 2013, $155,000[62]) or whose net worth at the date of expatriation equals or exceeds $2 million (not indexed). Certain dual nationals at birth who have not met § 7701(b)'s "substantial presence" residence test for more than ten of the fifteen taxable years ending with the year of expatriation and individuals losing U.S. citizenship before age 18 ½ who have not met the substantial presence test for more than ten years are excepted.

58. HEART Act § 301(a) (adding new § 877A).

59. HEART Act § 301(b) (adding new § 2801).

60. Treasury's 2012–2013 "Priority Guidance Plan," announced on November 19, 2012, lists a project on guidance under § 2801 regarding the tax imposed on U.S. citizens and residents who receive gifts or bequests from certain expatriates. It is believed that proposed guidance will be issued before the end of 2013.

61. Rev. Proc. 2012-41, *supra* note 46, § 3.16. For individuals expatriating in 2012, the comparable gain exclusion figure was $651,000. The annual gain exclusion figure is available in the Revenue Procedure that provides the annual inflation adjustments for each year, generally issued in October of each year for the succeeding tax year, or in Form 8854, applicable for a specific year. These forms are available at www.irs.gov/forms&publications.

62. Rev. Proc. 2012-41, *supra* note 46, § 3.15. Form 8854, the "Initial and Annual Expatriation Statement," now provides the indexed income tax liability amounts for all tax years since 2004.

Under the provision, a covered expatriate can irrevocably elect, on an asset-by-asset basis, to defer the payment of the mark-to-market tax attributable to an asset until the due date of the return for the year in which such property is sold or exchanged. (Guidance will be provided for dispositions in nonrecognition transactions.) In order to make the election, a taxpayer must provide "adequate security" (including a bond conditioned on the payment of tax and interest and meeting the conditions set forth in § 6325 or other security acceptable to the IRS) and irrevocably waive the benefit of any U.S. tax treaty that would preclude assessment of the tax. The election will terminate as to any property not sold or exchanged when a taxpayer dies or when the IRS determines that security is no longer adequate. Interest accrues on the deferred tax at the normal underpayment rate.

Certain property, including deferred compensation items, "specified tax deferred accounts" (i.e., individual retirement accounts and certain education and health savings accounts), and interests in nongrantor trusts are excepted from application of the mark-to-market tax.

"Deferred compensation items" include any interest in a qualified plan or other arrangement described in § 219(g)(5); interests in foreign pension, retirement, or similar plans or arrangements; any item of deferred compensation; and interests in property to be received in connection with the performance of services to the extent not previously taken into account in accordance with § 83. Deferred compensation attributable to services performed outside the United States while a covered expatriate was not a U.S. citizen or resident is not included.

Tax on the payment of an "eligible deferred compensation item" is deferred until a covered expatriate receives a taxable payment (i.e., a payment that would be taxable if the individual were a U.S. person), at which time tax is collected by means of a 30 percent withholding tax under rules similar to those of subchapter B of chapter 3 (i.e., § 1441 and following). However, no withholding tax is due under § 1441 or chapter 24 (i.e., wage withholding under § 3401 and following). Notwithstanding this, the tax is considered payable under § 871. An item is considered to be eligible deferred compensation if either the payor is a U.S. person or a foreign person who elects to be treated as a U.S. person for this purpose (and meets requirements to be established by the IRS), provided the covered expatriate notifies the payor of his status and makes an irrevocable waiver of any right to claim benefit under a U.S. income tax treaty.

In the case of deferred compensation items that are not eligible deferred compensation, an amount equal to the present value of an individual's account is treated as received and taxable on the day before expatriation. No early distribution tax is assessed, and appropriate adjustments will be made to subsequent distributions to reflect the prior taxation.

A covered expatriate's interest in a "specified tax deferred account" is treated as distributed on the day before expatriation. Again, no early distribution tax is assessed, and appropriate adjustments will be made to subsequent distributions to reflect such treatment.

The new law provides that a trustee shall withhold tax at 30 percent from the taxable portion of a direct or indirect distribution from a nongrantor trust to a covered expatriate. Again, the "taxable portion" is that part of a distribution that would be taxable if the expatriate remained a U.S. person. If a trust distributes appreciated property, gain is recognized to the trust as if it had sold the property to the expatriate. The provision does not distinguish between domestic and foreign trusts or U.S. or foreign trustees. Nor does it distinguish a nongrantor trust from a trust that is considered a grantor trust *as to a person other than the expatriate*. Thus, it imposes a withholding tax on post-expatriation taxable distributions to a covered expatriate from any trust of which the expatriate was a beneficiary immediately prior to expatriation to the extent that *the expatriate* was not also considered an owner, in whole or part, of such trust under the grantor trust rules. The fact that another person may have been treated as owner of the trust immediately prior to expatriation is irrelevant for this purpose. Withholding tax rules similar to those applicable to payments of eligible deferred compensation items are applied.

"Expatriation date" is defined to mean the date that a citizen relinquishes U.S. nationality or a long-term resident alien ceases to be a lawful permanent resident (i.e., green card holder). Section 7701(n), added to the Code by the AJCA, which provided that a covered expatriate is treated as a U.S. person for tax purposes until the later of the date he gives notice to the IRS on Form 8854 or to whichever of the DOS or the DHS is relevant, is repealed. However, § 7701(a)(50), added by the HEART Act, provides that an individual shall not cease to be treated as a U.S. citizen before the date on which the individual's citizenship is considered relinquished under § 877A(g)(4). That section provides that a citizen is considered to have relinquished U.S. citizenship at the earliest of the dates: (1) he renounces his nationality before a U.S. diplomatic or consular officer; (2) he provides a statement of voluntary relinquishment to the DOS; (3) the DOS issues the individual a Certificate of Loss of Nationality (CLN); or (4) a U.S. court cancels a naturalized citizen's certificate of naturalization.

Section 7701(b)(6), which generally defines who is a "lawful permanent resident," was amended to provide that an individual ceases to be a lawful permanent resident if he: (1) commences to be treated as a resident of a foreign country under the provisions of an applicable tax treaty with the United States; (2) does not waive tax benefits available under the treaty; and (3) notifies the IRS of the commencement of such treatment (e.g., by claiming treaty benefits on a Form 8833 filed with his U.S. income tax return on Form 1040NR).[63]

63. These provisions, added as "conforming amendments" by HEART Act § 301(c)(2), may eliminate some of the confusion caused under prior law by the interaction of §§ 877(e)(1) and 7701(n). The former section defined the act of tiebreaking residence to a foreign country under an applicable tax treaty as an expatriating act, but the latter section provided that a long-term resident had not expatriated until he notified *both* the IRS and the DHS. The latter notice frequently was not given by an individual who wanted to compute his U.S. tax liability as a nonresident alien but, at the

Finally, for purposes of the mark-to-market tax, all nonrecognition deferrals and extensions of time for the payment of tax are considered terminated as of the day before expatriation. In addition, solely for purposes of calculating the mark-to-market tax, the basis of property held when an individual first became a U.S. resident for tax purposes and still held when he expatriates will be stepped up (but not down) to its fair market value on such date. Such an individual can irrevocably elect not to have this basis rule apply.

B. Section 2801: Succession Tax

New § 2801 imposes a tax, at the highest applicable gift or estate tax rates, on the receipt by a U.S. person of a "covered gift or bequest," which is defined as a direct or indirect gift or bequest from a "covered expatriate" within the meaning of § 877A. Thus, the new succession (or inheritance) tax only applies to gifts and bequests from individuals who expatriate on or after June 17, 2008, the effective date of the new mark-to-market regime. The tax is assessed on, and intended to be paid by, the recipient of a covered gift or bequest. The succession tax will be reduced by any foreign gift or estate tax paid.

The new succession tax does not apply to gifts covered by the annual exclusion of § 2503(b), currently $14,000 per donee per annum.[64] Nor does it apply to gifts or bequests entitled to a marital or charitable deduction. Thus, for example, gifts or bequests to a U.S. citizen spouse will be exempt from the tax, while gifts to an alien spouse will be limited to the amount allowed by §§ 2503(b) and 2523(i), currently $143,000 per annum,[65] and bequests to an alien spouse will benefit from a marital deduction if left to a qualified domestic trust, per §§ 2056(d) and 2056A. The succession tax also will not apply to a taxable gift shown on a timely filed gift tax return or to property included in the estate of a covered expatriate that is shown on a timely filed estate tax return. Finally, from the interplay of relevant provisions of §§ 877A and 2801, it appears that the succession tax also will not apply to gifts and bequests made by a covered expatriate during any period following expatriation when the expatriate is again subject to tax as a citizen or resident of the United States (and, therefore, not treated as a "covered expatriate").[66]

Section 2801 creates a special rule for covered gifts and bequests made to trusts. In the case of such a transfer to a domestic trust, the succession tax will be

same time, wished to retain his lawful permanent resident status for immigration purposes. Note, however, that the termination of "lawful permanent resident" status described above, which is set forth in the flush language at the end of § 7701(b)(6), technically applies only to persons expatriating under the HEART Act changes, pursuant to the statute's effective date provisions. Thus, there could still be issues pertaining to the effective date of a treaty tiebreaker claim under prior law that must be addressed by guidance provided by Treasury and the IRS. However, as a matter of statutory construction, if a statute is clear on its face, a taxpayer is not required to look to the effective date provisions found in the statute's legislative history. As a result, § 7701(b)(6) likely can be applied as it appears.

64. Rev. Proc. 2012-41, *supra* note 46, § 3.19(1).

65. *Id.* § 3.19(2).

66. *See* §§ 877A(g)(1)(C) and 2801(e)(1)(A).

assessed on and paid by the trust. In the case of a covered gift or bequest made to a foreign trust, the succession tax will apply to the receipt by a U.S. person of a distribution, whether of income or capital, attributable to a transfer from a covered expatriate. A foreign trust is entitled to elect to be treated as a domestic trust solely for purposes of § 2801. Finally, in calculating his *income tax* liability on the receipt of a taxable distribution from a foreign trust attributable to a covered gift or bequest, a U.S. recipient will be entitled under § 164 to deduct the amount of tax imposed under § 2801 that is attributable to gross income of the recipient, but not to the capital portion of the distribution.

VI. Guidance under the HEART Act: Notice 2009-85

There are many issues that need to be addressed in public guidance under the expatriation tax provisions of the HEART Act. After a hiatus of some months, Treasury and the IRS issued Notice 2009-85 (the 2009 Notice or Notice),[67] which provides guidance for individuals subject to § 877A. The 2009 Notice does not expressly provide any new guidance regarding § 877. Nor does the Notice provide any guidance under § 2801, other than to confirm that satisfaction of the reporting and tax obligations for individuals receiving covered gifts or bequests is deferred until further guidance is provided. Additional guidance regarding § 877A can also be found in the substantially revised Form 8854 that was published most recently in December 2012 and Form W-8CE that was revised most recently in July 2012.[68]

A. Mark-to-Market Tax

Regarding the operative provisions of the HEART Act's central "mark-to-market" tax, the 2009 Notice generally confirms the statute's principles in a straightforward manner, clarifying and explaining those provisions most requiring it. In discussing the definition of "covered expatriate," the Notice confirms that certification of five-year tax compliance (the certification test) must be made on Form 8854 and filed on or before the due date of the taxpayer's tax return for the year of expatriation. The Notice also confirms that all U.S. citizens who relinquish citizenship and all long-term residents who cease to be lawful permanent residents within the meaning of amended § 7701(b)(6) will be treated as covered expatriates if they fail to certify five-year tax compliance, notwithstanding that they fail to meet the income tax liability or net worth tests at the date of expatriation.

67. Notice 2009-85, 2009-45 I.R.B. 598 (Oct. 15, 2009). Note that Treasury's "2012-2013 Priority Guidance Plan," issued on November 19, 2012, lists a project for a further notice under § 877A supplementing Notice 2009-85. It is not currently known what issues under the section are intended to be addressed in the proposed notice.

68. The revised Form 8854 (Expatriation Information Statement) and Form W-8CE (Notice of Expatriation and Waiver of Treaty Benefits) can be found under the forms and publications heading on the IRS's website, www.irs.gov.

The Notice parrots the statute's language regarding the exceptions to covered expatriate status for certain dual nationals at birth and individuals under age 18½ at the date of expatriation, but no effort is given to explain how the substantial presence test of § 7701(b)(3) should be applied to an expatriating citizen to determine if he was a U.S. resident in more than ten of the fifteen years preceding the year of expatriation. For example, does such an individual have the benefit of the "closer connection" exception to residence?[69]

Importantly, the 2009 Notice confirms that the date of cessation of lawful permanent residence by a long-term resident who "tiebreaks" his residence to a foreign country under the provisions of an applicable U.S. income tax treaty occurs when the individual's foreign residence "commences" for treaty purposes, and not on the date that notice of such commencement is provided to the IRS. That notice appears on Forms 8833 and 8854, filed with the individual's tax return for the year of expatriation (which frequently occurs as many as eighteen months after the foreign residence commencement" date).[70]

The 2009 Notice also confirms that the determination of whether an individual meets the income tax liability or net worth tests for "covered expatriate" status, as set forth in § 877A(g)(1)(A) (by reference to § 877(a)(2)), is done pursuant to the principles of Notice 97-19, the initial guidance issued under the 1996 HIPAA changes to the expatriation tax provisions.[71] Thus, for purposes of § 877A, an expatriating individual's net U.S. income tax liability is still determined under § 38 (with joint return filers each responsible for the total net income tax liability shown on a return), and, for purposes of determining his net worth at expatriation, an individual is considered to own property that would be taxable on a gratuitous transfer under the *gift tax* provisions of chapter 12 of subtitle B of the Code (disregarding available exemptions, etc.).

For purposes of computing a covered expatriate's tax liability under the mark-to-market provisions, the 2009 Notice states that an individual is considered to own any property that would be considered to be within his *estate* under the provisions of chapter 11 of subtitle B of the Code (with certain adjustments) were he to die on the day before his expatriation date. Property considered owned

69. The Code, at § 877A(g)(1)(B)(ii), refers to the § 7701(b)(1)(A)(ii) definition, so the full provisions of the substantial presence test presumably apply, other than, e.g., the "exempt individual" categories that could never have applied to a former U.S. citizen.

70. *See* Notice 2009-85, *supra* note 67, § 4, ex. 8. This is consistent with IRS practice under the HIPAA provisions, before the AJCA amendments introduced § 7701(n) and its "dual notice" requirement for expatriation to occur. The IRS's acknowledgment of this practice is important because it also permits taxpayers, in appropriate cases, to cease lawful permanent resident status before reaching the "eight out of fifteen" year threshold for long-term resident status. Note, however, that Notice 2009-85 also confirms that although the date of the expatriating act might establish whether an individual is subject to the provisions of the 2004 AJCA or 2008 HEART Act expatriation regimes, if the former, the ten-year alternative tax regime will run from the date of the *second notice* under former § 7701(n) rather than the effective expatriation date. *See* Notice 2009-85, *supra* note 67, § 4, ex. 7.

71. *See supra* note 33 and accompanying text. This is so notwithstanding that the original expatriation Notice has been obsoleted by Notice 2005-36, *supra* note 48.

through a *grantor* trust is included, but property considered owned through a nongrantor trust, pursuant to the principles set out in Notice 97-19 (which are applied for determining whether an individual meets the net worth threshold for covered expatriate status), is disregarded. This is because beneficial interests in nongrantor trusts as well as deferred compensation items and specified tax deferred accounts are expressly excepted from operation of the mark-to-market tax and subject to expatriation taxation under other provisions. Finally, the Notice provides that the valuation of property considered owned for purposes of the mark-to-market regime generally is to be made under estate tax principles. Thus, where appropriate, formal valuations are required.

In discussing § 877A's exclusion amount (currently $668,000), the 2009 Notice states that the amount must be allocated pro rata across all assets having built-in gain and without regard to a taxpayer's election to defer tax with respect to certain assets. Thus, the exclusion cannot be allocated to the highest taxed income first. Further, the Notice states that if the total built-in gain on all taxable assets is less than the exclusion amount, the exclusion amount that can be allocated across the property will be limited to the amount of built-in gain.[72] It is also clear from the Notice that built-in gain cannot always be reduced by built-in losses. The use of losses is generally limited by other applicable Code provisions (not including the wash sale rule of § 1091).[73] With respect to basis issues involved in the mark-to-market regime, the 2009 Notice makes it clear that the basis of an asset will be adjusted for purposes of determining gain or loss on a subsequent disposition by the amount actually taken into account in determining gain or loss without regard to the exclusion amount attributable to the asset. As regards the inbound basis step-up afforded to alien individuals at the time they become resident aliens (which is solely for purposes of the mark-to-market provisions), the Notice confirms that the basis in property is only stepped up (and not also down) and indicates that an individual can irrevocably elect *not* to have the automatic basis step-up to fair market value apply on an asset-by-asset basis. The 2009 Notice also indicates that Treasury and the IRS intend to exercise their regulatory authority to deny this basis step-up to U.S. real property interests and property used in a U.S. trade or business owned by a nonresident alien prior to becoming a U.S. resident.

With respect to a covered expatriate's right to defer the payment of the mark-to-market tax, the Notice establishes a thirty-day cure period in the event that an individual's proffered security for payment of the mark-to-market tax becomes inadequate. The Notice discusses the conditions of and procedures for entering into a deferral election agreement and, importantly, attaches a template of a tax deferral agreement as an appendix. The Notice also explains at some length the

72. Interestingly, the Notice indicates that each individual is eligible for only one lifetime exclusion amount, as may be adjusted for inflation. Prior expatriation regimes have never addressed the consequences of serial or multiple expatriations.

73. Thus, losses on personal use property not held for investment purposes (e.g., an individual's principal personal residence) cannot be taken.

calculation of the deferred tax considered attributable to each asset for which the election is made. Note, in particular, that the deferral election only applies to the tax arising as a result of § 877A and not to an individual's regular U.S. tax liability for the year of expatriation.[74]

Finally, the 2009 Notice discusses the interaction of § 877A with other Code provisions providing for the deferral of gain. In general, an expatriation under § 877A terminates any other prior tax deferrals, and all such deferral terminations must be accounted for before determining the consequences of expatriation under § 877A. In particular, the Notice discusses the expatriation tax consequences arising in respect of a terminated § 367(a) gain recognition agreement and § 684. The Notice states that if a covered expatriate's expatriation results in a deemed triggering event under a gain recognition agreement or in a transfer of assets comprised in a grantor trust to a foreign nongrantor trust, then the recognition of gain under §§ 367 or 684 will be considered to arise prior to the deemed sale under § 877A on the day before the taxpayer's expatriation date. The clear consequence of this ordering provision is that the income considered recognized under the busted gain recognition agreement or deemed transfer of assets to a foreign nongrantor trust cannot be offset by § 877A's gain exclusion amount.[75]

B. Tax on Deferred Compensation

As for the three exceptions to the general mark-to-market rule, the 2009 Notice first confirms the breadth of what constitutes an "item of deferred compensation." In particular, the Notice confirms that property received in connection with the performance of services is included whether or not such property is substantially vested, but only to the extent not previously taken into account in accordance with § 83. The Notice reiterates the statutory conditions for application of the deferred 30 percent withholding tax on the taxable portion of post-expatriation distributions of "eligible deferred compensation," but unfortunately only promises future guidance regarding the elective procedure for a non-U.S. person to be treated as a U.S. person so that otherwise "ineligible deferred compensation" may also benefit from the deferred 30 percent withholding tax regime. Absent such an election, the Notice confirms that the present value of a covered expatriate's accrued benefit will be treated as received by the taxpayer on the day before expatriation and must be included on the taxpayer's tax return for the portion of

74. The instructions to Form 8854 indicate that, in order to determine the maximum tax that can be deferred, a taxpayer is required to prepare two hypothetical tax returns, one reflecting all income, including the § 877A gain and loss, and the other including all income without the § 877A gain and loss.

75. Whether this ordering principle is justified is questionable, given that the event triggering gain under §§ 367 and 684 is the same event giving rise to a deemed sale of the individual's worldwide assets under § 877A's mark-to-market provisions.

the year preceding the expatriation date.[76] The Notice discusses at some length the appropriate adjustments that may be made to subsequent distributions from an ineligible deferred compensation plan to ensure that amounts included in future distributions will not be subject to income tax a second time.

The 2009 Notice confirms that the rules pertaining to deferred compensation items do not apply to any deferred compensation attributable to services performed outside the United States while a covered expatriate was not a U.S. citizen or resident, whether before or after expatriation. Until further guidance is issued, the Notice permits a taxpayer to use any reasonable method consistent with existing guidance pertaining to the sourcing and taxation of deferred compensation[77] to determine amounts that may be excluded.

C. Specified Tax-Deferred Accounts

Regarding "specified tax-deferred accounts," the 2009 Notice does little more than confirm the scope of the term (i.e., what statutory schemes are covered) and the manner of taxation for such items. The Notice also reiterates the provisions contained in the instructions to Form W-8CE.[78]

D. Interests in Nongrantor Trusts

In the case of "interests in nongrantor trusts," the 2009 Notice generally confirms the rules set forth in the statute, namely that the "taxable portion" of distributions to a covered expatriate who was a beneficiary but not also an owner of a trust on the day before the expatriation date are subject to a 30 percent withholding tax. The Notice also seeks to clarify who is a trust beneficiary in broad terms (i.e., a person permitted to receive a direct or indirect distribution under a trust's terms or local law having power to apply trust income or corpus for his own account, or *a person to whom income or corpus would be paid if current trust interests were terminated*), but does not address the obvious questions concerning beneficial interests in nongrantor trusts that may arise *after* the date of expatriation (e.g., pursuant to a discretionary trust power to add or exclude beneficiaries). The Notice does add that if a trust that was a nongrantor trust prior to expatriation

76. The taxation of ineligible deferred compensation is a particular hardship for, e.g., long-term resident employees of the World Bank and other international organizations who may wish to return to their countries of origin following retirement. Absent the ability for the former employer to elect to be treated as a U.S. person in order to operate the withholding tax regime, such retirees are subject to tax on the present value of their accrued benefit under a retirement plan but may not be entitled to take a distribution for purposes of paying the tax. The IRS is aware of this potential hardship and has indicated that it would be willing to enter into a contractual arrangement under which a foreign retirement plan administrator could operate the necessary withholding tax mechanism. Whether a foreign plan administrator would be willing to enter into such an arrangement or the IRS would be able to work out a satisfactory arrangement to secure future tax payments likely would be the principal obstacles reaching an agreement that would permit the election.

77. *E.g.*, Treas. Reg. § 1.861-4(b)(2); Rev. Rul. 79-388, 1979-2 C.B. 270; and Rev. Proc. 2004-37, 2004-1 C.B. 1099.

78. *See generally* discussion at pages 18–19, *infra*.

becomes a grantor trust as to a covered expatriate following expatriation, the conversion of status will be treated as a taxable distribution to the covered expatriate to the extent of his interest in the trust as "owner."

There is no statutory provision in § 877A that would permit a foreign trustee of a foreign trust to elect to be treated as a U.S. person for purposes of withholding the 30 percent tax on taxable distributions to a covered expatriate, as there is in the case of a foreign payor of deferred compensation (for which there is, as yet, no guidance). Further, Treasury and the IRS apparently have determined that they do not have sufficient regulatory authority to create such a parallel mechanism, which might actually aid in the collection of this tax, which otherwise appears to be largely unenforceable. (Such a provision may also afford foreign fiduciaries with U.S. operations a measure of relief against being caught up in a future U.S. tax enforcement action.) However, the Notice does confirm the existence of an elective procedure whereby a covered expatriate can apply to obtain a letter ruling from the IRS as to the value, if ascertainable, of his interest in a nongrantor trust as of the day before his expatriation date.[79] If a valuation ruling is forthcoming, the covered expatriate will be considered to have received the value of his trust interest immediately prior to expatriation, and tax will be due with his tax return for the period ending on his expatriation date. As a consequence, no subsequent trust distribution will be subject to the 30 percent withholding tax under § 877A(f),[80] and the covered expatriate will be entitled to claim treaty benefits vis-à-vis any distribution from the trust under an applicable income tax treaty.[81]

E. Filing and Reporting

Under broad regulatory authority contained in § 6039G, the 2009 Notice expands the reporting that is due from covered expatriates in years following the year of expatriation. Under prior law (in particular, the 2004 AJCA changes), a covered expatriate was required to file annual information returns on Form 8854 for the ten-year post-expatriation period that he remained subject to tax under the alternative tax regime, whether or not he had any income tax liability. In any year

79. This procedure was foreshadowed in a revision of Form 8854 that appeared prior to issuance of Notice 2009-85. In making a ruling request, a taxpayer is required to follow the procedures set out in Rev. Proc. 2009-4, 2009-1, C.B. 118.

80. Although a distribution may, of course, be subject to U.S. tax under other Code provisions, if carrying out U.S.-source income or income effectively connected with a U.S. trade or business.

81. It is difficult to predict whether expatriating U.S. taxpayers will consider the possible availability of such an elective procedure to be useful. The obvious advantage to making this election is to limit the taxation of distributions from nongrantor trusts to the value of the interest existing at the date of expatriation, if this can be determined. Otherwise, under § 877A, there could be a liability to pay the withholding tax forever, in which case it may be imposed on wealth that did not exist while the taxpayer was a U.S. person. This election might offer some advantages to expatriates having beneficial interests in domestic nongrantor trusts. Whether an expatriate would wish to make this election vis-à-vis a beneficial interest in a foreign nongrantor trust, against which the IRS may have no practical ability to collect the withholding tax, is doubtful.

that a covered expatriate had U.S.-source income on which tax due was not fully withheld at source, a covered expatriate was also required to file a Form 1040NR.

The Notice states that a covered expatriate having eligible deferred compensation items or interests in nongrantor trusts must annually file Form 8854 to certify either that no distributions have been received or to report distributions that have been received. Unlike under prior law, there apparently is no time limit on this obligation. The Notice also confirms that in accordance with Treas. Reg. § 1.6012-1(b), a covered expatriate having taxable income (i.e., eligible deferred compensation or distributions from nongrantor trusts) for which taxes are not fully withheld at source must file a tax return on Form 1040NR. Because foreign fiduciaries are unlikely to withhold and remit a 30 percent tax on distributions from nongrantor trusts, this creates an affirmative filing obligation for covered expatriates subject to all usual return filing rules. Any covered expatriate who has elected to defer payment of the mark-to-market tax must also file an annual Form 8854 through the year that the deferred tax and all interest is paid.

The 2009 Notice also confirms that a covered expatriate who has a deferred compensation item, a specified tax deferred account, or a beneficial interest in a nongrantor trust generally must file Form W-8CE with the relevant payor on or before the earlier of the day prior to the first distribution on or after the individual's expatriation date or thirty days after the expatriation date. With respect to a distribution of an eligible deferred compensation item or an interest in a nongrantor trust, the form generally provides notice to the payor that the individual has waived any otherwise applicable treaty benefits. However, in the case of a nongrantor trust, if the covered expatriate has indicated on the form that he will request a letter ruling from the IRS as to the value of his beneficial interest on the day before his expatriation date, the trustee is "required" to furnish the individual information necessary to calculate such value.[82] In the case of an ineligible deferred compensation item, Form W-8CE is notice to the payor that the individual is a covered expatriate who is treated as receiving an amount equal to the present value of his accrued benefit on the day before his expatriation date. This is also notice to the payor that adjustments may have to be made to future distributions to account for the tax required to be paid by the covered expatriate as a result of his expatriation. Finally, in the case of a specified tax deferred account, Form W-8CE is notice to a payor that the individual is a covered expatriate for whom adjustments may be required on future distributions from the account. Within sixty days of receiving the form, the payor is required to provide a statement to

82. The instructions to Form W-8CE indicate that the necessary information includes (but is not limited to): (1) a copy of the trust deed; (2) a list of the assets (and their values) held on the day before the expatriation date; (3) information regarding other potential trust beneficiaries; (4) birth dates for all measuring lives for the trust's perpetuity period; (5) policies followed by the trustees when making discretionary distributions that might constitute an "ascertainable standard"; and (6) any other relevant information.

the covered expatriate of the account balance on the day before the expatriation date.

VII. Additional Expatriation Issues Requiring Guidance

As indicated above, the 2009 Notice does not discuss the issues that may arise under § 2801, the succession tax provision introduced by the HEART Act, other than to say that guidance will be forthcoming and that satisfaction of the reporting and tax obligations for individuals receiving covered gifts or bequests is deferred until such guidance is provided.[83]

The 2009 Notice also does not address several other important issues, including: (1) whether, and on what terms, the deferred tax election can apply to property disposed of in nonrecognition transactions and (2) how the new rules are to be coordinated with U.S. tax treaties. In the case of the new tax mark-to-market tax, which is imposed on gains *deemed to arise* on the day before expatriation, the statute's inherent bias is that the income generally will be residence (i.e., U.S.) based and should not result in any double taxation. However, as a practical matter, gains arising from the subsequent *actual* disposition of a covered expatriate's assets, as well as deferred compensation and nongrantor trust distributions received subsequent to expatriation, are likely not to be U.S.-source income and generally will also be taxed by the expatriate's country of residence at realization or receipt.[84] Thus, there are likely to be *bona fide* treaty issues where a covered expatriate resides in a U.S. treaty partner following expatriation. Clearly, there will also have to be guidance on foreign tax credit issues that are bound to arise.[85]

In particular, there likely will be issues with the 30 percent withholding tax on payments of eligible deferred compensation and distributions from nongrantor trusts that is considered imposed under § 871. Section 906(b)(4), pertaining to the allowance of foreign tax credits to nonresident aliens (which a covered expatriate becomes), expressly provides that a foreign tax credit is not allowed against any tax imposed by § 871(a). This is reasonable, because § 871 generally imposes tax on certain U.S. source income of nonresident aliens. However, as indicated above,

83. The IRS is developing a new form, Form 708 (U.S. Return of Tax for Gifts and Bequests Received From Expatriates), for the purpose of making a return under the provisions of § 2801. The form is referred to in the latest version of Form 3520, part IV, issued in early 2010. The instructions to Form 3520, item 57, state that a taxpayer's tax payment obligations with respect to any § 2801 tax liability will not be due until the date indicated on Form 708, once issued. See Announcement 2009-57, 2009-29 I.R.B. 158 for additional information.

84. That an expatriate may have made what amounts to a coerced waiver of treaty benefits in order to try to comply with U.S. reporting obligations so that, *inter alia*, his expatriation might be considered complete under §§ 877(a)(2)(C) and 877A(g)(1)(A) should not be found to preclude him from claiming treaty benefits under otherwise applicable residence-based tax treaties.

85. Note that in the case of the § 2801 succession tax, the statute expressly provides that credit will be given for foreign gift and estate/inheritance taxes.

amounts subject to tax under § 877A(d)(1) and (f)(1) frequently will not be from U.S. sources and so should be entitled to foreign tax credits.

Two further points should be made about the need for additional guidance under the new expatriation tax rules. First, although the fundamental precept of the mark-to-market tax is that a covered expatriate is taxed on his wealth at the date of expatriation, there appears to be no income cap on taxable amounts received from nongrantor trusts. The new election to be treated as receiving the value of an individual's interest in such a trust, if ascertainable, is certainly an attempt to resolve or ameliorate this issue, but in many cases, it may not be possible to fairly ascertain the value of a beneficiary's contingent, discretionary interest in such a trust with sufficient precision for either the expatriate or the IRS to be comfortable. Nor is there a wealth cap on taxable amounts received from a covered expatriate that are subject to the succession tax. If it is even administrable, this tax might be imposed on individuals and wealth that are generations removed from the covered expatriate's expatriation date.

Finally, as with the 2004 AJCA that preceded it, the HEART Act does not address the so-called "Reed amendment" provision of immigration reform enacted in 1996.[86] That provision bars reentry to the United States of former citizens who expatriated for a principal tax avoidance purpose in the opinion of the Attorney General.[87] Because of certain statutory defects, it has never been implemented or enforced.[88] The 2003 JCT Report recommended changing the provision to bar U.S. reentry only to former citizens who have not fully complied with their expatriation tax obligations, but this unfortunately was not included with the AJCA's

86. The Reed amendment was contained in the Illegal Immigration Reform and Immigrant Responsibility Act of 1996, Pub. L. No. 104-208 (enacted Sept. 30, 1996).

87. Responsibility for administering and enforcing the provisions of the Reed amendment was formerly within the province of INS, an agency within the Department of Justice (DOJ). Because the role of the INS has now been transferred to USCIS, an agency of DHS, overall responsibility presumably has shifted from the Attorney General to the Director of DHS.

88. There are several apparent statutory flaws with the Reed amendment. First, it is unclear from the language of the statute whether it encompasses all acts of expatriation or only those expatriations accomplished by formal oath of renunciation. Second, it is unclear what the applicable tax avoidance standard is or should be; this is especially troublesome because tax avoidance has ceased to be relevant to enforcement of the expatriation tax provisions. Since the objective of the provision is to bar certain former citizens from reentering the United States and, therefore, effectively to penalize them, it is questionable whether due process would permit the necessary tax avoidance to be presumed based upon certain economic factors, as was the case under HIPAA's § 877 changes. More likely, USCIS, which now administers the provision, would be required to make a factual determination on a case-by-case basis. However, its ability to do this would be severely limited, since, under § 6103, the IRS is precluded from disclosing specific taxpayer information even to other federal agencies, except in limited circumstances that would not extend to enforcement of the Reed amendment. Notwithstanding these problems, it is known that USCIS (and, before it, INS) was working to develop regulations to implement the Reed amendment, and the project was on the DHS's regulatory agenda as recently as 2006. *See* 71 Fed. Reg. 22643 (Apr. 24, 2006). The current status of the regulation project is unknown, but the inability of the IRS to provide tax information pertaining to specific taxpayers may require tax legislation to amend § 6103 if the project is to move forward. Several of the former mark-to-market proposals would have done that.

expatriation changes, notwithstanding that its provisions generally followed the 2003 JCT Report recommendations and tax avoidance purpose is no longer relevant to tax expatriation. Several prior mark-to-market proposals, including some under consideration in 2007, also included provisions based on the 2003 JCT Report, but these provisions unfortunately were not part of the HEART Act. As the Reed amendment continues to have a chilling effect on U.S. citizens considering expatriation (notwithstanding that, in its present formulation, it likely is unenforceable), it is to be hoped that Congress will address this problem.[89]

VIII. Conclusion

Controlling the tax consequences of expatriation has attracted considerable attention and given rise to a spirited debate in Congress and elsewhere since the Clinton administration first proposed an exit tax in its fiscal 1996 budget.[90] The proposed solution contained in 1996's HIPAA, although no doubt affecting the actions of many wealthy individuals considering the potential tax benefits arising from expatriation, was not, in the opinion of the 2003 JCT Report, ultimately successful in deterring tax-motivated expatriation. Nor was it successful in raising the revenues envisioned by the 1996 scoring for the HIPAA provisions. The 2003 JCT Report concludes that this was attributable, in no small part, to the failure of the IRS to fully and properly administer and enforce the 1996 changes, although the report also acknowledges that the alternative tax regime has some inherent weaknesses.

The changes contained in 2004's AJCA were intended to facilitate easier administration and improved enforcement of the amended expatriation tax rules by removing the difficult and frequently uncertain and expensive (for both taxpayers and the Government) ruling program and requiring enhanced information reporting by expatriating taxpayers. In addition, the new short residence rule contained in § 877(g) was introduced to deter expatriation by many U.S. taxpayers. Whether this was sound fiscal or social policy is questionable, especially in the case of former long-term residents who may have left the United States in retirement to return to the countries from which they originally arrived. Many

89. On June 12, 2013, Senator Jack Reed, the author of the original "Reed amendment," joined by Senator Chuck Shumer, proposed an amendment to the current immigration bill being debated in Congress, the "Border Security, Economic Opportunity and Immigration Modernization Act of 2013," S. 744, 113th Cong. (2013). Their proposed amendment (S. Amend. 1233) would bar admission to the United States of any former citizen determined to have expatriated for a "tax avoidance purpose," as determined by the Secretary of DHS. However, individuals who are "covered expatriates" and expatriated under the HEART Act provisions would be presumed to have done so with such a purpose and would be inadmissible unless they can rebut the presumption with "clear and convincing evidence." The proposed amendment was not part of the final Senate bill that was sent to the House of Representatives for consideration.

90. Indeed, the actions of the United States even spurred the enactment of limited expatriation tax provisions in a number of other countries, including France, Germany, and the Netherlands.

such persons have children and grandchildren who have remained in the United States as well as continued U.S. vacation residences and other investments. Limiting their presence so drastically with the threat of renewed worldwide taxation seems shortsighted. However, in the final analysis, the alternative tax regime after the AJCA likely wasn't in place long enough to determine whether it achieved its intended goals.

Exactly what the goals of an expatriation tax should be is perhaps the core of the problem. Congress has several times indicated that tax neutrality is the correct policy—the law should serve neither as an inducement to leave U.S. tax solution nor as a bar to doing so. Unfortunately, the actions of Congress have not always followed this course.

The mark-to-market and succession tax regimes contained in the HEART Act are likely less a further philosophical or emotional onslaught against individuals who choose, for whatever reason, to leave full U.S. tax solution than a shortsighted and misguided effort to close the ever-present "tax gap." The several new taxing provisions—especially those pertaining to eligible deferred compensation, interests in nongrantor trusts, and the succession tax—are not even wholly consistent with the implicit objective to tax an individual's wealth as he leaves the U.S. tax system. Further, additional IRS resources likely will be required to efficiently administer and try to enforce the tax. However, even in an increasingly transparent financial world with greater cross-border cooperation among national tax administrations, it will be difficult to impose and collect tax on foreign income and assets from individuals who are no longer generally within the U.S. jurisdiction. Whether this is the final expatriation tax solution remains to be seen. The expatriation provisions found in the HEART Act are not sound tax policy, but they are scored to raise not insignificant revenue from a segment of the population for whom Congress—and likely many Americans—do not have much sympathy.[91]

91. In May 2012, news surfaced that Eduardo Saverin, a young immigrant from Brazil who was one of the founding owners of Facebook Inc., had renounced his U.S. citizenship and was residing in Singapore, where gains from an impending IPO of Facebook would not be taxed. Senators Charles Schumer (D-NY) and Bob Casey (D-PA), incensed by Saverin's action, coauthored a tax bill, the "Expatriation Prevention by Abolishing the Tax-Related Incentives for Offshore Tenancy Act (the Ex-PATRIOT Act), S. 3205, 112th Cong. (2012), that would impose a 30 percent capital gains tax (or twice the otherwise applicable tax rate under then existing law), collected by means of withholding, and also potentially bar Savarin or other similar "specified expatriates" (i.e., tax dodgers) from returning to the United States. After the fanfare accompanying its introduction subsided, the bill went nowhere. Ironically, when the Facebook stock plummeted soon after the IPO, it became apparent that the taxes Savarin incurred under the mark-to-market provisions of § 877A might possibly have far exceeded what he may have owed had he remained a U.S. citizen through the IPO (and likely insider "lock-up" period following it). Whether there was an element of poetic justice in this is beside the point. What the development reflected is that expatriation is a tax phenomenon that is likely driven more by emotion than well-considered and sound tax policy. *See, e.g.*, Jim Puzzanghera, *Two Senators Want to Stop Facebook's Saverin from Dodging Taxes*, L.A. Times, May 18, 2012.

PART V

U.S. Tax Treaties

Transfer Tax Treaties

11

Barbara R. Hauser

I. Overview

Once there is another country involved in the estate planning process, one must consider whether or not the other country (or countries) would impose an estate (or inheritance) or gift tax on the transfer of property. Although many countries do not have any death tax,[1] most of those in the so-called developed world do have such a tax.[2] Because Canada repealed its estate tax several years ago but replaced it with a tax at death under the income tax provisions, it will be considered separately.

If there would be two (or more) countries imposing a death (or gift) tax, then one will first want to see whether the United States has entered into an estate (or gift) tax treaty with that other country. Technically speaking, there are sixteen such treaties (although as a practical matter, the treaties with Australia and with Sweden no longer apply, because Australia and Sweden have abolished the death tax). It seems particularly disturbing that there is no treaty with Belgium in light of its importance in the European Union.[3] If there is no treaty, there would still be the United States credit for a foreign death tax that is paid.[4]

---

1. China has recently postponed the effective date of its new death tax, citing too many difficulties in determining correct ownership.

2. A notable exception is Australia, which repealed its death tax.

3. A treaty was negotiated and signed in 1954, but it was never ratified and is not in effect.

4. Except with respect to Canada, because the Canadian tax is an income tax and not a death tax, thus absent the Income Tax Protocol there would have been only a deduction in calculating the U.S. estate tax, and not a credit.

It is worth noting that most of the treaties are quite old and do not take into account changes in the United States estate taxes, particularly the restrictions on inheritances left to non-U.S. citizen spouses. With the exception of responding to Canada's changed system and negotiating one Protocol to the German treaty and one Protocol to the French treaty,[5] the United States has not negotiated any new or revised estate tax treaties in almost twenty years. This is true despite the fact that the United States' jurisdictional reach based upon mere citizenship presumably causes more multiple taxation than does any other country.[6] As stated by one leading authority: "States understandably put their treaty negotiating resources into the areas of greatest demand, that is income tax treaties between major trading states, but this should not be to the exclusion of death duties treaties."[7] Wolfe Goodman concurred: "While the seriousness of the problem has been recognized for over 70 years . . . there is a noticeable lack of energy on the part of governments in negotiating such conventions."[8] With the ever-changing domestic federal estate tax system in the United States, negotiating any treaty intended to have an enduring status would be an increasingly difficult challenge.

A. Pre-1966 Treaties

A total of nine estate tax treaties were negotiated by the United States after World War II, from 1951 to 1956. They are:

1. Australia (1954[9]) (not currently applicable)[10]
2. Finland (1952)—Estate and Inheritance
3. Greece (1953)—Estate
4. Ireland (1951)—Estate
5. Italy (1956)—Estate and Inheritance
6. Japan (1955)—Estate, Inheritance, and Gift
7. Norway (1951)—Estate and Inheritance
8. South Africa (1952)—Estate
9. Switzerland (1952)—Estate and Inheritance

Many countries impose a death tax (estate or inheritance) on property that is deemed to be situated in that country, even if the decedent was not a resident (or national, as in the case of the United States) of that country. Accordingly, the

5. The Protocol was signed by both countries on December 8, 2004. Apparently France had requested a Protocol since 1989 to restore benefits that were removed by the U.S. Tax Reform Act of 1988 (www.ambafrance-us.org/intheus/tax/009us.asp). Thus, the 2004 Protocol is effective retroactively to November 10, 1988.

6. The general rule is to impose worldwide taxation only on the basis of domicile or residency, not on citizenship.

7. J.F. Avery Jones, *A Comparative Study of Inheritance and Gift Taxes*, Eur. Tax'n 337 (Oct.–Nov. 1994).

8. Wolfe D. Goodman, *The OECD Model Estate Tax Convention*, Eur. Tax'n 339 (Oct.–Nov. 1994).

9. The year will refer to the year the treaty came into effect (which is after the exchange of instruments of ratification).

10. Because Australia abolished its estate tax, this treaty is not currently applicable.

general approach of these older treaties is to list categories of property and to establish in which single jurisdiction the property will be deemed to be located for purposes of imposing a tax that is based solely upon the situs of the property. These provisions, however, do not preclude the United States from taxing property deemed to have its situs in the other country if the owner was a U.S. citizen.

As an example of this approach, the treaty with Italy provides, in article III, that if a person who died was a citizen of or a domiciliary of either country, the situs of property for the purpose of imposing the tax will be determined exclusively as follows:

1. Real property is deemed located where the land is located;
2. Tangible personal property (except as otherwise specified in the treaty) and bank or currency notes are deemed to be situated where they are located at the time of death (or if in transit, at the place of destination);
3. Debts (including bonds and promissory notes) are deemed to be located where the debtor resides (and, if a corporation, at the place under whose laws it was created);
4. Stock in a corporation is deemed to be located at the place under whose laws the corporation was created;
5. Ships and aircraft (and shares thereof) are deemed to be located at the place of registration of the ship or aircraft;
6. Goodwill in a trade or business is deemed to be located where the trade or business is located;
7. Patents and trademarks are deemed to be located at the place where they are registered or used;
8. Copyrights, franchises, and licenses are deemed to be situated at the place where the rights arising from them are exercisable; and
9. All other property is deemed to be situated in the state in which the decedent was domiciled at the time of death.

Article IV of the U.S. treaty with Italy provides that if the only basis for imposing tax (in accordance with the above treaty provisions) is the situs of the asset (and not citizenship or residency of the decedent), then that taxing jurisdiction must allow a specific "exemption" for the assets subject to its tax at least in the amount of its regular "exemption" that is equal to the proportion those included assets bear to the entire estate (provided that the nontaxed property will not be included to determine the rate of tax).

Note that in 1981, the Internal Revenue Service ruled that the Italian[11] treaty reference to a specific "exemption" refers in the United States only to the limited credit allowed for nonresident aliens, i.e., $13,000, and not to the "unified credit" allowed for U.S. citizens and residents.[12] That ruling was revoked in Revenue

11. Also included were Australia, Finland, Greece, Japan, Norway, and Switzerland.
12. Rev. Rul. 81-303, 1981-2 C.B. 255.

Ruling 90-101 for estates of persons dying after November 10, 1988 (the effective date of the Technical and Miscellaneous Revenue Act of 1988). The meaning of "exemption" remains unclear, however, under several treaties.

Article V provides that if a state taxes based on domicile or nationality, it must allow against its tax a credit for the amount of the tax imposed by the other state on property that is deemed to be situated in that other state. In other words, the state in which the property is deemed to be located has the "first" right to impose its tax on that property. If the other state would also tax that same property, based on nationality or residency, then it must give a credit for the tax imposed by the state in which the property was located.

The treaty does not give exclusive taxation rights to only one country under any theory. The United States is free to impose its worldwide tax based on citizenship (or domicile). The main jurisdictional benefit of the treaty is the exclusive agreement as to the situs of various assets. If the situs country would otherwise impose a tax on those assets, it may still do so under the treaty.

The U.S. treaty with Switzerland illustrates how even treaties that are said to take the same "situs of assets" approach can vary considerably. Article IV of the Swiss treaty provides that if both the United States and Switzerland tax on the basis that the decedent was either a national or a domiciliary (i.e., imposition of worldwide taxation), then each must give the other a credit for the tax it imposes on the following assets:

1. stock in a corporation created under the laws of the other state;
2. debts (including bonds, promissory notes, and insurance[13]) if the debtor resides in the other state, or if a corporation was created under the laws of the other state;
3. "corporeal" movable property (including bank or currency notes) physically located in the other state at the time of death; and
4. any other property that the competent authorities of both states agree is located in the other state.

A summary of the U.S.-Japanese treaty will provide another contrast. This is primarily because in Japan, the jurisdictional basis for the tax (gift or inheritance) is the domicile of the recipient, not the transferor. In European countries that have an "inheritance" tax, as opposed to an "estate" tax, the jurisdictional base for taxation is nonetheless measured by the relationship of the transferor to the country (except in Spain). The "estate" tax in the United States follows the same approach.

The difference is that with an inheritance tax, once the transferor is within the tax jurisdiction, the actual rates are determined with reference to the relationship of the beneficiary to that jurisdiction. Thus, in a sense, what is being taxed is the inheritance itself. The domicile of the beneficiary is irrelevant (except in a few cases in which the rate is increased for gifts to "strangers").

13. Insurance is not listed in the Italian treaty.

In Japan (as in Spain, with whom the United States does not have a treaty) the domicile or nationality of the transferor is not what is used to impose the tax. It is the domicile of the recipient that is the jurisdictional base for the imposition of the Japanese tax. Japan has its own definition of "domicile" as well. Not only is it the intention to make Japan one's permanent home, but also domicile apparently is deemed to begin after only one year of living in Japan. Any Japanese nationals (except students and other dependents) who move out of japan can lose it.[14]

Article III of the treaty with Japan takes the approach of listing various categories of assets and specifying which is the country of situs with respect to that category:

1. immovable property (where it is located);
2. tangible movable property, including currency (where it is located or its place of destination);
3. debts, including bonds, promissory notes, bank deposits, and insurance, except bonds or other negotiable instruments in bearer form (where the debtor resides);
4. stock (where the corporation was created or organized);
5. ships and aircraft (where they are registered);
6. goodwill, for a business (where the business is carried on);
7. patents, trademarks, utility models, and designs (where they are registered or, if not registered, then where they are used);
8. copyrights, franchisees, licenses, etc. (where they are exercisable);
9. mining rights (where the mines are);
10. fishing rights (where they are exercisable); and
11. other property: if only one country claims to tax based on location, that tax regime will be followed. If neither is taxing it solely due to situs, then it is "deemed to be situated in accordance with the laws of each contracting state."

Because of the unusual jurisdictional base used by Japan, the treaty refers to the imposition of a tax by the United States for a decedent who was a national of or domiciled in the United States and to the imposition of a tax by Japan for a beneficiary who, at the time of death of the decedent, was domiciled in Japan.

There was then a gap of fifteen years when no new estate tax treaties were negotiated by the United States. As discussed below, the Organization for Economic Cooperation and Development (OECD) issued a Model Convention in 1966, and treaties negotiated after that date have been based in large part on the "domicile" approach of that Model Convention.

14. It was possible under the opposite systems that existed in Japan and the United States, to avoid taxation completely. If the beneficiary resided in the United States and received a gift or inheritance from a Japanese resident, the United States would not impose its gift or estate tax on the recipient (although there are now reporting rules applicable to the receipt of gifts),and Japan would not impose its inheritance or gift tax on the transferor who resided in Japan. Japan has since passed legislation to prevent that.

B. OECD Model Convention

The OECD was formed in 1961 (as a successor to the Organization for European Economic Cooperation (OEEC), which had been formed as part of the Marshall Plan to assist recovery after World War II). The mission was to work together to promote economic and social welfare.

The original twenty countries (Austria, Belgium, Canada, Denmark, France, Germany, Greece, Iceland, Ireland, Italy, Luxembourg, the Netherlands, Norway, Portugal, Spain, Sweden, Switzerland, Turkey, the United Kingdom, and the United States) have been joined by fourteen more since then: Australia (1971), Chile (2010), the Czech Republic (1995), Estonia (2010), Finland (1969), Hungary (1996), Israel (2010), Japan (1964), Korea (1996), Mexico (1994), New Zealand (1973), Poland (1996), the Slovak Republic (2000), and Slovenia (2010).

The OECD began its project of avoiding double taxation by addressing income taxes and issued a "model" convention for income and capital taxes in 1963. In 1966, it issued a "model" convention for avoiding double taxation on estates and inheritances.

The OECD revised the 1966 estate and inheritance tax convention in 1982. According to the report of their Committee of Fiscal Affairs, they hoped to "take account of recent trends in Member countries' attitudes towards the avoidance of double taxation with respect to taxes on estates and inheritances and on gifts" as well as to adapt it "where necessary" in light of the changes in the OECD 1977 income tax model. They noted that two of the member countries, Australia and Canada, would not be able to use the model inasmuch as they did not impose any taxes on estates or inheritances, and that Japan would be obliged to reserve its position due to its unusual domestic tax legislation.

Whereas the estate tax treaties negotiated by the United States during the period between 1946 and 1956 were based on a set of situs rules, with the intention of eliminating double taxation by allowing the situs state to have the primary right to tax, the OECD approach was to focus on domicile. (The U.S. treaty with the Netherlands, signed in 1971, was based on the 1966 OECD Model Convention.)

The 1966 Model Convention "closely" follows what the OECD had done in the income tax area. When one realizes how different an income tax regime is from an inheritance regime tax, it is easy to assume that simply following an income tax model may not work. One key distinction is that the income tax generally deals with only one person, the individual receiving the income. The inheritance tax, on the other hand, can and often does deal with two different parties: the one making the transfer and the one receiving the transfer. In addition, inheritance deals with ownership rights, which probably explains why the category of land is excluded from the general "everything is determined by domicile" approach that the model conventions try to take; states do feel "territorial" about land within their state.

The OECD did consider whether or not to work on a multilateral (as opposed to bilateral) estate tax model convention. It concluded, as it had in 1966 "that, in the present situation, this would meet with great difficulties."[15] Instead, it encouraged other groups of countries to try to work on one together.

Although the Model Convention does not have any legal effect, it can be helpful in understanding some of the treaties.[16] The 1966 OECD Model, entitled "Convention Between (State A) and (State B) for the Avoidance of Double Taxation with Respect to Taxes on Estates and Inheritances," can be summarized as follows.

1. The first article states that the Convention applies only to estates of deceased persons whose domicile at death was in one or both of the countries.
2. The second article provides a framework for listing the specific taxes covered.
3. The third article is a place to add definitions.
4. Article 4 is the all-important one dealing with domicile. If a person is deemed to be domiciled in both countries, the tiebreaker rules are: "permanent home"; or, if there is a permanent home in both countries, then "centre of vital interests"; or, if there is such a center in both countries, then "habitual abode"; or, if there is a habitual abode in both countries, then the country of citizenship; or, if there is dual citizenship, then by mutual agreement of the authorities of the two countries.
5. Article 5 allows the country where immovable property (which includes livestock, equipment, usufructs, mineral rights, and rights to payment for working on the land) is located to tax it.
6. Article 6 provides that business property of a permanent establishment may be taxed by the state in which the establishment is located.
7. Article 7 provides that ships, boats, and aircraft may be taxed in the state in which the effective management is located.
8. Article 8 is very important. It provides that all other property can be taxed only by the country of domicile.
9. Article 9 provides that debts "especially secured" on immovable property, as well as debts that are represented by the acquisition or repair of such property, may be deducted from the value of that property. Otherwise, debts are to be deducted "from the value of the property to which Article 8 applies."
10. Article 10 offers two options to eliminate any double tax: the exemption method and the credit method. Under the exemption method, the country of domicile "shall exempt" from its tax any property that under the Convention may be taxed by the other state. Under the credit method, the country of domicile must give a proportionate credit for the taxes paid to the other state.

15. Report of the OECD Committee on Fiscal Affairs, Doc. 93-31416, at ¶ 37.
16. *See also* the Commentaries to the Model Conventions.

The remaining articles are administrative and include provisions for the exchange of information.

In 1982, the OECD made revisions to the 1966 Convention. The OECD had updated the income tax model in 1977 and wanted to update the estate tax model in a similar way, stating that the only "major" change was the inclusion of gift taxes.

The OECD Model Convention continues to leave many questions unanswered. In fact, for those "seeking to avoid double taxation resulting from differing concepts of comprehensive tax liability, the Model Convention itself must be regarded as somewhat of a disappointment."[17]

The income tax models have been widely adopted; the estate tax models have not. Of the member countries of the OECD, most have fewer than six bilateral estate and inheritance treaties.

As mentioned at the beginning, the United States has sixteen treaties, but half of those were negotiated prior to the 1966 OECD model. Only those treaties with Austria, Denmark, and Sweden were negotiated after the 1982 revisions. Apart from addressing the critical gaps with Canada and negotiating a Protocol to the German estate tax treaty and to the French estate tax treaty, the United States has not had any new or revised estate tax treaties in almost twenty years.

Wolfe Goodman commented that although the OECD Committee on Fiscal Affairs has provided many useful guidelines, "a great many problems remain to be resolved by such countries before they arrive at a really workable convention."[18]

C. U.S. Treasury Department

The United States Treasury Department has also issued its own "model" estate tax treaties on several occasions.

1. The 1977 U.S. Model

The jurisdictional scope of the 1977 Model Convention, as set out in article 1, is for decedents and donors whose domicile was in one or both of the countries. However, the Convention goes on to say that except for the provision on credits, each country may tax its domiciliaries or its citizens (with "citizen" including for a ten-year period former citizens who had a principal purpose of avoiding tax when they lost their citizenship) as if the Convention did not exist.

The Convention will apply to specified taxes and to any future ones (on estates, inheritances, and gifts) that are in addition to or in place of the existing taxes.

The process to use to eliminate one of two domiciles follows the series of: permanent home, center of vital interests, habitual abode, citizenship, and mutual agreement. If the person was a citizen of one country and was domiciled in the

17. Goodman, *supra* note 8.

18. *Id.* at 343.

other for fewer than seven of the previous ten years, he or she would be treated as domiciled in the country of citizenship.

All immovable property may be taxed where it is located. All other property (including tangible property) may only be taxed by the country of domicile.

2. 1979 U.S. Model

The 1979 Model Convention adds generation-skipping transfers. The application to future taxes is limited to those that are "identical or substantially similar." Interests in partnerships that hold immovable or business property may be taxed where they are located.

3. 1980 U.S. Model

The United States Treasury Department also issued its revised model in 1980. Worthy of mention is the statement in its news release that: "The general principle underlying the model is to grant to the country of domicile the right to tax estates and transfers on a worldwide basis." Note, however, that "[t]he model also allows the country of citizenship the right to tax the estate or transfers of a decedent or transferor, but requires it to allow a credit for tax paid to the other State."

The 1980 Model Convention omits the specific treatment of ships and aircraft and redefines the treatment of interests of partnerships that hold immovable or business property. The title of the article "Credits" is changed to "Relief from Double Taxation." The Model also included a new marital deduction provision.

D. Post-1966 Estate Tax Treaties

The following treaties are based in large part on the above models:

1. Austria (1983)—Estate, Inheritance, and Gift
2. Denmark (1984)—Estate, Inheritance, and Gift
3. France (1980)—Estate, Inheritance, and Gift
4. Germany (1979)—Estate, Inheritance, and Gift
5. Netherlands (1971)—Estate, Inheritance, and Gift
6. Sweden (1984)—Estate, Inheritance, and Gift (terminated as of 2008)
7. United Kingdom (1979)—Estate and Gift

Note: A Protocol to the U.S.-German treaty was signed on December 14, 1998 (and became effective upon ratification by both countries on December 14, 2000), making several changes. This Protocol is important because it demonstrates the current U.S. approach to estate tax treaties. The most significant changes include:[19]

1. an increased U.S. unified credit (with a proportionate allowance).
2. a substantially revised marital deduction provision. At first, the Protocol appears to indicate that the United States is allowing an unlimited marital deduction. However, the last sentence of the applicable section provides

19. It also changed the five-year period of not being treated as being domiciled in the noncitizenship country to ten years.

that the allowable marital deduction will not exceed the lesser of that property or "the applicable exclusion amount" (in 2012, that amount was \$5,000,000).[20] The 2004 Protocol amending the estate tax treaty with France added a new provision aimed at disallowing a popular planning technique. It had been possible to remove a home located in France from being treated as taxable in France (under the situs rules) by creating a company that would own the home. The Protocol changed article 5 of the treaty to include the following:

> (3) The term "real property" shall also include shares, participations and other rights in a company or legal person the assets of which consist, directly or through one or more other companies or legal entities, at least 50 percent of real property situated in one of the Contracting States or of rights pertaining to such property. These shares, participations and other rights shall be deemed to be situated in the Contracting State in which the real property is situated.

The Convention between the United States of America and the French Republic for the Avoidance of Double Taxation and the Prevention of Fiscal Evasion with respect to Taxes on Estates, Inheritances, and Gifts will be summarized below, as an illustration of the post-1966 estate tax treaties, following the order of the articles.

The first article describes which estates and gifts are covered. These are:

- estates of decedents whose domicile at death was in France;
- estates of decedents that are subject to the taxing jurisdiction of the United States due either to the decedent's domicile or citizenship there at the time of death;
- gifts by donors whose domicile at the time of making the gift was in France; and
- gifts by donors that are subject to the taxing jurisdiction of the United States due either to the donor's domicile or citizenship there at the time of making the gift.

The second article specifies which taxes in each country are covered. For the United States, those are the federal gift tax, the federal estate tax, and the federal tax on generation-skipping transfers (GST) (note: the GST tax in effect at that time was subsequently retroactively repealed). For France, they are the duty on gifts and the duty levied on succession. Later taxes are also included if they are "identical or substantially similar taxes on estates, inheritances and gifts" and are imposed "in addition to, or in place of, the existing taxes."

20. This is similar to the approach in the Protocol to the Canada Income Tax Convention, discussed *infra* text accompanying footnotes 24–26.

The third article lists several definitions.

The fourth article reflects the major premise of the treaty, that of establishing one and only one domicile of the individual. The intention (also expressed in the 1966 Model Convention, described above) is that the country in which the person has his or her domicile will be the primary country to impose a tax.

The first step is for each country to follow its own internal rules relating to domicile. In the United States, for example, even though the estate and gift tax are imposed, under the Internal Revenue Code, for "residents," that term is defined in the regulations as "domicile." "Domicile" is defined in the regulations as follows:

> A person acquires a domicile in a place by living there, for even a brief period of time, with no definite present intention of later removing therefrom. Residence without the requisite intention to remain indefinitely will not suffice to constitute domicile, nor will intention to change domicile effect such a change unless accompanied by actual removal.[21]

If the result of the separate country application of its domicile test produces only one domicile, that will be the domicile for the rest of the treaty. If the result is two domiciles, the next test is that the person will be deemed to be domiciled in the country in which he or she "maintained his permanent home."

If the person had either a permanent home in both places or in neither place, the next test is the country "with which his personal relations were closest (centre of vital interests)."

If that center of vital interests cannot be determined, the next test is the country in which he or she had a "habitual abode."

If the person had a habitual abode in both places or in neither place, the next test is the country of which he or she was a citizen.

If the person was a citizen of both places, or of neither place, then the two countries need to resolve the domicile "by mutual agreement."

Unfortunately, what follows next in the treaty is a series of complete overrides to all of the above tests. These overrides provide that an individual who was domiciled in both countries but was a citizen of only one of them will be treated as domiciled in the country of citizenship if he or she:

1. had "a clear intention" to retain domicile in the country of citizenship, and
2. was domiciled in the other country "in the aggregate less than 5 years during the 7 year period" preceding the date of death or the date of the gift.

The above concept will also apply (without the "clear intention" test) to someone who was in the other country due to an assignment of employment in that other country (including being a "spouse or other dependent" of someone so employed). In that case, the five-years-out-of-seven test is still used, but if the

21. Treas. Reg. § 20.0-1(b)(1).

employment was renewed, the time is extended to "less than seven" of the preceding ten years.

The fifth article deals with "immovable (real) property." This article provides the primary exception to the premise that the country of domicile will be the main taxing country. It permits the country in which the property is located to tax the property. The country where it is located will define what "immovable (real) property" is, but it cannot include "mortgages or other claims secured by" it. It will, however, include "immovable (real) property" that is part of a "business property of a permanent establishment or is used for the performance of professional services or other independent activities of a similar character." The Protocol now defines "real property" to include rights in a company that owns at least 50 percent of real property (eliminating a common planning technique).

The sixth article covers business property (owned in the individual's name; thus it tends to have little application).

The seventh article covers "tangible personal property." Tangible personal property (which is defined to exclude currency) can be taxed by the country in which it is located, unless it can be taxed as "business property" by the other country (under article 6). Property that is "in transit" is considered to be located at its destination.

This general rule will not apply to property used for "normal personal use" by a person (or his or her family) who is domiciled in the country where he or she is not a citizen, has been there fewer than five of the seven preceding years, and either has the clear intent of going home or is in that country due to employment (increasing the time frame to fewer than seven of the preceding ten years if the employment was renewed).

Article 8 is very important. It provides that except for the immovable property (and business property) and tangible property dealt with above, all other property "including shares or stock in a corporation, debt obligations (whether or not there is written evidence of them), other intangible property, and currency" may be taxed by a country only if the person was at that time either a citizen of or domiciled in that county.

What this means for the United States is that it can continue to apply its worldwide tax on all of its citizens and on all of their property. The immovable property article allows the country where the property is located to tax it; the article does not prohibit the first country from taxing it also. Similarly, the article about tangible property gives permission to tax, but not an exclusive right.

This double taxation situation is sorted out in article 12, which provides, among other items, that France will not tax immovable property or tangible property that the United States can tax under articles 5 or 7. However, if France can tax those categories under articles 5 or 7, the United States can impose its own tax, but will give a credit against its tax for that portion of the French tax (but not in excess of the proportionate share of the United States tax that is attributable to that property).

This credit is in place of, not in addition to, the usual credit for foreign death taxes. Although the end of that article states that the treaty shall not increase the amount of tax either country would have imposed, it also states that if the treaty results in a smaller tax credit than there would have been without the treaty, that shall not be considered to be an increase in the tax.

The ninth article addresses the treatment of debts. The general rule (apart from businesses, ships, and aircraft) is that debts that would be deductible by the internal law of a country are deducted from the gross value of "the property that is taxable by that country," but only in the proportion that "such gross value bears to the gross value of the entire property wherever situated." As a practical matter, this requirement of full disclosure of all assets makes many taxpayers hesitant to claim the deduction.

The tenth article allows certain charitable deductions.

The eleventh article addresses community property (which is prevalent in France, although not required) and marital deductions. This is not a simple provision. Moreover, it was written prior to the major change in the United States in 1988 disallowing the marital deduction for property passing to a spouse who is not a citizen of the United States.

The only sentence that governs how the United States tax shall be "adjusted" applies solely to someone then domiciled in France (thus being taxed on a nearly worldwide basis) who is also taxed (on a full worldwide basis) by the United States, e.g., based on citizenship. It states that in such a case, the United States must allow "the same marital deduction in effect on the date of signature of this Convention, as if such individual were domiciled in the United States . . . ." That provision will not apply if the result would be to increase the tax.

On the date of treaty signature, November 24, 1978, the unlimited marital deduction was not yet in effect. So, to apply that sentence would have increased the tax, at least until 1988 when there might well be no deduction at all, unless the sentence is used to apply the limited deduction in force in 1978. The Protocol allows an exclusion up to 50 percent for certain property left to a spouse.

The twelfth article deals with exemptions and credits.

The balance of the treaty is administrative and includes the agreement to exchange information.

The Technical Explanation issued by the United States Treasury Department with respect to the U.S.-France treaty mentions that it is the second treaty signed after the sweeping changes made in the internal law in 1976, and that it is similar to the United States model convention published by the Treasury Department in 1977 and is also based "in part" on the OECD 1966 model.

The Explanation says that the general principle of the treaty is that the primary right to tax the worldwide assets "should lie with the country of domicile." At the end of that section, though, the Explanation acknowledges that the United States is contemplated to impose its tax on the worldwide property of its citizens, allowing a credit for a French tax.

E. Selected Issues under the Treaties

It may be helpful to examine how a few common issues are treated under each treaty. In each of the fifteen estate tax treaties (Australia is excluded), the right of the United States to impose worldwide taxation on its citizens notwithstanding other treaty provisions will be noted. With respect to a nonresident alien (NRA), whether or not the treaty follows the Internal Revenue Code provision allowing the United States to tax stock in a U.S. corporation will be noted. Finally the marital "allowance" provision for an NRA in the treaty will be noted. These examples assume that the NRA is domiciled in the other country.

1. Austria

Article 9 allows the United States to tax its citizens. An NRA cannot be taxed by the United States on U.S. stock, under article 7. No mention is made of a marital deduction.

2. Denmark

Article 1, § 3 provides that a country may tax based on citizenship "as if this Convention had not come into effect." An NRA cannot be taxed by the United States on U.S. stock, under article 8. The marital deduction for an NRA is addressed in article 9, § 2(a):

> The United States shall . . . allow the same marital deduction that would be allowed with respect to a decedent domiciled in the United States. . . . If the United States tax determined without regard to the preceding sentence is lower than that computed under the preceding sentence, the lower tax shall apply.

At the time of the treaty, 1984, the United States had an unlimited marital deduction. In 1988, however, the unlimited deduction was eliminated if the surviving spouse is not a U.S. citizen (unless the QDOT provisions are complied with). Accordingly if the NRA's spouse is not a U.S. citizen, it is likely that the first sentence of the quoted section would result in no marital deduction.

3. Finland

The right of the U.S. to tax based on citizenship seems to be assumed throughout. The United States can tax the U.S. stock owned by an NRA, under article III, § 2(d). The marital exemption is not addressed.

4. France

The right of the United States to tax based on citizenship seems to be assumed throughout. The United States cannot tax the U.S. stock owned by an NRA, under article 8. The somewhat difficult marital provision was discussed above in some detail.

5. Germany

The United States may tax its citizens, under article 11, ¶ 1 (a). The United States can tax the U.S. stock owned by an NRA, under article 9 (which refers to the exception of article 11, ¶ 1). The marital provision has been renegotiated in the Protocol, discussed above.

6. Greece

Under the original treaty, the United States was prevented from taxing, at all, immovable property located in Greece (article III). That provision was "deemed to be deleted" in the Protocol of 1964 (article I(b)). The United States may tax stock owned in a U.S. corporation (see article IV(2)(f)). Article V(a) provides that for an NRA, the United States "shall allow every . . . deduction . . . (except the marital deduction provided by the United States Revenue Act of 1948), which would be applicable under its law if the decedent had been domiciled in its territory in a [pro rata] amount . . . ."

7. Ireland

It seems to be assumed that the United States can tax based on citizenship. Under article III(2)(d), the United States can tax the U.S. stock owned by an NRA. The marital exemption is not addressed.

8. Italy

It seems to be assumed that the United States can tax based on citizenship. Under article III(1)(d), the United States can tax U.S. stock owned by an NRA. The marital exemption is not addressed.

9. Japan

It seems to be assumed that the United States can tax based on citizenship. Under article III(1)(d), the United States can tax U.S. stock owned by an NRA. The marital exemption is not addressed.

10. Netherlands

The right of the United States to tax its citizens is referred to in article 9: "If the decedent was a citizen of a State at his death that State may tax property in accordance with its laws, including property not enumerated in Article 6 [immovable] or 7 [business establishment], whether or not he was domiciled therein." Under article 8, the United States cannot tax the U.S. stock owned by an NRA. Article 10 does address the marital exemption from the Netherlands' perspective (and mentions community property) in paragraph one. Paragraph two could be read as continuing that theme, from the U.S. perspective, although "marital" is not mentioned. Paragraph two provides that if the United States taxes immovable or business property (articles 6 and 7), there shall be an exemption of $30,000, and if the tax is more than $30,000 "the tax imposed [by the United States] shall not exceed the lesser of (a) 50 percent of such value in excess of $30,000, or (b) the amount of the tax determined in accordance with the provisions of this Convention taking into account any exemptions allowable under the laws of the State."

11. Norway

It seems to be assumed that the United States can tax based on citizenship. Under article III(2)(e), the United States can tax U.S. stock owned by an NRA. The marital exemption is not addressed.

12. South Africa

It seems to be assumed that the United States can tax based on citizenship. Under article III(2)(d), the United States can tax U.S. stock owned by an NRA. The marital exemption is not addressed.

13. Sweden

It seems to be assumed that the United States can tax based on citizenship. Under article 7(1), the United States cannot tax "transfers and deemed transfers" of U.S. stock owned by an NRA. The marital exemption is addressed in article 8(8): for an NRA transferring property to a spouse, "such property shall be included in the taxable base only to the extent that the value of the property exceeds 50 percent of the value of all property . . . whose transfer may, under this Convention, be taxed by the United States." Note: this treaty was terminated in 2008.

14. Switzerland

It seems to be assumed that the United States can tax based on citizenship. Whether or not the United States can tax U.S. stock owned by an NRA is not addressed (article IV, which contains the "situs" categories, does not apply to NRAs). The marital exemption is not addressed.

15. United Kingdom

Article 5(1)(b) states a clear exception to the general rule that other than immovable and business property, only the country of domicile may tax: "[The general rule] shall not apply if at the time of the death or transfer the decedent or transferor was a national of that other State." The general rule, in article 5(1)(a), would prevent the United States from taxing the U.S. stock owned by an NRA. Article 8(2) provides that a marital deduction is allowable for an NRA "to the extent that a marital deduction would have been allowable if the decedent or transferor had been domiciled in the United States . . . ."

II. Canada—Income Tax Protocol

Since 1971,[22] the Canadian tax "at death" treats the deceased as if he or she had at that moment disposed of all of his or her assets, for income tax calculations. Unlike the income tax approach in the United States, which increases (steps up) the income tax basis at death to the current fair market value, thus eliminating any income tax on that capital gain, Canada chose to tax the increase in value at death.[23]

For United States persons (citizens or resident aliens) who do not reside in Canada but who own vacation homes (or cabins) in Canada, this rule meant that there would be a capital gains tax imposed by Canada at their death.[24]

The 1995 Protocol to the Income Tax Treaty will now allow the U.S. estate tax return to reflect a credit for that Canadian income tax. The result is much better than its previous treatment as a deduction.[25]

The Protocol also allows a proportionate share of the unified credit to be allowed against the U.S. tax (based on the proportion of assets in the United States). The severe change in 1988 in U.S. law regarding the marital deduction rules applicable to noncitizen spouses is also addressed. Under the Protocol, a marital "credit" is allowed by the United States when there is a noncitizen surviving spouse, but the marital credit cannot exceed, in general, an amount equal to the proportionate unified credit that is allowed under the Protocol.

Smaller estates are largely excluded from the double tax by a provision in the Protocol (¶ 8) that for gross estates of less than US$1.2 million, the only property that the United States would include, in the case of a Canadian resident, would be property, the sale of which would permit a United States income tax on the gain (under other provisions of the Income Tax Treaty). This will remain, however, a trap for those smaller estates that do own real property in the United States, since that property can be taxed regardless of the size of the estate.

For the larger estates, if a Canadian resident dies owning a large portfolio of U.S. securities, the U.S. estate tax will apply. The Canadian income tax could be small, depending on the amount of appreciation in the portfolio, in which case the ability to apply the U.S. estate tax as a credit against the Canadian income tax would be of limited benefit.

---

22. When Canada repealed its estate tax.

23. There is also recapture of prior depreciation.

24. Worse, the well-meaning transfer of those assets to a standard American revocable trust could trigger a current income tax in Canada.

25. For Canadians owning homes in the United States, the reverse is now true—an even more significant improvement for them, because the United States estate tax did not otherwise qualify even as a deduction from their income tax at death.

III. Conventions

The Hague Conference on Private International Law is the name of the intergovernmental organization formed to "work for the progressive unification of the rules of private international law." From 1951 to the present, it has adopted thirty-four international conventions. Four of those (#11, #21, #31, and #32) address topics in the multinational estate planning field.

Each convention can be ratified by the countries that were represented at the session at which the convention was adopted.

After three ratifications have been filed in the Netherlands, the convention becomes effective as to those that have ratified it. Subsequent ratifications by represented countries become effective as to those countries sixty days (or three full calendar months, depending on the convention) after their ratification. In addition, countries that were not represented may "accede" to the convention by filing an instrument of accession in the Netherlands. The convention will become effective as to those countries sixty days (or, again, three full calendar months) after their accession.

A. Convention of the Conflicts of Laws Relating to the Form of Testamentary Dispositions (Oct. 5, 1961)

Although this Convention has been ratified or acceded to by thirty-eight countries, the list does not include the United States. It could be a helpful reference nevertheless when dealing with several other countries. The list includes Australia, Belgium, Denmark, France, Germany, Italy, Japan, the Netherlands, Norway, Spain, Sweden, Switzerland, and the United Kingdom.

The purpose of the Convention is to recognize as valid the form of a testamentary instrument if its form complies with the internal law of any of the following:

1. the place where the testator made it;
2. the nationality of the testator either when he or she made it or at his or her death;
3. the place of domicile of the testator either when he or she made it or at his or her death;
4. the place of "habitual residence" either when he or she made it or at his or her death; or
5. for immovables, the place where they are physically located.

Unfortunately, one must also check whether a particular country chose not to recognize a number of permitted exceptions. For example, the general rule is that domicile is to be determined by the state that is under consideration as the domicile, but a country may also elect to use the law of the forum to determine the domicile. A discouragement of "forum shopping" is another provision allowing a state, at least with respect to property located within the state, not to recognize "foreign" documents if they were signed by one of its nationals who also was domiciled or had habitual residence in the "home" country and who did not die where the document was made.

B. Convention Concerning the International Administration of the Estates of Deceased Persons (Oct. 2, 1973)

This convention has not been as widely ratified or acceded to, with only three countries ratifying it (the Czech Republic, Portugal, and Slovakia), although it has also been signed by Italy, the Netherlands, and the United Kingdom (but not the United States).

The primary purpose of the Convention is to develop a recognized "international certificate" showing who is entitled to administer the moveable assets and what their powers are. It is unclear why this convention met with so little agreement.

C. Convention on the Law Applicable to Trusts and on Their Recognition (July 1, 1985)

This is the highly controversial convention. It attempts to address the confusion caused by the nonexistence of the trust entity under civil law (most European countries simply do not have the institution of a trust or laws designed to respond to trusts). This is an important subject, and the cause of many current planning problems.

A common trap for the U.S. practitioner is to transfer the ownership of assets in a civil law jurisdiction into a trust. The unintended results can be harsh: the current trigger of a taxable event; taxation at the rate determined by the relationship to the jurisdiction, if any, of the "trustee" who is treated as the new owner; and even potential liability to any creditors or heirs of the "trustee."

Ironically, these transfers are made the most often by well-meaning American lawyers who are trying to eliminate a foreign probate proceeding. Chances are, however, that the civil law jurisdiction that does not recognize trusts also has no probate proceeding.

Donovan Waters has reported that one Oxford scholar commented that the private international laws concerning trusts are "one of the most undeveloped and neglected areas of study that exist."[26]

This Convention has been ratified by the United States (and the United Kingdom, Australia, and Canada—all of which share the common law tradition that includes trusts), as well as by a slowly increasing number of European countries, which had not otherwise recognized trusts: the Netherlands (1995), Italy (1990),

26. Donovan Waters, *The Convention on the Law Applicable to Successions to the Estates of Deceased Persons*, Conference Papers of the Int'l Academy of Estate and Trust Law 18 (1989).

Luxembourg (2003), and Switzerland (2007). France "signed" it in 1991 but has not ratified it.

D. Convention on the Law Applicable to Succession to the Estates of Deceased Persons (Aug. 1, 1989)

This Convention has been signed by only four states (Argentina, Luxembourg, the Netherlands, and Switzerland) and ratified by only one of them, the Netherlands. Thus it is not in effect.

The purpose of this most recent Convention is to determine which law will apply for the actual inheritance. It is the author's opinion that this Convention is unlikely to be successful, since the determination of heirs is perhaps the single most basic cultural decision in this field.

Nonetheless, the Convention is a valiant attempt to make distinctions. They are not simple. At the outset, the Convention acknowledges that it will not deal with matrimonial property or any rights or interests "created or transferred otherwise than by succession."

Problems arise often in this area. If a person domiciled in one country owns homes in one or more other countries, the planning is difficult. The general rule is that the law of the country where the immovable is located will apply with respect to who will, or may, inherit that property. Many countries have forced heirship rules, many have differing marital property systems, and so on.

The basic premise is that the law of the "closest" state should govern, and its single law (without *renvoi*, as a general rule) should apply to the succession of all of the property. There is a system for determining the "closest" country.

The first priority is the state in which the decedent was both a national and also a habitual resident as of the time of death. But succession is "also governed" by a state in which he was only a habitual resident at the time of death if that residency had lasted more than five years. Even then, though, it is possible to prove that he was "manifestly more closely connected" with the state of nationality, in which case that law would govern.

The final general rule is that the law of nationality will apply—unless at the time of death the decedent was "more closely connected" with another state, in which case that law would apply. (This was apparently especially important for those who have clearly immigrated to a new country and settled down, but are in the process of obtaining the new citizenship.)

An interesting option included in the Convention is that a person may designate which law is to govern, so long as at the time of designation, or at the time of death, the person was either a national of the state or had his or her habitual residence there. If this statement is properly included in the testamentary document, it will be assumed to apply to any intestate property as well (other than those excluded from the scope of the Convention).

The Convention somewhat ambitiously proceeds to deal also with "agreements" as to succession rights by one or more persons. Near the end, on a less ambitious note, the Convention states that it does not affect any laws of states where particular categories of assets are located when those laws represent "a particular inheritance regime in respect of such assets because of economic, family or social considerations."

Donovan Waters, who participated in that Conference, was very hopeful about the prospects of this Convention, writing:

> This Convention . . . is probably one of the most interesting and potentially far reaching that has been adopted by The Hague Conference in recent years. . . . It is very much to be hoped that the enthusiasm . . . will be translated into an adoption . . . of this rather remarkable and unexpectedly successful Convention.[27]

The United States delegate to the Conference, Eugene Scoles, described it as "a genuine advance" and added: "It is particularly important that the United States respond to this opportunity by approval of the Convention."[28]

Waters' and Scoles' comments were both written in 1989. The United States has not signed the convention.[29] It has yet to be ratified by even three countries. It is not in effect.

IV. Conclusion

It is hoped that the foregoing review provides some insight into these difficult multinational tax issues. It is unfortunate, in the author's opinion, that so little attention and effort have been spent on harmonizing the substantial taxes imposed by countries on the accumulation of wealth throughout one's lifetime. As contacts an individual has with more than one country continue to increase, these multinational estate tax issues continue to increase in importance and, unfortunately, in complexity as well.

27. *Id.*

28. *Id.*

29. One difficulty in the United States is that probate matters would be under the jurisdiction of the U.S. federal courts.

Income Tax Treaties

12

William B. Sherman
Summer A. LePree*

I. Introduction

The United States, like most other countries, taxes its residents (both individual and corporate) on their worldwide income. The United States, unlike almost any other country in the world, also taxes its citizens on a worldwide basis, regardless of residence. Most countries, including the United States, also tax nonresidents on a limited basis where a sufficient connection exists between the income and the source (i.e., nonresidence) country.

Foreign (i.e., non-U.S.) individuals and businesses often make investments and/or conduct business activities in the United States. Many foreign individuals also at one time or another spend significant time in the United States. Acquiring such ties with the United States can cause such persons to become subject to U.S. tax under U.S. domestic tax law. Likewise, U.S. individuals and businesses continue to increase their economic and social ties outside the United States, which generally has tax implications under local law in those non-U.S. jurisdictions, though such persons also continue generally to be subject to U.S. tax as residents or citizens of the United States. With the increasing prevalence of such cross-border connections comes a heightened risk of double taxation. One significant tool in tax planning in this context is the utilization of the favorable provisions available in

* The authors would like to thank Len Schneidman, of WTAS in Boston, Massachusetts, for his assistance with portions of this chapter.

U.S. bilateral income tax treaties. Understanding these provisions and their potential impact is essential to the provision of competent advice in this area.

This chapter examines income tax treaties in general, including their constitutional and statutory authority from the U.S. perspective and their interpretation under U.S. and OECD (Organization for Economic Cooperation and Development) standards; describes the necessary qualifications to claim treaty benefits, including residence and limitations on benefits that are unique to U.S. treaties; discusses certain specific treaty benefits, including the taxation of business profits and the provisions relating to the taxation of nonbusiness income (e.g., dividends, interest and royalties); and, finally, discusses the procedural requirements necessary for the claiming of treaty benefits under U.S. law.

II. Tax Treaties in General

Most tax treaties are bilateral agreements in which the treaty partner countries agree to limit their respective taxation of residents of the other country. The United States currently has comprehensive income tax treaties with more than sixty countries.

In addition to income tax treaties, the United States, like many other countries, also has negotiated treaties relating to estate and/or gift tax and exchange of information. Those types of treaties are discussed in a separate chapter of this publication. Additionally, the U.S. Treasury Department periodically releases a "Model U.S. Treaty," which serves as a basis for the provisions the U.S. Treasury seeks to include in both new and renegotiated income tax treaties. The most recent U.S. Model Treaty, which is cited frequently throughout this chapter, was published in 2006. The OECD similarly publishes a Model Treaty periodically, with the most recent version of that Model Treaty published in 2010.

With respect to U.S. income tax treaties, with few exceptions (e.g., the U.S.-Canada income tax treaty, which also contains estate tax provisions), only federal income taxes are covered by the treaties. Thus, U.S. income tax treaties do not apply to federal wealth transfer taxes, state and local taxes, or federal social security taxes.

III. Constitutional and Other Authority

Treaties generally obtain their authority from the United States Constitution. Specifically, Article VI, clause 2, of the U.S. Constitution states as follows: "Laws of the United States which shall be made in Pursuance thereof; and all Treaties made, or which shall be made, under the Authority of the United States, shall be the supreme Law of the Land."

The United States Supreme Court previously interpreted this provision as generally placing federal statutes and treaties on equal footing.[1] In this way, when a statute and a treaty conflict, neither the statute nor the treaty automatically decides the issue. Instead, the conflict usually is resolved based on the most recently adopted of the two sources. This most recently adopted tenet comes from historical common law.

Recognizing that both treaties and statutes are important sources of U.S. law, U.S. courts considering these issues typically try to give effect to both the treaty and the statute, regardless of which was most recently adopted, to the extent this is possible.[2] According to the U.S. Supreme Court, "[a] treaty will not be deemed to have been abrogated or modified by a later statute unless such purpose on the part of Congress has been clearly expressed."[3]

U.S. tax treaties are negotiated by the U.S. Treasury Department's Office of Tax Policy on the one hand, and by the competent authority of the treaty partner country on the other hand.[4] The articulated goals of the tax treaty process are the "avoidance of double taxation" and the "prevention of fiscal evasion." In this way, treaties are intended to benefit both taxpayers and tax authorities.

After being fully negotiated and agreed upon by the respective tax authorities, on the U.S. side, income tax treaties are ratified by the Senate (with the House of Representatives having no role in this process) and are regarded as self-executing, which means they have the force of law even though they are not formally enacted as a statute.

IV. Interpreting Treaties[5]

A. General

U.S. income tax treaties generally provide that, unless the context otherwise requires or the competent authorities agree to a common meaning, any term contained in the treaty must be given the meaning that it has at that time under the

1. *See, e.g.*, Reid v. Covert, 354 U.S. 1 (1957).

2. *See* Whitney v. Robertson, 124 U.S. 190 (1888).

3. Cook v. United States, 288 U.S. 102, 120 (1933). *But see* S. Rep. No. 445, 100th Cong. 325 (1988) (stating that *Cook* does not require that "Congress must specifically advert to the treaties to have later statutes given effect," but mention of conflict in statute or legislative history is "dispositive" in favor of later statute).

4. For a somewhat critical analysis of the tax treaty process, see Patrick Drissen, *Is There a Tax Treaty Insularity Complex, Tax Analysts, Special Report*, Tax Notes Today 745 (May 7, 2012).

5. For a detailed discussion of tax treaty interpretation, see John A. Townsend, *Tax Treaty Interpretation*, 55 Tax Lawyer 219 (2002). In Report No. 1214, the New York State Bar Association Tax Section recommended that the IRS develop a program of providing guidance on generic issues that arise under U.S. income tax treaties. Daily Tax Rep. (BNA) (June 2, 2010).

laws of the country imposing the taxes to which the treaty applies.[6] The interpretation of U.S. income tax treaties therefore involves a multistep process. First, if the treaty explicitly defines a term, that definition clearly must be used. Second, if the treaty does not provide any specific definition for the term in question, the meaning of a term may be determined by reference to the context surrounding the negotiation and conclusion of the treaty, as illustrated by certain extrinsic evidence (e.g., Technical Explanations, Committee Reports, and other recorded evidence surrounding the treaty). The competent authorities may alternatively agree to a common meaning of the term. Finally, if the context does not require any particular meaning, and the authorities do not otherwise agree on a meaning, the term must be given its accepted meaning under the domestic law of the country imposing the tax at issue.[7]

B. Interpretation by U.S. Courts of Tax Treaties

According to the U.S. Supreme Court: "The clear import of treaty language controls unless 'application of the words of the treaty according to their obvious meaning effects a result inconsistent with the intent or expectations of its signatories.'"[8]

When the meaning of a particular treaty provision in a given case is unclear, extrinsic materials often are consulted for further guidance. For example, as further discussed below, each U.S. Income Tax Treaty is accompanied by a Treasury Technical Explanation to that treaty. The Technical Explanations typically are used by the Treasury during the Senate ratification proceedings. In addition, the Senate Foreign Relations Committee often releases a similar report after it completes its deliberations, interpreting or more fully explaining the specific provisions of the treaty in question. Beyond these typical materials, courts, the IRS and practitioners sometimes attempt to utilize other outside materials that may have a more distant or less formal connection to the final treaty as ratified. Debates have occurred over the issue of what extrinsic evidence is relevant and how forceful such materials are.

Many U.S. courts have taken into account interpretative materials that originated in the U.S. Treasury as the best available evidence, even where there is no evidence that the other country's tax authorities accepted or even were aware of the U.S. Treasury interpretation. In a given case, either of two types of unilateral Treasury material generally may be available. First, the Treasury issued regulations as Treasury Decisions under some older treaties, only a couple of which

6. *See* art. 3(2) of 2006 U.S. Model Treaty.

7. *See Construing U.S. Income Tax Treaties Under U.S. Law, in* ANDERSEN: ANALYSIS OF UNITED STATES INCOME TAX TREATIES, ¶ 1.05, [hereinafter ANDERSEN ON TREATIES].

8. Sumitomo Shoji Am., Inc. v. Avagliano, 457 U.S. 176, 180 (1982) (quoting Maximov v. United States, 373 U.S. 49, 54 (1963)). According to the Tax Court, "when interpreting a treaty, we begin with the text of the treaty and the context in which the written words are used. . . . The plain words of the treaty control unless their effect is contrary to the intent of the signatories. . . . The words of a treaty are to be interpreted according to their ordinary meaning as understood in the public law of nations." Park v. Comm'r, 136 T.C. 569 (2011).

remain in force today.[9] Specifically, the U.S. treaties with Pakistan and Greece were implemented by Treasury Decision.[10] More commonly, as discussed above, the Treasury prepares a technical explanation of each treaty for use in ratification deliberations in the Senate. The IRS often refers to the technical explanations,[11] as do taxpayers and their advisers, but judicial authority on the force of the technical explanations is limited.[12] For example, the Court of Federal Claims, referring to the technical explanation to a U.S.-U.K. treaty and a report of the Senate Foreign Relations Committee on the treaty, stated: "[T]he unilateral views of the U.S. are not controlling. . . . [T]he court must give meaning to the intent of the treaty partners, not simply the views of the U.S."[13]

C. OECD Commentary

The OECD Model Treaty, discussed above, is accompanied by extensive commentaries on each of the model's articles. Because the United States is a member of the OECD, U.S. courts also have relied on these commentaries in interpreting treaties between the United States and other OECD member countries.[14] Decisions of courts of the other country also have been cited in some instances.[15] According to the Supreme Court, "[t]he practice of treaty signatories counts as evidence of the treaty's proper interpretation, since their conduct generally evinces their understanding of the agreement they signed."[16]

---

9. *See* IRS Publication 901 (Apr. 2013).

10. T.D. 6431, 1954-2 C.B. 638 (Jan. 1, 1953) and T.D. 6109, 1960-1 C.B. 755 (Jan. 1, 1959), respectively.

11. *See*, e.g., Rev. Rul. 89-95, 1989-2 C.B. 131; Rev. Rul. 81-78, 1981-1 C.B. 604.

12. *See* Xerox Corp. v. United States, 14 Cl. Ct. 455 (1988) (inferring U.K. acceptance of Treasury Technical Explanation from the fact that it was made available to U.K. negotiators before treaty was ratified by U.K. parliament), *rev'd*, 41 F.3d 647 (Fed. Cir. 1994) (finding treaty text to be unambiguous on issue at hand). *See also* Mazurek v. United States, 271 F.3d 226, 233 (5th Cir. 2001) ("although the Commentary to the [OECD] Model Treaty provides guidance, the IRS's specific commentary and advice on the [particular treaty in the Technical Explanation] should be given greater weight").

13. Nat'l Westminster Bank v. United States, 58 Fed. Cl. 491 (2003), *aff'd*, 512 F.3d 1347 (Fed. Cir. 2008). *But see* Allchin v. Her Majesty, 2004 FCA 206 (Canadian Fed. Ct. of Appeal 2004) ("While technical explanations attached to treaties are not binding on the Court, they may be accepted as valid guidance").

14. *E.g.*, United States v. A.L. Burbank & Co., 525 F.2d 9, 15 (2d Cir. 1975), *cert. denied*, 426 U.S. 934 (1976); Nat'l Westminster Bank, PLC v. United States, 44 Fed. Cl. 120 (1999); PLC v. United States, 44 Fed. Cl. 120 (1999), *aff'd*, 512 F.3d 1347 (Fed. Cir. 2008) ("Commentaries . . . are important and helpful in determining the probable mutual understanding of countries which used the [Model] as the basis for a tax treaty. . . . Thus, [they are] appropriate for use in divining probable intent of countries adopting treaties based thereon"); Podd v. Comm'r, 76 T.C.M. (CCH) 906 (1998); Taisei Fire & Marine Ins. Co. v. Comm'r, 104 T.C. 535 (1995). *See* Rev. Rul. 86-145, 1986-2 C.B. 297.

The OECD frequently revises its Commentaries. One uncertain issue in this context is the probative value of additions to or revisions of Commentaries in interpreting treaties made before the additions or revisions were adopted. *See Nat'l Westminster Bank*, 58 Fed. Cl. 491 (discussing subsequent revisions and discussion drafts of proposed revisions).

15. *See* Donroy, Ltd. v. United States, 301 F.2d 200 (9th Cir. 1962).

16. United States v. Stuart, 489 U.S. 353, 369 (1989).

D. Application of Local Law

Most U.S. tax treaties also typically contain a provision similar to article 3(2) of the U.S. Model convention, which states as follows:

> As regards the application of the Convention at any time by a Contracting State any term not defined therein shall, unless the context otherwise requires, . . . have the meaning which it has at that time under the law of that State for the purposes of the taxes to which the Convention applies, any meaning under the applicable tax laws of that State prevailing over a meaning given to the term under other laws of that State.[17]

For example, article 13(2) of the U.S. Model Treaty authorizes the United States to tax residents of the other country on gains from the sale of any "United States real property interest." The quoted phrase is not defined in the Model Treaty, but it is clearly defined in the U.S. Internal Revenue Code[18] and accompanying regulations. Based on article 3(2) of the Model Treaty, the U.S. domestic law definition also is applicable for treaty purposes.

Under article 3(2), the focus is on the law of the taxing country as of the time the tax is applied, rather than the time that the treaty was concluded. For example, for purposes of article 13(2), the statutory definition of "United States real property interest" is applied as it exists for the taxable year for which the definition is relevant (i.e., the year with respect to which the tax is to be imposed), even if the definition has been amended since the treaty was adopted.

V. Qualification for Treaty Benefits

A. General

Tax treaties generally can only be used to help a taxpayer, not to make a taxpayer worse off than would be the case under domestic law in the absence of the treaty. In the words of the Treasury Technical Explanation to the 2006 U.S. Model Treaty, "the Convention may not increase the tax burden on a resident of a Contracting State beyond the burden determined under domestic law. Thus, a right to tax given by the Convention cannot be exercised unless that right also exists under internal law." In other words, treaties do not give the treaty partners any taxing rights that do not already exist under those countries' domestic laws; rather, they only reduce or eliminate those rights as to certain items in order to prevent double taxation. As a result, "a taxpayer's U.S. tax liability need not be determined under

17. For a discussion of the effects of a treaty country's right to apply its local law, see Lee Sheppard, *News Analysis: Treaty Countries' Right to Use Domestic Law, Tax Analysts*, TAX NOTES TODAY (Oct. 24, 2012).

18. Unless otherwise noted, all references to sections and the Code are to the U.S. Internal Revenue Code of 1986, as amended (the Code), and the U.S. Treasury Regulations promulgated under the Code.

the Convention if the Code would produce a more favorable result. A taxpayer may not, however, choose among the provisions of the Code and the Convention in an inconsistent manner in order to minimize tax."[19] In this sense, obtaining treaty benefits can be viewed as an "all or nothing" proposition, under which the taxpayer is not permitted to "cherry-pick" favorable treaty provisions and favorable code provisions and combine them to achieve the most advantageous result.

In order to secure treaty benefits, a taxpayer must first satisfy several requirements set forth under the treaties, as discussed immediately below.

B. Residence

1. General

Pursuant to the typical General Scope (or Personal Scope, depending on the specific treaty in question) articles of most U.S. treaties, treaty benefits generally are available only to persons who are "residents" of one or both Contracting States.[20] Thus, to be eligible to obtain treaty benefits, one must qualify under the relevant treaty definition of "resident."

In most U.S. treaties, including the 2006 U.S. Model Treaty, residence is defined in article 4 of the treaty. The 2006 U.S. Model Treaty provides:

> For the purposes of this Convention, the term "resident of a Contracting State" means any person who, under the laws of that State, is *liable to tax* therein by reason of his domicile, residence, citizenship, place of management, place of incorporation, or any other criterion of a similar nature, and also includes that State and any political subdivision or local authority thereof. This term, however, does not include any person who is liable to tax in that State in respect only of income from sources in that State or of profits attributable to a permanent establishment in that State.[21]

Thus, an individual who is considered a U.S. income tax resident pursuant to domestic U.S. law[22] generally also is considered a U.S. resident for purposes of an income tax treaty. This is because such persons are, under the tax laws of the United States, liable to U.S. federal income tax by reason of their residence, and this taxation is not limited to income from U.S. sources. For example, all residents of the United States, including U.S. lawful permanent residents (green card holders) and individuals who are considered U.S. residents under the "substantial presence test" (set forth in § 7701(b)(3)), are subject to worldwide income taxation by the United States. On this basis, such persons also generally are treated as U.S. residents for treaty purposes. Likewise, a corporation incorporated in the U.S. is classified as a "domestic corporation" and thus is liable to U.S. tax on its

19. Technical Explanation to art. 1, para. 2 of 2006 U.S. Model Treaty. *See, e.g.*, Rev. Rul. 84-17, 1984-1 C.B. 308.

20. *See, e.g.*, art. 1, 2006 U.S. Model Treaty.

21. Art. 4(1), 2006 U.S. Model Treaty (emphasis added).

22. *See* § 7701(b).

worldwide income pursuant to U.S. domestic tax law. Consequently, such domestic corporations also are U.S. residents for purposes of U.S. income tax treaties. Where a person (whether an individual or an entity) is a resident of one treaty country under the above definition, but is not a resident of the other treaty partner country, this ends the inquiry, and treaty benefits can be determined based on that unilateral residency classification.

2. Tiebreaker Rules

In many cases, particularly with respect to individuals who may be, for example, U.S. citizens or U.S. green card holders residing full-time in a treaty partner country, a person might be considered a resident of both countries under the countries' respective domestic law standards, and thus also for purposes of the treaty. In other words, an individual might be considered a U.S. income tax resident under U.S. law, and also an income tax resident of a foreign country under that nation's laws. Such persons generally are classified as "dual residents."

In the absence of treaty relief, dual residents are subject to a particularly high risk of double taxation, since both countries (unless one of the countries has a territorial tax system, for example) generally seek to tax that same person on worldwide income. While most countries that tax residents on a worldwide basis also provide a foreign tax credit mechanism that is intended to provide relief from this double taxation risk, such foreign tax credits are often an imperfect solution, largely because of differences in sourcing rules. For example, if both countries claim that a particular item is sourced to their country under domestic law, because the foreign tax credit generally is limited by the ratio of foreign source income to worldwide income, the foreign tax credit often will fail to provide relief.

With respect to dual residents, each U.S. treaty provides a "tiebreak" rule, usually found in article 4 of most treaties, under which a dual resident individual is classified as a resident of one, and only one, country for purposes of determining the individual's income tax liability under the income tax treaty.[23] In general, under a typical tiebreaker provision, exclusive residence is determined by applying the following tests in the following order:

- First, the individual is deemed to be a resident of the treaty country in which he has a permanent home available to him; if he has a permanent home available to him in both treaty countries, he is deemed to be a resident only of the treaty country with which his personal and economic relations are closer (center of vital interests);
- Second, if the country in which he has his center of vital interests cannot be determined, or if he does not have a permanent home in either country, he is deemed to be a resident of the country in which he has a habitual abode;

23. *See, e.g.*, art. 1(3), 2006 U.S. Model Treaty.

- Third, if he has a habitual abode in both treaty countries or in neither country, he is deemed to be a resident of the country of which he is a national; and
- Fourth, if the issue cannot be settled by the application of the tests set forth above, the competent authorities of the treaty countries, i.e., the IRS and its counterpart in the foreign treaty country, are required to make an effort to settle the issue by mutual agreement.[24]

A foreign individual who is treated as a U.S. resident under U.S. domestic tax law, but who is treated under an applicable income tax treaty's tiebreaker provision as a resident of a foreign treaty country, generally will be subject to U.S. federal income tax as a nonresident alien, provided that he timely and properly claims the relevant treaty benefits.[25] In this way, the double tax risk in such a case typically is minimized.

Importantly, the tiebreaker rules apply only to the computation of the individual's tax liability for the year, so that he pays the lesser of (1) the tax computed under U.S. domestic law or (2) the tax giving effect to the treaty rules. The individual nevertheless generally continues to be treated as a U.S. tax resident in applying all the other provisions of the Code other than those used in determining the individual's U.S. tax liability.[26]

For example, in determining the controlled foreign corporation (CFC) status of a corporation in which the individual owns stock, he continues to be treated as a U.S. person. In addition, for most U.S. information return filing purposes, such a tiebreaking individual may continue to be treated as a U.S. person and thus be subject to accompanying compliance obligations.[27]

Some newer U.S. income tax treaties also specifically provide a tiebreak provision applicable to companies. For example, article 1, para. 4 of the 2006 U.S. Model Treaty provides as follows:

> Where by reason of the provisions of paragraph 1 a company is a resident of both Contracting States, then if it is created or organized under the laws of one of the Contracting States or a political subdivision thereof, but not under the laws of the other Contracting State or a political subdivision thereof, such company shall be deemed to be a resident of the first-mentioned Contracting State. In all other cases involving dual resident companies, the competent authorities of the Contracting States shall endeavor to determine the mode of application of the Convention to such

24. *See, e.g.*, U.S. Model Income Tax Convention, art. 4.3 (Nov. 15, 2006).

25. *See* Treas. Reg. § 301.7701(b)-7(a)(1).

26. *But see* Prop. Treas. Reg. § 301.7701(b)-7(a)(4) (stating that a dual resident who makes a treaty tiebreak election for U.S. federal income tax purposes to be treated as a nonresident alien is not an eligible S corporation shareholder, and thus automatically causes an S corporation of which such individual is a shareholder to lose its S status.)

27. For further discussion of these issues, see Michael J.A. Karlin, *Now You See Them: U.S. Reporting Requirements for Tax Treaty Nonresidents*, 67(3) Tax Notes Int'l 267–77 (July 16, 2012).

company. If the competent authorities do not reach such an agreement, that company will not be treated as a resident of either Contracting State for purposes of its claiming any benefits provided by the Convention.

3. Transparent Entities

The 2006 U.S. Model Treaty and most newer U.S. income tax treaties contain provisions preventing fiscally transparent entities, such as partnerships or trusts, from qualifying as "residents" for treaty purposes unless the beneficial owners of the entity also qualify as treaty residents. For example, under the 2006 U.S. Model Treaty, income of an entity that is "fiscally transparent" under the laws of either country is considered "derived by a resident of a State to the extent that the item is treated for purposes of the taxation law of such Contracting State as the income, profit or gain of a resident."[28] Consequently, if an entity is a pass-through entity (such as a partnership) under the laws of both the United States and a country having a treaty with the United States that is based on the U.S. Model, income of the entity is considered income of a resident of one of the countries to the extent it is included in the distributive share of a partner or other owner that independently qualifies as a resident of that country for purposes of the treaty. If, on the other hand, the entity is treated as a pass-through entity (such as a partnership) under U.S. tax law but as a corporation under the laws of the other country, the treaty applies to the entity's U.S.-source income only if the other country taxes the partnership itself as a resident of that country.

In those instances in which a U.S. treaty does not follow the 2006 U.S. Model Treaty in looking through fiscally transparent entities for purposes of treaty residence, U.S. domestic law generally provides for a similar result, but only with respect to payments of fixed, determinable, annual, and periodic (FDAP) income. Specifically, § 894(c) provides that in certain cases, foreign persons are not entitled to a reduced rate of withholding under any income tax treaty with the United States on income derived through an entity that is treated as fiscally transparent (e.g., a partnership) for U.S. federal income tax purposes. This provision generally applies only to U.S.-source FDAP income, and only if (1) the item of income is not, under the tax laws of the other treaty country, considered income of the foreign person claiming the treaty benefit (for example, the partner); (2) the treaty does not contain a provision relating to "the applicability of the treaty in the case of an item of income derived through a partnership"; and (3) the other treaty country "does not impose tax on a distribution of such item of income from such entity to such person."[29]

28. Art. 1, para. 6 of 2006 U.S. Model Treaty.

29. § 894(c)(1). *See also* Treasury Regulations promulgated under this provision at Treas. Reg. § 1.894-1(d).

C. Limitation on Benefits

1. General

Even if a taxpayer qualifies as a resident of a treaty country under the above standards, under almost all U.S. treaties, that person must still successfully overcome one additional potential obstacle before being entitled to treaty benefits: the Limitation on Benefits, or LOB article of the treaty.

The United States has sought to include such LOB articles in its treaties since 1984 as a way to prevent treaty shopping by residents of third countries with which the United States does not have an income tax treaty. LOB provisions generally seek to limit the availability of treaty benefits to persons having a sufficient connection to the treaty countries. Without such provisions, for example, a resident of a country that does not have a tax treaty with the United States simply could form an entity in a country with which the United States does have such a treaty and claim whatever treaty benefits were being sought. The LOB provision of a treaty would prevent this result, for example, by requiring that a certain percentage of the ultimate ownership of such entity be held by persons who also are residents of the treaty country, or by requiring that an active business actually be conducted by such entity in the treaty partner country. There are still a few U.S. treaties that do not contain such LOB provisions (for example, the U.S. treaties with Pakistan, Greece, Egypt, and Romania), but the United States is actively seeking to renegotiate such treaties to include this limitation.[30]

According to the Treasury Technical Explanation of the 2006 U.S. Model Treaty under article 22, which is the LOB provision of that treaty,

> Article 22 contains anti-treaty-shopping provisions that are intended to prevent residents of third countries from benefiting from what is intended to be a reciprocal agreement between two countries. In general, the provision does not rely on a determination of purpose or intention but instead sets forth a series of objective tests. A resident of a treaty partner country that satisfies one of the tests will receive benefits regardless of its motivations in choosing its particular business structure.
>
> The structure of the Article is as follows: Paragraph 1 states the general rule that residents are entitled to benefits otherwise accorded to residents only to the extent provided in the Article. Paragraph 2 lists a series of attributes of a resident of a Contracting State, the presence of any one of which will entitle that person to all the benefits of the Convention. Paragraph 3 provides that, regardless of whether a person qualifies for benefits under paragraph 2, benefits may be granted to that person with regard to certain

30. For a discussion of tax planning techniques related to the ever-diminishing number of tax treaties that do not contain an LOB provision, see Jeffrey L. Rubinger, *Tax Planning With U.S. Income Tax Treaties Without LOB Provisions*, 36 Tax Mgmt. Int'l J. 123 (Mar. 9, 2007). Note that since the publication of that article, some of the treaties cited therein have been renegotiated to include such LOB provisions.

income earned in the conduct of an active trade or business. Paragraph 4 provides that benefits also may be granted if the competent authority of the State from which benefits are claimed determines that it is appropriate to provide benefits in that case. Paragraph 5 defines certain terms used in the Article.

2. Principal Tests

An individual taxpayer qualifies to claim treaty benefits under the typical LOB provision so long as the individual is a resident of the country, i.e., the individual is liable to tax in that country. Thus, an individual taxpayer typically does not present a challenge from the perspective of LOB provisions. Rather, the focus of such provisions is on entities that may qualify as "residents" of the treaty partner country, but which nonetheless are not viewed as deserving of treaty benefits.

LOB provisions typically provide three principal tests to determine whether an entity is entitled to claim treaty benefits:

1. *Public company test.* This test is based on the assumption (which is not necessarily true) that most of the shareholders of a public company will likely be residents of the country on whose public markets its shares are listed and traded. Article 22, para. 2(c) of the 2006 U.S. Model Treaty provides that a company is publicly traded for this purpose if all the shares in those classes of shares representing more than 50 percent of the voting power and value of the company are regularly traded on a recognized stock exchange.
2. *Ownership/base erosion test.* The ownership aspect of this test focuses on equity or beneficial ownership and establishes requirements relating to classes of shares, holding periods, and nature of the holders. For example, under Article 22, para. 2 of the 2006 U.S. Model Treaty, a taxpayer other than an individual will satisfy the LOB provision if at least 50 percent of the aggregate voting power and value of such person is owned by residents of the treaty partner country, and in cases of indirect ownership, each intermediary also is a resident of the treaty partner.

   The base erosion test focuses on deductible payments made by the entity claiming the treaty benefit. Its purpose is to determine whether income derived from the United States is, in fact, subject to tax in the other treaty jurisdiction. Thus, if at least half of the entity's income is paid out by deductible payments to persons who are not resident in either treaty partner country, and if those payments are not arm's length payments made in the ordinary course of the entity's business, this test will not be met.
3. *Active business test.* This test acts, in effect, as a substitute for a more subjective principal purpose test and is intended to establish a substantive connection between the entity and the treaty jurisdiction in which it is resident.

D. Other Limitations

In addition to the limitations imposed by the treaty itself under the residence and LOB articles thereof, two further inquiries may be needed to determine the availability of treaty benefits: beneficial ownership and economic substance.

In order to qualify for treaty benefits with respect to an item of income, the claimant must be the "beneficial owner" of such income. The exact contours of the beneficial ownership concept are unclear. The Technical Explanation of the 2006 U.S. Model Treaty, for example, in its discussion of dividends (art. 10) states:

> The term "beneficial owner" is not defined in the Convention, and is, therefore, defined as under the internal law of the country imposing tax (i.e., the source country). The beneficial owner of the dividend for purposes of Article 10 is the person to which the income is attributable under the laws of the source State. Thus, if a dividend paid by a corporation that is a resident of one of the States (as determined under Article 4 (Residence)) is received by a nominee or agent that is a resident of the other State on behalf of a person that is not a resident of that other State, the dividend is not entitled to the benefits of this Article. However, a dividend received by a nominee on behalf of a resident of that other State would be entitled to benefits. These limitations are confirmed by paragraph 12 of the Commentary to Article 10 of the OECD Model. See also paragraph 24 of the Commentary to Article 1 of the OECD Model.

A number of foreign law cases have attempted to define the term,[31] and the OECD has initiated a major project on the topic.[32]

In addition, the "economic substance" and other related anti-abuse doctrines may continue to apply to a claim of treaty benefits. In the view of the U.S. Treasury, satisfaction of the LOB provisions does not supersede anti-abuse doctrines under local law (e.g., business purpose, sham, substance over form, step transaction)—local law identifies the beneficial owner of the income and the application of the LOB provision determines if that person is entitled to the treaty benefit.

E. Saving Clause

Pursuant to the Saving Clause of most U.S. tax treaties,[33] U.S. citizens and U.S. residents (as determined under the residence article of the relevant treaty) generally may not enforce treaty concessions (such as reduced withholding tax rates on dividends, for example) against the United States, even if they have an otherwise sufficient connection with the treaty partner country. For example, a U.S. citizen

31. *See, e.g.*, Jakob Bundgaard, *Danish Case Law Developments on Beneficial Ownership*, *Tax Analysts*, Worldwide Tax, Daily (Oct. 1, 2012).

32. Clarification of the Meaning of "Beneficial Owner" in the OECD Model Tax Convention, Discussion Draft (Apr. 29, 2011).

33. *See, e.g.*, art. 1, para. 5 of 2006 U.S. Model Treaty.

living in the U.K. is not entitled to the reduced rate of tax on dividends otherwise allowed by the United States to residents of the United Kingdom.[34] Most Saving Clauses also are applicable to certain former U.S. citizens and former "long-term residents"[35] who expatriated from the United States, though the scope of this expatriation provision, particularly as applied to long-term residents, varies by treaty.

The Saving Clause is a provision that is uniquely found in U.S. income tax treaties. The United States, unlike almost any other country in the world,[36] asserts worldwide taxing jurisdiction not only on its residents but also on its citizens, regardless of where they are living. Thus, the purpose served by these clauses is a purpose that the United States alone seeks to fulfill. Originally, the Saving Clause was included in the Relief from Double Taxation article of treaties, but in most of the treaties the United States has entered into since the early 1970s, the Saving Clause appears in the Personal Scope or General Rules articles.

There are certain carve-outs from the Saving Clause under each treaty so that those provisions apply as though the Saving Clause did not exist. For example, under common exceptions, U.S. citizens may benefit from certain limited provisions, including an exemption for social security benefits paid by the other treaty country and a mutual agreement procedure under which the countries agree to resolve complaints about the construction of the treaty by either country.[37]

VI. Specific Treaty Provisions Providing Benefits

A. General

As noted above, treaties do not impose tax, but rather specifically limit the power of the treaty partners to tax a resident of the other country in certain defined respects. The specific benefits conferred by the various income tax treaties to which the United States is a party vary somewhat in their rates, their exemptions, and other details. However, in general, there are certain major categories of benefits conferred by all U.S. income tax treaties.

First, if a resident of one treaty country carries on business in the other treaty country, the other country may not tax the profits attributable to that business unless the taxpayer has a "permanent establishment" in the other country. This limitation is of substantial benefit as compared to U.S. domestic law applicable to residents of non-treaty countries conducting business in the United States.

34. *See* art. 1, para. 4 of U.S.-UK Income Tax Treaty.

35. For this purpose, a long-term resident generally is an individual who held a U.S. green card in at least eight of the prior fifteen tax years.

36. Eritrea also taxes its citizens on a worldwide basis regardless of where they live, but at a flat rate of 2 percent.

37. *See* art. 1, para. 5 of 2006 U.S. Model Treaty.

The permanent establishment concept and its implications are further discussed below.

Another primary benefit conferred by treaties is a series of provisions providing for reduced withholding tax rates on various categories of nonbusiness income. Under U.S. domestic law, subject to certain limited exceptions, U.S.-source fixed, determinable, annual, and periodic income (FDAP income) earned by a nonresident of the United States typically is subject to U.S. withholding tax at a rate of 30 percent of the gross amount. Treaties, however, typically reduce, or in some cases even eliminate, this 30 percent rate as to certain categories of income.

B. Permanent Establishment and Business Profits

1. General

Where a U.S. income tax treaty is applicable, a country may not impose tax on the business profits of a resident of the other treaty country (typically the business profits provision is found in article 7 of most treaties) unless the resident has a "permanent establishment" in the first country (this determination in turn is typically made under article 5 of most treaties).[38] The goal of the permanent establishment limitation is to prevent double taxation of an enterprise's income and to allocate taxing jurisdiction to the country that is deemed to have the most appropriate connection with the taxpayer.

The permanent establishment article is needed when one treaty country determines that the business profits of a resident of the other treaty country are taxable by the first country under its domestic tax law, for example, because the first country's source rules treat the income in question as being sourced to that country. In general, where a tax treaty applies, the business profits of an enterprise of one treaty partner derived from activities or sources in the other treaty partner cannot be taxed by the source country unless they are attributable to a permanent establishment in the source country. To the extent such business profits are so attributable, the profits (reduced by allocable deductions) may be taxed by the source country. On the other hand, if the enterprise does not have a permanent establishment in the source country, the source country may not tax any of the business profits of that enterprise, regardless of source or other connection to it. The definition of "permanent establishment" is, therefore, central to determining the respective taxing jurisdiction of the treaty partners.[39]

---

38. *See, e.g.*, art. 5, para. 1, 2006 U.S. Model Treaty. For a complete discussion of permanent establishments in U.S. treaties, see J. Ross MacDonald, *"Songs of Innocence and Experience": Changes to the Scope and Interpretation of the Permanent Establishment Article in U.S. Income Tax Treaties, 1950–2010*, 63 TAX LAWYER 285 (2010). For an earlier, exhaustive analysis of permanent establishments, see Robert L. Williams, *Permanent Establishments in the United States*, 29 TAX LAWYER 277 (1975–1976).

39. Although only two reported cases in the United States over the last thirty years deal in detail with the permanent establishment standard under a U.S. treaty (Taisei Fire & Marine Ins. Co. v. Comm'r, 104 T.C. 535(1995); Nat'l Westminster Bank, PLC v. United States, 44 Fed. Cl. 120 (1999)), the issue has become increasingly contentious outside the United States. *See, e.g.*, Philip Morris GmbH (Decision 7682/02) (Italy) and Seagate Singapore (AAR No. 831/2009) (India).

Treaties define a "permanent establishment" as a "fixed place of business" through which the business of an enterprise is carried on in whole or in part. Under this general rule, the taxpayer therefore must engage in business, and that business must happen at a fixed place. All treaties list some specific examples of what constitutes a permanent establishment (e.g., an office, place of management, or branch). Additionally, most U.S. income tax treaties include a provision that treats a construction site or installation project maintained by an enterprise of one treaty partner in the other country as a permanent establishment in the latter country only if the site or project exists for more than a specified term (e.g., twelve months). Some treaties also provide that income from an installation or drilling rig or ship used for the exploration or exploitation of natural resources is attributable to a permanent establishment if the activity continues for a certain term, for example, for more than thirty days in a year.[40]

All U.S. income tax treaties address the issue of when an agent's activities constitute a permanent establishment of the principal. Typically, the treaties treat an agent of an enterprise of one country that conducts activities in the other country, other than an independent agent acting in the ordinary course of its business, as a permanent establishment of the enterprise in the other country if the agent has and habitually exercises in the other country the authority to conclude contracts on behalf of the enterprise. In contrast, independent agents usually do not give rise to a permanent establishment of the principal.

Certain treaties also contain "services permanent establishment" provisions. For example, in some treaties, an enterprise that furnishes certain services in the other country can have a permanent establishment in the other country if a certain physical presence threshold is met. The United States, as a traditional net exporter of services, generally argues against such "services" permanent establishment provisions (note that the U.S. Model Treaty does not contain one), but some U.S. treaties, such as the U.S.-Canada Treaty, do contain one.

Certain treaties also treat the sale of goods in one country by an enterprise of the other country as giving rise to a permanent establishment if the goods were processed or purchased in the first country. Also, a limited number of treaties classify an enterprise's insurance of risks in the other country as resulting in a permanent establishment under certain circumstances.

U.S. income tax treaties typically exclude from the "permanent establishment" definition certain activities of a preparatory or auxiliary nature.[41] For example, excluded activities include the use of facilities or the maintenance of a stock of goods solely for storage, display, or delivery and the use of facilities solely for the purchase of goods or to collect information.

U.S. income tax treaties also usually clarify that an enterprise of one country does not have a permanent establishment in the other country merely by reason

40. Andersen on Treaties at ¶ 3.01. *See also* U.S.-Ireland treaty, which contains a similar provision, although with a 120-day threshold.

41. *See*, e.g., art. 5, para. of 2006 U.S. Model Treaty.

of controlling or being controlled by another company that might be engaged in business or have a permanent establishment in the other country.[42]

2. Partnerships

Under U.S. law, a foreign person who is a partner in a partnership that has a permanent establishment may be attributed that permanent establishment from the partnership.[43] This concept is consistent with U.S. domestic law, which likewise attributes the U.S. trade or business of a partnership to its partners.[44]

The U.S. and OECD Model Treaties tax business profits of an "enterprise" that is attributable to a permanent establishment of the enterprise. In the case of many U.S. income tax treaties, a partnership is considered an enterprise of a treaty country only to the extent that income derived by it is subject to tax in that country as the income of a resident.

3. Income Attributable to Permanent Establishment

If a resident of a treaty country carries on business in the United States through a permanent establishment, the United States may impose tax, pursuant to domestic law rates, on any business profits that are attributable to the permanent establishment.[45] The term "business profits" generally includes income of any trade or business. The profits attributable to a permanent establishment are those that "it might be expected to make if it were a distinct and independent enterprise engaged in the same or similar activities under the same or similar conditions."[46] This method of attribution is consistent with the arm's length principle that usually applies to associated enterprises.

For example, if a foreign corporation resident in a treaty country maintains a sales branch in the United States that sells goods produced by the corporation in a foreign country, the profits attributable to the U.S. branch are computed as though the branch purchased the goods from the foreign factory at an arm's length price.[47] In contrast, no business profits are attributed to a permanent establishment "by reason of the mere purchase" of goods.[48]

Under almost all U.S. income tax treaties, the business profits of a permanent establishment are expressly determined by taking deductions for all expenses

42. Art. 5, para. 7 of 2006 U.S. Model Treaty.

43. Rev. Rul. 90-80; *Unger*, 58 T.C.M. 1157 (1990), *aff'd*, 963 F.2d 1316 (D.C. Cir. 1991). *See also Donroy, Ltd. v. United States*, 301 F.2d 200 (9th Cir. 1962); *Johnston v. Comm'r*, 24 T.C. 920 (1955).

44. § 875(1).

45. Art. 7, para. 1 of 2006 U.S. Model Treaty.

46. 2006 U.S. Model Treaty, art. 7, para. 2. The OECD Model uses similar language, but adds the words "and dealing wholly independently with the enterprise of which it is a permanent establishment." OECD Model art. 7(2).

47. The OECD Model allows the profits of a permanent establishment to be determined by apportionment if the results are "in accordance with the principles" of the treaty. OECD Model art. 7(4). The OECD Model also requires the profits of a permanent establishment to be "determined by the same method year by year unless there is good and sufficient reason to the contrary."

48. Art. 7, 2006 U.S. Model Treaty.

"incurred for the purposes of the permanent establishment," whether those expenses are incurred in the United States or a foreign country.[49]

It is not completely clear whether the U.S. rules and standards applicable to income effectively connected with a U.S. trade or business, and the deductions allocated and apportioned to such income, may be used in computing business profits attributable to a U.S. permanent establishment.[50] The U.S. Model Treaty references these parallel rules in some places, but does not provide clarity on this point.

In *National Westminster Bank, PLC v. United States*,[51] the Court of Federal Claims held that a Treasury regulation that provides rules for determining interest deductions of foreign corporations engaged in trades or businesses in the United States did not apply under a prior version of the treaty between the United States and the United Kingdom. In that case, the taxpayer (NatWest), a U.K. corporation, carried on a banking business through several offices in the United States (the U.S. branch). The U.S. branch borrowed funds from NatWest's home office and from branches maintained by NatWest in other countries, and it sometimes loaned funds to foreign units of NatWest. Interest on these loans was reflected on the books of the U.S. branch, and the net interest paid was claimed as a U.S. tax deduction. The IRS instead demanded that the interest deduction be computed under Treasury Regulation § 1.882-5, which does not recognize intracompany loans and instead requires that the interest deduction be computed by complicated apportionment rules.

The court held in favor of NatWest, finding that the cited Treasury regulation was not consistent with the U.S.-U.K. treaty. The court relied in particular on two provisions of the treaty. First, paragraph 2 of article 7 states: "there shall in each Contracting State be attributed to that permanent establishment the profits which it might be expected to make if it were a distinct and separate enterprise engaged in the same or similar activities under the same or similar conditions and dealing wholly independently with the enterprise of which it is a permanent establishment." In addition, paragraph 3 of article 7 provides: "there shall be allowed as deductions those expenses which are incurred for the purposes of the permanent establishment, including a reasonable allocation of . . . interest . . . incurred for the purposes of the enterprise as a whole."

Based on the foregoing treaty provisions, the court reasoned that:

> [T]he Treaty contemplates that [the] profits [of a foreign banking corporation's U.S. branch] should be based on the books of account of such branch maintained as if the branch were a distinct and separate enterprise dealing wholly independently with the remainder of the foreign corporation, provided that the financial records of the branch, especially those

---

49. Art. 7, para. 3, 2006 U.S. Model Treaty.
50. *But see* Rev. Rul. 81-78.
51. 44 Fed. Cl. 120.

reflecting intra-corporate lending transactions, are subject to adjustment as may be necessary for imputation of adequate capital to the branch and to insure use of market rates in computing interest expenses. . . . [R]ather than treating the U.S. branch of foreign enterprises as separate entities, the regulation plainly treats each U.S. branch as a unit of a worldwide enterprise and, thus, is inconsistent with the "separate entity" provision of Article 7(2) of the Treaty. . . . [T]he regulation computes liabilities . . . , and from that figure the ultimate interest deduction . . . , on the basis of worldwide assets and worldwide liabilities of the entire foreign enterprise, rather than determining the interest deduction on the basis of the separate, independent operations of the U.S. branch.[52]

C. Provisions Relevant to Non-Business, FDAP Income

Under U.S. domestic tax law, nonresidents of the United States are taxable by withholding on certain types of passive income from U.S. sources labeled as "fixed determinable annual or periodic income" (FDAP). The rate of withholding on such amounts, including dividends paid by U.S. corporations, rents paid on U.S. property, and royalties paid for the right to use intellectual property in the United States, is a flat 30 percent of the gross amount paid. Thus, if a nonresident of the United States receives a dividend of $100 on stock of a U.S. corporation, the corporation must withhold $30 and pay that amount to the IRS, remitting to the shareholder the remaining $70.

Several provisions of each U.S. income tax treaty exist to reduce otherwise applicable rates of withholding tax by the source country applied to such FDAP items. For these provisions to apply, the items must not be attributable to a permanent establishment in the source country. If they are so attributable, then the Business Profits article of the treaty takes precedence, and such items are instead taxed on a net basis at graduated rates pursuant to that article. The discussion below assumes that such items are not connected with a permanent establishment of the taxpayer.

1. Dividends

Dividends paid by a company resident in one country to a person resident in the other country generally are subject to a reduced (generally 15 percent) rate of withholding tax by the source country, with the rate lowered further to 0 percent or 5 percent in certain instances relating to dividends paid to a parent company by a subsidiary (80 percent or more ownership is typically required by most such provisions). An increasing number of newer U.S. treaties provide for a 0 percent rate in some such cases, including the U.S. treaties with the following countries:

- United Kingdom
- Mexico

52. 44 Fed. Cl. at 128, 130.

- Australia
- Japan
- Netherlands
- Sweden
- Denmark
- Finland
- Germany
- Belgium
- France
- New Zealand

Thus, dividends paid by a U.S. resident corporation to a resident of one of the above countries generally should not be subjected to any U.S. withholding tax if certain requirements are met. Specifically, the 0 percent rate typically only applies to certain intercompany dividends between subsidiary and parent and dividends paid to certain tax-exempt pension funds. In the above-listed treaties, the dividends exemption usually will apply where the payor is a subsidiary of a company resident in the other treaty country, the parent owns at least 80 percent of the subsidiary, and certain holding period requirements are met (most frequently, the shares of the subsidiary must have been held for at least twelve months). For example, if a U.S. subsidiary of a U.K. parent that has owned 100 percent of the U.S. subsidiary's stock for three years pays a dividend to its U.K. parent, pursuant to the dividends article of the U.S.-U.K. treaty, the United States must not impose any withholding tax.[53]

The branch profits tax imposed by § 884, which is intended to equate branch taxation with tax imposed on dividends paid by a subsidiary corporation, acts, in effect, as a tax on dividends. As such, it often is similarly reduced, directly or indirectly, by an applicable treaty's dividends article. Section 884(e) can, however, effectively limit this branch profits tax relief by virtue of its requirement that the claimant be a "qualified foreign corporation."

2. Interest

Similarly, interest paid by a person resident in one country to a person resident in the other country generally is subject to a reduced or 0 percent rate of withholding tax by the source country. At least seventeen current U.S. treaties exempt interest from source-country withholding and grant the residence country the exclusive right to tax such interest. For example, the U.S. treaties with Austria, Canada, France, Denmark, Ireland, Luxembourg, and the Netherlands, as well as several other countries, provide for such an exemption. The exemption typically does not apply to contingent interest or certain interest paid to related parties.

The United States typically exempts fixed interest payments made to unrelated foreign recipients from U.S. withholding tax under its domestic law (pursuant to

53. Art. 10(3), U.S.-U.K. Treaty.

the "portfolio interest exception"[54]) in any case, and thus these treaty provisions generally do not grant any additional benefits from the U.S. perspective except in the case of certain related party and other loans that do not qualify as portfolio interest loans. However, the United States typically seeks to negotiate this 0 percent rate into its treaties so that the treaty partner will grant to U.S. residents the same benefits that the United States already provides to foreigners under U.S. domestic law.

For many years, tax authorities have grappled with the question of under what circumstances treaty benefits—in particular, reduced withholding rates on interest payments—should be permitted in the case of a company that is resident in a treaty country, but all or part of the share capital is owned by persons who are not treaty country residents. The IRS issued final regulations under § 7701(l), sometimes referred to as the "conduit financing regulations," which are designed to address multiple party financing arrangements that are designed to obtain the benefit of a reduction in U.S. withholding tax and that may not be affected by limitation on benefit restrictions. The regulations, which are effective for payments made on or after September 11, 1995, may recharacterize certain multiple-party financing transactions as directly among any two or more parties and thus may affect whether a reduction of the U.S. statutory rate of withholding tax is available either under a U.S. income tax treaty or under a statutory exemption. Although the primary focus of the conduit financing regulations is arrangements involving loans, the regulations also can apply to leases, licenses, and certain other transactions.

3. Royalties

Royalties paid by a person resident in one country to a person resident in the other country generally are subject to a reduced or 0 percent rate of withholding tax by the source country. Many treaties provide for a source state exemption on royalties (i.e., a 0 percent rate), including the U.S. treaties with Ireland, Luxembourg, the Netherlands, Norway, Switzerland, and the U.K. As with its policy with respect to interest, the United States seeks to include 0 percent withholding on royalties in all its treaties. This is because the United States is a net exporter of technology, just as it has historically been a net exporter of capital.

Many other U.S. treaties permit source-state withholding on royalties, at reduced rates of between 5 percent and 15 percent. Some U.S. treaties provide different source-state rates with respect to different types of royalties (see, for example, the royalties articles of the U.S. treaties with Italy and Israel). This creates difficulty in some cases when royalties are bundled and thus it is not easy to separate the component parts of the royalty payments.

Under the 2006 U.S. Model Treaty, gains from the sale of royalty-producing property are taxed as royalties where the sale amount is contingent on productivity, use, or disposition of the property. However, because neither sales income

54. § 871(h).

nor royalties are taxed under the Model Treaty, the distinction generally is not relevant. In many U.S. treaties, however, royalties are taxed, but sales income is not, in which case the distinction is obviously significant.

4. Gains

Gains realized by a person resident in one country attributable to the disposition of property located in the other country generally are not subject to tax in the source country unless the gain is real estate related or part of a permanent establishment in the source country. The U.S. domestic tax law typically does not tax nonresident foreign persons on such non-real estate or non-permanent establishment sale gains in any case, so resorting to a tax treaty is generally not necessary from the U.S. perspective, and thus from the U.S. perspective, this treaty provision typically is intended to obtain consistent benefits for U.S. taxpayers engaging in sales of property located in treaty partner countries.[55]

D. Employment/Services Income

Cross-border employment income generally is not subject to tax in the source country unless certain thresholds are met. For example, under the 2006 U.S. Model Treaty, source-country taxation of compensation paid by a resident of the source country to a resident of the other country is not permitted unless the recipient is present in the source country for a period or periods exceeding, in the aggregate, 183 days in any twelve-month period commencing or ending in the taxable year concerned.[56]

Most new treaties (*see, e.g.*, the U.S.-U.K. treaty) provide an "Income from Employment" article consistent with this principle. Most older treaties, on the other hand, distinguish between Independent and Dependent Personal Services, dealing with these types of income in two separate treaty articles. In most Independent Personal Services articles of U.S. treaties, the source country may tax income only if it is either attributable to a fixed base in that country and is derived from services performed in that country, or if certain presence thresholds are met. Most Dependent Personal Services articles, which deal with employees, reserve taxing rights for the residence country unless certain physical presence thresholds are exceeded (commonly 183 days) for services performed in the other country.

E. Miscellaneous

In addition, special rules typically apply under most treaties to real property, shipping and air transport, transactions between related parties, directors' fees,

---

55. Code § 871(a) (2) does, however, tax capital gains of nonresident aliens present in the United States for 183 days or more at a 30 percent rate. The enactment of the statutory definition of the term "nonresident alien" and the revision of the source rules for sales of personal property substantially reduce the practical effect of this provision.

56. Art. 14, para. 2, 2006 U.S. Model Treaty.

entertainers and athletes, pensions and social security, and students and trainees (and often teachers and researchers). It generally is necessary to consult the specific treaty in question to determine the precise treatment of these items, as they vary significantly from treaty to treaty.

F. Other Income[57]

Article 21 of the U.S. Model Treaty provides that any item of income not specifically covered in one of the treaty articles (e.g., business profits, interest, dividends, royalties, etc.) is taxable only in the country of the recipient's residence.

Examples of items of income covered by article 21 include income from gambling, punitive (but not compensatory) damages, and covenants not to compete. The article would also apply to income from a variety of financial instruments, where such income does not arise in the course of the conduct of a trade or business (e.g., notional principal contracts). As the kind of transactions potentially generating "other income" continues to expand (e.g., viatical settlement contracts), the importance of the "other income" article likewise expands.

VII. Claiming Treaty Benefits—Procedural Requirements

In order to claim benefits under a treaty, several procedural requirements generally must be met.

A. Forms W-8 and 8233

First, in order to prove to a payor of an item that would otherwise be subject to U.S. withholding tax under U.S. domestic law that treaty benefits apply to determine the withholding tax rates, a payee must generally provide the payor with a Form W-8BEN. This form is signed under penalties of perjury, must specify the treaty benefits in question and eligibility for those benefits, and generally must include a U.S. taxpayer identification number (TIN).

If the treaty benefits are claimed with respect to effectively connected income, then the payee instead should provide Form W-8ECI.

If the income is compensation for independent personal services performed in the United States, then Form 8233 should instead be provided by the payee.

B. IRS Reporting—Form 8833

In addition, to ultimately secure treaty benefits, a taxpayer must prove to the IRS that the treaty benefits are appropriate. Section 6114(a) requires that a taxpayer who "takes the position that a treaty of the United States overrules (or otherwise modifies) an internal revenue law of the United States" must disclose this

57. *See* Roger D. Lorence, *Why Other Income Tax Treaty Provisions are Important*, 22-4 J. Int'l Tax 44 (Apr. 2011).

position on a statement attached to the taxpayer's federal income tax return. The disclosure generally is made on IRS Form 8833, Disclosure of Treaty Based Return Position.

Form 8833 generally must be filed if any of the following treaty benefits are claimed:

1. A reduction or modification in the taxation of gain or loss from the disposition of a U.S. real property interest based on a treaty.
2. A change to the source of an item of income or a deduction based on a treaty.
3. A credit for a specific foreign tax for which foreign tax credit would not be allowed by the Internal Revenue Code.
4. Exemption of a foreign corporation from the branch profits tax or the branch-level interest tax.
5. Exemption of a foreign person's income effectively connected with a U.S. trade or business because it is not attributable to a permanent establishment.

Form 8833 also must be filed if a taxpayer makes the treaty tiebreak residency election away from the United States and receives payments or income items totaling more than $100,000.

Also, if the taxpayer's position under a treaty eliminates the need for the filing of a U.S. return, a return nevertheless must be filed in order to disclose the treaty position.[58] For example, if a foreign corporation engaged in a trade or business in the United States wishes to take the position that its effectively connected income is exempted by treaty from U.S. tax because the corporation has no permanent establishment in the United States, a return must be filed to make this claim, even if, assuming the position is valid, the corporation would not otherwise be required to file.

However, several treaty-based positions are exempt from disclosure. For example, disclosure is excused if the otherwise reportable payments or income do not exceed $10,000 ($100,000 if the issue is determination of the taxpayer's residence).[59]

In addition, Form 8833 is not required in the following situations:

1. To claim a reduced rate of withholding tax under a treaty on interest, dividends, rent, royalties, or other fixed or determinable annual or periodic income (FDAP income) ordinarily subject to the 30 percent rate.
2. To claim a treaty exemption that reduces or modifies the taxation of income from dependent personal services, pensions, annuities, social security and other public pensions, or income of artists, athletes, students, trainees, or teachers. This includes taxable scholarship and fellowship grants.

---

58. Treas. Reg. § 301.6114-1(a)(1)(ii).
59. *Id.* § 301.6114-1(c)(2).

3. To claim a reduction or modification of taxation of income under an International Social Security Agreement or a Diplomatic or Consular Agreement.
4. If the claimant is a partner in a partnership or a beneficiary of an estate or trust and the partnership, estate, or trust reports the required information on its return.

When Form 8833 is required but is not filed, a penalty of $10,000 generally applies if the taxpayer is a C corporation or $1,000 if the taxpayer is an individual, S corporation, partnership, trust, or estate. The penalty is separately imposed for each treaty-based position that is not disclosed. More than one penalty can thus be incurred by a taxpayer for one taxable year. However, no penalty is imposed if the taxpayer's failure is not "material," and the IRS may waive the penalty when shown that the failure to disclose was "not due to willful neglect."[60]

VIII. Conclusion

The benefits available under bilateral income tax treaties are often a critical component of tax planning. The higher tax presence threshold provided by the permanent establishment concept applicable to the taxation of business income as well as the reduction or elimination of withholding tax on nonbusiness income including dividends, interest, and royalties are some of the most significant treaty benefits. In order to qualify for those benefits, however, taxpayers must be aware of the qualification and compliance criteria that apply, including, from the U.S. perspective, meeting the residence and limitation on benefit requirements contained in the treaty as well as complying with certain procedural requirements contained in the Internal Revenue Code.

60. *Id.* § 301.6712-1(b).

PART

VI

Trusts and Alternative Vehicles for the International and Offshore Client

Introduction to Offshore Planning for the International Client

13

Alec R. Anderson

I. Introduction

Following high-profile cases of improper tax avoidance using undeclared bank accounts and offshore companies, as well as the financial crisis and consequent collapse of the Cypriot offshore banking industry, offshore activity has found itself increasingly under international scrutiny, particularly from the OECD, the EU, the G8 Financial Action Task Force, and the major developed countries. This has resulted in the eyes of some tax authorities and international press corps in an unfair blanket stigma around legitimate offshore planning activities for international clients. In the currently prevailing environment of minimal economic growth and significant government budget deficits, onshore governments seek to uncover any improper secrecy or tax evasion in order to increase tax revenues in part by making the offshore world of structuring more transparent to them and in part by minimizing opportunities for offshore tax planning.

The aim of this chapter on offshore structuring is to discuss the appropriate use of offshore entities for international families in pursuit of legitimate estate planning and other family and wealth preservation goals. Accordingly, this chapter considers the reasons for using offshore entities and then goes on to describe some of the most common offshore vehicles (and their characteristics). It also discusses the prevailing legal and regulatory environment for international clients who operate offshore entities.[1]

A. What Is Meant by "Offshore"?

The term "offshore" typically refers to a jurisdiction or country that has low levels of income tax on individuals and/or companies formed there by nonresidents. It heretofore also implied a low level of regulation. The common vernacular is to refer to these countries as "offshore financial centers" (OFCs). However, many OFCs are not, technically, offshore from major continents or G8 countries. For example, Alaska, Delaware, Nevada, Luxembourg, and Panama are all OFCs,[2] and the same has been said of Miami and Britain.[3]

There is no standard definition of an OFC. The OECD defines OFCs as:

> Countries or jurisdictions with financial centres that contain financial institutions that deal primarily with nonresidents and/or in foreign currency on a scale out of proportion to the size of the host economy. Nonresident-owned or -controlled institutions play a significant role within the centre. The institutions in the centre may well gain from tax benefits not available to those outside the centre.[4]

A recent IMF Working Paper[5] notes that conceptual definitions of OFCs have tended to focus on three key characteristics:

> (i) the primary orientation of business toward nonresidents; (ii) the favorable regulatory environment (low supervisory requirements and minimal information disclosure) and; (iii) the low-or zero-taxation schemes.

However, the Paper goes on to propose a simplified definition of an OFC:

> An OFC is a country or jurisdiction that provides financial services to nonresidents on a scale that is incommensurate with the size and the financing of its domestic economy.

The IMF Paper also develops "operational and measurable indicators of the OFC status of any given economy" and lists the countries that could be classified as

---

1. This author is primarily knowledgeable on Bermuda law, and so the commentary herein is naturally geared more toward that jurisdiction. This is not meant to suggest that other island jurisdictions are necessarily inappropriate for similar planning objectives or structures. The British Virgin Islands (BVI), Cayman, and Jersey (to name a few) are often able to provide similar juridical characteristics.

2. Geraint Thomas & Alastair Hudson, The Law of Trusts 1073 (2010).

3. *Onshore Financial Centres: Not a Palm Tree in Sight*, Economist (Feb. 16, 2013).

4. *See* OECD Glossary of Statistical Terms, http://stats.oecd.org/glossary/detail.asp?ID=5988.

5. Ahmed Zoromé, *IMF Working Paper: Concept of Offshore Financial Centers: In Search of an Operational Definition* (Apr. 2007).

OFCs. Interestingly, again, various "onshore" jurisdictions including Latvia, Uruguay, and the United Kingdom were classified as OFCs on the basis that "offshore financial entities are present in these countries and they cater to an extensive nonresident clientele."

It is clear that an OFC is not just a no-tax or nominal-tax jurisdiction. It may be a jurisdiction that provides one or more tax-favored entities. It may also be a jurisdiction, such as Panama and one or more other Latin American jurisdictions, that imposes tax on a territorial residential basis rather than on a worldwide income basis. Others may impose competitive tax practices designed to attract investment and economic activity in their country; for example, the United Kingdom employs a favorable system of income tax with regard to its remittance-based system for nondomiciled residents, and Delaware offers relatively low corporation tax rates.

In addition, the Netherlands' corporate tax regime (under which certain profits of foreign branches of Dutch holding companies are tax exempt) offers such favorable tax treatment to certain international companies that in 2009, the White House issued a press release in which the Netherlands was branded a tax haven.

Although, industrially and commercially, OFC activities are normally associated with financial services, several jurisdictions are now encouraging the establishment of different types of services. For example, an article in the *Economist* recently noted that Mauritius is hoping to become an international arbitration center, and Cayman has set up a special economic zone to promote medical tourism.[6] However, financial activities such as insurance, hedge funds, international estate planning with trusts, and debt financing are likely to remain the key focus of offshore structures for some time to come.

B. The Increasing Regulation of OFCs

In today's offshore environment, most serious OFCs are highly regulated and, in the majority of cases, more so than the onshore major economic powers, especially as regards anti-money-laundering rules, disclosure of beneficial ownership of private companies to regulators, and the ability to share information with foreign governments.

Following pressure from many major onshore economies (which created "blacklists" of low-tax jurisdictions where companies incorporated or operating would be subject to harsher tax rules and penal treatment), most of the major OFCs have now signed dozens of Tax Information Exchange Agreements (TIEAs) that are, essentially, designed to assist with the "enforcement" of onshore jurisdictions' tax laws[7] through information-gathering powers. Generally, as a result

6. *Prospects: Sunshine and Shadows*, Economist (Feb. 16, 2013).

7. For example, Bermuda has signed 35 TIEAs, including with the United States (1988) and the United Kingdom (2007).

of entering into a TIEA, the OFC is taken off of the blacklist designation.[8] Most of the major OFCs are now no longer blacklisted; for example, in 2009, Bermuda was the first country to be "white-listed" by the G20 during its 2009 London Summit.[9]

As a result of these developments, the regulators in most OFC jurisdictions have significant information-gathering powers. In fact, the more high-profile the OFC jurisdiction in the international business arena, the more action has been taken in order to cooperate on tax information exchange and transparency.[10] Also, most of the major OFCs have agreed and/or are negotiating to sign on to intergovernmental agreements (IGAs) with the U.S. Treasury in order to comply with the new Foreign Account Tax Compliance Act (FATCA). As an example, Bermuda announced in a press release dated April 2, 2013, that it has agreed to sign a Model 2 IGA with the U.S. Treasury and also that it will enter into a similar arrangement with the U.K. and also the G5 countries of the EU. FATCA requires information about U.S. taxpayers with foreign accounts or interests in foreign entities to be reported to the IRS and for foreign financial institutions to comply with the regulations under FATCA or become subject to a 30 percent withholding penalty tax on payments to be made to the noncompliant offshore entity.

As well as improved transparency, since the events of September 9, 2001, OFCs, like many onshore jurisdictions around the world, have been under considerable international pressure to tighten their anti-money-laundering legislation.[11] As a result, most OFCs now have money-laundering regulations that are as stringent as any in the world.

Bearing in mind the high level of scrutiny and regulation brought to bear on individuals using offshore structures and the structures themselves, it is mainly sophisticated, ultra-wealthy clients or businesses who tend to use top-tier OFCs. There is also a growing use of OFCs in emerging markets where the understanding of a need for disclosure and international compliance is culturally less developed, but which is moving toward this expected norm.

---

8. This happened in the case of Bermuda as regards Mexico, for example. Similarly, by virtue of Bermuda signing a TIEA with Canada, it has become a "designated treaty country," and therefore it is able to avail itself of benefits normally granted to double-taxation treaty countries (e.g., foreign profits can be accumulated tax free in Bermuda and remitted tax free to a Canadian parent company).

9. IFC Review (2011).

10. Bermuda was vice chair on the OECD Global Forum on Transparency and Exchange of Information for Tax Purposes and hosted a meeting of the same.

11. For example, in the last ten years, Bermuda alone has enacted a raft of anti-money-laundering legislation including the Anti-Terrorism (Financial and Other Measures) Act 2004, the Anti-Terrorism (Financial and Other Measures) (Businesses in Regulated Sector) Order 2008, the Financial Intelligence Agency Act 2007, the Proceeds of Crime (Anti-Money Laundering and Anti-Terrorist Financing Supervision and Enforcement) Act 2008, the Proceeds of Crime (Anti-Money Laundering and Anti-Terrorist Financing) Regulations 2008, and the Corporate Service Provider Business Act 2012.

II. Reasons for Using OFCs

There is a wide range of sensible commercial reasons for setting up international estate planning structures offshore; these reasons are often adapted to a particular family and their business interests. The key benefits are outlined below.

A. Tax Planning

Many clients wish to utilize OFCs for the purpose of carrying on operations or accumulating savings outside of their country of origin and outside the grasp of their own tax system. Persons who fall within this category are persons who reside in countries having a territorial system of taxation or a system that is effectively territorial, meaning a system of tax that primarily taxes only resident persons and/or income derived or received within that country.

Although political and economic change as well as pressure from the United States and the OCED has prompted legal changes in many major economies that have sought to make the potential tax advantages for moving capital offshore far more limited, there are still often tax benefits to be obtained through the use of OFCs. For example, offshore discretionary trusts are generally not subject, in the OFC, to tax on their capital gains, and most onshore jurisdictions do not tax the beneficiaries of the discretionary trust until their interest in the trust has vested (i.e., until a distribution has been made). This means that vast capital wealth can generally be maintained offshore in a tax-efficient manner until such time as distributions are desired.

Offshore structures may also offer estate tax savings if properly drafted (for example, see below with regard to grantor trusts).

Further, onshore jurisdictions do not generally impose estate taxes upon the estates of deceased persons by virtue of their status, before death, as a beneficiary of a discretionary trust. This will usually be the case, even if the only remaining discretionary beneficiaries of the trust are, effectively, the deceased person's heirs.

Additionally, there remain corporate tax benefits available to companies with offshore group entities, and although these are clearly under review, offshore jurisdictions remain popular locations to house special-purpose vehicles with shareholders in different taxing jurisdictions, in order to avoid double taxation.

B. Modern, Innovative, Flexible Legislation, Efficient Legal Systems, and Developed Infrastructure and Service Industries

Offshore legislation (e.g., in Bermuda, Cayman, BVI, and Jersey/Guernsey) is both modern and facilitative of succession planning and asset protection. It is often based on English law, meaning that there is a large body of precedent to rely upon.

Additionally, offshore jurisdictions often have innovative legal provisions not available in onshore jurisdictions. For example, the courts in Bermuda have an enhanced jurisdiction over trust management and administration (§ 47 of the

Trustee Act 1975), which affords trustees and beneficiaries of Bermuda trusts a unique procedure for amending trusts (beneficiary consent is not formally required).

In the trusts context, offshore perpetuity provisions are also often more flexible than onshore jurisdictions. At common law, the duration of a trust is limited to lives in being at the time when the trust is created plus twenty-one years. However, most OFCs have statutes that govern the rule against perpetuities. In some cases, this authorizes trusts that exist for a period in excess of 80 to 100 years.[12] Alternatively, the rule has been abolished, as in Bermuda, which recently amended its perpetuities legislation so that it is possible to establish perpetual trusts, whether for beneficiaries or purposes (and there is a flexible statutory provision to allow the Bermuda court to extend the perpetuity period of existing trusts even if they were originally created under the law of another jurisdiction). So a trust can be imported from another OFC or onshore jurisdiction and have its perpetuity period potentially removed.

Further, many offshore jurisdictions offer independent, efficient judicial systems. In some jurisdictions, such as Bermuda, the British Virgin Islands, and the Cayman Islands, the final court of appeal is to the U.K.-appointed Privy Council, essentially an offshoot panel of Lord Justices from the House of Lords in London, England.

The high-quality leading OFC jurisdictions (e.g., Bermuda, Jersey, Cayman, and Guernsey) also tend to have sophisticated service industries (offering top-quality legal, administrative, and accounting services), well-established infrastructure, and respected institutions. This is perhaps why, for example, approximately 75 percent of the Fortune 100 companies maintain a presence in Bermuda.[13]

C. Asset Protection

Offshore entities, particularly the offshore trust, can also offer considerable asset protection against unforeseen creditors, divorce-related attacks, mandatory succession laws, or concerns about spendthrift legatees.

1. Creditor Protection

Wealthy international private clients often wish to protect their assets from the claims of future unforeseen creditors—sort of a doomsday planning scenario. In some circumstances, a category of creditors might be anticipated, although there is no known cause of action existing, and there are no actual claimants in sight. The idea normally is to put a portion (less than half) of total wealth or liquid assets offshore as a risk diversification plan, including political risk challenges, which may occur due to volatile political environments in some emerging market countries. In this regard, asset protection is little different from seeking limited liability for a new business venture through the medium of a corporation.

12. *E.g.*, Barbados.
13. And more than 740 Bermuda companies are listed on stock exchanges around the world.

For the creditor-sensitive client, many OFCs have enacted specific legislation authorizing the existence of asset protection trusts (for example, Bermuda and the Cayman Islands). Asset protection legislation comes in various iterations and reflects the particular concerns of each OFC. Some jurisdictions have very aggressive anti-creditor laws, and others seek a more balanced approach. For example, the law in Bermuda protects "eligible creditors," i.e., creditors who become such before transfer of assets into trust or within the following two years. An "eligible creditor" may challenge a transfer to a trust in some cases where there was an intention to defeat legitimate creditor claims. However, provided there are no allegations of "sham," nor breach of this legislation or bankruptcy legislation relating to fraudulent preferences or improper dispositions at an undervalue, the courts in Bermuda and Cayman will recognize trusts as asset protection structures following settlor or beneficiary insolvency.[14]

In fact, most OFCs have some form of debtor-friendly legislation, for example, statutes containing a short limitations period, provisions for shifting of burden of proof or imposing a higher standard of proof to set aside conveyances into trust, and special provisions concerning whether a conveyance in trust was actually or constructively in fraud of creditors.[15]

At times, asset protection trusts involved in litigation disputes have been treated with some disdain by the courts both in the countries where creditors reside[16] and in the OFCs themselves.[17] Certainly, if trusts are established in such a way as to reflect the dominance of the settlors, or if there is nefarious conduct involved, the courts are unlikely to uphold asset protection trusts and to seek a way to pierce the veil of protection. However, in other cases, even where trusts have been created for asset protection purposes, they have been upheld if established a respectable period of time before the relevant claim arose.[18] Accordingly, great care must be taken when setting up any trust for asset protection purposes, but in appropriate cases, the offshore asset protection trust will very likely be enforced.[19]

2. Protection against Mandatory Succession Laws

In terms of inheritance, many persons reside in countries under which testamentary disposition is extremely circumscribed. Under Swiss law, for example, the property of a deceased automatically passes on death to his or her statutory heirs regardless of his or her wishes. This is an example of a legal culture that is relatively endemic to civil law countries, particularly in Europe and in Latin America. We normally refer to it as forced heirship or mandatory succession law. Wealthy

14. Kingate Global Fund Ltd. v Knightsbridge Fund Ltd. [2009] Bda LR 59.

15. *E.g.*, Bahamas, Cayman Islands.

16. *In re* Lawrence, 238 B.R. 498 (S.D. Fla. 1999).

17. 515 South Orange Grove Owners Ass'n v. Orange Grove Partners (Case No. 2), 1 O.F.L.R. 787 (Cook Islands 1995).

18. Reichers v. Reichers, 679 N.Y.S.2d 233 (App. Div. 1998).

19. *See, e.g.*, Kingate Global Fund Ltd. v Knightsbridge (USD) Fund Ltd. [2009] Bda LR 59, in which the court held that a Quistclose style of trust was effective to protect assets on insolvency.

international clients are usually interested in finding a way to freely choose how to dispose of their assets, whether during their life or on death, as they see fit, rather than being subject to constraints imposed by a system of law that may not be relevant to the situs of the assets or the ultimate residence of the client. Some countries apply these laws based on nationality rather than merely residence. Most OFCs have specific legislation barring forced heirship claims with regard to trusts established under their law where the assets are movable (i.e., not land), and situs is outside the forced heirship jurisdiction.[20]

For example, in Bermuda, § 11 of the Special Provisions Act (as amended) provides that a foreign judgment shall not be recognized, enforced, or give rise to any estoppel insofar as it purports to vary or set aside a trust validly created under Bermuda law, or deprive the trustee or any beneficiary of any rights, where that judgment arises out of a personal relationship.

This legislation was considered in *the Chief Justice of Bermuda in Garner v BTC and Schindler* [1992] BDA LR 34. In this case, the court considered whether the legislation prevented a forced heirship gift that was contrary to a Bermuda trust. The court ruled that the Act did not apply (because the trust predated the legislation), but held that the Act was declaratory of the common law of Bermuda, which applied to uphold the trust and bar the forced heirship gift made under foreign law. An appeal against this judgment was dismissed by the Bermuda Court of Appeal.

3. Protection against Divorce Judgments

While foreign divorce judgments may be enforceable in offshore jurisdictions under certain circumstances, they tend to be unenforceable against offshore trustees of discretionary trusts. This is because such beneficiaries are generally regarded as having no equitable interests capable of attachment or execution unless and until a distribution is made.

Further, offshore jurisdictions often have legislation designed to prevent the enforcement of certain foreign judgments in matrimonial proceedings against trusts, for example § 11 of the Bermuda Special Provisions Act, as outlined above.

However, unless there is strong evidence to the contrary, courts in foreign jurisdictions may assume that offshore trustees will comply with requests from beneficiaries for distributions to fund payment of orders made in foreign ancillary relief proceedings.[21] Hence, the courts in certain jurisdictions, especially the U.K., often strongly encourage offshore trustees to fund ancillary relief orders by regarding the trust assets as resources available to the discretionary beneficiary. In some cases, a bankruptcy order may be made against a beneficiary of an offshore trust to encourage the trustees of that trust to make a distribution to enable the judgment debt to be satisfied. It would clearly be difficult for a trustee to refuse a request from a beneficiary for a distribution in the face of a bankruptcy

20. *See, e.g.*, Bahamas Trusts (Choice of Governing Law) Act 1989, § 8(b).
21. *E.g.*, Charman v Charman (No. 4) [2007] 1 FLR 1246.

threat. Any trustees in this position should seek directions from the local courts before deciding on the appropriate course of conduct, especially given that other beneficiaries other than the divorcing parties have an interest to be protected (e.g., children and grandchildren).

4. Protection against Political Corruption

Additionally, for some clients, the mere presence of assets in a stable offshore jurisdiction offers protection to their assets, for example, from political risks in their countries of residence.

D. Confidentiality

Different jurisdictions have historically adopted different emphasis on the question of secrecy. For example, Switzerland underpinned its international banking industry with a statutory obligation of secrecy and, similarly, the Cayman Islands marketed their secrecy statute, the Confidential Relationships (Preservation) Law (originally enacted in 1976, and subsequently revised), which made disclosures of client information a criminal offense (albeit that the court could sanction disclosures pursuant to certain criminal investigations).

There are, of course, legitimate reasons for being protective of confidentiality, and keeping private wealth information confidential is still very much an important part of planning for very high net worth persons and their families. This is due to the risks of kidnapping, sophisticated cybercrime, political corruption leading to potential extortion, and other political pressure against wealthy business owners, as well as the real risk of confiscation in certain developing countries.

In light of the growing number of information-sharing treaties in place between offshore and onshore jurisdictions, the focus on secrecy, vis-à-vis domestic regulatory authorities, as a business driver is no longer a viable rationale for going offshore.

That is not to say that offshore activity cannot be carried out in a confidential manner vis-à-vis the public—for example, beneficial ownership of offshore trusts is not a matter of public record, and there are no public registration requirements for trusts in most offshore jurisdictions, meaning that execution of a trust is a private and confidential matter. This fact should not be seen as alarming given that, for example, private contracts dealing with financial arrangements between two commercial parties are not disclosed to the public as a general matter absent some regulatory or governmental connection. Normal bank-customer confidentiality also endures in offshore (as in onshore) jurisdictions, subject to international tax avoidance laws and relevant regulation of the "know-your-customer" record-keeping requirements for financial institutions.

E. Benefits to the Multi-Jurisdictional Family

OFCs are also beneficial to the multi-jurisdictional family with international assets and relatives located in different countries. It can be helpful to have a center for organizing international operations that is tax neutral and offers a developed legal system, such as that available in Bermuda or Cayman.

III. Common Offshore Vehicles

A. Trusts

The offshore trust is the most popular vehicle for the purpose of estate planning and the other planning objectives referred to above.

Such a trust will often be established as a capstone entity, and under it may be one or more holding corporations (or other entities) designed to hold and manage assets.

There are various types of offshore trust, which are outlined below.

1. The Key Types of Trust

(a) Private Discretionary Trusts. Discretionary trusts are probably the most common form of trust established offshore, offering, in most cases, the most flexible and efficient structure for the settlor and the beneficiaries.

Under the terms of a discretionary trust, the trustee is generally given wide discretionary powers over the trust fund and decides (according to the beneficiaries' best interests as a whole) when and to which beneficiary to distribute capital and income, and in what proportions. For this reason, the beneficiaries are not regarded as having a specific interest in the trust, but only a right to be considered when the trustee exercises its discretion.

After establishing the trust, the settlor will have divested himself of any ownership interest in the assets held in the trust, though he may retain certain powers, and the trustee will be entitled to take his or her wishes into account when making distributions. Further, the beneficiaries will have no "ownership" of the trust assets unless and until the trustees exercise their discretion to make an appointment or distribution. This unique feature of discretionary trusts permits the various tax and asset protection advantages outlined above.

Discretionary trusts can also serve family policy objectives, for example, keeping capital wealth out of the control of younger family members until they have the maturity to manage it.

(b) Revocable Grantor Trusts. A revocable grantor trust is a trust in which the settlor typically retains the right to income and/or a power to direct the income and a power to revoke the trust.

Because the settlor retains these controls over the fund, he or she may be treated by their domestic tax authorities (e.g., the United States) as "owning" the trust assets during their lifetime for income tax purposes.

However, the property in such a trust, if drafted appropriately, does not form a part of the settlor's estate on death and therefore is not subject to probate on the settlor's death (at which point the trust often becomes a discretionary trust). Depending on the domicile of the settlor, there may be savings on death taxes.

(c) Fixed-Interest Trusts. Under a fixed-interest trust, primary beneficiaries will normally be granted an automatic right to receive the income and/or capital of the trust fund (perhaps at certain ages), and the trustees will have little discretion over the nature and extent of distributions from the trust fund.

The fixed-interest form of trust is used for estate planning purposes or to ensure that certain property passes on stipulated terms and at stipulated times for the benefit of relevant family members in an orderly manner. It is often specially drafted to suit the particular planning goals contemplated by the settlor (e.g., the settlor of a fixed-interest trust can provide that the beneficiaries will not be able to sell off or otherwise dispose of their trust interests in the event of pressure from creditors).

(d) Purpose Trusts. Normally at common law, a trust must have a trustee, trust property, and beneficiaries. A trust will not fail for want of a trustee, because the courts are always willing to appoint a trustee for a trust that lacks one and does not have, within its provisions, a methodology for succession. However, a trust will normally fail for a lack of ownership of trust assets and/or a lack of a defined class of beneficiaries. A common law trust set up for a particular purpose, but without beneficiaries, is authorized in the case of charitable and other very limited circumstances.[22]

Several OFCs have enacted statutes to authorize noncharitable purpose trusts, for example, Bermuda, BVI, and the Cayman Islands. Essentially, a purpose trust has no specified beneficiaries with an enforceable claim or interest in the trust fund (although in some jurisdictions, for example Bermuda, a person or company may receive indirect or intangible benefits, without disqualifying the trust from the definition of a purpose trust).

Where OFC legislation authorizes purpose trusts, it generally specifies who will enforce the trust in the absence of beneficiaries. For example, in Bermuda, it is possible for any of the following people to petition the court to enforce a purpose trust: (1) a person appointed under the Trust Deed for this purpose, (2) the Grantor (unless the Trust Deed specifies otherwise), (3) a Trustee, (4) any person the court feels has sufficient interest in the enforcement of the trust, or, in the last resort, (5) the Attorney General,[23]

Aside from there being no beneficiaries, the other elements of the trust relationship are usually present in the statutory purpose trust. A trustee receives property from a settlor (or may declare a trust) and holds and distributes that

22. Paul Matthews, *The New Trust: Obligations Without Rights?*, *in* TRENDS IN CONTEMPORARY TRUST LAW 1, 2 (A.J. Oakley ed., 1996) (citing Morice v. Bishop of Durham, 9 Ves. 399, *aff'd,* 10 Ves. 522 (1804)).

23. *See* Bermuda Trusts (Special Provisions) Act 1989 (as amended).

property in accordance with fiduciary obligations. Those obligations are not to act in the best interests of beneficiaries, but to administer the trust property in fulfillment of the stated purposes.

Purpose trusts can offer creative solutions for philanthropic structures where a client's objectives reach beyond the fairly narrow scope of the traditional definition of "charity" (under Anglo-Saxon based laws) and extend to more philanthropic, benevolent, and socially useful purposes.

It is also common for purpose trusts to be set up to hold the shares in private trust companies, where it is desirable for such companies to be "orphans." Further, purpose trusts can provide for continuity of business ownership (e.g., their purpose could be the retention of certain shares), and it is possible to direct the recipients of the income earned to reinvest it in the trust fund.

Additionally, it is possible to create hybrid trusts for the benefit of pure purposes and beneficiaries. It would, for example, under Bermuda or Cayman law, be permissible to craft trust provisions that mandate, say, half of the income of a fund to a philanthropic purpose and the other half to be distributed for the benefit of individual beneficiaries.

There is a potential for legal arguments to be made, from the perspective of onshore tax law or under trust law principles, that if a purpose trust has the sole purpose of merely holding the shares of an underlying company, this is only an investment power and not a trust. Even though this structure may be seen as valid offshore, there are always onshore tax rules of interpretation to consider in jurisdictions that may not be bound by offshore laws. For this reason, drafting purpose trusts must involve careful thought and elaboration of proper purposes that are capable of enforcement and that are *bona fide* and substantive (i.e., more than an investment power or restriction on investment).

It is recognized that purpose trusts, just as any juridical vehicle, can be potentially used for improper purposes or attempted tax evasion. Such a trust would be invalid for being contrary to public policy and potentially voidable, as well as a money-laundering offense. The treatment of the purpose trust will be dependent on, *inter alia*, the terms of the trust and the fact pattern relating to distributions. For example, if there is a pattern of actual distributions to certain persons, the trust may be deemed a private trust or otherwise belonging in some proportion to the recipients.

(e) Charitable Trusts. In most offshore jurisdictions, charitable trusts will be trusts solely created for purposes recognized as charitable by the law of that jurisdiction. For example, a trust under Bermuda law, which follows English law, will be charitable if:

1. all of its purposes fall exclusively within one or more of the categories of charitable purposes recognized by law, being:
   - the relief of poverty;
   - the advancement of education;

- the advancement of religion;
- other purposes beneficial to the community at large; and

2. there is an element of public benefit.

(f) Unit Trusts. The concept of a unit trust is that investors contribute funds to the trustee to hold such funds in trust as trustee while they are managed by the manager for their benefit. Each investor is effectively a beneficial owner (and is possibly also a settlor) of a proportion of the assets held by the trustee.

The unit trust deed, as well as containing provisions for the constitution of a trust, will be similar to the bylaws of a mutual fund company, providing, among other things, for the calculation of net asset value per unit and setting out the terms for issue and redemption of units.

2. The Trust Protector

It is common for offshore trusts to provide for the appointment of a protector. Trust protectors have been recognized under common law and particularly in the United States for some time. There is now a well-known body of case decisions in offshore and onshore courts that deal with a variety of issues surrounding protectors.[24]

The protector may be a friend, relative, or adviser of the settlor and will be given certain powers of oversight over the trustee. Some settlors feel more comfortable having a protector to provide a check and balance on the wide discretionary powers often given to trustees. In fact, the concept of the trust protector was primarily a creature arising out of use of offshore trusts when onshore settlors were originally somewhat unsure (or were advised to be so) of the quality of the offshore professional trustee or bank. So the protector arrangement would bring comfort to the onshore settlor, knowing that his close adviser/protector could effect a change of trustee if the trust administration was not up to par.

Protectors will be subject to the powers, duties, and protections stipulated in the trust instrument. A protector will generally be treated as being subject to fiduciary duties.

The protector will often (depending on the terms of the trust documentation) have the following powers:

- to remove and appoint trustees;
- to consent to trustee remuneration;
- to consent to capital distributions (depending on whether this is advisable from a tax-planning standpoint; and
- to approve (or refuse consent to) the addition of new beneficiaries or the exclusion of beneficiaries.

24. *See* Andrew Holden, Trust Protectors (2011).

The protector may have the power to access trust documents and to review how the trust fund is managed. He or she may be in a position to advise the trustees on the financial needs of the beneficiaries or how to fulfill the purposes of a purpose trust.

It is important that the trust instrument does not give so many powers to the protector that he or she becomes a *de facto* trustee (and subject to a trustee's more stringent fiduciary duties). A court will look at the nature of a protector's powers under the trust deed when determining the extent of their liability. For example, the power to appoint and remove trustees has been deemed a fiduciary power by the Bermuda courts.

Revenue authorities have come to understand the role of protectors and, subject to the extent of powers and terms of the trust involved, may treat the protector as a fiduciary,[25] thereby possibly establishing a nexus of the trust to a country with adverse and unintended tax consequences. Accordingly, particular care must be taken when choosing a trust protector to make sure the location of the trust protector does not expose the trust to jurisdiction of an inappropriate tax authority or to increased exposure to creditors or vulnerability in divorce litigation.

3. Private Trust Companies

Private Trust Companies (PTCs) have become increasingly popular in offshore jurisdictions in recent times. The principal advantage of a PTC is that it allows clients to have more control over the administration of their trust assets. Where viable from a tax perspective, a settlor and his family (or their close advisers) can act as directors of the PTC or sit on subcommittees. This allows the family to take part in decision making regarding the trust. Involving a PTC may be less costly than a private trust company, and means that information regarding the family's affairs can be more restricted.

Using a PTC as trustee can also provide more flexibility on trustee decision making when the PTC's ownership is independent of a regulated institution (which can be more bureaucratic and rigid in relation to trustee services). The PTC also has a role to play in reducing the potential liability of professional trustees. Due to the increasing risk of being sued both by beneficiaries and third parties, professional trustees are increasingly reluctant to take ownership of assets in trust or participate in ventures where substantial risks may be present (such as owning commercial real estate in high-tax jurisdictions, venture capital investments, family trading companies, high-risk portfolios, unusual assets, or companies that own ships or aircraft). The professional trustee's preference is normally for a diversified portfolio of low-risk investment. In such circumstances, the incorporation of a PTC may be advisable. The professional trustee is then able to provide management and administration services to the trust company rather than acting as trustee directly.

25. *See, e.g.*, Steele v. Paz Ltd. [1993–95] Manx L.R. 102 (Isle of Man).

PTCs are also useful where a family has interests in a group of trusts in different jurisdictions since they can dispense with the need to have separate trustees in each country. Grouping assets into one structure can be a helpful planning tool for such international families.

When this approach was first used, the question of who would own the shares of the private trust company was always a problem. This is because clearly, if the beneficiaries of the trust also are the shareholders of the private trust company acting as trustee, issues as to the reality of the trust come into play. Recently, it has become common for the shares of the private trust company to be held by a purpose trust.

B. Trust Alternatives

1. Partnerships and Corporate Vehicles

Many people from civil law countries or who are otherwise unfamiliar with the trust concept, find it difficult to accept the trust. The idea that they will assign the legal ownership of their property to a stranger, even if that stranger is a well-established institution, is simply difficult for them to fathom. People coming from certain cultures and backgrounds are also concerned about surrendering control of their assets, even if they understand the concept of the trust in general terms. In these circumstances, OFCs offer alternatives. These will include partnerships (general and limited, as well as partnership funds) and ordinary limited companies, with which the reader will be familiar, as well as less common vehicles such as those outlined below.

(a) Companies Limited by Guarantee. Companies limited by guarantee are available in many offshore jurisdictions (e.g., Bermuda) where they are popular vehicles for philanthropic enterprises. Such companies issue no shares, and the liability of their members can be limited by the memorandum to a minimal amount, for example $1. A typical structure will provide that the members will also be the directors.

Companies limited by guarantee often also act as private trust companies, which is useful since there is no share ownership to deal with on the death of a family member or settlor. The bylaws may provide for the transfer of membership in the event of death.

(b) Mutual Fund Companies. Mutual fund companies are a popular form of investment fund used by high net worth families. The investment decisions of a mutual fund company may be made by its directors or by a separate management company. Alternatively, investment decisions may be delegated to an investment adviser, which is often a separate company incorporated for the purpose. Administration is usually delegated to a professional fund administration firm.

(c) Segregated Accounts Companies. Segregated Accounts Companies (SACs) are available in many offshore jurisdictions, for example, Bermuda, the BVI, and the Cayman Islands. They are, essentially, companies with the ability to segregate liabilities within separate accounts. It is noteworthy that a number of recent Supreme Court decisions in Bermuda have reinforced the confidence in and strength of the statutory segregation of assets and liabilities in a SAC.

A SAC affords greater protection against risks and losses and insulates investments without the need to establish corporate entities. Failure of one segregated account will not affect the solvency or viability of another segregated account unless the latter has undertaken to support the former.

A SAC may be useful to a private family as it can allow different branches of the family or different trusts to invest in separate types of investment through one SAC with general silos of segregated asset pools that are allocated among the branches of the family or among several trusts. For example, within one SAC, there might be one segregated account that invests in equities, one for distressed debt, one for private equity, and perhaps one segregated account that acts as a "bank account" to enable assets to be quickly deployed. Each of the subtrusts then invests in the cell (or cells) in which that particular family member has an interest (usually based on advice from a dedicated investment manager). This can be helpful where one family member may be younger than the others, or may wish to adopt a more aggressive investment approach—investments with respect to this person can be made in specific funds geared to his or her investment objectives. At the same time, the "risky" investment approach does not endanger the assets of other family members, and no separate corporate structure is necessary to contain the risk. Hence, the SAC can be a flexible investment holding structure for wealthy families with a variety of agendas and goals.

(d) Unlimited Liability Companies. Although unlimited liability companies have all the usual characteristics of a company (such as a board of directors, etc.), they have the partnership characteristic of unlimited liability. The members are liable for the liabilities of the company, and so these entities will typically be used only where liability is not a concern (e.g., as a passive investor vehicle with an owner vehicle that is not concerned with the company's liabilities, or where the member itself has limited liability).

Using an unlimited liability company as part of an international asset holding structure can provide tax-planning advantages in some jurisdictions as it may be treated as a transparent entity. For example, it can be advantageous to have an entity which, for U.S. tax purposes, has a default classification as transparent.

2. Wills and Will Trusts

There are circumstances when it is convenient or advisable for the high net worth individual client to create an offshore will. There may be real estate or other assets that are locally situated and cannot be held in a trust, for example, because there would be adverse tax consequences (e.g., substantive stamp duty may be charged). In such circumstances, it may be appropriate to deal with devolution under a will. Additionally, often the assets held in an estate are given a step-up in basis on death for capital gains tax calculations going forward, and this also may be advantageous.

However, the use of wills in this way has become less popular because ways have been found to craft *inter vivos* trusts so that they operate (for tax purposes) as if they were a will.

One relevant point to note is that the conflict of laws rules in Anglo-Saxon-based laws typically determine the validity of a will in accordance with the law of the domicile of the testator; on the other hand, trusts are governed by the governing law expressed to apply in the trust deed (this is the position, for example, under the Hague Convention on the Recognition of Trusts, which has been adopted by numerous onshore and offshore jurisdictions[26]).

The law of domicile may apply forced heirship rules or other principles affecting devolution of assets, which are not desired or which curtail freedom of disposition. This is a significant reason why trusts are typically employed instead of offshore wills. Additionally, wills are potentially a matter of public record in many jurisdictions, whereas the terms of a trust may remain private. However, wills may often be advisable where adverse tax treatment of trusts is the alternative.

If an international testator is not domiciled in a country in which he or she makes a will, there will typically be a requirement (in order to obtain an order for probate) that his or her estate contains property located in the relevant jurisdiction.[27] There may also be restrictive rules regarding the qualification of corporate executors who may be recognized by the court. Further, in some OFCs, private trust companies may not be eligible to act as an executor.

3. Family Foundations

Many European clients as well as clients from Central and South America who are uncomfortable with trusts are familiar with family foundations. Although the family foundation is known in many countries, it has found a most original expression under the Liechtenstein laws. A Liechtenstein *stiftung* may be established with a board of trustees that is a self-perpetuating body. It need not have members and can be established for the benefit of specific individuals, a family, or other defined group. Alternatively, the appointment of beneficiaries can be left to the directors. It functions very much like a trust. The founder exhausts all of his or her rights with respect to the property that he or she transfers to the foundation at the moment of transfer. Thereafter, the board of directors or trustees is in charge of managing the property and retains the discretion as to whether or when to

26. For example, Australia, Canada, Italy, Luxembourg, Malta, Monaco, the Netherlands, Switzerland, Liechtenstein, and San Marino have all ratified or acceded to the Convention.

27. For example, in Bermuda, § 2 of the Administration of Estates Act 1974 provides that the court has jurisdiction to grant probate if "the deceased person at the time of his death was ordinarily resident in Bermuda or . . . some property of the deceased person was then in Bermuda."

make distributions as required by the bylaws or other organic documents of the foundation.

Panama has adopted a family foundation law similar to that of Liechtenstein and therefore accords a corporate domicile in the Western Hemisphere. Recently, OFCs that have non-civil legal systems have adopted their own version of a foundations law, as in Bahamas, Jersey, Guernsey, and the Isle of Man.

Institutions similar to foundations are available, however, in common law jurisdictions, for example, the companies limited by guarantee referred to above.

Foundations are certainly an interesting wealth preservation vehicle, albeit that there is always the risk that a taxing jurisdiction will take the view that if there is a pattern of distributions to certain family members, they are deemed to be shareholders of the enterprise.

IV. The Future of OFCs

The 21st century has seen an unprecedented attack on OFCs (usually branded "tax havens" by their detractors). The media, OECD politicians, and NGOs have attacked them (often unfairly) for facilitating everything from tax evasion to money-laundering, and they have even been implicated in the global economic recession. As an illustration of the strength of feeling in some quarters, the French President recently stated that tax havens should be "eradicated."

As a result of the substantial pressure they have found themselves under, OFCs have had to adapt, as is evidenced by the deluge of tax information exchange agreements that have been entered into over the past few years, ushering in a new era of openness. The U.S. Foreign Account Tax Compliance Act (FATCA) will continue the trend toward ever greater transparency with onshore revenue authorities.

There is no evidence that the United States or the OECD wants (at the moment) to force any OFC to impose tax on its citizens and residents. From the tax perspective, it appears as if what is wanted is information so that the developed countries can be in an audit position to verify that transactions and financial accounts have been properly carried on or maintained under the rules of the country of residence of the principals. In the future, some of the international governmental associations may seek to establish a coordinated international tax system under which all persons, regardless of citizenship or residence, pay some material tax somewhere; but that is merely conjecture. For the present, transparency and exchange of tax information is the order of the day.

The net effect of these changes and of the underlying causes is likely to increase the incidence of fiscal migration. Increasing tax burdens and more efficient enforcement will provide powerful incentives for high net worth individuals to "follow their money" to more congenial OFC climes. Corporations and other business entities have also shown an increased tendency to migrate to business-friendly jurisdictions to enhance their pursuit of profit and benefit to their shareholders. It can be expected that this sort of regulatory and tax arbitage practice by businesses and international wealthy families will be pursued with greater frequency.[28]

OFCs' ability to serve as a tax-neutral jurisdiction for international joint ventures and their role in aiding international financial flows (acting as a buffer between different fiscal regimes) should be largely unaffected by the move toward increased transparency. They also serve other, non-tax-related purposes, such as offering neutral domiciles for international ventures with modern company law, light regulation, and reliable courts.

In conjunction with this strategy of tightened regulation and increased transparency, OFCs have also been seeking out new markets in the developing world, a sensible strategy given that, for example, Asia-Pacific is now home to more high net worth individuals than any other region, with a total of US$10.7 trillion investible wealth.[29] In fact, the *Economist*[30] has recently highlighted a 2012 academic study that found that OFCs' foreign-owned deposits rose during the period between 2007 and 2011 despite the growing pressure on them from the OECD. The author of the study, Mr. Sharman, attributed this to growth in business from Asia and other developing markets.

OFCs also continue to hone special areas of expertise, such as hedge funds (Cayman Islands), insurance and reinsurance (Bermuda), or incorporations (BVI).

In the medium term, increased transparency and stringent money-laundering regulations are here to stay, and onshore jurisdictions will continue to look for ways to increase tax revenues from multinational corporations and offshore structures for wealthy individuals.

In the longer term, the compliance role of OFCs in international tax planning may so change as to be beyond recognition. However, at the moment, owing to their balanced regulation, low-tax, flexible modern business laws and quality professional services and infrastructure, OFCs are likely to remain a highly important cog in the wheels of international finance, with a real role to play in the world's rapidly growing emerging markets.

---

28. *See, e.g.*, M.L. Gordon, Recent Public Inversion and Cross-Border Transactions, Structured Finance Institute, Maximizing Benefits from Offshore Structures (New York, July 24–26, 2000).

29. CapGemini Asia Pacific Wealth Report 2012.

30. *Storm Survivors*, ECONOMIST (Feb. 16, 2013) (referring to research by Mr. Sharman of Griffith University in Australia).

14

Letters of Wishes and Protectors as Devices to Further the Settlor's Purposes

Anne J. O'Brien
Cara M. Koss
David Hayton

I. Introduction

In international estate planning, considerations of flexibility and confidentiality have led to the use of exceptionally wide-ranging discretionary trusts.[1] Where there are flexible discretions that can be exercised in respect of a very wide class, even though the class may be certain (e.g., everyone in the world except the settlor, his spouse, and the trustees), then problems arise over the need for administrative workability and the ability of the court to adjudicate according to justiciable criteria whether the trustees have exercised their discretionary power "in a responsible

1. *E.g.*, "blackhole trusts," discussed by David Hayton, *English Fiduciary Standards and Trust Law*, 32 VAND. J. TRANSNAT'L L. 555, 606–09 (1999).

manner according to its purposes"[2] and not exercised it in an arbitrary, capricious manner perverse to any sensible expectation of the settlor.[3]

It is thus necessary to discern the settlor's purposes, which usually are not revealed on the face of the trust instrument. Many settlors justifiably are worried that the breadth of their trust provisions may result in the trustees not giving effect to the settlor's real purposes, especially where a new employee of a trust corporation takes over the running of the trust, or a new trustee takes over from an old trustee. Why not, therefore, have the settlor write a letter to his trustee setting forth the settlor's wishes or requesting that the trustee record the settlor's wishes in a memorandum? The expression "letter of wishes" will be used to cover both a settlor's letter and a trustee's memorandum; a court should treat them alike. Such a letter can also be used to provide guidance to a protector on exercise of the protector's discretions.

II. Three Types of Letters of Wishes

At one extreme, a *legally binding* letter of wishes is a document that must be read alongside the trust instrument and that will override such instrument insofar as the letter is inconsistent with it. Thus, if the settlor executes a discretionary trust instrument but the settlor contemporaneously provides a letter to the trustees, which the settlor insists the trustees sign to accept implementation of the letter, and in the letter the settlor directs the trustees to pay the income to the settlor for the rest of his life, then the terms of the letter are as much a part of the trust as those in the discretionary trust instrument. A *legally binding* letter of wishes, like the trust instrument, generally must be made available for inspection and copying by beneficiaries to the extent required under applicable law or the terms of the trust instrument.

At the other extreme from such a *legally binding* letter of wishes is *a morally binding* (as opposed to a *legally significant*) letter of wishes.[4] Such a letter may be prefaced by words such as:

> This letter is not to be regarded as indicating in a legally significant way the purposes for which the powers in my trust deed have been conferred on my trustees. I do not want my trustees to have extra legal obligations placed upon them by this letter, and I do not want my trustees to have to justify the exercise of their powers. I believe the imposition of such extra legal obligations would cause more difficulties than benefits to accrue, creating greater cost and proving likely to upset relationships between my

2. *In re* Hay's ST, [1982] 3 All E.R. 786, 792; *In re* Beatty's WT, [1990] 3 All E.R. 844, 846; *McPhail*, [1971] A.C. 424, 449.

3. *In re* Manisty's Settlement, [1974] Ch. 17, 26.

4. *See* Jeffrey A. Schoenblum, Multistate and Multinational Estate Planning § 18.18(C)(8) (2009); Paul Matthews, *Letters of Wishes*, 5 O.T.P.R. 181, 184 (1995).

> beneficiaries. Thus, my trustees are under a mere moral obligation to take into account the following wishes of mine and shall not be accountable by any beneficiary or before any court for taking into account or failing to take into account these wishes.

Although there is little authority on this, assuming that such preface is not a pro forma sham inserted by the settlor or the trustees without the settlor's approval, there seems to be no reason why effect should not be given to the settlor's intention to create a mere morally binding letter.[5] A *morally binding* letter of wishes does not need to be made available to beneficiaries. Taking or failing to take such a letter into account is not intended to be a justiciable issue where complaint can be made and a judicial adjudication made thereon.

In the middle of the spectrum is a letter of wishes intended to be legally significant[6] in revealing the purposes for which the settlor conferred an extensive range of powers on the trustees who, in turn, have to exercise any discretionary power "in a responsible manner according to its purpose."[7] The greater the range of discretionary powers conferred on the trustees by the trust instrument, the greater the need for some guidelines in a letter of wishes. To oust any possibility of any particular term of the letter being regarded as a legally binding letter containing part of the beneficial provisions of the trust instrument, it is standard practice to preface the letter with words such as:

> This letter is not to be legally binding upon the trustees and is not to be considered part of my trust.

The preface is then followed by detailed guidance on various matters, designed to help the trustees fulfill the settlor's purposes as much as possible. The trustees who rely on such prefatory words to protect themselves should assume that the settlor intended the letter of wishes to be *legally significant* in revealing the purposes for which the settlor conferred extensive discretionary powers upon the trustees.[8] Why else did the settlor go to such great lengths by setting forth his purposes in such detail? Wouldn't the settlor want the trustees to be under a legal obligation to take his wishes into account, without being slavishly bound

---

5. Some have suggested that a letter of wishes may be construed as a prior agreement between the settlor and the trustee, which could constitute ongoing control by the settlor over the trust assets. *See* Rahman v. Chase Bank (C.I.) Trust Co. Ltd., [1991] Jersey I.R. 103; BARBARA HAUSER, INT'L ESTATE PLANNING: A REFERENCE GUIDE § 10-5 (2006).

6. Where the trust is governed by foreign law, it is important to consider the effect of applicable law on the letter of wishes. The law of some jurisdictions automatically converts legally significant letters of wishes into morally binding letters. *E.g.*, Belize Trusts Act 1992 § 13(4).

7. *In re* Hay's ST, [1981] 3 All E.R. 786, 792 (per Megarry, V-C).

8. It is not always clear when a trustee is justified in acting contrary to a legally significant letter of wishes, although some courts have attempted to set forth a non-exhaustive list of such circumstances. *See* Breakspear v. Ackland, [2008] EWHC 220 (Ch).

to follow them, especially if circumstances have changed significantly since the letter of wishes was written?[9]

With respect to a *legally significant* letter of wishes, the settlor should have the express option to make the letter confidential to the trustees, especially if its contents may embarrass or embitter some beneficiaries.[10] This may also be preferred by the trustees, since a beneficiary who has the letter available to her could easily make a clamor requiring the trustees to justify any divergences from the settlor's wishes.[11] Confidentiality of the letter will provide the trustees with a zone of protection, with required disclosure of the letter only during civil litigation if some evidence of improper conduct by the trustees were produced that enabled a particularized statement of claim to be drawn up (and not struck down as a device to enable the discovery process to be used as a "fishing" expedition for evidence that might support the claim). Then, as Judge Robert Walker, J., states,[12] "If a decision taken by trustees is directly attacked in legal proceedings, the trustees may be compelled either legally (through discovery or subpoena) or practically (in order to avoid adverse inferences being drawn) to disclose the substance of the reasons for their decision."

Where the settlor has chosen to write a legally significant letter and has not chosen to make it expressly confidential to the trustees, the case law is unclear on whether beneficiaries have an unfettered right to see and copy the letter of wishes.[13] In principle, this must turn on the settlor's intention. In order for a beneficiary to demand access to the letter of wishes, the settlor must have intended the letter to be part of the trust and to be handed on with the trust deed from trustee to trustee.[14] After all, the trustee's discretionary duties and powers can

9. These circumstances may justifiably lead the trustee not to follow the letter of wishes. Bank of Nova Scotia Trust (Bahamas) Ltd. v. de Barletta, [1985] 11 March unreported, noted, [1994] 3 J. INT'L TR. & PLAN. 35 (1994), 1 B.O.C.M. 5 (1985).

10. *Hartigan Nominees Pty Ltd.*, [1992] 29 N.S.W.L.R. 405.

11. *See* Scott v. National Trust, [1998] 2 All E.R. 705, 719 (Walker, J.).

12. *Scott,* [1998] 2 All E.R. 705, 719. *See also* Buxton L.J. in Taylor v. Midland Bank Trust Co., 2 ITELR 439, 459–61 (2000).

13. In *Hartigan Nominees Party Ltd.*, [1992] 29 N.S.W.L.R. 405, the three court of appeal judges' views differed. More recently, in *In re Rabaiotti's 1989 Settlement*, [2000] J.L.R. 173, the Jersey Royal Court on May 31, 2000 held that a beneficiary normally has no right to see a legally significant letter of wishes, it is impliedly confidential and likely to reveal the reasons for the exercise of the trustee's discretion (which the trustee cannot be required to reveal), but, in the special circumstances, the court held the beneficiary could have a copy to use it against his wife's claims on divorce.

14. Even where the letter of wishes does not contain a confidentiality clause, it may be inferred from the terms of the letter of wishes that the letter was not intended by the settlor to be revealed to the beneficiaries. *See* Alexander A. Bove Jr., *The Letter of Wishes: Can We Influence Discretion in Discretionary Trusts?*, 35 ACTEC J. 38 (2009) (suggesting that the following hypothetical language in a letter of wishes, though helpful to trustees in exercising their discretion, would be hurtful to the beneficiaries and therefore should not be disclosed: Where distributions are to be made to my son, bear in mind that, although he is a fine person, he has demonstrated bad judgment, is of weak character, and could easily be adversely influenced by outside sources. I prefer that you place as little funds as possible under his direct control. Also consider that my daughter, who

only be exercised for the purposes that the settlor indicated[15] in the legally significant letter of wishes. The settlor also must intend for the beneficiaries to hold the trustees accountable in the exercise of the trustees' discretionary duties and powers.[16] If the settlor does intend for the beneficiaries to have the right to make the trustees account for exercise of their discretions, surely the beneficiaries need to be able to see the letter of wishes that indicates the purposes for which those discretions were conferred upon the trustee.[17] Without knowing such purposes, how can the beneficiaries possibly monitor the trustee's conduct and establish a prima facie case of improper exercise of powers? To the extent that legitimate expectations play a role in trust law, shouldn't the beneficiaries have a legitimate expectation of being able to see the letter of wishes in order to effectively protect their interests?[18] In our opinion, the settlor must, therefore, be taken to implicitly intend those with rights to the trust account[19] to have the right to see the letter of wishes. Thus, such persons have an unfettered right to see the letter unless the settlor made the letter confidential to the trustees.

III. Protectors

A protector is not a trustee because the trust property is not vested in the protector. Rather, a protector is some other person or entity vested with one or more powers affecting what the trustees do with the trust property.[20] The protectorship is an office with a protective function, normally served for the duration of the trust.

---

has never been gainfully employed and has been married three times, has obvious difficulty with responsibility and relationships. Accordingly, you should keep 'strings attached' to all distributions made to her.)

15. *In re* Hay's ST, [1981] 3 All E.R. 786, 792, *In re* Beatty's WT, [1990] 3 All E.R. 844, 846.

16. *See* David Hayton, *The Irreducible Core Content of Trusteeship*, *in* Trends in Contemporary Trust Law ch. 3 (A.J. Oakley ed., 1996); *In re* Murphy's Settlement, [1998] 3 All E.R. 1.

17. *Scally*, [1992] 1 A.C. 294, 306-07. The letter may or may not give the beneficiaries some insight into the reasons for the trustees' actions, but this should be immaterial as in the case of the provisions of the trust deed.

18. *Scott*, [1998] 2 All E.R. 705, 718 (per Robert Walker, J.); *see also Edge*, [1999] 4 All E.R. 546.

19. Beneficiaries (except temporarily under a blind trust, e.g., for the Prime Minister or Chancellor of the Exchequer or Director of Serious Fraud Office) must have a right to make the trustee account, and objects of a power will normally be intended to have such a right, Spellson v. George, [1987] 11 N.S.W.L.R. 300, 316–17, but the settlor could expressly exclude such a right of objects, the core trustee beneficiary duty-right relationship sufficing to validate a trust.

20. An individual who has only personal power and not any fiduciary power is not to be regarded as a protector (e.g., a settlor with a power of revocation, a settlor's widow with a power to appoint capital unequally amongst their children and grandchildren, or a beneficiary who is managing director of a company controlled by the trustees and who has power to veto any sale of the shares in that company). *See* Antony Duckworth, *Protectors—Fish or Fowl?*, 4 J. Int'l Tr. & Corp. Plan. 131 (1995) (part I); Antony Duckworth, *Protectors—Fish or Fowl?*, 5 J. Int'l Tr. & Corp. Plan. 18 (1996) (part II).

A protector may be called "protector," "guardian," "supervisor," or "advisory committee," and may be a committee, a board, a company, or an individual.[21]

The settlor may provide for a protector in the trust instrument when he does not completely trust the trustees to fulfill the trust purposes. The settlor, a member of the settlor's family, or an employee of or adviser to the settlor commonly serves as the first protector and will have whatever powers are conferred on the protector by the trust instrument (e.g., the power to replace the trustees with new trustees or to withhold consent over distributions or sales of trust property).

Here, it is appropriate to consider the wide-ranging powers that can be conferred on a protector. Such broad powers usually relate to the management of the trust fund but may relate to the distributive functions of trustees.[22] Examples of such powers[23] include the following:

- to remove and appoint trustees;
- to review the trust administration and to approve accounts;
- to appoint auditors;
- to agree to trustees' compensation or reimbursement;
- to approve self-dealing by trustees;
- to apply to the court at the expense of the trust fund, if *bona fide* believing this to be in the interests of any unborn or unascertained beneficiary;[24]
- to export the trust and change the governing law;
- to trigger or cancel flight arrangements in flee clauses for new trustees in a new jurisdiction;
- to withhold consent (generally or in specific areas) to investment or other managerial decisions of the trustees;

21. We recognize that many titles are available, but we shall refer to such person, group of people, or entity as "protector" for the remainder of this chapter.

22. As the name implies, the powers of a protector should be regarded as attached to an office-holder for the duration of the trust for the protection of those interested in the trust fund (i.e., as beneficiaries or as objects of powers). *See* Steele v. Paz Ltd., [1993–95] Manx L.R. 426 (so the court held that it had inherent jurisdiction to appoint a protector where no other mechanism was available). However, there can be circumstances where a particular power is intended by the settlor to be for her own protection for the rest of her life or for the personal protection of the protector for the rest of his life (e.g., where the settlor or the protector needs the protection of the trustees' voting rights as significant shareholder in a company of which the settlor or the protector is a director or chief executive). *See, e.g.*, Von Knierem v. Bermuda Trust, 1 B.O.C.M. 116 (Bermuda High Court 1994).

23. In a rare case, excessive powers may be given to a protector such that there is no true trust for beneficiaries, only a trust of capital and income for the settlor absolutely (albeit with power to benefit the beneficiaries really as simply objects of a power), e.g., if the powers prevent the beneficiaries having any enforceable rights against the trustees for wrongful conduct in the settlor's lifetime (the protector having power to release the trustees from any liability for breach of trust, such as returning the trust property to the settlor, and the beneficiaries having no right to know they are beneficiaries or to see the trust accounts unless the protector consents in his absolute uncontrollable discretion).

24. So far, courts have been prepared to assume that protectors have *locus standi*, presumably on the basis that recognition of their office and powers requires this.

- to direct (generally or in specific areas) the exercise of trustees' investment or other managerial discretions;
- to withhold consent over distributive decisions of the trustees;
- to direct the trustees to make particular distributions of income or principal or to accumulate income;
- to obtain and provide tax advice for the trustees;
- to veto the settlor's exercise of reserved powers in certain circumstances (e.g., where the protector believes the settlor to be acting under duress);
- to decide whether the settlor is suffering a disability so that his reserved powers should be suspended or terminated; and
- to make or approve additions to or deletions from the class of beneficiaries or of objects of powers of appointment.

Of course, the existence of such express powers conferred upon the protector will give rise to some necessarily implied rights, including the right to review the trust accounts and the right to an indemnity from the trust fund for properly incurred expenses if an express power to charge fees has been granted to the protector.[25] Frequently, the protector will also be given power to release any of the protector's powers.

Where the trust instrument is silent, how should the role of protector be defined? In ascertaining the applicable standards, one must consider who holds the office of protector. It may be the settlor, a designated relative or close friend, a beneficiary, a committee of beneficiaries, a professional adviser of the settlor, the firm in which the adviser is a partner, or a company, whether formed by the settlor or an independent professional company. One must also consider successor protectors. It is possible, for example, that the settlor may be the first protector, but upon the settlor's death, the settlor's spouse, the settlor's attorney, or an independent corporation is to take over as protector. In view of the infinite spectrum of possible protectors and protector powers, it is clearly impossible for legislation to define a protector and to prescribe the protector's powers and duties in any meaningful fashion. It is, however, possible for legislation to provide default standards such that, if a person is expressly appointed to be the protector, then such protector has certain statutory powers and duties, subject to contrary intention in the trust instrument, that may diminish or enlarge such powers and duties. Such legislation also could provide a mechanism for the appointment of successor protector should the office of protector become vacant, and could address the relationship between the protector and the trustee so as to protect the trustee from relying (unless the trust instrument provides otherwise) on the good faith action or inaction of the protector.[26]

25. Blampied v. Ram (Jersey Royal Ct. Jan. 28, 1994) (discussed in Paul Matthews, *Two Cases, Twenty Questions*, 9 Trust L. Int'l 108 (1995)).

26. *In re* Arnott, [1899] Irish R. 201, Royal Brunei Airlines v. Tan, [1995] 2 A.C. 378.

Although such legislation could help clarify the role of protector in certain contexts, the problem with statutory default rules is that they often are unworkable in unusual or complex situations. These cases require the skill of professional advisers to specify the requisite powers and duties of the protector, the rights of the protector (e.g., to remuneration and indemnity), and any exemption from liability, as well as the mechanism for succession to the office of protector on the death, incapacity, or insolvency of the protector, and the relationship between the protector and the trustee (e.g., meetings between them and trustee protection when relying upon the conduct of the protector). Offshore statutes[27] merely tend to provide that protectors (unless otherwise provided in the trust instrument) are not liable to the beneficiaries for the *bona fide* exercise of their powers.

The question often arises whether, in exercising their powers and in default of express or necessarily implied provisions in the trust instrument, the protector acts pursuant to a fiduciary duty. In default of clear intent articulated in the trust instrument, one must look to rules related to donees of powers.[28] In ascertaining duties attached to power holders, the first question is whether the power holder holds a particular office fundamental to the performance of the trust throughout the entire trust period. For example, in the case of a protector, provisions in the trust instrument for appointment of successor protectors and continuous involvement of the protector in the trustees' managerial and/or distributive functions suggests that the office of protector is tied to the ongoing administration of the trust.[29]

Where the powers were conferred on the protector *virtute officii*, they are presumed to be fiduciary powers.[30] Fiduciary powers, of course, must be exercised

27. *E.g.*, Bahamas Trustee Act 1998 § 81(3), British Virgin Islands § 86(3) Trustee Ordinance; *In re* Wills' Trust Deeds, [1964] Ch. 219.

28. Such rules need developing in light of modern trust practice, especially when, during the settlor's life, some of the protector's powers are intended not for the benefit of the beneficiaries nor the personal benefit of the protector, but for the sole personal benefit of the settlor (who is not one of the beneficiaries). For example, the settlor may transfer a particular shareholding to the trust but require that it not be sold nor its voting rights exercised, except to strengthen or preserve the settlor's own position as a director or employee of the company. As such, trustees are not to dispose of the shareholding without the protector's consent, and until then, must vote the shares as directed by the protector. A skilled draftsperson would incorporate a provision to the effect that, during the settlor's lifetime and so long as he is a director or employee of the company, the protector's powers with respect to shareholding in such company should be exercised with regard only to the interests of the settlor and to the exclusion of those beneficially interested under the trust. In the absence of some such provision, one would presume that an office holder with powers *virtute officii* has fiduciary powers which must be exercised exclusively in the interests of the beneficiaries under the trust. Without clarification in the trust instrument, it generally would be a fraud on the protector's power for the protector to exercise a power to benefit the settlor, as the settlor is not a beneficiary of the trust. However, where the settlor is named as the initial protector, a court reasonably could conclude that a particular power is a personal power, even if the other powers were fiduciary.

29. *Steele*, [1993-95] Manx L.R. 426, establishing that the court has inherent jurisdiction to appoint a person to the office of protector, which should also be the view of English judges.

30. This is also the case if the powers were conferred on him by name when, in the particular circumstances, he was selected as donee of the power because he was protector. *In re* Wills' Trust Deeds, [1964] Ch. 219.

bona fide for the purposes for which the settlor created the powers[31] and cannot be fettered, released,[32] or used for any personal benefit of the donee (unless authorized in the trust instrument expressly or by necessary implication).[33] Moreover, the protector must consider periodically whether or not to exercise his fiduciary powers.[34] If such powers relate not to the trustees' distributive functions but to their managerial functions, it seems likely that the protector will need to exercise such powers with the same degree of care as the trustees. For this reason, many offshore jurisdictions[35] have legislation preventing persons with fiduciary powers (but who are not trustees) from being liable to the beneficiaries for the *bona fide* exercise of such powers unless there is a contrary intention in the trust instrument.

A personal power may be one of two types. A general power is conferred on the donee by the settlor with the intent to confer full dominion on the donee over the property affected by the power to protect the donee's own position[36] or to further the donee's own interests.[37] Thus, the donee can discharge his own legal or moral obligations to objects of the power or exercise the power by taking into account exclusively the donee's own selfish interests. A special power is conferred on the donee by the settlor with the intent that the donee be wholly unaccountable in the courts for exercising or not exercising the power, so long as upon any exercise of the power, only proper objects of the power are to benefit.[38] In the case of a special power, it would be a fraud on such power if the donee exercises it to benefit himself.[39] Otherwise, "the donee is entitled to prefer one object to another from any motive he pleases, and however capriciously he exercises the power, the Court will uphold it."[40]

When the initial protector is the settlor with a power to promote a particular trust asset for the settlor's own benefit, it is likely that such power is personal. Likewise, when the first protector is a beneficiary with selfish interests that the settlor must have taken into account,[41] the beneficiary's power is likely also

31. *In re* Hay's ST, [1982] 1 W.L.R. 202, *Edge,* [1999] 4 All E.R. 546.

32. *In re* Gibson's ST, [1981] Ch. 179, *In re* Will's Trust Deed, [1964] Ch. 219, 228–29.

33. *Edge*, [1998] 2 All E.R. *547, aff'd,* [1999] 4 All E.R. 546, *In re Z* Trust, [1997] Cayman Islands L.R. 248.

34. *In re* Hay's ST, [1982] 1 W.L.R. 202.

35. *E.g.*, Bahamas Trustee Act 1998 § 81, British Virgin Island Ordinance § 86.

36. For example, this allows the donee to continue to live in a particular villa or to control a particular company: *In re Z* Trust, [1997] C.I.L.R. 248 (discussed in 2 The Chase J. 57 (1998)); Rawson Trust v. Perlman, 1 B.O.C.M. 135 (Bahamas Sup. Ct. Eq. 1984).

37. *In re* Wills' Trust Deeds, [1964] Ch. 219, 228.

38. *In re* Gulbenkian's Settlement, [1970] A.C. 508, 518; *In re* Hay's ST, [1982] 1 W.L.R. 202; *In re* Wills' Trust Deeds, [1964] Ch. 219; *In re* Somes, [1896] 1 Ch. 250.

39. Vatcher v. Paul, [1915] A.C. 372, *In re* Dick, [1953] Ch. 343, Palmer v. Locke, [1880] 15 Ch. D. 294, 299, 302.

40. *In re* Wright, [1920] 1 Ch. 108, 118 (per Lawrence, J.).

41. *Rawson Trust,* 1 B.O.C.M. 135.

personal.[42] Where the settlor or a beneficiary serves as protector, and the protector is given the power to withhold consent to proposed distributions of income or principal by the trustees to one or more beneficiaries, such power is also likely a personal power.[43] Such a power in the hands of a disinterested or professional trustee, however, usually will be deemed a fiduciary power. Even where the settlor or a beneficiary is a protector, the powers of such protector will be presumed fiduciary so far as they relate to the removal and appointment of trustees and the investment role of the trustees, because those powers will be presumed to be exercisable to promote the interests of the beneficiaries as a whole.[44]

Rather than rely on applicable default law, if any, a settlor should articulate in the trust instrument (with the benefit of professional advice) a mechanism for succession to the protectorship and the particular powers, duties, rights, and exemptions the settlor wishes to confer on the protector. The settlor who has reserved for himself personal powers as protector, which enable him to act capriciously and self-interestedly without being accountable before any court, will not expect to ever be accused, in fact, of acting capriciously or recklessly. To guard against such a legal claim, the settlor must ensure that his powers are exclusively and merely personal.

If the settlor can do this for himself, the question arises whether he can authorize others as protector to have exclusively personal powers so as to block any court challenges to the exercise of the protector's discretion. Such challenges can obviously be detrimental to the smooth running of the trust and provoke lengthy and costly litigation.[45] The answer to the question hinges on whether there is an irreducible core minimum content of protectorship in the same way that there is for trusteeship. In *Armitage v. Nurse*,[46] L.J. Millet stated:

> There is an irreducible core of obligations owed by the trustees to the beneficiaries and enforceable by them which is fundamental to the concept

42. Alternatively, a court may conclude that the beneficiary's power is a fiduciary power, but that there is a necessarily implied authorization of a conflict of interest in the trust instrument that allows the beneficiary, after due consideration of other beneficiaries' interests, to exercise the power for the power-holder's own benefit despite personal benefit accruing therefrom. *See In re* Z Trust, [1997] C.I.L.R. 248 (discussed in 2 THE CHASE J. 57 (1998)), where the judge held the beneficiary-protector's power was probably personal, but if it was fiduciary there was a necessarily implied authority to exercise the power and thereby benefit the beneficiary-protector, so upholding the consent of a protector committee to an amendment of the beneficial provisions of the trust fund so as to benefit beneficiary members of the protector committee at the expense of other beneficiaries.

43. *In re* Triffit's Settlement, [1958] Ch. 852; *In re* Penrose [1933] Ch. 793; *Palmer*, [1880] 15 Ch. D. 294.

44. Vestey's Executors v. IRC, [1949] 1 All E.R. 1108; IRC v. Schroder, [1983] Simons T.C. 480; *In re* Burton, [1994] 126 A.L.R. 557.

45. *E.g.*, *Von Knierem*, 1 B.O.C.M. 116. The problem can be avoided by employing a custodian trustee to hold the trust assets. A managing trustee sacked by the protector will not need to be informed of the identity of the new trustee and will have no cause to complain if the trust instrument provides that a sacked trustee cannot be liable for anything happening as a result of the appointment of the replacement trustee.

46. *Armitage*, [1998] Ch. 241, 253.

> of a trust. If the beneficiaries have no rights enforceable against the trustees there are no trusts. But we do not accept that these core obligations include the duties of care and skill, prudence and diligence. The duty of the trustees to perform the trusts honestly and in good faith for the benefit of the beneficiaries is the minimum necessary to give substance to the trusts.

Millet then held that exemption clauses cannot exempt trustees from liability for dishonest or reckless breaches of trust, but can exempt them from liability for negligence. It would seem to follow that, generally, the powers of the protector must be exercised honestly and in good faith for the benefit of the beneficiaries as a whole. However, if the settlor clearly intends that the protector's powers are to be exclusively personal and that their exercise is to be beyond challenge in the courts (unless proven that the protector has acted dishonestly and in the protector's own self-interest, thus committing a fraud upon the protector's powers), then the court should respect the settlor's intention.

Finally, it is important for a settlor to consider the various tax implications of granting particular powers to a protector. The protector's ability to exercise certain powers may, in some cases, result in the protector being deemed to have a general power of appointment over trust property and, therefore, such property being included in the protector's own estate for estate tax purposes.[47] Where a trust is settled under U.S. law with a U.S. trustee, but foreign trust status is desired for tax or other reasons, appointing a foreign person or entity as protector may be sufficient to achieve foreign trust status.[48] In addition, a foreign trust (such as a foreign asset protection trust) may be subject to U.S. jurisdiction if, *inter alia*, a U.S. protector has the power to remove and replace trustees, and the terms of the trust instrument do not explicitly prohibit appointment of a U.S. trustee.[49]

---

47. Where the power of the protector is a personal (rather than fiduciary) power, and where such personal power may be exercised in favor of the protector or for the protector's benefit, the power may be treated as a general power of appointment, which could result in the property being included in the protector's own estate for income and estate tax purposes. In theory, the same tax treatment would result where the power is a fiduciary power exercisable in favor of the protector or for the protector's benefit and is not limited by any ascertainable standard. Some have argued, however, that the power would not be deemed a general power of appointment, and adverse tax consequences would not result, where the power was in fact limited by a fiduciary duty, even if such duty was not explicit but was inferred from the trust instrument. See Alexander A. Bove Jr., *The Trust Protector: Trust(y) Watchdog or Expensive Exotic Pet?*, 30 ESTPLN 390, 395 (2003).

48. Under the so-called "control test," a trust will be characterized as a foreign trust where non-U.S. persons have control over any substantial decision of the trust. A foreign protector might meet this test depending on the powers granted to such protector. Treas. Reg. § 301.7701-7; James F. Gulecas & Alan S. Gassman, *Practical Considerations for Trust Protectorship Provisions in Foreign and Domestic Trusts*, Asset Protection J. (2001).

49. *See, e.g.*, United States v. Grant, No. 00-8986, 2005 U.S. Dist. LEXIS 22440 (S.D. Fla. Sept. 2, 2005).

15

The Inheritance and Gift Tax Treatment of Anglo-American Trusts

ESTATE PLANNING IN THE NETHERLANDS

Prof. Dr. Frans Sonneveldt
and Mike Vrijmoed LL.M.

I. General Law

A. Legal System

The Netherlands is a civil law country. Statutory law constitutes the most important source of Dutch law. The courts, however, also play an important role in the evolution of the law. It is certainly not true that the Dutch legal doctrine is purely legalistic. The law often refers to the open standard of "reasonableness and fairness" and thus imposes a considerable duty upon the courts. In order to determine what the requirements of reasonableness and fairness entail, the law requires that account be taken of generally approved legal principles, of legal convictions prevailing in the Netherlands, and of the social and personal interests involved in the given case. In the event of a dispute, the court decides what is reasonable and fair in a specific case.

All statutes are promulgated in the Bulletin of Acts and Decrees (*Staatsblad*) that is published by the government. This Bulletin is the formal source of all legislation.

B. Trusts

The trust concept is not known in Dutch law. However, the Convention on the Law applicable to trusts and on their recognition of July 1, 1985, came into effect in the Netherlands on February 1, 1996. This means that the Netherlands recognizes trusts insofar as they fall within the description of trusts given by the Convention. Such recognition is explicitly *not* made by applying or adapting rules applicable to other legal concepts known in the Dutch system.

In the Netherlands, trustees as such can act in and out of court. The law chosen by the settlor is applicable to the trust or, if the settlor has not made any choice, the law most closely related to the trust concerned. That law will usually be the law of the jurisdiction where the administration takes place. As a result of the recognition of the trust, the Netherlands will treat the trustee amongst others as (fiduciary) owner of the trust assets. The trustee will be able to register the Dutch trust assets in his name. At the time of the Convention coming into force, the Netherlands promulgated a statutory regulation that makes this possible where necessary. The trust assets constitute a ring-fenced fund against which the trustee's creditors have no recourse with respect to his personal debts. That estate does not fall under the trustee's bankruptcy. If and to the extent that applicability of the provisions in force for the recognized trust would result in infringement of rules of law that the Netherlands must also observe in international cases as mandatory provisions or as priority rules, such rules take precedence.

Dutch law recognizes the possibility of providing by will or gift that what is acquired by inheritance or gift is kept in administration (*bewind*). This has the effect that the property is not controlled by its owner but by a person called the administrator (*bewindvoerdei*), who is appointed for the purpose by the will or the gift. During the operation of the *bewind*, the owner's debts may not be recovered from the property concerned even though the property belongs to his estate. The duration of the *bewind* must be determined by will or by gift. A *bewind* ceases in any event upon the death of the person who acquired the property. In addition, after five years the entitled party can request the district court to terminate the *bewind*, provided that the entitled party can soundly manage the assets himself. The *bewind* is in some respects similar to a trust. One of the main differences compared to a trust is that property kept in *bewind* is held in the name of the owner and not in the name of the administrator. The taxation aspects of the trust will be discussed later in this chapter.

C. Matrimonial Property Law

In the Netherlands, marriage is open to people of different and same sexes. There are, however, some legal restrictions. Generally speaking, marriage is only open to persons

- who are not already married and who have not entered into a (or another) registered partnership (prohibition of bigamy);
- who are aged 18 or over;
- who are not closely related, e.g. parents and children, grandparents and grandchildren, brothers and sisters; and
- who have permission to reside in the Netherlands.

When a marriage takes place and Dutch law is applicable to the proprietary consequences of the marriage, a full community of property between the spouses (the statutory community of property) arises. This can be varied if the spouses to be draw up a marriage contract before their marriage.

All property contributed to the marriage by the spouses, being the property they already owned prior to their marriage, and all property they acquire during the marriage forms part of the statutory community of property.

There is an exception for property as regards to which it was provided by last will of the testator or when a gift was made stating that it would fall outside the community in which the beneficiary is married or may later marry. This condition is often declared applicable to gifts to children and in wills. The result is that the inherited or donated property remains the personal property of the spouse concerned and shall not become part of any community of property and, therefore, such property will not be divided between the spouses in case of divorce. Also, property and debts that have close (legal) affinity to one of the spouses do not fall into a community of property. This could possibly be a claim relating to the compensation of emotional damages. Finally, pension claims that, in the case of a divorce, will be equalized between the spouses do not fall into the community of property.

The spouses are equally entitled to the statutory community of property. Should the community be dissolved such as through divorce or on the death of one of the spouses, each spouse shall be entitled to 50 percent of the statutory community of property.

The spouse in whose name the property concerned is registered or who acquired the property by inheritance or gift manages the property forming part of the statutory community of property, unless the spouses have agreed otherwise in their marriage contract. With regard to other property, both spouses are entitled to manage that property. The spouse with managerial power is authorized to transfer the property to a third party. For some acts—for instance the sale of the conjugal residence, the taking out of a loan, or the making of gifts—a spouse requires the other spouse's permission. This permission requirement applies irrespective of the matrimonial property regime under which the spouses are married.

The debts of either spouse can be recovered from the community of property. Should one of the spouses contract a debt, the creditor can recover the debt from all property forming part of the community. In a case of bankruptcy of one of the spouses, the full community of property shall fall into the assets of the bankrupt spouse.

The spouses may deviate from the statutory community of property by drawing up a marriage contract. In the Netherlands a marriage contract has to be drawn up by notarial instrument.

There are many options as far as the content of the marriage contract is concerned. The spouses can choose a system by which each community of property is excluded (separation). Each spouse then keeps his or her own property, without either spouse getting any claim against the property of the other spouse. In the event of exclusion from every community of property, a spouse's debts can only be recovered from his property. The property of the other spouse is out of range. The spouses may choose all sorts of intermediate forms in the marriage contract, the community of property being one extreme and exclusion of each community of property the other. They can agree that only specific property—for instance the conjugal residence and/or furniture—shall form part of the community of property, while the other property continues to be their personal property. They can also that all property shall fall into the community of property, except for specific property which shall remain personal. The marriage contract must be registered in the matrimonial property register, which is kept at the registry of *rechtbank* (district court). Should the marriage contract not be registered, it cannot be invoked against third parties such as creditors who are not acquainted with the existence of the marriage contract.

In order to avoid the unfair result that can be the effect of a marriage contract, in the event of a separate property marital regime, the spouse gets no claim at all against property of the other spouse; a netting covenant is often added to this system. There are many varieties of such covenants. A distinction can be made between periodical and final netting covenants. In a periodical netting covenant, certain assets are settled at intervals. Regularly, spouses arrange that savings of income from work—i.e., the part of the income that has not been used for housekeeping expenses—are divided equally between the spouses on an annual basis.

In practice, a periodical netting covenant is often agreed upon. In most cases, however, spouses do not carry out the covenant. This omission can lead to various discussions at the end of a marriage by death of one of the spouses or in the case of a divorce. In most marriage contracts, a term of forfeiture for netting claims is included. Generally speaking, courts will decide that the term of forfeiture cannot be invoked against the debtor in accordance with the requirements of reasonableness and fairness. For cases where the periodical netting covenant has not been executed, the Dutch Civil Code determines that all property is deemed to be accrued from income liable to a periodical netting obligation. This will result in a 50-50 settlement at the end of the marriage. Finally, there are a lot of discussions possible on the definition of income liable to a periodical netting covenant, especially in cases where one spouse runs an enterprise in a private company with limited liability. In such cases, the question often arises as to whether deferred dividend payments and appreciation of shares/goodwill are subject to periodical settlement. From a tax perspective, the significance is whether the settlement of a claim arises from matrimonial property law or whether, for example, it can be seen as a taxable gift.

In a final netting covenant, the spouses arrange that settlement of the value of the assets shall take place at the end of the marriage. It is possible to provide that at the end of the marriage accounts are settled as if full community of property existed. It is also possible to provide that the netting covenant operates only if the marriage is dissolved on the death of one of the spouses; in such a case, the netting covenant does not apply in the event of divorce.

Spouses can draw up a marriage contract prior to or during their marriage and alter or annul a marriage contract that was drawn up prior to or during the marriage. However, the matrimonial property regime may not be altered during the first year of marriage. As of January 1, 2012, district court (*rechtbank*) approval is no longer required for making or altering marriage contracts during a marriage. A public notary will, however, not cooperate if there is a risk that creditors may be prejudiced or if one or more terms are in breach of the rules of mandatory law, bonos mores, or public policy.

D. Registered Partnership

As an alternative to the traditional marriage, Dutch law offers couples the possibility to register their partnership formally. The Act on registered partnership entered into force on January 1, 1998. The registered partnership (*geregistreerd partnership*) is equal to the marriage, not limited to persons of different sex. It is intended for couples who cannot or do not wish to marry. The same restrictions as to the marriage apply to the registered partnership. The property consequences of a registered partnership are equivalent to the consequences of a marriage as discussed in earlier. Thus, registered partners will share their property and their debts in full community, unless they have drawn up a registered partnership contract before registering their partnership.

The district court can terminate the partnership in the same way as a divorce in the case of a marriage. However, partners can also dissolve their partnership by mutual consent without involving the court, except for cases that involve minor children. If partners wish to dissolve their registered partnership without the intervention of the court, they may agree to terminate the registration, which agreement has to be acknowledged by at least one Dutch lawyer or Dutch civil law notary. The termination out of court has some disadvantages, the most important being the denial of such out-of-court procedure abroad and the absence of entitlement to enforcement, e.g., for alimony payments. In the case of a breach of payment obligations, one will need to go to court to enforce payment. The most important difference between a marriage and a registered partnership relates to the law of descent. A registered partnership of itself has no consequences for the relationship toward children of the other partner. A child born within a marriage automatically becomes blood relative of the husband/father. If the father is not a spouse but is instead a registered partner of the mother, he will have to acknowledge the child for it to be a blood relative.

As to the following paragraphs, it should be kept in mind that what is said of the spouse also applies to the registered partner, unless otherwise indicated.

E. Lifetime Gifts/Donations

The old Dutch law on donations (applicable until January 1, 2003) only recognized the formal donation. This was either a notarial contract or a gift from hand to hand. The previous Dutch civil code determined as follows: “A donation is an agreement whereby the donor, inter vivos, by gratuitous title irrevocably grants the full ownership of an asset to the donee who accepts the full ownership of the asset.” In addition to this formal donation, doctrine had developed the concept of the material donation. A material donation was defined as “any overt, liberal act effecting the enrichment of a person at the expense of another person”.

The new Dutch law (applicable as of January 1, 2003) makes a distinction between donations and gifts. A donation takes place if four conditions are met:

1. agreement,
2. gratuitous title,
3. enrichment/impoverishment, and
4. liberality (donative intent).

An active act is required to create a donation. Generally speaking, passiveness will not constitute a donation. For example, a debtor not (yet) reclaiming his debt will not make a donation. It is no longer required that a donation is made in the form of a notarial contract. However, under the new law it is possible to make donations "upon death" (*donatio mortis causa*) provided that the offer and the acceptance are made in a notarial deed. If the *donatio mortis causa* relates to personal goods such as clothes, personal jewelry, and household goods, a private deed will suffice. The requirement of the Dutch notarial contract serves to protect heirs, forced heirs, specific legatees, and also regular creditors. The requirement of a notarial contract does not only apply to donations but also applies to gifts that will be effected after the donor's death.

A gift is any act that enriches a person at the expense of one's own wealth. The donation is a specimen of the gift. The essential difference between the donation and the gift is the requirement of the legal title. The concept of the gift can also comprise reciprocal contracts with non-equivalent consideration. Furthermore, one-sided legal acts as, for example, waiving one's share in a community of property can be considered gifts.

Under the new Dutch law on donations, the possibility of revocation has been introduced. Under previous Dutch law it was only possible to revoke the offer to donate if the beneficiary had not accepted the offer. Revocation is only possible under the new law if this possibility has been stipulated. Revocation cannot only take place by means of a declaration to the donee, but it can also take place in a last will. This also means that it is allowed to make donations under "resolutive" or "suspensory" conditions. The conditions may, however, not conflict with essence of the obligation.

F. Estates of Deceased Persons

1. The Dutch Inheritance Law as Provided by Statute

As of January 1, 2003, the Dutch inheritance law has been radically changed. The new rules that will be discussed below have strengthened the position of the surviving spouse vis-a-vis the children. The inheritance law singles out four groups of heirs. An heir in a preceding group excludes the heirs in the later groups. The groups are

- first group: spouse, children and their descendants;
- second group: parents, brothers, sisters, and their descendants;
- third group: grandparents and their descendants; and
- fourth group: great-grandparents and their descendants.

Only the first two groups will be discussed hereinafter.

If a deceased person leaves a spouse and children, the spouse and children will inherit his estate, each for an equal part. This does not mean that the heirs receive all property from the estate. To protect the surviving spouse, as of January 1, 2003, the Dutch inheritance law stipulates that all property of the estate goes to the surviving spouse. The children will receive a pecuniary claim equal to their share in the estate. This so-called statutory division (*wettelijke verdeling*) applies automatically unless the deceased has provided otherwise in his last will. In principle, the children cannot effect their claim on the surviving spouse. The claim becomes eligible

1. upon the death of the surviving spouse;
2. if the surviving spouse goes bankrupt or if a debt rescheduling arrangement applies to the surviving spouse; or
3. in cases specifically mentioned in the deceased's last will, e.g., marriage, the entering into a registered partnership or migration abroad.

As shown earlier, the estate of a deceased person who was married in the community of property consists of his private capital and the undivided half of the community of property in which he was married. The other half of such dissolved communal estate belongs to the surviving spouse by virtue of the law of matrimonial property. If a married person dies without leaving descendants, the spouse will inherit the entire estate. If an unmarried person who does have children dies, the children will each inherit an equal portion of the estate.

In the event of succession of the estate according to the Dutch law, rules laid down in the law regarding substitution are applicable. Substitution implies that, in the event of prior death of a child, the children of such child will take his place in the event of succession. Those children will each inherit an equal portion of the inheritance that would have been due to the predeceased child, if a person dies without leaving a spouse and/or descendants, the heirs in the second group will inherit the estate. If there are no brothers and sisters, each of the parents will inherit half of the estate, or, if only one parent is alive, such a parent will inherit the entire estate. If there are one or more brothers or sisters, the parents and the brothers and sisters will each inherit an equal portion of the estate, taking into account that a parent is always entitled to a minimum portion of one-quarter of the estate. If a brother or sister has died before the deceased person, the rules regarding substitution are applicable. In the foregoing, it has been assumed that the deceased and brothers and sisters are all children from the same parents. The rules that apply in other cases will not be discussed here.

2. The Forced Share

A deceased may depart from the statutory division (*wettelijke verdeling*) as described earlier by will. However, when doing so the forced share portion due to forced heirs should be taken into account. The forced share is a part of the value of the estate of the deceased that the forced heir can claim contrary to any inter vivos gifts and testamentary dispositions by the deceased. The forced heir as such is (as of the introduction of the law of succession as per January 1, 2003) not entitled to a specific portion of the property belonging to the "estate" but has a pecuniary claim. A forced heir who wishes to receive his forced share must present a claim. The claim has to be presented within a reasonable period fixed by an interested party and no later than five years after the interested party became aware of his claim.

The forced heir has a pecuniary claim against the joint heirs or, if the estate has been distributed under the statutory division, against the deceased's spouse. The pecuniary claim will be increased with a percentage equal to the statutory interest rate, insofar as this is greater than six, calculated only on the principal debt and per annum as of the day on which a claim has been presented in respect of the forced share.

The forced share cannot be claimed within the first six months after the deceased's death. Furthermore, the surviving spouse has a preferential position towards the forced heirs. The claim can only be effected against the surviving spouse

- upon the death of the surviving spouse;
- if the surviving spouse goes bankrupt or if a debt rescheduling arrangement applies to the surviving spouse; or
- in cases specifically mentioned in the deceased's last will.

Also, if the deceased has chosen a different division from the statutory division in his last will, he can determine that a forced heir's claim can be effected only upon the death of the surviving spouse. Only descendants of a deceased person are entitled to a forced share either in their own right or in substitution for persons who have died prior to the devolution of the estate or who are unworthy at that time. Ascendants are not entitled to a forced share. The spouse of a deceased person is not entitled to a forced share. A testator may exclude his spouse as heir to his estate, without such spouse being able to challenge that on the basis of inheritance law. The spouse may, however, claim certain rights, like for example the right of usufruct of the conjugal residence.

The forced share is calculated on the basis of the statutory bulk (*egitimaire massa*). The statutory bulk consists of the value of the assets of the deceased's estate, increased by certain gifts made by the deceased during his lifetime. The forced share of a child amounts to one half of the statutory bulk divided by the number of heirs in the first group (spouse and descendants). Some examples will illustrate this:

- If a person dies leaving three children without leaving a spouse, the forced share of each of those children is a one-sixth portion of the statutory bulk.
- If a person dies leaving a spouse and a child, the forced share of the children is a one-fourth portion of the statutory bulk.

3. Formal Requirements of a Last Will

The making of a last will by two or more persons in one deed (mutual will) is not allowed under Dutch law. When drawing up a deed laying down the last will, a civil law notary must in principle be engaged under Dutch law. An exception applies only to the so-called "codicil," a holographic document written in its entirety by the testator by hand, dated and signed by the hand of its author, which document may or may not be supplementary to a last will made by notarial deed. In a codicil only specific dispositions can be made, like burial arrangements and legacies of clothing, certain jewelry, and furniture. A codicil is revoked in the same manner in which it is made. Destruction of the codicil is a more secure method of revocation.

Under certain conditions it is possible that a person makes a private last will and deposits this private last will with a Dutch civil law notary. The most common form of a last will, however, is the notarial last will. A notarial last will is executed before a Dutch civil law notary. The revocation of a last will is made in the same way as the last will is made. A notarial last will can be revoked by notarial deed. Reclaiming the last will from the Dutch civil law notary can revoke a deposited private last will. The restrictions that apply to the specific dispositions of a codicil do not apply to the notarial last will and the deposited private last will.

A Dutch civil law notary notifies the Central Register of Last Wills in The Hague of the fact that he has executed a deed in which a person has placed dispositions on record that must come into effect upon his death.

In the Taxation section, some last wills that are frequently made in the Netherlands are discussed. The Netherlands has ratified the Convention on the Conflicts of Laws relating to the Form of Testamentary Dispositions concluded in The Hague on October 6, 1961. On the basis of this convention, a testamentary disposition is valid as to form if it complies with the law of the state in which it was made or the national law of the testator or the law of his place of domicile or the law of his ordinary residence, any and all assessed at the moment at which the last will was made or at the moment of the testator's death. The Netherlands has made a reservation under article 10 of this convention to the effect that oral testamentary dispositions are not recognized.

4. Liquidation of the Deceased's Estate

The deceased's heirs—either testate or intestate—automatically enter into the rights of the deceased. Collectively they continue the "person" of the deceased. Judicial intervention is not required. The heirs shall in principle administer the estate collectively and they are only jointly authorized to dispose of the property belonging to the estate.

An heir, being a person who is entitled to a specific portion of the estate should be distinguished from a legataris (meaning both legatee and devisee, hereinafter called legatee). A legatee is a person to whom a specific property is devised or bequeathed.

Legatees are, unlike heirs, not automatically entitled to the property devised or bequeathed to them. Legatees are only entitled vis-a-vis the heirs to an action for transfer of the bequeathed or devised property. Upon such transfer the formal requirements applicable to the property concerned must be met.

An heir has the possibility to refuse an inheritance or to accept it subject to the privilege of an inventory (*beneficiaire aanvaarding*). Refusal implies that the heir renounces his inheritance. Acceptance subject to the privilege of an inventory means acceptance without any liability to debts beyond the assets descended. Making a statement to the clerk of the court, within whose district the deceased last resided, effects both refusal and acceptance subject to the privilege of an inventory. In Dutch law the declaration of inheritance (*verklaring van erfrectit*) has an important function in the winding up of an estate. A certificate of inheritance is a statement, issued by a Dutch civil law notary or the clerk of a court, showing who is or are authorized to dispose of the property belonging to the estate. The person with power of disposal identifies himself in judicial matters by means of the certificate of inheritance. If a testator has appointed an executor, a declaration of execution (*verklaring van executele*) can be issued in the same manner. By means of such a declaration, the executor can exercise the power granted to him.

There are no formal requirements for the division of an estate, if all persons who have to assist in the division have the free control of their property. If that is not the case, a description of the estate must be made and the division of it must be effected by notarial deed, after the draft of such deed has been approved by the Subdistrict Court (*kantonrechter*). The transfer of the bequeathed property concerned must follow each division. The transfer of a bequeathed property is subject to the same requirements as are applicable to the transfer of the property concerned. For immovable property, for example, this means that the property must be delivered by notarial deed and then be registered in the Public Registers. The liquidation and division of an estate is usually effected according to the law of the last residence of the deceased. The Netherlands is not a party to any conventions regulating the control of estates. Under Dutch law the court has jurisdiction to decide on disputes that have arisen with respect to the liquidation of an estate, if the last residence of the deceased was in the Netherlands. The Supreme Court, however, decided that the Dutch court also has jurisdiction, if the last residence was not in the Netherlands, but the immovable property belonging to the estate is in the Netherlands or the defendant to the dispute is resident in this state, provided that the action has sufficient connection with the jurisdiction of the Netherlands.

G. International Estate Planning Issues

1. Property Belonging to Spouses

(a) Convention on the Law Applicable to Matrimonial Property Regimes. The Convention on the Law applicable to Matrimonial Property Regimes (The Hague, March 1, 1978) entered into force September 1, 1992. Apart from the Netherlands,

France and Luxembourg are the only states that have ratified this Convention. The judicial authorities of the states that have ratified the Convention must apply it as from September 1, 1992. The Convention applies only to the law applicable to the spouses' matrimonial property regime if they were married after September 1, 1992, or if they have designated the applicable law after that date, even if they were married before such date.

The Convention's main rule is that the spouses are free to choose the law applicable. When the spouses make a designation before marriage, they may designate

- the law of a state of which either spouse is a national;
- the law of the state in which either spouse has his habitual residence; or
- the law of the state where one of the spouses establishes a new habitual residence after marriage.

If the spouses designate the law applicable during marriage, they may only designate the law of the state either of which either spouse is a national or in which either spouse has his or her habitual residence at that time. The Convention creates the possibility of making a designation with respect to immovable property for the law of the place where the immovable property is situated. The same formalities apply to a separate designation of the applicable law as prescribed for a marriage contract according to either the law that is designated or the law of the state where the designation is made (focus regit actum). In any event, the designation shall be made in a private document, dated and signed by both spouses.

The rules of the Convention that apply if no designation of law has been made are rather complicated. The principal rule is that the law of the state in which both spouses establish their first habitual residence after marriage governs the proprietary consequences of the marriage. However, under certain circumstances the law of the state of which both spouses are nationals at the time of their marriage prevails. These circumstances are where

- the state of the common nationality of the spouses has made a declaration in accordance with the Convention's rules that it is a nationality state. The Netherlands has made such a declaration; France and Luxembourg have not. However, if such spouses have had their habitual residence in an habitual residence state for five years before their marriage, the law of that state will be applicable;
- the state of which both spouses are nationals has not ratified the Convention and is a nationality state, and the spouses take their habitual residence there;
- the spouses do not establish their habitual residence in the same state shortly after marriage. If the spouses do not have a common nationality and do not establish a common habitual residence in one state shortly after marriage, the law of the state with which the matrimonial property regime is most closely connected applies.

The rule is that the applicable law at the beginning of the marriage does not change automatically during marriage. There are a couple of exceptions to this rule. The most important one is that, if the spouses have neither designated the applicable law nor made a marriage contract, the applicable law changes when the spouses have had their habitual residence in a state for a period often years.

2. Marriages Not Falling under the Convention

As stated before, the Convention only applies if the spouses were married after September 1, 1992, or have designated the applicable law after that date. Therefore the "old" conflicts of laws and rules are still relevant. Those rules were mainly defined in a judgment of the Supreme Court of December 10, 1976, *Chelouche v. Van Leer*, in which the Supreme Court held that the consequences for the property of a marriage would be governed by

- the law that the spouses had designated;
- if no designation of the applicable law had been made, the law of the state of which both spouses were nationals at the time of marriage or shortly after it;
- if the spouses did not have a common nationality, the law of the state in which both spouses established their habitual residence shortly after marriage; or
- if the spouses did not have an habitual residence, the law of the state with which the matrimonial property regime was most closely connected.
- The Supreme Court's judgment was inspired to a large extent by the Convention, which was being prepared at that time. The Chelouche-Van Leer rules do not apply:
- if the law applicable to the property of the marriage was governed by the Hague Convention on Matrimonial Property Regimes of 1905 (this Convention, according to which the law of the state of which the man was a national at the time of marriage applied, was revoked by the Netherlands on August 23, 1977); or
- if the spouses presumed on adequate grounds that a law other than the law that would be applicable according to those rules applied; or
- if those rules refer to a matrimonial property regime which the spouses could not have wanted.

3. Succession

The Netherlands has ratified the Hague Convention on the Law Applicable to Succession to the Estates of Deceased Persons of August 1, 1989 (the Convention). The Convention itself has not entered into force by this ratification as the ratification of two other states is required. The Netherlands incorporated the provisions of the Convention into Dutch legislation with effect from October 1, 1996. The Convention offers the possibility to designate the law of a particular state to govern the succession. Such a designation only has effect if the person concerned has designated the law of the state of which he was a national at the time of the designation or of his death, or of the state in which he was habitually resident at either of those times. A designation of the law applicable to the succession must be expressed in a statement that meets with the formal requirements for dispositions of property upon death. The law designated governs the existence and material validity of the act of designation. Choices of law made before the rules of the Convention became applicable in the Netherlands will, insofar as necessary, be recognised as valid.

If the deceased has not designated the law applicable to the succession, the following rules apply:

a. If a deceased at the time of his death was a national of the state of his habitual residence at that time, the law of that state is applicable to the succession.
b. If the nationality and the habitual residence did not coincide at the time of death, then the designation of the applicable law depends on the question of how long the deceased had already had this habitual residence.
c. If the deceased stayed in his habitual residence for a period of less than five years, then the law of the state of which the deceased was a national is applicable.
d. If the deceased stayed in this habitual residence for a period of five years or more, then the law of succession of the state of such habitual residence applies.

There are two exceptions to the rules outlined in c and d above. If the deceased had lived in his habitual residence for a period of less than five years and he was more closely connected with a state other than that of which he was a national, then the law of such state is applicable. The second exception only applies in exceptional circumstances. If the deceased had lived for a period of five years or more in a state other than that of which he was a national, but he was manifestly more closely connected with the state of which he was a national, then the law of the state of which he was a national applies. On the basis of the above, should the law of a non-contracting state be applicable, but that law refers to another non-contracting state that would apply its own law, then the Convention respects such referral. In short, the Convention has universal effect.

It is possible that a person entitled to an estate is prejudiced by the application of a law other than the one designated by the Convention to the inheritance of assets located abroad, measured according to the rules of the Convention. In that case, the statutory regulation gives the injured party the right to demand that the loss incurred be settled as far as possible on the liquidation of the remainder of the estate.

The law applicable to the succession governs the inheritance of the whole of the estate wherever the assets, movable or immovable, are located, such as the determination of the heirs, contribution and mitigation, and the legal portions. The applicable law does not govern the liquidation and the division of the estate.

The law incorporating the rules of the Convention includes a statutory regulation for the latter two subjects. This regulation means that Dutch law governs the liquidation of the estate, if the deceased had his last habitual residence in the Netherlands. Dutch law also governs the manner of division of such an estate, unless the participants together designate the law of another state.

4. Immovable Property

Dutch law does not have specific conflict of law rules with respect to immovable property, neither for matrimonial property law nor for succession law, with the exception of the rule discussed.

5. Movable Property

Dutch law does not have specific conflict of law rules with respect to movable property.

6. EU Regulation on Succession

Finally, mention should be made of the EU regulation on succession: Regulation (EU) No 650/2012 of the European Parliament and of the Council of 4 July 2012 on jurisdiction, applicable law, recognition and enforcement of decisions and acceptance and enforcement of authentic instruments in matters of succession and on the creation of a European Certificate of Succession (OJ n. L 201, p. 107 ff.). This regulation shall apply from August 17, 2015 to the succession of persons who die on or after that date. It will apply within the EU with the exception of Denmark, Ireland and the United Kingdom. Those three member states did not take part in the adoption of the instrument and are not bound by it. It must be noted that the Member States do not lose their authorities with regard to tax law and inheritance law.

In principle, the EU regulation on succession deals with two conflict of law matters. The first concerns which court is competent in case of a cross border succession. The second question is which law will be applied to the cross border succession. In short, the court of the State in which the deceased had his habitual residence at the time of death will be competent to the succession as a whole irrespective of the nature or the location of the assets. The same goes for the applicable law to the cross border succession. A person may also choose a law (and competent court) to govern his succession as a whole. The choice is limited to the law of the State whose nationality he possesses at the time of making the choice or at the time of death.

This is a big step ahead because currently in case of immovable property in a cross border succession the inheritance law (including the forced heirship rules) of the state of location may be applicable to the immovable property, namely if the system of scission applies. The other assets of the succession usually fall within the scope of the law of the last habitual residence or nationality State. If for example a testator residing in the Netherlands owns real estate in France, the French inheritance law and forced heirship rules will at the moment be applicable to the real estate in France, since France applies the schismatic approach. When the regulation takes effect, one single authority will be in charge of the succession and the schismatic approach will no longer apply. The EU regulation on succession has universal application. In other words, any law specified by this regulation shall be applied whether or not it is the law of a Member State.

II. Taxation

A. Inheritance and Gift Tax

As of January 1, 2010, the Dutch Inheritance and Gift Tax Act 1956 (IGTA 1956) was radically changed. The State Secretary of Finance had three main goals with the new amendments:

1. the lowering of tax rates;
2. the simplification of the IGTA 1956; and
3. the countering of tax structures.

In this current economic climate, it is government policy that amendments to tax acts be budget neutral. Also for this reason, the countering of tax structures is an important pillar of the 2010 amendments. In this section, the 2010 system will be discussed, unless expressly mentioned otherwise.

Inheritance tax is due on any values acquired on account of a person's death, if that person at the time of his death was residing in the Netherlands. A person who dies within ten years after leaving the Netherlands is deemed resident in the Netherlands if he still was a Dutch national at the time of his emigration and of his death. Inheritance tax is not only due on what is acquired directly from an estate. The IGTA 1956 holds various (fiction) provisions to prevent tax avoidance by transactions during lifetime. The most important are the following:

a. Everything a person has acquired out of a deceased's assets during his lifetime, in connection with a legal act to which the deceased was a party, is deemed an acquisition out of the inheritance if (i) the deceased has enjoyed either a usufruct or a periodical payment in connection with that legal act until his death or any related time, and (ii) this usufruct or periodical payment came to the debit of the other party. For instance, if a parent sells his house to his children but retains a lifetime usufruct, the house is deemed an acquisition out of the inheritance at the death of the parent. As of 2010 this rule also applies to goods in which the deceased acquired a usufruct during lifetime from his own wealth. For instance, if a parent acquires the usufruct of a new house whilst the children acquire the bare ownership of said house, both from own wealth, a deemed acquisition by way of inheritance is considered. For purposes of this regulation one is deemed to have enjoyed a usufruct if the usufructuary did not pay an amount equal to 6 percent of the value of the respective property annually for the benefit of that property.

b. Everything acquired on the death of a person on the basis of (i) a clause securing the assets to remain vested in the survivor, (ii) an assignment clause, or (iii) a takeover clause.

These provisions are only applicable if the deceased was married to or closely related to the beneficiary.

c. Everything donated by the deceased within 180 days prior to his death.
d. Everything acquired as a result of the death under a life insurance agreement or any third-party insurance, if and insofar as the premium has come to the expense of the deceased.
e. The appreciation of shares that constitute a substantial interest in a limited liability company, which appreciation is caused by the death of the deceased. For instance, if the company had the obligation to pay pensions or annuities to the deceased, upon his death the provision is (partially) released. If the shares were not held by the deceased himself but by a third party, without this deemed acquisition the increase in value would accrue to the third party free of inheritance tax.

To calculate the inheritance tax due, any value that is taxable as a result of one of the above-mentioned provisions will be added to the amount acquired by the same person from the estate.

1. Valuation

For calculation of inheritance tax, assets are valued at fair market value at the time of death. In respect to some specific properties, the IGTA 1956 provides special valuation rules. The value of a usufruct equals 6 percent of the estate value subjected to the usufruct, multiplied by a factor depending on the age of the usufructuary. These factors are:

Factor	Age of usufructuary
16	younger than 20
15	20 or older, but younger than 30
14	30 or older, but younger than 40
13	40 or older, but younger than 50
12	50 or older, but younger than 55
11	55 or older, but younger than 60
10	60 or older, but younger than 65
8	65 or older, but younger than 70
7	70 or older, but younger than 75
5	75 or older, but younger than 80
4	80 or older, but younger than 85
3	85 or older, but younger than 90
2	90 or older

The value of a periodical payment, depending on the life of a person, equals the annual amount multiplied by the factor prevailing for the person entitled, according to the table above.

2. Exemptions and Rates

All amounts mentioned apply for the year 2013. They are amended annually as from January 1. The applicable exemptions for inheritance tax are as follows:

a. For partners, €616,880. Deducted from this amount is half of the cash value of pension rights derived by a spouse from the death of the deceased. However, a minimum exemption of €159,361 always remains.
b. €58,604 for children whose costs of living were for the greatest part paid by the deceased and for whom it is expected that within the coming three years they will not be able to earn half of the income a physically and mentally healthy person would earn.
c. For other children and grandchildren, €19,535.
d. For parents, €46,266.
e. For others, €2,057.

Any inheritance of pension rights or certain annuities comparable to pension rights is exempt from inheritance tax.

3. Calculation of Inheritance Tax

Inheritance tax is imposed at progressive rates, depending on both the size of the acquisition and the relation between the deceased and the beneficiary. Before 2010, there were three groups, each with seven brackets. As of 2010, there are only two groups, each with two brackets. Inheritance tax in principle is for the account of the beneficiary. In the event that inheritance tax has to be paid by the estate, the acquisition has to be grossed up taking exemption and rate into account. Properties inherited by two partners as defined below are considered one acquisition for inheritance.

4. Relatives

The tax rates (2013) for partners and children are as follows (all amounts in Euro):

Taxable acquisition	Inheritance tax
€118,254 and more	20%
€0–118,254	10%

For descendants of the second (grandchildren) or further degree (great-grandchildren, etc.), percentages of the above-mentioned table should be multiplied by 1.8.

5. Other Beneficiaries

The tax rates (2013) for other beneficiaries (including brothers, sisters and relatives in the direct ascending line) are as follows:

Taxable acquisition	Inheritance tax
€0–118,254	30%
€118,254 and more	40%

6. Partners/Cohabitants

Besides spouses and registered partners, cohabitants may also qualify for partnership within the IGTA 1956 if they meet several requirements. Cohabitant partners must be of full age (18 or over) and must have shared a common household whilst being registered at the same address for (1) a minimum period of six months in the case of death, or (2) a minimum period of two years in the case of a donation. Additional requirements are that the cohabitant partners must have entered into a notarial cohabitation contract that contains reciprocal duty for care and that the cohabitant partners are not descendants. It is not possible to have multiple cohabitant partners. In case the cohabitation lasted for more than five years, the requirement of the notarial cohabitation contract no longer applies.

7. Bequests to Charitable and Other Bodies

An exemption is applicable to acquisitions by charities that have been classified by the Dutch tax authorities. The charity can be classified if it serves the public benefit for more than 90 percent and satisfies further requirements. The law defines public benefit by mentioning 12 categories that qualify as such. Examples are culture, animal welfare, education, science, and research.

8. Gift Tax

Gift tax is imposed on the value of all that is acquired by gift from an individual who was living in the Netherlands at the time of the gift.

In respect of gift tax, two residence fictions apply:

1. A Dutch national who has lived in the Netherlands and makes a gift within ten years of having left his residence in the Netherlands is deemed to have lived in the Netherlands at the time of making the gift. Consequently, gift tax is imposed in the Netherlands on such a gift.
2. Anyone who has lived in the Netherlands and makes a gift within one year of having left his residence in the Netherlands is deemed to have lived in the Netherlands at the time of making the gift. This fictional provision only has consequences for a non-Dutch national who, after having lived in the Netherlands, makes a gift within one year of departure.

Dutch gift tax is also an acquisition tax. It is levied on what the donee acquires, if need be, after deduction of charges and liabilities benefiting either the donor or a third party. Both donations and gifts (e.g., a sale at too low a price) are taxable for Dutch gift tax purposes. Furthermore, the execution or a void gift, the satisfaction of a "natural obligation," and the preferential treatment by a stipulation to the benefit of a third party are considered gifts.

As of 2010 a new fiction/anti-abuse provision for gift tax was introduced. The Supreme Court ruled in 1986 that an immediately claimable, interest-free loan to a solvent debtor is not a gift. In practice such loans were often used. To prevent these situations, as of 2010 immediately claimable loans are considered a gift of the usufruct from day to day of the nominal value of the loan if and insofar as the loan bears an interest lower than 6 percent. The gift is considered at December 31 of each year. For example if a father grants his solvent son an immediately claimable loan of €100,000 on February 1, 2010, at an interest rate of 2 percent, the son is deemed to acquire a gift of €3,660.

Like inheritance tax, gift tax in principle is for the account of the beneficiary. In the event that gift tax has to be paid by the donor, the acquisition has to be grossed up taking exemption and rate into account.

9. Natural Obligations

A natural obligation is a non-enforceable obligation that is based according to social standards on an acceptable urgent moral obligation of one person to forward a performance to another person.

It may, for instance, exist between spouses or cohabitants. The starting point is that the satisfaction of a natural obligation is a gift and hence subject to gift tax. However, the acquisition of what serves to satisfy a natural obligation is exempted from gift tax. This system was set up in order to put the burden of proof in respect of the existence of the natural obligation with the taxpayer.

10. Cancellation of a Limited Right

The cancellation or renunciation of a limited right is also considered to be a taxable gift. As an example the case may be mentioned where the usufructuary renounces the usufruct during his lifetime. The principal party entitled to the property shall then pay gift tax.

For the purpose of valuation of that which is acquired by gift, reference is made to the remarks made about valuation in the event of inheritance tax. The same rules apply.

11. Exemptions and Rates

The most important exemptions prevailing for the levy of gift tax in 2013 are as follows:

a. Acquisitions by children from parents: €5,141. A one time increase of this exemption is allowed if the child is aged 18 or over but younger than 40 at the time of the gift. The increase is permitted up to an amount of (1) €24,676 or (2) €51,407 if the donation was made for the acquisition of a Dutch principal residence or for an education that is more expensive than average studies.
b. For others, €2,057.

Gifts made by or to two partners are added up for the levy of gift tax. For the purpose of the rates the closest relation between two parties (one donor and one donee) is taken as basis.

Gift tax rates equal inheritance tax rates.

12. Transfer Tax

Before 2010, transfer tax used to be due for acquisitions of situs assets by virtue of gift or by virtue of the law of succession from an individual who at the time of the gift or on his death was neither living, nor deemed to be living, in the Netherlands. Transfer tax was also an acquisition tax against the same rates as inheritance and gift tax. As of 2010, the Netherlands no longer levies transfer tax. The two main reasons for the abolition of transfer tax are (1) the (possible) contravention with EC regulations and (2) the fact that implementation costs were high but yields were low. As a consequence, the Netherlands is in the unique position that acquisitions of situs assets by virtue of gift or by virtue of the law of succession are entirely free of gift or inheritance tax provided that the deceased or donor is not a (deemed) tax resident of the Netherlands.

13. Special Provisions

In connection with the relationship between the deceased or the donor and the beneficiary, it is important to note that the IGTA 1956 provides that some equations take place. A natural child is put on par with a legitimate child of the mother; a natural child is put on par with a legitimate child of the father, if the father has recognized the child. Furthermore, relatives by marriage, registered partnership, or cohabitant partnership are put on par with blood relatives. If a relative by marriage, registered partnership, or cohabitant partnership inherits from a blood relative of his spouse/partner after the marriage, registered partnership, or cohabitant partnership is dissolved, the relative is only put on par with a blood relative if the marriage, registered partnership, or cohabitant partnership by which the equation was created is dissolved on the death of one of the spouses/partners. Furthermore, foster children are put on par with the legitimate children of the foster parents. A foster child is anyone who was maintained and raised exclusively by the foster parent or exclusively by the foster parent and his spouse together as their own child for a period of not less than five years before the foster child reaches the age of 21. Finally, minors under guardianship of two joint guardians are treated as children in family relationship to those guardians.

B. Formalities in Respect of the Levy of Inheritance Tax and Gift Tax

1. Inheritance Tax

Any acquisition taxed with inheritance tax or gift tax must be declared. Tax returns for inheritance tax must be filed with the competent tax inspector. The inspector sets the period within which the declaration for inheritance tax must be filed. This period may not expire sooner than eight months from the demise.

2. Gift Tax

Declarations for gift tax must be filed with the competent tax inspector. The inspector also sets the period within which the declaration for gift tax must be filed. This period may not expire sooner than two months from the gift. An exception applies in respect of gifts by parents to children after the end of the calendar year in which the gift was made.

3. Assessments

Inheritance and gift tax are levied by way of assessment. The tax inspector must impose the inheritance tax assessment within three years from the day of registration of the death certificate of the deceased at the Registrar of Births, Deaths, and Marriages of a Dutch municipality. The tax inspector must impose the gift tax assessment within three years from the day of registration of the death certificate of the deceased at the Registrar of Births, Deaths, and Marriages of a Dutch municipality of a gift tax declaration was filed this rule does not apply. The inspector may impose a provisional assessment, preceding the final one. The final assessment must be imposed before the three-year period has passed. If the term is passed, any taxes paid on the provisional assessment must be refunded, with interest.

The tax due may be paid in cash or by transferring to the state works of art that belong to the estate. Such works of art are only accepted if they are considered of Dutch cultural interest. When such transfer is made, the transfer will be considered payment of inheritance tax equal to 120 percent of the value of the objects.

4. Appeal

Objections against an assessment may be raised with the inspector within six weeks after the date of the assessment. If objections are raised, a request for extension of payment with the collector of taxes can be made. The decision of the tax inspector on the objection may be appealed to the District Court within six weeks from the date of the decision. Secondly, the decision of the District Court may be appealed to the Court of Appeal within six weeks from the date of the decision of the District Court, by sending a note of appeal to the Court of Appeal. Finally, within six weeks from the date of the decision of the Court of Appeal, an appeal may be lodged with the Supreme Court. Contrary to the District Court and the Court of Appeal, the Supreme Court will only deal with legal issues and will not deal with questions of fact.

C. The Taxation of Trusts

The recognition of the trust for Dutch civil law purposes was discussed earlier. One of the most important changes of the IGTA 1956 (and also the Personal Income Tax Act 2001) concerns the tax treatment of trusts. In this respect the term "segregated private wealth" has been introduced. For a better understanding, we will first give a brief description of the complicated position of the trust in the Dutch tax system before 2010. Second, we will discuss the applicable legislation for segregated private wealth as of 2010.

Prior to 2010 the trust was not specifically mentioned in Dutch tax law. There were some court decisions on trusts that provided a general guideline of the tax treatment. Also, the State Secretary of Finance had published a decree on trusts. In practice, the tax treatment of a trust was a very delicate matter, especially since they were treated by the Dutch tax authorities with a great deal of suspicion. The Dutch tax authorities strove to treat a trust as transparent and to allocate the assets either to the settlor or to the beneficiaries (for income tax and inheritance/gift tax purposes). The most important guidelines for the tax treatment of trusts had been created by court decisions of the Supreme Court of November 1998. It ruled that an irrevocable discretionary trust could be qualified as an independent fund (*doelvermogen*). Acquisitions by way of inheritance and gift by such a trust made by a Dutch resident deceased or donor were as such subject to the high inheritance and gift tax rates. Distributions from such a trust situated outside the Netherlands could be exempt from inheritance and gift tax. In practice a doctrine had developed that transfers of property into an irrevocable discretionary trust by persons resident outside the Netherlands could not be taxed for Dutch gift tax purposes.

Possible distributions from such a trust were considered to be non-taxable for Dutch gift tax as long as the trust was resident outside the Netherlands. The trust itself was (considered) taxable for Dutch corporate income tax purposes only if the trust directly operated a Dutch enterprise (permanent establishment) or owned 5 percent or more of the shares in a limited liability company based in the Netherlands. The possession of Dutch real estate is hereby considered an enterprise. If, however, investment portfolios and shares in foreign companies were held in trust, the trust could in principle not be liable to Dutch corporate income tax for (income arising from) these assets. Assets of revocable and fixed trusts were generally allocated to the settlor or the beneficiaries. The Dutch tax authorities tended to ignore the above-mentioned court decisions regarding irrevocable discretionary trusts and tried to allocate the assets to the settlor or the beneficiaries for income tax and inheritance and gift tax purposes.

As of January 1, 2010, the IGTA 1956 changed at several points. As mentioned, transfer tax was abolished under the IGTA 1956. The exemptions of the IGTA 1956 were raised and the rates were lowered. They now vary from 10 percent to 40 percent. Additionally, the legislature has introduced several additional measures to combat tax avoidance as well as provisions to regulate the tax treatment of inter alia the Anglo-American trust. One of these measures is the introduction of the concept of segregated private wealth (*afgezonderd particulier vermogen*), which is defined in the Personal Income Tax Act 2001.

The new provisions in Dutch tax law basically result in tax transparency of the Anglo-American trust vis-à-vis the settlor. Hence, the trust assets are deemed to still form part of the property of the settlor. The tax transparency of the Anglo-American trust means that the setting up of an Anglo-American trust followed by a transfer of assets to this trust by a (deemed) Dutch resident is in principle no longer a taxable event for the IGTA 1956. However, if the beneficiary receives a legally enforceable right with regard to the trustee, which for example is the case with a life interest trust, the beneficiary is directly enriched and Dutch gift or inheritance tax will be levied concerning the contribution to the trust if the settlor is a (deemed) Dutch resident. In case of a payment from the trust, a taxable transfer for the IGTA 1956 occurs if the person to whom the trust assets are allocated—in first instance the settlor—is a (deemed) Dutch resident, since a payment from the trust is a deemed transfer from the person to whom the trust assets are allocated to the beneficiary for Dutch tax purposes. Upon the death of the settlor the assets in trust will, for tax reasons only, be deemed to form part of the estate of the settlor. His heirs will be deemed to have acquired those assets and will have to pay inheritance tax accordingly if the settlor was at the time of his death a (deemed) resident of the Netherlands. In other words the allocation shifts from the settlor to his heirs. The allocation to the heirs is based on their share in the inheritance. The applicable inheritance tax rates depend on the relationship to the contributor.

Many learned writers have made objections against these allocation rules. The main objection is that the discretionary character of the trust is disregarded and that the allocation rules may cause imbalances. The State Secretary of Finance responded that if an heir can prove that he will never acquire distributions out of the trust, he will not be deemed to have inherited (part of) the assets and will therefore not be taxed. In some cases it may be extremely difficult for an heir to prove this.

An example may explain how the new rules work. Mr. X, a resident of the Netherlands, has set up an irrevocable discretionary trust under the laws of Jersey. A number of charitable organizations are beneficiaries of this trust. Upon his death Mr. X's last will stipulates that his estate will go to his three children in equal shares. Under general law the estate does not comprise the assets in trust. Under the new tax rules, however, the trust assets will be considered the property of Mr. X. During his lifetime he will have to pay income tax with regard to income arising out of these assets. Upon his death his heirs will be deemed to inherit the assets from Mr. X. Only if they can prove that they will never acquire distributions out of the trust can they escape taxation. This proof could be supplied by showing that the trust deed contains an exclusion clause that mentions that the three children can never be beneficiaries of the Jersey trust.

For someone to prove that he is not a beneficiary and can never become one, he at least has to present the following information to the Dutch tax authorities: a description of the kind of trust, the place of residence, the trust deed, the letter of wishes, the annual financial statements of the last three years, name and address of the settlor and other heirs, and all other documents that state that the heir is not a beneficiary of the trust and can never become a beneficiary of the trust. Usually the trustee is the one who holds most of this information. However, beneficiaries of an irrevocable discretionary trust in principle have limited rights with regard to obtaining information from the trustee. It could therefore be very difficult for an heir to obtain the necessary information to prove he is not a beneficiary. Fiscal transparency does not apply for personal income tax purposes if the trust itself is subject to taxation at a rate of at least 10 percent based on an equal taxable base as under Dutch tax law. The trust assets will then not be allocated to someone else. It should be noted, however, that this exception has no effect on the IGTA 1956 provisions.

Although the changes with regard to the tax treatment of trusts are quite drastic, the tax legislator did not create comprehensive transitional arrangements. The earlier described transparency rules do not apply insofar the settlor has died before January 11, 2010, the value of trust assets on April 20, 2009, does not exceed €5.000, and the trust assets do not comprise a substantial interest (i.e. more than 5 percent of the shares in a company). Given the relatively small scope of this transitional provision, it does not apply often. More important is the transitional provision that provides that the gift tax that was levied based on the judgments of the Supreme Court in 1998 in case of contributions to an irrevocable discretionary trust before January 1, 2010, can be deducted from the inheritance tax due taxed on the new transparency rules. Finally, if for existing trusts (trusts established before January 14, 2010) a transparency agreement was concluded with the tax authorities, this agreement remains applicable. The limited transitional law states that the fiscal acquisition price of enterprises and substantial shareholdings as per January 1, 2010, is valuated at the original acquisition price of the contributor. This means that upon a disposition of such assets after January 1, 2010, a positive difference between that original acquisition price and the fair market value may be taxed for Dutch personal income tax purposes.

D. Principles of Estate Planning

1. Introduction

This section presents some options that are open to the taxpayer in order to reduce liability to inheritance tax in particular. Where relevant, attention will be given to income tax.

2. Avoidance of Dutch Inheritance Tax

As described above, inheritance tax is due in the Netherlands if property passes by virtue of the law of succession from an individual who on his death was living in the Netherlands or from a Dutch national who died as a resident abroad but who had been a resident of the Netherlands less than ten years. An individual may therefore avoid inheritance tax being due in the Netherlands in respect of the passing of his estate by ceasing to be resident in the Netherlands. To achieve that he must have been away from the Netherlands on his death for more than ten years or must have lost Dutch nationality prior to his death, while living abroad.

An individual having a nationality other than Dutch may avoid the levy of Dutch inheritance tax in respect of the passing of his estate by giving up his residence in the Netherlands. Then, even if he dies one week after having left the Netherlands, no inheritance tax will be levied in the Netherlands.

It must be noted that particularity during recent years, many wealthy Dutch nationals have left the Netherlands for tax reasons. Often cited are

- the high rate of Dutch income tax (maximum 52 percent); and
- Dutch tax on savings and investments (30 percent).

Dutch inheritance and gift tax usually only plays a minor part in the decision to abandon residence in the Netherlands, given the fact that in principle a person must wait another ten years before escaping those levies.

Many wealthy Dutch nationals have emigrated to Belgium in the past few years. Their most important fiscal motive used to be that by living in Belgium for a period of ten years after having left the Netherlands, one is able to dispose of one's shares forming a substantial shareholding without being liable to Dutch tax. Another important reason is that a Dutch national who has lived in Belgium for ten years can start making gifts from hand to hand in respect of which no gift tax is due in Belgium. After those ten years, gift tax is not imposed in the Netherlands either, as described above. After a large portion of the property has been given away from hand to hand, little stands in the way of a return to the Netherlands.

Other countries that attract much attention from Dutch nationals as potential countries of residence—albeit less than Belgium—are Curacao, the United Kingdom, Switzerland, and Monaco. To save inheritance and/or gift tax, emigration by Dutch citizens to Curacao is of particular interest. The inheritance and gift tax rates in Curacao are much lower than in the Netherlands. In Curacao the maximum rate applicable to inheritances by and gifts to the spouse and children is 6 percent. According to a tax agreement between the Netherlands, the Netherlands Antilles, and Aruba (the *Belastingregeling voor het Koninkrijk*), the ten-year period of the Dutch Inheritance Tax Act 1956 as discussed above is not applicable with regard to Dutch citizens who are resident in Curacao. If an emigrant dies shortly after having moved from the Netherlands to Curacao, no Dutch inheritance tax will be levied and the estate will only be taxed in Curacao. With respect to gifts, Dutch gift tax will be levied in addition to the gift tax in Curacao if a Dutch emigrant who is a resident of Curacao makes a gift within one year after having left the Netherlands. After this one-year period, gift tax will be levied in Curacao only. It should be noted, however, that the Netherlands and Curacao are preparing a new bilateral arrangement. Under this arrangement the country of former residence of the deceased or donor has a subsidiary taxing right for a period of five years from the moment the deceased or donor gave up residence in that country. If a Dutch resident emigrates to Curacao and dies there within five years of leaving the Netherlands, the Netherlands may tax the estate of the ex-resident, but it must give relief with regard to the tax levied in Curacao. It is expected that this bilateral arrangement will come into force on January 1, 2014.

E. Ways to Reduce Dutch Inheritance Tax

1. Law of Matrimonial Property: Statutory Community of Property

If spouses make no marriage contract, full community of property arises from marriage. Spouses are equally entitled to such community. If the community is dissolved for whatever reason, each spouse shall be entitled to 50 percent of the community.

If a community of property is dissolved on the death of one of the spouses, half of the community belongs to the surviving spouse by virtue of the law of matrimonial property. The other half of the community forms the deceased's estate. Inheritance tax is only levied in respect of the passing of the estate.

For reasons of succession, it may serve to be married in full community of property. The total assets of the spouses then pass in two halves; one half on the death of one of the spouses and the other half on the death of the surviving spouse. This means that exemptions from inheritance tax and the build-up of the bracket system can be used twice.

2. Cancellation of Marriage Contract

Spouses frequently cancel the marriage contract made before their marriage, so that the full community of property is created. If spouses are married under a marriage contract containing the exclusion of each community of property (i.e., separate property), it is often the case that one of the spouses has amassed assets while the other spouse has little or no property. If in that case the wealthier spouse dies, inheritance tax is levied in respect of the passing of his entire estate. If the poorer spouse dies first, little or nothing passes and no or a small amount of inheritance tax is imposed. If during the marriage the spouses cancel the marriage contract initially made, the property, as said, passes in two halves, which may entail a considerable saving of inheritance tax.

The disadvantage of cancelling a marriage contract is that, if the initially poorer spouse is to die first after the cancellation, inheritance tax is due that would not have been due at that time had the spouse maintained their marriage contract. Hence a liquidity disadvantage occurs. However, the advantage of spread out acquisitions as far as inheritance tax is concerned usually balances out this disadvantage.

By cancelling the marriage contract, the spouse who had fewer assets prior to the cancellation seems to be enriched. After all, after the cancellation the spouses are equally entitled to the entire property and upon dissolution of the community they are entitled to 50 percent each. In respect of this cancellation, no gift tax is imposed. This was confirmed several times by the Supreme Court. According to the Supreme Court, no definitive shifting of value is effected by the cancellation of the marriage contract because the final result at the end of the marriage is unknown, which means that no gift takes place. In a decree, the State Secretary of Finance has meanwhile also confirmed the Supreme Court decision.

3. Addition of Provisions to Marriage Contract

If spouses are married in community of property, half of the property also passes to each spouse in the event of divorce. This may prevent the wealthier spouse from cancelling the marriage contract. The inheritance tax consequences for a community of property may, however, also be attained by adding a final netting covenant to the marriage contract—containing the exclusion of each community of property—to the effect that, only if the marriage should be dissolved on the death of one of the spouses, settlement must take place as if entire community of property had existed. The result of this netting covenant is that on the death of a spouse, a distribution must be made out of the property of the wealthier spouse in favor of the property of the poorer spouse. If the wealthier spouse dies first, no inheritance tax is imposed on the distribution in favor of the property of the poorer spouse. Levy of inheritance tax then takes place on the property of the deceased spouse after deduction of the distribution. The tax benefits only apply if the covenant is obligatory and reciprocal. Therefore, it must always be operative on the death of a spouse, even if the poorer spouse dies first. The liquidity disadvantage described above in case of community of property may therefore also occur in the netting covenant.

If the netting covenant only operates in the event that the wealthier spouse dies first, inheritance tax will be imposed in respect of the acquisition of the distribution arising from such covenant. The same applies if the covenant is unilateral. Furthermore, a distribution under a netting covenant is also taxed with inheritance tax, if the covenant is indeed reciprocal but gives the right to demand settlement and thus is not obligatory.

4. Accrual of Interest on Children's Claims

As discussed above in the case of the statutory division, the surviving spouse obtains all the assets, while the children obtain a pecuniary claim against the spouse. According to the law of inheritance, such a claim will only be interest bearing once the statutory interest exceeds 6 percent. Therefore, currently, no interest will be payable. In order to optimize the inheritance tax advantage, a 6 percent compound interest can be stipulated on the claim.

An example may clarify the effect of such interest in the case of a statutory division.

Example

Suppose that spouses are married in the statutory community of property. The value of the community is 200. The couple has three children. If the husband dies, half of the dissolved matrimonial community of property belongs to the surviving spouse. The other half of the dissolved community forms the deceased's estate. The surviving spouse is 55 years old upon the death of her husband. Under the rules of the inheritance law, the surviving spouse and the children are each entitled to an equal part of the estate, i.e., one quarter. Under the statutory division, the entire estate is partitioned to the surviving spouse and the children get a claim on the surviving spouse in the amount of their portion, i.e., 25. The surviving spouse and the children are taxed with inheritance tax on an amount of 25. Let us presume that the deceased has stipulated in his last will that the surviving spouse has to pay a compound interest to the children of 6 percent. If the surviving spouse dies ten years after the deceased and the claims of the children have not been redeemed, the claims shall on the death of the surviving spouse have accrued to 44.7. These claims are deducted from the property of the surviving spouse, so that the surviving spouse's estate on balance is 65.9 (200 - (3 x 44.7)). On the death of the surviving spouse, inheritance tax is therefore only due on this 65.9.

In this example it is assumed that the value of the property remains the same between the death of the one spouse and the death of the surviving spouse, if the value of such property appreciates during that period the inheritance tax situation becomes less favorable. The value appreciation after all entirely benefits the surviving spouse. If the value of the property has appreciated to 150 percent, the inheritance tax due on the death of the surviving spouse is calculated on 165.9 (300 - (3 x 44.7)).

5. Limitation of Surviving Spouse's Portion

In order to enhance the effect of inheritance tax on the statutory division, the surviving spouse's portion from the estate of the deceased may be diminished, causing an increase of the children's portion. In any case, a certain portion must pass to the survivor, because otherwise a partitioning between spouse and children cannot be made. If in the example given the portion of the surviving spouse were to be limited to 1 percent, the claims of the children would on the death of the deceased become 33 per child. After ten years these claims will have accrued to 59.09. Taking into account the appreciation of the assets to 150 percent at the time of the death of the surviving spouse, the survivor's estate would then be 122.73 (300 - (3 x 59.09)).

Against the inheritance tax advantage arising as a result of the limitation of the survivor's portion, there may be a disadvantage on the death of the deceased. The result of the limitation of the portion may be that on the death of the deceased, the exemption of inheritance tax and the build-up of the bracket system prevailing for the surviving spouse cannot be used to full advantage. The inheritance tax disadvantage on the death of the deceased must be weighted against the inheritance tax advantage on the death of the surviving spouse.

6. Last Will: The Usufruct Last Will

Another form of last will thatis frequently made by Dutch testators in order to ensure that the surviving spouse in any case continues to have the control of the entire estate on the death of the deceased is the usufruct last will. In this last will the children are appointed as the sole heirs (the surviving spouse is usually excluded as heir) and the usufruct of the children's portions is bequeathed and devised to the surviving spouse. The surviving spouse as usufructuary has the authority to manage the estate of the deceased, to use it, and to enjoy its proceeds. The usufructuary may also be granted the authority to dispose of the property encumbered with usufruct independently. The usufructuary does not need the assistance of the principal parties entitled (the bare owners) for important decisions with respect to such property. The usufructuary may, in addition, be granted authority to consume the property encumbered with usufruct.

7. The Usufruct Last Will: Levy of Inheritance Tax

As regards the levy of inheritance tax, the rule is that on the death of one of the spouses, inheritance tax is imposed on the surviving spouse in respect of his acquiring the right of usufruct and on the children in respect of their acquiring property, encumbered with the right of usufruct (bare ownership). A clause can be provided in the last will, to the effect that all inheritance tax must be paid out of the estate. On the other hand, the IGTA 1956 provides that anyone to whom property is passed under encumbrance of usufruct passed under the same estate may demand that any inheritance tax due in respect of his portion is paid out of the property encumbered with usufruct or is advanced free of interest by the usufructuary. This provision does not apply if the testator has made other arrangements in his last will for the payment of inheritance tax.

For purposes of inheritance tax, the advantage of a usufruct last will is that no inheritance tax is due when the usufruct expires on the death of the usufructuary. On the demise of the usufructuary, the bare ownership of the children's property accrues to full ownership.

The result of the fact that no inheritance tax is due in respect of the expiry of the usufruct is that the value appreciation of the property encumbered with usufruct between the time of death of one of the spouses and that of the surviving spouse remains outside the levy of the inheritance tax. This may result in considerable inheritance tax advantages.

If, in the example given when discussing the statutory division, a usufruct last will had been made, on the death of a spouse inheritance tax would also be imposed on 100. If the valuation appreciation of the property between the time of death of a spouse and that of the surviving spouse takes place solely in the property encumbered with usufruct (say its value increases from 100 to 150 while the property belonging to the surviving spouse keeps a value of 100), then the levy of inheritance tax is limited on the death of the surviving spouse to the levy in respect of the passing of the latter 100. In connection with the above, it is recommended that goods should be encumbered with usufruct, which may be expected to increase in value following the death of one of the spouses. To that effect, one could consider such action with regard to the personal dwelling or shares in a private company with limited liability.

If shares in a private company with limited liability are accommodated under the property encumbered with usufruct, the effect is not just that the value appreciation of those shares remains outside the levy of inheritance tax, but it also results in the usufructuary being able to withdraw property from the company, should his sustenance so require. The testator will, after all, usually have granted the usufructuary the voting rights in the shares. Consequently, the usufructuary may decide to have the dividend distributed on the shares. This dividend in general belongs to the usufructuary for his free use. If the usufructuary should not need to withdraw property from the company because his sustenance is provided for in a different manner, dividend distribution will not be forthcoming. The value of the shares will increase as a consequence, and this value appreciation remains, as said, outside the levy of inheritance tax.

8. Gifts

As described above, the rates for inheritance tax also apply to gift tax. By making gifts on a regular basis, exemptions for gift tax and the build up of the bracket system can be employed several times.

If a testator were to leave €500,000 to his child in 2013, he would pay €84,267 in inheritance tax on such amount. Had the testator given an annual sum of €50,000 for five years preceding his death, gift tax would have to be paid in the amount of €4,485 in respect of each gift and the inheritance tax on the acquisition under the law of inheritance of the child (in the amount of €250,000) would be €34,267. The aggregate amount of gift tax and inheritance tax in this set-up is €56,692. Hence the saving is €27,575. Since gift tax is due at an earlier date than inheritance tax, there is a certain liquidity disadvantage. (All calculations are based on 2013 rates.)

Gifts can, of course, be made by transferring cash and other goods. Another possible arrangement is that goods are transferred to the donee at a real purchase price and that such purchase price remains due to the donor. The donor may then periodically discharge part of the debt due by the donee. In that way exemptions for gift tax and the build up of the bracket system can be employed several times. In the event that the donor, at the time of making the gift, does not have the required liquid means to make such gifts or he wishes to keep the given property in his possession, gifts may be made by way of admission of indebtedness. The admission of indebtedness means that the donor acknowledges a debt to the donee. This indebtedness becomes exigible only in agreed upon cases, the most important of which is the donor's death. The donated amount is subject to gift tax. It is safe to make an admission of indebtedness by notarial deed. In addition, the donor must pay the donee 6 percent interest on the amount he admitted to owe. This interest must actually be paid and may not be added to the debt. If the interest is not actually and annually paid, the amount admitted to owe will—if it has not been redeemed at the time of death of the donor—still be taxed with inheritance tax. The objective of the admission of indebtedness—i.e., spreading out the acquisitions by the donee in order to make use of exemptions for gift tax and the build up of the bracket system several times—is then not achieved. If inheritance tax is imposed on the amount admitted to be owed, the gift tax paid in the past at the time of the admission of indebtedness may be deducted from the inheritance tax.

9. Life Insurance Policies

As described above, payments from life insurance policies that are paid as a result of or on the death of the deceased are subject to inheritance tax by virtue of a fiction provision of the IGTA 1956. However, the levy of inheritance tax on these payments remains forthcoming if nothing has been withdrawn from the deceased's property to obtain the benefit. If the deceased did not contribute at all to the premiums due on the policy, but these premiums were debited to the account of the person entitled to the benefit of a third party, no inheritance tax shall be due on the payments. In the event that a person (the policyholder) takes out a life insurance policy on the life of another person (the insured) and the policyholder himself pays the premiums and designates himself as beneficiary of the benefit, levy of inheritance tax on the benefit remains forthcoming.

If the policyholder does not have the necessary means to pay the premiums, these may be donated to him by the insured. The benefit from the policy will then still remain outside the levy of inheritance tax. This has been decided by the Supreme Court. However, gift tax is due on the amounts donated by the insured to the policyholder to enable him to pay the premiums.

F. Business Succession

1. Inheritance and Gift Tax Facilities

In the case of a business succession (either by means of a gift or by means of inheritance), the IGTA 1956 provides for three main facilities:

1. The difference between the liquidation value of a business and the value as a going concern can be tax exempt conditionally.
2. The first €1,028,132 of the value as a going concern and 83 percent of the excess above the first €1,028,132 of the value as a going concern can be tax exempt conditionally.
3. For the remaining tax on the 17 percent of the remaining value as a going concern, a conditional extension for payment for a period of ten years can be obtained.

The first and second facility are conditional exemptions in the inheritance or gift tax assessment. The third facility is part of a separate conditional tax assessment.

All three facilities are conditional and upon request of the acquirer. The main condition is that the business must be continued for a period of five years after the gift or death of the deceased. For gifts, the donor also must have carried on the business for his own account for at least five years preceding the gift. For acquisitions by way of inheritance, the deceased must have carried on the business for his own account for at least one year. If the business is discontinued within the five-year period, as a whole or partially, the facilities are taken back as a whole or partially and taxes will be collected. If the five-year period is fulfilled, the conditional exemption(s) will become unconditional. The assessment for the taxable conserved value becomes claimable at the latest after a period of ten years. This last assessment is interest bearing during the ten-year period of the extension for payment. The conditional exemptions are not interest bearing.

For purposes of the above-mentioned facilities, business property consists of the following categories:

- privately owned business property;
- privately owned participations in (tax transparent) limited partnerships. An additional requirement is that the participation in the limited partnership must, as a business succession, have emanated from a privately owned business that has been run for the account of the deceased/donor. The business successor must in that case be general partner in the limited partnership;
- business property owned through a substantial interest in the form of common shares in a limited liability company that runs a business; and
- business property owned through a substantial interest in the form of preferential shares in a limited liability company that runs a business. An additional requirement is that the preferential shares must, as a business succession, have emanated from a regular shareholding in that limited liability company. The business successor must in that case already hold a substantial interest in the form of common shares in that limited liability company.

In the case of a limited liability company, there is often a structure with a holding company and several operating companies. The business property of the operating companies will in that case need to be allocated to the holding company. This allocation (consolidation) is allowed if a private shareholder indirectly holds a substantial (greater than or equal to 5 percent) interest in the operating company. Often, a company structure not only holds business assets but also holds excess cash or portfolio investments. For purposes of the IGTA 1956, the non-business assets may be taken into account for the business succession facilities up to a maximum amount equal to 5 percent of the value of the business assets owned by such company. If the value of the non-business assets exceeds this 5 percent, the excess value will be taxed according to the general rules. In practice, the question of whether or not an activity is a business activity is a question of fact. This question may lead to difficult discussions with the Dutch tax authorities, especially in the case of (the renting out of) real estate.

It should be noted that if the statutory division applies to business assets, then the claim on the surviving spouse does not qualify as a business asset. The business succession facilities do not apply to that acquisition. Therefore, a careful examination of the testamentary dispositions in the case of business assets is required. However, should the statutory division apply, Dutch tax law provides for a 10-year interest-bearing extension for payment for the inheritance tax due in respect of the claim acquired.

Lastly, a brief remark about whether or not the business succession facilities are contrary to the principle of equality because the (partial) exemption only applies to business property and not to private property. Currently there is a lawsuit pending dealing with this issue. The District Court of Breda granted the claim to the business exemption for private property based on this principle. The Dutch tax authorities have, as expected, lodged an appeal against this decision. The impact of this decision completely depends on the outcome of the appeal. It is possible that in the end it will have negative consequences for family businesses.

2. Personal Income Tax Facilities

The transfer of privately owned business assets by means of inheritance or gift in principle constitutes a taxable cessation of that business taxable against the progressive income tax rates (maximum 52 percent). The Personal Income Tax Act 2001 allows the heirs to continue the business with the acquisition price of the deceased upon request; in the case of a gift of (part of) the business, the successor can also continue with the acquisition value of the donor, provided that the successor had worked in the business as an employee for a minimum period of 36 months immediately preceding the gift or had formed a joint venture with the donor and was entitled to a share in the profits for at least 36 months immediately preceding the gift. In both cases the income tax claim on the business assets is passed on to the business successors. For business assets held through a substantial interest in a limited liability company, a transfer by means of inheritance or gift constitutes a taxable transfer taxable at a 25 percent rate. The Personal Income Tax Act 2001 provides for facilities in the case of an inheritance or gift. Both facilities only apply if and insofar as the limited liability company runs a business. Therefore, they do not apply if and insofar as the limited liability company owns excess cash or portfolio investments. As mentioned for the business succession facilities in the IGTA 1956, the definition of business is a matter of fact and can lead to discussions with the Dutch tax authorities, especially in the case of the renting out of real estate. The heirs/donees can continue with the acquisition price of the shares of the deceased and can as such take over the claim. For the facility in the case of a gift, an additional requirement is that the donee has worked (as an employee) for the limited liability company for a minimum period of three years preceding the gift. The latter requirement does not apply in the case of the acquisition by way of inheritance.

G. Tax Planning

To illustrate the foregoing, the following example is given in which several of the subjects discussed are combined in order to create optimal estate planning.

Example

A couple with children is married under a separate property regime. The property, mainly consisting of shares in a private company with limited liability, belongs for the main part to one of the spouses.

If, in this example, no estate planning measures were taken, the property would pass in one lump on the death of the spouse owning the bulk of the property. It is likely that if that spouse dies before the other spouse, the full ownership of part of the property must pass to the surviving spouse, so that such spouse gets the free disposal of any property. On the death of the surviving spouse, property passes again, so that once more inheritance tax is levied on that property. The spouses may decide to cancel their marriage settlement, thereby creating full community of property. By doing so they ensure that the property passes in two halves, so that use can be made twice of the exemptions for inheritance tax and the progression of the bracket system. Furthermore, under this arrangement it is less likely that on the death of one of the spouses the full ownership of property from his estate must pass to the surviving spouse. Afterall, the surviving spouse retains half of the community of property by virtue of the law of matrimonial property. Finally, the spouses may during life make periodic gifts to the children, in order to ensure by spreading the disposals that the exemptions for gift tax and the progression of the bracket system can be used several times.

The spouses make a usufruct last will. The surviving spouse acquires the usufruct of the estate by virtue of the last will and has the free use of it. The children acquire the bare ownership of the estate. For the payment of inheritance tax that is due in connection with the passing of the deceased's property, use can be made of the business succession facilities and/or the facilities for income tax. On the death of the surviving spouse, his/her own property will form the estate. Inheritance tax is paid on the property so passing. On the death of the surviving spouse inheritance tax is not levied on the accretion of the bare ownership of the children to full ownership as a consequence of the ending of the right of usufruct. As such, any value appreciation of the property subject to usufruct is free of inheritance tax.

It is self-evident that the foregoing is only a general example. Depending on the circumstances, other courses can be taken to achieve optimum estate planning.

H. Anti-Tax Avoidance

Various IGTA 1956 provisions aimed at avoiding taxation were discussed above. First, attention can be drawn to the residence fiction for inheritance and gift tax. In that way, avoidance of taxation is prevented, owing to the fact that a (Dutch) deceased or donor leaves the Netherlands shortly before he dies or makes the gift and takes up residence in a state with a more favorable inheritance or gift tax climate. Secondly, fiction provisions apply for inheritance tax. Under these fiction provisions, certain acquisitions that take place after or as a result of the death of the testator are taxed with inheritance tax, even though strictly speaking they are not acquisitions under the law of succession. The fiction provisions prevent the avoidance of the levy of inheritance tax by legal acts during an individual's lifetime.

1. *Fraus legis* and Due Levy

Furthermore, in Dutch tax law there are two doctrines on the prevention of tax avoidance. The first doctrine is called *fraus legis* (abuse of law). The doctrine of *fraus legis* is applicable if a(n artificial) course of action was followed with the apparent intention of tax avoidance. An apparent intention of tax avoidance is presumed to exist if the course of action, when fiscal consequences are left out, would result in a deficit. If *fraus legis* is accepted, taxes are levied as if the normal course had been followed instead of the other course. The second doctrine is called due levy that, unlike the *fraus legis*, has a legal basis. The relevant provision of the law says,

> For the levy of direct taxes no allowance is made for legal acts of which, by virtue of the fact that their objective was not a substantial change of actual relations, or by virtue of other specific facts and circumstances, it must be assumed that they would not have been done, if that would have made the levy of the tax henceforth in whole or in part impossible.

Should the tax authorities wish to apply the due levy doctrine, then the Minister of Finance must grant prior authorization; in practice, the doctrine of due levy is of little importance. The difference between the two doctrines is mainly of a theoretical nature. Since inheritance and gift tax are not direct taxes, due levy cannot be used in any case in respect of these taxes. The doctrine of *fraus legis* is not applied often in connection with inheritance and gift tax. It is invoked regularly, however, in connection with the levy of personal income and corporate income tax.

I. Double Taxation Relief

In connection with the prevention of international double taxation in the field of inheritance and gift tax, the following regulations are relevant to the Netherlands:

a. In respect of inheritance tax, the Netherlands has entered into double taxation conventions with Switzerland (1951), Sweden (1952), Finland (1954), Israel (1974), the United States (1969), the United Kingdom (1979), and Austria (2001). Only the conventions with the United Kingdom and Austria contain regulations for gift taxation. An inheritance tax treaty with France was initiated in 1991, but since then has not been signed and has not entered into force.
b. The Taxation Regulations for the Kingdom (*Belastingregeling voor het Koninkrijk*), to which the Netherlands, Curacao, and Aruba are currently still bound, is a state act that contains, inter alia, regulations for the avoidance of double taxation in the areas of acquisitions under the law of inheritance and gifts.
c. The decree on prevention of double taxation 2001 is a unilateral measure to prevent double taxation. It contains inter alia a regulation for inheritance and gift tax. The decree becomes applicable if prevention of double taxation has not been provided for in any other way.

1. Conventions

In conventions for the prevention of double inheritance and gift taxation, the influence of the OECD Estate and Inheritance Draft Model Convention (1966) and the OECD Estate, Inheritance and Gift Model Convention (1982) is usually evident. For the inheritance conventions entered into by the Netherlands, this is, however, only the case to a limited extent. In respect of the conventions with Switzerland (1951), Sweden (1952), and Finland (1954), this is not surprising. These conventions were concluded before the first model convention materialized. The convention with the United States dates back to 1969 and shows traces of the 1966 model. Nevertheless the convention deviates from that model on many points. The convention with Israel (1974) follows the 1966 convention model in broad outline. The convention with the United Kingdom (1979) shows an anticipation of the working of the model convention of 1982, but this convention, too, shows deviations from that model. The convention with Austria (2001) is based on the model convention of 1982 but shows certain differences.

2. Decree for Prevention of Double Taxation of 2001

By virtue of the decree for prevention of double taxation of 2001, a relief of Dutch inheritance tax is granted for inheritance tax imposed abroad on foreign situs goods, such as goods belonging to the property of foreign enterprises and immovable property situated abroad. The relief is based on the ordinary credit method. It is the amount of the foreign taxation (limited to the amount of the Dutch inheritance tax) that can be attributed to the foreign situs goods.

The decree provides a special regulation in the event that Dutch inheritance tax is imposed in connection with the residence fiction of the Dutch IGTA 1956. In this case a relief is also granted based on the ordinary credit method.

If neither of the regulations can be used and inheritance tax is also imposed abroad in respect of goods affected by Dutch inheritance tax, a relief is granted in the sense that the foreign tax may be deducted from the value of the acquisition.

Relief is computed for each individual recipient. The provisions concerning the relief of inheritance tax are applicable *mutatis mutandis* to gift tax.

J. Enforcement and Exchange of Information

The collection of inheritance and gift tax has already been discussed above. By virtue of the law, every individual is required to furnish the tax inspector with any data and information demanded by him that may be relevant to him for the purpose of taxation. In addition, every individual is required to surrender books and other documents, cognizance of which may be relevant to establish the facts that may affect taxation in his respect, for inspection to the inspector on demand.

Such obligations apply to any person other than the probable taxpayer, if matters of that other person are considered as relevant to the tax position of the person who is probably taxable. The requirements apply further to persons or bodies not resident in the Netherlands having interest of over 50 percent in a company established in the Netherlands whose capital or part of it is divided into shares, unless the relevant person or the relevant body is resident, or established in a Member State of the European Communities, a country with which the Netherlands has entered into a convention for the avoidance of double taxation in which an adequate provision concerning the giving of information has been incorporated, or the Netherlands Antilles and Aruba.

All inheritance conventions entered into by the Netherlands (with the exception of the convention with Switzerland) contain a provision on the basis of which the authorities of the parties to the conventions can exchange information that is relevant to the levy of inheritance tax. Also, the conventions that were entered into to prevent double taxation on income, property, and corporation tax usually contain an analogous provision. Furthermore, exchange of information can take place on the basis of the Directives of the Council of the European Communities.

The Dutch Act on international assistance in taxation provides further rules concerning the exchange of information. According to the legal provisions, the Dutch tax authorities may only furnish taxation relevant information at the request of a competent authority of another State, after having notified the person in whose respect a request for information was made (the interested party) in writing of its decision to furnish information. The interested party may appeal against this decision to the District Court. If urgent reasons so require, the information may be furnished before the interested party is so notified.

More recently the Netherlands has signed many exchange of information agreements relating to tax matters. These agreements have mainly been signed with tax havens such as Andorra, the British Virgin Islands, the Cayman Islands, the Cook Islands, Guernsey, Isle of Man, Jersey, Liechtenstein, St. Lucia, and Uruguay.

THE INHERITANCE AND GIFT TAX TREATMENT OF ANGLO-AMERICAN TRUSTS IN ITALY

Stefano Guiso Gallisay

I. Introduction

Italy is one of the few countries that ratified the 1985 Hague Convention on the law applicable to trusts and their recognition (the Convention).[1] Because of the Convention, Italy generally recognizes Anglo-America trusts. However, so that Italian courts do not invalidate or disregard a trust, the parties should make sure the trust deed complies with the applicable laws and does not contain terms and conditions that are contrary to Italian mandatory, public policy provisions.

Despite initial uncertainties and conflicting interpretations, the tax treatment of trusts is now, for the most part, sufficiently regulated. In addition to specific tax provisions, tax authorities have issued a number of guidelines and rulings. Furthermore, scholars and court cases have contributed to clarifying the taxation of trusts.

This section summarizes the inheritance and gift tax treatment of Anglo-America trusts in Italy. In addition, it briefly summarizes the income tax treatment of income arising from a trust and distributed or accrued to the beneficiaries.

II. Taxation

Italian tax law defines, and taxes accordingly, several steps during the life span of a trust, including (1) creating a trust, (2) conveying assets to a trust, (3) producing and distributing income to the beneficiaries, and (4) distributing the corpus to the beneficiaries.

A. Creating a Trust

In the event the settlor creates a trust with a notarial deed, and provided the trust deed does not convey assets in trust but limits itself to creating a trust, there is only a registration tax of EUR 168. If the settlor creates a trust with a will, there is no registration tax.

1. Law, Oct. 16, 1989, No. 364 (entered into force Jan. 1, 1992).

B. Conveying Assets to a Trust

The conveyance of Italian situs assets to a trust (whether by deed during the lifetime of the settlor or by will) may be subject to the following taxes:

- Estate and gift taxes, at rates varying according to the value of the assets conveyed in trust and the family relationship, if any, between the settlor and the beneficiary. Because of certain exemptions and exclusions, discussed below, not all conveyances are necessarily subject to estate and gift taxes;
- Mortgage and cadastral transfer tax at a combined rate of 3 percent. Mortgage and cadastral transfer tax applies only in the event of real estate conveyed in trust; and
- Income tax and value-added tax in the event the settlor is a business, and the assets conveyed in trust form part of the business. Here, the conveyance of assets to a trust may be treated as a transaction giving rise to recognition of gain.

Certain conveyances or assets are *not* subject to the estate and gift tax, including:

- Conveyances of assets not exceeding the threshold of EUR 1 million for each beneficiary, provided the beneficiary is specifically named and is a first-line descendant of the settlor. However, if the conveyance includes real estate, a combined 3 percent mortgage and cadastral transfer tax may still apply. Physically disabled beneficiaries have larger exclusion and family-relationship thresholds.
- Conveyances of controlling equity interests of companies (i.e., stocks and quotas) and unincorporated businesses (*aziende* and *rami d'azienda*), provided that: (1) the beneficiary, who must be named in the trust deed, is part of the immediate family (e.g., spouse, children, and first-degree relatives) of the settlor; (2) the trust has a term of at least five years; (3) the trust is not discretionary or revocable; and (4) the trustee keeps control of the transferred company or business or carries on the business for at least five years from the date of the conveyance.
- Conveyances to trusts whose beneficiaries are nonprofit entities or charities (including foreign charities subject to reciprocity); state, local government agencies, or political parties; and
- Conveyances of life insurances and social security proceeds, cars, artistic or "*cultural*" assets, government bonds.

Certain types of trusts (e.g., trusts to administer and manage assets in bankruptcy procedures and blind trusts) are not created with the purposes of gifting or bequeathing property. Therefore, the best view is that conveyance of assets to these types of commercial trusts should not be subject to estate and gift taxes.

Estate tax rates vary according to the value of the corpus and the degree of family relationship among the settlor and the beneficiaries, as follows:

- Direct ascendants and descendants (e.g., spouses, children, parents, grandparents, grandchildren): 4 percent on the value of the corpus exceeding EUR 1 million for each beneficiary;
- Brothers and sisters: 6 percent of the value of the corpus exceeding EUR 100,000 for each beneficiary;
- Collateral relatives (e.g., nieces and nephews, cousins, and other relatives of up to the forth degree): 6 percent;
- Others: 8 percent. The 8 percent rate applies to conveyances to trusts whose beneficiaries are not relatives of the settlor, or to trusts whose beneficiaries are unnamed or not identifiable by family relationship with the settlor.

In addition, if the conveyance includes real estate, there is a combined 3 percent mortgage and cadastral transfer tax.

C. Producing Income

1. Financial Income

Under Italian law, most financial type of income (e.g., interest, dividends, capital gains) is subject to a flat withholding tax, and neither the settlor, the trust, nor the beneficiaries have any additional filing obligations. However, special tax treatment may apply to certain types of financial income, and the trust and/or the beneficiaries may have filing obligations.

2. Other Income

With respect to other types of income, Italian tax law provides that either the settlor, the trust, or the beneficiaries are taxed, depending on the facts.

In the event the beneficiaries are specifically named, and provided they have the right to demand and receive distribution of income, then the trust is generally treated as a pass-through entity, and the beneficiaries (and not the trust) are taxed, on an accrual basis, at the beneficiaries' individual income tax rates.

In the event the beneficiaries of the trust are not named (e.g., secret trusts or purpose trusts), or in the event the trust accumulates income, the trust (and not the beneficiaries) is subject to corporate income tax, currently at the 27.50 percent income tax rate, plus regional and local taxes, if applicable.

In the event of grantor trusts or revocable trusts, tax authorities take the position that the trust is not a separate tax entity from the settlor, and thus the settlor (and not the trust) should be taxed on the income of the trust.

D. Distributing the Corpus to the Beneficiaries

The subsequent conveyance of the corpus from the trust to the beneficiaries is not taxed, even if the value of the corpus increases from the time of the original conveyance until the time of final distribution. The ratio, of course, is that the tax was already paid at the time of the conveyance from the settlor to the trust. However, in the event of distribution of real estate to the beneficiaries, a 3 percent combined mortgage and cadastral transfer tax is still due.

E. Residency Issues

Under Italian tax law, and subject to the tax rules indicated above, a resident trust is generally taxed on its worldwide income, while a nonresident trust is taxed only on the income sourced in Italy.

In general, the normal corporate residency rules are applicable to trusts, subject to certain special trust residency rules. Under these rules, trusts are deemed resident in Italy when, for most of the year, they have in Italy either: (1) the legal seat or registered office; (2) the place of management; or (3) the main business purpose. Special rules may apply if the trust holds controlling interests in Italian companies. In addition, special rules apply if a trust is created in a jurisdiction that does not have an exchange of information agreement with Italy (i.e., non-white list jurisdiction). In those cases, the trust will be deemed resident, until proved otherwise, if (1) at least one settlor and at least one beneficiary are Italian resident or (2) after the creation of the trust, an Italian resident conveys to the trust real estate or shares of real estate companies.

With respect to the place of management criteria, one should look at whether the trust has a fixed place of business (e.g., office, employees). If not, the place of management will be the residency of the trustee. With respect to the main business purpose of the trust, one should look at the relevant facts. For instance, if the trust has all or most of its assets in Italy, then the place of management is probably in Italy.

Finally, Italian tax authorities take the position that a trust should be treated as a person under article 4, paragraph 3 of the OECD Model Income Tax Treaty.

THE INHERITANCE AND GIFT TAX TREATMENT OF ANGLO-AMERICAN TRUSTS IN FRANCE

Line-Alexa Glotin

I. Civil Issues

A. Succession Law

1. Preliminary Comments

The French legal system is a codified system based on the Civil Code enacted by Napoleon Bonaparte in 1804. Civil law jurisdictions have based all or part of their legal system on that code, notably as it pertains to individuals. Since France is a unitary jurisdiction, it applies throughout France.

Under the Civil Code, the domicile of a person is where his or her *établissement principal* (principal establishment) is located.[2] In turn, principal establishment refers to the place where one resides permanently. *Résidence* is also a purely factual concept under civil law meaning the place where one lives at any given moment (e.g., summer residence). *Domicile* is sometimes a fiction of the law, for example when the Civil Code provides that a minor is deemed to have his or her *domicile* where the parents have their own *domicile*.

(a) General Principles of Inheritance Law. In the area of inheritance law, one of the most notable differences between the common law and civil law systems is that, generally, the latter do not recognize the concept of estate. This is true in France. The nearest conceptual equivalent is the notion of *masse successorale* or *succession*, which refers to the whole of the assets and liabilities of the deceased at the time of death.

Under French inheritance civil law (*droit des successions*), the conceptual approach is that the *succession* of an individual passes directly to the heirs upon death. The word *succession* also refers to the process whereby heirs and legatees follow in the steps of the deceased, from the moment of death. This moment is referred to as the "opening of the succession" (*l'ouverture de la succession*).

One further comment regarding civil law and *successions*: in the majority of cases, one is dealing with the *succession* of a person married under a so-called community property regime (*régime de communauté*). Under this system, to simplify greatly, the assets acquired by the spouses with funds generated by them during the marriage are in the nature of undivided property in equal shares. In that case, the *succession* is made up of the predeceased's undivided half of the community assets (the survivor keeps his or her half) and the predeceased's *biens*

2. Civil Code, art. 102 *et seq.*

propres (own assets), namely those assets that were the deceased's exclusive property.

When spouses are married under a so-called separation of assets regime (*régime de séparation de biens*), there are naturally no community assets and the predeceased's succession is made up of his or her own assets only.

(b) Forced Heirship and the Surviving Spouse Privilege. In France, issue of the deceased and, in the absence of issue, certain close relatives (together referred to as reserve heirs) and, in certain situations, the deceased's surviving spouse, enjoy special protection by operation of law, the effect of which is to guarantee that they receive a set portion of the *succession*, the so-called reserved portion.

The portion of the *succession* that exceeds the reserved portion is referred to as the free portion. What follows is a description of what happens when the deceased dies intestate. In a will, the deceased may naturally use the free portion to vary what would normally happen in an intestate situation.

The extent of the free and the reserved portions of the *succession* depends on the number of children of the deceased, if any, as follows: if there is one child, the reserved portion is one half; two children, two-thirds; and three or more children, three-quarters. In the event a child dies leaving issue, then the same rules apply *per stirpes*. Parents and siblings in limited cases are entitled to be part of the *succession*, but they can be deprived of it by will; in other words they are not reserve heirs. As to the surviving spouse, the intestate rule is that if the deceased leaves issue, the surviving spouse's share is calculated as follows:

- if all the children are children of both spouses, the surviving spouse can opt between a life interest on the whole *succession* (convertible to an annuity at the request of the surviving spouse or of any heir inheriting a remainder right, or an amount in capital if all parties are in agreement), or the full ownership of one quarter of the *succession*;
- if there are children of one but not the other spouse, the surviving spouse gets one quarter of the *succession* in full ownership; or
- if there is no issue, and if the parents of the deceased survive him or her, the surviving spouse receives one half of the *succession* and each of the parents receives one quarter.

When the surviving spouse inherits three-quarters of the *succession* or the whole of it, the surviving spouse is liable to a duty of maintenance in favor of any surviving ascendants of the deceased, other than the father or mother, if such ascendants are in need of assistance.

In addition, during the year following death, the surviving spouse is entitled to the free use of the family home and its furniture (rent is paid for that duration from the *succession* if the family home is leased). Moreover, the surviving spouse enjoys (1) a lifelong right of occupation of the family home (provided he or she occupied it effectively with the deceased at the time of death), if such home was owned by the spouses together or by the deceased alone; and (2) a right of use of the furniture in the home that is part of the *succession*. This is only true if the deceased, in a will, has not denied this right to the surviving spouse.

The strong protection of children and surviving spouse described above is also evident in French inheritance and gift tax rules.

Assets passed on to issue (or other close relatives) are subject to a much lower tax burden than when they are passed on to non-relatives.

Transfers to the surviving spouse on the occasion of death are treated even more favorably, as there is no tax at all.

The favoring of direct line succession is also apparent in the rule known as *rapport* (claw-back). The general idea of *rapport* is to forbid indirect violations of forced heirship rules through lifetime gifts or special will dispositions becoming effective upon death. Thus, if the total of lifetime gifts and bequests exceeds the free portion, the excess is notionally added back into the *succession*, for the purpose of computing the rightful share of each reserve heir. The purpose is to reinstate equality among reserve heirs. All lifetime gifts (including those that do not exceed the free portion) are subject to the claw-back rule unless the donor clearly indicated in the deed of gift that the donor's intention was to use the free portion. Conversely, all legacies by will of specific assets are deemed to have been intended by the deceased to deplete the free portion first. Similarly, lifetime gifts generally (including reserve heirs, surviving spouse, and non-family members) are subject to another claw-back rule known as *réduction*, which applies to the case where bequests or lifetime gifts exceed the free portion.

The effect of *réduction* is to nullify excess bequests or lifetime gifts to the extent that they exceed the reserved portion, so that the reserve heirs may receive their lawful share of the succession.

Under the Civil Code, an individual interested in estate planning can ask for an heir's consent to irrevocably waive the right to challenge violations of his reserved portion. This can be done by written deed in the presence of two French *notaires*.

(c) Entrusting Management and Control over Succession Assets to a Specific Heir, the Surviving Spouse, or a Third Party for a Limited Time. This is known as the power of attorney with posthumous effect, which survives the death of the principal. Under such a power of attorney, the principal can entrust to any person, including a legal entity, the management of certain designated assets for a limited duration (two or five years, renewable by court order). The power of attorney must be very precise in the description of the agent's powers and must designate the heir or heirs with respect to whom the document is written.

(d) Using "Gradual" and "Residual" Gifts and Bequests. An individual can make a lifetime gift or a bequest subject to the conditions that

- the transferee on his death leaves whatever remains of the gift or bequest to a named third party (residual gift or bequest); or
- the transferee keeps the gift or bequest during his lifetime and leaves it to a named third party on his death.

B. Private International Law

1. French Private International Law

In private international law terms, France is a schismatic (*scissionniste*) jurisdiction, in the sense that, when an international situation arises, French civil law takes into account the existence of the civil succession laws in jurisdictions, other than France, in which succession assets are located.

Estate planning within the European Union (EU) for EU nationals and residents is about to change deeply since the adoption of EC Regulation No. 650/2012 on June 7, 2012. The regulation is on jurisdiction, applicable law, recognition and enforcement of decisions, and acceptance and enforcement of authentic instruments in matters of succession and on the creation of a European Certificate of Succession. The term *succession* is defined by the Regulation as meaning "succession to the estate of a deceased person" and it "covers all forms of transfer of assets, rights and obligations by reason of death, whether by way of a voluntary transfer under a disposition of property upon death or a transfer through intestate succession." The Regulation will come into effect on August 17, 2015.

2. Jurisdiction

Jurisdiction is a matter that is more and more harmonized at EU level, by way of EU statutes and regulations. EU regulations have a direct and simultaneous effect in all the member states; there are a few exceptions to this general rule.

The so-called Brussels I and Brussels II (now Brussels II *bis*) Regulations were the precursors. They address the following matters:

- Council Regulation (EC) No 44/2001 of December 22, 2000 (Brussels I) deals with the issue of jurisdiction and the recognition and enforcement of civil and commercial judgments, notably with regard to trusts and maintenance before Council Regulation (EC) No 4/2009 came into effect on June 18, 2011.
- Council Regulation (EC) No 4/2009 of December 18, 2008, in effect as of June 18, 2011, deals with jurisdiction, applicable law, and the recognition and enforcement of decisions and co-operation in matters relating to maintenance obligations.
- Council Regulation (EC) No 2201/2003 of November 27, 2003 (Brussels II *bis*) concerns the issue of jurisdiction and the recognition and enforcement of judgments in matrimonial matters and parental responsibility.

- Also of great importance in all matters within the EU is Council Regulation (EC) No 1348/2000 of May 29, 2000, on the service in the member states of judicial and extra-judicial documents in civil or commercial matters.

II. Taxation

A. Criteria for Liability to Main Taxes

1. Territoriality Rules for Income Tax Purposes

The criteria that are generally applied in relation to income tax, subject to applicable tax treaties, if any, are embedded in Article 4A and 4B of the Tax Code:

> Article 4A: "Persons who have in France their tax residence [domicile fiscal] are subject to income tax by reason of all their income. Those who have their tax residence outside France are subject to such tax by reason only of their French source income."
>
> Article 4B: "Those persons regarded as having their tax residence in France within the meaning of article 4A are: 'a. Those persons who have in France their home [foyer] or [if that cannot be determined] the place of their principal abode; b. Those who have in France a professional activity, salaried or not, unless they can establish that such activity is conducted only on an ancillary basis; c. those who have in France the centre of their economic interests.'"

2. Territoriality Rules for Gift and Inheritance Tax Purposes

Liability to French gift (inheritance) tax depends, with reference to the time of gift, namely death (transfer) on the tax residence of the transferor (donor/deceased), of the transferee (donee, heir, or legatee), and of the assets for French tax purposes. If the transferor is a tax resident of France at the time of the transfer, the assets are subject to tax, irrespective of their location. If transferor and transferee are not tax residents of France at the time of the transfer, then only French-situs assets are subject to tax. If at the time of the transfer the transferor is resident outside France and the transferee is resident in France, the assets transferred irrespective of their location are subject to tax, excepting if the transferee was not a resident of France during six of the ten years preceding the transfer.

3. Territoriality Rules for Wealth Tax Purposes

Territoriality rules follow a rationale similar to that of gift and inheritance tax, so that, subject to tax treaty,

- if the owner of the wealth is a tax resident of France, the assets are subject to wealth tax irrespective of their location;
- if the owner is not a tax resident, only French situs assets are subject to tax; and

- assets situated outside France that an individual owns on January 1 of each of the five years following the calendar year in which he becomes a resident of France are not subject to wealth tax during those five years.

B. Taxes

The rates, thresholds, and ceilings mentioned below are 2013 numbers. All the rules below are subject to applicable international tax treaties, if any.

1. Personal Income Tax

A few preliminary comments:

- Dividends and interest received by residents and non-residents from French corporations are subject to personal income tax.
- French taxpayers are subject to social contribution taxes (referred to below as the "social tax") that operate as a personal income tax. Social contribution taxes, added together, are levied at the flat rate of 15.5 percent, as provided by the Revised Finance Bill 2012.
- Specific personal income tax rates apply when so-called non-co-operative jurisdictions and territories (*Etats et territoires non coopératifs*) are involved.
- A "tax shield" (*bouclier fiscal*), whereby the total amount of taxes due from a taxpayer, including personal income tax and wealth tax, may not exceed 75 percent of that person's annual income, was reintroduced in 2013.

Residents of France are subject to personal income tax according to a progressive brackets system with a marginal rate of 45 percent above EUR 150k on their worldwide income (wages, bonus, commissions, industrial or commercial profits, professional fees, rental income, etc.) plus social tax. An additional tax is due (1) at the rate of 3 percent between EUR 250k and EUR 500k and 4 percent above EUR 500k for tax payer who is single, or (2) at a rate of 3 percent between EUR 500k and EUR 1m and 4 percent above EUR 1m for married couples and members of a PACS (civil pact between different or same-sex couples).

Non-residents of France are subject to French personal income tax (sometimes payable at source) on their earned income on the basis of a brackets system with a minimum tax rate due at 20 percent. Artists and athletes who are not established in France are subject to personal income tax at the rate of 15 percent with respect to income earned in France, which could be increased to 75 percent when non-co-operative jurisdictions and territories are involved. Specific rules apply to income generated within life insurance vehicles as well as income withdrawn by the policy owner during the life of the policy.

2. Taxation of Capital Gains

Capital gains realized by tax residents of France on the sale of securities are subject to tax at the rate of 19 percent (plus social tax) or to the progressive brackets system. Non-residents of France are fully exempt on the condition that they have not held, during the five years preceding the sale, directly or indirectly, alone or with certain close relatives, more than 25 percent of the share capital of the relevant French entity. Some tax treaties can provide different rules for qualifying substantial or controlling participation in a French entity.

Capital gains realized on the sale of French real estate are taxed at a rate of 19 percent when the vendor resides in an EU Member State, 33.3 percent otherwise, and 75 percent when non-co-operative jurisdictions and territories are involved. Social contributions of 15.5 percent are due in addition to capital gains tax, plus a surtax between 2 percent and 6 percent depending of the amount of the gain (6 percent applies above EUR 260k).

3. Inheritance Tax and Gift Tax

Between parents and direct descendants, the tax is computed in accordance with a brackets system. The marginal rate is 45 percent above EUR 1,805k, subject to a basis reduction of EUR 100k (available every 15 years).

There is no inheritance tax between spouses or members of a PACS. Lifetime gifts between those couples are subject to tax at the marginal rate of 45 percent above EUR 1,805k subject to a basis reduction of EUR 80k.

Other rules apply to brothers and sisters (45 percent above EUR 24k) and non-relatives (60 percent).

4. Wealth Tax

Wealth tax is payable every year on the basis of the person's total wealth (subject to significant exceptions such as "professional assets" and works of art). Wealth tax was heavily reformed in 2011 and 2012.

The applicable wealth tax rates are progressive; for instance it amounts to 0.5 percent on net wealth comprised between €800k and €1.3m and 1.5 percent above €10m.

As regards tax residents of France, the taxable basis is made up of the individual's wealth worldwide, less personal income tax, local taxes, and the wealth tax itself. Non-residents are liable to wealth tax only as to their French-situs assets. Non-residents are not subject to wealth tax on their financial investments in France (e.g., bank accounts, receivables from French-based persons, assets held in a French life insurance vehicle, and certain non-controlling participations in the share capital of companies).

Wealth tax is subject to certain limitations other than those mentioned above, notably the following:

- A 30 percent rebate applies on the fair market value of the individual's first residence.
- The value of investments in business companies can be subject to a 75 percent rebate for the purpose of calculating the wealth tax basis.
- A similar 75 percent basis reduction applies to the value of shares of stock held by managers or salaried employees, on the condition that they

undertake to keep the same for at least six years. This also applies after retirement under certain conditions.

5. Corporation Tax

The standard corporation tax rate is 33.3 percent, irrespective of whether or not the profits are distributed. A surtax of 3.3 percent is applicable to all entities that are subject to corporate tax, including those that enjoy a reduced rate of 15 percent (small- and medium-sized businesses).

Capital gains realized by unlisted companies the assets of which are made up mainly of real estate (in excess of 50 percent) are subject to the standard corporate income tax rate noted above.

It is worth noting that the transfer of the registered office of a French corporation to another EU member state is no longer characterized as a cessation of business for tax purposes. As a consequence, the profits of the relevant year and latent capital gains are no longer immediately subject to corporate tax. In the event the transferred corporation leaves assets in France for the purpose of carrying out its business, the same becomes a permanent establishment and the profits of the establishment are liable to French corporate tax.

6. Withholding Tax

The branch withholding tax is equal to 30 percent. French branches of foreign entities are often exempt under intra-EU rules or tax treaties.

7. Property Tax

Property tax (*taxe foncière*) is assessed on the basis of a special, administratively set value. The land tax rate is set each year by the local government. Housing tax (*taxe d'habitation*) is due by anyone who owns, rents, or uses a furnished residence (be it his main residence or a secondary home). This tax is computed by applying the rate set by the local government to the rental value of the property. The reference is January 1 of each year. Therefore, whoever the occupant is on that date pays the tax.

8. Value-Added Tax

France has a value-added tax (*taxe sur la valeur ajoutée*) system and no sales tax. The basic rate is 19.6 percent, to be increased to 20 percent in 2014. The following specific reduced rates apply: 5.5 percent (non-refundable medical drugs, books, foodstuffs, water, public transport, transfer of intellectual property rights on works of art, and artistic interpretations), 7 percent on food immediately consumed to be increased to 10, and 2.1 percent on refundable medical drugs.

9. Registration Tax (*Droits d'Enregistrement*)

Sales of goodwill and leasehold rights are subject to tax above a threshold of EUR 23,000, namely 3 percent between EUR 23,000 and EUR 200,000, and 5 percent above this last figure.

Sales of real estate are subject to tax at the rate of 5.09 percent (excepting sales of buildings—not land—that are subject to VAT, acquisitions by realtors for the purpose of resale, and sales of certain types of rural buildings, which are subject to registration tax at the rate of 0.715 percent).

The sale of shares of a French or foreign company owning predominantly, directly or indirectly, French real estate must be registered in France through a French notary (*notaire*) within the month following the signature of the purchase deed. Registration duties are due on that occasion at the rate of 5 percent assessed on the sale price (from FY2012, only those loans granted for the purpose of acquiring the real estate may be considered for the purpose of determining shareholding interest values).

Sales of shares of stock are subject to tax at 3 percent on shares of *sociétés à responsabilité limitée* and (ii) 0.1 percent on shares of *sociétés anonymes*.

10. Annual 3 Percent Tax

Under Articles 990D to 990G, tax code, French situs real estate owned by unlisted foreign entities and trustees, directly or indirectly, is liable to an annual 3 percent tax based on the market value of the real estate. The following are exempt:

- companies located in jurisdictions that have a tax treaty with France that includes an administrative assistance clause ensuring co-operation in the area of fraud and tax evasion, on the condition that the relevant company discloses to revenue annually the location, nature, and market value of the real estate, the identity of company's shareholders, and the number of shares held by each; and
- legal entities that have their effective seat of management in France as well as legal entities abroad that enjoy equality of treatment under a treaty, providing there is the same disclosure of (or commitment to disclose) information as mentioned in the previous paragraph.

C. Enforcement and Collection of Taxes

1. Basic Procedures

The French revenue service is vested with wide-ranging investigative powers that include normal audits, investigations with special powers in the event of flagrancy, the right to search premises, and the right to obtain private and confidential information, notably from banks and accountants (persons listed as lawyers in the EU are protected to an extent insofar as the attorney-client privilege is at stake).

Audits can take the form of (1) a critical analysis by the revenue of the returns and documents prepared by the tax payer and collected from other sources, (2) an in-depth investigation of all aspects of the tax profile of the tax payer, or (3) an audit of specific aspects of a tax payer's tax position, at the taxpayer's request.

2. Late Payment Interest and Penalties

Late payment interest on past due or avoided taxes is levied at the rate of 0.4 percent per month. Interest comes in addition to penalties.

Unreported income gives rise to a penalty of 10 percent applied to the tax normally due. However, if the income was intentionally not reported, the penalty is at the rate of 40 percent. It reaches 80 percent when the taxpayer has acted fraudulently or when part of the price of a contract transaction was hidden.

3. Imprisonment

Criminal sanctions are meant principally to sanction the misdemeanor of tax fraud, i.e., the situation where the taxpayer, voluntarily, has used fraudulent means to evade tax or to attempt to evade tax.

Criminal fines of up to EUR 500,000 and jail sentencing of up to five years may be ordered by the judge. The fine reaches EUR 750,000 when the fraud was committed or facilitated through the use of purchases or sales without invoices or of invoices that do not reflect the underlying transaction, or if the purpose of the fraud was to improperly obtain payments from the state. The fine amounts to EUR 1,000,000 and a jail sentence of up to seven years when the fraud committed has a link with non-cooperative states and territories.

4. Flagrancy

Tax agents can act on the basis of flagrancy, a principle that is well known in the area of criminal law. The objective is to fight black market transactions and other fraudulent transactions, such as the issuance of fictitious invoices, carousel frauds, the use of software for fraudulent objectives, or the use of accounting methods with the purpose to impede tax collection efforts.

Revenue agents now can organize surprise visits of premises, confiscate goods and other assets, and initiate VAT audits without advance notice. Violations of tax law identified on the occasion of flagrancy proceedings involve special fines and penalties. The revenue can also rely on special taxation procedures, such as the right to apply VAT automatically to income identified during the audit. The revenue can also extend the audit period to six years and audit again a previously audited time period.

5. Fraud

Fraud encompasses all fictitious transactions or literal applications of the law or administrative precedents in contradiction with the intent of the lawmaker or of the courts, for no reason other than the avoidance of or the lowering of liability to tax.

The concept is applicable to all types of taxes without any restriction.

The principal instigator or beneficiary of the fraud is subject to penalty at the rate of 80 percent. All participants to the fraud are jointly answerable.

6. Recent Changes of Behavior by the Tax Authorities

At the initiative of the government, an exit tax has been re-introduced in the tax code. Subject to specific deferral rules, an individual who was a resident of France for income tax purposes during the six years preceding his exit date will be subject to exit tax on latent gains pertaining to direct or indirect participations (computed on the day preceding the exit date), to the extent that, alone or together with other members of the household, the individual's participation exceeds 1 percent of the outstanding shareholding or EUR 1.3m irrespective of whether the entity is French or not, provided it is subject to corporate tax or an equivalent tax.

An automatic payment deferral of the income tax component (the law does not provide for deferral of the social tax component), currently at a rate of 15.5 percent, without providing collateral in case the residence of the taxpayer, is transferred to another EU member state or EEA member state, which signs an administrative assistance agreement or mutual assistance agreement. Payment deferral may also be granted in other situations (transfer of residence for professional reasons, notably).

Statute bar periods have been extended from 3 to 10 years for failures to report controlled entities located in low-tax jurisdictions or the existence of bank accounts or life insurance wrappers outside France; and from 6 years to 10 years with respect to undisclosed transactions or situations of tax flagrancy.

Finally, the concept of deemed income was widened to include transfers of funds outside the European Union.

III. Asset Holding Vehicles

A. Trusts

The matter of trusts and France is a subject that would require lengthy discussion; hence the following is merely a summary of the system as it now stands under recently enacted statutes.

In those cases where a trust is settled by a French resident, a French resident is a beneficiary of a trust, or the trust fund contains French-situs assets, the following rules need to be taken into consideration.

- **Income tax**—distributions of capitalized income will be treated as distributions of arising income.
- **Gift and inheritance tax**—Trusts will be deemed transparent for gift and inheritance tax purposes. If the beneficiaries are identified individually, the relevant standard gift (namely inheritance tax) rate will apply. If the beneficiaries cannot be so identified but are all in the line of descent, the tax rate will be 45 percent. Otherwise, the tax will be levied at the rate of 60 percent. The 60 percent rate will apply if the settlor was a resident of France at the time the settlement was made.

- **Wealth tax/levy**—The assets in trust are includible in the settlor's taxable wealth if the settlor is a resident of France or to the extent that the trustees own French situs assets. If the tax cannot be levied at the settlor's level, a specific levy may be payable by the trustees or the French-resident beneficiaries, at the highest wealth tax rate (currently of 1.5 percent). The settlor and the beneficiaries will be jointly liable with the trustee for the payment of the tax. Recent immigrants to France (less than 5 years of residence) will be exempt of wealth tax in respect of trust assets located outside France.
- **Disclosure obligations**—The settlor, trustees, or informed beneficiaries (when either a French resident or French situs assets are involved) are subject to specific disclosure obligations pertaining to the settlement of the trust, trust deed modifications, termination of the trust, or characteristics of the trust (including the trust funds on a worldwide basis). Failure to disclose makes the settlor, trustees, and beneficiaries jointly liable for a 5 percent tax penalty assessed on the assets in trust including capitalized income.

B. Partnerships

France does not have partnerships properly speaking, but *sociétés civiles* (civil companies, SCIs) (as well as other types of structures) operate very much as partnerships. Notably, *sociétés civiles* are transparent for civil law purposes and semi-transparent for tax purposes.

SCIs can be used to enjoy full testamentary freedom, at least if the shareholder is resident in a jurisdiction that does not have similar rules. Indeed, shares are movables so that if the owner is a foreigner, the succession law of the place of his last domicile will apply. Movables are subject to the succession law of the place of last domicile. Hence, if the last domicile is in a non-forced-heirship jurisdiction, the succession law of that jurisdiction (generally testamentary freedom) applies.

IV. Transnational Giving

A. Obtaining Status as an Organization to which Tax Deductible Gifts Can Be Made

Deduction benefits have become significantly more attractive than they were not so long ago. Deductibility of gifts is dependent on whether the beneficiary of the gift is eligible under the relevant section of the revenue code. A distinction needs to be made between gifts made by individuals and gifts made by business enterprises.

The concept of a *fonds de dotation* (endowment fund) was introduced in French law under law number 2008–776 of August 4, 2008. Unlike foundations, endowment funds are quick and easy to establish, by way of a simple declaration to the prefecture in the area where the fund is to be established. The process of giving to a fund is subject to minimal rules. Endowment funds enjoy legal personality, i.e., legal capacity equivalent to any legal entity. As regards management, the only requirement is that a fund should have a board made up of three persons minimum.

Donors making gifts to a fund enjoy an income tax rebate equal to 66 percent of the donation, up to a ceiling of 20 percent of the taxable income. If the donor is a juridical entity, the rebate is of 60 percent, up to a ceiling of 5 per thousand of turnover. Gifts to a fund are exempt of registration tax.

Lastly, an endowment fund enjoys the general tax regime that applies to non-profit organizations.

Deductibility of gifts at the donor's level is dependent on whether the beneficiary of the gift is eligible under recognition of the public utility or of non-for-profit status. A distinction needs to be made between gifts made by individuals and those made by business enterprises.

As regards international giving, French domestic law provides for very limited flexibility in terms of permitting tax deductible gifts from a French tax resident to a foreign philanthropic body, except (rarely) when a treaty provides for more favorable rules. However, since a decision rendered by the European Union Court of Justice,[3] international giving within the EU is greatly facilitated. Under that case law, a donor who is a tax resident of one of the EU member states should enjoy the same tax benefits in that member state irrespective of whether he gives to a philanthropic body in that member state or in another member state.

The Revised Finance Law 2009 draws on the consequences of the *Persche* case to facilitate intra-EU giving.

V. Regulatory Environment

A. Anti-Money Laundering Legislation

In France, subject to the following, all transactions suspected of involving money laundering or terrorist financing are reported to a cell of the Ministries of Finance and Budget, the Intelligence processing and action against clandestine financial circuits cell, known under the acronym of its French name TRACFIN.

French lawyers do not report directly to TRACFIN; rather they must declare any suspicions of money laundering to the president (*Bâtonnier*) of the relevant bar. The president then passes on such declarations to TRACFIN, unless he or she considers the suspicions to be unfounded.

In addition, French lawyers are to an extent exempt from certain obligations under anti-money laundering laws when they act in the context of legal proceedings to defend a client or provide advice in the interest of the defense of a client,

3. 27 January 2009, *In re C318/07 Hein Persche.*

excepting naturally in the case of advice that would place the lawyer in the position of an accomplice.

B. EU Savings Tax Directive

The Savings Tax Directive establishes a system of systematic declaration of savings income paid to non-resident investors to facilitate taxation in the member state where the beneficial owner resides. Austria, Belgium, and Luxembourg have refused systematic declaration and have instead opted for the option available under the directive to maintain secrecy but to withhold tax on interest on savings and to transfer part of that to the state of residence of the beneficiary of the savings. France opted for the systematic declaration approach.

On regulatory matters it is worth noting that beyond the modernization of a number of bilateral treaties (e.g., with the United Kingdom, Luxembourg, and Switzerland), France has entered into a number of Tax Information Exchange Agreements (TIEAs) that, subject to some specifications, are in line with Article 26 of the OECD Model. These TIEAs are with Andorra, Anguilla, Belize, Brunei Darussalam, the Cayman Islands, Cook Islands, Costa Rica, Dominique, Gibraltar, Guernsey, Liberia, Liechtenstein, Netherlands Antilles, San Marino, and Uruguay. The British Virgin Islands, Jersey, and Bermuda were "blacklisted by the French government at the end of August 2013 and no longer qualify as cooperative countries for French tax purposes.

THE INHERITANCE AND GIFT TAX TREATMENT OF ANGLO-AMERICAN TRUSTS IN SPAIN

Sonia Velasco Menal
Carlos Ara Triadú

I. Introduction

Spain is not party to the Hague Convention of July 1, 1985, on the Law Applicable to Trusts and their Recognition, and does not have any substantive provisions relating to trusts under its legal system.[4] Thus, the trust is an unknown legal institution under Spanish law.

When analyzing the particular features of trusts, other legal institutions under Spanish law that might appear similar to trusts cannot be used in their place, as the grounds on which trusts are based do not allow an "equitable application" of any alternatives provided under Spanish law. The dissociation between legal and beneficial ownership that lies with the trust is unknown under Spanish civil law and, as a result, is unknown under Spanish tax law.

However, article 12 of the Spanish Civil Code establishes that foreign legal institutions validly and effectively incorporated under the provisions of the relevant legal system are recognized under Spanish law, so long as they are not contrary to the Spanish public order (*orden público*). For instance, the civil section of the Spanish Supreme Court (*Tribunal Supremo*) stated in the resolution of April 30, 2008, that *mortis causa* trusts validly incorporated under the legal system applicable to the settlor should be recognized by Spanish law under article 9.8 of the Spanish Civil Code,[5] so long as the claimant proves it is a valid institution under the foreign law applicable to it.[6]

Inter vivos trusts could be more difficult to accommodate within the Spanish legal system, because Spanish law views gifts granted during a person's life

4. The only Spanish legislation mentioning the word "trust" is Spanish Act 10/2010 of April 28, 2010, on the Prevention of Money Laundering and Terrorism Financing. The word "trust," as a clarification of the Spanish word "*fideicomiso*" or fiduciary agreement, is included on the list of legal agreements to be closely followed, which would be subject to special scrutiny when used.

5. The case analyzed by the Supreme Court involved a trust established by two U.S. nationals under U.S. law, under which their daughter (the plaintiff) was to become the beneficiary, acquiring, among other things, real estate located in Spain, which was held by the trust.

6. The case did not give effect to trusts in Spain because of formal procedural aspects (not proving the applicable law).

with suspicion. Article 34 of the Spanish Constitution only recognizes the right of incorporating public interest foundations. Thus, considering the traditional civil law principle of protection of creditors, it is challenging to recognize, from a civil law perspective, any effect in Spain of inter vivos trusts under article 12 of the Spanish Civil Code, because such trusts are likely to be contrary to the Spanish public order *(orden público).*

II. A Brief Approach to Spanish Civil Institutions Considered Similar to Trusts

The economic and family estate planning effects sought by *mortis causa* trusts could be obtained partially or fully using other institutions recognized by Spanish law, such as life interests, executorships, and fiduciary substitutions.[7]

Under Spanish law, it is possible to enjoy *in rem* rights (*derechos reales de disfrute*), such as life interest or usufructs (*usufructo*), which allows third parties to benefit from assets that belong to another party. Usufructs are often used to plan *mortis causa* transfers. For example, an asset's legal title (*nuda propiedad*) may remain with the original title holders (individually or jointly) until the beneficiaries reach a certain age. Meanwhile, the beneficiaries may receive the profits from the assets under the usufruct. However, although usufructs achieve differentiation between legal title and an enjoyment of *in rem* rights, their nature differs from trusts. Trusts dissociate property, while usufructs only enable enjoyment of *in rem* rights exercised over assets still belonging to another party.

Article 1,802 of the Spanish Civil Code establishes certain inter vivos agreements consisting of the transfer of assets (for instance, real estate) in exchange for life annuities (*contrato aleatorio de renta vitalicia*). Unlike trusts, under these agreements, the assets are transferred directly to the beneficiaries, who must pay a yearly annuity to the other party (normally an older relative).

Concerning *mortis causa* property transfers, the Spanish legal system also enables fiduciary substitutions (*sustitución fideicomisaria*), which are temporarily limited, though. Note that under Spanish law, the Roman *fiducia* differs from *fideicomisary* substitutions, which are a way to transfer assets in a *mortis causa* context. Under this institution, the fiduciary heir (*fiduciario*) acquires the property and must manage and keep the assets to transfer them upon his or her death to the *fideicomisary* heir (*sustituto fideicomisario*). There are different types of *fideicomisary* institutions, depending on the duties imposed on and powers granted to the fiduciary (first heir) regarding the assets to be transferred to the *fideicomisary*, ranging from managing assets to selling them.

7. The Spanish legal system is made up of general state legislation and the autonomous communities' legislation under section 149.1.8 of the Spanish Constitution. Certain autonomous communities, such as Aragon, the Basque Country, the Baleares Islands, Catalonia, Galicia, and Navarra, have particular civil institutions, which are treated similarly to *fideicomiso* for tax purposes under § 54 of the Spanish Inheritance and Gift Tax Regulation.

However, this institution differs from trusts. Fiduciary substitutions lead to a full transfer of property, that is, legal and economic ownership (even though, in the case of *fideicomiso de residuo*, there is an encumbrance limiting the power to dispose of the property), while trusts allow a disassociation of property. Under fiduciary substitutions, the *fideicomisary* acquires the assets when the fiduciary dies. Under article 781 of the Spanish Civil Code, fiduciary substitutions are moreover temporarily limited to only two generations (from the testator to the fiduciary and from the fiduciary to the *fideicomisary*).

Spanish law (especially in certain autonomous communities, such as Catalonia) also allows *mortis causa* gifts, which are gifts granted in life but whose effects are different until the donor dies. However, this institution does not coincide with the structure of trusts, because *mortis causa* gifts are granted directly in favor of the donees, whereas in trusts, the settlor gives the assets to the trustee to be held in the interest of the beneficiaries.

Finally, *mortis causa* trusts that aim to rationalize estate distributions to the heirs (e.g., until a certain age) are somewhat similar, but there are civil differences, such as the appointment of executorships or the creation of life interests relating to *mortis causa* usufructs. Executorships (*albaceas*) are considered *mortis causa* mandates in charge of executing testators' wills. Executors are individuals with legal capacity, appointed by testators to execute their wills. However, although the executor's role may lead to planning schemes similar to those sought by trusts, executors have no legal title over the estate. The heirs or beneficiaries of bequests would be considered to have acquired full ownership (both legal and economic) of the assets when the testators die. However, as in the case of trustees, executors agree to carry out the instructions in the wills and are responsible for managing and distributing the assets transferred under the decedent's specific instructions. Executors can be in charge of managing assets for as long as stated by testators in their wills. However, regarding the portion of the estate to which the forced heirship rules apply, the beneficiaries could claim full control of the assets managed by executors once they reach the age of eighteen.

A mandate could also be considered to play a role similar to a trustee in the sense that it involves managing an alien property for an equally alien interest.

This dogmatic point is relevant when considering the equitable application of civil and tax provisions under Spanish law regarding the institutions discussed above. Effectively, it is not possible to turn to other institutions under Spanish law, because their nature is different from trusts.

However, the civil analysis of the trust and its potential assimilation into Spanish institutions should be the first step in determining its taxation. Trustees should not trigger any wealth, or gift and inheritance tax if they do not gain any economic advantage from the trusts, except for a management or similar type of fee (similar to a mandate or an executor). This should not, in our view, lead automatically to the conclusion that the beneficiaries should always be subject to wealth or inheritance and gift tax, as analyzed below.

Considering the above, we analyze the Spanish administrative doctrine relating to the Spanish taxation of trusts.

III. The Trust from the Spanish Tax Authorities' Perspective

Spanish tax legislation does not contain any provisions on the taxation of trusts. This causes legal uncertainty when dealing with trusts, which the Spanish tax authorities are trying to reduce by issuing administrative doctrine (tax rulings).

Recent tax rulings regarding *mortis causa* trusts basically disregard trusts, as if they did not exist. The reason given to justify this approach is that Spain has not ratified the Hague Convention. The rulings do not mention whether the trusts were irrevocable or revocable trusts.

This "looking through" approach by the Spanish tax authorities on mostly *mortis causa* trusts could be summarized as follows, following the binding tax rulings V1991-08, V0010-10, V1016-10, and V2244-10:[8]

- Spain is not a party to the Hague Convention, and its legal system does not have any provision regarding trusts. Hence, the effects of trusts are not recognized, which means that irrespective of their particular features, they are fully disregarded for tax purposes.
- Thus, the assets held in trust only cease to be part of the settlor's wealth on the settlor's death. The date of the deed of trust is not relevant for tax purposes. Therefore, regardless of the provisions of each trust (mainly, whether it is revocable or not) and the trustee's powers (mainly, if it is a discretionary trust), for tax purposes, the settlor remains the owner of the assets held in trust. The property transfer for tax purposes only takes place on the settlor's death. Therefore, as a general rule, the establishment of the trust should not imply taxation in Spain for the settlor or the trust in Spain.[9]
- Consequently, based on the Spanish tax authorities' administrative doctrine, the income obtained from the assets held in trust should be allocated to the settlor during his or her life for Spanish tax purposes. In other words, until the settlor's death, the trust is disregarded. Although assets' legal title may have been transferred to the trustee under the law of the state incorporating the trust, the income still deemed to be obtained by the settlor.

8. Inconsistent with what has been the Spanish tax authorities' latest position, a recent tax ruling dated October 6, 2011, seems to recognize certain effects of a trust domiciled in a tax haven to recognize a right to apply an exemption. In our opinion, the Spanish tax authorities are taking advantage of the fact that trusts are not recognized under Spanish law, by taking a different approach in each case, depending on their interest.

9. As mentioned, tax authorities have not made any distinction between the contribution of assets to an irrevocable or revocable trust, even if they have completely different legal effects for all parties.

If the settlor is a tax resident in Spain, according to the Spanish tax authorities, the income obtained by the trust would be subject to Spanish corporate income tax or Spanish personal income tax (depending on whether the settlor is a legal company or an individual).

Although the tax rulings do not specify it, we understand that, because the assets held in trust are considered to stay in the settlor's wealth from the Spanish tax authorities' point of view, capital distributions to the settlor should not be subject to Spanish corporate or personal income tax.

Under the Spanish nonresident income tax, when the assets held in trust are located in Spain or can be exercised in Spain, settlors who are not tax residents in Spain would be taxed on their Spanish-source income.

Also, according to Spanish tax authorities, settlors that are tax resident in Spain would be subject to Spanish wealth tax, which applies to settlors' worldwide assets (notwithstanding the characteristics of the trust, since it has been fully disregarded for tax purposes). A nonresident settlor could become subject to wealth tax on the assets in trust located in Spain.[10]

- Regarding distributions made to the beneficiaries during the settlor's life, although not explicitly mentioned in any of the tax authorities' tax rulings, we understand that the tax authorities would consider these distributions a gratuitous transfer to the beneficiaries by the settlor.

If the beneficiaries were tax resident in Spain, they would be subject to Spanish inheritance and gift tax under the legislation of the autonomous community where they have lived for the previous five years. However, for real estate, the applicable law is the law of the place where the assets are located. In a number of autonomous communities in Spain, gifts between close relatives are exempt, or reduced tax rates apply if certain conditions are met.

If the beneficiaries are not tax resident in Spain, the Spanish inheritance and gift tax would only accrue if there are assets located in Spain or if there are that can be exercised in Spain, in which case the applicable law would be the general state legislation, which does not contemplate the exemptions or reduced tax rates mentioned above.[11]

---

10. Spain enacted Royal Decree-Law 13/2011, temporarily reestablishing wealth tax for the 2011 and 2012 tax years, abolishing the 100 percent relief that entered into force for the 2008 tax year onward. Nevertheless, certain autonomous communities, making use of their regulatory powers over wealth tax, have introduced a 100 percent relief for wealth tax that can be temporary (for 2011 and 2012) or permanent. Nonresidents in Spain are subject to the wealth tax as established in the general state wealth tax legislation (no relief for 2011 and 2012).

11. Spanish inheritance and gift tax was recently challenged vis-á-vis the EU Court of Justice in an appeal filed on March 7, 2012. It is claimed that its provisions, which are considered discriminatory, could be contrary to EU law, because nonresidents cannot benefit from the tax relief and reduced tax rates that residents benefit from. On October 27, 2011, the European Commission referred Spain to the EU's Court of Justice for discriminatory rules on inheritance and gift tax that require nonresidents to pay higher taxes than residents. The Commission had already formally

- On the death of the settlor,[12] it is considered that a *mortis causa* transfer of the trusts' assets to the beneficiaries has occurred, at which time, according to the Spanish tax authorities, the beneficiaries resident in Spain would be subject to the Spanish inheritance tax on all of the assets held in trust, wherever they are located.

In most autonomous communities in Spain,[13] inheriting an estate from close relatives is exempt or reduced tax rates apply, if certain conditions are met. The tax authorities have clarified in their rulings that because trusts are disregarded for Spanish purposes, beneficiaries inherit directly from the settlor.

The beneficiaries not resident in Spain would be subject only to Spanish inheritance and gift tax on the assets that are located or can be exercised in Spain.

If the settlor is not tax resident in Spain (and even if the beneficiaries are), the tax applied to the inheritance would be ruled by general state legislation, which does not establish as many exemptions as certain autonomous communities.

Finally, as mentioned, whether or not the beneficiaries have the power to dispose of the assets does not seem to be relevant for Spanish tax purposes since no legal effect is recognized to trusts. Hence, according to the Spanish tax authorities, inheritance and gift tax becomes due at the time of the testator/settlor's death.

- After the settlor's death, the beneficiaries should pay the tax on all of the income and capital gains obtained from the assets in trust, either under the Spanish personal income tax or the Spanish nonresidents income tax rules if the assets in trust are located or can be exercised in Spain.

In short, according to the Spanish tax authorities' administrative doctrine, transfers made by settlors to trusts are considered not carried out. Hence, there are no tax implications in Spain on the incorporation of trusts and subsequent transfers to trusts. Because settlors are considered to be the owners of assets held by trusts, all income obtained by trusts would be attributed directly to them and taxed accordingly. Transfers made from trusts to beneficiaries would be treated as if the transfers had been directly made between the settlors and beneficiaries. Depending on the nature of these transfers, they would be taxed as inter vivos gifts or as *mortis causa* transfers under the Spanish inheritance and gift tax rules. Once ownership of assets has passed from settlors to beneficiaries for Spanish tax purposes, the beneficiaries would be subject to tax on all of the income and capital gains obtained from the trust under the Spanish personal income tax

---

requested on May 5, 2010, and again on February 17, 2011, that Spain take action to ensure compliance with the EU rules regarding inheritance and gift tax provisions. However, no amendments have been made to the Spanish legislation on the matter.

12. Tax authorities have only issued their opinion on *mortis causa* transfers.

13. The autonomous communities in Spain have legislative power to partially modify the Spanish inheritance and gift tax legislation enacted by the Central Government. The applicable law would depend on the settlor's and the beneficiaries' tax residence. Where the settlor is tax resident in Spain, the applicable law would be that one of the autonomous community of its tax residence within the last five years before settlor's death.

or the Spanish nonresident income tax rules. Settlors (while considered the owners of the assets held by the trust) or beneficiaries (when the effective transfer is considered made, e.g., upon the settlors' death) would be subject to the Spanish wealth tax on the assets held by trust (as resident or nonresident).

IV. Comments on the Spanish Tax Authorities' Administrative Doctrine

We believe the Spanish tax authorities' administrative doctrine may be too simplistic and could lead to unfair taxation in certain situations that could take place in practice, although it provides guidance on how the use of a trust would be analyzed by tax authorities. Situations in which beneficiaries of a discretionary trust are subject to Spanish inheritance and gift tax, even though they do not have the power to dispose of the assets held in trust and are subject to tax on the income obtained by the assets held in trust, are particularly controversial.

We understand that the Spanish tax authorities should recognize an institution validly and effectively incorporated under the legal system of its origin and, hence, should recognize some, if not all, of its effects.

We also understand that it should be possible to argue in certain circumstances that Spanish inheritance and gift tax should not accrue on the settlor's death (as this should only occur if the beneficiaries do not only have an expectation but also the right to enjoy and dispose of the assets held in trust and income from those assets). As an alternative approach, as it is the case in other legal systems, the trust should be subject itself to taxation instead of the beneficiaries (if obtaining Spanish income), because the trustee is in charge of paying the due amounts, deducting them from the trust's wealth.

The same conclusion should be reached regarding Spanish wealth tax. The assets held in trust should be subject to tax in the hands of the beneficiaries if they exercise or are able to exercise the right to dispose of or control the assets. Alternatively, when determining the assets' value for wealth tax purposes, it should be taken into account that the beneficiaries do not have full control of the assets in trust.

The Spanish tax authorities' nonrecognition of trusts may also involve unfair taxation of the settlor, particularly when the settlor ceased to control the assets put in trust and has no right to receive income from the assets. In those circumstances, there might be arguments to avoid considering the settlor as the taxpayer on the income and wealth of the trust. For instance, the fact that the assets in trust do not belong any more to the settlor or that settlor's creditors cannot attach them.

V. Conclusion

Mainly because Spain is a civil law country, the Spanish legal system does not recognize the institution of trusts or any difference between formal and economic ownership. In addition, Spain has not ratified the Hague Convention on the Law of Trusts. Therefore, Spanish law does not contemplate the institution of trust.

Although trusts cannot be incorporated under Spanish law, there are other civil institutions, such as executorships, *fideicomisary* substitutions, and usufructs, that could have similar economic and estate planning effects.

Lack of regulation should not be the same as lack of recognition of any effects of an unknown institution validly incorporated under foreign law, so long as it is not contrary to Spanish public order. Some of the effects associated with *mortis causa* trusts should be recognized, provided that the trust was incorporated and validly exists under the applicable foreign law. Likewise, Spanish taxation should be adapted to specific cases. Otherwise, there is a risk of unfair taxation where beneficiaries have no control over the capital or income, as in the case of a discretionary trust.

Spanish tax authorities have come up with an administrative doctrine that simply disregards the trust and considers that the assets in trust belong either to the settlor or the beneficiaries. In our interpretation, this conclusion may be too simplistic in certain cases and may result in unfair situations, especially for discretionary trusts, where the trustee has full, exclusive discretionary powers to allocate or distribute the assets to beneficiaries, who have no control over them.

A case-by-case analysis should always be carried out to determine the tax implications of foreign trusts in Spain. Alternatively, an assessment of the institutions recognized under Spanish law could provide similar planning and economic solutions to those sought by the trust, with the advantage that there would be more legal certainty regarding the tax consequences.

THE GERMAN TAX AND INHERITANCE LAW TREATMENT OF TRUSTS

Gerd Kostrzewa

I. Introduction

With a population of over 82 million, Germany is the largest country in the European Union (EU). Although Germany is home to many large multinational companies, its economy is mainly characterized by small and medium-sized companies that account for about 85 percent of all enterprises. This creates a competitive and flexible economic environment, which has helped many highly specialized companies to attain a leading position on the world market. The international mobility of German entrepreneurs, executives, and their families has steadily increased due to this international orientation. At the same time, Germany is highly attractive for foreign investors. This leads to a steady increase of the number of individuals with a connection to German assets or sources of income.

In this context, it is not easy for international advisers to deal with the challenges of the German tax and legal system. Although German taxation is based on a restrictive concept of residence with taxation at relatively high tax rates of worldwide income and assets transferred by gift or inheritance, estate planning is determined by Germany's civil law system with forced heirship rules. It is also restricted by the fact that foreign trusts are generally not acknowledged.

The purpose of this section of the chapter is to give the international adviser an outline of the most relevant German rules that determine the German tax and inheritance law treatment of trusts.[14]

II. German Income Taxation

Germany generally taxes its residents on their worldwide income. Certain income from foreign sources may be exempted from German income taxation based on double-tax treaties, which Germany has concluded with many countries, among them several jurisdictions in which trusts are a common estate planning tool.

14. This chapter is based on the state of German law as of June 1, 2013.

Once an individual who is either the settlor or the beneficiary of a foreign trust becomes a German tax resident, he or she may face not only German taxation of transfers to or from a trust but also potential taxation of distributed and undistributed trust income. For this reason, it is crucial for the international adviser to understand how easily a client may become subject to German taxation.

A. German Income Taxation under National German Tax Law

The type of German jurisdiction applicable to income tax depends on residence, citizenship, and type and location of income sources. German income taxation may be limited by tax treaty provisions.

1. Unlimited Income Taxation

Individuals maintaining a residence or a habitual stay in Germany are subject to German taxation on their worldwide income.[15] This applies irrespective of citizenship.

(a) German Residence. A German residence is defined as an abode (house or apartment, owned or rented) that is used by the taxpayer under circumstances that indicate an intended continued use as a living place.[16] In the context of national German tax law, this residence does not need to constitute the center of the individual's vital interests.[17] The existence of one or more other foreign residences does not prevent the presumption of a German residence.

Such residence requires a place that is suitable as a permanent living place. This living place must be adequate in view of the personal and economic circumstances of the taxpayer. A living place needs to be furnished in a way that the taxpayer is able to use it at any time. In some cases, German tax authorities may even regard simple vacation homes, hunting cabins, or hotel rooms that are continuously at the disposition of the taxpayer as suitable living places.

Establishing German residence requires that the taxpayer must use the German living place with certain regularity. It is not required that the living place be used for a specific number of days during the calendar year. If the taxpayer owns or rents a German apartment, this will usually be regarded as an indication of the intention to use the apartment permanently as a living place.

(b) Habitual Stay in Germany. A habitual stay in Germany requires that the individual stay in Germany with certain regularity.[18] This regularity is always assumed if the stay continues for a period of more than six months. This period does not require completion within one calendar year. Short interruptions (e.g., for foreign travel) do not interrupt the six-month period.[19] However, even stays of less than

15. Sec. 1 Income Tax Act (Einkommensteuergesetz–EStG).
16. Sec. 8 Fiscal Code (Abgabenordnung–AO).
17. Federal Tax Court (BFH) decision of Jan. 28, 2004, I R 56/01, BFH/NV 2004, 917.
18. Sec. 9 Fiscal Code.
19. Federal Tax Court decision of June 22, 2011, I R 26/10, BFH/NV 2011, 2001.

six months may constitute a habitual stay if the individual originally intended to stay for more than six months.[20]

(c) General Consequences of Unlimited Income Taxation. Individuals who are subject to German unlimited income taxation are obliged to declare and be taxed on their worldwide income, but they may benefit from a variety of deductions (e.g., deduction of losses, special tax rates in case of a sale of business, deduction of social security contributions, etc.).

The income subject to unlimited income taxation is taxed at a progressive tax rate. The maximum tax rate presently is 45 percent plus 5.5 percent surcharge tax (Solidaritätszuschlag) on the assessed income tax.[21]

A flat tax rate of 26.375 percent (25 percent income tax plus 5.5 percent surcharge tax on the income tax) applies to income from capital and capital gains from shares, bonds, or other securities.[22] This taxation regime (Abgeltungssteuer) was introduced as of January 1, 2009.

Capital gains from the sale of securities acquired before January 1, 2009, are not subject to taxation if they were held for more than one year. However, this does not apply to capital gains from the sale of corporate shares of at least 1 percent. In such cases, 60 percent of respective capital gains are subject to taxation at a regular progressive tax rate of the individual.[23]

It is noteworthy that capital gains from the sale of privately held assets other than securities are still only taxable if the sale occurs less one year after the acquisition.[24] After a one-year holding period, the taxpayer can sell privately held assets, e.g., art, jewelry, gold, or vintage cars free of German capital gains taxation. For privately held real estate, the holding period is ten years.

Capital gains will always be taxable if they are to be qualified as business income. The sale of several privately held assets within a certain period of time may be regarded as a business transaction and consequently as being subject to taxation under the complex rules developed by the German courts and the German tax administration.[25]

(d) Taxation of Trust Income. If a person is subject to German unlimited income taxation, the special taxation rules under the Foreign Relations Tax Act (Aussensteuergesetz–AStG) pertaining to foreign trust or foundation income may apply.[26] Under these rules, the income of a foreign trust or foundation with family beneficiaries is allocated to German resident beneficiaries and taxed at their level

20. Federal Tax Court decision of Aug. 3, 1977, I R 210/75, BStBl. II 1978, 118.
21. Sec. 32a Income Tax Act.
22. Sec. 32d Income Tax Act.
23. Sec. 17, sec. 3 no. 40 c) Income Tax Act.
24. Sec. 22 no. 2, sec. 23 para. 1 Income Tax Act.
25. Federal Tax Court decision of Dec. 10, 2001, GrS 1/98, BStBl. II 2002, 291; Schmidt, EStG (2012), sec. 15 note 46.
26. Sec. 15 Foreign Relations Tax Act (Aussensteuergesetz–AStG).

proportionate to their "interest" in the trust or foundation. This taxation applies irrespective of actual distributions. A trust or foundation basically falls within the scope of this taxation if the settlor, the settlor's family, or their descendants (regardless of their residence) are entitled to more than half of the distributions of the foundation. In addition to the taxation of undistributed income, actual distributions will usually also be subject to income taxation at the level of a German resident recipient who may be entitled to a credit for the tax on the undistributed trust income. The details of this taxation on trust income are further outlined below.

(e) Controlled Foreign Companies. The Foreign Relations Tax Act also provides for a taxation of the income of a controlled foreign company (CFC) at the level of a German resident shareholder. This taxation also may apply if the CFC is held by a foreign foundation or trust.[27]

A CFC is defined as a foreign company that generates passive income and is subject to low taxation, i.e., a tax rate of less than 25 percent.[28] Instead of a definition of passive income, the Foreign Relations Tax Act contains a list of active income, e.g., income from a trade or service business.[29]

The passive income of a CFC is normally only allocated to a German resident if this resident alone or in association with other German residents holds more than 50 percent of the shares in the CFC.[30] If the income of the CFC is to be qualified as investment income (Einkünfte mit Kapitalanlagecharakter), this income is allocated to a German resident shareholder of the CFC, provided this shareholder holds at least 1 percent of the shares in the CFC.[31] The Foreign Relations Tax Act defines investment income as income resulting from the holding and administration of cash funds, shares, securities, investment funds, and so on, including the related capital gains.[32]

However, dividend income from corporations does not fall within the scope of the CFC taxation.[33] Such income is regarded as active income. The same applies to capital gains[34] resulting from the sale of shares in corporations, so long as this capital gain does not result from passive investment income of the respective corporation.

---

27. Sec. 15.5.3 Directive regarding the Application of the Foreign Relations Tax Act (AEAStG), May 14, 2004; BStBl I Special Edition 1/2004, 3. German lawmakers intend to introduce statutory law to this effect. *See* sec. 15 para. 9 Foreign Relations Tax Act according to the Annual Tax Bill 2013 (Jahressteuergesetz 2013), Oct. 24, 2012, BT-Drs. 17/11190 and Apr. 10, 2013, BT-Drs. 17/13033.

28. Sec. 8 Foreign Relations Tax Act.

29. Sec. 8 para. 1 no. 1, 10 Foreign Relations Tax Act.

30. Sec. 7 para. 1 Foreign Relations Tax Act.

31. Sec. 7 para. 6 Foreign Relations Tax Act.

32. Sec. 7 para. 6a Foreign Relations Tax Act.

33. Sec. 8 para. 1 no. 8 Foreign Relations Tax Act.

34. Sec. 8 para. 1 no. 9 Foreign Relations Tax Act.

(f) Exit Taxation. The German Foreign Relations Tax Act still provides for exit taxation.[35] This type of taxation applies if an individual who has been a German resident for at least ten years and holds at least 1 percent of a German or foreign cooperation relinquishes his or her German residence. In this case, the built-in gain contained in the corporate shares are taxed as a fictitious capital gain.

In March 11, 2004, the European Court of Justice (ECJ) passed the *de Lasteyrie du Saillant* ruling[36] with respect to the French exit tax rules, which were regarded as a violation of the freedom of establishment by the ECJ. Instead of abolishing the exit tax, Germany opted for an amendment of the existing rules. According to this amendment, the German exit tax is suspended so long as the taxpayer moves to a country within the European Union[37] or the European Economic Area (EEA)[38] in which he or she is subject to a taxation, which is equivalent to the German unlimited taxation for residents.

However, German lawmakers have used the amendment of the German exit taxation rules for a further complication through an introduction of extensive documentation requirements. In addition, the exit tax now also applies to cases in which the shares in the respective cooperation are passed from a resident taxpayer to a non-EU/EEA taxpayer by way of inheritance or to any transaction that would exclude the future German taxation of capital gains from a sale of the shares. A transfer of corporate shares by a German resident shareholder to a foreign trust could consequently also lead to German exit taxation.

The *de Lasteyrie du Saillant* decision has clearly made it easier for individual shareholders to take up residence in another EU/EEA country. However, the exit taxation still applies to individuals moving to non-EU countries.

2. Limited Income Taxation

(a) Income Sources Subject to German Limited Income Taxation. German limited income taxation applies to nonresidents who receive certain German-source income,[39] e.g., income resulting from:

- German real estate (rental income or capital gains generated within ten years upon acquisition);
- German business establishments;
- interests in German business partnerships;
- dividends from German corporations;
- capital gains from the sale of shares in German corporations (minimum share of 1 percent required);

35. Sec. 6 Foreign Relations Tax Act.

36. E.C.J. decision C-9/02.

37. EU countries: Austria, Belgium, Bulgaria, Cyprus, Czech Republic, Denmark, Estonia, Finland, France, Germany, Greece, Hungary, Ireland, Italy, Latvia, Lithuania, Luxembourg, Malta, Netherlands, Poland, Portugal, Romania, Slovakia, Slovenia, Spain, Sweden, U.K., but not the Channel Islands.

38. EEA countries: All twenty-seven EU countries plus Iceland, Liechtenstein, and Norway.

39. Sec. 49 Income Tax Act.

- interest from loans secured by German mortgages;
- German employment.

(b) Consequences of German Limited Income Taxation. The German-source income will be taxed at the same rates that are applicable under unlimited income taxation. This taxation can in principle also apply to a foreign trust with German-source income, since such trust would be subject to the limited corporate income taxation.[40] However, for German property law reasons, a trust will usually not directly hold German income sources (see below).

Deductions are limited under limited income taxation.[41] Losses can only be deducted if they are incurred in connection with German-source income. Deductions for items such as social security contributions are not available. Charitable donations can be deducted to the same extent as under unlimited income taxation. Expenses incurred in connection with income that is not subject to German taxation cannot be deducted.

(c) Extended Limited Income Taxation. Extended limited income taxation applies to individuals who have been subject to German unlimited taxation as German residents for at least five years while being German citizens and who have moved to a low-tax country (taxation of less than two-thirds of the German taxation under the normal rules of the respective country).[42]

The extended limited income taxation further requires that the taxpayer maintain significant economic interests in Germany (e.g., partnership shares). Shares in foreign corporations that would lead to an allocation of CFC income are to be regarded as significant economic interests in Germany.[43] However, the Directive regarding the Application of the Foreign Relations Tax Act suggests that foreign foundation or trust entitlements do not constitute such economic interests in Germany.[44] This raises the question as to whether the extended limited taxation would also include the income of a CFC held by a foreign foundation or trust (*see supra* Section II.A.1.e).

Extended limited taxation applies to all German-source income for a period of ten years after moving to the respective country. Such income is taxed at the rate applicable to the individual's worldwide income. This may lead to significantly higher taxation than the normal limited income taxation.

B. German Income Taxation under Tax Treaty Provisions

Both German unlimited and limited as well as extended limited taxation under German national tax law may be restricted by the provisions of a tax treaty

40. Sec. 2 para. 1 Corporate Income Tax Act (Körperschaftsteuergesetz–KStG).
41. Sec. 50 Income Tax Act.
42. Sec. 2 Foreign Relations Tax Act.
43. Sec. 2 para. 4 Foreign Relations Tax Act.
44. Sec. 2.4.2. Directive regarding the Application of the Foreign Relations Tax Act (AEAStG); *see also* Flick/Wassermeyer/Baumhoff/Schönfeld, AStG, sec. 2 note 55b.

concluded between Germany and the country in which the taxpayer is resident or the respective sources of income are located. For income tax purposes, Germany has tax treaties with more than ninety countries, among them the United States. Most of these treaties follow the OECD Model Tax Treaty.

1. Residence under Tax Treaty Provisions

Tax treaties commonly contain a tiebreaker provision that allocates the tax treaty residence to only one country if an individual maintains a residence under the respective national tax laws in both countries.[45] This also applies to the tax treaty between Germany and the United States.[46]

The respective treaty provisions allocate the tax residence to the country in which the individual maintains his or her center of vital interests. This center of vital interests is located in the country with which the individual has developed the closer personal, economic, and social ties. If the center of vital interests cannot be determined based on these aspects, the individual is deemed to be a tax treaty resident of the country in which he or she habitually stays. In case the habitual stay cannot be identified, the citizenship of the individual determines the tax treaty residence.

2. Consequences for Individuals Having Their Tax Treaty Residence in Germany

Individuals having their tax treaty residence in Germany are usually exempt from German taxation on certain sources of income located in the other tax treaty country. With respect to the tax treaty concluded with the United States, the income from the following sources is (with certain exceptions) exempted from German taxation:[47]

- rental income or capital gains from real estate located in the United States;[48]
- income from business establishments, including interests in business partnerships located in the United States.[49]

Interest income from U.S. sources, dividends resulting from U.S. corporate shares, or license income from the United States are taxed in Germany, although this income may be subject to U.S. withholding taxes.[50]

Income from sources in third countries will always be subject to German taxation, unless otherwise provided by a tax treaty concluded between Germany and the respective third country.[51]

45. Art. 4 OECD Model Tax Treaty.
46. Art. 4 U.S.-German Tax Treaty.
47. Art. 23 para. 3 a) U.S.-German Tax Treaty.
48. Arts. 6 and 13 U.S.-German Tax Treaty.
49. Art. 7 U.S.-German Tax Treaty.
50. Arts. 10 (dividend income), 11 (interest income), and 12 (license income) U.S.-German Tax Treaty.
51. Art. 21 U.S.-German Tax Treaty.

Foreign income is usually exempted from German taxation, however it is subject to an inclusion in the determination of the German tax rate (Progressionsvorbehalt). This means that tax-exempt income is added to taxable income in order to determine the tax rate. This increased tax rate is then applied to the taxable (nonexempted) income.

It is important to note that tax treaty provisions do not affect the German taxation of CFC income or undistributed income of a foreign trust at the level of a German resident shareholder, trust settlor, or beneficiary. The Foreign Relations Tax Act contains a specific treaty-override provision.[52] This is widely criticized in the professional literature.[53] This means that an individual with a dual tax residence under national tax law in Germany and, e.g., the United States but with a tax treaty residence in the United States, would—due to the German unlimited income taxation—nevertheless be subject to German taxation on undistributed trust income.

3. Consequences for Individuals Not Having Their Tax Treaty Residence in Germany

Individuals not having their tax treaty residence in Germany are commonly only subject to German taxation with income from certain German sources. This handling effectively limits the limited taxation under German national tax law. Most important, the tax treaties limit the German jurisdiction to taxing the following German sources:

- rental income and capital gains from German real estate
- income from German business establishments or business partnerships

As far as taxation in the United States is concerned, the U.S.-German Tax Treaty provides for a tax credit with respect to the German tax assessed on the respective German-source income.[54]

Under the U.S.-German Tax Treaty, dividends and interest payments from German sources are subject to U.S. taxation. However, such income may be subject to German withholding taxes at a maximum rate specified in the tax treaty. Not all German interest income is subject to German withholding tax. Interest income received by foreign residents will only be subject to German withholding tax in certain cases, most importantly if the interest income is paid for loans secured by German real estate.[55] Other income, particularly income from third countries, would be subject to taxation unless otherwise provided for by tax treaties between the United States and the respective third country.

52. Art. 20 para. 1 Foreign Relations Tax Act.
53. *See, e.g.*, Flick/Wassermeyer/Baumhoff/Schönfeld, AStG, sec. 20 note 47.
54. Art. 23 para. 1 US/German Tax Treaty.
55. Sec. 49 para. 1 no. 5 c Income Tax Act.

III. German Inheritance/Gift Taxation

The inheritance or gift taxation in Germany will depend on the residence and citizenship of the deceased or donor of gifts and the potential heirs or recipients of gifts as well as on the type, location and value of the respective assets and liabilities. Inheritances and gifts are generally treated in the same way for German tax purposes. Both fall within the scope of the German Inheritance Tax Act (Erbschaftsteuergesetz–ErbStG). Since transfers to a foreign trust by German resident settlors or trust distributions to German beneficiaries may lead to German inheritance or gift taxation, it is important for the international adviser to understand the main concepts of German inheritance or gift taxation.

A. German Inheritance/Gift Taxation under National German Tax Law

1. Unlimited Inheritance/Gift Taxation

An inheritance or a gift is subject to German unlimited inheritance taxation if the deceased, the donor of a gift, or the recipient of an inheritance or a gift maintains a German residence or habitual stay.[56] The requirements of a German residence or habitual stay for inheritance tax purposes are the same as for income tax purposes (see above). The German unlimited inheritance tax applies to all assets transferred by inheritance or gift regardless of their type or location (worldwide assets).

2. Extended Unlimited Inheritance/Gift Taxation

The extended unlimited inheritance/gift taxation applies to German citizens who have been German residents and who have given up their German residence less than five years before the inheritance or the gift. If a German citizen who has been a German resident moves to the United States, the five-year period is extended to ten years.[57] This type of taxation also applies to all assets transferred by inheritance or gift regardless of their type or location (worldwide assets). The extended unlimited inheritance taxation can be avoided by giving up German citizenship. However, this would require that the taxpayer acquires another citizenship.[58] The tax classes, rates, and tax-free amounts are the same as under the unlimited inheritance taxation.

The German extended unlimited taxation is an example of a regulation that has not yet been under review by the ECJ but may in fact violate EU law. This is because it discriminates against Germans moving to another EU country, which may potentially lead to a double taxation with respect to gifts or inheritances, while a non-German taxpayer would face no such risk. However, based on the

56. Sec. 2 para. 1 no. 1 a Inheritance Tax Act (Erbschaftsteuergesetz–ErbStG).
57. Art. 3 of the German Tax Treaty Transformation Act of Sept. 15, 2000.
58. Sec. 18, 25, 26 Citizenship Act (Staatsangehörigkeitsgesetz–StAG).

ECJ decisions *Van-Hilten*[59] and *Block*,[60] it is highly probable that the ECJ would not regard the German extended unlimited inheritance/gift taxation as a violation of EU law. In the *Van-Hilten* ruling, the ECJ concluded that a similar Dutch regulation did not violate the free movement of capital since the rule does not prevent nonresidents investing in assets located in the Netherlands. In the *Block* decision, the ECJ stated that the EU member states are to a certain extent autonomous with respect to taxation and are consequently not obliged to adjust their national taxes in a way that would avoid any potential double taxation in another EU member state. It is therefore not very likely that the German extended unlimited taxation will be abolished or amended in the near future.

3. Limited Inheritance/Gift Taxation

The limited inheritance taxation[61] only applies to individuals who are not subject to either unlimited or extended unlimited inheritance taxation and is limited to transfers of German situs assets[62] such as:

- German real estate;
- German tangible business assets or partnership interests;
- shares of at least 10 percent held directly or indirectly in a German corporation;
- copyrights, etc. registered in Germany;
- loan receivables secured by German mortgages, etc.;
- silent partnerships in a German business.

If these assets are held by foreign partnerships, these partnerships are regarded as transparent entities for German inheritance tax purposes. A limited inheritance taxation of German real estate could therefore, for instance, not be avoided by transferring the ownership of the real estate to a foreign partnership. However, if the transfer is made to a foreign corporation, a later transfer of the shares in this corporation by way of gift or inheritance may, under certain conditions, not qualify as a taxable transfer of German real estate. In this case, no German inheritance tax would arise.[63] However, it will not always be possible to transfer the real estate to the holding company free of income tax. Real estate transfer tax may also apply at 3.5 percent (5 percent in some German states) of the real estate value.

4. Extended Limited Inheritance/Gift Taxation

The extended limited inheritance taxation applies to testators and donors of gifts who—as German residents—have been subject to German unlimited taxation while being German citizens for at least five years before leaving Germany and who, at their death or at the time of the transfer of the gift, are residing in a

59. E.C.J. decision Feb. 23, 2006, C-513/03.
60. E.C.J. decision Feb. 12, 2009, C-67/08.
61. Sec. 2 para. 1 no. 3 Inheritance Tax Act.
62. Sec. 121 Valuation Act (Bewertungsgesetz–BewG).
63. Sec. 2.2 para. 3 Inheritance Tax Directive (Erbschaftsteuerrichtlinien–ErbStR).

low-income tax country.[64] The taxpayer cannot opt out of this type of taxation. The extended limited inheritance taxation expires ten years after leaving Germany. It cannot be prevented by an abandonment of German citizenship after leaving Germany. The tax rates and tax-free amounts are equivalent to the amounts granted under limited inheritance taxation.

All assets that would lead to income taxable in Germany if the testator had been subject to German unlimited income taxation (see above II.A.2.c.) at the time of his or her death or at the time of the transfer of the gift would fall within the scope of the extended limited inheritance taxation. This type of taxation would consequently apply to the assets subject to German limited inheritance taxation and also, e.g., to German bank accounts and shares in German corporations of less than 1 percent.

The Directive regarding the Application of the Foreign Relation Tax Act also lists foreign foundation or trust assets as assets that fall within the extended limited inheritance taxation.[65] However, since the extended limited inheritance taxation is linked to the extended limited income taxation, and foreign foundation or trust entitlements do not constitute economic interests in Germany,[66] it is arguable that only German situs assets held by foreign foundations or trusts are subject to the extended limited inheritance taxation.

B. German Inheritance/Gift Taxation under Tax Treaty Provisions

The inheritance and gift taxation under German national tax law may be limited by inheritance tax treaties. Germany has concluded inheritance tax treaties with Denmark, France, Greece, Sweden, Switzerland, and the United States.

1. Residence under Tax Treaty Provisions

The inheritance tax treaty between Germany and the United States basically allocates a tax treaty residence of an individual according to the same rules as the German-U.S. Income Tax Treaty (*see supra* Section II.B.1). However, if an individual is only a German citizen, and if this individual maintains a U.S. and German residence, he or she will be regarded as having a German inheritance tax residence if the U.S. residence was not maintained for more than ten years.[67]

2. Consequences for Individuals Having Their Inheritance Tax Treaty Residence in Germany

Individuals having their inheritance tax treaty residence in Germany are usually exempt from German inheritance taxation on inheritances or gifts consisting of assets located in the other tax treaty countries.

64. Sec. 4 Foreign Relations Tax Act.
65. Sec. 4.1.1. no. 9 Directive Regarding the Application of the Foreign Relations Tax Act.
66. *See supra* note 31.
67. Art. 4 para. 3 German-U.S. Inheritance Tax Treaty.

With respect to the Inheritance Tax Treaty[68] between Germany and the United States, the following assets would be exempt from German taxation:

- Real estate located in the United States;[69]
- Business assets located in the United States;[70] and
- Shares in partnerships to the extent the partnership owns U.S. real estate or U.S. business assets.[71]

All other German or worldwide assets would be subject to German inheritance or gift taxation. With respect to transfers to trusts, the Tax Treaty clarifies that Germany would not be hindered in applying its national tax law.[72]

Assets that are exempt from German inheritance or gift taxation under the tax treaty would be subject to an inclusion in the determination of the German tax rate (Progressionsvorbehalt).[73] This means that the tax-exempt assets are added to the taxable assets in order to determine the tax rate. The increased tax rate is then applied to the taxable (nonexempt) assets.

3. Consequences for Individuals Not Having Their Inheritance Tax Treaty Residence in Germany

Individuals not having their tax treaty residence in Germany are only subject to German inheritance or gift taxation with respect to German situ assets mentioned in above in Section III.B.2. Shares in German or foreign corporations or German bank accounts would consequently not be subject to a German inheritance or gift taxation.

C. Main Taxable Events

1. Transfers of Property by Reason of Death

The main taxable event under German inheritance and gift tax law is the transfer of property by reason of death (mortis *causa*).[74] Such taxable event includes inheritances as well as gifts, donations, or legacies upon the death of the donor and benefits directly acquired by a third person due to a contract(s) drawn up by the decedent (such as life insurance policies). Also, the funding of a German or a foreign foundation or foreign trust by the decedent's will is regarded as an acquisition of property by reason of death.[75]

It is important to note that transfers between spouses are generally taxable. However, spouses are regularly joint owners of the increase in capital value of their assets that are generated during the marriage. Upon the end of the marriage,

68. The Treaty also applies to gifts.
69. Art. 5 German-U.S. Inheritance Tax Treaty.
70. Art. 6 German-U.S. Inheritance Tax Treaty.
71. Art. 8 German-U.S. Inheritance Tax Treaty.
72. Art. 12 para. 1 German-U.S. Inheritance Tax Treaty.
73. Sec. 19 para. 2 Inheritance Tax Act.
74. Sec. 3 Inheritance Tax Act.
75. Sec. 3 para. 2 no. 1 Inheritance Tax Act.

such increase in capital value has to be equalized between the former spouses (Zugewinnausgleich).[76] If a marriage is terminated by the death of one spouse, the equalized amount does not form part of the taxable property transfer for inheritance tax purposes.[77] The same applies if the equalization of the increase in capital value takes place due to contractual arrangements between spouses about the applicable matrimonial property regime.

The net assets of a German family foundation (Familienstiftung) or other German association founded in the interest of one or more families is subject to inheritance tax every thirty years from the first funding of the foundation or association (Erbersatzsteuer).[78]

2. Lifetime Gifts

The second important taxable event under German inheritance and gift tax law is the granting of lifetime gifts.[79] Taxable lifetime gifts are also transfers of property to a German or foreign foundation or a foreign trust during the lifetime of the donor (settlor);[80] property received by a beneficiary upon the dissolution of a foundation or a foreign trust; and distributions during the existence of the trust.[81] Obligatory distributions from a foundation based on specific provisions in the deeds of the foundation are not subject to a gift tax.

D. Personal Tax-Free Allowances and Tax Rates

The inheritance tax is applied to a special tax base. This tax base is determined based on the fair market value of the transferred assets and liabilities according to a special Valuation Act (Bewertungsgesetz–BewG) and reduced by tax-free personal allowances. The following personal allowances are available in Germany for transfers by way of gift or inheritance:

Tax Class	Transferee	Current Law
I	Spouses, registered life partners	EUR 500,000
	Children	EUR 400,000
	Grandchildren, great grandchildren	EUR 200,000
	Parents and grandparents in the case of succession	EUR 100,000

76. Sec. 1371, 1372 Civil Code (Bürgerliches Gesetzbuch–BGB).
77. Sec. 5 Inheritance Tax Act.
78. Sec. 1 para. 2 Inheritance Tax Act.
79. Sec. 7 Inheritance Tax Act.
80. Sec. 7 para. 1 no. 8 Inheritance Tax Act.
81. Sec. 7 para. 1 no. 9 Inheritance Tax Act.

II	Parents and grandparents in the case of a gift; siblings, nieces, and nephews; stepchildren, children-in-law, divorced spouses, or life partners	EUR 20,000
III	Other	EUR 20,000

In case of more than one transfer from one person to one recipient, the tax base is determined by adding up the gifts and the inheritance received within a ten-year period.[82] The gift tax paid for previous gifts will be credited against the final inheritance tax to be paid on the accumulated ten-year tax base. As an effect of this procedure, the recipient can only make use of the above tax-free amounts once in a ten-year period.

Additional tax exemptions are granted in the case of an inheritance at EUR 256,000 for spouses and from EUR 10,300 to EUR 52,000 for children, depending on the age. These exemptions are reduced if the respective heir also receives pension benefits originating from the deceased.

The following inheritance and gift tax rates are applied to the tax base:

Value of the acquisition subject to tax up to and including Euro	Percentage rate in the tax class		
	I	II	III
75,000	7	30	30
300,000	11	30	30
600,000	15	30	30
6,000,000	19	30	30
13,000,000	23	50	50
26,000,000	27	50	50
in excess of 26,000,000	30	50	50

The tax rates under limited inheritance taxation are the same as the rates under unlimited inheritance taxation. However, the tax-free amounts available under unlimited inheritance taxation do not apply. Instead, the recipient of a gift or inheritance that is subject to limited inheritance taxation only has a tax-free amount of EUR 2,000.[83]

82. Sec. 14 Inheritance Tax Act.
83. Sec. 16 para. 2 Inheritance Tax Act.

The low tax-free allowance for nonresident taxpayers was subject to criticism under EU law. The ECJ has regarded it as a violation of the EU freedom of free movement of capital.[84] Germany has chosen a problematic approach to remedy this problem. Individuals not resident in Germany but resident in another EU/EEA country may now choose to be treated as resident individuals and thus qualify for the higher tax-free allowances for resident taxpayers.[85] However, the treatment as resident taxpayer can have undesirable effects since all gifts or inheritances received by the taxpayer from the same person within the last ten years would be added up irrespective of their location in order to determine the tax base. The EU Commission still regards the amended German rules as a violation of EU law and has initiated ECJ proceedings against Germany.

E. Special Tax Exemption for Business Transfers

If certain requirements are met, a tax relief is available for business transfers.[86] The relief amounts to 85 percent or even 100 percent of the inheritance/gift tax due on the fair market value of the transferred business assets.

Shares in a German or a EU/EEA corporation are regarded as business assets if they amount to more than 25 percent of the total shares in the company and if the company holds less than 50 percent passive assets. Passive assets are, e.g., securities not serving business purposes, art and other collectables, and shares in corporate subsidiaries of only 25 percent or less. The relief of 85 percent of the regular tax due on the market value of these shares is only available if the total amount of employee salaries paid at the level of the transferred business in the five years following the transfer will be no less than 400 percent of the average of the total annual salaries paid in the five years prior to the transfer. A reduction of the salary amount leads to a proportional reduction of the tax exemption. The tax reduction is also subject to a five-year holding period for the transferred shares at the level of the new owner. A sale prior to the end of the holding period leads to a proportional loss of the tax exemption (e.g., one-fifth of the 85 percent tax reduction for each year the shares are sold too early).

A 100 percent tax reduction applies if a total salary amount of 700 percent of the original average annual salary (see above) is maintained for seven years following the transfer. However, under this rule, the passive assets of the transferred business may only amount to 10 percent of the total business value. The holding period is also extended from five to seven years.

The rules pertaining to this tax exemption are extremely complex and were only introduced in 2008. There is consequently little experience on how the tax authorities will handle these rules. It is also highly uncertain how long these rules will remain in force. The Federal Tax Court has stated that the tax exemption for business transfers violates the constitutional principle of equality and has

84. E.C.J. decision Apr. 4, 2010 *Mattner*, C-510/08.
85. Sec. 2 para. 3 Inheritance Tax Act.
86. Secs. 13a, 13b Inheritance Tax Act.

therefore initiated a review procedure before the German Constitutional Court (Bundesverfassungsgericht).[87]

IV. German Inheritance Law Implications

A. Application of German Inheritance Law

From a German perspective, the German jurisdiction to the legal succession by way of inheritance is still governed by the provisions contained in the German Conflict of Laws Code (Einführungsgesetz zum BGB–EGBGB). According to this Code, the applicable laws for the legal succession by way of inheritance are determined by the laws of the country of which the decedent was a citizen.[88] German inheritance law therefore applies to the succession after German citizens regardless of where the deceased maintained his or her residence and regardless of the worldwide location of the assets belonging to the estate.

If a person has two citizenships, the applicable inheritance law is determined by the jurisdiction to which the person maintains the closest ties. However, if a person is a German citizen (besides having other citizenships), the German citizenship always has priority.[89] A German citizen cannot choose the jurisdiction applicable to his succession by inheritance.

With respect to certain assets, the legal succession by inheritance may be determined by foreign law. If the German citizenship of a person leads to the application of German inheritance law, this would not apply to assets located in another country and subject to special laws of that country with respect to the transfer of these assets by inheritance.[90] Such special laws are often relevant with respect to foreign real estate.

As of August 17, 2015, new rules will apply. Under the EU Inheritance Law Directive (Brussels IV), the succession by way of inheritance will be governed by the law of the country in which the decedent was resident at the time of his or her death unless the circumstances suggest a closer connection to another country.[91] Alternatively, a testator may choose the laws of any country of which he or she holds citizenship.[92]

B. German Testaments and Forced Heirship

In Germany, the decedent's property and his or her debts automatically accrue to the successor(s) at the time of the decedent's death.[93] The only requirement

87. Federal Tax Court decision of Sept. 27, 2012, II R 9/11.
88. Art. 25 para. 1 Conflict of Laws Code (Einführungsgesetz zum BGB–EGBGB).
89. Art. 5 para. 1 Conflict of Laws Code.
90. Art. 3a para. 2 Conflict of Laws Code.
91. Art. 21 EU Directive 650/2012 (Brussels IV).
92. Art. 22 EU Directive 650/2012 (Brussels IV).
93. Sec. 1922 Civil Code.

to become successor is that the person survives the death of the decedent for at least one second.

So far as no foreign inheritance law is to be applied with respect to certain foreign assets, all aspects of the legal succession by inheritance will be governed by German inheritance law. This also applies to the formal requirements of a testament. Under German inheritance law, a person is in principle free to determine the succession by testament. This testament must fulfill certain formal requirements. A handwritten testament must be completely handwritten and signed.[94] The testament can be written in English. A public testament is written and certified by a notary public.[95] A formally valid U.S. will would also be valid under German law.[96] However, this would have to be confirmed in each individual case.

Under German inheritance law, the testator cannot entirely disinherit a person who is entitled to a reserved portion of the inheritance under the German forced heirship rules (Pflichtteilsrecht).[97] This applies to the legal heirs, e.g., spouse and children, who would succeed the deceased if no testament was made. A testamentary heir can disclaim his or her testamentary portion and instead claim the reserved portion.

Under the legal succession rules, the spouse would receive 25 percent of the inheritance, which is subject to German inheritance law.[98] The children of the deceased would receive equal parts of the remaining 75 percent.[99] The reserved portion amounts to 50 percent of the normal legal portion.[100] The reserved portion of the spouse would consequently amount to 12.5 percent, while the children would only be able to claim 50 percent of 75 percent (i.e., in the case of three children, 12.5 percent each).

If spouses live in the German statutory joint property regime (Zugewinngemeinschaft),[101] the surviving spouse would be entitled to an increased reserved portion.[102] This additional reserved portion would require that the legal effects of the marriage are governed by German law. Assuming that spouses did not marry in Germany while being German residents, German law should not apply.[103]

Another part of the German forced heirship rules that is important to recognize is the add-back of gifts made by the decedent to others in the ten years prior to his or her death.[104] The add-back is reduced pro rata by one-tenth for each

94. Sec. 2247 Civil Code.
95. Sec. 2232 Civil Code.
96. This follows from art. 26 Conflict of Laws Code and art. 1 of the Hague Convention on the Conflict of Law Relating to the Form of Testamentary Dispositions.
97. Secs. 2303–2338 Civil Code.
98. Sec. 1931 Civil Code.
99. Sec. 1924 Civil Code.
100. Sec. 2303 Civil Code.
101. Sec. 1363 Civil Code.
102. Sec. 1371 Civil Code.
103. Art. 15 Conflict of Laws Code.
104. Sec. 2325 Civil Code.

year that has passed since the year following the gift. The difference between the values of the statutory share (with and without gift add-back) can be claimed as compensation from the heirs.

V. Trusts under German Civil and Tax Law

The general description of the German tax and inheritance law system presented above indicates that estate planning with the use of trust is highly complicated for German residents and will in most cases lead to adverse German tax effects.

A. Validity of Trusts under German Civil Law

Germany has a civil law system that does not contain any concept comparable to Anglo-American trusts and has not entered the Hague Convention on Trusts. The available legal concepts, such as the foundation or the continuous execution of an estate, cannot be used to achieve legal effects comparable to the effects of testamentary or inter vivos trusts.

1. Testamentary Trusts

As outlined above, German inheritance law is applicable to the estate of German citizens irrespective of their residence (*see supra* Section IV.A). From a German perspective, a German testator cannot circumvent the application of German inheritance law by establishing a testamentary trust under foreign law. For this reason, German courts would disregard any transfer of assets to a testamentary trust if one of the legal heirs (under German law) claimed the invalidity of the trust under German inheritance law. However, a legal heir (under German law) could not contest a transfer of assets to the trust if these assets only consisted of assets that fall within the scope of special legal rules in the jurisdiction of their location pertaining to a transfer of these assets by way of inheritance. This could apply in particular to foreign real estate and foreign companies.[105]

The invalidity of the establishment of a testamentary Anglo-American trust by a German testator does not lead to an invalidity of the entire testament.[106] In such a case, the German courts will try to reinterpret the testamentary instructions pertaining to the trust into instructions valid under German civil law (e.g., a continuous execution of the estate).

From August 17, 2015, on, a German citizen will be able to establish a valid testamentary trust under the new rules of Brussels IV so long as he or she is not resident in Germany at the time of death.[107] A U.S. citizen living in Germany can establish a valid testamentary trust under present German inheritance law and under the future rules of Brussels IV.

105. Federal Civil Court (BGH) Apr. 5, 1968, V ZR 18/67, BGHZ 50, 63.
106. Sec. 2084 Civil Code.
107. Art. 21 EU Directive 650/2012 (Brussels IV).

2. Inter Vivos Trusts

Within the concept of German civil law, the establishment of a foreign inter vivos trust is regarded as an obligatory transaction (*in personam*). Under German international private law, the parties to such an *in personam* transaction are free to choose the national law under which this transaction is agreed upon.[108]

Consequently, a German resident individual could establish a foreign inter vivos trust that would be valid under German civil law. Under this law, the settlor could only transfer foreign assets to the foreign trust (testamentary or inter vivos). Because the German legal system does not acknowledge trusts and their specific property regime, a trust cannot directly own German situs assets.[109] This is due to the restricted German property law system that does not provide for a trust-like distinction between legal title and equitable title. However, a trust could hold German assets indirectly, e.g., via a foreign holding corporation.

In certain cases, a formally valid foreign inter vivos trust may nevertheless be regarded as invalid by German courts. In a recent decision, the Higher District Court (OLG) Düsseldorf ruled a Liechtenstein foundation invalid because it was primarily established to evade German taxes.[110] In the underlying case, the heirs of a German testator successfully claimed the assets of a Liechtenstein foundation, which had been established to the benefit of the testator's wife. The testator had neither paid German gift tax on the transfer of the assets to the foundation nor did he tax the income of the foundation. The Court found that the establishment of the foundation violated the core principles of German law (ordre public)[111] and therefore regarded the entire foundation's structure as invalid under German civil law. It should also be mentioned that a similar approach would be applied to transfers to Anglo-American trusts that were primarily made to evade German taxes.

B. Taxation of Trusts

The local German tax offices will generally not have much experience in dealing with trusts. They often will assume that the trust was only established in order to avoid taxes. For this reason, it is extremely important that the adviser disclose all relevant facts and documents when negotiating trust taxation issues with the German tax authorities.

1. Establishment of a Trust

As stated above, the transfer of assets to a trust by a German resident taxpayer is subject to inheritance tax. This applies to the establishment of testamentary

108. Sec. 27 Conflict of Laws Code for transactions before December 17, 2009; sec. 3 EU Directive 593/2008 of June 17, 2008 (Rome I) for transactions after this date.

109. Federal Civil Court June 6, 1984, IV a ZR 196/82, NJW 1984, 2762; von Oertzen, Internationales Steuerrecht 1995, 149; Habammer, Deutsches Steuerrecht 2002, 425.

110. Higher District Court (OLG) Düsseldorf Apr. 30, 2010, I-22 U 126/06.

111. Art. 6 Conflict of Laws Code.

trusts[112] as well as to the establishment of inter vivos trusts.[113] The inheritance tax becomes due on all transfers to the trust made in connection with the establishment of the trust or at a later time.

The tax only arises if the trust gains the full right to the disposition of the assets. If the settlor retains substantial rights with respect to the assets so that he continues to exercise control over these assets, the German tax authorities may regard the trust as a transparent structure. As a consequence, the assets of the trust and the trust income would be allocated directly to the settlor and taxed at his or her level. No gift tax would become due on the transfer of the assets to the transparent trust structure. The Federal Tax Court has ruled that a taxable gift requires that the recipient is legally and factually able to gain full disposition with respect to the transferred assets.[114] This was further confirmed by a decision of the Federal Tax Court with respect to a transfer to a Liechtenstein foundation.[115]

In some cases, it might be preferable to argue that a formal transfer of assets to a trust did not in effect fulfill the requirements of a German gift taxation. This could be the case, for example, if a German resident taxpayer establishes a trust before he or she relocates to another country where he or she later gives up all rights with respect to the disposition of the trust assets. However, in such cases, the taxpayer needs to observe the effects of the extended unlimited inheritance taxation (*see supra* Section III.A.4.3.1.4).

So long as the taxpayer is not yet resident in Germany, he or she should make all intended transfers to a trust before becoming subject to German unlimited taxation.

2. Taxation of Undistributed Trust Income

As outlined above (Section II.A.1.d), a German resident settlor or beneficiary of a foreign family trust will be subject to the special German taxation on the undistributed trust income[116] As long as the settlor is resident in Germany, all undistributed trust income will be taxed at his or her level. After the death of the settlor or after the settlor is no longer a German resident, the trust income will be taxed at the level of the German resident beneficiaries according to their "interest" in the trust. The trust income attributed to the settlor or beneficiary is taxed at normal income tax rates (maximum marginal tax rate 47.475 percent).

German tax authorities will qualify a German resident taxpayer as a beneficiary of a trust if there is a probability of distributions to the taxpayer according to the deed of the trust.[117] This approach is widely criticized as being too rigid, particularly in cases in which the deed of the trust does not grant any concrete entitlements and the presumed "beneficiaries" have no influence on

112. Sec. 3 para. 2 no. 1 Inheritance Tax Act.
113. Sec. 7 para. 1 no. 8 Inheritance Tax Act.
114. Federal Tax Court Jan. 25, 2001, II R 39/98, BFH/NV 2001, 908.
115. Federal Tax Court June 28, 2007, II R 21/05, BStBl. II 2007, 669.
116. Sec. 15 Foreign Relations Tax Act.
117. Sec. 15.2.1. Directive regarding the Application of the Foreign Relations Tax Act.

the distribution policy.[118] However, the Federal Fiscal Court upheld the extensive definition of "beneficiaries" applied by the tax authorities.[119] As a result of this extensive approach, it is often almost impossible to determine the "share" of trust income to be allocated to German residents, particularly in cases in which the trust deed merely specifies the "issue" of the settlor as beneficiaries.

For purposes of this taxation, the income of the trust is determined according to the rules applicable to German resident entities.[120] For this reason, tax exemptions available to German entities would also be available to the trust, e.g., the 95 percent tax exemption for dividend income.[121] However, according to the Annual Tax Bill 2013, such deductions or exemptions will not be possible from 2013 onward.[122]

German taxation and reporting obligations with respect to the trust income can, under certain conditions, be avoided, so long as the income is generated by a corporate subsidiary of the trust and if the income of this subsidiary was neither distributed nor to be directly or indirectly attributed to the trust or the German resident settlor or beneficiaries. German tax authorities will attribute undistributed income generated by a corporate subsidiary of the foundation to the settlor or beneficiaries, if the subsidiary were to be qualified as a CFC (*see supra* Section I.A.1.e). However, so long as the subsidiary was subject to a taxation of at least 25 percent, its undistributed income could not be attributed to the trust and the settlor or beneficiaries. If the subsidiary was taxed at a rate of less than 25 percent, attributable income could be avoided if the subsidiary only generated active income. Since trusts commonly hold passive assets, such as cash accounts and securities, it is unlikely that passive income could be completely avoided.

If the trust is resident in an EU/EEA country, the taxation of undistributed income does not apply if the trust has unlimited rights with respect to the disposition of its assets and if its country of residence has entered into an extensive tax information exchange agreement with Germany.[123] EU law provides for a free movement of capital,[124] and this fundamental EU freedom also applies to investments in non-EU countries like the United States or the Channel Islands (Erga Omnes Effect). For this reason, the restriction of the exclusion of the taxation of undistributed trust income to EU/EEA trusts should violate EU law,[125] but so far, it has not been challenged in the German Tax Courts or in the ECJ.

118. *E.g.*, Flick/Wassermeyer/Baumhoff/Schönfeld, AStG, sec. 15 note 49.

119. Federal Tax Court Apr. 25, 2001, II R 41/98, BFH/NV 2001, 1457.

120. Sec. 15.1.1. Directive regarding the Application of the Foreign Relations Tax Act.

121. Sec. 8b para. 1 Corporate Income Tax Act.

122. *See* sec. 15 para 1 Foreign Relations Tax Act according to the Annual Tax Bill 2013 (Jahressteuergesetz 2013), Oct. 24, 2012, BT-Drs. 17/11190, and Apr. 10, 2013, BT-Drs. 17/13033.

123. Sec. 15 para. 6 Foreign Relations Tax Act, applicable since 2009.

124. Art. 63 Treaty on the Functioning of the European Union (TFEU).

125. Werder/Dannecker, Betriebs-Berater 2012, 2278.

3. Taxation of Trust Distributions

Actual distributions from trusts will be subject to income tax at the level of the German resident recipient.[126] This rule has been in effect since January 1, 2011. Prior to this, only recurrent trust distributions were taxable at the level of a German resident settlor or beneficiary. Although such recurrent distributions were taxed at the regular progressive tax rates, distributions received from 2011 onward are taxed at the special flat rate of 26.375 percent[127] if they are comparable to dividend payments. To the extent the distribution has already been taxed as undistributed trust income at the level of the recipient, there will be no tax on the actual distribution.[128]

Trust distributions to German residents will also be subject to gift tax at the tax rates of 30 to 50 percent applicable to unrelated parties (*see supra* Section III.C.2). Although obligatory distributions from a foundation based on specific provisions in the deeds of the foundation are not subject to gift tax, comparable trust distributions will always be regarded as taxable gifts according to the explicit wording of the Inheritance Tax Act.[129] This leads to an effective double taxation of trust distributions with income tax and gift tax.

4. German Tax Residence of the Trust

Under certain circumstances, the foreign trust itself may become subject to German corporation income taxation (Körperschaftsteuer). Under the German Corporation Income Tax Act (Körperschaftsteuergesetz—KStG), a trust is to be qualified as a special purpose fund (Zweckvermögen). Such a special purpose fund may be regarded as a German resident entity if it is managed by a German resident trustee.[130] This would lead to an unlimited German corporation income taxation of the trust on its worldwide income. For this reason, a trust should be managed exclusively by trustees who are not resident in Germany.

VI. Conclusion

Trusts are clearly not the ideal estate planning tool for German resident individuals. Not only the German taxation rules but also the restrictions of the German inheritance law make it extremely difficult to create and manage a family trust in a tax-efficient way if German residents are among the beneficiaries. These issues

126. Sec. 20 para. 1 no. 9 Income Tax Act.

127. Twenty-five percent income tax plus 5.5 percent surcharge tax on the income tax, sec. 32d Income Tax Act.

128. Sec. 15.1.5. Directive regarding the Application of the Foreign Relations Tax Act.; sec. 15 para. 11 Foreign Relations Tax Act according to the Annual Tax Bill 2013 (Jahressteuergesetz 2013), Oct. 24, 2012, BT-Drs. 17/11190, art. 6 no. 4 d).

129. Sec. 7 para. 1 no. 9 Inheritance Tax Act.

130. Sec. 1 para. 1 no. 5 Corporation Income Tax Act (Körperschaftsteuergesetz—KStG).

need to be addressed by the international adviser before a client moves to Germany. The adviser also needs to consider whether the estate planning objectives of the client can be reached with the aid of an alternative structure, such as an EU/EEA foundation.

PART VII

Considerations Pertaining to Particular Foreign Jurisdictions

Special Considerations in U.S.-Canada Estate Planning

16

Wolfe D. Goodman
Updated by
Mary Anne Bueschkens
Lucinda E. Main
Jason P. Trenton

I. Elimination of Canadian Federal Estate and Gift Taxes at the End of 1971

At the end of 1971, the government of Canada ceased to levy estate and gift taxes. At the same time, it instituted a system of taxation of capital gains, which had not previously been taxed in Canada, including deemed realization at fair market value of most forms of property at death and on the making of inter vivos gifts.[1] There were apparently two reasons for repealing estate and gift taxes. First, the federal government must have recognized that, although pre-1972 appreciation would not be taxed under its new system of capital gains taxation, as time went on and as post-1971

1. This major change was the federal government's response to the 1966 Report of the Royal Commission on Taxation (the Carter Report), but the government completely rejected the Commission's recommendation that gifts and inheritances be simply included in the recipient's income for tax purposes, and it accepted only partial taxation of capital gains, rather than their full inclusion in income, as the Commission had recommended.

appreciation became more significant, the combined incidence at death of estate taxes and taxes on capital gains was likely to become politically unpalatable. Second, under the complex federal-provincial arrangements that existed in 1971, about 75 percent of the estate tax revenues collected by the federal government were paid over to the provincial government, with only about 25 percent being retained.[2] At a time when a considerable number of articulate taxpayers were calling on the federal government to repeal estate and gift taxes, it was an astute political move for the federal government to abandon taxes for which it received almost all of the criticism but retained so little of the net revenue.

Commencing in 1972, six of the ten Canadian provinces—the four Atlantic provinces (Newfoundland, Nova Scotia, New Brunswick, and Prince Edward Island) and two Western provinces (Manitoba and Saskatchewan)—which had previously not levied their own death taxes and which had received 75 percent of the estate taxes collected by the federal government with respect to estates in their provinces, instituted new Succession Duty Acts. Three other provinces (Ontario, Quebec, and British Columbia), which previously had been levying their own succession duties, under federal-provincial arrangements, which involved the federal government forgoing 50 percent of the normal estate tax for estates in these provinces, doubled their rates of succession duties. Only Alberta declined to impose succession duties, becoming a sort of Canadian death tax haven.

The ultimate result of these moves was predictable. As the provincial governments began to realize that the combined effect of imposition of succession duties and income taxes on deemed realizations at death would become politically unwise, particularly when Alberta was not levying succession duties, they began to repeal their Succession Duty Acts. Some even cancelled them retroactively to the beginning of 1972. Ontario adopted, as a temporary relief measure, a dollar-for-dollar credit against its succession duties for income taxes imposed under the deemed realization rules. This measure was difficult to justify in principle and one that Quebec considered and rejected. Ontario and Quebec were the last to repeal their Acts: Ontario in 1979 and Quebec in 1986. As a result, none of the federal or provincial governments presently levy any form of traditional death taxes based on the net capital value of a decedent's estate. In retrospect, it might have been possible for the federal and provincial governments to have retained their former death taxes if, instead of providing for deemed realizations at death under the new system of taxing capital gains, they had provided for a carryover of cost basis from the decedent to his or her estate or heirs; however, it was clearly politically unpalatable for them to retain them indefinitely and, at the same time, to tax deemed realizations at death.

---

2. The pattern of federal and provincial death taxes in Canada is described in Wolfe D. Goodman, *Death Taxes in Canada: In the Past and in the Possible Future*, 43 CAN. TAX J. 1360 (1995).

II. Canadian Taxation of Capital Gains in Transferred Property after 1971

Under the system of taxation of realized capital gains, which began in 1972, 50 percent of realized capital gains were includable in income. There is no separate system of capital gains taxes. Only appreciation arising after 1971 was subject to tax unless the taxpayer elected to use the historic cost of the property where it exceeded its value at the end of 1971. The includable percentage was increased to 66 2/3 percent in 1988 and to 75 percent in 1990. In February 2000, the rate was reduced to 66 2/3 percent and in October 2000 to 50 percent, where it remains today. As part of this scheme, inter vivos gifts are treated as deemed realizations at fair market value with certain exceptions, including gifts to the donor's spouse, either directly or through a trust for the spouse's exclusive benefit during his or her lifetime, and gifts of farm and fishing businesses to children, both of which are subject to a carryover of cost regime.

Most property owned at death is also treated as being disposed of at fair market value with similar exceptions. In each case, the donee or beneficiary is treated as having acquired the property at a cost equal to the value at which the donor or the decedent is deemed to have disposed of it. Because it was recognized that retention of property in a trust could be a method of avoiding deemed realization at death, the legislation also provided for periodic revaluation of trust assets every twenty-one years, with tax then being payable on any appreciation except for trusts for the exclusive benefit of a spouse where deemed realization would occur only upon the spouse's death.

Another exception is for trusts established after 1999 by individuals aged sixty-five years or older for their exclusive benefit during their lifetime (alter ego trusts) or for the exclusive benefit of themselves and their spouses (married or common law) until the second death (joint spousal trusts). Both of these trusts are subject to deemed realization at fair market value at death (for alter ego trusts it is at the settlor's death, and for joint spousal trusts it is at the death of the second spouse).

Finally, when an individual ceases to be resident in Canada, he or she is deemed to have disposed of certain of his or her capital property at fair market value, and a tax is levied on the accrued gain.

III. The Canadian Approach to Life Insurance Taxation

A. Life Insurance Policies

Curiously, although there is nothing in the Canadian income tax legislation specifically exempting taxation of gains arising from the maturity of a life insurance policy on the death of the insured, such an exemption is clearly understood in Canada. The gain is specifically excluded from the definition of a capital gain in the

Income Tax Act (Canada), R.S.C. 1985, c.1 (5th Suppl.) (the ITA) by subparagraph 39(1)(a)(iii). Although it could conceivably be regarded as ordinary income, this is not a position that has ever been attempted in Canada.

Taxation of the "inside interest buildup" in a cash value life insurance policy has presented serious policy problems for Canadian tax authorities who have been concerned about the use of life insurance policies as vehicles for tax-sheltered savings. The authorities have had somewhat less reason to be concerned about situations in which a policy with substantial inside interest buildup is surrendered. In that event, the law provides that the excess of the proceeds of disposition of the policy over its adjusted cost basis have to be included in the policyholder's income in the year of surrender. However, to the extent that inside interest buildup, which is occurring annually, is taxed only on disposition of the policy, on surrender or maturity otherwise than on death, there is a significant tax deferral advantage for taxpayers in higher income brackets. In addition, because the interest accrual will never be taxed in the hands of the policyholder or the beneficiaries if the policy matures on the death of the life insured, an opportunity exists to avoid taxation at the policyholder level entirely.

The adjusted cost basis of a policy is defined basically as the aggregate of the cost of acquiring the policy and all amounts paid on account of premiums less dividends paid or credited (unless applied as premiums for additional insurance) and less the net cost of pure insurance.[3] This has the effect of restricting the adjusted cost basis to the savings element of the premiums. However, it allows the insurer's operating expenses to be charged entirely to the savings element. In addition, it does not attempt to deal with the tax advantage the policyholder gains by the deferral of taxation of the inside interest buildup until surrender of the policy.

ITA subsection 12.2(1) provides what appears to be a general rule: a policyholder is required to include in each year's income the amount by which the "accumulating fund" on the anniversary day of the policy in that year exceeds the adjusted cost basis of the policy. As a result, where this provision applies, the inside interest buildup is supposed to be taxed annually in the hands of the policyholder. Each year's buildup then increases the adjusted cost basis of the policy. However, certain policies—defined as "exempt policies"—are excluded from the operation of subsection 12.2(1). The definition of an exempt policy is contained in Regulation 306, a complicated provision requiring that in order for a policy to be exempt, the accumulating fund with respect to the policy cannot exceed the accumulation fund of a notional "exemption test policy," which is a level premium 20-pay endowment-at-85 policy for the same amount of insurance.

The accumulating fund of an exemption test policy (the ETP) is defined in two different ways under Regulation 307(1)(c), depending on the length of time since its notional issue date. If the actual policy was issued twenty or more years ago, the accumulating fund of the ETP is the present value of the future benefits that

3. *See* ITA § 148(9).

it is to provide. In other words, the accumulating fund is the net single premium that would have to be paid currently to purchase the ETP if it were an actual insurance policy with no expense loading in the premium. For policies that are less than twenty years old, the accumulating fund is the appropriate portion of what the accumulating fund will be twenty years after the notional issue of the ETP, that is, one-twentieth on the ETP's first anniversary, two-twentieths on its second anniversary, and so forth.

Another significant aspect of the exemption test is the way it treats increases in the death benefit of a policy after the policy has been issued. Increases in the face amount of up to 8 percent per year are treated as having been part of the policy since issue. This special rule has the effect of subjecting additions to a policy to a much less restrictive test than is applied to a new policy. Thus, policies that have these face amount supplements, which are mainly participating policies using policy dividends to pay for paid-up additions, are able to obtain greater tax benefits than other policies.

Since the inside interest build-up of a 20-pay endowment-at-85 policy is quite substantial, especially in later years, it would be unusual for an ordinary life policy to create an accumulating fund buildup that exceeded that of the ETP with which it had to be compared. In fact, Canadian insurers take care that the policies they issue qualify as exempt policies. It is rare for a policy that is not exempt at issue or that ceases to be exempt in later years to be issued unless it is owned by a tax-exempt entity, such as a charity or a tax-sheltered retirement savings plan.

A single-premium life insurance policy could usually not qualify as an exempt policy. For this reason, such policies are extremely unusual unless they are held by a tax-exempt entity. However, a policy that can become fully paid up in as few as five to seven years may be designed to qualify for exemption and to protect the policyholder from annual taxation of the inside interest buildup. Universal life policies can, with reasonable care, qualify for exemption from Canadian taxation even if they involve substantial savings elements. The advantages of such policies are vigorously promoted by the Canadian insurance industry.

As a method of indirectly attacking inside interest buildup, Canada imposes a flat 15 percent tax on the investment income of insurance companies that are accruing to the benefit of policyholders. This means that many individuals, for whose benefit this income is accruing in the hands of the insurance companies, would not be subject to a tax rate as high as 15 percent on their overall income if the accruing income were simply taxed currently in their hands. Other individuals, who are in higher tax brackets and who own exempt policies, benefit from both deferral of any further taxation until their policies are surrendered and complete exemption from any further taxation if the policy is held until death.

B. Annuity Contracts

The general tax rule requires annual taxation of the interest buildup of all kinds of investment contracts, including annuities. However, so long as the annuity contract qualifies as a "prescribed annuity contract," it is exempt from such taxation.[4] The prime requisite for qualification is that it is an immediate, rather than a deferred annuity, owned by an individual and providing for level payments. If the contract qualifies as a prescribed annuity contract, while the whole of the annuity received each year is includable in the annuitant's income, a deduction is permitted for the capital portion of each payment. The deduction is computed on a level basis by dividing the single premium by the estimated life expectancy of the annuitant. As a result, there is a tax-free recovery, in equal annual amounts, of the single premium over the annuitant's estimated lifetime.

Annuity/life insurance packages are quite attractive for elderly individuals. If an individual who has acquired a prescribed annuity contract has also purchased (in a separate transaction and preferably from a different insurance company) an exempt insurance policy with a death benefit that will replace the capital originally laid out to purchase the annuity, the inside interest buildup in this policy will be entirely exempt from tax so long as it is maintained until death. This absence of parallelism in the tax treatment creates an attractive tax advantage for elderly people whose capital would otherwise be invested in very conservative securities. If such a person uses part of his or her capital to purchase a single premium life annuity without guarantee, using the part of the annuity received each year to pay the premium on a life policy that will replace the original capital, the net after-tax sum available each year for living expenses will be significantly greater than the after-tax return on monies invested in very conservative securities.

IV. Valuation of Assets for Purposes of the Capital Gains Tax

The accepted definition of "fair market value" in Canada is that stated in *Minister of Finance v. Mann Estate*,[5] where Justice McIntyre of the Supreme Court of Canada approved a statement by an expert witness that "fair market value is the highest price available estimated in terms of money which a willing seller may obtain for the property in an open and unrestricted market from a willing; knowledgeable purchaser acting at arm's length."

When a shareholder owns a block of publicly traded securities that is larger than a normal trading lot, Canadian courts have not generally applied "blockage discounts" from stock market prices on the theory that if an attempt were made to sell a large block of stock in a normal securities market, the forces of supply and demand would drive the price down. In *Untermyer Estate v. Attorney General*,[6] a succession duty case, Justice Mignault commented in part as follows:

4. *Id.* § 12.2(1)(b).

5. Minister of Finance v. Mann Estate, [1972] 5 W.W.R. 23, 27, *aff'd*, [1973] C.T.C. 561 (BCCA), *aff'd*, [1974] C.T.C. 222 (SCC).

6. Untermyer Estate v. Attorney Gen., [1929] S.C.R. 84.

> I would not deduct anything from the market value of these shares on the assumption that the whole of them would be placed on the market at one and the same time; for I do not think that any prudent stockholder would pursue a like course. To make such a deduction in a case like the one at bar; would be to render the "sacrifice value" or "dumping value" of the shares the measure of valuation.[7]

However, in *Bank of New York v. M.N.R.*,[8] where the same blockage issue was scrutinized, the Minister of National Revenue apparently had arrived at a value of $8.00 per share by referring to the most recent closing price in the public market and discounting that amount by approximately 25 percent to allow for the delay, uncertainty, and inconvenience likely to occur if the shares were sold in an orderly manner over a reasonable period of time. In upholding the Minister's determination against an estate's argument that a larger discount was justifiable, this decision appears to indicate that a Canadian court will possibly accept blockage discounts if the value of unusually large blocks of securities is in question and, in addition, if a semi-organized market exists for large blocks of securities when the market may have particular significance in valuing such blocks.

In the United States, a common method of estate planning involves gifting partial interests in limited partnerships or limited liability companies to trusts for family members on a discounted basis. The gifted interests are valued at a substantial discount (e.g., a discount is taken for lack of control and for lack of marketability) from the pro rata value of such entity. It is less clear whether such discounts can be obtained from the pro rata value if such a partnership were actually formed in Canada. This involves consideration of a situation where a controlling interest in a corporation is held by a family group, but the taxpayer, a member of that group, has only a minority interest. In the United States, Revenue Ruling 93-12[9] acknowledged that "a minority discount will not be disallowed solely because the transferred interest; when aggregated with the interests held by family members; would be part of a controlling interest." However, in a number of Canadian cases, such as *Blank Estate v. M.N.R.*,[10] *Taylor Estate v. M.N.R.*,[11] and *The Queen v. Timmins*,[12] the court held that shares—which themselves represented only a minority interest when owned by a member of a family group that in the aggregate held a controlling interest in a company—had to be valued on the basis that a much smaller discount from their pro rata value, or, as in the *Timmins* case, no discount at all, should be applied than if they were held by nonmembers of the family group.

---

7. *Id.* at 91.
8. Bank of New York v. M.N.R., [1973] C.T.C. 636.
9. Rev. Rul. 93-12, 1993 C.B. 202.
10. Blank Estate v. M.N.R., 68 D.T.C. 759 (1968).
11. Taylor Estate v. M.N.R., 67 D.T.C. 405 (1967).
12. The Queen v. Timmins, [1939] Revue Legale 291.

The leading Canadian case on this question reached a rather inconclusive result. In *Littler v.* M.N.R.,[13] the appellant and his family owned 40.3 percent of the shares of a public company, and other relatives owned a 14.3 percent interest, with the balance being held by strangers. The appellant sold some of his shares to each of his sons at $24 per share at a time when the company's shares were trading at $23.50 per share on the Montreal Stock Exchange. At that time, however, a large public company was negotiating with him to purchase at least 67 percent of the company's shares. The company made its formal offer in the following month to buy them at $68.22 per share. The Minister assessed gift tax (which was then imposed) on the basis that by selling to his sons at $24 per share, Littler had made a gift to them equivalent to the difference between $68.22 and $24 per share. This assessment was reversed by the Federal Court, Trial Division on the grounds that the fair market value of the gifted shares was no more than the price at which they were trading on the Montreal Stock Exchange at the time of the gift.

When this decision was appealed by the Minister to the Federal Court of Appeal,[14] the appeal was dismissed in a two-to-one decision on purely technical grounds that the Minister had failed to plead a provision in the relevant statute which treated a non-arm's length sale at an under-valuation as a gift. However, Justice LeDain, who was one of the majority, went on to state the following in *obiter:*

> There is no doubt in my mind that at the time the respondent Littler sold his shares to his sons in April; 1968; for $24 per share; he had every reason to believe that they would be able to resell them to Standard Brands in the near future for the price of $68.22. It was not just a possibility; it was a probability—a virtual certainty. The respondent had been skillfully preparing the ground for the sale to Standard Brands for several months. As early as January; 1968; he had decided on the price that he would accept for the shares and he had reason to believe that it would be acceptable to the other members of his family . . . . At that price, in comparison with the price at which the stock was trading on the exchange, there was going to be no difficulty in obtaining the required 67 percent of the outstanding shares, whether or not the respondent and the members of his family could be said to be in effective control of the company . . . . In my view, it results from the evidence that at the time Littler sold the shares to his sons he conferred on them the benefit of transferring to them, at a price of $24, shares that were for all practical purposes worth $68.22, because of the virtual certainty they could be resold to Standard Brands at that price in a relatively short time.

While the statement is merely *obiter*, in light of the actual dismissal of the Minister's appeal, it cannot be ignored. Justice LeDain's view was that, because it was expected that at least 67 percent of the outstanding shares of the company would

13. Littler v. M.N.R., [1976] C.T.C. 379.
14. Littler v. M.N.R., [1978] C.T.C. 235.

be tendered in response to Standard Brand's anticipated offer, the fair market value of the rather small block of these shares that Littler sold to his sons a month earlier must have been the amount Standard Brands was negotiating to offer for 67 percent of the outstanding shares, rather than the price that could have been obtained for the small block at that time on the Montreal Stock Exchange. Contrary to the principle adopted in the United States in Revenue Ruling 93-12, this probably constitutes the strongest possible Canadian support for valuation of a minority interest in shares of a family-controlled company on the basis of their pro rata proportion of the value of the family's entire controlling interest.

The Canada Revenue Agency's Information Circular (IC) 89-3 reads as follows: "It is a rebuttable presumption that a family group has acted in concert to control a corporation. . . . In a situation where the existence of family control is recognized, the Department will employ a pro-ratable valuation for each family group member's shares."

V. The Concept of "Residence," the Jurisdictional Predicate to Canadian Taxation in Canadian Tax Law

Since neither the government of Canada nor any of its provinces or territories presently impose gift or estate taxes, domicile is not a relevant factor in Canadian taxation, though it previously was and still is the case in the United States.[15] Unlike the United States, which taxes an individual on his or her worldwide income if he or she is either a U.S. citizen or a U.S. resident, Canada taxes worldwide income only on the basis of residence in Canada.[16] A nonresident of Canada, generally speaking, is only taxable on his or her Canadian source income.

The term "resident" is not defined in the ITA. Subsection 250(3) of the ITA provides that a reference to a person resident in Canada in the ITA includes a person who was, at the relevant time, ordinarily resident in Canada. The term "ordinarily resident" is not defined in the ITA. An individual who is "ordinarily resident" in Canada is considered to be "factually resident" in Canada.

The leading case in determining residency for purposes of the ITA remains *Thomson* v. *M.N.R.*[17] The case is important because it establishes several key principles that are used to determine a taxpayer's residency status. First, for income tax purposes, it must be assumed that every person has at all times a residence. This will generally be the place where the person, in the settled routine of his or her life, regularly, normally, or customarily lives. Second, a person may be resident in more than one country at the same time. Third, while the intention of a taxpayer is relevant, it is not determinative of residence. Determining residency

15. *See, e.g.*, Treas. Reg. § 20.0-1(b)(1).
16. ITA, § 2(1).
17. Thomson v. M.N.R., 2 D.T.C. 812 (SCC 1946).

is essentially a question of fact, and in making a determination, all of the relevant facts of each case must be considered.

In applying these principles, courts have considered factors such as the following to determine residency:

- past and present habits of life;
- regularity and length of visits in the jurisdiction asserting residence;
- ties within that jurisdiction;
- ties elsewhere; and
- permanence or purposes of stay abroad.[18]

The Canada Revenue Agency (the CRA), Canada's taxing authority, generally follows the principles established in the jurisprudence to determine if an individual is resident in Canada for the purposes of the ITA.[19] According to the CRA, the most important factor in establishing residency for tax purposes is whether or not an individual maintains residential ties with Canada. The residential ties considered most significant are the existence of a spouse or common law partner located in Canada, dependents located in Canada, and/or a residential dwelling in Canada, whether owned or leased.

It is also important to note that the ties a Canadian makes to the other country are to be considered. If significant residential ties are not made to the other country, then the remaining residential ties to Canada receive greater attention by the CRA.[20]

Residency status could also be affected by the severing of secondary residential ties. Secondary residential ties include, but are not limited to, the following:

- personal property in Canada (e.g., furniture, clothing, cars, etc.);
- social ties with Canada (e.g., memberships in Canadian recreational and religious organizations);
- economic ties within Canada (e.g., employment with a Canadian employer and active involvement in a Canadian business; maintaining Canadian bank accounts, credit cards, retirement savings plans; etc.);
- landed immigrant status or appropriate work permits in Canada;
- a driver's license from a Canadian province or territory;
- a vehicle registration in a Canadian province or territory;
- hospital cards and Canadian provincial or territorial medical coverage;
- a Canadian passport;
- a seasonal dwelling place in Canada or a leased dwelling place; and
- memberships in Canadian unions or professional organizations.

18. The Queen v. Reeder, 75 D.T.C. 5160 (FCTD). *See also* Laurin v. The Queen, 2007 D.T.C. 236 (TCC), *aff'd,* 2008 D.T.C. 6175 (FCA).

19. Canada Revenue Agency Interpretation Bulletin IT-221R3 (Consolidated), *Determination of an Individual's Residence Status* (Oct. 2002).

20. *Id.* § 14.

The CRA has also noted that the following secondary residential ties are relevant, though are of lesser importance:

- a Canadian mailing address;
- a Canadian post office box;
- a Canadian safety deposit box;
- personal stationary (including business cards) with a Canadian address listing;
- a telephone listing(s) in Canada; and
- newspaper and magazine subscriptions delivered to a Canadian address.

All such connections with Canada must be considered collectively. It is unusual for a single secondary residential tie to be sufficient in and of itself to lead to the conclusion that an individual is factually resident of Canada.

Finally, the CRA will also consider the regularity and duration of an individual's visits to Canada. Where visits are more than occasional, particularly where the visits occur on a regular basis and secondary residential ties are maintained, this factor will be considered. However, this factor is stated to be a consideration in determining whether an individual has severed residential ties with Canada as opposed to the reacquisition of Canadian residency.

Pursuant to paragraph 250(1)(a) of the ITA, if an individual is determined not to be factually resident in Canada, he or she may be deemed to be resident in Canada throughout a tax year if the individual sojourned in Canada in the year for a period or periods amounting to 183 days or more in the year. The term "sojourned" is not defined in the ITA. It has been interpreted by the CRA and the courts to mean to be temporarily present in Canada. In *Thomson*, Justice Estey stated that "one "sojourns" at a place where he unusually, casually or intermittently visits or stays."[21]

Therefore, a person will be deemed to be resident in Canada under the ITA if he or she is present in Canada for 183 days or more in a taxation year.

An individual who is resident of Canada for tax purposes may also be resident of the United States for tax purposes under U.S. domestic law. Article IV(2) of the Convention between Canada and the United States of America with Respect to Taxes on Income and Capital (the Treaty) provides "tiebreaker" rules to determine in which country the individual will be resident for purposes of the other provisions of the Treaty. If at any time such tiebreaker rules apply, and it is determined that an individual is a resident of the United States for purposes of the Treaty, the individual who is otherwise resident in Canada (whether factual or deemed) will be deemed not to be resident of Canada at that time.[22]

The tiebreaker rules found in the Treaty are as follows:

21. *Supra* note 17, at 231.
22. ITA § 250(5).

1. A person is deemed to be a resident of the country in which he or she has a permanent home available to him or her. The home must be for more than occasional use.
2. If the person has a permanent home available to him or her in both countries or in neither country, he or she shall be deemed to be a resident of the country with which his or her personal and economic relations are closer (center of vital interests). This is a similar test to the factual residence test under Canadian common law (as discussed above).[23] The commentary in the Organization of Economic Cooperation and Development's (the OECD) Model Treaty provides that the test requires an examination of the individual's family and social relations; occupation; political, cultural, and other activities; place of business; and place where he or she administers his or her property. It further states the following:

   > The circumstances must be examined as a whole, but it would be nevertheless obvious that considerations based on the personal aspects of the individual must receive special attention. If a person who has a home in one State sets up a second in the other State while retaining the first, the fact that he retains the first in the environment where he has always lived, where he has worked, and where he has his family and possessions, can, together with other elements, go to demonstrate that he has retained his center of vital interests in the first State.[24]

   It is generally considered not to be easy to shift one's center of vital interests from one country to another.
3. If the country in which he or she has his or her center of vital interest cannot be determined, he or she shall be deemed to be resident of the country in which he or she has an habitual abode. This is the country to which the person frequently returned at regular and continual intervals and in which he or she spent considerable time.

The term "habitual abode" has been considered in very few Canadian cases. As set out in the recent *Lingle v. Her Majesty the Queen*[25] case, the habitual abode test "involves notions of frequency, duration and regularity of stays of a quality which are more transient. To put it differently, the concept refers to a stay of some substance in the jurisdiction as a matter of habit, so that the conclusion can be drawn that this is where the taxpayer normally lives."[26]

In *Lingle*, the taxpayer was a U.S. citizen and was a consultant for an Ontario company. His spouse and children lived in the United States. The parties agreed

23. *Supra* note 19 para. 26.
24. Article IV of OECD; Commentary of OECD's Model Treaty at para. 15.
25. Lingle v. Her Majesty The Queen, 2009 TCC 435, *aff'd*, 2010 FCA 152.
26. *Id.* para. 6 (FCA).

that Mr. Lingle was a dual resident, and, therefore, the Treaty's tiebreaker rules were to be considered. First, it was determined that he had a permanent home in both Canada and the United States. Second, it was determined that it was not possible to conclude in which country Mr. Lingle had his center of vital interests. Therefore, the third part of the tiebreaker test had to be looked at, and it was determined that his habitual abode was in Canada. He did not have any clients in the United States. He had spent only 69 out of the previous 623 days in the United States. During the relevant times, Mr. Lingle did not have a settled routine in the United States, but he had one in Canada, which showed that he regularly, customarily, or normally lived in Canada.

As set out in the Commentary on article IV(2) in the OECD's Model Treaty, "the comparison must cover a sufficient length of time for it to be possible to determine whether the residence in the two States is habitual and to determine also the intervals at which the stays take place."[27] While more is involved than just a simple computation of the number of days spent in each country, the country where the individual stays more frequently in such period will tip the balance.

4. If the person has an habitual abode in both countries or in neither country, he or she shall be deemed to be a resident of the country of which he or she is a citizen.
5. If the person is a citizen of both countries or of neither of them, the competent authorities of the countries shall settle the question by mutual agreement.

When an individual becomes a resident of Canada, paragraph 128.1(1)(b) of the ITA provides that the taxpayer is deemed to have disposed of all of his or her property immediately before that time for proceeds equal to the property's fair market value at the time of disposition. This provision operates together with paragraph 128.1(1)(c) of the ITA, which deems the taxpayer to have acquired at the particular time each property that was deemed disposed of at a cost equal to the proceeds of disposition of the property. The result is that properties held by the individual on becoming a resident of Canada receive a new basis equal to their fair market value for income tax purposes.

The following properties do not receive the new basis:

- property that is "taxable Canadian property";
- property that is described in the inventory of a business carried on by the taxpayer in Canada at the time of disposition;
- eligible capital property in respect of a business carried on by the taxpayer in Canada at the time of disposition; and
- an "excluded right or interest" of the taxpayer (other than an interest in a nonresident testamentary trust that was never acquired for consideration).

27. As set out *id.*, para. 8 (FCA).

These properties do not receive a new basis, and the full gain accrued from the date of acquisition by an individual of these properties is subject to tax under part I of the ITA regardless of whether the taxpayer is a resident of Canada. Accordingly, Canada taxes the entire increase in the value of the property when the individual eventually disposes of the property.

In circumstances where the property held by the immigrant has depreciated in value from the time of acquisition and prior to the immigrant becoming a Canadian resident, section 128.1(1) of the ITA will cause the taxpayer's cost base to be adjusted downward to the fair market value at the time of becoming a resident of Canada. In the case of an individual who is immigrating to Canada from the United States with capital property (other than taxable Canadian property) with a value below its original cost, the individual should consider selling such property if the individual can utilize the loss prior to entry into Canada.

When an individual leaves Canada and ceases to be regarded as a Canadian resident for tax purposes, he or she is generally treated for tax purposes as having disposed of most forms of his or her worldwide property (other than Canadian real estate and certain rights to receive future income) at their fair market value and immediately reacquired the property. The deemed capital gain, if any, in general, is the proceeds of disposition less the adjusted cost base of the capital property. This tax is commonly referred to as "departure tax" or "exit tax." One-half of the capital gain is the taxable capital gain. The taxable capital gain can, sometimes, first be offset by any capital losses. The taxable capital gain is payable in full on the person's departure from Canada.

Pursuant to subsection 220(4.5) of the ITA, an individual can postpone the payment of the departure tax by posting security with the Canadian taxing authority, regardless of the amount. The tax is paid later, without interest, when the individual sells (or otherwise disposes of) the property.

The individual should make the application by filing Form T1244, "Election, under Subsection 220(4.5) of the Income Tax Act, to Defer the Payment of Tax on Income Relating to the Deemed Disposition of Property," on or before April 30 in the year following the year of emigration. Subsection 220(4.51) of the ITA deems security on the first $100,000 of gains on the deemed disposition to be posted.

The Canadian taxing authority will generally accept the following types of security: bank letters of guarantee, bank letters of credit, bonds from the government of Canada or a province or territory of Canada, shares of private or publicly traded companies, certificates of precious metals, various other marketable securities, or a charge or mortgage on real property or valuable personal property.

It ought to be noted that whether security will be adequate will be determined on an annual basis; if it is determined to be insufficient, the individual must provide additional security within ninety days of notification by the Canadian taxing authority.

Subsection 128.1(6) of the ITA allows an individual who becomes resident in Canada for purposes of the ITA after departing Canada to "undo" the deemed disposition on departure of properties the individual still owns on his or her return to Canada. The mechanics for "taxable Canadian property" are slightly different than for other property. However, in both cases, the result is that the individual is no longer liable for departure tax on the properties. If the individual posted security for departure tax, the security will be released on making the election as the amount of departure tax owing will be reduced or eliminated. The election must be made on or before the filing due date for the year the individual returns to Canada.

Article XIII(5) of the Treaty contains a "clawback" provision that permits Canada to tax a former resident individual who emigrated to the United States on gains realized on the disposition of property owned when the individual emigrated if certain residency periods are met.

VI. Patterns of Death Taxation for Persons Having Contacts with Both the United States and Canada

Because Canada and the United States are contiguous and because they have so many economic contacts, their radically different systems of death taxation have created serious tax problems for many estates with cross-border interests.

A. U.S. Residents Owning Canadian Property

The fewest problems arise for U.S. resident decedents who own Canadian situs property. The disposition of all forms of "taxable Canadian property" can give rise to Canadian taxation under the provisions of the ITA. "Taxable Canadian property" is defined in section 248(1) of the ITA and includes, *inter alia*, real property situated in Canada, capital property used in carrying on business, in Canada and a capital interest in a trust resident in Canada. The definition was recently amended to narrow the types of properties that constitute taxable Canadian property. Previously, shares of a corporation resident in Canada (other than a mutual fund corporation) *that were not listed* on a designated stock exchange constituted taxable Canadian property. Now, such shares only constitute taxable Canadian property at a particular time if, at any time during the preceding sixty-month period, more than 50 percent of the fair market value of such shares was derived, directly or indirectly, from one or any combination of (1) real or immovable property situated in Canada; (2) Canadian resource properties; (3) timber resource properties; and (4) options or interests in respect of the foregoing. Similarly, previously, shares of a corporation resident in Canada *that were listed* on a designated stock exchange or shares of a mutual fund corporation constituted taxable Canadian property to a nonresident if, at any time during the preceding sixty-month period, 25 percent or more of the issued shares of any class or series of the corporation was owned by the nonresident, persons with whom the nonresident did not deal at arm's length, or the nonresident together with such persons. Now, such shares will only constitute taxable Canadian property if, in addition to the existing ownership test, at any time during the preceding sixty-month period, more than 50 percent of the fair market value of such shares was derived, directly or indirectly, from one or any combination of (1) real or immoveable property situated in Canada; (2) Canadian resource properties; (3) timber resource properties; and (4) options or interests in respect of the foregoing.

However, the ambit of Canadian taxation of U.S. residents owning such property is considerably narrowed by article XIII of the Treaty.[28] Paragraphs 1 and 3 of this article entitle Canada to tax the disposition of real property situated in Canada and the shares of any Canadian resident company, provided the value of those shares is derived principally from such real property. Paragraph 2 entitles Canada to tax the disposition of personal property forming part of the business property of a permanent establishment a U.S. resident has in Canada or part of a fixed base in Canada for independent personal services. Subject to these exceptions, paragraph 4 provides that gains from the disposition of any other forms of Canadian situs property of a U.S. resident are taxable only by the United States. As a result, U.S. residents who die owning most forms of Canadian property are exempt from Canadian taxation at death.

However, where a U.S. resident decedent dies owning property that may be taxed by Canada under paragraphs 1 and 2, the impact of such taxation may be significant. Before the coming into force of the Revised (Third) Protocol to the Convention in November 1995[29] (retroactive to November 1988), the applicable Canadian tax did not qualify for treatment as a foreign tax credit against estate tax under the U.S. Internal Revenue Code, because it was not a foreign death tax of the traditional sort.[30] Instead, the Canadian tax was merely a deduction in calculating the net value of the estate for estate tax purposes—a much less generous treatment. However, paragraph 7 of article XXIX B of the Treaty, inserted by the Third Protocol, treats the Canadian tax for U.S. foreign tax credit purposes as though it was a traditional form of death tax and allows it to be credited against U.S. estate tax.

In April 1995, the definition of "taxable Canadian property"[31] was expanded to include the shares of any company that was not resident in Canada, where more than 50 percent of the value of its properties consisted of Canadian real property or resource property. This change would have had the effect of subjecting to Canadian taxation the deemed realization on death of the shares of a U.S. or other non-Canadian company owned by a U.S. resident decedent, if the company derived more than 50 percent of its value from such Canadian property. However,

---

28. Canada-United States Income Tax Convention, T.I.A.S. No. 11087, 1469 U.N.T.S. 189. Entered into force August 16, 1984, the convention was effective January 1, 1985, except for certain taxes withheld on dividends, interest, and royalties, for which the effective date is October 1, 1984.

29. Entered into force November 9, 1995; effective date January 1, 1996.

30. Ballard v. Comm'r, 85 T.C. 300 (1985).

31. ITA § 115(1)(b).

it was subsequently recognized that this would lead to a serious double-taxation problem because the United States could not be expected to allow a foreign tax credit under paragraph 7 of article XXIX B for the Canadian tax levied on such property. As a result, the Fourth Protocol, signed on July 29, 1997,[32] amended paragraph 3(b)(ii) of article XIII to restrict Canada's right to tax only the shares of Canadian resident companies deriving their principal value from Canadian real property. As noted above, in 2010, changes to the definition of "taxable Canadian property" were made.

Under Canadian tax law, if a decedent has left property to a surviving spouse, that property is treated as having been disposed of at death at its cost basis rather than at fair market value, with the result that neither gain nor loss will be realized by reason of the death.[33] Any subsequent disposition during the spouse's lifetime or a deemed realization at the spouse's death will give rise to a deemed realization at fair market value. While section 70(6) of the ITA restricts this tax-deferred rollover to transfers by a Canadian resident to a spouse who was resident in Canada immediately before the decedent's death, paragraph 5 of article XXIX B of the Treaty extends the benefit of this provision by providing that where the decedent was a U.S. resident immediately before death, both the individual and the spouse are deemed to have been resident in Canada immediately before the death. This makes it possible for the U.S. estate to take advantage of this tax-deferred rollover with respect to its Canadian real property interest.

When Canadian situs property has been left to a trust for the decedent's spouse during the spouse's lifetime, paragraph 5 of article XXIX B provides that, if the trustees that were residents or citizens of the United States or domestic U.S. corporations request the Canadian competent authority, the authority may agree, subject to terms and conditions satisfactory to it, to treat the trust for the purposes of the ITA as being resident in Canada for such time and with respect to such property as it stipulates. Such a determination entitles the estate to the benefit of a tax-deferred rollover at the decedent's cost basis of the Canadian property, for Canadian tax purposes. Presumably, the Canadian competent authority will normally agree to treat the trust as being resident in Canada so long as it can be assured, by the lodging of appropriate security, that the applicable Canadian tax will be paid by the trustees when it becomes due.

Unlike the U.S. marital deduction, the transfer of property on death to the decedent's spouse or to a trust for the spouse's exclusive benefit during lifetime will defer Canadian income tax only until the *earlier* of the time of disposition of the property and the date of the spouse's death. Accordingly, if Canadian situs property of a U.S. citizen or resident is disposed of during the spouse's lifetime, the Canadian income tax liability will arise before the U.S. estate tax liability would normally come due. This situation will presumably be dealt with under paragraph

32. Tax Treaties (CCH) T 1949A (entered into force December 16, 1997; effective date varies).
33. ITA § 70(6).

3(g) of article XXVI, which provides that the competent authorities of the two countries may agree to provide relief from double taxation in cases where no relief is otherwise available.

B. U.S. Citizens Resident in Canada

Many thousands of U.S. citizens are Canadian residents, although some of them are also citizens of Canada. Their status as U.S. citizens subjects them to U.S. estate taxes on their worldwide estates, while their status as Canadian residents subjects them to Canadian taxes on deemed realizations at death in respect of their worldwide assets. Before the coming into force of the Third Protocol, the treatment of Canadian taxes on deemed realizations at death as a mere deduction in calculating the net value of the estate for U.S. estate tax purposes resulted in a serious problem for these estates, a problem that has largely been relieved by paragraph 7 of article XXIX B.

However, it must be noted that when the estate of a U.S. citizen resident in Canada includes U.S. situs property, the foreign tax credit that is allowed by paragraph 6 of article XXIX B against the Canadian tax on deemed realizations for the applicable U.S. estate tax is limited by this paragraph to the amount of U.S. taxes that would have been payable if the individual were not a U.S. citizen or former citizen. This may considerably reduce the amount of U.S. estate taxes that may be allowed by Canada as a foreign tax credit under this paragraph.

C. Canadian Resident Decedents (Non-U.S. Citizens) Owning U.S. Property

Before the Third Protocol to the Treaty, the double-taxation problems of Canadian resident decedents who were not U.S. citizens and who died owning U.S. situs property were extremely serious. The ITA provided no relief at all for U.S. estate taxes payable in connection with such property, because the foreign tax credit provision of the ITA allowed credits only for foreign income taxes; there was nothing in the ITA that provided any other form of allowance against the Canadian tax liability arising under the deemed realization provisions. The focus of Canadian complaints about this situation centered around, but was by no means confined to, estate taxes with respect to U.S. vacation homes, where the application of both U.S. estate taxes and Canadian income taxes on deemed realizations affected a large number of Canadians. The Third Protocol included a response to this problem and provided several types of tax relief for such Canadian estates:

1. The statutory U.S. unified credit against estate tax imposed on the estate of a decedent who was neither a citizen of nor domiciled in the United States was only $13,000, which effectively shielded from taxation only US$60,000 of U.S. situs property. However, paragraph 2 of article XXIX B provides for a unified credit equal to the greater of $13,000 and the amount that bears the same ratio to the credit allowed under U.S. law to the estate of a U.S.

citizen that the gross value of the U.S. situs property bears to the entire gross estate wherever situated. Pro rating the unified credit in this manner ensures that a Canadian estate with a gross value of not more than US$5.25 million in 2013 is completely exempt from estate tax with respect to its U.S. situs property. In fact, the amount of the estate that can be completely exempt may actually substantially exceed this figure because of the progressive nature of estate tax rates when this formula is applied.[34]

2. Paragraph 8 of article XXIX B provides that if the value of the entire gross estate of the Canadian resident, wherever situated, does not exceed US$1.2 million, the United States is restricted to imposing its estate tax on U.S. situs property only if any gain on the alienation of such property would be subject to U.S. tax under article XIII. This has the effect of restricting U.S. taxation to U.S. real property interests and personal property forming part of a U.S. permanent establishment, a very major concession on the part of the United States.

   However, because the gross value of an estate is calculated under U.S. estate tax rules, assets such as life insurance policies on the life of the decedent, which were owned by him or her and, in many cases, jointly held property and other assets that do not form part of the probate estate, must be taken into account in determining the gross value of the estate. This results in a number of estates, whose probate value is far less than US$1.2 million, being deprived of the benefit of this paragraph. In addition, it does not take into account any of the debts of the decedent. As a result, a Canadian estate with a gross value of, say, $2 million, but with debts of $800,000, cannot take advantage of this provision, although an estate that owns, as its only asset, all of the shares of a company with assets of $2 million and debts of $800,000 will qualify.

3. Under U.S. law, property that passes on death to a surviving spouse, either directly or by means of a trust for the spouse's exclusive benefit during the spouse's lifetime, is entitled to full exemption from estate tax, as a marital deduction, but only if the spouse is a U.S. citizen or the property is transferred to a qualified domestic trust (QDOT).[35] Since the spouse of a Canadian resident decedent who is not a U.S. citizen is, in most cases, also not a U.S. citizen, where the U.S. situs property of the estate is substantial, it is usually advisable for the estate to make use of a QDOT. However, this means that the assets in the QDOT will generally become subject to estate tax when the spouse dies or when they are withdrawn from the QDOT during the spouse's lifetime.

   As an alternative to establishing a QDOT, a Canadian estate can claim a further credit under paragraphs 3 and 4 of article XXIX B with respect to

34. Wolfe D. Goodman, *Cross-Border Estate Planning: The Canada-United States Income Tax Convention*, PROB. & PROP. 45 (July/Aug. 1996).

35. I.R.C. §§ 2056(d), 2056A.

the decedent's U.S. situs property as has been left to a surviving spouse. In lieu of the marital deduction, this additional credit cannot exceed the lesser of:

(i) the unified credit allowed under paragraph 2, described above; and

(ii) the amount of additional estate tax that would otherwise be imposed on the property left to the spouse, if such property were subject to estate tax.

4. Where, after taking into account the first three of these allowances, there is still a net liability for estate tax with respect to the estate of a Canadian resident, paragraph 6 of article XXIX B provides for Canada to allow a foreign tax credit against the Canadian income tax liability otherwise payable in respect of the estate's U.S. situs property that is equal to the lesser of the two taxes.

Where the U.S. situs property is worth considerably more than its cost basis, allowing a foreign tax credit against Canadian income taxes on deemed realization of U.S. situs property for U.S. estate tax in respect of such property can be exceedingly helpful in reducing the total tax burden at death. However, if the property is worth no more than its cost basis, so that there is no Canadian tax liability at death, the U.S. tax payable is simply an additional burden for the estate. As a result, it is often essential that measures be taken to shelter the U.S. situs property from estate tax. Some of the major measures that can be taken are described below.

Where the U.S. property consists of a valuable portfolio of U.S. securities, it is common for the Canadian resident to transfer the portfolio during his or her lifetime into a Canadian holding company so that on death, the decedent's property will consist of shares in and debt owing by the company, which will not be regarded as situated in the United States. If these securities are worth more than their cost basis, their transfer to the company on a tax-deferred basis is facilitated by section 85(1) of the ITA, which permits the parties to treat the securities as being transferred at an elected figure that is not less than their cost basis and not more than their fair market value. It seems to be generally acknowledged by the Internal Revenue Service that as long as the portfolio is treated by the parties as really belonging to the company, it will not be subject to estate tax upon the transferor's death.

U.S. real property acquisitions may be financed through a nonrecourse mortgage. This type of mortgage is netted against the value of the property for U.S. estate tax purposes. A nonrecourse mortgage is collectable only against a specific property and not against any other assets of the decedent, and, therefore, most arm's length lenders will not usually advance more than 50 percent to 60 percent of the value of the property. A nonrecourse mortgage could be obtained from a non-arm's length party to reduce the value of U.S. situs property, provided the terms of such mortgage were similar to commercial nonrecourse mortgages.

A Canadian resident's ownership of U.S. vacation property through a Canadian single-purpose corporation will avoid U.S. estate tax. This is because his or her interest in shares of a foreign corporation is not a U.S. situs asset. However, it is no longer a popular or recommended vehicle to use, because the shareholder must report a taxable benefit for the personal use of the property. Previously, the CRA, subject to particular conditions being met, permitted a single-purpose Canadian company to hold such property without imposing a taxable benefit on the Canadian resident shareholder(s). After 2004, the CRA changed its administrative position. Now, a shareholder benefit will be imposed in such circumstances. Qualifying companies incorporated and holding U.S. vacation property prior to this change in administrative policy are safe unless and until the property is sold or the company's shares are disposed of.

Regardless of the Canadian tax situation, there are U.S. tax issues that make this ownership vehicle unappealing. First, the income tax rate on the sale of the property would be much higher than if an individual or trust owned and sold the property. Second, when U.S. real property is owned by a corporation, it is feasible that the use of the property by the owner or his or her family will result in imputed rental income. There are additional tax considerations to review if the U.S. property is owned by an American subsidiary of a foreign corporation.

The most popular vehicle for the ownership of U.S. vacation property by Canadians today is the use of a Canadian resident irrevocable discretionary trust. There are two main advantages to this approach. First, U.S. estate tax can be avoided on the death of the Canadian resident. Second, if the real property is sold prior to the Canadian resident's death, any increase in value will be subject to the same capital gain as if the property had been owned personally by the Canadian resident.

There are two main disadvantages to using a Canadian resident irrevocable discretionary trust to hold U.S. vacation property. First, the Canadian resident has to accept that he or she is giving up control of the property for the benefit of his or her spouse and/or children. Second, pursuant to the ITA, certain trusts are deemed to dispose of all of their capital property for fair market value every twenty-one years. Tax on any accrued gain will be payable at that time, regardless of whether the trust has actually disposed of the asset and has the funds available to pay the tax. Therefore, typically, the asset is rolled out of the trust on a tax-deferred basis prior to the trust's twenty-first anniversary.

5. Where U.S. situs property of a Canadian resident is left at death to a surviving spouse, it will normally be treated, for Canadian tax purposes, as hav-

ing been disposed of by the decedent at its cost basis and as having been acquired by the spouse at the same figure so that no tax will be levied at the first death in respect of a deemed disposition. However, if this property is not exempt from estate tax, by reason of one or more of the provisions of article XXIX B, it will become subject to estate tax, unless the surviving spouse is a U.S. citizen or unless a QDOT is utilized. In some cases, it may be preferable for the estate to elect, under section 70(6.2) of the ITA, to treat the property as having been disposed of by the decedent at its fair market value and acquired by the spouse at the same figure. While this will lead to realization of a capital gain, if the property has appreciated while it was owned by the decedent, the resulting Canadian tax liability may, in some cases, be offset by a foreign tax credit in respect of the U.S. estate tax, thereby avoiding double taxation.

VII. Enforcement of Cross-Border Tax Liabilities

Article XXVII of the Treaty provides for the exchange of information between the competent authorities of Canada and the United States. Paragraph 1 of the article authorizes competent authorities to exchange the information necessary for carrying out the provisions of the Treaty or the domestic laws of the two countries concerning taxes covered by the Treaty insofar as taxation under those domestic laws is not contrary to the Treaty. This article is utilized to exchange information upon specific request, routinely and spontaneously.

Under paragraph 2, if information is requested by a state, the other state shall use its information-gathering measures to obtain the requested information, even though the other state may not need such information for its own tax purposes.

Paragraph 6 provides that if specifically requested by the competent authority of a state, the competent authority of the other state shall provide information in the form of depositions of witnesses and authenticated copies of unedited original documents (including books, papers, statements, records, accounts, and writings).

Paragraph 3 provides that in no case shall paragraphs 1 and 2 be construed so as to impose on a state the obligation to carry out administrative measures at variance with its own laws and administrative practice or that of the other state, to supply information that is not obtainable under the laws or in the normal course of administration of either state, or to supply information that would disclose any trade, business, industrial, commercial, or professional secret or trade process or information, the disclosure of which would be contrary to public policy.

The traditional Canadian legal rule is that the country's courts will not enforce a claim for taxes made by a foreign government; this rule was followed and expanded by the Supreme Court of Canada in *United States v. Harden*,[36] involving an action brought in the Province of British Columbia for enforcement of a judgment obtained in a U.S. court regarding U.S. taxes. Similarly, when it is the Canadian government seeking to enforce its tax claims outside Canada, it can face a similar obstacle in the foreign country. In *Attorney General for Canada v. William Schulze & Co.*,[37] the Canadian Controller of Customs had seized some of the Schulze company's goods in Canada for breach of customs law. The seizure was contested in the Canadian Exchequer Court, where it was upheld and the company was ordered to pay costs. However, when the Attorney General for Canada sued in Scotland, where the company conducted business, seeking to recover these costs, the claim was dismissed on the basis of the traditional rule.

This traditional rule is, however, overridden by article XXVI A of the Treaty (as amended by the Fifth Protocol), by which the two countries undertake to lend assistance to each other in the collection of all categories of taxes collected by or on behalf of the government of either of the countries. This assistance extends to interest, costs, additions to such taxes, and civil penalties.

Under paragraph 2 of this article, an application for assistance in the collection of such a revenue claim must include a certification by the competent authority of the applicant country that, under the laws of that country, the revenue claim has been finally determined, that is, when the applicant country has the right under its internal law to collect the revenue claim and all administrative and judicial rights of the taxpayer to restrain collection in the applicant country have lapsed or been exhausted.

Under paragraph 3, a revenue claim of the applicant country may be accepted for collection, but apparently need not necessarily be accepted for collection, by the competent authority of the requested country. It shall then be collected by the requested country as though it were its own revenue claim, finally determined in accordance with the laws applicable to the collection of the requested state's own taxes.

Under paragraph 7, a revenue claim of an applicant country does not have, in the requested country, any priority accorded to the revenue claims of the requested country.

There is an important exception to the application of article XXVI A contained in paragraph 8, which states that no assistance is to be provided for a revenue claim with respect to a taxpayer if the taxpayer can demonstrate that:

a. where the taxpayer is an individual, the revenue claim relates to a taxable period in which the taxpayer was a citizen of the requested country or, if the taxpayer became a citizen of the requested state at any time before

36. United States v. Harden, 63 D.T.C. 1276 (1963).
37. Attorney Gen. for Canada v. William Schulze & Co., [1901] 9 S.L.T. 4.

November 9, 1995, and is such a citizen at the time the applicant state applies for collection of the claim, to a taxable period that ended before November 9, 1995; and

b. where the taxpayer is an entity that is a company, estate, or trust, the revenue claim relates to a taxable period in which the taxpayer derived its status as such an entity from the laws in force in the requested country.

Since there are many Canadian residents who are dual citizens of Canada and the United States, paragraph 8 constitutes a major obstacle to the collection of U.S. taxes in Canada. It may also affect the collection of Canadian taxes from a U.S. citizen and resident.

VIII. Dangers in the Use of a U.S.-Style Revocable Inter Vivos Trust

Because the transfer of property by an individual to a revocable inter vivos trust has no immediate U.S. tax consequences, and because such a trust may be advantageous for non-tax reasons, it is not uncommon for U.S. residents to transfer the bulk of their property during their lifetime to such a trust. The income and gains of such a trust will be attributed to the transferor during his or her lifetime under the U.S. grantor trust rules. No gift tax will be payable upon such a transfer, but the property in the trust will be subject to estate tax on his or her death. Unfortunately, the transfer of property to such a trust is deemed, for Canadian tax purposes, to take place at fair market value with the result that any appreciation in such property before the transfer will give rise to deemed realization of a capital gain. This means that if appreciated Canadian real property is settled by a U.S. resident on such a trust, it will lead to a Canadian tax liability for which a foreign tax credit will not be available in the United States. Additionally, Canada imposes a deemed disposition of assets held in a trust on each twenty-one-year anniversary of such trust. Assets held in a revocable inter vivos trust will be subject to this "deemed disposition rule" and will give rise to tax liability on the deemed realization of capital gain every twenty-one years.

The alter ego trusts and joint spousal trusts permit an individual sixty-five years of age or older to transfer appreciated property to such a trust at the settlor's cost basis.

It is also common for U.S. residents to deal with their remaining property, which has not been transferred during their lifetime to such a trust, by providing in their wills for the residue of the probate estate to be poured over to the trust, to be dealt with as part of the trust property. This can cause difficulties of two sorts. First, although U.S. state laws generally validate such pour overs, no Canadian jurisdiction has similar legislation; they all apply the common law rule that invalidates any provision in a will that has the effect of allowing it to be amended after its execution otherwise than by a duly executed codicil or another will.[38] Since a revocable inter vivos trust can usually be amended quite simply, without the formalities attending the execution of a will or codicil, the pour over of Canadian situs property of a U.S. resident decedent to such a trust will be legally ineffective. In addition, because the trust will not have arisen on the decedent's death, the foreign tax credit provisions of paragraph 7 of article XXIX B of the Treaty will not be applicable.

IX. Conclusion

The recent protocols to the Treaty have considerably alleviated the tax problems associated with cross-border holdings by Canadian residents and by U.S. citizens. However, the radically different nature of the death tax systems of the two countries still creates many problems for the estate planner and for the client.

38. A.H. Oosterhoff, Wills and Succession 122 (3d ed. 1990), states, in discussing incorporation by reference in a will: "if the reference is to an existing document which is subject to change, as where the maker of it has a power of revocation, the document cannot be incorporated."

Advising the Client Who Has Ties with Mexico

17

Michelle B. Graham
Laura M. Nava

I. Nontax Considerations

A. Cultural Differences

If you practice in the area of international estate planning, you face or are likely to face people from different countries, with different cultures, different religions, different languages, different customs, and so forth. It is critical for the international estate planner to be aware and respectful of those differences. Unless the planner is already familiar with the particular country or culture with which he or she is dealing, the planner will be well advised to listen very carefully and say very little at first. As with all clients, it is critical that we understand the clients' objectives, or we run the risk of proposing the wrong plan. Make no assumptions, and do not pass judgment simply because someone is different.

B. Communication Challenges

In the realm of domestic estate planning, we may be more accustomed to having a client whom we have met for the first time simply provide us with a complete list of assets and any other information we care to request. With international clients, matters are not likely to progress the same way. The planner needs to explain to the client what the planner needs and why, and the planner needs to earn the client's trust—a process that is likely to take much longer when dealing with a non-U.S. client.

Among the additional communication challenges the international estate planner faces are the following:

1. If the planner is communicating with the client through an interpreter, much of the information being conveyed, including the kind of information we usually get from reading between the lines or observing body language when we speak with someone in our own language, is likely to be lost. The planner must ask many questions and attempt to satisfy himself or herself that he or she has the information needed to plan properly.
2. If the planner communicates with the client in English and English is the client's second language, the information the planner will get will be limited by the client's ability to communicate effectively in English. Do not be fooled by what appears to be an almost perfect command of conversational English. This facility does not always translate into effective communication of legal issues.
3. Unless the client already knows and has come to trust the planner, the client will likely provide only the information the client believes the planner needs to know. In most cases, the information received will be insufficient. It is important that the planner explain to the client in detail the information that will be needed and provide clear examples of how things can go wrong if a key piece of information is missed. The planner should also make sure that the client understands the attorney-client privilege and the planner's practices to ensure client information is kept confidential. In addition, the planner's advice should always be accompanied by a summary of the facts on which the planner relied.

C. Confidentiality

International clients are more likely to be sensitive about confidentiality. The planner would be well advised to be extremely sensitive to that need and to avoid making assumptions or judgments about why the client might be so interested in keeping personal matters confidential. It is not necessarily the case that the client has something to hide. In some cases, confidentiality is an integral part of the client's culture. In other cases, it can be a matter of life and death.

In Mexico, until relatively recently, financial information was traditionally controlled by the family's patriarch. Planners are still likely to encounter this family profile, though it is more likely to be found in older couples. Unless there is a responsible adult child who is already familiar with the family's affairs, a planner who represents the widow in such a family is likely to encounter someone who needs a significant amount of education and hand-holding and who is likely to have very little knowledge about the family's financial affairs. Planners who find themselves representing multiple clients, with different knowledge and awareness about the family's financial affairs, should be sensitive to the ethical dilemmas he or she is likely to face. If the person in control of the information and management of the family's assets intends to continue the same pattern and is really not interested in having the other person become aware or educated about the planning process, the planner may be better off representing only one client rather than undertaking multiple-client representation.

As a result of the recent increase in uncontrolled crime in Mexico (in particular, kidnappings), Mexican clients' concern about confidentiality is less driven by tax issues and more driven by personal and family safety issues. Information about a person's wealth, its whereabouts, and its magnitude, in the wrong hands, could be a death sentence for a family member. These same pressures have resulted in renewed interest on the part of well-educated and affluent families to leave Mexico and immigrate into other countries or to send children to study abroad. As a result, more and more international estate planning involves families with members in more than one jurisdiction.

D. Marital Property Regime

Mexico has two regimes for marital property, community property (*sociedad conjugal*) and separate property (*separación de bienes*). Couples who marry in Mexico must elect at the time of marriage which marital regime they want to apply. Such election will be noted on their marriage certificate. For the planner advising a couple married in Mexico, it will be important to determine which marital regime the couple elected. If the couple still reside in Mexico, it is important to note that most U.S. style pre- or post-nuptial agreements generally will not be recognized in Mexico. If a pre- or post-nuptial agreement is desired, it is recommended that a marital property agreement be drawn up and executed before a Mexican notary public.

Some states may not recognize the election of the marital regime as an effective means to change the characterization of property. For example, if a couple married in Mexico and elected to have the separate property regime (*separacion de bienes*) apply, the planner will need to consider whether the applicable state in the United States will apply its own marital property laws or whether it will apply the laws of Mexico. To avoid the potential conflict of law issues, the planner should consider a pre- or post-nuptial agreement drafted and executed in the United States.

E. Ownership Versus Title

Even after receiving a list of assets from the client, the planner must carefully review each asset with the client to determine whether the title of the assets matches the ownership of the assets. It is common in Mexican culture for a parent to add children or other family members to the title to assets even though the child or other family member contributed nothing to its acquisition. In most cases, the parent did not intend to make a completed current gift of a portion of the asset. In some cases, the parent simply intended for the asset to pass to the other person at the time of the parent's death. In many cases, however, the parent simply added the name to the title for convenience purposes and actually expects his or her will to control the disposition of the asset. A foreign will that attempts to dispose of joint or Totten Trust assets, for example, is litigation waiting to happen.

Transfers to minors have additional problems. Not uncommonly, a parent titles real estate, for example, in the name of minor children. When the parent needs to sell, refinance, collect insurance proceeds, or otherwise deal with the property, the parent learns that he or she cannot simply act on behalf of the minor(s) as the natural guardian. Accordingly, a more costly and time-consuming court proceeding becomes necessary.

The planner must explain to the client not only the non-tax consequences of the titling of assets and subsequent changes to such title, but also the actual and potential gift tax consequences of the resulting transfers. The gift tax issues that arise from the changes in the title of assets come as a complete surprise to Mexican clients for many reasons.

1. As explained in greater detail in the Section II below, "Summary of Mexican Tax Issues," there is no gift tax in Mexico, like the one in the United States. Accordingly, it rarely occurs to Mexican clients to ask whether a change in title has any tax consequences.
2. Frequently, when they do ask, they may not ask the right person, and they receive poor advice from presumably well-meaning but ill-informed friends, relatives, and even other professional advisers. For example, people who are aware that transfers between U.S. citizen spouses have no tax consequences may not be aware that the marital deduction is restricted in the case of non-U.S. citizen spouses.[1]
3. When taxable transfers are made in Mexico, they must be made through a *notario publico*, a person with far different qualifications, authority, and responsibility with respect to a transaction than a U.S. notary public. A Mexican *notario* is a licensed Mexican attorney with significant additional education and practical training to achieve the status of *notario*. Among other responsibilities, the *notario* must determine and collect any tax due as a result of a particular transaction. If the proper amount of tax is not collected, the *notario* is personally liable therefor. Accordingly, it is no wonder Mexican clients assume that because they signed a deed in front of a U.S. notary and paid the nominal recording fee, no further tax can possibly be due.

1. *See* discussion of transfer tax issues and Qualified Domestic Trusts, *supra* Chapters 2 and 9, respectively.

4. In the case of transfers to minors, parents are often completely unaware of the need for guardianship proceedings in certain cases because, in Mexico, they can simply act as the natural guardians of their children.

F. Recognition and Use of Trusts

Mexico is a civil law jurisdiction. Consequently, trusts are not as well known or used as they are in the common law jurisdictions. As set forth in the Summary of Mexican Tax Issues (*see infra* Section II), Mexico recognizes Mexican trusts or *fideicomisos*. However, only a Mexican bank or authorized institution can be the trustee of a Mexican trust. Mexican trusts, even if irrevocable, are not treated as separate taxpayers unless they are special business trusts. Instead, income of the trust is currently taxable to its beneficiaries if they are ascertainable or to the settlor if the beneficiaries are not ascertainable.

It is not clear whether Mexican tax authorities will apply the same tax principles to Mexican settlors or beneficiaries of foreign trusts as are applied to Mexican settlors or beneficiaries of Mexican trusts or whether, under certain circumstances, a foreign trust will be recognized as a separate taxpayer. Accordingly, the tax consequences of planning structures involving assets directly owned by a non-Mexican trust with Mexican resident settlor(s) and/or beneficiaries are uncertain. Therefore, most planning structures involving Mexican residents include one or more corporate or other better-recognized and understood entities.

G. Mexican Trusts for Mexican Real Property

Although Mexican trusts are not as commonly used by Mexican persons as part of their estate plan, the Mexican trust or *fideicomiso* is required to be used by non-Mexican nationals to acquire and hold land in the "restricted zone." The restricted zone includes 50 kilometers from all Mexican coastlines and 100 kilometers from all Mexican borders. Pursuant to the Mexican Constitution, real property located within the restricted zone that will be used for residential purposes may only be owned by Mexican nationals (those individuals who are Mexican by birth or naturalization) and Mexican entities, provided, however, that such Mexican entities may not be owned by non-Mexican persons. If, however, the real property is used for nonresidential purposes, the property may be owned by a Mexican entity, which in turn may be owned by non-Mexican persons.

For real property that is located within the restricted zone and is used for residential purposes, title to such property must be held in a Mexican trust or *fideicomiso*. By law, only a Mexican bank or financial institution may serve as trustee. Although the title to the real property is held in the name of the trustee, the beneficiary (i.e., non-Mexican national) has all the corresponding rights to use, lease, or sell the rights derived from the trust. The Mexican government must grant a special permit to establish these type of trusts. The permits are granted for a fifty-year renewable term.

Any individual or legal entity, whether Mexican or foreign, may be the beneficiary under a *fideicomiso*. This includes but is not limited to a U.S. person, a U.S. LLC, a U.S. trust, or a company (U.S. or Mexican). Most *fideicomiso* instruments do not contemplate U.S. estate taxes. Accordingly, care should be taken to review the instrument carefully and tailor the trust instrument to fit the particular family situation and to provide for an orderly succession and minimize or defer U.S. transfer taxes. At a minimum, the *fideicomiso* instrument should provide for successor beneficiaries. It is the authors' experience that a Mexican trustee generally will not designate successor beneficiaries based on a U.S. will or "pour over will" designating such beneficiaries. Rather, the Mexican trustee may well require a probate proceeding and a U.S. court order, which must then be domesticated under Mexican law before the beneficial property rights are passed to the successor beneficiary.

In the past, there was doubt whether a U.S. family trust could be named as the beneficiary of a Mexican *fideicomiso*. As noted above, it is now generally recognized that a U.S. family trust may be named as the beneficiary or successor beneficiary. In one such instance that the authors encountered, the Mexican trustee required an order from a U.S. court recognizing the authority of the successor trustee of the U.S. family trust in order to allow the transfer of interest under the Mexican trust.

As discussed in more detail in other chapters of this book, care must be taken to comply with all United States foreign reporting. U.S. taxpayers have long questioned whether *fideicomisos* are "trusts" for U.S. tax purposes. If a *fideicomiso* is considered a trust for U.S. tax purposes, an Annual Return to Report Transactions with Foreign Trusts and Receipt of Certain Foreign Gifts (Form 3520) and Annual Information Return with a U.S. Owner of Foreign Trust (Form 3520-A) likely will be required, along with a Statement of Specified Foreign Financial Assets (Form 8938) and possibly Report of Foreign Bank and Financial Accounts (Form TD F 90-22.1). In an important private letter ruling (I.R.S. Priv. Ltr. Rul. 201245003), the Internal Revenue Service ruled that the *fideicomiso* in the ruling was not a trust. Therefore, Form 3520 and Form 3520-A were not required. Although a private letter ruling cannot be cited as precedent, the ruling can be used as guidance to determine whether foreign trust reporting is required with respect to a particular *fideicomiso*.

One final note on *fideicomisos*. On April 23, 2013, the House of Representatives of Mexico approved an amendment to Article 27 of the Mexican Constitution that would allow foreigners to acquire real property within the Restricted Zone with fee simple title and thus avoid the need to use a *fideicomiso*. As of the time the authors submitted this chapter to the editors, the constitutional amendment still requires approval by the Mexican Senate, and, thereafter, if approved by the Mexican Senate, it will require approval of the majority of State Congresses of Mexico before becoming law. Furthermore, the respective Mexican foreign investment law and its regulations must also be amended to reflect the constitutional amendment and to provide the provisions applicable to the direct foreign ownership within the Restricted Zone.

II. Summary of Mexican Tax Issues

A. Overview

Mexico has federal, state, and local taxes. The main federal taxes are the income tax (*impuesto sobre la renta*), flat tax (*impuesto empresarial a tasa única* or IETU),[2] and the value added tax (*impuesto al valor agregado*). The main state taxes are the payroll tax and in some states the tax on the possession or use of vehicles. Typical local taxes are real estate taxes and real estate acquisition taxes.

Mexico does not have a gift tax, estate tax, or inheritance tax. In addition, the concept of income from the sale or other disposition of assets specifically excludes transfers due to death, donation, or merger of companies. However, transfers at death by a Mexican resident to a nonresident of Mexico of either shares in a Mexican company or in real estate located in Mexico will be subject to an income tax in general based on the gross value of the asset and will be taxable in the hands of the recipient. Care must be taken if the planner intends to use a trust to implement any transfers at death from a Mexican resident because such transfers could be subject to tax in Mexico if the trust agreement is not properly drafted.

Mexican income tax law recognizes only two types of taxpayers: corporations and individuals. Other entities are recognized but given a different treatment. For example, silent partnerships are taxed as corporations, and trusts are simply considered vehicles for final payment of the tax owed by the parties to the trust.

Individuals are taxed in Mexico on the basis of their residency. Unlike the United States, Mexico does not tax as residents its citizens residing outside of Mexico. Individuals who have established their home in Mexico are residents of Mexico unless they spend more than 183 calendar days in another country and can establish that they have acquired tax residence in the other country. Mexican citizens are presumed to be Mexican residents, but this is a rebuttable presumption. Entities established or created in accordance with Mexican laws, and those that are effectively administered or managed in Mexico, are residents of Mexico. An entity will be effectively administered or managed in Mexico if: (1) the meetings of shareholders and directors are held in Mexico, (2) the persons who, on a day-to-day basis, make control, direction, or management decisions are tax residents of Mexico or have offices in Mexico, or (3) its accounting records are kept in Mexico.

Residents of Mexico are subject to Mexican income tax with respect to their worldwide income, whether such income is derived in cash, credit, services, property, or in kind. Nonresidents of Mexico that have a permanent establishment in

2. A significant tax reform proposed in September 2013 includes the complete repeal of the flat tax law. If this part of the reform is approved, the flat tax law will not be in place as of January 1, 2014.

Mexico are taxed on all income that is attributable to such permanent establishment and on all Mexican-source income that is not attributable to such permanent establishment. Nonresidents of Mexico who do not have a permanent establishment are taxed only with respect to Mexican-source income.

In addition to the income tax, there is a flat tax (*impuesto empresarial a tasa única* or IETU) that applies to Mexican entities or permanent establishments of foreign residents on the sale, service, and lease activities of the entity. The IEUT is calculated by applying a 17.5 percent rate to the tax base, which is the excess of the total income derived from the taxable activities over the limited authorized deductions. The IETU is similar to the Alternative Minimum Tax (AMT) in the United States in that taxpayers are required to pay the higher between the income tax and the IETU. Currently, the IETU is recognized by the Internal Revenue Services as a type of tax similar in nature to the income tax. Thus, the IETU paid in Mexico by a Mexican subsidiary is eligible for a tax credit in the United States.[3]

B. The Mexican Tax Legislation

Before 1997, Mexico did not tax its residents with respect to earnings of corporate and other entities they owned so long as the Mexican resident owners had not yet received distributions of those earnings (in the form of dividends or otherwise). In other words, Mexico did not have a tax regime similar to the subchapter F regime of the U.S. Internal Revenue Code.[4] However, toward the end of 1996, the Mexican Congress started to implement a series of amendments to the Federal Income Tax Code and the Federal Fiscal Code in sweeping tax legislation, most of which became effective in 1997 and 1998, and more recently in 2002 and 2005. That legislation included a regime similar to I.R.C. subchapter F dealing with investments made through "tax havens," "low-tax jurisdictions," or now what are known as "preferential tax jurisdictions."

The legislation, as amended, provides that Mexican taxpayers must pay income tax on income subject to preferential tax jurisdictions that is received through entities or foreign legal institutions in which they participate and/or have effective control, directly or indirectly, in the proportion that corresponds to their participation in the entity, as well as for income that is obtained through entities or foreign legal institutions that are transparent in such foreign jurisdictions. The income subject to preferential tax jurisdictions is defined to mean income that is not taxed in the foreign jurisdiction, or, when it is subject to an income tax, it is lower than 75 percent of the income tax that would be caused and paid in Mexico. Such reportable income will be determined each calendar year in accordance with the provisions of the Mexican income tax law. In very general terms, if the taxpayer has effective control over the administration to a degree such that the taxpayer may decide the moment of payment or distribution of income, profits, or dividends, whether

3. *See, e.g., supra* note 2.
4. *See* I.R.C. §§ 951 *et seq.*

directly or through a third person, the income generated in such entity is now subject to income tax. For such purpose, it is presumed, unless proven otherwise, that the taxpayer has control over the entities in a foreign legal organization that generates income subject to a foreign preferential tax jurisdiction.

In addition, the legislation imposes on Mexican taxpayers the obligation to file, in the month of February of each year, an information declaration concerning the investments made or maintained in the immediately preceding tax year in preferential tax jurisdictions or in corporations or entities located or resident in such jurisdictions.

The comprehensive legislation amended the federal fiscal code to include as one of the crimes, punishable with imprisonment from three months to three years, the failure to file for more than three months the required information return of investments made or maintained in preferential tax jurisdictions or in corporations or other entities resident or located in such jurisdictions.

Finally, in 2004, the federal fiscal code was further amended to include provisions applicable to the definition of Mexican tax residency. The amended legislation provides that Mexican tax residents are those with their personal residence located in Mexico, and those with residences in two jurisdictions when their vital center of interests are in Mexico. Mexican citizens are presumed to be Mexican residents. Furthermore, Mexican citizens will not forgo their resident status if they reside in a county or territory where their income is subject to a preferential tax jurisdiction. Finally, the amendment requires that individuals file a notice of change of domicile if they cease to be Mexican tax residents.[5]

The transitory articles of the income tax law include the current countries and territories that require taxpayers to file an informative return; the respective countries and territories are listed below:

Albania	Brunei
American Samoa	Campione
Andorra	Canary Special Zone
Anguilla	Canary Islands
Antigua (and Barbuda)	Cape Verde
Aruba	Cayman Islands
Ascension	Channel Islands
Azores Islands	(Guernsey and Jersey)
Bahamas	Christmas Islands
Bahrain	Cook Islands

5. At the time of the writing this chapter (September 2013), an extensive law reform was presented to the Mexican Congress by the newly elected President Peña Nieto. The tax reform includes the complete revocation of the flat tax law, and amendments to the income tax law, the value added tax law, and the federal fiscal code. All the reforms and amendments that are approved after negotiations would be expected to go into effect on January 1, 2014.

Barbados
Belize
Bermuda
British Virgin Islands
French Polynesia
Gibraltar
Grenada
Greenland
Guam
Guyana
Honduras
Hong Kong
Isle of Man
Kiribati
Kuwait
Labuan
Liberia
Liechtenstein
Luxemburg
Macao
Madeira
Maldives
Malta
Marshall Islands
Mauritius
Monaco
Montserrat
Nauru
Netherland Antilles
Niue
Norfolk Island
Oman
Ostrava
Pacific Islands
Costa Rica
Cyprus
Djibouti
Dominican Republic
Panama
Patau
Pitcairn
Puerto Rico
Qatar
Salomon Islands
San Marino
Sark
Seychelles
Sri Lanka
St. Helena
St. Lucia
St. Kitts and Nevis
St. Pierre & Miquelon Islands
St. Vincent and the Grenadines
Svalbard
Swaziland
Tonga
Tokelau
Trieste Archipelago
Trinidad and Tobago
Tristan da Cunha
Turks and Caicos Islands
Tuvalu
Qeshm Island
United Arab Emirates
United States Virgin Islands
Uruguay
Vanuatu
Western Samoa

C. Tax Treaties

Mexico has an increasing network of income tax and information exchange treaties. Currently, Mexico has tax treaties with the following:

Argentina, Australia, Austria, Bahamas, Bahrain, Barbados, Belgium, Bermuda, Brazil, Canada, Cayman Islands, Chile, China, Czechoslovakia, Cook Islands, Costa Rica, Colombia, Denmark, Ecuador, Finland, France, Germany, Greece, Guernsey and Jersey Islands, Hong Kong, Hungary, Iceland, India, Indonesia, Ireland, Israel, Italy, Japan, Korea, Luxemburg, Lithuania, Marshall Islands, Netherlands, Netherlands Antilles, New Zealand, Norway, Panama, Poland, Portugal, Romania, Russia, Samoa, Singapore, Slovak Republic, South Africa, Spain, Sweden, Switzerland, United Kingdom, United States, Ukraine, Uruguay.

In addition, Mexico is currently negotiating income tax and information trade treaties with the countries listed below.

British Virgin Islands, Jamaica, Lebanon, Marshall Islands, Malaysia, Monaco, Morocco, Nicaragua, Pakistan, Saudi Arabia, St. Lucia, Slovenia, Thailand, Turkey, Turks and Caicos Islands, Vanuatu.

Treaties have been signed with the following countries but are not yet in effect:

Aruba, Belgium, Estonia, Gibraltar, Italy, Liechtenstein, Malta, Peru, United Emirates, Venezuela.

III. U.S. Tax Issues and Planning for Clients with Mexican Connections

A. Determining the Client's Tax Residence

As discussed above, whether you are planning for a Mexican resident or any other client, you first need to know your client. Among the most important issues to determine early on is the residential status of the clients and others connected to the client. Are they U.S. taxpayers or nonresident aliens? Other chapters of this book discuss the different rules that apply to nonresident aliens.[6] Before applying such rules or implementing any planning that depends upon the application of such rules, the planner must be certain that the appropriate persons are indeed nonresident aliens.

Relying on the client for the determination of residence for tax purpose is dangerous. When laypersons discuss the concept of residence, they are more likely referring to the immigration rather than the tax concept of residence, and, as shown in other chapters of this book, the two are not the same. Before anyone can make a correct determination of residence, all relevant facts must be known. As illustrated by the situations described below, to conclude that a particular client

6. *See, e.g., supra* Chapter 2.

is a nonresident alien, it is not sufficient for the planner to know that the client is a citizen and resident of Mexico.

1. The planner might be later surprised to learn that the client is a U.S. citizen. In light of the proximity of Mexico and Canada to the U.S. borders, there are many people in those countries who were born in the United States and immediately returned to their countries. Never having lived in the United States, such individuals may not consider themselves U.S. citizens and may be completely unaware of their tax obligations as U.S. citizens. Many individuals who were born in the United States but lived in Mexico all of their lives renounced their U.S. citizenship (most likely at their parents' insistence) when they attained age eighteen. In light of changing policy in the United States with respect to loss of U.S. citizenship, many of these individuals are now able to recover their U.S. citizenship. In addition, with Mexico's formal acceptance of dual nationality effective on March 20, 1998, planners are more likely than ever to encounter dual nationals of the United States and Mexico.
2. The planner might also be later surprised to learn that the client spends enough time in the United States to meet the substantial presence test and is, therefore, a resident alien for income tax purposes. The planner should consider in this circumstance whether it is appropriate and/or beneficial to take a position under the income tax treaty with Mexico that the client has closer connections to Mexico and thus is a resident of Mexico for income tax purposes. Note that if the client takes such a position, all U. S. reporting, as discussed below, still applies.
3. The planner might also be later surprised to learn that the client was once a green card holder and left the United States intending to give up residence in the United States but did not surrender the green card.

As shown herein, the client's status depends on many facts, including, in some cases, compliance with filing requirements. It is essential that the planner gather all necessary facts and perform a detailed analysis before proceeding with any planning. In addition, as more fully described in other chapters of this book, residence for tax purposes is defined differently for income tax purposes and for estate tax purposes. The subjective determination of domicile for estate tax purposes must be undertaken with significant care.

B. Investments in U.S. Situs Assets

Unless the U.S.-Mexico Income Tax Treaty applies, Mexican residents who are neither residents nor citizens of the United States are taxed as any other nonresident aliens. Accordingly, the same planning techniques described elsewhere in this book should generally be considered. In the case of structures involving the use of foreign corporations to hold assets otherwise deemed situated in the United States to avoid the imposition of U.S. estate tax on the transfer of those assets by the nonresident alien owner to his or her intended beneficiaries, the planner must now be aware of Mexico's rules dealing with the holding of investments in so-called preferential tax jurisdictions discussed above. Since the enactment of Mexico's preferential tax jurisdiction legislation, different strategies have emerged in an effort to deal with the new rules. Some of these strategies involve the formation of entities in jurisdictions not considered preferential tax jurisdictions under Mexican law, and some have involved efforts to fall within exceptions provided in the legislation itself. Some of the strategies originally developed have already been rendered obsolete by changes in either the Mexican legislation itself or by changes in legislation in the countries in which other entities were established. As noted above, there are continuing changes made to the Mexican legislation, and thus it will probably be some time before we can expect greater stability with respect to any planning done as it relates to this portion of the Mexican tax code.

C. Pre-immigration Planning

As set forth above, the current situation in Mexico is creating greater interest among Mexican families in moving to the United States or other countries. As more fully discussed elsewhere in this book, pre-immigration planning for these families is essential.[7] In addition, once a portion of more and more families immigrates to the United States, we will increasingly face clients whose families are partly in the United States and partly outside of the United States. As more fully discussed elsewhere in this book, this scenario presents many planning opportunities but also many traps for the unwary.[8]

As more fully discussed in the expatriation chapter of this book, long-term green card holders who give up their green cards are now treated as expatriates for purposes of the U.S. expatriation rules. Accordingly, persons wishing to immigrate into the United States may want to postpone as long as possible the acquisition of a green card. There are many other visas that will enable clients to spend long or even indefinite periods of time in the United States without a green card.

D. Compliance with the U.S. Foreign Trust Compliance Rules

The increase in families with connections to more than one jurisdiction, and in particular the increase in families with both U.S. and Mexican connections, makes it essential for planners to inform the U.S. persons in the family of the need to comply with the U.S. foreign trust compliance rules enacted in the United States at the end of 1996. As more specifically covered elsewhere in this book,[9] these rules deal primarily with tax and reporting obligations associated with the establishment of foreign trusts, the transfer of assets to foreign trusts, distributions from

7. *See supra* Chapter 8.
8. *See, e.g., supra* Chapter 7.
9. *Id.*

foreign trusts, gifts from foreign persons, and the taxation of persons related to the trust.

E. Compliance with Transfer Tax Reporting Obligations

Ignorance on the part of Mexican clients about the existence of U.S. estate, gift, and generation-skipping assets and their applicability to certain U.S. situs assets held by persons who are neither residents nor citizens of the United States[10] often results in poor compliance with U.S. transfer tax rules. Very often, when a death occurs in the family, family members are less likely to travel to their vacation home in the United States, which may have been titled in the decedent's name. The surviving family members are often completely unaware that an estate tax return is required to be filed within nine months of the decedent's death. If the property was titled in joint tenancy, someone may have already incorrectly advised the family that there is nothing to worry about because the property passes "automatically" to the survivors. So when the family finally comes to see you (sometimes many years later when they are trying to sell the property), they are facing not only the estate tax due but also interest and penalties. They may even be facing a second death. Although ignorance of the law is no excuse, a request for abatement of penalties should always be filed, especially if the executor (for tax purposes) is filing the return at the earliest opportunity after learning that a return needed to be filed. Interest, of course, will always be due.

10. *See supra* Chapter 2 dealing with the transfer tax rules as they apply to nonresidents.

18

Navigating the Treacherous Tax North Atlantic: Aspects of Anglo-American Estate Planning Updated

Barry McCutcheon
Richard Cassell
Dyke Davies
Updated by
Richard Cassell
Penelope Williams*

I. Introduction

The purpose of this chapter is to identify and comment on certain aspects of Anglo-American taxation and tax planning. The chapter does not attempt to provide exhaustive coverage either as to Anglo-American taxation and planning generally or as to all the technicalities. Rather, the authors have concentrated on identifying areas of symmetry and asymmetry that advisers should avoid, rectify, or exploit, as may be appropriate in

* Richard Cassell and Penelope Williams are partners in the London office of Withers LLP, with many thanks to Jaime McLemore who contributed significantly to this version.

attempting to navigate the treacherous tax waters of the North Atlantic. Initially, background matters are outlined from both jurisdictions and subsequently, outline planning options are described.

II. Background

A. Overview

Both the U.K. and the United States tax lifetime transfers, transfers on death, and capital gains.

Estate taxes are imposed by both the United States and the U.K. The U.K. has a single tax—"inheritance tax"—for both lifetime transfers and transfers on death, while the United States has a separate gift tax, generation-skipping transfer tax, and estate tax, although they share a unified rate schedule. For convenience, these three taxes will occasionally, both separately and together, be referred to simply as "transfer tax" or "transfer taxes."

So far as capital gains are concerned, the U.K. has a separate capital gains tax while the United States charges capital gains to income tax. For convenience, reference is made in this chapter simply to "capital gains tax." Capital gains tax applies to gains made during a person's lifetime, whether in the form of an actual gain on the sale of an asset or as the result of a deemed gain under circumstances specified in the relevant tax rules.

Generally speaking, both the U.K. inheritance tax regime and the U.K. capital gains tax regime afford taxpayers significantly greater exemptions and reliefs than their U.S. counterparts. At the time of writing, the U.S. tax on long-term capital gains is capped at 20 percent, and the maximum U.K. capital gains tax rate is 28 percent. The U.S. transfer tax rates are capped at 40 percent. U.K. inheritance tax is applied at two rates: 0 percent (applied in relation to the "nil rate band") and 40 percent applied above the "nil rate band." However the unified credit (or exempt) account for U.S. gift and estate tax is $5.25 million for 2013 and will increase annually in line with inflation.

B. Estate Taxes

1. Generally

U.K. inheritance tax is broadly charged on diminutions in value in a person's estate occasioned by dispositions he makes during his lifetime and on his death. This sometimes is referred to as "the loss to the donor" principle. This is the amount by which the value of a donor's estate is diminished by a transfer, not the value of that which he gives away nor, if it is different, the value to the donee of that which he is given. Special rules apply to property held in trust (see below). There are a large number of reliefs and exemptions, the most notable of which are discussed below, as well as a plethora of anti-avoidance rules.

In contrast, U.S. transfer taxes are imposed by reference to the value of the transferred property, rather than by reference to the diminution in the value of the transferor's estate. There are few tax preferences by reference to the type of property transferred (although an installment payment option is available with respect to certain closely held business properties). This means that much of U.S. estate planning focuses on leveraging values on lifetime transfers. For example, for U.S. transfer tax purposes, a gift of a partial interest in property that is subject to marketability restrictions or that represents a minority interest can result in a low value being ascribed to the property transferred compared with the value of the underlying property, although this has been heavily litigated by the Internal Revenue Service (IRS) over recent years. Given the U.K.'s loss to donor principle, this approach is generally ineffective for U.K. estate planning.

Despite the significant differences in the U.S. and U.K. estate planning regimes, there is an overall principle in common. In a domestic planning context, when planning for a married couple with children and descendants, the estate planner on both sides of the Atlantic will strive to: (1) preserve the tax-free amount that each taxpayer can transfer to children and others through the use of a bypass trust (note that both the United States and the U.K. have introduced transferability or portability of a spouse's unused tax free amount); (2) otherwise defer transfer tax until the later of the death of the taxpayer and his or her spouse through use of reliefs for transfers to spouses, and their using the foreign tax credit mechanism to offset one tax against the other; and (3) maximize the reliefs available for lifetime transfers to establish trusts to benefit children and descendants. Traps and opportunities arise as we seek to achieve similar planning goals for those with a transatlantic marriage, a same sex marriage or civil union, or transatlantic property or domicile issues.

2. Foreign Element

The territorial scope of the U.S. transfer taxes and U.K. inheritance tax is seriously askew. Both systems impose their estate taxes on assets situated domestically, but the similarity ends there. The United States taxes on a worldwide basis both U.S. nationals and individuals domiciled in the United States for federal tax purposes (which generally includes permanent residents or "green card" holders), wherever they may be resident. The U.K., on the other hand, adopts a radically different approach in which nationality plays no part (though it can be relevant under the 1979 U.S.-U.K. Estate and Gift Tax Treaty) and focuses on domicile.

(a) U.K. Inheritance Tax. The basic rule is that inheritance tax is imposed on a worldwide basis. This is subject to the important qualification that non-U.K. domiciliaries are liable to inheritance tax only on their U.K. situs assets. Therefore, a taxpayer's domicile is important for determining inheritance tax exposure. There are two domicile rules peculiar to the U.K. to keep in mind. First, a taxpayer who loses his domicile of choice will find that his domicile of origin revives automatically (broadly, the person's father's domicile at birth). Second, a taxpayer who has been tax resident in the U.K. for more than sixteen out of twenty U.K. tax years is treated as, or deemed to be, U.K. domiciled for inheritance tax purposes, regardless of the taxpayer's actual domicile. Non-U.K. situs assets held in a trust created by an individual who was domiciled outside the U.K. for inheritance tax purposes at the time he created the trust are generally outside the scope of inheritance tax, even though the beneficiaries are U.K. domiciliaries and notwithstanding the fact that the settlor subsequently becomes domiciled (or treated as domiciled) in the U.K.

(b) U.S. Transfer Tax. The U.S. approach is to tax all citizens regardless of domicile in addition to U.S. domiciliaries. It continues to tax its own nationals even after they have ceased to have any connection with the United States other than their nationality. As a result, U.S. citizens remain subject to U.S. transfer taxes even though subject to inheritance tax in the U.K. as a domiciliary (for example). Every U.S. estate and gift tax treaty includes a "savings" provision that enables the United States to tax its citizens without regard to the treaty provisions. The consequence is that planning with a U.S. treaty for a U.S. citizen is primarily based on using treaty and U.S. domestic foreign tax credit provisions to avoid double taxation. In determining a noncitizen's domicile for transfer tax purposes, the taxpayer's immigration status is relevant. Possession of a green card creates a rebuttable presumption of U.S. domicile, and so immigration status is a significant factor in determining domicile.

U.S. gift tax (and therefore generation-skipping transfer tax on lifetime transfers) operates differently from U.S. estate tax in relation to a non-U.S. citizen who is not a U.S. domiciliary. Estate tax is imposed on transfers of virtually all U.S. situs property, and for this purpose, conventional rules for determining situs apply. For gift tax and lifetime generation-skipping transfer tax, on the other hand, intangible property is treated as not being situated in the United States. This means that an individual who is neither a U.S. citizen nor domiciled in the United States for transfer tax purposes can give away, for example, shares in U.S. companies without being subject to gift tax. This can be particularly important to such an individual if he is planning to move to the United States; for example, a U.K. domiciliary with such plans should consider making gifts of intangible property before coming within the full ambit of the U.S. transfer taxes.

This limited exemption does not affect the general liability of a U.S. citizen for U.S. transfer taxes on a worldwide basis. The most drastic solution for escaping U.S. transfer tax liability for a U.S. citizen or long-term green card holder is to expatriate (long-term green card holders are individuals who have held a green card for eight or more of the prior fifteen years). However, expatriation can give rise to significant U.S. tax consequences. An expatriate with net assets over $2 million at the time of expatriation will be treated as a "covered expatriate" unless he meets certain limited exceptions. The principal exceptions relate to dual citizens (who must have been born dual citizens and be tax resident in the other citizenship country) and certain expatriates aged 18 to 18½ years. A covered expatriate is treated as recognizing gain on all appreciated assets (with an exemption for the first $668,000 of gain as adjusted for inflation in 2013) and taxed on the deemed disposition of assets.

Almost more significant than the expatriation "exit tax" is the additional transfer tax that applies to any future transfers by a covered expatriate to a U.S. person, whether by gift or bequest. In addition, complex rules seek to impose a 30 percent tax on distributions from certain foreign trusts to the expatriate if the trusts were not subject to gain recognition on expatriation.

The net, anomalous result is that although a U.S. citizen (or long-term green card holder) planning to become domiciled in the U.K. is in a position to arrange his affairs so that, notwithstanding the fact that he is to be domiciled and resident,[1] in the U.K., he will be virtually immune to inheritance tax, he will remain fully liable to U.S. transfer taxes on his worldwide assets as long as he retains his U.S. passport (or, in most cases, green card), and expatriation may not be possible prior to moving to the U.K.

3. Anti-avoidance Provisions

Both U.K. inheritance tax and U.S. transfer taxes contain a wide variety of specific anti-avoidance provisions designed to prevent certain mischief.

(a) U.K. Inheritance Tax. U.K. inheritance tax contains three wide anti-avoidance provisions that merit specific mention.

First, although generally lifetime transfers are not subject to inheritance tax if the transferor survives the beneficiary by seven years, virtually all lifetime transfers into trust are immediately taxable and may well trigger capital gains tax. This harsh tax result was introduced significantly to limit the use of trusts.

Second, where a taxpayer gives away property from which he can in the future benefit, the gift stands, but on his death, the property is clawed back into his estate under the reservation of benefit provisions and is charged accordingly. If the original transfer was also taxable, HM Revenue & Customs (HMRC) will generally impose tax only in respect of whichever of the two occasions produces the greater charge. The most obvious example of the provisions operating is in the case of a taxpayer settling property on discretionary trusts under which he can benefit. (There is, however, no inheritance tax objection to his wife being a beneficiary in his place.)

Third, the associated operations provisions broadly allow HMRC to telescope a series of transactions into a single transaction and to charge tax accordingly. In practice, the bark of these provisions is often worse than their bite, though

1. The concept of ordinary residence has been abolished as a concept from tax residence in the U.K. with effect from April 2013.

they do operate as something of a residual deterrent. The general anti-abuse rule (known as the GAAR) introduced in the UK with effect from July 17, 2013, extends to inheritance tax. However, at the time of writing it is not known how it will be applied in this context.

(b) U.S. Transfer Tax. For U.S. gift tax purposes, the principal test for whether a gift tax liability might arise is whether a donor has made a completed gift because the donor has ceased to have dominion and control over the transferred property. For U.S. estate tax purposes, the tests as to includability in a decedent's estate largely focus on whether the donor has retained any interest in or control powers over the property. In contrast to the position in the U.K., if a donor retains a power of appointment over the transferred property, it is likely to be includable in his estate. For U.S. generation-skipping transfer tax purposes, the test is dependent on whether a transfer has been made that was subject to either the U.S. gift or estate tax rules.

Although the transfer tax rates have been unified (between gift and estate tax), the tests summarized above are not unified. It is therefore possible for a donor to make a completed gift for U.S. gift tax purposes, but for the property still to be includable in the donor's estate (the ultimate estate planning disaster). This might occur if a donor created a trust over which he had ceased to retain dominion and control (for example, a typical English form discretionary trust), but in which the donor was regarded as retaining an interest, e.g., because he was within the class of beneficiaries.

A major focus of the U.S. anti-avoidance legislation in recent decades has been the special valuation rules contained in chapter 14 of the Internal Revenue Code. These are designed to prevent "value freeze" planning through the use of split interests in entities such as companies or trusts. The classic example of this is the division of the share capital of a company into common (or ordinary) stock and preferred stock so that future growth accrues to one class, thereby passing value to the next generation at minimal transfer tax costs. The anti-avoidance rules are complex, but in essence, this is a technique that can only be used in certain limited circumstances in accordance with methods accepted by the IRS. For example, it is still possible to undertake split interest planning with certain approved formats using charities or personal residences.

The United States has ensured that it collects transfer taxes from each generation by imposing a "generation-skipping transfer tax" at a flat rate equivalent to the highest U.S. transfer tax rate (currently 40 percent) on transfers from, for example, a grandparent to a grandchild. Each transferor has an exemption that, at present, protects up to $5,250,000 of value from this tax.

4. Pre-owned Assets

In addition to the anti-avoidance provisions that are contained in the inheritance tax rules, an income tax charge, "the pre-owned asset tax," was introduced with effect from April 6, 2005. This charge may arise where an individual uses, occupies, or benefits from certain assets he previously owned, or where he directly or indirectly provides finance for the purchase by another of property that the contributor then uses, occupies, or benefits from. Individuals may also be subject to a pre-owned assets charge in relation to trusts holding intangible property (such as stocks and shares or life policies) where they are, or would be, taxable on the income as the settlor.[2]

5. Capital Gains Taxes

(a) U.K. Capital Gains Tax. U.K. capital gains tax is charged on actual and notional gains realized by persons resident in the U.K. during any part of a tax year. Where property is disposed of otherwise than by way of arm's length bargain, it is deemed to have been disposed of for a market value consideration. It is thus possible in theory for the same gift to suffer both inheritance tax and capital gains tax. In some situations, it is possible to avoid an immediate charge to capital gains tax, e.g., where inheritance tax is chargeable in relation to the transfer or where the transfer is of certain business assets. However, this relief is not permitted in all cases; e.g., it is not allowed in relation to transfers to "settlor interested trusts" or where the transferee is not U.K. resident.

On an individual's death, unrealized gains and losses showing on the assets comprising his estate are generally erased, his personal representatives being treated as having acquired the assets free of capital gains tax at their market value on the date of the death.

The rate at which U.K. capital gains tax is charged is generally linked to the rate at which the individual in question is charged to income tax. The highest rate of capital gains tax is currently 28 percent.

(b) U.S. Income Tax on Capital Gains. As noted above, capital gains are subject to U.S. income tax rather than being subject to a separate tax system. Although ordinary income (other than qualified dividends) and short-term capital gains are taxed at graduated rates of up to 35 percent, long-term (where property has been held for more than one year) capital gains are currently capped at 20 percent (plus, 3.8 percent net investment income tax may apply), presenting a very significant rate advantage over the U.K. rate. An important difference from the U.K. capital gains tax is that capital gains are only taxed when recognized in a sale or exchange, and are not taxed on other disposals. Accordingly, a donor is not required to recognize gain on a gift or transfer into trust unless it is a foreign nongrantor trust. Conversely, a donee does not receive a step-up in basis and will take the donor's basis in the gifted asset. This can lead to a serious mismatch between the U.S. and U.K. gain recognition events and can work both to the taxpayer's advantage and disadvantage.

2. For this purpose, the interests of the settlor's spouse or civil partner are disregarded.

Another key distinction between the U.S. and U.K. rules relates to the timing of a recognition event on a sale or exchange: in the United States, gain is not recognized until completion of the sale rather than at the time of execution of a contract, whereas the reverse is true in the U.K. Moreover, the United States has a defined set of installment sale rules, whereby gain on a sale payable over more than one year can be recognized as each installment is received subject to anti-avoidance rules. Further, the United States has more generous definitions of nonrecognition events for gain recognition purposes, so that a transfer of property to a domestic corporation that is controlled by the transferor in exchange solely for stock will qualify for nonrecognition treatment. Although the rules are becoming stricter, it is still possible to construct a like-kind exchange transaction whereby property in one category can be exchanged for other property in the same category without gain recognition. Usually, this requires a third party in order to effect the transaction.

As in the U.K., assets comprising a decedent's estate will receive a tax-free step-up in basis at death. However, the rules are more restrictive than in the U.K. when the assets in question were comprised in a trust established by a non-U.S. person who was not subject to U.S. estate tax. This can mean that assets that pass from a U.K. trust and that may have been subject to U.K. inheritance tax at the relevant death will not receive a step-up in basis if they pass to a U.S. beneficiary, unless the trust life tenant has a qualifying interest in possession or income interest. It is also important to bear in mind that appreciated assets distributed from a trust to a beneficiary will not usually receive a step-up in basis, so that a distribution in kind from a U.K. trust to a U.S. beneficiary may result in the beneficiary unless the trust life tenant had a qualifying interest in possession or income interest receiving an asset with a very low basis, even though gain was recognized for U.K. purposes at distribution.

6. Foreign Element

(a) U.K. Capital Gains Tax. The basic rule is that an individual resident in the U.K. during part of a tax year is subject to capital gains tax on his worldwide gains. Provisions also exist to attribute gains of nonresident trusts to individuals who are resident if certain conditions are satisfied. Nonresidents are generally not chargeable to capital gains tax even though the gains are made on assets situated in the U.K. There are three exceptions to this rule.

First, a person carrying on a trade in the U.K. through a branch or agency can be charged on gains made on U.K. situs assets used in or held for the purpose of that trade. Second, where an individual ceases to be resident and ordinarily resident in the U.K. but resumes his U.K. residence within five tax years, certain gains by him (or trustees of trusts established by him) during his period of absence may be brought into charge to capital gains tax on his return, wherever the assets in respect of which the gains are realized are situated. Third, the U.K. government has introduced legislation to tax certain "nonnatural persons" (broadly, companies) on gains realized on the disposal of certain "high-value"[3] residential property regardless of the residence of the "nonnatural person." Gains on property left to third parties on a commercial basis are not caught by these new rules.

As with inheritance tax, foreign domiciliaries are given favored treatment. They are subject to capital gains tax on all gains realized by them in respect of assets situated in the U.K., but "remittance basis users" are taxed on gains realized on foreign situs assets only to the extent that such gains are remitted to the U.K. A remittance basis user is a nondomiciled resident who chooses to claim the remittance basis of taxation and who pays the appropriate remittance basis annual charge. Gains realized by trusts are taxed differently: although gains realized by trusts that are not resident in the U.K. for capital gains tax purposes are not generally taxable in the U.K., even if remitted by the trustees to the U.K., such gains can be attributed to beneficiaries who are resident and ordinarily resident in the U.K., who will be chargeable to tax in respect of such trust gains. Nondomiciled remittance basis users will only be taxable on such gains, however, if the benefit in respect of which the gains is attributed was received in the U.K. or is remitted to the U.K. at any time either by the trustees or the beneficiary. Care is needed if a remittance basis user transfers appreciate assets to a non-U.K. trust. The gain recognized on the transfer can effectively be treated as embedded in the asset settled, and a later remittance of the proceeds of sale of that asset could give rise to a capital gains tax charge in the hands of the settlor.

(b) U.S. Income Tax on Capital Gains. As with the U.K., the United States broadly taxes only its residents and citizens on capital gains and does not tax nonresident aliens on U.S.-source capital gains, except gains that are effectively connected with a U.S. trade or business and U.S. real estate gains. Some U.S. tax treaties change the domestic rules relating to gain taxation, but the current U.S.-U.K. treaty does not alter the domestic law position on taxation of capital gains. However, there is U.S. authority that a claim of nonresidence based on the dual residence resolving provisions of a treaty can be made to prevent a capital gains tax liability from arising.

There is a long-standing provision relating to residence purely for purposes of tax on capital gains: this provision (which predates the current U.S. tax residence rules) mandates that if an individual is present in the United States for more than 183 days during a tax year (that is the calendar year) or a calculated total of 183 days based on a specified percentage of actual days of presence in the current and two preceding tax years, he will be taxed on U.S. source capital gains. Because the primary test for U.S. residence is physical presence for 183 days or more during a tax year, this might be thought to be of no effect. However, it can apply in unexpected ways. For example, presence in the United States as a student does

3. "High value" is considered to be where the value amount or value of the consideration exceeds £2 million.

not count for the normal residence test, but does count for determining liability to tax on capital gains, and similarly, issues can arise for partial years of residence, typically when a taxpayer is entering or leaving the United States.

The source of income rules as they apply to gains recognized by U.S. persons can yield unexpected results. The general rule with respect to personal property sales is that the gain is sourced where the taxpayer is resident, so that a U.S. citizen resident in the U.K. who sells both U.S. and U.K. situate property will in each case be treated as receiving foreign-source capital gain income. The primary significance of this for a U.K. resident U.S. citizen is that he can then claim a credit against U.S. tax for foreign tax paid, which is generally a benefit for the nonresident U.S. citizen.

However, there is a trap with respect to low foreign taxed gain: if the effective foreign tax rate is less than 10 percent of the gain as computed for U.S. tax purposes, the gain is sourced in the United States. This means that a taxpayer with carry-forward foreign tax credits must ensure that a rate of at least 10 percent foreign tax is paid on capital gains on personal property. Because the U.K. rate is significantly higher than 10 percent, it might be thought that this should not present a problem; however, in practice, it frequently does due to the differences in the U.S. and U.K. definitions of gain recognition events. For example, a sale of a painting recently acquired by gift would result in little U.K. tax because of the basis step-up by virtue of the gift, but there would have been no basis step-up for U.S. purposes, which could result in a very significant U.S.-source gain. The mismatch in treatment of gains on personal residences between the United States and U.K. catches many taxpayers unawares: the U.K. exempts such gains, while the United States permits only a limited dollar exclusion.

III. Specific Planning Considerations

We turn now to consider various interactions of U.S. and U.K. tax of interest in practice when planning for the interaction of U.S. and U.K. tax systems.

A. The Estate Tax Spouse Exemption Mismatch

Assume that a taxpayer is within the scope of both U.K. inheritance tax and U.S. transfer taxes (as a U.S. citizen or domiciliary) and that his wife is domiciled (or treated as domiciled) in the U.K. for inheritance tax purposes, but is neither a U.S. citizen nor a green card holder. Typically, this would be a U.S. citizen married to a U.K. citizen and domiciliary residing in the U.K.

Assume also that the taxpayer is on his second marriage, has children from his first marriage but none from his second, and wishes his estate ultimately to pass to his children. Accordingly, by his will he establishes a trust under which his second wife takes a life interest that qualifies as an "immediate post-death interest" for U.K. inheritance tax purposes (discussed below) with remainders over to his children.

If this arrangement is allowed to stand, it will produce the following unhappy result. First, on his death, there will be a charge to U.S. estate tax, but not to U.K. inheritance tax. Second, on the widow's death, there will be a charge to U.K. inheritance tax, but not, given that she will be outside the scope of U.S. estate tax, a charge to U.S. estate tax (assuming there is no U.S. charge on a situs basis). No credit will be available under the U.S.-U.K. Estate and Gift Tax Treaty, because the charges arise on two different, unrelated occasions.

This problem derives from the nature of the spouse exemption under U.K. inheritance tax and U.S. estate tax rules.

1. U.K. Inheritance Tax Spouse Exemption

The general rule is that transfers between spouses are exempt transfers and so are outside the scope of inheritance tax. The U.K. recognizes civil partnerships between same-sex couples, and, accordingly, under U.K. tax law, civil partners are afforded the same exemptions and reliefs as are afforded to heterosexual spouses. Same sex marriages will be recognized in the UK. A spouse or civil partner who is entitled to an "immediate post-death interest" is treated as being entitled to the underlying assets of the trust, and so the interest qualifies for the spouse exemption. There is one important restriction on this rule. Where the transferor spouse or civil partner, but not the transferee spouse, is domiciled in the U.K. for inheritance tax purposes (be it as a matter of general law or under the inheritance tax deemed domiciled rules), the spouse exception is restricted to the amount of the nil rate band (currently £325,000) if the transfer of assets is from the domiciled to the nondomiciled spouse or civil partner. This exception is designed to prevent an individual within the scope of inheritance tax from transferring his assets to a foreign domiciliary and so placing them potentially outside the scope of inheritance tax.

The limitation on the spouse exemption does not mean that transfers in excess of that limit are necessarily chargeable to inheritance tax. A lifetime transfer in excess of the limit will be a potentially exempt transfer and so chargeable only if the transferor spouse dies within seven years of making the transfer; potentially exempt transfers are discussed below. As of April 6, 2013, a nondomiciled spouse can elect to be treated as deemed domiciled in the U.K. in order to secure an unlimited spouse exemption in relation to lifetime gifts or a transfer on the death of his or her U.K.- domiciled/deemed domiciled spouse. If a spouse makes this election his or her own estate will be within the scope of U.K. inheritance tax until the election lapses after four years of non-U.K. tax residence.

The U.S.-U.K. Estate and Gift Tax Treaty attempts to provide another solution to this problem, but it is a very imperfect solution. Further, it does not provide any relief with respect to the U.S. problem outlined below, because it predates the change in the U.S. rules, and Congress determined that there was no conflict with the Treaty (even though the Treaty was negotiated at a time when the U.S. rules were different and the Treaty specifically tried to address the restrictions on the U.K. spouse exemption). The terms of the Treaty benefit are narrowly drawn and generally only help a couple, if both are U.S. citizens and the transferee is not U.K. domiciled but the transferor spouse is U.K. domiciled. Even this circumscribed benefit is limited to a reduction in the rate of inheritance tax to 50 percent of the usual rate and does not provide a complete exemption. Thus, although each system of taxation envisages a single charge per marriage, the interaction of the systems will produce one charge per spouse.

2. U.S. Estate Tax Marital Deduction

The U.S. equivalent to the U.K. spouse exemption is referred to as the marital deduction and provides for a 100 percent deduction for outright transfers to U.S. citizen spouses. Civil unions are not recognized at the federal level, but the Supreme Court in 2013 ruled that same sex marriages will be respected for federal tax purposes. Certain types of transfers in trust for the benefit of a spouse also qualify for the marital deduction. In general terms, a transfer in trust must require all of the income to be payable to the spouse and must either give the spouse a general power of appointment over the trust (so that it is includable in the spouse's estate under U.S. estate tax rules) or provide for an election to be made to qualify as a marital deduction trust (known as a Qualified Terminable Interest Property trust, or QTIP).

In an international context, it is important to bear in mind that there are several critical requirements for a marital deduction trust. First, the surviving spouse must be able to require that nonproductive property be converted into productive property—not a provision typically included in most U.K. spouse exemption trusts. Second, inclusion of a trustee overriding power of appointment during the spouse's lifetime (a typical provision in the context of U.K. inheritance tax planning to allow potentially exempt transfers or "PETs" to be made to children from the marital trust) will disqualify the trust for the marital deduction unless power is restricted during the surviving spouse's life. Finally, property must pass "from the decedent," which can be a surprisingly difficult requirement as illustrated by the following example. If a testator leaves property on discretionary trusts and within two years of his death the trustees appoint an interest in possession to the surviving spouse, then, for U.K. inheritance tax purposes, the spouse is treated as having been entitled to an immediate post-death interest from the death so that the spouse exemption is retrospectively made available. However, because the property will not, as a matter of general law, have passed from the decedent to the spouse, such a trust can never qualify for the U.S. marital deduction. In addition, it should be noted that an outright transfer to the surviving spouse would be capable of being decanted into a qualifying marital trust under U.S. rules, but this would be treated as a lifetime settlement for U.K. inheritance tax giving rise to a potential 20 percent tax on a U.K.-domiciled spouse (or 40 percent if the spouse does not survive seven years).

The United States shared the concerns of the U.K. about the possibility of using the spousal tax reliefs to transfer assets irrevocably outside the domestic taxing jurisdiction, but this did not manifest itself in legislation until 1988. At that point, the United States withdrew the marital deduction for transfers to noncitizen spouses, ignoring the claims of U.S.-domiciled spouses (who are fully within the U.S. transfer tax system) for qualification for the marital deduction on the ground that a noncitizen can always leave the United States and thereby escape the U.S. taxing jurisdiction.

There are two important reliefs associated with the withdrawal of the marital deduction for transfers to noncitizen spouses. First, there is an annual gift tax exclusion for gifts to noncitizen spouses of $143,000 (as adjusted for inflation in 2013), but the gift must also meet the other requirements of the U.S. gift tax exclusion so that the spouse must generally receive the gift outright or in a trust over which the spouse has a withdrawal right (i.e., receipt of a present interest). Second, there is an estate tax deduction for gifts in trust for the benefit of a noncitizen spouse that would otherwise qualify for the marital deduction if it satisfies additional requirements designed to ensure that U.S. estate tax is ultimately paid. Such a trust is known as a Qualified Domestic Trust (QDOT).

3. Solving the Problem

Although the gift tax exclusion is important in estate planning for Anglo-American spouses, the QDOT provisions are critical in ensuring that the taxpayer in the above example does not suffer true double taxation. A QDOT preserves the U.S. estate tax charge at the death of the first (U.S.) spouse to die by postponing the imposition of the tax on the property comprising the QDOT. The importance of the QDOT in the context of the overall estate planning position is not, in itself, the deferral of U.S. estate tax achieved through the postponement of the tax until the death of the surviving spouse. Rather, the real tax saving derives from the matching of the U.S. transfer tax event with the U.K. inheritance tax event.

A non-U.S. tax imposed on the death of the surviving spouse is available as a credit against the QDOT tax due determined by reference to the death of the U.S. spouse but postponed through the QDOT mechanism. This achieves a real avoidance of double taxation because it enables a credit to be taken for U.K. tax due on the surviving spouse's estate against the notionally postponed tax due on the U.S. spouse's estate. Moreover, this result is achieved without reliance on the imperfect mechanisms of the U.S.-U.K. Estate and Gift Tax Treaty.

It should be noted at a time when U.S. estate tax rates have fluctuated significantly that the rates of tax and the exemption amount are fixed at the date of death of the U.S. spouse, and so there is no opportunity to benefit from a subsequent rate reduction.

The main requirements that a trust must satisfy to qualify as a QDOT are that a U.S. citizen and resident or a U.S. corporation serve as a trustee of the QDOT and have certain overriding powers over the QDOT. Further, it is required that no principal distributions can be made without withholding U.S. estate tax postponed through the use of the QDOT with respect to that property. For QDOTs with a value over $2 million at the date of death of the U.S. spouse, additional security requirements are imposed, which broadly require that a U.S. trust company (or the U.S. branch of a foreign trust company) be appointed as the controlling trustee of the QDOT or that other security be obtained.

Under the QDOT regulations, it is clear that a QDOT can be established that meets the security requirements of the IRS to ensure collection of the U.S. estate tax without necessarily being treated as a U.S. trust for U.S. income tax purposes. A QDOT is, by definition, required to pay all of its income to the surviving spouse, so that income will not necessarily be subject to U.S. tax if the spouse is not U.S. resident. However, a QDOT need not be subject to U.S. tax on capital gains recognized during the life of the surviving spouse. This may yield an overall tax saving if the children or other remainder beneficiaries are not U.S. citizens. However, if some of the remainder beneficiaries are U.S. taxpayers, then care must be taken with a non-U.S. trust to avoid the throwback tax discussed below.

B. The Joint Property Trap

An often-overlooked aspect of the current U.S. transfer tax rules applicable to a non-U.S. citizen spouse is the treatment generally of a non-U.S. citizen spouse as a non-spouse in the context of joint property transfers. Generally, U.S. citizen spouses are treated as owning joint property equally for tax purposes. However, on the death of an individual who owns property as a joint tenant with right of survivorship with a noncitizen spouse, the whole of the value of the property is included in the individual's estate except to the extent the surviving spouse can evidence financial contributions to the property acquisition. Furthermore, the splitting of a joint tenancy during the lives of the joint tenants can trigger an immediate charge to U.S. gift tax if the value of the noncitizen spouse's resulting tenant in common interest (or proceeds of sale) exceeds such spouse's financial contributions. Complex transitional and tracing rules apply to determine each spouse's total contributions.

1. The Family Home—A Potentially Costly Castle

An Englishman's or American's home may be his castle, but it can also contain an alligator-infested moat in relation to U.K. and/or U.S. planning.

2. Capital Gains Tax

For U.K. capital gains tax purposes, gains made on the family home are wholly exempt from capital gains tax, irrespective of the size of the gain, provided certain requirements are satisfied.

However, there is no equivalent exemption in the United States. Until 1997, U.S. taxpayers could roll over gain from the sale of one house into the purchase of the next house, but this has been replaced by an exclusion of $250,000 of gain for single taxpayers and $500,000 for married taxpayers, which can be used every five years. Therefore, this favors taxpayers who move every five years and discriminates against taxpayers who stay in the same house for decades before deciding to move.

When one spouse is a U.S. taxpayer and the other is not, depending on the size of the property in question, one way of coping with the U.S. cap on the property exemption is to arrange matters so that the U.S. taxpayer's interest in the property results in a gain that is likely to fall within the exclusion.

For U.K. inheritance tax purposes, the family home is an asset like any other. It does not qualify for special relief or adverse treatment, save that certain U.K. inheritance tax anti-avoidance rules have been extended to counteract certain tax-planning devices that attempt to enable individuals to give their homes away to the next generation but to continue to live in them without falling foul of the rules.

3. Estate Tax (and Income Tax)

Although no particular inheritance tax treatment is meted out to the family home, where a foreign domiciliary living in the U.K. is concerned, the family home suffers from one intrinsic shortcoming—it is, unavoidably, property situated in the U.K. After relief for the inheritance tax nil rate band and the spouse exemption, it is clearly subject to inheritance tax.

Foreign domiciliaries coming to live in the U.K. were historically advised to own their U.K. residences through offshore companies, the shares in which were held by offshore trusts. The relevant asset was thus the foreign situs shares, which were (and still are) effectively outside the scope of U.K. inheritance tax. Although such a structure may still be desirable for inheritance tax purposes, it comes with a significant U.K. stamp duty land tax cost, a U.K. capital gains tax, and a U.K. income tax health warning. The ongoing U.K. income tax risk arises because if the individual concerned is an actual or "shadow" director of the company, HMRC will seek to charge income tax annually on, in effect, the rent he should be paying in respect of the property. The new stamp duty land tax and capital gains tax change on corporate ownership of residential property valued at £2 million or more (other than third-party rental property) essentially rule out corporate ownership. To avoid the potentially penal charges, taxpayers are advised to adopt other approaches to solving the inheritance tax problem. For example, if the exposure is a short-term one, term life insurance may be a simple answer. Another possibility would be to reduce the value of the property with a mortgage, although care is required in this case to ensure that the debt will be deductible, as rules were introduced in the 2013 U.K. budget to restrict the deductibility of debts in certain cases.

Holding a house through a company also has the potential for generating significant U.S. income tax. When a U.S. taxpayer owns his house (directly or indirectly) through a foreign corporation, this triggers the application of the panoply of U.S. anti-avoidance rules applicable to controlled foreign corporations with passive assets and under the passive foreign investment company rules. The combination of these rules has the effect with this structure of attributing the gain recognition through to the taxpayer when the house is sold, and the gain will not qualify for the residence exclusion and may cause the gain to be taxed at ordinary income rates rather than capital gain rates.

The only way this structure can work from a U.S. tax perspective is if the taxpayer makes an entity classification ("check-the-box") election. This permits a taxpayer to elect to disregard the corporation for all U.S. tax purposes so that the taxpayer is treated as owning the house directly, and the gain will then qualify for both the exclusion and capital gain rates of tax. It is essential that the election be made from the commencement of the ownership of the house because the effect of the election is to cause a deemed liquidation of the company that would cause gain recognition with respect to the house.

Because the corporate ownership plan has significant adverse stamp duty land tax and other costs, a U.S. taxpayer may decide to deal with the inheritance tax risk with insurance and own the house in joint names with his U.K. wife. In this case, he will need to take into account the U.S. estate tax rules relating to property owned jointly between a U.S. citizen and a non-U.S. citizen spouse. As discussed above, the usual U.S. rule for property owned jointly between spouses with right of survivorship, which treats each spouse as owning 50 percent of the property for transfer tax purposes, does not apply if one spouse is not a U.S. citizen. Rather, the U.S. spouse is presumed to own all of the property unless the non-U.S. spouse can provide financial contributions.

In the context of a U.K. house owned by such a couple, this can lead to double taxation. For example, if the U.S. citizen spouse were to die first and it could not be proven that his spouse contributed any of the purchase cost of the house, all of the value would be included in the U.S. spouse's estate at his death for U.S. estate tax purposes. On the subsequent death of the non-U.S. spouse, the entire value would be included in her estate for U.K. inheritance tax purposes, with no offsetting credit for the prior U.S. estate tax credit.

The position may be helped with use of a QDOT, but it may still be advantageous to transfer ownership of the property to the U.K. spouse because of the U.S. tax exposure on capital gains. This can be achieved by severing the joint tenancy (with care not to trigger a U.S. gift tax liability) and using the U.S. annual $143,000 exclusion to transfer interests in the house to the U.K. spouse. Of course, severing the joint tenancy and declaring that the house is, as a matter of property law, owned 99 percent by the U.S. husband will be treated as a gift from the U.K.-domiciled wife to her nondomiciled spouse, which would be a potentially exempt transfer for

U.K. inheritance tax purposes. In addition, this transfer may not encourage marital harmony and may represent a significant transfer of property rights, depending on the value of the house. The U.S. husband can then make planned gifts of the annual exclusion amounts, or he might want to use part of his gift tax exemption.

C. The U.K. as a Tax Haven for Entrepreneurs

U.K. inheritance tax and capital gains tax contain many overlapping but far from identical reliefs for, in effect, trading activities, whether carried on by sole traders, partnerships, or certain companies. Each of these must be approached with caution by U.S. citizens who will remain subject to U.S. transfer tax. One effect of the U.K. relief could be simply to increase the tax payable in the United States.

1. Inheritance Tax Reliefs

Probably the most significant inheritance tax relief is business property relief, which takes out of charge to inheritance tax 100 percent of the value of shares in unquoted trading companies, the business of a sole trader, and the interest of a partner in a trading partnership, provided the transferor has owned the relevant asset for at least two years immediately preceding the chargeable event. Fifty percent relief is given in respect of certain land or building, or machinery or plant used by, but not owned by, the business in question.

No relief is available where the relevant activity consists wholly or mainly of dealing in securities, stock or shares, land or buildings, or making or holding investments. In order to prevent taxpayers "parking investments" in, e.g., their trading company, anti-avoidance provisions may operate to attenuate the relief where the value of the shares, etc., is attributable to nontrading assets; these provisions can sometimes be circumvented with careful structuring.

Although certain agricultural businesses can qualify for business property relief, a special relief—agricultural property relief—is also available for such businesses. This relief is given in priority to business relief, which, in some cases, operates as a backup. For example, no agricultural property relief is given to "hope value," but the owner of agricultural land ripe for development may qualify for business relief.

Provided certain conditions are satisfied, this relief is available at 100 percent to taxpayers who are landlords as well as to owner-occupiers. The relief is also available to shares in companies.

Inheritance tax can, in appropriate circumstances, be paid by installments over ten years, in which case the outstanding tax bears simple interest unless certain conditions are satisfied, when the installments are interest-free. It is easy to overlook this relief, which is extremely valuable. It is available in relation to land and buildings (e.g., the family home). It is also available in relation to certain business assets where its availability, in very broad terms, follows business relief, although in certain areas, it is, happily, subject to fewer restrictions.

2. Inheritance Tax Relief Clawbacks

Each of the above reliefs can be clawed back if the donee ceases to be the owner of the relieved assets within seven years of a lifetime transfer, e.g., because the donee sells the asset transferred to him. This clawback does not operate where the relief is given in respect of a transfer on death.

3. Capital Gains Tax Reliefs

The U.K. capital gains tax legislation contains a number of reliefs that allow taxpayers to sell or give away assets with very favorable tax results. The most noteworthy are Entrepreneurs' Relief, Holdover Relief, and Rollover Relief.

(a) Entrepreneur's Relief. Entrepreneurs' Relief is available to individuals (and in certain cases, trustees) and reduces the rate of capital gains tax to 10 percent for gains arising on "qualifying disposals."

A qualifying disposal is essentially a disposal of all or part of a trading business; assets in a business that used to trade; shares or securities in a trading company (if, immediately before the disposal, the taxpayer is an officer or employee of the company and holds at least 5 percent of the voting rights); or assets used by a company where that disposal is associated with a disposal of shares by someone who is withdrawing from the business. In all of these circumstances, the business or the shares must have been owned for at least one year prior to the disposal. It is worth noting that the business must "trade" because Entrepreneurs' Relief is not available in the context of investment businesses or companies.

Entrepreneurs' Relief gives each individual a lifetime allowance currently set at £10 million. An individual can make as many qualifying claims as he likes during his lifetime until their cumulative gains reach the £10 million limit. Any gains beyond that limit will be charged using the ordinary capital gains tax rates.

As mentioned above, Entrepreneurs' Relief may also apply to gains made on qualifying disposals by trustees. However, this applies only where there is a qualifying beneficiary who works in the business or, in the case of a company, is an employee or officer of the company and holds at least 5 percent of the voting rights.

(b) Holdover Relief. Where an individual gives away a business asset, any capital gains tax liability can be postponed until the person who received the gift disposes of the asset. Where the relief is available, the donor will have no liability to capital gains tax. Holdover relief may also be claimed where an asset is sold at an undervalue, but the relief will only be available on the "gift element," i.e., the difference between the price paid and the market value.

Holdover relief is also available, irrespective of the nature of the asset, where a transfer gives rise to an inheritance tax charge. This is available on transfers in and out of trusts to avoid double taxation. In this context, holdover relief means that an asset that has grown substantially in value can be placed in a trust and then appointed out to a beneficiary with relief again being claimed on the exit from the trust. This is particularly useful because although it only delays payment, it allows the beneficiary to use the proceeds of sale to pay the tax following the ultimate sale of the asset.

There are restrictions on the application of these reliefs; e.g., they are not available if the transferee is not tax resident in the U.K.; nor are they available in relation to gifts to settler-interested trusts.

(c) Rollover Relief. A taxpayer can avoid having to pay capital gains tax each time certain business assets are sold and replaced by electing to "roll over" the gain into the replacement asset. As a consequence, the acquisition cost of the replacement asset is reduced by the amount of the gain being rolled over. Therefore, tax is postponed until the replacement asset is sold, and no new replacement asset is acquired. It is possible to roll over gains indefinitely, provided the qualifying assets are acquired within the time limits (that is the period commencing one year before and ending three years after the disposal of the asset).

D. Making the Most of Exemptions

Exemptions are mundane but offer simple and predictable tax-planning possibilities.

1. Nibbling Away at an Estate: U.S. and U.K. Annual Gifts/Small Gifts Exemptions

For U.K. inheritance tax purposes, a taxpayer can make outright gifts each year of £250 to as many persons as he wishes (i.e., not into trust). In addition, he can give away £3,000 free of inheritance tax in a year, and if he does not use this facility in one year, he can carry it forward, but to the next year only. So, ignoring any carry forward of the £3,000 annual exemption, a taxpayer could give £3,250 free of inheritance to X and £250 free of inheritance tax to Y. If the gift to Y exceeded £250, it would not be exempt under these exceptions.

For U.S. gift tax purposes, each U.S. taxpayer is entitled to give away $14,000 per year per done (indexed for inflation), and so in a large family, this can be used to transfer fairly significant sums. It is important to note that the gift will only qualify for the annual gift tax exclusion if it is made outright or in a trust that qualifies as a "present interest" for the donee. It will qualify as a present interest if the donee has a withdrawal right (often referred to as a "Crummey power") over the amount of the gift for a reasonable period, and subject to certain notice provisions. Accordingly, gifts are frequently structured in trust, particularly for children, with lapsing withdrawal rights exercisable by the parent or guardian on the child's behalf. This exclusion can be leveraged to great effect. For example, a trust can acquire a life insurance policy that is outside the estate of the insured for U.S. estate tax purposes, and where the transfer of cash to pay premiums is sheltered by the annual gift tax exclusion through giving a lapsing withdrawal right to one or more beneficiaries under the trust.

2. U.K. Normal Expenditure Out of Income Exemption

An individual can make gifts free from U.K. inheritance tax of his income so long as, broadly speaking, there is an established pattern of giving, and the gifts do not force him to dip into his capital to maintain his standard of living. This is an extremely valuable exemption for wealthy individuals with substantial income that exceeds their needs. Use of this exemption through gifts in excess of the nil rate band amount requires reporting to HMRC, and it is necessary for the donor to keep records to assist his executors/personal representatives to claim this relief should he die within seven years of the gifts.

3. U.S. "Grandparent's" Exemption

While there is no U.S. equivalent to the gift out of income exemption, there is some hope for the wealthy grandparent who wants to provide benefits for grandchildren. There is a U.S. exclusion for gifts for educational and medical purposes, so a grandparent can pick up the school and university fees and medical expenses of a grandchild without any gift tax or generation-skipping transfer tax liability. It is important to note that in order to qualify for this exclusion, the gifts must be made directly to the educational or medical institution and cannot be given to the intended donee (or the donee's parent) even though the gift is earmarked for a particular qualifying expenditure. This exclusion can be combined well with the U.K. inheritance tax expenditure out of income exemption to enable a grandparent to pick up quite substantial school and university fees (particularly if the grandchild opts for college in the United States following boarding school in the U.K.) free of transfer taxes.[4]

4. U.K. Tax-Free Seven-Year Gifts

Gifts made to individuals and to certain trusts are chargeable to inheritance tax only if the donor fails to survive the gift by seven years. Such gifts are called "potentially exempt transfers" and have come to be known as "PETs," with various learned articles having been written on their care and feeding. They are obviously an extremely important tax-planning tool, not least because any charge imposed on the donor's death is imposed by reference to the value of the gift when the PET was made, not to the value of the gifted property when the donor died. A PET thus has an inherent estate freezing quality. There is no U.S. equivalent, but PETs will clearly have a role to play for a U.K. taxpayer who is about to become a U.S. taxpayer.

4. Note that some non-U.K.-domiciled persons may also be able to use "Section 529" plans established under relevant U.S. state law to establish trusts that both qualify for the gift tax exemption and offer certain U.S. income tax benefits. HMRC has indicated that it views such plans as trusts that could be excluded property trusts.

E. Bigger Bites into the Estate: The U.S. Unified Credit and the U.K. Nil Rate Band

Under both the U.S. transfer tax and U.K. inheritance tax, a taxpayer may make gifts not covered by his exemptions but that still do not occasion a charge to tax.

1. U.S. Transfer Tax

Although the rules relating to U.S. transfer tax are not unified, the tax rate is unified. It is imposed at graduated rates up to 40 percent, but in practice, U.S. citizens and domiciliaries are entitled to a unified credit amount that can be used to pass assets, which for 2013 is $5,250,000 and is inflation indexed.

2. U.K. Inheritance Tax

Generally speaking, inheritance tax is charged at 40 percent on transfers that are not covered by an exemption. This is subject to the qualification that every inheritance tax payer has a nil rate band—at present, £325,000. This figure is normally increased annually to keep it in line with inflation, although no increase is scheduled until April 6, 2015, when it is scheduled to increase to £329,000 and thereafter in line with the Consumer Prices Index. Transfers falling within this nil rate band are charged at a nil rate.

Whether or not a transfer falls within a taxpayer's nil rate band depends on the value of the transfers he has made within the previous seven years. The net effect is that a taxpayer can recycle his nil rate band every seven years.

3. Using that Bigger Bite for the U.K.-Domiciled U.S. Citizen

For the U.S. citizen who is treated as domiciled in the U.K., possibly because of his years of U.K. residence, if he leaves his planning until death, he will be restricted to using the lower of the U.S. unified credit amount and the U.K. inheritance tax nil rate band amount (for the foreseeable future circa £325,000). However, if he plans to use the nil rate band at least seven years before he dies, he can effectively take advantage of the full unified credit amount by making a lifetime gift that equals the difference between the two amounts and then either by using the amount of the nil rate band under his will, or by making a further lifetime gift.

For a U.S. citizen married to a U.K. domiciliary, the difference between the unified credit amount and the nil rate band amount can provide a good opportunity to get liquid assets to the surviving spouse outside the QDOT. For example, a will could provide for an outright gift to the surviving noncitizen spouse for the difference between the nil rate band amount and the unified credit amount. Instead of an outright gift, a gift in trust could be used, and the trust would not need to meet the restriction of a QDOT.

F. Post-Death Tax Planning

In the U.K., there are at least three opportunities for post-death inheritance tax planning: (1) deeds of variation (where beneficiaries "rewrite" the will in a more tax-efficient manner); (2) two-year discretionary trusts; and (3) disclaimers. In the

United States, a disclaimer that meets certain restrictions is the only device for post-death transfer tax planning. It is sometimes beneficial, however, to utilize a deed of variation for a U.S. beneficiary so long as the beneficiary avoids making a completed gift when agreeing to vary the interests in the estate.

G. Loans

Interest-free loans that are genuinely repayable on demand and that produce no income usually have no adverse U.K. tax consequences. In particular, the lender is not regarded as receiving any deemed interest. However, loans to trustees that might avoid the inheritance tax entry charge on transfers to trusts require careful planning.

In the United States, for the most part, a below-market interest rate loan in excess of $100,000 between related parties (broadly defined) is treated as giving rise to imputed interest income in the hands of the lender and (if the interest is not collected) to a deemed gift from the lender to the borrower. However, there is one particular opportunity for U.S. citizens married to non-U.S. citizen spouses: the general rule that there is no imputed interest on interspousal loans is not limited to citizen spouses and extends to loans between citizen and noncitizen spouses. This provides a valuable means to mitigate the harsh effects of the restrictions on gifts and other transfers to noncitizen spouses and offers valuable income and estate planning opportunities.

If an individual simply allows another individual the free use of property, there is no question of a deemed rent being attributed to that individual in either jurisdiction. Accordingly, if a wealthy individual wishes to benefit family members without eating into his U.S. unified tax credit, he could purchase properties or other assets that he allows them to occupy or use free of charge.

In the United States, the rules relating to personal use of corporate property do generally result in an income tax liability. In addition, there is now a specific provision that taxes U.S. beneficiaries of foreign nongrantor trusts on the rent-free occupancy and use of trust property.

If a U.S. beneficiary occupies or uses trust property without paying fair market rent, there is a deemed distribution to the U.S. beneficiary from the trust's distribution net income (including gains) equal to the amount of the foregone rent. If the trust is a grantor trust, or if the trust had no net income and gains (including accumulated income and gain), then there is only a reporting requirement and no tax due. These rules do not apply to a U.S. trust. Therefore, it is possible to plan around this by paying rent, suing a "dry" trust, or moving the property into a U.S. trust.

H. The Amount on Which Estate Tax Is Charged: Who Cares Who Pays the Tax?

A significant and easily overlooked disjunction of estate taxes is that there are very different consequences in the U.K. and the United States according to who pays the tax.

As was mentioned above, a special feature of U.K. inheritance tax is that lifetime charges are generally imposed on a "loss to donor" basis. One consequence of this approach is that where the transferor bears the inheritance tax on a transfer, the inheritance tax paid is itself regarded as diminishing the value of his estate, with the result that the amount of the gift must be grossed up to reflect this. Assume X's nil rate band is exhausted so that his effective rate of inheritance tax is 40 percent, and X wants to give Y £60,000 net of inheritance tax. X must either give Y £100,000, out of which Y will pay £40,000 to HMRC, or he must give Y £60,000 and himself pay £40,000 to the HMRC. There is no possibility of X giving Y £60,000 and only paying £24,000 (£60,000 x 40 percent) to the HMRC.

The U.S. position is exactly the reverse of the U.K. position, so that gift tax is calculated on the net transfer rather than the gross transfer. Estate tax is necessarily a gross calculation, and for U.S. transfer tax purposes, it is always advantageous to transfer property so that tax will be payable by way of gift rather than at death. For example, if X, having exactly used up his unified credit amount, decided to make a gift of $60,000 (net of gift tax) to Y, he would only pay U.S. gift tax of $22,200 and make a total transfer of $82,200. However, a legacy from X to Y would require a gross transfer amount of $95,238 (using a 35 percent marginal rate) to get $60,000 net of tax to Y.

IV. A Few Words about Trusts

Complicated rules exist for taxing property held in trust. Perhaps the basic point that emerges from these rules is that a trust that seems entirely harmless from a U.S. tax standpoint can be positively explosive as far as inheritance tax is concerned and vice versa. Some initial background is helpful.

A. U.K. Inheritance Tax—A Twin-Track System

Trusts generally fall into two categories for U.K. inheritance tax purposes—trusts in which there is a "qualifying interest in possession" and trusts in which there is no such interest. An individual has an interest in possession if he is entitled to such income as the trust produces. The fact that the trust does not actually produce any income is irrelevant; what matters is whether the individual would be entitled to the trust income if the trust produced any income. An interest in possession that came into effect prior to March 22, 2006, is a qualifying interest in possession, but an interest in possession that comes into effect after that date will only be a qualifying interest in possession if it is an "immediate post-death interest," a "disabled person's interest," or a "transitional serial interest."

An "immediate post-death interest" (IPDI) is essentially a post-March 21, 2006, interest in possession effected by will or intestacy and to which the relevant individual becomes entitled on the death of the testator/intestate. The interest will not qualify as an IPDI if it falls within the definition of a trust for bereaved minors' (in broad terms, a trust under a will or intestacy where a child of the deceased will become absolutely entitled to assets no later than his eighteenth birthday) or a "disabled person's trust."

A "disabled person's trust" is a trust that qualifies under a specific set of provisions contained within the U.K. inheritance tax rules under which assets can be held for a person who is disabled in accordance with criteria set out in the rules.

There are a number of forms of "transitional serial interest" (TSI, but essentially the interest is an interest in possession that immediately succeeds a pre-March 22, 2006, interest in possession. A successor interest will only qualify as a TSI in restricted circumstances, and it should not be assumed that all successor interests will be TSIs. An interest in possession that succeeds an IPDI will not qualify itself as an IPDI for inheritance tax purposes.

The basic rule is that an individual who has a qualifying interest in possession in a trust is treated as owning the trust fund.

A trust in which no such qualifying interest in possession subsists (e.g., a fully discretionary trust or an inter vivos interest in possession trust settled on or after March 22, 2006) is taxed on a completely different basis. Transfers into such a trust will give rise to an immediate charge to inheritance tax at 20 percent (over the nil rate band). In addition, such a trust is taxed every ten years on the value of the trust fund, with exit charges being imposed between ten-year anniversaries on distributions from the trust fund. Special rules apply for determining the rate of tax that applies to discretionary trusts. Under present legislation, the maximum rate of tax is 6 percent. Originally, the rates were much higher.

B. The U.S. Rules—Twin-Track Issues

For U.S. purposes, two entirely separate analyses must be undertaken of any gift into trust from a transfer tax standpoint. First, is the gift a completed gift for gift tax purposes? Second, is the transferred property includable in the transferor's estate?

In many cases, the transferor will want to make sure that the transfer is not a completed gift and may be creating a trust (sometimes referred to as a "living trust") purely for probate avoidance purposes and to preserve secrecy relating to transferred assets. The easy way to accomplish this from a U.S. tax perspective is to make the trust fully revocable so that it is clearly an incomplete transfer, and the trust assets remain includable in the transferor's estate.

For U.S. income tax purposes, trusts can be divided into three categories: (1) grantor trusts, where the grantor is taxed on the income and the trust is ignored by virtue of the control or other powers retained (or deemed retained) by the grantor; (2) simple (nongrantor) trusts, where there is a requirement to pay all of the trust's income to one or more beneficiaries on a current basis; and (3) complex (nongrantor) trusts, where the payment of income is wholly discretionary. Frequently, a U.S. adviser will want to plan so that a trust will qualify as a grantor trust.

If the trust is treated as a grantor trust because it is revocable, this will mean that the dispositive provisions can provide flexibility and need not require the trustees to distribute all trust income currently. Typically, such a revocable trust will give the settlor the power to direct income or capital and will provide for the trust to be discretionary if the settlor loses capacity, or will appoint someone to exercise the grantor powers for the grantor.

A separate set of rules governs whether trust property is includable in the estate of the settlor or another person for U.S. estate tax purposes. Generally, a settlor must retain a greater degree of control or a more defined interest in the trust for it to be includable in his estate than is required for it to qualify as a grantor trust. Spousal powers are not attributed to the settlor for estate tax purposes, because they are for determining grantor trust status, and trustee powers are attributed in more limited circumstances.

Trust property will be included in the estate of a person other than the settlor if such person holds directly or indirectly a general power of appointment over the trust.

C. Planning Implications: The Deadly Discretionary Grantor Trust

It follows from the foregoing U.K. inheritance tax analysis that a nonexempt transfer (which exceeds the transferor's nil rate band amount) to a grantor trust after March 21, 2006, although harmless from a U.S. tax standpoint, will produce an immediate charge to inheritance tax as well as a further periodic charge every ten years. Nor does the trouble stop there. Subsequent to the transfer, the property transferred will not only be subject to the special U.K. inheritance tax regime taxing trusts, but on the settlor's death will also be clawed back into his estate under the reservation of benefit rules, without any relief for the charges suffered in the interim. Finally, many U.S. citizens act as trustee of their own grantor trusts, which can undermine their ability to take advantage of the remittance basis of taxation following a move to the U.K.

Likewise, a settlor may make a transfer into trust intending to remove the property from U.K. taxation at death, perhaps in the context of the lifetime use of his nil rate band. He may discover though, that the trust property has not been removed from his estate for U.S. transfer tax purposes because of U.S. rules that deem him to have retained a sufficient interest as the trust property (for instance if he acts as co-trustee with an independent fiduciary or has the power freely to hire and to fire trustees).

D. Revocable Trusts

As described above, for U.S. tax planning, it is often desirable for a trust to be a revocable trust within the meaning of the U.S. grantor trust rules. Achieving this by giving the grantor of the trust certain rights to revoke the trust may have adverse inheritance tax implications under the reservation of benefit rules or, possibly, because the right of revocation may be considered by some commentators and by HMRC to be a valuable asset for inheritance tax purposes. In these contexts, it is important to bear in mind that whether or not a trust is a "revocable trust" for these purposes depends on express U.S. statutory provisions, and it may be possible for a trust to be a revocable trust for U.S. tax-planning purposes without being a revocable trust that offends the U.K. inheritance tax rules.

E. Penalties for Nondistributing Offshore Trusts

1. U.K. Capital Gains Tax on Non-U.K. Trusts

Trusts are subjected to capital gains tax under rules that differ considerably from those that relate to inheritance tax. The basic principle is to tax the trustees as a body, but various provisions operate to deem gains arising to certain trusts as arising to the person who created the trust or who receive benefits from it. The rules in relation to offshore trusts apply so that gains arising to the trustees of a trust under which a settlor's grandchildren can benefit can be attributed to the settlor, even though neither the settlor, his spouse, nor his children can benefit.

Gains of an offshore trust that are not deemed to arise to a settlor can be attributed to beneficiaries to the extent they receive benefits from the trust. Gains are treated as distributed on a last-in, first-out basis, and gains that are not so attributed on a timely basis will suffer a deemed interest surcharge to compensate HMRC for not having been able to charge tax in the year in which the gain arose. This surcharge can result in capital gains tax being charged at a rate of up to 44.8 percent. The surcharge operates where gains have not been deemed to have been attributed to beneficiaries by the end of the year of assessment (April 6–April 5) following that in which the gain was realized by the trust. The surcharge is currently at 2.8 percent for each year of nondistribution, up to a maximum surcharge of 16.8 percent so that the surcharge is capped after six years. The surcharge is, in effect, at simple interest, without any compounding. (The manner in which the U.K. remittance rules are overlaid in relation to remittance basis users are referenced above.)

As the law now stands, there is no U.K. surcharge on undistributed income. How long this continues to be the case remains to be seen.

2. U.S. Tax on Non-U.S. trusts

Generally, the additional U.S. tax on non-U.S. trust accumulations applies not only to capital gains but also to income, and the accumulation (or throwback) charge provides for daily compounding of the interest charge on the notional tax on accumulated income. Usually, for U.S. tax purposes in a U.S. domestic context, capital gains are not included in the ordinary income of a trust and are taxed separately, and tax is capped for long-term capital gains at 15 percent. However, for a non-U.S. trust, where capital gains are accumulated, they are added to the ordinary income of the trust, taxable at rates of up to 35 percent and subject to the accumulation charge. Therefore, the rate differential for capital gains taxed in a U.S. domestic trust, compared with those accumulated in a foreign trust, is dramatic.

In response to this penal tax, it is important for U.S. taxpayers with foreign trust interests to plan carefully with respect to any accumulations. Planning techniques include deferral of gain recognition, distribution of accumulated income, and gains to non-U.S. beneficiaries or charities and the creation of "mirror" settlements to wash out accumulated income and gains.

A related point is that although, generally, a transfer of an appreciated asset to a trust does not trigger gain recognition, a transfer to a foreign nongrantor trust is a gain recognition event that triggers taxable gain. This can interfere with transfers to U.K. trusts for wholly non-U.S. beneficiaries where holdover relief applies for U.K. capital gains tax purposes.

Note that a U.S. person can be subject to tax as a grantor with respect to non-U.S. trusts. In such a case, the "throwback tax" regime is inapplicable.

V. Common Investment Funds

In both the U.K. and the United States, there are special, complicated regimes for taxing gains realized on interests in common investment funds, e.g., units in a unit trust. Gains realized in respect of such interests are potentially subject to both U.K. and U.S. tax, and therefore such interests should be acquired only after very careful consideration of the likelihood that these will interact to impose tax on a highly asymmetrical basis. In particular, for U.S. tax purposes, it is likely that any non-U.S. common investment fund will be classified as a passive foreign investment company, or PFIC. These are subject to an interest charge on any tax deferred through accumulation of income and gains within the PFIC. Gains from sales on exchange of certain dispositions of PFIC interests are taxed at ordinary income rates, and many nonrecognition rules are inapplicable to transactions with respect to PFIC shares.

VI. Charities

Charitably minded taxpayers face frustration in the U.K./U.S. context because gifts to U.K. charities will not qualify for U.S. income tax relief, and gifts to U.S. charities will not qualify for any type of U.K. tax relief. What is needed is a structure to which charitable gifts can be made that will qualify for full tax relief in both jurisdictions. A structure has been approved that accomplishes this through use of a two-entity structure with a U.S. entity election (or check-the-box election).

The U.S. tax code also offers various tax-planning opportunities to taxpayers who, though charitably minded, also wish to secure some personal benefit from gifts made to charities. The key technique uses a split interest charitable trust whereby a charity receives either an income or a remainder interest, with the settlor retaining the other interest for himself or his family. For example, a donor with appreciated securities who wants to commit to make a gift to charity, but who also wants to retain some income, could create a charitable remainder trust. The donor would transfer the appreciated securities to a trust in which the settlor would retain an income interest and allocate the remainder interest to charity. The appreciated securities could then be sold without tax on the capital gains because this is allocable to the charity's remainder interest. In the meantime, the donor will receive income from the gross proceeds of sale, rather than the after-tax proceeds, yielding an additional advantage for the donor. Great care should be taken where the prospective donor is domiciled in the U.K. for inheritance tax purposes because the U.K. has no counterpart to the provisions in the U.S. Code, and disallows the inheritance tax exemption for gifts to charities if the gift is not an outright gift to charity. The living legacies campaign led by Philanthropy Impact seeks to introduce legislation in the U.K. that would permit U.K. charitable remainder trusts.

VII. Temporal Bermuda Triangles

The wheel of time turns differently under the two systems. The U.K. tax year runs from April 6 to the following April 5, and the U.S. tax year for most taxpayers is the calendar year. For many years, this mismatch combined with certain published concession by HMRC enabled U.K. taxpayers to realize gains either after ceasing to be U.K. taxpayers but before becoming U.S. taxpayers, or after ceasing to be U.S. taxpayers but before becoming U.K. taxpayers, or both, so that realized gains escaped both capital gains taxes. The position has recently been made considerably more difficult for U.K. taxpayers. Now, if they go abroad for fewer than five years, many of the gains they realize during their absence will be visited on them upon their return to the U.K. and charged accordingly. Taxpayers should be careful using split years to avoid gain because treaty provisions and other provisions may not apply for the period of a brief stay in a local tax jurisdiction. Given that the United States taxes all capital gains of U.S. citizens, it is impossible for U.S. citizens to avoid taxes by merely changing residence.

VIII. Breaking the Ties That Bind

Under U.K. law generally, domicile is a fairly artificial concept. It is possible for a person to be domiciled in a country in which he has never set foot; conversely, a person could be living in a country for a long time without being domiciled there. Indeed, many wealthy foreigners live in the U.K. on just that basis, enjoying to the full their favored U.K. tax status.

But there are three potential drawbacks. The first, which applies generally, is that the inheritance tax legislation contains provisions under which a person who has been tax resident in the U.K. for the last seventeen out of twenty tax years is deemed to be domiciled in the U.K. for inheritance tax purposes. Conversely, individuals not within this provision who have ceased to be domiciled in the U.K. as a matter of general law will cease to be domiciled in the U.K. for inheritance tax purposes only after the passage of three calendar years. Third, although the "deemed" domiciled rule applies for long-term U.K. residents, there is now a tax, or remittance basis charge, payable on an annual basis, for non domiciliaries to avoid worldwide U.K. tax on income and capital gains.

The second, which is of particular importance in relation to the United States (and other federal jurisdictions), is that under U.K. law generally, it is not possible to be domiciled in the United States; rather, one must be domiciled in a particular state. So a U.K. taxpayer who thinks he is emigrating to "the United States" is going nowhere fast for inheritance tax purposes, because his three-year "cooling off" period will begin to run only after he settles permanently or indefinitely in a particular state.

PART VIII

Considerations of Ethics, Transparency, and Asset Protection in a Global World

19 Ethics in International Estate Planning

Christopher M. Reimer

I. Introduction

International estate planning has grown in popularity in recent years. This trend can be attributed to a number of factors, including increased international mobility, widely available communications technology, and the importance of international wealth and finance to the world economy, all leading to increased demand for legal services across national boundaries. Wealthy clients are increasingly aware that they need not be limited to the professionals or laws provided by the jurisdictions in which they reside. One of the largest change occurred during the 1990s when many U.S. practitioners began to take advantage of offshore entities and trusts, typically located in so-called "haven" jurisdictions, such as the Cook Islands and the Cayman Islands, to safeguard their clients' wealth from creditor attack.[1] In addition to benefits from powerful asset protection laws and economic diversification, many such jurisdictions offered innovative, substantive laws that broke with the English common law of trusts. In recent years, the adoption of federal reporting requirements like FATCA (Foreign Account Tax Compliance Act) and favorable

1. Duncan E. Osborne, *New Age Estate Planning: Offshore Trusts*, 27TH HECKERLING INST. ON ESTATE PLANNING ¶¶ 1700.1–1700.5 (2001).

state trust legislation have made U.S. jurisdictions more competitive with traditional offshore jurisdictions for both domestic and international clients.[2] Estate planners who once concentrated their practices in their home jurisdictions have realized the possible financial opportunities offered by international clients. For example, a Wyoming estate planning attorney who once focused her practice on preparing wills and trusts for Wyoming residents may now find her services in demand by Chinese professionals who seek to take advantage of Wyoming structures to manage their U.S. investment portfolios.

Providing estate planning services on an international basis raises a variety of ethical issues. Some of these issues are not entirely different from those that commonly occur during domestic planning. For example, unauthorized practice of law in an offshore jurisdiction has an analogue in the commonplace situation in which U.S. attorneys practice law across state lines (including the offering of opinions on the law of states in which the attorneys are not licensed). Like domestic planners, international estate planners must address the possibility that they may assist others in the perpetration of crimes or fraud. In these situations, the primary difference between domestic and international estate planning ethical questions can often be one of degree, rather than kind.

However, international planning often raises the ethical stakes because of its sheer scale. International estate planning attorneys may not have long-term relationships with certain clients and may never meet with them face-to-face. A globalized client base introduces other problems not commonly experienced in small-town estate planning, such as the possibility that the planning involves the laundering of assets derived from criminal activities or is implemented to fund international terrorism. When attorneys provide advice and assistance in an international context, they may also be subjecting themselves to multiple, overlapping (and sometimes contradictory) ethical and legal obligations.[3] The problem can be intensified if an attorney is working with a legal system, economy, clientele, or culture with which the attorney is not familiar. For example, European Union courts may not provide the same protections for attorney-client confidentiality to which U.S. lawyers have grown accustomed.[4] Many such rules are beyond the scope of

2. Christopher M. Reimer, *International Trust Domestication: Migrating an Offshore Trust to a U.S. Jurisdiction*, 25 QUINNIPIAC PROB. L.J. 170 (2012).

3. For a discussion of international practice and the different possible rules to which an attorney may be subject, see Detlev F. Vagts, *Professional Responsibility in Transborder Practice: Conflict and Resolution*, 13 GEO. J. LEGAL ETHICS 677 (2000).

4. For example, the Court of Justice of the European Union may not extend the attorney-client privilege to communications with attorneys who have not received status and credentials from an EU member state. *See* Case 155/79, AM & S Europe Ltd. v. Comm'n, 1982 E.C.R. 1575. More recently, the court has ruled that certain communications with in-house lawyers are not protected because they are not "independent lawyers." Case C-550/07 P, Akzo Nobel Chems., Ltd. v. Comm'n [2010] (not yet published in E.C.R.) ("The Court therefore considers that the legal situation in the Member States of the European Union has not evolved, since the judgment in AM & S Europe v Commission was delivered, to an extent which would justify a change in the case-law and recognition for in-house lawyers of the benefit of legal professional privilege.").

this chapter. But attorneys are well advised to determine specific obligations that may arise from practice in a foreign jurisdiction.

This chapter focuses on major ethical issues that arise in international estate planning practice. First, it discusses some of the major sources for ethical rules applicable to international estate planning practice. Second, it briefly discusses the attorney's ethical duty of competence in relation to international planning. Third, it examines the risk of unauthorized practice of law, including relevant rules, penalties, and possible ways of avoiding liability, including the employment of and partnership with foreign counsel and legal consultants. Fourth, it discusses restrictions on advertising in regard to international practice. Finally, the chapter closes with a discussion of ethical and legal issues raised by the possibility that international estate planning services will be used to further criminal, fraudulent, or terrorist activities, including a discussion of how U.S. attorneys may use the voluntary recommendations of the Financial Action Task Force and its risk-based approach to due diligence, training, and bookkeeping regarding international clients.

II. Sources of Rules

A. Domestic and Foreign Professional Responsibility and Disciplinary Rules

As in domestic estate planning, ethical guidelines for international planners stem from a number of sources. The most relevant rules to many estate planners will be the professional conduct regulations adopted by the highest court of the jurisdiction in which they are licensed to practice. The majority of state rules are derived from the Model Rules of Professional Conduct (Model Rules),[5] although significant variations exist between states. Some states have adopted their own unique codes of ethical rules.[6] The Model Rules were preceded by the Model Code of Professional Responsibility (Model Code) and the Canons of Professional Ethics (the Canons).[7] In addition, attorneys should be aware of the disciplinary enforcement rules to which they are subject.[8]

5. Model Rules of Prof'l Conduct (1983); Jay L. Krystinik, *The Complex Web of Conflicting Disciplinary Standards in International Litigation*, 38 Tex. Int'l L.J. 815, 819 (2003).

6. *See, e.g.*, Cal. Rules of Prof'l Conduct (1992). California's professional conduct rules permit consideration of ethical rules, opinions, and standards issued by other jurisdictions. *Id.* R. 1-100(A).

7. The ABA adopted the Canons in 1908. Model Code of Prof'l Responsibility preface (1983). According to the Model Code,

> [The Canons] were based principally on the Code of Ethics adopted by the Alabama State Bar Association in 1887, which in turn has been borrowed largely from the lectures of Judge George Sharswood, published in 1854 under the title of *Professional Ethics*, and from the fifty resolutions included in David Hoffman's *A Course of Legal Study* (2d ed. 1836).

Id.

8. *See, e.g.*, Model Rules for Lawyer Disciplinary Enforcement (1989).

Regardless of what kind of international practice an estate planning attorney engages in, he or she should be aware of the possibility of facing discipline in his or her home state. Because very little transnational regulation of the legal profession exists,[9] the largest source of applicable ethical rules will come from the jurisdictions in which an attorney is licensed.[10] The rules of most U.S. jurisdictions in which a lawyer may be licensed will apply to the lawyer's extraterritorial conduct, even if the lawyer is practicing in a foreign nation or has been hired by a foreign client.[11] The Model Rules do not limit their application to political or geographic boundaries.[12] According to the amended version of Rule 8.5,

> A lawyer admitted to practice in this jurisdiction is subject to the disciplinary authority of this jurisdiction, regardless of where the lawyer's conduct occurs. A lawyer not admitted in this jurisdiction is also subject to the disciplinary authority of this jurisdiction if the lawyer provides or offers to provide any legal services in this jurisdiction. A lawyer may be subject to the disciplinary authority of both this jurisdiction and another jurisdiction for the same conduct.[13]

Local authorities have not been reluctant to discipline locally licensed attorneys for their extraterritorial misconduct. For example, the Hawaiian Disciplinary Counsel disciplined a Hawaiian lawyer for fraudulently converting a client's funds in California.[14] In 1978, the Minnesota Supreme Court recognized that the Model Code did not distinguish between an attorney's conduct in the jurisdiction in which he was licensed and conduct abroad.[15] The relevant provision of the Model Code provided that "[a] lawyer shall not . . . [e]ngage in conduct involving dishonesty, fraud, deceit, or misrepresentation."[16] As the court recognized, ethical codes are not to be strictly construed like criminal codes, but are to be liberally construed based on the "spirit" of the Code. The failure of the then existing ethi-

9. The European Union provides the most prominent exception. Rona R. Mears, *Ethics and Due Diligence: A Lawyer's Perspective on Doing Business with Mexico*, 22 St. Mary's L.J. 605, 611 (1991). In 1956, the International Bar Association drafted an International Code of Ethics, but it has received little attention. *Id.* at 611–12 (citing Roger J. Goebel, *Professional Qualification and Educational Requirements for Law Practice in a Foreign Country: Bridging the Cultural Gap*, 63 Tul. L. Rev. 443, 520 (1989)).

10. Mears, *supra* note 9, at 612.

11. *Id.*

12. *See, e.g.*, Model Rules of Prof'l Responsibility R. 8.4(c) ("It is professional misconduct for a lawyer to . . . engage in conduct involving dishonesty, fraud, deceit or misrepresentation . . . .").

13. *Id.* R. 8.5(a); *see also* Tex. Disc. Rules of Prof'l Conduct R. 8.05(a) (2005) (subjecting Texas attorneys to discipline for conduct occurring in another jurisdiction).

14. Office of Disciplinary Counsel v. Cashman, 629 P.2d 105, 108 (Haw. 1981) (per curiam); *see also In re* Wade, 526 A.2d 936 (D.C. 1987) (affirming discipline by the D.C. bar against a Massachusetts resident who converted client funds in Massachusetts because he was licensed by the District of Columbia).

15. *In re* Scallen, 269 N.W.2d 834, 839–40 (Minn. 1978) (suspending attorney for committing theft and circulating a false prospectus in Canada).

16. Model Code DR 1-102.

cal code to specify foreign misconduct as grounds for discipline did not prevent discipline for violating foreign criminal laws.[17] Other examples abound.[18]

Additionally, the Model Disciplinary Rules provide that it is a violation not only to violate the Professional Conduct rules of the local jurisdiction but also to "engage in conduct violating applicable rules of conduct of another jurisdiction."[19] The commentary explains:

> The agency's jurisdiction to investigate and to take whatever action is deemed to be appropriate is triggered by discipline imposed in another state. The imposition of discipline in one jurisdiction does not mean that every other jurisdiction in which the lawyer is admitted must necessarily impose discipline, but the burden is on the respondent to demonstrate that the imposition of the same discipline is inappropriate.[20]

For practical reasons, the most likely source of discipline for misconduct in a foreign jurisdiction will be the jurisdiction in which the attorney is licensed. Although this chapter does not specifically focus on any foreign jurisdiction's laws, an estate planning attorney who engages in or directs his or her practice to a foreign jurisdiction must be aware of that jurisdiction's laws and ethical requirements.[21] Most jurisdictions extend their ethical rules to lawyers who are not licensed to practice in the jurisdiction, although there are some exceptions.[22]

Lawyer may be subject to discipline for violating, attempting to violate, or assisting someone else in violating the applicable version of the Model Rules or other relevant code or set of rules of professional responsibility.[23] Discipline can give rise to a variety of sanctions, depending on the severity of the conduct, the lawyer's past misconduct, and other mitigating and aggravating factors.[24] Possible sanctions include the following:

---

17. *Id.*

18. *See* People v. Schindelar, 845 P.2d 1146, 1147 (Colo. 1993) (en banc) (per curiam); *In re* Howes, 940 P.2d 159, 163, 171 (N.M. 1997).

19. Model Rules for Lawyer Disciplinary Enforcement R. 9(1)(2).

20. *Id.* R. 9, cmt.

21. *See, e.g.*, Código de Etica Profesional de la Barra Mexicana Colegio de Abogados (Mex. 1948); Charter of Core Principles of the European Legal Profession & Code of Conduct for European Lawyers (2010) (European Union), *available at* http://www.ccbe.eu/fileadmin/user_upload/NTCdocument/EN_Code_of_conductp1_1306748215.pdf; Basic Rules on the Duties of Practicing Attorneys (2004) (Japan), *available at* http://www.nichibenren.or.jp/library/en/about/data/basic_rules.pdf.

22. Council of the Bars and Law Societies of the European Community, Common Code of Conduct, 25 The Law Society's Gazette art. 2.4 (1989), *reprinted in* The Lawyer's Responsibility for Foreign Law and Foreign Lawyers, *in* A.B.A. Sec. Int'l Law & Practice Committee Program (1990) (subjecting all attorneys practicing in the European Union to applicable ethical rules, even if they are not locally licensed). See Jeffrey L. Rensberger, *Jurisdiction, Choice of Law, and the Multistate Attorney*, 36 S. Tex. L. Rev. 799 (1995), for a discussion of different choice of law regimes.

23. Model Rules of Prof'l Conduct R. 8.4(a) & cmt. 1; Model Rules for Lawyer Disciplinary Enforcement 9, ¶ 1.

24. Model Rules for Lawyer Disciplinary Enforcement 10, ¶ 3.

- limitation on the lawyer's future practice,
- loss of fees,
- private reprimand,
- public reprimand,
- probation,
- suspension for a period of time, and
- disbarment.[25]

B. Additional Resources

Many possible ethical issues that confront estate planners are not adequately addressed by the Model Code or Model Rules. In such instances, attorneys may consult additional materials, including court decisions, formal and informal opinions issued by state bar organizations and disciplinary authorities, the commentaries on the Model Rules by the American College of Trusts and Estates Counsel (ACTEC Commentaries),[26] and the Third Restatement of the Law Governing Lawyers.[27] The ACTEC Commentaries note that a major problem with the Model Rules is that they are general principles applicable to all lawyers and often fail to address issues faced in trusts and estates practice.[28] The Model Rules often tend to presuppose litigation and an adversarial relationship, which are models that may not be applicable to many forms of estate planning practice.

Practitioners should also be aware of legal requirements to which they may be subject, including state laws, federal laws, court rules, and Treasury Regulations. As the Scope of the Model Rules recognizes, "[t]he Rules presuppose a larger legal context shaping the lawyer's role. That context includes court rules and statutes relating to matters of licensure, laws defining specific obligations of lawyers and substantive and procedural law in general."[29] Many of these laws do not alter or supplant other ethical standards to which a practitioner is subject, but they do create additional standards for certain types of practice, such as practice before the IRS, which is governed by Circular 230.[30]

III. Competence

U.S. attorneys remain subject to a basic duty of competence in representing their clients.[31] This is true regardless of whether the representation pertains to

25. *Id.* ¶ 1.
26. ACTEC Commentaries on the Model Rules of Prof'l Conduct (4th ed. 2006).
27. Restatement (Third) of the Law Governing Lawyers (2000).
28. ACTEC Commentaries on the Model Rules of Prof'l Conduct 4 (4th ed. 2006).
29. Model Rules of Prof'l Conduct scope (1983).
30. Treas. Dep't Circular No. 230 (rev. 8-2011).
31. *See* Model Rules of Prof'l. Conduct R. 1.1 ("A lawyer shall provide competent representation to a client. Competent representation requires the legal knowledge, skill, thoroughness and preparation reasonably necessary for the representation.").

domestic or international issues or whether the attorney provides the services at home or abroad.[32] First, the attorney must be able to recognize the existence of a question of foreign law.[33] Second, the attorney needs to determine whether he or she has the competence to address the issue of foreign law with the same speed, expertise, and cost as a foreign attorney.[34] Depending on the complexity of questions of foreign law and the reasonableness of the client's expectations, it may be advisable to consult foreign counsel[35] or even refer the client to a foreign attorney.[36] These options raise new ethical issues, which are discussed in Section IV.D.6.

IV. Unauthorized Practice of Law

With the explosive development of international legal practice, the problem of unauthorized practice of law has taken on new importance. International estate planners should be aware of the different ways in which they may (often inadvertently) engage in the unauthorized practice of law through multijurisdictional practice, its attendant consequences, and possible ways of avoiding the problem.

A. The Risk

Unauthorized practice of law emerged as a major issue for state bar associations during the early part of the 20th century.[37] The issue has traditionally arisen in the United States in the context of non-attorneys practicing law or attorneys practicing law in states in which they have not been licensed.[38] Commonly cited rationales for prohibiting unauthorized practice of law include the need to maintain local regulatory control over lawyer conduct and the protectionist impulse to safeguard local professionals from foreign competition.[39] Sovereign states have a substantial interest in regulating the practice of law within their jurisdictions and in protecting their citizenry from what they view as unauthorized legal practice.[40]

32. Robert E. Lutz, *Ethics and International Practice: A Guide to the Professional Responsibilities of Practitioners*, 16 FORDHAM INT'L L.J. (1993).

33. *See* MODEL RULES OF PROF'L CONDUCT R. 1.1 cmt. 2.

34. M.W. Janis, *The Lawyer's Responsibility for Foreign Law and Foreign Lawyers*, 16 INT'L LAW. 693, 703 (1982) ("[T]he lawyer is responsible to his client to recognize questions of foreign law. Once such a question is recognized . . . the lawyer is obliged either to deal competently with the foreign law point himself or to advise his client that foreign counsel should be retained.").

35. WILLIAM H. NEWTON III, INTERNATIONAL INCOME TAX & ESTATE PLANNING § 1:10 (2d ed. 2002); *see also* MODEL RULES OF PROF'L CONDUCT R. 1.1 cmt.; MODEL CODE OF PROF'L RESPONSIBILITY EC 6-1 n.1; Mears, *supra* note 9, at 620–21.

36. Lutz, *supra* note 32, at 61; MICHAEL SPIELMAN, U.S. INTERNATIONAL ESTATE PLANNING ¶ 2.04[2] (2012).

37. RESTATEMENT (THIRD) OF THE LAW GOVERNING LAWYERS ch. 1, topic 2, tit. B, introductory note (2000).

38. *Id.* §§ 3, 4.

39. *Id.* § 3.

40. Malini Majumdar, *Ethics in the International Arena: The Need for Clarification*, 8 GEO. J. LEGAL ETHICS 439 (1995).

In the contemporary era, U.S. jurisdictions typically allow a licensed attorney to maintain offices and practice anywhere within the jurisdiction in which he or she is licensed.[41] Sovereign states' strong interest in regulating the practice of law within their jurisdictions has resulted in groups of legal professional receiving a monopoly on providing certain legal services in nearly all nations.[42] In the United States, whether someone is authorized to practice law is a matter determined by law rather than professional responsibility guidelines or court rules.[43]

Modern estate planning practice often raises the issue of whether attorneys are engaging in the unauthorized practice of law. Even smaller boutique law firms now serve clients from multiple nation states, largely due to the globalized nature of modern business and finance.[44] Proper management of a single client's estate may require consideration of applicable laws from several jurisdictions. Clients have also come to demand the best attorneys in a given practice area, rather than the best that are available in their localities.[45] Meeting this demand may create ethical problems, especially if an attorney is asked to travel to a foreign nation to provide advisory and other legal services for non-U.S. clients.[46] Even an attorney who does not actually travel to a foreign jurisdiction may raise the issue of unauthorized practice of law if local planning raises issues of foreign substantive law.[47]

Many of the rules governing multijurisdictional practice were drafted at a time when there was little demand for interstate or international representation.[48] There have been calls for the practice of law to be federalized in some fashion to increase professional uniformity and diminish the importance of state boundaries in determining who may practice law.[49] However, national and state governments continue to limit the practice of law to those persons who have in some manner received permission from the relevant local authority to practice.

41. Restatement (Third) of the Law Governing Lawyers § 3 cmt. e.

42. Bryant G. Garth, *Transnational Legal Practice and Professional Ideology*, *in* Issues of Transnational Legal Practice 3, 7 (1985).

43. *See, e.g.*, N.Y. Jud. Law § 484 (prohibiting a natural person from appearing before a tribunal or preparing legal instruments for another person for compensation without being admitted to practice as an attorney, with some exceptions); Wyo. Stat. Ann. § 33-5-117 ("It shall be unlawful, and punishable as contempt of court, for any person not a member of the Wyoming state bar to hold himself out or advertise by whatsoever means as an attorney or counselor-at-law.").

44. Norman M. Krivosha, *The Case for Multijurisdictional Practice of Law in the United States*, 2001 ABA Prof'l Law. 45 (2001) (arguing that attorney regulation must find ways to adapt to the inevitable internationalization of legal practice).

45. *Id.*; *see also* ABA Ctr. for Prof'l Responsibility, Client Representation in the 21st Century: Report of the Commission on Multijurisdictional Practice (2002) [hereinafter ABA Report].

46. Joseph R. Lundy & Robert A. Creamer, *Private Practitioner Problems with Multijurisdictional Law Practice in Transactional and Litigation Matters*, 11 ABA Prof'l Law. 10 (2000).

47. Newton, *supra* note 35, § 1:10

48. ABA Report, *supra* note 45.

49. *See, e.g.*, Fred C. Zacharias, *Federalizing Legal Ethics*, 73 Tex. L. Rev. 335 (1994).

B. Relevant Rules

1. Model Rules

Few of the Model Rules offer express guidance regarding international legal practice.[50] This changed with amendments to Model Rule 5.5 in 1993. Additionally, several other rules continue to pose relevance to the issue of whether an attorney has engaged in the unauthorized practice of law in a foreign jurisdiction. In contrast to the Model Code's focus on interstate issues, the drafters of the Model Rules have sought to direct ethical guidelines to the international context.[51]

(a) Model Rule 5.5. Model Rule 5.5(a) prohibits a lawyer from practicing law in any jurisdiction or assisting another in practicing law if doing so violates that jurisdiction's applicable regulations. The Rule is extraterritorial in its application.[52] A lawyer who is subject to the Model Rules in his or her home jurisdiction will therefore be subject to discipline for practicing in a foreign jurisdiction in which he or she has not been authorized to practice law. Rule 5.5(a) may be violated indirectly by assisting someone else in practicing law in a jurisdiction in which that person is not licensed.[53]

Model Rule 5.5(b) prohibits the unauthorized practice of law in the local jurisdiction.[54] Unless otherwise authorized by the rules, a lawyer who has not been admitted to practice in the local jurisdiction shall not create an office or systematic and continuous presence as a legal practice in the jurisdiction or represent to the public that the lawyer is admitted to practice in the local jurisdiction.[55]

Following amendments in 2002, Model Rule 5.5(c) provides limited situations in which a lawyer admitted in a U.S. jurisdiction may practice law on a temporary basis.[56] Most states have adopted some form of amended Rule 5.5. Permissible limited multijurisdictional legal services include those that:

(1) are undertaken in association with a lawyer who is admitted to practice in this jurisdiction and who actively participates in the matter;

---

50. Krystinik, *supra* note 5, at 840.

51. *Compare* Model Code of Prof'l Responsibility EC 3-9 ("[T]he demand of business and the mobility of our society pose distinct problems in the regulation of the practice of law by the states.") *and* ABA Comm. on Prof'l. Ethics, Formal Op. No. 316 (1967) ("Much of clients' business crosses state lines. People are mobile, moving from state to state. Many metropolitan areas cross state lines. It is common today to have a single economic and social community involving more than one state. The business of a single client may involve legal problems in several states."), *with* Model Rules of Prof'l Conduct R. 8.5 cmt. ("In modern practice lawyers frequently act outside the territorial limits of the jurisdiction in which they are licensed to practice, either in another state or outside the United States.").

52. Model Rules of Prof'l Conduct R. 5.5(a).

53. *Id.* R. 5.5, cmt. 1.

54. *Id.* R. 5.5(b).

55. *Id.*

56. *Id.* R. 5.5(c). See *infra* Section IV.B.1.a for a discussion of how the 2002 amendments to Model Rule 5.5 can apply to isolated incidents of multijurisdictional practice by estate planning attorneys.

(2) are in or reasonably related to a pending or potential proceeding before a tribunal in this or another jurisdiction, if the lawyer, or a person the lawyer is assisting, is authorized by law or order to appear in such proceeding or reasonably expects to be so authorized;

(3) are in or reasonably related to a pending or potential arbitration, mediation, or other alternative dispute resolution proceeding in this or another jurisdiction, if the services arise out of or are reasonably related to the lawyer's practice in a jurisdiction in which the lawyer is admitted to practice and are not services for which the forum requires pro hac vice admission; or

(4) are not within paragraphs (c)(2) or (c)(3) and arise out of or are reasonably related to the lawyer's practice in a jurisdiction in which the lawyer is admitted to practice.[57]

These exceptions are discussed in more detail in Section IV.D.

Rule 5.5(d) allows a lawyer admitted to practice in another U.S. jurisdiction to practice in the local jurisdiction through an office or other systematic and continuous presence in the jurisdiction if the services are "(1) are provided to the lawyer's employer or its organizational affiliates and are not services for which the forum requires pro hac vice admission; or (2) are services that the lawyer is authorized by federal or other law or rule to provide in this jurisdiction."[58]

A lawyer would likely violate a foreign rule analogous to 5.5(b) (and consequently his or her home jurisdiction's version of Model Rule 5.5(a)) if he or she established an office or continuous presence or held himself or herself forth to the public that he or she was authorized to practice law in a jurisdiction in which he or she had not received a license.[59] A continuous and systematic presence need not be physical.[60] The situation is less clear when an attorney offers advice about foreign law, whether from his or her home state or while traveling to the foreign jurisdiction on a temporary basis.

Of course, attorneys should consult applicable unauthorized practice of law rules adopted by the local jurisdiction before undertaking a matter implicating foreign law. As noted above, these rules can differ from the Model Rules, Model Code, or Canons, yet a lawyer may still be subject to discipline by foreign or domestic authorities for the unauthorized practice of law.

(b) Model Rule 8.5. Prior to its amendment, Model Rule 8.5(a) provided for discipline of an attorney by the jurisdiction in which he or she was authorized to practice law. This gave disciplinary authorities extraterritorial enforcement of their professional responsibility and disciplinary rules, regardless of the location of the client or legal services. However, Rule 5.5 did not expressly state that an

57. Model Rule of Prof'l Conduct R. 5.5(b).
58. *Id.* R. 5.5(d).
59. *Id.* R. 5.5, cmts. 4 & 5.
60. *Id.* R. 5.5, cmt. 4.

attorney was subject to discipline in a jurisdiction in which the attorney provided legal services, but was not licensed.[61] This created the problem of lawyers not being subject to jurisdiction in jurisdictions in which they practiced law but were not licensed.[62]

Following 2002 amendments, Model Rule 8.5(a) gives states disciplinary authority over (1) locally licensed attorneys who practice in foreign jurisdictions and (2) foreign lawyers who are not licensed in the local jurisdiction but provide legal services in the local jurisdiction.[63] The same misconduct can cause an attorney to be subject to disciplinary authority of his or her home state and the state in which the conduct occurred.[64] Reciprocal enforcement of disciplinary rules protects a jurisdiction's residents.[65]

Model Rule 8.5(b) provides a choice of law framework for the exercise of jurisdiction over attorneys who engage in multijurisdictional practice. If conduct occurs in connection with a matter pending before a tribunal, the rules of the jurisdiction in which the tribunal sits will apply.[66] In other situations, the rules of the jurisdiction in which the conduct occurred or the jurisdiction in which the conduct has the predominant effect will apply.[67] The second situation is more likely to occur in most transactional arrangements. Lawyers are not subject to discipline if they engage in conduct that does not violate the professional responsibility rules of a jurisdiction in which they reasonably believe the conduct's predominant effect will occur.[68] A lawyer's belief is "reasonable" if it would be believed by a reasonably prudent and competent lawyer.[69]

If the home state and foreign state have differing ethical guidelines, a conflict of laws analysis is likely necessary. Commentary to Rule 8.5 clarifies application of the choice of law analysis in the international contest: "The choice of law provision applies to lawyers engaged in transnational practice, unless international law, treaties or other agreements between competent regulatory authorities in the affected jurisdictions provide otherwise."[70] Given the dearth of transnational agreements, practice, and law regarding professional responsibility, choice of law

61. Kathryn A. Ballsun, *Attorney Liability and Ethics*, *in* 1 Asset Protection: Domestic & Int'l Law & Tactics § 4:24 (2012).

62. Charles D. Fox IV, *The Top Ten Ethical Challenges Facing Estate Planning Practitioners Today and the Best Practices for Addressing Them*, 42 U. of Miami Law Center's Heckerling Inst. on Estate Planning 16, ¶ 1601.8 (2008).

63. Model Rules of Prof'l Conduct R. 8.5(a).

64. *Id.*

65. *Id.* R. 8.5 cmt. 1; *see also* Model Rules for Lawyer Disciplinary Enforcement Rs. 6, 22.

66. Model. Rules of Prof'l Conduct R. 8.5(b)(1).

67. *Id.* R. 5.5(b)(2).

68. *Id.*

69. *Id.* R. 1.

70. *Id.* R. 8.5 cmt. 7.

principles will likely apply to an attorney's international conduct.[71] One commentator suggests a choice of law analysis that proceeds by examining five factors to determine which jurisdiction has the greatest degree of contact with the practice of law in question: (1) where the advice is given, (2) where the client is located when receiving the advice, (3) the client's residence, (4) which jurisdiction's law is applicable to the advice, and (5) the duration of the lawyer's engagement by the client.[72] Despite the brevity of Rule 8.5(b), conflicts of law analyses can be very complex, resulting in uncertainty regarding which jurisdiction's rules will apply to international practice situations.[73]

An extraterritorial exercise of disciplinary jurisdiction by a U.S. authority must comply with the due process clause of the U.S. Constitution.[74] This requirement will probably be satisfied if the attorney purposefully avails himself of the local jurisdiction's laws by being licensed in or providing legal services with the jurisdiction such that the attorney can fairly and justly expect to be subject to that jurisdiction's courts.[75]

(c) Model Rule 7.5(b). Rule 7.5(b) permits a law firm with offices in multiple jurisdictions to use the same name or other professional designation in all jurisdictions.[76] However, "identification of the lawyers in an office of the firm shall indicate the jurisdictional limitations on those not licensed to practice in the jurisdiction where the office is located."[77] Foreign jurisdictions may provide additional restrictions on permissible names of foreign law firms. For example, Russia, China, and Indonesia have required foreign firms to practice through a local client, local firm, or the names of their resident foreign lawyers.[78]

2. Foreign Laws and Rules

As noted above, attorneys who engage in multijurisdictional practice must be careful to ensure that they do not violate the unauthorized practice rules of a foreign jurisdiction. In-depth treatments of specific foreign rules are beyond the scope of this chapter. However, international estate planning attorneys are advised that rules may differ between different jurisdictions.[79] Other than the

---

71. Martin Henssler & Laurel S. Terry, *Lawyers Without Frontiers—A View from Germany*, 19 Dick. J. Int'l L. 269, 290 (2001); Detlev F. Vagts, *Professional Responsibility in Transborder Practice: Conflict and Resolution*, 13 Geo. J. Legal Ethics 677, 690 (2000).

72. Osborne M. Reynolds, *Practice and Performance by the Out-of-State Attorney—The Jealous Mistress Becomes an Interstate Traveler*, 6 U. Tol. L. Rev. 63, 76 (1974) (citing Restatement (Second) of Conflict of Laws § 6 (1959)).

73. Laurel S. Terry, *An Introduction to the European Community's Legal Ethics Code Part I: An Analysis of the CCBE Code of Conduct*, 7 Geo. J. Legal Ethics 1, 3 (1993)

74. *Cf.* Int'l Shoe Co. v. Washington, 326 U.S. 310, 316 (1945).

75. *Cf.* Burger King Corp. v. Rudzewicz, 471 U.S. 462, 475 (1985).

76. Model Rules of Prof'l Conduct R. 7.5(b).

77. *Id.*

78. Richard L. Abel, *Transnational Practice of Law*, 44 Case W. Res. L. Rev. 737, 759 (1994).

79. *See* Olga M. Pina, *Systems of Ethical Regulation: An International Comparison*, 1 Geo. J. Legal Ethics 797, 800, 804 (1988).

European Union,[80] most jurisdictions' ethical guidelines are nationally specific.[81] As one commentator has observed:

> If the regulation of lawyers were optimally efficient, we would expect it to be similar across national boundaries, at least among the most developed countries. However, regulations are nationally specific; those that are essential to one legal profession are merely quaint or even bizarre to another. For example, barristers believe that the divided English profession and the ban on partnerships are indispensable to their "independence." Other legal professions, including many solicitor compatriots, find such a claim insulting. Solicitors believe that only they can perform conveyancing services honestly and efficiently. Yet in those American and Australian states where lawyers have lost the monopoly on conveyancing, prices are lower and quality unaffected. In the United States, lawyers believe only they can advise about the law of any nation. Few other professions agree with this proposition. The Dutch have few problems with multinational partnerships which most other professions still prohibit or tightly regulate. When the United States permitted lawyers to advertise, most other professions jeered. Today, many have dropped their own advertising bans.[82]

Many jurisdictions may offer fewer permissible means of practicing foreign law than are available in the United States.[83] Despite the substantial influence of American and English law on foreign transactional law, heightened restrictions on foreign practice may be found in nations like France, Singapore, or Japan.[84] Attorneys should consult local rules or foreign counsel before engaging in extensive multijurisdictional practice.

C. Penalties

1. Local or Foreign Discipline

It may be unlikely that an attorney will be sanctioned solely for engaging in the unauthorized practice of foreign law, especially if the attorney operates from his or her home jurisdiction and engages in foreign practice on an isolated or incidental basis. It is difficult to find cases in which an attorney has been disciplined

80. Rona R. Mears, *Ethics and Due Diligence: A Lawyer's Perspective on Doing Business with Mexico*, 22 St. Mary's L.J. 605, 611 (1991) (citing Council of the Bars and Law Societies of the European Community, Common Code of Conduct The Law Society's Gazette art. 2.4 (1989)).

81. Stephen M. Worth, *The Transnational Practice of Law: Staggering Growth in Spite of Economic and Regulatory Barriers to Entry*, 7 Gonz. J. Int'l L. 5 (2004).

82. Abel, *supra* note 78, at 751–52.

83. Newton, *supra* note 35, § 1:10. See Masako C. Shiono, *Foreign Attorneys in Japan: The International Practice of Law as a Question of Unfair Trade Practices*, 2 Am. Univ. Int'l Law Rev. 615 (1987) for a discussion of the development of rules regarding the unauthorized practice of law by foreign attorneys in Japan (citing Japanese Attorneys Law art. 72).

84. Abel, *supra* note 78.

by his or her home state for the unauthorized practice of law in another jurisdiction.[85] The number of sanctions has tended to be limited by the discretion of enforcement authorities, which may choose to ignore unauthorized practice until malpractice or a fee dispute results in a complaint or litigation of some kind. This has resulted in widespread multijurisdictional practice.[86] However, as discussed above, unauthorized practice likely violates the ethical rules of the attorney's home jurisdiction,[87] creating the risk of sanctions.[88] This is particularly true if the lawyer's conduct results in a complaint to a court or enforcement authority.[89] Additionally, the attorney may be subject to discipline in the foreign jurisdiction if it has adopted a rule or long-arm statute analogous to Model Rule 8.5(a).

2. Lost Fees

The largest practical risk from the unauthorized practice of law is the possibility that the practitioner will be unable to collect fees for his or her services.[90] This result may arise if there is a fee dispute of some sort or the client is unhappy with his or her services and the attorney commences proceedings to collect unpaid fees. In a number of cases, U.S. courts have prohibited attorneys from collecting fees for services performed in jurisdictions in which the attorneys were not licensed.[91] Given the high fees and heightened due diligence requirements associated with certain forms of international estate planning, such as the creation of offshore trusts, this may be a very undesirable consequence.

3. Voided Pleadings

Attorneys who engage in the unauthorized practice of law risk having pleadings and other documents that they prepared deemed void.[92] Under common law conflict of law principles, the validity of a living trust holding movable assets will typically be governed by the jurisdiction designated by the settlor if it has a substantial relationship to the trust and applying the law does not violate the strong public policy of the jurisdiction with the most significant relationship with the trust.[93] Otherwise, validity will be determined by the local law of the jurisdiction

---

85. Fox, *supra* note 62, ¶ 1601.3.

86. ABA Report, *supra* note 45, at 11–12.

87. Model Rules of Prof'l Responsibility R. 8.5(a); Model Rules for Lawyer Disciplinary Enforcement Rs. 9(1)(2), 22.

88. *See* Office of Disciplinary Counsel v. Mbakpuo, 652 N.E.2d 976, 977–78 (Ohio 1995) (affirming discipline of an Ohio attorney who, among other infractions, engaged in unauthorized practice of law in the District of Columbia).

89. Lundy & Creamer, *supra* note 46.

90. *Id.* at 15; Newton, *supra* note 35, § 1:10.

91. *See, e.g.*, Martin & Martin v. Jones, 541 So. 2d 1 (Ala. 1989); Spivak v. Sachs, 211 N.E.2d 329, 331 (N.Y. 1965).

92. Steven G. Nilsson, *Are Living Trusts Void When Commercially Formed through the Unauthorized Practice of Law?*, Fla. B.J., Apr. 1995, at 29–30; *cf., e.g.*, N.C. Nat'l Bank v. Va. Carolina Builders, 299 S.E.2d 629, 632 (N.C. 1983) (holding plaintiff's remedy was to move to strike an answer filed by an out-of-state attorney).

93. Restatement (Second) of Conflict of Laws § 270 (1971)(a).

with the most substantial relationship to the trust regarding the matter at issue.[94] Some commentators argue that trusts drafted by attorneys who are not authorized in the local jurisdiction are void because their formation was contrary to law, even if there was no other defect in the creation of the underlying trust as a matter of contact law.[95] This appears to be less of a risk in transactional engagements, such as preparing a will or trust, than in litigation.[96]

4. Other Penalties

An attorney who engaged in the unauthorized practice of law may be subject to other consequences, including contempt by a tribunal, criminal prosecution, malpractice claims, or disqualification from litigation.[97]

D. Solutions

1. Temporary Practice Related to Practice in Home Jurisdiction

One way to avoid engaging in the unauthorized practice of law is to limit the attorney's services to isolated, noncontinuous incidents. There has been some precedent for this in the context of multistate practice.[98] It has generally been expressed that merely providing incidental advice regarding foreign law does not necessarily constitute the practice of law in a foreign jurisdiction.[99] In 1967, the ABA issued Formal Opinion 316, which acknowledged the importance of multijurisdictional practice, but provided limited options for providing legal services across state lines.[100] While occasional multistate practice by attorneys has been has been widespread and has rarely resulted in sanctions, very few states expressly permitted isolated practice by out-of-state attorneys prior to 2002.[101]

As originally drafted, Model Rule 5.5 was similar to DR 3-101 of the Model Code.[102] It restricted an attorney from practicing law in a jurisdiction in violation of that jurisdiction's regulations or assisting a nonmember of the bar in committing unauthorized practice of law.[103] In 2000, the ABA's Commission on

---

94. *Id.* § 270(b).

95. Nilsson, *supra* note 92, at 24.

96. *See* Miller v. Miller, 744 N.E.2d 778 (Ohio Ct. App. 2000) (holding that although a living trust's preparation by a non-attorney constituted unauthorized practice of law, the subject matter remained legal, and the trust was validly executed).

97. *See* Lundy & Creamer, *supra* note 46, at 10–11.

98. *See, e.g.*, Spivak v. Sachs, 211 N.E.2d 329 (N.Y. 1965) (permitting "incidental and innocuous" multijurisdictional practice, but prohibiting a California attorney from recovering fees for work advising a client and local counsel in New York); Appell v. Reiner, 204 A.2d 146, 148 (N.J. 1964).

99. *See* John E. Martindale, *Attorney's Liability in Non-client and Foreign Law Situations*, 14 CLEV.-MARSHALL L. REV. 44, 56 (1965).

100. ABA Comm. on Prof'l Ethics, Formal Op. 316 (1967) (permitting multistate practice in association with licensed, local attorneys); Ballsun, *supra* note 61, § 4 (2012) (noting the limits of Formal Op. 316).

101. *See* MICH. COMP. LAWS ANN. § 600.916; VA. STATE BAR RULES pt. 6, § (1)(C).

102. Fox, *supra* note 62.

103. MODEL RULES OF PROF'L CONDUCT R. 5.5 (1983); *see also* MODEL CODE OF PROF'L RESPONSIBILITY DR 3-101.

Multijurisdictional Practice recommended amendments to Rule 5.5, which were adopted in 2002. Most states have adopted amendments identical or similar to amended Model Rule 5.5. The amendments' primary substantive change clarified situations in which attorneys admitted in other U.S. states could provide temporary representation in certain limited circumstances. The primary rationales for the amendments were to enable clients to utilize one lawyer or firm for all aspects of a transaction, maintain preexisting attorney-client relationships, and obtain the services of attorneys who have expertise in specific fields of law.[104]

Of the exceptions permitting isolated instances of temporary practice of foreign law, Model Rule 5.5(c)(4) is most directly relevant to estate planners. That exception permits transactional representation and other nonlitigation work on a temporary basis if it arises from or is reasonably related to the lawyer's practice in his or her home jurisdiction.[105] Several factors determine whether representation arises out of or is reasonably related to practice in the lawyer's home jurisdiction, including the lawyer's previous representation of the client, the client's residency in or contacts with the lawyer's home jurisdiction, and other significant involvement of the matter with the home jurisdiction.[106] Further,

> [t]he necessary relationship might arise when the client's activities or the legal issues involve multiple jurisdictions, such as when the officers of a multinational corporation survey potential business sites and seek the services of their lawyer in assessing the relative merits of each. In addition, the services may draw on the lawyer's recognized expertise developed through the regular practice of law on behalf of clients in matters involving a particular body of federal, nationally-uniform, foreign, or international law.[107]

The attorney's contact with the foreign jurisdiction must remain temporary. If the contact is temporary, the foreign jurisdiction has less of an interest in regulating the attorney's conduct.[108] But if the attorney establishes a more regular presence, the foreign jurisdiction has a much greater interest in regulating the attorney by requiring admission to the local bar.[109] No single test exists for determining whether an attorney's practice of law in a jurisdiction is "temporary."[110] "Services may be 'temporary' even though the lawyer provides services in this jurisdiction on a recurring basis, or for an extended period of time, as when the lawyer

---

104. ABA Report, *supra* note 45, at 27–28; *see also* Restatement (Third) of the Law Governing Lawyers § 3(3) (citing Cal. Sup. Ct. Adv. Task Force on Multijurisdictional Practice, Report and Recommendations 30 (Aug. 1, 2001).

105. Model Rules of Prof'l Conduct R. 5.5(c)(6).

106. *Id.* R. 5.5 cmt. 14.

107. *Id.*

108. ABA Report, *supra* note 45, at 29.

109. *Id.*

110. Model Rules of Prof'l Conduct R. 5.5 cmt. 6.

is representing a client in a single lengthy negotiation or litigation."[111] The ABA has acknowledged that amended Rule 5.5 cannot eliminate uncertainty regarding the permissible extent of multijurisdictional practice.[112] Individual opinion and judicial interpretation will necessarily shape application of the Rule and provide greater certainty over the permissible extent of temporary practice over time.[113]

For example, a Utah estate planner who has expertise in offshore trust planning may have a long-standing relationship with a Utah client who seeks to transfer assets to a Cook Islands trust. If the Utah attorney has sufficient expertise to assist the client and the assistance is directly related to legal services provided by the attorney in Utah, allowing the attorney to engage in limited multijurisdictional practice can increase the efficiency of the transaction and provide superior service to the client by allowing the client to receive services from an attorney in which he or she has confidence. The client has firsthand knowledge of the attorney's competence and the attorney has an additional incentive to provide quality service to retain the client's business.[114] In such a situation, the attorney's home state of Utah would be tasked with determining whether the attorney had the requisite character, fitness, and competence to provide the relevant services.[115] However, if the Utah attorney has no prior relationship with the client and lacks special expertise in the relevant area of law, it is less likely that the attorney's multijurisdictional practice will be considered related to the attorney's Utah practice.[116]

2. Restrict Advice to Nonlocal Matters

Another means of avoiding the unauthorized practice of law in multijurisdictional practice is to simply limit advice to matters regarding jurisdictions in which the attorney is licensed. Providing advice about nonlocal matters does not raise much of an issue of the unauthorized practice of law and is international only to the extent the client resides in, comes from, or has ancillary dealings with a foreign jurisdiction.[117]

Model Rule 1.2(d) permits an attorney to place reasonable limits on the scope of representation if the client provides informed consent.[118] The informed consent agreement must comply with the other terms of the Model Rules, including Model Rules 1.1 (competence), 1.8 (current conflicts of interest), and 5.6 (restrictions on rights to practice).[119] The lawyer and client have significant discretion in agreeing

111. *Id.* R. 5.5 cmt. 6.

112. ABA Report, *supra* note 45, at 23, 29.

113. *Id.*

114. *Id.* at 28.

115. *Id.* at 27.

116. *Id.* at 29.

117. Wayne J. Carroll, *Innocents Abroad: Opportunities and Challenges for the International Legal Adviser*, 34 Vand. J. Transnat'l L. 1097, 1100 (2001).

118. Model R. Prof'l Conduct R. 1.2(c).

119. *Id.* R. 1.2 cmt. 8.

to limit the scope of the representation, but the limit must be reasonable under the circumstances.[120] A limited scope of representation also does not waive an attorney's duty of competence.[121] There is a substantial risk that issues of foreign law will arise in an international engagement, such as the status of foreign fraudulent transfer laws or other laws protecting creditors' rights when transferring offshore assets to a trust in a U.S. jurisdiction.[122]

For example, a Colorado attorney providing U.S. tax planning services to Indonesian residents who plan to immigrate to the United States could limit her advice to matters of Colorado and U.S. federal law and provide that the client is solely responsible for retaining counsel regarding matters of foreign law from other jurisdictions. The client should be informed of the limited scope of the representation in the engagement letter, which the client should sign.[123] But the limited scope may not be reasonable if matters of foreign law will arise during the representation. If advice implicates local matters, the attorney may unwittingly engage in the unauthorized practice of law in the local jurisdiction.[124] If local matters have the possibility of arising from the representation, it may be preferable for the attorney to retain foreign counsel or legal consultants to address issues of foreign law.[125]

An attorney may opt to withdraw from the representation under appropriate circumstances if it becomes impossible to provide competent legal advice without opining on matters of foreign law.[126] Withdrawal from representation is appropriate if it will not have a "material adverse effect" on the clients' interests or if good cause for withdrawal exists.[127] Upon termination of the attorney-client relationship, the attorney must take reasonable steps to allow the client to protect his or her interests, including providing reasonable notice, allowing time for the client to retain replacement counsel, surrendering papers and property to which the client is entitled, and refunding advance payment of fees or expenses that have not yet been earned.[128]

---

120. *Id.* Rs. 1.2 cmt. 7, 1.1.

121. *Id.* See *infra* Section III for a brief discussion of competence as it relates to international estate planning.

122. Osborne, *supra* note 1, ¶ 1703.2.

123. Fox, *supra* note 62.

124. *In re Roel*, 3 N.Y.2d 224, 228–30 (1957) (holding that a Mexican attorney who advised clients about Mexican law while located in New York committed unauthorized practice of law despite providing no advice as to New York law). *But see* El Gemayel v. Seaman, 533 N.E.2d 245 (N.Y. 1988) (distinguishing *Roel* and holding that a Lebanese attorney who called New York clients to advise them about Lebanese law did not engage in unauthorized practice of law because of the attorney's incidental contacts with New York).

125. Newton *supra* note 35, § 1:10 n.4

126. *Id.*

127. Model Rules of Prof'l Conduct R. 1.16(b)(1), (7). Withdrawal is simpler in the nonlitigation context because the attorney is less likely to require permission of a tribunal to withdraw his or her appearance and terminate the representation. *See, e.g.*, *id.* R. 1.16(c); Local Rules of the U.S. Dist. Cts. for the S. & E. Dists. of N.Y. R. 1.4; Rs. of Ct. of Chancery of the State of Del. R. 5(aa).

128. Model Rules of Prof'l Conduct R. 1.16(d).

3. Narrow "Practice of Law"

Model Rule 5.5 depends on the definition of the phrase "practice of law." Lawyers are only prohibited from engaging in the unauthorized practice law. They are free to engage in conduct that falls short of that standard. According to the commentary to Model Rule 5.5, "[t]he definition of the practice of law is established by law and varies from one jurisdiction to another. Whatever the definition, limiting the practice of law to members of the bar protects the public against rendition of legal services by unqualified persons."[129]

Avoiding the authorized practice of law by narrowing the definition of "practice of the law" may be difficult given the broad manner in which courts and other authorities have defined that phrase, particularly in the realm of estate planning.[130] For example, the Arkansas Supreme Court has held that the practice of law includes "writing and interpreting wills, contracts, trust agreement, and the giving of legal advice in general."[131] Most forms of international estate planning will involve the preparation of legal documents and providing advice regarding those documents, making the success of this solution somewhat remote.

4. Provide Services from Home Jurisdiction

An estate planner may avoid discipline for the unauthorized practice of law by providing advice from jurisdictions in which he or she is licensed. Electronic communications technology has made it much easier to oversee legal matters without the need to physically meet with parties or other attorneys. In the past, U.S. courts, at least, have placed importance on the attorney's location when providing advice regarding foreign legal matters.[132] For example, a Nevada attorney who provides advice regarding Cayman Islands trusts to California residents may never actually visit the Cayman Islands or California. This approach may limit the attorney's practice by preventing him or her from visiting the foreign jurisdiction to meet with trust parties, examine property, or meet with foreign counsel. Additionally, physical presence in a jurisdiction may not be necessary to imposing

129. *Id.* R. 5 cmt. 2.

130. 1 Jeffrey A. Schoenblum, Multistate and Multinational Estate Planning § 5.02 (2009 ed., 2008).

131. Undem v. State Bd. of Law Examiners, 587 S.W.2d 563, 568 (Ark. 1979); *accord* Grievance Comm. of Bar v. Dacey, 222 A.2d 339 (Conn. 1966) (affirming a Superior Court's holding that drafting and preparing documents intended to have legal effect and providing advice regarding such instruments constitutes practice of law, rather than the provision of general information (such as a form book)). *But see* Lindsey v. Ogden, 406 N.E.2d 701, 708 (Mass. App. Ct. 1980) (holding that a well-regarded New York attorney who oversaw a will execution in Boston, but did not hold himself out as a Massachusetts attorney, did not draft the documents in Massachusetts, and did nothing else that would be considered the practice of law in Massachusetts, did not engage in unauthorized practice of Massachusetts law).

132. Worth, *supra* note 81 (citing *In re* Roel, 3 N.Y.2d 224, 228–30 (1957); El Gemayel v. Seaman, 533 N.E.2d 245 (N.Y. 1988)); *see also* Estate of Condon, 64 Cal. Rptr. 2d 789 (Ct. App. 1997) (holding a Colorado lawyer did not violate a California statute prohibiting practice of law "in" the state by providing advice about California law, directing communications to California, and visiting California to confer with clients and co-counsel and negotiate).

discipline for misconduct.[133] There do not appear to be any cases directly sanctioning this method as a safe harbor to unauthorized practice.[134]

5. Pro Hoc Vice Motions

Traditionally, attorneys have relied on the pro hoc vice motion to engage in limited practice of law in a jurisdiction in which they are not licensed.[135] These motions provide little utility in most estate planning contexts because they typically give the attorney the right to litigate a particular matter before a foreign jurisdiction's tribunal (such as a probate), but not the right to provide transactional services unconnected to litigation.[136] Pro hoc vice motions have additional drawbacks, including the requirement that the attorney associate with local counsel and the fact that foreign courts have wide latitude to reject a motion.

6. Employment of Foreign Counsel and Legal Consultants

Attorneys have a general duty to provide clients with competent representation and must provide appropriate knowledge, skill, thoroughness, and preparation to the matter.[137] In order to provide competent representation, it may be necessary to associate with or consult another attorney.[138] In the international estate planning context, this may require the assistance of foreign attorneys or legal consultants. Association and consultation can alleviate some of the risk of engaging in the unauthorized practice of law by allowing a locally licensed attorney to opine on matters of local law.[139]

This solution raises its own ethical issues. In addition to practical concerns, including the increased costs and inefficiencies introduced by foreign consultation,[140] the association must be conducted in a professionally responsible manner. First, if a U.S. attorney operates a foreign law office, the office should be staffed by locally licensed professionals, with nonlocal attorneys limited to carrying out transitory professional activities incidental to the firm's foreign operations in a coordinating/supervisory capacity.[141] Locally licensed attorneys must remain responsible for local legal matters.[142] Second, the U.S. attorney needs to ensure that foreign counsel and consultants conduct themselves in an ethical and

---

133. *See* MODEL RULES OF PROF'L CONDUCT R. 8.5 cmt. 1; MODEL RULES FOR LAWYER DISCIPLINARY ENFORCEMENT Rs. 6, 22.

134. Fox, *supra* note 62.

135. RESTATEMENT (THIRD) OF THE LAW GOVERNING LAWYERS § 3 cmt. e.

136. Fox, *supra* note 62; ABA Report, *supra* note 45; *see also* CHARLES W. WOLFRAM, MODERN LEGAL ETHICS § 15.4.3 (1986).

137. MODEL RULES OF PROF'L RESPONSIBILITY R. 1.1; *see also* MODEL CODE OF PROF'L RESPONSIBILITY DR 6-101(A)(1).

138. MODEL RULES OF PROF'L RESPONSIBILITY R. 1.1 cmt. 1.

139. *See* Fought & Co. v. Steel Eng'g & Erection, Inc., 951 P.2d 487 (Haw. 1998); *In re* Opinion 33, 733 A.2d 478 (N.J. 1999).

140. Fox, *supra* note 62; Lundy & Creamer, *supra* note 46.

141. Fla. Bar v. Savitt, 363 So. 2d 559, 560 (Fla. 1978).

142. *See* ABA Comm. on Prof'l Ethics, Formal Op. 263 (1944).

competent manner.[143] Third, if a firm employs foreign attorneys, it must ensure that prohibited information does not exist on the firm's letterhead, business cards, or other promotional materials,[144] such as misleading representations that attorneys can practice in jurisdictions in which they are unlicensed or representations that attorneys are specialists in areas of law that have not been recognized by the local licensing authority.[145] Fourth, U.S. attorneys must ensure that they do not assist foreign attorneys or legal consultants in committing the unauthorized practice of law.[146]

(a) Foreign-Domestic Partnerships and Employment of Foreign Attorneys. One possible solution to the problem of unauthorized multijurisdictional practice is to simply hire or form a partnership with foreign attorneys. The number of transnational law firms has grown significantly since the 1980s.[147] Such firms have typically taken two different approaches to establishing international offices. In the home office approach, a U.S. attorney establishes an office in a foreign jurisdiction and rotates U.S. attorneys through the foreign office.[148] In the franchise approach, a firm will open offices in a foreign jurisdiction and primarily staff that office with locally licensed attorneys.[149]

U.S. law firms must ensure that equity partnerships with foreign attorneys comply with applicable ethical guidelines. Most jurisdictions prohibit non-lawyers from having ownership interests in law firms.[150] That raises the issue of whether an attorney licensed in a foreign jurisdiction is an "attorney" for the purposes of determining a firm's permissible partners. The American Bar Association has approved the ability of U.S. attorneys to form partnerships with foreign attorneys.[151] The foreign partners must be members of a recognized legal profession in their home jurisdiction, and the arrangement must comply with the laws of

143. Am. Bar Found., Annotated Code of Professional Responsibility 136–39 (1979).

144. *Id.*

145. *Id.*; *see also* Model Rules of Prof'l Conduct R. 7.4(d) (setting standards for communicating specialization other than patent or admiralty law).

146. Model Rules of Prof'l Conduct R. 5.5(a).

147. Worth, *supra* note 81.

148. *Id.*

149. *Id.*

150. *See, e.g.*, Cal. Bus. & Prof'l Code § 6165 ("Except as provided in [other sections governing nonprofit public benefit corporations and officers of single-shareholder professional corporations] each director, shareholder, and each officer of a law corporation shall be a licensed person as defined in the Professional Corporation Act, or a person licensed to render the same professional services in the jurisdiction or jurisdictions in which the person practices."); N.Y. Bus. Corp. Law § 1507(a) (providing that a professional service corporation may not issues shares to individuals who are not authorized to practice the relevant profession in the state); *see also* Cal. Rules of Prof'l Conduct R. 1-310 (prohibiting lawyers from forming law partnerships with non-attorneys).

151. ABA Formal Ethics Op. 01-423 (2001); *see also* N.Y. State Bar Ass'n, Comm. on Prof'l Ethics, Op. 646 (1993) (stating that a member of the New York bar could enter into a partnership with a Japanese attorney if doing so did not interfere with the New York lawyer's ethical requirements and the attorneys complied with all substantive and legal requirements of both nations).

all jurisdictions in which the attorneys practice.[152] U.S. attorneys who are party to such arrangements have an ethical duty to ensure that foreign partners are duly licensed by the authority that governs authorization to practice law.[153] Additionally, U.S. attorneys should be careful to not assist a foreign attorney in the unauthorized practice of law in a U.S. jurisdiction.[154] U.S. attorneys must exercise due care and competency in their selection of foreign legal counsel.[155] Otherwise, negligent or incompetent conduct by foreign co-counsel may be imputed to the referring attorney.[156]

(b) Fee Splitting. In most U.S. jurisdictions, fee splitting is governed by Model Rule 1.5(e):

> A division of a fee between lawyers who are not in the same firm may be made only if:
>
> (1) the division is in proportion to the services performed by each lawyer or each lawyer assumes joint responsibility for the representation;
> (2) the client agrees to the arrangement, including the share each lawyer will receive, and the agreement is confirmed in writing; and
> (3) the total fee is reasonable.[157]

A division of fees occurs if a single bill to a client covers fees of multiple lawyers who are not employed by a single firm.[158] Commentary to the Rule reflects an understanding that there may be situations in which multiple attorneys providing joint service can provide superior representation, particularly when one attorney is a specialist in a particular legal field.[159]

Fee division is generally permissible if it is divided in proportion to each lawyer's services or if each lawyer assumes responsibility for the entire representation.[160] The client must agree to the arrangement, including the proportional division,[161] in writing, preferably through a signed engagement letter. Each attorney will be financially and ethically responsible for the representation as if he or she were in a partnership. Attorneys should not refer work to another attorney, including a fee-splitting arrangement, if the attorney does not reasonably believe that the other attorney has sufficient competence to handle his or her part of the

152. *Id.*
153. ABA Formal Ethics Op. No. 01-423.
154. Model Rules of Prof'l Conduct R. 5.5(a); N.Y. Ethics Op. 864 n.13 (May 10, 2011).
155. *See, e.g.*, Tormo v. Yormark, 398 F. Supp. 1159 (D.N.J. 1975).
156. *See generally* Note, 47 Harv. L. Rev. 1056, 1057 (1934).
157. Model Rules of Prof'l Conduct R. 1.5(e).
158. *Id.* R. 1.5 cmt. 7.
159. *Id.*
160. *Id.*
161. *Id.* Rs. 1.5(b), 1.5(e) cmt. 7.

representation.[162] Foreign counsel should be careful to draft a reasonably specific fee agreement to ensure that they will be entitled to their fees.[163]

The largest ethical question in determining the permissibility of splitting fees with foreign attorneys is the question of whether an attorney licensed in a foreign jurisdiction is considered an "attorney" for purposes of Model Rule 1.5(e). The Model Rules prohibit an attorney from splitting a fee with a non-lawyer.[164] Even if an attorney is licensed in a foreign state or nation, that lawyer may not be considered a lawyer under a jurisdiction's unauthorized practice of law rules. However, some authorities have shown a willingness to apply a broader definition to the term "lawyer" in the context of fee splitting than in the context of unauthorized practice.

ABA Formal Opinion 316 states that, for fee division purposes, "[i]t is not necessary that both lawyers be admitted to practice in the same state, so long as the division was based on the division of services or responsibility."[165] Although this opinion was issued prior to adoption of the Model Code, it has been used by some courts, including, most notably, the U.S. Court of Appeals for the Tenth Circuit,[166] to hold that a "lawyer" for fee-splitting purposes need not be a lawyer for general professional responsibility purposes.

Similarly, a New York ethics opinion determined that language in New York's comparable fee-splitting rule referred to any lawyer admitted to practice law by a United States jurisdiction.[167] While the Opinion limited its scope to U.S. attorneys, it provided a useful analysis of the rationale for free-splitting rules. The purpose of fee-splitting rules is to ensure that clients obtain quality representation and that attorneys adhere to their ethical responsibilities, including their duties of loyalty and confidentiality.[168] The opinion quoted an Annotation to the New York Rules of Professional Conduct for the proposition that "[u]nlike a disbarred lawyer or a lawyer disqualified due to a conflict of interest, the out-of-state lawyer could handle the matter personally if he came to New York to be admitted pro hac vice."[169] Although pro hac vice admission remains infeasible for most types of estate planning practice, as discussed above, amended Model Rule 5.5(b)(4) provides opportunities to provide limited legal services in connection with services provided in his or her home jurisdiction without engaging in unauthorized practice of law. Based on Rule 5.5 and the rationale articulated in the New York

162. *Id.* R. 1.5(b)

163. *See* ABA Comm. on Ethics and Prof'l Responsibility, Formal Op. 27 (1930) (holding a local attorney was free to fix the terms of the fee-splitting arrangement if the terms were reasonable and did not misappropriate client funds, because no agreement had reached before the representation began).

164. *See* Model Rules of Prof'l Responsibility R. 1.5.

165. ABA Formal Op. 316 (Jan. 18, 1967).

166. Dietrich Corp. v. King Res. Co., 596 F.2d 422 (10th Cir. 1979) (requiring fees be paid to a law professor who was not locally licensed but consulted regarding a bankruptcy matter).

167. N.Y. Ethics Op. 864 (May 10, 2011).

168. *Id.* (citing N.Y. Code of Prof'l Responsibility 447 (2008)).

169. *Id.* (citing Roy Simon, Simon's Code of Professional Responsibility Annotated 447 (2008)).

and ABA ethics opinions, an argument can be made that foreign attorneys who are licensed in their home jurisdiction and provide limited assistance in connection with international estate planning matters may qualify as "lawyers" under Rule 1.5(e).

Even if fee splitting with a foreign attorney is authorized, local counsel must ensure that that local and foreign counsel do not engage in or assist each other in engaging in the unauthorized practice of law. Additionally, the document providing for the client's informed consent should explain which responsibilities are shifted to the out-of-state attorney, the jurisdictions in which the services will be provided, and the amount and compensation of each estate planner.

(c) Foreign Legal Consultants. Foreign legal consultants offer an alternative to forming employment or partnership relationships with foreign attorneys. It may be more efficient and less expensive to simply consult foreign attorneys on questions of foreign law. New York led many states in allowing members of foreign legal professions to be licensed as legal consultants without being fully licensed to practice law in the state.[170] According to the state's "liberal rule," a foreign attorney may practice as a foreign consultant in New York

> if the applicant has been in good standing as a member of the bar in his or her home country for at least three of the five previous years, possesses good moral character, is over 26, and intends to practice as a legal consultant in the State of New York.[171]

A New York foreign legal consultant will be permitted to undertake limited tasks, including providing advice and drafting instruments involving the non-U.S. laws and international law.

In 1993, the ABA adopted a Model Rule for the Licensing of Legal Consultants to encourage states to allow limited practice by foreign legal consultants.[172] The Rule was adopted based on the perception that U.S. attorneys had wide latitude to practice in foreign nations without obtaining licenses, but foreign attorneys lacked similar rights in U.S. jurisdictions, even if limiting their advice to nonlocal matters. The Rule gives courts discretion to license a foreign legal consultant without examination if the applicant

> (a) is, and for at least five years has been, a member in good standing of a recognized legal profession in a foreign country, the members of which are admitted to practice as lawyers or counselors at law or the equivalent

170. N.Y. Ct. Rules § 521.1.

171. *Id.*

172. ABA Model Rules for the Licensing and Practice of Foreign Legal Consultants; Am Bar Ass'n, Interim Report of the Comm'n on Multijurisdictional Practice 32 (2001); *see also* Carol A. Needham, *The Licensing of Foreign Legal Consultants in the United States*, 21 Fordham Int'l L.J. 1126 (1998).

and are subject to effective regulation and discipline by a duly constituted professional body or a public authority;

(b) for at least five years preceding his or her application has been a member in good standing of such legal profession and has been lawfully engaged in the practice of law in the foreign country or elsewhere substantially involving or relating to the rendering of advice or the provision of legal services concerning the law of the foreign country;

(c) possesses the good moral character and general fitness requisite for a member of the bar of this jurisdiction; and

(d) intends to practice as a foreign legal consultant in this jurisdiction and to maintain an office in this jurisdiction for that purpose.[173]

The Model Rule allows licensed foreign legal consultants to provide a limited range of legal services in the local jurisdiction without requiring admission to practice law or being deemed to hold themselves forth as members of the local bar. Foreign legal consultants may not appear as lawyers before a tribunal, prepare instruments affecting title to U.S. real property, prepare certain legal instruments, provide professional legal advice regarding the law of the local jurisdiction or the United States unless based on the advice of locally licensed attorney, or carry on practice except under authorized names, titles, or designations.[174] Of particular importance to international estate planners is that foreign legal consultants may not prepare "(i) any will or trust instrument effecting the disposition on death of any property located and owned by a resident of the United States of America, or (ii) any instrument relating to the administration of a decedent's estate in the United States of America . . . ."[175]

Foreign legal consultants licensed in a different state may provide legal services in the local jurisdiction pursuant to the Model Rule for Temporary Practice by Foreign Attorneys.[176] But they may not establish an office or engage in systematic and continuous practice in the local jurisdiction or hold themselves out to the public as foreign legal consultants. Foreign legal consultants are generally subject to the local licensing authority's rules of professional responsibility and disciplinary rules.[177]

Many states have not adopted the proposed Model Rule. As of July 1, 2013, thirty-one states had adopted some version of the Rule.[178] States that have

173. ABA Model Rules for the Licensing and Practice of Foreign Legal Consultants § 1. The Model Rules state that subsection 1(b) is optional.

174. *Id.* § 3.

175. *Id.*

176. *Id.* § 4.

177. *Id.* §§ 5, 6.

178. ABA, *State Implementation of ABA MJP Policies*, July 1, 2013, http://www.americanbar.org/content/dam/aba/administrative/professional_responsibility/recommendations.authcheckdam.pdf. Those jurisdictions include Alaska, Arizona, California, Connecticut, the District of Columbia, Florida, Georgia, Hawaii, Idaho, Illinois, Indiana, Iowa, Louisiana, Massachusetts, Michigan, Minnesota, Missouri, New Jersey, New Mexico, New York, North Carolina, North Dakota, Ohio, Oregon,

adopted the Model Rule have not experienced significant problems, and the ABA Commission on Multijurisdictional Practice continues to urge states to adopt the Rule or a comparable alternative rule.[179]

V. Advertising in Foreign Jurisdictions

Advertising in connection with international estate planning raises a number of ethical issues. First, can a U.S. attorney or firm advertise expertise in foreign law? Second, can an attorney advertise in foreign publications offering assistance regarding legal matters in his or her home jurisdiction? As electronic communications have made it substantially cheaper to advertise one's services in different nations, these issues have gained prominence. Attorneys should be careful to adhere to these rules when engaging in any form of communication or solicitation of their services, including language on a law firm's letterhead.

A. Advertisement of Expertise

Model Rule 7.4 provides rules for most U.S. attorneys regarding claims or advertisements claiming specialization in certain fields of law.[180] Although a lawyer may communicate whether he or she does not practice certain types of law, other than certain intellectual property and admiralty attorneys, lawyers subject to Model Rule 7.4 may not

> state or imply that a lawyer is certified as a specialist in a particular field of law, unless: (1) the lawyer has been certified as a specialist by an organization that has been approved by an appropriate state authority or that has been accredited by the American Bar Association; and (2) the name of the certifying organization is clearly identified in the communication.[181]

Pennsylvania, South Carolina, Texas, Utah, Virginia, and Washington. ABA, CTR. FOR PROF'L RESP., POLICY IMPLEMENTATION COMM., FOREIGN LEGAL CONSULTANT RULES (2010), *available at* http://www.americanbar.org/content/dam/aba/migrated/cpr/mjp/for_legal_consultants.authcheckdam.pdf. See the website of the ABA Commission on Multijurisdictional Practice for useful resources concerning rules affecting foreign legal consultants in different states. ABA Comm'n on Multijurisdictional Practice, http://www.americanbar.org/groups/professional_responsibility/committees_commissions/commission_on_multijurisditional_practice.html (last accessed September 14, 2012).

179. ABA, INTERIM REPORT OF THE COMM'N ON MULTIJURISDICTIONAL PRACTICE 32 (2001). While the Model Rule provided for foreign attorneys to engage in regular legal consulting practice in the United States, the Rule was not considered practical for foreign attorneys who sought to practice in the United States on a limited basis. *Id.* The ABA Interim Committee on Multijurisdictional Practice thus recommended that states adopt a rule providing a means for foreign attorneys to practice in the United States on a temporary basis. *Id.* This recommendation was manifested in the form of amended Rule 5.5, which was discussed in Section IV.B.1.a, above.

180. MODEL RULES OF PROF'L CONDUCT R. 7.4(a).

181. *Id.* R. 7.4(d).

An attorney may thus indicate that he or she provides international estate planning services or will not accept matters in other fields.[182] The attorney may also state that he or she specializes in international planning if such claims are neither false nor misleading.[183] But an attorney cannot state or imply that he or she is *certified* as a specialist in an area of law unless the local licensing authority has approved such certification.[184]

The permissible extent of advertisement of foreign legal expertise has largely been determined by ethics opinions issued by various licensing authorities.[185] It is permissible for an attorney to advertise that he or she is authorized to practice law in jurisdictions in which he or she is actually licensed.[186] Such information cannot be misleading.[187] If an attorney is not licensed in the jurisdiction, he or she can be listed as an adviser regarding the law of a foreign nation, but there must be a statement that clearly indicates that he or she does not practice that nation's law and lists the locations of that attorney's offices.[188] If locally licensed attorneys have foreign offices, those offices may be listed, but the listing must identify the locally licensed attorney who is in charge of those offices and clarify that other attorneys are not licensed in that jurisdiction.[189] A foreign firm may also list a U.S. attorney, but must indicate that the U.S. attorney is not licensed in the foreign nation.[190]

B. Advertising in Foreign Jurisdictions

1. U.S. Laws and Rules

U.S. jurisdictions once imposed heavy restrictions on attorney advertising. According to former Canon 27: "It is unprofessional to solicit professional employment by circulars, advertisements, through touters or by personal communications or interviews not warranted by personal relations."[191] Informal Decision 513 therefore concluded that it would be unethical for attorneys to publish advertisements for their services in a foreign jurisdiction because doing so would constitute impermissible solicitation.[192] This rule extended to foreign attorneys advertising in the United States.[193]

In 1977, in the landmark *Bates v. State Bar of Arizona* case, the U.S. Supreme Court held that attorneys who advertise their services in a nonmisleading way are

182. *Id.* R. 7.4 cmt. 1.
183. *Id.* Rs. 7.4 cmt. 1, 7.1.
184. *Id.* R. 7.4 cmt. 3.
185. Schoenblum, *supra* note 130, § 6.05[B].
186. Los Angeles Bar Ass'n, Formal Op. 392 (1983).
187. Model Rules of Prof'l Conduct R. 7.5(b).
188. ABA Comm. on Ethics & Prof'l Responsibility, Informal Op. 181.
189. *Id.*; ABA Comm. on Ethics & Prof'l Responsibility, Informal Op. 182.
190. ABA Comm. on Ethics & Prof'l Responsibility, Informal Op. 182.
191. Model Code of Prof'l Responsibility Canon 27.
192. ABA Comm. on Ethics & Prof'l Responsibility, Informal Dec. 513 (1962).
193. *Id.*; ABA Comm. on Ethics & Prof'l Responsibility, Informal Op. C-105.

engaged commercial speech, which is entitled to some protection as free speech under the First Amendment to the U.S. Constitution.[194] However, the Court noted that states are free to regulate attorney advertising that is false, deceptive, or misleading or involves illegal transactions. States may also impose reasonable time, place, and manner restrictions on attorney advertising.[195]

The Model Rules take the *Bates* holding into account and, while not discussing geographic limitations, acknowledge the general right of attorneys to advertise their services through all channels of communication.[196] However, such advertising remains subject to other requirements, including the requirement that it not be false or misleading.[197] Additionally, courts have determined that states may regulate advertisements that pertain to the unauthorized practice of law within their jurisdictions, such as a New York attorney who advertises only New York or federal legal services in Florida.[198] A similar analysis would presumably apply to advertising by foreign attorneys in U.S. publications.

2. Foreign Laws and Rules

While specific foreign laws and rules of professional responsibility are beyond the scope of this chapter, international estate planning attorneys should be aware of rules restricting permissible advertising adopted by foreign nations. Such laws may be stricter than those in the United States and will likely not be subject to the same First Amendment free speech restrictions as laws in U.S. jurisdictions. For example, Belgium, Spain, and Italy allow very little attorney advertising other than providing brochures to preexisting clients.[199]

VI. Avoiding Providing Assistance to Criminal and Fraudulent Activities

International estate planners must be on guard and adhere to procedures to protect themselves from civil liability, criminal charges, or ethical sanctions arising from clients who seek to use the planners' services to further fraudulent or criminal conduct. Although all forms of legal practice provide the risk that an attorney will inadvertently provide assistance to unsavory activities, the risk is pronounced in international estate planning. Large international transfers of money and asset protection planning, in particular, are susceptible to abuse by those who are engaged in fraudulent or criminal enterprises. For example, revocable trusts can

194. 433 U.S. 350, 363 (1977).

195. *Id.* at 383.

196. Model. Rules of Prof'l Responsibility R. 7.2(a); *see also* Disc. R. 2-101(b) (allowing attorney advertising in the geographic areas in which the lawyer resides or maintains an office or where a significant part of his or her clients reside).

197. Model. Rules of Prof'l Responsibility Rs. 7.1, 7.2 cmt. 1.

198. *See* Gould v. Fla. Bar, 259 F. App'x 208, 210–11 (11th Cir. 2007).

199. Abel, *supra* note 78, at 758–59.

be useful at certain stages of the money-laundering process.[200] The problem is compounded by murky rules, reticence among estate planning attorneys in keeping abreast of recent developments in money-laundering practices, and overlapping and sometimes inconsistent legal and ethical regimes.[201] Additionally, in many international engagements, estate planners may never have face-to-face meetings with critical parties to a transaction.[202] This increases the susceptibility of the relationship to being utilized for fraudulent ends, especially if the attorney has no preexisting relationship with the client in question.

A. Ethical Restrictions

1. Model Rule 1.2(d)

The Model Rules make it clear that an attorney cannot knowingly counsel a client to commit fraudulent or criminal actions. According to Rule 1.2(d), in determining the scope of the attorney-client relationship,

> [a] lawyer shall not counsel a client to engage, or assist a client, in conduct that the lawyer knows is criminal or fraudulent, but a lawyer may discuss the legal consequences of any proposed course of conduct with a client and may counsel or assist a client to make a good faith effort to determine the validity, scope, meaning or application of the law.[203]

Model Rule 1.2(d) applies even if the defrauded party is not a participant in the transaction.[204] It thus includes both the client's third-party creditors and governments to which the client has tax liabilities.[205] Although an attorney may not advise a client to convey assets to an offshore trust for the purpose of evading known creditors, the attorney may discuss the consequences of such a transfer and can help the client to determine what will constitute a fraudulent transfer. Determining the validity of a statute or regulation may require conduct in violation of a statute, regulation, or government interpretation of a statute or regulation.[206]

Tax planning raises special ethical problems for international estate planners. The United States taxes the worldwide income of its citizens and permanent residents.[207] Some clients may seek to use international planning for the purpose of concealing assets from the jurisdictions in which they may be subject to income

200. Financial Action Task Force (FATF) 2001, at 10. For a detailed examination of the nature and context of the money laundering process, see OECD, Money Laundering Awareness Handbook for Tax Examiners and Tax Auditors (2009), *available at* http://www.oecd.org/tax/exchangeofinformation/43841099.pdf.

201. Bruce Zagaris, *Ethical Issues in Offshore Planning*, SP017 ALI-ABA 365, 2008.

202. Kevin L. Shepherd, *Guardians at the Gate: The Gatekeeper Initiative and the Risk-Based Approach for Transactional Lawyers*, 43 Real Prop. Tr. & Est. L.J. 607 (2009).

203. Model Rules of Prof'l Responsibility 1.2(d).

204. *Id.* R. 1.2 cmt. 12.

205. *Id.*

206. *Id.*

207. I.R.C. §§ 1, 2001(a), 2031, 2501(a); Treas. Reg. § 1.1-1(a)(1).

or transfer taxes. The United States uses a self-assessment system to ensure tax compliance, and attorneys face the constant risk that clients will not disclose all of their assets. Nations have generally stepped up enforcement of their revenue laws in the years following the 2007 financial crisis.[208] Tax attorneys thus need to be careful and exercise diligence to help clients minimize their tax burdens while adhering to their reporting requirements.[209]

One area of concern is the unclear line between legitimate methods of tax minimization and tax crimes. At one time, attorneys had at least some confidence that under the common law revenue rule, U.S. courts would not enforce foreign tax judgments or revenue laws against their clients.[210] That confidence was greatly shaken by the *Pasquantino* decision, in which the U.S. Supreme Court held that the common law revenue rule did not bar a wire fraud prosecution, despite the fact that the prosecution indirectly assisted enforcement of a foreign tax judgment.[211] If a technique for assisting a client in evading foreign tax liabilities violates the terms of a domestic criminal statute, such as RICO or the Computer Fraud and Abuse Act, it is possible that a client's conduct will be deemed fraudulent or criminal under U.S. law. If that is the case, the attorney's active assistance to such a scheme likely violates his or her ethical duties under Rule 1.2(d).

2. Model Rule 4.4(a)

Model Rule 4.4(a) prohibits an attorney from using methods that serve no substantial purpose other than to "embarrass, delay, or burden a third person" to represent a client.[212] It is therefore improper, for example, for an attorney to utilize an offshore estate planning structure in the Cook Islands for the sole purpose of delaying the claim of an existing creditor. Commentary to Model Rule 4.4 notes that attorneys' responsibilities to their clients do not authorize them to disregard the rights of third persons.[213] "It is impractical to catalogue all such rights, but they include legal restrictions on methods of obtaining evidence from third persons and unwarranted intrusions into privileged relationships, such as the client-lawyer relationship."[214]

3. Model Rule 8.4

Model Rule 8.4 specifies that it is professional misconduct for an attorney to:

> (a) violate or attempt to violate the Rules of Professional Conduct, knowingly assist or induce another to do so, or do so through the acts of another;

---

208. SPIELMAN, *supra* note 36, ¶ 2.01 n.1.

209. *Id.*

210. Attorney Gen. of Canada v. R.J. Reynolds Tobacco Holdings, Inc., 268 F.3d 103 (2d Cir. 2001); RESTATEMENT (THIRD) OF THE LAW OF FOREIGN RELATIONS § 483 (1987).

211. Pasquantino v. United States, 544 U.S. 349, 360–70 (2005).

212. MODEL RULES OF PROF'L RESPONSIBILITY R. 4.4(a).

213. *Id.* R. 4.4 cmt. 1.

214. *Id.*

(b) commit a criminal act that reflects adversely on the lawyer's honesty, trustworthiness or fitness as a lawyer in other respects;
(c) engage in conduct involving dishonesty, fraud, deceit or misrepresentation;
(d) engage in conduct that is prejudicial to the administration of justice;
(e) state or imply an ability to influence improperly a government agency or official or to achieve results by means that violate the Rules of Professional Conduct or other law; or
(f) knowingly assist a judge or judicial officer in conduct that is a violation of applicable rules of judicial conduct or other law.[215]

This Rule is broad and covers violations of other professional responsibility rules, in addition to criminal and fraudulent conduct not expressly identified by the Model Rules.

B. The Withdrawal Solution

1. Permissive Withdrawal

If the lawyer knows or reasonably should know that the client expects to receive advice disallowed by the Model Rules, such as assistance with a fraudulent transfer, the attorney must advise the client of the attorney's obligations.[216] The Model Rules provide four relevant circumstances in which an attorney may permissibly withdraw from the attorney-client relationship because of the client's misconduct.

- First, the attorney may withdraw if doing so will not have a materially adverse effect on the client's interests.[217]
- Second, if the client persists in engaging in actions that the lawyer reasonably believes are criminal or fraudulent, the attorney may withdraw from the relationship.[218] It is not necessary that the client's persistence in engaging in future services be directly connected to the lawyer's services, since "a lawyer is not required to be associated with such conduct even if the lawyer does not further it."[219]
- Third, the attorney may withdraw if the client has used the lawyer's services in the past to perpetrate fraudulent or criminal actions.[220] This criterion permits withdrawal even if withdrawal will materially prejudice the client's interests.[221]
- Fourth, the attorney may withdraw if the client insists in acting in a manner that "the lawyer considers repugnant or with which the lawyer has a fundamental disagreement."[222]

---

215. *Id.* R. 8.4.
216. *Id.* R. 1.2 cmt. 13; *see also id.* R. 1.4(a)(5).
217. *Id.* R. 1.16(b)(1).
218. *Id.* R. 1.16(b)(2)
219. *Id.* R. 1.16 cmt. 7.
220. *Id.* R. 1.16(b)(3).
221. *Id.*
222. *Id.* R. 1.16(b)(4).

2. Mandatory Withdrawal

If the attorney-client relationship necessitates violation of the Model Rules or any other law, then the attorney is obligated to not represent the client or to withdraw from representation.[223] But withdrawal is not mandatory simply because the client has suggested criminal or fraudulent conduct.[224] Of course, withdrawal must adhere to the lawyer's other duties under the Model Rules.[225] If a matter involves representation of the client before a tribunal, the tribunal may demand an explanation for the withdrawal. In light of an attorney's duty of confidentiality under Model Rule 1.6, attorneys may be permitted to simply state that the termination was required by professional considerations.[226]

C. Legal Restrictions, the Gatekeeper Initiative, and Voluntary Due Diligence Procedures

In addition to state professional responsibility and disciplinary rules, U.S. attorneys may be subject to other legal requirements. Many of these rules provide further restrictions on attorney conduct, particularly when such conduct risks providing assistance to fraudulent or criminal activities. Attorneys practicing before the IRS or bankruptcy courts have additional rules that they must follow.[227] Many attorneys have been referred to their state bars or sanctioned for assisting clients in committing bankruptcy fraud.[228] U.S. states have also adopted laws making it a crime to assist others in carrying out fraudulent activity.[229] Such assistance can result in discipline.[230]

Finally, attorneys should educate themselves about federal statutes, such as the Bank Secrecy Act, the Anti-Money Laundering Act, and the USA Patriot Act.[231] Such laws have grown in importance in the years since the September 11, 2001, terrorist attacks.[232] Despite the identification of attorneys by the Financial Action Task Force (FATF) as potential gatekeepers for fraudulent and criminal activity,[233] U.S. attorneys are not generally subject to the bank secrecy or anti-

---

223. *Id.* R. 1.16(aa)(1)

224. *Id.* R. 1.15 cmt. 2.

225. *See id.* R. 1.16 cmt. 3.

226. *Id.* R. 1.16 cmt. 3; *see also id.* Rs. 1.6, 3.3.

227. *See* 18 U.S.C. § 152; I.R.C. §§ 7701(a)(36), 6694; I.R.S. Circular 230.

228. *See, e.g.*, *In re* Delcorso, 382 B.R. 240 (Bankr. E.D. Pa. 2007).

229. *See In re* Frank, 556 N.W.2d 717 (Wis. 1996).

230. *See, e.g.*, *In re* Whitbeck, 727 N.Y.S.2d 414 (App. Div. 2001); *In re* Albrecht, 42 P.3d 887 (Or. 2002); Allen v. State Bar, 570 P.2d 1226, 1229 (Cal. 1977).

231. 31 U.S.C. §§ 5311–5332 (Bank Secrecy Act); 18 U.S.C. §§ 1956–1957 (Money Laundering Control Act); USA Patriot Act § 326; 31 C.F.R. pt. 103.

232. Gavin F. Leckie & Anthony E. Woods, Jr., *Ethical Issues in Offshore Planning*, SJ027 ALI-ABA 221; Am. Bar Ass'n, Task Force on Gatekeeper Regulation and the Profession, *Voluntary Good Practices Guidance for Lawyers to Detect and Combat Money Laundering and Terrorist Financing* 6 (2010); Terry Christensen III, *Developments in the Application to Lawyers of Anti-Money Laundering Initiatives Around the World*, 39 U. of Miami Law Center's Heckerling Inst. on Estate Planning 18 (2005).

233. FATF, 40 Recommendations (2004).

money-laundering statutes and regulations. However, given the other ethical and legal obligations of U.S. attorneys to not assist fraudulent or criminal activity, it is advisable for estate planning attorneys to engage in due diligence and put procedures in place to protect themselves from participation in illegitimate enterprises. Voluntary guidance can be found in the risk-based approach of the FATF's 2008 Lawyer Guidance.

1. FATF and the Gatekeeper Initiative

The FATF is a supranational organization composed of thirty-four member states and two regional organizations, representing most of the major world financial centers.[234] The United States is a founding member, but the Task Force is international in scope.[235] The FATF was initially created to fight international money-laundering activity, but has since broadened its focus to include the fight against terror financing.[236] It has created a number of recommendations and guidelines to assist practitioners in avoiding using their services to further money laundering and terrorism. Although such initiatives are not legally binding on member states, the recommendations have proven highly influential, especially in the United States, because members do not want to be excluded from the process.[237]

The FATF adopted the 40+9 Recommendations in 1990 and has amended them several times.[238] The recommendations generally involve high-level guidance to ensure that professionals do not assist others in engaging in money-laundering or terror-financing activities.[239] Attorneys generally fall within the scope of the initiative's "gatekeeper" recommendations, which are directed to professionals who are in a position to facilitate or prevent laundering and terror-financing activities. Compliance with the procedures is not mandatory for U.S. lawyers at this time.[240] However, in addition to demonstrating the growing intrusion of extra-disciplinary regulations on attorneys' conduct, the Recommendations provide helpful voluntary guidelines that attorneys may use to ensure that they adhere to their professional and legal obligations. Yet the recommendations remain somewhat abstract and are not readily applicable to specific situations faced by lawyers on a day-to-day basis.

2. Conflict between Confidentiality and Suspicious Activity Reporting

Model Rule 1.6 provides that "[a] lawyer shall not reveal information relating to the representation of a client unless the client gives informed consent, the disclosure is impliedly authorized in order to carry out the representation or the

234. Laurel S. Terry, *An Introduction to the Financial Action Task Force and its 2008 Lawyer Guidance*, 2010 Prof. Law. 3 (2010).

235. *Id.*

236. *Id.*

237. *Id.*

238. FATF, 40 Recommendations (2003) [hereinafter Recommendations].

239. *Id.*

240. Paul D. Paton, *Cooperation, Co-option or Coercion? The FATF Lawyer Guidance and Regulation of the Legal Profession*, 2010 Prof. Law. 165 (2010).

disclosure is permitted by paragraph (b)."[241] This prohibition includes disclosure not only of protected information but also of information that could allow a third party to reasonably discover protected information.[242] Additionally, state and federal rules of evidence generally provide that attorney-client communications are entitled to testimonial privilege, with some exceptions.[243]

Paragraph (b) provides a number of relevant exceptions to Model Rule 1.6's confidentiality rule, the most relevant of which to this topic include the so-called "crime fraud exception." Rule 1.6(b)(2) provides that disclosure is permissible if a lawyer reasonably believes disclosure is necessary

> to prevent the client from committing a crime or fraud that is reasonably certain to result in substantial injury to the financial interests or property of another and in furtherance of which the client has used or is using the lawyer's services.[244]

The exception applies to reasonably certain future misconduct.[245] Serious abuses of the attorney-client relationship generally forfeit protection by Rule 1.6.[246] In such situations, the client can prevent disclosure by not engaging in the problematic activity.[247]

Rule 1.6(b)d) provides that disclosure is permissible if a lawyer believes disclosure is necessary

> to prevent, mitigate or rectify substantial injury to the financial interests or property of another that is reasonably certain to result or has resulted from the client's commission of a crime or fraud in furtherance of which the client has used the lawyer's services . . . .[248]

This exception applies to conduct that the attorney discovers after it has already been committed.[249] At that point, the attorney has no means of dissuading a client from committing the misconduct, but disclosure may nonetheless prevent or miti-

241. Model Rules of Prof'l Conduct R. 1.6(a).

242. *Id.* R. 1.6 cmt. 4.

243. *Id.* R. 1.6 cmt. 3; *see also, e.g.*, Fed. R. Evid. 501 ("The common law—as interpreted by United States courts in the light of reason and experience—governs a claim of privilege unless any of the following provides otherwise: the United States Constitution; a federal statute; or rules prescribed by the Supreme Court."); Upjohn Co. v. United States, 449 U.S. 383, 388 (1981) ("The attorney-client privilege is the oldest of the privileges for confidential communications known to the common law. Its purpose is to encourage full and frank communication between attorneys and their clients and thereby promote broader public interests in the observance of law and administration of justice. The privilege recognizes that sound legal advice or advocacy serves public ends and that such advice or advocacy depends upon the lawyer's being fully informed by the client.") (citations omitted).

244. *Id.* R. 1.6(b)(2).

245. *Id.* R. 1.6 cmt. 7.

246. *Id.*

247. *Id.*

248. *Id.* R. 1.6(b)(3).

249. *Id.* R. 1.6 cmt. 8.

gate the resulting harm.[250] The lawyer may disclose confidential information to the extent necessary to prevent or mitigate the harm.[251] However, this exception does not apply to situations in which a client engages an attorney regarding an offense after it has already occurred.[252] It is therefore improper for an attorney to disclose information (without the client's informed consent) regarding a new client who is a U.S. citizen and hires the attorney to assist with the problem of offshore assets that have not been properly disclosed to the IRS.

These exceptions are permissive, not mandatory.[253] An attorney may break confidentiality to prevent a crime or fraud but is not ethically required to do so. However, an attorney is still prohibited from advising or assisting a client in committing criminal or fraudulent activity.[254] If an exception applies, the attorney may only disclose information to the extent necessary to rectify the purpose of the exception.[255] Before disclosing confidential information, the attorney should attempt to persuade the client to take action to prevent the necessity of disclosure.[256]

The primary source of controversy regarding the application of FATF recommendations to U.S. attorneys stems from the possible conflict between the gatekeeper recommendations and U.S. attorneys' professional obligation to maintain client confidentiality under Rule 1.6.[257] The Recommendations acknowledge the importance of attorney-client confidentiality and privilege.[258] However, they also require attorneys to engage in suspicious transaction reporting (STR).[259] A number of commentators, including the ABA, have expressed concern that STR obligations may require violations of Model Rule 1.6.[260]

---

250. *Id.*
251. *Id.*
252. *Id.*
253. *Id.* R. 1.6 cmt. 17.
254. *Id.* Rs. 1.6 cmt. 7, 1.2(d), 1.16.
255. *Id.* R. 1.6 cmt. 16.
256. *Id.*
257. Terry, *supra* note 234.
258. FATF, RBA Guidance for Legal Professionals ¶¶ 6 ("The provisions contained in this Guidance, when applied by each country, are subject to professional secrecy and legal professional privilege."), 16 ("The provisions in this Guidance are subject to applicable professional secrecy, legal professional privilege or rules of professional conduct, which are determined by each country.") (2008), *available at* http://www.fatf-gafi.org/media/fatf/documents/reports/RBA%20Legal%20 professions.pdf [hereinafter 2008 Lawyer Guidance].
259. Recommendations, *supra* note 238.
260. *E.g.*, ABA Policies Relevant to the FATF—The ABA's 2003 and 2008 Resolutions and the 2003 Joint Statement American Bar Association Task Force on Gatekeeper Regulation and the Profession Section of Real Property, Probate and Trust Law Criminal Justice Section, Section of Litigation Section of International Law and Practice Report to the House of Delegates Recommendation #104 (2003).

Mandatory STR mandated by Recommendations 13 through 16 has substantial tension with Model Rule 1.6.[261] Recommendation 13 requires that a financial institution that suspects or has reasonable grounds to suspect that funds are related to criminal or terrorist activity must notify a financial intelligence unit of its suspicions.[262] STR arguably interferes with the policy underlying Model Rule 1.6 by deterring clients from providing full and accurate information to their attorneys for fear that an attorney will disclose embarrassing or legally damaging information.[263] Without such information, attorneys cannot provide effective representation to their clients or be in a position to dissuade their clients from engaging in improper conduct.[264] Additionally, Recommendation 14 provides a "no tipping off" policy, which prevents an attorney from attempting to persuade a client to not engage in or rectify the consequences of misconduct.[265]

3. 2008 Lawyer Guidance and Due Diligence/ "Know Your Client" Procedures

In 2008, the FATF adopted the more specific 2008 Lawyer Guidance.[266] The 2008 Guidance focuses on risk-assessment techniques relevant to the attorney-client relationship. Rather than resolve the controversy of balancing STR obligations against attorney-client confidentiality and privilege, the 2008 Lawyer Guidance omitted STR requirements.[267]

U.S. attorneys are not currently required to adhere to the guidelines provided by the 2008 Lawyer Guidance. If an attorney adheres to all applicable statutes, court rules, regulations, and disciplinary and professional responsibility rules, he or she is generally safe from liability or sanctions. However, the Model Rules do not always provide specific advice for how attorneys should handle various situations in which it is unclear whether the representation violates the attorney's ethical or legal responsibilities. In an international estate planning context, an attorney may never directly meet with clients or other important parties to a transaction. Clients may also disclose information to the attorney on a "need-to-know" basis, making it more difficult for the attorney to assess whether his or her services are being used to commit fraud. In such situations, it may be helpful for U.S. attorneys to voluntarily adhere to procedures suggested by the FATF's 2008

261. *Id.*; Shepherd, *supra* note 202, at 636–37 (citing 40 Recommendations, at 8; 12 C.F.R. § 21.11 (mandating Suspicious Activity Reports, which are the corresponding requirement for depository financial institutions under Bank Secrecy Act)).

262. Recommendations, *supra* note 238, at 8.

263. *See* Model Rules of Prof'l Responsibility R. 1.6 cmt. 2.

264. *Id.*

265. *See* Recommendations, *supra* note 238, at 8.

266. See FATF, RBA Guidance for Legal Professionals (2008), *available at* http://www.fatf-gafi.org/media/fatf/documents/reports/RBA%20Legal%20professions.pdf [hereinafter 2008 Lawyer Guidance].

267. *Id.* ¶ 120 ("STRs are not part of risk assessment, but rather reflect a response mechanism—typically to an SRO or government enforcement authority—once a suspicion of money laundering has been identified."); Shepherd, *supra* note 202, at nn. 157–164.

Lawyer Guidance to ensure that their practice is consistent with their professional and legal obligations. These guidelines include the FATF's risk-based approach to due diligence (also known as "know your client" procedures), bookkeeping, training, and other practical procedures. These practices should minimize the risk of inadvertently violating Model Rule 1.2(d).

The 2008 Lawyer Guidance identifies two different approaches to the problem of how to prevent gatekeepers from assisting criminal and terrorist activities.[268] The rule-based approach requires the rote application of rules to situations and typically involves some form of "box ticking," in which a professional goes down a checklist to ensure the propriety of a professional engagement.[269] In contrast, a risk-based approach acknowledges that limited resources exist to combat money-laundering and terrorist activities and attempts to allocate resources based on the level of risk associated with different practices and situations.[270] The 2008 Lawyer Guidance provides a risk-based approach to lawyers as gatekeepers, using different variables to determine the appropriate level of due diligence, training, and record keeping necessary for each type of engagement, client, or transaction. Ideally, more resources will be focused on activities that have a higher probability of providing assistance to money-laundering activities or terrorism finance.

(a) Five Services to which Lawyer Guidance Applies. From the outset, the Lawyer Guidance is limited to attorneys who prepare for and carry out five types of activities:

1. buying and selling real estate;
2. managing client money, securities, or other assets;
3. managing bank, savings, or securities accounts,;
4. organizing contributions for the creation, operation, or management of companies; and
5. creating, operating, or managing legal persons or arrangements and buying and selling business entities.[271]

Many international estate planning attorneys will fall into one of these categories, particularly the fifth category, which includes the creation of and administration of trusts.[272]

(b) Three Risk Categories. As noted above, the necessary amount of due diligence, training, and record keeping for each firm, client, engagement, and transaction depends on a risk assessment of each situation, rather than the mechanical application of rules to facts. If an attorney falls into one of the covered categories,

268. 2008 Lawyer Guidance, *supra* note 266, ¶¶ 18–26.
269. *Id.*
270. *Id.*
271. *Id.*
272. Shepherd, *supra* note 202, at 648

he or she must then evaluate three risk categories for each engagement. These categories determine the general level of risk to which an attorney is subject by engaging in his or her practice. The major risk categories are (1) country/ geographic risk, (2) client risk, and (3) service risk. These categories, as well as the additional variables listed below, will determine what resources an attorney should commit to determining the legitimacy of a particular engagement.[273]

(i) Country/geographic risk. The level of risk may vary depending on the nations and geographic regions relevant to a transaction or engagement. Although the category is not absolute (legitimate transactions can emerge from high-risk countries and vice versa), the FATF has taken steps to identify lower- and higher-risk countries and areas. Some nations have been profiled as having higher risks of being the source or destination for funds derived from criminal activities. Such nations may be subject to U.N. sanctions, embargoes, or similar measures. Attorneys can utilize information from credible sources to determine whether a nation has inadequate bank secrecy or anti-money-laundering laws or has a higher prevalence of corruption, crime, or terrorist activity and financing.

(ii) Client risk. While every client has the potential to engage in money laundering or terror financing, certain clients are more likely to increase the risk of supporting criminal or terrorist activities than others. Examples of high-risk clients include the following:

- politically exposed persons residing in foreign nations,
- clients with cash-intensive businesses,
- unregulated nonprofit organizations,
- new clients,
- clients who have not had face-to-face meetings with the attorney,
- clients who have been convicted of or charged with criminal activities in the past,
- clients who request unusual legal services or legal structures that make it difficult to identify an asset's true beneficial owner or an entity's controlling interest,
- clients who request legal acts, entities, or arrangements that appear to lack any legal or legitimate tax, business, economic, or other motivation,
- clients who have multiple addresses without legitimate reasons, and
- clients who utilize professionals who are not subject to anti-money-laundering or bank secrecy laws or have little experience with the type of services being requested.

(iii) Service risk. Some services carry a higher risk of abuse than others. The riskiest services involve the international movement of funds, the concealment of

273. *Id.* at 651.

the beneficial ownership of assets from authorities, or both. Other services associated with increased risk include the following:

- those involving money transfer businesses and facilities,
- those involving attorneys who touch assets without knowing their source or destination,
- those in which the client knows the attorney lacks the relevant expertise and in which there is no referral to a specialist,
- those involving the transfer of real estate in an unusually short time, and
- transactions with no apparent business or economic purpose.

(c) Other Variables. After assessing the general level of risk based on the three risk categories, attorneys should then examine additional variables that may increase or decrease the risk of assisting criminal or terrorist activity. A transaction that initially seems safe might raise a greater risk based on these factors or vice versa. These factors include the following variables:

- the nature of the specific attorney-client relationship and the reason the client needs a lawyer,
- the level of regulation or oversight or the governance regime to which the client is subject,
- the reputation and publicly available information regarding the client,
- the regularity and duration of the attorney-client relationship, and
- the proportionality between the volume and longevity of the client's past business and the present use of the lawyer's legal services.

Asset Protection Trusts

20

Gideon Rothschild*

I. Introduction

Although the use of the so-called "offshore" trust as a vehicle to protect assets from creditors has often been cited as a relatively recent phenomenon, in fact, offshore jurisdictions have long been favored over domestic jurisdictions for various asset protection purposes. Most notably, offshore trusts have been used to escape domestic political strife, exchange controls, forced heirship provisions, and confiscatory government action or to obtain favorable tax benefits—all of which can, to some extent, be considered to be "asset protection" purposes. Today's offshore asset protection trusts, however, are at least as likely to be created for the purpose of obtaining leverage against future private creditors as for these other purposes because such trusts can provide significant procedural, substantive, and psychological barriers that impact upon a private creditor's ability to attach a debtor's assets. For individuals resident in stable political and economic jurisdictions, such as the United States, leverage against private creditors is probably the most common use of the offshore asset protection trust today. The offshore trust is

* Gideon Rothschild is a partner at Moses & Singer LLP. The author gratefully acknowledges Daniel S. Rubin, a partner at Moses & Singer LLP, for his assistance in preparing this chapter. A prior version of this chapter appears in TRUSTS IN PRIME JURISDICTIONS (3d ed. Globe Business Publishing Ltd.), and permission to reproduce is granted with all rights reserved.

unique to asset protection planning since, if established in one of a number of jurisdictions that have repealed the common law prohibition against self-settled spendthrift trusts, the settlor can name himself as a discretionary beneficiary of the trust while at the same time protecting the trust corpus from the claims of future creditors. Thus the settlor is relieved from the traditional dilemma inherent in having permanently and completely to divest himself of property in order to protect it from potential future creditors.

Although thirteen states in the United States to date have followed suit in repealing the self-settled trust rule, the U.S. Constitution and public policy considerations in those states that have not repealed the rule make it questionable whether trusts established under the law of such domestic jurisdictions will provide significant asset protection in the event of an aggressive creditor challenge. Of course, as an asset protection device, the more traditional domestic trust (as well as an outright transfer of property) remains viable where the settlor, for whatever reason, desires to transfer irrevocably his property for the benefit of another. Where the named beneficiaries include the settlor's spouse, the transferred property can potentially be used for the indirect benefit of the settlor, provided, of course, that neither a divorce nor the spouse's untimely death intervenes. In the past, however, such asset protection planning techniques were used because no viable alternative existed. Today, those who are at substantial risk (e.g., real estate developers, corporate directors, doctors, lawyers, and others who may be viewed as having "deep pockets") and who are willing to incur the greater costs associated with the offshore trust settlement have the viable alternative of protecting their assets in an offshore self-settled spendthrift trust.

As the use of offshore trusts for asset protection purposes has become increasingly prevalent in recent years, a basic understanding of the law governing such entities has become *de rigeur* for professionals practicing in this area of the law and providing advice across a broad spectrum of disciplines. This chapter provides the reader with a grounding in the law relating to offshore asset protection trusts.

II. Benefits of Offshore Asset Protection Trusts

A. Creditor Protection

A trust, whether foreign or domestic, is uniquely geared to providing asset protection to its beneficiaries since the very concept of the trust involves a division between the legal (i.e., administrative or managerial) and the beneficial ownership of property. Specifically, a trust imposes a fiduciary relationship with respect to property, subjecting the title holder (the trustee) to equitable duties to deal with the property for the benefit of another (the beneficiary). Pursuant to this important distinction, and in accordance with the legal maxim of *cujus est dare, ejus est disponere* (whose it is to give, his it is to dispose), most courts will recognize a trust provision purporting to restrain the alienation of the beneficial trust interest, either voluntarily by the trust beneficiary or involuntarily by his creditors. Such a provision is called a "spendthrift provision," and such a trust is called a "spendthrift trust," although it is important to note that whether the beneficiary is actually a spendthrift is immaterial to the protection afforded. Notwithstanding the wide recognition of spendthrift trust protections where one individual establishes a trust for the benefit of another, an exception is often made on public policy grounds for the so-called "self-settled" spendthrift trust, which is a trust in which the settlor retains for himself an interest as a beneficiary, even if it is only a potential to receive distributions from the trust within the discretion of an independent, third-party trustee. The principal underlying such limitation (where it exists) is that it is against public policy to allow an individual to tie up his property in such a way that he can still enjoy it but can prevent his creditors from reaching it. Significantly, this is the case whether the settlor's creditors are present or future, reasonably anticipated or impossible to foresee, as an intent in the settlor to defraud creditors is not required to invalidate a self-settled spendthrift trust in such jurisdictions. The settlor of a trust, however, may designate the law of any jurisdiction as governing the administration of his trust and hence may designate a jurisdiction that recognizes self-settled spendthrift trusts as valid even if the settlor's domicile does not. Moreover, under established rules relating to conflict of laws, including the Hague Convention on the Law Applicable to Trusts and on their Recognition and the Restatement (Third) of the Law of Conflict of Laws, the settlor's designation of governing law should be respected, both domestically and internationally, regardless of venue. Notwithstanding the foregoing, however, case law indicates that particularly egregious cases (generally those that implicate fraudulent conveyance or sham trust arguments) are unlikely to withstand a spirited attack on public policy grounds in the settlor's domicile.

Beyond having repealed the self-settled spendthrift trust rule, however, an offshore trust geared toward asset protection should be sited in a jurisdiction that has also statutorily modified the Statute of Elizabeth. The Statute of Elizabeth, which was enacted in England in 1571 and now forms the basis of fraudulent transfer law throughout most of the common law system, renders void any transfer made with an intent to defeat, delay, or hinder any creditor. Because the Statute of Elizabeth sets a very low threshold relating to the imputation of fraudulent intent and contains no set period of limitations within which a creditor must bring a fraudulent conveyance claim, no real asset protection can be obtained in a jurisdiction in which the Statute of Elizabeth is in force. In contrast, a jurisdiction that has statutorily repealed the Statute of Elizabeth will typically provide for a short limitations period and will limit the potential to impute, from the circumstances surrounding the transfer, the intent required for finding that the settlor has made a fraudulent conveyance.

It is also important that an offshore asset protection trust be sited in a jurisdiction which denies judicial comity to foreign judgments that conflict with the substantive law of the jurisdiction. In the absence of this facet of asset protection law, a judgment rendered in the trust settlor's domicile on fraudulent conveyance grounds could potentially be filed and then enforced in the offshore jurisdiction without ever implicating the otherwise protective asset protection laws of that offshore jurisdiction.

Finally, aside from the United States, most common law jurisdictions:

- do not allow attorneys to take matters based on a contingency fee; and
- provide that the losing party to a lawsuit must pay all of the prevailing party's expenses, including attorneys' fees.

Combined with an evidentiary standard in some asset protection jurisdictions that requires proof beyond a reasonable doubt on fraudulent conveyance claims, assets held in trust may, in the end, be unreachable. At a minimum, the process of litigating such a claim in an offshore jurisdiction may prove prohibitively expensive for a creditor when the potential reward is so uncertain. The aggregate of these factors will likely provide the settlor of an offshore asset protection trust with significant leverage against his creditors.

B. Estate Planning

Since the settlor of an offshore asset protection trust will almost always be named as a discretionary beneficiary of the trust (since preservation of the trust estate would generally be as well served onshore if the trust were not, in fact, self-settled), the trust will normally be structured so that its funding is an "incomplete gift" for U.S. transfer tax purposes. As an incomplete gift, no transfer tax is imposed upon the funding of the trust. A gift to the trust will be deemed complete for transfer tax purposes if the settlor has parted with dominion and control over the gifted property so as to leave the settlor with no power to change the disposition of the trust property. Conversely, U.S. Treasury Regulations provide that a gift will be deemed incomplete if and to the extent a reserved power gives the settlor the power to name new beneficiaries or to change the interest of the beneficiaries as between themselves (provided, however, that the power is not a fiduciary power limited by a fixed or ascertainable standard). Pursuant to this guidance, a self-settled, spendthrift trust structured so that its funding constitutes an incomplete gift will typically reserve a power of appointment to the settlor. The retained power should, however, be carefully circumscribed so that its existence does not have the inadvertent effect of opening up the trust to claims of the settlor's creditors. Therefore, the power should be limited to a select class of beneficiaries (i.e., the settlor's descendants) and to a testamentary exercise so as to avoid the potential argument that the settlor retained an excessive amount of control over the trust during life. If the settlor is not the sole beneficiary of the trust, then he should also retain a veto power over distributions to avoid a completed gift challenge.

In the alternative, if it is unlikely (although not impossible) that the settlor will ever need a distribution from the trust, the offshore asset protection trust would be better structured if its funding were a completed gift (albeit at a current gift tax cost for transfers exceeding the tax-exempt amount, which is currently $5 million). As a completed gift, the trust corpus as well as any post-transfer appreciation thereon will not be included in the settlor's estate when the settlor dies, notwithstanding that the settlor can, in the interim, receive distributions from the trust within the discretion of the trustees. Aside from the estate planning benefit, however, a trust structured in this manner gains an additional asset protection benefit since the settlor can then defend against a creditor's fraudulent conveyance attack by demonstrating that the trust was funded for an estate tax benefit rather than to hinder, delay, or defraud the settlor's creditors.

Most domestic trusts, however, cannot confer this estate planning benefit because the U.S. estate tax regime will deem a trust includable in the settlor's estate to the extent the settlor's creditors can access the trust. This is so the settlor is considered to have retained to himself, at least indirectly, the "use and enjoyment" of the transferred assets because his creditors can look to the trust corpus in satisfaction of their claims against the settlor. In the same vein, however, if the trust is sited in a jurisdiction where the settlor's creditors cannot reach the trust assets (i.e., a jurisdiction that has repealed the self-settled spendthrift trust rule), then the gift will be complete for U.S. federal transfer tax purposes notwithstanding the fact that the trustees have discretion to make distributions to the settlor.

Because many offshore trust jurisdictions have also repealed the common law rule against perpetuities, an additional estate planning benefit can be obtained by creating a perpetual offshore asset protection trust and then allocating a sufficient amount of the settlor's unused generation-skipping transfer tax exemption to the trust. Properly structured, such a "dynasty" trust will preserve the transferred assets as well as any accumulations thereto, free from creditors of both the settlor and the settlor's descendants, including all tax authorities. Generally, such a trust would provide that to the extent possible, the trust corpus would be preserved for the benefit of the beneficiaries rather than being distributed to the beneficiaries. For example, the trust could purchase a home for a beneficiary to live in rent-free rather than distribute corpus to that beneficiary and thus enable the beneficiary to purchase a home in his own name. In this manner, the home will never be subject to the beneficiary's creditors (including an ex-spouse of the beneficiary), and will not be taxed as a part of the beneficiary's estate when the beneficiary ultimately dies.

C. Foreign Investment

As noted in the previous section regarding estate planning, the question of whether an offshore asset protection trust will be able to withstand creditor attack will depend, in part, on the strength of the creditor's fraudulent conveyance claim, which in turn will depend, in part, on the settlor's intent in creating the trust. In this regard, any evidence the settlor can proffer that demonstrates an intent other than to avoid creditors may prove critical to preserving the trust. If the settlor cannot afford (or otherwise does not wish) to structure the offshore asset protection trust as a completed gift, the estate tax benefits of the trust may be insignificant. Therefore, the settlor may have to look to the unique opportunities that an offshore trust provides for foreign investment (which may not be available to U.S. residents) in order to provide the "good" intent necessary to defend against a fraudulent conveyance claim. The vast majority of offshore investment opportunities are unavailable to onshore entities because such investments choose not to meet the relatively strict U.S. regulatory requirements relating to public investments. As a consequence, certain offshore investments are arguably more attractive than domestic investments, in part because they have the potential to earn higher returns than similar onshore investments that must bear the substantial costs of complying with domestic regulation of public investments.

D. Confidentiality

A legitimate offshore asset protection trust need not operate by means of secreting assets. In fact, it is questionable whether any asset protection benefit is obtained by secreting assets, since concealment of assets from creditors is one of the badges of fraud that may be used to impute fraudulent conveyance intent. Notwithstanding the foregoing, however, confidentiality is often an important consideration in choosing to create an offshore asset protection trust or in choosing the particular jurisdiction in which to settle the trust. To the extent that a settlor's legitimate desire for confidentiality can be distinguished from an impermissible effort to secrete assets from creditors, this beneficent aspect of the offshore asset protection trust should not be deemed a badge of fraud. An offshore asset protection trust provides confidentiality to its beneficiaries primarily by reason of the natural division between the beneficial and legal ownership of the trust structure; since assets are held in the name of the trustees, in a fiduciary capacity, rather than in the name of any one or more of the beneficiaries, the beneficial ownership of the assets is hidden from casual observance. For the beneficial ownership of the assets to be discovered, generally, a copy of the trust document must be reviewed—and the trust document is not a public document. Onshore, the use of revocable living trusts as a substitute for a will is a common example of how a trust provides confidentiality to the settlor. Additional confidentiality can be obtained if the trust assets are held by a nominee on behalf of the trustees or in the name of a corporation or other business entity, which, in turn, is wholly owned by the trust.

In fact, the trust instrument could legitimately provide that the trustees have no obligation to furnish even the trust beneficiaries with any information relating to the trust's holdings (although it may be deemed to violate public policy to limit the trustees' obligation to provide such information to the settlor). Certainly, however, the trustees are under no obligation to reveal information concerning the trust to any nongovernmental third party (e.g., the settlor's creditors). In addition, offshore asset protection trusts will likely provide greater confidentiality than will onshore trusts since most offshore centers that wish to attract significant trust business have made it a criminal offense to divulge information relating to the establishment, constitution, or business affairs of an offshore trust.

E. Avoidance of Forced Heirship

"Forced heirship" (including a right of election in a surviving spouse) is the legal right of a family member to claim an interest in the estate of a decedent despite the fact that the decedent desired to exclude the family member under his dispositive testamentary documents. Even though property held in trust is, for most purposes, not considered to be part of the decedent's probate estate, many domestic jurisdictions will deem the trust a "testamentary substitute" subject to the jurisdiction's forced heirship provisions as though the trust corpus were, in fact, a part of the decedent's probate estate. Although an offshore asset protection trust will also likely be deemed a testamentary substitute in the decedent's domicile, assets held in an offshore trust may avoid a forced heirship if neither the trust nor the property held therein can be claimed subject to the jurisdiction of the domestic court. In addition, the law of the offshore jurisdiction will likely override the forced heirship claim in the deceased settlor's domicile.

III. Jurisdictional Issues

A. Common Law Versus Civil Law

The trust concept, rooted in equity, is a product of the common law legal system and is distinct from the civil law system, which does not generally recognize the trust concept. For this reason, the vast majority of asset protection trusts are created within a jurisdiction governed by common law principles. Notwithstanding the fact that the trust is not native to the civil law, several civil law jurisdictions have enacted legislation that attempts to append the trust concept to their legal system. Although these civil law jurisdictions will, ostensibly, recognize the offshore asset protection trust, complications that may arise by reason of a general unfamiliarity with the trust concept inherent in a civil law jurisdiction will likely warrant the use of a similarly protective jurisdiction with a common law tradition.

B. Effect of Retained Interests and Powers

Retained interests and powers, for various reasons—including an innate distrust of an unknown offshore trustee—often are made a prerequisite to the settlor's agreement to settle the trust. Unfortunately, the retention of control has a direct, inverse relationship to asset protection. For example, the most control (i.e., the settlor retaining the assets in his own name) provides the least amount of asset protection. At the other extreme, were the settlor to transfer his assets to a non-self-settled trust with an independent corporate fiduciary overseen by an independent corporate protector, he would obtain the most asset protection. Between these two extremes, the settlor's creditors are afforded various arguments with which to attack either the validity of the trust or the settlor himself. In this regard, to the extent the settlor remains within the jurisdiction of the domestic court rather than expatriating at the first sign of a creditor attack, the settlor must rely upon the trust's anti-duress clause and his own impossibility of performance to protect him from the specter of being held in contempt for failing to repatriate the trust's assets. Since the burden of proving impossibility of performance is upon the settlor, case law has demonstrated that to the extent the settlor has exercised control over the trust until entry of the court's order, the settlor will be hard-pressed to prove a current inability to the court in an effort to avoid punishment for contempt.

C. Effect of Statute of Elizabeth

The Statute of Elizabeth was enacted in England in 1571 as a compilation of prior English common law on fraudulent conveyance. More than four centuries later, the Statute of Elizabeth still provides the basis for the prohibition on fraudulent conveyances throughout the entire common law system, including the United States. The Statute of Elizabeth provides that transfers made with the intent to hinder, delay, or defraud creditors of the transferor are voidable. Although the statute requires that the debtor's actual intent be proved, it was recognized early on that very few debtors would admit to such an intent. The courts have therefore deemed a number of facts as so-called "badges of fraud," which, when aggregated in sufficient number, will be deemed to provide proof of the debtor's intent. Some badges of fraud heretofore recognized by the courts include:

- the transfer was to an insider;
- the debtor retained possession or control of the transferred property;
- the transfer was concealed;
- the debtor had been sued or threatened with suit prior to the transfer;
- the transfer consisted of all or substantially all of the debtor's assets;
- the debtor absconded;
- the debtor removed or concealed assets;
- the value of the consideration received by the debtor was not reasonably equivalent to the assets transferred;
- the debtor was insolvent at the time of the transfer, or the debtor was thereby rendered insolvent; and
- the transfer occurred at the same time that a substantial debt was incurred.

The Statute of Elizabeth does not distinguish between existing creditors and future creditors, provided, of course, that the requisite fraudulent intent exists and can be sufficiently proved. Similarly, the Uniform Fraudulent Conveyance Act and the Uniform Fraudulent Transfer Act (which in the aggregate form the law of fraudulent conveyance in the majority of the United States) both allow a fraudulent conveyance claim by a future creditor (again, provided the transfer was made with the actual intent to hinder, delay, or defraud, which is likely a more difficult proposition for future creditors to prove). A major difference between pure Statute of Elizabeth jurisdictions and Uniform Fraudulent Conveyance/Transfer Act jurisdictions exists, however, with regard to the limitations period within which a creditor must bring his claim: no limitations period exists under the Statute of Elizabeth, but Uniform Fraudulent Conveyance/Transfer Act jurisdictions generally provide for a limitations period of four years or one year from discovery, whichever is greater.

1. Comity Issues

Under principles of judicial comity, the courts of one jurisdiction will often give effect to the judicial decisions of another jurisdiction as a matter of deference and mutual respect. The "full faith and credit" clause of the U.S. Constitution—which provides, in pertinent part, that "Full Faith and Credit shall be given in each State to the public Acts, Records and judicial Proceedings of every other State"—is a clear example of a codification of the principle of judicial comity. Since the principle of judicial comity is effective both domestically and internationally, its potential application by an offshore asset protection jurisdiction in favor of the jurisdiction of the settlor's domicile would vitiate any certainty that asset protection can be achieved through the creation of an asset protection trust in such jurisdiction. Therefore, it is important that the trust be settled in a jurisdiction that has negated the potential application of judicial comity through a statute providing that foreign judgments are unenforceable when the foreign judgment conflicts with the substantive law of such jurisdiction. For example, the International Trusts Act 1984 of the Cook Islands provides that no proceedings for or in relation to the enforcement of a foreign judgment against a trust may be brought in a Cook Islands court if the judgment is based upon the application of law inconsistent with that Act.

2. Tax Laws and Exchange Controls

In the increasingly competitive market for offshore asset protection business, most (but not all) offshore asset protection jurisdictions exempt from taxation trusts settled by nonresidents; those jurisdictions recognize that the local services used by such trusts necessarily provide a much more lucrative benefit to the local economy than does a direct tax on the trusts themselves. Therefore, the offshore asset protection trust should be settled in a no-tax jurisdiction. Similarly, the trust should be settled in a jurisdiction that does not impose exchange controls.

3. Selected Offshore Jurisdictions with Favorable Asset Protection Laws

Many offshore jurisdictions have adopted legislation to obtain a piece of the asset protection trust pie, but considerable differences exist among jurisdictions. The first jurisdiction to enact such legislation was the Cook Islands (in the

South Pacific) when it passed the International Trusts Act 1984. With subsequent amendments to the Act made in 1985, 1989, 1991, 1995 to 1996, and 1999, the Cook Islands is generally considered to remain the foremost offshore asset protection jurisdiction, notwithstanding that its notoriety in this regard may, in the eyes of some planners, be considered to detract from the asset protection a Cook Islands asset protection trust can provide. At least twenty-two jurisdictions have either statutory or common law that encourages the use of trusts to protect assets from creditors, those jurisdictions being: Anguilla, Antigua, Bahamas, Barbados, Belize, Bermuda, Cayman Islands, Cook Islands, Cyprus, Gibraltar, Guernsey, Jersey, Labuan, Liechtenstein, Marshall Islands, Mauritius, Niue, Nevis, St. Vincent and the Grenadines, St. Lucia, Seychelles, and Turks and Caicos Islands.

The planner must select the jurisdiction in which to establish the trust by analyzing numerous factors about the jurisdiction, including:

- the jurisdiction's legal system and specific trust law;
- political and economic stability;
- tax laws;
- the existence of exchange controls;
- the availability of professional services;
- the presence of modern telecommunications facilities; and
- the existence or lack of language barriers.

D. Funding the Trust

1. Revocable and Irrevocable Trusts

Although a revocable trust with a spendthrift trust provision can provide asset protection to nonsettlor beneficiaries, the settlor's retention of such direct control over the trust will vitiate any asset protection with respect to the settlor's own creditors even if the settlor is not named as a beneficiary of the trust. This is because the right to revoke the trust is tantamount to the retention of a general power of appointment over the trust's assets. In fact, an irrevocable self-settled trust (in the appropriate jurisdiction) provides a greater degree of asset protection because the settlor cannot, by his will alone, receive back the trust assets.

2. Control Issues

Even though it is almost universally recognized that a settlor should not retain control of assets transferred to an offshore asset protection trust either by naming himself as co-trustee of the trust or as "trust protector," or by establishing an underlying entity such as a limited partnership in which the settlor is the general partner, or a limited liability company in which the settlor is the manager, there are a number of other ways a settlor can be made comfortable with the idea of the trust. In the first instance, it should be understood that the named trustee need not be adverse to the settlor's wishes in order to be deemed "independent." Even a corporate fiduciary should prove amenable to the settlor's wishes, provided that the settlor's wishes are not unreasonable or in violation of the trust agreement. Further, a corporate fiduciary will likely be especially receptive to acting in accordance with the settlor's requests where the settlor's counsel has a long-standing relationship with the corporate fiduciary and a track record of making valuable referrals. Finally, where a trust protector has authority to remove and replace the trustee with or without cause, not only can a more compliant trustee be substituted in the unlikely event of intransigence on the part of the current trustee, but also the likelihood of such intransigence is almost certainly reduced. And although the trust protector should also be an independent, offshore corporate body, the same factors that suggest that an offshore corporate trustee will be amenable to the settlor's wishes should also prove relevant in assuaging concerns about the trust protector acting in the desired fashion, according to the settlor's best interests and receptive to the settlor's reasonable requests.

3. Asset Situs and Related Issues

Since most offshore asset protection jurisdictions do not require any local investment by the trust, an offshore asset protection trust need not invest its assets in the jurisdiction of the governing law of the trust. Moreover, although an offshore investment might strengthen the settlor's defense to allegations that the trust was funded to avoid creditors, many settlors wish to have the trust retain their original, domestic investments following settlement of the trust. However, since conflict of laws rules are generally considered too esoteric to engender a consistent favorable application by the domestic courts, it is highly advisable to have the trustees position assets outside of the jurisdiction of the domestic courts at the earliest possible opportunity and, in all events, prior to any creditor problem. Provided that the trust's assets are located offshore (whether in the jurisdiction of the trust's governing law or an established financial center such as Switzerland or Luxembourg), a creditor with a domestic judgment will still be faced with significant hurdles before actually being able to levy on any of the trust's assets. In fact, since most offshore asset protection jurisdictions will not recognize foreign judgments, the creditor may be forced to relitigate its entire case against the trust if the trust's assets are appropriately sited in a timely manner.

E. Protective Trust Clauses

1. Discretionary Distributions

A provision in the trust agreement giving the trustees sole discretion to distribute any amount, or all or none of the trust corpus, to any one or more of a number of beneficiaries is deemed protective of the trust corpus since no one beneficiary (or his potential creditors) has any vested interest in the trust corpus. In the alternative, were the settlor entitled to a set amount of the trust corpus, a court could potentially order the distribution of such vested amount to the settlor's creditors. Even if the settlor were not necessarily entitled to a set amount of the trust corpus, but was the sole trust beneficiary entitled to trust corpus within the discretion of the trustees, a court might mistakenly deem the entire trust corpus as vested in the settlor and command its distribution to the settlor (or his creditors). Therefore, a trust provision allowing the trustees to distribute trust corpus, within their discretion, to one or more of the settlors and one or more other persons is most protective. Such a discretionary distribution provision can provide unfettered discretion to the trustees, for example, as follows:

> The Trustees may pay to, appropriate, or apply for the benefit of one, more, or all of the beneficiaries so much of the net income and/or capital of the trust fund as the trustees in the trustees' sole and absolute discretion may think fit for any purpose.

Alternatively, such a discretionary distribution provision can limit the trustees' discretion to distribute trust corpus. A provision limiting the trustees' discretion to make distributions might be desirable if the interest of a particular beneficiary (e.g., the settlor) is particularly likely to be the subject of a creditor attack, since a distribution in satisfaction of a creditor's claim might be outside of the trustees' discretion and hence less likely to be compelled by a court with jurisdiction over the trustees. An example of a discretionary distribution provision that limits the trustees' discretion might read as follows:

> The trustees may pay to, appropriate, or apply for the benefit of the settlor, the net income or capital of the trust fund only to the extent reasonably necessary or appropriate, as determined in the sole and absolute discretion of the trustees, for the settlor's needs for health, support, or maintenance in the settlor's accustomed standard of living, after considering the settlor's other income or resources.

2. Spendthrift Provision

Asset protection is not exclusively within the domain of foreign trusts. There are currently thirteen states whose laws provide for the validity of self-settled spendthrift trusts. Even outside of those states, however, one of the more common uses of trusts in the United States is for protection from creditors (albeit a protection afforded only to nonsettlor beneficiaries). Consider, for example, the spendthrift trust provision included in most trust agreements. Such provisions have been upheld in most jurisdictions, except where the settlor retains excessive control over the trust or benefits from the trust. A sample spendthrift clause might read as follows:

> Subject to the applicable law, no beneficiary shall have any right, power, or authority to sell, assign, pledge, mortgage, or in any other manner to encumber, alienate, or impair all or any part of his interest in the Trust Fund or otherwise under this Settlement. The beneficial and legal interest in, and the capital and income of, the Trust Fund and every part of it shall be free from interference or control of any creditor of any beneficiary, and shall not be subject to the claims of any such creditor, including

> claims for the payment of alimony, nor liable to attachment, execution, bankruptcy, or any other legal or equitable process. No creditor of any beneficiary shall be entitled to obtain an order for attachment of the Trust Fund or any part thereof by way of execution, in bankruptcy proceedings, or otherwise. No benefit devolving on any beneficiary under this Settlement shall be subject to seizure, attachment, or lien by any creditor.

3. Anti-duress Provision

If an offshore asset protection is drafted so that the settlor retains certain powers (e.g., to remove and replace trustees), a creditor may attack the trust by moving to compel the settlor to exercise such retained power so as to discharge the foreign trustee and repatriate trust assets held offshore into the hands of a domestic receiver appointed as "trustee." Accordingly, an anti-duress clause should be included in the trust so as to direct the foreign trustee to ignore any order or instructions given by the settlor if made under duress. The purpose of such a clause is to protect the settlor against acts of coercion by a domestic court because impossibility of performance, if proven, should be an absolute defense to coercive civil contempt. The following is a sample anti-duress clause:

> The Settlor directs that this Settlement be administered consistent with its terms, free of judicial intervention and without order, approval, or other action of any court. To the extent any person is granted the power hereunder to compel any act on the part of the Trustee, or has the authority to render advice to the Trustee, or to otherwise approve or compel any action or exercise any power that affects or will affect this Settlement, the Trustee is directed, to the extent the Trustee would not be subject to personal liability or personal exposure (for example, by being held in contempt of court or other such sanction by a court having jurisdiction over the Trustee): (1) to accept or recognize only instructions or advice or the effects of any approval or compelled action or the exercise of any power, which are given by or are the result of persons acting of their own free will and not under compulsion of any legal process or like authority; and (2) to ignore any advice or any directive, order, or like decree, or the results or effects thereof, of any court, administrative body, or any tribunal whatsoever, or of past or present Trustees, or of any Protector hereunder, or of any other person, where (a) such has been instigated by directive, order, or like decree of any court, administrative body or other tribunal, or where (b) the person attempting to compel the act, or attempting to exercise the authority to render advice, or otherwise attempting to compel any action or exercise any power that affects or will affect this Settlement, is not a person either appointed or so authorized, or the like pursuant to the terms and conditions of this Settlement.

4. Change of Situs Provision

There may come a time when a change of situs may be desired to protect assets from the claims of creditors, the threat of political instability, or a change in the law. The trust agreement can include various provisions to permit a change of trustees, the situs of the trust, or the situs of the trust's assets. These provisions (often referred to as flee clauses) can give the trustee or a trust protector a discretionary power to change the situs by appointing new trustees, removing trust assets to another jurisdiction, or amending the trust to comply with the laws of a new jurisdiction. A sample flee clause follows:

> The Trustees may, by a signed declaration in writing, at any time or times and from time to time during the Trust Period as the Trustees shall deem advisable in the Trustees' discretion for the benefit or security of this Trust Fund or any portion hereof, remove (or decline to remove) all or part of the assets and/or the situs of administration thereof from one jurisdiction to another jurisdiction and/or declare that this Settlement shall, from the date of such declaration, take effect in accordance with the law of some other state or territory in any part of the world, and thereupon, the courts of such other jurisdiction shall have the power to effectuate the purposes of this Settlement to such extent. In no event, however, shall the law of some other state or territory be any place under the law of which: (1) substantially all of the powers and provisions herein declared and contained would not be enforceable or capable of being exercised and so taking effect; or (2) this Settlement would not be irrevocable. From the date of such declaration, the law of the state or territory named therein shall be the Applicable Law, but subject always to the power conferred by this paragraph and until any further declaration be made hereunder. So often as any such declaration as aforesaid shall be made, the Trustees shall be at liberty to make such consequential alterations or additions in or to the powers, discretions, and provisions of this Settlement as the Trustees may consider necessary or desirable to ensure that the provisions of this Settlement shall (*mutatis mutandis*) be so valid and effective as they are under the Applicable Law governing this Settlement at the time the power contained herein is exercised. The determination of the Trustees as to any such removal or change in Applicable Law shall be conclusive and binding on all persons interested or claiming to be interested in this Settlement.

5. Trust Protector Provision

The use of a trust protector (alternatively called a "trust adviser" or a "trust enforcer") is common among foreign trusts, although it is only recently becoming commonplace among domestic trusts. This person (or a committee of such persons) generally has the power to replace trustees and, perhaps, to veto certain discretionary actions by the trustees. With the exception of the power to remove and replace trustees, the protector's powers should generally be drafted as negative powers so as to protect against an order compelling the protector to exercise his control over the trust in a manner adverse to the beneficiaries' interests. A sample trust protector provision might provide:

> Notwithstanding anything to the contrary herein contained, and in particular anything conferring an absolute or uncontrolled discretion on the Trustees hereof, all and every power and discretion vested in the Trustees by this Settlement and incorporated herein by this reference shall only be exercisable by the Trustees subject always to the power of the Protector to veto any exercise by the Trustees of such power or discretion, and accordingly, the Trustees shall be required to provide the Protector with reasonable prior notice before any such powers or discretions may be exercised so as to allow the Protector reasonable advance opportunity within which to veto or refrain from vetoing the exercise of the power or discretion. The Protector's exercise or nonexercise of this veto power shall be communicated in writing to the Trustees, and failure to so communicate in a timely fashion, provided notice is actually received by the Protector, shall be treated by the Trustees as a veto by the Protector of the proposed exercise of the power or discretion; however, if one or more of the Trustees reasonably believe that failure by the Protector to so communicate is due to the Protector being restrained or enjoined from doing so, then such failure to communicate shall be treated by the Trustees and deemed for all purposes hereof as acquiescence by the Protector to the proposed exercise of the power or discretion. It is further provided that, notwithstanding anything to the contrary otherwise herein expressed or implied, no discretion or power conferred upon the Protector, or upon any other person by this Settlement, or by any rule of law, or arising in consequence of the exercise of any power conferred upon the Protector or any other person by this Settlement, shall be exercised, and nothing contained herein shall operate, so as to cause the Protector to be successful in ordering any action or causing any result that is not of the Protector's own free will or that is otherwise the result of the Protector acting under the duress or influence of an outside force.

IV. Selective Jurisdictional Review

A. The Bahamas

The Bahamas is a group of islands located in the western Atlantic Ocean, just off the east coast of Florida. Although completely independent of the United Kingdom since 1973, the Bahamas remains a member of the British Commonwealth. The Bahamas has strict bank secrecy laws. Under Bahamian secrecy laws, it is a crime for a banker (or other person) who, in a professional capacity, has acquired information about the identity, assets, liabilities, transactions, or accounts of a customer to reveal such information to another person unless such disclosure is required by Bahamian law or unless the customer consents to the disclosure. Moreover, although the Bahamas requires the reporting of large currency transactions in certain situations, it excepts customers who have an existing relationship with a Bahamian bank as well as transactions by customers who have the recommendation of a "reputable" party.

Fraudulent dispositions are addressed in the Bahamas under the Fraudulent Disposition Act 1991. Under that statute, dispositions are voidable by the creditor prejudiced by the disposition if the transferor made the disposition with an intent to defraud. Under the statute, an "intent to defraud" means an intention to defeat willfully an obligation owed to a creditor. The burden of proof for establishing such intent is on the creditor, and the statute of limitations is two years from the date of the applicable disposition.

The Trusts (Choice of Governing Law) Act 1989 provides, in pertinent part, that if Bahamian law is designated as the trust's governing law, such designation will be binding and effective regardless of any other circumstances. The Trustee Act (1998) provides that a trust shall not be invalidated by the settlor's having retained any powers to revoke the trust, power to appoint the property, power to remove the trustees, protectors, or beneficiaries, or right to be appointed protector or retain a beneficial interest. The Perpetuities Act (2004) increased the period for trusts from 80 years to 150 years. Pursuant to general principles of trust law, a settlor may name himself as a discretionary beneficiary of his trust, and the settlement will be protected against the settlor's creditors provided the settlement does not violate the provisions of the Fraudulent Disposition Act 1991.

Finally, the Bahamas is essentially a "no-tax" jurisdiction. It has no personal income tax, corporate income tax, value added tax, capital gains tax, withholding tax, gift tax, estate tax, or employment tax, and does not tax offshore trusts in any manner.

B. Bermuda

Bermuda is a group of islands in the Atlantic Ocean approximately 1,000 kilometers east of North Carolina. It is an English-speaking dependent territory of the United Kingdom and has a common law legal system. Strict privacy laws prevail with regard to Bermuda trusts. Significantly, Bermuda trusts need not be registered or filed with any public agency. The Statute of Elizabeth does not apply in Bermuda. However, certain types of transfer are likely to be recognized as fraudulent in Bermuda and therefore may defeat a transfer of assets to a trust. These transfers generally equate to recognized badges of fraud; for instance, the following are all recognized badges of fraud under Bermuda law:

- the transfer of most of the settlor's assets;
- the settlor's continued possession of the assets or continuation of enjoyment of their use or income;
- the settlor's secrecy or haste in disposing of the assets;
- the settlor's disposition of assets while litigation is pending; and
- the settlor retaining an advantage under the trust.

In addition, there must be a two-year period after the trust's creation or after any transfers are made to the trust, during which the settlor has no knowledge or reasonable notice of any creditor or action. If there is a problem during that two-year period, the creditor has six years to bring an action to declare a transfer to a trust void or fraudulent.

Bermuda law recognizes the settlor's choice of governing law expressed in a trust as well as the trust's ability to change its governing law to or from that of Bermuda. Questions of capacity and the validity of the trust are therefore determined under the law of Bermuda. Bermuda law allows full delegation of powers of investment and management of the trust fund. A Bermuda trust may accumulate income, and the trust term can extend to 100 years. The trust laws in Bermuda protect a trust from application of the laws of another jurisdiction with respect to marital rights, forced heirship claims, and creditors' rights. Similarly, subject to the Judgments (Reciprocal Enforcement) Act 1958 whereby judgments rendered in the United Kingdom and certain other Commonwealth nations may be enforced in Bermuda, Bermuda courts generally do not recognize foreign court awards. A Bermuda trust may be validly self-settled.

C. Cayman Islands

The Cayman Islands is located in the western Caribbean Sea, approximately 750 kilometers south of Miami, Florida. The Cayman Islands is an English-speaking dependent territory of the United Kingdom and has a common law legal system strongly influenced by English case law. The Cayman Islands has strict secrecy laws that provide for substantial penalties for revealing confidential information. In general, a foreign government cannot obtain assistance from the Cayman Islands in pursuing criminal matters unless the offense is also an offense under Cayman Islands law. For instance, tax crimes are not an offense under Cayman Islands law (since the Cayman Islands is a no-tax jurisdiction). Notwithstanding the foregoing, however, the United States and the Cayman Islands entered into a Mutual Legal Assistance Treaty in 1988 under which the Cayman Islands promised to provide U.S. authorities with information in investigations involving either drugs or certain white-collar crimes, including bank fraud. However, the person who is required to give evidence or make a disclosure must still receive permission for such action from the Cayman Islands' Grand Court.

The trust law of the Cayman Islands comprises the Trusts Law (2009 Revision), the Fraudulent Dispositions Law (1996 Revision), the Perpetuities Law (1999 Revision), the Property (Miscellaneous Provisions) Law 1994, and the Special Trusts (Alternative Regime) Law 1997. As it relates to fraudulent transfers, Cayman Islands law provides that a disposition is voidable by a creditor prejudiced by the disposition only if the disposition was made with an intent to defraud. An "intent to defraud" is defined as an intention of the transferor willfully to defeat an existing obligation owed to a creditor. The burden of proof for establishing an intent to defraud is on the creditor. If a fraudulent disposition is proved, it will set aside the disposition only to the extent necessary to satisfy the claim of the creditor bringing the action. Finally, the statute of limitations on proving a fraudulent disposition is six years from the date of the disposition.

As it relates to asset protection, Cayman Islands trust law provides that the Cayman Islands will use the choice of governing law provision that the settlor sets forth in the trust instrument so that all questions regarding the trust will be determined by the laws of the Cayman Islands (unless and until amended under the trust instrument). Moreover, a Cayman Islands trust may not be set aside due to the fact that the laws of a foreign jurisdiction prohibit or do not recognize the trust concept or due to the fact that the trust defeats certain rights conferred by foreign law. In addition, there is no limitation on the accumulation of income within the trust and no restriction on permissible investments by trustees. A settlor may name himself as a discretionary beneficiary of his trust, and the settlement will be protected against the settlor's creditors (except in the case of a bankruptcy), provided that the settlement does not violate the Fraudulent Dispositions Law (1996 Revision).

The Cayman Islands is a no-tax jurisdiction.

D. Cook Islands

The Cook Islands, located in the Pacific Ocean east of New Zealand and south of Hawaii, is a self-governing democracy with a parliamentary system of government and a common law legal system. The Cook Islands' closest link is with New Zealand, which retains responsibility for defense and foreign affairs since the islands became self-governing in 1965. English is the official language.

The Cook Islands enacted the world's first comprehensive asset protection trust legislation with the International Trusts Act 1984. The legislation addresses "international trusts" and the effect thereon of fraudulent dispositions and bankruptcy. With respect to fraudulent dispositions, a creditor seeking to set aside a disposition must prove beyond a reasonable doubt that the disposition was made with an intent to defraud that particular creditor and that the transferor was rendered insolvent by the transfer. As a bright-line rule, if the fair market value of the settlor's property after the transfer to the trust exceeds the value of the creditor's claim at the time of the transfer, an intent to defraud necessarily cannot be found. Even if the creditor meets the heavy burden necessary to prove a fraudulent disposition, the transfer is not void or voidable; instead, the transferor must pay the creditor's claim from property that would have been subject to its claim but for the transfer. Further, the statute expressly states that an international trust will not be deemed void by virtue of the settlor's bankruptcy. Another section of the legislation sets forth certain circumstances that will not be deemed badges of fraud: fraudulent intent cannot be imputed from a transfer to an international trust within two years of the accrual of a creditor's cause of action or the retention of powers or benefits by the settlor, or the designation of the settlor as a beneficiary, trustee, or protector.

With regard to fraudulent conveyance claims, if a creditor's cause of action accrues more than two years before a transfer to an international trust, the transfer will not be deemed to be fraudulent. If a creditor's cause of action accrues less than two years before a transfer to a trust, the creditor must bring an action within one year of the date the transfer to an international trust occurs, unless an action has been commenced in a court of competent jurisdiction before the expiration of one year from the date of transfer. Further, if the transfer (whether initial or subsequent) to an international trust occurs before a creditor's cause of action accrues, such a disposition will not be fraudulent as to that creditor. A "cause of action" is defined as the first cause of action capable of assertion against a settlor. Finally, as regards redomiciled trusts, the limitations period commences at the time of original transfer, even though the transfer was to an offshore center other than the Cook Islands.

An international trust cannot be declared void or be affected in any way because the settlor:

- has the power to revoke or amend the trust, dispose of trust property, or remove or appoint a trustee or protector; or
- retains, possesses, or acquires any benefit, interest, or property from the trust.

The rule against perpetuities has also been repealed in the Cook Islands. Other provisions of trust legislation in the Cook Islands:

- make selection of Cook Island law binding and conclusive;
- ensure that an international trust is not subject to forced heirship laws of other countries; and
- mandate the nonrecognition of a foreign judgment against an international trust, its settlor, trustee, and protector.

The Cook Islands is a no-tax jurisdiction.

E. Gibraltar

Gibraltar is a British territory located at the southern tip of the Iberian Peninsula. Gibraltar generally follows the English common law system. The Trusts (Recognition) Ordinance 1989 incorporates the 1984 Hague Convention on the Law

Applicable to Trusts and their Recognition, which expressly provides that a trust shall be governed by the law chosen by the settlor. In conjunction with its trust law, Gibraltar's Bankruptcy Amendment Ordinance 1990 provides that a creditor cannot reach the assets of a trust properly registered in Gibraltar (as an asset protection trust is required to do, in any event) by claiming that the settlement was a fraudulent conveyance if, at the date of settlement of the trust, the settlor:

- was solvent,
- did not render himself insolvent by reason of the transfer of property to the trust, and
- was not then subject to any outstanding litigation.

However, Gibraltar does not provide for the nonrecognition of foreign judgments, nor does it provide for a statute of limitations on fraudulent conveyance claims. It should also be noted that the registration requirement of an asset protection trust in Gibraltar is required, upon criminal offense, to be kept confidential.

Offshore trusts established in Gibraltar are not subject to Gibraltar income tax, notwithstanding the fact that the trustees are resident in Gibraltar, provided that the trust has no Gibraltar residents as beneficiaries.

F. Jersey

Jersey is the largest of the Channel Islands, a group of islands located in the English Channel. Jersey, together with the other Channel Islands, is a possession of the British Crown and is self-governing for all internal matters, including all tax matters. Jersey is a common law jurisdiction with a number of civil law aspects because of historical ties to France (in particular relating to inheritance and family rights). As a partially civil law jurisdiction, Jersey had no trust law until 1984 when it enacted the Trusts Law, codifying English common law principles relating to trusts. The Trusts Law specifically allows the settlor to be a beneficiary of the trust. The 2006 amendments to the Trusts Law protect Jersey trusts from foreign laws being applied to issues of forced heirship and creation of marital rights. Also, the amendments allow Jersey trusts of unlimited duration. Jersey does not, however, have an asset protection trust law, but instead provides that the law of another jurisdiction (that does have an asset protection trust law) may be validly designated as controlling. Trust information is kept confidential by Jersey law, which provides that, in the absence of a court order, no one is entitled to information about the trust if he does not have an interest in the trust.

A trust established by a nonresident of Jersey for the benefit of a nonresident of Jersey is taxed only on local source income (excluding local bank deposits and excluding capital gains).

G. United States

Of the fifty states comprising the United States, thirteen states have enacted legislation providing spendthrift protections to a settlor-beneficiary of a discretionary trust. Those states are: Alaska, Delaware, Hawaii, Missouri, Nevada, New Hampshire, Ohio, Rhode Island, South Dakota, Tennessee, Utah, Virginia, and Wyoming. A thirteenth state, Oklahoma, permits the creation of a protective revocable trust for the benefit of the settlor's spouse and dependents with up to $1 million. In all cases, however, "foreign" trusts will likely offer more substantive barriers to creditors than will "domestic" trusts, at least where the trust fund is invested outside of the United States, since a U.S. judgment should not be enforceable offshore, whereas the "full faith and credit" clause of the U.S. Constitution may result in a court's enforcement of a sister state's judgment against a settlor's U.S. situs trust. Nevertheless, domestic trusts remain relevant, in particular where illiquid U.S. situs assets exist and are therefore reviewed in some detail below.

1. Alaska

The Alaska Trust Act (1997) modified Alaska's previously undistinguished body of trust law in an effort generally touted as making Alaska an onshore alternative to offshore asset protection trusts. In contrast to the general state of domestic spendthrift trust law at the time the Alaska statute was enacted (as exemplified by Restatement (Second) of Trust §156(2)), Alaska law permitted a settlor to create a trust for his own benefit that would be protected from the settlor's future creditors. As subsequently amended, the law provides for protection so long as:

- the settlor has not retained the right to revoke or terminate the trust;
- the settlor has not been in default by thirty days or more in making a child support payment;
- the settlor's ability to receive distributions from the trust is within the discretion of the trustees rather than mandatory. However, the trustee may permit a beneficiary the use of property, and the settlor may retain an annuity or unitrust interest in a charitable remainder trust. The settlor may also retain the right to receive a percentage of the trust each year not to exceed the unitrust amount provided under Internal Revenue Code § 643(b); and
- the transfer of property to the trust was not intended to hinder, delay, or defraud creditors (i.e., a "fraudulent conveyance").

Furthermore, the law requires at least one trustee to be a trust company or bank in Alaska or an individual resident of Alaska; some of the trust assets must be deposited with a bank in Alaska; and part or all of the trust administration must occur in Alaska.

Moreover, under Alaska law, a creditor of the settlor existing at the time the trust is created must bring suit on a fraudulent conveyance claim within the later of four years from the transfer or one year after the transfer is, or reasonably could have been, discovered. A creditor arising after the transfer to the trust must bring suit within four years of the transfer. Notwithstanding the foregoing, in *Battley v. Mortensen*, Case No. A09-00565-DMD (D. Alaska May 26, 2011), despite the settlor's transfer of property to what he intended to qualify as an asset protection trust under Alaska law four-and-a-half years prior to filing for bankruptcy, the bankruptcy court found that the transfer by the settlor should be void under § 548(e) of the Bankruptcy Code because they found that the settlor had the actual intent to hinder, delay, or defraud his creditors, and the transfer fell within the ten-year statute of limitations of that section. *See also In re Huber, supra.*

2. Delaware

The avowed purpose of the Delaware self-settled trust law is to allow settlors to reduce estate tax by excluding creditors' claims against self-settled trusts. Under the Delaware Qualified Dispositions in Trust Act, a trust must be irrevocable and have a trustee resident in Delaware. It can include one or more of the following provisions:

- The settlor may retain the power to veto distributions;
- The settlor may retain a special power of appointment;
- The settlor may receive income, principal or both in the sole discretion of a trustee who is neither the settlor nor a related or subordinate party; and
- The settlor may even retain:
    - current income distributions;
    - payments from a charitable remainder trust;
    - annual payments of up to 5 percent of the initial value of the trust or of its value as determined from time to time; and
    - principal distributions under an ascertainable standard (e.g., health, maintenance, education, or support).

Provided that the transfer of property to the trust was not intended to hinder, delay, or defraud creditors, no action to enforce a judgment can be brought for attachment against such transfer. Under Delaware law, a creditor existing at the time a transfer to a trust is made must commence an action to enforce a judgment within the later of four years or one year after the transfer was or could reasonably have been discovered by the creditor. If the creditor's claim arose after the transfer, the action must be brought within four years of the transfer. Moreover, a trust that is redomiciled to Delaware will tack on the time during which it was located elsewhere for purposes of the statute of limitations regarding creditor claims.

Finally, addressing the "full faith and credit" clause problem, the trustee's authority will be immediately terminated upon the occurrence of another state court's attempt to exercise jurisdiction over a trustee if that other state's court declines to apply Delaware law with respect to the validity, construction, or administration of the trust. If the trust instrument does not provide for a successor trustee, the Delaware Court of Chancery will appoint a successor trustee (and presumably one who would be subject to the Delaware court's jurisdiction only).

3. Hawaii

Hawaii enacted the Permitted Transfers in Trust Act on June 28, 2010. The Act permits the creation of self-settled spendthrift trusts and excludes those trusts created under the Act from the statutory rule against perpetuities. However, for a self-settled spendthrift trust provision to be enforceable, the Act requires the transfer to be to a Hawaii resident trustee of only "permitted property." In addition, the amount of the permitted property must be equal to or less than 25 percent of the transferor's net worth. "Permitted property," which is a concept unique to Hawaii, is defined as cash (only U.S. currency), marketable securities (only securities that are exchanged on a governmentally regulated exchange within the United States, provided it does not include real estate or any interest in corporations, partnerships, and limited liability companies that are not publicly traded), life insurance contracts, and nonprivate annuities.

Under Hawaii law, a self-settled trust must be irrevocable but can include one or more of the following provisions:

- The settlor may retain the power to veto distributions;
- The settlor may retain a testamentary special power of appointment;
- The settlor may retain the right to remove a trustee or advisor and to appoint a new trustee or adviser; and
- The settlor may receive income, principal or both under certain circumstances, including:
    - current income distributions;
    - annual payments of up to 5 percent of the initial value of the trust or of its value as determined from time to time; and
    - principal distributions due to the discretionary action of a permitted trustee, provided that no provision in the trust instrument shall confer upon the settlor a substantially unfettered right to the receipt or use of the principal.

Under the Act, a claim or judgment that arises after a permitted transfer may not be brought unless the permitted transfer was found to have been made with actual intent to defraud, hinder, or delay the creditor, and in all events, a claim will be extinguished unless: (1) the creditor's claim arose before the permitted transfer was made and the action is brought before the date of the permitted transfer, or (2) the creditor's claim arose concurrent with or subsequent to the permitted transfer and the action is brought within two years thereafter. As in other states, there is a class of exception creditors, including the settlor's spouse, former spouse, and children who have a judgment against the settlor for support or maintenance; any person who suffers death, personal injury, or property damage on or before the date of a permitted transfer by reason of the tortuous act or omission of the settlor; a lender who extended a secured or collateralized loan to the settlor based on the settlor's representation that the assets transferred to the trust would be available as security; and the State of Hawaii in connection with tax liabilities.

4. Missouri

Missouri law provides for the validity of a self-settled spendthrift trust with respect to the settlor's creditors, provided the settlor is not the sole beneficiary of a trust and does not retain the power to revoke or amend the trust or retain a portion of the income or principal of the trust. Excepted from the foregoing protection, however, are the settlor's spouse, former spouse, and children who have a judgment against the settlor for support or maintenance or a judgment creditor that provided services for the protection of a beneficiary's interest in the trust. Of course, the conveyance of assets to the trust must also not have been fraudulent as to creditors.

5. Nevada

Similar to the Alaska and Delaware laws, Nevada law provides that a person may create a spendthrift trust for his own benefit (or for the benefit of the settlor and another), provided that the writing establishing the trust:

- is irrevocable;
- does not mandate the distribution of income or principal to the settlor; and
- was not intended to hinder, delay, or defraud known creditors.

Moreover, the settlor may be given the power to prevent a distribution from the trust and/or may hold a testamentary special power of appointment or similar power over the trust without affecting the validity of the self-settled trust under Nevada law.

Unlike Alaska and Delaware, however, Nevada law provides for a substantially shorter period within which a creditor must commence a fraudulent transfer claim against the trust. If the creditor existed at the time the transfer to the trust was made, the creditor must commence an action within two years of the transfer, or within six months of the date on which the creditor discovered or reasonably should have discovered the transfer; if, however, the creditor's claim arose after the transfer to trust, the action must be brought within two years of the transfer to the trust. In 2011, Nevada enacted a law allowing trusts set up in other jurisdictions to be moved to Nevada without re-starting the applicable statute of limitations.

6. New Hampshire

New Hampshire enacted legislation effective January 1, 2009, which is substantially similar to that of South Dakota.

7. Ohio

Ohio enacted the Ohio Legacy Trust Act on December 20, 2012, and it became effective March 20, 2013. Ohio Revised Code Section 5816 provides that the settlor may create a self-settled spendthrift trust provided that

- the governing law must be Ohio;
- the trust must be irrevocable; and
- the trust must prohibit voluntary or involuntary assignment;

The settlor may retain the following:

- a power to veto trust distributions;
- a limited power of appointment;
- the right to current income distributions;
- payments from a charitable remainder trust;
- annual payments of up to 5 percent of the initial value of the trust or of its value as determined from time to time;
- principal distributions under an ascertainable standard (*i.e.*, health, maintenance, education, or support); and
- a power to remove and appoint advisors and trustees.

A creditor's claim against property that was the subject of a qualified disposition in trust is extinguished unless the creditor's claim arose before the qualified disposition was made and the action is brought within the later of 18 months after the qualified disposition or 6 months after the transfer is or reasonably could have been discovered if the creditor files suit or makes a written demand that asserts a claim based on an act or omission that occurred before the qualified disposition and that suit is filed within 3 years after the transfer. However, any person to whom the settlor was indebted on account of an agreement or court order for support, alimony, or property distribution in favor of a spouse, former spouse, or children may avoid the transfer.

8. Oklahoma

Oklahoma enacted the Family Wealth Preservation Trust Act on June 9, 2004. The Act provides that up to $1 million placed into a revocable trust for the sole benefit of the settlor's spouse, issue, and one or more 501(c)(3) charities would not be deemed available to the settlor's creditors, and no court would have authority to compel the settlor to exercise the settlor's power to revoke the trust. In order to come under the act, however, the following requirements must be met:

- The trustee must be a bank or trust company located in Oklahoma. Notably, an individual trustee, even though he may be resident in Oklahoma, will not suffice; and

- The corpus must consist of assets in Oklahoma-based banks, real estate located in Oklahoma, and securities issued by Oklahoma-based companies (including corporations, limited liability companies, and limited partnerships formed in Oklahoma and having a principal place of business in Oklahoma).

Transfers to the trust remain subject, of course, to the provisions of Oklahoma's version of the Uniform Fraudulent Transfer Act. Moreover, a transfer of property into trust within three years of the settlor filing a voluntary petition in bankruptcy is presumed to be a fraudulent conveyance.

9. Rhode Island

Rhode Island law provides that a person may create a spendthrift trust for his own benefit provided that:

- the trust is irrevocable;
- the trust does not require the distribution of income or principal to the settlor; and
- the trustee is neither the settlor nor a related or subordinate party.

Moreover, a trust will not be deemed invalid simply because the settlor has retained the power to veto a distribution from the trust or because the settlor holds a testamentary special power of appointment or similar power over the trust.

Notwithstanding the foregoing, however, a transfer to a self-settled Rhode Island trust is ineffective in certain circumstances. Specifically, the trust will not protect against:

- the court-ordered payment of support or alimony in favor of the transferor's spouse, former spouse, or children, or for a division of distribution of property in favor of the transferor's spouse or former spouse (provided the transferor was married to the person at the time the transfer is made); or
- any person who suffers death, personal injury, or property damage on or before the date of the transfer, by reason of the transferor's act or omission or the act or omission of another person for whom the transferor is or was vicariously liable.

With regard to the statutes of limitation applicable under Rhode Island law, if the creditor existed at the time the transfer to trust was made, the creditor must commence an action within four years of the transfer or, if later, within one year after the date on which it discovers or reasonably could have discovered the transfer; if, however, the creditor's claim arose after the transfer, the action must be brought within four years of the transfer.

10. South Dakota

The Act to Authorize Qualified Dispositions, effective for trusts settled on or after July 1, 2005, permits self-settled spendthrift trusts to be created under the law of South Dakota. In order to qualify, the trust must meet the following requirements:

- The governing law must be South Dakota;
- The trust must be irrevocable; and
- The trust must prohibit voluntary or involuntary assignment.

In addition to the receipt of income, principal, or both, in the discretion of a trustee who is neither the settlor nor a related or subordinated party within the meaning of § 672(c) of the U.S. Internal Revenue Code, the settlor may also retain the following rights and powers:

- the power to veto trust distributions;
- a limited testamentary power of appointment;
- the right to receive distribution of current income;
- the right to receive payments under a charitable remainder trust;
- the right to receive annual payments of up to 5 percent of the initial value of the trust, or of its value as determined from time to time;
- the right to receive principal distributions under an ascertainable standard (e.g., health, maintenance, education, or support); and
- the power to remove and appoint trustees.

The trustee must be either an individual resident of the state of South Dakota or a South Dakota bank or trust company. In either case, the trustee is required to:

- maintain or arrange for custody of some or all of the property in the state of South Dakota;
- maintain records on an exclusive or nonexclusive basis;
- prepare or arrange for the preparation of the trust's tax returns; or
- otherwise materially participate in the administration of the trust.

The Act also permits the appointment of a nonresident trust adviser, including a trust protector, who may hold one or more trust powers. The settlor may even be designated as the trust adviser.

Transfers are subject to provisions of South Dakota's version of the Uniform Fraudulent Transfer Act. Moreover, certain additional creditors can avoid qualified dispositions even though these may not be a fraudulent transfer. They are:

- any person to whom the settlor is indebted on account of an agreement or court order for support, alimony, or property distribution in favor of a spouse, former spouse, or children; or
- any person who suffers death, personal injury, or property damage on or before the qualified disposition, which was caused by the transferor or another person for whom the transferor is liable.

11. Tennessee

The Tennessee Investment Services Act permits self-settled trusts to be created after July 1, 2007. The Act has provisions similar to those of South Dakota's law.

Under the Act, the trust does not provide asset protection until four years after a transfer of assets thereto.

12. Utah

The state of Utah permits self-settled spendthrift trusts created after May 5, 2003, to qualify as valid with respect to the settlor's creditors if the trust meets the following requirements:

- At least one trustee is a trust company resident in Utah;
- Only personal property or interests therein are transferred to the trust;
- The settlor does not retain the right to revoke the trust;
- The settlor can receive income or principal only in the discretion of the trustee; and
- The settlor was not in default by thirty days or more under a child support order at the time of the creation of the trust.

The trust will be subject to Utah's governing law if:

- some or all of the assets are deposited in the state in a bank, brokerage, or trust company;
- the trust has at least one resident trustee; and
- some administration (e.g., maintaining of trust records or arranging for tax return preparation) occurs in the state.

A creditor existing at the time the trust is settled must bring suit within the later of three years after the transfer is made or one year after the transfer is or reasonably could have been discovered. A creditor arising after the transfer has two years from the transfer date to bring a suit.

13. Virginia

Effective July 1, 2012, Virginia enacted legislation permitting the creation of self-settled spendthrift trusts. Virginia's legislation is substantially similar to that of the other jurisdictions and includes the following requirements:

- the trust must be irrevocable;
- some or all of the assets must be maintained in the Commonwealth of Virginia;
- the trust must have at least one qualified resident trustee;
- some administration (e.g., maintaining of trust records or arranging for tax return preparation) must occur in the commonwealth;
- the settlor must be entitled only to discretionary distributions of income and principal; and
- the transfer to the trust must not be a fraudulent transfer.

Virginia's statutes also include some provisions that are less favorable than other domestic jurisdictions, including:

- There is a five-year period in which creditors at the time of the creation of the trust may bring a claim;
- The settlor may not retain a veto power over trust distributions; and
- The person or entity who approves distributions may not be related or subordinate to the settlor.

14. Wyoming

Wyoming provides for creation of a "qualified spendthrift trust." The statute is substantially similar to that of the other jurisdictions. It further provides that the trusts would not be protected if the trust property is listed on an application or financial statement used to obtain credit other than for the benefit of the trust, or the settlor transferred property that was received in a fraudulent transfer.

V. Legal Challenges to Offshore Asset Protection Trusts

Although a self-settled spendthrift trust, valid under the law designated by the settlor as governing the trust, should be held similarly valid by all courts, wherever situate, a self-settled spendthrift trust may yet be tested against concepts of fairness and good faith if the settlor is ultimately forced to obtain judicial sanction of the trust in a jurisdiction that does not, under its own law, recognize self-settled spendthrift trust protections as valid. Although the heavy costs of litigation, when weighed against the likelihood of a successful recovery against assets held in an offshore asset protection trust, have severely limited the number of cases that have been decided in this area, a few reported decisions do exist that may provide insight into how the courts, both in the United States and internationally, are likely to view the offshore asset protection trust.

The first reported case involving an offshore asset protection trust, *In Re 515 South Orange Grove Owners Association v. Orange Grove Partners*, was decided in 1994. The *Orange Grove Case*, as it is commonly known, involved a California real estate developer sued by the purchasers of its condominiums under allegations of faulty construction and breach of warranty. Between the commencement of suit and the entry of a multimillion-dollar judgment against them, the defendants transferred a substantial amount of their assets to a self-settled Cook Islands asset protection trust. The plaintiffs were therefore forced to bring suit in the Cook Islands in an attempt to enforce their California judgment.

The defendants argued to the Cook Islands court that the plaintiffs' claim was barred by the applicable statute of limitations because more than two years had elapsed since the condominiums were sold to the plaintiffs. The Cook Islands court, however, found for the plaintiffs under an argument that a cause of action to enforce a foreign judgment accrues upon the entry of the foreign judgment. Since less than two years had elapsed since the entry of the California judgment, the Cook Islands court allowed the plaintiffs' action to proceed. Notwithstanding the plaintiffs' success on this statute of limitations argument, the case was ultimately settled before any finding on the merits. Moreover, on November 21 1996, the International Trusts Amendment Act was passed into law, in part to clarify that a cause of action on a foreign judgment accrues upon the earliest act or omission forming the basis for the underlying claim.

In *Brown v. Higashi*, a 1996 U.S. Bankruptcy Court case, the debtors, husband and wife, argued that certain assets sought by their tort judgment creditor were protected from attachment by reason of the debtors' self-settled spendthrift trust (which they had created under the laws of Belize). The court, however, found the potential application of the law of Belize to be "inappropriate" and the law of Alaska as controlling. The court therefore determined that the trust assets were includable in the debtors' bankruptcy estate. The court, however, was clearly not disposed to limit itself to the law cited by the debtors as governing under the trust instrument since, at all times, the trust was administered as a mere alter ego of the debtors rather than as a legally distinct entity. Specifically, the trust was a common law business trust that incorporated features found in corporations and trusts, and the debtors were the president and secretary of the trust. In such capacity, the debtors exercised complete control over the trust's assets to the total exclusion of their named trustee. For this reason, the court called the trust a "sham" and cited the settlors' retention of direct control over the trust's assets as the "primary reason" for its finding that the settlors' transfers to the trust were fraudulent.

In the 1996 U.S. Bankruptcy Court case of *In re Portnoy*, the debtor placed virtually all of his assets into an offshore asset protection trust at a time when the debtor knew that his personal guarantee of the indebtedness of his corporation was about to be called. Against this backdrop, the creditor argued that the debtor should be denied a discharge in bankruptcy on the basis that the debtor had failed to disclose a retained interest in the trust as an asset of the bankruptcy estate. The debtor's position was that under Jersey (Channel Islands) law, he had not retained a property interest in the trust. In its conflict of laws analysis, however, the court concluded that the domestic jurisdiction had the weightier concern in determining whether the debtor's retained rights in the trust could be considered to constitute a property interest that should have been disclosed in his bankruptcy schedules. Moreover, the court held that application of the substantive law of Jersey would offend strong domestic public policies were it to be applied. The court therefore denied the debtor a discharge in bankruptcy.

In the 1998 U.S. Bankruptcy Court case of *In re BV Brooks*, the issue before the court was whether to apply domestic law or foreign law (here, the laws of Bermuda and Jersey) to an exemption for spendthrift trusts under the U.S. Bankruptcy Code. The creditor argued that the trusts were property of the bankruptcy estate, because they were self-settled and invalid as a matter of domestic law. The debtors argued that the trusts were not property of the estate, because they were enforceable spendthrift trusts under the laws of the offshore jurisdictions. Citing *Portnoy* as precedent, the court found the trusts' assets includable in the bankruptcy estate on the basis of domestic public policy considerations.

In *In re Stephan Jay Lawrence*, a later 1998 U.S. Bankruptcy Court case, following a forty-two-month arbitration and just sixty-six days before an award in excess of $20 million was entered against him, the settlor funded an offshore trust citing first the law of Jersey and about a month later the law of Mauritius as governing. Citing both *Portnoy* and *BV Brooks* as precedent, the court found that the sole purpose of the trust was to shield the settlor's assets from a creditor who was about to obtain an arbitration award against him in the amount of $20. Although the basis of the court's judgment against the settlor was seemingly well grounded in fraudulent conveyance law, the *Lawrence* court purported to base its holding on an analysis of the conflict of laws issue. However, the *Lawrence* court's entire analysis as to the conflict of laws between the domestic forum and the trust's designated law of Mauritius was a statement that the court was persuaded by the decisions in *Portnoy* and *Brooks* and that the domestic jurisdiction had an overriding interest in the trust. Following the court's refusal to grant the settlor his discharge in bankruptcy, the creditors sought to collect their judgment by obtaining a court order compelling the settlor to repatriate the trust's assets. The settlor alleged that because the trustee would not accept the settlor's direction if made under duress, the settlor had no ability to repatriate the trust's assets. Based upon an extremely spare analysis of the settlor's alleged impossibility of performance defense, the court found the settlor in contempt and jailed him for noncompliance with the court's order.[1] On a subsequent appeal, the appellate court suggested that a self-created impossibility of performance would vitiate the impossibility of performance defense to a finding of civil coercive contempt, although this should probably be qualified as referring only to an impossibility of performance that is self-created shortly before or in reasonable anticipation of the court order.

Grupo Torras, Grupo Torras, SA v. SFM Al Sabah, Chemical Bank & Trust (Bahamas) and Private Trust Corp, a 1995 case adjudicated by the Bahamian Supreme Court, stands for the seemingly obvious proposition that the courts will not uphold a trust funded with illegally obtained assets. In *Grupo Torras*, creditors brought suit in the Bahamas to challenge a Bahamian trust on various grounds, including the fact that the trust was funded with assets the settlor had obtained by defrauding the plaintiffs. Citing long-standing principles of English common law, the Bahamian Supreme Court held that the spendthrift trust protections afforded by Bahamian law do not apply to illegally obtained assets.

1. The settlor in this case remained incarcerated for six years until the court held that the coercive effect of the contempt order had run its course.

FTC v. Affordable Media, LLC,[2] a 1999 case heard in the U.S. Court of Appeals for the Ninth Circuit, dealt with a tangential yet important issue concerning the use of offshore trusts: specifically, the potential for the settlor to be deemed in contempt of court in the settlor's domicile by reason of being unable to convince the court that the settlor truly divested himself of control over the trust's assets. In *FTC v. Affordable Media*, the settlors were found to be in contempt of court for failing to comply with a court order to repatriate trust assets invested offshore. Specifically, the settlors, who were also co-trustees of their own trust as well as the trust protectors, were ordered to instruct their foreign co-trustee to repatriate more than $6 million in profits collected under an alleged Ponzi-type investment scheme. In attempting to comply with the court order, however, the settlors either intentionally invoked (or at least intentionally failed to preclude the invocation of) an anti-duress clause in the trust agreement, thereby resulting in their removal as trustees and ensuring that the assets would not be repatriated pursuant to the order. When the assets were not timely repatriated, the settlors were held in civil contempt for failing to comply with the court order and were jailed pending repatriation of the assets. On appeal, the Ninth Circuit considered the settlors' claimed defense of impossibility of performance. Although the U.S. Supreme Court has repeatedly held that impossibility of performance constitutes an absolute defense to civil coercive contempt because the remedy is permissible only as a coercive measure presumed necessary to obtain compliance with the order, the Court of Appeals for the Ninth Circuit held the defense inapposite to the facts of the case since the settlors had retained actual control, in part because they were the protectors of their trust, with the authority to remove and replace the trustee.

A similar basis for a finding of control was made in *United States v. Grant*.[3] In 1983 and 1984, Raymond Grant created a Bermuda trust and a Jersey, Channel Islands, trust. Raymond was the beneficiary of the Bermuda trust, and his wife, Arline Grant, was the beneficiary of the Jersey trust. In 1991 and 1993, the IRS assessed millions of dollars in back taxes against the Grants for the years 1977 through 1982 and 1984 through 1987. In 2003, judgment was entered against the Grants for more than $36 million, and a motion was made to order Arline to repatriate the trust funds. Arline had the power to remove and replace any acting trustee. The court set forth its query in simple terms:

> [I]s this a trust over which the beneficiary lacks any control, such that the beneficiary is simply that and nothing more, and regardless of what she does or says, she lacks the power to repatriate these assets to the United States?—or, does the beneficiary retain such control that she has the power vested in her in some way by the terms of the trust to repatriate the corpus? If she has such power, then this asset is no different from any other asset.

2. 179 F.3d 1228 (9th Cir. 1999).
3. 2008 U.S. Dist. LEXIS 51332 (S.D. Fla. May 27, 2008).

Although the court found that "by giving Arline Grant total unreviewable authority over discharge and appointment of the Trustees, she in actuality controls the corpus of the trust," and the court determined there was evidence that Arline took steps to have the trustees remit the funds or resign in favor of a U.S. trustee, which were unsuccessful, the court denied the government's motion to hold Arline in contempt because her impossibility to comply was a complete defense to contempt. But see the follow up decision wherein the Court, after further discovery revealed trust distributions indirectly benefiting Arlene, compelled her to turn over all future distributions and prohibited her from informing the trustees that she was under a Ccourt order.[4]

In *Rush University Medical Center v. Sessions*,[5] the plaintiff, Rush University Medical Center, sued the defendant's estate to enforce a charitable pledge. Upon obtaining a successful judgment, plaintiff learned that the deceased settlor transferred his assets to a Cook Islands trust one year prior to making the pledge. Defendant argued that Cook Islands law governed the trust and any transfers thereto while the plaintiff argued that the transfers were fraudulent under Illinois law and that Illinois law does not recognize self-settled trusts as against the settlor's creditors. The Supreme Court, in reversing the lower court, held in favor of plaintiff. Unfortunately, the trust held limited partnership interests in Illinois real property and therefore will likely be subject to attachment.

In re Huber[6] involved the creation of an Alaska asset protection trust by a Washington developer at a time when he "was or had to be aware of the 'gathering storm clouds,'" including "the threat of a collapsing housing market," and when his prospects for repayment of several substantial loans was "fragile at best." *Huber* held the trust invalid under a conflict of laws analysis, which, if correct, would invalidate every self-settled spendthrift trust created by a Washington resident, irrespective of circumstances. Whether *Huber*'s analysis was correct, however, is subject to dispute. It is unfortunate that the first case to address the conflicts of law issue with regard to a domestic asset protection trust involved fraudulent transfers that seemingly impacted the Court's decision on the conflicts of law issue.

The Court in *Huber* cited to § 270 of the Restatement (Second) of Conflict of Laws (1971), which speaks to the validity of an inter vivos trust in movables. After finding that the trust had its most significant relationship with Washington, partially based on the debtor's residence, *Huber* held, without real analysis, that Washington had a strong public policy against "asset protection trusts." Indeed, it is not clear why the Court even felt compelled to address the conflicts of law issue, since the same result was obtainable by reference to the fact that the trust's funding was a fraudulent transfer. Thus, the question left after *Huber* is whether

4. U.S. v. Grant, 2013 WL 1729380 (S.D. Fla., April 22, 2013).
5. 2012 WL 4127261.
6. 201 B.R. 685 (Bankr. W.D. WA May 17, 2013).

another court would rule similarly on the conflicts of law question absent the fact of the fraudulent transfer.

As many of these cases illustrate "bad facts make bad law." Based on the facts presented, the trusts were created after the debt was incurred, and accordingly, the Court, in each instance, reached the right decision. Notwithstanding the results obtained (and without condoning such transfers), in many cases the debtors apparently even benefited by their wrongful transfers.

In the end, the best results will be obtained where trusts are settled sufficiently in advance and properly structured and administered. A decision recognizing the validity of a foreign trust arose in the context of a divorce proceeding. In *Riechers v. Riechers*, heard in the courts of New York State, the settlor was sued for divorce two years following his establishment of an asset protection trust sited in the Cook Islands. According to the settlor, the trust (which named the settlor's wife as a beneficiary only by designation as the "spouse of the settlor") was established following the resolution of several medical malpractice suits against the settlor (a doctor) in order to guard against the likelihood of future medical malpractice claims. Although the parties were having marital difficulties at the time the trust was created, the settlor's wife was apparently aware that the trust was being established. In the divorce proceeding, the settlor's wife sought to have the trust included in computing an equitable distribution award, because domestic law did not recognize the validity of a self-settled trust. The domestic court, however, noted that since the trust was established for a legitimate purpose of protecting family assets, it did not have jurisdiction over the trust. The court therefore determined that issues such as whether the settlor's wife was entitled to any trust property should be left to a Cook Islands court to decide. The beneficent view of offshore asset protection trusts under the moderate facts of the *Riechers* case suggests that the predecessor cases, which flout established conflict of laws principles relating to the settlor's ability effectively to designate the controlling law of a trust, were decided pursuant to the axiom that "bad facts make bad law."

Ultimately, however, whether a domestic court gives credence to the application of offshore trust law is unlikely to affect the asset protection that such trust provides. So long as the trust's assets are located offshore (whether in the jurisdiction of the trust's governing law or in an established offshore financial center such as Switzerland), a creditor with a domestic judgment will still be faced with significant hurdles before actually being able to levy on any of the assets of an offshore asset protection trust. For example, notwithstanding the bankruptcy court having denied the respective debtors their desired discharge in bankruptcy, reliable sources have reported that the creditors in *Brooks* settled for approximately 50 cents on the dollar and that the creditor in *Portnoy* settled for approximately 20 cents on the dollar. Contrast, however, the case of *Nastro v. D'Onofrio*,[7] in which the court, in order to maintain jurisdiction over at least some of the assets of a

7. 263 F. Supp. 2d 446 (D. Conn. 2003).

foreign asset protection trust pending a decision on the merits, entered a preliminary injunction against a U.S. corporation with respect to stock in the corporation that was held in the name of the trust.

In any event, these reported cases obviously represent a tiny fraction of all offshore asset protection trust controversies; based on the author's experience, most controversies are never reported, because a favorable settlement is entered into prior to judgment.

The fact that the determination of the courts of the settlor's domicile may ultimately not impinge upon the asset protection afforded by an offshore trust does not mean, however, that the trust should not be structured with an eye toward obtaining a favorable domestic judicial decision should the need arise. In this regard, the reported cases provide some important guidance. First, the trust should be as separate as possible from its settlor. This requires an independent, if friendly, trustee who has control of the trust's assets exclusive of the settlor. Additionally, it would be advisable to give the trustee discretion to distribute trust assets to persons in addition to the settlor (called a "sprinkling power"), such as the settlor's spouse and descendants. Second, the circumstances surrounding the creation or funding of the trust must be as distant as possible from a potential creditor's claim. This means that the trust should be set up as early as possible for the purpose of guarding against future, rather than current, creditors.

VI. Ethical Considerations with Asset Protection Planning

There is little force behind the argument that asset protection planning is per se unethical. In this regard, there are at least two state bar association advisory opinions that provide that asset protection planning, in the appropriate circumstances, is ethical. In fact, it can be argued with some merit that an attorney or other professional adviser who fails to counsel his clients as to opportunities to structure their planning in a manner that maximizes asset protection has committed malpractice. Most pointedly, imagine an attorney who counsels his client to operate a business as a sole proprietorship rather than as a corporation solely because the attorney regards the limitation of liability provided by the corporate form as unethical. Notwithstanding the foregoing, asset protection planning as to any particular client may be deemed unethical depending on that client's particular situation. Whether asset protection planning in any particular situation is an ethical pursuit depends primarily on the application of local fraudulent conveyance law since, for example, the American Bar Association's Model Rules of Professional Conduct provide that an attorney "shall not counsel a client to engage, or assist a client, in conduct that the lawyer knows or reasonably should know . . . is fraudulent." Therefore, if an offshore asset protection trust is established during the pendency of litigation, it may result in disciplinary claims against the attorneys who assisted in the establishment of the trust, since the trust's funding will likely be seen locally as a fraudulent conveyance. The best way for an adviser to avoid violating applicable disciplinary rules and unethical behavior in the practice of asset protection planning is to perform a due diligence check on each client who requests such planning. If appropriate due diligence is conducted prior to any planning, the adviser should be insulated from liability, even if the client's transfer does, in fact, constitute a fraudulent conveyance since the *scienter* requirement necessarily cannot be met.

The Financial Action Task Force, the Gatekeeper Initiative, and the Risk-Based Approach to Client Due Diligence

21

Kevin L. Shepherd

I. Introduction

Most lawyers view client due diligence (CDD) as an administrative exercise to confirm the client's ability to pay the lawyer's fees and the absence of ethical conflicts. If the client passes muster during the intake stage, the lawyer then performs the legal services desired by the client. This process has served the legal profession well for decades, but there is something missing from this equation.

Although the lawyer has performed the level of CDD that most lawyers would perform under similar circumstances, the lawyer has not undertaken a risk-based analysis of the client to assess whether that client presents a risk of money laundering or terrorist financing. At first blush, that may seem to be a far-fetched notion. But efforts by the international community and federal authorities to impose anti-money-laundering (AML) and counter-terrorist-financing (CFT)[1] obligations on lawyers portend significant changes in their client intake and monitoring and potential encroachments on the attorney-client relationship, including the attorney-client privilege and the duty of client confidentiality. These efforts are referred to as the "Gatekeeper Initiative."

This chapter will describe the background and status of the Gatekeeper Initiative, trace the development of risk-based guidance for the legal profession, review the development of voluntary, risk-based good practices guidance for the U.S. legal profession, and analyze the application of the good practices guidance to a business transaction. This chapter will highlight the need for transactional and other lawyers to embrace the voluntary good practices guidance, both from the perspective of performing responsible and effective CDD and deflecting federal legislative efforts to impose onerous AML and CFT obligations on the legal profession. This chapter will conclude by assessing the likely impact recent revisions to the international AML and CFT standards will have on the voluntary, risk-based guidance for the legal profession.

II. FATF and the FATF Recommendations

Nearly a quarter century ago French President Francois Mitterrand hosted a spectacular celebration commemorating the 200th anniversary of the French Revolution. President Mitterrand, joined by leaders from thirty-two countries, viewed a Bastille Day parade along the Champs-Elysees, Paris's grand ceremonial boulevard, that featured tanks, 5,000 troops, and a mobile nuclear missile unit.[2] Later that afternoon, President Mitterrand, joined by President George H.W. Bush and leaders from other Western democracies,[3] repaired to the newly built I.M. Pei-designed pyramid at the Louvre to kick off the G-7 World Economic Summit.[4]

---

1. CFT is sometimes referred to as counter-terrorist financing, or CTF. For consistency, this chapter will use the acronym CFT.

2. R.W. Apple Jr., *Days of Wine and Bunting: 200th Anniversary for France*, N.Y. TIMES, July 15, 1989.

3. The leaders of these democracies were Prime Minister Brian Mulroney (Canada), Chancellor Helmut Kohl (West Germany), Prime Minister Ciriaco De Mita (Italy), Prime Minister Sosuke Uno (Japan), Prime Minister Margaret Thatcher (United Kingdom), and Jacques Delors (President of the Commission of the European Communities). *Summit of the Arch*, DEP'T OF STATE BULL. (Sept. 1, 1989) [hereinafter State Dep't Bulletin].

4. The G-7 (also known as the Group of Seven) summit originated fifteen years earlier in November 1975 when French President Valéry Giscard d'Estaing invited the heads of government from West Germany (Helmut Schmidt), Italy (Aldo Moro), Japan (Takeo Miki), the United Kingdom (Harold Wilson), and the United States (Gerald R. Ford) to a summit in Rambouillet, the summer residence of the presidents of France. These leaders agreed to an annual meeting organized under a rotating presidency, forming the Group of Six (G-6). In 1976, President Gerald R. Ford invited Canada to join the group, thereby forming the Group of Seven (G-7). *See* http://www.cbc.ca/canada/story/2006/12/27/ford-canada.html?ref=rss. The United Kingdom invited the European Union to attend the annual economic meetings with the G-7 leaders beginning in 1977. The European Union is represented by the President of the European Commission and the leader of the country that holds the Presidency of the Council of the European Union. *See* http://ec.europa.eu/external_relations/g7_g8/intro/index.

Known formally as the Summit of the Arch,[5] the leaders met to discuss a number of pressing economic issues.

After meeting for two days, the leaders issued a fifty-six-paragraph Economic Declaration covering topics such as international monetary developments and coordination, trade issues, environmental matters, and drug issues.[6] Toward the end of the lengthy Economic Declaration, the G-7 leaders agreed to the creation of a Financial Action Task Force on Money Laundering (FATF),[7] primarily for the purpose of coordinating efforts to prevent money laundering in the international and domestic financial systems.

A decade after the creation of FATF, the G-8 interior and justice ministers[8] met during three snowy days in Moscow in mid-October 1999 and adopted what is known as the Moscow Communiqué.[9] Then United States Attorney General Janet Reno represented the United States at this "little-noticed conference,"[10] which was hosted by then Russian Prime Minister Vladimir V. Putin.[11] The Moscow Communiqué, which specifically employed the term "gatekeeper," gave rise to the

---

htm. President Bill Clinton invited Russia to join this informal alliance of states in 1998, thereby creating the Group of Eight (G-8). *See* http://www.g7.utoronto.ca/what_is_g8.html. All URLs cited in this chapter were last visited on March 14, 2013.

5. The G-7 summit was referred to as the Summit of the Arch because of the newly constructed four-dimensional hypercube in Paris known variously as the Arche de la Défense and La Grande Arche. Built to resemble a 20th-century version of the Arc de Triomphe, the monument was nearly complete in time for the 1989 Bastille Day parade. *See* http://en.wikipedia.org/wiki/Grande_Arche.

6. *See* State Dep't Bulletin. Environmental issues consumed about a third of the paragraphs contained in the Economic Declaration, thereby underscoring the importance of that issue at the G-7 summit in Paris.

7. *See* para. 53 of the Economic Declaration. The pertinent provision of this paragraph states as follows:

> Convene a financial action task force from Summit Participants and other countries interested in these [drug] problems. Its mandate is to assess the results of cooperation already undertaken in order to prevent the utilization of the banking system and financial institutions for the purpose of money laundering, and to consider additional preventative efforts in this field, including the adaptation of the legal and regulatory systems so as to enhance multilateral judicial assistance. The first meeting of this task force will be called by France and its report will be completed by April 1990.

8. The G-7 became the G-8 when Russia became formally involved in the summit process starting with the 1998 Birmingham Summit. The G-7 Group of Finance Ministers and Central Bank Governors continues to exist and is distinct from the G-8. *See* http://ec.europa.eu/economy_finance/international/forums/g7_g8_g20/index_en.htm.

9. Ministerial Conference of the G-8 Countries on Combating Transnational Organized Crime (Moscow, Oct. 19–20, 1999)—Communiqué. *See* http://www.justice.gov/ag/events/g82004/99MoscowCommunique.pdf; *see also* Rebecca Gregory, *The Lawyer's Role: Will Uncle Sam Want You in the Fight Against Money Laundering and Terrorism?*, 72 UMKC L. Rev. 23, 31 (2003) (describing Gatekeeper Initiative and Moscow Communiqué).

10. Editorial, *The Wall Street Journal* (Oct. 27, 1999), *available at* http://www.apnewsarchive.com/1999/Editorial-Roundup/id-9cb25f2b0110265e5655f9b2a6c3b9e1.

11. Judith Ingram, *Russia Joins U.S. to Fight Bank Crime, Reno Says*, Miami Herald, Oct. 21, 1999, at 1.

Gatekeeper Initiative.[12] The Gatekeeper Initiative, as will be discussed in greater detail in this chapter, is an effort by governmental authorities to enlist the support of "gatekeepers" to combat money laundering and terrorist financing.[13] "Gatekeepers" include lawyers, notaries, trust and company service providers (TCSPs),[14] real estate agents, accountants, auditors, and other designated nonfinancial businesses and professions (DNFBPs) who assist with transactions involving the movement of money in the domestic and international financial systems.[15]

The grand celebration in Paris in July 1989 seems an incongruous and inauspicious beginning of a chain of events that would eventually cast a long and ominous shadow over the American legal system. The Paris and Moscow meetings, separated by a decade but rooted in the core desire to combat money laundering, together have spawned a multifaceted effort by foreign and domestic governmental authorities to impose AML and CFT obligations on the legal profession. This effort took on increased urgency in reaction to the cataclysmic terrorist attacks on the United States on September 11, 2001.

A. What Is Money Laundering?

AML and CFT lie at the heart of the Gatekeeper Initiative and FATF's existence. By way of background, money laundering "is the criminal practice of filtering ill-gotten gains, or 'dirty' money, through a series of transactions; in this way the funds are 'cleaned' so that they appear to be proceeds from legal activities."[16] Money laundering involves three distinct stages: the placement stage, the layering

---

12. Bruce Zagaris, *The Gatekeeper Initiative: An Emerging Challenge for Professional Advisors of International Business and Tax Matters*, 2002 ABA/ABA Money Laundering Enforcement Seminar at 3 (Oct. 27–29, 2002).

13. Paragraph 32 of the Moscow Communiqué contains the "gatekeeper" provision:

> 32. We recognize that many money-laundering schemes involve the corruption of financial intermediaries. We will therefore consider requiring or enhancing suspicious transaction reporting by the "gatekeepers" to the international financial system, including company formation agents, accountants, auditors and lawyers, as well as making the intentional failure to file the reports a punishable offense, as appropriate.

http://www.justice.gov/ag/events/g82004/99MoscowCommunique.pdf. *See* John W. Brooks & Roberta Vassallo, *Attorney Cathy's Continuing Quandary, Or, Can the Gatekeeper Initiative Be Reconciled with the Multi-Jurisdictional Practice of Law?*, 42 Int'l Law. 59, 59–60 (2007) (providing overview of Gatekeeper Initiative).

14. The Gatekeeper Initiative and FATF have employed the extensive use of acronyms. See http://www.fatf-gafi.org/pages/glossary.

15. Bruce Zagaris, *Gatekeepers Initiative: Lawyers and the Bar Ignore it at Their Peril*, 23 Criminal Just. 28 (Summer 2008); *see* Kevin L. Shepherd, *USA PATRIOT Act and the Gatekeeper Initiative: Surprising Implications for Transactional Lawyers*, Prob. & Prop. 26, 29 (Sept./Oct. 2002).

16. Fed. Fin. Insts. Examination Council, Bank Secrecy Act Anti-Money Laundering Examination Manual 12 (Apr. 29, 2010), *available at* http://www.ffiec.gov/bsa_aml_infobase/documents/BSA_AML_Man_2010.pdf. The Federal Financial Institutions Examination Council comprises the following agencies: Board of Governors of the Federal Reserve System, Federal Deposit Insurance Corporation, National Credit Union Administration, Office of the Comptroller of the Currency, Office of Thrift Supervision, and State Liaison Committee. *See* Steven V. Melnik, *The Inadequate Utilization of the Accounting Profession*

stage, and the integration stage.[17] The placement stage is the stage at which funds from illegal activity, or funds intended to support illegal activity, are first introduced into the financial system. The layering stage involves further disguising and distancing the illicit funds from their illegal source through the use of a series of frequently complex financial transactions. This stage may include the creation of tiered entities and complicated entity structures designed to conceal the illicit funds. The integration phase of money laundering results in the illicit funds, now laundered, returning to "a status of expendability in the hands of the organized crime group that generated them."[18]

B. Background of FATF

FATF is an intergovernmental policy-making body formed to develop and promote national and international policies to combat money laundering, terrorist financing, and other related threats to the integrity of the international financial system.[19] FATF, which is based in Paris, by its own admission seeks to "generate the necessary political will to bring about legislative and regulatory reforms" in the money-laundering and terrorist-financing areas.[20] FATF thus has no independent ability to enact laws but instead relies on its political muscle to achieve reforms in these areas. Since its creation in 1989, FATF has operated under various mandates. The most recent mandate, issued in 2012, identifies nine tasks.[21] These tasks include the following: (1) identifying and analyzing money laundering, terrorist financing, and other threats to the integrity of the financial system, (2) developing and refining the "FATF Recommendations,"[22] which are the international standards for combating money laundering and the financing of terrorism and proliferation of weapons of mass destruction,[23] (3) ensuring effective compliance with the FATF

---

in the United States Government's Fight Against Money Laundering, 4 N.Y.U. J. LEGIS. & PUB. POL'Y 143, 146 (2000/2001). *See* Cuellar v. United States, 553 U.S. 550 (2008) (the common meaning of money laundering is the taking of steps to make funds appear legitimate).

17. *See* Christopher Boran, *Money Laundering*, 40 AM. CRIM. L. REV. 847, 848 (2003) (explaining three stages of money laundering); Mariano-Florentino Cuellar, *The Tenuous Relationship between the Fight Against Money Laundering and the Disruption of Criminal Finance*, 93 J. CRIM. L. & CRIMINOLOGY 311, 324–30 (Winter/Spring 2003) (same); http://www.fatf-gafi.org/pages/faq/moneylaundering (same).

18. George A. Lyden, *Note: The International Money Laundering Abatement and Anti-Terrorist Financing Act of 2001: Congress Wears a Blindfold While Giving Money Laundering Legislation a Facelift*, 8 FORDHAM J. CORP. & FIN. L. 201, 208 (2003); *see* http://www.fincen.gov/news_room/aml_history.html (explaining three stages of money laundering).

19. *See* http://www.fatf-gafi.org/pages/aboutus/.

20. *Id.*; *see* Andrew de Lotbinère McDougall, *International Arbitration and Money Laundering*, 20 AM. U. INT'L L. REV. 1021 (2005) (discussing origins of FATF).

21. FATF Mandate (2012–2020), ¶ 3 (Apr. 20, 2012), *available at* http://www.fatf-gafi.org/media/fatf/documents/FINAL%20FATF%20MANDATE%202012-2020.pdf [hereinafter, FATF Mandate].

22. The FATF Recommendations, adopted by FATF in February 2012, are officially known as the "International Standards on Combating Money Laundering and the Financing of Terrorism & Proliferation." *See* http://www.fatf-gafi.org/media/fatf/documents/recommendations/pdfs/FATF_Recommendations.pdf.

23. In 2008, FATF's mandate was expanded to include dealing with the financing of proliferation of weapons of mass destruction.

Recommendations by assessing and monitoring the FATF members through peer review or "mutual evaluations," and (4) engaging and consulting with the private sector on FATF matters.[24]

FATF consists of thirty-four members, comprising thirty-two countries and territories and two regional organizations.[25] The United States, along with the United Kingdom, France, Italy, and Germany are charter members of FATF along with eleven other members. In the early 1990s, FATF nearly doubled its membership from the original sixteen members to twenty-eight members.[26] Between 2000 and 2010, FATF gradually increased its membership by adding eight new members.[27] Eight FATF-style regional bodies serve as associate members of FATF.[28] FATF members must commit in writing at the political level to endorse and support FATF's recommendations and policies and agree to undergo periodic mutual evaluations and attain acceptable ratings.[29]

In terms of governance, FATF is led by a president who serves for a one-year term. The position is held by a high-level government official from one of the FATF jurisdictions.[30] The FATF Secretariat, based at the headquarters of the Organization for Economic Cooperation and Development (OECD)[31] in Paris, supports the work of FATF and its president. This work includes interaction with FATF working groups and ad hoc groups to ensure coordination and consistency.[32] FATF, however, is an independent international body, and its operations are funded through

24. *See supra* note 22.

25. Argentina, Australia, Austria, Belgium, Brazil, Canada, China, Denmark, European Commission, Finland, France, Germany, Greece, Gulf Co-operation Council, Hong Kong, China, Iceland, India, Ireland, Italy, Japan, Republic of Korea, Kingdom of the Netherlands (comprises the Netherlands, the Netherlands Antilles, and Aruba), Luxembourg, Mexico, New Zealand, Norway, Portugal, Russian Federation, Singapore, South Africa, Spain, Sweden, Switzerland, Turkey, United Kingdom, and United States. *See* FATF MEMBERS AND OBSERVERS, http://www.fatf-gafi.org/pages/aboutus/membersandobservers/#d.en.3147 [hereinafter FATF Report].

26. *See* FATF, WHO WE ARE, http://www.fatf-gafi.org/pages/0,3417,en_32250379_32236836_1_1_1_1_1,00.html.

27. *Id.* Argentina, Brazil, and Mexico were added in 2000; Russia and South Africa in 2003; China in 2006; Korea in 2009; and India in 2010. *Id.*

28. The associate members are the Asia/Pacific Group on Money Laundering, the Caribbean Financial Action Task Force, the Council of Europe Committee of Experts on the Evaluation of Anti-Money Laundering Measures and the Financing of Terrorism, the Eurasian Group, the Eastern and Southern Africa Anti-Money Laundering Group, the Financial Action Task Force on Money Laundering in South America, the Inter Governmental Action Group against Money-Laundering in West Africa, and the Middle East and North Africa Financial Action Task Force. *Id.*

29. FATF, FATF MEMBERSHIP POLICY, http://www.fatf-gafi.org/pages/aboutus/membersandobservers/fatfmembershippolicy.html.

30. The FATF president for the period July 1, 2012, to June 30, 2013, was Bjørn Skogstad Aamo, Special Advisor in Norway's Ministry of Finance. Vladimir Nechaev of the Russian Federation became the President of FATF as of July 2013. *See* http://www.fatf-gafi.org/pages/aboutus/fatfpresidency.

31. The OECD, made up of thirty-four members, is an international organization designed to assist governments in tackling the economic, social, and governance challenges of a globalized economy. *See* http://www.oecd.org/about/membersandpartners.

32. FATF Mandate, ¶ 24.

the OECD with member contributions in line with OECD contribution formulas.[33] For fiscal year 2012, FATF's annual budget was over EUR $3.3 million.[34] FATF organizationally does not have an unlimited mandate or duration. Unless member states otherwise agree, FATF is scheduled to sunset on December 31, 2020.[35]

C. The FATF Recommendations

The FATF Recommendations reflect an evolution in the development and refinement of the international standards for AML and CFT. As the global AML and CFT standard setter, FATF has developed and modified these recommendations since their initial development in 1990. The following discussion will trace this evolutionary development.

Less than a year after the G-7 directed the formation of FATF, FATF issued in 1990 a comprehensive action plan for combating money laundering known as the Forty Recommendations.[36] The Forty Recommendations represented the basic framework for AML efforts and were designed to be of universal application.[37] In FATF's view, the Forty Recommendations are "neither complex nor difficult, nor do they compromise the freedom to engage in legitimate transactions or threaten economic development."[38] The Forty Recommendations, as initially developed, consisted of four major sections: (1) the framework of the Forty Recommendations, (2) the role of national legal systems in combating money laundering, (3) the role of financial systems in combating money laundering, and (4) international cooperation.[39]

Since 1990, FATF has revised the Forty Recommendations several times.[40] Shortly after the September 11, 2001, terrorist attacks in the United States, FATF expanded its mandate to address terrorist financing and issued eight (later nine) Special Recommendations on Terrorist Financing.[41] The Forty Recommendations

---

33. *Id.* ¶ 25.

34. FATF Report 2011–2012, at 38, *available at* http://www.fatf-gafi.org/media/fatf/documents/brochuresannualreports/FATF%20annual%20report%202011%202012%20website.pdf. As of March 10, 2013, this amount equated to over US$4.2 million.

35. FATF Mandate, ¶ 8

36. *See* The Financial Action Task Force on Money Laundering, The Forty Recommendations, at 1, http://www.fatf-gafi.org/media/fatf/documents/recommendations/pdfs/FATF%20Recommendations%201990.pdf [hereinafter Forty Recommendations].

37. *Id.*

38. *See* http://www.fatf-gafi.org/document/28/0,3343,en_32250379_32236930_33658140_1_1_1_1,00.html.

39. *See* Forty Recommendations.

40. FATF revised the Forty Recommendations in 1996 and 2003. The 1996 version of the Forty Recommendations, *available at* http://www.fatf-gafi.org/media/fatf/documents/recommendations/pdfs/FATF%20Recommendations%201996.pdf, contained revisions reflecting evolving money-laundering trends and techniques and extending their reach beyond drug-money laundering. The 2003 revisions are *available at* http://www.fatf-gafi.org/media/fatf/documents/recommendations/pdfs/FATF%20Recommendations%202003.pdf.

41. FATF adopted the FATF IX Special Recommendations in October 2001. *See* http://www.fatf-gafi.org/media/fatf/documents/reports/FATF%20Standards%20-%20IX%20Special%20Recommendations%20and%20IN%20rc.pdf.

and the Nine Special Recommendations are sometimes collectively referred to as the "40+9 Recommendations."

On February 15, 2012, FATF adopted a major revision to the 40+9 Recommendations by updating and renumbering the 40+9 Recommendations.[42] Now referred to simply as the "FATF Recommendations" or the "FATF Standards" (the FATF Standards refer collectively to the FATF Recommendations, Interpretative Notes, and Glossary), they represent the international standard for AML and CFT. The FATF Recommendations, which now number forty, represent "a comprehensive and consistent framework of measures which countries should implement in order to combat money laundering and terrorist financing, as well as the financing of proliferation of weapons of mass destruction.[43] To date, over 180 countries have endorsed the FATF Recommendations. For ease of reference and to avoid confusion in the numbering conventions used in the superseded 40+9 Recommendations and the new FATF Recommendations, this chapter will refer to the new numbering of the FATF Recommendations.

Specific recommendations are referred to as "Recommendations."[44] Organizationally, section A sets forth Recommendations 1 and 2. Importantly, Recommendation 1 embodies the risk-based approach to ensure that measures to prevent or mitigate money laundering and terrorist financing are commensurate with the risks identified. This chapter will discuss the risk-based approach in greater detail. Section C, which covers Recommendations 5 through 8, deals with terrorist financing and the financing of proliferation. Section D, entitled "Preventive Measures," addresses areas of intense interest to the legal profession. The Recommendations included in section D cover Recommendations 10 and 11 (CDD and record keeping), Recommendation 12 (politically exposed persons, or PEPs), Recommendations 20 and 21 (reporting of suspicious transactions and tipping-off and confidentiality), Recommendations 22 and 23 (DNFBPs), and Recommendations 24 and 25 (transparency and beneficial ownership of legal persons and arrangements).

The CDD and record-keeping requirements set forth in Recommendations 10, 11, 12, 15, and 17 apply to lawyers "when they prepare for or carry out transactions for their client concerning" certain "activities" specified in Recommendation 22(d). These activities comprise the following: (1) buying and selling of real estate; (3) managing of client money, securities, or other assets; (3) management of bank, savings, or securities accounts; (4) organization of contributions for the creation, operation, or management of companies; and (5) creation, operation, or management of legal persons or arrangements, and buying and selling of business entities.

---

42. Officially styled as the "International Standards on Combating Money Laundering and the Financing of Terrorism & Proliferation: The FATF Recommendations," they can be found at http://www.fatf-gafi.org/dataoecd/49/29/49684543.pdf.

43. *Id.*

44. "Recommendations" is a bit of a misnomer. They are actually standards, not mere "recommendations."

Recommendation 20 deals with suspicious transaction reporting (STR).[45] This Recommendation, which articulates the general STR rule, states that if a "financial institution" suspects or has reasonable grounds to suspect that funds are the proceeds of a criminal activity or are related to terrorist financing, the financial institution must report its suspicions to the appropriate authority by filing an STR. Recommendation 21 embodies the corollary "no tipping off" or "NTO" rule. Under the NTO rule, if the financial institution files an STR, it cannot inform its customer that it has made such a report. The STR requirement and the NTO rule have been a controversial aspect of the application of the FATF Recommendations to the legal profession. Although Recommendations 20 and 21 refer to "financial institutions," Recommendation 23 makes clear that those Recommendations apply to all DNFBPs, including lawyers. Lawyers are not required to file an STR "if the relevant information was obtained in circumstances where they are subject to professional secrecy or legal professional privilege."[46]

Recommendations 24 and 25 deal with transparency and beneficial ownership issues. FATF has made clear that it is "essential" that countries have in place measures to enhance the transparency and availability of beneficial ownership information on legal persons and legal arrangements. To that end, Recommendation 24 states that countries should "ensure that there is adequate, accurate and timely information on the beneficial ownership and control of legal persons that can be obtained or accessed in a timely fashion by competent authorities." Recommendation 25, which governs transparency and beneficial ownership of "legal arrangements,"[47] states that countries should "ensure that there is adequate, accurate and timely information on express trust, including information on the settlor, trustee and beneficiaries, that can be obtained or accessed in a timely fashion by competent authorities."

III. Background of Gatekeeper Initiative

Now entering its second decade of existence, the Gatekeeper Initiative traces its origin to the Moscow Communiqué issued at the 1999 meeting of the G-8 Finance Ministers. It calls on countries to consider various means to address money laundering through the efforts of professional gatekeepers of the international financial system, including lawyers, accountants, company formation agents, and others. Following the Moscow Communiqué, FATF created a working group that identified several professions as "gatekeepers" (including lawyers and accountants) with respect to money laundering. On May 31, 2002, FATF identified several

45. Domestically, STRs are known as "suspicious activity reports" (SARs).

46. Interpretive Note to Recommendation 23 (DNFBPs—Other Measures). *See* FATF Recommendations.

47. FATF defines "legal arrangements" as "express trusts or other similar legal arrangements." *Id.* (General Glossary).

areas where possible changes could be made to FATF's AML framework. The broad topics covered concern CDD and STRs, beneficial ownership and control of corporate vehicles, and the application of AML obligations to DNFBPs, including the legal profession.

The American Bar Association's Task Force on Gatekeeper Regulation and the Profession (Gatekeeper Task Force) was formed in February 2002 to address certain issues arising from the Gatekeeper Initiative. At the time the Gatekeeper Task Force was established, its principal focus with regard to federal AML policy was whether the federal government would impose a mandatory STR requirement on lawyers, i.e., filing with federal government regulators or law enforcement personnel reports on suspicious activity by clients and being prohibited from informing clients that such a report had been filed. This would have made lawyers subject to reporting obligations that are similar to what banks and other financial institutions have for reporting suspicious financing transactions to Treasury's Financial Crimes Enforcement Network (FinCEN). In more recent years, the focus of the Gatekeeper Task Force has turned to the risk-based approach to combat money laundering and terrorist financing and to address efforts by federal legislators to impose mandatory AML obligations on the legal profession. To date, the Gatekeeper Task Force has been instrumental in seeking the adoption of three ABA House of Delegates resolutions on Gatekeeper Initiative issues. House of Delegates Resolution 104 was adopted in 2003,[48] Resolution 300 was adopted in 2008,[49] and Resolution 116 was adopted in 2010.[50]

IV. Risk-Based Approach and Development of Lawyer Guidance

The risk-based approach permeates the FATF Recommendations. The risk-based approach is grounded in the premise that the limited resources (both governmental and private sector) available to combat money laundering and terrorist

48. Resolution 104 supported the enactment of reasoned and balanced initiatives to detect and prevent money laundering and terrorist financing, but also opposed any law or regulation that would compel lawyers to disclose privileged or confidential information to government officials based on "suspicious" activity of the client, or otherwise compromise the attorney-client relationship or independence of the bar. *See* http://www.americanbar.org/content/dam/aba/directories/policy/2003_my_104.authcheckdam.pdf.

49. Resolution 300 provided that states, and not the federal government, should retain the authority to regulate those who form certain business entities. Resolution 300 also urged U.S. lawyers to develop voluntary risk-based guidance for client due diligence and directed the ABA to develop this guidance and to engage with the federal government and other interested parties in this process. *See* http://www.americanbar.org/content/dam/aba/directories/policy/2008_am_300.authcheckdam.pdf.

50. Pursuant to Resolution 116, the ABA adopted as its official policy the voluntary good practices guidance that is discussed in more detail in this chapter. *See* http://www.americanbar.org/content/dam/aba/migrated/leadership/2010/annual/pdfs/116.authcheckdam.pdf.

financing should be employed and allocated in the most efficient manner possible so that the sources of the greatest risks receive the most attention. A risk-based approach is intended to ensure that measures to prevent or mitigate money laundering and terrorist financing are commensurate with the risks identified, thereby facilitating an efficient allocation of this limited pool of resources. By contrast, a "rules-based" approach ignores risk and mechanically applies the governing standards in a rote, box-ticking manner.

The proportionate nature of the risk-based approach means that higher risk areas should be subject to enhanced risk-based procedures, such as enhanced CDD and enhanced transaction monitoring. By contrast, simplified, modified, or reduced risk management procedures may apply in lower risk areas. An effective risk-based approach involves identifying and categorizing money-laundering and terrorist-financing risks and establishing reasonable controls based on the risks identified.

FATF has been active in developing risk-based guidance for financial institutions and DNFBPs, including legal professionals. In June 2007, FATF adopted risk-based guidance for financial institutions.[51] Three months later, in September 2007, FATF and representatives from the DNFBPs agreed to develop risk-based guidance for their respective sectors, using the same structure and style as that for the financial institution guidance. During the course of over a year, representatives from the legal profession from around the world met with FATF to develop the risk-based guidance. After intensive negotiations between the legal profession and FATF, FATF adopted the RBA [Risk Based Approach] for Legal Professionals (Lawyer Guidance or Guidance) at its October 2008 plenary in Rio de Janeiro. Guidance for each of the other DNFBP sectors was published separately in 2008.[52] The newly adopted FATF Recommendations expressly incorporate the risk-based approach.[53]

The Lawyer Guidance, which contains 126 separately numbered paragraphs, is a complex document that addresses different audiences (e.g., private sector and public authorities), undertakes to identify the AML/CFT issues specific to the legal profession, and outlines the risk factors that lawyers need to consider in developing a risk-based system. It is "high-level" guidance intended to provide a broad framework for implementing a risk-based approach for the legal profession. It does not offer detailed direction on the application of this approach to specific factual situations, nor does it take into account the practical realities of the practice of law in an increasingly complex environment or attempt to address

51. Guidance on the Risk-Based Approach to Combating Money Laundering and Terrorist Financing (June 2007). *See* http://www.fatf-gafi.org/media/fatf/documents/reports/RBA%20ML%20and%20TF.pdf.

52. For a detailed analysis of the development of the Lawyer Guidance, see Kevin L. Shepherd, *Guardians at the Gate: The Gatekeeper Initiative and the Risk-Based Approach for Transactional Lawyers*, 43 Real Prop. Tr. & Estate L.J. 607 (Winter 2009).

53. FATF Recommendation 1 states, in part, that "countries should apply a risk-based approach (RBA) to ensure that measures to prevent or mitigate money laundering and terrorist financing are commensurate with the risks identified." *See* http://www.fatf-gafi.org/dataoecd/49/29/49684543.pdf.

jurisdictional variations among FATF member countries. For those reasons, the Lawyer Guidance urges the legal profession generally, or in different countries, to develop "good practice in the design and implementation of an effective risk-based approach."

Importantly, the Lawyer Guidance is limited to those lawyers who "prepare for and carry out specified activities."[54] The Guidance focuses on the services performed by the lawyer, meaning that all lawyers are not automatically subject to the Guidance. It does not define "prepare for and carry out," but it does define "specified activities," as described below. Thus, even if the lawyer is subject to the Guidance, CDD may not be required because of the particular nature of the proposed engagement.

The "specified activities" consist of the following five categories: (1) buying and selling of real estate, (2) managing of client money, securities, or other assets, (3) management of bank, savings, or securities accounts, (4) organization of contributions for the creation, operation, or management of companies, and (5) creation, operation, or management of legal persons or arrangements, and buying and selling of business entities. The Guidance does not further define the specified activities, thereby creating ambiguity about the scope and coverage of each specified activity. If a lawyer performs or carries out one or more of the specified activities, that lawyer is subject to the Guidance.

V. Risk Categories

The Lawyer Guidance identifies three major risk categories with regard to legal engagements: (1) country/geographic risk, (2) client risk, and (3) service risk.[55] Lawyers need to determine their exposure to each of these risk categories. The relative weight to be given to each category in assessing the overall risk of money laundering and terrorist financing will vary from one lawyer or firm to another because of the size, sophistication, location, and nature and scope of services offered by the lawyer or the firm. Based on their individual practices and judgments, lawyers will need to assess independently the weight to be given to each risk factor. These factors are subject to variables that may increase or decrease the perceived risk posed by a particular client or type of work.

With respect to the first major risk category, country/geographic risk, no universally adopted listing of countries or geographic areas that are deemed to present a lower or higher risk exists. The Lawyer Guidance itself identifies the profile of those countries that in FATF's view pose a higher risk of money laundering. These higher-risk countries include those that are subject to sanctions, embargoes, or similar measures issued by certain bodies, such as the United Nations,

54. *See* FATF Recommendation 22(d).

55. Interpretive Note to Recommendation 10 elaborates on the service risk factor by characterizing it as "product, service, transaction or delivery channel risk factors[.]"

and those identified by credible sources as having significant levels of corruption or other criminal activity or a location from which funds or support are provided to terrorist organizations.

The second major risk category, client risk, entails an analysis of various factors to assess the potential money-laundering or terrorist-financing risk posed by a client. Clients encompass a broad spectrum, ranging from individuals to global enterprises. This breadth of clients presents challenges to the lawyer to determine whether a particular client poses a higher risk and, if so, the level of that risk and whether the application of any mitigating factors influences that determination. The Lawyer Guidance identifies about a dozen categories of potentially higher-risk clients, such as PEPs. Not all high-level political officials are PEPs; rather, PEPs are high-level political officials in *foreign* countries.[56] Other categories of potentially higher-risk clients include (1) clients conducting their relationship or requesting services in unusual or unconventional circumstances (as evaluated in light of all the circumstances of the representation), (2) legal structures that make it difficult to identify in a timely manner the true beneficial owner or controlling interests, (3) clients having convictions for "proceeds generating crimes" (such as embezzlement) who instruct the lawyer (who has actual knowledge of these convictions) to undertake specified activities on their behalf, and (4) the use of legal entities and arrangements without any apparent legal or legitimate tax, business, economic, or other reason.

The third major risk category, service risk, identifies those services at higher risk for money laundering and terrorist financing. Typically, those services involve the movement of funds and/or the concealment of beneficial ownership. For example, a lawyer who "touches the money" while performing or carrying out a specified activity creates a higher risk for potential money laundering if the lawyer does not know the sources and destination of the funds. Others services considered to present a higher risk of money laundering or terrorist financing include (1) services that conceal improperly beneficial ownership from competent authorities, (2) services requested by the client for which the client knows the lawyer does not have expertise except where the lawyer refers the request to an appropriately trained professional for advice, and (3) transfer of real estate between parties in a time period that is unusually short for similar transactions with no apparent legal, tax, business, economic, or other legitimate reason.

Once a lawyer performs CDD based on the factors identified within the three major risk categories described above, the lawyer needs to take into account a number of risk variables. These variables may either require the lawyer to perform enhanced due diligence or lead the lawyer to conclude that standard CDD can be reduced. In FATF's view, however, every client, without exception, presents some

56. In an important development, the newly adopted FATF Recommendations extend the definition of PEPs to *domestic* PEPs. See FATF Recommendation 12. FATF Recommendation 12 states that its requirements apply to "family members or close associates of such PEPs." The FATF Recommendations do not define "family members" or "close associates."

level of potential money laundering or terrorist financing. This view has been the subject of considerable criticism.

The risk variables include (1) the nature of the client relationship and the client's need for the lawyer to provide specified activities, (2) the level of regulation or other oversight or governance regime to which a client is subject, (3) the reputation and publicly available information about a client, (4) the regularity and duration of the relationship, and (5) the proportionality between the magnitude or volume and longevity of the client's business and its use of the lawyer for its legal requirements, including the nature of the professional services sought.

VI. Development of Good Practices Guidance

The Lawyer Guidance, self-styled as "high-level guidance," offers little practical guidance to U.S. lawyers. The risk factors lack elaboration, the Guidance itself is laced with often impenetrable jargon, and no practical insights are offered into the application of the risk factors to real-life CDD scenarios. In light of these shortcomings, and taking a cue from the Guidance suggesting that the legal profession develop good practices guidance, the Gatekeeper Task Force and representatives from other ABA sections and specialty bar associations collaborated to develop a paper entitled "Voluntary Good Practices Guidance for Lawyers to Detect and Combat Money Laundering and Terrorist Financing" (Good Practices Guidance).[57] Dated April 23, 2010, the Good Practices Guidance is designed to implement the Lawyer Guidance by providing practical and understandable guidance to the legal profession for the development of a risk-based approach to CDD. The goal of the Good Practices Guidance is to assist members of the legal profession in the United States in designing and implementing effective risk-based approaches consistent with the broad contours of the Lawyer Guidance. The ABA House of Delegates, the policy-making body of the ABA, endorsed the Good Practices Guidance as official ABA policy at the 2010 annual meeting in San Francisco.

It is important to understand the premise underlying the Good Practices Guidance. The Good Practices Guidance is not intended to be a statement of the standard of care governing the activities of lawyers in implementing a risk-based approach to combat money laundering and terrorist financing. Rather, given the vast differences in practices, firms, and lawyers throughout the United States, the Good Practices Guidance seeks only to serve as a resource that lawyers can use in developing their own voluntary risk-based approaches. At the same time, the Good Practices Guidance is not intended to be an academic exercise. The federal government is under pressure from FATF and others to adopt legislation implementing some or all of the provisions of the Lawyer Guidance. An overarching purpose of the Good Practices Guidance is to encourage and empower lawyers to

57. *See* www.americanbar.org ("Good Practices Guidance").

develop and implement voluntary, but effective, risk-based approaches consistent with the Lawyer Guidance, thereby negating the need for federal regulation of the legal profession.

The first section of the Good Practices Guidance provides an overview of the mechanics of money laundering and terrorist financing so that practitioners can better understand and achieve the goals of the United States' and FATF's AML/CFT efforts. The sections that follow then describe the risk-based approach and recommended CDD, identify those lawyers who are subject to the Lawyer Guidance, describe the specified activities that are addressed by the Lawyer Guidance, list and analyze the risk categories and risk variables, and conclude with a suggested protocol for client intake and assessment and a discussion of the importance of ongoing education and continuing legal education efforts in this area.

The Good Practices Guidance is best viewed as "gloss" on the Lawyer Guidance. The Good Practices Guidance distills the concepts and principles of the Lawyer Guidance in easy-to-understand language, which is particularly helpful given the sometimes syntactically challenged nature of the Lawyer Guidance. The "practice pointers" appearing throughout the text, which take the form of hypothetical fact patterns to highlight specific issues or points, are designed to provide practical guidance and insights to practitioners. They may also elaborate on a statement or concept contained in the Lawyer Guidance.

In an unprecedented action, U.S. Treasury issued a statement in support of the Good Practices Guidance. Treasury views the Good Practices Guidance as a significant step in implementing an effective risk-based approach for legal professionals in the United States. Federal legislators have encouraged the ABA to issue guidance to its members prohibiting the use of any financial account to accept suspect funds involving PEPs, conceal PEP activity, facilitate suspect transactions involving PEPs, or circumvent AML or PEP controls at U.S. financial institutions. The Good Practices Guidance is an effort to address these concerns.

VII. Application of Good Practices Guidance to CDD

The Lawyer Guidance applies to lawyers when they "prepare for or carry out specified activities." The Guidance does not define "prepare for and carry out," but it does define "specified activities" as including the buying and selling of real estate and the creation of legal persons and arrangements.

The first and perhaps most fundamental task of any lawyer's CDD process is to identify the client and verify its identity. Beyond obtaining the prospective client's name, address, and telephone number, it may be necessary to obtain additional information on the new client. This information may include some or all of the client's employment background, place of birth, prior residential addresses, current residential address, business address, telephone numbers, date of birth, marital status, names of prior or current spouses and/or children, dates of birth and social security numbers of any such spouses and/or children, the name and contact information of the client's certified public accountant, prior criminal convictions, pending lawsuits, and status of tax filings with governmental authorities. Obviously, all of this information may not be necessary to verify the client's identity, but it reflects the scope of possible sources of inquiry to enable a lawyer to verify the client's identity.

As part of the lawyer's risk-based CDD protocols, the lawyer should as a matter of course check the client's name against the Specially Designated Nationals list (SDN List), maintained by Treasury's Office of Foreign Assets Control.[58] The lawyer may also conduct an Internet search of the client's name to see if that yields any additional insights. Depending on the information the lawyer knows about the client, there may not be a need to conduct a more exhaustive analysis of the client, such as obtaining a background check.

The following will illustrate how to perform a risk-based assessment during the CDD process based on a hypothetical real estate transaction. Kristen, a junior partner with a ninety-lawyer law firm in a Midwest city, specializes in commercial real estate and corporate law. Her clients are principally local real estate developers with a sprinkling of domestic institutional pension funds. Kristen receives a call from Brittany, a former law school classmate on the West Coast, who wants to refer a potential client to Kristen to handle a real estate transaction in Kristen's city. In a bad economy, Kristen is thrilled to receive the referral. Brittany relates to Kristen that Brittany has been representing the client, an operator of a local warehouse distribution center, for a few months in labor and employment law matters, but now the client wants to acquire a strip shopping center in Kristen's city. Brittany informs Kristen that the potential client has a good payment record with Brittany's firm and thinks that Kristen and the potential client would be good match for the new real estate matter. Brittany mentioned in passing that the client is somewhat of a local celebrity because his spouse is the daughter of a high-ranking cabinet minister of a South American country. Brittany noted that she does not know too much about the client's other businesses or investments and is mildly curious why the client would like to acquire a real estate investment in the Midwest. Kristen thanks Brittany for the referral and tells Brittany that she will call the potential client as soon as she runs a conflicts check. To assist Kristen in that effort, Brittany e-mails the potential client's name, address, and telephone number to Kristen.

The conflicts check is clear, and Kristen promptly calls the potential client. Kristen asks the name of the shopping center owner so she can complete her conflicts check. The potential client indicates that a domestic insurance company now owns the shopping center pursuant to a foreclosure that occurred last year. Kristen immediately runs the owner's name through conflicts and confirms that

58. This list was formerly known as the "Specially Designated Nationals *and Blocked Persons List*." http://www.ustreas.gov/offices/enforcement/ofac/sdn/.

no conflict exists. Kristen then informs the client that the conflicts are clear and that Kristen's firm can handle the new engagement.

Kristen and her client then discuss the terms of the proposed shopping center acquisition. Kristen learns the deal is on a fast-track and that she is to review the draft contract of sale later that day, which the client will immediately forward to her. The client informs Kristen that a new entity will need to be formed to enter into the contract and to take title to the asset, and Kristen and the client discuss the pros and cons of the various forms of entities before deciding on a limited liability company (LLC). The LLC will be managed by the client but will have a number of "silent" investors. The client insists that the LLC be formed in Nevada, but does not offer much of an explanation. Kristen assures the client that she can form the entity quickly and prepare a standard member-managed operating agreement. Kristen does not push the client to identify the investors in the LLC or to form the LLC in the state in which Kristen and the real estate are located. Kristen concludes the call by expressing her appreciation for the client's business and that she looks forward to working with him on this transaction.

The above scenario has played out countless times with transactional lawyers across the United States. Kristen is pleased to have the new business, and the client is delighted to have a lawyer recommended by Brittany, his regular attorney. Kristen feels she has discharged her ethical obligations by running the standard conflicts check. Based on Brittany's assurances that the client is creditworthy, Kristen waived the need for a credit report on the client or the need for a retainer.

But what is wrong with this scenario? Although Kristen has performed the level of CDD that most lawyers would perform under similar circumstances, she has not undertaken a risk-based analysis to assess whether that client presents a risk of money laundering or terrorist financing. The following will analyze the risk-based CDD assessment Kristen should have adopted at the inception of the new client relationship.

The Lawyer Guidance applies to lawyers when they "prepare for or carry out specified activities." The Guidance does not define "prepare for and carry out," but it does define "specified activities" as including the buying and selling of real estate and the creation of legal persons and arrangements. Here, Kristen will be preparing for or carrying out the specified activity of buying and selling real estate (i.e., the shopping center) and the specified activity of creating a legal arrangement (i.e., the formation of the new LLC that will own the shopping center).[59]

59. Note, though, that if the client engaged Kristen to handle the leasing work at the shopping center, it is not clear whether that work, standing alone, would constitute performing or carrying out one of the five enumerated specified activities. Buying and selling real estate is a specified activity, but the Lawyer Guidance does not address whether the leasing of real property would fall within the ambit of one of the specified activities. *See* Financial Action Task Force, RBA Guidance for Legal Professionals ¶ 12 (2008), http://www.fatf-gafi.org/fr/themes/recommandationsgafi/documents/riskbasedapproachguidanceforlegalprofessionals.html,.

The first and perhaps most fundamental task of any lawyer's CDD process is to identify the client and verify its identity. Brittany, the lawyer who referred the new client to Kristen, provided Kristen with the potential client's name, address, and telephone number. Based on that elementary information, Kristen performed no other analysis to verify the identity of the client. Kristen has never met the client in person, and her only contact with the client has been through a telephone call. She knows from her discussions with Brittany that Brittany and the client have worked together for a relatively short time, about five months. She recalls that Brittany remarked favorably on the client's payment track record with Brittany's firm. Thus, this is not a situation where a potential new client enters a lawyer's office without any referrals or recommendations. Because the referral was from a trusted source (i.e., Brittany), Kristen likely would have no need to obtain additional information on the new client. But there are a few aspects of the client that should be of concern to Kristen.

As discussed in greater detail below, the client is a PEP, or politically exposed person. For this reason alone, Kristen needs to conduct a more exhaustive analysis of the client. As part of Kristen's risk-based CDD protocols, she should, as a matter of course, check the client's name against OFAC's (U.S. Treasury Office of Foreign Assets Control) SDN List. Kristen might also conduct an Internet search of the client's name to see if that yields any additional insights. Kristen also plans to call Brittany to obtain more information about the client.

After having verified the identity of the new client, from a risk-based perspective, should Kristen identify the beneficial owners of the new LLC and verify their identity? Based on the information Kristen has gotten from Brittany and from the client, Kristen may ask the client to identify the other members of the LLC so that she can confirm that no conflicts of interest exist. But is this enough? Assuming the client will provide this information, should Kristen then seek to verify the identity of the "silent investors" in the new LLC? The cost and time to perform these activities may be significant, and, in some instances, verification may be difficult to achieve.[60] From a risk perspective, Kristen should investigate the identity of the other members of the LLC. Although the transaction is a relatively straightforward commercial real estate deal, including the need to form a typical

60. The provisions governing the identification and verification of beneficial ownership are contained in FATF Recommendation 24 and currently represent one of the most controversial provisions in the FATF Recommendations. Many FATF countries consistently fall short of complying fully with this Recommendation. Most recently, in February 2010, FATF gave Germany a "noncompliant' rating for Recommendation 33 (now Recommendation 24) in connection with FATF's mutual evaluation of that country. *See* Mutual Evaluation Report, Anti-Money Laundering and Combating the Financing of Terrorism, http://www.fatf-gafi.org/dataoecd/44/19/44886008.pdf. In the last session of Congress, federal legislators introduced a bill obligating the identification of beneficial ownership information for certain entities. Incorporation Transparency and Law Enforcement Assistance Act, S. 1483, 112th Cong. (2011). The ABA opposed S. 1483 on a number of grounds. *See* letter dated December 16, 2011, from ABA President Wm. T. (Bill) Robinson to The Honorable Joseph Lieberman and The Honorable Susan Collins, *available at* http://www.americanbar.org/content/dam/aba/uncategorized/2011/gao/2011dec16_incorptransparency_l.authcheckdam.pdf.

member-managed LLC to take title to the asset, Kristen should not ignore identifying and verifying the identity of the other members of the LLC. Particularly since her client is a PEP, Kristen needs this information to ensure no conflicts of interest exist and to understand whether any of the other investors are PEPs.

In light of the Good Practices Guidance, how should Kristen perform CDD on her new client? Once Kristen has identified and verified the identity of her client, Kristen should then evaluate the new client based on the three major risk categories (i.e., country/geographic risk, client risk, and service risk) and the risk variables set forth in the Lawyer Guidance to determine whether the client is higher risk and, if so, perform enhanced CDD. As far as Kristen knows, the client is a U.S. citizen with a domicile in Brittany's home state. These facts do not point to any meaningful country/geographic risk.

Client risk, the second major risk category, merits critical attention by Kristen. The client's father-in-law is a high-ranking cabinet member of a South American country. The father-in-law is thus a PEP. PEPs include senior politicians of foreign countries as well as their family members. The FATF Recommendations do not define the contours of "family members," but the relationship here is not attenuated or distant.[61] The Lawyer Guidance is clear that the representation of PEPs inherently poses a greater risk of money laundering or terrorist financing. In dealing with PEPs, such as the client, Kristen needs to perform a more exacting level of CDD. She needs to know the foreign country involved and its reputation for political corruption. Kristen should also seek to understand the level of scrutiny to which the PEP would be subjected in the PEP's home country.[62] Based on discussions with the client and with Brittany and a review of a website maintained by Transparency International,[63] Kristen learns that the client's father-in-law serves in a politically stable South American country that does not have a reputation for political corruption.

Her client is an individual and has asked Kristen to form a new LLC to take title to the shopping center. From an ethics standpoint, Kristen needs to make clear whether she will be representing the interests of the individual or the LLC in

61. In the newly adopted FATF Recommendations, FATF did not accept the invitation to define "family members." The FATF explained that "the definition of family member and close associates of PEPs could differ substantially with the culture and risks in a country, and that any useful definition has to be sufficiently broad and flexible for countries, financial institutions and DNFBPs to adapt to the appropriate local circumstances, and the precise nature of the business relationships. The decision was taken, therefore, not to define these terms as part of the revised Recommendations." *See* FATF's Response to the Public Consultation on the Revision of the FATF Recommendations, ¶ 25, http://www.fatf-gafi.org/dataoecd/50/26/49693324.pdf.

62. The Financial Action Task Force of South America Against Money Laundering (GAFISUD) may be able to shed light on this issue. *See* http://www.fatf-gafi.org/document/35/0,3746,en_32250379_32236869_34355875_1_1_1_1,00.html.

63. Since 1995, Transparency International has published a Corruption Perceptions Index (CPI) that ranks about 200 countries by their perceived levels of corruption, as determined by expert assessments and opinion surveys. Here is a link to Transparency International's website for the CPI: http://www.transparency.org/policy_research/surveys_indices/cpi.

the proposed transaction. Kristen does not suspect the client is using a member-managed LLC structure to mask beneficial ownership, and the structure itself is not particularly complicated or convoluted, but Kristen wonders why the client insists on using a Nevada LLC. Kristen asks the client why he wants to form the LLC in Nevada, and the client responds by stating that his other business interests are formed under Nevada law, and he would prefer, from an administrative standpoint, to deal with a single state for formation purposes. Kristen is satisfied with that response.

Kristen has no knowledge of whether the client has any criminal convictions for proceeds-generating crimes, such as embezzlement. Based on a review of the client risk factors, and after evaluating the background and nature of the father-in-law's PEP classification and the need to use a Nevada LLC, Kristen does not discern that the client presents a higher risk of money laundering or terrorist financing.

Service risk, the third major risk category, focuses on those services involving the movement of funds or the concealment of beneficial ownership. Kristen plans to use an escrow agent to hold the earnest money deposit and to act as the closing agent, meaning that Kristen and her firm will not be "touching the money" in the shopping center transaction. In some jurisdictions, however, it is customary for lawyers to hold the deposit and to receive and transmit the settlement proceeds. Lawyers in those jurisdictions need to make sure that, in this higher-risk scenario, they know the source and disposition of the settlement funds. Because a single transfer of the shopping center is contemplated, this is not a situation where a higher-risk scenario arises because of accelerated transfers of real estate. Based on Kristen's knowledge, this transaction involves nothing unusual or out of the ordinary, other than the client investing in real estate distant from his home state. The client appears knowledgeable about commercial real estate transactions, investments, and protocols, and states that he feels this investment opportunity allows him an opportunity to diversify his assets.

Kristen's evaluation of the client in light of the three major risk categories leads her to conclude that the client does not present a higher risk of money laundering or terrorist financing. Still, Kristen must assess her client based on the risk variables contained in the Lawyer Guidance to determine whether the client or the proposed work would be unusual, risky, or suspicious. One risk variable is the nature of the client relationship. Kristen is dealing with a new client referred to her by Brittany, a trusted source. Given the lack of any prior relationship with this client, it may be prudent for Kristen to run a Google search on the client's name and any known investors in the transaction. Another risk variable deals with the "one shot" transaction, meaning that the client has instructed the lawyer to undertake a single transaction-based service (as opposed to an ongoing advisory relationship), and one or more other risk factors are present.[64] To be sure, the cli-

64. Lawyer Guidance ¶ 112 (ninth bullet).

ent has engaged Kristen to perform a single transaction, but Kristen has evaluated the other risk factors and has obtained a comfort level that the client's PEP status does not present a higher risk of money laundering or terrorist financing. By way of contrast, suppose the client had requested Kristen to form a limited liability company for the sole purpose of receiving the funds from the proceeds of a sale. That narrow representation, which is described in one of the Practice Pointers in the Good Practices Guidance, may pose a higher risk factor.[65]

Kristen has not met the new client in person, but has spoken with him on the telephone and has corresponded with him via e-mail. This situation, which is not at all unusual in our technologically dependent profession and economy, calls into play risks that may arise from the use of new or developing technologies that permit non-face-to-face relationships that could be used to favor or promote anonymity.[66] FATF perceives that anonymity in specified activities is conducive to potential money-laundering and terrorist-financing risks. Here, Kristen's electronically facilitated communications with her client are typical and do not suggest any nefarious activity. Finally, one risk variable focuses on the origination of the referral.[67] Brittany, a law school classmate of Kristen's, referred the client to Kristen. Kristen trusts Brittany's judgment, which militates in favor of performing a standard CDD process for the client, but the client's status as a PEP warrants an enhanced level of CDD.

Once Kristen has performed the CDD, she should document her findings and maintain the records. FATF Recommendation 10 directs that financial institutions and DNFBPs maintain these records for a period of at least five years after the business relationship is ended. The scope and degree of documentation will vary from case to case, and Kristen may find it prudent to summarize her risk assessment process in those situations where she has performed enhanced CDD.

VIII. Recent Revisions to the FATF Recommendations May Trigger Revisions to Good Practices Guidance and Lawyer Guidance

The revisions to the FATF Recommendations adopted by FATF in February 2012 will likely lead to a revision of the Good Practices Guidance as well as the Lawyer Guidance. The FATF noted in a paper issued simultaneously with the adoption of the revised FATF Recommendations that FATF remains committed to continuing its engagement with the private sector and that this engagement may take the

65. Good Practices Guidance § 4.9.

66. *See* Lawyer Guidance ¶ 112 (tenth bullet).

67. *See id.* (eleventh bullet).

form of "updating the relevant guidance to the specific sectors[.]"[68] The reorganization and renumbering of the FATF Recommendations will obviously entail revisions to the Good Practices Guidance and the Lawyer Guidance, but it remains to be seen the extent to which FATF otherwise desires to modify the Lawyer Guidance. But the revised FATF Recommendations are consistent with the Good Practices Guidance and the Lawyer Guidance by their strong emphasis on the risk-based approach.

IX. Conclusion

U.S. lawyers should embrace the Good Practices Guidance and implement it in their client intake, CDD, and ongoing client monitoring processes.[69] This common sense approach will signal to FATF and federal regulators and legislators that the legal profession can take steps to ensure that the services they provide will not promote or facilitate money laundering or terrorist financing, thereby obviating the need for a federally imposed, rules-based AML/CFT regime. Such a regime could dangerously encroach on the attorney-client relationship, including the attorney-client privilege and the duty of client confidentiality.

68. *See* FATF's Response to the Public Consultation on the Revision of the FATF Recommendations, ¶ 44, http://www.fatf-gafi.org/media/fatf/documents/publicconsultation/FATF%20Response%20to%20the%20public%20consultation%20on%20the%20revision%20of%20the%20FATF%20Recommendations.pdf.

69. A formal opinion issued on May 23, 2013 by the ABA Standing Committee on Ethics and Professional Responsibility on the Good Practices Guidance underscores the importance of lawyers adopting the Good Practices Guidance in their client intake and on-going monitoring activities. *See* Kevin L. Shepherd, *Ethically Speaking. . . Just What Are My Obligations under the Gatekeeper Initiative*, PROB. & PROP. 43 (Sept./Oct. 2013).

United States Tax: International Compliance Considerations for the Individual Client

22

Marianne Kayan
Ben S. Wright
Ashley A. Weyenberg
Caryn Gross*

I. Introduction

The other chapters of this book focus on technical rules and planning opportunities with regard to advising individual clients with assets located in, and income earned from, multiple jurisdictions. This chapter focuses on the reporting requirements and burdens placed on these taxpayers by the United States (U.S.) tax compliance system as a result of holding assets or earning income from

* Marianne Kayan, Ben S. Wright, Ashley Weyenberg, and Caryn Gross are members of the Individual Global Tax Planning group in Ernst & Young LLP's National Tax Department's Personal Financial Services practice, located in Washington, D.C. The authors would like to thank both Justin Ransome, who is a partner in Ernst & Young LLP's National Tax Department's Personal Financial Services practice, and also Elvin Hedgpeth, who is an executive director in Ernst & Young LLP's National Tax Controversy practice, for their reviews and comments to this chapter. The views expressed herein are those of the authors and do not necessarily reflect the views of Ernst & Young LLP.

outside the U.S. or as a nonresident alien. U.S. reporting obligations may arise due to an individual's U.S. residency or citizenship, the entity or structure an individual chooses to employ for non-U.S. investment, or the jurisdiction where an individual lives or invests. U.S. tax compliance obligations for reporting foreign income and assets are complex and growing. Since 2008, the Internal Revenue Service (IRS) has increased its enforcement efforts with respect to foreign reporting, and Congress has introduced several new reporting requirements for U.S. citizens and residents with foreign assets and for foreign entities that receive U.S.-source income.

Any non-U.S. investment or income—including investment in foreign entities, life insurance policies, pension benefits from a current or previous employer, bank accounts, and interests in foreign estates or trusts—may trigger one or more U.S. reporting requirements. Failure to file the required forms can lead to the tolling of the statute of limitations,[1] reductions of foreign tax credits, civil fines, and even criminal penalties. The purpose of this chapter is to provide an introduction and high-level overview of these complex compliance matters, and separately describe each reporting requirement, including who may be required to file, a general description of the information that must be included, the due date to file each form, and the consequences of the failure to file. This chapter also explains the options taxpayers have to disclose previous noncompliance. The primary goal is to provide advisors with the necessary information to alert clients of the number of forms required and the types of information that must be reported and leave advisors better prepared to assist clients with navigating these complex requirements.

II. Residency

Nonresident aliens are taxed differently for U.S. income tax purposes than U.S. citizens and U.S. residents. Therefore, the first step to determine an individual's U.S. income tax liability is to establish whether the individual is a U.S. resident.

An individual is a U.S. resident if the individual satisfies one of two tests, either the lawful permanent resident test (also known as the "green card test") or the substantial presence test (SPT).[2] First, under the green card test, any lawful permanent resident of the United States, as evidenced by possession of a U.S. green card, is a U.S. income tax resident. Second, under the SPT, an individual is a U.S. resident if she: (1) is present for at least thirty-one days during the calendar year; and (2) was present in the United States for at least 183 days in the current year and two previous calendar years. To calculate the 183 days of presence, a weighted average is

1. Enacted in 2010, § 6501(c)(8) of the Internal Revenue Code tolls, or suspends, the statute of limitations to assess additional tax with respect to the assets that should have been reported on the information returns described herein until three years after those returns are filed. Unless otherwise noted, all references to Code or Section citations herein are references to the Internal Revenue Code of 1986 and the Regulations thereto, as amended.

2. In certain situations, an individual may elect to be treated as a U.S. resident. *See* § 7701(b)(4).

used in which all days of physical presence in the determination year, one-third of the days of presence in the preceding calendar year, and one-sixth of the days of presence in the second preceding calendar year are aggregated. However, certain individuals, including foreign government-related individuals, teachers or trainees, students, and professional athletes may be eligible to exclude days of presence from the weighted average calculation.[3] Furthermore, certain individuals may be able to exclude days of presence in which an individual was unable to leave the United States because of a medical condition that arose while the individual was in the United States.[4] Additionally, individuals who satisfy the SPT but are present in the United States for less than 183 days in the current calendar may avoid U.S. residency status if they have a tax home in a foreign country and a closer connection to that foreign country than to the United States. Note, however, that the closer connection exception is not available for U.S. green card holders or those who have applied for, or taken steps to apply for, a green card. Individuals who are dual-resident taxpayers pursuant to the laws of the United States and another country with which the United States has an income tax treaty in force may be treated as nonresidents of the United States pursuant to the residency article in an applicable treaty. However, qualifying as a nonresident under an income tax treaty may not relieve the taxpayer of filing U.S. informational returns.[5]

A. Terminating U.S. Citizenship and Residency

Individuals who terminate their U.S. residency or citizenship may be subject to an exit tax. Section 877A, enacted in the Heroes Earnings Assistance and Relief Tax Act of 2008 (HEART) to replace the prior expatriation regime under § 877, requires "covered expatriates" to pay an exit tax upon relinquishing their U.S. citizenship or terminating their U.S. residency. An expatriate is either: (1) a U.S. citizen who renounces his or her citizenship or (2) a long-term resident, defined as a U.S. green card holder for eight of the last fifteen taxable years, who ceases to be a lawful permanent resident of the United States. A covered expatriate is an expatriate: (1) with a net worth in excess of $2 million; (2) an average U.S. income tax liability for the previous five taxable years of $155,000 (for 2013 expatriates, indexed for inflation);[6] or (3) an individual who fails to certify that he or she has complied with

3. *See* § 7701(b)(5).

4. *See* § 7701(b)(3)(D).

5. *See* Treas. Reg. § 301.7701(b)-7(a)(3) ("Generally, for purposes of the Internal Revenue Code other than the computation of the individual's United States income tax liability, the individual shall be treated as a United States resident. Therefore, for example, the individual shall be treated as a United States resident for purposes of determining whether a foreign corporation is a controlled foreign corporation under section 957 or whether a foreign corporation is a foreign personal holding company under section 552.").

6. §§ 877(e)(2)(A), 877A(g)(1)(A). The average tax liability threshold is adjusted for inflation annually. The amount provided is in effect for 2013. Rev. Proc. 2012-41, 2012-45 I.R.B. 539.

all of his or her federal tax obligations for the five tax years preceding the date of expatriation. There are exceptions from covered expatriate status for certain dual citizens and minors.[7] All expatriates must document their expatriation on Form 8854, whether or not they are covered expatriates.

The exit tax includes different tax regimes for different assets. The mark-to-market regime treats a covered expatriate as having sold all of her worldwide assets on the day prior to the expatriation date. Each covered expatriate may exclude up to $668,000 (for 2013 covered expatriates, indexed for inflation) of gain from the deemed sale of his or her assets.[8] Alternative tax regimes apply to certain items of deferred compensation, certain specified deferred tax accounts, and certain interests in nongrantor trusts; the gain exclusion is not applicable to these assets.[9]

HEART also introduced a new wealth transfer tax under § 2801 that imposes a tax on U.S. persons who receive a gift or bequest from a covered expatriate.[10] Generally, § 2801 requires the recipient of a gift or bequest from a covered expatriate to pay tax on the fair market value of the property received at the highest gift or estate tax rate in effect on the date of receipt. As a result, § 2801 imposes primary tax liability on the recipient of the gift, which diverges from the traditional rule imposing primary responsibility on the transferor.

B. Residency Reporting

1. Form 8833

Form 8833, Treaty-Based Return Position Disclosure under Section 6114 or 7701(b), is required for individuals who claim treaty-based return positions, including positions under income, gift, and estate tax treaties, and for dual-resident taxpayers to claim to be a nonresident of the United States based on the residency provisions of a treaty. Generally, treaty-based modifications of the Internal Revenue Code (the Code) that result in a reduction of tax are reportable.[11] However, there are several exceptions. For example, individuals are not required to report the re-sourcing of income (for foreign tax credit limitation purposes) or report any reduction of tax if payments that would be reportable on the Form 8833 do not exceed $10,000 in the aggregate.[12] Form 8833 is due with the individual's tax return. If the individual is not otherwise required to file an income tax return, Form 8833 is due at the IRS service center where the individual would normally file a tax return.

---

7. § 877A(g)(1)(B). Dual citizens and minors must certify that they have complied with their federal tax obligations for the five years preceding the date of expatriation.

8. § 877A(a)(3). The gain exclusion is adjusted for inflation annually. The amount provided is in effect for 2013. Rev. Proc. 2012-41, 2012-45 I.R.B. 539.

9. See I.R.S. Notice 2009-85, 2009-85 I.R.B. 598, for a detailed explanation of the exit tax.

10. Compliance with § 2801 is deferred until the IRS issues guidance. I.R.S. Notice 2009-85, 2009-45 I.R.B. 598. At the time of publication, § 2801 guidance has not been issued, but is anticipated to be issued in 2013.

11. Treas. Reg. § 301.6114-1(b).

12. *See* Treas. Reg. § 301.6114-1(c).

Key considerations with respect to Form 8833: (1) both residents and non-residents may be required to file Form 8833; (2) consider whether to file Form 8833 whenever an individual relies on an income tax treaty to reduce U.S. tax due under the Code; (3) determine whether any of the exceptions listed in Treas. Reg. § 301.6114-3(c) apply; and (4) if a U.S. resident is a dual-tax resident, she may claim to be a nonresident using Form 8833. There are two important caveats for dual-resident taxpayers who choose to be treated as nonresidents for U.S. income tax purposes based on the application of a treaty: (1) a long-term green card holder who takes the treaty position that she is an income tax resident of a foreign country may be deemed to have expatriated and could be subject to an exit tax if she qualifies as a covered expatriate;[13] and (2) filing as a non-U.S. person based on a determination under the residency article of an income tax treaty may not relieve the individual from U.S. information-reporting requirements, e.g., Form 3520, Form 8938, and Form TD F 90-22.1.

2. Form 8840

Form 8840, "Closer Connection Exception Statement for Aliens," is used to claim the statutory closer connection exception to U.S. residency under the SPT. Individuals must identify on Form 8840 the location of their non-U.S. tax home and the significant contacts they have with the foreign country or countries with which they are claiming a closer connection. The closer connection test is subjective, and the individual must indicate, among other facts, the location of the individual's permanent home, family, personal belongings, bank accounts, driver's license, and voter registration on the Form 8840 to establish a closer connection. Form 8840 must be attached to the individual's Form 1040NR.

Form 8840 is due with the individual's Form 1040NR for the year the return is due. If the individual does not have to file Form 1040NR, the individual should file Form 8840 with the IRS Service Center in Austin, Texas, by the due date for the individual's income tax return. If an individual does not file Form 8840, she is not eligible to claim the closer connection exception and may be treated as a U.S. resident.

Key considerations with respect to Form 8840 include: (1) determine whether the individual was present in the United States for less than 183 days in the current year; (2) determine whether the taxpayer has a tax home in a foreign country; and (3) compare the individual's contacts with the non-U.S. tax home country with the individual's U.S. contacts to determine to which country the individual appears closer.

3. Form 8843

Form 8843, "Statement for Exempt Individuals and Individuals with a Medical Condition," is used by individuals to exclude days of U.S. physical presence from

13. §§ 877A(g)(b)(3) and 7701(b)(6) (flush language).

counting toward calculation of the substantial presence test. Certain individuals, including teachers/trainees, students, professional athletes, or patients with a medical condition, may exclude days of presence from counting toward the residency requirements based on the substantial presence test.

Form 8843 must be filed with the individual's Form 1040NR or, if the individual is not required to file Form 1040NR, filed alone by the due date for filing Form 1040NR. Failure to timely file Form 8843 prevents professional athletes and individuals with a medical condition from excluding their days of presence. In contrast, this rule regarding failure to file does not apply to teachers and students, and these individuals may be able to exclude days of presence in a particular year by filing a Form 8843 after the due date for the return.[14]

Key considerations with respect to Form 8843 include: (1) exempt persons should file a timely Form 8843 if they intend to be treated as nonresident aliens; (2) teachers, trainees, and students are limited with regard to the total number of years they may claim to be exempt from the substantial presence test;[15] and (3) individuals with a medical condition must consider whether their condition was preexisting prior to coming to the United States.[16]

4. Form 8854

Expatriates are required to file Form 8854, "Initial and Annual Expatriation Statement," to report their initial expatriation, and to fulfill any ongoing reporting obligations. Form 8854 consists of five parts: part I requests general information; part II is for persons who expatriated after June 3, 2004, and before June 17, 2008; part III is for persons who expatriated after June 17, 2008, and elected to defer the exit tax; part IV is to be completed by individuals who expatriated during the current year; and part V requires the expatriate to include an income statement and balance sheet for the current year.

Parts I, IV, and V must be completed by expatriates to document their initial expatriation, even if the individual is not a covered expatriate, if the individual expatriated in the current tax year. Parts I, II, and V must be filed by certain expatriates who are subject to the prior tax regime under § 877 for individuals who expatriated after June 3, 2004, and before June 17, 2008.[17] Finally, parts I and III must be filed by covered expatriates who expatriated after June 16, 2008, and elect to defer paying tax on mark-to-market assets or who had

14. The Instructions to Form 8843 state that "if you do not file Form 8843 on time, you may not exclude the days you were present in the United States as a *professional athlete* or because of a *medical condition* or medical problem that arose while you were in the United States" (emphasis added); *see also* Treas. Reg. § 301.7701(b)-8(d) (consistent with instructions).

15. *See* § 7701(b)(5)(E).

16. The medical exemption is only available to an individual who was prepared to leave the United States and then became unable to leave due to a medical condition that arose while the individual was present in the United States.

17. Section 877 imposes an alternative tax regime for all taxable years ending with the ten-year period following the individual's expatriation date.

interests in eligible deferred compensation or nongrantor trusts. Individuals who expatriated after June 16, 2008, must file Form 8854 as an attachment to the expatriate's Form 1040 or Form 1040NR for the tax year that includes the date of expatriation. In addition, a copy of Form 8854 must be sent to the IRS Service Center in Philadelphia by the due date for the expatriate's Form 1040 or Form 1040NR.

Part V of Form 8854 includes a balance sheet and income statement. Current year expatriates must complete the balance sheet as of the individual's expatriation date. The income statement must be completed for the partial tax year ending on the date of expatriation. It may be useful for the expatriate to complete her final Form 1040 before completing the income statement.

Key considerations with respect to Form 8854 include: (1) determine the expatriate's date of expatriation, which will be the date listed on a long-term resident's Form I-407, "Abandonment of Lawful Permanent Resident Status," or U.S. citizen's Oath of Renunciation; (2) determine whether the expatriate's net worth exceeded $2 million on the day prior to expatriation, whether the expatriate's five-year average tax liability exceeded $155,000 (in 2013), and whether the expatriate is capable of certifying that she has complied with all of her federal tax obligations for the five tax years preceding the date of expatriation; (3) determine whether the expatriate qualifies for the dual-citizen or minor exception; (4) determine the expatriate's basis in mark-to-market property, including any adjustments for nonresidents who became U.S. residents; (5) determine the present value of ineligible deferred compensation and specified tax-deferred accounts on the day prior to expatriation; and (6) for individual's considering expatriation, determine whether the individual may be able to reduce his or her net worth to less than $2 million prior to expatriation and whether the individual can afford to pay the exit tax.

III. Foreign Financial Assets

A. FinCen 114

FinCen 114, formerly Form TD F 90 22.1, "Report of Foreign Bank and Financial Accounts," commonly known as the FBAR (and referred to in this chapter as the FBAR), is authorized by Title 31, Section 5314 of the United States Code (which is not part of the Internal Revenue Code). That law requires U.S. persons holding a financial interest in or signatory authority over foreign financial accounts to file an FBAR if the aggregate value of all foreign financial accounts exceeded $10,000 at any point during the year. In this case, "U.S. persons" means citizens, resident individuals, and resident entities. Financial accounts include banking, brokerage, securities, checking, deposit, or any other type of account held at a foreign financial institution. It also includes commodities, futures, and options accounts; life insurance policies with a cash-value component; and certain mutual funds or similar pooled funds. A financial account is foreign if the account is physically located outside the United States,[18] e.g., funds held on deposit with a bank located in Paris or even a branch of a U.S. incorporated bank located in Toronto.

A financial interest includes direct and indirect interests in the account. Thus, a U.S. resident may indirectly own accounts that are directly owned by a corporation in which the individual is a shareholder, a partnership in which she is a partner, or a trust of which she is an owner or beneficiary. Signatory authority is the right of an individual to control the disposition of the assets by direct written communication to the financial institution. This requirement may cause the CFO of a corporation or trustee of a trust to report financial accounts owned by the corporation or the trust on his or her personal FBAR, even if the CFO or trustee has no personal financial interest in the entity or entity's accounts.

The FBAR is administered by the IRS, but is not authorized in the Code; the FBAR is designed by the Financial Crimes Enforcement Network (FinCEN)[19] of the Department of the Treasury. Prior to July 1, 2013, the FBAR was not due with the income tax return, but rather was due each year by June 30 at the Department of the Treasury office in Detroit, Michigan. Additionally, in contrast with federal income tax returns, paper filings of the FBAR were deemed to be timely filed when *received* by the Department of the Treasury office in Detroit.[20]

As of July 1, 2013, electronic filing of the FBAR is required using FinCen's Bank Secrecy Act (BSA) E-Filing system. The newly designed FBAR for completion in

18. For FBAR purposes, the United States includes the states, the District of Columbia, all U.S. territories and possessions (e.g., American Samoa, the Commonwealth of the Northern Mariana Islands, the Commonwealth of Puerto Rico, Guam, and the U.S. Virgin Islands), and Indian lands as defined in the Indian Gaming and Regulatory Act.

19. In addition to the more widely known FBAR, FinCEN has other filing requirements, including but not limited to Form 104 and Form 105. FinCEN Form 104, "Currency Transaction Report," requires financial institutions to report each deposit, withdrawal, exchange of currency, or other payment or transfer, by, through, or to the financial institution that involves a transaction in currency of more than $10,000. Multiple transactions must be treated as a single transaction if the financial institution has knowledge that: (1) they are by or on behalf of the same person; and (2) they result in either currency received or currency disbursed by the financial institution totaling more than $10,000 during any one business day. FinCEN 104 is required to be filed electronically through the Bank Secrecy Act E-filing System. FinCEN Form 105, "Report of International Transportation of Currency or Monetary Instruments," must be filed by (1) a person who transmits, mails, or ships, or causes to transmit, mail, or ship currency or other monetary instruments in an aggregate amount exceeding $10,000 at one time from the United States to any place outside the United States, or into the United States from any place outside of the United States; and (2) each person who receives in U.S. currency or other monetary instruments in an aggregate amount exceeding $10,000 at one time, which have been transported, mailed, or shipped to the person from any place outside the United States. A transfer of funds through normal banking procedures, which does not involve the physical transportation of currency or monetary instruments, is not required to be reported. FinCEN 105 is filed with the Commissioner of Customs, and not with the IRS.

20. This means the "mailbox rule" does not apply, and the FBAR must be *received* by the Detroit Treasury office by June 30.

the electronic filing system has a field to enter reasons for late filing. FinCen 114a (Record of Authorization to Electronically File FBAR) is a form that a third-party preparer must keep in their files to reflect a client's authorization for the third party to electronically file the FBAR on the client's behalf. Since FBARs pertaining to calendar year 2012 were due by June 30, 2013, the electronic filing requirement impacts calendar year 2013 FBARs, which will be due June 30, 2014. Upon completion of the online FBAR, the system will generate a confirmation of filing.

Finally, there is no extension of time to file a FBAR. Failure to file the FBAR may subject an individual to a civil penalty of $10,000, which may be abated for reasonable cause. Furthermore, a willful failure to file the FBAR may result in a civil penalty equal to the greater of $100,000 or 50 percent of the balance of the account at the time of the violation and potential criminal penalties.

B. Form 8938

Section 6038D, enacted as part of the Foreign Account Tax Compliance Act (FATCA) rules in 2010, requires individuals who directly own interests in "specified foreign financial assets" (SFFA) to include a report of such assets with their tax returns. This rule became effective for tax years beginning after March 18, 2010.[21] The regulations[22] provide that any "specified person" with any interest in a SFFA during the tax year must attach Form 8938, "Statement of Foreign Financial Assets," to that person's annual return for the tax year if the aggregate value of all such assets exceeds the relevant threshold. The thresholds are: $50,000 ($100,000 for married taxpayers filing a joint return, "MFJ") on the last day of the tax year or $75,000 ($150,000 for MFJ) at any time during the tax year for individuals living in the United States, and $200,000 ($400,000 for MFJ) on the last day of the tax year or $300,000 ($600,000 for MFJ) at any time during the tax year for individuals living abroad. In this case, "living abroad" is defined by reference to § 911(d)(1) and requires that the individual maintain a tax home in a foreign country and that either the individual has been a resident of the foreign country for a year, or has been living outside the United States for at least 330 days in twelve consecutive months.

As of the date of publication of this book, specified persons include only U.S. citizens or resident aliens; however, proposed regulations have been issued to expand Form 8938 filing to specified domestic entities.[23] These regulations originally were to take effect for tax years beginning after December 31, 2011,[24] but reporting for specified domestic entities has been suspended pending future

21. 2011 was the first tax year Form 8938 was due for calendar year taxpayers.
22. *See* Treas. Reg. §§ 1.6038D-1T *et seq.*
23. *See* Prop. Treas. Reg. § 1.6038D-6(a).
24. Prop. Treas. Reg. § 1.6038D-6(e).

guidance.[25] Specified individuals are required to report SFFAs held by a disregarded entity or grantor trust in which the individual is treated as an owner.

Specified foreign financial assets are (1) financial accounts maintained by a foreign financial institution and (2) other foreign financial assets held for investment if they are not held at a foreign financial institution, including (a) stock or securities issued by a non-U.S. person, (b) any interest in a foreign entity, and (c) any financial instrument or contract that has a non-U.S. person issuer or counterparty. Generally, other foreign financial assets include direct ownership of equity or debt securities of a foreign entity; interests in a foreign pension plan, trust or estate; foreign life insurance plans, options, futures, forwards; and other financial instruments. Physical assets such as real estate or gold are generally not required to be reported on Form 8938 if legally owned directly by the individual.

Some SFFAs, including financial accounts maintained by a foreign financial institution and certain interests in foreign mutual funds or similar pooled interest funds, will also meet the requirements for reporting on the FBAR. The IRS does not consider the two reporting requirements duplicative, and both forms must be filed if required. In contrast, SFFAs reported on other required information returns, such as a foreign corporation reported on Form 5471 or a foreign trust reported on Form 3520 must be noted, but need not be reported directly, on Form 8938.[26]

Form 8938 is required to be filed with the individual's income tax return and is due by the due date of the income tax return, including extensions. Failure to file Form 8938 may result in a fine of $10,000 or up to $50,000 after the taxpayer has received notice of the failure to file from the IRS. Furthermore, any underpayment of tax involving an undisclosed specified foreign financial asset may result in an underpayment penalty of 40 percent of that underpayment. Finally, the statute of limitations for the tax year may remain open for all or part of the income tax return until three years after all specified foreign financial assets are reported on a properly filed Form 8938.

Key considerations with respect to Form 8938: (1) all SFFAs owned individually, jointly, or indirectly through a disregarded entity or grantor trust in which the individual is considered an owner for U.S. tax purposes are considered as being owned by the individual to determine whether the individual meets the filing threshold; (2) individuals with SFFAs in excess of the threshold amount must report all SFFAs on Form 8938; (3) foreign financial accounts reported on the FBAR must also be reported on the Form 8938; (4) SFFAs reported on other information forms, such as Form 5471 or Form 8621, are technically exempt, but the number of such forms in the individual's return must be noted on the Form 8938; (5) only directly owned[27] SFFAs must be reported on Form 8938, and the individual

---

25. *See* I.R.S. Notice 2013-10, 2013 I.R.B. 503.

26. *See* part IV of Form 8938 (revised Nov. 2012) and the instructions thereto.

27. For this purpose, "directly owned" includes amounts owned by a foreign or domestic disregarded entity or grantor trust in which the individual is considered an owner.

need not report additional SFFAs owned, for example, by a foreign partnership in which the individual is a partner; (6) as of the time of publication, U.S. entities are not required to file Form 8938, however Treasury has proposed regulations that will require certain specified domestic entities to file Form 8938 in the future; and (7) the requirement to file Form 8938 began in 2011 for calendar year filers, and failure to file Form 8938 can result in civil fines and the suspension of the statute of limitations with regard to the SFFAs that should have been reported.

C. Form 8891

Form 8891, "U.S. Information Return for Beneficiaries of Certain Canadian Registered Retirement Plans," must be filed by U.S. persons to report interests in Canadian registered retirement savings plans (RRSPs) and registered retirement income funds (RRIFs).[28] Article XVIII(7) of the U.S.-Canada Income Tax Treaty provides that U.S. residents may elect to defer tax on amounts contributed to or earned through these accounts until the individual receives a distribution. Form 8891 was created to simplify the filing procedures for U.S. individuals with interests in these tax-deferred Canadian retirement accounts.[29] Individuals who own an RRSP or RRIF should file Form 8891 to make the election to defer reporting undistributed earnings of an RRSP or RRIF in the first year that the individual is considered a U.S. resident and the owner of such an account. Furthermore, U.S. persons must annually report contributions, undistributed earnings, and distributions from RRSPs and RRIFs. If an individual fails to make a timely deferral election, late election relief may be available through a private letter ruling.

Alternatively, at the time of publication, individuals in the 2012 Offshore Voluntary Disclosure Program (OVDP), 2011 Offshore Voluntary Initiative, or the 2009 Offshore Voluntary Disclosure Program may seek streamlined relief to make a late election to defer taxation of income earned through these Canadian retirement accounts. The requirements to request streamlined relief are described in the OVDP Frequently Asked Questions and Answers #54.[30]

Form 8891 must be filed annually as an attachment to the individual's Form 1040. Failure to file does not result in a penalty; however it may result in inclusion on the individual's income tax return of the amounts contributed to and income earned in these Canadian retirement accounts during the year.

Key considerations with respect to Form 8891 include: (1) if an individual is or ever has been employed in Canada, then the individual may own an RRSP or RRIF and should file Form 8891 to preserve tax deferral on the accounts; and (2) if

28. These are tax-deferred retirement accounts in Canada, with taxation similar to a U.S. Individual Retirement Account (IRA) or § 401(k) account. Other types of Canadian tax-deferred accounts may not be eligible for the treaty exception.

29. Previously, RRSPs and RRIFs were subject to more onerous reporting on Form 3520. For additional guidance on Form 8891, see I.R.S. Notice 2003-75, 2003-2 C.B. 1204.

30. Offshore Voluntary Disclosure Program Frequently Asked Questions and Answers, Question 54, *available at* http://www.irs.gov/Individuals/International-Taxpayers/Offshore-Voluntary-Disclosure-Program-Frequently-Asked-Questions-and-Answers.

an individual has failed to file Form 8891 to make the election available under the U.S.-Canada Income Tax Treaty in the past, at the time of publication there is a procedure available in the 2012 OVDP to make a late election, or relief may be available through a private letter ruling.

IV. Income Tax Reporting, Generally

In the United States, both entities and individuals are subject to federal income tax annually, but the application of that tax differs based on the residency, citizenship, or place of organization of the taxpayer. U.S. individuals and entities (e.g., nongrantor trusts and corporations) are subject to tax on their worldwide income. U.S. individuals report their income on Form 1040, while domestic estates and nongrantor trusts, partnerships, and U.S. corporations file an annual income tax return on Form 1041, Form 1065, and Form 1120, respectively.

Non-U.S. entities and individuals are subject to federal income tax on U.S.-source income and certain limited types of foreign-source income. U.S.-source income includes both nonbusiness income and business income; each is treated differently. Non-U.S. individuals and nongrantor trusts report their U.S.-source-income on Form 1040NR.

Nonbusiness income is generally subject to 30 percent withholding tax on gross income, which may be reduced based on an applicable treaty-based return position.[31] For these purposes, nonbusiness income is defined as fixed and determinable, annual or periodical income (FDAP), which includes interest (certain bank and portfolio interest is exempt), dividends, rents, royalties, and other passive income. Nonresident aliens are generally not subject to tax on the gain on the sale of capital assets unless those assets are U.S. real estate or assets used in a U.S. trade or business.

Income effectively connected with the conduct of a U.S. trade or business (ECI) is subject to tax on net income based on graduated rates.[32] ECI includes income earned from (1) business performed from a fixed base in the United States (similar to permanent establishment); (2) compensation for personal services rendered; (3) partnership distributions from a partnership that is engaged in a U.S. trade or business; and (4) selling/renting real estate.

A. Withholding Requirements

Withholding agents are the persons responsible for withholding tax on payments made to foreign persons. Withholding agents are U.S. or foreign persons—individuals, partnerships, corporations, trusts, associations, or any other entity—that have control, receipt, custody, disposal, or payment of any item of income to a

31. § 871(a). To take a treaty position, Form 8833 is generally required.
32. § 871(b).

foreign person that is subject to withholding. A withholding agent that can reliably associate the payment with documentation from a U.S. person is not required to withhold tax.[33] A withholding agent may apply a reduced rate of withholding if it can reliably associate documentation from a beneficial owner that is a foreign person that is entitled to a reduced rate of withholding. The withholding agent is personally liable for the tax that should be withheld.

To effectively administer the withholding requirements, prior to making any payment, a withholding agent should request documentation, a withholding certificate, from each payee that may be a foreign person. Upon request, the foreign payee should provide the proper withholding certificate (see below for an explanation of the various withholding certificates) indicating the foreign person's status and claiming any treaty benefit to which that person may be entitled. The documentation is not valid if the withholding agent knows, or has reason to know, that it is unreliable or incorrect. In the absence of documentation, the withholding agent may apply certain presumption rules[34] to avoid liability for tax, interest, and penalties for tax that should have been withheld. In addition, the withholding agent has annual reporting requirements with respect to its withholding obligations (see Form 1042, below).

1. Form W-8

Generally, U.S. persons are required to withhold tax on payments of U.S.-source income to nonresident aliens, foreign corporations, foreign partnerships, foreign trusts, estates, and other foreign payees.[35] The W-8 series of forms are withholding certificates used to certify the U.S. tax status of the foreign payee to the U.S. withholding agent and ensure proper withholding. Foreign payees who are beneficial owners of U.S.-source payments should provide one of the Forms W-8 to a U.S. withholding agent to notify the payor of the payee's status as a foreign resident and to assist the payor with the determination of the proper withholding on payments of U.S.-source income. U.S. residents should not provide Form W-8, but should provide Form W-9 if a U.S. payor requests documentation of the U.S. resident's tax status or Taxpayer Identification Number (TIN) (see Form W-9 below). A Form W-8 should be provided to a withholding agent with respect to payments of FDAP income. To claim an exemption from withholding with respect to compensation income, a different withholding certificate is required (see Form 8233 below).

The most common form is the W-8BEN, "Certificate of Foreign Status of Beneficial Owner for United States Tax Withholding.[36] This form is used to establish for-

33. The payor may, however, have information-reporting requirements with regard to the payment, i.e., the Form 1099 series.

34. See Publication 515, *Withholding of Tax on Nonresident Aliens and Foreign Entities*, and the regulations to § 1441 for more information.

35. *See* §§ 1441–1446.

36. Other forms in the W-8 series include Form W-8ECI, "Certificate of a Foreign Person's Claim that Income Is Effectively Connected with the Conduct of a Trade or Business in the United States," for use by a nonresident alien or corporation that has made an election pursuant to

eign status, to claim that the foreign person is the beneficial owner of the payment for which the form is furnished, and to claim a reduced rate of, or exemption from, withholding under an income tax treaty. Form W-8BEN should be sent to the U.S. payor upon initiation of the payor-payee relationship and will remain in effect for three years (for foreign persons without a U.S. Taxpayer Identification Number) or until a change in circumstances makes the information incorrect.

Key considerations with respect to Form W-8 include: (1) foreign payees/payors should identify U.S.-source income/non-U.S. payees; (2) categorize the non-U.S. payee as a beneficial owner entitled to a reduction in withholding, engaged in a U.S. trade or business, as a foreign government or organization or as an intermediary to determine the appropriate type of Form W-8 to be filed; (3) non-U.S. payees should analyze the appropriate U.S. treaty to determine whether a reduced rate of withholding is available with respect to each type of income received; and (4) payees should provide a new Form W-8 whenever a current withholding certificate expires or circumstances change to make the previous certificate invalid.

2. Form W-9

U.S. residents, including resident aliens, should complete Form W-9, "Request for Taxpayer Identification Number and Certification," to provide a Taxpayer Identification Number to a U.S. payor to ensure that the U.S. payor can properly report payments to the U.S. resident on required information returns, such as a Form 1099. Foreign persons should not provide Form W-9, but should provide the proper Form W-8 if a U.S. payor requests a TIN (see Forms W-8 above).

3. Form 8233

Form 8233, "Exemption from Withholding on Compensation for Independent (and Certain Dependent) Personal Services of a Nonresident Alien Individual," is the withholding certificate used to claim a treaty exemption from withholding with respect to independent and certain dependent services compensation income. In general, § 1441 requires a 30 percent tax to be withheld from compensation payments for independent personal services performed by nonresident aliens. However, a nonresident alien may be exempt from U.S. tax, and the required withholding, on income earned for the performance of certain services based on the

§ 871(d) or § 882(d) to be treated as engaged in a U.S. trade or business with respect to its real property income; Form W-8EXP, "Certificate of Foreign Government or Other Foreign Organization for United States Tax Withholding," for use by foreign governments, foreign central banks of issue, foreign foundations, international organizations, and foreign tax-exempt organizations; and Form W-8IMY, "Certificate of Foreign Intermediary, Foreign Flow-Through Entity, or Certain U.S. Branches for United States Tax Withholding," used to indicate, among other things that the foreign entity is a qualified intermediary that will assume responsibility for U.S. withholding upon payment to the ultimate beneficial owner of the income. See Publication 515, *Withholding of Tax on Nonresident Aliens and Foreign Entities*, for more information. Furthermore, covered expatriates may be required to provide Form W-8CE, "Notice of Expatriation and Waiver of Treaty Benefits," to certain payors of deferred compensation, custodians for specified deferred tax accounts, and trustees of nongrantor trusts. *See* I.R.S. Notice 2009-85, 2009-85 I.R.B. 598.

application of a treaty. For dependent personal services compensation for which a nonresident alien is not claiming a treaty exemption to withholding, the nonresident should provide Form W-4, "Employee's Withholding Allowance Certificate" (for other types of income, see Form W-8 series above).

Independent personal services are services performed by an independent contractor in the United States by a nonresident alien who is self-employed rather than an employee. Common types of independent personal services include payments for contract labor and professional services including, but not limited to, attorneys, accountants, physicians, consultants, visiting professors and other speakers, and public entertainers. Certain treaties do not have an independent personal services article, and payments for independent personal services are covered under the business profits article. Dependent personal services are services performed as an employee.

Key considerations with respect to Form 8322 include: (1) categorize the compensation income as from dependent or independent personal services; (2) review the appropriate treaty to determine whether the nonresident alien individual is eligible for an exemption from U.S. tax and withholding for compensation of that type of services; and (3) promptly notify the withholding agent if circumstances change that may impact the U.S. taxation of the compensation income.

4. Form 1042

Form 1042, "Annual Withholding Tax Return for U.S. Source Income of Foreign Persons," and Form 1042-S, Foreign Person's U.S. Source Income Subject to Withholding," are required to be filed by U.S. withholding agents to withhold and remit payment on U.S.-source FDAP payments to nonresident aliens, foreign corporations, foreign partnerships, foreign trusts, estates, and other foreign payees.[37] Withholding agents are personally liable for tax that is required to be withheld. Form 1042-S is used to report payments to non-U.S. person payees. Form 1042 is used to summarize a withholding agent's total withholding for the preceding calendar year.

Form 1042-S, Copy A, must be filed with the IRS by March 15 of the year following the reporting year. Withholding agents are encouraged to file Form 1042-S electronically. If it is filed on paper, Form 1042-T, "Annual Summary and Transmittal of Forms 1042-S," must be filed as well. Copies B, C, and D of Form 1042-S must be sent to the income recipient by March 15.

Form 1042 must be filed with the Ogden, Utah, IRS Service Center by March 15 to report amounts for the preceding calendar year. An extension of time to file may be granted by filing Form 7004, although this does not extend the time for remitting payment. Payments must be deposited through the Electronic Federal

37. See Form 941, "Employer's Quarterly Federal Tax Return, and Form 945, "Annual Report of Withheld Federal Income Tax," for information on income tax withholding on wages, pensions, annuities, and certain other deferred compensation of nonresident aliens.

Tax Payment System (EFTPS).[38] Failure to file Form 1042 when due may result in a late filing penalty of 5 percent of the unpaid tax for each month the return is late (up to a maximum of 25 percent). Failure to pay the tax when due may result in a penalty of 0.5 percent of the unpaid tax for each month the tax is unpaid (up to a maximum of 25 percent of the unpaid tax). Interest charges may be imposed on the late payment of tax and on penalties. The Instructions for Form 1042 note that the computation of interest and penalties is complex, and the filer may have the IRS perform these calculations.

Key considerations with respect to Form 1042 and Form 1042-S include: (1) request withholding certificate from foreign payee; (2) determine whether a payment made to a foreign payee is subject to withholding and the amount of withholding; (3) file Forms 1042 and 1042-S annually by March 15.

V. Foreign Entity Ownership

A. Taxation and Reporting of Passive Foreign Investment Companies

The Code seeks to prevent taxpayers from shifting income to low-tax foreign jurisdictions by immediately taxing some types of foreign income. For example, U.S. shareholders must pay ordinary income tax rates and interest on distributions from and dispositions of passive foreign investment companies (PFIC). A foreign corporation is a PFIC if either 75 percent or more of its gross income is passive in nature,[39] or if 50 percent or more of its assets produce passive income.[40] A classic example of a PFIC is a foreign mutual fund, although many other corporations may meet the income or the asset test during the corporation's existence, and PFICs may arise in other unexpected situations. For example, an active manufacturing corporation with an operating loss may be a PFIC if the corporation generates even a small amount of passive income, such as interest or dividends. Furthermore, that active corporation will continue to be a PFIC in subsequent years even if it subsequently fails the income and asset tests because of the "once a PFIC, always a PFIC" rule.[41] Another example of an unexpected PFIC is an active sales or services corporation with little overhead and few nonpassive assets to offset its cash and other passive assets, which qualifies as a PFIC under the asset test

38. Deposits made through EFTPS are timely so long as they are made by 8:00 p.m. EST the day before the deposit is due. See www.eftps.gov/eftps for enrollment and additional information on EFTPS. See Publication 515, *Withholding of Tax on Nonresident Aliens and Foreign Entities*, for additional information.

39. § 1297(a)(1).

40. § 1297(a)(2). Passive income is defined as interest, dividends, rents, royalties, and gains from the sale of assets that produce this type of income. For example, cash is generally considered a passive asset. § 1297(a)(2).

41. § 1298(b)(1). The "once a PFIC, always a PFIC" rule may be avoided if the taxpayer makes a timely QEF election.

despite the fact that it generates substantial active income and does not qualify as a PFIC under the income test.

There are three separate taxation regimes for U.S. persons holding PFIC stock: (1) the excess distribution regime, which imposes a tax and interest charge on the deferred accumulation of income when excess distributions are made; (2) the qualified electing fund (QEF) regime, which allows the U.S. shareholder to treat all of the earnings of the PFIC as income distributed to the individual annually; and (3) the mark-to-market regime, which allows the U.S. shareholder to mark the PFIC to market every year and report the annual gain as ordinary income. Absent an election made by filing Form 8621, "Information Return by a Shareholder of a Passive Foreign Investment Company or Qualified Electing Fund," the U.S. person is subject to tax under the default excess distribution regime.

B. Taxation of Controlled Foreign Corporations

A controlled foreign corporation (CFC) is a foreign corporation with U.S. shareholders that own directly, indirectly, or constructively[42] more than 50 percent of (1) the total combined voting power of all classes of its voting stock or (2) the total value of the stock of the foreign corporation.[43] A U.S. shareholder is a U.S. person that owns 10 percent or more of the voting power of a foreign corporation.[44] U.S. shareholders pay U.S. federal income tax at ordinary rates on certain types of income, including dividends, interest, and gain on sale, earned by the CFC as if such income were currently distributed to the U.S. shareholders. Form 5471 is often associated with reporting interests in a CFC, although the filing requirements often extend to other foreign corporations that do not satisfy the definition of a CFC.

C. Attribution Rules

The foreign information-reporting rules are complex because U.S. residents may be required to report indirect and constructive interests in foreign entities in addition to their direct interests. Furthermore, the ownership attribution rules vary depending on the type of entity and information being reported. An individual must address an entity's ownership structure as a whole to determine whether she has a filing requirement for a lower-tier entity or even for an entity in which the individual is merely a constructive owner.

Individuals should be aware of the variations in attribution rules. For example, § 1298 provides specific attribution rules to determine a U.S. shareholder's interest in a PFIC. Alternatively, § 958 provides specific attribution rules, including constructive ownership rules incorporated through § 318(a), to determine

42. *See* § 958(a) and (b) for ownership rules.

43. § 957(a). To determine whether a foreign corporation is a CFC, the constructive ownership rules under § 318(a) apply except that stock owned by a nonresident alien individual is not considered as owned by a U.S. person. § 958(b)(1).

44. § 951(b).

whether a U.S. person is a U.S. shareholder for CFC purposes. On the other hand, the constructive ownership rules under § 267 are applicable, with modification, to determine whether an individual has an interest in a foreign partnership. The attribution rules in these sections are similar, but not identical; for example, § 267 will include stock held by an individual's siblings as constructively owned by the individual, whereas § 318 does not. Thus, it is essential for the filer to have a clear understanding of her entity structure as well as any structures in which she may have a constructive ownership interest and the particular set of attribution rules and modifications to those rules that apply.

D. Foreign Entity Reporting

1. Form 8621

Form 8621 must be filed by U.S. persons who receive certain direct or indirect distributions from a PFIC, recognize gain on a direct or indirect disposition of PFIC stock, or elect QEF or mark-to-market treatment. In addition, § 1298(f) imposes an annual reporting requirement on U.S. owners of PFICs regardless of whether the PFIC is disposed of or makes distributions. *However, at the time of publication of this book, the annual reporting requirement under § 1298(f) is suspended until the IRS releases a revised Form 8621.*[45] U.S. persons who are otherwise required to file Form 8621 are not relieved from their filing obligations. Form 8621 must be attached to the person's income tax return.

Key considerations with respect to Form 8621 include: (1) whether the foreign entity is categorized as a corporation for U.S. income tax purposes; (2) whether a foreign corporation meets one of the PFIC income or asset tests; (3) whether the foreign corporation may also be a CFC (in which case the CFC taxation rules would trump the PFIC rules); (4) whether the individual has made any prior elections on Form 8621 or would like to elect QEF or mark-to-market treatment for the current and subsequent tax years; and (5) whether the taxpayer has received any indirect distributions from lower-tier PFICs. In addition, many individuals may acquire PFICs inadvertently, e.g., by becoming a U.S. resident while owning interests in foreign mutual funds, and should consider whether the benefits of owning the foreign investment are reasonable given the additional tax and increased cost of compliance.

2. Form 5471

Form 5471, "Information Return of U.S. Persons With Respect to Certain Foreign Corporations," is required to report beneficial interests in foreign corporations and should be considered whenever a U.S. person acquires an interest in a foreign corporation, controls a foreign corporation, or owns any interest in a CFC. Generally, Form 5471 requires the U.S. individual to report ownership interests of the shareholders of the corporation, the corporation's financial information according

45. Instructions for Form 8621, page 1 (Dec. 2012). *See also* I.R.S. Notice 2011-55, 2011-29 I.R.B. 53.

to U.S. tax and accounting standards, and transfers to and from the corporation to related persons and entities. The specific information required depends on which of the five filing categories the U.S. shareholder meets during the tax year. Keep in mind that some filers may be subject to the filing requirements of multiple categories. The Category 1 filing requirement, which was repealed by the American Jobs Creation Act of 2004, is now obsolete.

Categories 2 and 3 focus on whether a U.S. person has acquired an interest in a foreign corporation. Category 2 filers include U.S. officers or directors of foreign corporations in which any U.S. person acquires 10 percent (in one or more transactions) or more of the voting power or value of the corporation. Category 3 filers include U.S. persons who acquire stock in a foreign corporation which, when added to any stock owned on the date of acquisition, is at least 10 percent of the outstanding stock as well as a U.S. person who acquires stock which, without regard to stock already owned on the date of acquisition, is at least 10 percent of the outstanding stock.

Categories 4 and 5 focus on U.S. persons with interests in U.S.-controlled foreign corporations. Category 4 filers include U.S. persons who had "control"[46] of a foreign corporation for an uninterrupted period of at least thirty days during the annual accounting period of the foreign corporation. To determine a U.S. person's total voting power or value, direct, indirect, and constructive ownership must be considered.[47] Category 5 filers include "U.S. shareholders"[48] who own stock in a foreign corporation that is a CFC for an uninterrupted period of thirty days or more during any tax year of the foreign corporation, and who owned that stock on the last day of that year.

U.S. persons described in any one of the four categories enumerated on Form 5471 must complete and attach Form 5471 to their income tax return in respect

46. A U.S. person has "control" of a foreign corporation if, at any time during that person's tax year, she owns, directly, indirectly, or constructively, stock possessing (1) more than 50 percent of the total combined voting power of all classes of stock of the foreign corporation entitled to vote or (2) more than 50 percent of the total value of shares of all classes of stock of the foreign corporation. It is possible for a U.S. person to control a corporation for purposes of § 6038 without the foreign corporation satisfying the definition of a CFC in § 957. For purposes of § 6038, stock of a non-U.S. person may be attributable to a U.S. person. § 6038(e)(2). However, for purposes of § 957, stock of a non-U.S. person may *not* be attributed to a U.S. person. § 958(b)(1).

47. Treas. Reg. § 1.6038-2(b). To determine control, an individual is deemed to constructively own stock according to the attribution rules of § 318(a), except that: (1) stock owned by or for a partner or a beneficiary of an estate or trust is not attributable to the partnership, estate, or trust when the effect is to consider a U.S. person as owning stock owned by a person who is not a U.S. person; (2) a corporation will not be considered as owning stock owned by or for a 50 percent or more shareholder when the effect is to consider a U.S. person as owning stock owned by a person who is not a U.S. person; and (3) if 10 percent or more in value of the stock in a corporation is owned, directly or indirectly, by or for any person, § 318(a)(2)(C) shall apply, which attributes stock from the corporation to its shareholders. *See* Treas. Reg. § 1.6038-2(c); § 318(a)(1)(A)(ii).

48. *See* § 951(b).

of any applicable foreign entity that is treated as a foreign corporation for U.S. federal income tax purposes. Some taxpayers may be relieved from filing Form 5471. For example, one person may file on behalf of multiple members of the same category. Also, certain constructive stock owners may be relieved from filing. For example, a Category 4 or 5 filer is not required to file Form 5471 if the U.S. person (1) does not own a direct or indirect interest in the foreign corporation; (2) is required to file Form 5471 solely because of constructive ownership from a nonresident alien; and (3) the U.S. person through which the indirect shareholder constructively owns an interest in the foreign corporation properly files Form 5471. Failure to file Form 5471 may result in a penalty of $10,000 with the potential for additional penalties if the failure to file continues for more than ninety days from the receipt of the IRS notice.

Key considerations with respect to Form 5471 include: (1) understand the entity's entire ownership structure in order to properly determine whether a U.S. person indirectly or constructively owns an interest in a foreign corporation through interests in other entities or through interests of family members, whether the U.S. person has control of a foreign corporation, or whether the foreign corporation is a CFC; (2) if a U.S. individual is an officer or director of a foreign corporation, that individual must be aware of the fluctuations in ownership of other U.S. persons; and (3) once a U.S. person has determined the applicable Form 5471 categories, gather the relevant information and translate financial statements into U.S. figures according to U.S. tax and accounting methods.

3. Form 926

Taxpayers who file Form 5471 should also consider whether they must file Form 926, "Return by a U.S. Transferor of Property to a Foreign Corporation," because Form 926 targets U.S. shareholders who contribute property to or participate in reorganizations with respect to foreign corporations. Specifically, U.S. persons are required to report on Form 926 transfers of property to a foreign corporation if the transfer (1) is part of a nonrecognition transaction pursuant to a corporate formation, liquidation, or a tax-free reorganization;[49] (2) includes the transfer of intangible property in a nonrecognition transaction pursuant to a corporate formation;[50] or (3) includes certain distributions to a foreign distributee on liquidation or spinoff.[51] There are also special rules for reporting transfers of cash to a foreign corporation.[52]

Form 926 must be filed with the U.S. individual's income tax return for the year of the transfer. Generally, the U.S. transferor must provide information identifying and describing the transferee, value and basis of property transferred, and the

49. *See* § 6038B(a)(1)(A).
50. *See* § 367(d).
51. *See* § 367(e).
52. *See* § 6038B(c).

overall transaction.[53] Failure to file Form 926 may result in a penalty of 10 percent of the fair market value of the property transferred not to exceed $100,000.

Key considerations with respect to Form 926 include: (1) determine whether there has been a transfer of property to a foreign corporation; (2) a requirement to file Form 926 may arise inadvertently if a person makes an election to change the classification of an entity (discussed further in Form 8832, below) to a corporation; and (3) U.S. persons should also be aware that it is possible to have a Form 926 filing requirement without a Form 5471 filing requirement.

4. Form 8865

Form 8865, "Return of U.S. Persons with Respect to Certain Foreign Partnerships," may be required where a U.S. person owns an interest in a foreign partnership. Certain U.S. persons are required to provide information with respect to certain other U.S. partners and the foreign partnership's financial information according to U.S. tax and accounting standards. Specifically, Form 8865 requires U.S. persons to report interests in foreign partnerships where the U.S. person (1) controls the partnership; (2) owns an interest in a partnership that is controlled by other U.S. persons; or (3) contributes property to the partnership. Furthermore, the IRS requires information reporting for certain acquisitions and dispositions of partnership interests. As with Form 5471, Form 8865 must be filed by any U.S. person described in one or more of the four categories of filers. Note, however, that the categories of filers for Form 8865 differ from the categories of filers for Form 5471.

Category 1 filers include U.S. persons who controlled[54] a foreign partnership at any time during the partnership's tax year. Category 2 filers include U.S. persons who owned 10 percent or more of the foreign partnership while the foreign partnership was controlled by U.S. persons each owning at least a 10 percent interest.[55] Category 3 filers include U.S. persons who contributed property to a foreign partnership if (1) the U.S. person owned directly or constructively at least a 10 percent interest immediately after the contribution; (2) the U.S. person (or a related person) contributed property exceeding a total value of $100,000 to the partnership within the twelve-month period ending on the date of the transfer; or (3) the U.S. person previously transferred appreciated property to the partnership and the foreign partnership disposed of the property while the U.S. person remained a direct or indirect partner. Category 4 filers include U.S. persons who (1) acquired at least a 10 percent interest or became a 10 percent interest holder; (2) disposed of at least a 10 percent interest or made a disposition causing the U.S. person to own less than a 10 percent interest; or (3) increased or decreased direct proportional interests in the partnership by at least 10 percent. Unlike

53. Advisers should consult Treas. Reg. §§ 1.6038B-1(c) and 1.6038B-1T(c) to determine whether any supplemental information is required to be reported in part III.

54. Control is defined as owning an interest in the foreign partnership of more than 50 percent of the capital, profits, or deductions or losses.

55. A 10 percent interest is defined as owning an interest in the foreign partnership equal to 10 percent of the capital, profits, or deductions or losses.

other foreign reporting forms, Form 8865 uses the constructive ownership rules of § 267(c), excluding § 267(c)(3), to determine whether a U.S. person has an interest in a foreign partnership. A notable consequence is that individuals are deemed to constructively own the partnership interests of their siblings, which is not the case under the § 318(a) constructive ownership rules.

U.S. persons described in any one of the four categories enumerated on Form 8865 must complete and attach Form 8865 to their income tax return in respect of any applicable foreign entity that is treated as a foreign partnership for U.S. federal income tax purposes. However, some U.S. partners may be relieved from filing Form 8865. For example, one Category 1 filer may file on behalf of multiple Category 1 filers, subject to certain requirements.[56] Also, certain individuals with constructive interests in a foreign partnership may be relieved from filing Form 8865.

Failure to file Form 8865 may result in different penalties, depending on the individual's Form 8865 category. For example, Category 1 and 2 filers may be subject to a penalty of $10,000 (with the potential for additional penalties if the failure to file continues for more than ninety days from the receipt of an IRS notice), a 10 percent reduction in foreign taxes available for foreign tax credits (with the potential for additional reduction), and potential criminal penalties. Category 3 filers may be subject to a penalty for failure to file equal to 10 percent of the fair market value of the property contributed to the partnership (up to $100,000) as well as losing nonrecognition of gain on the contribution. Category 4 filers may be subject to a failure to file penalty of $10,000 with the potential for additional penalties if the failure to file continues for more than ninety days from the receipt of the IRS notice.

Key considerations with respect to Form 8865 include: (1) establish whether the foreign entity is a partnership for U.S. income tax purposes; (2) determine all of the ownership interests in the foreign partnership and the specific U.S. filer's actual and constructive ownership interests; and (3) determine whether the partnership interest has been affected by any new or recently departed partners. Furthermore, as with Form 5471, the U.S. person must be prepared to gather the relevant information, which could require substantial time and effort, and translate financial statements into U.S. figures according to U.S. tax and accounting methods, which could be significantly different from the accounting standards common in the foreign partnerships country of residence.

5. Form 8858

Form 8858, "Information Return of U.S. Persons with Respect to Foreign Disregarded Entities," is required to report a U.S. person's ownership of a foreign entity that is disregarded as separate from its owner for U.S. income tax purposes. The U.S. person's requirement to file Form 8858 often arises after the U.S. person has made an election to change the default foreign entity classification

56. *See* Instructions for Form 8865.

from a corporation to a disregarded entity. Generally, U.S. persons are required to report a foreign disregarded entity's financial information according to U.S. tax and accounting standards and to report § 987 foreign currency gain or loss on any remittances from the foreign disregarded entity. U.S. persons who are treated as owning the assets and liabilities of a foreign disregarded entity are responsible for filing Form 8858. Furthermore, U.S. persons may also be required to report foreign disregarded entities in which the person indirectly owns an interest in the disregarded entity through a foreign corporation or foreign partnership.

Form 8858 must be filed at the same time as the U.S. person's income tax return. Failure to file Form 8858 may result in a penalty of $10,000, with the potential for additional penalties if the failure to file continues for more than ninety days from the receipt of IRS notice. Furthermore, failure to file may also result in a 10 percent reduction of foreign taxes available for credit, with the potential for additional reduction if the failure continues for more than ninety days from the receipt of IRS notice.

Key considerations with respect to Form 8858 include: (1) determining whether the entity is a foreign disregarded entity; (2) determining whether the U.S. owner has properly elected such treatment on Form 8832 (see below); (3) determining whether a U.S. person with an interest in a foreign corporation or foreign partnership is required to report a foreign disregarded entity owned by that foreign corporation or foreign partnership; (4) as with Forms 5471 and 8865, the U.S. owner must be prepared to gather the relevant information and translate financial statements into U.S. dollars according to U.S. tax and accounting methods; and (5) Form 8858 requires U.S. owners to track foreign currency gains and losses on certain remittances of cash or property to the U.S. owner.

6. Form 8832

Form 8832, "Entity Classification Election," is used to make an election to make an initial entity classification or to change the entity classification for an eligible entity. To avoid confusion with regard to an entity's classification for U.S. income tax and reporting purposes, advisors should address changing default entity classification when a U.S. person forms or acquires an interest in a foreign entity, or when a non-U.S. individual becomes a U.S. resident, at which point foreign entities owned by that individual will usually become relevant for U.S. income tax and information reporting purposes.

To address whether an entity classification should be changed, advisors must understand the default classification rules. The default classification of a domestic eligible entity[57] is a partnership if there are two or more members and a disregarded entity if there is a single owner. The default classification for a foreign eligible entity is treated as follows: (1) a partnership if there are two or more members and at least one member does not have limited liability; (2) an

57. An eligible entity is a business entity that is not classified as a per se corporation under Treas. Reg. § 301.7701-2(b)(1), (3), (4), (5), (6), (7), or (8).

association taxable as a corporation if all members have limited liability; and (3) a disregarded entity if there is a single owner that does not have limited liability. Generally, an eligible entity may elect to change its default classification between twelve months before and seventy-five days after the date the election is to take effect. Each member of the electing entity who is an owner at the time the election is filed must sign a consent statement included in Form 8832. Alternatively, any officer, manager, or member of the electing entity who is authorized to make the election may sign the consent statement.

U.S. persons who fail to make a timely entity classification election may seek relief by filing Form 8832, and completing part II, pursuant to Revenue Procedure 2009-41.[58] Any entity that does not satisfy the requirements of Revenue Procedure 2009-41 may seek relief for a late entity classification election by requesting a private letter ruling.

Key considerations with respect to Form 8832 include: (1) determining each foreign entity's default classification at creation or upon the date the entity becomes relevant for U.S. income tax purposes; (2) determining whether the entity is a per se corporation pursuant to Treas. Reg. § 301.7701-2(b)(8) that is ineligible to make a change to its default classification; (3) determining the preferred treatment for the foreign entity; (4) ascertaining the persons who must consent to change an entity classification; (5) determining when the election should take effect; (6) if the filing date will be more than seventy-five days after the effective date, then the election may need to meet the additional requirements of Rev. Proc. 2009-41 or a private letter ruling; (7) an election to change entity classification could trigger a taxable event, such as a deemed liquidation or reorganization; and (8) an election to change entity classification may also necessitate filing Form 5471, Form 926, or Form 8865 to report an additional investment in a foreign corporation or partnership.

VI. Taxation and Reporting for Foreign Trusts

A. Background

A trust is considered "foreign" if the entity fails either the "court test" or the "control test" in Treas. Reg. § 301.7701-7. Under the court test, a U.S. court must be able to exercise primary supervision over the administration of the trust.[59] Under the control test, one or more U.S. persons must have the authority to control all substantial decisions of the trust. A person may have control of substantial decisions without being a trustee or acting in a fiduciary capacity.[60] Specifically, in many non-U.S. drafted trusts, additional fiduciary relationships are included in the

58. Rev. Proc. 2009-41, 2009-39 I.R.B. 439.
59. Treas. Reg. § 301.7701-7(a)(1)(i), (c)(3)(iv).
60. Treas. Reg. § 301.7701-7(d)(3).

trust instrument, e.g., a trust protector. A "trust protector" is a person other than the trustee who is responsible for monitoring and overseeing the operations of the trust under specified terms. A trust protector who is given sufficient authority has *de facto* control over the trust for this purpose.

As with U.S. trusts, for U.S. federal tax purposes, a foreign trust[61] is taxable as either: (1) a wholly grantor trust, which is an entity not separate from its owners where the tax attributes flow through to such owner or owners;[62] (2) a wholly non-grantor trust, which is an entity separate from its owners where the tax attributes are shared between the trust and the beneficiaries based on annual income and distributions; or (3) a partially grantor, partially nongrantor trust.[63]

B. Classification as a Foreign Grantor Trust

U.S. federal tax law views a grantor and a grantor trust as a single taxpayer,[64] and all tax items of the grantor trust flow to the grantor's personal income tax return. A grantor is typically a person who both (1) makes a gratuitous transfer to a trust and (2) retains certain powers over the trust or trust property.

In addition to the general grantor trust rules, a U.S. person who makes a gratuitous transfer (directly, indirectly, or constructively) to a foreign trust is automatically treated as the owner of the trust under the grantor trust rules if the trust has a U.S. beneficiary for the year in question.[65] This is true without regard to whether a U.S. person retained any traditional grantor trust powers over the trust.

Further, a U.S. beneficiary includes not only a person who was a U.S. person at the time of the transfer, but also a person who was a non-U.S. person at the time of the transfer and later becomes a U.S. person within five years of making the transfer.[66] Therefore, if a trust beneficiary becomes a U.S. person more than five years after a U.S. person makes a gratuitous transfer to the trust, the trust is not treated as having a U.S. beneficiary.[67] The presumption of a U.S. beneficiary will apply, without proof to the contrary, even if the trust instrument prevents the presence or subsequent appointment of U.S. beneficiaries, if the trust could be amended by its terms, under local law or pursuant to oral agreements or implied understandings between the parties.[68]

---

61. A foreign trust is generally a trust that is either (or both): (1) not subject to primary supervision by a U.S. court; (2) non-U.S. trustees/persons control one or more of the operations/substantial decisions of the trust. Treas. Reg. § 301.7701-7. Determination of the presence of an ordinary trust requires analysis of the trust instrument and all surrounding facts and circumstances. Treas. Reg. § 301.7701-4.

62. § 671.

63. § 643.

64. §§ 671–679.

65. § 679.

66. § 679(a)(4) (residency begins on the same date as for the SPT of § 7701(b)(2)(A), and the transfer will include any retroactively calculated undistributed net income of the trust from the date of the original transfer through the residency start date).

67. § 679(c)(3).

68. Treas. Reg. § 1.679-2(a)(4) (applicable to transfers after Mar. 10, 2010).

C. Classification as a Foreign Nongrantor Trust

A foreign nongrantor trust is taxed in much the same manner as a non-U.S. person.[69] A non-U.S. person is only taxed under the U.S. federal income tax regime on (1) U.S.-source FDAP income;[70] and (2) ECI.[71] A U.S. beneficiary of a nongrantor trust is subject to U.S. federal income taxation on distributions to the extent of the beneficiary's pro rata share of the trust's distributable net income (DNI) for the year of the distribution.[72]

A distribution in any year in excess of DNI is generally deemed to carry out trust undistributed net income (UNI)—"accumulation distribution"—unless the distribution in excess of DNI is not in excess of the trust accounting income for the year.[73] Typically, distributions (wholly or partially) comprised of UNI to a U.S. beneficiary have the following consequences to the U.S. beneficiary for U.S. federal income tax purposes: (1) capital gains are taxed at ordinary income rates; (2) an interest charge is imposed on the tax amount due on the distribution of accumulated income;[74] and (3) a "throwback tax" also applies to the accumulation distribution, whereby income is taxed at the beneficiary's tax rate over the years the income recognition and accompanying tax were deferred. To the extent distributions exceed DNI and UNI, they are treated as being distributed from principal on a tax-free basis to beneficiaries. Note, too, the sixty-five-day election may be used to mitigate some distributions of UNI in the first quarter of a new taxable year.[75]

An alternative method of approaching nongrantor trust distributions is the default method of calculating accumulation distributions, which is a more standardized and predictable method. The calculation can be found within the Instructions to Form 3520.

D. Foreign Trusts Reporting Forms

1. Form 3520

U.S. persons (and executors of estates of U.S. decedents) file Form 3520, "Annual Return To Report Transactions With Foreign Trusts and Receipt of Certain Foreign Gifts," to report (1) certain reportable events or transactions with foreign

---

69. §§ 641(b), 871(a)(2). For this purpose, non-U.S. person means nonresident, noncitizen of the United States. For additional information on tax risks of foreign trusts, see Eileen Caufield Schwab & Dyke M. Davies, *Tax Risks When U.S. Fiduciary Acts as Trustee of Foreign Trust*, N.Y.L.J. (Jan. 7, 1997)

70. §§ 861, 871.

71. § 871(b).

72. § 643; *see* Treas. Reg. § 1.662(b)-1 (exemption to proportionate allocation of DNI). Note that DNI is calculated differently for foreign nongrantor trusts when compared to U.S. nongrantor trusts, e.g., allocation of capital gains to income, etc.

73. § 665(b).

74. This interest charge applies to tax years after December 31, 1995, and the rate imposed is the compounded floating rate applicable to the underpayment of tax. This is computed based on an averaging method—UNI is retroactively deemed distributed in each year of income accumulation.

75. § 663(b).

trusts; (2) ownership of foreign trusts under the grantor trust rules in §§ 671–679; (3) receipt of distributions from a foreign trust; and (4) the receipt of certain large gifts or bequests from certain foreign persons.[76] A separate Form 3520 must be filed for transactions with each foreign trust. Note that various exceptions to filing exist, e.g., transfers to Canadian RRSPs and RRIFs (addressed further in Form 8891, above) and foreign trusts described in §§ 402(b), 404(a)(4), or 404A.

First, reportable events with respect to foreign trusts include: (1) the creation of a foreign trust by a U.S. person (U.S. grantor), whether or not the trust has U.S. beneficiaries; (2) the transfer of money or property (directly or indirectly) to a foreign trust by a U.S. person; and (3) the death of a U.S. citizen or resident, if the foreign trust was treated as a grantor trust, in whole or in part with respect to the U.S. decedent, or if the trust was included in the U.S. decedent's gross estate, in whole or in part.[77] Reportable transactions do not, however, include transfers for fair market value or transactions entered into with certain tax-exempt or tax-deferred arrangements, such as 501(c)(3) entities and U.S. pension plans.

Second, the mere status as an owner of a foreign trust under the grantor trust rules requires reporting on Form 3520 (see Form 3520-A, below).

Third, a U.S. person who directly or indirectly received a distribution from a foreign trust during the current tax year or a related foreign trust held an outstanding obligation issued by the U.S. person treated as a qualified obligation during the current tax year must complete part III. A distribution may include both the receipt of cash or assets outright, indirect receipt through a separate entity, or the right to uncompensated use of trust property during the year, e.g., use of a Bahamian property owned by the trust for a two-week vacation without paying the trust fair value rent. An extension of credit from a U.S. person to a foreign trust is a qualified obligation only if it is (1) in writing; (2) denominated in U.S. dollars; (3) for a term of five years or less; (4) the yield to maturity of the obligation is not less than 100 percent of the applicable federal rate and not greater than 130 percent of the applicable federal rate;[78] (5) the U.S. person extends the period for assessment of any income or transfer tax attributable to the transfer and any consequential income tax changes for each year that the obligation is outstanding to a date not earlier than three years after the maturity date of the obligation;[79] and (6) the U.S. person reports the status of the obligation, including principal and interest payments, on Form 3520 for each year that the obligation is outstanding.[80]

Fourth, an individual must report large gifts on part IV of Form 3520 if one (or both) of the applicable thresholds is met. One threshold requires a U.S. individual

---

76. §§ 6048(a)-(b), 6677 (HIRE Act amended provision to create a $10,000 minimum penalty); I.R.S. Notice 97-34, 1997 C.B. 422; *see* Form 3520 and accompanying instructions and Form 3520-A and accompanying instructions.

77. § 6048.

78. *See* § 1275(d) (applicable federal rate).

79. Treas. Reg. § 301.6501(c)–1(d)

80. I.R.S. Notice 97-34, 1997 C.B. 422.

who receives gifts from a non-U.S. individual or estate that exceed $100,000 during the year in question to report such gifts on Form 3520. This is determined on an aggregate basis, whereby gifts from multiple recipients must be added together to determine whether the threshold is met if the donee knows or has reason to know the donors are related.[81] Once the $100,000 threshold has been satisfied, the donee must separately identify each gift in excess of $5,000, but need not identify the donor. The other threshold requires a U.S. person who receives gifts from foreign corporations or foreign partnerships to report such gifts on Form 3520 if the aggregate amount of gifts from all entities exceeds $15,102 (for 2013, indexed for inflation).[82] Note, that the definition of a gift does not include payments from a foreign person or entity paid directly to a medical or educational institution on behalf of the U.S. person.

To report a reportable foreign gift properly, the donee must provide the date of the gift (or bequest), a description of the property received, and the value of the property received from a nonresident alien or foreign estate. If the donor is a foreign corporation or partnership, the donee must provide the name and address of the donor, the donor's identification number, as well as additional situational information.

Penalties generally apply if Form 3520 is not timely filed or if the information is incomplete or incorrect. Generally, the initial penalty is equal to the greater of $10,000 or (1) 35 percent of the gross value of any property transferred to a foreign trust for failure by a U.S. transferor to report the creation of or transfer to a foreign trust; (2) 35 percent of the gross value of the distributions received from a foreign trust for failure by a U.S. person to report receipt of the distribution; or (3) 5 percent of the gross value of the portion of the trust's assets treated as owned by a U.S. person for failure by the U.S. person to report the U.S. owner information. No penalties will be imposed if the taxpayer can demonstrate that the failure to comply was due to reasonable cause and not willful neglect.

Key considerations with respect to Form 3520 include: (1) classification of a trust as a foreign trust; (2) determination of trust ownership; (3) presence of certain reportable transactions with the trust, e.g., loan or contribution; (4) notification to beneficiaries of amount and character of distributions received; and (4) consider whether foreign bequests and gifts from individuals, entities and/or related parties should be aggregated to determine whether the reporting threshold for gifts and bequests from foreign individuals is met

2. Form 3520-A

Form 3520-A, "Annual Information Return of Foreign Trust With a U.S. Owner," is required to report the income and expenses arising in a foreign grantor trust that may be reported on the grantor's personal U.S. income tax return. If a U.S. person is the grantor of a foreign trust, additional reporting requirements may

81. I.R.S. Notice 97-34, 1997 C.B. 422; *see* § 643(i)(2)(B).
82. Rev. Proc. 2012-41, 2012-45 I.R.B. 539.

be imposed on the grantor and/or trustee. For example, bank accounts in foreign jurisdictions held through a foreign trust may create an FBAR or Form 8938 filing requirement.

Form 3520-A is generally due March 15 (the fifteenth day of the third month after the end of the trust's fiscal year). A six-month extension of time to file is available by filing Form 7004. Merely extending a taxpayer's individual income tax return is not sufficient to extend the due date for Form 3520-A.

A foreign trust deemed to be owned by a U.S. person can appoint a U.S. agent to facilitate IRS communications, records requests, production of testimony, or other items the IRS may request. Any U.S. citizen, resident alien, or domestic corporation (including a U.S. grantor or U.S. beneficiary of a foreign trust) may be named as the trust's U.S. agent. The appointment of a U.S. agent requires that the trust and the agent enter into a binding agreement in "substantially" the form prescribed by the IRS in Notice 97-34. The responsible parties must execute the agreement appointing a U.S. agent before the due date of the Form 3520-A for the reporting period the agent will serve and remains in effect for as long as the statute of limitations remains open for the U.S. owner's taxable year. When executing a U.S. agent appointment, it is important to reference Notice 97-34 for precise language and requisite formalities.

A U.S. owner is subject to a penalty of the greater of $10,000 or 5 percent of the gross value of the portion of the trust she is deemed to own if the trust does not furnish the proper information.[83] Failure to file a timely and complete return that continues for more than ninety days after the IRS mails notice of the failure to the person required to pay the penalty results in an increase in the penalty by an additional $10,000 for each thirty-day period (or fraction thereof) during which the failure continues. These penalties cannot, however, exceed the gross reportable amount that is determinable by the Secretary, and any excess is to be refunded to the taxpayer.[84]

The "gross reportable amount" with respect to the 5 percent penalty for failure to file Form 3520-A is defined the same as it is for purposes of the 35 percent penalty for failure to file Form 3520, except that it applies only to that portion of the trust deemed owned by the U.S. person. The penalties for failure to file Form 3520-A are not imposed if the failure to file is shown to be due to reasonable cause and not due to willful neglect, on the same basis as penalties for failure to file Form 3520.

Key considerations with respect to Form 3520-A include: (1) classification of a trust as a foreign trust; (2) detailed compilation of trust transactions during the year, including value of contributions; (3) cash basis income statement; (4) balance sheet reflecting assets at fair market value; (5) trust owner is generally responsible for foreign asset and entity reporting for foreign assets legally

83. § 6048(b)(1).
84. § 6677(a)(2).

owned by the trust; (6) provide name and contact information of trustee(s) and other fiduciaries; and (7) consider U.S. agent appointments to ease administrative burden.

E. Taxation of U.S. Grantor Trusts (Owned by a Non-U.S. Person)

Non-U.S. persons are generally not treated as grantors of U.S. trusts, with two specific exceptions. A non-U.S. person will be treated as the grantor of a U.S. trust if (1) the non-U.S. person has the power to revest title to trust property in herself without the approval or consent of any other person or only with the consent or approval of a related or subordinate party subservient to the non-U.S. person; or (2) the non-U.S. person (and/or her spouse) is entitled to all distributions from that trust for life.[85] If a non-U.S. person is treated as the grantor of a U.S. trust, the income and deductions attributable to the trust's assets will flow through to the non-U.S. grantor who will be subject to U.S. tax on the trust's income like any other nonresident alien.

VII. Transfer Tax Reporting

A. Form 709

Both U.S. and non-U.S. persons use Form 709, "United States Gift (and Generation-Skipping Transfer) Tax Return," to report (1) transfers subject to federal gift and generation-skipping transfer (GST) taxes and (2) allocation of GST exemption to property transferred during the U.S. person's lifetime.

Non-U.S. persons are subject to U.S. federal gift tax on transfers of U.S. situs property in excess of the per-donee gift tax annual exclusion ($14,000 in 2013, as indexed for inflation).[86] U.S. situs property generally includes U.S. real estate and tangible property located in the United States.[87] The transfer by a nonresident alien of real property and tangible property physically located outside the U.S. does not trigger a U.S. gift tax liability. Additionally, under the gift tax rules, non-U.S. situs property generally includes intangible property comprising (1) stocks and bonds in U.S. and foreign corporations; (2) partnership interests;[88] (3) cash deposits at a foreign bank or foreign branch of a U.S. bank; (4) interests in pensions, IRAs and stock options, whether domestic or foreign; and (5) goodwill in a

85. § 672(f)(2)(A).

86. §§ 2503(b), 2511.

87. This may include cash located in U.S. bank accounts (including a domestic branch of foreign bank). *See, e.g.*, I.R.S. Priv. Ltr. Rul. 200748008 and I.R.S. Priv. Ltr. Rul. 200340015. Private letter rulings may not be cited as precedent, however they provide some insight into the IRS's view on a particular issue.

88. Caution is advised in the case of partnership interests holding property that would be treated as having a U.S. situs, particularly U.S. real property, as the IRS has a "no-rule" policy on the issue of whether a partnership interest will be treated as having a U.S. or foreign situs.

company. Gift tax treaties executed between the U.S. and foreign countries may alter the impact of U.S. gift taxes to transfers made by non-U.S. persons.

B. Form 706

The executor of a decedent's estate uses Form 706, "United States Estate (and GST) Tax Return," to calculate the estate tax imposed and to compute the generation-skipping transfer tax imposed on certain transfers.

C. Form 706NA

Executors of nonresident alien decedents use Form 706-NA, "United States Estate (and Generation-Skipping Transfer) Tax Return Estate of Nonresident Not a Citizen of the United States," to compute estate and generation-skipping transfer tax liabilities.

U.S. estate tax applies to the estates of non-U.S. persons with respect to their U.S. situs assets.[89] For purposes of the estate tax, U.S. situs property includes: (1) real and tangible personal property located in the U.S.; (2) stock and stock options of U.S. corporations; (3) debt of a U.S. person (except portfolio debt);[90] (4) certain U.S. trusts and deferred compensation; (5) pensions and deferred compensation obligations payable by U.S. persons; and (6) annuity contracts enforceable against U.S. obligors.[91] The assets of nonresident aliens generally exempt from the reach of U.S. estate tax include: (1) real and tangible personal property located outside of the U.S.; (2) securities that generate portfolio interest; (3) cash in U.S. bank accounts (to the extent not used in connection with a U.S. trade or business); and (4) proceeds of a life insurance policy from a domestic or foreign carrier.[92] Estate tax treaties executed between the U.S. and foreign countries may alter the impact of U.S. estate taxes to the estate of a non-U.S. person.

VIII. FATCA Withholding and Reporting Obligations

Congress enacted the FATCA provisions in the Hiring Incentives to Restore Employment ("HIRE) Act passed on March 18, 2010, and introduced a new information reporting and withholding regime that will begin to take effect on July 1, 2014. The FATCA provisions generally require foreign entities to disclose information regarding their U.S. person account holders and substantial U.S. owners. Beginning after June 30, 2013, U.S. payors are required to withhold 30 percent of "withholdable payments," which include U.S. source fixed and determinable annual payments and gross proceeds from sales, made to foreign entities unless

89. § 2101(a).

90. §§ 2104(c), 2105(b). Generally, registered U.S. debt obligations owned by nonresident alien investors are excluded for estate tax purposes.

91. §§ 2103, 2104; Treas. Reg. § 20.2104-1(a).

92. §§ 2104, 2105; Treas. Reg. §§ 20.2103-1 and 20.2105-1(a).

that foreign entity is in compliance with its reporting obligations or otherwise qualifies for an exemption. Final FATCA regulations explaining the reporting and withholding provisions were released in January 2013. Many of the planning techniques and structures described throughout this book involve the use of one or more foreign entities, and these entities will be required to comply with the FATCA reporting regime beginning in 2013 and 2014.

The goal of FATCA is to require foreign entities to report information regarding their U.S. person account holders; including any substantial U.S. owners of each U.S.-owned foreign entity that is an account holder. FATCA categorizes non-U.S. entities as either foreign financial institutions (FFIs) or non-financial foreign entities (NFFEs). Generally, if a non-U.S. entity is not an FFI, it is categorized as an NFFE. FFIs include (1) depository institutions that accept deposits in the ordinary course of business; (2) custodial institutions that hold financial assets for the benefit of one or more other persons; (3) investment entities that manage financial assets on behalf of customers; and (4) insurance companies that issue or are obliged to make payments with respect to a cash value insurance or annuity contract.

The reporting requirements for FFIs are more stringent than the reporting requirements for NFFEs. For example, FFIs must report all U.S. owners with a more than 0 percent (yes, zero!) equity interest in the entity, while NFFEs must report U.S. owners with a more than 10 percent equity interest in the entity. Generally, to avoid withholding on withholdable payments, an FFI must enter into an FFI agreement with the IRS and comply with U.S. information reporting requirements. The regulations allow specified FFIs, known as deemed compliant FFIs and exempt FFIs, to avoid withholding without entering FFI agreements. Exempt FFIs include, among others, specified foreign governments, central banks, and retirement funds. Deemed-compliant FFIs are low-risk FFIs that include registered deemed compliant FFIs, certified deemed compliant FFIs, and owner-documented FFIs. A registered-deemed compliant FFI must register with the IRS or with its own tax authority under a Model 1 Intergovernmental Agreement. Certified deemed compliant FFIs do not need to register with the IRS but are required to provide withholding agents with specified documentation. Owner-documented FFIs are limited to investment entities with a withholding agent that is a participating FFI or U.S. financial institution that agrees to satisfy the owner-documented FFIs reporting requirements, and the owner-documented foreign entity must provide that withholding agent with certain specified information.

The U.S. has signed Intergovernmental Agreements (IGAs) with several foreign governments regarding the FATCA reporting requirements for entities in those jurisdictions. These IGAs provide eligible entities located in those countries with an alternative to the FATCA withholding and reporting regime. There are two models of IGA. Under the Model 1 IGA, FFIs report FATCA information directly to their home taxing authority, and the taxing authority will share information regarding U.S. account holders directly with the IRS. Under the Model 2 IGA, FFIs request permission from account holders to share information with the IRS. If account holders refuse, FFIs can report information on all non-consenting account holders in aggregate to the IRS. In summary, an IGA will alter the reporting requirements for entities located in jurisdictions that have signed an IGA with the U.S. Entities in these jurisdictions should refer to the IGA for the specific reporting and compliance requirements and procedures in that jurisdiction. According to Notice 2013-43 certain jurisdictions will be treated as having an IGA in effect even if that particular IGA is not completed before July 1, 2014.

A. Form 8957

Form 8957, Foreign Account Tax Compliance Act (FATCA) Registration, is intended to be used by foreign entities to register with the IRS for FATCA purposes. Form 8957 has been released in draft form and is available on the IRS website. However, at the time of publication, the IRS has advised that registration can be accomplished most efficiently and effectively by registering through the online registration portal that opened August 19, 2013. The questions required for online registration will be similar to those on the draft Form 8957. Online registrants will receive electronic notification of registration acceptance and obtain the Global Intermediary Identification Number (GIIN) used to demonstrate FATCA compliance. Failure to register by April 25, 2014, may result in application of the 30 percent withholding tax on withholdable payments to the foreign entity beginning July 1, 2014.

B. Form 8966

Beginning March 31, 2015, for the 2013 and 2014 tax years, FFIs and NFFEs will be required to file Form 8966, FATCA Report. The Form is due on March 31, annually, thereafter. Each reporting entity will be required to provide the name, address, and TIN of each U.S. person who is an account holder, and each substantial U.S. owner of any account holder that is a U.S.-owned foreign entity, the account number, account balance or value, and potentially the gross receipts and withdrawals or payments from the account. At the time of publication, Form 8966 is not available in draft form.

C. Forms W-8

New expanded versions of the Forms W-8 are under development and will be used to identify the foreign entity's status for FATCA reporting purposes. Form W-8BEN-E (for entities) is available in draft form on the IRS website. New draft Form W-8 (for individuals), W-8ECI, W-EXP, and W-IMY are also available. After these forms become final they will eventually make existing Forms W-8 obsolete.

IX. Offshore Voluntary Disclosure Program

At the time of publication, the IRS provides a program for U.S. persons with undisclosed foreign income, accounts, or other assets to become compliant with U.S. tax laws. The 2012 OVDP is similar to programs that came before it in 2009 and 2011. The 2012 OVDP currently remains open indefinitely, although the IRS may change the terms of the program or close the program at any time. Like the programs before it, the OVDP also provides an opportunity for U.S. persons who had properly reported taxable income in prior years but failed to file certain information returns to file such late information returns without penalty.

The ability to participate in the 2012 OVDP depends on whether the disclosing taxpayer has previously unreported income or assets and missed information reporting. IRS Frequently Asked Question(s)[93] (FAQ) 17[94] and 18[95] address the filing procedure for U.S. residents who reported and paid tax on all of their taxable income but failed to file certain information returns, such as Forms 5471, 3520, and FBAR.[96] These taxpayers may be able to file missed information returns

93. Offshore Voluntary Disclosure Program Frequently Asked Questions and Answers, posted June 26, 2012, *available at* http://www.irs.gov/Individuals/International-Taxpayers/Offshore-Voluntary-Disclosure-Program-Frequently-Asked-Questions-and-Answers.

94. Question: "I have properly reported all my taxable income but I only recently learned that I should have been filing FBARs in prior years to report my personal foreign bank account or to report the fact that I have signature authority over bank accounts owned by my employer. May I come forward under this new program to correct this?" Answer: "The purpose for the voluntary disclosure practice is to provide a way for taxpayers who did not report taxable income in the past to come forward voluntarily and resolve their tax matters. Thus, if you reported, and paid tax on all taxable income but did not file FBARs, do not use the voluntary disclosure process. For taxpayers who reported, and paid tax on all their taxable income for prior years but did not file FBARs, you should file the delinquent FBAR reports according to the instructions . . . and attach a statement explaining why the reports are filed late. The IRS will not impose a penalty for the failure to file delinquent FBARs if there are no underreported tax liabilities and you have not previously been contacted regarding an income tax examination or a request for delinquent returns. Nonresident taxpayers should also review the Filing Compliance Procedures for Non-Resident U.S. Taxpayers if they do not qualify for the procedures described in this FAQ."

95. Question: "Question 17 states that a taxpayer who only failed to file FBAR should not use this process. What about a taxpayer who only has delinquent Form 5471s or Form 3520s but no tax due? Does that taxpayer fall outside this voluntary disclosure process?" Answer: "A taxpayer who has failed to file tax information returns, such as Form 5471 for controlled foreign corporations (CFCs) or Form 3520 for foreign trusts but who has reported, and paid tax on, all their taxable income with respect to all transactions related the CFCs or foreign trusts, should file delinquent information returns with the appropriate service center according to the instructions for the form and attach a statement explaining why the information returns are filed late. (The Form 5471 should be submitted with an amended return showing no change to income tax liability.) The IRS will not impose a penalty for the failure to file delinquent Forms 5471 and 3520 if there are no underreported tax liabilities and you have not previously been contacted regarding an income tax examination or a request for delinquent returns. Non-resident taxpayers should also review the New Filing Compliance Procedures for Non-Resident U.S. Taxpayers if they do not qualify for the procedures described in this FAQ."

96. Although only Forms 5471 and 3520 are specifically mentioned in FAQ 18, the answer to FAQ 18 implies that other information returns may be filed without penalty.

without the imposition of penalties. Taxpayers filing pursuant to FAQ 17 and 18 are directed not to use the traditional voluntary disclosure process. Instead, they are directed to file their delinquent information returns with the appropriate IRS service center specified on each form.[97] In addition, the disclosing taxpayer should attach a statement explaining why the information returns are late. Furthermore, if the information return must be attached to an income tax return, the taxpayer should attach the information return to an amended income tax return showing no change in income tax liability.

Taxpayers who do not satisfy the requirements for filing under FAQ 17 or 18 may be able to come into compliance through the general OVDP. Generally, all taxpayers with undisclosed foreign accounts or assets who are not under civil or criminal examination are eligible to participate in the 2012 OVDP. Taxpayers should first submit a pre-clearance request to participate in the program in accordance with FAQ 23. The IRS Criminal Investigation unit will send a letter of acceptance to the requesting taxpayer indicating that the taxpayer has ninety days to complete and submit all voluntary disclosure materials. An additional ninety days may be requested if the taxpayer satisfies the requirements listed in FAQ 25.1. The voluntary disclosure materials required for a complete submission are set forth in FAQ 25.

At any time prior to signing a closing agreement, a taxpayer may choose to opt out of the 2012 OVDP and submit to a traditional disclosure and audit. The most critical factor necessary to make the decision to opt out in favor of the traditional disclosure and audit process is to understand the differences between the potential penalties available to the IRS under the traditional disclosure and audit process and the 2012 OVDP penalty framework. Under the 2012 OVDP, the 20 percent accuracy-related penalty, failure to file, and failure to pay penalties may apply. The revenue agent administering the taxpayer's case does not have authority to exercise any discretion or to negotiate the penalties. In addition, the revenue agent is required to asses an offshore penalty of 27.5 percent, which may be reduced to 12.5 percent or 5 percent if the taxpayer satisfies specific requirements set forth in FAQ 52[98] and 53.[99] The offshore penalty is applied to the highest aggregate value of all of the taxpayer's undisclosed foreign accounts and undisclosed

97. IRS Policy Statement 5-133, I.R.M. 1.2.14.1.18 suggests that taxpayers should file six years of delinquent returns. However, the IRS retains the right to extend the enforcement period beyond six years.

98. FAQ 52 sets out three categories of taxpayers that may qualify for the reduced 5 percent penalty. Generally, these taxpayers have had minimal contact with their undisclosed accounts, or minimal contact with the United States, and have complied with the foreign tax reporting requirements in the country in which they reside. In addition, taxpayers who are foreign residents and were unaware that they were U.S. citizens may qualify for the reduced penalty.

99. FAQ 53 provides a reduced 12.5 percent penalty for taxpayers whose highest aggregate undisclosed account balance (including the fair market value of any undisclosed assets) is less than $75,000 for each year covered by the OVDP.

foreign assets (if the assets generated unreported income or were purchased with unreported income during the disclosure period) in the years at issue.

If the taxpayer opts out of the 2012 OVDP, the IRS may assert all penalties in the Code including willful and nonwillful FBAR penalties, penalties for failure to file various information returns, civil fraud penalties, and even criminal penalties. Under a traditional audit, the revenue agent has some discretion to determine whether to apply penalties based on the taxpayer's facts and circumstances, and penalties may be abated for reasonable cause. However, in a traditional audit, the revenue agent also has discretion to assert additional penalties outside the OVDP disclosure period if the statute of limitations has not run.

A. Streamlined Compliance Procedure for Nonresident U.S. Taxpayers

Following the announcement of the 2012 OVDP, the IRS introduced an alternative, streamlined voluntary disclosure procedure for current nonresidents including, but not limited to, dual citizens who have not filed U.S. income tax returns or information returns.[100] The streamlined procedure is generally available to nonresident U.S. taxpayers who have resided outside of the United States since January 1, 2009, and who have not filed a U.S. tax return during that time. Taxpayers are required to file delinquent tax and information returns for the past three years and delinquent FBARs for the past six years, as well as any payment for tax and interest, if applicable. In addition, taxpayers must also submit a questionnaire that is used to determine the taxpayer's level of compliance risk.

Taxpayers with low compliance risk submissions will be subject to an expedited review, and the IRS will not assert penalties or pursue follow-up action. Submissions with higher risk may be subject to applicable penalties and a full examination. One of the key risk factors that should be considered to determine a taxpayer's compliance risk is whether the taxpayer's tax liability is less than $1,500 for each of the three years under review. Other risk factors that may be considered include: whether the taxpayer is already under audit or investigation by the IRS, whether a refund is claimed on any of the returns, whether there is material economic activity in the United States, whether the taxpayer has declared all income in the taxpayer's country of residence, whether FBAR penalties have been previously assessed against the taxpayer or if the taxpayer has received an FBAR warning letter, whether the taxpayer has a financial interest in or authority over financial accounts outside the taxpayer's country of residence, whether the taxpayer has a financial interest in an entity located outside the taxpayer's country of residence, whether the taxpayer has U.S.-source income, and whether there any other indications of sophisticated tax planning or avoidance. Taxpayers who are deemed high-risk may consider entering the 2012 OVDP.

---

100. *See* New Filing Compliance Procedures for Non-Resident U.S. Taxpayers, *available at* http://www.irs.gov/Individuals/International-Taxpayers/New-Filing-Compliance-Procedures-for-Non-Resident-U.S.-Taxpayers.

Table of Cases

C

D

E

F

In re Estate of Clark, 281 N.Y.S.2d 180 (1967), *aff'd*, 236 N.E.2d 152 (N.Y. 1968) 10n.37
In re Estate of Crichton, 267 N.Y.S.2d 706 (Sur. Ct.), *aff'd*, 272 N.Y.S.2d 987 (App. Div. 1966), *aff'd*, 288 N.E.2d 799 (N.Y. 1967) 91, 91n.29, 92n.31
In re Estate of Georg, 298 F. Supp. 741 (D.V.I. 1969) 13n.48
In re Estate of Gould, 1 Ohio Op. 2d 366 (Hamilton County Prob. Ct. 1956), *aff'd*, 140 N.E.2d 801 (Ohio Ct. App. 1956) 87n.6, 91, 91n.24
In re Estate of Janney, 446 A.2d 1265 (Pa. 1982) 12n.43
In re Estate of Jones, 588 P.2d 960 (Kan. Ct. App. 1979) 60n.2
In re Estate of Massaglia, 113 Cal. Rptr. 751 (1974) 60n.5
In re Estate of Nelson, 475 N.Y.S.2d 194 (Sur. Ct. 1984) 7n.21
In re Estate of Renard, 417 N.Y.S.2d 155 (Sur. Ct.), *aff'd*, 418 N.Y.S.2d 553 (1979) 8n.29, 70, 70n.48
In re Estate of Renard, 437 N.Y.S.2d 860 (Sur. Ct. 1981), *aff'd*, 447 N.Y.S.2d 573 (App. Div. 1981), *aff'd*, 439 N.E.2d 341 (N.Y. 1982) 94, 94n.40, 95
In re Estate of Rougeron, 217 N.E.2d 639 (N.Y.) *cert. denied*, 385 U.S. 899 (1966) 7n.23
In re Estate of Siegel, 373 N.Y.S.2d 812 (Sur. Ct. 1975) 8n.28
In re Estate of Swanson, 397 So. 2d. 465 (Fla. Dist. Ct. App. 1981) 87n.4
In re Estate of Taylor, 391 A.2d 991 (Pa. 1978) 15n.59
In re Estate of Turton, 15 N.Y.S.2d 131 (Sur. Ct. 1961) 8n.27
In re Estate of Vischer, 280 N.Y.S.2d 49 (Sur. Ct. 1967) 7n.23, 68, 68n.39
In re Estate of Wachman, 238 N.Y.S.2d 112 (Sur. Ct. 1963) 7n.25
In re Estate of Withington, 140 P.2d 482 (Cal. Ct. App. 1943) 60n.4
In re Estrem's Estate, 107 P.2d 36 (Cal. 1940) 6n.19
In re Frank, 556 N.W.2d 717 (Wis. 1996) 678n.229
In re Gibson's ST, [1981] Ch. 179 481n.32
In re Gifford's Will, 18 N.E.2d 663 (N.Y. 1939) 72, 72n.52
In re Goldstein's Will, 310 N.Y.S.2d 602 (App. Div. 1970) 7n.21
In re Gulbenkian's Settlement, [1970] A.C. 508 481n.38
In re Hahnel, 389 N.Y.S.2d 970 (Sur. Ct. 1976), *aff'd*, 395 N.Y.S.2d 395 (App. Div. 1977) 71, 71n.50
In re Hay's ST, [1982] 1 W.L.R. 202 481nn.31, 34, 38
In re Hay's ST, [1982] 3 All E.R. 786 474n.2, 475n.7, 477n.15
In re Heller-Baghero, 310 N.Y.S.2d 313 (1970) 68, 68n.38, 70n.45
In re Howes, 940 P.2d 159 (N.M. 1997) 651n.18
In re Huber 201 B.R. 685 (Bankr. W.D. WA May 17, 2013) 719, 719n.6
In re Lawrence, 238 B.R. 498 (S.D. Fla. 1999) 459n.16
In re Manisty's Settlement, [1974] Ch. 17 474n.3
In re Nevai, 788 N.Y.S.2d 843 (Sur. Ct. 2005), *aff'd*, 28 A.D.3d 561 (N.Y. App. Div. 2006) 70n.46
In re Panousseris' Will, 151 A.2d 518 (Del. 1959) 66, 66n.26
In re Penrose [1933] Ch. 793 482n.43
In re Portnoy, 201 B.R. 685 (S.D.N.Y. Bkrpt 1996) 716–717, 717

J

K

L

M

Madorin v. Comm'r, 84 T.C. 667 (1985) 138, 198n.267
Maharaj v. Maharaj, 1996 Ont. C.J. Lexis 2676 (Ont. Ct. S. July 7, 1996) 109n.58
Martin-Montis Trust v. Comm'r, 75 T.C. 381 (1980) 75n.63
Maximov v. United States, 373 U.S. 49 (1963) 80, 80n.81, 428n.8
Mazurek v. United States, 271 F.3d 226 (5th Cir. 2001) 429n.12
McPhail, [1971] A.C. 424 474n.2
Meltzer v. Commonwealth Unemployment Compensation Bd. of Review, 471 A.2d 157 (Pa. Commw. Ct. 1984) 5n.9
Miller v. Miller, 744 N.E.2d 778 (Ohio Ct. App. 2000) 661n.96
Miltenberger v. Miltenberger, 78 Mo. 27 (1883) 67n.33
Minister of Finance v. Mann Estate, [1972] 5 W.W.R. 23, *aff'd*, [1973] C.T.C. 561 (BCCA), *aff'd*, [1974] C.T.C. 222 (SCC) 580n.5
Montgomery v. Nat'l Sav. & Trust, 356 F.2d 806 (D.C. Cir. 1966) 7, 7n.21
Morice v. Bishop of Durham, 9 Ves. 399, *aff'd,* 10 Ves. 522 (1804) 463n.22
Moultrie v. Hunt, 23 N.Y. 394 (1861) 13n.49
Murphy's Heirs v. Murphy, 5 Mart. (o.s.) 83 (La. 1817) 104n.25

N

Nahar v. Nahar, 656 So. 2d 225 (Fla. Dist. Ct. App. 1995) 94n.43, 96n.49
Nat'l Shawmut Bank v. Cumming, 91 N.E.2d 337 (Mass. 1950) 96n.51
Nat'l Westminster Bank, PLC v. United States, 44 Fed. Cl. 120 (1999) 429n.14, 439n.39
Nat'l Westminster Bank v. United States, 58 Fed. Cl. 491 (2003), *aff'd*, 512 F.3d 1347 (Fed. Cir. 2008) 429n.13
N.C. Nat'l Bank v. Va. Carolina Builders, 299 S.E.2d 629 (N.C. 1983) 660n.92

O

Office of Disciplinary Counsel v. Cashman, 629 P.2d 105 (Haw. 1981) (per curiam) 650n.14

P

Palmer v. Locke, [1880] 15 Ch. D. 294 481n.39, 482n.43
Park v. Comm'r, 136 T.C. 569 (2011) 428n.8
Pasquantino v. United States, 544 U.S. 349 (2005) 676n.211
People v. Schindelar, 845 P.2d 1146 (Colo. 1993) (en banc) (per curiam) 651n.18
Pershadsingh v. Pershadsingh, [1987] 40 D.L.R. (4th) 681 109n.58
Pierre v. Comm'r, 133 T.C. No. 2 (Aug. 24, 2009) 336n.16
PLC v. United States, 44 Fed. Cl. 120 (1999), *aff'd*, 512 F.3d 1347 (Fed. Cir. 2008) 429n.14
Podd v. Comm'r, 76 T.C.M. (CCH) 906 (1998) 429n.14
Proschek v. Proschazka, [1973] C.A. 410 116, 116n.111
Pullman's Palace Car v. Pennsylvania, 141 U.S. 18 (1891) 6n.19

Index

J

K

L